The Consumer Credit and Sales
Legal Practice Series

COLLECTION ACTIONS

Defending Consumers and Their Assets

First Edition

WITH COMPANION WWW WEBSITE

See *page ix* for information about the companion website.

Jonathan Sheldon
Carolyn Carter
Chi Chi Wu

Contributing Authors: Dwain Alexander, Lynn Drysdale, Joanne S. Faulkner, Robert J. Hobbs, Mary Kingsley, Richard Rubin

National Consumer Law Center
7 Winthrop Square, 4th Floor   Boston, MA 02110   www.consumerlaw.org

About NCLC	The National Consumer Law Center, a nonprofit corporation founded in 1969, assists consumers, advocates, and public policy makers nationwide who use the powerful and complex tools of consumer law to ensure justice and fair treatment for all, particularly those whose poverty renders them powerless to demand accountability from the economic marketplace. For more information, go to www.consumerlaw.org.
Ordering NCLC Publications	Order securely online at www.consumerlaw.org, or contact Publications Department, National Consumer Law Center, 7 Winthrop Square, 4th Floor, Boston, MA 02110, (617) 542-9595, FAX: (617) 542-8028, e-mail: publications@nclc.org.
Training and Conferences	NCLC participates in numerous national, regional, and local consumer law trainings. Its annual fall conference is a forum for consumer rights attorneys from legal services programs, private practice, government, and nonprofit organizations to share insights into common problems and explore novel and tested approaches that promote consumer justice in the marketplace. Contact NCLC for more information or see our website.
Case Consulting	Case analysis, consulting and co-counseling for lawyers representing vulnerable consumers are among NCLC's important activities. Administration on Aging funds allow us to provide free consulting to legal services advocates representing elderly consumers on many types of cases. Massachusetts Legal Assistance Corporation funds permit case assistance to advocates representing low-income Massachusetts consumers. Other funding may allow NCLC to provide very brief consultations to other advocates without charge. More comprehensive case analysis and research is available for a reasonable fee. See our website for more information at www.consumerlaw.org.
Charitable Donations and Cy Pres *Awards*	NCLC's work depends in part on the support of private donors. Tax-deductible donations should be made payable to National Consumer Law Center, Inc. For more information, contact Suzanne Cutler of NCLC's Development Office at (617) 542-8010 or scutler@nclc.org. NCLC has also received generous court-approved *cy pres* awards arising from consumer class actions to advance the interests of class members. For more information, contact Robert Hobbs (rhobbs@nclc.org) or Rich Dubois (rdubois@nclc.org) at (617) 542-8010.
Comments and Corrections	Write to the above address to the attention of the Editorial Department or e-mail consumerlaw@nclc.org.
About This Volume	*Collection Actions* is a 2008 First Edition, with a companion website. Continuing developments can be found in periodic supplements to this volume and in NCLC REPORTS.
Cite This Volume As	National Consumer Law Center, Collection Actions (2008).
Attention	*This publication is designed to provide authoritative information concerning the subject matter covered. Always use the most current edition and supplement, and use other sources for more recent developments or for special rules for individual jurisdictions. This publication cannot substitute for the independent judgment and skills of an attorney or other professional. Non-attorneys are cautioned against using these materials to conduct a lawsuit without advice from an attorney and are cautioned against engaging in the unauthorized practice of law.*

Copyright

ISBN: 978-1-60248-029-2 (this volume)
ISBN: 978-0-943116-10-5 (Series)

Library of Congress Control Number 2008932330

About the Authors

Jonathan Sheldon has been an NCLC staff attorney writing and consulting on a number of consumer law topics since 1976. Previously he was a staff attorney with the Federal Trade Commission. His publications include *Unfair and Deceptive Acts and Practices* (6th ed 2004), *Consumer Warranty Law* (3d ed. 2006), *Consumer Arbitration Agreements* (5th ed. 2007), *Consumer Class Actions* (6th ed. 2006), and *Repossessions* (6th ed. 2005).

Carolyn L. Carter is NCLC's deputy director for advocacy and was formerly co-director of Legal Services, Inc., in Gettysburg, Pennsylvania, and director of the Law Reform Office of the Cleveland Legal Aid Society. She is the editor of *Pennsylvania Consumer Law*, editor of the first edition of *Ohio Consumer Law*, co-author of *Consumer Warranty Law* (3d ed. 2006), *Unfair and Deceptive Acts and Practices* (6th ed. 2004), *Repossessions* (6th ed. 2005), and *Automobile Fraud* (3d ed. 2007), and a contributing author to *Fair Debt Collection* (6th ed. 2008) and other NCLC publications. She is a past member of the Federal Reserve Board Consumer Advisory Council and a recipient of the Vern Countryman Consumer Law Award.

Chi Chi Wu is an NCLC staff attorney working on medical debt collection, consumer credit, and credit reporting issues. She is co-author of *Fair Credit Reporting* (6th ed. 2006) and *Credit Discrimination* (4th ed. 2005) and a contributing author to *The Cost of Credit* (3d ed. 2005) and *Truth in Lending* (5th ed. 2003). She was formerly an assistant attorney general with the Consumer Protection Division of the Massachusetts attorney general's office and an attorney with the Asian Outreach Unit of Greater Boston Legal Services.

Dwain Alexander is a Navy Judge Advocate, practicing in Norfolk, Virginia, and Reserve Navy Legal Assistance Attorney. He has provided legal advice and representation to servicemembers for 18 years.

Lynn Drysdale for over 20 years has been a consumer protection attorney with Jacksonville Area Legal Aid, Inc., is on the Board of the National Association of Consumer Advocates, and has contributed to a number of NCLC publications and to the *Consumer Financial Services Law Repor*t. She is co-author of *The Two-Tiered Consumer Financial Services Marketplace*, 51 S.C. L. Rev. (Spring 2000) a member of the Small Claims Rules Committee of the Florida Bar Association, and a presenter at the FTC Workshop on Collecting Consumer Debts.

Joanne S. Faulkner has a private consumer law practice in New Haven, Connecticut, with a major focus on representing consumer under the FDCPA and other consumer protection laws. Previously, she was an attorney at New Haven Legal Assistance for many years. She has served as chair of the Consumer Law Section of the Connecticut Bar Association and as a member of the FRB's Consumer Advisory Council. She has contributed to a number of NCLC publications, including *Fair Credit Reporting* and *Credit Discrimination*. She received the Vern Countryman Award in 2002 for her contributions to the well-being of low-income consumers.

Robert J. Hobbs is NCLC's deputy director. He has written and consulted since 1972 on debt collection and other consumer credit issues. Prior to that, he was a staff attorney with New Orleans Legal Assistance. He is the author of *Fair Debt Collection* (6th ed 2008), co-author of *The Practice of Consumer Law* (2d ed. 2006), and editor of *Consumer Law Pleadings on CD-Rom* (2007). He advises attorneys on their clients' fair debt collection claims, was counsel to amicus curiae in *Heintz v. Jenkins*, 514 U.S. 291 (1995), has served on the FRB's Consumer Advisory Council, is a founder and former board member of the National Association of Consumer Advocates, and worked on the enactment of the Fair Debt Collection Practices Act.

Mary Kingsley is a 1971 graduate of Harvard Law School and a Massachusetts attorney. She has contributed to a number of NCLC publications in addition to this volume, including *Fair Debt Collection* (6th ed. 2008) and *Repossessions* (6th ed. 2005).

Richard Rubin is a private attorney in Santa Fe, New Mexico whose practice is limited to representing consumers in federal appeals and consulting for other consumer rights advocates. He is chair emeritus of the National Association of Consumer Advocates, has taught consumer law at the University of New Mexico School of Law, and presents continuing legal education and attorney training programs throughout the country. He is the 2000 recipient of the Vern Countryman Award.

Acknowledgments

We want to thank a number of attorneys for their work in this area and for contributing ideas for this volume: Ian Lyngklip, Robert Murphy, Neil Fogarty, and Brian Bromberg. Thanks also to Sharon Dietrich and Margot Saunders for assistance with chapter 12; Dwain Alexander for drafting chapter 7; John Rao and Geoff Walsh for bankruptcy issues; and Nathanael Player, Charlene Kjobstad, Gillian Feiner, and Kurt Terwilliger for legal research.

Finally, we are grateful to Eric Secoy for editorial supervision; Katherine Hunt for editorial assistance; Michael Trudeau for both editorial and website assistance; Shirlron Williams for assistance checking citations; Shannon Halbrook and Microsearch for designing and implementing the companion website; Mary McLean for indexing; and Xylutions for typesetting services.

What Your Library Should Contain

The Consumer Credit and Sales Legal Practice Series contains 18 titles, updated annually, arranged into four libraries, and designed to be an attorney's primary practice guide and legal resource in all 50 states. Each manual includes one year of access to a companion website, containing the manual appendices, sample pleadings, primary sources, and other practice aids, allowing pinpoint searches and the pasting of text into a word processor.

Debtor Rights Library

2006 Eighth Edition (Two Volumes), 2007 Supplement, and Companion Website, Including Law Disks' Bankruptcy Forms

Consumer Bankruptcy Law and Practice: the definitive personal bankruptcy manual, from the initial interview to final discharge, including consumer rights when a company files for bankruptcy. The eighth edition and supplement fully incorporate the 2005 Act in the text and include such practice aids as a redlined Code, the latest Bankruptcy Rules, a date calculator, over 150 pleadings and forms, software to compute the initial forms, means test data, and a client questionnaire and handout.

2008 Sixth Edition and Companion Website

Fair Debt Collection: the basic reference, covering the Fair Debt Collection Practices Act and common law, state statutory and other federal debt collection protections. Unique case summaries list reported and unreported FDCPA cases by category. The Companion Website contains sample pleadings and discovery, the FTC Commentary, an index to and the full text of *all* FTC staff opinion letters, and other practice aids.

2007 Second Edition, 2008 Supplement, and Companion Website

Foreclosures: examines RESPA and other federal and state rights to challenge servicer abuses, as well as details on work out agreements for VA, FHA, Fannie Mae, subprime, and other types of mortgages. The volume also covers rights to stave off foreclosure and tactics after the foreclosure sale. Special chapters cover tax liens, land installment sales contracts, mobile home foreclosures, and other topics.

2005 Sixth Edition, 2007 Supplement, and Companion Website

Repossessions: a unique guide to motor vehicle and manufactured home repossessions, threatened seizures of household goods, statutory liens, and automobile lease and rent-to-own default remedies. The volume examines UCC Article 9 and hundreds of other federal and state statutes regulating repossessions.

2006 Third Edition, 2007 Supplement, and Companion Website

Student Loan Law: collection harassment; closed school, disability, and other discharges; tax intercepts, wage garnishment, and offset of social security benefits; repayment plans, consolidation loans, deferments, and non-payment of loan based on school fraud.

2004 Third Edition, 2007 Supplement, and Companion Website

Access to Utility Service: consumer rights as to regulated and unregulated utilities, including telecommunications, terminations, billing errors, low-income payment plans, utility allowances in subsidized housing, LIHEAP, and weatherization.

Credit and Banking Library

2007 Sixth Edition with Companion Website

Truth in Lending: detailed analysis of *all* aspects of TILA, the Consumer Leasing Act, the Fair Credit Billing Act, and the Home Ownership and Equity Protection Act (HOEPA). Appendices and the website contain the Acts, Reg. Z, Reg. M, and their Official Staff Commentaries, numerous sample pleadings, rescission notices, two programs to compute APRs, TIL legislative history, and a unique compilation of *all Federal Register* notices and supplementary information on Regulation Z.

2006 Sixth Edition, 2007 Supplement, and Companion Website

Fair Credit Reporting: the key resource for handling any type of credit reporting issue, from cleaning up blemished credit records to suing reporting agencies and creditors for inaccurate reports. Covers the new FACTA changes, identity theft, creditor liability for failing to properly reinvestigate disputed information, credit scoring, privacy issues, the Credit Repair Organizations Act, state credit reporting and repair statutes, and common law claims.

2005 Third Edition, 2008 Supplement, and Companion Website

Consumer Banking and Payments Law: covers checks, telechecks, electronic fund transfers, electronic check conversions, money orders, and credit, debit, payroll, and stored value cards. The title also covers banker's right of setoff, electronic transfers of federal and state benefit payments, and a special chapter on electronic records and signatures.

2005 Third Edition, 2008 Supplement, and Companion Website

The Cost of Credit: Regulation, Preemption, and Industry Abuses: a one-of-a-kind resource detailing state and federal regulation of consumer credit in all 50 states, numerous types of predatory lending, federal preemption of state law, credit math calculations, excessive credit charges, credit insurance, and numerous other topics.

2005 Fourth Edition, 2008 Supplement, and Companion Website

Credit Discrimination: analysis of the Equal Credit Opportunity Act, Fair Housing Act, Civil Rights Acts, and state credit discrimination statutes, including reprints of all relevant federal interpretations, government enforcement actions, and numerous sample pleadings.

Consumer Litigation Library

2008 First Edition and Companion Website

Collection Actions: Defending Consumers and Their Assets is a complete guide to consumer defenses and counterclaims to collection lawsuits filed in court or in arbitration, with extensive discussion of setting aside default judgments and limitations on a collector's post-judgment remedies. Special chapters include the rights of active duty military, and unique issues involving medical debt, government collections, collector's attorney fees, and bad check laws.

2007 Fifth Edition and Companion Website

Consumer Arbitration Agreements: successful approaches to challenge arbitration agreements' enforceability and waivers of class arbitration, the interrelation of the Federal Arbitration Act and state law, class actions and punitive damages in arbitration, collections via NAF arbitration, the right to discovery, and other topics.

2006 Sixth Edition, 2008 Supplement, and Companion Website

Consumer Class Actions: makes class litigation manageable even for small offices. Includes numerous sample pleadings, class certification memoranda, discovery, class notices, settlement materials, and much more. Also includes a detailed analysis of the Class Action Fairness Act, class arbitration, state class action rules and case law, and other topics.

2007 CD-Rom with Index Guide and Companion Website: ALL pleadings from ALL NCLC Manuals, including Consumer Law Pleadings Numbers One through Thirteen

Consumer Law Pleadings on CD-Rom: over 1300 notable recent pleadings from all types of consumer cases, including predatory lending, foreclosures, automobile fraud, lemon laws, debt collection, fair credit reporting, home improvement fraud, student loans, and lender liability. Finding aids pinpoint desired pleading in seconds, ready to paste into a word processor. The December 2007 version is presented *both* on a CD-Rom and on a Companion Website.

Deception and Warranties Library

2004 Sixth Edition, 2007 Supplement, and Companion Website

Unfair and Deceptive Acts and Practices: the only practice manual covering all aspects of a deceptive practices case in every state. Special sections on automobile sales, the federal racketeering (RICO) statute, unfair insurance practices, the FTC Holder Rule, telemarketing fraud, attorney fees, and many other topics.

2007 Third Edition, 2008 Supplement, and Companion Website

Automobile Fraud: examination of title transfer law, "yo-yo" sales, odometer tampering, lemon laundering, sale of salvage and wrecked cars, undisclosed prior use, and prior damage to new cars. The website contains numerous sample pleadings and title search techniques.

2006 Third Edition, 2008 Supplement, and Companion Website

Consumer Warranty Law: comprehensive treatment of new and used car lemon laws, the Magnuson-Moss Warranty Act, UCC Articles 2 and 2A, mobile home, new home, and assistive device warranty laws, FTC Used Car Rule, tort theories, car repair and home improvement statutes, service contract and lease laws, with numerous sample pleadings.

NCLC's Companion Websites

Every NCLC manual includes a companion website, allowing rapid access to appendices, pleadings, primary sources, and other practice aids. Search for documents using a table of contents or various keyword search options. All documents are in PDF format, and all pleadings are also in Word format, to facilitate copying onto a word processor. One year free access is included with each manual. The initial one year service is automatically renewed at no charge when a manual update is ordered.

2008 Website

Consumer Law on the Web: combines *all* pleadings, software, practice aids, agency interpretations, statutes, and other documents from the 18 other NCLC companion websites. Using *Consumer Law on the Web,* instead of multiple individual companion websites, is the fastest and most convenient way to pinpoint and retrieve key documents among the thousands available on our 18 individual companion websites.

Other NCLC Publications for Lawyers

Issued 24 times a year

NCLC REPORTS covers the latest developments and innovative ideas in the practice of consumer law. This four page report, issued 24 times a year, provides the practice implications and new opportunities presented by recent court rulings, agency interpretations, statutes, and industry developments.

2007 First Edition and Companion Website

Bankruptcy Basics: A Step-by-Step Guide for Pro Bono Attorneys, General Practitioners, and Legal Services Offices: provides everything attorneys new to bankruptcy need to file their first case, with a companion website that contains software, sample pleadings, and other practice aids that greatly simplify handling a bankruptcy case.

2006 Second Edition with CD-Rom

The Practice of Consumer Law: Seeking Economic Justice: contains an essential overview to consumer law and explains how to get started in a private or legal services consumer law practice. Packed with invaluable sample pleadings and practice pointers for even experienced consumer attorneys.

2007 First Edition with CD-Rom

Foreclosure Prevention Counseling: Preserving the American Dream: explains how to obtain a workout, with advice specifically tailored for Fannie Mae, Freddie Mac, subprime, FHA-insured, VA, and Rural Housing Service loans. The book also includes homeowner strategies for reducing and prioritizing debt and options after the sale.

2007 Second Edition with CD-Rom

STOP Predatory Lending: A Guide for Legal Advocates: provides a roadmap and practical legal strategy for litigating predatory lending abuses, from small loans to mortgage loans. How to analyze the documents, spot issues, raise legal claims, select defendants, and even how to craft a community response.

National Consumer Law Center Guide Series are books designed for consumers, counselors, and attorneys new to consumer law:

2008 Edition

NCLC Guide to Surviving Debt: a great overview of consumer law. Everything a paralegal, new attorney, or client needs to know about home foreclosures, debt collectors, managing credit card debt, whether to refinance, credit card problems, evictions, repossessions, credit reporting, utility terminations, student loans, budgeting, and bankruptcy.

2006 Edition

NCLC Guide to the Rights of Utility Consumers: explains consumer rights concerning electric, gas, and other utility services: shut off protections, rights to restore terminated service, bill payment options, weatherization tips, rights to government assistance, and much more.

2006 Edition

NCLC Guide to Consumer Rights for Domestic Violence Survivors: provides practical advice to help survivors get back on their feet financially and safely establish their economic independence.

2002 Edition

NCLC Guide to Mobile Homes: what consumers and their advocates need to know about mobile home dealer sales practices and an in-depth look at mobile home quality and defects, with 35 photographs and construction details.

2000 Edition

Return to Sender: Getting a Refund or Replacement for Your Lemon Car: find how lemon laws work, what consumers and their lawyers should know to evaluate each other, investigative techniques and discovery tips, how to handle both informal dispute resolution and trials, and more.

Visit **www.consumerlaw.org** to order securely online or for more information on all NCLC manuals and companion websites, including the full tables of contents, indices, and **web-based searches of the manuals' full text**.

About the Companion Website, Other Search Options

The Companion Website

This volume includes one year of free access to its companion website. Continued subscription to this title includes continued free access to the website. NCLC companion websites supersede, update, and improve upon NCLC's former companion CD-Roms. The same documents are presented in the same PDF and Microsoft Word formats, but with more flexible access, more powerful search capabilities, and more frequent updates.

Nevertheless, older CD-Roms can be retained for situations where Internet access is unavailable or unusually slow, or to insure permanent access to files after a subscription lapses. CD-Roms may continue to be a good source for historical information, but should never be relied upon for current law.

Accessing the Companion Website

One-time registration is required to access NCLC's companion websites. One email address and password allows continual access to *all* NCLC companion websites that a subscriber has authorization to use. For example, the one email address and password allows a subscriber to four NCLC titles to access all four companion websites.

To register, go to www.consumerlaw.org/webaccess, and click on "New users click to register." Enter the "Companion Website Registration Number" found on the packing statement or invoice accompanying this publication. (This step is *not* necessary if an email address and password have been selected for another NCLC companion website; registering a second time overrides the prior email address and password.)

Once registered, click on the login link at www.consumerlaw.org/webaccess, enter the email address and password, and select the desired companion website from the list of authorized websites.

Locating Documents on the Companion Website

The companion website provides three options to locate documents.

1. The search page (the home page) uses keyword searches to find documents—full text searches of all documents on the website or searches just on the documents' titles.

- Narrow the search to documents of a certain type (such as federal statutes or pleadings) by making a selection from the "Document Type" menu, and then perform a full text or document title search.
- If unsure of a keyword's spelling, type the first few letters and click "see choices."
- To locate a specific appendix section, select the appendix section number (e.g. A.2.3) or a partial identifier (e.g. A) at the search page's "Appendix" drop-down field.
- Click Search Hints for a quick reference to special search operators, wildcards, shortcuts, and complex searches.

2. The contents page (click on the "contents" tab at the top of the page) is a traditional "branching" table of contents. Clicking on a branch expands to a list of sub-branches or documents. Each document appears one place on this contents "tree."

3. The pleading finder page (click on the "pleading finder" tab at the top of the page, *if available*) allows pleadings to be located using one or more menus, such as "Type of Pleading" or "Subject." Select more than one item from one menu by using the Ctrl key. For example, make one selection from "Type of Pleading–General," one from "Subject," and three from "Legal Claims" to locate all pleadings of that type and subject that contain one or more of the three legal claims selected. If this search produces insufficient results, de-select "Subject" and/or "Legal Claims" to find pleadings of that type in any subject area or based upon any legal claim.

Additional software, related websites, and other information can be located by clicking on links found at the left hand toolbar or on the "search" page. These links bring you to credit math software, search tips, other websites, the tables of contents and indices of all NCLC manuals, and other practice aids.

Finding Word Versions of Website Documents

All documents on the website are in PDF format, and can be cut and pasted into a word processor. All pleadings and certain other documents also are available in Word format, facilitating the cutting and pasting of large portions of a documents into a word processor. After opening the selected PDF file, click at the top of the page on "Word Version, if available." If a Word version is listed as available, click on "DOC Download Document" to save the Word file to your computer.

Documents Found on the Website

This website contains 70 files relating to collection actions on consumer debt, including all of the manual's appendices and other pleadings and primary resources. All files are in PDF format and the sample pleadings are also in Word format.

The website contains federal statutes and summaries of state statutes providing consumers with important exemptions from creditor post-judgment remedies, federal legislation governing federal collection actions, and the Servicemembers Civil Relief Act, the Fair Debt Collection Practices Act and the FTC Credit Practices Rule all providing protections from collection actions. More than 50 pleadings relate to consumer defenses to collection actions or consumer claims against collectors for litigation misconduct.

The website does *not* contain the full text of the manual chapters. See below about using Internet-based keyword searches to pinpoint page numbers in the manual where topics are discussed.

Locating Topics in This Manual

Go to www.consumerlaw.org/keyword to electronically search the full text of every chapter and appendix of this title's main volume and supplement. Select this title and enter a search term or combination of search terms: a case name, a regulation cite, or other keywords. Instantly, the page numbers containing that term or terms are listed. These "hits" are shown in context, facilitating selection of the most relevant pages. The chapters' text is *not* available online; keyword search locates text to be read in the print book.

This title also contains a detailed table of contents and a detailed index, located in the hard copies. These can be searched electronically at the companion website by following the link at the "Search" page.

Locating Topics in the Seventeen Other NCLC Manuals

Current tables of contents, indices, and other information for all eighteen NCLC manuals and supplements can be found at www.consumerlaw.org/shop. Click on *Publications for Lawyers* and scroll down to the book you want.

The full text of all NCLC manuals and supplements can also be electronically searched to locate relevant topics. Go to www.consumerlaw.org/keyword, and enter a search term or combination of search terms, in a similar fashion to performing a keyword search on one title.

The Quick Reference at the back of this volume lets you pinpoint the correct manual and manual sections or appendices that discuss over 1000 different subject areas. These subject areas are listed in alphabetical order and can also be electronically searched at www.consumerlaw.org/qr.

Finding Pleadings

Pleadings relating to this title are found in PDF and Word format on the companion website; search options are discussed above at "Locating Documents on the Website." Over 1000 other pleadings are available at NCLC's *Consumer Law Pleadings* and can be located on the *Consumer Law Pleadings* companion website, using the same web-based search techniques discussed above at "Locating Documents on the Website." Pleadings can also be located using *Consumer Law Pleadings*' hard copy index guide, which organizes pleadings by type, by subject area, by title, and by other categories.

Summary Contents

Contents

Chapter 3 Dismissal Before Reaching the Merits

Chapter 4 The Collector's Proof of the Merits

Chapter 5 Defenses and Counterclaims

Chapter 6 State Restrictions on the Recovery of Attorney Fees and Other Collection Expenses

Chapter 7 Defending Military Personnel in Collection Actions

Chapter 8 Creditor's Use of Arbitration to Collect Consumer Debts

Chapter 10 Medical Debt

Chapter 11 Defending Consumers Against Collection by Federal Administrative Agencies

Chapter 12 Protecting Debtors from Creditors' Post-Judgment Remedies

Chapter 13 Setting Aside or Discharging a Judgment

Chapter 14 Prevailing Consumers' Post-Judgment Actions

Chapter 1 Introduction

1.1 About This Manual

This manual assists attorneys in the representation of consumers sued on credit card, medical, and other debts. Much of this manual is new, but a number of the chapters and appendices originally were found in NCLC's *Fair Debt Collection* and have been moved to this manual.

Recent years have seen an explosion in not just the number of consumer debts being enforced in the courts, but also in the number of such actions in which the consumer does not owe the debt or has substantial defenses, or in which the collector has no reliable evidence whether the consumer owes the debt or not. Moreover, the entities bringing most consumer collection actions today are not the original creditor but a debt buyer represented by a collection law firm that brings huge numbers of cases in state courts. These realities color all aspects of consumer collection actions, and point to the need for a comprehensive manual to assist attorneys in representing consumers in such cases.

This manual examines consumer defenses, the elements of the collector's causes of action, evidentiary issues, and other practical considerations. It also contains chapters covering a number of specialized issues: the rights of active duty military personnel, the use of arbitration proceedings to collect a debt, and the collection of medical debt, debts owed the federal government, and debts arising from dishonored checks.

The manual also details consumer protections when the collector seeks to enforce the judgment, and consumer rights to set aside or discharge that judgment. Finally, this manual presents steps a prevailing consumer should consider taking after the judgment is issued.

This manual will be updated annually with either cumulative supplements or revised editions. Continuing developments are also reported throughout the year in NCLC REPORTS *Debt Collection and Repossessions Edition.*

1.2 This Manual's Organization

1.2.1 Chapters 2–6: General Consumer Defenses

Chapter 2, *infra*, is a practical chapter focusing on the reasons why attorneys should represent consumers in collection actions, tips on setting up a practice in this area, and pointers on conducting the client interview and other preliminary investigative steps. The chapter details case selection considerations, litigation tactics, and alternatives to representing the consumer in the collection action.

Chapter 3, *infra*, examines defenses to a collection action that are not based upon the merits of the collector's claims. These defenses can be used to support a motion to dismiss and can also be used later in the proceeding. The most important such defense is the statute of limitations, which has taken on increasing importance as debt buyers bring collection actions years after a consumer defaults on the credit account. Another important group of defenses relate to the adequacy of the complaint and the supporting documents, because a number of states require the complaint to be verified or to include certain documentation. Other defenses discussed: that the collector has brought the action in the wrong court, and that the case must be removed to arbitration.

Chapter 4, *infra*, covers the collector's proof of the merits of its allegations, both the elements of its causes of action and the evidentiary requirements as to the proof of those elements. Collectors often seek to prove their case not with their own evidence but by sending lengthy requests for admissions to the consumer, that are deemed admitted if the consumer fails to timely respond. The chapter provides advice on how to respond to such requests for admissions and how to withdraw an admission based upon the consumer's failure to answer.

Collectors also seek to prove their case at summary judgment with documentary evidence. The chapter examines the admissibility and weight to be given to two types of documentary evidence commonly submitted with such motions—affidavits and business records.

A key issue in many collection actions is whether the collector in fact owns the debt and has the right to collect on it. With the advent of debt buyers who aggressively buy and sell portfolios, the consumer's account may have passed through two, three, or even more hands before it is sold to the entity bringing the collection action. Chapter 4, *infra*, also examines the collector's burden to prove that a continuous chain of ownership has properly transferred the debt to that entity.

The chapter then turns to the elements of the collector's cause of action. Collectors often bring claims for breach of contract or for the balance owed on a credit card or other open-end account. Another common collector cause of action is "account stated," which is not based upon the contract but upon a consumer's implicit promise to pay an amount delineated in a statement of account. Other possible causes of action treated in the chapter are *quantum meruit*, money lent, goods and services, and sworn account.

Chapter 5, *infra*, focuses on basic consumer defenses and counterclaims to the collector's action. These defenses include that the debt has already been paid, settled, or discharged in bankruptcy. Other defenses relate to when someone else owes the debt (such as when the collector mistakenly sues the wrong consumer), when the consumer is the victim of identity theft or other unauthorized charges, when the consumer is only an authorized user, or when the consumer's spouse owes the money, not the consumer. The chapter also examines defenses related to the consumer's incapacity based upon minority, mental incompetence, or intoxication.

The chapter also considers an important consumer defense when the collector seeks a deficiency action after a car's repossession and sale—that the collector has offered insufficient proof of a commercially reasonable sale of the repossessed vehicle. The chapter also looks at defenses to unreasonable charges imposed after default.

A consumer may have numerous counterclaims to a collection action. Chapter 5, *infra*, focuses on what types of counterclaims are available, and tactical considerations as to whether they should be raised in the collection action or brought as affirmative claims in a separate lawsuit brought by the consumer. The chapter looks in particular at such considerations when the counterclaim relates to the collector's litigation misconduct. The chapter concludes with a discussion of some advantages to bringing a counterclaim on a classwide basis.

Chapter 6, *infra*, reviews the collector's attempt in the collection action to recover attorney fees and other collection expenses. The chapter analyzes whether the collector has a contractual right to those fees and whether state law overrides that contract. The chapter also examines state law that allows prevailing collectors to recover attorney fees regardless of the contract terms, and also considers state law that limits the size of an attorney fee award.

1.2.2 Chapters 7–11: Special Topics

Chapter 7, *infra*, looks at special rights that the Servicemembers Civil Relief Act provides for active duty military personnel in defending collection actions. The Act limits the ability of a collector to take a default judgment and also gives the servicemember the right to stay a collector's action. Military service tolls statutes of limitations, reduces the interest rate to six percent on obligations incurred before active duty, and restricts a creditor's right to self-help repossession, foreclosure, and lien enforcement. Other special rights for active duty personnel relate to automobile and residential leases. The Act provides consumer remedies for violations.

Chapter 8, *infra*, examines the increasingly common practice of a collector suing the consumer not in court, but in an arbitration proceeding. The chapter explains how collection using arbitration works and the consumer's options after receiving a notice of arbitration. The chapter also covers the consumer's ability to vacate an arbitration award entered against the consumer, and what defenses the consumer has when the collector seeks to confirm the arbitration award in court. The chapter concludes with a brief review of a consumer's or government agency's separate court action challenging the use of the arbitration process to collect consumer debts.

Chapter 9, *infra*, looks at criminal and civil proceedings against consumers concerning dishonored checks, including limitations on criminal prosecutions for a consumer presenting a check with insufficient funds. The chapter also looks at the operation of civil dishonored check laws and details the consumer's remedies for a collector's abuse of dishonored check laws.

Chapter 10, *infra*, is a thorough analysis of a consumer's defenses to a medical debt collection action. It examines a number of federal and state statutes that provide special rights for medical debtors and that provide defenses to medical collection actions. The chapter also looks at a number of other defenses in medical debt cases, including duress, charges in excess of a reasonable value, discriminatory pricing, and overbilling and billing errors. The chapter also considers the applicability of family necessaries statutes that would impose liability on other family members.

Chapter 11, *infra*, examines federal agency collection actions, including such non-litigation collection methods as administrative offset, wage garnishment, tax refund intercepts, and other remedies under the Claims Collection Act. Federal law often limits federal collection actions and provides consumers with the right to obtain an installment plan, compromise of the debt, or even suspension or discharge of the debt. The chapter also considers private remedies for illegal government collection actions, and government prejudgment and post-judgment remedies under the Federal Debt Collection Practices Act. While the chapter considers collection by most federal agencies, a more thorough discussion of student loan collections is found in NCLC's *Student Loan Law*.[1]

1 (3d ed. 2006 and Supp.).

1.2.3 Chapters 12–14: Collector and Consumer Post-Judgment Rights

Chapter 12, *infra*, may be the most important chapter in the manual. It considers consumer protections against the collector's post-judgment remedies. These include federal and state limits on wage garnishment, and exemption laws that prevent seizure of the consumer's property to satisfy a court judgment. These exemptions may apply to the consumer's homestead, personal property, benefit payments, and other assets. An important discussion is the protection from seizure of exempt funds deposited into the consumer's bank account. Also covered are limits to a collector's ability to seize funds in a joint bank account, and prohibitions on a consumer's waiver of exemptions. The chapter also reviews interstate collection efforts, debtor's examinations, and imprisonment for debt.

Chapter 13, *infra*, details approaches consumers can take to set aside or discharge the collector's judgment. It reviews the grounds to set aside both default and stipulated judgments and then considers the relief a bankruptcy filing can offer a judgment debtor. The chapter concludes with a discussion of the advisability of an affirmative action challenging collector litigation misconduct after a judgment for the collector.

Chapter 14, *infra*, reviews actions a consumer can take after the consumer prevails in the collector's collection action. The chapter discusses various theories allowing the consumer to recover attorney fees from the collector. It also examines how consumers can improve their credit reports after prevailing in the collection action. The chapter also considers the consumer's remedies when the collector refuses to abide by the judgment. In a surprising number of cases collectors either sell the debt to another debt buyer or continue to seek collection on the debt even though the court has dismissed the collector's action with prejudice. The chapter concludes with a discussion of what types of litigation the consumer should consider to challenge the collector's litigation misconduct in a dismissed collection action.

1.2.4 The Appendices

This manual contains six appendices. Appendix A, *infra*, reprints selected portions of the Servicemembers Civil Relief Act. Appendix B, *infra*, reprints the federal statute and regulations protecting a portion of a consumer's wages from garnishment. Appendix C, *infra*, excerpts provisions from various federal statutes that exempt federal benefit payments from seizure to satisfy a debt, including Social Security, SSI, veteran's benefits, and civil service and federal employee retirement and disability payments.

Appendix D, *infra*, reprints the Federal Trade Commission's Credit Practices Rule that limits certain creditor remedies, such as cognovit notes, non-purchase money security interests in certain household goods, certain co-signer practices, and the waiver of exemptions. Appendix E, *infra*, reprints the Debt Collection Improvements Act that regulates the collection of debts owed to the federal government. Appendix F, *infra*, summarizes each state's exemption statutes, which protect property and income from a collector's post-judgment remedies.

1.2.5 Finding Aids

A number of finding aids can help pinpoint a particular issue in this manual. The detailed table of contents and the index are obvious examples. The volume has a quick reference at the end that provides cross-references to issues discussed in other NCLC manuals.

The complete text of this manual can also be searched electronically on the Internet, using individual keywords or combinations of keywords (for example, "account stated within 10 words of affidavit"). This website, located at www.consumerlaw.org/keyword, is open to the general public at no charge. Search results are shown in context, and the page number is also listed, allowing the user to quickly find the exact page in the manual where the topic is discussed. Alternatively, appendix material can be searched using the search feature of the companion website.

A number of unreported cases are cited in this manual, and the text of these decisions can be found at www.consumerlaw.org/unreported. The cases are reprinted at that web address in Adobe Acrobat (PDF) format, and are listed there in alphabetical order by the first party's name.

1.2.6 The Companion Website

The companion website to this manual contains the appendices and a number of other documents relevant to consumer collection actions. These documents are in Adobe Acrobat (PDF) format and, in certain cases, also in Microsoft Word format. All files can be searched, printed, and copied and pasted into a word processing program. Advice on how to access and use the website is provided on page ix, *supra*, and also on the inside back cover of this manual. Documents can be found using the website's table of contents or by searching for key words, type of document, or appendix number. The website will be updated periodically.

1.3 Topics Covered in Other NCLC Manuals

This manual comprehensively covers a consumer's rights when the consumer is sued in a collection action. But the manual can not cover in detail all areas of consumer law. Consequently, this manual should be read in conjunction with other NCLC manuals, which cover in far more detail certain types of collections or consumer rights.

A common collection lawsuit seeks a deficiency, that is, the remaining balance after a creditor forecloses on the consumer's home, repossesses the consumer's car or manufactured home, or otherwise seizes and sells the consumer's property. The creditor sells the property and deducts the sale price from the amount due on the loan. The creditor (or a debt buyer) then sues for the remainder of the original balance due, called a deficiency.

Deficiency actions raise many unique defenses and counterclaims that are examined in detail in two other NCLC manuals. *Foreclosures*[2] focuses on foreclosure of real property, including a chapter on manufactured homes. *Repossessions*[3] comprehensively covers repossessions of motor vehicles, manufactured homes, and household goods.

Chapter 11, *infra*, reviews consumer defenses to a collection action brought by the federal government. Collection actions on student loans are so pervasive, and involve so many special issues, that they require a volume of their own: *Student Loan Law*.[4]

This manual frequently refers to the federal Fair Debt Collection Practices Act, state debt collection law, and tort law in discussing consumer counterclaims and independent affirmative actions against the collector or collection attorney. These subjects are examined in great detail in NCLC's *Fair Debt Collection*.[5] Reference should also be made to NCLC's *Unfair and Deceptive Acts and Practices*[6] and *Consumer Class Actions*.[7]

One of the recurring themes in this manual is the importance of the consumer's credit report in a collection action. The credit report is a key investigative tool and can be particularly helpful in cases involving identity theft, mistaken identity, or disputes over the amount owed. A review of the consumer's credit report can also indicate if it has been reviewed by the collector. If so, this information will reveal what the collector should have known about the debt, and can thus help prove that a collector was seeking payment on a debt it should have known was not owed (for example, because the debt was discharged in bankruptcy). Moreover, consumers being sued upon a debt will invariably have negative information on their report. An important step for a consumer prevailing in the collection action will be to try to clean up that credit report. These issues are examined in more detail in NCLC's *Fair Credit Reporting*.[8]

Bankruptcy can be an important consumer strategy in dealing with a collection action and a court judgment. In addition, a complete defense on a debt is that the debt has been discharged in bankruptcy. For a complete analysis of all consumer bankruptcy issues, see NCLC's *Consumer Bankruptcy Law and Practice*.[9] For a step-by-step guide to assist an attorney in filing a first bankruptcy case, see NCLC's *Bankruptcy Basics*.[10]

The federal Fair Credit Billing Act and other Truth in Lending Act provisions have an impact on a collection action involving credit cards or other open-end credit. These issues are discussed in Chapters 4 and 5, *infra*, but are described in more detail in another NCLC manual, *Truth in Lending*.[11]

Chapter 8, *infra*, examines collection actions using arbitration. Several of the issues discussed in that chapter, such as whether an arbitration requirement is enforceable, standards to vacate an arbitration award, and what law applies to a state court action to confirm an award, are reviewed in more depth in NCLC's *Consumer Arbitration Agreements*.[12]

1.4 Debt Buyers and Collection Lawsuits

1.4.1 Dramatic Growth in Debt Buying

Attorneys representing consumers in collection cases must consider the implications of the dramatic growth of the debt buying industry. In the early 1990s debt buying was a minor enterprise, but by 2000 it had reached almost $40 billion in face value of consumer debt purchased, the overwhelming majority of which was seriously delinquent credit card debt. By 2005, debt buyer purchases of consumer debt had more than tripled to $128 billion, with credit card debt accounting for $88 billion of that total.[13] In 2005 debt buyers held about $170 billion in credit card debt less than five years old.[14]

Debt buyers paid card issuers in 2005 about $3 billion to buy these defaulted accounts.[15] One major debt buyer reports paying a little under 2 cents a dollar for debt involving California, Arizona, and Florida residents, but slightly over 2.5 cents a dollar for debt from Tennessee, Georgia, Ohio, Michigan, and Virginia.[16] Another source estimates that all debt buyers paid card issuers in 2006 on average 5.3 cents on the dollar.[17]

2 (2d ed. 2007 and Supp.).
3 (6th ed. 2005 and Supp.).
4 (3d ed. 2006 and Supp.).
5 (6th ed. 2008).
6 (6th ed. 2004 and Supp.).
7 (6th ed. 2005 and Supp.).
8 (6th ed. 2006 and Supp.).
9 (8th ed. 2006 and Supp.).
10 (2007).
11 (6th ed. 2007).
12 (5th ed. 2007).
13 *See* R. Hunt, *Collecting Consumer Debt in America*, Philadelphia Fed. Reserve Bank Bus. Rev. (Q2 2007).
14 *Id.*
15 *Id.*
16 As listed in Portfolio Recovery Associates's 2007 10K statement.
17 *See* Collecting Consumer Debts: The Challenges of Change, Testimony before the Federal Trade Commission (Oct. 10, 2007) (statement of R. Hunt, Fed. Reserve Bank of Philadelphia).

1.4.2 Debt Buyers Identified

Debt buyers are often large corporations that do business on an enormous scale, often collecting debts under a variety of names. In 2006 the ten largest debt buyers accounted for 81% of all bad debts purchased.[18] Major debt buyers with revenues over $100 million (well over $100 million in many cases) include Sherman Financial Group, Unifund, Asset Acceptance Corp, Firstcity Financial, Encore Capital Group, Portfolio Recovery Associates, and Asta Funding.

1.4.3 Resulting Explosion in Collection Litigation

Debt buyers aggressively use state courts to collect on their purchased debt. In 2006 approximately 320,000 consumer debt cases were filed in New York City alone, seeking almost $1 billion.[19] A study has found that 89.3% of these cases were filed by debt buyers.[20] Consumer debt cases are clogging up state courts, making up over 50% of some courts' dockets.[21] Just one debt buyer, Encore Capital Group, in 2007 filed over 350,000 lawsuits around the country. Asset Acceptance has 350 employees in its legal collections department.

Most of these debt buyer collection actions are for credit card debt, but other types of debt also result in collection actions. When AT & T Wireless merged with Cingular in 2004, it sold a significant amount of its debt to debt buyers, including Palisades Collection. This purchased AT & T debt was a major source of court filings in New York City in 2006.[22]

18 *See id.*

19 Urban Justice, Debt Weight, the Consumer Credit Crisis in New York City and Its Impact on the Working Poor (Oct. 2007).

20 *Id.*

21 *Id.*; Richard M. Hynes, *Broke But Not Bankrupt: Consumer Debt Collection in State Courts*, 60 Fla. L. Rev. 1 (Jan. 2008).

22 Urban Justice, Debt Weight, the Consumer Credit Crisis in New York City and Its Impact on the Working Poor (Oct. 2007).

1.4.4 Characteristics of Debt Buyer Collection Lawsuits

Eighty percent of consumer collection actions in New York City in 2006 resulted in default judgments against unrepresented consumers,[23] with an average award of $3063.[24] The same 80% default judgments statistic was reported in a study of collection actions in Massachusetts.[25] Only about 2% of the default judgments in New York City were later set aside.[26] The collectors recovered about $800 million of the almost $1 billion sought.[27]

The New York City study also found that in 99% of the cases in which default judgments were entered, the materials underlying those applications constituted inadmissible hearsay and did not meet New York's standards for the entry of a default judgment.[28] In 85% of the cases the supporting evidence was an affidavit from the debt buyer's own employee, and in another 12% it was from an employee of an unidentified entity.[29]

The New York City study looked at a sample of 600 collection cases and found that only two of the 600 consumers were represented by counsel.[30] On the other hand, over 70% of the 320,000 collection actions brought in New York City in 2006 were brought by just four law firms: Pressler & Pressler, Cohen & Slamowitz, Mel S. Harris & Associates, and Wolpoff & Abramson.[31] This means that *each week*, on average, in New York City alone, *each* of these four firms filed over 1000 new cases and obtained over 800 default judgments in other cases.

23 *Id.*

24 *Id.*

25 *Dignity Faces a Steamroller: Small-Claims Proceedings Ignore Rights, Tilt to Collectors*, The Boston Globe, July 31, 2006.

26 Urban Justice, Debt Weight, the Consumer Credit Crisis in New York City and Its Impact on the Working Poor (Oct. 2007).

27 *Id.*

28 *Id.*

29 *Id.*

30 *Id.*

31 *Id.*

Chapter 2 Case Selection, Advising the Client, and Litigation Strategy

2.1 Ten Reasons to Defend Consumer Collection Actions

2.1.1 Consumers Often Have Dispositive Defenses

Many people, including some judges, assume that when a collector sues on a debt the consumer almost always owes the money. Whatever the accuracy of this view in times past, changed practices in the marketplace have dramatically altered the facts. Today, consumers have complete defenses in a significant number of collection cases.

The major reason for this development is the explosive expansion of the multi-billion dollar distressed debt buying industry, in which debt collectors purchase literally millions of old debts for pennies on the dollar that the original creditors have written off. The debt buyers receive minimal information on each account, and certainly do not receive the contract or copies of any communications in which the consumer might have disputed the amount owed. In addition, after having unsuccessfully attempted to collect the accounts, these debt buyers regularly resell repackaged portfolios of uncollectable debts to other debt buyers whose connection to the original creditor—and to original documentation and proof—is even more attenuated.

Because debt buyers purchase very old debt, the statute of limitations is an important consumer defense. Debt buyers who can not produce the written contract often bring the case on a claim not based upon that contract.[1] In many states, such causes of action have a shorter limitations period than a claim based upon a written contract.[2] Moreover, the credit contract's choice of law provision may select a state whose limitations period is shorter than the forum state's period.[3]

Because the debts are old, the consumer often will have moved after the credit account was closed, and the debt buyer must first try to locate the consumer's present residence. Debt buyers may try to serve the consumer at the wrong address or evens sue the wrong consumer. Debt buyers rely on credit reports to locate the consumer but the credit reports themselves are filled with errors, including "mismerged" information that mixes the credit reports of two or more people with similar names and other identifying information and that results in the collector then suing the wrong person.

Creditors also may commit billing errors which may be the reason the creditor stopped collection efforts—the consumer did not owe all or part of the money claimed. When these debts are sold the debt buyer does not receive or retain this information concerning consumer defenses. The consumer can then defend the collection action based upon the original dispute the consumer had with the creditor.

Too often debt buyers will bring actions against spouses and other parties knowing these defendants do not owe the debt, but hoping to either pressure them into payment or obtain a default judgment against them. The debt buying business model is to cast a wide net without consideration as to whether the consumer owes the money, and see what money is recovered.

At the same time that debt buyers are suing people without sufficient knowledge whether they actually owe the money or whether the statute of limitations has run, there has also been an explosion of identity theft and unauthorized use of credit cards. While federal law states that consumers in these situations do not owe the money, the collector may still sue the consumer.

Another factor leading to the recent increase in valid consumer defenses is that creditors have aggressively offered credit to almost anyone, including college and even high school students. Credit is being thrust upon not only the young but also upon others who traditionally would not have been eligible. This practice leads to the increased relevance of the defense of lack of capacity, including that the consumer was underage, had mental disabilities, or was intoxicated at the time of the credit offer.

Another change in the marketplace is that many creditors base their profitability on consumers *not* paying their debts. Creditors are content to load up interest charges and fees on those who pay less than the minimum amount due. Collectors also seek enormous extra charges when suing on the debt, including finance charges at jacked up rates and un-

1 *See* Ch. 4, *infra*.

2 *See* § 3.7.3.1, *infra*.

3 *See* § 3.7.2, *infra*.

reasonable or even illegal attorney fees. Because most cases end in unexamined default judgments, there is little incentive for the collector to limit the amount requested over and above the original debt.

The bottom line is that attorneys, judges, and the public must readjust their expectations. When consumers are sued the operating assumption should be that they owe either nothing or less than is being sought. Certainly the assumption should not be that they owe the amount the collector is seeking.

2.1.2 Stopping Systematic Abuse of the Justice System

Debt buyers today are using the courts to engage in wholesale litigation abuse. They sue huge numbers of consumers with no real knowledge whether the consumer owes the debt or whether the statute of limitations has run. Debt buyers sue with little or no evidence to prove that the consumer owes the money, that the debt buyer in fact owns the debt, or even that they are suing the right consumer. This litigation strategy is effective because very few consumers obtain legal representation, and the overwhelming majority of consumer defendants default in the collection action.

When the consumer contests an action the collector utilizes various techniques to win without having to produce admissible evidence to prove its claim. The collector may take advantage of the unrepresented consumer by working out a stipulated judgment without disclosing that the collector can not prove the debt. Another technique is to send the consumer a long list of requests for admission to which the consumer does not timely respond. The requests are deemed admitted, and the collector needs no other evidence to prove its case.[4] Alternatively, collectors seek summary judgment on junk evidence—attachments that are not attached, affidavits from debt buyer employees (or even non-employees) who state conclusory facts about which the affiant has no personal knowledge, or about pretend business records created years after the fact.

Consumers fare much better in court when they obtain legal representation. Many debt buyers will not even pursue the case once they realize the consumer has legal representation. Such an individual consumer victory has no adverse impact on a debt buyer that has purchased the debt for pennies on the dollar. But that strategy may educate the court as to the shoddy practices of certain debt buyers and collection attorneys. The next time the collector or collection attorney brings a series of cases asking that court to enter default judgments the court may look more closely at the collector's evidence, throw out large numbers of uncontested collection actions, or establish standards for when default judgments will be allowed in uncontested consumer collection matters.

4 *See* § 4.2.2, *infra.*

Individual collection litigation can be the vehicle that creates a jurisdiction's controlling standards. A collector or collection attorney who brings cases that are clearly not actionable under those established standards runs a significant risk that a Fair Debt Collection Practices Act (FDCPA) class action will succeed in producing a large award for the class.

For example, individual litigation in a collection case may establish the state's rule recognizing, for example, a three-year limitations period for an account stated claim or barring an account stated claim on an "account statement" that the debt buyer created and sent to the consumer years after the creditor wrote off the account, thereby resulting in FDCPA liability for future actions.[5]

2.1.3 Counterclaims Can Result in the Recovery of Damages and Attorney Fees

In many collection actions the consumer will have significant counterclaims. Being able to raise consumer claims as counterclaims has both advantages and disadvantages. Some of the advantages are that filing fees are avoided and federal claims can stay in state court. Disadvantages include that the collector may be less willing to dismiss its claims and may prosecute the collection case more aggressively in order to vigorously contest the counterclaim.

A good example of a collection case that raises numerous potential counterclaims is when the collector is seeking to recover a deficiency after a car repossession and sale. The consumer may have counterclaims under Uniform Commercial Code (UCC) Article 9 and other state laws relating to the repossession and sale or to the original sale and performance of the vehicle. Consumers can also raise in many collection cases counterclaims based upon the FDCPA and related debt harassment theories. It may even be possible to raise counterclaims related to the collector's litigation misconduct. Legal representation can thus result not only in dismissal of the collector's case but also in the consumer's recovery of significant damages and attorney fees.

2.1.4 Prevailing in the Collection Action Can Improve a Consumer's Credit Rating

Consumers are rightfully concerned about their credit rating, and prevailing in the collection action can have an impact on their credit record. If the case is dismissed the consumer can take action to insure that credit reports indicate that the current balance of that debt is now reported as

5 *See* § 14.4, *infra.*

zero.[6] If the judge also rules that the consumer never owed the money (for example, because the collector sued the wrong consumer), then the consumer can seek to delete information in their consumer report that the debt had been in default in the past.[7] In addition the attorney can help the consumer dispute inaccurate information in a credit report, and the consumer has a cause of action under the Fair Credit Reporting Act (FCRA) if that information is not properly investigated and corrected.[8]

2.1.5 Alleviation of Emotional Distress

Being sued can be extremely upsetting for some clients, particularly older and other especially vulnerable consumers. Some may never have been sued in their whole lives and can become very distressed over a suit, even for a relatively minor debt. That distress can have medical consequences, which can be accentuated when the consumer can not obtain legal representation to explain to them what is happening and to defend the consumer's interests.

2.1.6 Protection of the Consumer's Assets and Income

A judgment for a collector can have serious consequences for the consumer's assets and income, particularly for lower-income consumers.[9] Bank accounts, even those containing only exempt funds, can be frozen for days or even weeks, and may eventually be seized unless exemptions are properly pursued. Wages can be garnished. Cars and other property can be seized. Defeating a collection action eliminates these threats. Even if a default judgment has already been entered, an attorney can assist the consumer either in setting aside the default judgment or in minimizing the impact of these creditor remedies.

2.1.7 Collection Clients Often Have FDCPA, FCRA, and Other Consumer Claims

Representing consumers in collection actions can lead to subsequent affirmative actions under the FDCPA, FCRA, and other federal and state statutes, resulting in significant actual and statutory damages and attorney fees, either on an individual or classwide basis. Investigating the facts relating to the collection action will often uncover various systematic law violations.

The consumer's attorney should normally not pursue these affirmative claims without first resolving the individual collection action, as there will be legal and tactical reasons to complete the collection action first.[10] Moreover, the client is unlikely to be interested in retaining an attorney to handle an affirmative action while that attorney turns down the request for representation in the collection action.

2.1.8 Development of Expertise and a Name in the Community

Collection actions, particularly those brought by debt buyers, are often not difficult to win for practitioners who develop expertise in this area. That capability in turn enhances one's reputation as a consumer attorney among judges, other attorneys, and the community at large, thus leading to increased referrals of other collection cases and also other consumer law matters.

2.1.9 Debt Collector May Have to Pay the Consumer's Attorney Fees

Attorneys often shy away from collection cases for fear their time will be uncompensated. The consumer may be willing to offer a modest retainer, which still may not cover the attorney's time and expenses. Nevertheless, there are a number of ways that a prevailing consumer can recover attorney fees from the collector, as set out in § 14.1, *infra*. Fees may be recovered for prevailing on certain counterclaims, or as a result of the collector's vexatious litigation, or by statute in about one-third of the states.

2.1.10 Defending a Collection Action Allows for a Class Action to Stay in State Court

The Class Action Fairness Act (CAFA) has resulted in many state court consumer class actions being removed to federal court.[11] Class actions can only avoid removal and stay in state court if they allege state law causes of action and contain fewer than 100 class members or seek less than $5 million. Otherwise they can be removed to federal court unless two-thirds of the class members and all the primary defendants are residents of the state.[12]

Defense of a consumer collection action provides an exception. A class counterclaim can not be removed to federal court even if it could be removed if brought as an

6 *See* § 14.2, *infra*.
7 *Id.*
8 *Id.*
9 *See* § 2.4, Ch. 12, *infra*.
10 *See* § 5.5, *infra*.
11 *See* § 5.5.4, *infra*.
12 *See* National Consumer Law Center, Consumer Class Actions § 2.4 (6th ed. 2006 and Supp.).

affirmative action.[13] CAFA allows the defendant to remove a case, not the plaintiff. Class counterclaims thus can stay in state court even if they allege federal causes of action.[14]

2.2 Setting Up a Consumer Collection Defense Legal Practice

2.2.1 *Obtaining Clients*

There seems to be an almost unlimited number of consumers being sued in collection actions needing representation. With effective marketing attorneys wishing to take these cases will typically find they have too many consumers seeking representation, not too few. Traditional sources of marketing are effective, such as the yellow pages, websites, and the like. Bar associations also have referral panels. Legal aid offices may welcome volunteers for consumer representation.

Other attorneys are particularly happy to provide referrals. Most attorneys will view such cases as economic drains and have no interest in either pursuing them or receiving compensation for the referral. They are thrilled to be able to refer the consumer to someone who makes known a willingness to take these cases.

Consumers who have been sued may try to consult lawyers in general practice, family law attorneys, personal injury attorneys, and others. Getting one's name around to these attorneys should produce a steady supply of clients. Advertising or placing articles in the local bar association periodical can heighten the attorney's exposure.

A key referral source is bankruptcy attorneys, whom it often makes sense to contact in person, individually. Consumers being sued or with serious debt delinquencies often go to bankruptcy attorneys, and many of these are dissuaded from proceeding with a bankruptcy because their debt load is too low, the cost of filing bankruptcy is too high, or bankruptcy is not a good option for some other reason. Bankruptcy attorneys should be only too happy to refer such cases to a consumer attorney willing to explore other debt defense options. Bankruptcy trustees are another potential referral source.

Other sources of referrals are court clerks and even judges who on a daily basis see unrepresented consumers unable to adequately represent their interests in court. Effectively handling a few cases in a court can lead to many others. It is also worth exploring whether you can assist the local court in providing education to consumers and court personnel about collection actions. An attorney can even offer to hold a debtors' defense clinic.

13 *See* § 5.5.4, *infra*.
14 *Id.*

2.2.2 *Office Resources*

The attorney should obtain copies of all court rules for the courts where collection actions are traditionally brought. The attorney should also start collecting and organizing copies of all relevant statutes and case law. This library will slowly grow and will pay enormous dividends in the long run. Also included should be selected law treatises, including any state-specific manual on collection cases. Other particularly good choices are NCLC's *Fair Debt Collection*[15] and *Fair Credit Reporting*.[16] For deficiency cases following repossessions, an essential resource is NCLC's *Repossessions*.[17] For student loan cases, NCLC's *Student Loan Law*[18] is indispensable.

2.3 Steps Prior to Representation

2.3.1 *When the Consumer Has Not Yet Been Sued*

Consumers may seek legal representation before they are sued on a debt. Debt collection contacts can be stopped by the consumer sending a "cease communication" letter to a collection agency or a debt buyer.[19] If that fails, an attorney letter should succeed.[20] The consumer can also be advised about how to document abusive collection contacts.[21]

The attorney should also explain to the consumer what a summons and complaint look like and how they are served. It is probably a good idea to advise the consumer to accept all certified mail, because failure to do so will likely shorten the time the consumer has to respond to a summons and increase the likelihood of a default. Upon receipt of a complaint the consumer should be advised to contact the attorney immediately.

2.3.2 *What the Client Should Bring to the First Interview*

The decision whether to take a case will be greatly facilitated by the consumer bringing to the first interview all relevant documentation. When talking to a prospective client on the phone, before almost anything else, tell the consumer not to write on any documents relating to the case. Too often consumers will have the original of such documents in front of them when calling the attorney, and use them to take notes!

15 (6th ed. 2008).
16 (6th ed. 2006 and Supp.).
17 (6th ed. 2005 and Supp.).
18 (3d ed. 2006 and Supp.).
19 National Consumer Law Center, Fair Debt Collection § 5.3.8 (6th ed. 2008).
20 *Id.* § 5.3.3.
21 *Id.* § 2.4.1.

Consumers should be told to bring in absolutely everything that has been sent to them regarding the matter, including envelopes. Consumers should also bring in all debt collection correspondence, any answering machine that has messages from collectors, any and all statements and paperwork relating to the account, any canceled checks or bank statements reflecting payments, and even the credit card itself. Consumers who have already received a credit report should bring it in too; but consumers who have not yet obtained their report should be told to wait to do so until they come to the attorney's office, when the report can be accessed using the precautions discussed in the next subsection.

A consumer who has defaulted on one debt likely has others. The attorney should consider having the consumer bring in this information concerning *all* of the consumer's debts. Such an over-inclusive request may also be the only way to insure that the consumer brings in all the documents related to the debt at issue, as the consumer is unlikely to have separate files for each debt. Finding out about all of the consumer's debts also will help the attorney formulate a strategy to protect the consumer's assets. Fighting off one judgment will not do much good for consumers who already have, or in the near future will have, other judgments entered against them. The documents relating to other debts may also uncover Fair Debt Collection Practices Act or other consumer law violations that the attorney may decide are worth pursuing.

2.3.3 Reviewing the Consumer's Credit Report

A consumer's credit report is a key document that can help the attorney unravel many aspects of a case. It will usually show the current status of an account, the amount owed, and who provided that information. It will also show the history of the account and who reported that historical information.

The report will show the last payment date, which can help determine if the statute of limitations has run, and will indicate public record information, such as bankruptcies. The report can provide evidence of identity theft, or that the collector has mistakenly sued the wrong consumer. The credit report itself will also disclose who has obtained it in the past year. As a result the report may show that a particular collector knew or should have known of the exculpatory information reported and that the collector still pursued its predetermined course of action, thus proving that it engaged in the misconduct willfully, intentionally, and with full knowledge of its wrongdoing.

The consumer is entitled to one free report a year from each of the three major reporting agencies, most easily accessed over the Internet. Details on obtaining a report are found in § 14.2.3, *infra*. A good strategy may be to obtain only one free report at first, and save the other two free reports for a later time.

It makes sense for the consumer to obtain the report in the attorney's office with the assistance of the attorney or the attorney's staff, and with the aid of the attorney's Internet connection and printers. Unskilled consumers who attempt to access their reports on their own may mistakenly purchase extra services that the credit bureaus foist on them, seek more than one credit report, or fail to properly print out the report or save it electronically. If the attorney seeks to do this with the consumer's permission, but without the consumer present, the attorney may not know various identifying information that is required to pull the report. Obtaining the report with the consumer shows the consumer how to do it in the future, and also eliminates any question as to whether the attorney had authority to obtain the report.

2.3.4 The Client Interview

An attorney should develop a system to obtain basic information from the client without taking up too much of the attorney's time, so that the attorney can focus on the important parts of the interview. This habit is particularly important when the attorney follows the useful practice of obtaining information not just about the debt in question, but about all of the consumer's debt issues. While all that information may be invaluable in effectively representing the consumer, it can also take a long time to review all of this information.

One approach is to have a paralegal or office assistant work with the consumer in recording basic information. Another approach is to develop a standard questionnaire that the consumer can be asked to fill out with or without the assistance of office staff. Some questions can be sent to the consumer in advance, or asked over the telephone.

The attorney can then focus on the more important parts of the interview. An essential part of any client interview is to lower client expectations if they are too high. It is much better for a client to be pleasantly surprised by an outcome than to be disappointed by an outcome that the consumer's own attorney believes to be a good one.

Another key issue is to determine the procedural status of a case. Besides talking to the consumer and reviewing the documents the consumer brings in, this task may require contacting the opponent's attorney or the court. Has the consumer just been served with the complaint? Is an answer or response to admissions due imminently or overdue? Has the collector moved for summary judgment? Has the consumer defaulted? Has the collector obtained a default judgment? How long ago? Has the collector begun instituting post-judgment remedies?

Some collection actions are not even brought in court, but in arbitration. What stage is that proceeding? Has notice been given to the consumer about the arbitration? Has an award been issued? Is there still time under state law to vacate the award or oppose its confirmation?

In particular note all deadlines, such as those to answer the complaint or respond to requests for admissions. Determine whether the court where the action is brought is in the judicial district where the consumer resides or where the contract was signed. Otherwise venue may not be proper.[22]

Also listen to and hear everything the consumer has to say. Potentially material information includes anything about the consumer's health, job, and age, as well as any debt collection contacts prior to the collection action, and even the nature of the transaction underlying the debt. Look for any evidence of identity theft, and anything that might lead to a counterclaim. Check to see if the consumer is in, or recently was on, active duty in the military, as this status provides special defenses.[23]

A collection case can drag on for some time, and can be further extended if there is any follow-up litigation.[24] It is important for the attorney to be able to communicate with the client over that period, so it is useful to obtain additional contact information for the client, such as all telephone and cell phone numbers, e-mail addresses, and work and home addresses, as well as contact information for two or three other people who will always know how to reach the consumer.

A key issue in any collection action will be the consequences for the consumer of a judgment for the collector. In particular, what assets and wages can the collector seize pursuant to the judgment? This issue is explored in § 2.3.5, *infra*.

Carefully read the complaint and all attachments. If attachments are missing, do not assume the consumer lost them. Debt buyers frequently fail to attach those attachments referenced in the complaint. Note whether the plaintiff is the original creditor or a debt buyer. See what evidence is attached to the complaint that a debt buyer in fact owns the debt. If a contract is available review the choice of law provision.

Compute whether the limitations period has run. A key factor will be determining when the last payment was made on the account. Another factor will be whether the forum state's limitations period applies or whether a shorter limitations period from the state chosen in the contract's choice of law provision applies. Also determine from the complaint exactly what causes of action the collector is alleging, and see what evidence the collector may have for each cause of action. Look at the attorney fees and finance charges being sought and determine if they are legal under existing law and whether the collector can justify them.

Ask the consumer in detail about the underlying transaction that resulted in the debt. Did it involve medical debt, a student loan, a dishonored check, a credit card, a cell phone bill, or the like? Each different type of debt may present different defenses and counterclaims.[25] For example, if the collector is seeking a deficiency after an automobile repossession, then the attorney should explore with the consumer the nature of the default (did the creditor suddenly repossess after customarily allowing late payment, thus possibly waiving default), whether the creditor complied with a state right to cure or right to reinstate law, whether the repossession breached the peace, what notices of sale and of a deficiency the consumer received, and other aspects of the repossession. The attorney should even ask about the underlying sale of the vehicle to see if there were unfair sales tactics, credit violations, or problems with the vehicle.

Explore whether the consumer was the principal owner of a credit account, or only an authorized user. What is the basis for the consumer's alleged liability? Does the consumer believe payments were made that are not reflected in the account balance? Are there unauthorized charges involved?

2.3.5 Follow-Up Investigation

A key factor in any collection action will be the normal litigation tactics of both the collector and the collector's attorney. Do the collector and collection attorney typically pursue cases aggressively or do they drop them upon the first hint that the matter will be contested? Is the collector's attorney even familiar with what is necessary to prevail in a contested action?

Other attorneys are probably the best source of information on the litigation tendencies of the collector and the collector's attorney. The collector and collector's attorney can also be the subject of a Westlaw or Lexis search, or a search of a state-specific litigation database, similar to the federal PACER system.

2.3.6 Do Judgment-Proof Debtors Need Representation?

An important part of a client interview is to understand the client's assets and income that are at risk if the collector prevails in the court action. A debtor who possesses *only* exempt assets is referred to as "judgment proof" or "collection proof." While a judgment may be taken against such a person, the creditor can not compel collection of the judgment from the debtor's income or assets, unless the debtor fails to properly claim the exemption or circumstances change.

Judgment-proof debtors formerly were unlikely to be sued except by high-volume collection firms that do not make any pre-suit assessment of the prospects of collection.

22 *See* § 3.3, *infra*.
23 *See* Ch. 7, *infra*.
24 *See* Ch. 14, *infra*.

25 *See, e.g.*, Chs. 4, 9–11, *infra*.

The growth of the bad debt buying industry, however, is making suits against judgment-proof debtors more common.

In addition a creditor may pursue a judgment because the debtor's or the exempt property's status may change in the future. For example, in many states a homestead loses that status when the owner-occupant dies, and a judgment lien will generally be paid by the decedent's estate to clear the title. The debtor may receive training that makes employment viable. Also the creditor may need to obtain a judgment in order to protect the debt from being barred by the statute of limitations.

A client's limited vulnerability to judgment is often the key factor in devising a strategy of representation. The advocate must first determine which of the low-income client's assets are available to creditors. A debtor who has nonexempt wages may want to consider a chapter 7 (liquidating) bankruptcy if there are substantial debts and little other property available to creditors.[26] Nonexempt equity in a home threatened by creditors presents yet a different scenario and suggests that consideration should be given to a chapter 13 (installment payment plan) bankruptcy.[27] While property exemption laws are fundamental to bankruptcy cases, many exemptions are also available outside of bankruptcy and a truly judgment-proof debtor is not likely to need bankruptcy at all.

Some attorneys consider defense of a debt collection suit brought against a judgment-proof client to be a low priority unless there is a substantial potential counterclaim. It is important to remember, however, that judgment-proof individuals are sometimes targets for debt collection abuse. Because ordinary legal tactics are not effective, collectors attempt to scare these judgment debtors into paying "voluntarily." Representing a consumer in an affirmative suit against a debt collector for collection abuse may remove a source of grave stress for the client and provide some relief for the client's financial hardship.[28] In addition an unsatisfied judgment can stay on the consumer's credit record until the statute of limitations for the judgment has expired, but no less than seven years.[29] Finally, the growth of the debt buyer industry means that judgment debts are rarely abandoned. Debt buyers may invoke post-judgment remedies repeatedly over a period of years until they find some asset that the debtor can not protect or fails to protect.

In addition, in a particularly disturbing and growing development, bank accounts are often being frozen even though they contain only exempt funds. This practice means that for a period of days or even weeks, or even permanently, the consumer loses access to funds to pay for the basic necessities of life, even though under federal law these funds are exempt from garnishment.

2.3.7 *Case Selection*

2.3.7.1 Procedural Status of the Case

2.3.7.1.1 Collection actions filed in court

The first criterion in deciding whether to take a case is the procedural status of the litigation. Sometimes the consumer comes to the attorney years after a default or stipulated judgment was entered, when the collector is just getting around to garnishing wages or bank accounts. The first step will require the consumer to set aside a default judgment and then successfully defend the collection action. Most jurisdictions establish special hurdles to set aside a default judgment entered more than one year earlier, but even then relief is still possible.[30] At this point the attorney will have to decide whether setting aside the judgment is the appropriate approach, whether the consumer should file bankruptcy, or whether the attorney should help the consumer resist the creditor's remedies.[31] If a default judgment has not been entered in a case, then the factors discussed in the succeeding subsections will determine case selection.

2.3.7.1.2 Collection actions filed with an arbitration provider

With increasing frequency collection actions are being brought as an arbitration proceeding, in which event the attorney may have different views on taking a case, based upon the stage of that proceeding. Sometimes there is still time to respond to the arbitration action and participate in the proceeding, and then the attorney must decide if the consumer should participate *pro se*, whether the attorney should represent the consumer in the arbitration proceeding, or whether the consumer should not participate at all.[32] If the consumer does participate *pro se* the attorney can help the consumer understand how the proceeding works, help map out a defense, and advise the consumer to put in writing an objection to the proceeding, based on the lack of an enforceable arbitration agreement. Another option is to seek a court order enjoining the arbitration proceeding.[33]

If an arbitration award has been issued against the consumer the consumer has ninety days in most states, and less in some, to seek to vacate the award. An attorney's repre-

26 *See generally* National Consumer Law Center, Consumer Bankruptcy Law and Practice Ch. 3 (8th ed. 2006 and Supp.).

27 *See* National Consumer Law Center, Consumer Bankruptcy Law and Practice Ch. 4 (8th ed. 2006 and Supp.).

28 *See* National Consumer Law Center, Fair Debt Collection Ch. 10 (6th ed. 2008); § 12.4.1.5, *infra* (tort remedies for excessive wage garnishment).

29 15 U.S.C. § 1681c(a)(2); *see* National Consumer Law Center, Fair Credit Reporting § 5.2.3.4 (6th ed. 2006 and Supp.).

30 *See* § 13.2, *infra*.

31 *See* Ch. 12, §§ 13.2, 13.4, *infra*.

32 *See* § 8.2.4, *infra*.

33 *See* § 8.2.3, *infra*.

sentation at this stage is critical because the consumer's defenses are sharply narrowed if this deadline is missed, and because the potential defenses are quite specialized at this stage of the proceeding. An unrepresented consumer seeking to relitigate the same issues that were arbitrated is unlikely to get far.

If the deadline to seek to vacate the arbitration award is missed, the next stage will be the collector seeking to confirm the award in court. An attorney's participation will be critical at this stage, because the consumer's defenses here are quite limited and quite technical, such as that there is no arbitration agreement and thus no jurisdiction to hear the confirmation proceeding. These defenses are examined in § 8.4.4, *infra*.

2.3.7.2 The Client

An important consideration in the decision whether to take the case is the client. Is the client likely to stay in touch throughout the whole length of the case, or is the client likely to lose interest and fail to attend a critical hearing? Are the client's expectations unreasonably high, indicating it may be difficult to conclude the case to the client's satisfaction?

Of course the client's credibility will be important when the client is a witness. Beware of the client who believes he understands the law, particularly when that understanding includes some popular but bizarre legal theories, such as "no money lent," "illegally monetized" debt, or "vapor money" or when the client thinks he can pick a bogus arbitration company to rule the debt is not owed. The client may aggravate not only his own attorney but also the court.

The attorney must also warn the client of the risks of litigation, including the fact that the collector's attorney fees may be higher if the collector wins after a contested case than if the collector prevailed without a contest. A potential client's response to that warning should be a factor in case selection.

2.3.7.3 The Collector

Probably no factor will be as determinative of the nature of the litigation as the identity of the collector and, in particular, whether the collector is a debt buyer or the original creditor. A debt buyer will have purchased a debt for pennies on the dollar that the original creditor had decided was not worth pursuing. The debt buyer instead is using the state's courts to play a numbers game. A high percentage of cases will proceed to default judgment without the collector having to expend time marshalling evidence or otherwise incurring significant expenses. The debt buyer is betting that post-judgment remedies for all those cases will bring in more money than the debt buyer expended on purchasing and litigating all its debts. Such a debt buyer is unlikely to expend significant resources either coming to court with solid evidence or actually trying the case. The debt buyer may not even be able to prove it owns the debt with admissible evidence, if challenged by the consumer.

The original creditor, on the other hand, may have easy access to employee affidavits, and will usually be able to produce account statements and the credit contract, though not always.[34] The creditor should have no problem proving it owns the debt.

2.3.7.4 Other Factors

Good facts make good law. Do not try to make new law in a case in which the consumer clearly owes the money. It is much better to raise new legal theories when there is a good argument that the consumer does not owe the money and when the consumer is otherwise sympathetic.

Obviously the strength of the consumer's defense and the availability of counterclaims will be factors in taking a case, as will the availability of an attorney fee award for a prevailing consumer. An attorney must consider how much time a case will require in traveling to the court, and waiting around for the case to be heard. The attorney must also consider how many court appearances will be necessary and how often those court dates will be put off at the last minute by the collector. On the other hand, the consumer may be able to attend certain hearings instead of the attorney, depending on state procedure. For example, a consumer might attend an initial hearing to see if the action is disputed and merely state that a defense will be raised, with the court setting a later trial date.

Related to those factors is the type of court which will hear the action. In a small claims court pleadings may be minimal or nonexistent and the consumer or attorney can just appear at the trial date. A key question then is whether the court customarily grants the collector's continuance motions when someone appears for the defense, and whether the particular collection attorney routinely asks for a continuance only if an attorney shows up, or if even a consumer makes an appearance. In some situations one solution might be for the client to attend and obtain a definite trial date, at which the attorney can attend.

Another factor that varies depending on the court and a state's court system is the nature of the appeal from the trial court's decision. In some states there is the right to an appeal de novo to a higher court, meaning there is less incentive for the attorney to attend the first trial.

34 *See, e.g.*, Johnson v. MBNA, 357 F.3d 426 (4th Cir. 2004); *In re* Vee Vinhnee, 336 B.R. 437 (B.A.P. 9th Cir. 2005).

2.4 Minimizing the Impact of Creditor Post-Judgment Remedies

2.4.1 Introduction

Whether or not an attorney takes a case, the attorney can offer basic advice concerning minimizing the impact of the collector's post-judgment remedies. This advice will have immediate utility if a default or other judgment has already been entered and can also educate the consumer as to the stakes involved in defending a collection action *pro se* and steps to take to avoid the worst consequences of losing the case.

There sometimes can be a fine line between exemption planning and fraudulent transfers, and this line may vary from jurisdiction to jurisdiction. To the extent that the exemption planning is legal and ethical, the attorney can explore with the client converting nonexempt assets into exempt assets or transferring assets to others. The discussion in the rest of this section considers consumer actions that can protect income or property without involving such transfers.

2.4.2 Bank Accounts

A collector with a judgment can seize nonexempt funds from the consumer's bank account. Although some banks scrutinize accounts to determine whether they are comprised exclusively of exempt funds—in which case the bank declines the attachment order—the majority of banks do not. Upon receipt of a judgment creditor's request for attachment, most banks ignore even clear evidence of exempt funds—such as electronic deposit from the Social Security Administration—and simply freeze the recipient's bank account, depriving the consumer of the means to pay for the most basic of necessities. Subsequent monthly deposits into the account will also be subject to the freeze and inaccessible to the recipient. The funds will remain frozen for a time, and then turned over to the collector unless the consumer prevails in an objection.

Procedures to "unfreeze" an account will vary by state. For example, in some states the consumer will have to fill out, file, and serve a form stating that the funds in the account are exempt and provide accompanying proof—letters from the Social Security Administration and bank statements. A collector agreeing to release the funds sends a release to the bank, and it often takes days or even weeks before the funds are actually released. If the collector does not agree to release the funds, the consumer must seek a court hearing. The collector may later seek to seize funds from the same account again, requiring the consumer to repeat the same process.

One new approach to avoid these problems is to ask the Social Security Administration, the Veterans Administration, or whatever federal agency is sending the consumer exempt funds to sign the consumer up for the Direct Express card, a stored value card on which the funds will be electronically deposited and which can be used like a debit card to access cash and to make purchases. Funds deposited onto the Direct Express card will not be subject to garnishment *or* freezing.[35] This arrangement is generally a better alternative than a consumer taking a paper check and paying a check casher to cash the payment.

If the consumer is going to deposit exempt funds into a bank account it is safest to set up a separate account just to receive those funds. Exempt funds usually remain exempt even when commingled with nonexempt funds, but there can be tracing problems, plus in some states the funds are more likely to be frozen if they are commingled.

If all the funds in an account are exempt, and the collector already knows about an account or is likely to discover it, the consumer can deter the collector from seizing the funds by notifying the collector and its attorney of that fact. Consumers should also notify their attorney if the account is frozen. This precaution may also lead to a Fair Debt Collection Practices Act (FDCPA) claim against the collector and the collector's attorney if they do try to seize the funds. Nevertheless, recent FDCPA case law recommends providing more than mere notice, in favor of sending the collector actual proof of the exempt status of the funds, such as sworn statements with documentary evidence. Even then an actionable FDCPA claim may require showing that the collector employed an actual false statement in connection with the garnishment.[36]

Of course, if funds are not deposited in a bank, they can not be seized. Thus a consumer can immediately cash small checks or endorse them over to others, for consideration. Consumers should avoid highly priced check cashers.

Collectors will also seek to seize any bank account with the consumer's name on it. Consumers who have or expect to have a judgment entered against them should remove their names from any account that holds someone else's money (for example, accounts containing funds owned by another family member, such as an elderly parent or a child). If the owner of the funds needs the consumer to manage the account, a power of attorney should be used or the account should be clearly designated as a trust.

---

35 There are very narrow situations in which these funds may be garnished. Social Security—but not SSI—funds may be garnished to pay child support and alimony, and can also be administratively offset to satisfy debts owed to the federal government, such as taxes or student loans. Administrative offsets are deducted from the funds before payment is even made, whether it is made by direct deposit, by paper check, or onto the Direct Express card.

36 *Compare* Beler v. Blatt Hasenmiller Leibsker Moore, L.L.C., 480 F.3d 470 (7th Cir. 2007) *with* Todd v. Weltman Weinberg Reis Co., L.P.A., 348 F. Supp. 2d 903 (S.D. Ohio 2004), *aff'd*, 434 F.3d 432 (6th Cir. 2006).

2.4.3 Wages

The attorney can explain to the consumer when wages are at risk and the amount that can be seized. State law may provide for more protections beyond the minimum limits on garnishment that federal law imposes.[37] Until July 23, 2009, no garnishment can be made if an employee's disposable earnings are $196.50 or less for the week in question. When an employee's disposable earnings exceed $196.50 but are less than $262.00, only the amount over $196.50 can be garnished. For example, if an employee's gross earnings in a particular week are $250.00, and disposable earnings are $220.00, only $23.50 may be garnished and $196.50 must be paid to the employee. Twenty-five percent of an employee's disposable earnings can be garnished if those earnings are $262.00 or more in a given week.

After July 23, 2009, when the minimum wage increases to $7.25 per hour, no garnishment will be allowed if an employee's disposable earnings are $217.50 or less for the week in question. If an employee's disposable earnings exceed $217.50 but are less than $290.00, only the amount over $217.50 will be allowed to be garnished. When an employee's disposable earnings are $290.00 or more in a given week, up to twenty-five percent of those earnings will be subject to garnishment.

The wages that are exempt are the "disposable earnings," that is, the wages available after applicable taxes and other "amounts required by law to be withheld" are deducted.[38] As a result, consumers who under-withhold taxes expose themselves to greater garnishment while at the same time do not pay down their tax liability. Consumers who pay child support should consider having those payments made by way of wage deduction. Each dollar of a child support wage deduction reduces the consumer's disposable earnings that could otherwise be subject to garnishment by judgment creditors.

2.4.4 Property

A consumer's property can be seized to pay a judgment to the extent to which the equity in that property is not exempt. For example, if a state has a $100,000 homestead exemption and the consumer's home is valued at $200,000 and is subject to a $105,000 mortgage, then the home is exempt from seizure. The consumer has $95,000 in equity in the home and there is a $100,000 exemption.

Some states require that a homestead declaration be recorded before the exemption is effective.[39] This declaration should be recorded before judgment is entered, at the first meeting with the attorney. Whether this declaration will be effective as to preexisting debts that have not yet been reduced to a judgment is a question of state law, but the sooner the homestead declaration is recorded the better.

If a judgment is against one spouse, the attorney can make sure that assets that are in fact held as tenancies by the entirety are properly labeled as such. Property held in such a tenancy by the entirety can not be seized to pay the debts of only one of the owners.[40] Although an attorney may not advise a consumer to fraudulently transfer assets, property that is in fact owned by another should not have the consumer's name associated with that property.

2.5 The Bankruptcy Alternative

A chapter 7 bankruptcy filing wipes out unsecured debts and eliminates the need to defend the collection action. Because nonexempt assets will be lost in a chapter 7 bankruptcy and because of the cost involved, bankruptcy may not make sense to discharge one small debt. It is a powerful remedy when a consumer has a significant amount of unsecured debt and minimal nonexempt assets. When a consumer has significant nonexempt assets, filing under chapter 13 may be a better alternative as it typically will significantly reduce the portion of an unsecured debt that must be repaid and allows that amount to be paid out over a period of years.

There is no rush to file bankruptcy, as the bankruptcy can discharge the obligation even after a judgment has been entered, and often can even avoid liens that a creditor places on the consumer's property after judgment. Bankruptcy will not discharge debts incurred after the bankruptcy filing, so the timing of a bankruptcy filing is important. Absent the immediate loss of property or income, it is usually premature to file bankruptcy until the consumer's financial picture has stabilized. Any additional debts that are expected to mount up can only be discharged by waiting to file bankruptcy. Probably the best course of action is to consider the bankruptcy option early, but let the bankruptcy attorney determine the appropriate time to actually file. The consumer might consider starting credit counseling, which is a precondition to filing bankruptcy (cost ranges from $30 to $50, but can be waived for indigency), but counseling must be completed no more than 180 days before the bankruptcy filing.

More on the bankruptcy option is found in § 13.4, *infra*. A good chapter explaining bankruptcy to the consumer is found in *NCLC Guide to Surviving Debt*[41] and a brochure on bankruptcy rights may be found at www.consumerlaw.org. Other NCLC publications provide information on bankruptcy for the consumer attorney, as described below.

If bankruptcy is an option, the attorney can refer the consumer to a bankruptcy specialist or to a bar association pro bono bankruptcy program. A relationship between a

37 *See* § 12.4.3, *infra*.
38 *See* 15 U.S.C. § 1672(b).
39 *See* § 12.5.2, *infra*.
40 *See* §§ 12.5.3.4, 12.7, *infra*.
41 Ch. 19 (2008).

bankruptcy attorney and a consumer attorney can be mutually beneficial. The bankruptcy specialist can refer clients to the consumer attorney when a bankruptcy is not appropriate or when the consumer has substantial consumer law claims. The consumer attorney refers clients to the bankruptcy attorney when bankruptcy may be the best course of action.

The consumer attorney can also handle the bankruptcy for the client. An initial intake interview has already been conducted and a relationship established. Bankruptcy is not nearly as intimidating as many think. NCLC's *Bankruptcy Basics*[42] takes the attorney through all the necessary steps with clear guidance. Software available on the companion website to that manual facilitates the attorney filling out the initial forms on the attorney's own computer. NCLC's *Consumer Bankruptcy Law and Practice*[43] is an even more comprehensive practice manual.

2.6 *Pro Se* Representation

Attorneys who determine not to represent the consumer can still give the consumer information on *pro se* representation. The attorney can explain the importance of not missing court dates and of responding to requests for admission.

A strict warning can be given about communications with the collector's attorney. Sample settlement language can be spelled out. The consumer should be advised to check with the court clerk regarding the status of a case, particularly after settlement, in order to prevent the collector's attorney from obtaining a default judgment after the consumer believed the case was settled.

The consumer will also need specific information on how to appear and defend a collection action for the particular court and the particular jurisdiction. In many states the bar association or a legal services office may have already created a step-by-step written guide that can be given to the consumer. If the collection action has been filed in a small claims court that does not require pleadings, then the attorney may be able to provide sufficient advice during a brief interview.

2.7 Scams to Avoid

Attorneys should advise consumers as to certain scams to avoid. The marketplace is rife with companies preying on those in debt, and consumers compound their difficulties by signing up for one of these pitches.

One common scam is the debt elimination company that, for a fee, promises to explain how to eliminate debt. Some offer various instruments, such as a "bond for discharge of debt" or a "redemption certificate" that the debtor is to present to the creditor supposedly to force the creditor to relinquish the debt. These scams are not only ineffective, but their use may be a federal crime. Another useless scheme sets up an arbitration proceeding that is programmed to produce a ruling that the debt is invalid.

Just as problematical are debt settlement companies that require consumers to make their payments to the debt settlement company and not the creditor. The company takes an up-front fee and a percentage of each payment and puts the rest of the payment in a segregated account. At a later point, if enough money is accumulated, the debt settlement company promises to negotiate with creditors and satisfy the debt with part payment using the accumulated sums. Typically the fees are so high that the consumer never accumulates enough money, and the only winner is the debt settlement company. Even when settlements are arranged, the fees are so high that consumers might have been better off negotiating settlements on their own.

Other scams involve debt consolidation and home equity loans that result in large fees, high interest rates, and eventually the consumer losing far more than would have been lost based upon the simple collection action. Payday and auto title loans also will just sink the consumer deeper in debt and are not a solution. Consumers should be warned about overdrawing their bank account through use of a check, debit card, or ATM withdrawal, which results in astronomical bank fees, and effective interest rates that exceed even payday loan rates.

2.8 Collection Litigation

2.8.1 Tactical Considerations

Different consumer attorneys utilize very different tactics in collection defense cases, depending on their jurisdiction, the applicable court, and the attorney's own preferences. One approach is to litigate the case aggressively from the start, sending extensive discovery to the collector, filing motions, and raising counterclaims. This approach will often lead to the collector either leaving the case in limbo or, at some point, bringing a summary judgment motion, seeking to dispose of the case without a trial. This summary judgment motion is examined in § 2.8.4, *infra*. When the summary judgment motion fails, the collector may stop pursuing the case.

The opposite approach is to minimize the attorney's time and pre-trial discovery, and just appear at trial and see if the collector is prepared to prove its case. Collectors usually show up with either insufficient or inadmissible evidence, because they are used to an unrepresented consumer either defaulting or presenting an ineffective challenge at trial.

In choosing between these two models one factor will be local rules. For example, some court rules require the con-

42 (2007).

43 (8th ed. 2006 and Supp.).

sumer's attorney to file an appearance prior to trial. The necessity to respond to requests for admissions or to file an answer may force the consumer attorney to expend resources prior to the trial, as will the necessity to move to set aside a default judgment.

A consumer's litigation tactics will also be shaped by the nature of the collector. A debt buyer is unlikely to have access to the credit contract or to affidavits from the original creditor's employees to authenticate business records. On the other hand, the original creditor may have access to this evidence, yet the creditor's cost-benefit determination may still prevent it from producing this information at trial.

Another factor affecting litigation tactics will be the probability of the consumer recovering an attorney fee. When the likelihood is low, then the attorney may wish to minimize the number of hours devoted to the case, including minimizing pre-trial motions.

2.8.2 First Litigation Steps

The consumer's answer should admit as little as possible because the collector will have trouble proving facts on its own.[44] Depending on local rules, failure to plead an affirmative defense in the consumer's answer may constitute waiver of that defense. It is thus critical in many courts to affirmatively plead that the statute of limitations has expired and the like. These defenses may also lead to the consumer filing a motion to dismiss. A motion to dismiss is appropriate if the collector's own pleadings indicate the date of default and that the applicable limitations period has expired.

The plaintiff's failure to obey local rules that require it to append to the complaint documents substantiating its claim can also lead to a motion to dismiss. One example is when a collector pleads breach of contract and fails to attach a copy of the contract as required by local rule. On the other hand, the consumer can raise this objection later at trial. Making the motion at the start of the trial may just educate the collector and help the collector prepare its case.

It is critical to determine from the collector's complaint exactly what legal theories are being pleaded in order to know, among other things, the elements the collector must prove, the applicable statute of limitations, whether the collector is entitled to attorney fees or finance charges, and which state's law applies.[45] The consumer should request a more definite statement or seek dismissal for failure to state a claim if there is any uncertainty or if there is sufficient ambiguity that the collector may try to swap theories midway through the case.

Pay careful attention to a collector's request for admissions. If the consumer fails to timely respond, the statements will be deemed admitted. If the time to respond has already passed, then immediately ask the collector's attorney for an extension and, if denied, then make a request to the judge. An unrepresented consumer should be in a strong position to withdraw such an admission and ask for additional time to respond.[46] If the time period to respond has not been missed, then § 4.2.2.2, *infra*, provides advice as to responses to the collector's requests for admissions. When the consumer's memory and the facts allow, there is little additional risk to denying core requests to admit liability in cases in which collectors who successfully prove the debt would in any event be entitled to recover reasonable attorney fees and costs under the contract or substantive law to the same extent as they would be as a consequence of the consumer's denial of a request for admission.

2.8.3 The Consumer's Discovery

Discovery in a collection case has much broader implications than just developing facts for the litigation. Refraining from taking discovery at all may be appropriate when the collector assumes the case will result in a default judgment or a simple trial and therefore may not be prepared with sufficient evidence to meet its burden of proof. Discovery may in fact force the collector to pull together its evidence and be more prepared for trial, when it otherwise would not be.

On the other hand, sending extensive discovery can delay a case or even convince the collector that the case is not worth pursuing. The collector may ignore the discovery request and refrain from prosecuting the case. The consumer can attempt to compel discovery, send a series of letters to the collector reminding the collector that discovery is overdue, or just do nothing and wait for developments.

This standoff between the parties can keep a case in limbo for years. In this situation, it is important for the attorney to make sure that the consumer keeps in touch with the attorney the whole time. The consumer will still need legal representation if the same or another collector revives the old case or brings a new case. Bringing a second case on the same debt without first resolving the first case may be a Fair Debt Collection Practices Act (FDCPA) violation, emphasizing the need for the consumer to stay in touch with the attorney. One technique is for the consumer's attorney to periodically update the client as to the status of the case, even if it is just by a form letter stating that the case is still pending.

Discovery in a collection case can also be used to develop evidence as to the nature of collection contacts and related actions that may lead to FDCPA claims. Ask for collection notes and communications from the debt collector to the consumer. In other words, the collector's lawsuit can provide the vehicle to find evidence to determine whether an FDCPA case is worth bringing separately.

44 *See* § 4.2, *infra*.

45 *See* § 4.4, *infra*.

46 *See* § 4.2.2.3, *infra*.

2.8.4 The Collector's Summary Judgment Motion

In an attempt to avoid a time-consuming trial, collectors may resort to a summary judgment motion. The motion may be based on statements deemed admitted by the consumer because the consumer failed to timely respond to a request for admissions. Or the motion can be based on an affidavit from an employee of the collector and various "business records" attached to the motion.

When the consumer's discovery requests are outstanding, the consumer should argue that summary judgment is premature until the consumer receives all of the requested discovery. The collector can not argue that there are no facts in dispute if the consumer has not had a chance to obtain all the facts.

Carefully review the affidavits and records supporting a summary judgment motion. Look for inconsistencies between the affidavits and documents and even between the facts alleged in the summary judgment motion and in the attachments. Of course documents referenced in the motion but not attached should have no weight. For example, debt buyers often seek to prove they own a debt by attaching a bulk transfer agreement and then reference a computer tape or document that allegedly shows that the contract at issue was part of that bulk transfer, but no computer tape or document is in fact attached.[47]

Determine if attached records meet all of the requirements of the business records exception to the hearsay rule. In particular there must be an affidavit from someone who on personal knowledge can attest that the record was made at or near the time of the occurrence set forth in the record and that the record was kept in the regular course of business.[48] Debt buyer employees should not be able to introduce business records produced by the original creditor.[49] Debt buyers also often seek to prove a fact by a conclusory affidavit, which is no substitute for the actual business records.

The consumer can present counter-affidavits and documents to create a factual dispute to defeat the summary judgment motion. Certainly the court should not utilize a different standard for acceptable affidavits from the consumer than from the collector.

A court should not order summary judgment for the total amount the collector seeks if there are factual disputes as to certain elements. The consumer can present facts showing that some or the entire amount sought has been paid, that the collector agreed to accept payments in full satisfaction of the debt, that certain charges were unauthorized, that the consumer never received a proffered contract, and the like.

2.8.5 The Trial

Sometimes the best course of action is for only the consumer's attorney and not the consumer to appear at trial. A common collector technique when it has insufficient evidence to prove its case is to call the consumer to the stand and to try to prove its case using the consumer's own testimony. For example, it can ask the consumer to authenticate various documents when it has not brought its own witness to trial. If it is unclear whether the consumer will be needed to testify in his own defense, one option is for the consumer to wait nearby, but not so close that the collector can call the consumer to the stand in the case in chief.

If the case is to be heard by a jury or before certain judges, it may be better to have the consumer testify or at least appear in the courtroom, even if the result is that the collector can then prove some of the elements of its case through the consumer. Otherwise the jury will be wondering why the consumer did not appear. Even if the consumer's attorney does not plan to call the consumer as a witness, if the consumer does appear in the courtroom the consumer should be prepared to testify. The consumer's attorney should explain how cross-examination works and what are proper responses to such questioning (in other words, yes or no answers).

When the collector produces a witness make sure the hearsay rules are enforced and that the witness testifies based upon firsthand knowledge. Business records should be introduced only if they meet the exceptions to the hearsay rules. The consumer's attorney may even come into court with a few short "pocket briefs" arguing why certain business records or testimony is inadmissible as hearsay. The attorney should be prepared with a copy of the applicable rules of evidence, particularly the rules regarding admissibility of documents, hearsay, and the business records exception to the hearsay rule.

The consumer's attorney should give some consideration to having a court reporter present. Some courts automatically provide a court reporter, but in others arrangements have to be made for a court reporter to be hired. A number of factors must be weighed in deciding whether to incur this expense. When an appeal is possible, there may be little for the appellate court to review if there is no transcript.[50] The trial court decision may simply specify the amount the collector is to recover.

If the consumer has a right to a trial de novo, the trial transcript will be useful as a tool to remind the consumer's attorney as to testimony and argument in the first trial and for impeachment. A trial transcript may also have the effect of formalizing the proceeding so that it is more likely that the collector will have to follow the rules of evidence in

47 *See* § 4.3, *infra*.
48 *See* § 4.2.4, *infra*.
49 *Id.*

50 *Cf.* Asset Acceptance L.L.C. v. Lemon, 2007 WL 3408304 (Ohio Ct. App. Nov. 5, 2007).

introducing records and the like, and the court may be more detailed in its rulings.

2.9 Settlement, the Court's Decision, Post-Judgment Actions

2.9.1 The Court's Order for the Consumer

Consumers who assert that they never owed the debt—for example, because of identity theft, because the wrong consumer has been sued, or because of a valid dispute on the debt—should seek more than just dismissal of the case with prejudice. The consumer ultimately will want to clean up their credit report so that it contains no evidence of the debt. It will not be enough to show that the current balance is zero. The report should delete all historical record of the debt being overdue.

A decision that states that the consumer never owed the debt will facilitate deleting this historical information[51] The court might even order the collector to correct the consumer's credit report as part of its judgment.

2.9.2 Settlement

Dismissing the consumer's counterclaims with prejudice along with the collector's claims will constitute res judicata, barring a subsequent action. If the consumer wishes to bring the counterclaims in a subsequent action, the settlement must dismiss the collector's claim with prejudice, but not the counterclaims.

Any settlement of the action should dismiss the lawsuit with prejudice using a court order or a document filed with the court. There can be a written consent order to judgment; the parties can agree to a voluntary or involuntary dismissal; the court can issue a written order, or orally state "on the record" that the case is dismissed. The case can be dismissed with conditions, which can presented to the court or not; the court can include the conditions in an order; or the conditions can just be filed with the court. The important point is that the case has been formally dismissed, the consumer can not be sued on the debt again, and the consumer has a certified document to use in cleaning up the credit report.

Any settlement of the debt should also include a provision requiring the collector to clean up the consumer's credit report. Reproduced below is a sample settlement provision that requires the creditor to withdraw the entire report of the disputed debt. This withdrawal is sometimes referred to as a "hard delete." The credit record will then be altogether silent about the debt and will not even provide a basis for another creditor, interested in the creditworthiness of the consumer, to inquire further. This approach is often the simplest solution for the consumer and the safest. When a debt buyer brings the action, the language will have to be modified to only require deletion of information provided by that entity.

> It is further agreed that [*name of creditor*] shall take all steps necessary to ensure that no credit report or credit reference that is unfavorable or that may be construed unfavorably to [*name of consumer*] shall be made by it or to any consumer reporting agency with regard to any debts or claims as between [*creditor*] and [*consumer*]. Without limiting the effect of the foregoing obligation, [*creditor*] shall also within ten days hereof send notice [*in writing or electronically or both*] [*in the form attached hereto as Appendix A*], to each consumer reporting agency to which the creditor has reported any information about [*consumer*], deleting from its files all references to the [*alleged*] debt which is the subject of this settlement agreement. To that end, [*creditor*] shall submit a [*Metro II form coded with "DA" (delete account)*] [*and/or*] [*a Universal Data Form with the "Delete Tradeline" option box checked*] to each consumer reporting agency to which the creditor has reported any information about the consumer. Prior to any execution of any release of claims by [*consumer*], [*creditor*] shall submit to counsel for [*consumer*] clear and complete copies of these forms (with [*creditor's*] subscriber/password code redacted if [*creditor*] chooses) and proof that [*creditor*] has submitted these forms. Each required "Universal Data Form" or the equivalent must contain [*creditor's*] certification that it has modified its internal records so that the information to be deleted is not re-reported. In the event Plaintiffs discover, more than forty-five days following [*creditor's*] submission of the [*Metro II form*] [*Universal Data form*] as described, that any consumer reporting agency still reports the alleged debt, [*consumer*] may notify [*creditor*] in writing, and [*creditor*] will within ten business days resubmit a request for deletion of all reference to the debt.
>
> [*Creditor*] shall adjust its relevant internal records in a manner that will permanently reflect the agreed-upon status of the debt. [*Creditor*] agrees to take all steps necessary or appropriate to prevent the re-reporting of any information about the [*alleged*] debt. In the event any such information is re-reported to any consumer reporting agency, [*creditor*] agrees to take all steps necessary or appropriate to ensure that the re-reported information is deleted from the files of every consumer reporting agency to which the information was re-reported. Further, should a consumer reporting agency ever notify [*creditor*] that [*consumer*] is disputing the tradeline, [*creditor*] will not verify the tradeline or will confirm that the

51 *See* § 14.2, *infra*.

> tradeline should be deleted; in such an event, [*creditor*] will also submit to counsel for [*consumer*], within forty-five days after receiving the notification of the dispute from the consumer reporting agency, clear and complete copies of the notification of the dispute and any and all forms (including electronic forms) by which it responds to such notification (with [*creditor's*] subscriber/password code redacted if [*creditor*] chooses). [*Creditor*] further agrees that it will not assign, hypothecate, or transfer the [*alleged*] debt to another creditor, a collection agency, or any other third party, and that it will not alter the account number or otherwise relabel the account. The parties agree that time is of the essence of this contract. This release shall not extend to the obligations created by this Agreement or to any claim or cause of action based in whole or in part upon a communication to a consumer reporting agency after the date of this agreement.

Sometimes the consumer wishes to keep information about an account in the credit report to show a history of payments, and only wishes to delete adverse information supplied about the account. To accomplish this goal the settlement provisions must carefully delineate what information can not be furnished to an agency because it might be construed unfavorably to the client. Relevant sample settlement language is found in NCLC's *Fair Credit Reporting* Appx. J.9.3.[52] Even so, there is always the risk that even the limited information reported, though accurate in a narrow sense, will permit another creditor using the report to fill in the gaps incorrectly or to draw its own negative inferences. For example, if there was a dispute a creditor might suppose there was a default as well.

2.9.3 Attorney Fees

The prevailing consumer's attorney should file a request for attorney fees, when available, together with adequate documentation. Procedures will vary by state, and may also depend on the basis for the attorney fee award.

As described in § 14.1, *infra*, there are a number of bases on which a prevailing consumer can recover fees in a collection action. Surprisingly some contracts actually call for fees, not just for the collector, but for the prevailing party. About one-third of the states have statutes that allow the consumer to recover fees, at least in certain collection actions. Another basis may be a counterclaim under the Fair Debt Collection Practices Act (FDCPA), a deceptive practices (UDAP) statute, or other statute with fee provisions. A collector's vexatious litigation conduct may also provide a basis to recover fees. In addition, the consumer may recover fees as actual damages in follow-up litigation under the FDCPA or a related claim for the collector's litigation misconduct.[53]

---

52 (6th ed. 2006 and Supp.).

53 *See* § 14.4, *infra*.

Chapter 3 Dismissal Before Reaching the Merits

3.1 Introduction

This chapter focuses on consumer defenses that do not deal with the merits of the collector's claim: whether the action is brought in the proper court, whether pleading requirements have been met, whether the collector is qualified to bring the action, and whether the action is brought within the applicable statute of limitations. Typically these defenses are raised at the beginning of litigation, before the merits are decided. But sometimes they are raised later in the proceeding.

For example, the statute of limitations may be raised immediately in a motion to dismiss, if the defect is apparent from the pleadings, but may also be raised later in a summary judgment motion after the facts have been clarified. Moreover for tactical reasons, as discussed in Chapter 2, *supra*, the consumer may wish to wait until trial before raising defenses. But, no matter when the defense is raised, if it does not go to the merits of the collector's claims, then it is treated in this chapter.

One exception is service of process. Typically, when process is defective, the consumer never even becomes aware that a suit has been brought until after a default judgment has been entered. Setting aside a default judgment based upon defective service of process is examined in § 13.2.4, *infra*.

Standing to sue is another preliminary issue that is treated elsewhere. This chapter examines whether a collector is properly licensed or otherwise eligible to use a state's courts to bring a collection action. Chapter 4, *infra*, considers whether the collector bringing the lawsuit in fact has proven that it owns the debt or that the plaintiff on whose behalf it is bringing the action owns the debt.

3.2 Jurisdiction

Only rarely is a collection action brought in a court that does not have jurisdiction to hear the case. Consumer collection actions are rarely brought in federal court, so the consumer can not challenge that there is no federal jurisdiction. Similarly, the consumer is seldom able to remove the action to federal court, as the case will not involve federal jurisdiction.

Issues occasionally do arise as to whether the selected state court has jurisdiction over the claim. In some states, collectors prefer to bring actions in a small claims court or a similar, less formal court. Check to make sure that the action seeks an amount below any jurisdictional maximum for the court selected. If a collection action seeks to confirm an arbitration award, a state may also limit which court the confirmation proceeding may be brought in.[1]

3.3 Venue

A collector's action must comply with state venue rules. In addition, the action should comply with the Fair Debt Collection Practices Act (FDCPA), and also with Federal Trade Commission and state deceptive practices standards that similarly limit proper venue.

The FDCPA requires that any debt collector bring a lawsuit only in the judicial district in which the consumer signed the contract or resides at the time of the lawsuit.[2] The judicial district refers to the state district and not the federal district.[3]

The FDCPA provision applies to actions brought by debt buyers and also by collection attorneys and collection agencies bringing the court action on behalf of a creditor. The provision does not apply to the original creditor bringing an action *pro se*. Nevertheless, violating this provision has been defined as unfair and deceptive under the Federal Trade Commission Act and state deceptive practices statutes,[4] so that creditors should not be able to sue in an inconvenient venue either. Moreover, if the creditor files *pro se* but an attorney enters an appearance retaining control over the case, the FDCPA provision applies to that attorney.[5]

---

1 *See* § 8.5.5.2, *infra*.

2 15 U.S.C. § 1692i.

One exception is that an action to enforce an interest in real property securing the consumer's obligation must be brought in the district where the real property is located.

3 *See* Fox v. Citicorp Credit Services Inc., 15 F.3d 1507 (9th Cir. 1994); Nichols v. Byrd, 435 F. Supp. 2d 1101 (D. Nev. 2006).

4 *See* National Consumer Law Center, Unfair and Deceptive Acts and Practices § 5.1.1.4 (6th ed. 2004 and Supp.).

5 John F. LeFevre, Att'y, Fed. Trade Comm'n, Informal Staff Letter to Milton P. Goldfarb, Att'y, Newman, Goldfarb, Freyman & Stevens, P.C. (Nov. 23, 1988) (available on the companion website to this manual).

Although the collector can sue where the consumer signed the contract, if the collector is not suing on the contract and does not present the contract in evidence, the collector would be limited to suing in the judicial district where the consumer presently resides. If there are joint debtors on an obligation, residing in different judicial districts, the collector would have to bring two separate actions, each complying with the FDCPA venue rule. More on the FDCPA and venue requirements is found in NCLC's *Fair Debt Collection* § 5.9.[6]

If a collection action is brought in an improper venue, violating the FDCPA, the consumer has an action for actual and statutory damages and attorney fees.[7] But that does not resolve the question whether the federal law violation can be grounds to dismiss or move an action brought in an illegal venue.

First, determine whether there is any language in the state's venue statute or rules that would make it improper to bring an action in a venue prohibited by federal law. Even if there is not, the case can still be dismissed or moved pursuant to the common law notion of *forum non conveniens.* The United States Supreme Court has stated that a case can be dismissed on *forum non conveniens* grounds "when an alternative forum has jurisdiction to hear [the] case and. . . . trial in the chosen forum would establish . . . oppressiveness and vexation to the defendant . . . out of all proportion to plaintiff's convenience."[8] This reasoning should certainly apply to a case brought in violation of federal or state law in an inconvenient judicial district. The case can easily be refiled in the judicial district where the consumer resides, the consumer is harmed by the action brought in a distant forum, and the collector's convenience can not be considered when it seeks to bring a case in violation of federal law. The Supreme Court has made clear that *forum non conveniens* applies to damages actions in law and not just actions in equity.[9]

3.4 Forcing the Action into Arbitration

Most creditors today insert binding arbitration agreements in their credit agreements with the intent of preventing consumers from pursuing class actions and cases before juries seeking punitive damages. The agreements force consumers to arbitrate their disputes with the creditor, but most collectors prefer to bring collection actions in court, not in arbitration.[10] It may be that the consumer wishes to turn the tables on a collector, and force the collector to drop its lawsuit in court and instead bring the collection action in an arbitration proceeding.

Often arbitration clauses will give a defendant the option of requiring that an action proceed using arbitration. The creditor will avail itself of this option if the consumer initiates litigation, and is counting on the consumer not to raise this right when the creditor brings a court action. Consequently a simple appearance in the case, requesting the matter be referred to arbitration, will provide a surprise to the creditor, who may be unprepared to arbitrate the dispute. The creditor may not be geared up to submit the claim to arbitration, or high arbitration fees may discourage the creditor from pursuing the claim in arbitration.

In a bizarre turn of events, some collectors are so put off by consumer demands that collection actions be removed to arbitration, that they are inserting change-in-terms notices in their collection letters. The change-in-terms notice purports to nullify the arbitration clause in the original credit contract. Such a unilateral change is unlikely to be legally binding; among other reasons, the consumer is probably no longer allowed to use the card, so the collector can not rely on the consumer's continued use of the card to signify acceptance of the changed terms.[11] The collector's attempt to change the terms does indicate the consternation that some collectors feel when required to arbitrate, instead of going to court, to collect on a debt.

On the other hand, if the collector does proceed to arbitration, the consumer may be worse off. The creditor has selected the arbitration service provider and that provider has a greater incentive to please the creditor that selected it, and that will select it in the future, than it has to please an individual consumer. The arbitration service provider in turn selects the panel of arbitrators from whom the arbitrator is selected. Arbitration also involves very high payments to the arbitrator, and the consumer may have to share in those payments. Arbitration will significantly abbreviate the consumer's discovery. Moreover, the arbitrator need not even follow the law or the facts, and there is very limited judicial review of an arbitration decision.[12]

If the consumer does decide to try to force the case into arbitration, review the arbitration clause to see if it covers creditor disputes with the consumer, and not just consumer disputes with the creditor. If it covers any lawsuit brought by

6 (6th ed. 2008).

7 *See* National Consumer Law Center, Fair Debt Collection § 5.9 (6th ed. 2008).

8 Sinochem Int'l Co., Ltd. v. Malaysia Int'l Shipping Corp., 127 S. Ct. 1184, 167 L. Ed. 2d 15 (2007) (quoting Am. Dredging Co. v. Miller, 510 U.S. 443, 114 S. Ct. 981, 127 L. Ed. 2d 285 (1994)).

9 Quackenbush v. Allstate Ins. Co., 517 U.S. 706, 116 S. Ct. 1712, 135 L. Ed. 2d 1 (1996).

10 A number of credit card issuers and debt buyers are bringing collection actions in arbitration proceedings, and Chapter 8, *infra*, examines how a consumer should respond to such a proceeding.

11 *See* National Consumer Law Center, The Cost of Credit: Regulation, Preemption, and Industry Abuses § 11.7.2.4 (3d ed. 2005 and Supp.).

12 *See* National Consumer Law Center, Consumer Arbitration Agreements Ch. 11 (5th ed. 2007).

the creditor, it should also cover any lawsuit brought by an assignee of the creditor.[13] Watch out for any exceptions in the arbitration requirement for actions under a certain dollar amount or cases brought in small claims court. The motivation of such an exception is to force class actions and punitive damages claims into arbitration, while allowing small collection actions to remain in court. Any ambiguity must be interpreted against the drafter and *in favor of* arbitration.[14]

To force a collection action into arbitration the consumer's attorney should appear before the court hearing the collection action and file a motion with the court to either dismiss the case or stay the judicial action until after the creditor has submitted its case to arbitration. In either case the consumer's attorney should do so immediately, before any extensive participation in the court action. Participation in the court case may be viewed as waiving the right to arbitrate the dispute.[15]

3.5 Defects on the Face of the Complaint

Defects in the complaint and its attachments may be grounds to dismiss the case, although perhaps not with prejudice. In some states the proper response is not a motion to dismiss, but a motion for a more definite statement.[16] In reviewing the requirements for the appropriate form of pleading, be sure to look at the rules of procedure for the court where the action is being brought. For example, a small claims court may have its own rules as to the form of the complaint and required attachments that are different from the state's general rules of civil procedure.

Debt buyers in particular may make clearly false statements in their pleadings. For example, the pleadings may allege that the contract was between the consumer and the debt buyer, instead of between the consumer and the original creditor. The debt buyer may also allege that it supplied goods and services to the consumer.

Some states require that a complaint be verified, and specify how a corporation is to verify the complaint. Failure to meet such state requirements as to verification should suffice to get the case dismissed. For example, facts stated in a complaint may have to be stated as true upon the signer's personal knowledge or information and belief.[17] This requirement is not met when the complaint is signed with an unreadable signature by an otherwise unnamed paralegal for the collector with no personal knowledge of the facts and not an officer of the plaintiff.[18] Affidavits from out-of-state affiants also may have to meet special requirements as to notarization.[19]

Some states and municipalities require that, if the plaintiff is required to have a license, the plaintiff must allege in its complaint that it is licensed and include its licensing information in its complaint.[20] For example, if state or local law requires a debt buyer to be licensed, then the debt buyer's complaint is only proper in some states if the complaint alleges that the debt buyer is licensed, and attaches the licensing information to the complaint.[21]

Besides meeting normal pleading requirements, a collection action often has to comply with state procedural statutes or rules dealing with what documents must be attached to the complaint. Debt buyers in particular are often sloppy, indicating documents are attached when they are not. If rules require a document to be attached, and it is not, this may be grounds to dismiss the case.[22]

A number of states' court rules specify that if a claim is based upon a written document then a copy of the document shall be attached to the complaint; if the writing is not accessible to the pleader, then it is sufficient to state the reason it is not accessible and the substance of the writing.[23] These rules thus require, if a collection case is based upon a credit agreement, that the agreement be attached to the complaint.[24] This requirement can not be met by a report

13 *See id.* § 7.4.5.

14 *See id.* § 3.1.

15 *See id.* Ch. 8.

16 Ohio Civ. R. 12(E); Capital One Bank v. Toney, 2007 WL 969420 (Ohio Ct. App. Mar. 28, 2007).

17 *See* Fla. R. Civ. P. 1024.

18 Atl. Credit & Fin., Inc. v. Giulliana, 829 A.2d 340 (Pa. Super. Ct. 2003); *see also* Worldwide Asset Purchasing, L.L.C. v. Stern (Pa. C.P. Allegheny County May 13, 2005), *available at* www.consumerlaw.org/unreported.

19 *See* § 4.2.3, *infra*.

20 *See* N.Y. C.P.L.R. 3015(e) (McKinney).

21 Centurion Capital Corp. v. Druce, 828 N.Y.S.2d 851 (Civ. Ct. 2006); *see also* PRA III, L.L.C. v. MacDowell, 841 N.Y.S.2d 822 (Civ. Ct. 2007).

22 Worldwide Asset Purchasing, L.L.C. v. Stern (Pa. C.P. Allegheny County May 13, 2005), *available at* www.consumerlaw.org/unreported.

23 *See, e.g.*, Fla. Small Cl. R. 7.050(a); Fla. R. Civ. P. 1.1.30; N.J. R. Civ. P. 6:6-3(a); N.M. R. Civ. P. 1-009(I); Ohio Civ. R. 10(D); Pa. R. Civ. P. 1019(i).

24 Fla. Credit Research, Inc. v. Felicien (Fla. County Ct. Duval County Apr. 15, 2008), *available at* www.consumerlaw.org/unreported; N. Star Capitol Acquisition, L.L.C. v. Lewis (Fla. County Ct. Duval County Oct. 23, 2007), *available at* www.consumerlaw.org/unreported (illegible contract, without the defendant's name or other indication that it relates to the complaint, no dates, and exhibit not attached); LVNV Funding L.L.C. v. Matthews (Fla. County Ct. Duval County Oct. 4, 2007), *available at* www.consumerlaw.org/unreported; LVNV Funding L.L.C. v. Moeherlin (Fla. County Ct. Volusia County Aug. 2006), *available at* www.consumerlaw.org/unreported; New Century Fin. Services, Inc. v. Sanchez (N.J. Super. Ct. Law Div. Apr. 12, 2002), *available at* www.consumerlaw.org/unreported; Citibank (S.D.) v. Martin, 11 Misc. 3d 219 (Civ. Ct. 2005); Capital One Bank v. Toney, 2007 WL 969420 (Ohio Ct. App. Mar. 28, 2007); Atl. Credit & Fin., Inc. v. Giuliana, 829 A.2d 340 (Pa. Super. Ct. 2003); Palisades Collection, L.L.C. v. Grassmyer (Pa. C.P. Blair County Jan. 15, 2008), *available at*

and affidavit from a legal specialist of the plaintiff debt buyer, when that person is not familiar with the business records of the original creditor.[25]

There must also be more than just an unsigned, standard form contract attached to the complaint. Some connection between that form contract and the defendant and the defendant's account number must be provided. For example, credit card issuers utilize different standard form contracts and these are often amended over time. The collector has not attached the operative contract when the contract attached is the original version that does not include any subsequent amendments applicable to the consumer.[26] Similarly, appending the current contract should not suffice if that contract only applies to new accounts, and not to the consumer defendant in the case. Thus a court had little problem finding inadequate an unsigned and undated ledger card that did not reference the account number, the name of the plaintiff, or the original account holder.[27]

Clearly it is not adequate to refer to exhibits "A" and "B," when there is only one illegible attachment, labeled neither "A" nor "B," that does not contain the defendant's name or relate in any other way to the case.[28] Look for inconsistencies between the complaint and attached documents to further demonstrate their inadequacy. For example, make sure an alleged credit account number has the same number of digits as are typically found on VISA, Mastercard, or American Express cards. When the collector is suing on the contract or on an "open account" theory, then the collector should also attach to the complaint monthly statements or other documentation showing how the amount owed was computed.[29]

Collectors often seek to recover based upon an account stated cause of action.[30] The claim is that the consumer has been sent a statement of the account, and the consumer has implicitly agreed to pay that amount. Thus the action is not upon the original contract or the individual charges making up the statement of account, but on the promise to pay the amount included in the statement.

An account stated claim may allow the plaintiff to avoid having to prove each of the underlying obligations making up the statement of account, but it does not mean the plaintiff can avoid the obligation to show that there is in fact a statement of account that has been agreed to. This proof must be more than just an account number and a dollar amount. When state rules require that the statement be attached to the complaint,[31] the statement must be more than a mere memorandum, but should show on its face that it was intended to be a final settlement up to that date,[32] and show individual items, amount due, and dates.[33]

An important document that should be attached to the complaint is a written assignment from the original creditor to the assignee bringing the action (or a series of assignment documents, if there is a more extensive chain of ownership of the account).[34] Section 4.3.3, *infra*, examines what a proper documentation of assignment must include.

---

www.consumerlaw.org/unreported; FIA Card Services, Nat'l Ass'n v. Kirasic (Pa. C.P. Allegheny County Nov. 7, 2007), *available at* www.consumerlaw.org/unreported; Preston State Bank v. Jordan, 692 S.W.2d 740 (Tex. App. 1985); *see also* eCast Settlement Corp. v. Tran, 369 B.R. 312 (Bankr. S.D. Tex. 2007). *But see* Nat'l Check Bureau v. Buerger, 2006 WL 3702638 (Ohio Ct. App. Dec. 18, 2006).

25 PRA III, L.L.C. v. MacDowell, 841 N.Y.S.2d 822 (Civ. Ct. 2007).

26 FIA Card Services, Nat'l Ass'n v. Kirasic (Pa. C.P. Allegheny County Nov. 7, 2007), *available at* www.consumerlaw.org/unreported; Worldwide Asset Purchasing, L.L.C. v. Stern (Pa. C.P. Allegheny County May 13, 2005), *available at* www.consumerlaw.org/unreported.

27 LVNV Funding, L.L.C. v. Matthews (Fla. County Ct. Duval County Oct. 4, 2007), *available at* www.consumerlaw.org/unreported; *see also* Fla. Credit Research, Inc. v. Stromberg (Fla. County Ct. June 22, 2007), *available at* www.consumerlaw.org/unreported; Worldwide Asset Purchasing, L.L.C. v. Stern (Pa. C.P. Allegheny County May 13, 2005), *available at* www.consumerlaw.org/unreported.

28 N. Star Capital Acquisition, L.L.C. v. Lewis (Fla. County Ct. Duval County Oct. 23, 2007), *available at* www.consumerlaw.org/unreported.

29 Fla. Credit Research, Inc. v. Felicien (Fla. County Ct. Duval County Apr. 15, 2008), *available at* www.consumerlaw.org/unreported; Worldwide Asset Purchasing, L.L.C. v. Stern (Pa. C.P. Allegheny County May 13, 2005), *available at* www.consumerlaw.org/unreported.

30 This cause of action is examined in more detail in § 4.7, *infra*.

31 *See, e.g.*, Fla. R. Civ. P. 1.9333; Ohio Civ. R. 10(D).

32 *See* Ahlbin v. Crescent Commercial Corp., 100 Cal. 2d 646 (1950); Capital One Bank v. Toney, 2007 WL 969420 (Ohio Ct. App. Mar. 28, 2007). *But see* Citibank (S.D.) v. Kessler, 2004 WL 795689 (Ohio Ct. App. Apr. 15, 2004).

33 *See* Nevilles v. Citigroup, Inc., 2007 WL 1879427 (S.D. Fla. June 27, 2007); Fla. Credit Research, Inc. v. Felicien (Fla. County Ct. Duval County Apr. 15, 2008), *available at* www.consumerlaw.org/unreported; N. Star Capital Acquisition, L.L.C. v. Lewis (Fla. County Ct. Duval County Oct. 23, 2007), *available at* www.consumerlaw.org/unreported; LVNV Funding, L.L.C. v. Matthews (Fla. County Ct. Duval County Oct. 4, 2007), *available at* www.consumerlaw.org/unreported; Capital One Bank v. Gelsey (Fla. County Ct. Duval County July 3, 2007), *available at* www.consumerlaw.org/unreported; New Century Fin. Services, Inc. v. Sanchez (N.J. Super. Ct. Law Div. Apr. 12, 2002), *available at* www.consumerlaw.org/unreported; Palisades Collection, L.L.C. v. Grassmyer (Pa. C.P. Blair County Jan. 15, 2008), *available at* www.consumerlaw.org/unreported; FIA Card Services, Nat'l Ass'n v. Kirasic (Pa. C.P. Allegheny County Nov. 7, 2007), *available at* www.consumerlaw.org/unreported.

34 New Century Fin. Services, Inc. v. Sanchez (N.J. Super. Ct. Law Div. Apr. 12, 2002), *available at* www.consumerlaw.org/unreported; Palisades Collection, L.L.C. v. Grassmyer (Pa. C.P. Blair County Jan. 15, 2008), *available at* www.consumerlaw.org/unreported; Worldwide Asset Purchasing, L.L.C. v. Stern (Pa. C.P. Allegheny County May 13, 2005), *available at* www.consumerlaw.org/unreported.

3.6 Is Plaintiff Qualified to Bring the Action?

3.6.1 *Introduction*

There are a number of reasons why the collector may not be qualified to bring the collection action in a state's courts. The entity bringing the action may not be entitled to bring any type of action in the state's courts. Or the entity may not be qualified specifically to bring debt collection actions.

A third reason why the collector may have no right to pursue the action is examined in the next chapter: that the collector does not own the obligation or is not properly bringing the action for the owner. This contention will often turn on whether there is proof that the original creditor has assigned the debt to that particular debt buyer.

3.6.2 *Is the Collector Qualified to Bring Any Action in the State's Courts?*

States often have requirements that companies incorporated out-of-state obtain certain certification, registration, or licensure before they can bring actions in the state's courts.[35] Moreover, some statutes even require that the assignor of the collector be qualified to bring an action in the state's courts.[36] This rule prevents a non-qualifying corporation from merely assigning the action to another. These rules have important implications for collection actions, because what is at issue is not only whether the collector is qualified to bring an action, but whether every owner up the chain of ownership is qualified.

For example, if a creditor is qualified, and assigns the debt to unqualified debt buyer A that assigns the debt to qualified debt buyer B, then B can not bring an action in the state's courts, even though it could have if it had been assigned the debt directly from the creditor. The consumer's attorney in such a state should look not just at the collector's qualification to sue, but at the qualifications of every entity in the chain of ownership.

3.6.3 *Is the Collector Qualified to Bring a Collection Action?*

Some states prohibit debt collectors from bringing an action on behalf of others.[37] A collector not owning an obligation can not bring the action for the creditor that does own the obligation. If a collector is to successfully pursue the collection action, it must prove that it owns the debt in its own right.[38]

State law may also prohibit a licensed collection agency from purchasing or receiving assignments of an obligation with the purpose of collection or instituting suit on the obligation.[39] This provision in effect prevents licensed collection agencies from becoming debt buyers and bringing collection actions on the debts they purchase.

In some states only licensed collectors can bring suit, and the failure of a debt buyer to be licensed as a debt collector prevents it from bringing suit[40] (at least when state law considers a debt buyer to be a debt collector). Debt buyers argue that they are not debt collectors, but debt owners, and need not be licensed as debt collectors. But courts reject this argument, finding a legislative intent to require licensure of those who purchase debts after the obligations are in default.[41] The result may be different when a debt buyer has no contact with the consumer, and all collection activity is performed by another entity or by a collection attorney hired by the debt buyer.[42] Another issue may be whether debt buyers not licensed as debt collectors can still bring actions if they do so represented by a licensed attorney.

35 *See, e.g.*, 15 Pa. Cons. Stat. § 4141(a); Golt v. Phillips, 308 Md. 1, 517 A.2d 328 (1986); DeReggi Constr. Co. v. Mate, 130 Md. App. 648, 747 A.2d 743 (2000); Atl. Credit & Fin., Inc. v. Giuliana, 829 A.2d 340 (Pa. Super. Ct. 2003).

36 *See, e.g.*, 15 Pa. Cons. Stat. § 4141(a).

37 *See, e.g.*, Conn. Gen. Stat. § 36a-805(1); *see also* National Consumer Law Center, Fair Debt Collection § 11.5.2 (6th ed. 2008).

38 *See* § 4.3, *infra*.

39 *See, e.g.*, Conn. Gen. Stat. § 36a-805(3). *But see* Asset Acceptance Corp. v. Robinson, 625 N.W.2d 804 (Mich. Ct. App. 2001).

40 *See* Commercial Serv. of Perry, Inc., 856 P.2d 58 (Colo. Ct. App. 1993); PRA III, L.L.C. v. MacDowell, 841 N.Y.S.2d 822 (Civ. Ct. 2007) (interpreting N.Y.C. Admin Code § 20-489(a)); Centurion Capital Corp. v. Druce, 828 N.Y.S.2d 851 (Civ. Ct. 2006) (same); Rushmore Recoveries XI, L.L.C. v. Morninstar (N.Y. Civ. Ct. May 7, 2007) (same), *available at* www.consumerlaw.org/unreported; *see also* Great Seneca Fin. Corp. v. Dowd, No. 12627-05 (N.Y. Civ. Ct. Richmond County Jan. 24, 2008), *available at* www.consumerlaw.org/unreported; Dep't of Consumer Affairs v. Asset Acceptance L.L.C. (N.Y.C. Dep't of Consumer Affairs July 24, 2006), *on appeal* (N.Y.C. Dep't of Consumer Affairs Feb. 23, 2007), *both available at* www.consumerlaw.org/unreported.

41 Commercial Serv. of Perry, Inc., 856 P.2d 58 (Colo. Ct. App. 1993); Centurion Capital Corp. v. Druce, 828 N.Y.S.2d 851 (Civ. Ct. 2006); *see also* Great Seneca Fin. Corp. v. Dowd, No. 12627-05 (N.Y. Civ. Ct. Richmond County Jan. 24, 2008), *available at* www.consumerlaw.org/unreported; PRA III, L.L.C. v. MacDowell, 841 N.Y.S.2d 822 (Civ. Ct. 2007); Rushmore Recoveries XI, L.L.C. v. Morninstar (N.Y. Civ. Ct. May 7, 2007), *available at* www.consumerlaw.org/unreported; Dep't of Consumer Affairs v. Asset Acceptance L.L.C. (N.Y.C. Dep't of Consumer Affairs July 24, 2006), *on appeal* (N.Y.C. Dep't of Consumer Affairs Feb. 23, 2007), *both available at* www.consumerlaw.org/unreported.

42 *See* Kuhne v. Cohen & Slamowitz, L.L.C., 2008 WL 608607 (S.D.N.Y. Mar. 5, 2008).

3.7 Statute of Limitations

3.7.1 Raising the Defense

Particularly when a debt buyer is bringing a collection action, a key consumer defense is often the statute of limitations. A statute of limitations defense can be raised early in a proceeding through a motion to dismiss, if the failure to timely file is apparent on the face of the complaint and the complaint's attachments. Another option is to raise the failure to timely file as an affirmative defense in the consumer's answer, and raise it again through a summary judgment motion or at the trial. The consumer may also bring a Fair Debt Collection Practices Act (FDCPA) counterclaim or a separate affirmative action based upon the collector's filing of a lawsuit whose statutes of limitations has already run.[43] This section focuses on what statute of limitations apply to a case and how the limitation period is computed—irrespective of whether expiration of the limitations period is raised in a motion to dismiss, at trial, or in an FDCPA action.

3.7.2 Which State's Law Applies?

3.7.2.1 The Forum State or the State Selected in the Credit Agreement?

Credit card agreements and other consumer credit contracts typically specify that the contract will be governed by the law of a particular state, such as Delaware. Whether the statute of limitations should be determined by the law of the forum state or by the law of the state specified in the contract thus becomes an issue.

Surprisingly, the law selected in the contract may have a shorter limitations period than the forum state. Creditors, in selecting which state's law should be used to interpret the credit agreement, typically have other legal issues in mind than the statute of limitations—which has more significance for those purchasing debts than it does for the original creditor. As a result the consumer, in some cases, may wish to argue for the applicability of the statute of limitations of the state selected in the contract, not that of the forum state. The consumer need not admit to the enforceability of the contract in arguing for the use of the contractual choice of law. The consumer can simply state that, if the contract is enforceable then, by its own terms, the limitations period has expired.

Courts are divided whether they will utilize the forum's limitations period or that of the state selected in the contractual choice of law provision. At least some states view the statute of limitations as procedural and thus decide, despite the choice of law provision, to use the forum state's limitation period,[44] or simply rule that the forum state's statute of limitations is always to be applied.[45]

Other jurisdictions find that a contractual choice of laws clause refers to all of the chosen state's laws (not just substantive laws), and thus includes the statute of limitations.[46] Moreover, some courts question the supposed distinction between substantive and procedural laws, and find it hard to determine which category to place the statute of limitations in.[47] Having decided that the contractual choice of law includes that state's statute of limitations, courts generally find no fundamental state policy to use their own statute of limitations, which might override the contractual choice of law provision, and therefore utilize the chosen state's limitation period.[48]

---

43 *See* §§ 5.5, 14.4, *infra*.

44 MedCap Corp. v. Betsy Johnson Health Care Systems, Inc., 16 Fed. Appx. 180 (4th Cir. 2001) (N.C. law); Cole v. Mileti, 133 F.3d 433 (6th Cir. 1998) (Mich. law); Phelps v. McClellan, 30 F.3d 658 (6th Cir. 1994) (Mich. law); Telular Corp. v. Mentor Graphics Corp., 282 F. Supp. 2d 869 (N.D. Ill. 2003) (Illinois law treats the statute of limitations as procedural, requiring use of the forum's law); Sharp-Richardson v. Boyds Collection, Ltd., 1999 WL 33656875 (N.D. Iowa Sept. 30, 1999) (interpreting Iowa law as to choice of laws); Hemar Ins. Corp. of Am. v. Ryerson, 108 S.W.3d 90 (Mo. Ct. App. 2003); Educ. Res. Inst., Inc. v. Piazza, 17 A.D.3d 513 (2005); Educ. Res. Inst., Inc. v. Czarnik, 8 Misc. 3d 136(A) (App. Term 2005) (table).

45 Nez v. Forney, 783 P.2d 471 (N.M. 1989).

46 Wang Laboratories, Inc. v. Kagan, 990 F.2d 1126 (9th Cir. 1993); Avery v. First Resolution Mgmt. Corp., 2007 WL 1560653 (D. Or. May 25, 2007) (but court refused to use non-forum state's law when court's odd interpretation of non-forum state's tolling rules would mean there would never be a limitations period); Jahn v. 1-800-Flowers.Com, Inc., 2002 WL 32362244 (W.D. Wis. Oct. 21, 2002); W. Group Nurseries, Inc. v. Ergas, 211 F. Supp. 2d 1362 (S.D. Fla. 2002); W. Group Nurseries, Inc. v. Adams, 2000 WL 34446155 (D. Ariz. July 3, 2000); ABF Capital Corp. v. Costello & Lanahan, 2005 WL 3514288 (Cal. Ct. App. Dec. 23, 2005); Hambrecht & Quist Venture Partners v. Am. Med. Int'l, Inc., 38 Cal. App. 4th 1532 (1995); Fla. Credit Research, Inc. v. Felicien (Fla. County Ct. Duval County Apr. 15, 2008), *available at* www.consumerlaw.org/unreported; Fla. Credit Research, Inc. v. Stromberg (Fla. County Ct. Duval County Feb. 20, 2008), *available at* www.consumerlaw.org/unreported; Capital One Bank v. Gelsey (Fla. County Ct. Duval County July 3, 2007), *available at* www.consumerlaw.org/unreported; L.W.T. v. Brodsky, 14 Fla. L. Weekly Supp. 188a (Fla. County Ct. Broward County Dec. 8, 2006); Discover Bank v. Eschwege (N.Y. Sup. Ct. Mar. 5, 2008), *available at* www.consumerlaw.org/unreported; *see also* Maxcess, Inc. v. Lucent Technologies, Inc., 433 F.3d 1337 (11th Cir. 2005) (Fla. law); Boracchia v. Biomet, Inc., 2008 WL 512721 (N.D. Cal. Feb. 25, 2008); Hughes Electronics Corp. v. Citibank Del., 120 Cal. App. 4th 251 (2004).

47 Jahn v. 1-800-Flowers.Com, Inc., 2002 WL 32362244 (W.D. Wis. Oct. 21, 2002); W. Group Nurseries, Inc. v. Ergas, 211 F. Supp. 2d 1362 (S.D. Fla. 2002); Hambrecht & Quist Venture Partners v. Am. Med. Int'l, Inc., 38 Cal. App. 4th 1532 (1995).

48 W. Group Nurseries, Inc. v. Ergas, 211 F. Supp. 2d 1362 (S.D. Fla. 2002); Hambrecht & Quist Venture Partners v. Am. Med. Int'l, Inc., 38 Cal. App. 4th 1532 (1995); *see also* Maxcess, Inc.

This split in the cases is mostly along state lines, and reflects a difference between state courts following the traditional approach (using the forum state's limitation period) and those following a more modern approach (using the limitations period of the state selected in the contract). The 1971 version of *The Restatement (Second) of Conflict of Laws* took the position that the forum state's limitations period always applies.[49] The 1988 version uses the forum state's period when it is shorter, but uses a more flexible standard when the forum state's limitations period is longer.[50]

3.7.2.2 Consumer, But Not the Collector, Can Use the Contractually Chosen Limitations Period

A collector may attempt to use the limitations period of the state selected in the contract when it is longer than that of the forum state. Even assuming a state takes the more modern view that the contractual choice of law clause determines the statute of limitations, the collector will run into problems. The collector will have to prove the terms of the contract containing the choice of law clause—otherwise there is no basis for that state's law being applied to any of the collector's causes of action. As described in § 4.5.3, *infra*, collectors in consumer collection cases may have difficulty producing such proof.

In addition, forum states have an important interest in avoiding limitations periods that extend the time period beyond that established by their own legislature. The limitations period not only protects defendants, but also the state's courts from having to hear stale evidence. Even the modern version of the *Restatement (Second) of Conflicts of Laws* uses the forum state's limitations period when that period is shorter, even if does not use the forum state's limitations period when it is longer than the contractually chosen period.[51] States also have policies that a contract can not extend the limitations period, even if the courts allow contracts to shorten the limitations period.[52]

As a result, the consumer is in a stronger position than the collector to claim that the contractually chosen state's laws determine the statute of limitations. Nor is this consumer claim inconsistent with a defense that there is no binding contract. The consumer is just taking the position that, if the contract is enforceable then, by its own terms, the count for breach of contract should be dismissed.

The same result should apply even to the collector's causes of action that are not based upon the contract, as long as the collector alleges there is a contract. By alleging that there is a contract the collector is estopped from arguing that the contract, and the contract's choice of law, do not apply. By choosing to allege that a binding contract exists, the collector can not avoid application of the contract's choice of law provisions and the statute of limitations chosen in this document.[53] The plaintiff is the "master of its complaint" and can not avoid the choice of law provision found in the contract referenced in its complaint. If the non-forum state's limitations period has clearly expired, then the consumer should also consider introducing the contract into evidence if the collector does not.

3.7.2.3 Borrowing Statutes

If a consumer enters into a credit contract in one state, and then moves and is sued in a second state with a longer limitations period, the consumer may be able to take advantage of the first state's shorter limitations period. A number of states have borrowing statutes that require use of the statute of limitations where an action arose, if that limitations period is shorter.[54] On the other hand, if the statute of limitations is shorter in the forum state, the borrowing statute will not apply and the forum state's limitations period will control. For example, Delaware's borrowing statute reads:

> Where a cause of action arises outside of this State, an action can not be brought in a court of this State to enforce such cause of action after the expiration of whichever is shorter, the time limited by the law of this State, or the time limited by the law of the state or country where the cause of action arose, for bringing an action upon such cause of action.[55]

v. Lucent Technologies, Inc., 433 F.3d 1337 (11th Cir. 2005) (Fla. law); Burroughs Corp. v. Suntogs of Miami, Inc., 472 So. 2d 1166 (Fla. 1985) (contractual provision shortening the period of time for filing a suit was not contrary to a strong public policy).

49 Restatement (Second) of Conflict of Laws § 142 (1971).

50 Restatement (Second) of Conflict of Laws § 142 (1988); *see also* W. Group Nurseries, Inc. v. Adams, 2000 WL 34446155 (D. Ariz. July 3, 2000).

51 Restatement (Second) of Conflict of Laws § 142 (1988); *see also* W. Group Nurseries, Inc. v. Adams, 2000 WL 34446155 (D. Ariz. July 3, 2000).

52 *See* § 3.7.4, *infra*.

53 Fla. Credit Research, Inc. v. Felicien (Fla. County Ct. Duval County Jan. 17, 2008), *available at* www.consumerlaw.org/unreported; Capital One Bank v. Gelsey (Fla. County Ct. Duval County July 3, 2007), *available at* www.consumerlaw.org/unreported.

54 *See* Del. Code Ann. tit. 10, § 8121; Fla. Stat. § 95.10; 735 Ill. Comp. Stat. § 5/13-210; N.Y. C.P.L.R. 202 (McKinney).

55 Del. Code Ann. tit. 10, § 8121.

3.7.3 *Differing Statutes of Limitation Within a State*

3.7.3.1 General

States typically establish several statutes of limitations, of varying lengths, that are applicable to different causes of action. These statutes of limitations are often found in the state's code section governing courts and judicial proceedings for personal actions, or in the state's version of the Uniform Commercial Code (UCC).

There is enormous variation in statutes of limitations from state to state, not only in the number of years, but how the state organizes and applies its statutes of limitations. The one exception are the statutes of limitations found in the UCC, described in §§ 3.7.3.2–3.7.3.3, *infra*. Although there are some state variations even in UCC provisions, in general, there is uniformity among the states as to the limitations period for cases related to the sale of goods, leases, dishonored checks, and promissory notes, which are found in the state's version of the UCC.

Every state also has a limitations periods for claims based on a written contract, but the time periods vary significantly from state to state: three years in Delaware, the District of Columbia, Maryland, Mississippi, New Hampshire, North Carolina, and South Carolina;[56] four years in California, Pennsylvania, and Texas;[57] five years in Arkansas, Florida, Idaho, Kansas, Nebraska, Oklahoma, and Virginia;[58] six years in Alabama, Alaska, Arizona, Colorado, Connecticut, Georgia, Hawaii, Maine, Massachusetts, Michigan, Minnesota, Nevada, New Jersey, New Mexico, New York, North Dakota, Oregon, South Dakota, Tennessee, Utah, Vermont, Washington, and Wisconsin;[59] eight years in Montana;[60] ten years in Illinois, Indiana, Iowa, Louisiana, Missouri, Rhode Island, West Virginia, and Wyoming;[61] and fifteen years in Kentucky and Ohio.[62]

Statutes of limitations for a claim on a non-written contract are usually shorter than those for a written contract, varying by state from three to ten years.[63] In a number of states, though, the limitations period is the same for non-written and written contracts.[64]

In states in which the period is shorter for non-written than written contracts, an important issue is whether a collector's claim—for example, for account stated or an open account—should be characterized as a written or a

56 Del. Code Ann. tit. 10, § 8106; D.C. Code § 12-301; Md. Code Ann., Cts. & Jud. Proc. § 5-101 (West); Miss. Code Ann. § 15-1-29; N.H. Rev. Stat. Ann. § 508:4; N.C. Gen. Stat § 1-52(1); S.C. Code Ann. § 15-3-530; Wash. Rev. Code § 4.16.040.

57 Cal. Civ. Proc. Code § 337 (West); 42 Pa. Cons. Stat. § 5525(1); Tex. Civ. Prac. & Rem. Code Ann. § 16.004 (Vernon).

58 Ark. Code Ann. § 16-56-111; Fla. Stat. § 95.11(2)(b); Idaho Code Ann. § 5-216; Kan. Stat. Ann. § 60-511; Neb. Rev. Stat. § 25-205; Okla. Stat. tit. 12, § 95; Va. Code Ann. § 8.01-246(2).

59 Ala. Code § 6-2-34; Alaska Stat. § 09.10.050; Ariz. Rev. Stat. Ann. § 12-548; Colo. Rev. Stat. § 13-80-103.5; Conn. Gen. Stat. § 52-576; Ga. Code Ann. § 9-3-24; Haw. Rev. Stat. § 657-1; Me. Rev. Stat. Ann. tit. 14, § 752; Mass. Gen. Laws ch. 260, § 2; Mich. Comp. Laws § 600.5807; Minn. Stat. § 541.05; Nev. Rev. Stat. § 11.190; N.J. Stat. Ann. § 2A:14-1; N.M. Stat. § 37-1-3; N.Y. C.P.L.R. 213 (McKinney); N.D. Cent. Code § 28-01-16; Or. Rev. Stat. § 12.080; S.D. Codified Laws § 15-2-13; Tenn. Code Ann. § 28-3-109; Utah Code Ann. § 78-12-23; Vt. Stat. Ann. tit. 12, § 511; Wis. Stat. § 893.43.

60 Mont. Code Ann. § 27-2-202.

61 Ill. Code of Civ. Proc. § 110-13-205; Ind. Code § 34-1-2-1; Iowa Code § 614.1(5); La. Civ. Code art. 3499; Mo. Rev. Stat. § 516.110(1); R.I. Gen. Laws § 9-1-13(a); W. Va. Code § 55-2-6; Wyo. Stat. Ann. § 1-3-105.

62 Ky. Rev. Stat. Ann. § 413.090 (West); Ohio Rev. Code Ann. § 2305.06 (West).

63 *See* Ariz. Rev. Stat. Ann. § 12-543 (three years instead of six years for written contracts); Ark. Code Ann. § 16-56-111 (three years instead of five); Cal. Civ. Proc. Code § 339 (West) (two years instead of four); Conn. Gen. Stat. § 52-581 (three years instead of six); Fla. Stat. § 95.11(3)(k) (four years instead of five); Ga. Code Ann. § 9-3-25 (four years instead of six); Idaho Code Ann. § 5-217 (four years instead of five); Ill. Code of Civ Proc. § 110-13-205 (five years instead of ten); Ind. Code § 34-1-2-1 (six years instead of ten); Iowa Code § 614.1(4) (five years instead of ten); Kan. Stat. Ann. § 60-511 (three years instead of five); Ky. Rev. Stat. Ann. § 413.120 (West) (five years instead of fifteen); Mo. Rev. Stat. § 516.120 (five years instead of ten); Mont. Code Ann. § 27-2-202 (five years instead of eight); Neb. Rev. Stat. § 25-205 (four years instead of five); Nev. Rev. Stat. § 11.190 (four years instead of six); N.M. Stat. § 37-1-4 (four years instead of six); Ohio Rev. Code Ann. § 2305.06 (West) (six years instead of fifteen); Okla. Stat. tit. 12, § 95 (three years instead of five); Utah Code Ann. § 78-12-25 (four years instead of six); Va. Code Ann. § 8.01-246(4) (three years instead of five); Wash. Rev. Code § 4.16.080 (three years instead of six); W. Va. Code § 55-2-6 (five years instead of ten); Wyo. Stat. Ann. § 1-3-105 (eight years instead of ten).

64 Ala. Code §§ 6-2-34, 6-2-37 (six years for both); Alaska Stat. § 09.10.050 (six years for both); Colo. Rev. Stat. § 13-80-103.5 (six years for both); Del. Code Ann. tit. 10, § 8106 (three years for both); D.C. Code § 12-301 (three years for both); Haw. Rev. Stat. § 657-1 (six years for both); La. Civ. Code arts. 3498, 3499 (ten years for both); Me. Rev. Stat. Ann. tit. 14, § 752 (six years for both); Md. Code Ann., Cts. & Jud. Proc. § 5-101 (West) (three years for both); Mass. Gen. Laws ch. 260, § 2 (six years for both); Mich. Comp. Laws § 600.5807 (six years for both); Minn. Stat. § 541.05 (six years for both); Miss. Code Ann. § 15-1-29 (three years for both); N.H. Rev. Stat. Ann. § 508:4 (three years for both); N.J. Stat. Ann. § 2A:14-1 (West) (six years for both); N.Y. C.P.L.R. 213 (McKinney) (six years for both); N.C. Gen. Stat § 1-52(1) (three years for both); N.D. Cent. Code § 28-01-16 (six years for both); Or. Rev. Stat. § 12.080 (six years for both); 42 Pa. Cons. Stat. § 5525 (four years for both); R.I. Gen. Laws § 9-1-13(a) (ten years for both); S.C. Code Ann. § 15-3-530 (three years for both); S.D. Codified Laws § 15-2-13 (six years for both); Tenn. Code Ann. § 28-3-109 (six years for both); Tex. Civ. Prac. & Rem. Code Ann. § 16.004 (Vernon) (four years for both); Vt. Stat. Ann. tit. 12, § 511 (six years for both); Wis. Stat. § 893.43 (six years for both).

non-written contract claim.[65] Sometimes this issue will be resolved by the statute's language, such as when there is an explicit limitations periods for a claim based upon an account stated,[66] an open account,[67] or a contract implied in law (for example, *quantum meruit* or unjust enrichment).[68] States also have default limitations periods that apply when no other limitations period is applicable—in some states a claim for *quantum meruit* may be covered under this general limitations period.[69] Default limitation periods can be quite short,[70] but can be quite long in other states.[71]

3.7.3.2 UCC Limitations Period for Merchant Credit Cards, Installment Sales of Goods, and Leased Goods

Every state but Louisiana has adopted UCC Article 2,[72] which provides that an action for breach of any contract for the sale of goods must be brought within four years after the cause of action accrues.[73] Eight states have adopted variations to this period, most of these eight lengthening the period to five or six years.[74] UCC section 2A-506(1) also provides for a four-year limitations period after the cause of action accrues on default of a lease.

These UCC statute of limitations periods are important because they generally take precedence over other state limitations periods, such as for a written contract. When a seller or lessor of goods (or that entity's assignee) is seeking to collect on a debt, the UCC four-year limitations period generally controls, even when some other statute of limitations could apply.[75]

3.7.3.3 UCC Limitations Period for Dishonored Checks and Defaulted Promissory Notes

If a consumer pays for goods or services with a personal check that is later dishonored, the collector can sue for the nonpayment of the goods or services and/or for the nonpayment of the check. Each of these claims will have a separate statute of limitations. If a creditor sues for nonpayment of goods, the four-year UCC Article 2 limitations period applies.[76] If the creditor sues on the dishonored check, UCC section 3-118(c) requires that the action be commenced within three years after the check's dishonor.[77]

A separate UCC Article 3 statute of limitations applies to actions to collect on promissory notes that are negotiable instruments. A promissory note is a negotiable instrument if it meets certain UCC Article 3 requirements.[78] (Installment sales agreements will not meet these requirements because they include too many duties in addition to the duty to pay.) Typically a note evidencing a direct loan from a credit union or a bank will qualify as a negotiable instrument—even if the proceeds are used to purchase goods. But even a loan note will not qualify as a negotiable instrument if it does not meet the UCC's strict requirements.[79] In that case, the Article 3 limitations period will not apply.

If the note does qualify as a negotiable instrument, then UCC section 3-118(a) states that an action to enforce the obligation of a party to pay a note payable at a definite time must be commenced within six years of the due date. If the note is accelerated, then the six years commences with the accelerated due date. Arkansas and Louisiana shorten both six-year periods to five years; Montana, Oregon, and Washington shorten it to three years; and Illinois and Iowa omit this provision entirely.

3.7.4 The Statute of Limitations Can Not Be Extended by Contract

It would be unusual for a consumer credit agreement to *lengthen* a statute of limitations, and any such attempt

65 *See* § 3.7.5, *infra*.

66 Ariz. Rev. Stat. Ann. § 12-543 (three years); Cal. Civ. Proc. Code § 337 (West) (four years); Del. Code Ann. tit. 10, § 8106 (three years).

67 Ala. Code § 6-2-37(1) (three years); Ariz. Rev. Stat. Ann. § 12-543 (three years); Cal. Civ. Proc. Code § 337(2) (West) (four years); Conn. Gen. Stat. § 52-576 (six years); La. Civ. Code art. 3498 (three years); 42 Pa. Cons. Stat. § 5527 (six years); Utah Code Ann. § 78-12-25 (four years); *see also* Ayers v. Cavalry SVP, L.L.C., 876 So. 2d 474 (Ala. Civ. App. 2003).

68 Cal. Civ. Proc. Code § 339 (West) (two years); 42 Pa. Cons. Stat. § 5525(a)(4) (four years).

69 *See* Capital One Bank v. Gelsey (Fla. County Ct. Duval County July 3, 2007), *available at* www.consumerlaw.org/unreported.

70 *E.g.*, Va. Code Ann. § 8.01-248 (two years).

71 *E.g.*, 42 Pa. Cons. Stat. § 5527(b) (six years).

72 Although U.C.C. Article 2 was amended in 2003, no state has adopted this revised version, so the pre-2003 version of Article 2 that is enacted in every state but Louisiana is discussed here.

73 U.C.C. § 2-725.

74 The following states have variations that would affect consumer collection actions: The Colorado U.C.C. refers to Colo. Rev. Stat. § 13-80-101, which imposes a three-year period for U.C.C. actions, but also in turn refers to Colo. Rev. Stat. § 13-80-103.5, which imposes a six-year period for actions to recover a liquidated debt or an unliquidated determinable amount; Florida omits the section; Iowa omits the four-year period; Mississippi substitutes six years for four; Oklahoma substitutes five years for four; South Carolina substitutes six years for four; South Dakota deletes the provision prohibiting lengthening of the period by agreement; and Wisconsin substitutes six years for four.

75 *See* § 3.7.5.2, *infra*.

76 *See* § 3.7.3.2, *supra*.

77 There are unusual situations in which the three-year period can be even further shortened when the collector holds onto the check for a number of years before it seeks to cash it. The U.C.C. Article 3 limitations period for dishonored checks has been uniformly adopted in every state but Iowa.

78 *See* U.C.C. § 3-104(a), (b), (e).

79 See National Consumer Law Center, Unfair and Deceptive Acts and Practices § 6.7.2 (6th ed. 2004 and Supp.) for a discussion of when a note qualifies as a negotiable instrument.

should be unenforceable. The statute of limitations is the legislature's attempt to achieve a balance between protecting the courts and defendants against stale claims and providing plaintiffs a reasonable period in which to bring an action. A contract provision seeking to extend that period should be unenforceable.[80] In fact, the UCC Article 2 statute of limitations explicitly states that its limitations period may not be extended by agreement.[81]

3.7.5 Determining Which Statute of Limitations in a State Applies

3.7.5.1 General

As described in § 3.7.3, *supra*, a state may have a number of different statutes of limitations, such as for written contracts, oral contracts, accounts stated, open accounts, implied contracts, sales of goods, leases, dishonored checks, and promissory notes. These limitations periods may be of differing lengths, so it is critical in many cases to determine which limitations period applies.

Doing so poses several issues. One occurs when two limitations periods appear to apply to the same cause of action, such as when a merchant sues for breach of a written agreement to pay for goods purchased. Does the limitations period for written contracts apply or that for the sale of goods? Another issue is determining which limitations period applies to a claim when the scope of a statute is not precise. For example, is a claim on an open account or an account stated a claim on a written contract or on a non-written contract?

It is important to analyze each cause of action in a collection lawsuit separately, to determine which statute of limitations applies to that cause of action. An action being brought on just one debt can have multiple statutes of limitations apply, each applying to a different cause of action, and each specifying a different time period.

When the collector's complaint has not sufficiently clarified the nature of a claim so as to allow the consumer to determine which limitations period applies, the consumer should ask the court to require a more definite statement or seek the claim's dismissal for failure to state a claim. Ambiguity in the nature of the claim being sued upon not only confuses what elements the collector must prove, but also confuses the applicable limitations period. In fact, the collector's ambiguity as to the nature of its claim may be a deliberate attempt to seek to prove one cause of action while adopting the longer limitations period of a different cause of action.

80 W. Gate Vill. Ass'n v. Dubois, 761 A.2d 1066 (N.H. 2000).

81 U.C.C. § 2-725.

3.7.5.2 UCC Limitations Period for Sale of Goods Overrides the Period for Written Contracts

The UCC Article 2 four-year limitations period for the sale of goods overrides a state's limitations period for a claim based upon a written contract, which is often longer than UCC Article 2's four-year period.[82]

The official comment to UCC section 2-725 states:

> **Purposes:** To introduce a uniform statute of limitations for sales contracts, thus eliminating the jurisdictional variations and providing needed relief for concerns doing business on a nationwide scale whose contracts have heretofore been governed by several different periods of limitation depending upon the state in which the transaction occurred. This Article takes sales contracts out of the general laws limiting the time for commencing contractual actions and selects a four year period as the most appropriate to modern business practice. This is within the normal commercial record keeping period.

Thus, the UCC's Article 2 four-year limitations period and not the period for written contracts applies to installment agreements for the sale of goods, such as automobile installment sales initiated by a dealer and sold to a bank.[83] This rule applies even when the vehicle is repossessed and the creditor is seeking a deficiency, and when the state's limitations period for a written contract is more than four years.[84] Creditors sometimes argue that they are suing upon a "secured transaction," or a "deficiency suit," and not on a contract for the sale of goods. This argument has long been rejected.[85]

The UCC Article 2 limitations period also applies to a collection action on a store credit card,[86] or when a merchant

82 *See* Taylor v. Unifund Corp., 2001 WL 1035717 (N.D. Ill. Sept. 1, 2001) (applying four-year U.C.C. period instead of ten-year period for written contracts, including promises to pay).

As described in § 3.7.3.1, *supra*, most states have limitations periods for written contracts that are five years or longer, but three states have four-year limitations periods and six (plus the District of Columbia) have three-year periods for written contract claims.

83 When a credit union, for example, makes a direct loan to the consumer to pay for a vehicle, and the loan note qualifies as a negotiable instrument, then U.C.C. Article 3's six-year limitations period for notes would apply.

84 *See* National Consumer Law Center, Repossessions § 12.7 (6th ed. 2005 and Supp.); *see also* Jackeskett Lincoln-Mercury, Inc. v. Metcalf, 158 Cal. App. 3d 38 (1984); D.A.N. Joint Venture, III v. Clark, 218 S.W.3d 455 (Mo. Ct. App. 2006); Ford Motor Credit Co. v. Arce, 348 N.J. Super. 198 (Super. Ct. App. Div. 2002).

85 *See* Associates Discount Corp. v. Palmer, 219 A.2d 858 (N.J. 1966) (Pa. law); Ford Motor Credit Co. v. Arce, 348 N.J. Super. 198 (Super. Ct. App. Div. 2002).

86 *See* Hamid v. Blatt, Hasenmiller, Leibsker, Moore & Pellettieri,

otherwise agrees to defer payment.[87] This transaction is a contract for the sale of goods, with payment deferred. The same logic may not, however, apply to a bank credit card, when the bank is loaning money to the consumer to make a purchase with a third party.[88] Fine distinctions may be drawn when the store credit card is actually originated by a corporation affiliated with the store, and when the card is only used to make purchases at that store. The UCC limitations period should apply to an action to collect on a Sears credit card used to purchase goods at Sears. But what about goods purchased at Sears with a Discover Card during the years when Sears owned the Discover Card?

The UCC Article 2 limitations period does not apply to the sale of services. UCC section 2-102 states "unless the context otherwise requires, this Article applies to transactions in goods." When a series of sales, some for goods and some for services or cash advances, is combined in the same open-end account with a merchant, then two different statutes of limitations may apply. If an action is brought after the four-year period has expired, but before the limitations period for sale of services has expired, the collector should only be able to collect on the amount owed for the services, if it can collect anything.

If a purchase is a mixed sale of goods and services (for example, the sale of flooring which is also installed as part of the purchase), then UCC Article 2 case law has developed rules as to how the purchase is to be treated—as the sale of goods, services, or both. These rules are set out in NCLC's *Consumer Warranty Law* § 19.3.[89]

UCC case law also holds that water, electricity, and gas are goods,[90] so that the UCC Article 2 four-year limitations period applies to actions to collect delinquent utility bills for water, electricity, and gas. Cell phone delinquencies, on the other hand, are made up primarily of monthly usage charges, although they may include purchases of cell phones or other goods. In any action on a cell phone delinquency, the limitations period in a state applicable to the action for the usage charges should be identified. However at least for the portion of the amount due that relates to the purchase of goods, the UCC four-year limitations period should apply.

2001 WL 1035726 (N.D. Ill. Sept. 4, 2001); Taylor v. Unifund Corp., 2001 WL 1035717 (N.D. Ill. Sept. 1, 2001); Gimbel Bros., Inc. v. Cohen, 46 Pa. D. & C.2d 747 (C.P. 1969); *see also* Sliger v. R.H. Macy & Co., 59 N.J. 465 (1971) (store charge account is a contract for sale of goods).

87 Fallimento v. Fischer Crane Co., 995 F.2d 789 (7th Cir. 1993); Ford Motor Credit Co. v. Arce, 348 N.J. Super. 198 (Super. Ct. App. Div. 2002); May Co. v. Trusnik, 375 N.E.2d 72 (Ohio Ct. App. 1977).

88 Harris Trust & Sav. Bank v. McCray, 316 N.E.2d 209 (Ill. App. Ct. 1974).

89 (3d ed. 2006 and Supp.).

90 *See* National Consumer Law Center, Consumer Warranty Law § 1.5.6 (3d ed. 2006 and Supp.).

3.7.5.3 What Limitations Period Applies to Actions on Bank-Issued Credit Card Debt?

An important issue is the applicable statute of limitations for a collection action on bank-issued credit cards. Occasionally collectors will claim that the credit card obligation is based upon a promissory note, and that the UCC's six-year limitations period applies.[91] There is no merit to this argument, as a credit card obligation is not a negotiable instrument, because there is not a promise to pay a fixed amount and there are conditions on the promise to pay.[92]

More commonly collectors argue that a state's limitations period for written contracts applies to a credit card debt. This is advantageous to the collector in about half the states because the period applicable to written contracts is longer than other limitations periods in the state.[93] (In the other half, the limitations period for claims based upon a written contract is the same as for a claim based upon a non-written contract or an open account, so that this issue does not arise.[94])

The statute of limitations for written contracts may not be applicable to collection on a credit card debt for a number of reasons. First, it only applies to causes of action for breach of a written contract. Because they can not produce the written credit card agreement, debt buyers often look for causes of action to include in their collection complaints that are not based upon that agreement. If a cause of action is not based upon a written contract, the statute of limitations for a written contract does not apply to that cause of action.[95] This rule applies even if the cause of action relies in part upon the existence of a written contract, when the written instrument is a link in the chain of evidence to prove the

91 *See* § 3.7.5.3, *supra*.

92 *See* McLane v. MRC Receivables Corp., 2007 WL 19435 (Ky. Ct. App. Jan. 5, 2007).

93 *See* § 3.7.3.1, *supra*.

94 *See id.*

Every state listed in that section as having the same limitations period for both written and non-written contracts also has the same limitations period for open accounts, with the exception of two states, Alabama and Louisiana. Ala. Code §§ 6-2-34, 6-2-37 (the same six-year limitation period for written and non-written contract claims, but three years for claims on open accounts); La. Civ. Code arts. 3498, 3499 (ten years for written or non-written contracts, but three years for claims on open accounts).

95 *See* Rawson v. Credigy Receivables, Inc., 2006 WL 418665 (N.D. Ill. Feb. 16, 2006); *see also* Union Labor Life Ins. Co. v. Sheet Metal Workers Nat'l Health Plan, 1991 WL 212232 (D.D.C. Sept. 30, 1991); Capital One Bank v. Creed, 220 S.W.3d 874 (Mo. Ct. App. 2007) (failure to produce agreement signed by consumer precluded creditor from bringing action based on a "writing for the payment of money or property," which has a ten-year statute of limitations under Missouri law, versus a breach of implied contract claim, which has a five-year limitations period).

cause of action but does not on its face establish all of the elements of plaintiff's claim.[96]

A collector's counts for *quantum meruit* or money lent are not based on a written contract,[97] and this limitations period will not apply. *Quantum meruit*, by its very nature, is a claim based upon a contract implied in law, not an actual contract.

A claim for account stated is not a claim based upon a written contract either, but instead is based on a statement of account to which the consumer has implicitly assented.[98] Instead of a written, signed contract, there is only a statement identifying an account, itemizing certain charges. The statement of account supersedes the contract and the collector is suing not upon the contract, but upon the consumer's implicit promise to pay the statement. In fact, some states have an explicit limitations period for an account stated.[99] Other states use the limitations period for a non-written contract or a contract implied in law.[100]

If a collector's cause of action is based upon a written contract, then an essential element of the collector's case must be proof of a binding written contract. The collector can not fudge the two and claim that its cause of action is founded on a written contract, when in fact the collector can not produce the written contract or can only produce a form contract that may not even apply to the consumer. Thus one court has found:

> The "Customer Agreement" attached to the Complaint does not identify the Defendant or his account, show the amount lent to Defendant or the terms of repayment, or otherwise establish that Defendant is liable to Plaintiff. When a document does not on its face establish all the elements of Plaintiff's claim, that claim is not "founded on a written instrument" so as to extend the statute of limitations.[101]

Even if the collector is able to produce the agreement, a credit card agreement may not qualify as a written agreement.[102] Credit card agreements are subject to change unilaterally, are generally not signed by either party, and there often is not a "complete writing," but an initial writing plus a series of standard form amendments whose enforceability is contingent on the consumer's continued use of the credit card.[103]

In addition, credit card obligations are open ended, and the amount owed is not fixed in the contract, but is instead determined by a series of charges and payments. As such, a shorter limitations period for non-written contracts is most appropriate:

> "[S]tatute of limitations are designed to prevent undue delay in bringing suit on claim and to suppress fraudulent and stale claims from being asserted, to the surprise of parties or their representatives, when all the proper vouchers and evidence are lost, or the facts have become obscure from the lapse of time or the defective memory or death or removal of [a] witness" citing *Foremost Properties, Inc. v. Gladman*, 100 So. 2d 669 (Fla. 1st DCA 1958), *cert den.* 102 So. 2d 728 (Fla. 1958). A review of the statute shows, consistent with common sense, that those actions on which proof is less likely to deteriorate over time are subject to longer limitation periods; those actions on which proof is more likely to deteriorate because of faulty memory or otherwise are subject of shorter limitations periods. Unlike a written contract containing all the terms sued on, proof of the balance due under a store credit card depends on the correctness of the store's books. We know, though, that record keepers come and go; purchased items are returned or exchanged; and partial payments are made. Proof of the amount due under a store credit card is simply not as secure as proof of the amount due on, for example, a promissory note that contains in writing all the terms of the parties' undertakings. *See Nardone v. Reynolds,* 333 So. 2d 25, 36 (Fla. 1976), *mod. on other grds., Tanner v. Hartog,* 618 So. 2d 177 (Fla. 1993) (unfair to allow one who has slept on his rights to sue a party " ' . . . who is left to shield himself from liability with nothing more than tattered or faded memories, misplaced or discarded records, and missing or deceased witnesses' "); *Allie v. Ionata,* 503 So. 2d 1237 (Fla. 1987).[104]

---

96 Kersten v. Cont'l Bank, 628 P.2d 592 (Ariz. 1981); ARDC Corp. v. Hogan, 656 So. 2d 1371, 1374 (Fla. Dist. Ct. App. 1995).

97 *See* Tao of Systems Integration, Inc. v. Analytical Services & Materials, Inc., 299 F. Supp. 2d 565 (E.D. Va. 2004); Union Labor Life Ins. Co. v. Sheet Metal Workers Nat'l Health Plan, 1991 WL 212232 (D.D.C. Sept. 30, 1991); Capital One Bank v. Gelsey (Fla. County Ct. Duval County July 3, 2007) (Flower, J.), *available at* www.consumerlaw.org/unreported.

98 *See* § 4.7, *infra.*

99 *See* § 3.7.3.1, *supra.*

100 Richburg v. Palisades Collection L.L.C., 247 F.R.D. 457 (E.D. Pa. 2008); Capital One Bank v. Gelsey (Fla. County Ct. Duval County July 3, 2007) (Flower, J.), *available at* www.consumerlaw.org/unreported; Nicolai v. Mason, 454 N.E.2d 1049 (Ill. App. Ct. 1983).

101 Capital One Bank v. Sawyer, 15 Fla. L. Weekly Supp. 170a (Fla. County Ct. Duval County Dec. 17, 2007) (Cox, J.); *see also* Capital One Bank v. Gelsey (Fla. County Ct. Duval County July 3, 2007) (Flower, J.), *available at* www.consumerlaw.org/unreported.

102 *See* Rawson v. Credigy Receivables, Inc., 2006 WL 418665 (N.D. Ill. Feb. 16, 2006). *But see* Hill v. Am. Express, 2008 WL 204623 (Ga. Ct. App. Jan. 24, 2008).

103 *See* Rawson v. Credigy Receivables, Inc., 2006 WL 418665 (N.D. Ill. Feb. 16, 2006); Capital One Bank v. Gelsey (Fla. County Ct. Duval County July 3, 2007) (Flower, J.), *available at* www.consumerlaw.org/unreported.

104 Portfolio Recovery Associates, L.L.C. v. Fernandes, 13 Fla. L. Weekly Supp. 506a (Fla. Cir. Ct. Palm Beach County Mar. 6, 2006) (Perez, J.); *cf.* ARDC Corp. v. Hogan, 656 So. 2d 1371 (Fla. Dist. Ct. App. 1995) (when writing does not contain all the terms the statute of limitations for a written contract does not apply).

3.7.6 When Does the Limitations Period Start Running?

3.7.6.1 The Date Triggering the Limitations Period

Typically, the limitations period will begin from the date of default.[105] This approach is consistent with the rule that, for a breach of contract action, the statute of limitations "runs from the time of the breach, although no damage occurs until later."[106]

UCC Article 2's limitations period explicitly states that it begins running when the breach occurs, regardless of the aggrieved party's lack of knowledge of the breach.[107] In other words, the four years begin running as soon as the consumer has breached the agreement, even if the creditor has not realized the breach has occurred, and certainly not when the creditor decides to declare a breach or when the debt buyer acquires an account. UCC Article 3's limitations period for suit on a dishonored check begins to run from the date of dishonor.[108] The limitations period for promissory notes begins on the date of acceleration.[109]

A state's statute of limitations may have explicit language as to when the limitations period starts running. For example, California's limitations period for an account stated specifies that the time period begins running "from the date of the last item,"[110] indicating that it begins to run not from the occurrence of any default, but from the date the last charge was incurred. When a contract for services indicates that payment is due when the services are completed, then the statute of limitations should begin running when the services are completed.[111]

New Hampshire has a very short three-year limitations period for breach of contract, and its period begins when the collector discovers or should have reasonably discovered the act or omission.[112] Nevertheless, even New Hampshire typically considers the date of reasonable discovery in a contract case to be the date of breach.[113]

Debt buyers and collection attorneys often claim that the date of default for purposes of the statute of limitations is when the creditor unilaterally decides to accelerate the debt. This claim is not supported by law and may even be inconsistent with the credit card agreement (that may be attached to the complaint), which will *not* require notice of acceleration as a prerequisite to declaring a default in the terms of the agreement or as a condition precedent to filing a lawsuit to collect the debt. A common credit card agreement's default provision states: "You will be in default under this agreement upon: (a) your failure to make at least the minimum payment by the date specified on your statement; (b) your violation of any other provision of this agreement. . . ." Default clauses generally provide that a party has a right to sue immediately upon the occurrence of any of the "default contingencies," and thus the default should be the trigger date for the starting of the running of the limitations period.

Collectors may also claim that the statute of limitations begins to run on the charge-off date. But this date is a matter of accounting practice dictated by banking regulators, such as the Office of the Comptroller of the Currency (OCC).[114] For example, the OCC defines "charge off" as the date when a company using the accrual method must stop recording putative income from the loan and treat it as nonperforming. In open-end credit accounts such as credit cards, the account must be "charged off" 180 days after the delinquency. The charge-off date is not the date of default because a creditor would not take the position that it would have to wait 180 days after the debtor stopped making payments before it could file a lawsuit.[115] Do not confuse the Fair Credit Reporting Act calculation rules as to when information is obsolete (which do reference when a debt is charged off) from a state's statute of limitations calculation, for which the charge-off date has no relevance.

Finally, some debt buyers go so far as to claim that the limitations period begins to run when they purchase the debt. This position is clearly wrong, bacause the date of default generally triggers the limitations period, not the date the collector discovers the default. And even if a limitations period begins to run when the creditor discovers the default, this rule applies to the original creditor's discovery. Subse-

105 Isaacson, Stolper & Co. v. Artisan's Sav. Bank, 330 A.2d 130, 132 (Del. 1974).

106 18 Richard A. Lord, Williston on Contracts § 2021A (3d ed. 1978); *see also* Med. Jet, S.A. v. Signature Flight Support—Palm Beach, Inc., 941 So. 2d 576 (Fla. Dist. Ct. App. 2006).

107 U.C.C. § 2-725(2).
In contrast, the U.C.C. Article 2A limitations period for leases accrues when the default occurs or when the lessor should have discovered the default, whichever is later. U.C.C. § 2A-506(2).

108 U.C.C. § 3-118(c).

109 U.C.C. § 3-118(a).

110 Cal. Civ. Proc. Code § 337 (West).

111 Person Earth Movers, Inc. v. Buckland, 525 S.E.2d 239 (N.C. Ct. App. 2000).

112 N.H. Rev. Stat. Ann. § 508:4.

113 W. Gate Vill. Ass'n v. Dubois, 761 A.2d 1066 (N.H. 2000).

114 Office of the Comptroller of the Currency, OCC 2000-20, OCC Bulletin; Fed. Fin. Institutions Examinations Council, Uniform Retail Credit Classification and Account Management Policy, 65 Fed. Reg. 36,903 (June 12, 2000); Fed. Fin. Institutions Examinations Council, Uniform Retail Credit Classification and Account Management Policy, 64 Fed. Reg. 6655 (Feb. 10, 1999).

115 *See* Rochholz v. Farrar, 547 F.2d 63, 64 n.2 (8th Cir. 1976) ("A 'charge off' occurs when a loan is determined to be uncollectible. The amount charged off is then carried in the bad debt account and not as a general ledger asset on the books of the bank."); Fla. Credit Research, Inc. v. Felicien (Fla. County Ct. Duval County Apr. 15, 2008), *available at* www.consumerlaw.org/unreported.

quent purchases of the debt do not start the period running anew. In that case the limitations period would go on forever.

3.7.6.2 Determining the Date of Default

In computing whether the statute of limitations has run, it is not always easy to determine the date of default. Because the date occurred years ago, the consumer is unlikely to have records as to the first date of default. A debt buyer may not have records showing this date either. This is a reason why the collector's proof should include billing statements.[116]

The consumer can start developing the case by closely examining the collector's pleadings and any attached documents. Even if the collector is claiming a later date of default, its own pleadings, affidavits, and other documents may indicate an earlier date.[117] Never underestimate the sloppiness of debt buyer documentation. The date of default can also be inferred from the charge-off date,[118] if the collector provides that date in any of its documents—something collectors do surprisingly often. The charge-off date, under OCC standards, is supposed to be 180 days after the account becomes delinquent. Thus a reasonable assumption of a default date is 180 days before the charge-off date.[119]

Another approach is to look at the consumer's credit report to see what is the last payment on the account reflected in the report. Again, do not confuse the charge-off date which may be indicated there with the date when the debt went into default.[120]

3.7.7 *Is the Limitations Period Tolled or Revived?*

3.7.7.1 Terminology

Although courts use different terminology, this chapter will use the term "tolling" to mean suspension of the running of the limitations period, and "reviving" to mean restarting the running of the limitations period from the beginning. When the limitations period is five years, and two years remain on the period, and the period is tolled, then two years continue to remain before the action is barred. When the occurrence that tolled the period ends the counting begins anew, with only two years left in the period. If the action is revived, then the counting goes back to zero, and the limitations period does not expire for five more years.

3.7.7.2 Tolling the Limitations Period

3.7.7.2.1 Military service

Federal law specifies that the period of a servicemember's military service may not be included in the computing any limitations period under federal or state law.[121] The provision applies to those on active duty military service, and applies to debts incurred before and during the period of active duty military service. This increased risk of a collection lawsuit is offset to some extent by the fact that servicemembers have certain protections against collection actions not available to others, examined in Chapter 7, *infra*. Of course, an individual no longer on active duty loses these special protections, but the statute of limitations is extended because of the tolling effect of the individual's active duty status.

The tolling provision applies to the servicemember and the servicemember's heirs, executors, administrators, or assigns. It does not, by its terms, apply to those jointly liable with the servicemember.[122] Thus the statute of limitations may run against a spouse while it is still tolled against the servicemember.

3.7.7.2.2 Bankruptcy

A bankruptcy proceeding can toll the limitations period, but this will have practical effect only in certain situations. A successful chapter 7 or chapter 13 bankruptcy makes moot the tolling effect of the bankruptcy proceeding on a collection action for an unsecured debt. The successful bankruptcy discharges the debt and there can be no collection action. But, if a chapter 7 filing is dismissed or if a chapter 13 plan fails, then the collector can sue for the unpaid portion of a debt, and the statute of limitations will be tolled during the pendency of the bankruptcy.[123] As soon as the bankruptcy is dismissed or the plan fails, then the statute of limitations starts running again.[124]

116 *See* § 4.6, *infra*.

117 *See* Fla. Credit Research, Inc. v. Felicien (Fla. County Ct. Duval County Apr. 15, 2008), *available at* www.consumerlaw.org/unreported; Capital One Bank v. Gelsey (Fla. County Ct. Duval County July 3, 2007), *available at* www.consumerlaw.org/unreported.

118 *See* § 3.7.6.1, *supra*.

119 *See* Fla. Credit Research, Inc. v. Felicien (Fla. County Ct. Duval County Apr. 15, 2008), *available at* www.consumerlaw.org/unreported; Capital One Bank v. Gelsey (Fla. County Ct. Duval County July 3, 2007), *available at* www.consumerlaw.org/unreported.

120 *See* § 3.7.6.1, *supra*.

121 50 U.S.C. app. § 526(a).

122 50 U.S.C. app. § 526(a).

123 11 U.S.C. § 108(c); *see also* Person Earth Movers, Inc. v. Buckland, 525 S.E.2d 239 (N.C. Ct. App. 2000).

124 Person Earth Movers, Inc. v. Buckland, 525 S.E.2d 239 (N.C. Ct. App. 2000).

3.7.7.2.3 *Time spent out of state*

Other grounds for tolling the statute of limitations will be based on state law. A common ground for such tolling is if the consumer moves out of state for some of the period. The time of the absence is not part of the time limit.[125] The burden will be on the collector to show the dates the consumer was absent from the state. If the collector can not meet this burden, then the limitations period will not be tolled.

A number of courts have also found that the tolling rule for time out of state does not apply when service of process is available out of state.[126] The premise of the tolling statute is that the defendant's personal absence from the jurisdiction makes service on the defendant difficult. When this premise is no longer applicable because of modern notions of long-arm statutes and the like, then the tolling statute should not apply.[127] Some courts simply define "absent" or "out of state" as meaning a defendant who is beyond personal jurisdiction and process of the court, thus denying tolling when an action is possible against the out-of-state defendant.[128]

Moreover, it is very possible that a rule tolling the limitations period when the defendant is out of state is unconstitutional. The courts seem to be in agreement that leaving the state to engage in commerce should not be discriminated against, and that lengthening a statute of limitations period for those engaging in interstate commerce would be unconstitutional.[129] Courts have found the tolling to be unconstitutional when the consumer went out of state for employment,[130] or to change residences,[131] but not for a vacation.[132]

When the law of the state selected in the credit agreement controls the statute of limitations, collectors sometimes point to the non-forum state's provision that the limitations period does not run when the consumer does not reside in that state. As the consumer has never resided in the non-forum state, the limitations period never begins to run. Courts have no problem rejecting this argument that would otherwise make a sham of the limitations period.[133]

3.7.7.3 Reviving the Limitations Period

3.7.7.3.1 *Part payment*

Certain actions by the consumer can revive the statute of limitations—that is start the statute running again from the beginning. In many states, one such action is making a payment on the debt.[134] Of course the payment must be directed at the debt in question. For example, if a collector seeks payment on two different accounts, even two accounts with the same creditor, payment on one account does not revive the limitations period on the other account.[135]

Moreover the consumer's intent must be, in making part payment, to acknowledge that the remainder is also due. If the consumer intended a payment to be the final amount, even if the collector believes more is due, then the statute of limitations continues to run for the balance the collector is seeking.[136] Payment of principal does not revive the limitations period for interest payments that are disputed.[137] If the consumer makes a payment indicating an obligation for part of the debt alleged, but disputing the remainder of the

125 Alaska Stat. § 09.10.130; Cal. Civ. Proc. Code § 351 (West); Idaho Code Ann. § 5-229; Me. Rev. Stat. Ann. tit. 14, § 866; Miss. Code Ann. § 15-1-63; Mo. Rev. Stat. § 516.200; Neb. Rev. Stat. § 25-214; Ohio Rev. Code Ann. § 2305.15(A) (West); Or. Rev. Stat. § 12.150; S.C. Code Ann. § 15-3-30; S.D. Codified Laws § 15-2-20; Tenn. Code Ann. § 28-1-111; Tex. Civ. Prac. & Rem. Code Ann. § 16.063 (Vernon); Utah Code Ann. § 78-12-35; Wash. Rev. Code § 4.16.180; Wyo. Stat. Ann. § 1-3-116.

126 Kuk v. Nalley, 166 P.3d 47 (Alaska 2007); Shin v. McLaughlin, 967 P.2d 1059 (Haw. 1998); Meyer v. Paschal, 498 S.E.2d 635 (S.C. 1998). *But see* Dew v. Appleberry, 23 Cal. 3d 630 (1979); Couts v. Rose, 90 N.E.2d 139 (Ohio 1950); Vaughn v. Deitz, 430 S.W.2d 487 (Tex. 1968); Olseth v. Larson, 153 P.3d 532 (Utah 2007).

127 Kuk v. Nalley, 166 P.3d 47 (Alaska 2007).

128 Peters v. Tuell Dairy Co., 35 So. 2d 344 (Ala. 1948); Byrne v. Ogle, 488 P.2d 716 (Alaska 1971); Meyer v. Paschal, 498 S.E.2d 635 (S.C. 1998).

129 Bendix Autolite Corp. v. Midwesco Enterprises, 486 U.S. 888, 108 S. Ct. 2218, 100 L. Ed. 2d 896 (1988); Abramson v. Brownstein, 897 F.2d 389 (9th Cir. 1990); Tesar v. Hallas, 738 F. Supp. 240 (N.D. Ohio 1990); Heritage Mktg. & Ins. Services, Inc. v. Chrustawka, 2008 WL 542185 (Cal. Ct. App. Feb. 29, 2008); McFadden v. Battifora, 2004 WL 103353 (Cal. Ct. App. Jan. 23, 2004); Filet Menu, Inc. v. Cheng, 71 Cal. App. 4th 1276 (1999); State *ex rel.* Bloomquist v. Schneider, 244 S.W.3d 139 (Mo. 2008).

130 Tesar v. Hallas, 738 F. Supp. 240 (N.D. Ohio 1990); McFadden v. Battifora, 2004 WL 103353 (Cal. Ct. App. Jan. 23, 2004); *see also* Filet Menu, Inc. v. Cheng, 71 Cal. App. 4th 1276 (1999).

131 Heritage Mktg. & Ins. Services, Inc. v. Chrustawka, 2008 WL 542185 (Cal. Ct. App. Feb. 29, 2008); Filet Menu, Inc. v. Cheng, 71 Cal. App. 4th 1276 (1999); State *ex rel.* Bloomquist v. Schneider, 244 S.W.3d 139 (Mo. 2008).

132 Johnson v. Rhodes, 733 N.E.2d 1132 (Ohio 2000).

133 Harwitch v. Adams, 155 A.2d 591 (Del. 1959); L.W.T. v. Brodsky, 14 Fla. L. Weekly Supp. 188a (Fla. County Ct. Broward County Dec. 8, 2006).

134 *See* Kan. Stat. Ann. § 60-520(a); Martindell v. Bodrero, 256 Cal. App. 2d 56 (1967); Citibank S.D. v. Cramer, 139 Wash. App. 1089 (2007); Annotation, *Payment on Account, or Claimed to be on Account, as Removing or Tolling Statute of Limitations*, 156 A.L.R. 1082 (1945).

135 H.A. Wood, Annotation, *Necessity and sufficiency of identification of part payment with the particular debt in question, for purposes of tolling, or removing bar of, statute of limitations*, 142 A.L.R. 389 (1943).

136 Huntingdon Fin. Corp. v. Newtown Artesian Water Co., 659 A.2d 1052 (Pa. Super. Ct. 1995).

137 *Id.*

debt, the payment does not revive the limitations period for the disputed portion of the debt.[138]

There must also be proof that payment was in fact made. A debt buyer wishing to revive the limitations period can not just claim that a part payment has been made recently. It must provide evidence of that payment, particularly if the consumer denies making the payment. Some states disallow an alleged payment whose only proof is a note in the creditor's books, requiring additional proof.[139]

Payment by one co-debtor may not revive the limitations period in an action against the other co-debtor.[140] The same is the case for a payment by a bankruptcy trustee. This payment does not revive the limitations period against the consumer.[141] The reason that payment revives the limitation period is that it implies that the consumer acknowledges the debt. If the consumer did not make the payment, or if the consumer made the payment with a different intent, then the payment does not imply this acknowledgment.[142]

Because the collector has the burden of proof to show that a consumer's action has revived the limitations period, the collector will have the burden of proof to show that a payment was made, that the consumer being sued in fact made the payment, that the payment was directed to the account in question, and that the payment was made with the intent to acknowledge the remainder of the debt.[143]

3.7.7.3.2 Acknowledgment of the debt

The consumer's acknowledgment of the obligation may revive the statute of limitations. But here states establish standards as to what type of acknowledgment is sufficient to revive the limitations period. Typically an oral statement that the money is owed is *not* enough. Some states require the acknowledgment be in writing and signed.[144] Other states find that it is not enough that the debtor recognize the debt. The debtor must also admit liability and agree to pay the remainder due.[145] For example, in Pennsylvania, a simple declaration of an intent to discharge an obligation is not enough. There must be more than a willingness to pay at a future time, but a willingness to pay upon demand.[146]

The acknowledgment must be "clear, distinct, and unequivocal."[147] An acknowledgment of the principal amount due on a debt may not be an acknowledgment that the claimed finance charges and other fees are also owed.[148] In addition, when there are joint debtors and one of the debtors admits to the debt sufficient to restart the limitations period, that admission may not be sufficient to restart the limitations period for claims against the other debtor.[149]

3.7.7.3.3 Intersection with Fair Credit Reporting Act obsolescence rules

Under the Fair Credit Reporting Act (FCRA), most negative information must be removed from a consumer's credit history file after seven years.[150] For debts that are charged off or in default, this seven-year period begins 180 days after the date of first delinquency.[151] Unlike the statute of limitations, part payment or acknowledgment of the debt does not restart the seven-year period under the FCRA.[152] Debt collectors have been known to "re-age" a debt by reporting an incorrect date of first delinquency, which is a potential violation of the FCRA (albeit without a private right of action),[153] as well as the Fair Debt Collection Practices Act.

138 O'Malley v. Frazier, 49 P.3d 438 (Kan. 2002).

139 *E.g.*, N.J. Stat. Ann. § 2A:14-25 (West).

140 *See* N.J. Stat. Ann. § 2A:14-24 (West); Elmore v. Fanning, 117 P. 1019 (Kan. 1911).

141 Person Earth Movers, Inc. v. Buckland, 525 S.E.2d 239 (N.C. Ct. App. 2000).

142 *Id.*

143 Huntingdon Fin. Corp. v. Newtown Artesian Water Co., 659 A.2d 1052 (Pa. Super. Ct. 1995).

144 *See* Cal. Civ. Proc. Code § 360 (West) (no acknowledgment or promise is sufficient evidence of a new or continuing contract, by which to take the case out of the operation of this title, unless the same is contained in some writing, signed by the party to be charged thereby); Kan. Stat. Ann. § 60-520(a); N.J. Stat. Ann. § 2A:14-24 (West); Asset Acceptance, L.L.C. v. Morgan, 2007 WL 949251 (Mich. Ct. App. Mar. 29, 2007).

145 A & B Lumber Co., L.L.C. v. Vrusho, 871 A.2d 64 (N.H. 2005); Gurenlian v. Gurenlian, 595 A.2d 145 (Pa. Super. Ct. 1991).

146 Gurenlian v. Gurenlian, 595 A.2d 145 (Pa. Super. Ct. 1991); *see also* Pagnotti v. Lehigh Valley Coal Sale Co., 269 B.R. 326 (Bankr. M.D. Pa. 2001).

147 Gurenlian v. Gurenlian, 595 A.2d 145 (Pa. Super. Ct. 1991).

148 Huntingdon Fin. Corp. v. Newtown Artesian Water Co., 659 A.2d 1052 (Pa. Super. Ct. 1995).

149 N.J. Stat. Ann. § 2A:14-24 (West); A & B Lumber Co., L.L.C. v. Vrusho, 871 A.2d 64 (N.H. 2005).

150 *See* National Consumer Law Center, Fair Credit Reporting § 5.2 (6th ed. 2006 and Supp.).

151 *See id.* § 5.2.3.3.1.

152 *See id.* § 5.2.3.3.4.

153 *See id.* § 5.2.3.3.5.

Chapter 4 The Collector's Proof of the Merits

4.1 Introduction

This chapter examines the debt collector's proof as to the merits of its causes of action. As the burden is on the plaintiff to prove its claims no recovery can be had, either at trial or on summary judgment, unless the debt collector presents proper evidence satisfying the elements of the collector's cause of action. As a general rule, debt buyers assume virtually all complaints will end in a default judgment. As a result debt buyers will not produce this level of evidence, and the consumer is in a strong position to defend against the claim.

This chapter first analyzes various general challenges to a collector's offer of evidence.[1] Then the chapter turns to the application of these evidentiary rules to the various elements of the collector's claims. When a debt buyer is bringing the action, the first and often most important issue is whether the collector can prove that it owns the debt being sued upon.[2]

Assuming the collector can establish standing, it can only recover under one or more delineated causes of action. Section 4.4, *infra*, explains that the collector must clearly specify which causes of action it is bringing in a case, and that the court should rule only on those claims and not on any others.

The chapter then turns to the collector's proof of the nature of the credit contract. The collector's failure to produce this proof will not only defeat its breach of contract cause of action, but will also limit its recovery under other causes of action.[3] Proof of the balance due is then examined, being essential to any claim on an open-end account for breach of contract, "on account," or "open account."[4] "Account stated" is another common collector cause of action, being based not upon the contract or proof of individual charges, but upon the allegation that the consumer has explicitly or implicitly agreed to pay an amount owed.[5] The chapter concludes with a brief analysis of other possible causes of action, such as *quantum meruit*, money lent, or materials and services supplied.

1 *See* § 4.2, *infra*.
2 *See* § 4.3, *infra*.
3 *See* § 4.5, *infra*.
4 *See* § 4.6, *infra*.
5 *See* § 4.7, *infra*.

4.2 Sufficiency of the Collector's Evidence

4.2.1 Introduction

Most contested consumer collection actions do not involve extensive testimony, but are largely decided based upon documents submitted to the court. The collector may move for summary judgment, attaching admissions, affidavits, and purported business records. Even when small claims court rules do not allow for summary judgment motions, the collector will typically seek to prevail at trial using similar documentation, without relying on witness testimony.

This section focuses on three forms of evidence collectors commonly use: the consumer's admissions, affidavits in support of a summary judgment motion, and business records. This section provides merely an overview of the subject as it relates to collection actions. It does not replace a thorough knowledge of a state's rules of evidence. The discussion should also be supplemented with review of general treatises on evidence.

4.2.2 Collector's Request for Admissions

4.2.2.1 General

Debt buyers in particular may have little evidence to establish their case, and little interest in obtaining the evidence. Instead they may try to win their case using the consumer's own admissions. Along with the complaint, or shortly thereafter, the collector will send the consumer a lengthy list of statements, asking the consumer to admit to them, hoping the consumer will not respond in a timely manner. Failure to respond is treated as an admission of all the requested statements.[6] The collector then appends those statements to a summary judgment motion and seeks to

6 *See* McLane v. MRC Receivables Corp., 2007 WL 29435 (Ky. Ct. App. Jan. 5, 2007); Great Seneca Fin. Corp. v. Lee, 2006 WL 1132473 (Ohio Ct. App. Apr. 26, 2006); Asset Acceptance, L.L.C. v. Rees, 2006 WL 416373 (Ohio Ct. App. Feb. 23, 2006); Luke v. Unifund CCR Partners, 2007 WL 2460327 (Tex. App. Aug. 31, 2007).

prevail in the case although presenting little or none of its own evidence.[7] By serving requests for admission collectors prey on unrepresented consumers' lack of legal knowledge, attempting to prove their cases by sleight of hand when they can not do so by evidence.

This section examines two related questions: first, how to respond to requests for admission when there is still an opportunity to timely do so;[8] second, what should be done if the consumer has failed to timely respond to the requests.[9]

The rules as to requests for admissions vary by state and even by court within the same state. This section focuses on the rules set out by Federal Rules of Civil Procedure 36 and 37, as many state rules of procedure are patterned after the federal rules. But practitioners must compare the federal rule with their own state's rules and the procedures that apply for the court in which the action is brought. For example, small claims courts may not even allow requests for admission or will not provide for any negative consequences if the consumer fails to respond. If a court's rules do not establish any negative consequences, there will be little reason to respond.

Federal Rule of Civil Procedure 36 states that parties can seek admissions as to the facts, the application of law to the facts, and the genuineness of described documents. Matters are admitted unless there is a response within thirty days.[10] If the consumer admits to the statement then the collector need not prove that statement in court by its own evidence, and the matter is deemed proven. If the consumer timely responds to the requests but denies the statement without good cause to do so, Federal Rule of Civil Procedure 37(c)(2) provides that, if the collector later proves the statement to be true, the consumer is liable for the reasonable expenses of the collector's proof—which would include attorney fees and other expenses.

4.2.2.2 How to Respond to Requests for Admissions

If a request for admissions contains statements meeting all the elements of the causes of action the collector is raising, the collector can prevail on summary judgment based solely upon the consumer's failure to respond.[11] Consequently, the worst thing that the consumer can do is fail to respond to the request for admissions. The consumer's options as to each requested admission are to admit (in whole or in part), deny (in whole or in part), neither admit nor deny (with explanation), or object.

In responding, the consumer does not want to admit to matters that are not true or that the collector could not prove or will not seek to prove. On the other hand, there is risk in denying matters which are true and that the collector will be able to prove to be true. The consumer can be ordered to pay the costs required to prove those matters—both attorney fees and other costs associated with developing that evidence.

One option is to neither admit nor deny the matter. Federal Rule of Civil Procedure 36 allows the consumer to state in detail why the answering party can not truthfully admit or deny the matter, such as no records or no recollection. Lack of knowledge can be a basis for the inability to admit or deny only if the party states he or she has first made a reasonable inquiry and that the information known or readily obtainable by the party is insufficient to enable the party to admit or deny the matter.[12] The consumer can not be expected to admit or deny information outside the consumer's control, or about which the consumer has no personal knowledge.[13]

If the lack of knowledge is reasonable, then the consumer is not liable under Rule 36 for the collector's expenses in proving that fact.[14] For example, the consumer does not have to go to the trouble or expense of trying to get records from the original creditor; that is up to the debt buyer that has to prove its case.

The consumer can also reasonably state she is neither admitting nor denying that a debt buyer is the owner of an indebtedness, because to do so would require knowledge of facts not known to the consumer. The consumer can also deny that the collector's "predecessor in interest" made the loan, because the consumer does not know who is being referred to or even if the collector has an interest in the debt. The consumer should also be able to reasonably refuse to admit or deny that a standard form contract is identical to the one the consumer received, if the consumer no longer possesses the consumer's copy. Likewise, the consumer can also state that she is neither admitting nor denying that various documents generated by the debt buyer are genuine business records of the debt buyer. For all of these requests, the consumer has no ability to obtain sufficient information on which to base a response.

The consumer is also allowed to object to a request for admissions, stating the grounds for the objection.[15] At that point, the collector can request that the court determine the sufficiency of the objection and the court, if it overrules the

7 *See* Great Seneca Fin. Corp. v. Lee, 2006 WL 1132473 (Ohio Ct. App. Apr. 26, 2006).

8 *See* § 4.2.2.2, *infra*.

9 *See* § 4.2.2.3, *infra*.

10 Fed. R. Civ. P. 36; *see also* McLane v. MRC Receivables Corp., 2007 WL 29435 (Ky. Ct. App. Jan. 5, 2007); Great Seneca Fin. Corp. v. Lee, 2006 WL 1132473 (Ohio Ct. App. Apr. 26, 2006); Asset Acceptance, L.L.C. v. Rees, 2006 WL 416373 (Ohio Ct. App. Feb. 23, 2006); Luke v. Unifund CCR Partners, 2007 WL 2460327 (Tex. App. Aug. 31, 2007).

11 *See* Great Seneca Fin. Corp. v. Lee, 2006 WL 1132473 (Ohio Ct. App. Apr. 26, 2006); Luke v. Unifund CCR Partners, 2007 WL 2460327 (Tex. App. Aug. 31, 2007).

12 Fed. R. Civ. P. 36.

13 United States *ex rel.* England v. Los Angeles County, 235 F.R.D. 675 (E.D. Cal. 2006).

14 Fed. R. Civ. P. 36.

15 Fed. R. Civ. P. 36(a)(5); *see also* ADC Telecommunications Inc. v. Telect, Inc., 143 F.R.D. 214 (D. Minn. 1992).

objection, can then order that an amended answer be made.[16] Possible grounds for objection are that the statement calls for a purely legal opinion, or that the requested statement is irrelevant or burdensome.[17] The consumer can also object to vague or ambiguous requests. The Third Circuit has said that requests for admissions "should not be used unless a statement of fact sought to be admitted is phrased so that it can be admitted or denied without explanation."[18]

Local state rules may specify additional grounds to object. In New York a request for admission must ask about information within the party's knowledge and can not ask about matters that go to the ultimate issue of the case.[19] For example, it would be objectionable to ask the consumer to admit that the debt has been assigned to the plaintiff (no firsthand knowledge) or to admit that the consumer is liable for the amount sought (ultimate issue of the case).

When good faith permits, the consumer can deny a request for admission. However good faith may require that the consumer admit to a specific part of a statement, and deny the rest. Even if the statement is later proven to be true, the consumer is not liable for the collector's expenses of proof if there were reasonable grounds for the consumer to deny the matter.[20] The consumer need not win the case but, for the particular statement requested, the consumer need only have reasonable grounds for believing that the statement is not true. For example, the consumer can safely deny a statement that a $5000 amount is due even when $4950 is clearly owed, if there is a reasonable issue as to the remaining $50, and even if the full $5000 is eventually proven.

When it is not certain beyond a doubt that the consumer has reasonable grounds to deny a statement, tactical considerations come into play as to the safest response. If the consumer denies the statement, what are the odds that the collector will in fact try to prove that statement, and what are the odds that it will in fact prove that statement? If the statement is proven, will the collector go back to court to seek the expenses of proving that statement, necessitating a showing that the consumer did not have reasonable grounds for the denial, and also requiring proof of the amount of the expenses involved?

The answer to these questions may depend very much on whether the collector is the original creditor or a debt buyer. The original creditor will have access to much more information about the account, and will be more likely to pursue a case to completion. A debt buyer, on the other hand, having purchased the debt for pennies on the dollar and not possessing much information about the account, may have a business model that relies on either default judgments or on consumers failing to respond to requests for admissions. The debt buyer may have a policy of not pursuing contested cases. Other factors include the size of the debt, the difficulty of proof, and the typical practices of the particular collection attorney who brought the suit.

Even if the consumer has to pay the collector's expenses necessary to prove a statement, those expenses may not be as costly as one might suppose. If the consumer loses the case the consumer may be liable for the collector's attorney fees and for costs in any case. Of course, these fees and costs may be lower if the consumer admits to certain matters, shortening the trial. In addition certain expenses to prove a statement may be recoverable under Federal Rule of Civil Procedure 37 that would not otherwise be awarded as court costs.

In general, the consumer must be wary admitting to anything that the collector can not easily prove on its own. The consumer does not want to lose a case that the collector would not have been able to prove if it had been forced to develop its own evidence at trial. Nevertheless, the consumer can admit to certain aspects of a statement, but deny other aspects that are central to the collector's proof. For example, the consumer might admit to applying for and using a credit card, but deny the amount being sought on the card on the grounds that payments were not credited, that fees were unfair or improperly assessed, or that the finance charges are not accurate.

4.2.2.3 When Time Period to Respond Has Lapsed

A consumer who has failed to respond to admissions in a timely manner is in peril. The request specifies a due date and the court has discretion, if there is no response by that date, to deem the requested statements to be admitted.[21] But there are still a number of steps a consumer can take to withdraw or limit the impact of the admissions.

First, do not assume that a collector has sent the requests for admissions just because it says it has, or that it sent the requests on the date it specifies. Many debt buyers and collection attorneys work more on volume than on precision.

Once it is discovered that a deadline for responding has been missed, immediately approach the collector's attorney and request additional time. If the request is denied, promptly seek relief from the court. Waiting will only lessen the chances that the court will grant the requested relief, because delay may increase the prejudice to the collector of withdrawing the admissions.

Under Federal Rule of Civil Procedure 6(b), the court can extend time to respond because of excusable neglect. But Rule 36(b) offers a standard that courts are more likely to

16 Fed. R. Civ. P. 36(a)(6).

17 Federal Rule of Civil Procedure 36 incorporates Federal Rule of Civil Procedure 26(b), which indicates that a request's burden should not outweigh its likely benefit.

18 United Coal Companies v. Powell Constr. Co., 839 F.2d 958 (3d Cir. 1988).

19 N.Y. C.P.L.R. 3123 (McKinney).

20 Fed. R. Civ. P. 37(c)(2).

21 *See* § 4.2.2.1, *supra*.

utilize in deciding when to grant a party leave to submit otherwise untimely answers to requests for admission.[22] Rule 36(b) deals with withdrawal of admissions, and its provisions apply to admissions based upon the failure to answer.[23] The standard set out in Rule 36(b) is also more advantageous to consumer defendants than the standard found in Rule 6(b).

Rule 36(b) provides: "[T]he court may permit withdrawal or amendment if it would promote the presentation of the merits of the action and if the court is not persuaded that it would prejudice the requesting party in maintaining or defending the action on the merits."[24] The consumer has the burden of showing that leave to file an untimely answer will promote the presentation of the merits, and the collector will have the burden of showing prejudice from the delay.[25] When the consumer shows the answer will promote presentation of the merits, and the collector fails to prove prejudice, the court must allow withdrawal of the admission. This is not a matter of court discretion.[26]

The collector's prejudice the Rule refers to is not that the collector will now have to prove to the fact finder that the statement previously admitted is true. Instead, the prejudice must concern how the delay will make it more difficult for the collector to prove its case, because of the sudden unavailability of key witnesses or the difficulty to obtain evidence for trial at short notice.[27] Prejudice to the collector is more likely to be present when the admission is withdrawn during trial than before trial.[28]

The consumer's burden to show that withdrawal of the admission will promote the presentation of the merits is "satisfied when upholding the admissions would practically eliminate any presentation of the merits of the case."[29] The Eleventh Circuit required that admissions be withdrawn when a party uses the rule "with the wild-eyed hope that the other side will fail to answer and therefore admit essential elements."[30] The Rule's purpose is to establish uncontested facts in order to narrow the issues at trial, not to be used as a weapon to take advantage of unrepresented consumers.[31]

Always explain the reason for the consumer's neglect. In one case, the consumer asked for a more definite statement of the complaint, and did not respond while waiting for that more definite statement.[32] In another case, the consumer had consistently disputed the bill over a period of years and had requested information from the creditor.[33] The unrepresented consumer may have thought a response was unnecessary because the consumer already had so clearly disputed many of the statements. Of course courts also consider the fact that the consumer was unrepresented at the time.[34]

If admissions can not be withdrawn, there are still steps to take. Carefully review all the statements that are being treated as admitted. Debt buyers and other collectors may be sloppy in their drafting of admissions. See if any of the statements requested to be admitted conflict with each other. If the request asks the consumer to admit "X" and also "not X," and the consumer fails to respond to the requests, then the collector can not rely on the admissions to prove either X or not X.[35] Contradictory admissions are a nullity. Similarly, if a matter to be admitted is not drafted well or contains a typographical error, so that its meaning is unclear, the failure to respond should not be taken as an admission of anything.[36]

4.2.3 Collector's Use of Affidavits As Evidence

This subsection focuses on collectors' use of affidavits to proffer evidence found in the affidavits themselves. The following subsection examines the use of affidavits to authenticate or certify business records that are introduced into evidence. Thus this subsection examines affidavits meant to constitute evidence, rather than those used just to authenticate other documentary evidence. With rare exceptions these affidavits are not admissible at trial, but collectors often use them to aid a motion for a summary or default judgment.

22 *See* 8A Charles A. Wright et al., Federal Practice and Procedure § 2257 (2008) (preferring the Rule 36 standard over the Rule 6 standard).

23 Perez v. Miami-Dade County, 297 F.3d 1255 (11th Cir. 2002); Gutting v. Flastaff Brewing Corp., 710 F.2d 1309 (8th Cir. 1983); McLane v. MRC Receivables Corp., 2007 WL 29435 (Ky. Ct. App. Jan. 5, 2007).

24 *See also* Asset Acceptance L.L.C. v. Lemon, 2006 WL 2474355 (Ohio Ct. App. Aug. 25, 2006) (citing Balson v. Dodds, 62 Ohio St. 2d 287 (1980)).

25 Revlon Consumer Products Corp. v. L'Oreal S.A., 170 F.R.D. 391 (D. Del. 1997).

26 Perez v. Miami-Dade County, 297 F.3d 1255 (11th Cir. 2002).

27 *Id.*

28 *Id.*

29 Hadley v. United States, 45 F.3d 1345, 1348 (9th Cir. 1995); *see also* Perez v. Miami-Dade County, 297 F.3d 1255 (11th Cir. 2002).

30 Perez v. Miami-Dade County, 297 F.3d 1255, 1268 (11th Cir. 2002).

31 Capital One Bank v. Toney, 2007 WL 969420 (Ohio Ct. App. Mar. 28, 2007) (time extended because consumer had requested a more definite statement of the complaint, which was not forthcoming); Asset Acceptance L.L.C. v. Lemon, 2006 WL 2474355 (Ohio Ct. App. Aug. 25, 2006) (consumer had consistently disputed the amount owed); *see also* Human Res. Dev. Press, Inc. v. IKON Office Solutions, Inc., 246 F.R.D. 82 (D. Mass. 2007); McLane v. MRC Receivables Corp., 2007 WL 29435 (Ky. Ct. App. Jan. 5, 2007).

32 Capital One Bank v. Toney, 2007 WL 969420 (Ohio Ct. App. Mar. 28, 2007).

33 Asset Acceptance L.L.C. v. Lemon, 2006 WL 2474355 (Ohio Ct. App. Aug. 25, 2006).

34 Spencer v. Dearborn County Sheriff's Dep't, 2007 WL 1729752 (S.D. Ind. June 6, 2007).

35 Luke v. Unifund CCR Partners, 2007 WL 2460327 (Tex. App. Aug. 31, 2007).

36 *Id.*

Debt buyers in particular may seek to conceal their inability to produce the best evidence of a factual allegation by having an employee state in an affidavit that the fact is true. Affidavits must be made on personal knowledge and show affirmatively that the affiant is competent to testify as to the matters stated therein.[37] Thus, when an affiant asserts that a statement was mailed to the consumer, the affiant must either attest to personal knowledge that the statement was mailed or describe a regular office practice for mailing documents of that type.[38] It is clearly inadequate for a debt buyer's employee to state in an affidavit, without more, that the creditor assigning it the debt had mailed out a contract to the consumer, as the debt buyer's employee has no personal knowledge whether the contract was mailed to the consumer.

The affidavit should not be conclusory.[39] General statements in an affidavit which are only conclusions of law or fact do not prove a case.[40] Good examples of inadequate affidavits are those that state that the consumer owes a certain amount without attaching any documentation to support that conclusion,[41] and an affidavit claiming that an assignment has been made without attaching the actual assignment document.[42]

An affidavit clearly provides no evidence as to the nature of account statements, contracts, or other documents that are allegedly attached to the affidavit, when the documents in fact are not attached.[43] Such omissions occur surprisingly often, particularly with debt buyers.

When documents are in fact attached to the affidavit, look for inconsistencies between the documents and the affidavit itself, which will call into question the evidence being proffered both by the affidavit and by the documents.[44] Similarly, look for inconsistencies between the affidavit, the complaint, a collector's summary judgment motion, and other affidavits and documents in the case.

See if the affidavit also contains false statements. Look for statements that the affiant is employed by the plaintiff when in fact the affiant is employed by a collection agency hired by the plaintiff. Does an affiant employed by a debt buyer claim to have personal knowledge of the practices of the original creditor, when it would be impossible for that affiant to have that knowledge?

Also look for technical deficiencies in an affidavit. Is the name of the individual signing the affidavit disclosed on the affidavit? Is the affidavit properly signed and notarized?

A number of state laws require that sworn pleadings from other states be accompanied by a certificate authenticating the oath giver's authority[45] and courts may reject sworn pleadings submitted without that certificate,[46] particularly if the consumer objects.[47] Indiana's law, which is typical of such statutes, requires out-of-state affidavits sworn before judges and notaries to be certified under the seal of the clerk of court in the county where such judge or notary practices.[48] Other states may be more liberal in accepting out-of-state affidavits, when they are properly notarized in that state,[49] or even when the witness just affirms under the penalties of perjury.

The consumer should consider submitting an affidavit to counter facts alleged in the collector's affidavit, thus placing those facts in dispute. This response should be enough to defeat the collector's summary judgment motion.[50] If the court finds the consumer's affidavit conclusory or lacking in

37 Palisades Collection, L.L.C. v. Gonzalez, 809 N.Y.S.2d 482 (Civ. Ct. 2005) (table) (text available at 2005 WL 3372971); Citibank (S.D.) v. Martin, 807 N.Y.S.2d 284 (Civ. Ct. 2005); Luke v. Unifund CCR Partners, 2007 WL 2460327 (Tex. App. Aug. 31, 2007).

38 Palisades Collection, L.L.C. v. Gonzalez, 809 N.Y.S.2d 482 (Civ. Ct. 2005) (table) (text available at 2005 WL 3372971); *see also* Norfolk Fin. Corp. v. MacDonald, 2003 Mass. App. Div. 153 (Dist. Ct. 2003) (debt buyer's employee could not prove that contract had been sent by creditor to consumer).

39 Luke v. Unifund CCR Partners, 2007 WL 2460327 (Tex. App. Aug. 31, 2007).

40 Thomas v. OSI Funding Group, Inc., 2004 WL 541519 (Fla. Cir. Ct. Feb. 2, 2004).

41 *See* Suggs .v. Sherman Acquisition Ltd. P'ship, 13 Fla. L. Weekly Supp. 301a (Fla. Cir. Ct. Sept. 28, 2005); Capital One Bank v. Toney, 2007 WL 969420 (Ohio Ct. App. Mar. 28, 2007); Luke v. Unifund CCR Partners, 2007 WL 2460327 (Tex. App. Aug. 31, 2007).

42 Powers v. Hudson & Keyse, L.L.C., 656 S.E.2d 578 (Ga. Ct. App. 2008); PRA III, L.L.C. v. MacDowell, 841 N.Y.S.2d 822 (Civ. Ct. 2007) (table) (text available at 2007 WL 1429026); Palisades Collection, L.L.C. v. Gonzalez, 809 N.Y.S.2d 482 (Civ. Ct. 2005) (table) (text available at 2005 WL 3372971).

43 Cole Taylor Bank v. Corrigan, 595 N.E.2d 177 (Ill. App. Ct. 1992); Luke v. Unifund CCR Partners, 2007 WL 2460327 (Tex. App. Aug. 31, 2007). *But see* Citibank (S.D.) v. Kessler, 2004 WL 795689 (Ohio Ct. App. Apr. 15, 2004) (recovery allowed even though affidavit did not attach billing statements).

44 *See* § 4.2.4.2, *infra*.

45 *See, e.g.*, Ind. Code § 34-37-1-7; Minn. Stat. § 600.09; N.Y. C.P.L.R. 2309(c) (McKinney).

46 *See* First Nat'l Bank of Dillsboro v. Mulford, 95 N.E. 432 (Ind. Ct. App. 1911); Citibank (S.D.) v. Suen, 11 Misc. 3d 126(A), 814 N.Y.S.2d 889 (App. Div. 2005) (table); Discover Bank v. Kagan, 803 N.Y.S.2d 18 (Sup. Ct. 2005); Citibank (S.D.) v. Martin, 807 N.Y.S.2d 284 (Civ. Ct. 2005). *But cf.* Raynor v. Raynor, 108 N.Y.S.2d 20 (App. Div. 1951) ("the lack of an authenticating certificate was a defect or irregularity which could be corrected *nunc pro tunc*").

47 *See* MBNA Am. Bank v. Stehly, 2008 WL 141675 (N.Y. Sup. Ct. Jan. 11, 2008).

48 Ind. Code § 34-37-1-7.

49 *See, e.g.*, Fla. Stat. § 92.50; Ga. Code Ann. § 9-10-113; 5 Ill. Comp. Stat. § 255/6; La. Rev. Stat. Ann. § 13:3719; Mich. Comp. Laws § 565.262; N.J. Stat. Ann. § 41:2-17 (West); Wash. Rev. Code § 887.01; W. Va. Code § 57-5-9; *cf.* Haston v. Gen. Motors Corp., 678 So. 2d 1164 (Ala. Civ. App. 1996) (witness affidavit was void and could not be considered in connection with manufacturer's motion for summary judgment in products liability action when Michigan notary public who had signed affidavit had failed to affix seal of office).

50 *See, e.g.*, Bozeman v. CACV of Colorado, L.L.C., 282 Ga. Ct. App. 256 (2006); Colonial Credit Corp v. Dana, 2007 WL 446033 (Ohio Ct. App. Feb. 12, 2007).

personal knowledge, the court should apply the same standard to the collector's affidavit.

4.2.4 *Proof Using Documents—the Business Records Exception*

4.2.4.1 The Business Records Exception

Business records used to prove a collector's causes of action are hearsay,[51] and must fit within the business records exception to the rules prohibiting hearsay evidence in order to be admitted into evidence. Most state rules of evidence are similar to Federal Rule of Evidence 803(6), which establishes that a business record is exempt from the hearsay rule if it is:

> [M]ade at or near the time by, or from information transmitted by, a person with knowledge, if kept in the course of a regularly conducted business activity, and if it was the regular practice of that business activity to make the . . . record or data compilation, all as shown by the testimony of the custodian or other qualified witness, or by certification that complies with [federal requirements as to such certification] unless the source of information or the method or circumstances of preparation indicate lack of trustworthiness.[52]

One requirement is that the record be contemporaneous, that is, that the record was created at the same time as the event the record is documenting occurred. The record is not admissible if it was created years later, by either the original creditor or by a debt buyer.

The document must be kept in the regular course of a business activity, as part of a regular practice of conducting that activity. Thus the collector can not create the record for use in litigation.[53] It must have been created as part of the creditor's regular business of extending credit and receiving payments.

The record also can not lack trustworthiness. Inconsistencies between the record and collector affidavits, pleadings, or other documents can suggest a lack of trustworthiness in the records themselves. If the documents are introduced as true copies of what was sent to the consumer, they should not contain handwritten notes that were added after the document was sent to the consumer.

51 Federal Rule of Evidence 801(c) provides that: "Hearsay is a statement, other than one made by the declarant while testifying at the trial or hearing, offered in evidence to prove the truth of the matter asserted."

52 *See also* Great Seneca Fin. Corp. v. Felty, 869 N.E.2d 30 (Ohio Ct. App. 2006); Citibank S.D. v. Cramer, 139 Wash. App. 1089 (2007).

53 Rae v. State, 638 So. 2d 597 (Fla. Dist. Ct. App. 1994); Reach Out, Inc. v. Capital Associates, Inc., 336 S.E.2d 847 (Ga. Ct. App. 1985).

4.2.4.2 Requirements for Affidavits Certifying Business Records

When business records are introduced at trial, they are introduced by the testimony of the custodian of those records or some other qualified witness.[54] When they are utilized as attachments to a summary judgment motion, they must be certified by an affidavit.[55] The witness or affiant must be familiar with how the business records were prepared. The federal rule concerning this certification states that the business record should be:

> [A]ccompanied by a written declaration of its custodian or other qualified person . . . certifying that the record—
> (A) was made at or near the time of the occurrence of the matters set forth by, or from information transmitted by, a person with knowledge of those matters;
> (B) was kept in the course of the regularly conducted activity; and
> (C) was made by the regularly conducted activity as a regular practice.[56]

Documents must be accompanied by an affidavit that is made on personal knowledge, sets forth facts as would be admissible in evidence, and shows that the affiant is competent to testify to the matters stated in the affidavit.[57] Some states also require that the affidavit disclose the affiant's employer, and at least some collection affidavits fail to do so.

Business records can not be the basis for the collector's summary judgment motion if they are unaccompanied by any affidavit swearing to or certifying the records.[58] A debt buyer can not merely file documents received from the original creditor, even if they are retained in the debt buyer's regular course of business.[59] They must have been kept in the original creditor's regular course of business, and an affidavit must authenticate that fact.

An employee of a debt buyer typically will be unable to certify records created by the original creditor.[60] To certify

54 Fed. R. Evid. 803(6).

55 *Id.*

56 Fed. R. Evid. 902(11).

57 *See* Great Seneca Fin. Corp. v. Felty, 869 N.E.2d 30 (Ohio Ct. App. 2006).

58 *See* Unifund CCR Partners v. Harrell (Conn. Super. Ct. Aug. 3, 2005), *available at* www.consumerlaw.org/unreported; Suggs v. Sherman Acquisition Ltd. P'ship, 13 Fla. L. Weekly Supp. 301a (Fla. Cir. Ct. Sept. 28, 2005).

59 Palisades Collection L.L.C. v. Haque, 2006 N.Y. Misc. LEXIS 4036 (N.Y. Civ. Ct. Apr. 13, 2006).

60 Rushmore Recoveries X, L.L.C. v. Skolnick, 841 N.Y.S.2d 823 (Dist. Ct. 2007); PRA III, L.L.C. v. MacDowell, 841 N.Y.S.2d 822 (Civ. Ct. 2007) (table) (text available at 2007 WL 14290261); Palisades Collection, L.L.C. v. Gonzalez, 809 N.Y.S.2d 482 (Civ. Ct. 2005) (table) (text available at 2005 WL 3372971); Martinez v. Midland Credit Mgmt., Inc., 2008 WL

business records the affiant must be familiar with the original creditor's record keeping practices.[61] The affiant must be able to state from personal knowledge that the records were created at or near the time of the occurrence. A debt buyer's affidavit has no probative value when the affiant's claimed familiarity with the assignor's business records is derived solely from the affiant's review of those records after they came into the debt buyer's possession.[62]

The affiant instead must be familiar with the habits and customary practices and procedures utilized in making the documents. The affiant must be able to certify that the documents were made in the original creditor's regular course of business, that it was the original creditor's regular practice to make the documents, and that the original creditor created the documents contemporaneously with the facts that were recorded.[63] Otherwise, courts will not allow business records into evidence.[64]

Similarly, an affidavit can not certify documents if the substance of the affidavit conflicts with the documents themselves.[65] For example, an affidavit may state a total dollar amount owed, while component numbers in the attached business records may add up to a different number.

704206 (Tex. App. Mar. 13, 2008). *But cf.* Wamco XXVIII Ltd. v. Integrated Elec. Environments, Inc., 903 So. 2d 230 (Fla. Dist. Ct. App. 2005); Great Seneca Fin. Corp. v. Felty, 869 N.E.2d 30 (Ohio Ct. App. 2006) (finding, in the circumstances, that the original creditor's records were trustworthy).

61 C & W Asset Acquisition, L.L.C. v. Somogyi, 136 S.W.3d 134 (Mo. Ct. App. 2004); Rushmore Recoveries X, L.L.C. v. Skolnick, 841 N.Y.S.2d 823 (Dist. Ct. 2007); Palisades Collection, L.L.C. v. Gonzalez, 809 N.Y.S.2d 482 (Civ. Ct. 2005) (table) (text available at 2005 WL 3372971); Martinez v. Midland Credit Mgmt., Inc., 2008 WL 704206 (Tex. App. Mar. 13, 2008); *see also* Dan Med., Prof'l Corp. v. N.Y. Cent. Mut. Fire Ins. Co., 14 Misc. 3d 44, 829 N.Y.S.2d 404 (App. Div. 2006).

62 C & W Asset Acquisition, L.L.C. v. Somogyi, 136 S.W.3d 134 (Mo. Ct. App. 2004); Rushmore Recoveries X, L.L.C. v. Skolnick, 841 N.Y.S.2d 823 (Dist. Ct. 2007).

63 C & W Asset Acquisition, L.L.C. v. Somogyi, 136 S.W.3d 134 (Mo. Ct. App. 2004); Rushmore Recoveries X, L.L.C. v. Skolnick, 841 N.Y.S.2d 823 (Dist. Ct. 2007); Banc One Asset Solution Corp. v. Thomas, 2001 WL 259140 (Tex. App. Mar. 16, 2001).

64 *See, e.g.*, C & W Asset Acquisition, L.L.C. v. Somogyi, 136 S.W.3d 134 (Mo. Ct. App. 2004); Palisades Collection, L.L.C. v. Gonzalez, 809 N.Y.S.2d 482 (table) (Civ. Ct. 2005) (table) (text available at 2005 WL 3372971); Banc One Asset Solution Corp. v. Thomas, 2001 WL 259140 (Tex. App. Mar. 16, 2001). *But cf.* Bozeman v. CACV of Colorado, 638 S.E.2d 387 (Ga. Ct. App. 2006) (affirming summary judgment for creditor and rejecting consumer's hearsay argument because consumer failed to present evidence contradicting creditor's affidavit); Cockrell v. Republic Mortgage Ins. Co., 817 S.W.2d 106 (Tex. App. 1991) (assignee's affidavit comprised business records of the assignor if the assignee verifies the accuracy of the information generated by the assignee; receipt of records in the regular course of business sufficed to show the accuracy and trustworthiness of the loan histories).

65 Palisades Collection, L.L.C. v. Gonzalez, 809 N.Y.S.2d 482 (Civ. Ct. 2005) (table) (text available at 2005 WL 3372971).

4.2.4.3 Electronic Records

Business records must also be authentic. Ordinarily, the same proof as required to qualify for the exception from the hearsay rule is sufficient to show authenticity.[66] But electronic records create special authentication issues. Has the record been preserved during the time it was in the electronic file so as to assure that the document being proffered is the same as the document that was originally created? This issue raises questions not only about the computer equipment and programs used, but policies for use of the equipment, database and programs, how access is controlled, how changes are recorded, what the audit system is, and the like.[67] Thus the affiant must have special knowledge of the computer system, database, access and related issues before electronic records can be admitted.[68]

Courts have viewed with favor[69] an eleven-step foundation for computer records suggested by E. Imwinkelried, *Evidentiary Foundations*:

1. The business uses a computer.
2. The computer is reliable.
3. The business has developed a procedure for inserting data into the computer.
4. The procedure has built-in safeguards to ensure accuracy and identify errors.[70]
5. The business keeps the computer in a good state of repair.
6. The witness had the computer readout certain data.
7. The witness used the proper procedures to obtain the readout.
8. The computer was in working order at the time the witness obtained the readout.
9. The witness recognizes the exhibit as the readout.
10. The witness explains how he or she recognizes the readout.
11. If the readout contains strange symbols or terms, the witness explains the meaning of the symbols or terms for the trier of fact.[71]

66 5 Jack B. Weinstein & Margaret A. Berger, Weinstein's Fed. Evidence § 900.06[2][a] (Joseph M. McLaughlin ed., 2d. ed. 2005).

67 Am. Express Travel Related Services Co. v. Vinhnee, 336 B.R. 437 (B.A.P. 9th Cir. 2005).

68 *Id.*

69 *See, e.g., id.*

70 One court has elaborated on this element by mentioning details regarding computer policy and system control procedures, including control of access to the database, control of access to the program, recording and logging changes, backup practices, and audit procedures to assure the continuing integrity of the records. *See* Am. Express Travel Related Services Co. v. Vinhnee, 336 B.R. 437 (B.A.P. 9th Cir. 2005).

71 E. Imwinkelried, Evidentiary Foundations § 4.03[1] (5th ed. 2002).

4.3 The Collector's Proof That It Has Standing to Collect on the Debt

4.3.1 General

Chapter 3, *supra*, examines situations in which the entity collecting the debt does not have authority to use the state's courts—such as when the entity is not properly licensed to collect on a debt or has not properly registered with the state as an out-of-state corporation.[72] This section examines the common situation in which the collector is not the original creditor, but alleges that it has been assigned the right to collect on a debt owed to the original creditor. In some cases, the collector may be an assignee of the original collector. In other cases it may be an assignee of an assignee, or an assignee of an assignee of an assignee.

Another common scenario that should be distinguished is when the entity collecting the debt has merged with or purchased the lender who originally extended the credit, or when the creditor has simply changed its name. For example, on January 1, 2006, MBNA Corp. merged with and into Bank of America Corp., with MBNA America Bank becoming a subsidiary of Bank of America. On June 10, 2006, MBNA changed its name to FIA Card Services. A successor corporation to the original creditor (such as FIA Card Services) will have an easier time establishing that it has standing to sue the consumer than will a debt buyer who purchased the obligation as part of a bulk sale from another debt buyer.[73]

A collector seeking to recover on an obligation has the burden of proof to show that it has the right to seek collection on the obligation because it owns the consumer's obligation or state law gives it the right to sue on behalf of the owner.[74] A consumer defendant should always put the plaintiff to its proof that it has standing to collect on the debt, partly because the plaintiff often can not meet this burden. The consumer also should not have to litigate a debt with one party, only to find out later that another party is the true owner and that the consumer must now litigate the same claim with this second party.[75]

A characteristic of debt buyer collections is that the debt has often been sold a number of times, creating a complex chain of ownership. In one case, the successor company to Providian assigned a debt to Vision Management Services, which then assigned it three days later to Great Seneca Financial Corp., which a month later assigned it to Account Management Services. Four months later, Account Management Services (which shortly thereafter changed its name) assigned the account to Madison Street Investments, which then assigned the account five months later to Jackson Capital which, on that same day, assigned the account to Centurion Capital. Three weeks later Centurion hired Wolpoff and Abramson as their attorneys to collect on the debt. After the transfer to Jackson Capital, but before the transfer to Centurion Capital, the consumer was sued on the account by Melville Acquisitions Group (which appears nowhere in the above chain of ownership).[76]

This example has a number of implications. It shows that the consumer is correct to be concerned that proof of the complete chain of ownership be produced. As entities transfer large batches of accounts, it is easy for there to be confusion as to who owns an individual account, and more than one entity can end up seeking collection on the same debt.

The example also shows that for a collector to prove it owns an obligation, it may have to establish proper assignments between multiple entities, something a debt buyer collecting on a relatively small matter is unlikely to do with precision. Debt buyers' business model is to purchase debt for pennies on the dollar and then seek payments with a minimal investment of effort. The debt buyer is unlikely to put much effort into establishing proper documentation of an assignment when it is suing the consumer. On the other hand, if the debt buyer is being sued by a class of consumers who allege it has sought judgments without proper assignments of the debt, the collector may invest considerable time and effort into obtaining proper documentation.

4.3.2 Debt Buyer Must Prove a Complete Chain of Ownership

While collectors may have difficulty proving even one assignment, the collector may have to prove a whole series of assignments on the same debt. The collector can not merely show that it received an assignment of the obligation, if the assignor was not the original creditor. Instead, the collector must show a continuous, unbroken chain of assignments from the original creditor to the entity collecting

72 *See* § 3.6, *supra*.

73 *But see* FIA Card Services, Nat'l Ass'n v. Thompson, 2008 WL 624904 (N.Y. Dist. Ct. Mar. 10, 2008) (case dismissed when MBNA obtained arbitration award but sought confirmation under the name FIA Card Services).

74 Great Seneca Fin. Corp. v. Leanna, 2006 WL 2536275 (Conn. Super. Ct. Aug. 15, 2006); Midwestern Health Mgmt., Inc. v. Walker, 208 S.W.3d 295 (Mo. Ct. App. 2006); C & W Asset Acquisition, L.L.C. v. Somogyi, 136 S.W.3d 134 (Mo. Ct. App. 2004); New Century Fin. Serv. v. Sanchez (N.J. Super. Ct. Law Div. Apr. 12, 2002), *available at* www.consumerlaw.org/unreported; Palisades Collection L.L.C. v. Haque, 2006 N.Y. Misc. LEXIS 4036 (N.Y. Civ. Ct. Apr. 13, 2006); Palisades Collection, L.L.C. v. Gonzalez, 809 N.Y.S.2d 482 (Civ. Ct. 2005) (table) (text available at 2005 WL 3372971); Citibank (S.D.) v. Martin, 807 N.Y.S.2d 284 (Civ. Ct. 2005).

75 *See* Miller v. Wolpoff & Abramson, LLP, 2007 WL 2694607 (N.D. Ind. Sept. 7, 2007).

76 *See id.*

on the debt.[77] An earlier debt buyer can assign to the current collector only the rights it itself acquired from its assignor.[78] In fact, the language of the typical bill of sale assigning rights will specify that the assignor is assigning only those rights that it has in the account. Such language does not prove that it has rights in the account.

At each link in the chain of ownership, the entity that has been assigned a debt must be identical to the entity that subsequently assigns it to the next buyer in the chain. For example, there is a break in the chain when evidence is offered of a transfer from Discover Bank to Vision Nevada, Inc. followed by a transfer from Vision Management Services to the collector.[79] The collector must provide evidence that the two Vision entities are the same or that Vision Nevada, Inc. assigned the debt to Vision Management Services.

Also look for inconsistencies in the collector's pleadings, affidavits, and documents as to the identity of an entity in the chain. For example, in one case the entity was first described as a Delaware limited liability company and later described as a New Jersey corporation.[80] Even if a collector provides assignment documents for each assignee, the chain is broken when one of the assignment documents is not signed by the assignor.[81]

4.3.3 Proving Transfer of Ownership

The collector must prove the assignment through tender of proper documentation specifically relating to the particular account at issue.[82] Mere affirmation of the assignment in an affidavit is insufficient; the collector must submit actual contracts of assignment identifying the accounts at issue,[83] with proper authentication of those accounts using affidavits.[84] Certainly a collector's affidavit can not be used as evidence that an assignment was made from the original creditor to the collector's assignor.[85]

Debt buyers usually can produce a quite detailed contract or bill of sale delineating the relationship between the debt buyer's assignor and the debt buyer, but the document will make reference only generally to thousands of accounts being purchased at the same time, and will not identify the consumer's account. This evidence is not enough. The assignment document must indicate that one of the thousands of accounts the collector has purchased is the account at issue in the lawsuit. The debt buyer's documentation must reference the specific account at issue.[86]

Debt buyer documentation instead will often refer to a particular computer tape containing thousands of accounts, but will not attach the computer tape or offer any evidence that the particular consumer's account being sued on is on that computer tape. This evidence is not sufficient to prove assignment.[87] Other times, an affidavit or documentation will refer to a schedule or appendix that allegedly will identify the account, but no schedule or appendix will be attached.[88] The debt buyer must also prove a proper assignment of the particular account at issue to each entity in the chain of ownership prior to the account being assigned to the debt buyer.

---

77 *In re* Leverett, 378 B.R. 793 (E.D. Tex. 2007); Wright v. Asset Acceptance Corp., 2000 WL 33216031 (S.D. Ohio Jan. 3, 2000); *In re* Kendall, 380 B.R. 37 (Bankr. N.D. Okla. 2007); Rushmore Recoveries X, L.L.C. v. Skolnick, 841 N.Y.S.2d 823 (Dist. Ct. 2007); Nat'l Check Bureau, Inc. v. Cody, 2005 WL 174762 (Ohio Ct. App. Jan. 27, 2005) (dissent); *see also* PRA III, L.L.C. v. MacDowell, 841 N.Y.S.2d 822 (Civ. Ct. 2007) (table) (text available at 2007 WL 1429026). *But cf.* Nat'l Check Bureau, Inc. v. Cody, 2005 WL 174762 (Ohio Ct. App. Jan. 27, 2005) (majority opinion) (finding sufficient evidence of the chain of title).

78 Munoz v. Pipestone Fin., L.L.C., 397 F. Supp. 2d 1129 (D. Minn. 2005); Wright v. Asset Acceptance Corp., 2000 WL 33216031 (S.D. Ohio Jan. 3, 2000); Rushmore Recoveries X, L.L.C. v. Skolnick, 841 N.Y.S.2d 823 (Dist. Ct. 2007).

79 *Cf.* Great Seneca Fin. Corp. v. Leanna, 2006 WL 2536275 (Conn. Super. Ct. Aug. 15, 2006) (not reaching the issue but implying this proof is inadequate).

80 Palisades Collection L.L.C. v. Haque, 2006 N.Y. Misc. LEXIS 4036 (N.Y. Civ. Ct. Apr. 13, 2006).

81 Rushmore Recoveries X, L.L.C. v. Skolnick, 841 N.Y.S.2d 823 (Dist. Ct. 2007).

82 New Century Fin. Serv. v. Sanchez (N.J. Super. Ct. Law Div. Apr. 12, 2002), *available at* www.consumerlaw.org/unreported; Citibank (S.D.) v. Martin, 11 Misc. 3d 219 (County Ct. 2005); Gonzalez v. Palisades Collections, 10 Misc. 3d 1058A (County Ct. 2005) (table); Zwick v. Suburban Constr. Co., 134 N.E.2d 733 (Ohio Ct. App. 1956).

83 New Century Fin. Serv. v. Sanchez (N.J. Super. Ct. Law Div. Apr. 12, 2002), *available at* www.consumerlaw.org/unreported; PRA III, L.L.C. v. MacDowell, 841 N.Y.S.2d 822 (Civ. Ct. 2007) (table) (text available at 2007 WL 1429026); Palisades Collection, L.L.C. v. Gonzalez, 809 N.Y.S.2d 482 (Civ. Ct. 2005) (table) (text available at 2005 WL 3372971); Citibank (S.D.) v. Martin, 807 N.Y.S.2d 284 (Civ. Ct. 2005).

84 *See* § 4.2.4.2, *supra.*

85 Wright v. Asset Acceptance Corp., 2000 WL 33216031 (S.D. Ohio Jan. 3, 2000).

86 *In re* Kendall, 380 B.R. 37 (Bankr. N.D. Okla. 2007); Velocity Investments v. Bailey, 2007 WL 1828037 (Conn. Super. Ct. June 5, 2007); Palisades Collection L.L.C. v. Haque, 2006 N.Y. Misc. LEXIS 4036 (N.Y. Civ. Ct. Apr. 13, 2006); Palisades Collection, L.L.C v. Grassmyer (Pa. C.P. Jan. 15, 2008), *available at* www.consumerlaw.org/unreported.

87 Wright v. Asset Acceptance Corp., 2000 WL 33216031 (S.D. Ohio Jan. 3, 2000); New Century Fin. Serv. v. Sanchez (N.J. Super. Ct. Law Div. Apr. 12, 2002), *available at* www.consumerlaw.org/unreported; Nat'l Check Bureau, Inc. v. Cody, 2005 WL 174762 (Ohio Ct. App. Jan. 27, 2005) (dissent); Palisades Collection, L.L.C v. Grassmyer (Pa. C.P. Jan. 15, 2008), *available at* www.consumerlaw.org/unreported. *But see* Nat'l Check Bureau, Inc. v. Cody, 2005 WL 174762 (Ohio Ct. App. Jan. 27, 2005) (majority opinion).

88 Velocity Investments v. Bailey, 2007 WL 1828037 (Conn. Super. Ct. June 5, 2007); Palisades Collection L.L.C. v. Haque, 2006 N.Y. Misc. LEXIS 4036 (N.Y. Civ. Ct. Apr. 13, 2006); Nat'l Check Bureau, Inc. v. Cody, 2005 WL 174762 (Ohio Ct. App. Jan. 27, 2005) (dissent).

Carefully review all documents of assignment, because they are often incomplete or illegible. In one case the court found an assignment to be improper when the debt buyer submitted only four pages of a twenty-plus page loan sale agreement.[89] The court observed: "The first page, entitled "Loan Sale Agreement" merely identifies the parties and states the effective date of the transaction. The second page contains a pair of signatures, third page contains a redacted table of four accounts. These three pages do not appear to have any relationship to one another given that they were respectively numbered "i," "7," and "19 of 28."[90]

In another case, the debt buyer produced a series of exhibits that showed the defendant's name, address, and account number on a blackened-out photocopy, that purported to evidence several transfers of the debt. The court found this evidence inadequate without a supporting affidavit.[91]

Another factor is the date of an assignment. Watch for assignments that are either back-dated or dated well after the actual assignment. Consider a case in which Debt Buyer A assigns a debt to Debt Buyer B in 2006 who assigns it without proper documentation to Debt Buyer C in 2007. Debt Buyer C can not rectify this mistake by obtaining a new assignment in 2008 directly from Debt Buyer A. In 2008, Debt Buyer A no longer had any ownership interest in the account, having assigned it to Debt Buyer B in 2006. Always be skeptical of assignment documents dated after the collector began seeking payment on the debt.

Any business records showing the assignment must be properly authenticated by an affidavit.[92] If the collector's employee is the affiant attesting to a document assigning the debt to that collector, the affidavit must meet all the requirements necessary to satisfy the business records exception to the hearsay rule.[93] Moreover an affidavit should be given weight only if it is signed by an employee of one of the entities involved in the transfer. A collector's employee's affidavit is insufficient when the assignment document covers the transfer between two prior entities in the chain of ownership.[94]

It is also insufficient to introduce a notice from the assignor to the consumer that it is assigning the debt to the assignee.[95] There must be evidence of the actual assignment. A memorandum from the assignee stating that it has received assignment of the account at issue is also insufficient.[96] A statement by the purported assignee that it has been assigned an account is no evidence that this transfer has actually occurred.[97] There must be evidence linking that document to the actual assignment.[98]

4.3.4 *Determining What Rights Have Been Assigned*

Carefully check along the complete chain of ownership what rights are being assigned to each assignee. For example, an assignment can be for receivables, account receivables, rights under a contract, or choses in action. If owner A assigns only receivables to owner B and owner B assigns only rights under the contract to owner C, then owner C does not have rights under the contract, and may not even have rights to receivables.

Assignment of a "receivable" has been interpreted as an assignment to collect what was owed at the time of assignment, but not interest accruing after the assignment or the right to seek contractual attorney fees incurred after the assignment.[99] Conversely, if only rights under the contract are assigned, the collector will have difficulty recovering on a theory not based upon the contract, such as *quantum meruit*.

4.4 Collector's Legal Theory in Its Pleadings Controls the Case

The collector's pleadings or amended pleadings establish the collector's legal theory to collect on the debt. A court should rule only on the theory delineated in those pleadings, and should not find for the collector on a different theory.[100] For example, if a collector seeks recovery on an "open account" theory, and the court finds the collector has not proven the elements of that claim, the court should not rule for the collector on an "account stated" theory,[101] when the consumer has not been given an opportunity to present evidence and law opposing an account stated claim.

Some states' rules of civil procedure may allow the legal theory to be amended, even after trial, if this does not prejudice the other party. In these states the consumer's

89 C & W Asset Acquisition, L.L.C. v. Somogyi, 136 S.W.3d 134, 140 (Mo. Ct. App. 2004).

90 *Id.*

91 Great Seneca Fin. Corp. v. Leanna, 2006 WL 2536275 (Conn. Super. Ct. Aug. 15, 2006); *see also* Great Seneca Fin. Corp. v. Felty, 869 N.E.2d 30 (Ohio Ct. App. 2006).

92 *See* § 4.2.4.2, *supra.*

93 *See id.*

94 Wright v. Asset Acceptance Corp., 2000 WL 33216031 (S.D. Ohio Jan. 3, 2000); *see also* § 4.2.4.2, *supra.*

95 Wright v. Asset Acceptance Corp., 2000 WL 33216031 (S.D. Ohio Jan. 3, 2000).

96 *Id.*; New Century Fin. Serv. v. Sanchez (N.J. Super. Ct. Law Div. Apr. 12, 2002), *available at* www.consumerlaw.org/unreported.

97 Wright v. Asset Acceptance Corp., 2000 WL 33216031 (S.D. Ohio Jan. 3, 2000).

98 *Id.*

99 Munoz v. Pipestone Fin., L.L.C., 397 F. Supp. 2d 1129 (D. Minn. 2005).

100 *See* Wiltel Communications, L.L.C. v. Sunrise Int'l Leasing Corp., 2005 WL 354030 (Minn. Ct. App. Feb. 15, 2005); Citibank v. Miller, 222 S.W.3d 318 (Mo. Ct. App. 2007); Palisades Collection, L.L.C. v. Gonzalez, 809 N.Y.S.2d 482 (Civ. Ct. 2005) (table) (text available at 2005 WL 3372971).

101 Citibank v. Miller, 222 S.W.3d 318 (Mo. Ct. App. 2007).

attorney, at the start and throughout the case, should clarify with court the collector's causes of action, and object to evidence or argument relating to a different theory.

The collector should not be able to amend its complaint informally. The collector must seek permission from the court. The amended complaint must be in writing and state its legal theory of recovery with specificity. If there is any ambiguity as to the collector's legal theory in its complaint, the consumer should obtain, under a state's rules of procedure, a more definite statement, a bill of particulars, or some similar specification of the causes of action.

For example, a collector's pleadings may be vague as to whether the collector is pleading based upon an "open account," "on account," "statement of account," or contract theory. Each of these causes of action may have different elements of proof.[102] Other times the complaint will allege facts relating to nonpayment, but not specify the exact theory of the case.

A state's rules of procedure often require that the complaint attach documents supporting the cause of action, such as the credit contract or a statement of the account.[103] If these documents, which will help the consumer understand the collector's legal theory, are not attached, the consumer should move for either a more definite statement or for dismissal of the case.

The legal theory specified in the complaint does more than just establish what elements the collector must prove. It can also determine which state's law controls, what statute of limitations applies, and whether and how interest and attorney fees are to be computed.

Credit contracts will often specify a choice of law—for example, Delaware law. Collector claims often are *not* based on the contract—debt buyers may have little evidence of the contract between the original creditor and the consumer. In that case the collector can not argue for the contractual choice of law. The forum state's law will apply.

The theory pleaded will also determine the statute of limitations.[104] A collection action based on the contract may have a longer limitations period than one based upon an account stated. The applicable statute of limitations can only be determined once the collector's legal theory is clearly established.

An interest rate and the right to attorney fees may be specified in the contract. But if the collector's claim is not based on the contract, then the contract is not a valid basis for the award of attorney fees and interest. The collector may have to rely on state law regarding pre-judgment interest and the collection of attorney fees.

Collectors, in an attempt to avoid these restrictions, may plead multiple theories in the alternative. This approach should *not* prevent a careful analysis of each theory to determine the required elements for that individual cause of action, the applicable statute of limitations, and the applicable theories for the collector to recover interest and fees. When these alternatives conflict with each other, the court can not award a recovery under both theories, but instead must select one theory and determine if the collector has met all the elements of that legal theory.

For example, a court should not issue an award for a collector on a breach of contract and a *quantum meruit* theory. *Quantum meruit* is only available when there is no contract.[105] If the court adopts a *quantum meruit* theory, it must hold there was no binding contract, and then the consumer should not be liable for interest and attorney fees based upon the contract.

4.5 Proof of a Written Contract

4.5.1 Introduction

A common collector cause of action is breach of contract. The consumer entered into a credit agreement and defaulted, and the creditor has incurred damages. In a closed-end credit obligation—when the total obligation is spelled out in the contract—this claim is relatively straightforward. The collector, after establishing its standing, must prove the existence of a binding contract, the consumer's default, and the collector's right to damages.

Matters are more complex in an open-end credit obligation, when the contract establishes the terms of the relationship but the consumer's indebtedness varies over time, as obligations are incurred and payments are made. Moreover, the contract itself may have been amended over time. A credit card is the most common example of an open-end credit obligation, but there are many other examples, including obligations for cell phone, cable television, landline telephone, water, gas, and electric service. In such open-ended arrangements the collector must prove the balance owed on the open-ended account.

Proof that a credit card account was opened is not proof of the balance due upon default. Conversely, if the collector provides detail showing the charges and credits that resulted in the balance due, this is not proof of a contract, which is a necessary element of a breach of contract action. This section will focus on proof of the existence of a contract.

Proof of the balance due in an open-end transaction is examined in § 4.6, *infra*. This fact, of course, is important to establish in order to recover on a breach of contract claim. It may also be an important issue even when the collector does not prove a written contract, but still seeks to recover the account balance under some other theory of liability.

102 *See* §§ 4.5–4.7, *infra*.
103 *See* § 3.5, *supra*.
104 *See* § 3.7.5, *supra*.

105 *See* § 4.8, *infra*.

4.5.2 What State Law Applies?

Many consumer credit contracts specify what state's law that is to apply to the contract, which often is not the law of the consumer's residence or the state where the consumer entered into the contract. The decision whether to use the contractually specified state's law or the forum state's law has practical significance when the elements of a contract claim vary between the states.

In general, courts apply the contractually chosen state's laws to interpret the contract instead of the forum state's law, as long as the issue is viewed neither as purely procedural nor as impinging on a fundamental state interest.[106] A prior section examined whether a court will apply the forum state's statute of limitations (treating this issue as procedural in nature) or that of the state chosen in the contract.[107] A court is likely to apply the law of the state chosen in the contract to interpret more substantive aspects of the contract.

But which state's law applies to determine whether an enforceable contract was ever consummated? If the contract was never consummated, then the choice of law provision is not enforceable either. Nevertheless, at least some courts rule that when the contract would be consummated under the law of the state selected in the contract, then the contract is enforceable even if it would not be found to be consummated under the forum state's laws.[108]

4.5.3 Proof of the Contract's Terms

Proof of the terms of a written contract typically requires the collector to produce a written agreement that is binding on the parties.[109] Surprisingly, this will often be difficult for the collector. Debt buyers will usually not possess this documentation when they purchase the debt, and may be unable or unwilling to obtain the required documentation from the original creditor. Even more surprising, the original creditor may not retain this documentation.[110]

The creditor can not excuse this lapse by pointing to federal or other legal requirements[111] that such documents be kept for a certain number of years.[112] Such requirements establish minimum requirements and do not require destruction of the documents after that period of time. Minimum retention requirements do not excuse a creditor from providing proof that a contract exists. If the creditor wishes to prove the contract, it merely retains the documents for a longer period of time.[113]

Collectors of credit card and other open-end debt must produce not just a standard form contract, but the version of the contract that the particular consumer agreed to. Courts have dismissed cases when the collector submits a generic, undated and unsigned "customer agreement" that does not even contain the consumer's name or any indicia relating the document to the consumer.[114] The collector's burden is further increased when the consumer disputes that an unsigned and undated form contract was ever received.[115]

The collector should produce the version of its standard form contract that was sent to the consumer at the time of consummation of the contract, and must also produce all subsequent amendments to that contract. If the initial contract has been superseded by an entirely new contract, then that new contract must be produced.

This requirement will pose many practical problems for a collector. Credit card issuers over time change their agreements, send out various bill stuffers amending the agreements, and may even send different versions of a standard form agreement to different categories of card holders. Moreover, when Bank A purchases or merges with Bank B, Bank A's agreement with its preexisting card holders will certainly be different from Bank B's agreement with its preexisting card holders.

There must be some linkage between the form contract and the consumer to indicate that this contract does in fact apply to the consumer. To prove that a contract was the one sent to the consumer and to whose terms the consumer

106 *See* Restatement (Second) of Conflict of Laws § 187 (1971).

107 *See* § 3.7.2, *supra*.

108 *See* Jackson v. Pasadena Receivables, Inc., 921 A.2d 799 (Md. 2007).

109 *See* Fla. Credit Research Inc. v. Felicien (Fla. County Ct. Apr. 15, 2008), *available at* www.consumerlaw.org/unreported.; Fla. Credit Research, Inc. v. Stromberg (Fla. County Ct. Duval County June 22, 2007), *available at* www.consumerlaw.org/unreported; LVNV Funding L.L.C. v. Moehrlin (Fla. County Ct. Volusia County Aug. 2006) (Green, J.) (count dismissed when no contract proven and affidavit was not proper), *available at* www.consumerlaw.org/unreported; Citibank (S.D.) v. Martin, 807 N.Y.S.2d 284 (Civ. Ct. 2005); Palisades Collection, L.L.C v. Grassmyer (Pa. C.P. Jan. 15, 2008), *available at* www.consumerlaw.org/unreported; Williams v. Unifund CCR Partners, 2008 WL 339855 (Tex. App. Feb. 7, 2008); *cf.* Roberson v. Ocwen Fed. Bank, 553 S.E.2d 162 (Ga. Ct. App. 2001) (describing an acceptable substitute for production of the contract when the contract was over ten years old and had been destroyed). *But see* Discover Bank v. Poling, 2005 WL 737404 (Ohio Ct. App. Mar. 31, 2005)

110 Johnson v. MBNA Am. Bank, 357 F.3d 426 (4th Cir. 2004) (card issuer only retained documents for five years).

111 *See* 12 C.F.R. § 226.25 ("[a] creditor shall retain evidence of compliance with this regulation . . . for 2 years").

112 Johnson v. MBNA Am. Bank, 357 F.3d 426 (4th Cir. 2004).

113 *See* Fla. Credit Research Inc. v. Felicien (Fla. County Ct. Apr. 15, 2008), *available at* www.consumerlaw.org/unreported.

114 Capital One Bank v. Mullis, 15 Fla. L. Weekly Supp. 370a (Fla. County Ct. Feb. 13, 2008); N. Star Capital Acquisition, L.L.C. v. Lewis, 15 Fla. L. Weekly Supp. 72a (Fla. County Ct. Duval County Oct. 23, 2007), *available at* www.consumerlaw.org/unreported. *But cf.* Capitol One Bank v. Hardin, 178 S.W.3d 565 (Mo. Ct. App. 2005) (when original contract not produced, sufficient to produce signed application, revised agreement, two years of billing statements, and telephone log of calls between consumer and card issuer).

115 Palisades Collection L.L.C. v. Haque, 2006 N.Y. Misc. LEXIS 4036 (N.Y. Civ. Ct. Apr. 13, 2006).

consented to by using the card, the collector's summary judgment motion will have to attach an affidavit from someone familiar with the contracts sent out to card holders at a particular point in time in the past.[116] A debt buyer will have difficulty providing such proof.[117] None of its employees will have any idea what contract was sent to which card holders. Even the original creditor may be unable to rely on an affidavit of its own employee when the contract was sent out by a third-party mailing service.

The collector also must do more than just produce the contract and prove that it was mailed to the consumer. It must show that the consumer assented to that contract and to any subsequent amendments to that contract. Often a collector will claim that the consumer's use of a credit card or use of a cell phone is sufficient assent to the contract and to any subsequent amendments.[118] This argument should not apply to amendments sent to the consumer after the consumer has stopped using the credit card or when a cell phone has been deactivated. When an account is seriously delinquent, the consumer will either voluntarily stop using the account or the creditor will cut the consumer off. The collector thus must produce the version of the creditor's contract originally assented to, and as subsequently amended up until the time the account stopped being used.

Nevertheless, for credit card accounts, the collector need not produce a contract containing the consumer's signature in order for the contract to be binding[119] Even if a forum state's laws would appear to require a signature,[120] the court may apply the law of the state chosen in the credit card agreement,[121] and that state's law may not require a signature.[122] However, proof of the consumer's signature—on the application but not the actual contract—will be important in credit card cases in two circumstances: when identity theft is alleged, or when the collector is seeking to hold a consumer liable as a joint borrower when the consumer is actually a mere authorized user.

4.5.4 *Proof of Contractually Established Finance Charges and Other Fees*

A collector who proves the existence of a contract has additional proof requirements if it is to obtain finance charges and other fees, as allegedly specified by that contract. The creditor's proof of the terms of a contract must include those provisions that entitle the creditor to interest in a specified amount.[123] It is not enough just to point to some monthly statements with an interest rate disclosure.[124]

Assuming a collector establishes its right to include finance charges and other fees, the question arises whether it is entitled to finance charges and fees based upon the contract for the period *after* the account is closed. Any such charges can not be based on a contractual amendment sent after the account is closed.[125] For example, a debt buyer can not increase the interest rate after the account stopped being used,[126] because the consumer has not assented to this unilateral change in terms. There is also an issue whether the contract specifies finance charges and fees for the period after the account is closed, or only for the period while the account is open. This question is one of contractual interpretation, whose answer will depend solely on the contract language.[127]

Many, but not all, credit card issuers are national banks. Federal law preempts state limits on finance charges and related fees that national banks can charge.[128] Non-bank credit card issuers are not entitled to this preemption. If interest charges and other fees are illegal under state law, the collector has the burden of demonstrating that the card issuer can charge these fees because it is a national bank.[129] One court has stated:

> In credit card cases, the first concern of any court is whether the amount at issue is a lawful claim,

116 *See* Wincheck v. Am. Express Travel Related Services Co., 232 S.W.3d 197 (Tex. App. 2007).

117 *See* Rushmore Recoveries X, L.L.C. v. Skolnick, 841 N.Y.S.2d 823 (Dist. Ct. 2007); Palisades Collection, L.L.C. v. Gonzalez, 809 N.Y.S.2d 482 (Civ. Ct. 2005) (table) (text available at 2005 WL 3372971).

118 Wincheck v. Am. Express Travel Related Services Co., 232 S.W.3d 197 (Tex. App. 2007).

119 Davis v. Discover Bank, 627 S.E.2d 819 (Ga. Ct. App. 2006) (consumer's use of credit card constituted his acceptance of card member agreement); Jackson v. Pasadena, 921 A.2d 799 (Md. 2007); Am. Express Travel Related Services v. Redner, 2006 WL 664698 (Mich. Ct. App. Mar. 16, 2006) (corporate officer could be found to be individually liable on corporate credit card, even though he never sign an application or other document for the card, because his use of the card manifested an intent to be bound by the card member agreement, which imposed individual liability on him); Citibank S.D. v. Santoro, 150 P.3d 429 (Or. Ct. App. 2006) (following *Davis v. Discover Bank*); MBNA Am. Bank v. Goodman, 140 P.3d 589 (Utah Ct. App. 2006) (noting Utah Statute of Fraud specifically provides that a credit card agreement is binding without a signature of the consumer when it states that use of the card constitutes acceptance).

120 *See, e.g.*, Md. Code Ann., Com. Law § 12-503(e) (West).

121 *See* Jackson v. Pasadena, 921 A.2d 799 (Md. 2007).

122 *See* S.D. Codified Laws § 54-11-9 (South Dakota law, chosen in many credit card contracts, provides that use of a credit card and failure to cancel the card creates acceptance); *see also* Jackson v. Pasadena, 921 A.2d 799 (Md. 2007).

123 Williams v. Unifund CCR Partners, 2008 WL 339855 (Tex. App. Feb. 7, 2008).

124 Tully v. Citibank (S.D.), 173 S.W.3d 212 (Tex. App. 2005).

125 *See* First Select Corp. v. Grimes, 2003 WL 151940 (Tex. App. Jan. 23, 2003).

126 *Id.*

127 Citibank (S.D.) v. Martin, 807 N.Y.S.2d 284 (Civ. Ct. 2005) (can not charge contract rate after the account is closed unless the contract so specifies).

128 *See* National Consumer Law Center, The Cost of Credit: Regulation, Preemption, and Industry Abuses § 3.4.6 (3d ed. 2005 and Supp.).

129 Citibank (S.D.) v. Martin, 807 N.Y.S.2d 284 (Civ. Ct. 2005).

> which brings up for consideration whether the credit card's interest rate and related charges are subject to this State's usury limits. [footnote omitted] The information upon which a court may make that determination generally requires no more than (1) an identification of the organizational character of the credit card issuer, and (2) a statement and description of the law which governs the interest rate and related charges.[130]

Given the various names under which card issuers operate, it may not always be simple for a debt buyer to prove that the card issuer is in fact a national bank. It will have to prove the name of the original card issuer. But this creditor's name, as stated in the assignment document, may not make it obvious that it is a national bank. The collector will have to provide credible evidence that the entity is wholly owned by a national bank and thus allowed to exceed state interest caps.

Another issue is whether an assignee of a national bank that itself is not a national bank is entitled to assess finance charges in excess of a state maximum during the time when the assignee owns the obligation. Several courts have held the assignee may do so.[131]

4.5.5 Implications If Contract Not Proven

The existence of a contract is an essential element in a cause of action for breach of contract. Failure to prove the existence of a contract will result in the claim being denied. The collector may be able to prevail on alternative claims not based upon the contract, but these alternative claims must have been clearly pleaded. The collector can not change directions and switch theories, unless the court gives it leave to amend its pleadings.[132] The court should not deny the breach of contract claim but render judgment for the collector on a different theory not pleaded.[133]

In pursuing alternative theories of recovery, because no contract has been proven, the collector can not claim that those alternative causes of action should be decided using the state's law chosen in the contract. The statute of limitations for the other claims should not be based upon the statute of limitations for a written contract, again because no written contract has been proven. The contract also can not be the basis for the collector to seek attorney fees. There may be a statutory entitlement to recover attorney fees,[134] but there can be no contractual recovery of attorney fees without a contract.[135]

If there is no contract, then there is no entitlement to contractual finance charges or other fees. It is not enough just to point to some monthly statements containing an interest rate disclosure.[136] A cause of action may allow for the recovery of pre-judgment interest, but not finance charges at a rate specified by contract because there is no contract. A collector seeking to recover the balance due on a credit card without proving a contract can recover no more than the balance owing, adjusted downward to delete finance charges and other fees, with past payments being applied to cash advances or purchases, but not to finance charges and fees.[137] Even when permitted by state law, the collector can only receive pre-judgment interest at the statutory rate.

4.6 Seeking the Balance Due on Open-End Accounts

4.6.1 General

Proof of a written contract is not enough for a collector to recover on an open-end account, such as one involving a credit card, or cell phone, cable, water, gas, or electricity service. The collector must also prove its damages—that is, the unpaid credit balance. Causes of action for the unpaid balance of an open account often are termed "on account" or "open account," but may use different terminology in other states. The cause of action may not even require proof of a written contract, but only proof of entitlement to the unpaid balance of the open-end account.[138]

The action for "on account" or "open account" allows the collector to prove in one action a series of charges and payments, resulting in a balance due, instead of having to bring a separate action for each individual charge.[139] As described in § 4.6.3, *infra*, though, there must still be some proof of each charge.

"Account stated" (examined in § 4.7, *infra*) is an entirely different cause of action than "on account," with different

130 *Id.* at 287.

131 *See* Munoz v. Pipestone Fin., L.L.C., 513 F. Supp. 2d 1076 (D. Minn. 2007); *see also* Olvera v. Blitt & Gaines, Prof'l Corp., 431 F.3d 285 (7th Cir. 2005) (assignee debt buyer permitted to collect same interest as original creditor under Illinois Interest Act); PRA III, L.L.C. v. Hund, 846 N.E.2d 965 (Ill. App. Ct. 2006) (same). *But see* Citibank (S.D.) v. Martin, 807 N.Y.S.2d 284 (Civ. Ct. 2005) (holding that non-national bank assignee can not charge interest in excess of state law cap).

132 *See* § 4.4, *supra*.

133 *Id.*

134 *See* § 6.2, *infra*.

135 *See* Citibank (S.D.) v. Martin, 807 N.Y.S.2d 284 (Civ. Ct. 2005).

136 Tully v. Citibank (S.D.), 173 S.W.3d 212 (Tex. App. 2005).

137 *See* FIA Card Services Nat'l Ass'n v. Kirasic (Pa. C.P. Allegheny County Nov. 7, 2007) (Wettick, J.), *available at* www.consumerlaw.org/unreported.

138 *See, e.g.*, Berlin v. Pickett, 221 S.W.3d 406 (Mo. Ct. App. 2006).
On the other hand, if characterization of an account as open-ended is spurious, then the collector must prove a written contract in the closed-end transaction. Hurley State Bank v. Pickens, 861 So. 2d 846 (La. Ct. App. 2003).

139 *See* Capital One Bank v. Toney, 2007 WL 969420 (Ohio Ct. App. Mar. 28, 2007); Great Seneca Fin. Corp. v. Felty, 869 N.E.2d 30 (Ohio Ct. App. 2006).

elements of proof.[140] It is easy to confuse the two, as both seek to prove a statement of account, and proof of the elements of "on account" sometimes involve proof of a preliminary account stated. Nevertheless, these are two separate causes of action and will be examined in two different sections of this chapter. Neither the collector nor the court should mix up the elements of these two causes of action or allow recovery on one when the collector only pleads the other.[141]

Historically, the causes of action for "on account" and "open account" involved a merchant and a consumer engaging in a series of purchases and payments, with no involvement of a third-party lender. Some courts question whether these common law causes of action even apply to a credit card debt, in which a lender finances a series of purchases from different merchants.[142] In other states "on account" or "open account" may not apply when there is a written contract. For example, California courts hold that an "open account" is "an unsettled debt, arising from items of work and labor, goods sold and delivered, and other open transactions, not reduced to writing," the sole record of which is usually the account books of the owner of the demand. The cause of action does not include express contracts or obligations reduced to writing.[143] In these states a collector seeking to recover on credit card debt or other open-end debt based upon a written contract will have to utilize a different cause of action.

However a state labels the cause of action, this section examines the proof a collector must produce to recover the balance on an open-end account. The section also considers the implications of a failure to prove a written contract in conjunction with proof of the balance owed.

4.6.2 Implications of Failure to Prove a Written Contract

Even if state law allows the collector to recover on an open-end account without proof of a written contract, the failure to prove that contract has a dramatic effect on the collector's recovery. The collector's entitlement to finance charges and other fees are established by written contract. Without proof of such a contract, the collector is not entitled to recover finance charges or other fees as part of the balance due.[144] The collector's proof of the account balance should include only charges for cash advances and for goods and services purchased, but should *not* include charges for finance charges, late fees, over the limit fees, and other fees.[145] Moreover, consumer payments on the account should be applied to the cash advances and the purchases of goods and services, not toward finance charges and fees.[146] This lowers the amount the collector can recover, and makes it difficult for the collector to compute the balance due.

If the collector offers no proof of a written contract, it can not recover attorney fees based upon that contract,[147] and it can not seek to use another state's law based upon a contractual choice of law.[148] Similarly, the statute of limitations can not be one based upon a written contract, but must be some other applicable limitations period established by state law.[149]

4.6.3 Required Proof As to the Balance Due

One court has described how to prove the balance due:

> [A]n account must show the name of the party charged. It begins with a balance, preferably at zero, or with a sum recited that can qualify as [a specified amount that the consumer has previously agreed to pay], but at least the balance should be a provable sum. Following the balance, the item or items, dated and identifiable by number or otherwise, representing charges, or debits, and credits, should appear. Summarization is necessary showing a running or developing balance or an arrangement which permits the calculation of the balance claimed to be due.[150]

140 Moreover, an action in Texas on a sworn account has different elements than either an action on an "account stated" or "on account." *See* § 4.9, *infra*.

141 *See* § 4.4, *supra*.

142 *Cf.* Citibank v. Whiteley, 149 S.W.3d 599 (Mo. Ct. App. 2004) (recognizing but not reaching the issue).

143 *See* Los Angeles County v. Cont'l Corp., 113 Cal. App. 2d 207, 212, 248 P.2d 157 (1952) (quoting People v. Magee, 41 Cal. App. 727 (1919)).

144 *See* § 4.5.5, *supra*; *see also* FIA Card Services Nat'l Ass'n v. Kirasic (Pa. C.P. Allegheny County Nov. 7, 2007) (Wettick, J.), *available at* www.consumerlaw.org/unreported; Target Nat'l Bank v. Samanez (Pa. C.P. Allegheny County Dec. 19, 2007) (Wettick, J.), *available at* www.consumerlaw.org/unreported.

145 *See* FIA Card Services Nat'l Ass'n v. Kirasic (Pa. C.P. Allegheny County Nov. 7, 2007) (Wettick, J.), *available at* www.consumerlaw.org/unreported; *see also* Target Nat'l Bank v. Samanez (Pa. C.P. Allegheny County Dec. 19, 2007) (Wettick, J.), *available at* www.consumerlaw.org/unreported.

146 *See* FIA Card Services Nat'l Ass'n v. Kirasic (Pa. C.P. Allegheny County Nov. 7, 2007) (Wettick, J.), *available at* www.consumerlaw.org/unreported; *see also* Target Nat'l Bank v. Samanez (Pa. C.P. Allegheny County Dec. 19, 2007) (Wettick, J.), *available at* www.consumerlaw.org/unreported.

147 Of course, state law can still provide for such fees. *See, e.g.*, Miss. Code Ann. § 11-53-81 (establishing the right to attorney fees if the collector first sends written demand correctly setting forth the amount owed with an itemized statement of the account in support of that demand).

148 *See* § 4.5.5, *supra*.

149 *See* § 3.7.5.1, *supra*.

150 Asset Acceptance Corp. v. Proctor, 804 N.E.2d 975, 977 (Ohio Ct. App. 2004) (quoting Brown v. Columbus Stamping & Mfg. Co., 223 N.E.2d 373 (Ohio Ct. App. 1967)); *see also In re* Leverett, 378 B.R. 793 (E.D. Tex. 2007); Citibank (S.D.) v. Ogunduyile, 2007 WL 2812969 (Ohio Ct. App. Sept. 28, 2007); Capital One Bank v. Toney, 2007 WL 969420 (Ohio Ct. App.

Courts require the collector to prove the amount of the charges for goods and services that are part of the claim, the dates of the charges, credits for payments, dates and amounts of interest charges, and dates and amounts of other charges (assuming there is proof of contractual entitlement to such interest and related charges).[151] This requirement does not mean that the collector must prove each individual charge with signed sales slips or the like (unless the consumer disputes that charge),[152] but the collector must provide an itemized, running balance. Courts, for example, may accept as evidence a series of monthly statements relating to the charges at issue, but should not accept just the most recent monthly statement[153] that does not reflect charges and payments from earlier months. When the terms of the written contract are not proven the collector should specify as charges only cash advances and purchases of goods and services, but not finance charges or other fees.[154]

Wisconsin's Consumer Act provides that, upon the consumer's written request, the collector must submit copies of writing evidencing any transaction in an open-end credit account, and no recovery can be had if the collector does not do so.[155] This provision is interpreted as requiring the collector to provide writings evidencing each and every transaction in the account.[156]

Proof of the balance due on an open-end account may require proof of the reasonableness of each separate charge.[157] For example, if there is no proof as to an agreed price for a service, a collector seeking to recover for medical, cell phone, cable, utility, or other services may have to show that the charges were reasonable.[158]

Courts have even suggested that a collector suing on an open-end account must prove the reasonableness of charges found on a credit card statement.[159] On the other hand, because a third-party credit card statement is just a list of credit extensions made to various merchants on the consumer's behalf, it may be that the court will find that the consumer requested extensions in those amounts, and that they are thus reasonable. Of course, this rationale does *not* apply to charges assessed by the card issuer, such as finance charges, late fees, over the limit fees, and the like. If it can not be proved that the consumer agreed to these charges, then the collector will have to show some basis for its right to charge for those fees, and that the amount of each is reasonable.

Finally, the Truth in Lending Act requires that for a credit card obligation "the burden of proof is upon the card issuer to show the use was authorized."[160] This federal requirement implies that a collector in proving an account balance on a credit card debt must present some evidence that the consumer applied for the card and that card charges were authorized by the consumer.[161] The consumer's failure to dispute the charges earlier does not shift the burden of proof from the collector.[162]

4.6.4 Inadequate Evidence Presented by Collectors

In evaluating a collector's evidence on a claim based upon an open-end account, the first step is to determine if there is evidence of a written contract. If there is not, then any counts based upon breach of a written contract must be dismissed.[163] The collector also has no basis to seek finance charges and other fees, and must then produce itemizations of the account that do not include such charges.[164]

Even as to evidence of the balance due, collectors often present far less evidence than is required. It should not be enough for a debt buyer to obtain summary judgment by producing an affidavit from one of its employees and a computer printout with a dollar amount owed.[165] The printout does not qualify as an admissible business record[166] and

Mar. 28, 2007); Great Seneca Fin. Corp. v. Felty, 869 N.E.2d 30 (Ohio Ct. App. 2006).

151 *See* LVNV Funding L.L.C. v. Matthews, 15 Fla. L. Weekly Supp. 65a (Fla. County Ct. Oct. 4, 2007), *available at* www.consumerlaw.org/unreported (citing Fla. R. Civ. P. Form 1.932); FIA Card Services Nat'l Ass'n v. Kirasic (Pa. C.P. Allegheny County Nov. 7, 2007) (Wettick, J.), *available at* www.consumerlaw.org/unreported; *see also* Target Nat'l Bank v. Samanez (Pa. C.P. Allegheny County Dec. 19, 2007) (Wettick, J.), *available at* www.consumerlaw.org/unreported; Palisades Collection, L.L.C v. Grassmyer (Pa. C.P. Jan. 15, 2008), *available at* www.consumerlaw.org/unreported; 1 Am. Jur. 2d *Accounts and Accounting* § 17 (2007).

152 *See* Cavalry SPV, L.L.C. v. Anderson, 99 Ark. App. 309 (2007); 1 Am. Jur. 2d *Accounts and Accounting* § 17 (2007).

153 *See* FIA Card Services Nat'l Ass'n v. Kirasic (Pa. C.P. Allegheny County Nov. 7, 2007) (Wettick, J.), *available at* www.consumerlaw.org/unreported; *see also* Target Nat'l Bank v. Samanez (Pa. C.P. Allegheny County Dec. 19, 2007) (Wettick, J.), *available at* www.consumerlaw.org/unreported.

On the other hand, an action for "account stated" may rely only on the most recent account statement. But do not confuse the elements of "account stated" with "on account."

154 *See* § 4.6.2, *supra*.

155 Wis. Stat. § 425.109(2).

156 Newgard v. Bank of Am., 735 N.W.2d 578 (Wis. Ct. App. 2007).

157 Citibank v. Whiteley, 149 S.W.3d 599 (Mo. Ct. App. 2004); *see also* Midwestern Health Mgmt., Inc. v. Walker, 208 S.W.2d 295 (Mo. Ct. App. 2006); 1 Am. Jur. 2d *Accounts and Accounting* § 8 (2007).

158 *See* § 10.5.5, *infra*.

159 *See* Citibank v. Miller, 222 S.W.3d 318 (Mo. Ct. App. 2007).

160 15 U.S.C. § 1643(b).

161 *See* Danner v. Discover Bank, 99 Ark. App. 71 (2007); *see also* Bank of N.Y.—Del. v. Santarelli, 491 N.Y.S.2d 980 (County Ct. Greene County 1985). *See generally* National Consumer Law Center, Truth in Lending § 5.9.4.8 (6th ed. 2007).

162 *See* § 4.7.6, *infra*.

163 *See* § 4.5.5, *supra*.

164 *See* § 4.6.2, *supra*.

165 New Century Fin. Serv. v. Sanchez (N.J. Super. Ct. Law Div. Apr. 12, 2002), *available at* www.consumerlaw.org/unreported.

166 *See* § 4.2.4, *supra*.

it lacks sufficient detail as to the individual charges. The printout is usually created well after the consumer's default, on a computer system not belonging to the original creditor.[167] Moreover, an affidavit from a debt buyer employee is hardly sufficient evidence as to the nature of the original creditor's bookkeeping.

In addition, no affidavit or summary sheet can satisfy the requirement that, to prevail on an open account claim, the collector must produce the actual statements or some other itemization of individual charges and payments.[168] Summary sheets do not itemize each charge and each payment.

The collector must produce not just the most recent statement, but all monthly statements going back to a zero balance or a dollar amount to which the consumer has previously agreed.[169] The collector does not meet its burden by showing a series of monthly statements, when those statements start already with a substantial balance.[170] Nevertheless, there are limits to how far back a collector need go. One court indicated that the collector need not go back thirty years to show each monthly statement, but it was sufficient to provide more than four years of statements.[171]

When the collector does submit a series of monthly statements, either at trial or accompanying a summary judgment motion, those business records must be properly authenticated.[172] Discussion of proper authentication of business records is examined in § 4.2.4.2, *supra*.

For the consumer to admit to being in default is not inconsistent with a dispute about the size of the balance owing. The collector must still prove the exact amount due, and how that amount was derived.[173] The fact that the consumer did not exercise rights under the Fair Credit Billing Act to dispute charges does not mean that the consumer has admitted to the amount due claimed by the collector.[174]

167 *See id.*

168 Capital One Bank v. Toney, 2007 WL 969420 (Ohio Ct. App. Mar. 28, 2007).

169 H & H Design Builders v. Travelers, 639 So. 2d 697 (Fla. Dist. Ct. App. 1994).

170 Great Seneca Fin. Corp. v. Felty, 869 N.E.2d 30 (Ohio Ct. App. 2006).

171 Am. Express Travel Related Services v. Silverman, 2006 WL 3491741 (Ohio Ct. App. Dec. 5, 2006).

172 Unifund CCR Partners v. Harrell, 2005 WL 2082731 (Conn. Super. Ct. Aug. 3, 2005); Asset Acceptance L.L.C. v. Lemon, 2007 WL 3408304 (Ohio Ct. App. Nov. 5, 2007); Great Seneca Fin. Corp. v. Felty, 869 N.E.2d 30 (Ohio Ct. App. 2006); *cf.* Am. Express Travel Related Services v. Silverman, 2006 WL 3491741 (Ohio Ct. App. Dec. 5, 2006) (affidavits found adequate to authenticate the records); Citibank (S.D.) v. Ogunduyile, 2007 WL 2812969 (Ohio Ct. App. Sept. 28, 2007) (same).

173 Asset Acceptance Corp. v. Proctor, 804 N.E.2d 975 (Ohio Ct. App. 2004).

174 This Fair Credit Billing Act defense is described in more detail in § 4.7.6, *infra*.

4.7 Account Stated

4.7.1 General

Collectors suing on credit card or other open account debts commonly allege a cause of action for an "account stated" because it may not require proof of the written contract or itemization of each individual charge in an open-end account. Avoiding such proof is especially attractive for a debt buyer that may have little documentation of the credit contract or of individual charges. Nevertheless there are a number of difficulties a collector will encounter using the account stated theory, as will be detailed in this section.

A claim for account stated is *not* based upon a written credit agreement or even the various individual transactions contributing to a current balance owing on a debt. Instead, it is based upon an agreement, either explicit or implicit, between the creditor and the consumer as to the current account balance due of a series of prior charges and payments, and the consumer's agreement to pay that amount.[175] The collector must prove that there is an adequate statement of account that was presented to the consumer, and that the consumer assented to the statement.

An account stated is an independent cause of action, superseding a cause of action based upon the credit agreement and the individual charges. In effect, the cause of action states that the parties have come to a new agreement that the consumer will pay a certain amount. The action then seeks to enforce this later agreement, and is not based upon the original contract or charges.

Consequently, the collector is not required to produce the original contract or evidence of individual charges. Instead, it produces evidence as to the statement of account that forms the basis for the new agreement, and evidence that the consumer consented to pay the amount indicated in this statement. Nevertheless, courts may require that there be an independent basis for liability, and may treat the accounting as merely establishing the amount of the debt.[176]

An account stated claim differs in a number of ways from a claim on a contract or on an open account. A contractual

175 Ahlbin v. Crescent Commercial Corp., 100 Cal. App. 2d 646 (1950); LVNV Funding L.L.C. v. Moehrlin (Fla. County Ct. Volusia County Aug. 2006) (Green, J.), *available at* www.consumerlaw.org/unreported; Bank of N.Y.—Del. v. Santarelli, 491 N.Y.S.2d 980 (County Ct. Greene County 1985); Morrison v. Citibank, 2008 WL 553284 (Tex. App. Feb. 28, 2008); Restatement (Second) of Contracts § 282 (1981).

176 Dreyer Med. Clinic v. Corral, 591 N.E.2d 111 (Ill. App. Ct. 1992) (account stated is method of proving damages; creditor must first prove liability; creditor failed to prove several essential elements); Nelson v. First Nat'l Bank Omaha, 2004 WL 2711032 (Minn. Ct. App. Nov. 30, 2004); Citibank (S.D.) v. Martin, 807 N.Y.S.2d 284 (Civ. Ct. 2005) (account stated can not create a liability where none existed).

choice of law provision is not applicable to a claim for account stated, because the new agreement between the parties does not contain such a provision, and the preexisting contract has not been proven.

Because an account stated claim typically is not founded upon a written contract between the parties, but rather is based upon the consumer's implicit assent, the applicable statute of limitations is not one based upon a written contract. Instead, the applicable limitations period may be one for non-written contracts or one that is explicitly applicable to claims based upon account stated. In many states such limitations periods are shorter than for a written contract.[177]

An important implication of the account stated cause of action not being based upon the original written contract is that the collector is not entitled to contractual attorney fees. The collector can only recover attorney fees based upon a statute, if one is applicable.

If the collector can prove that the consumer agreed to a statement of account, that statement will typically include finance charges and various fees. The collector can recover those amounts because there has been proof that the consumer has consented to pay those amounts. Including in the statement of account such charges and fees creates a risk for the collector that it will be unable to recover anything on the account stated cause of action. As described in § 4.7.5, *infra*, at least one court has found that it will be difficult for a collector to show that the consumer assented to finance charges and fees, and thus the collector's proof of the consumer's assent to the statement of account as a whole is undermined.

In any event, the account stated cause of action will provide no right to contractual finance charges or fees assessed *after* the agreed-upon statement of account.[178] The agreed-upon statement of account sets out a balance owed at that point in time, and does not include amounts owed later. If the collector seeks interest after that date, it can only do so based on a right to statutory pre-judgment interest, if allowed by state law.

4.7.2 Limits on the Account Stated Cause of Action

The account stated claim developed historically when a consumer entered into a series of transactions with a merchant and the merchant kept an accounting of those transactions. The cause of action was not developed with credit card transactions in mind, and may be difficult to use for this type of debt, particularly in certain states. Therefore consumers must examine the law in their state as to the availability of an account stated cause of action and should note any limits on that cause of action for the type of debt at issue.

For example, Wisconsin, by statute, has sharply limited the account stated cause of action in consumer credit transactions. Wisconsin's Consumer Act provides that, upon the consumer's written request, the collector must submit copies of writings evidencing any transaction in an open-end credit account, and no recovery can be had for the collector if it does not do so.[179] This provision has been interpreted as requiring the collector to provide written evidence of each and every transaction in the account,[180] and applies even to claims based upon an account stated.[181] In other words, even when the collector presents a statement of account and the consumer consents to that account, the consumer, when sued, can still demand evidence of each and every charge, and the collector can not recover on any charges if it does not produce that evidence.[182]

New York law states that: "No agreement between the issuer and the holder shall contain any provision that a statement sent by the issuer to the holder shall be deemed correct unless objected to within a specified period of time. Any such provision is against public policy and shall be of no force or effect."[183] While not explicitly prohibiting account stated causes of action for credit card debt, it does indicate a legislative intent that liability should not be built upon the consumer's silence upon receiving an account. At least one New York court has rejected an account stated claim on this basis.[184]

Connecticut at one point had a statute specifying the elements of a claim for account stated, but has since repealed that statute.[185] Nevertheless, courts in Connecticut apparently allow a common law claim for account stated.[186]

Courts may limit the account stated cause of action to the sale of goods or services and not to a third-party relationship involving a credit card issuer.[187] Account stated claims also may not be available for credit cards because such claims conflict with a federal right. The federal Truth in Lending Act states that the collector has the burden of proving that the credit card charges are authorized.[188] An account stated claim, on the other hand, is based upon the consumer's implied consent to a statement of account, and the collector

177 *See* § 3.7.3.1, *supra*; *see also* Richburg v. Palisades Collection, L.L.C., 247 F.R.D. 457 (E.D. Pa. Jan. 28, 2008).

178 Citibank (S.D.) v. Martin, 807 N.Y.S.2d 284 (Civ. Ct. 2005).

179 Wis. Stat. § 425.109(2).

180 Newgard v. Bank of Am., 735 N.W.2d 578 (Wis. Ct. App. 2007).

181 *Id.*

182 *Id.*

183 N.Y. Gen. Bus. Law § 517 (McKinney).

184 Bank of N.Y.—Del. v. Santarelli, 491 N.Y.S.2d 980 (County Ct. Greene County 1985).

185 Conn. Gen. Stat. § 52-113 was repealed in 1978, by 1978 Conn. Pub. Acts 379, §§ 26, 27.

186 *See* Citibank (S.D.) v. Moniz, 2008 WL 714134 (Conn. Super. Ct. Feb. 27, 2008); Citibank v. Strumpf, 2006 WL 2773540 (Conn. Super. Ct. Sept. 13, 2006); Citibank v. Morgan, 2006 WL 574211 (Conn. Super. Ct. Feb. 27, 2006).

187 *Cf.* Morrison v. Citibank (S.D.), 2008 WL 553284 (Tex. App. Feb. 28, 2008) (need not reach the issue whether account stated applies to credit card debt).

188 15 U.S.C. § 1643(b).

does not have to prove that the charges making up the account are authorized.[189]

4.7.3 What Document Qualifies As a Statement of Account?

The account stated cause of action depends on the consumer assenting to a statement of account that details a balance due. The collector thus must present into evidence the statement upon which the cause of action depends; in some states the statement must be appended to the complaint.[190] Failure to produce a statement of account should be grounds to dismiss the action.[191]

The statement must be more than just a memorandum and must indicate that it is intended to be a final settlement of an account up to date.[192] It should include more than a mere summary number, but should indicate individual items, the accrual of each item, and the amount of each item. A debt buyer's letter indicating a balance due without more is certainly not a statement of account, even if it has been made to look like a billing statement.

When the collector seeks summary judgment, the affidavit describing the statement of account must be consistent with the document it is authenticating. In one case the affiant described the items as purchases when they were monthly charges for cell phone usage, negating the affidavit's credibility.[193]

4.7.4 Has the Account Statement Been Reviewed by the Consumer?

For the consumer to assent to a statement of account, the consumer must receive it. "An account stated has been defined as an account in writing, examined and expressly or impliedly accepted by both parties thereto, as distinguished from a simple claim or a mere summary of accounts."[194]

At a minimum, the collector must prove that the statement was sent to the consumer.[195] Debt buyers can get into trouble trying to prove that the creditor mailed the account statement when the debt buyer produces an affidavit to the effect from a debt buyer employee, not from the original creditor that sent the statement.[196]

But merely sending the statement is not enough. This cause of action is not one in which a party is just showing compliance with a notice requirement. The collector must show that the consumer assented to the account, at least implicitly. Implicit consent can not be proved if the consumer never received the statement of account.

Consequently there must be proof not only that the account statement was sent to the consumer, but that it was received by the consumer.[197] If the consumer has not seen a statement, the consumer can not have either explicitly or implicitly agreed to it.[198] In one case, the statements were sent to the husband's business address and the wife did not use the card and had no knowledge of the charges and payments. The account stated claim against the wife could not survive.[199]

189 Bank of N.Y.—Del. v. Santarelli, 491 N.Y.S.2d 980 (County Ct. Greene County 1985). *But see* Citibank (S.D.) v. Poynton, 187 Misc. 2d 397 (Sup. Ct. 2000).

190 *See* § 3.5, *supra*.

191 Ayers v. Cavalry SVP, L.L.C., 876 So. 2d 474 (Ala. Civ. App. 2003); *see* Fla. Credit Research Inc. v. Felicien (Fla. County Ct. Apr. 15, 2008), *available at* www.consumerlaw.org/unreported; Capital One Bank v. Mullis, 15 Fla. L. Weekly Supp. 370a (Fla. County Ct. Feb. 13, 2008); N. Star Capital Acquisition, L.L.C. v. Lewis, 15 Fla. L. Weekly Supp. 72a (Fla. County Ct. Duval County Oct. 23, 2007), *available at* www.consumerlaw.org/unreported; Capital One Bank v. Gelsey, 15 Fla. L. Weekly Supp. 64a (Fla. County Ct. Duval County July 3, 2007), *available at* www.consumerlaw.org/unreported; LVNV Funding L.L.C. v. Moehrlin (Fla. County Ct. Volusia County Aug. 2006) (Green, J.), *available at* www.consumerlaw.org/unreported; Wiltel Communications, L.L.C. v. Sunrise Int'l Leasing Corp., 2005 WL 354030 (Minn. Ct. App. Feb. 15, 2005); Grandell Rehab. & Nursing Home v. Devlin, 809 N.Y.S.2d 481 (Sup. Ct. 2005); Citibank (S.D.) v. Lesnick, 2006 WL 1670257 (Ohio Ct. App. May 18, 2006); Asset Acceptance Corp. v. Proctor, 804 N.E.2d 975 (Ohio Ct. App. 2004) (setting forth type of accounting required for account stated action); Mercy Franciscan Hosp. v. Willis, 2004 WL 2244809 (Ohio Ct. App. Sept. 24, 2004). *But see* Citibank (S.D.) v. Kessler, 2004 WL 795689 (Ohio Ct. App. Apr. 15, 2004) (lender entitled to summary judgment against *pro se* defendant on account stated claim based on affidavit of its keeper of records; no indication that an accounting or billing statements were provided).

192 Ahlbin v. Crescent Commercial Corp., 100 Cal. App. 2d 646 (1950).

193 Palisades Collection, L.L.C. v. Gonzalez, 809 N.Y.S.2d 482 (Civ. Ct. 2005) (table) (text available at 2005 WL 3372971).

194 13 Pa. Law Encyclopedia (Second) Contracts § 512.

195 Ayers v. Cavalry SVP I, L.L.C., 876 So. 2d 474 (Ala. Civ. App. 2004); LVNV Funding L.L.C. v. Moehrlin (Fla. County Ct. Volusia County Aug. 2006) (Green, J.), *available at* www.consumerlaw.org/unreported; Nelson v. First Nat'l Bank Omaha, 2004 WL 2711032 (Minn. Ct. App. Nov. 30, 2004); Morrison, Cohen, Singer & Weinstein, LLP v. Brophy, 798 N.Y.S.2d 379 (App. Div. 2005); Rushmore Recoveries X, L.L.C. v. Skolnick, 841 N.Y.S.2d 823 (Dist. Ct. 2007); Citibank (S.D.) v. Martin, 807 N.Y.S.2d 284 (Civ. Ct. 2005); *see also* Erickson v. Johnson, 2006 WL 453201 (D. Minn. Feb. 22, 2006).

196 *See* Palisades Collection, L.L.C. v. Gonzalez, 809 N.Y.S.2d 482 (Civ. Ct. 2005) (table) (text available at 2005 WL 3372971).

197 Morrison v. Citibank (S.D.), 2008 WL 553284 (Tex. App. Feb. 28, 2008).

198 Ayers v. Cavalry SVP I, L.L.C., 876 So. 2d 474 (Ala. Civ. App. 2004); Nelson v. First Nat'l Bank Omaha, 2004 WL 2711032 (Minn. Ct. App. Nov. 30, 2004); *see also* First Merit Bank v. Wilson, 2007 WL 1827589 (Ohio Ct. App. June 27, 2007).

199 First Merit Bank v. Wilson, 2007 WL 1827589 (Ohio Ct. App. June 27, 2007); *see also* Erickson v. Johnson, 2006 WL 453201 (D. Minn. Feb. 22, 2006).

4.7.5 Consumer's Implied Consent

4.7.5.1 General

Consumers rarely agree in writing to pay a specified amount after reviewing a statement of account. The collector's action for account stated generally must rely on the consumer's implied consent to pay the amount found in the statement. The law is far from clear as to what actions by the consumer imply consent, and the law may be different for transactions between businesses than for consumer obligations.

Implied consent has been found when there are discussions between the parties or other back and forth communications as to the amount that is due, resulting in agreement as to the amount due.[200] A communication from the consumer accepting responsibility for payment, but professing an inability to make that payment, might be found to be enough to show implied consent.[201] Similarly, in one case the defendant did not object to periodic invoices and acknowledged the existence of the outstanding debt.[202] Consent can also be found implicit in other affirmative actions by the consumer.[203]

On the other hand, if the consumer objects to a statement of account, then the collector can not prevail because the consumer has not consented to pay the amount found in the statement.[204] The result should be the same even if the dispute was made over the telephone.[205] Companies routinely indicate that a call may be recorded, so consumers should be able to reasonably rely on a phone call as a means of documenting their dispute.[206]

Federal law places the burden on the collector to prove that charges are authorized.[207] This burden is not met merely by referencing a statement of account and the consumer's silence.[208] Some courts apply this federally created burden of proof only to claims for breach of contract, and not to a claim for account stated.[209] But that approach does not comport with the actual language of the federal statute that applies the burden to "*any* action by a card issuer to enforce liability for use of a credit card" [emphasis added].[210]

When there are joint owners of an account, no implied consent should be found if it can be shown that this particular joint owner did not see the statements and was not knowledgeable about the charges and payments. Such a joint owner can hardly be found to assent in that situation.[211]

In many cases the decisive question will be whether the consumer's silence after receipt of a statement of account signifies implicit consent to pay that amount. Federal law appears to indicate that silence is not enough when a debt collector or debt buyer sends a demand for payment along with notice of the consumer's Fair Debt Collection Practices Act right to request verification of the debt. The FDCPA provides that a court may not treat a consumer's failure to dispute a debt in this situation as an admission of liability.[212]

The consumer's silence does not signify consent when the context of the submission of the statement of account to the consumer fails to suggest that the consumer should object. For example, the consumer would not be expected to object to a debt buyer's dunning letter made to look like a statement, and sent years after the account was closed. If there is no existing relationship between the parties, assent should not be implied from silence.[213]

The collector should not prevail when the consumer, during the litigation, raises the defense that the consumer never had an account with the collector. Merely receiving statements regarding an account that the consumer believes does not belong to the consumer can not show assent to a statement of account.[214] The collector may have to also offer proof that the consumer agreed to the relationship between the parties.[215]

Some courts also require that there be more than just silence on the part of the consumer to indicate consent.[216]

200 *Cf.* Target Nat'l Bank v. Samanez (Pa. C.P. Allegheny County Dec. 19, 2007), *available at* www.consumerlaw.org/unreported.

201 Obermayer, Rebmann, Maxwell & Hippel v. Banta, 28 Pa. D. & C.4th 225 (C.P. 1996), *aff'd in part, vacated in part*, 687 A.2d 866 (Pa. Super. Ct. 1996).

202 Residential Services Validated Publications v. Carus, 2006 WL 1026660 (E.D.N.Y. Apr. 19, 2006).

203 *See* 15 Samuel Williston, Treatise on the Law of Contracts § 566 (Walter H. Jaeger, ed., 3d ed. 1972); 13 Pa. Law Encyclopedia (Second) Contracts §§ 512, 513.

204 *See* Discover Bank v. Walker, 787 N.Y.S.2d 677 (Sup. Ct. 2004); Palisades Collection L.L.C. v. Haque, 2006 N.Y. Misc. LEXIS 4036 (N.Y. Civ. Ct. Apr. 13, 2006).

205 Palisades Collection L.L.C. v. Haque, 2006 N.Y. Misc. LEXIS 4036 (N.Y. Civ. Ct. Apr. 13, 2006).

206 *See id.*

207 15 U.S.C. § 1643(b).

208 *See* § 4.7.5.2, *infra*.

209 Citibank v. Poynton, 723 N.Y.S.2d 327 (Sup. Ct. 2000).

210 15 U.S.C. § 1643(b); *see also* Bank of N.Y. v. Santarelli, 491 N.Y.S.2d 980 (County Ct. 1985).

211 First Merit Bank v. Wilson, 2007 WL 1827589 (Ohio Ct. App. June 27, 2007).

212 *See* 15 U.S.C. § 1692g(c); *see also* National Consumer Law Center, Fair Debt Collection § 5.7 (6th ed. 2008).

213 Nelson v. First Nat'l Bank Omaha, 2004 WL 2711032 (Minn. Ct. App. Nov. 30, 2004).

214 *Id.*

215 *Id.*

216 *See, e.g.*, Braude & Margulies, Prof'l Corp. v. Fireman's Fund Ins. Co., 468 F. Supp. 2d 190 (D.D.C. 2007); Dreyer Med. Clinic v. Corral, 591 N.E.2d 111 (Ill. App. Ct. 1992); Target Nat'l Bank v. Samanez (Pa. C.P. Allegheny County Dec. 19, 2007), *available at* www.consumerlaw.org/unreported; Morrison v. Citibank (S.D.), 2008 WL 553284 (Tex. App. Feb. 28, 2008); *see also* LVNV Funding L.L.C. v. Moehrlin (Fla. County Ct. Volusia County Aug. 2006) (Green, J.), *available at* www.consumerlaw.org/unreported; C-E Glass v. Ryan, 70 Pa. D. & C.2d 445 (C.P. 1975); Ryon v. Andershonis, 42 Pa. D.& C.2d 86 (C.P. 1967); 13 Arthur Linton Corbin, Corbin on Contracts §§ 1312, 1313 (1962–2002 interim ed.); 13 Pa. Law Encyclopedia (Second) Contracts § 513.

"Something more than mere acquiescence by failing to take exception to a series of statements of account received in the mail is required to create an account stated."[217]

Other courts though, particularly for transactions between two businesses, create an obligation on the defendant to inspect a statement of account when presented to the defendant, and agreement is implied if the defendant does not object within a reasonable time, unless fraud, mistake, or other equitable considerations are shown.[218]

4.7.5.2 Special Considerations for Credit Card Obligations

A perceptive 2007 opinion examines why a consumer's silence is insufficient to show implied consent in the credit card context, when the consumer can not be expected to understand and thus does not assent to the computation of finance charges and other fees shown on the statement.[219] Its analysis is so cogent, it will be excerpted at length:

> Credit cardholders who do not pay the full amount of the new balance usually do not know whether any charges, other than the charges for purchases and cash withdrawals, are correct. It is reasonable to assume that most credit cardholders have never attempted to read the entire initial cardholder agreement. Furthermore, even if they attempted to do so, it is unlikely that they would fully understand what they have read. Also, most agreements provide that they can be amended upon fifteen days notice, and frequently the monthly statements are accompanied by amendments to the initial agreement that can not be understood unless the credit cardholder has access to and does review the initial agreement, subsequent amendments, and the newest amendment. This does not occur.
>
> In the present case, for example, the annual percentage rates in the monthly statements from October 25, 2005 through September 25, 2007 frequently differed from month-to-month. In January 2006, the annual percentage rate for purchases was 20.99%; in May 2006, the annual percentage rate for purchases was 21.74%; in August 2006, the annual percentage rate for purchases was 22.24%; in December 2006, the annual percentage rate for purchases was 22.24%; and in March 2007, the annual percentage rate for purchases was 28.24%.
>
> For several months, there was a late payment fee charge of $35.00.
>
> While the credit cardholder, looking at the statement, can see the amount of the charges that were imposed, he or she is unlikely to know whether the charges are consistent with the writings governing the cardholder's obligations. Consequently, he or she is not in a position to either agree or disagree with the amount of the balance in any monthly statement that does not begin with a $0.00 balance.
>
> The above description of the cardholder and issuer relationship is consistent with the findings in a September 2006 108-page report prepared by the United States Government Accountability Office titled *Credit Cards—Increased Complexity in Rates and Fees Heightens Need for More Effective Disclosures to Consumers,* www.gao.gov, Document GAO-06-929 (912006) (the "Report").
>
> The portion of the Report titled *Results in Brief,* states that disclosures are too complicated for many consumers to understand. *Id.* at 4–6. In addition, the disclosures are often poorly organized, burying important information in the text, and scattering information about a single topic in numerous places. *Id.* at 6. The design of the disclosures often makes the disclosures hard to read with large amounts of the text in small, condensed typefaces and poor, ineffective headings. *Id.* at 6. The cardholder is not in a position to agree or disagree with the charges on a monthly statement that are unrelated to the cash withdrawals and purchases shown on the monthly statement because the obligations imposed on the cardholder are not easily understood.
>
> Prior to 1990, most issuers charged a fixed interest rate and imposed few other charges. Thus, furnishing an adequate disclosure was relatively easy. Today, credit cards feature complex pricing structures. *Id.* at 13. Most cards now assess one interest rate on balances from the purchase of goods, another on balances that are transferred from another credit card, and a third on balances that result from using the card to obtain cash. Also, the cards usually provide for payments to be allocated first to the balance assessed at the lowest interest rate. *Id.* at 14–15, 27.
>
> In addition to having separate rates for the different transactions, the cards increasingly impose interest rates that vary periodically as market interest rates change. Issuers typically establish these variable rates by taking the prevailing level of a base rate, such as the prime rate, and adding a fixed percentage amount. They frequently reset the interest rates on a monthly basis. *Id.* at 15.
>
> Most credit cards provide for a penalty fee, described as a late fee, which issuers assess when

217 13 Pa. Law Encyclopedia (Second) Contracts § 513.

218 *See* Ayers v. Cavalry SVP I, L.L.C., 876 So. 2d 474 (Ala. Civ. App. 2003); Wiltel Communications, L.L.C. v. Sunrise Int'l Leasing Corp., 2005 WL 354030 (Minn. Ct. App. Feb. 15, 2005); Nelson v. First Nat'l Bank Omaha, 2004 WL 2711032 (Minn. Ct. App. Nov. 30, 2004); Gross v. Empire Healthchoice Assur., Inc., 819 N.Y.S.2d 210 (Sup. Ct. 2006).

219 Target Nat'l Bank v. Samanez (Pa. C.P. Allegheny County Dec. 19, 2007), *available at* www.consumerlaw.org/unreported; *see also* National Consumer Law Center, The Cost of Credit: Regulation, Preemption, and Industry Abuses § 11.7 (3d ed. 2005 and Supp.).

they do not receive at least a minimum required payment by the due date. Most of the cards have a tiered fee structure depending upon the amount of the balance held by the cardholder (e.g., $15.00 late fee when the balances are between $100.00 and $250.00; $25.00 to $29.00 fee on accounts with balances up to $1,000.00; and $34.00 to $39.00 fee when the balance exceeds $1,000.00). *Id.* at 19–20.

Most issuers also assess cardholders a penalty fee for exceeding the credit limit, with the over limit fee also involving the use of a tiered structure. *Id.* at 20–21. Cards frequently have total credit limits at a lesser limit for cash. *Id.* at 22. Also, issuers do not reject purchases during the sale authorization even though the transaction puts the cardholder over the card's credit limits, thereby exposing the cardholder to an over limit fee and a higher interest rate. *Id.* at 30.

Many cards provide for higher interest rates to be assessed if cardholders make late payments or exceed the credit limit. *Id.* at 24. Many cards also provide for increased rates when cardholders fail to make payments to other creditors. *Id.* at 24–25.

Most of the cards also provide for the cardholder to pay fees for certain services (e.g., 3% of cash advance amounts, 3% of transfer of a balance from another creditor, 3% of purchases made in a foreign country). *Id.* at 23.

The Report concluded that the disclosures which provide information about the costs and terms of using credit cards "had serious weaknesses that likely reduce their usefulness to consumers;. . . . The disclosures . . . [were] written at a level too difficult for the average consumer to understand, and [had] design features, such as text placement and font sizes, that did not conform to guidance for creating easily readable documents. When attempting to use these disclosures, cardholders were often unable to identify key rates or terms and often failed to understand the information in [the] documents." *Id.* at 33.

The pricing structures depend upon the circumstances of the cardholder, and credit card disclosures are inadequate to inform cardholders as to the interest rates, fees, penalties, and other costs that may be imposed. The Report stated that the "disclosure documents were written such that understanding them required a higher reading level than that attained by many U.S. cardholders; . . . nearly half of the adult population in the United States reads at or below the eighth-grade level." *Id.* at 38. Accordingly, the Securities and Exchange Commission recommends that disclosure materials be written at a sixth-to eighth-grade level. *Id.* Disclosures of credit card issuers on average were written "at a reading level commensurate with about a tenth-to twelfth-grade education." *Id.* at 37. An understanding of the disclosures in the solicitation letters would require "an eleventh-grade level of reading comprehension, while understanding the cardmember agreements would require about a twelfth-grade education. *Id.* In addition, certain portions of the typical disclosure documents required even higher reading levels to be understandable. For example, information about annual percentage rates, grace periods, balance computation, and payment allocation methods required "a minimum of a fifteenth-grade education, which is the equivalent of 3 years of college education." *Id.* at 38.

The Report described additional problems that also prevented cardholders from understanding the transactions, even assuming that the relevant documents were available. The disclosure documents do not use effective organizational structures and formatting. *Id.* at 38. The typical credit card disclosure lacks effective organization. *Id.* at 39. Many of the disclosure documents use font sizes that are difficult to read and thus hinder the consumer's ability to find information. *Id.* at 41. The typical disclosure documents are overly complex and present the relevant information in too much detail, "such as by using unfamiliar or complex terms to describe simple concepts." *Id.* at 46.

4.7.6 The Fair Credit Billing Act Fallacy

Collectors sometimes argue that federal law provides that a credit card holder consents to an account stated if the card holder does not dispute the statement in writing within sixty days. A number of Connecticut trial court decisions and even an Ohio appellate court have agreed that Truth in Lending Act Part D, commonly referred to as the Fair Credit Billing Act (FCBA),[220] creates an affirmative obligation for consumers, if they believe a credit card statement is inaccurate, to send a written dispute letter within sixty days. Failure to do so admits the accuracy of the charges.[221]

---

220 15 U.S.C. § 1666; *see also* National Consumer Law Center, Truth in Lending § 5.8.3 (6th ed. 2007).

221 Citibank v. Strumpf, 2006 WL 2773540 (Conn. Super. Ct. Sept. 13, 2006); Citibank (S.D.) v. Lovell, 2006 WL 1229922 (Conn. Super. Ct. Apr. 13, 2006); Citibank (S.D.) v. Currea, 2006 WL 1229919 (Conn. Super. Ct. Apr. 13, 2006); Citibank (S.D.) v. Babuscio, 2005 WL 3667343 (Conn. Super. Ct. Dec. 21, 2005); Citibank (S.D.) v. Todd, 2005 WL 3666353 (Conn. Super. Ct. Dec. 21, 2005); Citibank (S.D.) v. Kilberg, 2005 WL 3665805 (Conn. Super. Ct. Dec. 21, 2005); Citibank (S.D.) v. Forcinelli, 2005 WL 3665635 (Conn. Super. Ct. Dec. 21, 2005); Citibank (S.D.) v. Gemske, 2005 WL 3665083 (Conn. Super. Ct. Dec. 21, 2005); Citibank (S.D.) v. Kessler, 2004 WL 795689 (Ohio Ct. App. Apr. 15, 2004); *cf.* Asset Acceptance Corp. v. Proctor, 804 N.E.2d 975 (Ohio Ct. App. 2004) (finding no consent, because consumer never received statements). *But see* DBI Architects, Prof'l Corp. v. Am. Express Travel-Related Services Co., 388 F.3d 886 (D.C. Cir. 2004); Danner v. Discover Bank, 2007 WL 1428987 (Ark. Ct. App. Aug. 16, 2007); People's Bank v. Scarpetti, 1998 WL 61925 (Conn. Super. Ct. Feb. 5, 1998);

This approach is clearly unfounded and wrongheaded, with no basis in the statutory language, the regulation or official staff commentary interpreting the statute, or the congressional history. This interpretation would turn a consumer protection statute on its head into a debt buyer's protection statute. The FCBA's congressional intent is to protect consumers, not creditors.[222]

In fact, a careful reading of the FCBA's language shows that it creates no affirmative obligation on the consumer to do anything. Not one sentence requires a consumer to take any action. The FCBA instead details actions the *creditor* can and can not take if a consumer sends a particular written notice of dispute. Nor is there any legislative history that would indicate any congressional intent to limit the rights of a consumer who does not send written notice within sixty days.

Collectors often refer to a sentence in the Act that states: "Nothing in this section shall be construed to prohibit any action by a creditor to collect any amount which has not been indicated by the obligor to contain a billing error."[223] Even taken out of context, this sentence merely states that the FCBA does not prohibit the creditor from filing a suit to collect on a debt when the consumer has not raised a billing error dispute. The sentence does not prevent the consumer from raising defenses and counterclaims in such an action. Numerous defenses apply to a collection action—for example, the statute of limitations, full payment, and accord and satisfaction. This FCBA provision does not eliminate all these consumer rights if the consumer fails to send a billing error dispute. In fact, the Federal Reserve Board's official staff commentary to the Truth in Lending Act explicitly states that the consumer can raise claims and defenses on a debt pursuant to 15 U.S.C. §§ 1666i and 1643, even though the consumer does not send a written notice of dispute under the FCBA.[224]

Moreover, when this sentence is taken *in context*, its meaning is even clearer. The FCBA requires a creditor, in response to the consumer's written notice about a billing error, to refrain from taking any action to collect the amount until certain steps are taken.[225] The "nothing in this section" sentence simply means that this prohibition on taking action to collect on that portion of a debt under dispute does not apply to portions of a debt not in dispute.

Also, the collector's position is inconsistent with another section of the Truth in Lending Act, which provides that the credit card issuer has the burden of proof to show use was authorized[226] (unauthorized use is one of the billing errors to which the FCBA explicitly relates[227]). If the card issuer has the burden of proof, then a consumer's failure to send a written notice within sixty days can not be treated as consent to the unauthorized use.

The FCBA dispute procedures do not even apply to many areas in which a consumer may dispute a statement of account. The billing errors covered by the Act are set out in Regulation Z.[228] Not defined as a billing error, for example, are certain disputes relating to the goods or services purchased, such as disputes as to the quality of property or services that the consumer accepts.[229] How can the failure to send a billing dispute notice be treated as consent to certain charges, when a billing notice can not be sent to dispute those charges?

Taken to its extreme, the collector's argument concerning the FCBA also means that a consumer is treated as consenting to an account stated when the consumer objects to the account orally or even when the consumer objects in writing on the payment stub or on the statement itself and sends that back to the creditor. The FCBA allows the creditor to specify the procedure for sending in written disputes, and if the consumer fails to follow that procedure, the creditor need not comply with the creditor's FCBA obligations.[230]

The collector's argument also conflicts with another Truth in Lending Act section which states that "this subchapter[231] and the regulations issued thereunder do not affect the validity or enforceability of any contract or obligation under State or Federal law."[232] Clearly the collector's interpretation of the FCBA would affect the enforceability of the contract under state law. In addition, state law may even specify that there can be no agreement between a credit card issuer and card holder that a credit card account is to be deemed correct unless objected to within a specified period of time.[233]

4.8 *Quantum Meruit* or Unjust Enrichment

Some collectors routinely add a *quantum meruit* or unjust enrichment claim to their collection action, perhaps in recognition that they will have difficulty proving either a

Crestar Bank v. Cheevers, 744 A.2d 1043 (D.C. 2000) (need not bring FCBA dispute to claim charges are unauthorized); Citibank (S.D.) v. Mincks, 135 S.W.3d 545 (Mo. Ct. App. 2004).

222 *See* McSherry v. Capital One Fed. Sav. Bank, 236 F.R.D. 516 (W.D. Wash. 2006); Thomas D. Mangelsen, Inc. v. Heartland Payment Systems, Inc., 2005 WL 2076421 (D. Neb. Aug. 26, 2005); Symeonidis v. Paxton Capital Group, Inc., 220 F. Supp. 2d 478, 480 n.3 (D. Md. 2002).

223 15 U.S.C. § 1666(c).

224 Fed. Reserve Bd., Official Staff Commentary to Regulation Z, 12 C.F.R. §§ 226.12(c)-1, 226.12(b)(3)-3.

225 15 U.S.C. § 1666(a).

226 15 U.S.C. § 1643(c).

227 *See* 12 C.F.R. § 226.13(a)(1).

228 12 C.F.R. § 226.13(a).

229 Fed. Reserve Bd., Official Staff Commentary to Regulation Z, 12 C.F.R. § 226.13(a)(3)-1.

230 15 U.S.C. § 1666(a).

231 Subchapter in this context means the Truth in Lending Act, including the Fair Credit Billing Act.

232 15 U.S.C. § 1610(d).

233 *See* N.Y. Gen. Bus. Law. § 517 (McKinney).

contract or an account stated. A debt buyer who has paid pennies on the dollar should not be able to claim unjust enrichment as a means of collecting the entire amount of the account.

In addition, *quantum meruit* and unjust enrichment claims are based upon an implied contract, and most courts find a claim upon an implied contract is *not* available when there is an existing contract.[234] Often the collector's own pleadings, affidavits, or submitted documents will allege an explicit contract, so that the collector's own case will be inconsistent with the cause of action for *quantum meruit* or unjust enrichment.[235]

Moreover, any case on a credit card debt against the principal card holder must involve an existing contract. Federal law requires, before a credit card account is opened, that the creditor send the consumer extensive written disclosures as to the terms of relationship[236] and also requires, with each monthly statement, additional statements as to the terms of the transaction.[237] Clearly, a credit card transaction involves an explicit contract. The fact that the collector can not prove the terms of the contract does not alter the fact that a contract exists, and thus an action can not be brought on such debts for *quantum meruit* or unjust enrichment.

When there is no contract between the collector and consumer (for example, when an authorized user on a credit card was provided only a card and no terms of use), there are certain logical limits to an action on *quantum meruit* or unjust enrichment. By definition there is no contract, and thus there can be no recovery for finance charges, late fees, and the like. A contractual choice of law can not exist. There can be no recovery for contractual attorney fees.[238] In many states, pre-judgment interest is not even allowed because there is no liquidated amount in an implied contract.[239]

Also carefully examine any assignment to a debt buyer. Is the assignment only of the contractual rights or is there an assignment of any chose in action the original creditor possesses? If the former, than the assignee has no right to bring a *quantum meruit* or unjust enrichment claim, as its rights are based solely on contract, and there can be no *quantum meruit* action when there is a contract.

Moreover, the collector will have to prove what money, goods, or services were received by the consumer that form the basis of its claim, and prove the value of those items received. In the credit card context, when a *quantum meruit* action is brought against an authorized user or someone else not obligated by contract, the collector will have to show which charges were for the benefit of that party, and not for the benefit of the principal card holder.

4.9 Other Causes of Action

Depending on state law there are any number of other causes of action a collector may raise to collect on a debt. Often these claims will be in lieu of a claim for breach of contract, because the collector is concerned it can not prove a contract. In selecting alternative claims the collector will look to those that provide attorney fees, interest, or other benefits to maximize the collector's recovery. When shoehorning the facts into such a claim, the collector may be more concerned with the potential amount it can ask the court to award than whether such claims are legally viable. Most actions end in a default judgment, and the fact that the claim does not fit the facts may never be raised.

In defending against such causes of action, the consumer should first ascertain if the collector's complaint clearly states what causes of action are being alleged. For example, a claim for "credit card" may be meaningless under a state's jurisprudence. If the cause of action is not clearly stated, request a more definite statement or move to dismiss the count.

If the cause of action has a statutory basis, carefully parse the statutory language to determine its application and elements of proof. Even if a cause of action does not have a statutory basis, carefully consider the nature of the cause of action under the state's common law to see if it even applies to the debt. For example, does a claim for "materials and services supplied" apply to an action on a third-party credit card debt, when the lender did not supply materials and services, but an extension of credit?

Determine if the collector has proven all the elements of the cause of action. Consider the applicable limitations

234 Banner Iron Works, Inc. v. Amaz Zinc Co., 621 F.2d 883 (8th Cir. 1980); Owen v. Gen. Motors Corp., 2006 WL 2808632 (W.D. Mo. Sept. 28, 2006); May v. Sessums & Mason, P.A., 700 So. 2d 22 (Fla. Dist. Ct. App. 1994); N. Star Capital Acquisition, L.L.C. v. Lewis, 15 Fla. L. Weekly Supp. 72a (Fla. County Ct. Duval County Oct. 23, 2007), *available at* www.consumerlaw.org/unreported; Capital One Bank v. Gelsey, 15 Fla. L. Weekly Supp. 64a (Fla. County Ct. Duval County July 3, 2007), *available at* www.consumerlaw.org/unreported; Am. Express Travel Related Services Co. v. Seidenfeld, 781 N.Y.S.2d 622 (Sup. Ct. 2003); Truly v. Austin, 744 S.W.2d 934 (Tex. 1988); Tully v. Citibank (S.D.), 173 S.W.3d 212 (Tex. App. 2005); Pioneer Roofing, Inc. v. Westra/Const., Inc., 241 Wis. 2d 50 (Ct. App. 2000) (table).

See also § 10.5.4, *infra*, for additional supporting cases.

235 *See* N. Star Capital Acquisition, L.L.C. v. Lewis, 15 Fla. L. Weekly Supp. 72a (Fla. County Ct. Duval County Oct. 23, 2007), *available at* www.consumerlaw.org/unreported; Capital One Bank v. Gelsey, 15 Fla. L. Weekly Supp. 64a (Fla. County Ct. Duval County July 3, 2007), *available at* www.consumerlaw.org/unreported.

236 15 U.S.C. § 1637(a); *see also* National Consumer Law Center, Truth in Lending § 5.5 (6th ed. 2007).

237 15 U.S.C. § 1637(b); *see also* National Consumer Law Center, Truth in Lending § 5.6 (6th ed. 2007).

238 *See* Mclain v. W. Side Bone & Joint Ctr., 656 So. 2d 119 (Miss. 1995).

239 *See* 22 Am. Jur. 2d *Damages* § 468 (2008); *see also* George v. Double-D Food, Inc., 155 Cal. App. 3d 36 (1984); Mclain v. W. Side Bone & Joint Ctr., 656 So. 2d 119 (Miss. 1995); Farmah v. Farmah, 348 N.C. 586 (1998).

period for such a cause of action,[240] and whether the cause of action is consistent with recovery of finance charges, pre-judgment interest, fees, and attorney fees. For example, in a claim for materials and services supplied, it is unlikely that state law allows for finance charges and other fees, and state law would only allow attorney fees if explicitly stated in a statute.[241]

In some jurisdictions, money lent is a cause of action to recover funds. The creditor must show that money was delivered to the defendant, intended as a loan, and not repaid.[242] In some states the cause of action for money lent contemplates a loan of a definite amount, not an indefinite open-end agreement under which the amount lent could increase and decrease with time, such as a credit card obligation. In addition, in many states, to recover on a money lent claim, the plaintiff must show either a contractual relationship or an account proving the amount lent.[243]

In Texas collectors may attempt to recover credit card debts using a "sworn account" theory, even though Texas courts have found this cause of action inapplicable to third-party credit cards. Collectors favor this cause of action because the collector need not provide a particularization or description of the nature of the component parts of an open account or claim, unless the trial court sustains special exceptions to the pleadings. The collector just files an affidavit, which is prima facie evidence unless the consumer files a written denial under oath. If the denial is not timely, the consumer can not later deny the claim.[244]

Nevertheless, the action on a "sworn account" is founded on an open account or other claim for goods, wares, and merchandise or for personal services furnished. Because of this basis, Texas courts find that the cause of action does not apply to credit card debt owed to a third-party lender.[245]

---

240 *See, e.g.*, Slayter v. Slayer, L.L.C. v. Ryland, 953 So. 2d 1000 (La. Ct. App. 2007) (La. Civ. Code art. 3494(3) establishes a three-year limitations period for the cause of action of money lent).

241 *See* Neb. Rev. Stat. § 25-1801 (providing for limited attorney fees for actions under $2000 for materials and services supplied).

242 *See* McIntyre v. Nice, 786 A.2d 620 (Me. 2001).

243 *See* LVNV Funding L.L.C. v. Moehrlin (Fla. County Ct. Volusia County Aug. 2006) (Green, J.), *available at* www.consumerlaw.org/unreported.

244 Tex. R. Civ. P. 185.

245 Williams v. Unifund CCR Partners, 2008 WL 339855 (Tex. App. Feb. 8, 2008); Sherman Acquisition II Ltd. P'ship v. Graham, 2006 WL 2978570 (Tex. App. Oct. 18, 2006); Tully v. Citibank, 173 S.W.3d 212 (Tex. App. 2005). *But cf.* McManus v. Sears, Roebuck & Co., 2003 WL 22024238 (Tex. App. Aug. 28, 2003) (sworn account applies when merchant issues the credit card).

Chapter 5 Defenses and Counterclaims

5.1 About This Chapter

5.1.1 What This Chapter Covers

This chapter analyzes a number of basic defenses that apply to actions to collect credit card and other consumer debts. Depending on a state's procedures, some of these issues must be raised as affirmative defenses in the consumer's answer, or they will be waived. For others, a simple denial of allegations in the collector's complaint will suffice. The defenses considered in this chapter include:

- The debt has already been paid, settled, or discharged in bankruptcy;
- The collector is suing the wrong consumer in a case of mistaken identity;
- Identity theft or other unauthorized use;
- The consumer is only an authorized user, and not an account holder;
- The consumer is not liable for debts of a spouse;
- The consumer is not liable for the debts of a deceased family member;
- A credit protection product should pay off the debt;
- The consumer was incapacitated because of minority, mental incompetence, or intoxication;
- A collector seeking a deficiency judgment after selling the collateral has failed to meet its burden of proving that all aspects of the sale were commercially reasonable; and
- Certain post-default charges are unconscionable or otherwise unenforceable.

The chapter also examines consumer counterclaims in a collection action: what types of counterclaims are available, the advantages and disadvantages of making counterclaims in a collection action, and certain special considerations that apply when the counterclaim relates to the collector's own conduct in the collection litigation. A final topic is the advantages of bringing a class counterclaim in an individual collection action.

5.1.2 Defenses and Counterclaims Analyzed Elsewhere

A full discussion of all possible consumer defenses and counterclaims is beyond the scope of this chapter and, in fact, beyond the scope of this manual. Other chapters in this manual, however, do examine certain additional defenses and counterclaims. The statute of limitations is an important defense in many collection actions, particularly those brought by debt buyers, and is examined in § 3.7, *supra*. Chapter 3, *supra*, also considers defenses related to jurisdiction, venue, an agreement that disputes will be resolved by arbitration, defects in the complaint, and the plaintiff's qualifications to use the state's courts. Chapter 4, *supra*, considers the collector's burden of proof to show it owns the debt and that its proof meets the elements of its causes of action. Chapter 4, *supra*, also considers the collector's right to finance charges and related fees.

Those on active duty military have certain special defenses, examined in Chapter 6, *infra*. A significant part of a collector's case is usually a request for attorney fees, and the consumer's defenses to that request are considered in Chapter 7, *infra*. Collection actions for dishonored checks and for medical debt also provide special defenses which are examined in Chapters 9 and 10, *infra*, respectively. Chapter 10, *infra*, also includes a discussion of the defense that the contract was entered into under duress. Collections by federal agencies of debt owed to the United States implicate special government collection remedies and special consumer defenses, and are analyzed in Chapter 11, *infra*.

Other NCLC manuals consider other important consumer defenses and counterclaims:

- Defenses and counterclaims to deficiency actions on automobile and other secured personal property loans are analyzed in NCLC's *Repossessions* manual.
- Defenses and counterclaims to deficiency actions relating to home foreclosures are analyzed in NCLC's *Foreclosures*.
- Defenses related to student loan debt are comprehensively treated in NCLC's *Student Loans*.
- Defenses and counterclaims related to utility debt are analyzed in NCLC's *Access to Utility Service*.
- Counterclaims relating to abusive debt collection prac-

tices are more thoroughly treated in NCLC's *Fair Debt Collection*.

- Fair Credit Reporting Act counterclaims relating to an entity's impermissible use of a consumer report or inaccurate furnishing of information to a reporting agency are covered in NCLC's *Fair Credit Reporting*.
- Truth in Lending Act, Home Ownership Equity Protection Act, and Consumer Leasing Act counterclaims are analyzed in NCLC's *Truth in Lending*.
- Counterclaims regarding credit charges and terms are analyzed in NCLC's *Cost of Credit*.
- Counterclaims regarding credit discrimination, notice of credit denials, co-signers, and other violations of the Equal Credit Opportunity Act are found in NCLC's *Credit Discrimination*.
- Defenses and counterclaims regarding electronic transfers, checks, money orders, and other payment devices are analyzed in NCLC's *Consumer Banking and Payments Law*.
- Counterclaims under a state's unfair amd deceptive practices (UDAP) statute can relate to almost any aspect of the transaction: pre-sale representations, sales techniques, product defects, credit terms, collection practices, and more. Both UDAP and Racketeer Influenced Corrupt Organizations Act (RICO) counterclaims are analyzed in NCLC's *Unfair and Deceptive Acts and Practices*.
- Counterclaims can also relate to defective products or the consumer's revocation of acceptance of a product, as examined in NCLC's *Consumer Warranty Law*.
- Deficiency actions on car loans can also involve counterclaims relating to odometer rollbacks, undisclosed adverse prior history of a vehicle, or other fraudulent practices, as described in NCLC's *Automobile Fraud*.

An important issue affecting the raising of counterclaims in a collection action is the collector's derivative liability for the misconduct of others. For example, can the consumer raise counterclaims in a debt buyer's collection action based upon the conduct of the original creditor or a seller related to that creditor? While these issues are touched upon in § 5.5.1, *infra*, they are more thoroughly treated in other NCLC manuals, particularly *Unfair and Deceptive Acts and Practices* Chapter 6.[1]

5.2 Debt Already Paid, Settled, or Discharged in Bankruptcy

5.2.1 Proving Debt Already Paid

Particularly when a debt is sold and resold or when a creditor has hired multiple collection agencies to collect the same debt, consumer payments may not be properly credited, resulting in the collector claiming an excessive amount owed. For example, Debt Buyer C may purchase a consumer's account as part of a bulk purchase from Debt Buyer B shortly after B purchased the consumer's account as part of another bulk purchase from Debt Buyer A. Consumers, having been dunned until recently by Debt Buyer A, may make payments to A even after ownership of the account has been transferred to C.

The record of payments can become lost if Debt Buyer A does not properly forward payment information to Debt Buyer B or if Debt Buyer B does not properly forward this information to Debt Buyer C. Moreover, it is very likely that none of the three debt buyers have accounting systems to track consumer payments that are as reliable as the system in place with the original creditor.

The consumer's problem will be one of proof, as the collector will deny that the payments were ever made. Ask the client how payment was made—by check, money order, or by refinancing or consolidation when another entity was to pay off the debt as part of a new loan. Then try to obtain a record of the payment—a canceled check, a record of the money order, or evidence from the third party that it paid off the debt. If the consumer's bank does not cooperate, a subpoena can be issued. The third party that was to make payments for the consumer also can be brought into the case if it did not make the payment or refuses to verify that it made the payment.

Examine the consumer's credit report from one or more of the major credit reporting agencies. Details on how to obtain and decipher that report are found in NCLC's *Fair Credit Reporting*.[2] Entries indicating payment or showing an account balance lower than that claimed by the collector are support for the consumer's position. Of course, the difference between the report and the amount the collector seeks might reflect newly added interest and fees after the report was issued.

On the other hand, the report's failure to reflect the payment should *not* be taken adversely. It is no surprise when a debt buyer who refuses to acknowledge a payment does not report that payment to a reporting agency. While the original creditor will regularly furnish information about its accounts to reporting agencies, debt buyers and collection agencies are less likely to do so. Moreover, even the original creditor may stop furnishing data about an account after the account has been sold or charged off.

A third approach is to locate other consumers who claim their payments have not been properly credited with the same debt buyer or collector. This pattern or practice evidence showing habit or routine custom can be used to discredit the reliability of a collector's records or bolster the consumer's evidence.

1 (6th ed. 2004 and Supp.).

2 (6th ed. 2006 and Supp.).

In the final analysis, when the consumer states that a payment has been made and the collector states the contrary, the question will be one for the fact finder. Sometimes just putting the question in controversy with admissible evidence, and thereby defeating the collector's summary judgment motion, is a victory, as many collectors have a business model that relies on default and summary judgments and will not pursue the matter at trial. At trial the burden to show the balance due will be on the collector.

5.2.2 Proving Debt Already Settled

Often consumers make a payment on a debt in reliance on a collector's representation that the partial payment will be in full settlement of the amount owed. Try to obtain a copy of the canceled check, to see if the consumer noted on the check "payment in full" or the like, and look for other contemporaneous writings that may prove helpful. The consumer may also seek to discover any telephone recordings or other collector notations reflecting the settlement conversation. Also useful are affidavits from other consumers who similarly made a partial payment in full satisfaction of a debt with the same creditor or collector, who then denied that their payment was in full satisfaction of the debt.

The consumer's case will be bolstered by proof of a large payment made well after the account became delinquent. While such payment need not have been in full satisfaction of the debt, the fact of the payment is consistent with the consumer's version of events. Note also to whom the payment was made, because the current debt owner will have no evidence that a payment to a prior owner was not made in full satisfaction of the debt.

Distinguish a debt being settled from a debt being charged off or written off. Charging off or writing off a debt is merely an accounting procedure whereby the debt is moved from one category of receivables to another. The purpose of this accounting procedure is to allow investors evaluating a company's balance sheet to have an accurate assessment as to the chances of payment on that debt.[3] Charging off or writing off a debt does not mean that the creditor has agreed to cancel the debt. Similarly, the fact that the collector has not pursued a debt for some time does not mean that the creditor has canceled the debt, although at some point the statute of limitations will have run, making the debt uncollectible. A consumer arguing settlement of the debt should not allege that the debt was charged off, written off, or left dormant for years, but instead should point to a representation that a partial payment would be accepted as full satisfaction of the debt.

That representation need not be in writing, and need not meet all the requirements of the original contract formation. The essential elements of equitable estoppel are conduct by which one induces another to believe in certain material facts, resulting in justifiable reliance, causing injury to the consumer. Similarly, waiver of a right is enforceable when the consumer relies on that waiver. The common law theory of accord and satisfaction is based upon the creditor's acceptance of payment with the agreement (which can be oral) that it constitutes full payment. These types of oral modifications and waivers are enforceable even if the underlying contract purports to require that all changes be made in writing.[4] The issue thus becomes whether there was, in fact, a representation that the debt would be canceled upon partial payment, and whether the consumer relied upon this promise.

The consumer who states that there was such a representation and reliance is raising a factual dispute over whether the debt is still due. This evidence should be enough to defeat the collector's summary judgment motion, and create a question of fact for trial.

5.2.3 Debts Discharged in Bankruptcy

The discharge of a debt in bankruptcy is a complete defense to that debt. The typical bankruptcy is a no-asset chapter 7 case, and all that need be shown in such a case is that the debt was incurred before the bankruptcy filing, and that there was a bankruptcy discharge.[5] The consumer will often have a copy of the discharge and the consumer may also have a copy of the initial notice showing the date the bankruptcy was filed. If not, the consumer's complete bankruptcy file is accessible electronically over the Internet through a system called PACER,[6] including the discharge and the date the bankruptcy was filed. Finding the consumer's file on PACER is simplified with the bankruptcy file number, but the case can also be found using the consumer's name and the district where the bankruptcy case was filed.

In a no-asset chapter 7 case, most courts hold that the consumer need not have listed the individual debt in the bankruptcy schedules, and there is no problem if the debt is listed in a different amount than the collector claims or if the account number or other description in the bankruptcy schedules differs from the actual debt.[7] The debt is still discharged. On the other hand, for a bankruptcy discharge to be effective in a chapter 13 case or a chapter 7 case

3 The charge-off date also starts the clock running as to when information in a credit report is obsolete and must be deleted. *See* National Consumer Law Center, Fair Credit Reporting § 5.2.3.3 (6th ed. 2006 and Supp.).

4 *See In re* R & D Contracting, L.L.C., 383 B.R. 890 (Bankr. E.D. Mich. 2008); Hanley v. MacDonald, 971 So. 2d 998 (Fla. Dist. Ct. App. 2008); Fleming v. J.E. Merit Constr., Inc., 2008 WL 762541 (La. Ct. App. Mar. 11, 2008).

5 *See* National Consumer Law Center, Consumer Bankruptcy Law and Practice § 3.6 (8th ed. 2006 and Supp.).

6 Located at http://pacer.psc.uscourts.gov.

7 *See* National Consumer Law Center, Consumer Bankruptcy Law and Practice § 14.4.3.3 (8th ed. 2006).

involving assets, the consumer must list the account in the bankruptcy schedules. Even in a no-asset chapter 7 case, it is safest to show that the debt was listed on the consumer's bankruptcy schedules. The consumer may have retained a copy of the schedules, and they are also available on PACER.

It is also important to check whether a consumer filing under chapter 13 eventually received a discharge. The consumer may have been making payments under a chapter 13 plan for several years, but may never have completed the plan and thus never received a discharge. In that case the debt is not discharged, but payments under the plan should be credited on the account. If there is a dispute, the chapter 13 trustee will have records of the payments.

If the collector alleges that the individual debt was not discharged, because of fraud or some other reason, this allegation can be easily undermined by looking at the bankruptcy case records on PACER. Exceptions from discharge must be raised as an adversary proceeding. Whether an adversary proceeding was ever filed and brought to a conclusion will be apparent in the file. No adversary proceedings need be filed for certain exceptions to discharge, such as for student loans, but these exceptions will not apply to credit card debt or most other consumer debt.[8] In any event the burden is on the collector to show why a debt was not discharged in bankruptcy.

Similarly, if the collector claims that a debt has been reaffirmed, a reaffirmation is only enforceable if the reaffirmation agreement was filed with the court.[9] A review of the file on PACER will indicate whether a reaffirmation agreement was filed with the court and whether that agreement was disapproved by the court. In any event the burden should be on the collector to produce a valid reaffirmation agreement.

5.3 Someone Else Owes the Debt

5.3.1 When Collector Mistakenly Identifies the Consumer As the Debtor

Sometimes a collector will sue the consumer on a debt about which the consumer has no knowledge. One explanation, discussed in the next subsection, is that an identity thief opened up an account in the consumer's name. Another possibility is that the collector mixed up the consumer's identity with that of the real debt owner. This latter explanation is far more common than many realize, particularly with the explosive growth in accounts purchased by debt buyers. Not only do the debt buyers have minimal information on the account holder, but they are seeking to collect very old debt, when the debtor often has moved one or more times since the account was closed.

Debt buyers who can not find a consumer's present address often use a consumer report from a credit reporting agency to locate the consumer. This practice results in a significant number of cases of mistaken identity because the consumer reports themselves are fraught with error—as many as twenty-five percent of consumer reports contain serious errors.[10]

The mistaken identity phenomenon is so common that it has a name: mismerge.[11] Merging is the process whereby billions of pieces of information received each month by each of the three national credit reporting agencies gets properly sorted and inserted into the correct consumer's file, by matching individual identifiers associated with the information: name, address, date of birth, and Social Security numbers.[12] Mismerging occurs when the files of two or more consumers are improperly mixed because of the over inclusive matching programming used by the reporting agencies that do not require a perfect match of identifiers, but only a close match.[13]

Consider a debt buyer looking to locate John A. Smith, Jr. to sue Mr. Smith on VISA account number 12345678, and who comes across information on that very account in a consumer report for John B. Smith. The debt buyer assumes the two John Smiths are the same, because VISA account number 12345678 is in John B. Smith's report, and sues John B. Smith on the account.

Mismerging explains how John A. Smith Jr.'s account information got into John B. Smith's file. All three major credit reporting agencies sort information from a creditor into a particular consumer's file even when only two of the four designated identifiers associated with the data match. Moreover, partial matches suffice for even unique identifiers, so that seven of nine Social Security number digits are considered a match. Same state of residence may be considered a match for address. Names are considered a match even though variations in spelling, middle names, initial, nicknames, and generational designations (Jr., Sr., III, and so forth) are found. For example, James McKeown went through an extensive ordeal to convince the reporting agencies that debts belonging to James N. McOwen were not his.[14] Even completely different last names (to accommodate name changes after marriage) are allowed.[15]

Because debt buyers do not have to notify consumers when they use their consumer report for skip tracing, a

8 *Id.* Ch. 14.

9 *Id.* § 14.5.2.

10 Nat'l Ass'n of State PIRGs, Mistakes Do Happen: A Look at Errors in Consumer Credit Reports 11 (2004).

11 *See* National Consumer Law Center, Fair Credit Reporting §§ 4.3.3, 4.4.6.5 (6th ed. 2006 and Supp.).

12 *Id.* § 4.3.3.2.

13 *Id.* § 4.3.3.

14 McKeown v. Sears, Roebuck & Co., 335 F. Supp. 2d 917 (W.D. Wis. 2004).

15 *See* Apodaca v. Discover Fin. Services, 417 F. Supp. 2d 1220 (D.N.M. 2006).

consumer caught up in a case of mistaken identity will have no notion why it is happening, and will either ignore collection contacts or simply tell the collector they have the wrong person. The collector's next action might be a lawsuit filed against the wrong person for the debt.

When consumers are sued on a debt with which they have no connection, it is useful to distinguish between identity theft and a mismerged credit report, as both look the same from the consumer's perspective, but should be handled differently. For example, an attempt to collect on a credit account opened within the last year may involve identity theft; an attempt to collect on an account opened several years ago will more likely involve a mismerged credit report. A consumer who is the victim of identity theft typically learns of the scam when contacted by the creditor collecting the debt once the identity thief disappears. Even then, victims discover the identity theft on average after fifteen months, and at least twenty percent learn of the problem only after two years.[16] On the other hand, in the case of a mismerged file, the real account owner is likely to have paid on the account for some time and, even after that owner's default, there will be a period of time before assignment to a debt buyer. So the account will likely have been opened some time ago.

In defending a case of a mistaken identity, an obvious first step is to look at the way the defendant is identified in the complaint and accompanying documents. If the defendant is listed as James McOwen, then James McKeown has a good case that he should not have been served with the complaint and is not liable on the account. Also seek through informal or formal discovery from the original creditor and the collector all identifying information about the account owner—previous addresses, Social Security number, age, employment, and so forth. This information may show that the individual owning the account is not the same one as the individual being sued.

Another step is to order consumer reports from the three major reporting agencies.[17] The inquiries section on each report will indicate who has pulled the report, and this information will allow the consumer to identify which report the collector utilized to locate the consumer. Look to see if the same debt is found in the consumer's report at the other two reporting agencies. A debt found in the files of only one agency is a good indicator of mismerging, because the three agencies receive almost identical information from creditors, but may have differing systems to match credit data to a particular individual.

Also look for an indication that the account has only recently been added to the consumer's file. Information on an account having been inserted into the consumer's file for many months can be explained by consistent mismerging over that period of time, but the sudden appearance of an account in the report with no history of payments may indicate a recent instance of mismerging.

Beside defending the collection action the consumer, in the case of a mismerged file, should also send a dispute letter to the reporting agency, with copies sent to the original creditor. Include the consumer's identifying information and state that the account does not belong to the consumer. Failure to properly reinvestigate may give the consumer a claim under the Fair Credit Reporting Act against the creditor and the reporting agency.[18]

5.3.2 Unauthorized Charges Due to Identity Theft and Other Causes

5.3.2.1 General

There are a number of situations in which a consumer can be wrongfully sued on charges that the consumer did not authorize. An identity thief can open an account in the consumer's name, or make charges on an account opened by the consumer. Someone finding a lost credit card can use it without authorization. There are also situations involving marital separation or other family discord when one family member uses another family member's account without proper authorization, or obtains or renews a credit card on the consumer's account without authorization.[19]

5.3.2.2 Credit Card Protections

The federal Truth in Lending Act contains strong consumer protections against unauthorized use of a credit card. These protections are examined in more detail in NCLC's *Truth in Lending* § 5.9.4[20] and also in NCLC's *Consumer Banking and Payments Law* § 6.3.[21] In brief, consumers are not liable for unauthorized charges on their own accounts, but under some circumstances may be liable for up to $50.[22] Even $50 can not be assessed for unauthorized transactions conducted by telephone, mail, or Internet.[23]

Federal law specifies that the creditor has the burden of proof to show that a charge is authorized.[24] "Unauthorized

16 *See* Fed. Trade Comm'n, Identity Theft Victim Complaint Data, Figures and Trends November 1999 through March 2001, *available at* www.consumer.gov/idtheft/reports/rep-mar01.pdf *and* www.consumer.gov/idtheft/charts/nov99-mar01.pdf.

17 *See* National Consumer Law Center, Fair Credit Reporting Ch. 3 (6th ed. 2006 and Supp.).

18 *Id.* §§ 10.2.2.2, 10.2.4.2.

19 *See* Citibank (S.D.) v. Hauff, 668 N.W.2d 528 (S.D. 2003); Dillard Dep't Stores, Inc. v. Owens, 951 S.W.2d 915 (Tex. App. 1997) (card holder's estranged spouse obtained credit card on card holder's account after separation).

20 (6th ed. 2007).

21 (3d ed. 2005 and Supp.).

22 15 U.S.C. § 1643.

23 *See* National Consumer Law Center, Truth in Lending § 5.9.4.4 (6th ed. 2007).

24 15 U.S.C. § 1643(b); *see also* Minskoff v. Am. Express Travel

use" means the use of the credit card by a person other than the card holder who does not have actual, implied or apparent authority for such use, and from which the card holder receives no benefit.[25]

The consumer need not have notified the card issuer at the time of the unauthorized use in order for unauthorized use to be a defense in a collection action.[26] The consumer also need not have first complied with the Fair Credit Billing Act's notice requirements before raising unauthorized use as a defense in a collection action.[27]

These protections for unauthorized use apply only to credit cards, defined as "any card, plate, coupon book, or other credit device existing for the purpose of obtaining money, property, labor, or services on credit."[28] The protections apply to all types of credit cards, including store credit cards and telephone calling cards, and not just third-party cards, such as those with the VISA or Mastercard logos.

When an identity thief opens an account in the consumer's name the consumer is not in fact the card holder and will not owe anything, whether for purchases, finance charges, or fees. Matters are more complicated when certain charges on the consumer's actual account are unauthorized, but the consumer should not be liable for those unauthorized charges or any finance charges or other fees flowing from those unauthorized charges.

5.3.2.3 Fair Credit Reporting Act Protections

Both to protect the consumer from future unauthorized charges and to bolster the consumer's defense in a collection action, the consumer should report the identity theft to local law enforcement, and also to at least one reporting agency, to put the account on a fraud alert. That agency is obligated to inform others of the identity theft.[29]

When an identity thief opened an account, rather than the consumer, the consumer has a right to obtain information about that application and related business records to help demonstrate that the consumer did not open the account. The consumer, as an identity theft victim, has the right under federal law to obtain from the original creditor a copy of the application and business transaction records in control of that creditor, whether maintained by that entity or by another for that entity.[30] The request must be in writing,[31] and the creditor must first obtain proof of positive identification of the identity theft victim.[32] The creditor can not charge for this information,[33] and must respond within thirty days after receiving the consumer's request.[34]

Federal and state law provide other protections for identity theft victims. About half the states have security freeze laws that allow consumers to freeze access to their consumer reports.[35] This freeze prevents identity thieves from opening accounts in the consumer's name because there is no access to a consumer report. Under the Fair Credit Reporting Act consumers can also have a credit reporting agency block fraudulent information from their reports, and the credit reporting agency must notify the furnisher of that information, who must take steps so as not to furnish the same information again.[36]

5.3.3 Liability of Authorized Users

5.3.3.1 Distinguishing Authorized Users from Joint Account Holders

Those using open-end credit can be put into two different categories—account holders and authorized users. A credit account is in the name of one or more account holders, who applied for and agreed to be obligated on that account. The account holder can authorize others, who are called authorized users, to use the account. The account holder is the one who contacts the creditor to add the authorized user—others can not add themselves to an account as either an authorized user or as a joint account holder, without the account holder's consent.[37] As described in the Federal Reserve Board's official staff commentary to Regulation Z, "cards may be sent to consumer A on A's request, and also (on A's request) to consumers B and C, who will be authorized users on A's account."[38]

In theory, it should be straightforward to determine who is an account holder and who is an authorized user. But a credit card issuer's electronic record-keeping may compli-

---

Related Services Co., 98 F.3d 703 (2d Cir. 1996); Citibank (S.D.) v. Gifesman, 773 A.2d 993 (Conn. App. Ct. 2001); Crestar Bank v. Cheevers, 744 A.2d 1043 (D.C. Ct. App. 2000).

25 15 U.S.C. § 1602(o).

26 Danner v. Discover Bank, 2007 WL 1428987 (Ark. Ct. App. May 16, 2007); People's Bank v. Scarpetti, 1998 WL 61925 (Conn. Super. Ct. Feb. 5, 1998); Crestar Bank v. Cheevers, 744 A.2d 1043 (D.C. Ct. App. 2000); Universal Bank v. McCafferty, 624 N.E.2d 358 (Ohio Ct. App. 1993); Fifth Third Bank/Visa v. Gilbert, 478 N.E.2d 1324 (Ohio Mun. Ct. 1984); Mich. Nat'l Bank v. Olson, 723 P.2d 438 (Wash. Ct. App. 1986); *see also* 15 U.S.C. § 1643(b) (burden on creditor to show use was authorized in a collection action).

27 *See* § 4.7.6, *supra.*

28 15 U.S.C. § 1602(k).

29 National Consumer Law Center, Fair Credit Reporting § 9.2 (6th ed. 2006 and Supp.).

30 15 U.S.C. § 1681g(e)(1).

31 15 U.S.C. § 1681g(e)(3).

32 15 U.S.C. § 1681g(e)(2).

33 15 U.S.C. § 1681g(e)(4).

34 15 U.S.C. § 1681g(e)(1).

35 *See* National Consumer Law Center, Fair Credit Reporting § 9.4 (6th ed. 2006 and Supp.).

36 *Id.* § 9.2.1.

37 *Cf.* Citibank (S.D.) v. Hauff, 668 N.W.2d 528 (S.D. 2003) (authorized user can not apply for a renewal card).

38 Fed. Reserve Bd., Official Staff Commentary to Regulation Z, 12 C.F.R. § 226.12(a)(1)-6; *see also* Cleveland Trust Co. v. Snyder, 380 N.E.2d 354 (Ohio Ct. App. 1978).

cate rather than help resolve this inquiry. If a card issuer mistakenly (or deliberately) codes an authorized user as an account holder, that card issuer and all subsequent debt buyers will treat that person as an account holder. Surprisingly, the card issuer may have little or no documentation to support its designation of an individual as an account holder instead of an authorized user. In *Johnson v. MBNA*,[39] the card issuer was unable to show whether the consumer, the wife of the card holder, was an authorized user or joint account holder, because it did not have the original account agreement, having destroyed it pursuant to its document retention policy. The mere fact that the card issuer mailed statements jointly to the account holder and the wife did not prove that the wife was a joint account holder.[40]

Federal law requires that a credit card be issued only in response to a request or application for a card.[41] The question then is whether another person (the account holder) requested the card for the consumer (meaning the consumer is an authorized user) or whether the consumer requested the card (making the consumer an account owner). Evidence from the real account holder that he or she requested the card for the consumer indicates that the consumer is an authorized user. If the collector has not retained a contemporaneous record of the credit card request that shows the consumer's application as an account owner, the collector may not be able to refute the consumer's evidence that the consumer is an authorized user. Certainly a debt buyer will have difficulty doing so when its only evidence is a printout from a prior debt buyer or creditor listing the consumer as an account owner, and the debt buyer has no firsthand knowledge how that designation came about.

The collector, in alleging that the consumer is an account holder, is claiming that the consumer authorized the card issuer to make the consumer responsible for all charges on the card. The consumer is saying that the consumer did not agree to be responsible for such charges. Federal law states that "[i]n any action by a card issuer to enforce liability for the use of a credit card, the burden of proof is upon the card issuer to show the use was authorized."[42] The collector thus has the burden of proof to show that a consumer authorized the card issuer to make the consumer liable on the account.

5.3.3.2 Liability of Authorized User for Account Owner's Obligations

The Federal Reserve Board's official staff commentary to Regulation Z indicates that only the account holder and not authorized users have any liability for unauthorized use.[43] In general, state law follows this federal rule and limits authorized users' liability, holding that an authorized user, without more, is not liable for debts incurred by the account holder or others.[44]

The collector has the burden of proving that an agreement exists by which an authorized user consents to be liable for the charges of others on the account. If there is such an agreement, any ambiguity is construed against the creditor. Silence certainly does not create liability.[45]

Typically, there will be no provision making an authorized user liable for the debts of others and some standard contracts explicitly provide that the authorized user is liable only for that user's own charges, but not for charges incurred by the account holder or others.

If a provision in a standard form contract creates liability for the user,[46] then the collector still must prove that the authorized user agreed to that provision. It is not sufficient to have sent that contract to the account holder. There must be proof that the version of the standard form contract which contains the liability provision was sent to the authorized user who agreed to be bound by its terms.

Even if it can be shown that the authorized user was sent a contract containing such a provision, this may not be enough to create a binding contract providing for such liability. Can such liability be created by the fine print buried in the boilerplate of a standard form contract, when an authorized user's expectation is so different? In effect, the card issuer is sending not the requested authorized user card, but an unsolicited joint owner card. The federal Truth in Lending Act prohibits issuance of a credit card other than in response to a request or application.[47] Neither the consumer nor the account holder requested or applied for a card that in effect converts the account into joint ownership.

5.3.3.3 Authorized User's Liability for Own Charges

Collectors who seek to hold an authorized user liable for that user's own charges create an immediate practical problem for themselves. Some credit cards have separate numbers for each user, allowing segregation of charges by user

39 357 F.3d 426 (4th Cir. 2004).
40 *Id.*
41 15 U.S.C. § 1642.
42 15 U.S.C. § 1643(b).
43 Fed. Reserve Bd., Official Staff Commentary to Regulation Z, 12 C.F.R. § 226.12(a)(1)-6.

44 Sears, Roebuck & Co. v. Ragucci, 203 N.J. Super. 82, 495 A.2d 923 (Special Civ. Pt. 1985); Cleveland Trust Co. v. Snyder, 380 N.E.2d 354 (Ohio Ct. App. 1978); State Home Sav. Card Ctr. v. Pinks, 540 N.E.2d 338 (Ohio Mun. Ct. 1988); Sears, Roebuck & Co. v. Stover, 513 N.E.2d 361 (Ohio Mun. Ct. 1987); *cf.* FCC Nat'l Bank v. Laursen (*In re* Laursen), 214 B.R. 378 (Bankr. D. Neb. 1997) (court noted that there would have been no contractual liability even if husband had been an authorized user).
45 *See* Citibank (S.D.) v. Hauff, 668 N.W.2d 528 (S.D. 2003).
46 *See In re* Garberg, 2006 WL 1997415 (Bankr. E.D. Pa. June 7, 2006); Am. Express Travel Related Services Co. v. Seidenfeld, 781 N.Y.S.2d 622 (Sup. Ct. 2003) (table).
Sears's contracts also provide that the authorized user has the same liability as the account holder.
47 15 U.S.C. § 1642.

(however a debt buyer may not have access to that information). But other credit card accounts keep the same number for all users and it may be impossible for the card issuer to then segregate charges relating to one particular user from other charges on the account. Remember that federal law puts the burden of proving that the use was authorized on the card issuer.[48] In addition, the authorized user should not be liable for finance charges and other fees, because these are computed based upon all charges on the account, not just upon the authorized user's charges.

If the collector does succeed in segregating only the authorized user's charges, then the collector must establish a basis for liability. *Quantum meruit* should not be applicable because there is an explicit contract covering the charges.[49] Because federal law requires that there be a request or application for the card and disclosure of the terms of the card,[50] there should always be an explicit contract covering the charges, making *quantum meruit* inapplicable.

For that reason, liability instead must be based upon an agreement sent to the authorized user, usually with the card, making the authorized user liable for his or her own charges. Some agreements with authorized users do not specify that the authorized user is liable for the user's own charges,[51] and any ambiguity is to be construed against the drafter.[52] Even if the creditor's standard form agreement specifies that the authorized user is liable for that user's own charges, the collector will have to produce this contract and prove that this contract was sent to the authorized user.[53] The collector alternatively may be able to produce a charge slip signed by the user, that includes an agreement to pay for the charges. But the collector may not have that slip, the slip may not be signed, or it may not include that agreement.

48 15 U.S.C. § 1643(b).

49 *See* § 4.7, *supra*; *see also* Sears, Roebuck & Co. v. Stover, 513 N.E.2d 361 (Ohio Mun. Ct. 1987).

50 *See* § 4.8, *supra*.

51 *See* Alabran v. Capital One Bank, 2005 WL 3338663 (E.D. Va. Dec. 8, 2005); *cf.* First Nat'l Bank of Findlay v. Fulk, 566 N.E.2d 1270 (Ohio Ct. App. 1989) (authorized user not liable for own charges when no agreement that user would be liable).

52 Because many credit card agreements are to be interpreted using South Dakota law, a significant case for the proposition that ambiguities are to be interpreted against the drafter is the South Dakota Supreme Court's decision in Citibank (S.D.) v. Hauff, 668 N.W.2d 528 (S.D. 2003).

53 *See* § 4.5, *supra*; *see also* Am. Express Travel Related Services Co. v. Seidenfeld, 781 N.Y.S.2d 622 (Sup. Ct. 2003) (table); *cf. In re* Garberg, 2006 WL 1997415 (Bankr. E.D. Pa. June 7, 2006) (sufficient evidence that American Express agreement holding authorized user liable for own charges was accepted by the user); Am. Express Travel Related Services v. Redner, 2006 WL 664698 (Mich. Ct. App. Mar. 16, 2006) (card use manifested user's intent to be bound by agreement which imposed liability).

5.3.4 Liability of Spouses

5.3.4.1 General

Consumers who are not liable as account owners or as authorized users may still be liable for their spouses' debts, based upon state statutory or common law theories. There is significant variation in this law, particularly between community property states and other states.

An important question is which state's law applies—the forum state's law, the law of a state specified in the credit agreement, or some other state, such as the one where the debts were incurred or where the parties lived at the time the debts were incurred. Because spousal liability is not based upon the contract, a choice of law clause in the contract should be of no effect and the forum state's choice of law rules should apply.

Using a contractually chosen choice of law would have very odd results in this context. A state's community property law would not apply to contracts consummated in that state if the law selected in the contract was that of a non-community property state. The result would be even odder if the law selected in the contract was that of a community property state when the forum was not a community property state.

5.3.4.2 Community Property States

This section discusses only a few general concepts applicable to community property jurisdictions. In community property states debts incurred after marriage and before separation are generally treated as community debts, even if only one spouse is obligated on the contract. If a credit card is issued in one spouse's name only, a collector can reach community property to pay for charges incurred during the marriage.

Two exceptions are worth noting. The married partners can enter into an agreement that they are not responsible for each others' debts.[54] A creditor also can only reach community property in recovering on the obligated spouse's account, not property belonging to the other spouse individually. Property separately held by the other spouse can not be seized to pay the community debt.[55] Non-community property typically includes property brought into the mar-

54 *E.g.*, Schlaefer v. Fin. Mgmt. Serv., 196 Ariz. 336, 996 P.2d 745 (Ct. App. 2000) (debts for necessary medical care presumed to be community debts, but presumption rebutted by proof of valid premarital agreement that each spouse would be responsible for own debts).

55 *See* Samaritan Health Sys. v. Caldwell, 191 Ariz. 479, 957 P.2d 1373 (Ct. App. 1998) (health care debts are community debts, which may be satisfied from community property, but not from separate property of non-debtor spouse).

riage or received during marriage by bequest or gift, as long as those assets are not commingled with community property.

5.3.4.3 Necessaries Statutes and Liability for Spouses' Debts in Non-Community Property States

In non-community property states, one spouse's property can not generally be taken to pay the other spouse's debts. However, many non-community property states have necessaries statutes that make spouses liable for certain of each others' debts. These statutes are examined in more detail in § 10.6, *infra*, in the context of medical debt, to which they are most applicable.

A necessaries statute typically will *not* provide a basis for holding a consumer liable on the other spouse's credit card, cell phone, or most other consumer debts. Necessaries statutes apply only to the purchase of necessaries—usually considered to be medical services, food, and shelter.[56] It will be hard to argue that a cell phone bill, for example, is for a necessity. In the typical credit card case, the collector will have a difficult time isolating individual charges that are in fact necessaries. The burden is on the collector to show that a particular charge is a necessary.[57]

Moreover, any finance charges, late charges, attorney fees, collection costs, and other fees the account holder may have incurred are certainly not necessaries, and the other spouse should not be obligated for those charges.[58] There is even a question whether a credit card issuer, as a lender, can take advantage of these necessaries statutes, as the card issuer is not supplying a necessary but is supplying a loan, which is not a necessary.[59]

State law may provide additional defenses for the non-account holder spouse. Separation may be a defense.[60] Some states require the collector to prove that the secondarily liable spouse had failed to support the primarily liable spouse.[61] It may be a defense that the financial resources of the spouse who incurred the expenses were sufficient;[62] that the creditor did not rely on the non-debtor spouse's credit to furnish the necessaries;[63] or that, as at common law, the non-debtor spouse's inability to pay the spouse's debts limits his or her responsibility to do so.[64] The secondarily liable spouse may also raise any defenses available to the other spouse.[65]

Furthermore, only certain states currently recognize the necessaries doctrine. Necessaries statutes evolved from Married Woman Acts that many states passed at the turn of the century. As originally written, these statutes imposed liability on husbands for wives' bills, but not *vice versa*. Some states have abolished this doctrine or ruled the nec-

56 *See* Nelson v. First Nat'l Bank Omaha, 2004 WL 2711032 (Minn. Ct. App. Nov. 30, 2004); Fifth Third Bank/Visa v. Gilbert, 478 N.E.2d 1324 (Ohio Mun. Ct. 1984) (father not liable for his minor daughter's unauthorized charges under necessaries doctrine, because none of purchases were for "necessaries").

57 See Nelson v. First Nat'l Bank Omaha, 2004 WL 2711032 (Minn. Ct. App. Nov. 30, 2004) (credit card lender failed to show that items purchased on account were household necessaries, and thus lender not entitled to summary judgment on spouse's liability).

58 *See* N.A.R., Inc. v. Elmer, 141 P.3d 606 (Utah Ct. App. 2006) (interest and attorney fees, provided for in contract for medical services, are not necessaries within the meaning of the Utah Family Expense statute).

59 *See* N. Shore Cmty. Bank & Trust Co. v. Kollar, 710 N.E.2d 106 (Ill. App. Ct. 1999) (bank loan, even if the proceeds are spent for household needs, was not a "family expense" within the meaning of the Illinois family expense statute; widow not liable on loan taken by deceased husband; attorney fees to the widow).

60 Yale Univ. Sch. of Med. v. Scianna, 701 A.2d 65 (Conn. Super. Ct. 1997); Allen v. Keating, 517 N.W.2d 830 (Mich. Ct. App. 1994); Balyeat Collection Professionals v. Garland, 51 P.3d 1127 (Mont. 2002) (Montana statute provides exception if non-debtor has been abandoned by debtor); Doctors Laves, Sarewitz & Walko v. Briggs, 613 A.2d 506 (N.J. Super. Ct. Law Div. 1992); Roach v. Mamakos, 764 N.Y.S.2d 539 (Sup. Ct. 2003). *But cf.* Bartrom v. Adjustment Bureau, 618 N.E.2d 1 (Ind. 1993); Forsyth Mem'l Hosp. v. Chisholm, 467 S.E.2d 88 (N.C. 1996); Mercy Health Sys. Corp. v. Gauss, 639 N.W.2d 803 (Wis. Ct. App. 2001) (table) (text available at 2001 WL 1632549); St. Mary's Hosp. Med. Ctr. v. Brody, 519 N.W.2d 706 (Wis. Ct. App. 1994).

61 Allen v. Keating, 517 N.W.2d 830 (Mich. Ct. App. 1994) (spouses were separated); Smith v. Hernandez, 794 P.2d 772 (Okla. Civ. App. 1990).

62 *In re* Olexa, 476 F.3d 177 (3d Cir. 2007) (Pennsylvania necessaries statute); Foster v. DBS Collection Agency, 463 F. Supp. 2d 783 (S.D. Ohio 2006); St. Francis Reg'l Med. Ctr., Inc. v. Bowles, 251 Kan. 334, 836 P.2d 1123 (1992); Bethany Med. Ctr. v. Niyazi, 890 P.2d 349 (Kan. Ct. App. 1995); Hawley v. Hawley, 904 S.W.2d 584 (Mo. Ct. App. 1995); Med. Bus. Associates Inc. v. Steiner, 183 A.D.2d 86, 588 N.Y.S.2d 890, 897 (1992); Roach v. Mamakos, 764 N.Y.S.2d 539 (Sup. Ct. 2003); Promenade Nursing Home, Inc. v. Lacey, 814 N.Y.S.2d 564 (Civ. Ct. 2005) (table) (text available at 2005 WL 3592001); Landmark Med. Ctr. v. Gauthier, 635 A.2d 1145 (R.I. 1994).

63 Kent Gen. Hosp., Inc. v. Russell, 1997 Del. Super. LEXIS 336 (Del. Super. Ct. July 14, 1997), *aff'd*, 705 A.2d 244 (Del. 1998) (table); Med. Bus. Associates Inc. v. Steiner, 183 A.D.2d 86, 588 N.Y.S.2d 890, 897 (1992) (citing Our Lady of Lourdes v. Frey, 152 A.D.2d 73, 75 (1989)); Promenade Nursing Home, Inc. v. Lacey, 814 N.Y.S.2d 564 (Civ. Ct. 2005) (table) (text available at 2005 WL 3592001).

64 *In re* Olexa, 317 B.R. 290 (Bankr. W.D. Pa. 2004), *aff'd*, 476 F.3d 177 (3d Cir. 2007); Med. Bus. Associates Inc. v. Steiner, 183 A.D.2d 86, 588 N.Y.S.2d 890, 897 (1992) (citing Our Lady of Lourdes v. Frey, 152 A.D.2d 73, 75 (1989)); Promenade Nursing Home, Inc. v. Lacey, 814 N.Y.S.2d 564 (Civ. Ct. 2005) (table) (text available at 2005 WL 3592001); *see also* Porter Mem'l Hosp. v. Wozniak, 680 N.E.2d 13 (Ind. Ct. App. 1997) (remanded to trial court to determine husband's ability to pay); MRI Coop. v. Berlin, 1993 WL 257078 (Ohio Ct. App. June 30, 1993); Ohio State Univ. Med. Ctr. v. Calovini, 2002 WL 31953905 (Ohio Ct. Cl. Oct. 8, 2002).

65 St. Francis Reg'l Med. Ctr., Inc. v. Bowles, 251 Kan. 334, 836 P.2d 1123 (1992).

essaries statute unconstitutional.[66] In states that have not yet ruled on extending the statute to wives, the non-debtor wife can argue that extending the doctrine to her is a task for the legislature, not the court.[67] But in other states, the legislature or courts have rewritten the necessaries statutes in gender-neutral terms,[68] and some courts enforce liability not under a statute, but under a common law theory.[69] Even when a state recognizes the doctrine under a gender-neutral statute, that statute may be subject to challenge under the Equal Credit Opportunity Act, which prohibits creditors from requiring that both spouses obligate themselves for one spouse's transaction.[70]

5.3.5 Liability of Family Members for Decedent's Debts

A decedent's estate is liable for the decedent's debts, and those debts may have to be paid ahead of distributions to those inheriting from the estate. But family members, even those who inherit from an estate, do not become liable for the debts of an individual just because that individual is deceased. Nevertheless, some creditors contact family members after the debtor's death and then, without a written agreement, create a new account in that family member's name, transferring the decedent's account obligation to the new account. The creditor may then begin dunning the family member, and even sue on the debt. Other times the creditor may sell the debt, and a debt buyer, having no knowledge of the "account's" origin, will sue on the debt.

The family member's defense is clear—the family member was never obligated on the decedent's debt and there is no written agreement under which the family member agreed to pay that debt. Even if a creditor sent a contract to the family member, the family member never signed the contract. Because the family member never used the account, the collector can not imply assent on that basis.

When the collector behaves in such fashion and the debt is from a credit card account, the amount sought on the "account" may be an unauthorized charge, and the collector has the burden of proving it was authorized.[71] In addition, if the collector alleges the new account is a credit card account, then there is a Truth in Lending violation because the card was issued without the family member's request.[72]

66 *See* § 10.6, *infra*.
67 *See id.*
68 *See id.*
69 *See id.*
70 15 U.S.C. § 1691(a)(1); 12 C.F.R. §§ 202.7(d)(1), 202.11(b)(1)(ii); *see* Edwards v. McCormick, 136 F. Supp. 2d 795, 803 n.9 (S.D. Ohio 2001) (stating in dicta that imposition of liability upon spouse probably violates Equal Credit Opportunity Act). *See generally* National Consumer Law Center, Credit Discrimination § 9.3 (4th ed. 2005 and Supp.).
71 15 U.S.C. § 1643; *see also* § 5.3.2, *supra*.
72 15 U.S.C. § 1642.

5.3.6 Should Creditor's Protection Product Pay the Balance Due?

The collector should not seek a credit balance from the consumer if the creditor's protection product should pay off the balance due. Credit card issuers and other creditors aggressively market products that pay off an account balance if the consumer becomes unemployed, disabled, or dies. If this product is purchased and a covered event occurs, the consumer should seek payment from the creditor.[73] If the collector argues that the consumer does not qualify for the product benefits (because of age, disability, or employment status upon applying for the product, and so forth), then the consumer should not have been paying for the product, and should receive a rebate of all charges and related finance charges.[74] Moreover, if the consumer's non-qualification was evident from information submitted to the creditor, then the creditor should be estopped from refusing to pay benefits.[75]

5.4 Debt Not Legal or Not Owed

5.4.1 The Consumer's Incapacity—Minority, Mental Incompetence, or Intoxication

5.4.1.1 General

An otherwise valid contract may be voidable because the consumer does not have the capacity to make the contract.[76] Parties must be capable of intelligent assent in order to make a valid contract, and there can be no contract when there is no capacity to understand or agree.[77] There are three conditions which give rise to questions about a person's capacity to contract: minority, mental disability, and intoxication. When the party with the defective capacity seeks to cancel the contract, that person is entitled to have the creditor return whatever the incompetent gave under the contract and must usually restore to the creditor what they received under the contract.[78]

In a credit card situation, this principle would imply that the consumer's obligation on the account is canceled and all past payments for purchases, finance charges, and fees must be returned to the consumer. The consumer in turn must

73 *Cf.* Discover Bank v. Owens, 129 Ohio Misc. 2d 71, 822 N.E.2d 869 (Mun. Ct. 2004).
74 *See* National Consumer Law Center, The Cost of Credit: Regulation, Preemption, and Industry Abuses § 8.5.5.1 (3d ed. 2005 and Supp.).
75 *Id.*
76 Dan B. Dobbs, Dobbs Law of Remedies § 13.4.1 (2d ed. 1993).
77 17A Am. Jur. 2d *Contracts* § 28 (2004).
78 *Id.* §§ 28, 580.

return to the card issuer all credit extended. On balance, this nets out to the cancellation of all current and past finance charges and other fees.

5.4.1.2 Minority

The legal age of minority is determined by the law of the state in which the contract is made. A minor may void a contract whether or not the other party knew of the minority and whether or not the minor understood the nature of the contract.[79] Among other things, this rule protects the minor from being bound by contracts he or she may not understand, or may have entered into at the insistence of an overzealous or intimidating creditor.

One notable exception is that federal law states that the United States and guaranty agencies are not subject to a claim of minority for Federal Family Education Loans and Federal Direct Loans.[80] It appears that this exception does not apply to Perkins Loans, and it certainly does not apply to private student loans.

Other than this exception for federal student loans, a contract may be disaffirmed by the minor during his or her minority. It also may be disaffirmed within a reasonable period after the minor reaches majority, unless ratified when of legal age.[81] The minor disaffirms by giving the seller notice of his age or by offering to return to the seller any goods the minor may still have. A disaffirming minor need only return the goods in their present condition. If the goods have been damaged or dissipated, the seller must bear the loss.[82] Some states have modified this result by statute, requiring the minor to restore the value received.[83]

Despite the general rule about contracts entered into by minors, a minor may be liable for the fair market value of goods that are necessaries.[84] The disaffirming minor is not liable for the contract price of these goods, but only for their fair market value. Whether goods are necessaries is determined by the facts of each case, depending upon the person and the circumstances, being relative to the minor's actual needs and status in life.[85]

Courts generally limit necessaries to food or clothing of a reasonable kind purchased for the minor or the minor's family and to medical and dental services. It has generally been held that an automobile is not a necessary.[86] If goods are not necessaries then the general rule applies and the contract can be disaffirmed, as per the general rule for minors.

5.4.1.3 Mental Incompetence

The general rule for a mentally incompetent person is that the incompetent person may avoid the contract upon proof of mental incapacity at the time of contracting, provided the incompetent can fully restore the other party to its position before the contract.[87] If the incompetent no longer has the consideration received, the incompetent can not rescind the contract.[88] However the result would be different if the person was under guardianship when the contract was made, as such a contract is totally void.[89] In addition, if the seller is aware of the incompetency, the incompetent person may rescind the contract upon returning whatever is left of the consideration.[90]

The *Restatement (Second) of Contracts* finds a person mentally incompetent if that person is unable to understand in a reasonable manner the nature and consequence of a transaction *or* if the person is unable to act in a reasonable manner in relation to the transaction and the other party has reason to know of the condition.[91] An important difference between incapacity due to mental incompetence and incapacity due to minority is that the mental incompetence defense requires a showing that the party did not have the capacity to understand the nature and consequences of the contract.[92] As with minors, though, a person deemed mentally incompetent is still liable for the fair market value of necessaries.[93]

---

79 *See* Keser v. Chagnon, 159 Colo. 209, 410 P.2d 637 (1966) (minor's absolute right to disaffirm is not diminished by minor's false representation of age); Gillis v. Whitley's Discount Auto Sales, Inc., 70 N.C. App. 270, 319 S.E.2d 661 (1984) (fraudulent misrepresentation would not be valid defense to minor's action to disaffirm).

There seems to be some move away from this rule in some jurisdictions. *See, e.g.*, A. D. Kaufman, Annotation, *Infant's Misrepresentation as to His Age as Estopping Him from Disaffirming His Voidable Transaction*, 29 A.L.R.3d 1270 (1970).

80 20 U.S.C. § 1091a(b)(2).

81 Keser v. Chagnon, 159 Colo. 209, 410 P.2d 637 (1966); *see also* Gillis v. Whitley's Discount Auto Sales, Inc., 70 N.C. App. 270, 319 S.E.2d 661 (1984).

82 Restatement (Second) of Contracts § 14 cmt. (c) (1981).

83 *Id.*

84 Webster Street P'ship, Ltd. v. Sheridan, 220 Neb. 9, 368 N.W.2d 439 (1985) (liability based not on contractual but on quasi-contract theory); *see also* Joseph M. Perillo, Calamari and Perillo on Contracts § 8-8 (5th ed. 2003).

85 Webster Street P'ship, Ltd. v. Sheridan, 220 Neb. 9, 368 N.W.2d 439 (1985).

86 Star Chevrolet Co. v. Green, 473 So. 2d 157 (Miss. 1985) (car usually not a necessary for a minor).

87 Dan B. Dobbs, Dobbs Law of Remedies § 13.4(3) (2d ed. 1993).

88 *Id.*; *see, e.g.*, Young v. Lujan, 11 Ariz. App. 47, 461 P.2d 691 (1969); Davis v. Colo. Kenworth Corp., 156 Colo. 98, 396 P.2d 958 (1964); Sjulin v. Clifton Furniture Co., 241 Iowa 761, 41 N.W.2d 721 (1950); Lawson v. Bennett, 240 N.C. 52, 81 S.E.2d 162 (1954).

89 Restatement (Second) of Contracts § 13 (1981).

90 Dan B. Dobbs, Dobbs Law of Remedies § 13.4(3) (2d ed. 1993); Sjulin v. Clifton Furniture Co., 241 Iowa 761, 41 N.W.2d 721 (1950).

91 Restatement (Second) of Contracts § 15 (1981).

92 *In re* Estate of Hendrickson, 248 Kan. 72, 805 P.2d 20 (1991) (courts will apply presumption in favor of mental capacity to contract and place burden of proof on those claiming incapacity to rebut that presumption); Restatement (Second) of Contracts § 15 (1981); *see also* 17A Am. Jur. 2d *Contracts* § 28 (2004); 53 Am. Jur. 2d *Mentally Impaired* §§ 155–166 (1996).

93 Samuel Williston, Treatise on the Law of Contracts § 10.7

One who is no longer deemed incompetent because of mental illness or other disability may ratify a contract by indicating assent to it.[94] In addition, if the person, upon regaining legal competence, is aware of the contract made while legally incompetent and delays in disaffirming, this delay may constitute ratification.[95]

5.4.1.4 Intoxication

Persons who make contracts when they are so intoxicated that they can not understand the nature and consequences of their act may be treated in the same manner as mentally disabled persons.[96] Disaffirmance and ratification would occur in the manner described in § 5.4.1.3, *supra*. Presumably, drug abusers will be treated similarly to intoxicated persons and, in jurisdictions following the *Restatement* view, contracts they make when incompetent by reason of drug use will be voidable.

5.4.2 No Deficiency When Insufficient Proof of Commercially Reasonable Sale

A common collection action seeks a "deficiency" on an auto loan or other secured debt after the creditor has sold the collateral. The amount due on the loan plus certain expenses to prepare and sell the collateral is offset by the collateral's sale price, and the difference is called a deficiency.

This subsection focuses on one simple but very effective defense to a deficiency action, particularly when a debt buyer has purchased the right to bring the deficiency action. If the consumer denies that a repossession sale was conducted in a commercially reasonable manner,[97] the collector has the burden of proving the reasonableness of all aspects of the collateral's sale before the court will award a deficiency.[98]

The original secured party will have some difficulty proving that all aspects of a repossession sale were commercially reasonable, including the notice provided to the consumer, the advertising made to the public, the sale's timing, and the method of disposition. A debt buyer without knowledge of any of these facts will have great difficulty meeting its burden of proof.

This requirement that the collector prove that all aspects of the sale were commercially reasonable makes perfect sense. Repossession and repossession sales are extraordinary remedies, allowing seizure and sale of the consumer's property with no court supervision and few judicial standards. The collector need not even show that the purchase price at the repossession sale was a good one. One of the few standards regulating this process is that, if the collector seeks to recover a deficiency after selling the consumer's property, it must show that the sale price resulted from a commercially reasonable sale of the property.

The collector must produce more evidence than just the resale price.[99] The issue is not whether the car or other property was in fact sold for the price used in the deficiency computation. The issue is whether that sale price was the result of a commercially reasonable sale that would produce a reasonable price to use in that deficiency computation. A conclusory affidavit from the secured party that it sold the collateral for the best possible price is insufficient.[100]

It is certainly insufficient for a debt buyer (who will have little if any knowledge of the actual sale) to produce an affidavit from one of its employees that the secured party sold the collateral for the best possible price. The collector's burden is not met by evidence that the price obtained at the sale was reasonable, if the collector can not prove that the sale itself was conducted in a commercially reasonable manner.[101] The Uniform Commercial Code does not look to whether the sale price is reasonable, but whether the method of disposition was reasonable. (States differ as to the remedy if a sale is not proven to be commercially reasonable. Some states bar the deficiency absolutely. Others put the burden of proof on the collector to prove the collateral's value by some measure other than the sale price.[102])

The consumer also has numerous other possible defenses and counterclaims to a collection action for a deficiency. Was there a valid security interest? Was there a default? Did the repossession breach the peace? Was other property seized with the collateral? Were notices proper? Was the consumer offered the required opportunity to cure or reinstate? Were the secured party's expenses reasonable, and was the deficiency correctly computed? Other counterclaims relate to deception in the original sale of the property to the consumer, defects in the product's subsequent performance, the terms of the financing, and the creditor's debt collection conduct. These defenses and counterclaims are examined in another NCLC manual, *Repossessions*.[103]

(Richard A. Lord ed., 4th ed. 1990).

94 Joseph M. Perillo, Calamari and Perillo on Contracts §§ 8.12, 8.4 (5th ed. 2003).

95 Samuel Williston, Treatise on the Law of Contracts §§ 10.5, 10.12 (Richard A. Lord ed., 4th ed. 1990).

96 *Id.* § 16.

97 In at least California, the District of Columbia, and Maine, the consumer may not even have to deny that the sale was commercially reasonable; the collector still has the burden to show that it was conducted in such a manner. *See* National Consumer Law Center, Repossessions § 12.6.1.1 (6th ed. 2005 and Supp.).

98 *See* National Consumer Law Center, Repossessions § 12.6.1.1 (6th ed. 2005 and Supp.).

99 *Id.*

100 Boles v. Tex. Nat'l Bank, 750 S.W.2d 879 (Tex. App. 1988).

101 Hall v. Owen County State Bank, 370 N.E.2d 918 (Ind. Ct. App. 1977).

102 *See* National Consumer Law Center, Repossessions § 12.6 (6th ed. 2005 and Supp.).

103 (6th ed. 2005 and Supp.).

5.4.3 Post-Default Charges

5.4.3.1 General

Some of the most suspect charges that collectors seek to recover involve those imposed upon the consumer after default. When a collection action results in a default judgment, there is little inspection of the amount the collector seeks. Because most such actions result in a default judgment, the collector has an incentive to seek an inflated amount, often through additional post-default charges. Important examples are collection and attorney fees, both examined in some detail in Chapter 6, *infra*.

Other examples are post-default finance charges, late fees, and over the limit fees. Chapter 4, *supra*, considers the collector's right to various finance charges and fees. On a cause of action for account stated, the collector should not be entitled to any contractual finance charges and fees incurred after the statement of account that forms the basis for the claim.[104] If a contract has not been proven, the collector is not entitled to contractual finance charges and fees.[105] Even if the collector is entitled to contractual finance charges, the contract may be drafted so as not to authorize them after default.[106] A unilateral amendment to the credit agreement after default should not be enforceable because the consumer has not used the account, and thus has taken no action to assent to the change in terms.[107] A contract that calls for a higher interest rate or fees after default may be challenged as an unenforceable penalty clause under basic contract notions.

5.4.3.2 Charges for Extra Services That Are No Longer Necessary

Credit card issuers and other creditors increasingly market other services as a profit center—default insurance, various plans to protect against identity theft or lost cards, and the like. When those services offer no benefit after default, collectors should not charge for them after default. For example, after card privileges have been revoked, the consumer should not be paying for theft protection. If default insurance does not cover losses after an account has been delinquent for sixty days, there should be no charges for this insurance after the account has been delinquent for sixty days.

104 *See* § 4.7, *supra*.
105 *See* § 4.5.5, *supra*.
106 *See* § 4.5.4, *supra*.
107 *See* § 4.5.3, *supra*.

5.4.3.3 When Collector Sits Back and Lets Finance Charge and Other Fees Accrue

Collectors sometimes sit back and let finance charges and fees accrue, to increase the amount owed so that it is substantially more than the amount that was due when the consumer first started getting behind. For example, in one case a consumer had paid $3492 over six years on a $1900 debt, but was still faced with a $5564.28 balance as a result of all the fees and accrued finance charges. The court stated:

> Discover kept Owens's account open and active long after it was painfully obvious that she was never going to be able to make payments at the expected level. Under the law, an injured party has a duty to mitigate his damages and may not recover those damages that he could reasonably have avoided. . . . Even if plaintiff was technically within its rights in its handling of defendant's account, it was unreasonable and unjust for it to allow defendant's debt to continue to accumulate well after it had become clear that defendant would be unable to pay it. Unjust enrichment occurs when one retains money or benefits that, in justice and equity, belong to another. . . . Because of its failure to even minimally pay attention to Owens' circumstances, and for allowing the debt to accumulate unchecked, the court finds that Discover would be unjustly enriched if this court were now to grant judgment in its favor. The court further finds the repeated six-year accumulation of over-limit fees to be manifestly unconscionable.[108]

The last sentence of the above quotation is particularly interesting. There is a question whether over-limit fees are unconscionable when the consumer makes no purchases to cause the account to go over the limit, but when instead the creditor's own finance charges, late fees, and the like cause the account to go over the limit.

5.5 Counterclaims

5.5.1 Available Counterclaims

In most courts counterclaims can be brought challenging the collector's own misconduct. For example, a collector's improper debt collection phone calls or third-party contacts are viable counterclaims under federal and state debt collection statutes. Counterclaims related to the collector's improper litigation conduct are considered in § 5.5.3, *infra*. When the collector is the original creditor, numerous counterclaims may be available relating to the original credit transaction.

108 Discover Bank v. Owens, 822 N.E.2d 869 (Ohio Mun. Ct. 2004).

When the collector is a debt buyer, counterclaims relating to the original creditor can also be brought in the collection action, but the claim in most states can only be raised by way of recoupment or defense, offsetting the amount owed. Unless an exception applies they may not be used to produce an affirmative recovery against the collector. Consider a debt buyer seeking $3000, when the consumer has a $5000 counterclaim relating to the original creditor's conduct. The consumer can use that counterclaim to offset the $3000 owed. But, at least in many situations in which the action is being brought by a debt buyer, the consumer can not also affirmatively recover the remaining $2000 on the counterclaim.

There are a number of exceptions to this rule. The Truth in Lending Act and the Consumer Leasing Act create affirmative assignee liability for violations apparent on the face of the contract, if the counterclaim can be brought within the applicable one-year statute of limitations.[109] In addition, many car loans and other closed-end credit agreements contain a contract provision often referred to as the "FTC Holder Notice," which states that the holder of the credit obligation is subject to all *claims* and defenses that the consumer could bring against the seller.[110] In such situations the consumer can raise seller-related claims as counterclaims in the collection action, and most courts will allow the consumer to recover affirmatively over and above the amount required to cancel out the debt, but the consumer's recovery is limited to the amount of the remaining debt plus a return of any amount the consumer paid.[111]

The contract language as specified by the FTC Holder Rule makes holders liable for the consumer's claims against a "seller" and thus allows consumers to bring counterclaims in the collection action relating to the conduct of car dealers, home improvement contractors, and other credit sellers—both their conduct in the sales transaction and their conduct in extending credit. But the notice does not provide a basis to bring claims against banks and other lenders as to their conduct in extending loans, as they are not "sellers." On the other hand, the notice allows for seller-related counterclaims to be brought against the lender or the lender's assignee, even when the seller did not assign the loan to that lender, but only referred the consumer to the lender.

Another exception to the "no affirmative recovery" rule applies in certain states that have enacted a statute specifically providing for such an affirmative recovery. Most states have statutes providing for a certain level of assignee liability in consumer transactions, and some of these allow consumers to recover affirmatively against an assignee for the assignor's conduct.[112]

5.5.2 Tactical Considerations in Raising Counterclaims

Some counterclaims are so closely related to the collection action that they are compulsory, and therefore will be lost if not brought in that action. In such cases the consumer's attorney will have to determine if counterclaims are tactically better abandoned or brought in the action. Other counterclaims are permissive, in which case the issue will be whether it is better to bring a separate affirmative action or bring the claim as a counterclaim in the collection action.

Raising permissive counterclaims in a collection action may encourage the collector to settle—many collectors are suing to obtain default judgments, and have no interest in pursuing a case through trial. On the other hand, bringing counterclaims may tip off the collector that the matter will be aggressively contested, and the collector may then put more effort into its offers of proof. The collector also will be less willing to dismiss its complaint because the counterclaim will remain.

On the other hand, if the consumer does not bring counterclaims or otherwise tip off the fact that the case will be contested, the collector's case preparation may not be sufficient to prevail when the consumer later challenges the proffered evidence. After the collection action is dismissed with prejudice, if a counterclaim is permissive, the consumer can bring it affirmatively in a new action.

One advantage of raising certain counterclaims in the collection action is that they provide a basis for an attorney fee award for the consumer. In many states, without such counterclaims, a prevailing consumer receives no attorney fee award. Section 14.1, *infra*, lists several exceptions to this rule but, when these exceptions do not apply, the best way to recover fees, making consumer representation practical, is to bring a counterclaim for violation of a statute that awards fees to a successful consumer. Examples include the state deceptive practices (UDAP) statute, the federal Fair Debt Collection Practices Act, an installment sales act, and the Truth in Lending Act.

Another advantage of a counterclaim is that it can be raised by way of a recoupment defense to offset the debt

109 National Consumer Law Center, Truth in Lending §§ 7.2, 7.3, 10.7 (6th ed. 2007).

After the one-year limitations period has expired, in every jurisdiction except Louisiana, the claim can still be brought by way of recoupment in the collection action, but the consumer will not be able to recover affirmatively, only offset the amount being sought by the collector.

110 For more about the Federal Trade Commission's Holder Notice, see National Consumer Law Center, Unfair and Deceptive Acts and Practices § 6.6 (6th ed. 2004 and Supp.).

111 A number of courts have misinterpreted Federal Trade Commission language and limit recoveries under the FTC Holder Rule to the amount required to offset the amount owed on the debt. See National Consumer Law Center, Unfair and Deceptive Acts and Practices § 6.6.3 (6th ed. 2004 and Supp.).

112 But see National Consumer Law Center, Unfair and Deceptive Acts and Practices § 6.6.3 (6th ed. 2004 and Supp.) for a discussion of state law that may provide rights to an affirmative recovery.

even when the statute of limitations on an affirmative claim would otherwise have expired.[113] Often collection actions are brought years after a debt goes into default, while consumer statutes often have short statutes of limitations—Truth in Lending Act and Fair Debt Collection Practices Act claims both have one-year limitations periods. If a claim is not brought in the collection action by way of recoupment, it may not be available at all.

A counterclaim in a collection action is also more likely to avoid an arbitration requirement than if the action were brought on its own, affirmatively. The collector may waive its ability to require arbitration when it proceeds with the litigation for at least some period after the counterclaim is raised. And a court may find it unconscionable that the collector can proceed in court, but the consumer must bring his counterclaims separately in arbitration.

Whether to bring a counterclaim or a separate litigation may be determined by which court the consumer wishes to litigate a federal claim. If the consumer prefers to bring a federal claim in the state court system, then a counterclaim is an excellent option. If the federal claim were brought instead as an affirmative state court action, it could be removed to federal court. But the collector can not remove a state court action to federal court just because the consumer raises a federal counterclaim—under the well-pleaded complaint doctrine, the collector's complaint determines whether there is federal court jurisdiction.[114] As examined in § 5.5.4, *infra*, this rule applies as well to class counterclaims, meaning they can not be removed to federal court. On the other hand, if the consumer prefers to bring a federal claim in federal court, that claim obviously should not be raised as a counterclaim in state court.

5.5.3 FDCPA Counterclaims Relating to Collector's Litigation Conduct

The consumer can bring a federal Fair Debt Collection Practices Act (FDCPA) counterclaim based upon a collector's litigation misconduct in the collection case, particularly when the collector's action is egregious, such as when it knowingly filed the action outside the statute of limitations, knowingly sued on a debt discharged in bankruptcy, or when it was not licensed to bring collection actions in the state. Too often debt buyers abuse the court system by bringing inadequate claims, knowing they will prevail by default and so do not need to present a viable case.

Attorneys who regularly collect consumer debts, including through litigation, are covered by the FDCPA, as are debt buyers who purchase debt after default.[115] It is also clear that the FDCPA applies to the collector's conduct in the litigation.[116] But the fact that an FDCPA counterclaim is available for such conduct does not mean bringing such counterclaims is in the consumer's best interests. This subsection just focuses on whether the FDCPA claim for litigation misconduct should be brought as a counterclaim in the collection case itself. Section 14.4, *infra*, examines not only the advantages of bringing the FDCPA action after the consumer prevails in the collection action, but also considers the types of litigation conduct that may lead to such an FDCPA action.

An FDCPA counterclaim for litigation misconduct is unlikely to recover damages beyond the FDCPA's $1000 maximum statutory damages plus the consumer's attorney fees. Dismissal of the collection case will eliminate many of the consumer's potential damages. Of course, the ability to obtain attorney fees from the collector may be key to an attorney's ability to represent the consumer, and the FDCPA will provide two theories for such a recovery of attorney fees. The FDCPA provides statutory attorney fees to a prevailing consumer; and the consumer's attorney fees to defend the collection action will be treated as actual damages if the collector improperly brought the action.[117]

This main justification for an FDCPA counterclaim must then be weighed against a number of countervailing factors. First, a consumer prevailing in the collection case may be able to recover attorney fees even without the FDCPA counterclaim for litigation misconduct. A successful defense of the collection action in some states may result in an attorney fee award for the consumer, as described in § 14.1, *infra*. In addition, statutory attorney fees are often available for state unfair and deceptive practices act (UDAP), retail installment sales act (RISA), and other state and federal statutory causes of action brought as counterclaims. The same is the case for FDCPA counterclaims based not upon litigation conduct, but upon illegal collector actions prior to the litigation. When such attorney fees are available under other theories, there may be little benefit in bringing an FDCPA counterclaim for litigation misconduct.

Instead, consumers are often better off bringing the FDCPA claim for the litigation misconduct *after* prevailing in the underlying collection case. Raising the counterclaims in the collection case will alert the collector to weaknesses in its case, and may result in the collector making unusual efforts to substantiate its case, when it would not do so without the counterclaim. While it is true the collector may drop the case in the face of this resistance, it would likely

113 *See* National Consumer Law Center, Truth in Lending § 7.2.5 (6th ed. 2007).

114 *See, e.g.*, Shamrock Oil & Gas Corp. v. Sheets, 313 U.S. 100, 61 S. Ct. 868, 85 L. Ed. 1214 (1941); Chase Manhattan Mortgage Corp. v. Smith, 507 F.3d 910 (6th Cir. 2007).

115 *See* National Consumer Law Center, Fair Debt Collection § 4.2.8 (6th ed. 2008).

116 Heinz v. Jenkins, 514 U.S. 291, 115 S. Ct. 1489, 131 L. Ed. 2d 395 (1995); *see also* National Consumer Law Center, Fair Debt Collection § 4.2.8 (6th ed. 2008); § 14.4.3.1, *infra*.

117 *See* National Consumer Law Center, Fair Debt Collection §§ 2.5.2.2.3, 6.3.2 (6th ed. 2008).

have done the same with any other counterclaim or serious defense. And other collectors may work up a case far more when an FDCPA claim for litigation misconduct is involved, particularly when the collector's attorney is concerned about his or her own exposure.

Waiting to bring a separate FDCPA action for litigation misconduct after the collection action is concluded will generally strengthen the case. Even when the FDCPA violation is manifest at the time the collector first files the collection suit waiting is advisable. Suing on a known time-barred debt and suing without standing or proper authorization under state law are prime examples of violations that are complete upon filing. Nevertheless, even such FDCPA claims as those can only become more appealing as the collection case proceeds.

Some of the core false representation violations do not occur upon filing of the collection complaint, or even if they appear to, may initially be of marginal quality. However those deceptive, unsubstantiated, and sham allegations in the collection complaint are almost always repeated or ratified at a later point in the proceedings under circumstances that strengthen the resulting FDCPA claim.

For example, the Sixth Circuit has held that a debt buyer's routine practice of filing a collection suit without having immediate means of proving the collector's allegations is not unfair or an unlawful deception in violation of the FDCPA.[118] However, the same court later held that a collector who submitted an affidavit with the complaint which falsely stated that the plaintiff was entitled to the relief sought did violate the FDCPA.[119] The federal courts appear to be more receptive to FDCPA violations based, for example, on false verifications attached to a pleading or false affidavits submitted in support of summary judgment, default judgment, or post-judgment proceedings than they are to finding FDCPA violations based on essentially the same misrepresentation when merely recited in the pleading itself.

Moreover, suing immediately gives the collector the opportunity to try to undermine the federal claim with contentions, such as that the falsehood was misunderstood, a mistake, or never intended to be acted upon. Res judicata and issue preclusion flowing from a final judgment in the state case are potentially dispositive in some derivative cases. In that event, knowing the outcome of the state case before filing the federal claim is a powerful advantage available to the federal plaintiff.

One possible advantage of bringing the FDCPA action as a counterclaim is that, pursuant to the well-pleaded complaint doctrine,[120] the case can stay in state court. But the consumer also can stay in state court by limiting the consumer's claims in a subsequent affirmative action to those under state law. In many states, almost any conduct violating the FDCPA is arguably also unfair and deceptive in violation of a state deceptive practices act (UDAP) statute, leading in some of these states to multiple or punitive damages.[121] State tort claims can lead to punitive damages for unreasonable collection practices,[122] including such litigation abuses as suing or continuing to sue the wrong person once put on notice.[123] Nevertheless, when the consumer needs to utilize the FDCPA, the only way to insure that federal court jurisdiction is avoided is to bring the counterclaim in the state court collection action.

Bringing FDCPA violations as counterclaims in the collection action also has the advantage of avoiding the FDCPA's short one-year limitations period—even after the period has expired, the counterclaim should be able to be raised by way of recoupment. On the other hand, when the FDCPA claims relate to current litigation misconduct and the collection case may be completed within one year, there should be sufficient time to bring the FDCPA claim as part of a separate affirmative action. In addition, that one-year period can be extended in federal and many state courts by filing the FDCPA action within the one-year period, but delaying service of the complaint on the collector for four months.[124] At least for those additional months the collector may not be aware of its exposure, and may continue to pursue its collection action under its normal procedures. Another option is to bring a subsequent action using state law UDAP, tort, or other theories that have longer limitations periods.

5.5.4 Class Counterclaims

An interesting option is to bring a class action counterclaim in the individual collection lawsuit. The class counterclaim stays in state court, and can not be removed to federal court—which may be a significant advantage in some jurisdictions. The Class Action Fairness Act of 2005 (CAFA) significantly expanded the grounds to remove a state court class action to federal court. A class counterclaim has the double advantage of staying in state court even when federal causes of action are raised,[125] and even when CAFA would otherwise allow removal of an original class action to federal court on diversity grounds.

CAFA substantially broadens the diversity grounds to remove a state court class action to federal court, as long as there are more than 100 class members, and the amount in

118 Harvey v. Great Seneca Fin. Corp., 453 F.3d 324 (6th Cir. 2006).

119 Gionis v. Javitch Block, Rathbone, LLP, 238 Fed. Appx. 24 (6th Cir. 2007) (unpublished), *cert. denied*, 128 S. Ct. 1259 (2008).

120 *See, e.g.*, Shamrock Oil & Gas Corp. v. Sheets, 313 U.S. 100, 61 S. Ct. 868, 85 L. Ed. 1214 (1941); Chase Manhattan Mortgage Corp. v. Smith, 507 F.3d 910 (6th Cir. 2007).

121 *See* Russey v. Rankin, 911 F. Supp. 1449, 1461–1462 (D.N.M. 1995); *see also* National Consumer Law Center, Unfair and Deceptive Acts and Practices § 5.1.1.1.1 (6th ed. 2004 and Supp.).

122 *See* Billsie v. Brooksbank, 525 F. Supp. 2d 1290, 1297 (D.N.M. 2007).

123 *See* Montgomery Ward v. Larragoite, 467 P.2d 399 (N.M. 1970).

124 *See* Fed. R. Civ. P. 4(m).

125 *See* § 5.5.2, *supra*.

controversy exceeds $5 million.[126] CAFA though is drafted to allow only a "defendant" to remove a class action,[127] and courts find CAFA does not provide a basis for a plaintiff to remove a class counterclaim to federal court.[128] The rule applies even when the consumer brings additional counterclaim defendants into the case and then brings class counterclaims against those defendants. These additional counterclaim defendants can not remove the class counterclaim to federal court.[129]

For example, in one case a debt buyer brought a collection action to recover on an unpaid cell phone obligation. The consumer added the cell phone carrier as an additional counterclaim defendant and brought a class counterclaim against the carrier for its early termination charge policy. The class counterclaim otherwise met the standards for CAFA removal. But, when the carrier removed the case to federal court, the federal court remanded the case to state court. The court found CAFA did not authorize additional counterclaim defendants to remove cases to federal court.[130]

126 *See* 28 U.S.C. § 1332(d); National Consumer Law Center, Consumer Class Actions Ch. 2 (6th ed. 2006 and Supp.).

127 28 U.S.C. § 1453(b).

128 *See* Palisades Collections L.L.C. v. Shorts, 2008 WL 163677 (N.D. W. Va. Jan. 16, 2008); CitiFinancial, Inc. v. Lightner, 2007 WL 1655225 (N.D. W. Va. June 6, 2007); *see also* Unifund CCR Partners v. Wallis, 2006 WL 908755 (D.S.C. Apr. 7, 2006).

129 Palisades Collections L.L.C. v. Shorts, 2008 WL 163677 (N.D. W. Va. Jan. 16, 2008); Ford Motor Credit Co. v. Jones, 2007 WL 2236618 (N.D. Ohio July 31, 2007).

130 Palisades Collections L.L.C. v. Shorts, 2008 WL 163677 (N.D. W. Va. Jan. 16, 2008).

Chapter 6 State Restrictions on the Recovery of Attorney Fees and Other Collection Expenses

6.1 Overview

When a debtor fails to make timely payment of a debt, the common law strictly limits the damages a creditor may recover to the interest provided in the contract or by statute.[1] This general rule of damages law is justified by two considerations. Creditors set interest rates at levels that take into account that a certain portion of debtors necessarily default. Thus the rate of interest already compensates the creditor for collection expenses and losses, so any separate recovery of collection expenses would be duplicative. The other consideration is that almost all consumer credit defaults result from the debtor's financial distress, and the imposition of collection fees would only exacerbate the debtor's financial distress and hinder the debtor's financial recovery.

Dissatisfied with this limitation on their profits, creditors and collectors have through adhesion contracts and legislation sought additional charges from consumers in order to allegedly compensate them for their collection expenses. The most common inroad on the common law rule prohibiting recovery of more than interest for the failure of a consumer to pay a debt on time is the allowance by some courts of an attorney fee award for a creditor if it is authorized by the contract. In addition some states have adopted statutes that authorize creditors to recover attorney fees from debtors. States tend to be considerably more restrictive with respect to collection agency fees.

This chapter first examines the award of attorney fees to the prevailing party pursuant to a contract term. The chapter analyzes whether states allow this method of fee shifting, the creditor's need to establish that the consumer has in fact agreed to the contract containing the clause, and the interpretation of such clauses.

The chapter then turns to the question whether a state has overridden the "American rule" (that attorney fees are not recoverable as damages) by statute for certain types of actions, whether the creditor is the prevailing party, and courts' varying approaches for determining the amount of attorney fees to award. It concludes with an analysis of whether collection agency fees can be passed on to debtors.

1 Loudon v. Taxing Dist., 104 U.S. 771, 774, 26 L. Ed. 923 (1881); 22 Am. Jur. 2d *Damages* § 81 (2003).

Dishonored check charges are addressed in a different chapter,[2] and late charges and judgment interest are discussed in a different manual.[3]

The implications of these issues go beyond defeating a creditor's claim for attorney fees or a collector's claim for collection expenses. Collecting or attempting to collect expenses beyond those allowed by law can subject the party to liability under the Fair Debt Collection Practices Act (FDCPA), the state deceptive practices (UDAP) statute, or a state debt collection statute.[4]

2 *See* Ch. 9, *infra*.

3 National Consumer Law Center, The Cost of Credit: Regulation, Preemption, and Industry Abuses § 7.2.4, Appx. A (3d ed. 2005 and Supp.).

4 *See, e.g.*, Picht v. Jon R. Hawks, Ltd., 236 F.3d 446 (8th Cir. 2001) (use of Minnesota pre-judgment procedure to collect bad check penalties violated Minnesota law, and thus FDCPA, when procedure usable only for sum certain, and penalties were discretionary); Adams v. A. & S. Collection Associates, Inc., 2007 WL 2206936 (D. Conn. July 30, 2007) (mag.) (recommending award of punitive damages against collector that required creditor to add 49% collection fee and 18% interest to claims before forwarding them to agency; Connecticut Creditors' Collection Practices Law forbids agency to add such fees); Munoz v. Pipestone Fin., L.L.C., 513 F. Supp. 2d 1076 (D. Minn. 2007) (creditor liable under FDCPA for seeking fees at outset of collection suit, before they had been incurred); Fields v. W. Mass. Credit Corp., 479 F. Supp. 2d 287 (D. Conn. 2007) (FDCPA violation to add collection agency fee to deficiency after motor vehicle repossession; Connecticut motor vehicle loan law allows fees only for attorney, not collection agency); Barrows v. Chase Manhattan Mortgage Co., 465 F. Supp. 2d 347 (D.N.J. 2006) (FDCPA claim against lender's law firm; fact issue whether legal fees demanded for mortgage reinstatement complied with New Jersey court rule limiting costs and fees in foreclosure actions); Thineson v. JBC Legal Group, Prof'l Corp., 2005 WL 2346991 (D. Minn. Sept. 26, 2005) (consumers stated FDCPA class action claims over misstated amount of dishonored check service charge); Stolicker v. Muller, Muller, Richmond, Harms, Myers & Sgroi, 2005 WL 2180481 (W.D. Mich. Sept. 9, 2005) (law firm's affidavit in support of default judgment violated FDCPA by claiming 25% attorney fee when state law required judicial determination of reasonable fee); Semper v. JBC Legal Group, 2005 WL 2172377 (W.D. Wash. Sept. 6, 2005) (law firm that purchased bad check debts for purpose of collection was not "seller" within meaning of Washington bad check law, not entitled to statutory damages meant to reimburse merchants for collecting dishonored checks,

6.2 Is the Creditor Entitled to Recover Attorney Fees?

6.2.1 American Rule Denies Fees

The "American rule" is that attorney fees are not recoverable as damages, and attorney fees will not be awarded in the absence of a statutory or contractual authorization, except for vexatious, frivolous litigation.[5] The rule's common justification is that it discourages litigation.

Some states go beyond the American rule, and codify a prohibition against or restrictions on fee shifting regardless

and demand for those statutory damages violated FDCPA); Hansen v. Ticket Track, Inc. 280 F. Supp. 2d 1196 (W.D. Wash. 2003) (Washington collection agency statute, Wash. Rev. Code § 19.16.250(18), forbade collector, but not creditor, to add collection fee to debt; fee here was added by collector, and thus unlawful, when collector's contract with creditor-parking lot operator required it to include fee provision in its contract with customers); Adair v. Sabharwal, 2002 WL 31243019 (S.D. Ind. Aug. 16, 2002) (patients stated claim under Indiana deception statute against doctor whose collector demanded 50% collection fee under contract making patient liable for sums "paid or incurred," when there was no evidence of amounts actually incurred); Brooks v. Auto Sales & Services, Inc., 2001 WL 686950 (S.D. Ind. June 15, 2001) (allowing consumer to go forward with FDCPA action against attorney who routinely added 33.33% attorney fee to amount claimed in small claims actions for deficiency on repossessed cars when contract clause allowed "reasonable" fees but did not specify a percentage); Padilla v. Payco Gen. Am. Credits, Inc., 161 F. Supp. 2d 264 (S.D.N.Y. 2001) (collector violated FDCPA by seeking to collect more than the 18% collection fee permitted by federal regulations; no defense that collector relied on figures given to it by creditor guarantee agency); Ballard v. Equifax Check Services, Inc., 158 F. Supp. 2d 1163 (E.D. Cal. 2001) (FDCPA and California Unfair Business Practices Act); Campion v. Credit Bureau Services, 2000 U.S. Dist. LEXIS 20233 (E.D. Wash. Sept. 19, 2000) (creditor violated FDCPA and state collection agency and consumer protection acts by claiming certain fees for which it had not followed required state procedure); *In re* Machnic, 271 B.R. 789 (Bankr. S.D. W. Va. 2002) (credit card issuer violated West Virginia Consumer Credit and Protection Act when it sought to collect fees authorized by contract but not explicitly permitted by Act); Ai v. Frank Huff Agency, Ltd., 607 P.2d 1304 (Haw. 1980) (placing clause allowing 33.33% attorney fees in note, when statute only allowed 25%, was a misrepresentation and violated state UDAP statute); State *ex rel.* Hatch v. JBC Legal Group, P.C., 2006 WL 1388453 (Minn. Dist. Ct. Apr. 13, 2006) (FDCPA and Minnesota Collection Act Claims against law firm that collected NSF checks; FDCPA violations sufficiently alleged; question whether lawyers at large-volume collection firm were acting "as lawyers" within meaning of the attorney exemption in state collection agency act); Collection Bureau Services, Inc. v. Morrow, 87 P.3d 1024 (Mont. 2004) (collector made required demand for NSF check amount plus service charge, then negotiated a payment plan; when consumer later missed payments, state law required new notice letter; FDCPA violation to demand statutory damages without new notice); Davis Lake Cmty. Ass'n v. Feldman, 530 S.E.2d 865 (N.C. Ct. App. 2000) (creditor would violate UDAP statute by attempting to collect attorney fees in excess of 15% allowed by law); Evergreen Collectors v. Holt, 60 Wash. App. 151, 803 P.2d 10 (1991) (attempt to collect fees to which collector is not entitled violates state debt collection law); *see also* Gostony v. Diem Corp., 320 F. Supp. 2d 932 (D. Ariz. 2003) (judicial proceeding was prerequisite for award under lease provision allowing "prevailing party" to recover attorney fees and collection costs; inclusion of fees in initial demand letter was unlawful); Nance v. Ulferts, 282 F. Supp. 2d 912 (N.D. Ind. 2003) (Indiana's civil bad check statute explicitly excludes postdated checks; FDCPA violation when payday lender sought treble damages under that statute; no claim under civil theft statute when consumer failed to allege pecuniary loss). *But see* Johnson v. Riddle, 2007 WL 528719 (D. Utah Feb. 15, 2007) (judicial proceedings privilege bars all common law and statutory claims, including UDAP, arising from attempt to apply Utah's shoplifting civil damages statute to NSF check); Tate v. NationsBanc Mortgage Corp. (*In re* Tate), 253 B.R. 653 (Bankr. W.D.N.C. 2000) (state UDAP and debt collection statutes preempted by bankruptcy law when creditor charged improper "bankruptcy fee" to evade rules for claiming attorney fees in bankruptcy); Bowman Plumbing, Heating & Elec. v. Logan, 59 Va. Cir. 446 (2002) (violation of statute limiting late fees not per se UDAP violation; when late fee provision not part of contract, no violation of UDAP provision forbidding certain penalties); *cf.* Singer v. Pierce & Associates, Prof'l Corp., 383 F.3d 596 (7th Cir. 2004) (when mortgage provided for "reasonable attorney fees" servicer could include $2250 attorney fees in pay-off amount, even though court in foreclosure action, dismissed when borrower arranged to sell to third party, had awarded half that amount); Cook v. Hamrick, 278 F. Supp. 2d 1202 (D. Colo. 2003) (attorney fees demanded in eviction action were not consumer debt within the meaning of FDCPA); Reid v. Ayers, 531 S.E.2d 231 (N.C. Ct. App. 2000) (lawyer collectors fall within UDAP statute's exemption for "learned professions"). *See generally* National Consumer Law Center, Fair Debt Collection §§ 5.5.4.3, 5.6.3, 5.7.2.6.4, 11.2.4.4, 11.3.3, 11.3.4 (6th ed. 2008).

5 Alyeska Pipeline Serv. Co. v. Wilderness Soc'y, 421 U.S. 240, 95 S. Ct. 1612, 44 L. Ed. 2d 141 (1975); Vill. of Glenview v. Zwick, 826 N.E.2d 1171 (Ill. App. Ct. 2005) (village ordinance that provided for one-sided attorney fees in actions arising from violations of ordinance was beyond village's powers, noting strong public policy in favor of American rule); Roan v. Murray, 556 N.W.2d 893 (Mich. Ct. App. 1996) (applying American rule to deny attorney fees to seller suing for repossession of motor vehicle; Michigan statute allowing secured parties to recover certain "costs" allowed attorney fees only "to the extent provided for in the agreement"); *In re* Estate of Vayda, 875 A.2d 925 (N.J. 2005) (explaining rationale for American rule and reiterating New Jersey's "strong public policy against the shifting of costs"; no fee shifting in action to remove executor); Green Harbor Homeowners' Ass'n, Inc. v. G.H. Dev. & Constr., Inc., 763 N.Y.S.2d 114 (App. Div. 2003) (reiterating American rule and narrowly construing fee-shifting clauses in agreements between home owners and developer); Westhaven Associates, Ltd. v. C.C. of Madison, Inc., 652 N.W.2d 819 (Wis. Ct. App. 2002) (Wisconsin follows American rule; attorney fees only if contract "clearly and unambiguously provides"); Dan B. Dobbs, Dobbs Law of Remedies § 3.10 (2d ed. 1993); *cf.* Van Der Stork v. Voorhees, 866 A.2d 972 (N.H. 2005) (seller of land, who had lied about buildability, sued buyer who stopped payment on check after discovering the truth; buyer entitled to attorney fees under vexations litigation exception to American rule).

of the parties' contract. Other states, however, provide by statute for fee awards, or allow the parties to agree to fee shifting. These variations are discussed in the following subsections.

6.2.2 Whether a Contractual Attorney Fee Is Permissible

The primary means by which a creditor may seek to create a right to recover attorney fees is by inserting a clause to this effect in the contract.[6] In some states courts hold that such clauses are permissible even in the absence of a specific authorizing statute, on a freedom of contract theory.[7]

Other states, however, limit or prohibit a creditor's recovery or attempted recovery of its attorney fees from the debtor regardless of the terms of any contract. These restrictions may be contained in statutes that apply only to specific creditors (for example, small loan companies or debt collection agencies) or only to certain types of credit (for example, small loans or retail installment sales).[8]

For example, West Virginia allows only those fees explicitly permitted by the state Consumer Credit and Protection Act.[9] Alabama prohibits attorney fee clauses in consumer credit contracts when the amount financed is $300 or less, and restricts the amount of fees that can be charged when the amount financed exceeds $300.[10] Iowa prohibits attorney fee clauses altogether in consumer credit transactions.[11] South Dakota prohibits contractual attorney fees unless specifically authorized by statute.[12]

6 Secondary sources citing to case law on the validity and limitations of contractual provisions for collection expenses and attorney fees include: 17A Am. Jur. 2d *Contracts* §§ 288–290, 402–404, 489–490 (2004); Joan Kirshberg Davis, Annotation, *When may federal court decline to award to prevailing party attorneys' fees authorized by contract*, 56 A.L.R. Fed. 871 (1982); A. Della Porta, Annotation, *Validity of provision in promissory note or other evidences of indebtedness for payment as attorneys' fees, expenses and costs of collection, of specified percentage of note*, 17 A.L.R.2d 288 (1951); 11 Decennial Digest, *Bills and Notes* §§ 471, 529, 533, 534.

7 *See, e.g.*, Leamon v. Krajkiewcz, 132 Cal. Rptr. 2d 362 (Ct. App. 2003) (parties are free to define conditions for fee shifting; provision denying fees to party who sues without first seeking mediation applied to buyer who had contract declared voidable on grounds of duress); Butler v. Lembeck, 2007 WL 4336229 (Colo. Ct. App. Dec. 13, 2007) (one-sided attorney fee provision enforceable as written; not against public policy and not unenforceable as a penalty); Roberts v. Row, 743 So. 2d 1145 (Fla. Dist. Ct. App. 1999) (trial court had no discretion to refuse to enforce attorney fee provision in contract); Himebaugh v. Weber Inv. Corp., 700 So. 2d 19 (Fla. Dist. Ct. App. 1997) (court had no discretion to refuse to enforce clause in subdivision covenant which provided for award of attorney fees incurred in collecting assessments); Mirar Dev. Inc. v. Kroner, 720 N.E.2d 270 (Ill. App. Ct. 1999) (attorney fee provision in construction contract is enforceable in mechanic's lien action, even though mechanic's lien statute is silent as to attorney fees); Lea v. Jarrott, 750 So. 2d 1098 (La. Ct. App. 1999) (provision in residential lease for attorney fees at an hourly rate would be enforced even though landlord recovered much less than the amount sought and fee would amount to 90% of sum recovered); First Sec. Sav. Bank v. Aitken, 573 N.W.2d 307, 320 (Mich. Ct. App. 1997) ("contractual provisions for the payment of reasonable attorney fees are judicially enforceable"); Garner v. Hubbs, 17 S.W.3d 922 (Mo. Ct. App. 2000) (court must enforce attorney fee clause in separation agreement which is treated as a contract); *In re* Marriage of Pfennigs, 989 P.2d 327 (Mont. 1999) (when contract language is clear as to attorney fees and costs, court must enforce as written; fees properly denied when neither party clearly prevailed); Parkert v. Lindquist, 693 N.W.2d 529 (Neb. 2005) (citing freedom of contract in declining to extend its policy against fee shifting in the courts to non-judicial foreclosures); West v. Gladney, 533 S.E.2d 334, 338 (S.C. Ct. App. 2000) (non-consumer case; when contract specifies attorney fees as a percentage of the debt, court has no discretion to consider reasonableness; "It is not for us to determine whether the parties' agreement was reasonable or wise, or whether they carefully guarded their rights."); Fletcher Hill, Inc. v. Crosbie, 872 A.2d 292 (Vt. 2005) (when contract specifically provides for attorney fees, Vermont courts are loathe to revise the agreement and deny the parties the benefit of their bargain); Schlesinger v. Woodcock, 35 P.3d 1232 (Wyo. 2001) (commercial loan; contractual attorney fee clauses will be enforced, but court will determine reasonableness using federal lodestar test); *see also* R.T.C. Mortgage Trust 1994-S2 v. Shlens, 72 Cal. Rptr. 2d 581 (Ct. App. 1998) (when both promissory note and deed of trust included attorney fee provisions, and one party clearly prevailed, court could not deny attorney fees on equitable grounds).

8 *See, e.g.*, Cheshire Academy v. Lee, 112 Misc. 2d 1076, 448 N.Y.S.2d 112 (Civ. Ct. 1982) (denying attorney fees when statute governing retail installment obligations specifically voids any provision for payment of attorney fees). *See generally* National Consumer Law Center, The Cost of Credit: Regulation, Preemption, and Industry Abuses (3d ed. 2005 and Supp.).

9 W. Va. Code §§ 46A-2-128(d) (prohibiting collection agencies from attempting to collect charge, fee, or expense unless it is expressly authorized by the agreement and by statute), 46A-3-101 (listing charges that may be included in consumer credit sale); *see In re* Machnic, 271 B.R. 789 (Bankr. S.D. W. Va. 2002) (credit card issuer violated West Virginia Consumer Credit and Protection Act when it sought attorney fees for collection when not explicitly permitted by Act, even though authorized by contract).

10 *See, e.g.*, Ala. Code § 5-19-10 (attorney fees forbidden on debts of $300 or less; permitted, with certain limitations, on larger debts).

11 Iowa Code § 537.2507.

12 *See, e.g.*, S.D. Codified Laws § 15-17-39 (prohibiting contractual attorney fees except as authorized by specific statute); Orion Fin. Corp. v. Am. Foods Group, Inc., 281 F.3d 733 (8th Cir. 2002) (S.D. law) (contract for services not covered by statute forbidding fee-shifting clauses in "evidence of debt"); Vanderwerf Implement, Inc. v. McCance, 561 N.W.2d 24 (S.D. 1997) (construing South Dakota statute that makes attorney fee clauses in certain contracts void); *cf.* Kimball Inv. Land, Ltd. v. Chmela, 604 N.W.2d 289 (S.D. 2000) (specific South Dakota statute allowing attorney fees for mortgage foreclosure is exception to general prohibition of contractual fees). *But cf.* Credit Collection Services, Inc. v. Pesicka, 721 N.W.2d 474 (S.D. 2006) (South Dakota law forbids fee shifting in "note, bond, mortgage or other evidence of debt," but hospital's patient

Even in the absence of an explicit statutory prohibition, some courts hold that contract clauses providing for the recovery of collection attorney fees are invalid unless there is specific statutory authorization of such fees. These courts look to a variety of legal theories to justify that conclusion. The most straightforward approach is that of the Kentucky and Nebraska courts, which hold such clauses to be contrary to public policy and invalid in the absence of statutory authorization.[13] A decision interpreting North Carolina law also holds that there must be a statutory basis for recovery of attorney fees, even when the parties' contract provides that attorney fees may be recovered.[14] Ohio had also been in this group,[15] but appears to be retreating. Several recent Ohio cases hold that contractual attorney fee clauses are enforceable, at least when the parties are of equal sophistication and the contract is not an adhesion contract.[16]

consent form was not "evidence of debt"; fee-shifting provision enforced).

13 Ranier v. Gilford, 688 S.W.2d 753 (Ky. Ct. App. 1985) (noting legislative changes broadening the availability of attorney fees in Kentucky, but refusing to award fees to creditor for conversion claims); Riley v. W. Ky. Prod. Credit Assoc., 603 S.W.2d 916 (Ky. Ct. App. 1980); Stewart v. Bennett, 727 N.W.2d 424 (Neb. 2007) (attorney fee clause in lease void as against public policy; public policy embodied in legislation that explicitly allows attorney fees for frivolous action, but is silent as to other litigation; legislature presumed to know American rule); Chambers-Dobson, Inc. v. Squier, 472 N.W.2d 391 (Neb. 1991) (contractual fee shifting contrary to public policy and void); First Nat'l Bank v. Schroeder, 218 Neb. 397, 355 N.W.2d 780 (1984). *But cf.* Parkert v. Lindquist, 693 N.W.2d 529 (Neb. 2005) (contractual provision for fee shifting in litigation would be void, but citing freedom of contract in declining to extend public policy against fee shifting to non-judicial foreclosures).

14 Sunbelt Rentals v. Corbridge, 171 F. Supp. 2d 14 (D. Me. 2001) (N.C. law).

15 Clarklift, Inc. v. Clark Equip. Co., 869 F. Supp. 533 (N.D. Ohio 1994) (Ohio will not enforce attorney fee clauses in promissory notes as being against public policy; despite a Michigan choice of law clause in a commercial contract, refusing to award attorney fees when the collateral was located in Ohio, and the creditor relied on Ohio law in its action), *aff'd*, 117 F.3d 1420 (6th Cir. 1997); Worth v. Aetna Cas. & Sur. Co., 32 Ohio St. 3d 238, 513 N.E.2d 253 (Ohio 1987) (attorney fee clause inserted by creditor into ordinary contract or lease is contrary to public policy, but agreement between company and its executives for indemnification of their legal expenses was enforceable); Glouster Cmty. Bank v. Winchell, 659 N.E.2d 330 (Ohio Ct. App. 1995) (inclusion of attorney fees and court costs provision in contract violated Ohio retail installment sales act and was a "willing violation" invalidating both the contract and the security interest); Telmark, Inc. v. Schierloh, 658 N.E.2d 43 (Ohio Ct. App. 1995) (denying enforcement of attorney fee clause in commercial lease on Ohio public policy grounds, despite New York choice of law clause; attorney fee clause generally disapproved, but may be allowed in agreements between "competent parties with equal bargaining positions" who engage in "free and understanding negotiations").

16 Davidson v. Weltman, Weinberg & Rice, 285 F. Supp. 2d 1093 (S.D. Ohio 2003) (requirement that borrower pay attorney fees as condition for reinstatement of mortgage after acceleration does not violate public policy even if Ohio cases still hold these clauses unenforceable in other contexts); Scotts Co. v. Cent. Garden & Pet Co., 256 F. Supp. 2d 734 (S.D. Ohio 2003) (former rule has been "revisited but not eviscerated"; fee-shifting clauses enforceable if "arrived at though free and understanding negotiation"; clause preprinted on back of non-consumer invoice not enforceable); Crown Food Serv. Group, Inc. v. Hughes, 1999 U.S. Dist. LEXIS 21701 (S.D. Ohio July 12, 1999) (contractual attorney fees are now enforceable under Ohio law); *In re* Shaffer, 287 B.R. 898 (Bankr. S.D. Ohio 2002) (fee-shifting clause in mortgage securing promissory note for less than $100,000, between parties of unequal bargaining power, is against public policy and void; distinguishing *Nottingdale*); Nottingdale Homeowners Ass'n v. Darby, 33 Ohio St. 3d 32, 514 N.E.2d 702 (Ohio 1987) (attorney fee provision in non-commercial condominium documents was enforceable, and was not against public policy as long as amount of fee is fair, just and reasonable; noting exception for adhesion contracts); Hagans v. Habitat Condo. Owners Ass'n, 851 N.E.2d 544 (Ohio Ct. App. 2006) (Ohio permits fee-shifting provisions in condominium declarations; construing declaration to allow fees for lien to collect unpaid assessments, but not unpaid fines); Wash. Mut. Bank v. Mahaffey, 796 N.E.2d 39 (Ohio Ct. App. 2003) (Ohio Rev. Code Ann. § 1301.21(A)(2) (West) which bars "a commitment to pay attorney fees" included in "a contract of indebtedness," not violated by requirement that borrower pay lender's attorney fees as condition of reinstatement; borrower not required to seek reinstatement, so attorney fee obligation did not arise "in connection with the enforcement of the contract of indebtedness"; distinguishing cases barring attorney fees after foreclosure); Furnier & Thomas, L.L.P. v. Bus. Info. Solutions, Inc., 2002 WL 31094472 (Ohio Ct. App. Sept. 20, 2002) (fee-shifting clause in unaltered form contract was enforceable, when party attacking it was a law firm "of some sophistication in the interpretation of business contracts" and no evidence that it "did not or could not participate in a free and understanding negotiation if it chose"); Kitchen v. Lake Lorelei Homeowners' Ass'n, 2002 WL 1274256 (Ohio Ct. App. June 10, 2002) (provision enforceable if fees are "fair, just and reasonable"; allowing fees to home owners' association in action to collect fine for violation of association rule); Vermeer, Inc. v. Argo Constr. Co., 760 N.E.2d 1 (Ohio Ct. App. 2001) (fee-shifting clauses disfavored, enforceable only if the product of "free and understanding negotiation" between "parties of equal bargaining power and similar sophistication"; not shown when provision of commercial equipment lease was part of two-page "unaltered form agreement provided by the advantaged party," presented and signed at the worksite when machine was delivered); First Capital Corp. v. G. & J. Industries, Inc., 131 Ohio App. 3d 106, 721 N.E.2d 1084 (1999) (contractual attorney fee clause enforced between commercial parties, but result may be different if parties lack equal sophistication and bargaining power); Stults & Associates, Inc. v. United Mobile Homes, Inc., 1998 Ohio App. LEXIS 5097 (Ohio Ct. App. Oct. 14, 1998) (commercial case) (contractual attorney fee provisions are enforceable absent a showing of unequal bargaining positions, misunderstanding, deception or duress; strong freedom of contract language); *see also* Taylor v. Luper, Sheriff and Niedenthal Co., L.P.A., 74 F. Supp. 2d 761 (S.D. Ohio 1999) (collection attorney who demanded attorney fees protected by FDCPA bona fide error defense in light of changing Ohio law). *But see* K & A Cleaning, Inc. v. Materni, 2006 WL 1047477 (Ohio Ct. App. Apr. 21, 2006) (unpublished) (attorney fee provision unenforceable if parties do not share an equal bargaining position, or terms

A few courts have held that a contract clause providing for attorney fees is a penalty prohibited by general contract law.[17] In distinguishing a forbidden penalty from an enforceable liquidated damages clause, courts will consider the difficulty of determining actual damages, the disparity between the actual and predicted damages, and any indicia of unconscionability, such as disparity of bargaining power and provisions highly unfavorable to the weaker party.[18] Other fee provisions have been found to be a cloak for usury,[19] unconscionable,[20] or against equity under the particular facts of a case.[21] Unauthorized practice of law statutes may also be construed to prohibit recovery of attorney fees from a debtor when the creditor represents itself or acts through individuals not licensed to practice law in the jurisdiction.[22]

Some state statutes can also be construed to prohibit collection attorney fees by implication. For example, the fees and charges permitted by state small loan statutes are construed by some courts to be the exclusive listing of

of provision not freely negotiable, or provision promotes litigation or illegal acts *or* acts as a penalty; unilateral attorney fee clause in cleaning woman's employment contract was so one-sided it encouraged litigation and acted as penalty).

17 *See, e.g.*, El Escorial Owners' Ass'n v. DLC Plastering, Inc., 65 Cal. Rptr. 3d 524 (Ct. App. 2007) ("inadequately documented or overbilled" fees were "penalties disguised as attorney fees"); Equitable Lumber Co. v. IPA Land Dev. Co., 38 N.Y.2d 516, 381 N.Y.S.2d 459, 344 N.E.2d 391 (1976) (30% fee not unconscionable between commercial parties; remanding for determination whether 30% was reasonable forecast of actual collection costs or commensurate with actual fees, and whether it was unreasonably large); Wasserbauer v. Marine Midland Bank-Rochester, 92 Misc. 2d 388, 400 N.Y.S.2d 979 (Sup. Ct. 1977) (refusing to dismiss claim that percentage attorney fees were illegal as a penalty); Exch. Bank v. Appalachian Land & Lumber Co., 38 S.E. 813 (N.C. 1901) (provision for 10% attorney fee in case suit is necessary is void as a penalty and as a cover for usury); K & A Cleaning, Inc. v. Materni, 2006 WL 1047477 (Ohio Ct. App. Apr. 21, 2006) (unpublished) (unilateral attorney fee clause in cleaning woman's employment contract so one-sided that it acted as a penalty and encouraged litigation). *But see* Butler v. Lembeck, 2007 WL 4336229 (Colo. Ct. App. Dec. 13, 2007) (provision requiring tenants to reimburse landlord for "reasonable attorney fees if legal action is required due to [tenant's] actions" was enforceable and not a penalty); McIntire v. Cagley, 37 Iowa 676 (1873) (10% attorney fee reasonable and not a penalty as it was not disproportionate to expected injuries).

18 *See, e.g.*, Auto. Fin. Corp. v. Ridge Chrysler Plymouth L.L.C., 219 F. Supp. 2d 945 (N.D. Ill. 2002) (penalty unenforceable even if negotiated by sophisticated parties); Easton Telecomm Services, L.L.C. v. CoreComm Internet Group, Inc., 216 F. Supp. 2d 695 (N.D. Ohio 2002) (liquidated damages clauses enforceable if reasonable compensation for actual damages is the legitimate objective, but not when "manifestly inequitable and unrealistic" and "one-sided boilerplate provision" not the subject of bargaining); Dist. Cablevision Ltd. P'ship v. Bassin, 828 A.2d 714 (D.C. 2003) (disparity of bargaining power significant, also disproportion between fee and actual cost of collection, and fact that same fee applied to all breaches, that is, whether additional collection effort required); Grunwald v. Quad City Quality Serv., Inc., 662 N.W.2d 370 (Iowa Ct. App. 2003) (liquidated damages clause in employment contract was penalty; "[A] party seeking to recover for breach of contract is entitled only to be placed in as good a position as the party would have occupied had the contract been performed. . . . A party is not entitled to use the breach to better its position by recovering damages not actually suffered."); Truck Rent-A-Center, Inc. v. Puritan Farms 2d, Inc., 361 N.E.2d 1015 (N.Y. 1977) (measure of damages in contract is just compensation for loss sustained; contractual penalties and forfeitures are against public policy; enforcing early termination provisions of commercial lease when actual damages unpredictable, contractual provision a reasonable estimate, and, although found in preprinted contract, no evidence of disparity of bargaining power or unconscionability); Lake Ridge Academy v. Carney, 613 N.E.2d 183 (Ohio 1993) (provision requiring payment of full tuition for withdrawal after August 1 would be enforced when actual damages difficult to calculate but estimate reasonable, no evidence of duress or unconscionability, and parties' intention clear); Phillips v. Phillips, 820 S.W.2d 785 (Tex. 1991) (measure of damages in contract is just compensation; liquidated damages enforced only if actual damages unpredictable and contract amount is "reasonable forecast").

19 Merchants Nat'l Bank v. Sevier, 14 F. 662, 663 (E.D. Ark. Cir. Ct. 1882) (refusing to enforce 10% attorney fee provision as a penalty, usurious, and at the time beyond the power of a national bank); Exch. Bank v. Appalachian Land & Lumber Co., 38 S.E. 813 (N.C. 1901) (provision for 10% attorney fee in case suit is necessary is void as a penalty and as a cover for usury); Campen Bros. v. Stewart, 145 S.E. 381,382 (W. Va. 1928); *see also* A. Della Porta, Annotation, *Validity of provision in promissory note or other evidences of indebtedness for payment as attorneys' fees, expenses and costs of collection, of specified percentage of note*, 17 A.L.R.2d 288, 313 (1951); National Consumer Law Center, The Cost of Credit: Regulation, Preemption, and Industry Abuses § 7.3.3.2 (3d ed. 2005 and Supp.).

20 *See, e.g.*, Consumers Time Credit, Inc. v. Remark Corp., 259 F. Supp. 135 (E.D. Pa. 1966) (reducing attorney fee to 5%; 15% provision in contract was an unconscionable penalty), *aff'd*, 377 F.2d 553 (3d Cir. 1967). *But cf.* Helm Fin. Corp. v. Iowa N. Ry. Co., 214 F. Supp. 2d 934 (N.D. Iowa 2002) (one-sided attorney fee provision not unconscionable, when commercial lease was product of "tedious" negotiations, lessee's principals were experienced businessmen, and lessee failed to present evidence of alleged market shortage that made lessor only source of necessary equipment).

21 *See* Healy v. Carlson Travel Network Ass'n, Inc., 227 F. Supp. 2d 1080 (D. Minn. 2002) (boilerplate provision in franchising contract is enforceable, but denying attorney fees "in consideration of the equities and of the nature of the contract" because of franchisor's superior bargaining power and failure to adhere strictly to the contract, and fact that franchise "never got off the ground"); Costas v. First Fed. Sav. & Loan Ass'n, 321 S.E.2d 51 (S.C. 1984) (declining to enforce contractual attorney fee clause in light of the creditor's failure to timely discover that its loan file was incomplete and in view of parties' conduct).

22 Cheshire Academy v. Lee, 112 Misc. 2d 1076, 448 N.Y.S.2d 112 (Civ. Ct. 1982) (refusing to award attorney fees pursuant to contract clause when creditor's attorney, although licensed in New York, did not maintain an office there and thus was not allowed to practice law there); Tenn. Att'y Gen. Op. No. 14, Pov. L. Rep. ¶ 25,494 (Sept. 7, 1977); *see also In re* Thompson, 174 N.Y. L.J. No. 52, p.8, Clearinghouse No. 16,597 (N.Y. Civ. Ct. 1975) (bank could not recover and retain attorney fees on default judgments obtained by its staff attorneys without engaging in the unauthorized practice of law).

permitted charges, and thus prohibit attorney fees or other collection charges if they are not listed.[23] Similarly, courts may allow attorney fees or collection fees to be added to regulated consumer debts, but only to the extent that the interest provided in the contract is less than the statutory maximum.[24]

6.2.3 Is There a Contract with the Consumer?

When the creditor claims a right to attorney fees based on a contract, a key initial question—assuming that such a clause is valid under state law—is whether the consumer has actually entered into a contract with the creditor. For example, the creditor may be asserting a claim based on *quantum meruit* that is not based on the existence of a contract. In that case, the creditor will not need to prove the existence of a contract—and in fact may have chosen the *quantum meruit* claim because it can not prove that a contract existed.[25]

Contractual attorney fees can not be awarded on a *quantum meruit* claim when the creditor has not proven that the consumer entered into a contract.[26] (In addition, even if the creditor proves the existence of a contract, the clause may not apply to claims that are not based on that contract.[27]) Likewise, if a debt buyer relies on a claim such as account stated or open account[28] without proving the existence of a written contract, it will not be able to hold the consumer liable for attorney fees under a clause in that contract.[29]

Even if the creditor can show that the consumer agreed to a contract, it may not be able to establish that the consumer agreed to the fee-shifting provision.[30] For example, a clause printed on the back of an invoice or a sign posted at a store may be insufficient to create a contract.[31] An attorney fee

23 *See In re* Machnic, 271 B.R. 789 (Bankr. S.D. W. Va. 2002) (collector violated state debt collection statute by seeking attorney fees on credit card debt; only fees explicitly permitted by West Virginia Consumer and Credit Protection Act may be charged, so collection agency's attempt to collect attorney fees and costs in addition to credit card debt violates state debt collection statute); New Fin., Ltd. v. Ellis, 225 So. 2d 784 (Ala. 1969); Harbour v. Arelco, Inc., 678 N.E.2d 381 (Ind. 1997) (attorney fee provision in car rental contract was unenforceable because such fees were not on list of fees permitted by Indiana Vehicle Rental Act); Elsea, Inc. v. Stapleton, 1998 WL 391943 (Ohio Ct. App. July 2, 1998) (when attorney fees are not among permitted fees enumerated in retail installment sales act (RISA), inclusion of attorney fee clause in preprinted RISA contract was willful violation which barred seller from enforcing contract or repossessing home; inclusion also violated UDAP statute); Missouri Dep't of Consumer Affairs, Regulation & Licensing, Ruling No. 31 (Dec. 5, 1974); *cf.* Keokuk State Bank v. Eckley, 354 N.W.2d 785 (Iowa Ct. App. 1984) (Iowa forfeiture notice statute does not entitle recovery of attorney fees as part of the reasonable cost of serving notice because the statute makes no express mention of attorney fees). *But cf.* Westinghouse Credit Corp. v. Walters, 17 B.R. 644 (Bankr. S.D. Ohio 1982) (retail installment sales act prohibition of other charges did not prohibit a provision for collection attorney fees because the focus of the statute was charges imposed at the time of the contract).

24 Valley Bank & Trust Co. v. Hall, 1980 Mass. App. Ct. 169 (1980).

25 *See* § 4.5, *supra.*

26 Uncle Henry's, Inc. v. Plaut Consulting, Inc., 270 F. Supp. 2d 67 (D. Me. 2003) (denying contractual attorney fees for company that recovered in *quantum meruit*; did not "recover under the contract"); Lubkey v. Compuvac Sys., Inc., 857 So. 2d 966 (Fla. Dist. Ct. App. 2003) (party who claims fees pursuant to written agreement entitled to fees only on claims based on that agreement; claimant failed to show that successful claims arose under settlement agreement with fee-shifting clause); Am. Prop. Maint. v. Monia, 59 S.W.3d 640 (Mo. Ct. App. 2001) (reversing award of fees pursuant to contract clause when creditor prevailed on mechanic's lien and *quantum meruit* claims but lost on contract claim).

27 *See* § 6.2.4, *infra.*

28 *See* § 4.6, 4.7, *supra.*

29 Norfolk Fin. Corp. v. MacDonald, 2003 Mass. App. Div. 153 (Dist. Ct. 2003) (denying summary judgment for attorney fees; no evidence that consumer received credit card agreement providing for fees); Citibank v. Martin, 807 N.Y.S.2d 284 (Civ. Ct. 2005) (debt buyer must prove an agreement to pay fees). *But cf.* Christy v. Smith Mountain, Inc., 855 So. 2d 1103 (Ala. Civ. App. 2003) (allowing creditor to go forward with claim for late charges and attorney fees disclosed in credit application and charge account agreement); Stan's Lumber, Inc. v. Fleming, 538 N.W.2d 849 (Wis. Ct. App. 1995) (fee-shifting clause in application for open account became contractual obligation once seller/creditor approved the account and debtor began making purchases). *See generally* § 4.5.5, *supra.*

30 Roberts v. Adams, 47 P.3d 690 (Colo. Ct. App. 2001) (real estate sale contract included attorney fee clause for "litigation arising out of this contract"; promissory note silent as to attorney fees, but when note existed only as result of payment terms of sales contract, attorney fees available in suit on note); Lazy Flamingo, U.S.A., Inc. v. Greenfield, 834 So. 2d 413 (Fla. Dist. Ct. App. 2003) (in action to enforce mediated settlement agreement, failure to include fees in agreement barred attorney fees, despite fee-shifting clause in underlying contract; fees could, however, be awarded as sanction for violating settlement agreement); Stevens v. Zakrzewski, 826 So. 2d 520 (Fla. Dist. Ct. App. 2002) (real estate purchase contract contained fee-shifting clause for "any litigation arising out of" the contract, but stated that no provision would survive the closing unless "expressly provided"; fee-shifting clause did not survive the closing; no attorney fees for buyer who sued for failure to disclose oil tank).

31 Scotts Co. v. Cent. Garden & Pet Co., 256 F. Supp. 2d 734 (S.D. Ohio 2003) (non-consumer contract; fee-shifting clause preprinted on back of invoice not enforceable; late fees disclosed in price list furnished before ordering were enforceable); Ballard v. Equifax Check Serv., 27 F. Supp. 2d 1201 (E.D. Cal. 1998) (no contract for $20 bad check charge when holder failed to show that merchant had posted signs [statute has since been amended to authorize $25 to $35 charges]); *In re* Dixie Produce & Packaging, L.L.C., 368 B.R. 533 (Bankr. E.D. La. 2007) (printed statement on bottom of delivery ticket or invoice providing for interest and attorney fees in case of default does not constitute a written agreement to pay, absent a showing that the buyer knew or should have known of the statement); Braylor Corp. v. MTES Operations, Inc., 2002 WL 1614115 (Cal. Ct.

clause in a contract with one party may not bind a different party.[32] A sometimes difficult issue is whether an attorney fee clause will survive the termination or rescission of the contract that included it.[33]

App. July 23, 2002) (fee-shifting clause printed on packing slips unenforceable); Ricci Drain-Laying Co. v. Baskin, 744 A.2d 406 (R.I. 1999) (home owner never agreed to provision which was preprinted in small type at the bottom of blank form on which parties' contract was typewritten); Agway Inc. v. Brooks, 790 A.2d 438 (Vt. 2001) (attorney fee provisions not binding, when they were written on back of tallies or receipts, not intended as contracts; if no one home when goods delivered, tallies left at farm unsigned; attorney fee provisions in personal account not binding on corporation). *But see* Monsanto Co. v. David, 516 F.3d 1009 (Fed. Cir. 2008) (attorney fee provision on back of contract between farmer and manufacturer of genetically modified seed was valid, in absence of showing of fraud).

32 Whiteside v. Tenet Healthcare Corp., 124 Cal. Rptr. 2d 580 (Ct. App. 2002) (attorney fee clause in contract between hospital and Blue Shield did not authorize award of attorney fees against patient); McCarthy Bros. Co. v. Tilbury Constr., Inc., 849 So. 2d 7 (Fla. Dist. Ct. App. 2003) (surety not liable for attorney fees pursuant to fee-shifting clause in contract between general contractor and subcontractor); Fielder v. Weinstein Design Group, Inc., 842 So. 2d 879 (Fla. Dist. Ct. App. 2003) (buyer's spouse, who did not sign contract, could neither claim nor be held liable for contractual attorney fees); Snedeker v. Lighthouse Realty Group, Inc., 773 So. 2d 109 (Fla. Dist. Ct. App. 2000) (attorney fee clauses in Florida contracts strictly construed; when contract for sale of realty provided for prevailing party fees for buyer, seller and brokers, fee award reversed as to developer); MSI Fin. Group v. Veterans Constr., 645 So. 2d 178 (Fla. Dist. Ct. App. 1994) (contract provision for "all court costs and reasonable attorneys fees" covered an action for a deficiency judgment against debtor's estate, but not an action against the guarantor); White v. Marshall, 83 S.W.3d 57 (Mo. Ct. App. 2002) (roommate who never signed lease not bound by fee-shifting provision); Green Harbor Homeowners' Ass'n, Inc. v. G.H. Dev. & Constr., Inc., 763 N.Y.S.2d 114 (App. Div. 2003) (fee-shifting clause in home owners' association covenant did not apply in litigation between owners and developer); Windsor Park Nursing Home, 850 N.Y.S.2d 342 (Sup. Ct. Jan. 10, 2008) (fee-shifting provision in contract between cooperative and members not part of contract between cooperative member and his subtenant); Prairie Hills Water & Dev. Co. v. Gross, 653 N.W.2d 745 (S.D. 2002) (action to enforce subdivision covenants that included fee-shifting clause; fees allowed against lot owners but not non-owner co-defendants); Fericks v. Lucy Ann Soffe Trust, 100 P.3d 1200 (Utah 2004) (realtors not entitled to attorney fees by fee-shifting clause in real estate contract as realtors were not a party to the contract, and the agency relationship to a party did not confer right to enforce clause for the agent's own benefit). *But cf.* Jefferson Door Co. v. Lago Dev., L.L.C., 848 So. 2d 101 (La. Ct. App. 2003) (credit application and guarantee contract, read together, made guarantor liable for attorney fees); Spokoiny v. Wash. State Youth Soccer Ass'n, 117 P.3d 1141 (Wash. Ct. App. 2005) (bylaws of social club, including provision for attorney fees if member sued without exhausting internal dispute-resolution procedure, were valid contract between club and member).

33 PM Group, Inc. v. Stewart, 64 Cal. Rptr. 3d 227 (Ct. App. 2007) (party who successfully claimed that no contract had been formed entitled to fees under provision of purported contract; reciprocal fees law provides that party is entitled to fees if other party, had it prevailed, would have been entitled); MBNA Am. Bank v. Gorman, 54 Cal. Rptr. 3d 724 (Ct. App. 2006) (California's reciprocal fees law requires attorney fees for party who prevails on the ground that contract is unenforceable if other party, had it prevailed, would have been entitled to fee award); Young v. Vlahos, 929 A.2d 362 (Conn. App. Ct. 2007) (fee-shifting clause for actions based upon default survived landlord's termination of lease for tenant's default); Tarr v. Honea, 959 So. 2d 780 (Fla. Dist. Ct. App. 2007) (prospective purchaser terminated real estate contract, as permitted by provision for inspection period, then changed mind and sought to enforce; contractual attorney fees proper when contract had existed and litigation "arose out of" it; distinguishing cases in which no contract formed); Fabing v. Eaton, 941 So. 2d 415 (Fla. Dist. Ct. App. 2006) (fee-shifting clause survives if contract found unenforceable, but not if contract never existed, for example, because of mutual mistake); Overton v. Kingsbrooke Dev., Inc., 788 N.E.2d 1212 (Ill. App. Ct. 2003) (land contract with broad fee-shifting clause; consumers successfully disaffirmed on grounds of breach of warranty of habitability; no attorney fees because consumers disaffirmed whole contract); Fici v. Koon, 642 S.E.2d 602 (S.C. 2007) (party who prevailed on statute of frauds defense to real estate contract entitled to contractual attorney fees; statute barred enforcement but did not void the contract); Bilanzich v. Lonetti, 160 P.3d 1041 (Utah 2007) (contractual attorney fees for party who invalidated contract; reciprocal fees statute requires fee award if other party, had it prevailed, would have been entitled to fees); Labriola v. Pollard Group, 100 P.3d 791 (Wash. 2004) (collection of cases awarding fees pursuant to Washington's reciprocal fees statute in cases when contract was invalidated); Castleberry v. Phelan, 101 P.3d 460 (Wyo. 2004) (attorney fee clause in contract for deed continued in force after contract terminated by buyer's default, when seller did not rescind but used the remedies provided in the contract); *see also* C. & L. Enterprises v. Citizen Band Potawatomi Tribe of Okla., 72 P.3d 1 (Okla. 2002) (Oklahoma statute allowing attorney fees in action on contract for labor or services applies only if labor or services provided; no fee shifting when contract was repudiated before contractor started work).

6.2.4 Interpreting Contractual Provisions for Collection Attorney Fees

Because contractual attorney fee clauses are an exception to the generally applicable American rule, and are harsh in effect, most courts construe them strictly.[34] Another basis for

34 U.S. Fid. & Guar. Co. v. Baspetro Oil Services Co., 369 F.3d 34, 74–78 (2d Cir. 2004) (N.Y. law) (contract clause allowing attorney fees must be strictly construed; construing contractual clause allowing "legal costs" not to include attorney fees); Coastal Power Int'l, Ltd. v. Transcontinental Capital Corp., 182 F.3d 163 (2d Cir. 1999) (under New York law, contractual attorney fee clause must be "unmistakably clear"); *In re* Parker, 269 B.R. 522 (D. Vt. 2001) (construing fee-shifting clause strictly against the writer; no attorney fees when residential lease ambiguous and adhesive); Islander Beach Club Condo. v. Skylark Sports, L.L.C., 975 So. 2d 1208 (Fla. Dist. Ct. App. 2008) (fee-shifting clause in commercial lease unenforceable; when clause as written was "incomprehensible," attempt to salvage it was error; "the right to contractual attorney fees is limited by the terms of the provision, and should be strictly construed"); Wendel v. Wendel, 852 So. 2d 277 (Fla. Dist. Ct.

a narrow construction is any ambiguity in the contract language. The general rule is that an ambiguity in a contract is construed against the drafter, and it is strictly construed against the drafter if a contract of adhesion is involved.[35]

Some courts refuse to award attorney fees when the contract only allows "costs and expenses" or "costs of collection" and does not specifically mention attorney fees.[36] A number of courts have held that the creditor is not

App. 2003) (strictly construing contractual fee-shifting provision; words "costs or expenses" in marital settlement agreement do not include attorney fees, when other paragraphs specifically refer to attorney fees); Snedeker v. Lighthouse Realty Group, Inc., 773 So. 2d 109 (Fla. Dist. Ct. App. 2000) (attorney fee clauses in Florida contracts strictly construed; when contract for sale of realty provided for prevailing party fees for buyer, seller and brokers, fee award reversed as to developer); LaGuardia v. Tompkins Inv. Group, 715 So. 2d 1057 (Fla. Dist. Ct. App. 1998) (contractual provisions shifting responsibility for attorney fees must be strictly construed); Pici v. First Union Nat'l Bank of Florida, 705 So. 2d 50 (Fla. Dist. Ct. App. 1997) (attorney fee provisions are to be strictly construed; "If you hire an attorney to collect what I owe, I agree to pay our reasonable fees" did not authorize fees for a replevin action based on a non-monetary default); Chapman v. Engel, 865 N.E.2d 330 (Ill. App. Ct. 2007) (fee shifting clauses strictly construed; when contract required fee shifting "in the event of default by seller or buyer," court's finding that neither party to failed real estate sale had breached contract meant fee-shifting clause was never triggered); Negro Nest L.L.C. v. Mid-Northern Mgmt., Inc., 839 N.E.2d 1083, 1085 (Ill. App. Ct. 2005) (contract provision for "all collection costs incurred" does not include attorney fees as cost shifting provisions narrowly construed; attorney fees allowed only if specified); Powers v. Rockford Stop'n'Go, Inc., 761 N.E.2d 237 (Ill. App. Ct. 2001) (contractual fee-shifting clauses enforceable, but will be "strictly construed and enforced at the discretion of the trial court"; reversing fee award when claims and counterclaims resulted in "essentially a draw"); *In re* Estate of Vayda, 875 A.2d 925 (N.J. 2005) (explaining rationale for American rule and reiterating New Jersey's "strong public policy against the shifting of costs"; no fee shifting in action to remove executor); N. Bergen Rex Transp., Inc. v. Trailer Leasing Co., 730 A.2d 843 (N.J. 1999) (New Jersey law disfavors shifting of attorney fees; shifting may be authorized by contract, but provision will be strictly construed and court will evaluate reasonableness of claimed fees); Kellam Associates, Inc. v. Angel Projects, L.L.C., 814 A.2d 642 (N.J. Super. Ct. App. Div. 2003) (fee shifting disfavored; clauses narrowly construed, but allowed when landlord got 75% of amount requested in dispute over construction of rent-escalator clause); Hatch v. T & L Associates, 319 N.J. Super. 644, 726 A.2d 308 (Super. Ct. App. Div. 1999) (fee-shifting provisions will be strictly construed); Green Harbor Homeowners' Ass'n, Inc. v. G.H. Dev. & Constr., Inc., 763 N.Y.S.2d 114 (App. Div. 2003) (reiterating American rule and narrowly construing fee-shifting clauses in agreements between home owners and developer; fee shifting denied); Westhaven Associates, Ltd. v. C.C. of Madison, Inc., 652 N.W.2d 819 (Wis. Ct. App. 2002) (Wisconsin follows American rule; attorney fees only if contract "clearly and unambiguously provides"); Cowardin v. Finnerty, 994 P.2d 335 (Wyo. 1999) (contractual provision for attorney fees must be explicit; clauses in purchase and sale agreement allowing non-defaulting party to "recover such damages as may be proper" and requiring return of earnest money "less costs incurred by sellers" if sale fell through, not specific enough to support award of attorney fees); *see also* Metroplex Indus. v. Thompson Industries, Inc., 2002 WL 27295 (10th Cir. Jan. 10, 2002) (denying attorney fees; American rule requires contractual fee-shifting clause to be unambiguous); *In re* I-Mind Educ. Sys., Inc., 269 B.R. 47 (Bankr. N.D. Cal. 2001) (clause in commercial lease allowing attorney fees to prevailing party in any "suit or arbitration" did not entitle lessor to attorney fees for its motion to lift the automatic stay); Vill. 45 Partners, L.L.C. v. Racetrac Petroleum, Inc., 831 So. 2d 758 (Fla. Dist. Ct. App. 2002) (fee-shifting clause must be unambiguous and must clearly identify the matters to which it applies); Anest v. Audino, 773 N.E.2d 202 (Ill. App. Ct. 2002) (attorney fee provisions strictly construed, but when language is clear, no further inquiry needed; when contract referred to fees "incurred," creditor need not prove he paid bills, which were mailed to him in care of a corporation).

35 Gray v. Am. Express Co., 743 F.2d 10 (D.C. Cir. 1984); *In re* Cmty. Med. Ctr., 623 F.2d 864 (3d Cir. 1980); Benderson-Wainberg, Ltd. P'ship v. Atl. Toys, Inc., 228 F. Supp. 2d 584 (E.D. Pa. 2002) (commercial lease; "all costs charged to or incurred by lessor in the collection of any amounts owed pursuant to the lease" was ambiguous; attorney fees not included); Banca Della Svizzera Italiana v. Cohen, 756 F. Supp. 805 (S.D.N.Y. 1991); *In re* Stark, 242 B.R. 866 (Bankr. W.D.N.C. 1999) (when mortgage documents were ambiguous as to lender's right to charge inspection fee, they must be construed against lender); *In re* EWI, Inc. 208 B.R. 885 (Bankr. N.D. Ohio 1997) (denying fees; New York law allowed recovery of attorney fees only when provided for by "express language"; contract allowing "out of pocket expenses" is ambiguous at best and is construed against the drafter); *In re* Woodham, 174 B.R. 346 (Bankr. M.D. Fla. 1994) (attorney fee clauses in Florida contracts are narrowly construed; ambiguous clauses are to be construed against the drafter, especially in contracts of adhesion; when provision in mortgage was ambiguous on whether it covered bank's attorney fees in debtor's bankruptcy, fees denied); Pioneer Peat, Inc. v. Quality Grassing & Services, Inc., 653 N.W.2d 469 (Minn. Ct. App. 2002) (commercial contract; ambiguous provision allowing "any/all attorney fees and collection agency fees in amount of 25% or $500 whichever was applicable" construed against drafter; seller gets $500 after trial). *But see* Sholkoff v. Boca Raton Cmty. Hosp., 693 So. 2d 1114 (Fla. Dist. Ct. App. 1997) (rejecting rule of strict construction for attorney fee clauses, although these must be "unambiguous" and "clearly identify the matter in which fees are recoverable").

36 U.S. Fid. & Guar. Co. v. Baspetro Oil Services Co., 369 F.3d 34, 74–78 (2d Cir. 2004) (N.Y. law) (construing contractual clause allowing "legal costs" not to include attorney fees); Lockett v. Freedman, 2004 WL 856516 (N.D. Ill. Apr. 21, 2004) ("costs" does not include attorney fees; consumer stated a claim for FDCPA violation against attorney who demanded attorney fees for deficiency when deficiency provision in contract referred to costs but was silent as to attorney fees); Benderson-Wainberg, Ltd. P'ship v. Atl. Toys, Inc., 228 F. Supp. 2d 584 (E.D. Pa. 2002) ("all costs . . . incurred . . . in the collection of any amounts owed" did not include attorney fees); Linebarger v. Owenby, 83 S.W.3d 435 (Ark. Ct. App. 2002) (statutory provision for "costs" does not include attorney fees); Wendel v. Wendel, 852 So. 2d 277 (Fla. Dist. Ct. App. 2003) (words costs or expenses in marital settlement agreement do not include attorney fees, when other paragraphs specifically refer to attorney fees); Zosman v. Schiffer\Taxis, Inc., 697 So. 2d 1018 (Fla. Dist. Ct. App. 1997) (clause in contract providing for "all costs

entitled to fees for work that its attorney anticipates having to perform but has not yet performed, and to demand such fees may violate the Fair Debt Collection Practices Act (FDCPA).[37] Creditors may not be allowed to recover expenses of non-attorneys working for the collection attorney[38] or dunning activities by an attorney.[39]

---

actually incurred in collecting overdue accounts," did not provide for attorney fees); Arbor Station Homeowners' Services, Inc. v. Dorman, 567 S.E.2d 102 (Ga. Ct. App. 2002) (attorney fees not recoverable under provision allowing "costs of collection"); Negro Nest L.L.C. v. Mid-Northern Mgmt., Inc., 839 N.E.2d 1083 (Ill. App. Ct. 2005) (contract provision for "all collection costs incurred" does not allow recovery of attorney fees as cost shifting provisions narrowly construed and attorney fees allowed only if specified); *see also* Fontana v. TLD Builders, 840 N.E.2d 767 (Ill. App. Ct. 2005) (contract authorizing party to "retain an attorney to assist in the enforcement" and authorizing recovery from "the party at fault" of "any and all reasonable expenses related to enforcement" did not authorize the recovery of attorney fees); Cowardin v. Finnerty, 994 P.2d 335 (Wyo. 1999) (contractual provision for attorney fees must be explicit; clauses in purchase and sale agreement allowing non-defaulting party to "recover such damages as may be proper" and requiring return of earnest money "less costs incurred by sellers" if sale fell through, not specific enough to support award of attorney fees). *But see* Casey v. Cohan, 740 So. 2d 59 (Fla. Dist. Ct. App. 1999) (provision in promissory note for "costs of collection" including reasonable attorney fee was specific enough to cover lender's attorney fees in defending against borrower's unsuccessful counterclaim for rescission, because lender could collect only if rescission was denied).

37 Munoz v. Pipestone Fin., L.L.C., 513 F. Supp. 2d 1076 (D. Minn. 2007) (contingent fee agreement between creditor and collection firm not binding on debtor, who agreed in contract only to pay reasonable fees; creditor liable under FDCPA for seeking fees at outset of collection suit, before they had been incurred); Stolicker v. Muller, Muller, Richmond, Harms, Myers & Sgroi, 2005 WL 2180481 (W.D. Mich. Sept. 9, 2005) (when state law required a court to award attorney fees, pre-judgment claim for a percentage fee violated FDCPA); Meriweather v. Taylor, 2004 WL 1146495 (S.D. Ind. May 13, 2004) (when mortgage agreement provided for "foreclosure costs" and attorney fees "properly associated with the foreclosure proceeding" fees could not be charged for reinstatement prior to suit); Gostony v. Diem Corp., 320 F. Supp. 2d 932 (D. Ariz. 2003) (judicial proceeding was prerequisite for award under lease provision allowing "prevailing party" to recover attorney fees and collection costs; inclusion of fees in initial demand letter was unlawful); McDowall v. Leschack & Grodensky, Prof'l Corp., 279 F. Supp. 2d 197 (S.D.N.Y. 2003) (demand for attorney fees in dunning letter violated FDCPA; fees could be awarded only after court proceeding); *In re* WCS Enterprises, 381 B.R. 206 (Bankr. E.D. Va. 2007) (entire 10% attorney fee did not become due when matter referred to attorney; "an attorney's fee provision in a contract, even though measured as a percentage of the amount due, entitles the creditor only to reasonable fees based on the work performed"; debtor liable only for the $180 billed by attorney before petition date); Wiginton v. Pac. Credit Corp., 2 Haw. App. 435, 634 P.2d 111 (1981) (claim for $1000 by a collection agency as the "probable expense of legal process" was deceptive because it was not due when the dunning letter was sent); Cox v. Hagan, 100 S.E. 666, 673 (Va. 1919) (creditor is entitled to attorney fees only if services of an attorney are in fact employed, even though contract allowed "costs of collection, or 10% attorney's fee" in event of nonpayment); *cf.* Ahwatukee Custom Estates Mgmt. v. Bach, 973 P.2d 106 (Ariz. 1999) (fee-shifting statute allows creditor to recovery only for work of attorney or surrogates that reflect and depend on attorney's training and legal skill). *But cf.* Fields v. Wilber Law Firm, Prof'l Corp., 383 F.3d 562 (7th Cir. 2004) (inclusion of pre-suit attorney fees in dunning letter proper when credit contract allowed "any and all collection costs and attorney fees," but demand for lump sum without breaking out attorney fee amount was misleading); Gonzalez v. Codilis & Associates, 2004 WL 719264 (N.D. Ill. Mar. 31, 2004) (inclusion of attorney fees in pay-off amount for reinstatement of mortgage proper when fees authorized by contract and already incurred; distinguishing cases forbidding demand for future fees or those that can only be awarded by court); Whaley v. Shapiro & Kreisman, L.L.C., 2003 WL 22232911 (N.D. Ill. Sept. 16, 2003) (mortgage provided for reasonable attorney fees and costs; attorney fees may be included in pay-off amount when house sold before foreclosure completed, even though court had not approved them; distinguishing case of statutory attorney fees that must be awarded by court); James v. Olympus Servicing, Ltd. P'ship, 2003 WL 21011804 (N.D. Ill. May 4, 2003) (when fee shifting permitted by contract, and fees actually incurred, lender may claim them without court order; no UDAP or FDCPA claim for demanding fees); Hage v. Gen. Serv. Bureau, 306 F. Supp. 2d 883 (D. Neb. 2003) (Nebraska statute allows attorney fees in suits for $2000 or less for debts for necessaries if claimant establishes the claim and secures judgment; no statutory authorization for fees without a judgment, but court finds genuine issue of fact whether there is "a recognized and accepted uniform course of procedure" that allows attorney fees when consumers settle before judgment).

38 *See* Walton v. Franklin Collection Agency, Inc., 1999 WL 33537147 (N.D. Miss. May 5, 1999) (consumers stated FDCPA claim with allegation that collector demanded and obtained judgments for attorney fees when in fact most of the work was done by collector's non-lawyer employees, who prepared and filed complaints that retained attorney signed; no discussion of whether fee claim was based on statute or contract); *cf.* Blair v. Ing, 31 P.3d 184 (Haw. 2001) (attorney fees may include hours for law clerks' or paralegals' legal work, such as research and cite checking, but not their secretarial work, such as phone calls and document preparation); All Seasons Window & Door Mfg., Inc. v. Red Dot Constr., 181 S.W.3d 490 (Tex. App. 2005) (to recover for paralegals' and legal assistants' work, must show "substantive legal work" under supervision of attorney, hours worked, and hourly rate); N. Coast Elec. Co. v. Selig, 151 P.3d 211 (Wash. Ct. App. 2007) (fees recoverable for legal work by legal assistants working under supervision of lawyer but not for "purely clerical" secretarial services). *But see* Armada Bulk Carriers v. ConocoPhillips Co., 505 F. Supp. 2d 621 (N.D. Cal. 2007) ("all costs and expenses (including reasonable attorney fees)" was broad enough to include expert witness fees).

39 Wetherbee v. Kusterer, 41 Mich. 359, 360 (1879) ("the clause in the contract relative to costs and expenses does not apply to ordinary dunning"); Cox v. Hagan, 100 S.E. 666, 673 (Va. 1919) (creditor is entitled to attorney fees only if services of an attorney are in fact employed, even though contract allowed "costs of collection, or 10% attorney's fee" in event of nonpayment); *see also* Mechanics'-American Nat'l Bank v. Coleman, 204 F. 24 (8th Cir. 1913) (contractual attorney fees would not be awarded when the attorney only provided advice to the creditor, and there was no suit; note, however that the Eighth Circuit held, in *In re* Morris, 602 F.2d 826 (8th Cir. 1979)

Another question is whether attorney fees are available for an appeal or other post-judgment legal work. After a judgment is rendered, the cause of action on the contract may be considered to have merged with the judgment, so that the creditor can no longer avail itself of an attorney fee clause in the contract, but instead is limited to the post-judgment remedies, such as post-judgment interest, that are provided by statute.[40] However, a number of courts have awarded fees for appeals under a contract clause, usually without considering this theory.[41]

Some courts refuse to award fees when a creditor represents itself, either *pro se* or through in-house counsel, rather than hiring an outside attorney.[42] In a commercial case applying New York law, the court held that the fees sought for settlement negotiations and for defending the attorney fee petition were not recoverable under the terms of the note.[43] An advance award of fees to take into account possible difficulties in collecting the judgment is error when the contract makes the debtor liable for fees that are "paid or incurred" by the creditor.[44]

Questions may also arise as to the scope of an attorney fee clause.[45] For example, it may only apply to contract claims, not to tort claims.[46] If the clause specifies certain types of

---

that this decision wrongly relied on federal common law instead of Arkansas law); Myer v. Hart, 40 Mich. 517 (1879) (refusing to enforce such a clause for an attorney's expenses incurred prior to a power of sale foreclosure). *But see* Shapiro v. Riddle & Associates, Prof'l Corp., 351 F.3d 63 (2d Cir. 2003) (no FDCPA violation for attorney collector to demand $98 for collection letter when contract allowed the reasonable costs of collection); Monroe v. Staser, 6 Ind. App. 364, 33 N.E. 665 (1893) (requiring reimbursement for attorney's efforts short of suit); *cf.* Dole v. Wade, 510 S.W.2d 909 (Tenn. 1974) (assuming that fees for pre-suit work can be allowed when note provides for fees if placed in hands of attorney for collection, but rejecting claim for fees based on percentage of debt).

40 *See, e.g.*, Citizens Bank v. Landers, 570 S.W.2d 756, 765 (Mo. Ct. App. 1978) (bank's cause of action on note was merged with the judgment).

41 Butler-Rupp v. Lourdeaux, 65 Cal. Rptr. 3d 242 (Ct. App. 2007) (appellate attorney fees permitted by California law and contractual fee-shifting clause); First State Bank of St. Charles, Mo. v. Frankel, 86 S.W.3d 161 (Mo. Ct. App. 2002) (remanding to determine amount of attorney fees on appeal when contract provided for reasonable attorney fees incurred in enforcement); Bechtle v. Tandy Corp., 77 S.W.3d 689 (Mo. Ct. App. 2002) (commercial lease provision for attorney fees "incurred in enforcing this lease" required award of fees for post-trial motions and appeal); R.C. Hobbs Enterprises, L.L.C. v. J.G.L. Distrib., Inc., 104 P.3d 503 (Mont. 2004) (if contract provided for attorney fees, prevailing party entitled to appellate attorney fees if attorney fees awarded below); Prof'l Credit Collections v. Smith, 933 P.2d 307 (Okla. 1997) (consumer who prevailed on appeal is entitled to appellate fees under fee-shifting statute); Pannos v. Olson & Associates Constr., Inc., 123 P.3d 816 (Utah Ct. App. 2005) (real estate contract that provided for costs and reasonable attorney fees in "litigation to enforce this contract" included attorney fees on appeal); *cf.* LINC Fin. Corp. v. Onwuteaka, 129 F.3d 917 (7th Cir. 1997) (fee-shifting clause in commercial lease covering "all commercially reasonable costs and expenses incurred by [lessor] in enforcing [its] rights under this lease . . . including reasonable attorney's fees" enforced to allow costs and attorney fees at trial and on appeal).

42 Fed. Deposit Ins. Corp. v. Bender, 182 F.3d 1 (D.C. Cir. 1999) (fees not available for in-house counsels' service as liaison with Justice Department attorneys who actually tried case); *In re* Gebhard, 140 F. 571 (M.D. Pa. 1905); Lambert v. Byron, 650 So. 2d 1201 (La. Ct. App. 1995) (note provided for attorney fees only if "placed in the hands of" or "referred to" an attorney); Stream v. CBK Agronomics, 48 A.D.2d 637, 368 N.Y.S.2d 20 (1975); Thompson v. Chem. Bank, 84 Misc. 2d 721, 375 N.Y.S.2d 729 (Civ. Ct. 1975) (statute prohibiting all additional charges except "actual expenditures" for attorney fees did not allow attorney fee award to bank using in-house counsel). *But see* Main St. Bldg. P'ship v. Hernandez, 844 N.Y.S.2d 617 (Dist. Ct. 2007) (fee shifting proper when landlord, a general partnership, was represented by attorney-partner).

43 Banca Della Svizzera Italiana v. Cohen, 756 F. Supp. 805 (S.D.N.Y. 1991).

44 Agri Credit Corp. v. Liedman, 337 N.W.2d 384 (Minn. 1983) (court should consider time expended and difficulty of work as well as amount of debt); Naugatuck Sav. Bank v. Gross, 625 N.Y.S.2d 572 (App. Div. 1995) (should not include fees "for anticipated future services which may be performed in enforcing the judgment").

45 *See, e.g.*, Gibson v. Decatur Fed. Sav. & Loan Ass'n, 508 S.E.2d 788 (Ga. Ct. App. 1998) (standard fee-shifting clause in mortgage note allowed lender to shift fees only when it was protecting itself from actions over which it had no control, such as borrower's default or bankruptcy; no fee shifting in declaratory judgment action which resulted from lender's independent contractor's mistake in marking loan "paid in full" when it was not, but fees awarded pursuant to statute due to borrowers' vexatious and harassing conduct); Lamprecht v. Jordan, L.L.C., 75 P.3d 743 (Idaho 2003) (fee-shifting clause for disputes among members of limited liability company; no fees when former member sued company); Chapman v. Engel, 865 N.E.2d 330 (Ill. App. Ct. 2007) (when contract required fee shifting "in the event of default by seller or buyer," court's finding that neither party to failed real estate sale had breached contract meant fee-shifting clause was never triggered); Chase v. Bearpaw Ranch Ass'n, 133 P.3d 190 (Mont. 2006) (provision for fee shifting in action "for the enforcement of these covenants" broad enough to require fees in proceeding seeking attorney fees); Weter v. Archambault, 61 P.3d 771 (Mont. 2002) (fee-shifting clause in contract for deed broad enough to allow attorney fees to seller regardless of which remedy for default chosen); Kellam Associates, Inc. v. Angel Projects, L.L.C., 814 A.2d 642 (N.J. Super. Ct. App. Div. 2003) (clause allowed fees incurred to collect past-due rent or enforce other term breached by tenant; attorney fees allowed in dispute over construction of rent escalator clause); Jedon Corp. v. Indus. Paint Services, 811 N.Y.S.2d 195 (App. Div. 2006) (note incorporated security agreement which required fees if creditor seized collateral; no fee shifting when creditor simply sued on note); FLCT Loans, Ltd. P'ship v. Estate of Bracher, 93 S.W.3d 469 (Tex. App. 2002) (fee shifting if suit is filed to collect on a default; fees awarded in action against borrowers' executors, challenging certain transfers of estate funds).

46 *In re* Chen, 345 B.R. 197 (N.D. Cal. 2006) (narrow fee-shifting clause did not apply to "independent" fraud claims raised in nondischargeability proceeding; distinguishing cases of tort claims "closely associated" with contract); El Escorial Owners' Ass'n v. DLC Plastering, Inc., 65 Cal. Rptr. 3d 524 (Ct. App. 2007) (provision for attorney fees "in any action or proceeding

proceedings or remedies, a court may refuse to award fees when the creditor pursues a different type.[47] The clause may not apply when the debtor sues the creditor.[48] (Note, how-

brought to construe or enforce the terms of this subcontract" did not apply to tort claims); David v. Bosi Productions, Ltd., 2003 WL 769365 (Cal. Ct. App. Mar. 6, 2003) (no fee shifting on tort claim for fraud in the inducement, which alleges a duty separate from the contract; contract required fees to prevailing party in "legal proceedings . . . to enforce the terms hereof, or to declare rights hereunder, as the result of a breach of any covenant or condition of this agreement"); Walters v. Luloff, 176 P.3d 1034 (Mont. 2008) (fee-shifting clause in contract for deed did not authorize fees in non-contract action; here tort claim alleging misrepresentations by sellers); Ulloa v. QSP, Inc., 624 S.E.2d 43 (Va. 2006) (fee-shifting clause for "action relating to this agreement" applied to contract claim but not statutory trade secrets claim, which was independent of contract; remanding to give plaintiff opportunity to show "with specificity" which fees attributable to claim); N. Coast Elec. Co. v. Selig, 151 P.3d 211 (Wash. Ct. App. 2007) (provisions for fee shifting "if it becomes necessary to refer any account to an attorney" not applicable to tort counterclaims alleging that creditor had filed lien on wrong building; counterclaims were independent of contract and not a defense to contract liability); Norris v. Church & Co., 63 P.3d 153 (Wash. Ct. App. 2002) (contractual attorney fees not available when consumers sued builder for fraudulent concealment of defects, a tort, not breach of contract). *But see* Caufield v. Cantele, 837 So. 2d 371 (Fla. 2002) (fee-shifting clause for litigation "arising out of" contract broad enough to cover claim of fraud in the inducement); *cf.* Cruz v. Ayromloo, 66 Cal. Rptr. 3d 725 (Ct. App. 2007) (fee award proper in tort action by group of tenants, some with leases providing fee shifting in "any civil action in connection with the lease," others with no lease; provision broad enough to include tort claims, and "incidental" benefit to no-lease tenants did not require reduction, when issues were identical); Thompson v. Miller, 4 Cal. Rptr. 3d 905 (Ct. App. 2003) (buyer sued claiming fraud and elder abuse; whether contractual fee-shifting agreement applies in tort claim between parties depends on specific language of provision; "any dispute under this agreement" is sufficient; distinguishing case construing "action to enforce the contract or declare rights under it"); Filmland Dev., Inc. v. Turner Constr. Co., 2002 WL 31693595 (Cal. Ct. App. Dec. 3, 2002) ("any litigation between the parties hereto to enforce any right or obligation hereunder or with respect to the subject matter hereof" was broad enough to apply to professional negligence action by building owner against engineer); Morris v. Edmonds, 2002 WL 31631005 (Cal. Ct. App. Nov. 22, 2002) (clause in purchase agreement providing for fee shifting "in any action, proceeding or arbitration between [sellers] and [buyers] arising out of this agreement" was broad enough to apply to tort actions, here a dispute over removal of a monument); Erlenbush v. Largent, 819 N.E.2d 1186 (Ill. App. Ct. 2004) (consumer who sued in tort for fraud in the inducement was entitled to fees when real estate contract provided for attorney fees in "an action . . . with respect to this contract"); Stratakos v. Parcells, 915 A.2d 1022 (Md. Ct. Spec. App. 2007) (real estate contract provided fee shifting for "actions arising out of this contract"; fees properly awarded when buyers unsuccessfully sued sellers alleging misrepresentations in disclosure statement; claim would not exist in the absence of the contract); Sheppard v. East, 192 S.W.3d 518 (Mo. Ct. App. 2006) (attorney fee provisions for "litigation between the parties" applied to tort and contract claims by buyers against sellers); Ft. Knox Self-Storage, Inc. v. W. Technologies, Inc., 142 P.3d 1 (N.M. Ct. App. 2006) (fee shifting for "any action in connection with" contract covered negligence claim, even though contract not breached); Rigney v. McCabe, 842 N.Y.S.2d 34 (App. Div. 2007) (real estate contract allowed fees for action or proceeding "arising out of the contract"; fees properly awarded in fraud action alleging misrepresentations about flood risk); Robbins v. Capozzi, 100 S.W.3d 18 (Tex. App. 2002) (purchase agreement for condominium provided for attorney fees for "the prevailing party in any legal proceeding brought under or with respect to the transaction described in this contract"; fees awarded to seller after buyer unsuccessfully sued for UDAP violation and common law fraud, alleging misrepresentations by seller; misrepresentations and transaction "go hand in hand").

47 *See, e.g., In re* Hatala, 295 B.R. 62 (Bankr. D.N.J. 2003) (contract provision allowing for fees in foreclosure action did not cover fees incurred in bankruptcy case after foreclosure); Pici v. First Union Nat'l Bank of Fla., 705 So. 2d 50 (Fla. Dist. Ct. App. 1997) (attorney fee provisions are to be strictly construed; "If you hire an attorney to collect what I owe, I agree to pay our reasonable fees." did not authorize fees for a replevin action based on a non-monetary default). *But cf.* O'Malia v. Regency Builders, Inc., 662 N.W.2d 373 (Iowa Ct. App. 2003) (table) (text available at 2003 WL 289412) (when contract with fee-shifting provision also referred to warranties implied by law or specifically tendered by contractor, consumers entitled to attorney fees in action for breach of express and implied warranties), *aff'd*, 668 N.W.2d 568 (Iowa 2003); Harsch Properties, Inc. v. Nicholas, 932 A.2d 1045 (Vt. 2007) (fees properly awarded in action alleging breach of implied covenant of good faith and fair dealing when contract's fee-shifting clause applied to actions to enforce the "terms and conditions" of contract).

48 Kellogg Co. v. Sabhlok, 471 F.3d 629 (6th Cir. 2006) (employee separation agreement required attorney fees if "employee files charges"; no fee shifting when employee filed counterclaim in employer's declaratory judgment action); Vill. 45 Partners, L.L.C. v. Racetrac Petroleum, Inc., 831 So. 2d 758 (Fla. Dist. Ct. App. 2002) (fee-shifting clause must identify matters to which it applies; no attorney fees when contract specified "in case of any violation or attempted violation" and buyer sought declaratory judgment on question whether its proposed use of property was lawful); Hamilton v. Hopkins, 834 So. 2d 695 (Miss. 2003) (real estate contract provided attorney fees if buyer initiated litigation; no fee shifting when seller sued); Adams v. Wash. Group, L.L.C., 2008 WL 809085 (N.Y. App. Div. Mar. 25, 2008) (lease provision for fees for tenant's default "in connection . . . with its performance of tenant's obligations under the lease" did not authorize fees when landlord successfully defended against claim of breach of implied covenant of good faith and fair dealing); Dupuis v. 424 E. 77th Owners' Corp., 821 N.Y.S.2d 173 (App. Div. 2006) (lease provided for fee shifting in case of lessee's default; no fees when co-op member sued board alleging failure to abate nuisance); Conley v. KCA Fin. Services, Inc., 931 P.2d 808 (Or. Ct. App. 1997) (attorney fee clause in consumer contract which imposed fees "if we start a collection action" did not entitle collector to attorney fees when debtors sued it for improper collection practices, and their action was dismissed for failure to state a claim); *see also* Madden v. Alaska Mortgage Group, 54 P.3d 265 (Alaska 2002) (provision in deed of trust for "costs, fees and expenses of the trustee" did not entitle beneficiary to attorney fees in action to determine amount owed); Greenway, Inc. v. Lynn, 2004 WL 1635881 (Ky. Ct. App. July 23, 2004) (interpreting attorney fee clause not to allow fees to party who prevailed on counterclaim rather than on complaint); *cf.* Rand v.

ever, that some states have reciprocal fee statutes that apply one-way attorney fee clauses equally to both parties.[49]) The exact language of the clause will be critical in making these distinctions.

Some courts have held that a contractual provision allowing "attorney fees and costs" must be construed to be consistent with a state statute that specifies what court costs the losing party must bear.[50] Thus, such clauses can not shift costs such as expert witness fees and mailing, faxing, and photocopying expenses which the statute does not require the losing party to pay.

6.3 State Statutes Allowing Recovery of Attorney Fees Regardless of Contract Terms

A few states permit recovery of collection attorney fees in certain circumstances even when such fees are not authorized by the consumer credit contract. Because statutes allowing attorney fees are in derogation of the common law rule, courts may construe them strictly.[51]

A few states allow an attorney fee award in a suit on an "account stated" or "open account," often specifically providing that this rule applies only when the creditor sends a pre-suit demand.[52] The creditor may lose its right to fees

Porsche Fin. Services, 167 P.3d 111 (Ariz. Ct. App. 2007) (automobile lease provided attorney fees if lessor hires lawyer "to collect what you owe"; fees properly awarded on lessor's counterclaim for deficiency in lessee's tort and civil rights action alleging repossession misconduct). *But see In re* Patchell, 344 B.R. 8 (Bankr. D. Mass. 2006) (mortgage provided fees for "enforcing the note"; when adversary proceeding put validity of note and mortgage in question, defending it was necessary to enforcement, so fees properly awarded); Coe v. Crady Davis Corp., 60 P.3d 794 (Colo. Ct. App. 2002) (fee-shifting clause in real estate purchase agreement for "any . . . litigation arising out of this contract" required award of fees to seller who defended against buyer's claim for reduced price on grounds that property was smaller than described); Sholkoff v. Boca Raton Cmty. Hosp., 693 So. 2d 1114 (Fla. Dist. Ct. App. 1997) (patient who voluntarily dismissed lawsuit challenging amount of hospital bill liable for attorney fees; contract provided for fee shifting "in the event it is necessary to refer this account to . . . an attorney"). *But cf.* Leamon v. Krajkiewcz, 132 Cal. Rptr. 2d 362 (Ct. App. 2003) (provision denying fees to party who sues without first seeking mediation applied to buyer who had contract declared voidable on grounds of duress).

49 *See* § 14.1, *infra*; National Consumer Law Center, Consumer Warranty Law § 13.9 (3d ed. 2006 and Supp.).

50 First Nationwide Bank v. Mountain Cascade, Inc., 92 Cal. Rptr. 2d 145 (Ct. App. 2000) (expert witness fees may not be awarded pursuant to attorney fee clause in contract); Ripley v. Pappadopoulos, 28 Cal. Rptr. 2d 878 (Ct. App. 1994) ("reasonable attorney fees and costs" do not include expert witness fees, mailing, faxing or copying expenses); *cf.* Ahwatukee Custom Estates Mgmt. v. Bach, 973 P.2d 106 (Ariz. 1999) (construing fee-shifting statute to allow award only of attorney fees and taxable costs, not other litigation expenses). *But see* Monsanto Co. v. David, 516 F.3d 1009 (Fed. Cir. 2008) (parties free to contract for fees in excess of what court could award under federal statute); Chase v. Scott, 38 P.3d 1001 (Utah Ct. App. 2001) (when contract included provision for costs and attorney fees, costs not limited to those available under court rules; contractual provision for costs would be superfluous if it allowed only those costs already available by court rule).

51 Negro Nest L.L.C. v. Mid-Northern Mgmt., Inc., 839 N.E.2d 1083, 1085, 1090 (Ill. App. Ct. 2005); Savant Ins. Services, Inc. v. Cent. Oil & Supply Corp., 821 So. 2d 623 (La. Ct. App. 2002) (statute allowing attorney fees for open account is penal and must be strictly construed); Jefferson Door Co. v. Lewis, 713 So. 2d 835 (La. Ct. App. 1998) (because award of attorney fees is "exceptional and penal," statute allowing attorney fees for open account must be strictly construed); Heritage Worldwide, Inc. v. Jimmy Swaggart Ministries, 665 So. 2d 523 (La. Ct. App. 1995) (strictly construing statute that allowed attorney fees in suit on an open account after demand that "correctly set[s] forth the amount owed"; denying fee shifting when demand included a sum which was not owed).

52 *ARKANSAS*: Ark. Code Ann. § 16-22-308 (prevailing party is entitled to fees in any civil action to recover on, *inter alia,* an open account, statement of account, or account stated).

CALIFORNIA: Cal. Civ. Code § 1811.1 (West) (requiring award of reasonable attorney fees to prevailing party in any action on a contract or installment account, whether instituted by the seller, holder, or buyer).

IDAHO: Idaho Code Ann. § 12-120(3) (prevailing party entitled to attorney fees in any civil action to recover on an open account, account stated, note, bill, negotiable instrument, guaranty, or contract relating to sale of goods or services and in any commercial transaction unless otherwise prohibited by law); *cf.* Bingham Mem'l Hosp. v. Boyd, 8 P.3d 664 (Idaho Ct. App. 2000) (reversing award of attorney fees because hospital won judgment on *quantum meruit* rather than on open account).

LOUISIANA: La. Rev. Stat. Ann. § 9:2781(A) (allowing fees when debtor fails to pay open account within thirty days after claimant sends written demand correctly setting forth amount owed; if claimant and its attorney have agreed on fixed or determinable amount of attorney fees, the claimant is entitled to that amount); *see, e.g.*, Gold, Weems, Bruser, Sues & Rundell v. Metal Sales Mfg. Corp., 236 F.3d 214 (5th Cir. 2000) (La. law) (attorney fees allowed for appeals and for representation by lawyer-employees under state open account statute); *In re* Troth Corp. v. Deutsch, Kerrigan & Stiles, L.L.P., 951 So. 2d 1162 (La. Ct. App. 2007) (when amount owed correctly stated and supported by invoices, creditor entitled to fees; amount discretionary with court; criteria include liable party's ability to pay); Indus. Screw & Supply Co. v. WPS, Inc., 926 So. 2d 134 (La. Ct. App. 2006) (when amount due was correctly stated in petition, though not in original demand letter, and not timely paid, attorney fees properly awarded for open account); Wright & Moreno L.L.C. v. Clement, 891 So. 2d 704 (La. Ct. App. 2004) (Louisiana allows attorney fees for account stated thirty days after demand or fifteen days after filing petition, before which debtor may pay without incurring fees); Paddison Builders, Inc. v. Newpark Square One Condo. Ass'n, 848 So. 2d 750 (La. Ct. App. 2003) (contract for single project not open account; Louisiana requires "running or current" dealings or expectation of future work); Acadian Services, Inc. v. Durand, 813 So. 2d 1142 (La. Ct. App. 2002) (allowing $2000 collection attorney fees for obtaining judgment and $500 for appeal based on time and effort; transactions were open account when demolition contractor performed two jobs for home owner, sent

altogether if its demand for payment of the open account includes any charges that are not in fact owed.[53] In addition, some states have statutorily overruled the American rule on attorney fees by generally permitting courts to award attorney fees to prevailing parties in civil suits generally or in contract actions.[54] Some states also have statutes or court

invoices but did not expect immediate payment, and anticipated further work on the same ongoing project); Hayes v. Taylor, 812 So. 2d 874 (La. Ct. App. 2002) ($1000 collection attorney fee for a default judgment on an open account); Sears, Roebuck & Co. v. Richardson, 759 So. 2d 190 (La. Ct. App. 2000) (credit card account was open account, so 25% attorney fees allowed); Jefferson Door Co. v. Lewis, 713 So. 2d 835 (La. Ct. App. 1998) (seller's compliance was adequate when seller sent demand by certified mail to address given in credit application; 18% service charge, which is allowed only for "commercial," that is, non-consumer, transactions was permissible when consumer did not inform seller, a wholesaler, that building products were to be used for consumer's residence); Salley v. Colonial Marine Indus., 680 So. 2d 1242 (La. Ct. App. 1996) (under Louisiana's open account statute, a seller to whom the court awarded the invoiced amount, and who had complied with all requirements of the statute, must be awarded attorney fees); Broussard v. Guilbeaux, 640 So. 2d 509 (La. Ct. App. 1994); Irwin Brown Co. v. Morton's Auction Exch., 446 So. 2d 403 (La. Ct. App. 1984) (Louisiana statute authorizes award of reasonable attorney fees for collection of a claim on open account provided the claimant furnished a written demand correctly stating the amount owed and a copy of the invoices).

MISSISSIPPI: Miss. Code Ann. § 11-53-81 (person who fails to pay open account within thirty days of written demand setting forth correct amount with an itemized statement is liable for reasonable attorney fees; alleged debtor who prevails is also entitled to fees); *see, e.g.*, Franklin Collection Serv., Inc. v. Stewart, 863 So. 2d 925 (Miss. 2003) (medical bill was open account for which statute allowed attorney fee; one-third contingent fee presumptively reasonable); Par Indus. v. Target Container Co., 708 So. 2d 44 (Miss. 1998) (attorney fees available on an open account must be reasonable; one-third of the amount of a non-consumer debt was reasonable).

NEW MEXICO: N.M. Stat. § 39-2-2.1 (allowing reasonable attorney fee to prevailing party in any civil action in district court, small claims court, or magistrate court on open account).

OKLAHOMA: Okla. Stat. tit. 12, § 936 (allowing reasonable attorney fee to prevailing party in civil action to recover on open account, statement of account, account stated, note, bill, negotiable instrument, or contract relating to purchase or sale of goods or services); *see* Prof'l Credit Collections v. Smith, 933 P.2d 307 (Okla. 1997) (consumer was prevailing party entitled to fees when creditor dismissed collection action after consumer won motion to vacate default judgment).

TEXAS: Tex. Civ. Prac. & Rem. Code Ann. § 38.001 (Vernon) (allowing recovery of attorney fees for valid claim for, *inter alia*, rendered services, performed labor, furnished materials, a sworn account, or any oral or written contract); *see, e.g.*, Williams v. Unifund Partners, 2008 WL 339855 (Tex. App. Feb. 7, 2008) (action on "sworn account" will lie only for sales of personal property, not "special contracts," here a bank credit card, when no personal property passed from bank to consumer); Pennwell Corp. v. Ken Associates, Inc., 123 S.W.3d 756 (Tex. App. 2003) (elements of account stated are goods or services provided, price is either agreed upon or "usual, customary and reasonable," and account unpaid); Elhamed v. Quality Oil Trucking Serv., Inc., 2003 WL 22211543 (Tex. App. Sept. 25, 2003) (open account; burden on creditor to show reasonable charges; sufficient if it charged same amount to others for same services and materials at same time and place); Andrews v. E. Tex. Med. Ctr., 885 S.W.2d 264 (Tex. App. 1994) (open account shown when hospital provided itemized bill and testimony that charges were customary).

53 Dixie Produce & Packaging, L.L.C., 368 B.R. 533 (Bankr. E.D. La. 2007) (attorney fees under open account statute only if demand "strictly and exactly" states amount due; denying fee shifting when seller demanded interest to which it was not entitled); Salley & Salley v. Stoll, 864 So. 2d 698 (La. Ct. App. 2003) (account stated shown, but attorney fees denied, when statute required demand for correct amount and creditor demanded late charges and interest not provided for in contract); Heck v. LaFourche Parish Council, 860 So. 2d 595 (La. Ct. App. 2003) (open account shown when contract called for services over a period of time, and provided formula for calculating price, but attorney fees denied because invoice and demand letter included work done in another parish); Contractors' Supply v. Caldarera & Co., 734 So. 2d 755 (La. Ct. App. 1999) (no attorney fees pursuant to open account statute when amount specified in demand letter was not correct, and there was some further question whether there ever was a meeting of the minds sufficient to establish an open account); Heritage Worldwide, Inc. v. Jimmy Swaggart Ministries, 665 So. 2d 523 (La. Ct. App. 1995) (strictly construing statute that allowed attorney fees in suit on an open account when prior demand had been made "correctly setting forth the amount owed"; denying fee shifting when demand included a sum which was not owed); Wayne v. A.V.A. Vending, Inc., 52 S.W.3d 412 (Tex. App. 2001) (unreasonable demand may bar statutory or contractual attorney fees and pre-judgment interest; "if the claiming party makes an unreasonable demand, the other party should not be forced to pay the demand or else risk suffering the opposing party's attorney's fees"); Pennington v. Gurkoff, 899 S.W.2d 767 (Tex. App. 1995) (statute which allowed award of attorney fees in action on contract did not justify fees when creditor made excessive demand of more than twice the actual recovery); *see also* Savant Ins. Services, Inc. v. Cent. Oil & Supply Corp., 821 So. 2d 623 (La. Ct. App. 2002) (no attorney fees permitted when creditor demanded more than court found to be due). *But cf.* S. Nights, Inc. v. Barnett, 881 So. 2d 1225 (La. Ct. App. 2004) (attorney fees properly awarded for open account, even though judgment was for $1400 less than creditor demanded); Guidry's Seafood Distributors, Inc. v. Farmers Seafood Co., 759 So. 2d 806 (La. Ct. App. 1999) (attorney fees properly awarded in default judgment on open account even though amount awarded not same as amount demanded when changes made to reflect payments made in the meantime, and amount was correct at various stages of the proceedings); Hernandez v. Lautensack, 201 S.W.3d 771 (Tex. App. 2006) (merely requesting more than jury determines is due is insufficient to deny fees, unless demand was made in bad faith).

54 These statutes include:

ALASKA: Alaska Stat. § 09.60.010 (authorizing court fee-shifting rules in certain civil actions); Alaska R. Civ. P. 82 (prevailing party in civil action entitled to attorney fee award except as otherwise provided by law or agreed by the parties; setting fee schedule); *see* Alaska Constr. & Eng'g, Inc. v. Balzer, 130 P.3d 932 (Alaska 2006) (Alaska R. Civ. P. 79 and 82 authorize prevailing party fees in civil actions; commercial lessor who prevailed on claim and all but one counterclaim was prevailing party).

ARIZONA: Ariz. Rev. Stat. Ann. § 12-341.04 (court may award attorney fees in any contested action arising out of contract); *see* Ahwatukee Custom Estates Mgmt. v. Bach, 973 P.2d 106 (Ariz. 1999) (construing fee-shifting statute to allow award only of attorney fees and taxable costs, not other litigation expenses); Hanley v. Pearson, 61 P.3d 29 (Ariz. Ct. App. 2003) (statute allowing fee shifting in contract case does not apply when contract is "factual predicate" but not "essential basis" of claim; no fee shifting in dispute between foreclosure purchaser and junior lien-holder over payment of real estate taxes); Robert E. Mann Constr. Co. v. Liebert Corp., 60 P.3d 708 (Ariz. Ct. App. 2003) (Arizona statute allowing fee shifting in contract case applies only in suit to enforce duty that would not exist but for contract; no fee shifting in common law product liability action); Pelletier v. Johnson, 937 P.2d 668 (Ariz. Ct. App. 1996) (statute allows fees for contested contract actions; allowing fees when vinyl siding seller prevailed in *quantum meruit*, after its contract was held invalid for failure to comply with door-to-door sales law).

ARKANSAS: Ark. Code Ann. § 16-22-308 (prevailing party is entitled to fees in any civil action to recover on an open account, statement of account, account stated, promissory note, bill, negotiable instrument, or contract relating to the purchase or sale of goods, wares, or merchandise, or for labor or services, or breach of contract, unless otherwise provided by law or the contract); *see* Curry v. Thornsberry, 128 S.W.3d 438 (Ark. 2003) (Arkansas law provides fee shifting in contract actions; attorney fees properly awarded against consumers who unsuccessfully sued builder for breach of implied warranty of habitability); Millwood-RAB Mktg., Inc. v. Blackburn, 236 S.W.3d 551 (Ark. Ct. App. 2006) (Ark. Code Ann. § 16-22-308 allows prevailing party attorney fees in civil action; whether to award fees, and amount, discretionary with court).

CALIFORNIA: Cal. Civ. Code § 1811.1 (West) (requiring award of reasonable attorney fees to prevailing party in any action on a contract or installment account, whether instituted by the seller, holder, or buyer).

HAWAII: Haw. Rev. Stat. § 607-14 (requiring attorney fees, capped at 25%, to be taxed as costs to losing party in actions in the nature of *assumpsit* and in all actions on a promissory note or other contract in writing that provides for attorney fees); *see* Blair v. Ing, 31 P.3d 184 (Haw. 2001) (Haw. Rev. Stat. § 607-14 allows fee shifting in contract cases; maximum of 25% of the judgment or of the amount sought).

IDAHO: Idaho Code Ann. § 12-120(3) (prevailing party entitled to attorney fees in any civil action to recover on an open account, account stated, note, bill, negotiable instrument, guaranty, or contract relating to sale of goods or services, and in any commercial transaction unless otherwise prohibited by law); *see* Champion Produce, Inc. v. Ruby Robinson Co., 342 F.3d 1016 (9th Cir. 2003) (fees may be awarded to prevailing party in contract action under Idaho Code Ann. § 12-120(3), but here neither party prevailed); Haight v. Dale's Used Cars, Inc., 87 P.3d 962 (Idaho Ct. App. 2003) (Idaho statute provides fee shifting in action to recover on contract for sale of goods; consumer who unsuccessfully sued to revoke acceptance of vehicle was liable for attorney fees at trial and on appeal).

At least some portions of the statute are limited to non-consumer transactions. *See* Bajrektarevic v. Lighthouse Home Loans, Inc., 155 P.3d 691 (Idaho 2007) (fee-shifting statute covering "any commercial transaction," defined as any transaction except one "for personal or household purposes," did not authorize attorney fees in borrower's action for breach of lock-in agreement in refinance of home loan); Karterman v. Jameson, 980 P.2d 574 (Idaho Ct. App. 1999) (Idaho statute allowed attorney fees in case involving commercial transactions, defined as all transactions except for personal or household purposes; no attorney fees under this provision in case arising from sale of personal residential property).

NEBRASKA: Neb. Rev. Stat. § 25-1801 (creditor prevailing on claim for $2000 or less for, *inter alia,* services rendered, labor performed, material furnished, or necessaries of life is entitled to recover attorney fees, subject to cap); *see* Hage v. Gen. Serv. Bureau, 2002 WL 1796575 (D. Neb. Aug. 5, 2002) (Nebraska statute allows costs and attorney fees if contract is for services or necessities, but consumers stated claim for UDAP violation when collection letter demanded costs and attorney fees in absence of judgment).

OKLAHOMA: Okla. Stat. tit. 12, § 936 (allowing reasonable attorney fee to prevailing party in civil action to recover on open account, statement of account, account stated, note, bill, negotiable instrument, or contract relating to purchase or sale of goods or services); *see* C. & L. Enterprises v. Citizen Band Potawatomi Tribe of Okla., 72 P.3d 1 (Okla. 2002) (Oklahoma statute allowing attorney fees in action on contract for labor or services applies only if labor or services provided; no fee shifting when contract was repudiated before contractor started work); Usrey v. Wilson, 66 P.2d 1000 (Okla. Civ. App. 2002) (Oklahoma statute allowing fee shifting in "civil action to recover for labor or services rendered or . . . relating to the purchase or sale of goods" applied in negligence action against contractor who built allegedly defective wall; contract related to the sale of goods because contractor furnished the stone); Meredith v. Smith, 35 P.3d 1002 (Okla. Civ. App. 2001) (Oklahoma statute allows fee shifting in suit for compensation for personal services; capped at 10% of judgment in uncontested small claims court case; cap did not apply when case contested); *see also* Robey v. Shapiro, Marianos & Cejada, L.L.C., 434 F.3d 1208 (10th Cir. 2006) (Okla. Stat. tit. 42, § 176 permits prevailing mortgagee to recover reasonable attorney in mortgage foreclosure action).

RHODE ISLAND: R.I. Gen. Stat. § 9-1-45 (attorney fees may be awarded in contract action for default judgment or in "a complete absence of a justiciable issue of either fact or law raised by the losing party").

TEXAS: Tex. Civ. Prac. & Rem. Code Ann. § 38.001 (Vernon) (allowing recovery of attorney fees for valid claim for, *inter alia*, rendered services, performed labor, furnished materials, a sworn account, or any oral or written contract); *see* DP Solutions, Inc. v. Rollins, 353 F.3d 421 (5th Cir. 2003) (Tex. law) (award of attorney fees mandatory to party who prevails in contract action; amount discretionary with trial judge); Scherer v. Angell, 2007 WL 4224383 (Tex. App. Nov. 30, 2007) (prevailing party that lost on contract claim and won on liability only, without damages, on promissory estoppel claim can not recover fees under fee shifting statute applicable to oral and written contracts); Charette v. Fitzgerald, 213 S.W.3d 505 (Tex. App. 2006) (comparing various provisions of Texas law allowing attorney fees; for open account, court may take judicial notice of customary and usual fees; for violation of property code, reasonableness must be shown); Time Out Grocery v. The Vanguard Group, 187 S.W.3d 41 (Tex. App. 2005) (plaintiff store sought attorney fees, pursuant to Texas statute allowing fees in contract action, against check writer who stopped payment; payee was third party who cashed check in plaintiff store; fees denied because no contract between store and check writer); Marker v. Garcia, 185 S.W.3d 21 (Tex. App. 2005) (Texas statute allowing attorney fees in action on contract for deed allows fees only for purchaser); G.R.A.V.I.T.Y. Enterprises, Inc. v. Reese Supply Co., 177 S.W.3d 537 (Tex. App.

rules allowing attorney fee awards for particular types of actions such as enforcement of liens.[55]

6.4 Is the Creditor the Prevailing Party?

Whether allowed by statute or by contract, attorney fees are generally available only to the prevailing party.[56] Voluntary dismissal of a collection action may bar the collector from recovering the costs associated with that action,[57] and in fact a collector who dismisses the action may be liable for fees.[58]

Further, the collector may not be considered the prevailing party if it receives substantially less relief than it sought.[59] Simply demanding an excessive amount before

2005) (fees available to party who prevails and recovers damages; no fees for party who successfully defends against contract claim); Cordova v. S. Bell Yellow Pages, Inc., 148 S.W.3d 441 (Tex. App. 2004) (Texas statute allows prevailing party attorney fees in certain contract actions; when claims are "interrelated," here collection of commercial debt and various counterclaims arising from same facts, fees may be awarded on all claims); Burnside Air Conditioning & Heating, Inc. v. T.S. Young Corp., 113 S.W.3d 889 (Tex. App. 2003) (Texas allows attorney fees to prevailing party in contract action); Mobil Producing Tex. & N.M., Inc. v. Cantor, 93 S.W.3d 916 (Tex. App. 2002) (Texas law provides for attorney fees and prejudgment interest in contract actions, but denied when plaintiff prevailed on unjust enrichment, not contract, claim); Wallace v. Ramon, 82 S.W.3d 501 (Tex. App. 2002) (attorney fees allowed in breach of contract action, if proper demand made and debtor does not pay with thirty days).

55 *See, e.g.*, Solution Source, Inc. v. LPR Associates Ltd. P'ship, 652 N.W.2d 474 (Mich. Ct. App. 2002) (detailed discussion of attorney fee provisions of construction lien statute); Stewart Title Guar. Title Co. v. Lewis, 788 A.2d 941 (N.J. Super. Ct. App. Div. 2001) (New Jersey court rules permit a small collection attorney fee in mortgage foreclosure cases, for example, 1% of debts exceeding $7500, and provide for downward, but not upward, adjustment).

56 *See In re* Hoopai, 369 B.R. 506 (B.A.P. 9th Cir. 2007) (creditor who unsuccessfully argued that foreclosure sale extinguished debtor's private sale of home was not prevailing party despite recovering debt from debtor's sale of home); *In re* Parker, 269 B.R. 522 (D. Vt. 2001) (landlord did not prevail); Fulton Homes Corp. v. BPP Concrete, 155 P.3d 1090 (Ariz. Ct. App. 2007) (affirming award of fees under statute allowing fees to "successful party" in contract action; party was successful when opponent stipulated to dismissal of its claim); Scherer v. Angell, 2007 WL 4224383 (Tex. App. Nov. 30, 2007) (award of statutory attorney fees in contract action requires showing of damages; fee shifting was error when jury awarded no damages on contract count, in case alleging tort and contract claims); Chang v. Soldier Summit Dev., 82 P.3d 203 (Utah Ct. App. 2003) (prevailing party is one who prevails on major issues and most expensive aspects); *see also* Gostony v. Diem Corp., 320 F. Supp. 2d 932 (D. Ariz. 2003) (judicial proceeding was prerequisite for award under lease provision allowing "prevailing party" to recover attorney fees and collection costs; inclusion of fees in initial demand letter was unlawful). *But see* Trull v. Cent. Carolina Bank & Trust, 478 S.E.2d 39 (N.C. Ct. App. 1996) (adopting strained interpretation of statute to allow contractual fees even if creditor does not prevail; failing to give weight to statutory provision allowing fees only if the debt "be *collected* by or through an attorney"), *aff'd*, 490 S.E.2d 238 (N.C. 1997) (table).

57 Pope v. Man-Data, Inc., 209 F.3d 1161 (9th Cir. 2000) (collection agency sued in small claims court, but failed to pursue action and was defaulted; when debtor made partial payment, collector deducted the amount of its filing fee, etcetera, in the small claims action; because collector was not a prevailing party, it was not permitted to charge debtor for costs).

58 Morris v. Edmonds, 2002 WL 31631005 (Cal. Ct. App. Nov. 22, 2002) (allowing contractual attorney fees against parties who voluntarily dismissed; California statute would forbid this result in contract action, but here fee-shifting clause applied in tort case arising from land sale); Trugreen Landcare, L.L.C. v. Elm City Dev. & Constr. Services, Inc., 919 A.2d 1077 (Conn. App. Ct. 2007) (landlord whose eviction action was non-suited is liable for tenant's attorney fees under contract clause requiring "nonprevailing party" to pay fees); Landry v. Countrywide Home Loans, Inc. 731 So. 2d 137 (Fla. Dist. Ct. App. 1999) (when lender initiated and then voluntarily terminated foreclosure proceeding, home owners were prevailing party entitled to attorney fees); Bardon Trimount, Inc. v. Guyott, 49 Mass. App. Ct. 764, 732 N.E.2d 916 (2000) (defendant who won dismissal on procedural grounds is prevailing party); Prof'l Credit Collections v. Smith, 933 P.2d 307 (Okla. 1997) (consumer was prevailing party entitled to fees when creditor dismissed collection action after consumer won motion to vacate default judgment). *But see* Kraffert v. Shea Homes, 2002 WL 44262 (Cal. Ct. App. Jan. 14, 2002) (consumer sued seller of home for UDAP and fraud, but voluntarily dismissed before seller answered; no attorney fees for seller under provision allowing fees to "the party in whose favor the award or final judgment shall be entered"); Nat'l Check Bureau v. Patel, 2005 WL 3454694 (Ohio Ct. App. Dec. 15, 2005) (consumer not entitled to attorney fees as sanctions against assignee of credit card debt who voluntarily dismissed; no evidence that assignee was acting in bad faith when it asserted written card agreement would be produced and assignee dismissed when it failed to find one); Wachovia SBA Lending v. Kraft, 158 P.3d 1271 (Wash. Ct. App. 2007) (for Washington's reciprocal fees statute, prevailing party is one in whose favor "final judgment" is entered; when lender voluntarily dismissed after losing summary judgment motion, no final judgment and no reciprocal fees), *review granted*, 2008 Wash. LEXIS 292 (Wash. Apr. 1, 2008).

59 *See* Bowen Inv., Inc. v. Carneiro Donuts, Inc., 490 F.3d 27 (1st Cir. 2007) (denying fee shifting when franchisor who demanded $120,000 got $12,000 on one claim and $1 on another); Tannenbaum v. Petrokowitz, 2003 WL 327475 (Cal. Ct. App. Feb. 13, 2003) (borrower was prevailing party when he "substantially achieved litigation objectives" by stopping foreclosure and significantly reducing amount due); Fielder v. Weinstein Design Group, Inc., 842 So. 2d 879 (Fla. Dist. Ct. App. 2003) (buyer who lost on counterclaims was nonetheless prevailing party, when seller who demanded $25,000 was required to pay buyer $5600 and accept return of goods); Trilogy Network Sys., Inc. v. Johnson, 172 P.3d 1119 (Idaho 2007) (denying statutory fee shifting; when plaintiff proved liability but failed to prove damages, no one prevailed); Flamingo Pools, Spas, Sunrooms & More Store v. Penrod, 993 S.W.2d 588 (Mo. Ct. App. 1999) (when seller was awarded barely one-third of the amount it

suit may preclude a fee award altogether. As one court has reasoned, "if the claiming party makes an unreasonable demand, the other party should not be forced to pay the demand or else risk suffering the opposing party's attorney's fees."[60]

In addition, the creditor may not be the prevailing party when there are several claims and counterclaims and the debtor prevails on some of them.[61] In the alternative, if the

demanded and amount due was key issue, seller did not prevail and was not entitled to fees); Fletcher Hill, Inc. v. Crosbie, 872 A.2d 292 (Vt. 2005) (mobile home installer could not recover fees pursuant to contract it had breached; no statutory fees because neither party clearly prevailed); *see also* Eckhardt v. 424 Hitnze Mgmt., L.L.C., 969 So. 2d 1219 (Fla. Dist. Ct. App. 2007) (fees should be substantially reduced for limited success; landlord demanded $17,000, awarded only $4250 because of failure to mitigate); McClain v. Papka, 108 S.W.3d 48 (Mo. Ct. App. 2003) (no abuse of discretion to reduce fees from $18,000 to $1000 because buyers prevailed on only one of three claims and received about one-third of recovery sought); *cf.* McCarthy Bros. Co. v. Tilbury Constr., Inc., 849 So. 2d 7 (Fla. Dist. Ct. App. 2003) (fee-shifting clause defined prevailing party as one who recovered at least 75% of sum demanded or was required to pay not more than 25% of that amount); Powers v. Rockford Stop'n'Go, Inc., 761 N.E.2d 237 (Ill. App. Ct. 2001) (party may prevail even if it receives less than amount claimed, but reversing fee award when result was "essentially a draw"); Kellam Associates, Inc. v. Angel Projects, L.L.C., 814 A.2d 642 (N.J. Super. Ct. App. Div. 2003) (landlord who got 75% of amount requested in dispute over construction of rent escalator clause was prevailing party; amount of fee should be adjusted to reflect partial success). *But see* King v. Brock, 646 S.E.2d 206 (Ga. 2007) (recovery of nominal damages sufficient to confer prevailing party status pursuant to contractual fee shifting clause); Allco Enterprises, Inc. v. Goldstein Family Living Trust, 51 P.3d 1275 (Or. Ct. App. 2002) (equipment lessor was prevailing party even though it received only half of amount claimed); Crowley v. Black, 167 P.3d 1087 (Utah Ct. App. 2007) (landlord's recovery of less than amount claimed not significant victory for tenant; landlord recovered something on all claims, and tenant consistently denied all liability).

60 Wayne v. A.V.A. Vending, Inc., 52 S.W.3d 412, 418 (Tex. App. 2001) (unreasonable demand may bar statutory or contractual attorney fees); *see also* § 6.2.4, *supra* (demanding charges not owed as part of open account may preclude statutory fee award to creditor).

61 *See* Alaska Constr. & Eng'g, Inc. v. Balzer, 130 P.3d 932 (Alaska 2006) (commercial lessor who prevailed on claim and all but one counterclaim was prevailing party; party who wins on "main issue" prevails; usually, as here, party who receives larger monetary award, but may be party who defeats potentially costly claim); Wheeler v. T.L. Roofing, Inc., 74 P.3d 499 (Colo. Ct. App. 2003) (multiple claims and counterclaims; applying net judgment rule to award fees to party with substantial recovery); Fielder v. Weinstein Design Group, Inc., 842 So. 2d 879 (Fla. Dist. Ct. App. 2003) (buyer who lost on counterclaims was nonetheless prevailing party, when seller who sought $25,000 was required to pay buyer $5600 and accept return of goods); Lasco Enterprises, Inc. v. Kohlbrand, 819 So. 2d 821 (Fla. Dist. Ct. App. 2002) (neither party was prevailing party and neither was entitled to fees when jury rejected both the claims and the counterclaims); Sampson v. DCI of Alexandria, 970 So. 2d 55 (La. Ct. App. 2007) (claims and counterclaims between home owners and building contractor; fee award to home owners when contractor found to owe money to them); First Sec. Sav. Bank v. Aitken, 573 N.W.2d 307 (Mich. Ct. App. 1997) (when commercial loan contract allowed attorney fees "in connection with the loan agreement," lender was entitled to fees both for its claim, and for successful defense against borrowers' counterclaim, when defeating counterclaim was necessary in order to prevail on complaint); Whipps L.L.C. v. Kaufman, Vidal, Hileman & Remilow, P.C., 156 P.3d 11 (Mont. 2007) (no prevailing party, so no contractual fee shifting, when tenant gave up counterclaim and landlord accepted offer of 20% of the amount demanded); Stanley v. Lemire, 148 P.3d 643 (Mont. 2006) (no prevailing party when landlord prevailed on claim for possession and tenant on claim for back rent); Grenfell v. Anderson, 56 P.3d 326 (Mont. 2002) (commercial tenant prevailed when landlord received small amount of back rent, which was uncontested, and tenant prevailed on other contested claims); *In re* Marriage of Pfennigs, 989 P.2d 327 (Mont. 1999) (no prevailing party); Wilkes v. Zurlinden, 328 Or. 626, 984 P.2d 261 (1999) (when plaintiff prevailed on claim and defendant on counterclaim and no damages awarded for either, both were prevailing parties and owed one another attorney fees); Barbara Parmenter Living Trust v. Lemon, 159 P.3d 1174 (Or. Ct. App. 2007) (landlord-tenant statute requires prevailing party fees except under unusual circumstances; such circumstances shown here when both parties presented small meritorious and large unmeritorious claims, unreasonably prolonged the litigation, and sought fees "highly disproportionate" to results obtained), *review granted*, 168 P.3d 1153 (Or. 2007); Robert Camel Contracting, Inc. v. Krautschied, 134 P.3d 1065 (Or. Ct. App. 2006) (claims and counterclaims between home builder and consumers; recently enacted Oregon statute, Or. Rev. Stat. § 20.077, requires that prevailing party be determined, and fees assessed, on a claim-by-claim basis—net judgment not proper standard); Jakab v. Gran Villa Townhomes Ass'n, Inc., 149 S.W.3d 863 (Tex. App. 2004) (home owners' association not prevailing party, because no net recovery as amount awarded on counterclaim for improper dues increase exceeded amount of home owner's missed payments); R.T. Nielson Co. v. Cook, 40 P.3d 1119 (Utah 2002) (when recovery on claim greatly exceeded recovery on counterclaim, plaintiff was prevailing party); Villeneuve v. Beane, 933 A.2d 1139 (Vt. 2007) (although both lease and landlord-tenant statute provided for fee shifting, denial of fees proper when net result of claims and counterclaims was "a wash"); Fletcher Hill, Inc. v. Crosbie, 872 A.2d 292 (Vt. 2005) (modular home installer could not recover fees pursuant to contract it had breached; no statutory fees because neither party clearly prevailed); *see also* Anglia Jacs & Co. v. Dubin, 830 So. 2d 169 (Fla. Dist. Ct. App. 2002) (discussion of prevailing party; question is who in fact prevailed on "significant issues"); Chang v. Soldier Summit Dev., 82 P.3d 203 (Utah Ct. App. 2003) (prevailing party is one who prevails on major issues and most expensive aspects; party who prevailed on two-thirds of matters was entitled to two-thirds of fees reasonably incurred); McGuire v. Lowery, 2 P.3d 527 (Wyo. 2000) (fees properly denied when no party "clearly prevailed on all issues"). *But cf.* Mantia v. Hansen, 77 P.3d 1143 (Or. Ct. App. 2003) (employee who lost on tort and retaliatory discharge claims was prevailing party when he received substantial net monetary recovery on his wage claims and defeated employer's counterclaims); Republic Bank v. Shook, 653 S.W.2d 278 (Tex. 1983) (reversing appellate ruling that $29,779.51 attorney fee pursuant to 10% contractual provision was unreasonable when defendant showed creditor only spent five hours of attorney time to collect the debt;

creditor prevails on only one of several claims, it may be entitled to fees only for work on that claim.[62]

6.5 Determining the Amount of Attorney Fees a Creditor May Recover

In cases in which the creditor is entitled to recover attorney fees, the next question is the amount the creditor may recover. Some states cap the amount of a fee award by statute. Hawaii, for example, forbids collection agencies from recovering any collection expenses, except for attorney fees after filing suit, and it caps those fees at twenty-five percent of the debt.[63] North Carolina limits contractual attorney fees to fifteen percent, if a note is collected by an attorney after maturity, and requires that the debtor be given a final five-day notice to pay without incurring fees.[64] These limits apply even when the parties' contract provides for greater fees.[65] (In addition, a decision interpreting North Carolina law holds that there must be a statutory basis for recovery of attorney fees, even when the parties' contract provides that attorney fees may be recovered.[66])

Georgia places a percentage cap on contractual attorney fees, and requires a final demand for payment of collection attorney fees, with a ten-day grace period to avoid them.[67] New Jersey court rules regulating the fees that may be charged in foreclosure actions override contractual provisions allowing for larger fees; courts have discretion to reduce but not increase fees calculated by the formula in the rules.[68]

If there is no statutory guidance some courts, taking a rigid freedom of contract approach, enforce attorney fee clauses that set a particular amount or formula for fees

attorney time spent defending a usury claim may be counted toward indemnification of creditor, because creditor had to overcome debtor's defenses to recover).

62 Indus. & Mech. Contractors of Memphis, Inc. v. Tim Mote Plumbing, L.L.C., 962 So. 2d 632 (Miss. Ct. App. 2007) (party who prevailed on only one of four claims entitled to fees only on that claim); Gullett v. VanDyke Constr. Co, 111 P.3d 220 (Mont. 2005) (court properly reduced attorney fees by denying fees for claims on which party did not prevail, and for party's "shared responsibility for this dispute"); Varner v. Cardenas, 218 S.W. 3d 68 (Tex. 2007) (attorney fees available only for work necessary to recover on contract or statutory claim allowing them, but not for claims "intertwined with" claims for which fees available; allowed here when seller must defeat counterclaim to recover on contract); Ulloa v. QSP, Inc., 624 S.E.2d 43 (Va. 2006) (remanding to allow "marginally successful" plaintiff to show "with specificity" which fees attributable to claim on which it prevailed). *But cf.* Erlenbush v. Largent, 819 N.E.2d 1186 (Ill. App. Ct. 2004) (consumer who won suit against home seller for fraud in the inducement was prevailing party, although she lost on some claims, and was entitled to award of attorney fees under the sales agreement).

63 Haw. Rev. Stat. § 443B-9 (collection agency may not collect or attempt to collect any collection fee, except attorney fee up to 25% after filing suit); *see, e.g.*, Ai v. Frank Huff Agency, Ltd., 607 P.2d 1304 (Haw. 1980) (it was a deceptive practice for a collection agency to attempt to collect attorney fees of one-third of the debt once matter was referred to attorney, when attorney fees were limited by statute to 25% and allowed only after suit filed).

64 N.C. Gen. Stat. § 6-21.2; *see* Sunbelt Rentals v. Corbridge, 171 F. Supp. 2d 14 (D. Me. 2001) (N.C. law) (attorney fees only as permitted by statute; allowed for collection by attorney after maturity, capped at 15%; debtor must be given final five-day notice to pay without incurring fees); Old Republic Surety Co. v. Reliable Hous., Inc., 603 S.E.2d 168 (N.C. Ct. App. 2004) (table) (text available at 2004 WL 1965603) (enforcing 15% cap); Reid v. Ayers, 531 S.E.2d 231 (N.C. Ct. App. 2000) (North Carolina statute limited attorney fees in debt collection matter to 15%); Davis Lake Cmty. Ass'n v. Feldman, 530 S.E.2d 865 (N.C. Ct. App. 2000) (North Carolina statute required that before creditor could claim attorney fees it must notify consumer and provide a five-day grace period; statute also limited fees to 15% of debt); *see also In re* Jones, 2000 Bankr. LEXIS 1741 (Bankr. E.D.N.C. Dec. 22, 2000) (statutory cap on attorney fees, as applied to alternative mortgage, not preempted by Federal Alternative Mortgage Transaction Act); N.C. Indus. Capital v. Clayton, 649 S.E.2d 14 (N.C. Ct. App. 2007) (North Carolina statute allowing attorney fees of 15% of "the outstanding balance" applied to lease; "outstanding balance" was amount actually awarded, not larger sum demanded by landlord); WRI/Raleigh, Ltd. P'ship v. Shaikh, 644 S.E.2d 245 (N.C. Ct. App. 2007) (affirming award of attorney fees under N.C. Gen. Stat. § 6-21.2 against commercial tenant; statute's reference to "note, conditional sale contract or other evidence of indebtedness," applies to real estate lease); FNB Southeast v. Lane, 586 S.E.2d 530 (N.C. Ct. App. 2003) (guarantee contract is evidence of indebtedness covered by this statute); *cf.* Trull v. Cent. Carolina Bank & Trust, 478 S.E.2d 39 (N.C. Ct. App. 1996) (adopting strained interpretation of statute to allow contractual fees even if creditor does not prevail; failing to give weight to statutory provision allowing fees only if the debt "be *collected* by or through an attorney"), *aff'd*, 490 S.E.2d 238 (N.C. 1997) (table).

65 Sunbelt Rentals v. Corbridge, 171 F. Supp. 2d 14, 18 (D. Me. 2001) (N.C. law).

66 *Id.*

67 Ga. Code Ann. § 13-1-11(a)(3); *see* GMAC Commercial Mortgage Co. v. Maitland Hotel Associates, Ltd., 218 F. Supp. 2d 1355 (M.D. Fla. 2002) (Georgia statute validates attorney fees provisions in promissory note if collected by attorney after maturity, subject to a cap; prevailing party must prove that it incurred fees in specific amount in order to recover the maximum); RadioShack Corp. v. Cascade Crossing II, L.L.C., 653 S.E.2d 680 (Ga. 2007) (state law placing 10% to 15% cap on percentage attorney fees provided for in "a note or other evidence of indebtedness" applies to real estate lease); Trust Associates v. Snead, 559 S.E.2d 502 (Ga. Ct. App. 2002) (discussion of cases construing Ga. Code Ann. § 13-1-11(a)(3); demand letter inadequate when it failed to specify that grace period ran from date of receipt, and to specifically identify the note and holder; award of attorney fees reversed).

68 N.J. Rule of Court 4:42-9 (restricting amount of attorney fees that may be awarded in foreclosure action); *see* Barrows v. Chase Manhattan Mortgage Co., 465 F. Supp. 2d 347 (D.N.J. 2006) (FDCPA claim against lender's lawyer; fact issue whether legal fee demanded for mortgage reinstatement complied with New Jersey rule); *In re* Hatala, 295 B.R. 62 (Bankr. D.N.J. 2003) (discussion of New Jersey law concerning fee shifting).

without regard to the reasonableness of the fees.[69] However some of these courts, though enforcing the clause in the particular case, qualify their opinions by indicating that a different result may be reached if there is proof that the clause is oppressive, unconscionable, or so disproportionate to foreseeable expenses as to be penal (violating the general contract law prohibition of penalty clauses in contracts).[70]

On the other hand, most courts read a requirement of reasonableness into any fee-shifting clause, regardless of its terms.[71] This position is consistent with the traditional authority of the courts to supervise the charging of fees for

69 Layfield v. Southeastern Constr. Coordinators, Inc., 492 S.E.2d 921 (Ga. Ct. App. 1997) (proof of reasonableness not required when clause made party liable for legal fees "incurred" and contractor presented evidence of amount of fees incurred); W.K. Henderson Iron Works & Supply Co. v. Meriwether Supply Co., 152 So. 69 (La. 1934) (enforcing 10% attorney fee clause; clause represents liquidated damages and is due regardless of extent or value of attorney's services); West v. Gladney, 533 S.E.2d 334 (S.C. Ct. App. 2000) (when contract specifies attorney fees as a percentage of the debt, court has no discretion to consider reasonableness; non-consumer case); Waller, Lansden, Dortch, Davis v. Hansey, 851 S.W.2d 131 (Tenn. 1992) (note's provision for 15% attorney fee if suit brought is an explicit and unconditional commitment to pay this amount, therefore is due even though attorneys represented themselves); Sturgis Nat'l Bank v. Smyth, 30 S.W. 678 (Tex. App. 1895) (clause for 10% attorney fee enforceable despite no charge for attorney services).

70 McIntire v. Cagley, 37 Iowa 676 (1873) (10% attorney fee reasonable and not a penalty as it was not disproportionate to expected injuries); Leventhall v. Krinsky, 90 N.E.2d 545 (Mass. 1950) (clause in note for percentage attorney fee is valid unless it is so unconscionable and oppressive as to amount to a penalty or a usurious device); Equitable Lumber Co. v. IPA Land Dev. Co., 38 N.Y.2d 516, 381 N.Y.S.2d 459, 344 N.E.2d 391 (1976) (30% fee not unconscionable between commercial parties; remanding for determination whether 30% was unenforceable as a penalty because it was unreasonably large, not a reasonable forecast of actual collection costs, or not commensurate with actual fees); Wilson Sewing Mach. Co. v. Moreno, 7 F. 806 (Or. Cir. Ct. 1879) (parties have right to make contract for attorney fees, but "court should be slow to enforce it" if it is a device to secure illegal interest or unconscionable advantage).

71 *See, e.g.*, Fed. Deposit Ins. Corp. v. Bender, 127 F.3d 58, 63 (D.C. Cir. 1997) (under District of Columbia law, attorney fee provisions enforced "only as indemnity for reasonable fees necessarily and properly paid or incurred"); Armada Bulk Carriers v. ConocoPhillips Co., 505 F. Supp. 2d 621 (N.D. Cal. 2007) (N.Y. law) (court awarding contractual fees must "make its own determination whether the request is justified by the time and labor expended"); Comi v. D.S.C. Fin., 994 F. Supp. 121 (N.D.N.Y. 1998) (under Texas law, contractual attorney fees must be reasonable in amount and bear a reasonable relationship to the amount in controversy; reducing fee request to reasonable amount even though contract clause did not require reasonableness); Consumers Time Credit, Inc. v. Remark Corp., 259 F. Supp. 135 (E.D. Pa. 1966) (amount specified in contract may not be reasonable; court may use its equitable powers to protect the borrower and deny or reduce fees), *aff'd*, 377 F.2d 553 (3d Cir. 1967); *In re* Coates, 292 B.R. 894 (Bankr. C.D. Ill. 2003) (standard of reasonableness implied in all contractual fee-shifting clauses; court sets forth requirements for proof, which include terms of creditors' contract with their lawyers); Smith v. Snyder, 839 A.2d 589 (Conn. 2004) (party claiming fees must state amount claimed, and present evidence of hours worked, opposing party may contest, and court may use its general knowledge in determining reasonableness); Marquard & Roche/Meditz & Hackett, Inc. v. Riverbend Executive Ctr., Inc., 812 A.2d 175 (Conn. App. Ct. 2003) (commercial landlord-tenant; abuse of discretion to award full amount of fees when some resulted from tenant's having initially sued former landlord; remanding to determine amount of fees attributable to this mistake); Mahani v. Essex Media Group, 935 A.2d 242 (Del. Super. Ct. 2007) (when awarding contractual attorney fees, court should apply criteria of Delaware Lawyers' Rules of Prof'l Conduct to determine reasonableness); Powers v. Rockford Stop'n'Go, Inc., 761 N.E.2d 237 (Ill. App. Ct. 2001) (fee-shifting clauses enforceable, but will be "strictly construed and enforced at the discretion of the trial court"; criteria similar to federal lodestar test); Bruno v. Wells Fargo Bank, 850 N.E.2d 940 (Ind. Ct. App. 2006) (fee-shifting clauses enforceable, but amount must be reasonable); Franklin College v. Turner, 844 N.E.2d 99, 105 (Ind. Ct. App. 2006) (awarding $420 to collection attorney who requested $4375; "the question presented is not how much [creditor] paid to its counsel, but what is a reasonable attorney fee"); Berkemeier v. Rushville Nat'l Bank, 459 N.E.2d 1194 (Ind. Ct. App. 1984) (contingent fee contract between obligee and his attorney not binding upon debtor; obligee is limited to reasonable fee based on other factors); Leenerts Farms, Inc. v. Rogers, 421 So. 2d 216 (La. 1982) (courts may inquire into reasonableness of claimed attorney fee regardless of provisions of note); Vignette Publications, Inc. v. Harborview Enterprises, Inc., 799 So. 2d 531, 538 (La. Ct. App. 2001) (courts may inquire into reasonableness of attorney fees as part of their inherent authority to regulate the practice of law); Custom-Bilt Cabinet & Supply, Inc. v. Quality Built Cabinets, Inc., 748 So. 2d 594 (La. Ct. App. 1999) (prohibition against excessive attorney fees can not be avoided by setting fees as a percentage of the debt; detailed criteria for setting reasonable fees; but note that court approved 25% attorney fees); Ford Motor Credit Co. v. Blanchard, 620 So. 2d 286 (La. Ct. App. 1992) (prohibition against attorney's acceptance of clearly excessive fee can not be abrogated by provision in note; remanding for evidentiary hearing when there was insufficient evidence that 25% fee required by note was reasonable); Myers v. Kayhoe, 892 A.2d 520 (Md. 2006) (interpreting fee-shifting provisions to allow reasonable fees; party claiming fees must provide court with information necessary to determine reasonableness; court has broad discretion, but abuse of discretion here as fees wholly denied); Allfirst Bank v. Dep't of Health & Mental Hygiene, 780 A.2d 440, 463–464 (Md. Ct. Spec. App. 2001) (regardless of whether fees are governed by statute or contract, only reasonable fees are allowable); Rauch v. McCall, 761 A.2d 76 (Md. Ct. Spec. App. 2000) (even though clause did not require fees to be reasonable, court must evaluate reasonableness); B. & P. Enterprises v. Overland Equip. Co., 133 Md. App. 583, 758 A.2d 1026 (2000) (when fees provided for by contract, prevailing party must prove amount due; detailed records required); Windemere Commons I Ass'n v. O'Brien, 713 N.W.2d 814 (Mich. Ct. App. 2006) (denial of fees was abuse of discretion when statute and condominium declaration require prevailing party fees; remanding to determine reasonable amount); Zeeland Farms v. JBL Enterprises, 555 N.W.2d 733, 736 (Mich. Ct. App. 1996) (recovery of contractual attorney fees limited to a reasonable amount); Sheppard v. East, 192 S.W.3d 518 (Mo. Ct. App. 2006) (enforcement of attorney fee clause not discretionary, but court must "hear from the parties"

legal services under the courts' inherent and statutory power to regulate the practice of law.[72] Some of these courts explicitly adopt an indemnification theory, limiting the enforcement of the clause "only as indemnity for reasonable fees necessarily and properly paid or incurred."[73] Courts that read a requirement of reasonableness into attorney fee clauses allow reimbursement only for fees actually incurred,[74] and refuse to indemnify unnecessary expenses.[75]

and apply its expertise to determine reasonable fees); Alcoa Edgewater No. 1 Fed. Credit Union v. Carroll, 210 A.2d 68 (N.J. 1965) (contractual fee-shifting provisions are enforceable, but fees must be reasonable); SO/Bluestar v. Canarsie Hotel Corp., 825 N.Y.S.2d 80 (App. Div. 2006) (fee-shifting clause entitled plaintiff to fees "to the extent that the amount is reasonable and warranted for the services actually rendered"; court has inherent power to regulate practice of law, including fees); McMullen v. Kutz, 925 A.2d 832 (Pa. Super. Ct. 2007) (requirement of reasonableness is read into contractual attorney fee provision), *review granted*, 934 A.2d 1162 (Pa. 2007); Dole v. Wade, 510 S.W.2d 909 (Tenn. 1974) (court is not bound by contractual provision for particular amount of fees and will only enforce reasonable amount); F.R. Hernandez Constr. v. Nat'l Bank of Commerce, 578 S.W.2d 675 (Tex. 1979) (agreement to pay attorney fees based on percentage of unpaid balance and interest on a promissory note was a contract to indemnify the holder of the note for reasonable attorney's expenses actually incurred in collection, not a promise to pay contractual amount); R.T. Nielson Co. v. Cook, 40 P.3d 1119 (Utah 2002) (contractual attorney fees provisions enforced, but court has discretion to determine reasonable fee; detailed documentation required); McGuire v. Lowery, 2 P.3d 527 (Wyo. 2000) (although contract provision for attorney fees is valid, court must exercise discretion to award only reasonable fees and may disallow if award would be inequitable; fees properly refused when neither party clearly prevailed on all issues); McLain v. Anderson, 933 P.2d 468 (Wyo. 1997) (requiring showing that attorney fees were reasonable even though contract clause did not require reasonableness; attorney fees are a form of punitive damages which must be proven to have been incurred and reasonable; fees denied when proof of reasonableness was insufficient).

72 Leenerts Farms, Inc. v. Rogers, 421 So. 2d 216 (La. 1982) (courts may inquire into reasonableness of attorney fees as part of their inherent authority to regulate the practice of law); *In re* First Nat'l Bank of E. Islip v. Brower, 368 N.E.2d 1240, 1242 (N.Y. 1977).

73 Fed. Deposit Ins. Corp. v. Bender, 127 F.3d 58, 63 (D.C. Cir. 1997); *see also In re* Gebhard, 140 F. 571 (M.D. Pa. 1905) (clause in note providing for 5% collection fee merely allows indemnification for reasonable attorney fees up to 5%; as the creditor-attorney pursued the confession of judgment *pro se*, there were no out-of-pocket expenditures to indemnify); F.R. Hernandez Constr. v. Nat'l Bank of Commerce, 578 S.W.2d 675 (Tex. 1979) (agreement to pay attorney fees based on percentage of unpaid balance and interest on a promissory note was a contract to indemnify the holder of the note for attorney's expenses actually incurred in collection, not a promise to pay contractual amount); Island Block Corp. v. Webster, 17 V.I. 29 (V.I. Terr. Ct. 1980) ("[S]uch a provision is a contract of indemnity . . . [and] should be enforced only to the extent that it reflects the cost of services actually rendered, whether by an attorney or by another legal representative. The 25% stipulation here has absolutely no relation to the services actually rendered.").

74 Chestertown Bank v. Walker, 163 F. 510 (4th Cir. 1908) (upholding lower court's decision to award less than the "five percent commission for collecting" required by note when bank did not prove that an attorney was hired or took steps to collect the debt); *In re* Gebhard, 140 F. 571 (M.D. Pa. 1905) (clause in note providing for 5% collection fee merely allows indemnification for reasonable attorney fees up to 5%; as the creditor-attorney pursued the confession of judgment *pro se*, there were no out-of-pocket expenditures to indemnify); *In re* WCS Enterprises, 381 B.R. 206 (Bankr. E.D. Va. 2007) ("an attorney's fee provision in a contract, even though measured as a percentage of the amount due, entitles the creditor only to reasonable fees based on the work performed"); *In re* Mathews, 208 B.R. 506, 514 (Bankr. N.D. Ala. 1997) (Alabama treats contractual attorney fee clauses as intended to indemnify the creditor against any necessity for employing an attorney, but not to secure the payment of a fee for unnecessary services, or services required because of some wrongful act by the creditor; party claiming contractual attorney fees must have acted reasonably in employing counsel, and services must be reasonable under the circumstances); Bank of Woodland v. Treadwell, 55 Cal. 379 (1880) (creditor not entitled to $100 counsel fees provided in contract when it used an employee attorney and the cost of the attorney's services could not be apportioned to this suit); Mix v. Tumanjan Dev. Corp., 126 Cal. Rptr. 2d 267 (Ct. App. 2002) (fees not "incurred" unless litigant liable to pay out of pocket; attorney who represented self not entitled to fees for own time, but could claim fees for other attorney who assisted him); Kamco Supply Corp. v. Annex Contracting, Inc., 261 A.D.2d 363, 689 N.Y.S.2d 189 (1999) (contractual provision setting attorney fees as a percentage of the debt should be enforced only if the amount is reasonable and warranted for services actually rendered; remanding for determination of reasonable fee); F.R. Hernandez Constr. v. Nat'l Bank of Commerce, 578 S.W.2d 675 (Tex. 1979) (agreement to pay attorney fees based on percentage of unpaid balance and interest on a promissory note was a contract to indemnify the holder of the note for attorney's expenses actually incurred in collection, not a promise to pay contractual amount); Island Block Corp. v. Webster, 17 V.I. 29 (V.I. Terr. Ct. 1980) ("[S]uch a provision is a contract of indemnity . . . [and] should be enforced only to the extent that it reflects the cost of services actually rendered, whether by an attorney or by another legal representative. The 25% stipulation here has absolutely no relation to the services actually rendered."); Mullins v. Richlands Nat'l Bank, 403 S.E.2d 334 (Va. 1991) (when contract provided for attorney fees but did not fix the amount, court's award of 10% was unreasonable as it bore no relation to time consumed, effort expended, or nature of services rendered); A. Della Porta, Annotation, *Validity of provision in promissory note or other evidences of indebtedness for payment as attorneys' fees, expenses and costs of collection, of specified percentage of note*, 17 A.L.R.2d 288, 304–305 (1951); *see also* Spencer v. Hendersen-Webb, Inc. 81 F. Supp. 2d 582 (D. Md. 1999) (lease that allowed legal costs and expenses does not allow collection of fees when none have been incurred).

75 Hog Slat, Inc. v. Ebert, 2002 WL 535061 (8th Cir. Apr. 11, 2002) (reducing fees from $62,000 to $38,000; court has discretion to determine reasonable amount); Cable Marine, Inc. v. M/V Trust Me II, 632 F.2d 1344 (5th Cir. 1980) (no recovery of contractual collection fees needlessly incurred by pursuing suit after generous settlement offer); *In re* Jones, 366 B.R. 584 (Bankr. E.D. La. 2007) (lender would not be reimbursed for

When reasonableness is required (whether by case law, by statute, or by the terms of the contract itself), some courts do not require proof of actual expenditures by the plaintiff, but hold that the amount stated in the contract is prima facie recoverable subject to the defendant's proof of unreasonableness[76] or a finding by the court of excessiveness.[77] But other courts require the creditor to submit evi-

unnecessary inspections); El Escorial Owners' Ass'n v. DLC Plastering, Inc., 65 Cal. Rptr. 3d 524 (Ct. App. 2007) ("inadequately documented or overbilled" fees sharply reduced); First Nat'l Bank v. Union Tavern Corp., 794 P.2d 261 (Colo. Ct. App. 1990) (collection attorney fees may not be awarded for pursuing an erroneous claim); Marquard & Roche/Meditz & Hackett, Inc. v. Riverbend Executive Ctr., Inc., 812 A.2d 175 (Conn. App. Ct. 2003) (commercial landlord-tenant; abuse of discretion to award full amount of fees when some resulted from tenant's having initially sued former landlord; remanding to determine amount of fees attributable to this mistake); Mahani v. Essex Media Group, 935 A.2d 242 (Del. Super. Ct. 2007) (when awarding contractual attorney fees, court should apply criteria of Delaware Lawyers' Rules of Prof'l Conduct to determine reasonableness); Soles v. Sheppard, 99 Ill. 616 (1881) (denying attorney fees to second mortgagee that filed unnecessary cross-bill in first mortgagee's foreclosure action); Franklin College v. Turner, 844 N.E.2d 99, 105 (Ind. Ct. App. 2006) ("the question presented is not how much [creditor] paid to its counsel, but what is a reasonable attorney fee"; awarding $420 to collection attorney who requested $4375); H. & G. Ortho v. Neodontics Int'l, Inc., 823 N.E.2d 734 (Ind. Ct. App. 2005) (court has discretion as to reasonableness and may apply "personal expertise" and "look to the responsibility of the parties in incurring the attorney's fees"; affirming award when there was expert testimony as to reasonableness of hours and hourly rate); Holstead v. Lewis, 160 So. 834 (La. Ct. App. 1935) (no recovery of attorney fees when debt was not in default and attorney was hired unnecessarily); B. & P. Enterprises v. Overland Equip. Co., 133 Md. App. 583, 758 A.2d 1026 (2000) (detailed discussion of criteria for reasonable attorney fees; burden on party seeking fees); TAL Fin. Corp. v. CSC Consulting, Inc., 844 N.E.2d 1085 (Mass. 2006) (when case should have been resolved "long before [lessor] hired counsel," any fee award would be unreasonable; lessor, relying on unenforceable penalty provision, had sought $86,000 damages and received $9500, which was less than pre-trial settlement offer); *see also* Coop. Fin. Ass'n v. Garst, 927 F. Supp. 1179 (N.D. Iowa 1996) (fee-shifting provision will be enforced, but court will determine reasonableness of attorney fees). *But see* A.B.C. Supply Co. v. Edwards, 952 P.2d 286 (Ariz. Ct. App. 1996) (court properly reduced amount of contractual attorney fees from $22,892 to $2500 when hours billed were unreasonable relative to the amount in controversy and borrowers presented evidence of what would be reasonable fees for collection of a debt, the existence and amount of which were not contested).

76 Fed. Deposit Ins. Corp. v. Bender, 127 F.3d 58 (D.C. Cir. 1997) (under District of Columbia law attorney fees enforced "only as indemnity for reasonable fees necessarily and properly paid or incurred"; may be enforced as written if debtors do not challenge reasonableness but when issue was properly raised, trial court to determine reasonable fee), *after remand*, 182 F.3d 1 (D.C. Cir. 1999) (party challenging reasonableness of fees is entitled upon request to see time records of other party's attorneys; fees for in-house counsel denied when their hours were insufficiently documented and part of their work was for liaison with Justice Department, an activity for which fees may not be charged); Webster Drilling Co. v. Walker, 286 F.2d 114 (10th Cir. 1961); *In re* Hathaway, 364 B.R. 220 (Bankr. E.D. Va. 2007) (percentage attorney fee presumed reasonable; burden on debtor to show unreasonableness; not shown here when actual attorney fees exceeded 25% of debt); *In re* Bowden, 326 B.R. 62 (Bankr. E.D. Va. 2005) (20% attorney fee in note presumed reasonable when neither side introduced evidence of amount and value of attorney services); McDowell Mtn. Ranch Cmty. Ass'n v. Simons, 165 P.3d 667 (Ariz. Ct. App. 2007) (home owners' association covenant provides for "all attorney fees and costs"; reasonableness of contractual fees presumed; burden on home owner to show unreasonableness); Roberts v. Adams, 47 P.3d 690 (Colo. Ct. App. 2001) (losing party entitled to hearing on fees, if timely requested); Theobald v. Nosser, 752 So. 2d 1036 (Miss. 1999) (when commercial promissory note allowed reasonable attorney fees and non-prevailing-party did not contest reasonableness of amount, court should allow attorney fees in amount claimed); Citicorp v. Morrisville Hampton Realty, 662 A.2d 1120 (Pa. Super. Ct. 1995) (Pennsylvania law permitted "reasonable" attorney fees in foreclosures; finding 10% of amount due to be reasonable when debtor offered no evidence of unreasonableness); Dole v. Wade, 510 S.W.2d 909 (Tenn. 1974) (amount stated in contract is prima facie recoverable, subject to reduction by the court if sum is unreasonable); F.R. Hernandez Constr. v. Nat'l Bank of Commerce, 578 S.W.2d 675 (Tex. 1979) (obligor must plead and prove contractual fee was unreasonable and lesser amount was reasonable under the circumstances); Hinojosa v. Citibank, 2008 WL 570601 (Tex. App. Mar. 4, 2008) (unpublished) (trial court must determine reasonableness of fees if opponent submits non-conclusory affidavit challenging reasonableness); O'Kehie v. Harris Leasing Co., 80 S.W.3d 316 (Tex. App. 2002) (25% fee provided by lease is prima facie reasonable, and losing party has burden of showing the contrary); Spring Branch Bank v. Mengden, 628 S.W.2d 130 (Tex. App. 1981) (incumbent upon payor to challenge the reasonableness of the amount demanded); *see also* Page v. Checkrite, Ltd., Clearinghouse No. 45,759 (D. Neb. 1984) ($8 service charge for bounced check commercially reasonable and lawfully recoverable by a check guarantee service which provided retailers with a decal for each cash register advising customers of the charge); Cabrera v. First Nat'l Bank of Wheaton, 753 N.E.2d 1138 (Ill. App. Ct. 2001) (complex commercial litigation; losing party entitled to hearing on reasonableness of attorney fees, but right waived if not timely claimed); Franklin Collection Serv., Inc. v. Stewart, 863 So. 2d 925 (Miss. 2003) (medical bill was open account for which statute allowed attorney fee; one-third contingent fee presumptively reasonable; default judgment was res judicata as to bill and fee); A. Della Porta, Annotation, *Validity of provision in promissory note or other evidences of indebtedness for payment as attorneys' fees, expenses and costs of collection, of specified percentage of note*, 17 A.L.R.2d 288, 303–304 (1951); *cf.* A & E Int'l Enterprises, Inc. v. Gold Credit Co., 450 So. 2d 1166 (Fla. Dist. Ct. App. 1984) (statute creates presumption that attorney fee award was reasonable so long as the amount of the fee in the instrument did not exceed 10% of the principal amount).

77 *See, e.g.*, Hog Slat, Inc. v. Ebert, 2002 WL 535061 (8th Cir. Apr. 11, 2002) (commercial contract; fees reduced from $62,000 to $38,000); S.N.A., Inc. v. Array, 173 F. Supp. 2d 347 (E.D. Pa. 2001) (discussion of reasonableness of counsel's hourly rate and number of hours; claimed fees reduced as excessive), *aff'd*, 2002 WL 1900053 (3d Cir. Aug. 19, 2002); Coop. Fin. Ass'n

dence showing the expenditure of time reasonably necessary to collect the debt.[78] Some courts require detailed affidavits

v. Garst, 927 F. Supp. 1179 (N.D. Iowa 1996) (although prevailing creditor opted for "Rolls Royce class" representation, court awarded fees only for "Chevrolet class," because contractual fee-shifting provisions "should not be used to justify gouging losers with the excuse that the losers agreed to them"); First Union Bank v. Kaskel, 847 F. Supp. 961 (S.D. Fla. 1994) (Fla. Stat. § 687.06 provided that it was unnecessary for a court to "adjudge an attorney's fee to be reasonable and just" if it did not exceed 10% of the amount due; court may review the reasonableness of any attorneys fees; fees actually incurred, which totaled less than 10%, were reasonable); Fleet Bank v. Steeves, 793 F. Supp. 18 (D. Me. 1992) (billing for excessive hours; fee reduced from $25,603.21 to $13,434.31); Grant Road Lumber Co. v. Wystrach, 682 P.2d 1146 (Ariz. Ct. App. 1984) (contingent fee agreement between creditor and collection agency insufficient to show reasonable collection expenses of the agency without evidence such as usual rate and practices in community, but when fee claimed was based on a percentage agreed to in the original loan contract no other evidence was necessary to recover collection agency and attorney fees up to that percentage); McKeever v. Fiore, 829 A.2d 846 (Conn. App. Ct. 2003) (court may reduce fees in foreclosure case *sua sponte* or after a hearing if opponent objects; sharply reducing attorney fees when delay resulted from "outrageous" lack of diligence by lender and one year was reasonable time to dispose of case); Capitol Light & Supply Co. v. Dan Charles Elec., 2001 Conn. Super. LEXIS 3098 (Conn. Super. Ct. Oct. 26, 2001) (attorney fees excessive; court considered, among other things, amount of debt and whether certain charges were duplicative); Brandner v. New Orleans Office Supply, 654 So. 2d 858 (La. Ct. App. 1995) (court had discretion to reduce excessive attorney fees set by contract; 10% fees approved, court cited case approving 25% fees); City Bank & Trust Co. v. Hardage Corp., 449 So. 2d 1181 (La. Ct. App. 1984); McClain v. Papka, 108 S.W.3d 48 (Mo. Ct. App. 2003) (trial judge is expert on attorney fees and presumed to know "duration, zeal and ability" of the services and their value according to "time, place and circumstances"; no abuse of discretion when fees reduced from $18,000 to $1000 because buyers prevailed on only one of three claims and received about one-third of recovery sought); Granada Condo. I v. Morris, 639 N.Y.S.2d 91 (App. Div. 1996) (condominium entitled to attorney collection fees in suit to foreclose lien for common facility charges when bylaws specifically provided for fee recovery; requested amount would be significantly reduced when case was "a simple collection matter" and much of collection attorney's time was spent on defending counterclaim on which unit owner prevailed); Marine Midland Bank v. Scallen, 161 A.D.2d 103, 554 N.Y.S.2d 541 (1990) (court not bound to award contractual 15% as attorney fees if court determined it not reasonable); Meredith v. Smith, 35 P.3d 1002 (Okla. Civ. App. 2001) (fee shifting permitted but $3300 attorney fee for $458 default judgment in small claims court appeared unreasonable; remanding to determine reasonable fee). *But see* Franklin College v. Turner, 844 N.E.2d 99, 105 (Ind. Ct. App. 2006) ("the question presented is not how much [creditor] paid to its counsel, but what is a reasonable attorney fee"; awards $420 to collection attorney who requested $4375); Sheppard v. East, 192 S.W.3d 518 (Mo. Ct. App. 2006) (when enforcing attorney fee clause, court must "hear from the parties" and apply its expertise to determine reasonableness).

78 Student Loan Mktg. Ass'n v. Hanes, 181 F.R.D. 629 (S.D. Cal. 1998) (in order to recover attorney fees under California law, creditor must show that contract permitted attorney fees, and evidence of reasonableness, including billing rates, hourly rate, and proof that this rate was reasonable for lawyer of counsel's skill and experience practicing in that geographic area); Garden State Auto Park Pontiac GMC Truck, Inc. v. Elec. Data Sys. Corp., 31 F. Supp. 2d 378 (D.N.J. 1998) (Tex. law) (burden is on party seeking fees; detailed explanation of why court reduced requested fee by 50% and denied certain requests, for example, because illegible photocopying made it impossible to determine whether claimed hours were for issue on which party prevailed); *In re* Jones, 366 B.R. 584 (Bankr. E.D. La. 2007) (lender failed to show reasonableness of attorney or inspection fees); *In re* Coates, 292 B.R. 894, 904 (Bankr. C.D. Ill. 2003) (standard of reasonableness implied in all contractual fee-shifting clauses; lender has burden of proving what expenses and attorney fees it incurred and their reasonableness); El Escorial Owners' Ass'n v. DLC Plastering, Inc., 65 Cal. Rptr. 3d 524 (Ct. App. 2007) ("inadequately documented or overbilled" fees sharply reduced); Greeley Nat'l Bank v. Sloan, 677 P.2d 409 (Colo. Ct. App. 1983) (plaintiff had burden to show reasonableness of attorney fees); Smith v. Snyder, 839 A.2d 589 (Conn. 2004) (party claiming statutory fee must state amount claimed and present evidence of hours worked, and court may apply its general knowledge in determining whether claim excessive); Murray v. Barrett, 571 S.E.2d 448 (Ga. Ct. App. 2002) (award of attorney fees not supported by evidence when party estimated fees as "about $6000" and judge noted that attorney was in good standing and "experienced"; party claiming fees must present evidence of actual amount and reasonableness); Sterling Homes, Ltd. v. Rasberry, 759 N.E.2d 163 (Ill. App. Ct. 2001) (lawyer's affidavit sufficient to show fees were "reasonable and warranted by existing law"); J. B. Esker & Sons v. Cle-Pa's P'ship, 757 N.E.2d 1271 (Ill. App. Ct. 2001) (party claiming fee must itemize services provided, hours expended, and hourly rate); First Midwest Bank v. Sparks, 682 N.E.2d 373, 382 (Ill. App. Ct. 1997) (fee petition must specify services performed, by whom, amount of time, and hourly rate; trial court did not abuse discretion by awarding about half the sum requested when bank presented detailed billing records and testified that these were normal and customary rates); Heller Fin. Inc. v. Johns-Byrne Co., 637 N.E.2d 1085 (Ill. App. Ct. 1994) (to establish reasonable attorney fees authorized in a lease, attorney must document the hours, services performed skill, difficulty of the case, "reasonable connection between the fees and the amount involved in the litigation"); Decatur Imaging Ctr. v. Ames, 608 N.E.2d 1198, 1202 (Ill. App. Ct. 1992) (dicta) (collection attorney who seeks fees must show that the fees sought are reasonable); Bruno v. Wells Fargo Bank, 850 N.E.2d 940 (Ind. Ct. App. 2006) (party seeking fees must present evidence; insufficient here when affidavit showed only total hours and range of hourly rates); Holliday v. Crooked Creek Villages Homeowners' Ass'n, 759 N.E.2d 1088 (Ind. Ct. App. 2001) (amount within trial court's discretion, but must be supported by evidence; counsel's representations to court regarding his hours and rate sufficient); Allfirst Bank v. Dep't of Health & Mental Hygiene, 780 A.2d 440 (Md. Ct. Spec. App. 2001) (when percentage fee not specified, burden on party claiming fees to show reasonableness); Rauch v. McCall, 761 A.2d 76 (Md. Ct. Spec. App. 2000) (court must evaluate reasonableness; evidence required; similar to federal lodestar); Solution Source, Inc. v. LPR Associates Ltd. P'ship, 652 N.W.2d 474 (Mich. Ct. App. 2002) (statutory attorney fees; construction lien; burden on claimant to show reasonableness; sufficiently shown by detailed billing statements and attorney's testimony); Zeeland Farms v. JBL Enter-

of time and activity by attorneys seeking fees in collection actions when indemnification is sought.[79]

An important issue underlying the indemnification approach is whether a fee must be reasonable in relation to the efforts expended to collect the particular debt, or whether the fee is reasonable if it is set as a percentage of the debt. Courts are divided on this question.[80] The latter approach

---

prises, 555 N.W.2d 733, 736 (Mich. Ct. App. 1996) (recovery of contractual attorney fees limited to a reasonable amount, party seeking fees has burden of introducing evidence of reasonableness; testimony of creditor's credit manager was probative when manager's duties included hiring lawyers and approving their invoices); Indus. & Mech. Contractors of Memphis, Inc. v. Tim Mote Plumbing, L.L.C., 962 So. 2d 632 (Miss. Ct. App. 2007) (entitlement to fees depends on specific proof; fees properly denied when party failed to allocate fees between successful and unsuccessful claims); SO/Bluestar v. Canarsie Hotel Corp., 825 N.Y.S.2d 80 (App. Div. 2006) (affidavit "wholly insufficient"; must provide breakdown of rates and hours); Citibank (S.D.) v. Martin, 807 N.Y.S.2d 284 (Civ. Ct. 2005) (debt buyer must show fee arrangement, services actually rendered, time spent, nature of issues and other "relevant factors"); Usrey v. Wilson, 66 P.2d 1000 (Okla. Civ. App. 2002) (detailed time records preferred but not mandatory; may be possible to reconstruct basis for fees; but fees denied when attorney gave only "general estimate" of his hours); Y-12 Credit Union v. Wiseman, 1986 WL 5240 (Tenn. Ct. App. May 6, 1986) (contract clause allowed reasonable fee of attorney or collection agency; reversing award of 40% collection fee to collection agency when it failed to prove reasonableness); Chang v. Soldier Summit Dev., 82 P.3d 203 (Utah Ct. App. 2003) (listing criteria, including hours worked, and whether work was necessary, and remanding for determination of reasonable fee); Anderson v. Meier, 641 P.2d 187 (Wyo. 1982) (proof of reasonableness of attorney fee must be introduced); *see also* Troth Corp. v. Deutsch, Kerrigan & Stiles, L.L.P., 951 So. 2d 1162 (La. Ct. App. 2007) (open account; amount of fees discretionary with court; criteria include liable party's ability to pay; fee request adequately supported when lawyer provided billing records, and court had opportunity to observe amount and quality of work); Charette v. Fitzgerald, 213 S.W.3d 505 (Tex. App. 2006) (comparing various provisions of Texas law allowing attorney fees; for open account, court may take judicial notice of customary and usual fees; for violation of property code, reasonableness must be shown; reversing award of fees to tenants because evidence of reasonableness not presented); Burnside Air Conditioning & Heating, Inc. v. T.S. Young Corp., 113 S.W.3d 889 (Tex. App. 2003) (court need not receive evidence on all factors; reasonableness shown when lawyer testified to hours worked, work done, and hourly rate); Brown v. Bank of Galveston, 930 S.W.2d 140 (Tex. App. 1996) (when creditor's attorney testified as to amount of attorney fees, and debtor had the opportunity to attempt to discredit or disprove this testimony but did not do so, fees were established "as a matter of law"), *aff'd*, 963 S.W.2d 511 (Tex. 1998); R.T. Nielson Co. v. Cook, 40 P.3d 1119 (Utah 2002) (attorney's affidavit acceptable when it provided legal basis for award, nature of work performed, hours worked by attorneys and non-attorneys, hourly rates, affirmation that rates comparable to those for similar services; submission not ideal because did not include contemporary billing records); Lee v. Mulford, 611 S.E.2d 349 (Va. 2005) (upholding jury's determination that parties to a promissory note should bear their own attorney fees despite fee-shifting clause in the note in the absence of proof of attorney fees incurred); O'Connell v. O'Connell, 694 N.W.2d 429 (Wis. Ct. App. 2005) (court erred in awarding each party amount requested without making findings of fact, and skimpy record failed to disclose hours worked, usual fee, lawyers' experience, and so forth, and one party demanded much larger fee than the other). *But see* Layfield v. Southeastern Constr. Coordinators, Inc., 492 S.E.2d 921 (Ga. Ct. App. 1997) (proof of reasonableness not required when contractor, in residential construction agreement containing attorney fee clause, proved actual amount of attorney fees).

79 *See, e.g.*, Fleet Bank v. Steeves, 793 F. Supp. 18 (D. Me. 1992); *In re* Coates, 292 B.R. 894 (Bankr. C.D. Ill. 2003) (Illinois standard similar to federal lodestar); El Escorial Owners' Ass'n v. DLC Plastering, Inc., 65 Cal. Rptr. 3d 524 (Ct. App. 2007) ("inadequately documented or overbilled" fees sharply reduced); Rockford Stop'n'Go, Inc., 761 N.E.2d 237 (Ill. App. Ct. 2001); Cabrera v. First Nat'l Bank of Wheaton, 753 N.E.2d 1138 (Ill. App. Ct. 2001); Bruno v. Wells Fargo Bank, 850 N.E.2d 940 (Ind. Ct. App. 2006) (fee affidavit insufficient when it showed only total hours and range of hourly rates and did not break down hours and rates for each attorney); Allfirst Bank v. Dep't of Health & Mental Hygiene, 780 A.2d 440 (Md. Ct. Spec. App. 2001) (when no percentage fee specified, burden on party claiming fees to show reasonableness; must provide "detailed records that contain the relevant facts and computations undergirding the computation of charges"); B. & P. Enterprises v. Overland Equip. Co., 133 Md. App. 583, 758 A.2d 1026 (2000) (number of hours multiplied by hourly rate insufficient; detailed time records required); SO/Bluestar v. Canarsie Hotel Corp., 825 N.Y.S.2d 80 (App. Div. 2006) (affidavit "wholly insufficient"; must provide breakdown of rates and hours); Citizens & S. Nat'l Bank v. Easton, 427 S.E.2d 640 (S.C. 1993) (when contract provided for 15% of outstanding principal and interest as attorney fees, collector must introduce evidence of attorney fees actually incurred); Hardaway Concrete Co. v. Hall Contracting Corp., 647 S.E.2d 488 (S.C. Ct. App. 2007) (award of contractual or statutory attorney fees requires "specific findings of fact on the record": (1) nature extent and difficulty of legal services; (2) time and labor; (3) professional standing of counsel; (4) contingency of compensation; (5) fee customarily charged in the area for similar services; (6) beneficial results obtained); McLain v. Anderson, 933 P.2d 468 (Wyo. 1997) (party claiming contractual attorney fees must provide itemized billing plus proof of reasonableness).

80 *Percentage fee permitted*: Taylor v. Luper, Sheriff, & Niedenthal, 74 F. Supp. 2d 761 (S.D. Ohio 1999) (collection attorney fee of one-third of debt not excessive when this was the amount the creditor would have to pay the collection attorney); Indus. Screw & Supply Co. v. WPS, Inc., 926 So. 2d 134 (La. Ct. App. 2006) (enforcing contractual 25% attorney fee in open account claim; statute provides that if claimant and its attorney have agreed on fixed or determinable amount of attorney fees, the claimant is entitled to that amount); Franklin Collection Serv., Inc. v. Stewart, 863 So. 2d 925 (Miss. 2003) (medical bill was open account for which statute allowed attorney fee; one-third contingent fee presumptively reasonable); West v. Gladney, 533 S.E.2d 334 (S.C. Ct. App. 2000) (when contract specifies attorney fee as a percentage of the debt, court has no discretion to consider reasonableness; non-consumer case); NationsBank v. Scott Farm, 465 S.E.2d 98 (S.C. Ct. App. 1995) (enforcing 10% attorney fee clause in non-consumer contract; when clause provides for specific rate, it governs and no finding of reasonableness is required); Waller, Lansden, Dortch, Davis v. Hansey, 851 S.W.2d 131 (Tenn. 1992) (note's provision for

results in awards higher than justified by the actual value of collection efforts on average, particularly when the debt is

15% attorney fee if suit brought is an explicit and unconditional commitment to pay this amount, and therefore is due even though attorneys represented themselves); *see also* Stolicker v. Muller, Muller, Richmond, Harms, Myers & Sgroi, 2005 WL 2180481 (W.D. Mich. Sept. 9, 2005) (when state law required a court to award attorney fees, pre-judgment claim for a percentage fee violated FDCPA); Brandner v. New Orleans Office Supply, 654 So. 2d 858 (La. Ct. App. 1995) (La. Civil Code makes agreement to pay attorney fees in a fixed or determinable amount enforceable, but court still may deny "clearly excessive" fees; upholding 10% fee); Trull v. Cent. Carolina Bank & Trust, 478 S.E.2d 39 (N.C. Ct. App. 1996) (upholding contractual 15% attorney fee, even though it exceeded actual fees incurred, and creditor bank was only partially successful, that is, it foreclosed but was denied a deficiency), *aff'd*, 490 S.E.2d 238 (N.C. 1997) (table); Stewart v. Indus. Nat'l Bank, 458 A.2d 675 (R.I. 1983) (approving of entry of default judgments for amount due plus one-third attorney fee pursuant to contract clause for reasonable attorney fees when creditor submitted affidavit in each case).

Percentage fee forbidden: Fed. Deposit Ins. Corp. v. Bender, 127 F.3d 58, 63 (D.C. Cir. 1997) (D.C. law) (contract clause for fixed percentage fees will not be enforced according to its terms; party only entitled to indemnity for reasonable fees necessarily and properly paid or incurred); Munoz v. Pipestone Fin., L.L.C., 513 F. Supp. 2d 1076 (D. Minn. 2007) (contingent fee agreement between creditor and collection firm not binding on debtor, who agreed in contract only to pay reasonable fees; creditor liable under FDCPA for seeking fees at outset of collection suit, before they had been incurred); Marine Midland Bank v. Kilbane, 573 F. Supp. 469 (D. Md. 1983) (N.Y. law) (creditor only entitled to reasonable fees, even if note specifies a percentage; otherwise, creditor and its attorney "would have a tremendous incentive to negotiate an extremely large contingency fee, since that fee would simply be collected from the debtor, in addition to the underlying debt"); *In re* WCS Enterprises, 381 B.R. 206 (Bankr. E.D. Va. 2007) (entire 10% attorney fee did not become due when matter referred to attorney; "an attorney's fee provision in a contract, even though measured as a percentage of the amount due, entitles the creditor only to reasonable fees based on the work performed"; debtor liable only for the $180 billed by attorney before petition date); Spears v. Brennan, 745 N.E.2d 862 (Ind. Ct. App. 2001) (contingency fee agreed to between creditor and its attorney can not be added to a judgment against the debtor under a "reasonable attorney fee" clause without other objective evidence of reasonableness); Berkemeier v. Rushville Nat'l Bank, 459 N.E.2d 1194 (Ind. Ct. App. 1984) (contingent fee contract between obligee and his attorney not binding upon debtor; obligee is limited to reasonable fee based on other factors); Leenerts Farms, Inc. v. Rogers, 421 So. 2d 216 (La. 1982) (provision of note fixing attorney fee at 20% is not binding on court; court may inquire into reasonableness); Ford Motor Credit Co. v. Blanchard, 620 So. 2d 286 (La. Ct. App. 1992) (prohibition against attorney's acceptance of clearly excessive fee can not be abrogated by provision in note; remanding for evidentiary hearing when there was insufficient evidence that 25% fee required by note was reasonable); Trustees of Tufts College v. Ramsdell, 554 N.E.2d 34 (Mass. App. Ct. 1990) (attorney fees are limited to reasonable amount, and court is not bound by creditor's one-third contingent fee contract with collection attorney); Alcoa Edgewater No. 1 Fed. Credit Union v. Carroll, 210 A.2d 68 (N.J. 1965) (percentage recovery fixed by note is allowable only if it is reasonable); Kamco Supply Corp. v. Annex Contracting, Inc., 261 A.D.2d 363, 689 N.Y.S.2d 189 (1999) (contractual provision setting attorney fees as a percentage of the debt should be enforced only if the amount is reasonable and warranted for services actually rendered; remanding for determination of reasonable fee); Cheshire Academy v. Lee, 112 Misc. 2d 1076, 448 N.Y.S.2d 112 (Civ. Ct. 1982) (20% attorney fee authorized by statute stated a maximum which would not be allowed for default judgment when the services performed were unrelated to the amount claimed, and the claim was for the tuition of a student who had withdrawn from the school after paying more than half of the tuition); *see also* Richmond v. Malad, 2001 U.S. Dist. LEXIS 10505 (S.D. Ind. July 6, 2001) (denying motion to dismiss claim that seeking percentage-based attorney fee was deceptive and breach of statutory and contractual provisions allowing "reasonable" fee); Brooks v. Auto Sales & Services, Inc., 2001 WL 686950 (S.D. Ind. June 15, 2001) (allowing consumer to go forward with FDCPA action against attorney who routinely added 33.33% attorney fee to amount claimed in small claims actions for deficiency on repossessed cars when contract clause allowed "reasonable" fees but did not specify a percentage); Kojetin v. C.U. Recovery, Inc., 1999 U.S. Dist. LEXIS 1745 (D. Minn. Feb. 17, 1999) (mag.) (stating in dicta that Minnesota prohibits percentage attorney fee clauses, and allows fees only to extent of reasonable value of services actually performed), *adopted by* 1999 U.S. Dist. LEXIS 10930 (D. Minn. Mar. 29, 1999), *aff'd*, 212 F.3d 1318 (8th Cir. 2000) (per curiam); Harrison County Bd. of Supervisors v. Carlo Corp. Inc., 833 So. 2d 582 (Miss. 2002) (statute allows attorney fee not to exceed 25%; county board acted arbitrarily and capriciously in imposing attorney fee of 25% of corporate tax debt when this resulted in $79,000 fee for writing one letter; fee violated both common sense and rule of professional responsibility that required fees to be reasonable; remanding to determine fee applying standards in rule); Y-12 Credit Union v. Wiseman, 1986 WL 5240 (Tenn. Ct. App. May 6, 1986) (contract clause allowed reasonable fee of attorney or collection agency; fact that collection agency charged creditor 40% of debt is insufficient to show that this fee is reasonable); F.R. Hernandez Constr. v. Nat'l Bank of Commerce, 578 S.W.2d 675 (Tex. 1979) (agreement to pay attorney fees based on percentage of unpaid balance and interest on a promissory note was a contract to indemnify the holder of the note for reasonable attorney's expenses actually incurred in collection, not a promise to pay contractual amount); *cf.* Newman v. Checkrite Cal., Inc., 912 F. Supp. 1354, 1368 (E.D. Cal. 1995) (amount that collector charges to merchant is not per se reasonable to impose on debtor); *In re* Hathaway, 364 B.R. 220 (Bankr. E.D. Va. 2007) (percentage attorney fee presumed reasonable; burden on debtor to show unreasonableness; not shown here when actual attorney fees exceeded 25% of debt); *In re* First Nat'l Bank of E. Islip v. Brower, 368 N.E.2d 1240, 1242 (N.Y. 1977) (trial court properly awarded fees on *quantum meruit* basis rather than 15% provided by contract, even though statute allows contracts to provide for fees up to 15%; "the reasonable value of legal services rendered incident to the recovery of a default judgment will not automatically and always be equal to a particular percentage of the debt being collected"); Best Bldg. Supply & Lumber Corp. v. Mastercraft Homes & Renovations, Inc., 835 N.Y.S.2d 355 (App. Div. 2007) (error to award attorney fees as percentage of debt without evaluation of reasonableness; remanding for recalculation on *quantum meruit* basis); Coniglio v. Regan, 186 A.D.2d 708, 709, 588 N.Y.S.2d 887 (1992) (error to award fees based solely on fixed rate set forth in promissory note; remanding for evidence of the reasonableness of the fee sought); Wasserbauer

large and recovery occurs with little effort.[81] As one court has pointed out, if percentage fees were allowed without regard to actual expenditure of time, the creditor and its attorney "would have a tremendous incentive to negotiate an extremely large contingency fee, since that fee would simply be collected from the debtor, in addition to the underlying debt."[82]

Creditors often argue that a percentage of debt recovery is necessary and appropriate because they do not unduly profit from these awards. This is because high fees in successful or simple collection cases pay for the expenses of unsuccessful or complex cases. The few cases that examine the extent of actual collection efforts reject the percentage of debt calculation. But in most cases there is no such examination, and the court may accept a percentage figure if it is reasonable in relation to customary charges. Consequently, consumer attorneys may be well served to present evidence of the minimal amount of the collection attorney's actual efforts, to draw the court's attention to the issue. Decisions examining the excessiveness of other fees of financial institutions as unconscionable[83] or in breach of the duty of good faith and fair dealing may also provide support.[84] There is no reason that one consumer should pay for the attorney expenses incurred against other consumers.[85]

6.6 Collection Agency Fees

While there is a fair amount of case law on the limitations applicable to the recovery of attorney fees for collection, there is little case law regarding collection agency fees. The traditional rule is that collection agencies are compensated by their contingent or flat-fee arrangements with creditors. Creditors, in turn, are compensated for losses due to a debtor's default by state laws that allow them to charge interest, and sometimes late charges as well, on overdue debts. Such interest rates are established by consumer credit legislation or more general statutes setting a "legal" interest rate that may be charged in the absence of a contractual agreement for post-maturity, pre-judgment interest.[86]

As collection agencies are hired and paid by creditors, they do not have any contractual relationship with the debtors they pursue. Thus collectors do not have any independent basis for claiming collection fees from the debtor. The only possible basis they might have for such a claim is a statute or the consumer's contract with the creditor.

Outside of the context of debts owed to governmental entities,[87] most decisions have held collection agencies not entitled to recover fees from consumers for their collection efforts, regardless of any clause in the contract.[88] Of the few

v. Marine Midland Bank-Rochester, 92 Misc. 2d 388, 400 N.Y.S.2d 979 (Sup. Ct. 1977) (percentage attorney fees can not be deemed automatically reasonable); Cox v. Hagan, 100 S.E. 666 (Va. 1919) (construing contract providing that the "makers . . . pay costs of collection or ten per cent attorney's fee in case payment shall not be made at maturity" to mean only "the same in substance as if it had been to pay such reasonable attorney's fee for collection actually incurred by the lawful holder of the note, up to but not exceeding 10 per cent of the amount due"); HCA Health Services of Va., Inc. v. Peters, 16 Va. Cir. 76 (1989) (refusing to enforce 25% collection attorney fee clause in medical services adhesion contract; awarding reasonable fee based on hours worked); Island Block Corp. v. Webster, 17 V.I. 29 (V.I. Terr. Ct. 1980) ("[S]uch a provision is a contract of indemnity . . . [and] should be enforced only to the extent that it reflects the cost of services actually rendered, whether by an attorney or by another legal representative. The 25% stipulation here has absolutely no relation to the services actually rendered.").

81 Harrison County Bd. of Supervisors v. Carlo Corp. Inc., 833 So. 2d 582 (Miss. 2002) (county board acted arbitrarily and capriciously in imposing attorney fee of 25% of corporate tax debt when this resulted in $79,000 fee for writing one letter; fee violated both common sense and rule of professional responsibility that required fees to be reasonable; remanding to determine fee applying standards in rule).

82 Marine Midland Bank v. Kilbane, 573 F. Supp. 469, 471 (D. Md. 1983) (N.Y. law).

83 *See* Perdue v. Crocker Nat'l Bank, 38 Cal. 3d 913, 702 P.2d 503, 216 Cal. Rptr. 345 (1985); National Consumer Law Center, The Cost of Credit: Regulation, Preemption, and Industry Abuses § 12.7 (3d ed. 2005 and Supp.); National Consumer Law Center, Unfair and Deceptive Acts and Practices § 4.4.9 (6th ed. 2004 and Supp.).

84 National Consumer Law Center, The Cost of Credit: Regulation, Preemption, and Industry Abuses § 12.8 (3d ed. 2005 and Supp.).

85 *See* Bondanza v. Peninsula Hosp., 23 Cal. 3d 260, 590 P.2d 22, 152 Cal. Rptr. 446 (1979) (unfair business practice to allocate all collection costs to the subset of accounts that collection agency successfully collects); Beasley v. Wells Fargo Bank, 1 Cal. Rptr. 2d 446, 458–459 (Ct. App. 1991) (upholding challenge to amount of insufficient funds fee; bank not allowed to spread costs of collection across all late debtors).

86 National Consumer Law Center, The Cost of Credit: Regulation, Preemption, and Industry Abuses §§ 2.2, 2.3.3, 2.4 (3d ed. 2005 and Supp.).

87 Black v. Educ. Credit Mgmt. Corp., 459 F.3d 796 (7th Cir. 2006) (upholding Dep't of Education regulations permitting assessment of collection costs as percentage of debt); City of New Haven v. Bonner, 863 A.2d 680 (Conn. 2005) (collection agency fees that statute authorizes municipality to add to tax debt may be based on percentage of debt regardless of actual work performed); *see also* Lawrence Mall of New Haven, Inc. v. W. Haven, 37 Conn. L. Rptr. 903 (Super. Ct. 2004) (percentage of debt is reasonable as fee to private collector of municipal tax debts, regardless of amount of work done in individual case, because it compensates agency for risk that many stale tax debts were uncollectible, and places cost of unsuccessful collections on delinquent rather than timely taxpayers), *later decision at* 2006 WL 853211 (Conn. Super. Ct. Mar. 20, 2006) (due process did not require that landowners be given advance notice that 15% collection fee would be imposed on late payments).

88 *Refusing to allow recovery of collection fees*: Fields v. W. Mass. Credit Corp., 479 F. Supp. 2d 287 (D. Conn. 2007) (collector not entitled to fee when debt arose from retail installment sale; statute prohibits collection fees for retail installment sales, and consumer's contract with creditor conformed to this statute);

decisions that might be construed as assuming that collection fees are allowable, most deny fees on grounds other than their illegality, or treat some question as a fact issue for trial.[89]

Restrictions on collection fees may be found in state statutes regulating collection agencies.[90] Hawaii, for ex-

---

Ozkaya v. Telecheck Services, Inc., 982 F. Supp. 578 (N.D. Ill. 1997) (state collection agency law prohibits fees unless "expressly authorized by law"; collection agency not entitled to fee for check on which consumer stopped payment when state law allows fees for certain dishonored checks but is silent as to stop-payments); Patzka v. Viterbo College, 917 F. Supp. 654 (W.D. Wis. 1996) (Wisconsin prohibits collection fees, even if separately negotiated; even in absence of statutory prohibition, fees here would be impermissible because not disclosed on face of consumer's contract with creditor); Teemogonwuno v. Todd, Bremer & Larsen, Inc., Clearinghouse No. 45,946B (N.D. Ga. 1991) (under Georgia law non-legal expenses are not recoverable as collection costs); Bolden v. G.H. Perkins Assoc., Inc., Clearinghouse No. 31,470 (D. Conn. 1981) (finding collection agency's claims for collection expenses excessive; no challenge as to recoverability of a more reasonable claim for collection expenses); Bondanza v. Peninsula Hosp., 23 Cal. 3d 260, 590 P.2d 22, 152 Cal. Rptr. 446 (1979) (enjoining collection agency's addition of one-third collection fee to hospital debt; finding fee to be a penalty unrelated to the actual anticipated expense of collection when the contract provided for reasonable attorney fees and collection expenses); Beasley v. Wells Fargo Bank, 235 Cal. App. 3d 1383, 1 Cal. Rptr. 2d 446 (1992) (illegal for bank to charge customers the fixed percentage fee it pays debt collectors); Y-12 Credit Union v. Wiseman, 1986 WL 5240 (Tenn. Ct. App. May 6, 1986) (refusing to award 40% collection fee when creditor did not prove that it was reasonable); *see also* Akalwadi v. Risk Mgmt. Alternatives, 336 F. Supp. 2d 492 (D. Md. 2004) (refusing to grant summary judgment for collection fee under lease that required renter to pay collection expenses incurred by owner; fact question whether owner actually incurred expenses); Gostony v. Diem Corp., 320 F. Supp. 2d 932 (D. Ariz. 2003) (interpreting lease clause allowing "prevailing party" to recover "collection agency fees" to allow recovery only when party prevails in judicial proceeding; collection agency violated FDCPA by seeking fee without having filed suit); Adair v. Sabharwal, 2002 WL 31243019 (S.D. Ind. Aug. 16, 2002) (refusing to dismiss claim that creditor added illegal collection fee, in absence of evidence that creditor actually paid or incurred fee, when contract obligated debtor to pay collection fees "paid or incurred" by creditor); Kojetin v. C.U. Recovery, Inc., 1999 U.S. Dist. LEXIS 1745 (D. Minn. Feb. 17, 1999) (mag.) (creditor could not pass on to consumer the percentage fee that the collection agency charged it when percentage was not related to actual costs of collection effort and contract made debtor liable for "costs of collection"), *adopted by* 1999 U.S. Dist. LEXIS 10930 (D. Minn. Mar. 29, 1999), *aff'd*, 212 F.3d 1318 (8th Cir. 2000) (per curiam).

Allowing recovery of collection fees: Talbott v. G.C. Services Ltd. P'ship, 53 F. Supp. 2d 846 (W.D. Va. 1999) (telephone company's tariff filed with FCC authorizes reasonable collection costs, so consumer can be required to pay collector's 35% fee); Decatur Imaging Ctr. v. Ames, 608 N.E.2d 1198 (Ill. App. Ct. 1992) (debt collection statute allows collection fee if expressly authorized by contract; statement in contract here was sufficient, but creditor must prove not only that fees were incurred but also that they were reasonable).

89 *See, e.g.*, Akalwadi v. Risk Mgmt. Alternatives, 336 F. Supp. 2d 492 (D. Md. 2004) (refusing to grant summary judgment for collection fee under lease that required renter to pay collection expenses incurred by owner; fact question whether owner actually incurred expenses); Gostony v. Diem Corp., 320 F. Supp. 2d 932 (D. Ariz. 2003) (interpreting lease clause allowing "prevailing party" to recover "collection agency fees" to allow recovery only when party prevails in judicial proceeding; collection agency violated FDCPA by seeking fee without having filed suit); Adair v. Sabharwal, 2002 WL 31243019 (S.D. Ind. Aug. 16, 2002) (refusing to dismiss claim that creditor added illegal collection fee, in absence of evidence that creditor actually paid or incurred fee, when contract obligated debtor to pay collection fees "paid or incurred" by creditor); Kojetin v. C.U. Recovery, Inc., 1999 U.S. Dist. LEXIS 1745 (D. Minn. Feb. 17, 1999) (mag.) (creditor could not pass on to consumer the percentage fee that the collection agency charged it when percentage was not related to actual costs of collection effort and contract made debtor liable for "costs of collection"), *adopted by* 1999 U.S. Dist. LEXIS 10930 (D. Minn. Mar. 29, 1999), *aff'd*, 212 F.3d 1318 (8th Cir. 2000) (per curiam); Y-12 Credit Union v. Wiseman, 1986 WL 5240 (Tenn. Ct. App. May 6, 1986) (refusing to award 40% collection fee when creditor did not prove that it was reasonable).

90 *See, e.g.*, Mich. Comp. Laws § 339.915a(e) (prohibiting licensees from demanding or obtaining a share of the compensation for services performed by an attorney in collecting a claim or demand or collecting or receiving a fee or other compensation from a consumer for collecting a claim, other than a claim owing the creditor pursuant to the provisions of the original agreement between the creditor and debtor); N.H. Rev. Stat. Ann. § 358-C:3 (prohibiting collection agencies from adding charges to debt, other than court costs, unless charge is expressly authorized by the agreement creating the obligation and legally chargeable to the debtor); N.C. Gen. Stat. § 75-55(2) (prohibiting debt collectors from attempting to collect charges to which they are not legally entitled); W. Va. Code §§ 46A-2-128(d) (prohibiting collection agencies from attempting to collect charge, fee, or expense unless it is expressly authorized by the agreement and by statute), 46A-3-101 (listing charges that may be included in consumer credit sale); *see also* Fields v. W. Mass. Credit Corp., 479 F. Supp. 2d 287 (D. Conn. 2007) (Connecticut motor vehicle loan law allows the addition only of attorney, not collection agency, fees to deficiency after repossession); Adams v. A. & S. Collection Associates, Inc., 2007 WL 2206936 (D. Conn. July 30, 2007) (mag.) (collector's requirement that creditor add 49% collection fee and 18% interest to claims before forwarding them to agency violates Connecticut Creditors' Collection Practices Law); Hansen v. Ticket Track, Inc. 280 F. Supp. 2d 1196 (W.D. Wash. 2003) (Washington collection agency statute, Wash. Rev. Code § 19.16.250(18), forbade collector, but not creditor, from adding collection fee to debt; fee here was added by collector, and thus unlawful, when collector's contract with creditor-parking lot operator required creditor to include fee provision in its contract with customers); Ozkaya v. Telecheck Services, Inc., 982 F. Supp. 578 (N.D. Ill. 1997) (state collection agency law prohibits fees unless "expressly authorized by law"; collection agency not entitled to fee for check on which consumer stopped payment when state law allows fees for certain dishonored checks but is silent as to stop-payments); Patzka v. Viterbo College, 917 F. Supp. 654 (W.D. Wis. 1996) (Wisconsin prohibits collection fees, even if separately negotiated; even in absence of statutory prohibition, fees here would be impermissible because not disclosed on face of consumer's contract with creditor). *But cf.*

ample, forbids collection agencies to recover any collection expenses, except for attorney fees after filing suit.[91] Iowa allows a collection agency to collect a fee from the debtor only if the fee is reasonably related to the actions taken by the collector and the collector is legally authorized to collect it.[92]

In many cases, the debt will arise from a transaction that is governed by a statute that lists the charges that may be imposed on the debtor. If collection agency fees are not specifically listed, courts consider them forbidden.[93]

While a number of states recognize attorney fee clauses by statute, or impose fee shifting for certain types of litigation even in the absence of a contractual clause,[94] it is rare for a state to have specific statutory authority for collection agency fees. Even if there is no prohibition against imposing the fee, the creditor must show that the consumer actually agreed to it,[95] and courts usually require the collector or creditor to show that the fee was actually incurred and is reasonable.[96]

When there is little case law, the law limiting recovery in other contexts (for example, contractually authorized attorney fees) may provide the rule of decision either directly or by analogy.[97] As with attorney fees clauses,[98] a collection fee clause may be unenforceable as a penalty[99] or may be held unconscionable.[100]

By analogy to attorney fee clauses, collection fee clauses should be strictly construed.[101] Indeed, courts should look on collection fee clauses with even greater disfavor, as attorneys must be licensed, must complete extensive professional training, are governed by rules of professional responsibility, and are subject to the inherent authority of courts to regulate the practice of law. Collection agencies are not subject to equivalent checks and balances and in many states need not even be licensed, so any purported authority to impose collection fees on the debtor should be even more strictly construed than in the case of attorney fees.

Decatur Imaging Ctr. v. Ames, 608 N.E.2d 1198 (Ill. App. Ct. 1992).

91 Haw. Rev. Stat. § 443B-9 (collection agency may not collect or attempt to collect any collection fee, except attorney fee up to 25% after filing suit); *see* Wiginton v. Pac. Credit Corp., 2 Haw. App. 435, 634 P.2d 111 (1981) (claim for $1000 by a collection agency as the "probable expense of legal process" was deceptive as it was not due when the dunning letter was sent); *cf.* Ai v. Frank Huff Agency, Ltd., 607 P.2d 1304 (Haw. 1980) (it was a deceptive practice for a collection agency to attempt to collect attorney fees of one-third of the debt when attorney fees were limited by statute to 25%).

92 Iowa Code § 537.7103(5)(c).

93 *See, e.g.*, Fields v. W. Mass. Credit Corp., 479 F. Supp. 2d 287 (D. Conn. 2007) (collector not entitled to fee when debt arose from retail installment sale; statute prohibits collection fees for retail installment sales, and consumer's contract with creditor conformed to this statute); Ozkaya v. Telecheck Services, Inc., 982 F. Supp. 578 (N.D. Ill. 1997) (state collection agency law prohibits fees unless "expressly authorized by law"; collection agency not entitled to fee for check on which consumer stopped payment when state law allows fees for certain dishonored checks but is silent as to stop-payments).

94 *See* §§ 6.2.2, 6.3, *supra.*

95 *Cf.* Alexson v. Hudson Valley Cmty. College, 125 F. Supp. 2d 27 (N.D.N.Y. 2000) (denying creditor's motion for summary judgment; fact question whether college violated state UDAP statute by seeking collection fee without having disclosed it fully in college catalog).

96 Bolden v. G.H. Perkins Assoc., Inc., Clearinghouse No. 31,470 (D. Conn. 1981) (finding collection agency's claims for collection expenses excessive; no challenge as to recoverability of a more reasonable claim for collection expenses); Decatur Imaging Ctr. v. Ames, 608 N.E.2d 1198, 1202 (Ill. App. Ct. 1992); Y-12 Credit Union v. Wiseman, 1986 WL 5240 (Tenn. Ct. App. May 6, 1986).

97 *See* Y-12 Credit Union v. Wiseman, 1986 WL 5240 (Tenn. Ct. App. May 6, 1986) (relying on attorney fee decisions by analogy; refusing to award 40% collection fee when creditor did not prove that it was reasonable).

98 *See* § 6.2.2, *supra.*

99 Bondanza v. Peninsula Hosp., 23 Cal. 3d 260, 590 P.2d 22, 152 Cal. Rptr. 446 (1979) (enjoining collection agency's addition of one-third collection fee to hospital debt; finding fee to be a penalty unrelated to the actual anticipated expense of collection when the contract provided for reasonable attorney fees and collection expenses; rejecting argument that collection agency may apportion all of its collection costs to those debtors from whom it successfully collects); Beasley v. Wells Fargo Bank, 235 Cal. App. 3d 1383, 1 Cal. Rptr. 2d 446 (1992) (illegal for bank to charge customers the fixed percentage fee it pays debt collectors).

100 *See* § 6.2.2, *supra.*

101 *See* § 6.2.4, *supra.*

Chapter 7 Defending Military Personnel in Collection Actions

7.1 Introduction

The Servicemembers Civil Relief Act (SCRA)[1] limits collection tactics and enforcement of claims against active duty military personnel. This law should be reviewed in detail whenever a current or former member of the military, or a dependent, is represented in a debt collection matter.

Among the Act's most significant features are protections against default judgments,[2] tolling of statutes of limitations,[3] a reduction of the interest rate on pre-active duty obligations to six percent,[4] prohibitions against self-help repossession and non-judicial foreclosure,[5] restrictions on eviction from residential premises,[6] and the right to terminate residential or vehicle leases.[7] The Act also contains a variety of protections relating to matters such as taxes, life and health insurance, professional liability insurance, and powers of attorney that are beyond the scope of this chapter.

The Act must be liberally construed to protect members of the armed forces.[8] An excellent and detailed Judge Advocate General (JAG) Corps manual analyzing the amended version of the Act may be found on-line.[9] The American Bar Association also has an on-line collection of materials on the Act,[10] including a judge's guide with sample stay motions.[11]

A number of states have similar laws.[12] These statutes are summarized on a state-by-state basis in the note below.[13]

1 50 U.S.C. app. §§ 501–596.

2 50 U.S.C. app. §§ 521, 522; *see* § 7.5, *infra*.

3 50 U.S.C. app. § 526; *see* § 7.6, *infra*.

4 50 U.S.C. app. § 527; *see* § 7.7, *infra*.

5 50 U.S.C. app. § 532; *see* § 7.8, *infra*.

6 50 U.S.C. app. § 531; *see* § 7.11, *infra*.

7 50 U.S.C. app. § 535; *see* §§ 7.9, 7.11, *infra*.

8 Boone v. Lightner, 319 U.S. 561, 63 S. Ct. 1223, 87 L. Ed. 1587 (1943); Engstrom v. First Nat'l Bank, 47 F.3d 1459, 1462 (5th Cir. 1995); Bank of Nova Scotia v. George, 2008 WL 501263 (D. V.I. Feb. 15, 2008); Johnson v. City of Philadelphia, 2007 U.S. Dist. LEXIS 82563 (E.D. Pa. Nov. 7, 2007) (in evaluating whether to grant a stay, a servicemember's absence when his rights or liabilities are being adjudged is usually prima facie prejudicial); Merrill v. Beard, 2007 WL 461469 (N.D. Ohio Feb. 7, 2007) (in setting aside default judgments courts strictly construe requirements of Act in favor of servicemembers); Sprinkle v. SB & C Ltd., 472 F. Supp. 2d 1235 (W.D. Wash. 2006) (acknowledging expansive purpose of protections under Act; construing requirement for affidavit of non-military service to apply to garnishment proceeding); Atkins v. County of Alameda, 2004 WL 444105 (N.D. Cal. Mar. 8, 2004) ("Courts have long construed the 'stay' provisions of the Act liberally, retaining broad discretion to consider any and all stay-related factors."); Antioch Co. v. Scrapbook Borders, Inc., 210 F.R.D. 645 (D. Minn. 2002); Cathey v. First Republic Bank, 2001 U.S. Dist. LEXIS 13150, at *12 (W.D. La. July 6, 2001) ("Any doubts that arise as to the scope and application of the Act should be resolved in favor of the military person."); *In re* Burrell, 230 B.R. 309 (Bankr. E.D. Tex. 1999); Lenser v. McGowan, 191 S.W.3d 506 (Ark. 2004); State *ex rel.* Estate of Perry, 168 S.W.3d 577 (Mo. Ct. App. 2005) (Act's provisions on tolling of statutes of limitations are to be liberally construed); Bernhardt v. Alden Café, 374 N.J. Super. 271, 864 A.2d 421 (Super. Ct. App. Div. 2005) (Act liberally construed to mandate appointment of counsel before default or default judgment may be entered against absent servicemember); Murdock v. Murdock, 338 S.C. 322, 526 S.E.2d 241 (Ct. App. 1999). *But see In re* Marriage of Bradley, 282 Kan. 1, 137 P.3d 1030 (2006) (recognizing rule of liberal construction of Act, but denying stay when servicemember did not provide documentation required by section 522(b)(2) in support of request for stay); *cf.* Chace v. Lopez, 89 S.W.3d 788 (Tex. App. 2002) (Act to be liberally construed but can not be stretched to prohibit prejudgment interest on tort claim when nothing in Act addresses this topic).

9 Available at www.jagcnet.army.mil/TJAGSA (Publication JA 260) (Mar. 2006).

10 Available at www.abanet.org/family/military.

11 Mark E. Sullivan, A Judge's Guide to the Servicemembers Civil Relief Act, *available at* www.abanet.org/family/military.

12 *See* Douglas W. Buchanan, *Complying with the Federal Servicemembers Civil Relief Act and Similar State Laws*, 60 Consumer Fin. L.Q. Rep. 286 (2006) (describing current and pending legislation in several states).

13 *ALABAMA*: Ala. Code §§ 31-12-1 to 31-12-10 preserve many servicemember rights and benefits during military service. They apply to National Guard and reserves called up to serve in armed conflict or a state of emergency for thirty days or more. They incorporate federal law into state law, preserve educational status, and require state and local governmental employers to pay their employees who are called into active duty the difference between military pay and the salary the employee would have received in the governmental job.

ALASKA: Alaska Stat. § 26.05.135 extends the protections of the federal act to National Guard and naval militia on active duty.

ARIZONA: Ariz. Rev. Stat. Ann. § 6-1260(L) restricts payday lending ("deferred presentment transactions") to servicemembers and spouses. It applies primarily to collection methods.

7.2 History of the Act and Amendments

The SCRA was originally adopted in 1940 as the Soldiers' and Sailors' Civil Relief Act. In 1991 Congress

---

Ariz. Rev. Stat. Ann. § 23-1390(B) tolls the six-month limitation period for filing unfair labor practice complaint for agricultural worker if service in the armed forces prevented the worker from filing the charge. Ariz. Rev. Stat. Ann. § 33-1413(F) excuses a mobile home park tenant who is a member of armed forces from the requirement to give two weeks' notice before terminating a rental agreement requirement if he or she receives reassignment orders that do not allow such prior notification.

ARKANSAS: Ark. Code Ann. §§ 12-62-701 to 12-62-718 apply to National Guard members called into active military service for the state by the governor for more than 180 continuous days. The state act provides extensive protections including prohibition against termination of installment contracts for the purchase of real or personal property for any breach that occurs during military service; prohibition against self-help repossession; extension of the statute of limitations; reduction of the interest rate on pre-active duty obligations to six percent; restriction on eviction; and prohibition of non-judicial foreclosure.

CALIFORNIA: Cal. Mil. & Vet. Code §§ 400 to 409.13 (West) apply to National Guard members ordered into active state service by the governor or into active federal service by the President, and to reservists called into active federal duty. The law provides extensive protections, including stay of court actions; restrictions on eviction; deferral of financial obligations, foreclosure, and repossession; reduction of the interest rate on pre-active duty obligations to six percent; prohibition against non-judicial foreclosure; extension of redemption periods after foreclosure or tax sale; and tax deferral.

COLORADO: Colo. Rev. Stat. §§ 1401 to 1407 provide protections for reservists and National Guard members when called to active duty in excess of thirty days. Protections include: stay of civil proceedings and enforcement of security interests; court intervention in eviction, distress, and rent payments; and modification of installment contracts.

CONNECTICUT: Conn. Gen. Stat. § 36a-737 provides a procedure to freeze the terms and conditions of pending mortgage applications from reservists and the National Guard during service.

FLORIDA: Fla. Stat. §§ 250.5201 to 250.5205 prohibit termination of installment contracts for the purchase of real or personal property for any breach that occurs during military service; allow a court to order a stay of proceedings; restrict eviction; and prohibit non-judicial foreclosure. These protections apply to persons called into state active duty by the governor for more than seventeen days.

GEORGIA: Ga. Code Ann. § 46-5-8 provides the procedure for servicemembers to terminate their wireless telecommunication service contracts prior to the contract's expiration, that is, when transferred, released from service, etcetera. Ga. Code Ann. § 44-7-22 provides for the termination of residential leases for military personnel with terms that are more liberal than the federal act. This 2007 statute relates back to leases entered into on or after July 1, 2005.

HAWAII: Haw. Rev. Stat. §§ 657D-1 to 657D-63 constitute a comprehensive law similar to the federal act, including a prohibition against non-judicial foreclosures and a reduction of pre-active duty interest rates to six percent. It applies to persons called to active state duty.

IDAHO: Idaho Code Ann. § 46-409 applies the provisions of the federal act and the Uniform Services Employment and Reemployment Rights Act (USERRA) to the air and army National Guard when called to active duty for thirty or more days.

ILLINOIS: 330 Ill. Comp. Stat. § 60/5.1 allows a court to order a stay of proceedings if state or federal military service directly results in failure to meet pre-service obligations.

IOWA: Iowa Code §§ 29A.90 to 29A.105 are similar to the federal act. Among other things, they bar a creditor from self-help repossession for breach, before or during military service, of an installment contract to buy real or personal property entered into before entry into service; reduce interest rates to six percent; and prohibit non-judicial foreclosure. They also provide for stays and reopening of default judgments. They apply to state military and reserve on full-time active duty and their dependents.

LOUISIANA: La. Rev. Stat. Ann. § 9:3261 provides that servicemembers may terminate residential leases (in case of transfer, and so forth). La. Rev. Stat. Ann. §§ 29:401 to 29:426 incorporate the SCRA and USERRA into Louisiana law (§ 29:422) and provide extensive provisions regarding servicemember health insurance, re-employment, occupational licenses, and so forth.

MAINE: Me. Rev. Stat. Ann. tit. 37-B, § 387 provides servicemember protections against evictions; Me. Rev. Stat. Ann. tit. 37-B, § 389-A provides servicemembers with the opportunity for stays of court proceedings, electronic testimony and evidence, expedited hearings, and so forth; Me. Rev. Stat. Ann. tit. 37-B, § 390 defers motor vehicle insurance coverage; Me. Rev. Stat. Ann. tit. 37-B, § 390-A provides extensions of professional licenses.

MARYLAND: Md. Code Ann., Pub. Safety § 13-705 (West) applies the protections of the federal act to members of the National Guard or Maryland Defense when ordered into military duty under state law for fourteen consecutive days or more. In addition, Md. Code Ann., Pub. Safety §§ 14-201 to 14-218 (West) apply many protections similar to those provided by the federal act to emergency management personnel during emergency periods and to people who suffer serious personal injury, family injury, or property damage during a declared emergency. These protections include stays of proceedings, and provisions concerning installment contracts, mortgages, evictions, and taxes.

MICHIGAN: Mich. Comp. Laws § 32.517 applies to those in active state service. It exempts the servicemember's property from execution, seizure, or attachment for debts incurred prior to or during state service, provides for stays of proceedings, and restricts termination of heat, water, electricity, or gas for unpaid bills for the servicemember or his or her household during the first ninety days of service.

MINNESOTA: Minn. Stat. § 72A.20(8)(b) and (c), the state's Unfair Insurance Practices (UNIP) statute, provides protections regarding denial of life insurance and health insurance (or reinstatement after period of service) to servicemembers and their families (including the National Guard). Minn. Stat. § 325E.027 prohibits termination of utility service for certain servicemembers, and Minn. Stat. §§ 325G.53 and 325G.54 allow servicemembers to cancel wireless service contracts, rental contracts, club contracts, service contracts, and membership travel contracts without penalty.

amended the Act to provide extra protections for military personnel called to active duty during the Desert Storm campaign.[14]

In 2003 Congress rewrote the law completely and renamed it the Servicemembers Civil Relief Act.[15] The 2003 law preserved most of the features of the previous Act, so decisions under the former law remain relevant. In addition, it expanded some protections, modernized the language,

---

MISSISSIPPI: Miss. Code Ann. § 37-103-19 provides in-state tuition for the spouse and child of the servicemember while on active duty if stationed in the state. Miss. Code Ann. § 75-24-5(2)(m) provides protections regarding reinstatement of motor vehicle insurance for returning servicemembers.

MISSOURI: Mo. Rev. Stat. § 41.944 allows active duty service members to terminate residential leases when transferred, released, and so forth; Mo. Rev. Stat. § 430.140 protects servicemembers from chattel liens for small repair bills.

NEW HAMPSHIRE: N.H. Rev. Stat. Ann. § 540:11-a provides protections regarding the termination of a residential lease when the servicemember is transferred, called up, and so forth.

NEW JERSEY: N.J. Stat. Ann. §§ 38:23C-1 to 38:23C-26 (West) constitute a comprehensive law similar to the federal act. Among other things it prohibits non-judicial foreclosure and provides that the period of military service is not included in any redemption period. It applies to those on active federal duty or in state military service pursuant to an order of the governor.

NEW YORK: N.Y. Mil. Law §§ 301-a to 328 (McKinney) constitute a comprehensive law similar to the federal act. It applies to those on federal active duty or those in the military service of the state pursuant to an order of the governor. Among other things, it prohibits non-judicial foreclosure and provides that the period of military service is not included in any redemption period.

OHIO: Ohio Rev. Code Ann. §§ 5919.29, 5923.12 (West) extend the protections of the federal act to those ordered by the governor into National Guard active duty or training; Ohio Rev. Code Ann. § 317.322 (West) exempts servicemembers from paying for a recording fee for a power of attorney; Ohio Rev. Code Ann. § 125.021 (West) provides that the office of information technology may purchase bulk phone service for the use of active duty servicemembers and families; Ohio Rev. Code Ann. § 1343.031 (West) addresses interest rates; Ohio Rev. Code Ann. § 1349.02 (West) addresses motor vehicle leases; Ohio Rev. Code Ann. § 1349.03 (West) addresses cell phone contracts; Ohio Rev. Code Ann. § 1923.062 (West) addresses residential evictions, including mobile homes; Ohio Rev. Code Ann. § 4933.12(F) (West) addresses gas utility shutoffs; Ohio Rev. Code Ann. § 4933.121 (West) addresses electricity utility shutoffs; Ohio Rev. Code Ann. § 323.122 (West) extends the amount of time to pay property taxes; Ohio Rev. Code Ann. § 3770.07 (West) provides that certain active duty personnel may make delayed claims for lottery prizes; Ohio Rev. Code Ann. § 3915.053 (West) addresses insurance policies, providing that there is no lapse for nonpayment during active duty; Ohio Rev. Code Ann. § 5747.026 (West) extends the period of time for filing income tax returns or paying taxes, for National Guard members and reservists called into active duty.

OKLAHOMA: Okla. Stat. tit. 44, § 208.1 provides civil relief for National Guard members; adopts SCRA and USERRA as state law and makes them applicable to National Guard members.

PENNSYLVANIA: 51 Pa. Cons. Stat. § 4105 makes National Guard members on active state service exempt from civil process, and suspends all presumptions arising from the lapse of time. 51 Pa. Cons. Stat. §§ 7301 to 7319 provide employment protections and allows courts to stay proceedings; extend the redemption period after a tax sale; provide for the maximum interest rates and rescheduling of debt payments to account for reduced income during service period for National Guard on active federal or state duty of thirty or more consecutive days; restrict eviction; and include other protections.

TENNESSEE: Tenn. Code Ann. § 26-1-111 addresses foreclosure of home mortgages and motor vehicle retail installment sales contracts.

TEXAS: Tex. Civ. Prac. & Rem. Code Ann. § 16.022 (Vernon) tolls statute of limitations for actions to recover or defend title to real property for servicemembers on active duty in time of war. Tex. Fin. Code Ann. § 342.602 (Vernon) addresses payday loans. Tex. Gov't Code Ann. § 466.408 (Vernon) addresses claiming lottery prizes. Tex. Labor Code Ann. § 101.116 (Vernon) addresses union dues. Tex. Prop. Code Ann. § 92.017 (Vernon) addresses residential leases and a tenant's right to terminate. Tex. Tax Code Ann. § 31.02(b) (Vernon) addresses extension of time to pay property taxes.

UTAH: Utah Code Ann. §§ 39-7-101 to 39-7-119, which are similar to the federal act, apply to National Guard members called into active full-time service by the governor for at least thirty days. The provisions of this law include suspension of the statute of limitations; restrictions on termination of contracts and self-help repossession; and prohibition of non-judicial foreclosure.

VERMONT: Vt. Stat. Ann. tit. 12, § 553 suspends the statute of limitations but does not provide other protections.

VIRGINIA: Va. Code Ann. § 8.01-15.2 addresses default judgments and non-military affidavits; Va. Code Ann. § 38.2-508.1 addresses life insurance; Va. Code Ann. § 38.2-2205.1 addresses car insurance; Va. Code Ann. §§ 43-34 and 46.2-1200.2 require the state Department of Motor Vehicles to notify lien holders of the military status of vehicle owners and requires those disposing of abandoned vehicles to comply with the federal act; Va. Code Ann. § 55-248.21:1 addresses early termination of residential leases.

WASHINGTON: Wash. Rev. Code § 4.16.220 suspends the statute of limitations; Wash. Rev. Code § 31.48.210 addresses payday lending; Wash. Rev. Code §§ 38.42.010 to 38.42.903 provide protections similar to the federal act, addressing waivers, default judgments, stays, fines and penalties under contracts, and business loan interest rates.

WEST VIRGINIA: W. Va. Code § 21-1A-6 extends the time allowed for filing unfair labor practice complaints.

WISCONSIN: Wis. Stat. § 21.74 suspends the enforcement of some tax liabilities, waives interest and penalties on some taxes, and terminates mobile telephone service for servicemembers in federal service; Wis. Stat. § 21.75 is a comprehensive law similar to the federal act. It applies to members of the National Guard or a state defense force who are called into active state service by order of the governor. It limits interest rates similarly to the federal act; provides for stays of proceedings; and restricts foreclosure, actions to resume possession of personal property, and enforcement of storage liens.

WYOMING: Wyo. Stat. Ann. §§ 19-11-101 to 19-11-124 address employment and re-employment, benefits, insurance, professional licenses, and so forth. The SCRA and USERRA are made applicable to certain National Guard members.

14 Soldiers' and Sailors' Civil Relief Act Amendments of 1991, Pub. L. No. 102-12, 105 Stat. 34.

15 Pub. L. No. 108-189, 117 Stat. 2835 (2003).

updated the caps on coverage of certain types of obligations, and applied existing protections to new situations. It also added a requirement that the military services give written notice to servicemembers of the protections provided by the Act.[16] Portions of the Act were again amended for clarification in 2004,[17] and a 2006 amendment provided further detail about the duty of the armed forces to notify servicemembers of their rights under the Act.[18]

The relevant portions of both the pre-2003 and post-2003 versions of the law are reproduced on the companion website to this manual.

7.3 Prohibitions Against Retaliation and Waivers

The Act prohibits issuing an adverse credit report, denying, revoking, or changing the terms of a credit transaction, or taking certain other specified adverse actions because of the assertion of rights under the Act.[19] It also restricts waivers of the protections relating to modification, termination, or cancellation of contracts, leases, bailments, or mortgage debts, or to repossession, retention, foreclosure, sale, or forfeiture of property. A waiver of any of these protections is ineffective unless made by a written agreement signed during or after active duty.[20]

7.4 Who Is Protected by the Act?

The Act applies to those in military service, defined to include the armed forces and the commissioned corps of the National Oceanic and Atmospheric Administration and the Public Health Service.[21] To be entitled to the Act's protections, the servicemember must be in "military service," defined as active duty.[22] All servicemembers on active duty are entitled to the benefits of the Act, whether or not they are stationed in a war zone, and whether they enlisted or were mobilized.

Active duty includes full-time training duty, annual training duty, and attendance at a military school while in active military service.[23] National Guard members called to active service by the President or Secretary of Defense for more than thirty consecutive days for the purposes of responding to a national emergency declared by the President and supported by federal funds are also considered to be on active duty and entitled to the Act's protections.[24] The similar language of the pre-2003 version of the Act was held to include reservists during periods of active duty.[25] Active duty includes periods of time that a servicemember is absent from duty on account of sickness, wounds, leave, or other lawful cause,[26] but not periods of time the servicemembers is absent without leave (AWOL) or confined to military prison.[27]

---

16 50 U.S.C. app. § 515 (compare to former 50 U.S.C. app. § 515); *see also* 50 U.S.C. app. § 515a (effective Jan. 6, 2006) (establishing general requirement for notifying servicemembers of rights under the Act during orientation and trainings and authorizing outreach to adult dependents of servicemembers).

17 Veterans Benefits Improvement Act, Pub. L. No. 108-454, 118 Stat. 3598 (2004).

Highlights of the amendments include defining "judgment" in 50 U.S.C. app. § 511, strengthening the safeguards against waiver in 50 U.S.C. app. § 517, clarifying that 50 U.S.C. app. § 522 allows both plaintiffs and defendants to obtain stays of civil actions and proceedings, and adding clarification and definitions to 50 U.S.C. app. § 535 regarding the servicemember's right to terminate a residential or motor vehicle lease.

18 Pub. L. No. 109-163, 119 Stat. 3337 (2006).

19 50 U.S.C. app. § 518; *see* Cathey v. First Republic Bank, 2001 U.S. Dist. LEXIS 13150 (W.D. La. July 6, 2001) (provision of former version of Act barring changes in credit terms does not forbid new loan to cover cost overruns that occur while commercial borrower is serving abroad).

20 50 U.S.C. app. § 517.

21 50 U.S.C. app. § 511(1) (cross-referencing 10 U.S.C. § 101(a)(5)). *But cf. In re* Gaddy, 2004 WL 2044107 (Bankr. D. Kan. Apr. 12, 2004) (SCRA protections do not apply to civilian employees of private contractor engaged in support of uniformed servicemembers in Iraq).

22 50 U.S.C. app. § 511(2)(i)) (cross-referencing 10 U.S.C. § 101(d)(1)).

23 10 U.S.C. § 101(d)(1). *But cf.* Donahou v. Presidential Limousine & Auto Sales, Inc., 2007 WL 1229342 (W.D. Ark. Apr. 24, 2007) (active duty does not include eight-month "Delayed Entry" period between time servicemember enlisted and time he reported for duty; he had no military duties during this time and was able to maintain civilian employment).

24 50 U.S.C. app. § 511(2)(A)(ii).

The Act was amended in 2002 to cover National Guard members who have been called up. *See* Pub. L. No. 107-330, § 305, 116 Stat. 2821 (2002).

25 Marin v. U.S. Postal Serv., 2003 WL 22427938 (2d Cir. Oct. 23, 2003) (reservist entitled to Act's benefits only when ordered to report for active duty); *In re* Marriage of Brazas, 662 N.E.2d 559 (Ill. App. Ct. 1996) (Soldiers and Sailors Civil Relief Act applies to reservists while on reserve duty; vacating default judgment entered on day when trial court and opposing counsel had actual notice that reservist was out of state on reserve duty); Sung Man Min v. Avila, 991 S.W.2d 495 (Tex. App. 1999) (statute of limitations is tolled only during active duty; annual two-week reserve duty is active duty but weekend reserve duty is not); *cf.* Bowen v. United States, 292 F.3d 1383 (Fed. Cir. 2002) (two weeks of National Guard training, ordered by state but paid for with federal paycheck, is not "federal service on active duty" under pre-2003 version of Act, so statute of limitations not tolled).

26 50 U.S.C. app. § 511(2)(C); *see* Sec'y of Hous. & Urban Dev. v. McClenan, 4 Misc. 3d 1027(A) (Civ. Ct. 2004) (table) (text available at 2004 WL 2187568) (active duty servicemember receiving medical treatment pending deployment is protected by Act).

27 *In re* Marriage of Hampshire, 934 P.2d 58 (Kan. 1997) (interpreting pre-2003 version of Act not to protect soldier who was absent without leave or in military prison at the time of proceedings which led to default judgment for child support); Reed v. Albaaj, 723 N.W.2d 50 (Minn. Ct. App. 2006) (Act does not apply to servicemember while incarcerated in military prison for crime committed while on active duty).

United States citizens serving with allied forces are also entitled to the protections of the Act.[28] Many of the Act's protections also apply to reservists between the date of receipt of orders to report for active duty and the reporting date, and to draftees between the date of the induction notice and the date of induction.[29]

Some protections of the SCRA cover the dependents and co-obligors of servicemembers. In many cases, however, the dependent or co-obligor must obtain a court order for protections that are automatic for servicemembers.[30] Rights under the Act may be enforced by the servicemember directly, or by a lawyer or an individual with a power of attorney who is acting for the servicemember.[31]

7.5 Protections in Court Proceedings

7.5.1 Introduction

The SCRA gives servicemembers important protections in civil judicial and administrative proceedings. It divides these protections into two main categories: cases in which the servicemember has not been notified of the proceeding,[32] and cases in which the servicemember has been notified of the proceeding.[33]

The 2003 revisions made both these protections applicable to administrative as well as judicial proceedings.[34] Types of administrative proceedings potentially affected include driver's license revocation hearings, proceedings to revoke business or professional licenses, zoning hearings, unemployment compensation and Social Security claims, and administrative child support proceedings. All of these proceedings are now subject to the same rules about stays and defaults as judicial proceedings.

28 50 U.S.C. app. § 514.

29 50 U.S.C. app. § 516; *see also* 50 U.S.C. app. § 517(c).

30 50 U.S.C. app. §§ 513 (stay, postponement, suspension, vacation of judgments, and bail bonds), 531(a)(1)(A) (evictions), 535(b) (termination of real property and vehicle leases), 538 (general extension to dependents), 561 (tax sales); Umstead v. Chase Manhattan Mortgage Group, 2005 WL 2233554 (W.D. Va. Sept. 13, 2005) (servicemember's mother qualified as dependent under the Act and could proceed with her own action to seek stay and modification of mortgage obligation on grounds that her ability to pay was materially impaired by son's active duty); *see* Tucson Telco Fed. Credit Union v. Bowser, 451 P.2d 322 (Ariz. Ct. App. 1969) (extending protections of former version of law to serviceman's wife with respect to pre-marriage debt incurred solely in her name when her ability to pay was impaired by serviceman's induction); *see also* § 7.7, *infra* (interest rate reduction).

31 50 U.S.C. app. § 519.

32 *See* § 7.5.2, *infra*.

33 *See* § 7.5.3, *infra*.

34 50 U.S.C. app. §§ 511(5) (defining "court" to include state and federal administrative agencies), 512(b) (Act applies to any judicial or administrative proceeding commenced in any court or agency), 521 (default judgments), 522 (stays).

The Act also restricts execution upon assets of the servicemember.[35]

7.5.2 Cases in Which the Servicemember Has Not Been Notified of the Proceeding

One section of the Act[36] governs cases in which the servicemember has not been notified of the proceeding. Courts are prohibited from entering default judgments in cases in which the defendant has not appeared, unless the plaintiff files an affidavit.[37] By virtue of a 2004 amendment, "judgment" is defined to include "any judgment, decree, order or ruling, final or temporary."[38]

The affidavit must either state whether the defendant is in military service and show facts in support of the statement,[39] or state that the plaintiff is unable to determine whether the defendant is in military service.[40] If it appears that the defendant is in military service, the court may not enter a

35 *See* § 7.5.4, *infra*.

36 50 U.S.C. app. § 521.

37 *See* Merrill v. Beard, 2007 WL 461469 (N.D. Ohio Feb. 7, 2007) (because Act requires a written affidavit, a verbal statement on the record in open court upon request for default judgment can not be substituted); *see also* Maredia v. Philip Morris USA Inc., 2007 WL 2462093 (E.D. Cal. Aug. 27, 2007) (affidavit requirement applies only if defendant has not appeared).

38 Veterans Benefits Improvement Act, Pub. L. No. 108-454, § 701, 118 Stat. 3598 (2004) (codified at 50 U.S.C. app. § 511(9)).

39 *See* Bank of Nova Scotia v. George, 2008 WL 501263 (D. V.I. Feb. 15, 2008) (affidavit that defendant is not in military service must state facts in support; mere review of creditors' records insufficient).

40 50 U.S.C. app. § 521(b)(1) (former 50 U.S.C. app. § 520).

As the 2003 revision did not make any substantive changes to this requirement, courts are likely to continue to follow decisions under the former version of the law: United States v. Nicholson, 2000 U.S. Dist. LEXIS 11028 (E.D. Cal. July 11, 2000) (denying application for default judgment for unpaid taxes because of numerous faults in application, including failure to file required affidavit stating that defendant is not serving in the military), *adopted by* 2000 U.S. Dist. LEXIS 13630 (E.D. Cal. Aug. 14, 2000); Murdock v. Murdock, 338 S.C. 322, 526 S.E.2d 241 (Ct. App. 1999) (failure to comply with Act's protections against default judgment renders judgment voidable); *see also In re* T.M.Y., 725 N.E.2d 997 (Ind. Ct. App. 2000) (failure to comply with Act renders judgment voidable but defendant must show prejudice and a meritorious defense); U.S. Bank v. Coaxum, 2003 WL 22518107 (N.Y. Sup. Ct. Oct. 31, 2003) (affidavit must establish that respondent is not in United States or ally's military service and that the investigation was done after default occurred and shortly before affidavit submitted, and must set forth facts in a manner sufficient for court to evaluate); *cf.* MNF Bank v. Thompson, 1999 Ohio App. LEXIS 5072 (Ohio Ct. App. Oct. 29, 1999) (judgment not voidable when it was entered more than thirty days after defendant left military service, even though suit was filed during the period of service; note that the 2003 revisions

judgment until it appoints an attorney to represent the defendant,[41] and there are special provisions for stays.[42] If the court can not determine whether the defendant is in military service, the court may require the plaintiff to post a bond.[43] An affidavit of non-military service must also accompany a creditor's request for entry of judgment in an attachment proceeding even though the defendant may not have been an active duty servicemember when the initial judgment was entered.[44]

A certificate as to military service may be obtained from the Defense Manpower Data Center (DMDC).[45] One court has held that obtaining the report provided in response to a query to the DMDC satisfies the plaintiff's duty to investigate for an affidavit of non-military service.[46] However in some instances courts have noted that the DMDC reports were inaccurate.[47]

With ongoing deployment of servicemembers in distant areas of conflict, several courts have recently articulated specific standards for the preparation of affidavits of non-military service under section 521 of the Act.[48] Counsel who submit inaccurate affidavits may be subject to sanctions or other forms of reprimand.[49] The Act authorizes criminal sanctions, including fines and imprisonment, against a person who knowingly makes or uses a false affidavit of non-military service or supporting document.[50]

A default judgment entered without complying with these protections is voidable.[51] In addition, the Act gives courts authority to vacate any default judgment entered while a servicemember is on active duty, or within sixty days of release from active duty.[52] The servicemember must apply to have the judgment vacated within ninety days after termination of or

extended these protections to judgments entered up to sixty days after termination or release from active duty).

41 50 U.S.C. app. § 521(b)(2).

42 50 U.S.C. app. § 521(d).

43 50 U.S.C. app. § 521(b)(3).

44 *See* Sprinkle v. SB & C Ltd., 472 F. Supp. 2d 1235 (W.D. Wash. 2006) (entry of judgment to garnish servicemember's bank account without submitting affidavit of non-military service violated SCRA, the Fair Debt Collection Practices Act, and state consumer protection statutes); Palisades Acquisitions, L.L.C. v. Ibrahim, 12 Misc. 3d 340, 812 N.Y.S.2d 866 (Civ. Ct. 2006) (in proceeding to garnish a joint bank account, creditor must submit affidavit for joint tenant who is not a judgment debtor as well as an affidavit for judgment debtor).

45 Active duty status information for compliance with the SCRA is free from the DMDC and can be obtained at https://www.dmdc.osd.mil/scra/owa/home or by writing to Defense Manpower Data Center, Military Verification, 1600 Wilson Blvd., Suite 400, Arlington, VA 22209.

46 363 Associates, L.L.C. v. Sharhan, 2 Misc. 3d 928, 774 N.Y.S.2d 907 (Civ. Ct. 2003).

47 *See In re* Templehoff, 339 B.R. 49 (Bankr. S.D.N.Y. 2005) (counsel's good faith but mistaken reliance on DMDC record mitigated against imposition of Rule 9011 sanctions); Sec'y of Hous. & Urban Dev. v. McClenan, 4 Misc. 3d 1027(A) (Civ. Ct. 2004) (table) (text available at 2004 WL 2187568) (counsel acted in bad faith in claiming to rely on DMDC report when counsel was aware of other substantial evidence of defendant's active military service).

48 *See, e.g.*, *In re* Templehoff, 339 B.R. 49 (Bankr. S.D.N.Y. 2005) (as an "essential step" in preparing affidavit of non-military service in relief from stay proceeding, creditor must examine the bankruptcy debtor's schedules to check for any information related to military employment); Water Pollution Control Auth. v. Mendes, 2004 WL 2165866 (Conn. Super. Ct. Sept. 1, 2004) (affidavit of non-military service must contain statement of personal knowledge and specify sources of information); New Century Fin. Services, Inc. v. Sanchez, Docket No. CD-2747-98 (N.J. Super. Ct. Law Div. Apr. 12, 2002), *available at* www.consumerlaw.org/unreported (affidavit must be based on personal knowledge; if creditor can not do so, it must either post a bond or show good cause for not being required to do so); Sunset 3 Realty v. Booth, 824 N.Y.S.2d 766 (Sup. Ct. 2006) (under local practice affidavit will be rejected if it does not set forth facts supporting conclusions, and facts must have been ascertained within thirty to sixty days of submission of affidavit); Heritage East-West, L.L.C. v. Chung & Choi, 6 Misc. 3d 523, 758 N.Y.S.2d 317 (Civ. Ct. 2004) (affidavits must be based on communication with defendant or Department of Defense database search and may not rely solely on recent physical observation of defendant); Citibank v. McGarvey, 196 Misc. 2d 292, 765 N.Y.S.2d 163 (Civ. Ct. 2003) (affidavit must be based on investigation concluded after commencement of the action and after the default in appearance by the party against whom creditor seeks entry of judgment); *see also* Merrill v. Beard, 2007 WL 461469 (N.D. Ohio Feb. 7, 2007) (because Act requires a written affidavit, a verbal statement on the record in open court upon request for default judgment can not be substituted).

49 *See* Heritage East-West, L.L.C. v. Chung & Choi, 6 Misc. 3d 523, 758 N.Y.S.2d 317 (Civ. Ct. 2004) (plaintiffs' counsel in eviction cases fined $1000 for each of six cases in which he sought default judgments without conducting investigations to support non-military affidavits); Sec'y of Hous. & Urban Dev. v. McClenan, 4 Misc. 3d 1027(A) (Civ. Ct. 2004) (table) (text available at 2004 WL 2187568) (finding counsel in eviction case acted in bad faith by ignoring ample evidence of defendant's active military service).

50 50 U.S.C. app. § 521(c).

51 Davidson v. Gen. Fin. Corp., 295 F. Supp. 878 (D. Ga. 1968); *cf.* Shatswell v. Shatswell, 758 F. Supp. 662 (D. Kan. 1991) (Act does not give federal court authority to order state court case stayed; judgment must be attacked in the court that rendered it); Scheidegg v. Dep't of Air Force, 715 F. Supp. 11 (D.N.H. 1989) (federal court lacks authority to vacate or impede order or judgment of state court; judgment must be attached in court that rendered it), *aff'd*, 915 F.2d 1558 (1st Cir. 1990) (mem.); Citibank v. McGarvey, 196 Misc. 2d 292, 765 N.Y.S.2d 163 (Civ. Ct. 2003); Goshorn v. Brown, 2003 WL 22176976 (Tex. App. Sept. 23, 2003). *But cf.* Pellegrini v. Silva, 2005 WL 3036321 (Mass Land Ct. Nov. 14, 2005) (party's failure to comply with Act's affidavit requirement will not invalidate a foreclosure action when objecting individuals never alleged they had been in military service); PNC Bank v. Kemenash, 335 N.J. Super. 124, 761 A.2d 118 (Super. Ct. App. Div. 2000) (incarcerated servicemember who was not protected by Act could not challenge default judgment entered without affidavit of non-military service); Dep't of Hous. Preservation & Dev. v. W. 129th St. Realty Group, 9 Misc. 3d 61, 802 N.Y.S.2d 826 (Civ. Ct. 2005) (irregularity in non-military affidavit is not jurisdictional defect, so defaulting party who makes no claim of active military duty can not proceed under Act to challenge judgment).

52 50 U.S.C. app. § 521(g).

release from military service,[53] and must show a meritorious or legal defense and that military service materially affected the servicemember's ability to make a defense.[54] State law limits on vacating judgments are inapplicable.[55]

7.5.3 Cases in Which the Servicemember Has Been Notified of the Proceeding

7.5.3.1 Automatic Stay of at Least Ninety Days

The Act also gives a servicemember who has been notified of a civil action or proceeding other than an eviction[56] the right to an automatic, non-discretionary stay of not less than ninety days upon request.[57] The 2004 amendments clarified that the stay under section 522 is applicable whether the servicemember is the defendant or plaintiff.[58]

The stay request must: (1) set forth facts explaining why current military duty requirements materially affect the servicemember's ability to appear; (2) state a date when the servicemember will be able to appear; and (3) include a letter or other communication from the servicemember's commanding officer stating that the servicemember's current military duty prevents appearance and that military leave is not authorized.[59] The application does not constitute an appearance for jurisdictional purposes and is not a waiver of any substantive or procedural defenses.[60] The Act does not specify any formal requirements for the stay request, so it should not have to be in the form of an affidavit or motion. While the initial stay must be for at least ninety days, it may be for the entire anticipated period of military service, plus ninety days.[61]

One of the first courts to consider the scope of the stay under the amended Act held that it did not prevent a trial court from issuing a temporary child custody order in a divorce suit that a servicemember had commenced while he was on leave.[62] The child had been with the servicemember's mother prior to the temporary order, and the servicemember argued that the stay prevented the court from restoring custody to the child's mother. The appellate court held that the stay could only be used to shield a servicemember from the adverse effects of judicial proceedings, not to be used as a sword for tactical advantage. Other courts have expressed similar concerns about the calculated use of the stay as a tactic in contested child custody litigation.[63] However, the Act was amended in 2008 to make it explicit that the rules about stays apply to child custody proceedings.[64]

When the servicemember requests a stay but has not provided the documentation required by section 522(b)(2), the court has the discretion to respond in several ways. The court may deny the motion.[65] The court may allow the servicemember an opportunity to cure the deficiency and then consider the request.[66] The court may grant the stay on its own motion under section 522 without the documentation as long as the party is a servicemember.[67] Finally, in exercising control over its own docket or acting in accordance with other procedural rules, the court may grant a stay without regard to the SCRA requirements.[68]

---

53 50 U.S.C. app. § 521(g()2); *see* Collins v. Collins, 805 N.E.2d 410 (Ind. Ct. App. 2006) (under former 50 U.S.C. app. § 520(4) (current 50 U.S.C. app. § 521(g)(2)) servicemember precluded from moving under the Act to set aside default judgment because he did not do so within ninety days of termination of military service).

54 50 U.S.C. app. § 521(g)(1); *see* Bernhardt v. Alden Café, 374 N.J. Super. 271, 864 A.2d 421 (Super. Ct. App. Div. 2005) (although trial court's decision to vacate default judgment under 50 U.S.C. app. § 521(g) is discretionary, it abused that discretion when it refused to set aside default for servicemember whose military status was undisputed and who alleged a meritorious defense).

55 *In re* Marriage of Thompson, 666 N.W.2d 616 (Iowa Ct. App. 2003); *In re* B.T.T., 156 S.W.3d 612 (Tex. App. 2004).

56 50 U.S.C. app. § 522(f).
See § 7.11, *infra*, for protections in eviction actions.

57 50 U.S.C. app. § 522; *see* Hernandez v. Hernandez, 169 Md. App. 679, 906 A.2d 429 (2006) (when servicemember has complied with documentation requirements of 50 U.S.C. app. § 522(b)(2), statute leaves no room for judicial discretion and court must grant initial ninety-day stay).

58 Veterans Benefits Improvement Act, Pub. L. No. 108-454, § 703, 118 Stat. 3598 (2004) (codified at 50 U.S.C. app. § 522(a)).

59 50 U.S.C. app. § 522(b); *see In re* Walter, 234 S.W.3d 836 (Tex. App. 2007) (no abuse of discretion to deny stay when application for stay did not include letter from commanding officer).

60 50 U.S.C. app. § 522(c).

61 *See* 50 U.S.C. app. § 525(a); Davenport v. Richards, 2006 WL 3791369 (W.D. Wash. Dec. 21, 2006) (granting stay for duration of active duty as indicated by commanding officer in statement provided to court); Mawer v. Daimlerchrysler Corp., 2006 WL 2253119 (S.D. Tex. Aug. 7, 2006); Hunt v. U.A.W. Local 1762, 2006 WL 572805 (E.D. Ark. Mar. 7, 2006) (administratively closing plaintiff servicemember's lawsuit pursuant to 50 U.S.C. app. § 522(a) and 50 U.S.C. app. § 525(a), with permission to reopen case within ninety days of return from active duty).

62 Lenser v. McGowan, 191 S.W.3d 506 (Ark. 2004).

63 *See* George P. v. Super. Ct., 127 Cal. App. 4th 216, 24 Cal. Rptr. 3d 919 (2005) (dependency action); *In re* Marriage of Grantham, 698 N.W.2d 140 (Iowa 2005); *In re* Marriage of Bradley, 282 Kan. 1, 137 P.3d 1030 (2006).

64 Nat'l Defense Authorization Act for Fiscal Year 2008, Pub. L. No. 110-181, § 584, 122 Stat. 3 (2008).

65 *See* King v. Irvin, 273 Ga. App. 64, 614 S.E.2d 190 (2005); *In re* Marriage of Bradley, 282 Kan. 1, 137 P.3d 1030 (2006); Mirisloff v. Monroe, 16 A.D.3d 1161, 791 N.Y.S.2d 255 (2005); *see also* City of Pendergrass v. Skelton, 278 Ga. App. 37, 628 S.E.2d 136 (2006) (trial court abused its discretion in granting indefinite stay when servicemember had not provided documentation of deployment dates and unavailability of leave).

66 *See* Davenport v. Richards, 2006 WL 3791369 (W.D. Wash. Dec. 21, 2006) (granting stay after allowing servicemember thirty days to provide documents from commanding officer showing that current military duty prevents appearance).

67 Advanced Litig., L.L.C. v. Herzka, 2004 WL 1949292 (Del. Ch. Ct. Aug. 20, 2004).

68 Sottoriva v. Claps, 2006 WL 3775945 (C.D. Ill. Dec. 21, 2006)

7.5.3.2 Discretionary Additional Stay

Either along with or after the initial nondiscretionary stay of not less than ninety days, the servicemember may seek an additional stay. This additional stay is not automatic. The court is to grant it if it determines that military duty continues to have a material effect on the servicemember's ability to appear.[69] This "material effect" standard is identical to the standard for all stays under the previous version of the statute, and the legislative history endorses the decisions that interpreted it.[70] Cases interpreting the standard under the old law are therefore relevant when the court rules on an application for an additional stay.[71] Relevant factors to consider when evaluating such requests as identified by courts under the former version of the law include whether the party seeking the stay and that party's counsel have acted with diligence, whether the servicemember is represented by competent counsel who has had sufficient time to prepare the case, and whether there are alternate ways to accommodate the servicemember's schedule.[72]

If the court denies an application for an additional stay, it must appoint counsel for the servicemember.[73] Leave of court is required for a plaintiff to proceed against co-defendants who are not in service.[74]

7.5.3.3 Co-Signers

Whenever a court enters a stay or vacates a judgment, it has discretion to grant the same relief to any surety, guarantor, endorser, accommodation maker, co-maker, or other person who may be primarily or secondarily liable.[75] Any pre-active duty waiver of these protections becomes invalid once a person enters active duty.[76]

(granting stay for servicemember under court's general authority to set schedule for summary judgment proceedings under Fed. R. Civ. P. 56(f)); United States v. Smith, 2006 WL 2338267 (W.D. Okla. Aug. 10, 2006) (granting stay under discretionary power to control docket when defendant servicemember mistakenly applied for stay under wrong statutory section).

69 50 U.S.C. app. § 522(d); *see* KCF v. TLSF, 839 N.Y.S.2d 433 (Sup. Ct. Apr. 12, 2007) (balancing factors and denying stay when servicemember stationed overseas was able to take leave if necessary to attend custody hearing in New York).

70 H.R. Rep. No. 108-81 (2003), at 36 (explaining why committee decided not to add a definition of "materially affected" to the Act).

71 Former 50 U.S.C. app. §§ 521, 522, 532; *see* Comer v. City of Palm Bay, 265 F.3d 1186 (11th Cir. 2001) (no abuse of discretion to deny stay when serviceman had nearly a year to do discovery before being called up and had entered the service while case was pending); White v. Black, 190 F.3d 366 (5th Cir. 1999) (court may stay proceedings on its own motion and has broad discretion); Dalenberg v. City of Waynesboro, 221 F. Supp. 2d 1380 (S.D. Ga. 2002) (burden of proving need for stay is imposed on neither party, but court is to use its sound sense; no stay of discovery when defendant was stationed near court and discovery could be accommodated to his schedule); Antioch Co. v. Scrapbook Borders, Inc., 210 F.R.D. 645 (D. Minn. 2002) (ordering accommodation of servicemember's schedule rather than stay; no stay for servicemember's co-defendant, at least for pre-trial proceedings); Branch v. Stukes, 2001 U.S. Dist. LEXIS 19985 (S.D.N.Y. Nov. 30, 2001) (motion for stay denied without prejudice; servicemember must provide affidavit and memorandum of law, showing how service will materially interfere with ability to participate in case); Allfirst Bank v. Lewis (*In re* Lewis), 257 B.R. 431 (Bankr. D. Md. 2001) (adversary proceedings regarding dischargeability of debt stayed while debtor-husband serving abroad, but additional stay denied after his return to United States because no showing that military service would interfere with ability to defend); *In re* Burrell, 230 B.R. 309 (Bankr. E.D. Tex. 1999) (not granting stay *sua sponte* when absent serviceman neither moved for stay nor presented evidence on the question; allowing secured creditor to foreclose on collateral); *Ex parte* K.N.L., 2003 WL 21848949 (Ala. Civ. App. Aug. 8, 2003) (no abuse of discretion in denying stay of temporary custody order; specific findings unnecessary); Harris v. J.B. Hunt Transp., Inc., 2003 WL 22300305 (Ark. Ct. App. Oct. 8, 2003) (affirming denial of motion for stay); Amber L. v. Super. Ct., 2003 WL 21967266 (Cal. Ct. App. Aug. 19, 2003) (finding no material effect); *In re* Brianna L., 2003 WL 220559 (Cal. Ct. App. Feb. 3, 2002) (denial of stay in neglected child case not error when soldier was represented by counsel throughout the proceedings); Louis J. v. Super. Ct., 103 Cal. App. 4th 711, 127 Cal. Rptr. 26 (2002) (denying stay in neglected child case); Christine M. v. Super. Ct., 69 Cal. App. 4th 1233, 82 Cal. Rptr. 2d 220 (1999) (affirming trial court's discretion in denying stay of neglected child case); King-Coleman v. Geathers, 795 So. 2d 1092 (Fla. Dist. Ct. App. 2001) (court that denies a stay pursuant to SSCRA must make explicit findings, supported by the record, as to why servicemember's ability to defend will not be materially affected by military service); Ensley v. Carter, 245 Ga. App. 453, 538 S.E.2d 98 (2000) (affirming trial court's discretion in denying stay); Greco v. Renegades, Inc., 307 A.D.2d 711, 761 N.Y.S.2d 426 (2003) (proper to stay action unless plaintiff proves that servicemember defendant is assigned to location that will not materially affect ability to defend); *In re* Day, 2003 WL 1194244 (Ohio Ct. App. Mar. 12, 2003) (trial court can deny stay only if it makes finding of fact that ability to defend is not materially affected by military duties); Henneke v. Young, 761 N.E.2d 1140 (Ohio Ct. App. 2001) (trial court erred in staying proceedings pursuant to prior federal act; officer was unable to obtain leave during two months, but otherwise could be available, and was able to communicate with counsel; case concerned child visitation orders).

72 Dalenberg v. City of Waynesboro, 221 F. Supp. 2d 1380 (S.D. Ga. 2002); Antioch Co. v. Scrapbook Borders, Inc., 210 F.R.D. 645 (D. Minn. 2002); *see, e.g.*, George P. v. Super. Ct., 127 Cal. App. 4th 216, 24 Cal. Rptr. 3d 919 (2005) (affirming denial of additional stay in dependency action in which servicemember was represented and had testified on pertinent issues before deployment); *In re* Marriage of Grantham 698 N.W.2d 140 (Iowa 2005) (affirming denial of stay in custody modification action when servicemember was represented by counsel, witnesses were available, and servicemember failed to present evidence as to why his personal appearance was needed).

73 50 U.S.C. app. § 522(d)(2).

74 50 U.S.C. app. § 525(b) (former 50 U.S.C. app. § 524).

75 50 U.S.C. app. § 513.

76 50 U.S.C. app. § 513(d)(1); *see also* 50 U.S.C. app. § 516 (applicability during period between reservist's receipt of orders or draftee's receipt of induction order and date of reporting for duty).

7.5.4 *Protections Against Property Executions*

The Act allows the court to stay execution of any judgment against a servicemember and to vacate or stay any pre-judgment or post-judgment attachment or garnishment of property.[77] In addition, the personal assets of a servicemember are not available for satisfaction of a trade or business debt for which the servicemember is personally liable.[78]

7.6 Tolling of Statutes of Limitations

The Act prohibits counting the period of active duty toward any time limit for bringing any action or proceeding in a court, board, bureau, commission, department or other agency of a state, a political subdivision of a state, or the federal government.[79] Thus, the statute of limitations is tolled not only for lawsuits but also for zoning appeals, unemployment compensation appeals, and similar administrative matters while the servicemember is on active duty.[80]

The period of active duty is also not to be included in computing any period for redeeming real property sold or forfeited to enforce any obligation, tax, or assessment.[81] Limitations periods prescribed by the Internal Revenue Code are not, however, subject to tolling under the Act.[82]

Tolling is unconditional and automatic.[83] Tolling applies to federal statutes of limitations regardless of whether they expressly refer to the Act.[84] The statute of limitations is tolled even if the defendant is stationed in the judicial district where the suit would be filed.[85] The Act has no provision allowing for servicemembers to waive the tolling of limitation periods.[86]

The tolling of the statute of limitation preserves claims both by[87] and against[88] the servicemember. However one court has held that an attorney's period of active duty military service does not toll time periods in a case he was handling for a non-servicemember.[89]

As the pre-2003 and post-2003 statutory language is similar, courts are likely to follow decisions under the former version of the statute.[90]

7.7 Interest Rate Reduction

7.7.1 *Reduction to Six Percent for Pre-Active Duty Obligations*

One of the most powerful provisions of the Act is the requirement that creditors reduce the interest rate to six

77 50 U.S.C. app. § 524 (former 50 U.S.C. app. § 513); *see* Sprinkle v. SB & C Ltd., 472 F. Supp. 2d 1235 (W.D. Wash. 2006) (requirement of 50 U.S.C. app. § 521 that creditor file affidavit of non-military service "before entry of judgment for plaintiff" applies to creditor's post-judgment entry of garnishment order against a bank); Palisades Acquisitions, L.L.C. v. Ibrahim, 12 Misc. 3d 340, 812 N.Y.S.2d 866 (Civ. Ct. 2006) (before creditor may execute against joint bank account, it must file affidavit of non-military service applicable to non-judgment debtor who has interest in account). *But cf.* World Tire Corp. v. Webb, 2007 WL 2812946 (Ohio Ct. App. Sept. 17, 2007) (unpublished) (not abuse of discretion to deny stay of execution under 50 U.S.C. app. § 524 when servicemember did not provide evidence, such as affidavits from his superiors, that he was in military and was deployed).

78 50 U.S.C. app. § 596; *see, e.g.*, Linscott v. Vector Aerospace, 2006 WL 1310511 (D. Or. May 12, 2006).

79 50 U.S.C. app. § 526(a); *see, e.g.*, State *ex rel.* Estate of Perry, 168 S.W.3d 577 (Mo. Ct. App. 2005) (50 U.S.C. app. § 526 tolls one-year statute of limitations for servicemember to file petition for presentment and application for letters testamentary in county probate court); *see also* Lowe v. United States, 79 Fed. Cl. 218 (Fed. Cl. 2007) (statute of limitations is tolled during period servicemember was confined in military prison while still in the service); Lazarski v. Archdiocese of Philadelphia, 926 A.2d 459 (Pa. Super. Ct. 2007) (statutes of limitations are tolled only during active duty, not entire period of enlistment). *But see* Kegley v. City of Fayetteville, 170 N.C. App. 656, 613 S.E.2d 696 (2005) (Act does not extend time for servicemember/property owner to challenge municipal annexation plan when his objection was to entire municipal plan and not specifically to treatment of his own property).

80 Giel v. Winter, 503 F. Supp. 2d 208 (D.D.C. 2007) (SCRA tolls Administrative Procedure Act's time period for appealing administrative decision).

81 50 U.S.C. app. § 526(b); *see* Conroy v. Aniskoff, 507 U.S. 511, 113 S. Ct. 1562, 123 L. Ed. 2d 229 (1993) (under prior version of Act, soldier is entitled to extension of redemption period without need to show that military service caused hardship that should excuse the failure to act within the normal time); *see also* Small v. Kulesa, 90 Ark. App. 108, 204 S.W.3d 99 (2005) (two-year limitation period for payment of overdue property taxes to prevent tax sale began with date servicemember left military service); Farran v. Wayne County, 2005 WL 2219417 (Mich. Ct. App. Sept. 13, 2005) (50 U.S.C. app. § 526(b), unlike 50 U.S.C. app. § 561(a), tolls period for servicemember to redeem non-residential property from tax sale).

82 50 U.S.C. app. § 526(c).

83 Lowe v. United States, 79 Fed. Cl. 218 (Fed. Cl. 2007) (statute of limitations is tolled even when servicemember is in military prison, up until the time of his dishonorable discharge).

84 Bretherick v. Crittenden County, 2007 WL 890200 (E.D. Ark. Mar. 21, 2007).

85 *Id.*

86 Sedler v. Select Properties, Inc., 2004 WL 3392897 (Va. Cir. Ct. June 18, 2004) (servicemember's prior filing of suit on same cause of action against wrong defendant did not deprive servicemember of Act's tolling benefit when he filed second action).

87 *E.g.*, Baker v. England, 397 F. Supp. 2d 18 (D.D.C. 2005) (tolling extended limitations period for member's action to amend military record); *see also* Murphree v. Communication Technologies, Inc., 460 F. Supp. 2d 702 (E.D. La. 2006) (tolling allows servicemember to file state law tort claim in employment case).

88 *E.g.*, Vincent v. Longwater, 245 Ga. App. 516, 538 S.E.2d 164 (2000) (limitations tolled in personal injury action against member).

89 Kethley v. Jack & Kethley, 961 So. 2d 559 (La. Ct. App. 2007).

90 Former 50 U.S.C. app. § 525.

percent on any obligation or liability incurred by a servicemember before active duty.[91] The interest rate reduction lasts as long as the servicemember is on active duty.[92] These provisions are substantively unchanged from the former version of the law.[93]

The application of the interest rate reduction to any "obligation or liability,"[94] means that it applies to all types of debt, including car loans, mortgages, credit cards, and business debts.[95] It even applies to debts when a corporation is the primary obligor, as long as the servicemember is personally liable.[96]

Because the interest rate reduction applies to "liabilities" as well as "obligations," post-judgment interest on a judgment debt must also be reduced to six percent.[97] The rate reduction even applies to the interest paid on obligations under a confirmed chapter 13 bankruptcy plan.[98]

The interest rate reduction only applies to debts incurred *before* the servicemember entered active duty.[99] It also does not apply to student loan debts.[100] A student loan debtor can, however, apply for a deferment due to military service.[101]

The term "interest" includes service charges and late payment fees related to the obligation.[102] In the 2003 revision Congress codified case law[103] holding that the interest must be forgiven, not just deferred.[104] Congress also added an explicit requirement that the periodic payment due from the servicemember must be reduced by the amount of the forgiven interest, thus foreclosing creditors from requiring the same payment amount but just applying a greater portion of the payment to principal.[105] Continuing the regular monthly payment, but applying a greater portion of the payment to principal, would be inconsistent with the statute's goal of providing short-term relief to servicemembers.[106] The legislative history indicates that Congress intended to allow lenders to reamortize the loan using a six percent interest rate, so that the monthly payment is consistent from month to month.[107]

For high-rate loans, lowering the interest rate can save thousands of dollars. Consider a servicemember who entered into a thirty-year, $80,000 mortgage at sixteen percent just before being called to active duty for a year. A six percent interest rate lowers monthly payments from $1075 to $479, while paying off $864 *more* in principal, with $8018 in interest savings for that one year. Paying off more principal provides additional benefits when the interest rate returns to sixteen percent, saving $3171 more in interest over the remainder of the loan. The total savings in interest paid over the life of the loan is $11,189.

When the servicemember and his or her spouse are jointly liable on an obligation, the statute explicitly requires the interest rate to be reduced for both of them.[108] The same result should be reached when there are other co-obligors, as the statute requires the interest rate on the "obligation or liability," not the interest rate paid by the servicemember, to be reduced. As a court interpreting the former law noted, forcing co-obligors to pay the contract rate would place pressure on the servicemember to pay the contract rate.[109]

To take advantage of the interest rate reduction, the Act as revised in 2003 requires the servicemember to give written notice to the creditor and a copy of the military orders calling the servicemember to military service and any orders further extending military service.[110] This notice must be given no later than 180 days after the servicemember leaves active duty.[111] Once this requirement is met, the interest rate reduction is self-executing and is effective, retroactive to the

91 50 U.S.C. app. § 527.

92 50 U.S.C. app. §§ 527(a)(1) (interest rate reduction applies during "the period of military service"), 511 (defining "period of military service").

93 *See* former 50 U.S.C. app. §§ 526, 511(2).

94 50 U.S.C. app. § 527(a)(1).

95 *See* Cathey v. First Republic Bank, 2001 U.S. Dist. LEXIS 13150 (W.D. La. July 6, 2001) (business debt); Moll v. Ford Consumer Fin. Co., 1998 U.S. Dist. LEXIS 3638 (N.D. Ill. Mar. 23, 1998) (mortgage debt).

96 *See* Linscott v. Vector Aerospace, 2006 WL 1310511 (D. Or. May 12, 2006) (granting preliminary injunction against enforcing foreign judgment against corporation, which included interest in excess of the six percent allowed by Act, when corporation's obligations were personally guaranteed by servicemember), *later opinion at* 2007 WL 2220357 (D. Or. July 27, 2007) (denying relief under SCRA because servicemember failed to send creditor a copy of his military orders); *see also* Cathey v. First Republic Bank, 2001 U.S. Dist. LEXIS 13150 (W.D. La. July 6, 2001) (decided under comparable language of pre-2003 version of Act).

97 Linscott v. Vector Aerospace, 2006 WL 1310511 (D. Or. May 12, 2006) (granting preliminary injunction against enforcing foreign judgment against corporation, which included interest in excess of the six percent allowed by Act, when corporation's obligations were personally guaranteed by servicemember), *later opinion at* 2007 WL 2220357 (D. Or. July 27, 2007) (denying relief under SCRA because servicemember failed to send creditor a copy of his military orders).

98 *E.g.*, *In re* Watson, 292 B.R. 441 (Bankr. S.D. Ga. 2003).

99 50 U.S.C. app. § 527(a)(1).

100 20 U.S.C. § 1078(d).

101 34 C.F.R. § 682.211(i).

102 50 U.S.C. app. § 527(d); *see* Koenig v. Waukesha State Bank, 2006 WL 2334841, at *4 (E.D. Wis. Aug. 10, 2006).

103 Moll v. Ford Consumer Fin. Co., 1998 U.S. Dist. LEXIS 3638, at *4 (N.D. Ill. Mar. 23, 1998).

104 50 U.S.C. app. § 527(a)(2).

105 50 U.S.C. app. § 527(a)(3).

106 Office of the Comptroller of the Currency, Advisory Letter AL 2001-10 (Oct. 25, 2001) (interpreting former version of statute).

107 Cong. Rec. H12,877 (Dec. 8, 2003) (statement of Rep. Smith of New Jersey); Cong. Rec. H12,876 (Dec. 8, 2003) (statement of Rep. Evans).

108 50 U.S.C. app. § 527(a)(1).

109 Cathey v. First Republic Bank, 2001 U.S. Dist. LEXIS 13150, at *14 (W.D. La. July 6, 2001).

110 50 U.S.C. app. § 527(b)(1).

111 50 U.S.C. app. § 527(b)(1).

date the servicemember was called to military service.[112] The Act does not require the servicemember to go to court to obtain this relief.

There is only one exception to the rate reduction. If the creditor proves to a court that the ability of the servicemember to pay interest on the debt at a rate over six percent is not materially affected by reason of the debtor's military service, the court may allow a higher rate.[113] The debtor does not have to prove a material effect: the duty is on the creditor to go to court to seek a ruling allowing it a higher rate and, if it does not do so, it must reduce the interest rate.[114]

The Act prohibits creditors from cutting off credit, changing the terms of credit, denying credit, or making an adverse credit report because a servicemember exercises rights under the Act.[115] Even without this specific prohibition, it would be clear that adverse actions such as acceleration, repossession, or a negative credit report were wrongful: as a matter of contract law, because the obligation now bears interest at six percent, a servicemember who pays six percent is simply not in default.

7.7.2 *Thirty-Six Percent Cap on Certain Obligations Incurred During Active Duty*

As part of the 2007 defense authorization legislation, Congress enacted new restrictions on credit extended to active duty servicemembers and their dependents.[116] This legislation was effective October 1, 2007. As implemented by regulations of the Department of Defense, it prohibits payday lenders, auto title lenders, and refund anticipation loan (RAL) lenders from charging more than thirty-six percent (including fees) on loans to servicemembers and their families. It is not part of the SCRA, and unlike the SCRA it applies to credit extended *after* rather than *before* the servicemember has entered active duty. This law is discussed in detail in another NCLC manual.[117]

7.8 Prohibition Against Self-Help Repossession, Foreclosure, and Lien Enforcement

The Act forbids self-help repossession if a servicemember made a payment under a purchase contract prior to entering active duty.[118] This prohibition applies regardless of whether there are cosigners, and regardless of whether the servicemember is the principal obligor, and it applies whether the delinquency arose prior to or during the servicemember's active duty.

If the creditor files a replevin or similar action to regain possession of the property, the court may, as a condition of allowing repossession, order the creditor to return the servicemember's payments. The court may also stay the proceedings if it finds that the servicemember's ability to comply with the contract is materially affected by military service, and may make other dispositions as are equitable to preserve the interests of all parties.[119]

These protections apply to all contracts for the purchase, lease, or bailment of real or personal property, including motor vehicles.[120] The 2003 revisions expanded the scope of the former statute by including all leases, whether or not the lease includes a purchase option.[121]

Similar protections apply in the case of foreclosure. The Act forbids non-judicial foreclosure on real or personal property owned by a servicemember based on an obligation incurred prior to entering active duty, and allows the servicemember to obtain a similar stay or other equitable order.[122] It also prohibits non-judicial tax sales of personal property and certain real property, and extends the servicemember's period for redemption until 180 days after the end of active duty.[123] The restrictions on self-help repossession and non-judicial foreclosure are especially important because a creditor or debt collector who threatens such action is likely to be in violation of the Fair Debt Collection Practices Act or a state debt collection or deceptive practices (UDAP) statute.

The 2003 revisions also broadened the protections against the enforcement of liens. The former law prohibited enforcement of liens for storage of a servicemember's house-

112 50 U.S.C. app. § 527(b)(2); *see* Rodriguez v. Am. Express, 2006 WL 908613 (E.D. Cal. Apr. 7, 2006) (lender does not comply with 50 U.S.C. app. § 527 by making offer to servicemember to adjust interest rates; upon notice of debtor's military service creditor must proceed to adjust account and credit any sums overpaid since date of entry into active duty).

113 50 U.S.C. app. § 527(c).

114 50 U.S.C. app. § 527(c).
The phrasing of the revised version of the Act is even clearer than the former version in this regard, in that it separates the creditor's right to seek relief from a court into a separate subsection, 50 U.S.C. app. § 207(c).

115 50 U.S.C. app. § 518 (former 50 U.S.C. app. § 518); *see* Marin v. Armstrong, 1998 U.S. Dist. LEXIS 22792 (N.D. Tex. Sept. 1, 1998) (recognizing private cause of action for violations); Office of the Comptroller of the Currency, Advisory Letter AL 2001-10 (Oct. 25, 2001).

116 10 U.S.C. § 987.

117 National Consumer Law Center, The Cost of Credit: Regulation, Preemption, and Industry Abuses § 2.3.3.12 (2007 Supp.).

118 50 U.S.C. app. § 532 (former 50 U.S.C. app. § 531(1)); *see* Donahou v. Presidential Limousine & Auto Sales, Inc., 2007 WL 1229342 (W.D. Ark. Apr. 24, 2007) (Act prohibits self-help repossession of car servicemember bought during eight-month "Delayed Entry" period between time of enlistment and reporting for duty).

119 50 U.S.C. app. § 532(c)(2), (3) (former 50 U.S.C. app. § 531(3)).

120 50 U.S.C. app. § 532(a)(1).
See § 7.9, *infra*, for a discussion of automobile leases.

121 H.R. Rep. No. 108-81 (2003), at 40, 47.

122 50 U.S.C. app. § 532(a) (former 50 U.S.C. app. § 532).

123 50 U.S.C. app. § 561.

hold goods, furniture or personal effects during any period of active duty or for ninety days thereafter, except by court order.[124] The revised law covers any and all liens on the property or effects of a servicemember, so it prohibits enforcement of landlords' liens, mechanics' liens, repair liens, drycleaners' liens, and materialmen's liens in addition to storage liens.[125] The language is also broad enough to cover water and sewer liens and the like, although those liens may also be governed by the similar protections that the law affords against sale of property to enforce a tax or assessment.[126]

7.9 Automobile Leases

The Act as revised in 2003 gives the servicemember the option of terminating a vehicle lease upon entering active duty.[127] This right applies if, after executing the lease, the lessee enters active duty under a call or order for 180 days or more.[128]

To terminate a vehicle lease, the servicemember must give the lessor written notice with a copy of the military orders, and then return the vehicle within fifteen days.[129] Termination of the lease is effective once these two steps are accomplished. The lessor is prohibited from imposing an early termination charge, but may charge for taxes, summonses, title and registration fees, and excess wear, use, or mileage.[130] The lessor must refund any lease payments that the servicemember paid in advance.[131] Upon application by the lessor before the termination date, however, a court may modify the relief granted the servicemember as justice and equity require.[132]

A particularly significant protection added in 2003 is the right to cancel vehicle leases executed during active duty if the lessee receives military orders for a permanent change of station outside the continental United States or to deploy with a military unit for 180 days or more.[133] The continental United States is defined as the forty-eight contiguous states and the District of Columbia.[134] The servicemember then has the same right to terminate the lease without penalty as if the lease had been signed before active duty began. This provision makes vehicle leasing a more attractive option than buying for servicemembers who anticipate being posted overseas and do not have family members back home who will need the vehicle in that event.

As an alternative, if the servicemember does not want to return the car, the servicemember can ask a court to stay enforcement of the payment obligation under the lease during the period of active duty, under a general provision of the law applicable to all obligations.[135] Then, upon leaving the service, the servicemember will have a period equal to the period of active duty to make up the deferred payments, with no interest or penalties. This option is discussed in the next subsection.

7.10 Deferring Enforcement of Obligations During Active Duty

Servicemembers have the right to apply to a court to stay enforcement of an obligation for the period of active duty, plus a period of time after the servicemember is released from military service.[136] In the case of a contract to purchase real estate or a contract secured by a mortgage on real estate, the post-military service stay may last for a period equal to the remaining loan term plus the length of the military service period, and the balance must be paid in equal installments at the contract interest rate during this combined period.[137] For any other obligation, a servicemember leaving military service may be granted a period equal to the period of active duty to make up the deferred payments plus any accumulated interest.[138] These protections are substantively unchanged from the pre-2003 version of the law.[139]

The obligee is not allowed to impose any penalties because of failure to comply with an obligation that has been stayed.[140] Nor can the obligee make an adverse credit report, deny additional credit, or change the terms of an existing credit arrangement.[141]

This option is particularly attractive for vehicle leases. Because vehicle leases do not bear interest, the person's obligation would be just to pay the deferred payments upon

124 Former 50 U.S.C. app. § 535.

125 50 U.S.C. app. § 537.

Even under the old law, the Fifth Circuit gave a broad interpretation to "personal effects," finding that it included a car. United States v. Bomar, 8 F.3d 226 (5th Cir. 1993); *see* Linscott v. Vector Aerospace, 2006 WL 240529 (D. Or. Jan. 31, 2006) (servicemember has private right of action for damages under 50 U.S.C. app. § 537 against creditor who enforced mechanic's lien against servicemember's property despite notice of servicemember's active duty status).

126 50 U.S.C. app. § 561.

127 50 U.S.C. app. § 535(a); *see also* 50 U.S.C. app. § 511(2) (defining "military service").

The vehicle must be used or intended to be used by the servicemember or dependents for personal or business transportation.

128 50 U.S.C. app. § 535(b)(2)(A).

129 50 U.S.C. app. § 535(c).

The notice must be delivered by hand delivery, private business carrier, or U.S. mail return receipt requested.

130 50 U.S.C. app. § 535(e).

131 50 U.S.C. app. § 535(f).

132 50 U.S.C. app. § 535(g).

133 50 U.S.C. app. § 535(b)(2).

134 50 U.S.C. app. § 535(i)(2).

135 50 U.S.C. app. § 591 (former 50 U.S.C. app. § 590).

136 50 U.S.C. app. § 591 (former 50 U.S.C. app. § 590).

137 50 U.S.C. app. § 591(b)(1)(B).

138 50 U.S.C. app. § 591(b)(2)(B).

139 Former 50 U.S.C. app. § 590(2).

140 50 U.S.C. app. § 591(c).

141 50 U.S.C. app. § 518.

leaving military service.[142] For example, a person who had a $600 vehicle lease payment and was called to active duty for eight months, could stop making payments while on active duty. Upon leaving the military, the person would have eight months to catch up on the eight deferred payments, in equal installments.

Unlike the six percent interest reduction, payment deferments are neither automatic nor self-executing. Servicemembers must apply to a court for this relief,[143] and the statute only says that the court "may" grant it if the ability of the servicemember to pay is materially affected by their military service.[144] The application for a stay or modification of an obligation must be made to the court during or within 180 days of the termination of military service.[145] The court has discretion to stay enforcement of the lease not only for the person in military service but also for any co-signers.[146]

Student loans may be also be deferred during active military duty under laws applying to student loans.[147]

7.11 Residential Leases

7.11.1 Eviction

The pre-2003 version of the Act prohibited non-judicial eviction of servicemembers or their dependents from rental property if the rent did not exceed $1200 per month, and allowed the court to stay such an eviction up to ninety days.[148] As revised in 2003, the law covers leases up to $2400 per month, and includes an annual inflation adjustment.[149] It also allows the court to "adjust the obligation under the lease to preserve the interests of all parties," presumably meaning that the court can order rent to be deferred, order that a security deposit be applied to rent, allow subletting despite a prohibition in the lease, or make other orders that will preserve the tenancy.[150]

7.11.2 Right to Break a Lease

Servicemembers also have the right to break a lease of premises that they or their dependents occupy or intend to occupy for residential, professional, business, agricultural, or similar purposes.[151] This right applies to leases signed before the servicemember enters active duty.[152] In addition it applies to leases signed after entering active duty if the servicemember receives military orders for a permanent change of station or to deploy with a military unit for ninety days or more.[153] "Military orders," as defined by the 2004 amendments, means official military orders from the Bureau of Naval Personnel or any notification, certification, or verification from the servicemember's commanding officer.[154] The servicemember is entitled to a refund of the unused portion of any rent that was paid in advance.[155]

7.12 Remedies for Violations

Courts have held that the former version of the Act creates a private cause of action for violations.[156] There is no

142 Of course, an implicit rate of return for the lessor is built into a vehicle lease. If the lessor argues that this rate of return is analogous to an interest rate and should accumulate while the servicemember is on active duty, the rejoinder is that if it is analogous to an interest rate it should be automatically reduced to six percent.

143 50 U.S.C. app. § 591(a) ("servicemember may . . . apply to a court"); *see* Koenig v. Waukesha State Bank, 2006 WL 2334841 (E.D. Wis. Aug. 10, 2006) (in absence of application by servicemember to court, 50 U.S.C. app. § 591 does not impose any enforceable duty upon creditor to negotiate a modification of obligation).

144 50 U.S.C. app. § 591(b).

145 50 U.S.C. app. § 591(a); *see* Rodriguez v. Am. Express, 2006 WL 908613 (E.D. Cal. Apr. 7, 2006) (servicemember must not only file a complaint with court within the statutory time frame, but must also file separate motion for stay before end of 180-day post-discharge period).

146 50 U.S.C. app. § 513(a); *see* Umstead v. Chase Manhattan Mortgage Group, 2005 WL 2233554 (W.D. Va. Sept. 13, 2005) (servicemember's mother qualified as a dependent under Act and could bring her own application for modification of mortgage payments under 50 U.S.C. app. § 591). *But see In re* Cockerham, 336 B.R. 592 (Bankr. S.D. Ga. 2005) (when servicemember had agreed in chapter 13 plan to surrender collateral, court would not grant request of non-servicemember co-debtor for a stay under the Act).

147 *See* 34 C.F.R. §§ 682.210(i), 674.34(c); National Consumer Law Center, Student Loan Law §§ 3.2.5, 3.2.6 (3d ed. 2006 and Supp.).

148 Former 50 U.S.C. app. § 530; *see* Mill Rock Plaza Associates v. Lively, 580 N.Y.S.2d 815 (Civ. Ct. 1990) (in response to Desert Storm, court would look seriously at "non-military" affidavits in eviction cases: must show sufficient facts to support a trustworthy conclusion that the tenants involved were neither in the military, nor dependents of military personnel); *cf.* Taylor v. Raabe-Manupule, 2003 WL 21782681 (Haw. Ct. App. July 29, 2003) (no right to stay when servicemember was the son and dependent of the tenant and had not signed lease).

149 50 U.S.C. app. § 531(a).

The maximum rent level effective January 1, 2007 is $2720.95 as set by the Department of Defense Housing Price Inflation Adjustment. 72 Fed. Reg. 1319 (Jan. 11, 2007).

150 50 U.S.C. app. § 531(b)(1)(B); *see also* 50 U.S.C. app. § 591 (allowing court to defer servicemember's liability on any obligation during the period of active duty).

151 50 U.S.C. app. § 535.

152 50 U.S.C. app. § 535(b)(1)(A).

153 50 U.S.C. app. § 535(b)(1)(B).

154 Veterans Benefits Improvement Act, Pub. L. No. 108-454, § 704, 118 Stat. 3598 (2004) (codified at 50 U.S.C. app. § 535(i)(1)).

155 50 U.S.C. app. § 535(f).

156 Marin v. Citibank, 208 F.3d 203 (2d Cir. 2000) (table) (text available at 2000 U.S. App. LEXIS 3789) (reversing dismissal of affirmative suit and remanding for consideration of existence of private cause of action); Cathey v. First Republic Bank, 2001

indication that, in renewing the Act, Congress intended to change this result.[157] One United States district court recently reviewed decisions under the former Act and held that, as under the prior law, a servicemember may assert a private right of action to enforce the SCRA.[158] The court ruled that the servicemember could sue a creditor for monetary relief related to the creditor's retention of the servicemember's property to enforce a mechanic's lien in violation of the Act.[159] The debtor is not confined to raising the violation of the Act defensively, in response to a foreclosure or collection suit, but can sue affirmatively.[160]

The revised Act also expressly preserves the servicemember's right to pursue conversion or wrongful eviction claims that are available for a violation of a number of its prohibitions.[161] A class action may be appropriate if a creditor follows a general practice of enforcing obligations in violation of the Act.[162]

Violations of the SCRA may also lead to Fair Debt Collection Practices Act (FDCPA) violations. For example, a debt collector violated the SCRA, the FDCPA, and state consumer protection statutes when it entered judgment against a garnishee bank and seized a servicemember's military pay without the filing of an affidavit of non-military service.[163] The court held that by doing so the collector was proceeding with an action it had no lawful right to take and using false representations and deceptive means to collect a debt in violation of the FDCPA.[164] In addition, the FDCPA prohibits debt collectors from misrepresenting the amount of a debt, and requires affirmative disclosure of the amount as part of the validation notice.[165] Dunning the servicemember or a co-obligor for a pre-active duty debt without having reduced the interest rate to six percent as required by the SCRA[166] is likely to violate this prohibition. As another example, using self-help repossession to recover property in violation of the SCRA[167] may violate the FDCPA prohibition against taking non-judicial action to effect dispossession of property when there is no present right to possession.[168] If the creditor itself rather than an independent debt collector is collecting the debt, the FDCPA does not apply, but in many jurisdictions a state debt collection law will impose similar requirements.[169]

If a creditor violates the prohibition against making an adverse credit report because of the failure to pay the interest that should have been forgiven,[170] the debtor may also have a claim under the Fair Credit Reporting Act (FCRA). Before a consumer can sue a creditor under the FCRA for making an inaccurate report, the consumer must dispute the report with the credit reporting agency. The credit reporting agency is then required to ask the creditor who made the report to reinvestigate the debt. The creditor can be sued under the FCRA if it does not conduct a reasonable reinvestigation of the disputed item.[171] However, these preliminary steps are unnecessary when the consumer sues under the Civil Relief Act itself.[172]

The Civil Rights Division of the Department of Justice (DOJ) will consider taking action on a violation of the SCRA. However the servicemember must first seek the assistance of his or her military legal assistance office. If that office can not resolve the complaint, it may choose to forward the complaint to the DOJ. The DOJ then will review the matter to determine whether DOJ action is appropriate.[173]

U.S. Dist. LEXIS 13150, at *14 (W.D. La. July 6, 2001); Moll v. Ford Consumer Fin. Co., 1998 U.S. Dist. LEXIS 3638 (N.D. Ill. Mar. 23, 1998). *But see* Batie v. Subway Real Estate Corp., 2008 WL 413627 (N.D. Tex. Feb. 15, 2008) (stating in dictum that SCRA does not create private cause of action).

157 Linscott v. Vector Aerospace, 2006 WL 240529 (D. Or. Jan. 31, 2006) ("There is no indication that in enacting and renewing the Act, Congress intended to create rights without remedies.").

158 *Id.*

159 *See* 50 U.S.C. app. § 537.

160 Moll v. Ford Consumer Fin. Co., 1998 U.S. Dist. LEXIS 3638 (N.D. Ill. Mar. 23, 1998).

161 50 U.S.C. app. §§ 531(c)(2) (evictions and distress), 532(b)(2) (installment contracts), 533(d)(2) (mortgages and trust deeds), 535(h)(2) (vehicle leases), 536(e)(2) (life insurance), 537(c)(2) (foreclosure on storage liens).

162 *See, e.g.*, Moll v. Ford Consumer Fin. Co., 1998 U.S. Dist. LEXIS 3638 (N.D. Ill. Mar. 23, 1998).

163 15 U.S.C. § 1692e(5), (10).

164 Sprinkle v. SB & C Ltd., 472 F. Supp. 2d 1235 (W.D. Wash. 2006).

165 15 U.S.C. §§ 1692(e)(2)(a), 1692g(a)(1); *see* National Consumer Law Center, Fair Debt Collection §§ 5.5.4, 5.7.2.6.5 (6th ed. 2008).

166 *See* § 7.7, *supra.*

167 *See* § 7.8, *supra.*

168 15 U.S.C. § 1692f(6).

169 *See* National Consumer Law Center, Fair Debt Collection § 11.2, Appx. E (6th ed. 2008).

170 50 U.S.C. app. § 518.

171 15 U.S.C. § 1681s-2(b); *see* National Consumer Law Center, Fair Debt Collection §§ 9.6.6, 9.6.3.4 (6th ed. 2008); National Consumer Law Center, Fair Credit Reporting § 6.10.4 (6th ed. 2006 and Supp.).

The 2003 amendments to the Fair Credit Reporting Act place some additional duties upon creditors, but communicating the dispute to the credit reporting agency is still a precondition of a private cause of action.

172 *See* Koenig v. Waukesha State Bank, 2006 WL 2334841 (E.D. Wis. Aug. 10, 2006) (50 U.S.C. app. § 518(3) prohibits negative reporting of a request for a stay or modification of an obligation, but creditors may make adverse reports of failure to make payments lawfully due during a stay period); *cf.* Rodriguez v. Am. Express, 2006 WL 908613 (E.D. Cal. Apr. 7, 2006) (50 U.S.C. app. § 518(3) does not prohibit negative credit reporting that is based on actual credit problems unrelated to the servicemember's exercise of rights under the SCRA).

173 See www.usdoj.gov/crt/military.

Chapter 8 Creditor's Use of Arbitration to Collect Consumer Debts

8.1 How Collection Using Arbitration Works

With astonishing frequency, creditors are placing mandatory arbitration clauses in their consumer agreements or stuffing in their billing envelopes notice of such a change of terms.[1] These clauses purport to force disputes between the consumer and the creditor into binding arbitration.

Until recently these clauses have been used primarily to compel arbitration of consumer class actions and other suits brought *against* the creditor. However some creditors, including MBNA[2] and buyers of MBNA debts, use arbitration clauses as a means of collecting consumer debts. Nonpayment of the debt is viewed as a dispute, and the arbitration clause allows a party to settle disputes through arbitration. While some credit card agreements permit the party initiating the action to choose between two or more arbitration service providers, most clauses specify a particular service provider. The service provider establishes procedural rules and fees for the arbitration proceeding and handles administrative tasks.

MBNA's credit card agreement provides that all disputes will be arbitrated by the National Arbitration Forum (NAF). NAF is widely recognized for handling a significant number of arbitrations on behalf of creditors against debtors.[3] More than half of all consumer arbitrations conducted by NAF in California are claims filed by MBNA or assignees of MBNA, and NAF typically conducts over 1000 arbitrations per quarter on behalf of MBNA in California.[4] NAF has advertised to creditors that requiring all disputes to be arbitrated by NAF not only avoids creditor exposure to class actions and punitive damages, but also provides an efficient means to collect debts, saving the creditor up to 60% of collection costs.[5] In less than two years First USA Bank initiated over 40,000 collection actions through NAF, paying NAF $5.3 million.[6] Other data on NAF arbitration of MBNA and other collection actions is found in a September 2007 report by Public Citizen, *The Arbitration Trap, How Credit Card Companies Ensnare Consumers*.[7] Among the report's findings are that:

- 99.6% of NAF cases are brought by creditors, not consumers;
- 94.7% of awards were in favor of businesses;
- In California the top five NAF arbitrators handled an average of 1000 cases each, and ruled for businesses almost 97% of the time;
- The highest volume NAF arbitrator issued as many as sixty-eight awards in a single day—in which he awarded every penny the creditor sought in all sixty-eight cases; on his six busiest days, when he issued 332 awards, businesses sought $3,432,919 and he awarded them $3,432,919;
- Arbitrators ruling for consumers are blackballed;
- Excessive fees are charged for a written decision and for other aspects of the arbitration; and

1 See National Consumer Law Center, Consumer Arbitration Agreements §§ 5.2.3, 5.6.3, 5.7 (5th ed. 2007) for further discussion about when bill stuffers are sufficient to form an agreement to arbitrate.

2 According to a filing with the Securities and Exchange Commission by Bank of America: "[O]n January 1, 2006, MBNA Corporation merged with and into Bank of America Corporation. As a result of the merger, MBNA America Bank, National Association ('MBNA') became a wholly-owned subsidiary of Bank of America Corporation. On June 10, 2006, MBNA changed its name to FIA Card Services, National Association ('FIA')." BA Credit Card Funding, L.L.C., Current Report (Form 8-K) (Oct. 20, 2006). Although it is doubtful that MBNA is still a proper claimant in any debt collection case, creditors and debt collectors attempting to enforce MBNA arbitration clauses are referred to in this manual as "MBNA" for the sake of simplicity.

3 *See* Caroline Mayer, *Win Some, Lose Rarely? Arbitration Forum's Rulings Called One-Sided*, Wash. Post. Mar. 1, 2000, at E1 (explaining that, of nearly 20,000 arbitration awards entered by the NAF in arbitrations filed by First USA between early 1998 and March 2000, "not only has the company sought arbitration far more often than consumers, it has also won in 99.6 percent of the cases that went all the way to an arbitrator").

4 Nat'l Arbitration Forum, California CCP 1281.96 Reports, *available at* www.adrforum.com/main.aspx?itemID=563&hideBar=False&navID=188&news=3.

5 *See* Plaintiff's Response to Defendant First USA's Motion to Dismiss and/or Stay Proceedings and to Compel Arbitration, Marsh v. First USA Bank, Clearinghouse No. 52,494 (N.D. Tex. Dec. 3, 1999).

6 *Id.*

7 Available at www.citizen.org/documents/Final_wcover.pdf.

- Consumer attorneys are frustrated by NAF's failure to follow its own procedures and its seeming pro-business bias in case administration.

Because NAF handles such a large number of debt collection cases for its creditor clients, much of the discussion in this chapter will focus on arbitration proceedings before the NAF.[8]

Often the first step in the collection using arbitration process is for the creditor, collector, or law firm hired by the creditor/collector to threaten that the matter will be turned over to arbitration. Then, when the creditor decides to go forward with arbitration, it files a claim with the NAF. NAF rules provide that the creditor may mail or even e-mail minimal paperwork to NAF to initiate the arbitration collection action.[9] Claims filed by creditors generally request an arbitration award in the amount of the principal allegedly owed, plus interest, arbitration fees, attorney fees, and other fees, such as "process of service" fees.

According to current NAF rules, the creditor is required to send notice of the proceeding to the consumer, giving the consumer thirty days to respond to the claim.[10] The notice must be substantially the same as set out in Appendix A of the NAF Code of Procedure. After the notice from the creditor is served, NAF is supposed to send a second notice, substantially the same as set out in Appendix B of the NAF Code of Procedure, giving the consumer up to fourteen more days to respond.[11] The notices are supposed to describe consumers' options, which include submitting a written response with supporting documents, demanding an in-person participatory hearing, or demanding a hearing online or by telephone. The notice does not typically indicate whether or not requests for hearings will be granted. In addition, in some cases, the consumer may never receive a copy of the claim filed by the creditor and may not learn that an arbitration was filed until she receives a notice of arbitration from NAF.

After an NAF employee determines the type of proceeding to be held, NAF assigns an arbitrator to the case. If either party has requested a participatory hearing, the arbitrator assigned must be available in the consumer's state. Either party may strike one arbitrator for any reason. If the consumer does not respond to the notice of arbitration, the arbitrator will reach a decision based solely on documentation provided by the creditor and will enter a default award against the consumer. The vast majority of NAF arbitrations in debt collection cases result in a default award.[12]

Once the arbitrator issues an award, a copy of the award is supposed to be delivered by the arbitrator to the consumer. The date of delivery determines the timeliness of future actions in court to vacate or confirm the award. Until and unless the creditor obtains judicial confirmation of the award, the award is not enforceable and the creditor has no right to garnish wages, place liens on the consumer's property, or subject the consumer to a debtor's examination.

The prevailing party generally has one year or even more to confirm the award. However, the losing party has only a very short time frame within which to challenge the award in court, usually ninety days (or even less in some states) from when the consumer receives notice of the arbitration award.

This chapter will explain some of the consumer's options for responding to a notice of arbitration, participating in an arbitration proceeding, challenging an arbitration award that has been entered against her, resisting confirmation of the award, and bringing an independent action for arbitration-related debt collection harassment.

8.2 Options After Receiving a Notice of Arbitration

8.2.1 Introduction

Many consumers do not seek legal advice until after an arbitration award has been entered against them on behalf of the creditor. But, in some cases, the consumer does contact an attorney soon after being served with notice of the arbitration proceeding. This section examines the advice that an attorney can give the consumer in this situation.

A consumer has several options upon receiving a notice of arbitration. Some consumer advocates in certain jurisdictions advise their clients to simply ignore the notice and then challenge the arbitration award later in court. However, as discussed in § 8.5.4, *infra*, this option may foreclose arguments against the enforcement of the award in some jurisdictions, and is therefore a risky strategy.

If the consumer has a valid argument that she is not bound by an arbitration clause (for example, she is a victim of identity theft or mistaken identity, she opted out of the arbitration clause, or she never received any bill stuffer containing an arbitration clause), she may respond by objecting that the arbitrator has no jurisdiction. This option is discussed in § 8.2.2, *infra*. After objecting, the consumer may either participate in the arbitration under protest or refuse to otherwise participate in the proceeding, and then later seek to vacate the award or oppose confirmation of the

8 For discussion of whether a creditor's selection of a particular arbitration service provider to handle thousands of collection actions, resulting in millions of dollars of business for that provider, could subject the arbitration service provider to a bias challenge, see National Consumer Law Center, Consumer Arbitration Agreements § 6.5.7 (5th ed. 2007).

9 Nat'l Arbitration Forum, Code of Procedure, Rules 2(M), 7, *available at* www.arb-forum.com.

10 Nat'l Arbitration Forum, Code of Procedure, Rule 6(A).

11 Nat'l Arbitration Forum, Code of Procedure, Rule 7(C).

12 National Arbitration Forum, California CCP 1281.96 Reports, *available at* www.adrforum.com/main.aspx?itemID=563&hideBar=False&navID=188&news=3.

award. Alternatively, the consumer may also go to court to seek a stay of arbitration in order to challenge the validity of the arbitration clause. This option is discussed in § 8.2.3, *infra*.

Of course, the consumer may choose to participate in the arbitration while preserving any objections to the existence or enforceability of the arbitration agreement. This option is discussed in § 8.2.4, *infra*. The consumer may also file counterclaims against the creditor, either in arbitration or in court. This option is discussed in § 8.3, *infra*.

Whichever option is chosen, the consumer can send a complaint to the agency regulating the creditor, describing any unfair practices by the creditor, collector, collection attorney, arbitration service provider, or arbitrator. MBNA and virtually all credit card issuers are national banks regulated by the Office of the Comptroller of the Currency. Government enforcement is discussed in § 8.8, *infra*.

8.2.2 Objecting to Arbitration When No Agreement to Arbitrate Exists

Whether or not the consumer chooses to participate in the arbitration, many practitioners advise their clients to raise any objection to the enforceability of the arbitration agreement at the beginning of the arbitration proceeding.[13] While a consumer's objection to arbitration on the ground that no agreement exists is unlikely to have much impact on the arbitration itself, in some jurisdictions it is necessary to object at this stage in order to preserve the right to dispute the validity of the arbitration clause in a later court proceeding.[14]

In most jurisdictions raising this objection before the arbitrator should be sufficient to preserve the argument, and the consumer need not also raise this objection by seeking a stay of arbitration in a court proceeding.[15] In addition, some courts may treat a consumer's argument that she was a victim of identity theft as an objection that the consumer was not bound by an arbitration requirement.[16]

Because the arbitration is likely to move forward as if the consumer had not objected, many practitioners also find it advisable to file any other defenses or counterclaims in the arbitration, within the original time limits, in order to avoid a default award, being careful to make clear that the alleged debtor is participating only under protest and that she does not waive her argument that she is not bound by a valid arbitration clause.

8.2.3 Seeking a Stay of Arbitration

Federal and state law provide the consumer the right to go to court to seek a stay of an arbitration proceeding in order to determine whether there is a binding arbitration agreement between the parties. The Uniform Arbitration Act (UAA) (enacted in forty-nine states) provides that: "[O]n application, the court may stay an arbitration proceeding commenced or threatened on a showing that there is no agreement to arbitrate. Such an issue, when in substantial and bona fide dispute, shall be forthwith and summarily tried and the stay ordered if found for the moving party."[17] The application may be made in any state court of competent jurisdiction where venue is proper.[18] The UAA was revised in 2000, and twelve states have adopted this version, but the revised UAA provides the consumer similar rights to seek a court order staying the arbitration.[19] Jurisdiction is almost never appropriate in federal court.[20]

Thus, when a consumer receives notice of an arbitration action to collect on a credit card debt, one option many practitioners recommend is to file an action in state court seeking to stay the arbitration proceeding until the court resolves whether the consumer is bound by a valid arbitration agreement. These practitioners believe that a court is more likely than an arbitrator to require the creditor to produce the arbitration agreement and show that the consumer agreed to it.[21] In addition there is some risk that, if the consumer does not seek a stay of arbitration, the creditor may argue in a subsequent confirmation proceeding that the consumer can no longer raise the issue of the existence or enforceability of the arbitration agreement.[22]

Such a court action may be frustrating for a collector seeking to use the arbitration proceeding as an inexpensive

13 *See, e.g.*, Garner v. MBNA Am. Bank., 2006 WL 2354939 (N.D. Tex. Aug. 14, 2006) (confirming award against consumer who could not prove he had objected to arbitration, on grounds that he had participated in the proceeding); MBNA Am. Bank v. Felton, 2004 WL 2898632 (Conn. Super. Ct. Nov. 8, 2004).

14 *See* § 8.5.4, *infra*.

15 Holcim (Tex.) Ltd. P'ship v. Humboldt Wedag, Inc., 211 S.W.3d 796 (Tex. App. 2006). *But see* Garner v. MBNA Am. Bank., 2006 WL 2354939 (N.D. Tex. Aug. 14, 2006).

16 Boran v. Columbia Credit Services, Inc., 2006 WL 3388400 (D. Conn. Nov. 21, 2006).

17 Unif. Arbitration Act § 2(b) (1955).

18 Unif. Arbitration Act § 2(c) (1955); *see also* Unif. Arbitration Act § 18 (1955).

19 Unif. Arbitration Act § 7(b), (c), (e) (2000).

20 *See* National Consumer Law Center, Consumer Arbitration Agreements § 11.2.1 (5th ed. 2007).

21 *See* Creech v. MBNA Am. Bank, 2008 WL 216311 (Mo. Ct. App. Jan. 28, 2008).

22 *See* Garner v. MBNA Am. Bank., 2006 WL 2354939 (N.D. Tex. Aug. 14, 2006) (proper way to raise objection that no agreement to arbitrate exists is to move for a stay of arbitration).

N.Y. C.P.L.R. 7503(c) (McKinney) specifies that a party seeking arbitration can provide a notice to the other party specifying the agreement pursuant to which arbitration is sought and the name and address of the party serving the notice, and stating that unless the party served applies to stay the arbitration within twenty days after such service he shall thereafter be precluded from objecting that a valid agreement did not exist. Such notice or demand shall be served in the same manner as a summons or by registered or certified mail, return receipt

alternative to a court proceeding. In addition, creditors may have difficulty producing the credit agreement and arbitration clause agreed to by the particular consumer.[23] This requirement will be even more difficult for a debt buyer, who may even have difficulty providing evidence that the debt was in fact assigned to the debt buyer.[24] Without a proper assignment, the debt buyer can not utilize the arbitration clause and can not seek to enforce the debt. And of course the consumer can raise all the issues, discussed elsewhere in this manual, why an arbitration agreement that was in fact entered into is still unenforceable.

8.2.4 Participating in the Arbitration Proceeding

8.2.4.1 Introduction

The consumer can, of course, participate in the arbitration proceeding that the creditor initiates to collect on the debt, and raise any defenses in arbitration. However, if the consumer contests the validity of the arbitration clause itself, it is essential to preserve this argument by making clear that the consumer did not agree to arbitration, does not concede that the arbitrator has authority to decide the dispute, and is participating in the arbitration only to make sure the consumer's rights are protected. The implications of participation on a later attempt to vacate or oppose confirmation of an award are discussed in § 8.5.4, *infra*. As described there, at least in Pennsylvania, Kansas, Kentucky, and Virginia, there may be advantages to *not* participating until ordered to do so by a court.

The nature of the consumer's participation will be shaped by the rules of the arbitration service provider selected by the creditor. NAF's rules may be found at www.arb-forum.com. It is essential that an attorney representing a consumer in an NAF arbitration carefully read the NAF rules concerning document hearings, discovery, subpoenas, exchange of information before a participatory hearing, participatory hearing procedures, evidence, and so forth.

The NAF rules permit it to charge several different kinds of fees, including filing fees, commencement fees, and administrative fees; fees for hearings; penalties for late requests; fees for non-dispositive orders, discovery orders, and dispositive orders; and objection processing fees. In addition, a party wishing to request that the arbitrator issue "written findings" must pay a fee.

8.2.4.2 Filing a Response

Under present NAF rules, a consumer defending a debt collection claim is not required to pay a fee in order to simply submit a response to the creditor's claims. The response should include any documentation supporting the consumer's defenses. A sample response and counterclaim may be found in NCLC's *Consumer Arbitration Agreements* Appendix K.[25] In general, there are no up-front arbitration fees that the consumer must pay merely to submit documentation. A simple letter documenting identity theft or why certain charges were unauthorized may occasionally be enough for the consumer to prevail, if the consumer is fortunate with the choice of arbitrator.

8.2.4.3 Requesting a Hearing

Requesting a hearing may require certain up-front payments from the consumer. A consumer opting for an in-person or telephone hearing in response to a collection action must pay the fee for a participatory hearing, unless the arbitration agreement or state law require otherwise.[26] If the amount in dispute is $5000 or less, the hearing fee is $150 (and the consumer's portion would be $75) for each sixty-minute session. If the amount in dispute is over $5000 but under $15,000, the fee is $300 (and the consumer's portion would be $150) for each ninety-minute session. For larger disputes, the consumer pays $250 per session.[27] Some practitioners have reported that NAF hearing fees can be has high as $950 depending on the type of dispute. The NAF rules specify a procedure to request a waiver of hearing fees for indigent consumers.[28] As described in § 8.2.4.5, *infra*, it appears that, under the MBNA arbitration clause, a consumer can request that MBNA advance or reimburse these fees.

8.2.4.4 Risk That Consumer Will Be Ordered to Pay Creditor's Arbitration and Attorney Fees

If the consumer does not prevail, NAF rules allow the arbitrator to order the consumer to pay *all* of the creditor's arbitration fees and attorney fees, even if the consumer meets the federal poverty standards.[29] For starters this means that the arbitrator can require even an indigent consumer to pay the creditor's filing fees, which can amount to

---

requested. But if the notice is not proper, the provision is not effective. Lucas v. MBNA, 2008 WL 44325 (N.Y. Sup. Ct. Jan. 2, 2008).

23 *See* § 8.4.4.2, *infra*; *see also* Creech v. MBNA Am. Bank, 2008 WL 216311 (Mo. Ct. App. Jan. 28, 2008).

24 *See* § 8.4.4.2, *infra*.

25 (5th ed. 2007).

26 Nat'l Arbitration Forum, Fee Schedule, *available at* www.arb-forum.com (fees for common claims consumer respondents).

27 *Id.*; *see also* Nat'l Arbitration Forum, Code of Procedure, Rule 34(B), *available at* www.arb-forum.com.

28 Nat'l Arbitration Forum, Code of Procedure, Rule 45.

29 *See* Nat'l Arbitration Forum, Code of Procedure, Rule 44(A).

hundreds of dollars. Thus, even if the consumer received a waiver of hearing fees because of indigence, if the consumer loses the case the arbitrator can order the consumer to pay 100% of the hearing fees.

Non-prevailing consumers may also have to pay all other arbitration fees assessed to the creditor. On a $6000 debt, for example, when there are two hearing sessions and various objections to various requests by parties, the non-prevailing consumer may have to pay almost $2000 in arbitration costs. Nevertheless, as described in § 8.2.4.5, *infra*, at least the current version of the MBNA arbitration clause provides that the consumer will not have to pay more than what he or she would have been required to pay in a state court action.

Perhaps more significantly, the arbitrator can award the creditor its attorney fees in almost any amount. The arbitrator also has discretion to decide if such attorney fees will be assessed in the same amount whether the consumer defaults, participates through a documentary hearing, or insists on a participatory hearing. Whatever the attorney fee award assessed, there are very narrow grounds for challenging an arbitration award, even when there is a clear error of law.[30] Consequently, one risk of contesting the creditor's collection action is that the arbitrator may assess a significant attorney fee against the consumer, and the consumer may have little recourse to challenge the size of that fee.

8.2.4.5 Can the Consumer Avoid Costs Under the MBNA Clause?

A great deal of collection using arbitration today, either in a collection action brought in MBNA's name or by a debt buyer purchasing an MBNA debt, involves the MBNA arbitration clause. MBNA's arbitration clause provides that in no case will the cost of arbitration to the consumer exceed what he or she would have had to pay if the action had been filed in state court.

The clause appears to limit the consumer's exposure to arbitration costs and fees. In particular the clause provides: "At [the consumer's] written request, [the creditor] will advance any arbitration filing fee, administrative and hearing fees which you are required to pay to pursue a claim in arbitration." When the consumer defends against a collection action brought before an arbitrator, the consumer must pay for the right to have a participatory hearing. This clause appears to allow the consumer to make a written request that the creditor advance those fees. "To pursue a claim in arbitration" should be interpreted as also applying to defending against the collection action.

The MBNA clause also provides that "[i]n no event will [the consumer] be required to reimburse [the creditor] for any arbitration filing, administrative or hearing fees in an amount greater than what [the consumer's] court costs would have been if the Claim had been resolved in a state court with jurisdiction." This unambiguously limits the amount an arbitrator can assess against the consumer. Left uncertain is whether the amount to be assessed is capped at a level established by the state court with jurisdiction that assesses the *highest* costs or by the state court with jurisdiction (such as a small claims court) that assesses the *lowest* costs. However, any ambiguities should be resolved in the consumer's favor, especially given that MBNA has used this provision of its arbitration clause to argue that the clause is not unconscionable.[31]

8.3 Filing Counterclaims Against the Creditor in Court or in Arbitration

One possible approach is to file counterclaims in the arbitration action. Filing the counterclaim may prevent the creditor or arbitrator from dismissing the case without prejudice, thus leaving the creditor free to initiate a lawsuit or an arbitration to collect the debt at a future date, when the consumer may not be able to seek or obtain legal representation.

Most practitioners prefer to raise substantive consumer claims in a separate court action rather than in a NAF arbitration proceeding. Filing the counterclaim in the arbitration would be most appropriate when collateral estoppel would prevent the consumer from raising the claim later in a separate court proceeding. While an arbitration proceeding may have as much of a preclusive effect as a court proceeding,[32] often an action to collect on a consumer debt does not preclude a separate action on consumer debt harassment claims.[33] Another factor in deciding whether to bring counterclaims in the arbitration or separately is whether that separate action could also be forced into arbitration.

Filing a counterclaim under NAF rules requires use of special forms that need be obtained from the NAF, which must then be delivered to the NAF and the creditor. NAF Rule 14 calls for a filing fee when making a counterclaim. Given that MBNA's arbitration agreement provides that the consumer will not be required to pay costs greater than she would in court, and that there is typically no fee to make a counterclaim, the consumer can request that the creditor pay all costs associated with filing the counterclaim.

30 *See* National Consumer Law Center, Consumer Arbitration Agreements § 11.5 (5th ed. 2007).

31 *See* Jaimez v. MBNA Am. Bank, 2006 WL 470587 (D. Kan. Feb. 27, 2006) (MBNA's clause not unconscionable based on unreasonable arbitration costs, given that it "provides that in no case will the cost of arbitration exceed the costs if the action were filed in state court").

32 *See* National Consumer Law Center, Consumer Arbitration Agreements § 11.8 (5th ed. 2007).

33 *See* National Consumer Law Center, Fair Debt Collection § 7.4.2 (6th ed. 2008).

8.4 Seeking to Vacate the Award

8.4.1 Introduction

The procedure and statutory grounds for seeking *vacatur* of an arbitration award are discussed in National Consumer Law Center, *Consumer Arbitration Agreements* Chapter 11.[34] This section will highlight issues particularly relevant to *vacatur* of a debt collection arbitration award.

8.4.2 Timeliness

A consumer may challenge an arbitration award by seeking a court order vacating or modifying the award. In many jurisdictions waiting for the creditor to seek confirmation of the award in court is not advisable, because some courts have held that they have no discretion to refuse to confirm an award unless a timely motion to vacate has been filed.[35]

In federal court and virtually all state courts, the consumer must seek to vacate or modify the award within ninety days of the delivery of that award to the consumer,[36] but there are variations. Connecticut, Maryland, and Massachusetts provide only thirty days to vacate an award;[37] Michigan allows only twenty-one days.[38] On the other hand, Arizona law provides a ninety-day period to modify an award, but imposes no time limit to vacate the award, so that the consumer can seek to vacate the award at any time up through the confirmation proceeding.[39] California law provides for one-hundred days.[40] The Seventh Circuit, in computing the ninety-day period under the Federal Arbitration Act (FAA), started the period when the arbitration award was sent (not received) and ended it when the notice to vacate was served upon the other party.[41]

Whatever the time period specified, equitable tolling may apply to extend this period,[42] and some states have rules that restart the time period if a case timely brought in federal court is dismissed because of a lack of federal jurisdiction.[43] Courts have also found the motion to vacate timely when an improper motion was timely filed but a later, proper motion was filed after the time period had expired.[44] The Uniform Arbitration Act (UAA) and revised UAA also extend the time period when the grounds are "predicated upon corruption, fraud, or other undue means." In that case the action to vacate "shall be made within ninety days after such grounds are known or should have been known."[45] Corruption, fraud, or undue means may be difficult to prove in the typical arbitration case.[46]

While there are generally strict time deadlines for the consumer to seek to vacate an award, the creditor typically has much longer to confirm an award. Thus creditors often wait to seek confirmation of an award until after the deadline for *vacatur* has passed. While many practitioners believe that every effort should be made to bring the action to vacate within the applicable time period, all is not lost if the consumer fails to do so. Section 8.5, *infra*, sets out a number of grounds on which to challenge the creditor's confirmation action even after the ninety-day or other applicable time period has expired.

Two of those grounds relate directly to the ability to vacate an award even beyond ninety days after an award is issued. As set out in § 8.5.3.3, *infra*, a growing number of

34 (5th ed. 2007).

35 *See, e.g.*, MBNA Am. Bank v. Swartz, 2006 WL 1071523 (Del. Ch. Ct. Apr. 13, 2006) (confirming award despite "barely adequate paperwork provided by MBNA" on grounds that court was "without power to do otherwise"); MBNA Am. Bank v. Tackleson, 720 N.W.2d 192 (Iowa Ct. App. 2006) (table) (text available at 2006 WL 1229935) ("the court may deny confirmation of an arbitration award under the statute only if relief is granted under the accompanying vacation and correction statutes"); Asset Acceptance, L.L.C. v. Stancik, 2004 WL 2930997 (Ohio Ct. App. Dec. 16, 2004) (confirming award when no motion to vacate had been filed within state's ninety-day period, but holding that counterclaims are not subject to the same time limit); *see also* National Consumer Law Center, Consumer Arbitration Agreements § 11.2.3 (5th ed. 2007).

36 *See, e.g.*, Occidental Chem. Corp. v. Local 820, Int'l Chem. Workers Union, 614 F. Supp. 323 (W.D. Mich. 1985); Kutch v. State Farm Mut. Auto. Ins. Co., 960 P.2d 93 (Colo. 1998); Musser v. Wolpoff & Abramson, L.L.P., 2008 WL 451844 (Colo. Ct. App. Feb. 21, 2008); MBNA Am. Bank v. Leslie, 2005 WL 2277252 (Conn. Super. Ct. Aug. 25, 2005); Walter A. Brown Inc. v. Moylan, 509 A.2d 98 (D.C. 1986); Broward County Paraprofessional Ass'n v. Sch. Bd. of Broward County, 406 So. 2d 1252 (Fla. Dist. Ct. App. 1981); Bingham County Comm'n v. Interstate Elec. Co., 105 Idaho 36 (Idaho 1983); MBNA Am. Bank v. Tackleson, 720 N.W.2d 192 (Iowa Ct. App. 2006) (table) (text available at 2006 WL 1229935); Local 589, Amalgamated Transit Union v. Mass. Bay Transp. Auth, 397 Mass. 426 (1986); MBNA Am. Bank v. Belleleslie, 2005 Mont. Dist. LEXIS 1119 (Mont. Dist. Ct. Apr. 26, 2005); MBNA Am. Bank v. Hart, 710 N.W.2d 125 (N.D. 2006); MBNA Am. Bank v. McArdle, 2007 WL 1229214 (Ohio Ct. App. Apr. 27, 2007); CACV v. Kogler, 2006 WL 2790398 (Ohio Ct. App. Sept. 29, 2006); Garner v. MBNA Am. Bank, 2007 WL 499646 (Tex. App. Feb. 16, 2007); MBNA Am. Bank v. Miles, 2007 WL 1711803 (Wash. Ct. App. June 14, 2007).

37 Conn. Gen. Stat. § 52-417; Md. Code Ann., Cts. & Jud. Proc. § 3-224 (West); Mass. Gen. Laws ch. 251, § 12.

38 Mich. Ct. R. 3.602(J)(2).

39 Morgan v. Carillon Investments Inc., 207 Ariz. 547 (Ct. App. 2004).

40 Cal. Civ. Proc. Code § 1288 (West).

41 Webster v. A.T. Kearney, Inc., 507 F.3d 568 (7th Cir. 2007).

42 *See* Bauer v. Carty & Co., 2005 WL 948641, at *4 (W.D. Tenn. Mar. 9, 2005).

43 *See* Fischer v. MBNA Am. Bank, 2007 WL 779295 (Ky. Ct. App. Mar. 16, 2007).

44 Bonar v. Dean Witter Reynolds, Inc., 835 F.2d 1378 (11th Cir. 1988); Dealer Computer Services v. Dub Herring Ford, 489 F. Supp. 2d 772 (E.D. Mich. 2007).

45 Unif. Arbitration Act § 12(b) (1955).
Revised Uniform Arbitration Act § 23(b) (2000) contains similar, but not identical language.

46 *See* MBNA Am. Bank v. Hart, 710 N.W.2d 125 (N.D. 2006).

courts find that the lack of a binding arbitration agreement can be raised as ground to vacate an award at a later date, in the confirmation proceeding. The lack of an arbitration agreement goes to the court's jurisdiction to confirm the award. In addition, as examined in § 8.5.3.2, *infra*, the time period to vacate an award does not begin to run until the consumer is properly notified of the award, and a number of questions can be raised concerning notice of an award relating to a debt collection arbitration.

8.4.3 Applicable Law, Jurisdiction, and Venue

Jurisdiction for the consumer's action to vacate or modify the award is almost always in state, not federal court.[47] Actions to vacate an award in state court will be governed by state law, not the FAA.[48] State law in forty-nine states concerning *vacatur* is patterned on the Uniform Arbitration Act (UAA),[49] but as of May 2008, thirteen of these states have adopted the revised UAA.[50]

A state court action to vacate an award usually can be brought in any court of competent jurisdiction in the state.[51] There is no requirement to bring an action to vacate an award issued by NAF in Minnesota, despite the fact that the NAF is located in Minnesota and notices from the NAF contain a Minnesota address. If there had been an in-person proceeding, it would have been held near the consumer's residence.[52]

There is almost never federal court jurisdiction to bring a motion to vacate an arbitration collection award, because the Federal Arbitration Act (FAA) does not provide federal court jurisdiction and consumer collection actions rarely satisfy diversity or federal question jurisdictional requirements.[53] In the rare case in which a federal court has jurisdiction over a consumer's petition to vacate an award (or a creditor's petition to confirm an award),[54] the proceeding would be governed by the FAA. The FAA requires application in the court specified in the agreement, or if no court is specified, then in the federal district court for the district where the arbitration was held.[55] The Supreme Court has held that venue is proper under the FAA either in the district where the award was made or in any district proper under the general venue statute.[56]

8.4.4 Grounds for Vacating an Award in a Debt Collection Case

8.4.4.1 Introduction

Chapter 11 of NCLC's *Consumer Arbitration Agreements*[57] examines generally the right of any party to seek to vacate, modify, or oppose confirmation of an award. This section focuses on the grounds to vacate an award and the applicability of these grounds to a creditor's arbitration collection award.

8.4.4.2 When Arbitration Award Not Binding on the Consumer

If the consumer never assented to the arbitration agreement, or for some other reason the arbitration agreement is not enforceable as to that consumer, then the arbitration award is not enforceable, unless the consumer participated in the arbitration without objection.[58] The UAA states that

47 *See* National Consumer Law Center, Consumer Arbitration Agreements § 11.2.1 (5th ed. 2007).

48 *See id.* § 11.2.2.

49 Unif. Arbitration Act (1955), *available at* www.law.upenn.edu/bll/ulc/fnact99/1920_69/uaa55.pdf.

50 Unif. Arbitration Act (2000), *available at* www.law.upenn.edu/bll/ulc/uarba/arbitrat1213.pdf.

States adopting the revised UAA include Alaska, Colorado, District of Columbia, Hawaii, Nevada, New Jersey, New Mexico, North Carolina, North Dakota, Oklahoma, Oregon, Utah, and Washington.

51 Unif. Arbitration Act § 17 (1955); Unif. Arbitration Act § 1(3) (2000).

See National Consumer Law Center, Consumer Arbitration Agreements § 11.2.2 (5th ed. 2007), for a discussion of these statutes.

52 *See* § 8.5.5.2, *infra*.

53 Fisher v. MBNA Am. Bank, 422 F. Supp. 2d 889 (S.D. Ohio 2006); Turner v. MBNA Am. Bank, 2006 W.L. 825991 (N.D. Ga. Mar. 29, 2006); Watson v. MBNA Am. Bank, 2005 WL 1875778 (W.D.N.C. Aug. 1, 2005); Garcia v. MBNA Am. Bank, 2005 WL 1653639 (D. Or. July 6, 2005); Stafford v. Chase Manhattan Bank U.S.A., 2005 WL 1330874 (M.D.N.C. June 3, 2005); Miles v. MBNA Am. Bank, 2005 WL 1220842 (E.D. Wash. May 23, 2005); Fischer v. MBNA Am. Bank, 2005 WL 1168388 (W.D. Ky. May 17, 2005); Mesdag v. MBNA Am. Bank, 2005 WL 418549 (D. Or. Feb. 17, 2005); Mellado v. MBNA Am. Bank, 2004 WL 2937224 (N.D. Tex. Dec. 17, 2004); Kearns v. MBNA Am. Bank, 2004 WL 2512742 (N.D. Tex. Nov. 5, 2004); MBNA Am. Bank v. Shnitzer, 2004 WL 1717670 (D. Or. July 30, 2004).

54 *See* National Consumer Law Center, Consumer Arbitration Agreements § 11.2.1 (5th ed. 2007); § 8.5.5.2, *infra*.

55 9 U.S.C. § 10.

56 Cortez Byrd Chips, Inc. v. Bill Harbert Constr. Co., 529 U.S. 193, 120 S. Ct. 1331, 146 L. Ed. 2d 171 (2000).

57 National Consumer Law Center, Consumer Arbitration Agreements Ch. 11 (5th ed. 2007).

58 McKenzie v. MBNA Am. (D. Mont. Sept. 20, 2007), *available at* www.consumerlaw.org/unreported; MBNA Am. Bank v. Blanks, 2007 WL 2713361 (Ark. Ct. App. Sept. 19, 2007); MBNA Am. Bank v. Felton, 2004 WL 2898632 (Conn. Super. Ct. Nov. 8, 2004); MBNA Am. Bank v. Phoenix, 2004 WL 2166955 (Conn. Super. Ct. Sept. 9, 2004); MBNA Am. Bank v. Credit, 132 P.3d 898 (Kan. 2006); MBNA Am. Bank v. Barben, 111 P.3d 663 (Kan. Ct. App. 2005) (table) (text available at 2005 WL 1214244); MBNA Am. Bank v. Cornock, No. 03-C-0018 (N.H. Super. Ct. Mar. 20, 2007), *available at* www.consumerlaw.org/unreported; MBNA Am. Bank v. Engen, 2005 WL 1754169 (Wash. Ct. App. July 25, 2005).

an award shall be vacated when there is no arbitration agreement unless a court had previously ruled that there was an arbitration agreement or the consumer participated in the arbitration proceeding without raising an objection.[59] The revised UAA has a similar provision.[60] The Supreme Court has stated: "Arbitration is a matter of contract and a party can not be required to submit to arbitration any dispute that he has not agreed so to submit. This axiom recognizes the fact that arbitrators derive their authority to resolve disputes only because the parties have agreed in advance to submit such grievances to arbitration."[61]

The consumer should argue that the creditor or collector is required to produce evidence that the consumer agreed to arbitration. Creditors often can not produce evidence that the particular consumer assented to or even was sent a particular arbitration agreement. If the company can not produce evidence of an agreement, then it should not be allowed to enforce an arbitration award based on that purported agreement.[62] Debt buyers in particular will have difficulty showing the existence of a credit agreement, or an assignment from the creditor of the debt.[63] It is not enough to introduce an undated and unsigned standard form contract, with no proof that the contract applies to the consumer.[64] Of course a debt buyer can not use arbitration to collect on a debt when it can not even present evidence that it has the right to enforce the credit agreement, including the arbitration clause.

A recent case in which MBNA sought to confirm an arbitration award discussed this problem in some detail:

> Petitioner must tender the *actual* provisions agreed to, including any and all amendments, and not simply a photocopy of general terms to which the credit issuer may currently demand debtors agree. For example, Petitioner's Exhibit A which is labeled "Credit Card Agreement and Additional Terms and Conditions" lacks Respondent's signature. Neither does it contain a date indicating when these terms were adopted by MBNA nor how the terms were amended or changed, if at all, over the years appear anywhere on the document. Furthermore, the contract does not contain any name, account number or other identifying statements which would connect the proffered agreement with the Respondent in this action. In fact, petitioners appear to have attached the exact same photocopy, which as noted is not specific to any particular consumer, to many of its confirmation petitions. While on its face there is nothing necessarily unusual about a large commercial entity such as MBNA providing a standard form contract that all credit card consumers agree to, the burden nevertheless remains with MBNA to tie the binding nature of its boiler-plate terms to the user at issue in each particular case and to show that those terms are binding on each Respondent it seeks to hold accountable (the Respondent's intent to be bound *after notice of terms is established* can be shown via card use. The fact that MBNA issues a particular agreement with particular terms with the majority of its customers is of little relevance in determining the actual terms of the alleged agreement before this Court, if not linked directly to respondent in some way shape or form. Just because a petitioner provides a photocopy of a document entitled "Additional Terms and Conditions," certainly does not mean those terms are binding on someone who could have theoretically signed a completely different agreement when they were extended credit. Whether the physical card itself or some solicitation agreement with Respondent's signature referenced the terms and conditions, or whether the terms were made readily accessible to Respondent by e-mail or the internet, and Respondent was in fact aware of this, may all be relevant to an inquiry into constructive notice but such notice must still be established. At bar, MBNA Bank has failed to establish that the provided terms and conditions were the actual terms and conditions agreed to by Nelson. As such, applying *Kaplan,* the Court does not find objective intent on the part of the Respondent to be bound to the contractual statements proffered by MBNA requiring the question of arbitrability to be decided by the arbitrator or that arbitration is the required forum for either party to bring claims against the other.

N.Y. C.P.L.R. 7503(c) (McKinney) specifies that a party seeking arbitration can provide a notice to the other party specifying the agreement pursuant to which arbitration is sought and the name and address of the party serving the notice, and stating that unless the party served applies to stay the arbitration within twenty days after such service he shall thereafter be precluded from objecting that a valid agreement did not exist. Such notice or demand shall be served in the same manner as a summons or by registered or certified mail, return receipt requested. But if the notice is not proper, the provision is not effective. Lucas v. MBNA, 2008 WL 44325 (N.Y. Sup. Ct. Jan. 2, 2008).

59 Unif. Arbitration Act § 12(5) (1955).

60 Unif. Arbitration Act § 23(5) (2000).

61 AT & T Technologies, Inc. v. Communications Workers of Am., 475 U.S. 643, 106 S. Ct. 1415, 89 L. Ed. 2d 648 (1986).

62 Acher v. Fujitsu Network Communications, 354 F. Supp. 2d 26 (D. Mass. 2005); Owen v. MBPXL Corp., 173 F. Supp. 2d 905, 922 (N.D. Iowa 2001); Alltell Corp. v. Sumner, 203 S.W.3d 77 (Ark. 2005); Am. Express Centurion Bank v. Frey, 2004 WL 1676465 (Mich. Ct. App. July 27, 2004); Creech v. MBNA Am. Bank, 2008 WL 216311 (Mo. Ct. App. Jan. 28, 2008); Lucas v. MBNA, 2008 WL 44325 (N.Y. Sup. Ct. Jan. 2, 2008). *But see* MBNA Am. Bank v. Tackleson, 720 N.W.2d 192 (Iowa Ct. App. 2006) (table) (text available at 2006 WL 1229935).

63 *See* Koch v. Compucredit Corp., 2007 WL 991070 (E.D. Ark. Mar. 29, 2007); NCO Portfolio Mgmt., Inc. v. Chouest, 2008 WL 1970319 (La. Ct. App. Apr. 29, 2008); § 4.5.3, *supra*.

64 NCO Portfolio Mgmt., Inc. v. Chouest, 2008 WL 1970319 (La. Ct. App. Apr. 29, 2008); FIA Card Services, Nat'l Ass'n v. Thompson, 2008 WL 624904 (N.Y. Dist. Ct. Mar. 10, 2008); *see also* § 4.5.3, *supra*.

> While these deficiencies of proof are fatal to Petitioner's claim, such a problem is not without a solution. Since the credit card issuer is the party in the best position to maintain records of notification it may provide an affidavit from someone with knowledge of the policies, procedures and practices of its organization affirming (1) when and how the notification of the original terms and conditions was provided, including any solicitations or applications containing the Respondent's signature, (2) what those terms and conditions were *at the time of the notification,* (3) whether the mandatory arbitration clause, and any other additional provisions Petitioner now treats as binding, were included in the terms and conditions of card use at the time Respondent entered into the retail credit agreement, and if they were not, then when they were added, as well as a statement certifying that (a) such addition was made pursuant to the applicable law chosen by the parties to apply to the agreement, not limited to but especially including mandatory opt-out requirements, and (b) a statement indicating that upon reasonable and diligent inspection of the records maintained by the Petitioner, and to the best of Petitioners' knowledge Respondent never opted out of said clause, and the basis for this determination. The use of such affidavits to support confirmation of arbitration awards is not novel.[65]

Moreover, in many states, if an affidavit is used to support the company's evidence, additional requirements may exist if the affiant is out of state. In New York, the affidavit must be accompanied by a certificate of conformity, and a certificate of authority may also be required.[66]

Even if the collector does produce evidence of a binding arbitration agreement, the consumer can challenge the enforceability of the agreement on many bases. NCLC's *Consumer Arbitration Agreements* Chapter 5[67] examines whether arbitration agreements sent in bill stuffers are enforceable. Chapter 6 of NCLC's *Consumer Arbitration Agreements*[68] examines whether various aspects of the arbitration agreement are unconscionable. Other grounds are also examined throughout chapters 7 and 8 of that manual.[69]

65 MBNA Am. Bank v. Nelson, 15 Misc. 3d 1148(A) (Civ. Ct. 2007) (table) (text available at 2007 WL 1704618) (footnotes omitted); *see also* Owen v. MBPXL Corp., 173 F. Supp. 2d 905, 922 (N.D. Iowa 2001) (rejecting affidavit as not sufficiently based on personal knowledge).

66 MBNA Am. Bank v. Nelson, 15 Misc. 3d 1148(A) (Civ. Ct. 2007) (table) (text available at 2007 WL 1704618).

67 National Consumer Law Center, Consumer Arbitration Agreements Ch. 5 (5th ed. 2007).

68 *Id.* Ch. 6.

69 *Id.* Chs. 7, 8.

8.4.4.3 Lack of Notice of the Arbitration Proceeding

Lack of notice of the arbitration proceeding is a sufficient basis for vacating or refusing to confirm an award.[70] The revised Uniform Arbitration Act (UAA) states that one basis on which to vacate an award is that "the arbitration was conducted without proper notice of the initiation of the arbitration . . . so as to prejudice substantially the rights of a party to the arbitration proceeding."[71] The UAA, likewise, provides grounds for *vacatur* when the arbitrators failed to provide notice of the hearing, so as to prejudice substantially the rights of a party.[72] NAF rules require both the creditor and the NAF to send form notices of the proceeding. Failure to do so or sending the notice to the wrong address may be grounds to vacate the award.[73]

In addition, NAF arbitration may run afoul of the UAA and revised UAA if NAF notices are sent via regular mail. The UAA states that, "[u]nless otherwise provided by the agreement . . . [t]he arbitrators shall appoint a time and place for the hearing and cause notification to the parties to be served personally or by registered mail."[74] Similarly, revised UAA section 9(a) requires notice "in the agreed manner between the parties or, in the absence of agreement, by certified or registered mail, return receipt requested and obtained, or by service as authorized for the commencement

70 Cas. Indem. Exch. v. Yother, 439 So. 2d 77 (Ala. 1983); CACV v. Miller, No. 845316 (Cal. Super. Ct. July 13, 2005) (petition to confirm NAF award denied when bank "failed to present sufficient, admissible evidence" that respondent was adequately served with notice of the arbitration proceedings); CACV v. Corda, 2005 WL 3664087 (Conn. Super. Ct. Dec. 16, 2005) (noting that NAF rules provide "no procedure by which the arbitrator makes any determination of whether the defendant has received actual notice of the demand for arbitration"); MBNA Am. Bank v. Nelson, 15 Misc. 3d 1148(A) (Civ. Ct. 2007) (table) (text available at 2007 WL 1704618) (denying without prejudice petition to confirm, when creditor failed to provide necessary evidence, including notice of arbitration and proof of service of notice of arbitration); MBNA Am. Bank v. Pacheco, 12 Misc. 3d 1194(A) (Civ. Ct. 2006) (table); MBNA Am. Bank v. Straub, 815 N.Y.S.2d 450 (Civ. Ct. 2006) (to confirm award creditor must show notice of arbitration was properly served, either as provided under state law or as provided in the arbitration agreement); Worldwide Asset Purchasing v. Karafotias, 801 N.Y.S.2d 721 (Civ. Ct. 2005) (explaining that a petition to confirm an arbitration award must be accompanied by proof of notice of arbitration); *see also* CACV of Colo., L.L.C. v. Ryan, 2005 WL 2981680 (Conn. Super. Ct. Oct. 19, 2005); *cf.* Cavalry Investments, L.L.C. v. Grasson, 2005 WL 2981691 (Conn. Super. Ct. Oct. 19, 2005).

71 Unif. Arbitration Act § 23(a)(6) (2000).

72 Unif. Arbitration Act § 12(a)(4) (1955).

73 MBNA Am. Bank v. Pacheco, 12 Misc. 3d 1194(A) (Civ. Ct. 2006) (table).

74 Unif. Arbitration Act § 5 (1955); *cf.* Fodor v. MBNA Am. Bank, 34 A.D.3d 473 (2006) (when notice sent by certified mail, with a signed mail return receipt, this created presumption of proper notice).

of a civil action." It is an open question whether notice by first class U.S. Mail is proper, when the arbitration agreement selects NAF, and NAF rules allow delivery via first class U.S. Mail.[75]

8.4.4.4 Lack of a Required In-Person Hearing

The consumer has a right under the UAA and revised UAA to an in-person hearing. UAA section 5 states that "the parties are entitled to be heard, to present evidence . . . and to cross-examine witnesses," unless otherwise provided for by agreement.[76] Failure to provide such a hearing is grounds to vacate an award.[77]

The Supreme Court of Virginia, interpreting that state's version of the UAA, held that a trial court erred by failing to vacate an arbitration award issued without a hearing, when the arbitration clause did not specify that a hearing was not required.[78] At least one state trial court has interpreted the hearing requirement as barring confirmation of a creditor's action to confirm an arbitration award on behalf of an MBNA debt buyer, when the award was issued without a hearing.[79]

8.4.4.5 Failure to Follow the Arbitration Agreement or Arbitration Service Provider Rules

The arbitration agreement and the arbitration service provider will spell out rules for the conduct of its hearings, and violation of those rules may be grounds for *vacatur*.[80] For example, under NAF rules, even if the consumer fails to participate, the most an arbitrator can award is the amount initially sought by the creditor, plus fees and costs.[81] Awarding interest not sought in the original claim, for example, would violate this rule. The MBNA arbitration clause itself also appears to limit the amount of arbitration costs that may be assessed by the arbitrator.[82] Costs in excess of this amount should be sufficient grounds to vacate, or at least modify, the award.

8.4.4.6 Arbitrator Improperly Selected

Improper selection of the arbitrator should be a basis on which to vacate an award,[83] and the method of selection should be carefully reviewed, particularly when the consumer does not participate in the selection. State and federal arbitration law specify that, when the consumer does not participate, selection of the arbitrator must be referred to a court, unless the arbitration service provider has established a procedure in the absence of the consumer's participation.[84]

However, the NAF and American Arbitration Association (AAA) rules *do* provide procedures for the selection of an arbitrator when the consumer does not participate in the proceeding.[85] The arbitration service provider creates a list of arbitrators, and each side *that makes an appearance* has the right to strike arbitrators from the list, and then the arbitration service provider selects an arbitrator.

If an arbitration agreement does not provide that the AAA or NAF rules apply, and the arbitrator is neither chosen with the consumer's consent nor by the court, then the arbitration award should be void.[86] The award should be void even if the creditor selects the AAA or NAF to conduct the arbitration, because the consumer has not consented to use of this service provider or its method of selecting an arbitrator. The consumer's failure to participate in the arbitration does not waive the consumer's right to have an arbitrator selected properly.[87]

---

75 Revised Uniform Arbitration Act § 9, comment 3, states that the NAF, AAA and other arbitration organizations allow service by regular mail, and this is acceptable if the parties agree.

76 Unif. Arbitration Act § 5 (1955).

77 Unif. Arbitration Act § 12(a)(4) (1955).

78 Bates v. McQueen, 270 Va. 95, 102–103, 613 S.E.2d 566, 569–570 (2005) ("In short, the failure to conduct 'the hearing' clearly intended by [the UAA], unless otherwise provided by an agreement, and by the provisions of [the UAA] was tantamount to no arbitration. Unless parties agree otherwise, a hearing is a fundamental part of the arbitration process because '[t]he arbitrators are the final judges of both law and fact, their award not being subject to reversal for a mistake of either.' " (citations omitted)).

79 CACV of Colo., L.L.C. v. Rubin, No. GV06-004208-00 (Va. Dist. Ct. Apr. 21, 2006), *available at* www.consumerlaw.org/unreported.

80 *See* National Consumer Law Center, Consumer Arbitration Agreements §§ 11.4.2, 11.5 (5th ed. 2007).

81 Nat'l Arbitration Forum, Code of Procedure, Rules 37(B), 37(C), *available at* www.arb-forum.com.

82 *See* § 8.2.4.5, *supra.*

83 Improper selection can be viewed as an award procured by undue means, or that the arbitrator exceeded his powers. *See* Brook v. Peak Int'l Ltd., 169 F. Supp. 2d 641, 645 (W.D. Tex. 2001) ("arbitrators are without power to arbitrate a dispute when they are not chosen in accordance with the parties' arbitration agreement"), *rev'd*, 294 F.3d 668 (5th Cir. 2002) (party failed to object properly and waived right to do so); Martinez v. Master Prot. Corp., 118 Cal. App. 4th 107 (2004); *see also* Alan v. Super. Ct., 111 Cal. App. 4th 217 (2003).

84 *See* 9 U.S.C. §§ 4, 5; Unif. Arbitration Act § 3 (1955); Unif. Arbitration Act § 11 (2000); *see also* Hugs & Kisses, Inc. v. Aguirre, 220 F.3d 890 (8th Cir. 2000).

85 Val-U Constr. Co. v. Rosebud Sioux Tribe, 146 F.3d 573 (8th Cir. 1998).

86 Hugs & Kisses, Inc. v. Aguirre, 220 F.3d 890 (8th Cir. 2000); *see also* R.J. O'Brien & Associates, Inc. v. Pipkin, 64 F.3d 257 (7th Cir. 1995); Cargill Rice, Inc. v. Empresa Nicaraguense Dealimentos Basicos, 25 F.3d 223 (4th Cir. 1994); Szuts v. Dean Witter Reynolds, Inc., 931 F.2d 830 (11th Cir. 1991); Avis Rent A Car Sys., Inc. v. Garage Employees Union Local 272, 791 F.2d 22 (2d Cir. 1986).

87 Hugs & Kisses, Inc. v. Aguirre, 220 F.3d 890 (8th Cir. 2000).

8.4.4.7 Arbitration Award Is Contrary to the Law or Facts

That an arbitration award is clearly contrary to the law or the facts is not listed in state or federal arbitration statutes as a basis on which to vacate an award. But the United States Supreme Court has recognized that there is some opportunity for courts to review the merits of an arbitrator's decision.[88] While great deference is paid to the arbitrator's decision, courts do have some role in reviewing the merits of that decision, although the exact nature of that role is still unsettled. For a more detailed discussion of when an award may be contrary to the law or facts, see National Consumer Law Center, *Consumer Arbitration Agreements* § 11.5.[89]

8.4.4.8 Arbitrator Bias

Arbitrator bias, as described in National Consumer Law Center, *Consumer Arbitration Agreements* § 11.4.3,[90] is another basis on which to vacate an award. It may be difficult to prove bias in a particular case, as discussed in NCLC's *Consumer Arbitration Agreements* §§ 6.5.7, 11.4.3.[91] Nevertheless, a California statute specifies that the court "shall" vacate an award if the arbitrator fails to make certain disclosures concerning relationships the arbitrator has to the parties.[92]

8.4.4.9 Inconvenient Venue

Consumer attorneys often focus on inconvenient venue of the arbitration proceeding itself as a possible basis on which to vacate an award, noting NAF's Minnesota address. It is important to understand that, while NAF is headquartered Minnesota, any in-person hearing should take place at a location near the consumer's residence, not in Minnesota. While a Minnesota venue would be inconvenient for an in-person hearing, a document hearing administered from Minnesota may not raise the same concerns.[93]

A venue challenge certainly makes sense when the consumer requested an in-person hearing, and that hearing was offered at a significant distance from the consumer's residence. NAF rules require that the hearing occur in the same federal judicial district where the consumer resides, and at "a reasonably convenient location."[94] In addition, to comply with the Fair Debt Collection Procedures Act (FDCPA), the Federal Trade Commission Act, and state deceptive practices (UDAP) statutes, the location must be within the county where the consumer resides.[95] Consequently it should be improper to conduct an in-person hearing, even if it is within the federal judicial district where the consumer resides, if it is not also within the county where the consumer resides. There is no reason to establish a different standard as to venue for consumer collection actions utilizing arbitration proceedings than for those utilizing judicial actions. Courts will strike down an arbitration agreement if it requires an inconvenient venue to arbitrate the case,[96] and this should also provide grounds to vacate an award, particularly when the consumer did not participate in the arbitration.

8.5 Opposing Confirmation of the Award

8.5.1 Introduction

An arbitration award is not an enforceable judgment on the debt. The creditor can not use the arbitration award to seize property or institute wage garnishment. Instead, the creditor must go to court to "confirm" the award, at which point the court enters a judgment that can be enforced like any other judgment in a civil action.[97] This allows the creditor to garnish wages, place liens on property, and conduct a debtor's examination.[98]

88 *See* First Options of Chicago, Inc. v. Kaplan, 514 U.S. 938, 942, 115 S. Ct. 1920, 131 L. Ed. 2d 985 (1995); Wilko v. Swan, 346 U.S. 427, 436, 745 S. Ct. 182, 98 L. Ed. 168 (1953).

89 (5th ed. 2007).

90 *Id.*

91 *Id.*

92 Cal. Civ. Proc. Code § 1286.2(a)(6) (West) (discussed in National Consumer Law Center, Consumer Arbitration Agreements § 11.4.3.2 (5th ed. 2007)).

93 *See* Lamb v. Jovitch, Block & Rathbone, L.L.P., 2005 WL 4137778 (S.D. Ohio Jan. 24, 2005) (no Fair Debt Collection Practices Act violation when NAF administered the arbitration from Minnesota, but when consumer was entitled to an in-person hearing in a convenient location).

94 Nat'l Arbitration Forum, Code of Procedure, Rule 32(A), *available at* www.arb-forum.com.

95 *See* National Consumer Law Center, Fair Debt Collection § 5.9 (6th ed. 2008).

The Federal Trade Commission and numerous state unfair and deceptive practices (UDAP) cases have found it to be unfair and deceptive to bring consumer collection suits in inconvenient venues; also unfair are credit agreements that waive the consumer's right to a convenient venue. *See* National Consumer Law Center, Unfair and Deceptive Acts and Practices § 5.1 (6th ed. 2004 and Supp.).

96 *See* Patterson v. ITT Consumer Fin. Corp., 14 Cal. App. 4th 1659 (1993); Philyaw v. Platinum Enterprises, Inc., 54 Va. Cir. 364 (Va. Cir. Ct. 2001); *see also* Bailey v. Ameriquest Mortgage Co., 2002 WL 100391 (D. Minn. Jan. 23, 2002), *rev'd*, 346 F.3d 821 (8th Cir. 2003) (issues should first be presented to the arbitrator); Bolter v. Super. Ct., 87 Cal. App. 4th 900 (2001); Brower v. Gateway 2000, 246 A.D.2d 246, 676 N.Y.S.2d 569 (1998); *cf.* Bank v. Worldcom, Inc., 2002 N.Y. Misc. LEXIS 33 (Sup. Ct. Jan. 24, 2002).

97 Unif. Arbitration Act § 14 (1955); Unif. Arbitration Act § 25 (2000).

98 *See* Chauffers, Teamsters, Warehousemen and Helpers Local No. 135 v. Jefferson Trucking Co., 628 F.2d 1023 (7th Cir. 1980); MBNA Am. Bank v. Leslie, 2005 WL 2277252 (Conn.

While it is traditionally thought that there are few grounds on which to resist confirmation of an award, particularly after the time to seek modification or vacation of the award has expired,[99] this section explores a number of promising approaches to challenging confirmation of an award on a debt. This is particularly important because consumers often do not participate in the arbitration process and only respond when they receive notice of a court proceeding to confirm the award.

In deciding whether an attorney should represent the consumer in a confirmation proceeding the availability of attorney fees paid by the other side will be a factor. At least in California a consumer successfully resisting a confirmation proceeding may recover attorney fees from the party seeking confirmation.[100]

8.5.2 The Confirmation Process

As described in NCLC's *Consumer Arbitration Agreements* § 11.2,[101] actions to confirm an arbitration award on a consumer collection matter will be brought in state court and governed by state law, patterned on either the Uniform Arbitration Act (UAA) or revised UAA. The confirmation process is generally governed by the Federal Arbitration Act (FAA) only when the action is brought in federal court. Despite this fact, state courts are often confused on this matter, and often refer to the FAA's provisions regarding confirmation.

This generally makes no difference because the UAA, revised UAA, and the FAA have similar provisions relating to award confirmation. The UAA and revised UAA provide that a court "shall" confirm the award unless "grounds are urged for vacating or modifying or correcting the award."[102] The FAA provides that a court "must" confirm an award upon a proper motion "unless the award is vacated, modified, or corrected" as provided in the statute.[103]

The court must give the consumer the opportunity to respond to a motion to confirm an award.[104] The deadline to file such an opposition to a motion to confirm varies by state and may be shorter than the deadline for responding to a regular civil complaint.[105]

The consumer should have a right to a hearing to oppose the motion.[106] The consumer must have received proper service concerning the confirmation proceeding,[107] and the creditor must supply an affidavit that the debtor is not in the military[108] and must have also properly moved to seek confirmation. At least in some states it is not enough for the creditor to successfully resist the consumer's action to vacate the award—the creditor must also affirmatively move to confirm the award.[109]

8.5.3 Lack of Arbitration Agreement or Defective Arbitration Proceeding As Grounds to Oppose Confirmation

8.5.3.1 General

Important challenges to confirmation actions include whether there is a binding arbitration agreement allowing arbitration in the first place, and whether the arbitration proceeding was properly conducted. These are both grounds to vacate an award, as described in § 8.4.4, *supra*. As long as these challenges are timely brought, the consumer can raise either of these grounds for *vacatur* in response to the confirmation action. While one line of cases allows motions to vacate to be filed in response to a confirmation proceeding even after the time limits have expired,[110] most cases rule otherwise.[111] Because confirmation actions are invariably brought well over three months after the arbitration award,

Super. Ct. Aug. 25, 2005); Bernstein v. Gramercy Mills, Inc., 452 N.E.2d 231 (Mass. App. Ct. 1983).

99 *See* Unif. Arbitration Act § 11 (1955); Unif. Arbitration Act § 22 (2000).

100 MBNA Am. Bank v. Gorman, 147 Cal. App. 4th Supp. 1 (2007).

101 (5th ed. 2007).

102 Unif. Arbitration Act § 11 (1955); Unif. Arbitration Act § 22 (2000).

103 9 U.S.C. § 9.

104 *See, e.g.*, Vogt v. Liberty Mut. Fire Ins. Co., 900 A.2d 912 (Pa. Super. Ct. 2006).

105 *Compare* Cal. Civ. Proc. Code § 1290.6 (West) (providing ten days to respond to petition to confirm arbitration award) *with* Cal. Civ. Proc. Code § 412.20(3) (West) (providing thirty days to file answer to complaint).

106 MBNA Am. Bank v. McArdle, 2007 WL 1229214 (Ohio Ct. App. Apr. 27, 2007); MBNA Am. Bank v. Anthony, 2006 WL 1063752 (Ohio Ct. App. Apr. 18, 2005).

107 MBNA Am. Bank v. Dimario, 2006 WL 2349201 (Conn. Super. Ct. Aug. 2, 2006); Cavalry Investments, L.L.C. v. Grasson, 2005 WL 2981691 (Conn. Super. Ct. Oct. 19, 2005); Vogt v. Liberty Mut. Fire Ins. Co., 900 A.2d 912 (Pa. Super. Ct. 2006); *see also* CACV of Colo., L.L.C. v. Ryan, 2005 WL 2981680 (Conn. Super. Ct. Oct. 19, 2005).

108 MBNA Am. Bank v. Nelson, 15 Misc. 3d 1148(A) (Civ. Ct. 2007) (table).

109 MBNA Am. Bank v. Mackey, 343 F. Supp. 2d 966 (W.D. Wash. 2004). *But see, e.g.*, Mass. Gen. Laws ch. 251, § 12(d) (if application to vacate is denied, the court shall confirm the award).

110 *See* Paul Allison v. Minkin Storage of Omaha, Inc., 452 F. Supp. 573 (D. Neb. 1978); Riko Enterprises, Inc. v. Seattle Supersonics Corp., 357 F. Supp. 521 (S.D.N.Y. 1973); Milwaukee Police Ass'n v. City of Milwaukee, 285 N.W.2d 119 (Wis. 1979).

111 *See, e.g.*, MBNA Am. Bank v. Leslie, 2005 WL 2277252 (Conn. Super. Ct. Aug. 25, 2005); Kutch v. State Farm Mut. Auto. Ins. Co., 960 P.2d 93 (Colo. 1998); Walter A. Brown Inc. v. Moylan, 509 A.2d 98 (D.C. 1986); Broward County Paraprofessional Ass'n v. Sch. Bd. of Broward County, 406 So. 2d 1252, 1253 (Fla. Dist. Ct. App. 1981); MBNA Am. Bank v. Tackleson, 720 N.W.2d 192 (Iowa Ct. App. 2006) (table) (text available at 2006 WL 1229935); Local 589, Amalgamated Transit Union v. Mass. Bay Transp. Auth., 491 N.E.2d 1053 (Mass. App. Ct. 1986); MBNA Am. Bank v. Belleleslie, 2005 Mont. Dist. LEXIS 1119 (Mont. Dist. Ct. Apr. 26, 2005); MBNA Am. Bank v. Cooper, 2006 WL 1519640 (Ohio Ct. App. June 5, 2006); Burst v.

this is a significant impediment to bringing a motion to vacate in the confirmation proceeding.

The remainder of this subsection examines three ways in which the consumer can still raise, in the confirmation proceeding, substantive issues as to the existence or enforceability of an arbitration agreement or the nature of the arbitration proceeding and award, even well after the arbitration award is issued: (1) improper notice of the award means that the time period to vacate has not expired (thus allowing the consumer to raise the non-existence of an arbitration agreement or any other grounds to vacate); (2) lack of a binding arbitration agreement can be raised at any time because it goes to the court's jurisdiction; and (3) the creditor has not complied in the confirmation proceeding with state requirements including proof of the arbitration agreement and that the creditor owns the debt.

Section 8.5.4, *infra*, examines the effect on confirmation when the consumer objects to, or fails to participate in, the arbitration. Section 8.5.5, *infra*, considers certain defects in the confirmation application that may result in denial of that application.

8.5.3.2 Time Period to Vacate Does Not Start Running When Notice of Award Is Defective or Not Sent

Delivery to the consumer of the arbitration award triggers the running of the time period to move to vacate the award. Thus, a motion to vacate in a confirmation proceeding is timely if the consumer never received notice of the award.[112] Furthermore, the burden is on the party claiming that *vacatur* is untimely to prove that the motion to vacate was not made within the ninety-day (or other applicable) time period, and therefore this party also has the burden of proving that notice of the award was delivered.[113]

The nature of the required notice is very different under the UAA (adopted in most states) than under the revised UAA (adopted in twelve states).[114] The UAA states: "[T]he award shall be in writing and signed by the arbitrators joining in the award. The arbitrators shall deliver a copy to each party personally or by registered mail, or as provided in the agreement."[115]

The UAA thus has two requirements, only the second of which can be altered "as provided in the agreement." The first requirement is that the arbitrator sign a written award and deliver a copy of the award to the consumer. (The "or as provided in the agreement" language modifies the mode of delivery and not the requirement that the arbitrator deliver the award.) The second requirement is that delivery be personally or by registered mail, or as provided in the agreement.

In the typical NAF documentary hearing, the arbitrator mails the award to the NAF director of arbitration. The NAF then mails notice of the award to the parties. The notice also must include the actual award, not the NAF's summary or translation of the award.

It appears that the arbitrator must also deliver the award directly to the consumer, and not send the award to someone else, who then delivers the award to the consumer.[116] At least one court has noted that NAF's method of delivering awards to consumers may fall short of compliance with its own rules: "The award identifies Larry Rute as the arbitrator, but he makes no certification or acknowledgment of service in the form. We question whether delivery by the [NAF] Director of Arbitration fulfills the arbitrator's duty to deliver a copy of the Award."[117]

Moreover, NAF awards state that the award has been "duly entered and delivered to the parties on this date," followed by the date of the award. One court noted that such a statement is "patently false" in the case of a document hearing, because the consumer was not present on that date and the award was mailed to the director of arbitration and only then mailed to the consumer.[118] Thus any notice was delivered at some later date, not on the date of the award. If nothing else, the date an award is entered should not be considered evidence of when the NAF delivered it.

As for the form of delivery, in collection arbitrations, the award is almost never delivered personally or by registered mail. So the question is whether an alternative form of delivery is "provided in the agreement." Typical creditor arbitration agreements do not specify an alternative form of delivery but will specify that the arbitration will be administered by the NAF or pursuant to NAF rules, usually those in effect at the time of the arbitration. NAF rules permit delivery by U.S. mail,[119] and courts in other contexts have generally held that the rules of an arbitration provider specified in an agreement are deemed to be incorporated by reference into the contract.[120] A court may hold that incorporation of such rules in this context is sufficient. On the

MBNA Am. Bank, 2005 Tex. App. LEXIS 3461 (Tex. App. May 5, 2005).

112 *See* NCO Portfolio Mgmt. v. B.A. Williams, 2006 WL 2939712 (Ohio Ct. App. Oct. 13, 2006).

113 MBNA Am. Bank v. Barben, 111 P.3d 663 (Kan. Ct. App. 2005) (table) (text available at 2005 WL 1214244); NCO Portfolio Mgmt. v. Williams, 2006 WL 2939712 (Ohio Ct. App. Oct. 13, 2006).

114 *See* National Consumer Law Center, Consumer Arbitration Agreements § 11.2.2 (5th ed. 2007).

115 Unif. Arbitration Act § 8(a) (1955).

116 MBNA Am. Bank v. Barben, 111 P.3d 663 (Kan. Ct. App. 2005) (table) (text available at 2005 WL 1214244).

117 *Id.*

118 *Id.*

119 Nat'l Arbitration Forum, Code of Procedure, Rules 39(D), 2(M), *available at* www.arb-forum.com.

120 *See, e.g.*, Val-U Constr. Co. v. Rosebud Sioux Tribe, 146 F.3d 573 (8th Cir. 1998) (*ex parte* arbitration award enforceable when contract incorporated AAA rules that allow an arbitration hearing to proceed in a party's absence if that party is given notice of the hearing and an opportunity to have it postponed).

other hand, there is an argument that a reference to NAF rules is too attenuated and thus insufficient to show that the alternative form of delivery is "provided in the agreement."[121] This is especially true because a consumer would have to first note NAF Rule 39(D), which then refers the consumer to Rulc 2(M).

The revised UAA dramatically loosens the UAA notice requirement, making it much more difficult to challenge the arbitrator's notice of the award. The revised UAA requires that the arbitrator or arbitration organization give notice of the award, including a copy of the award.[122] Notice is "taking action that is reasonably necessary to inform the other person in ordinary course, whether or not the other person acquires knowledge of the notice."[123] Even the signature requirement is loosened, allowing the arbitrator to make a "record" of an award, that is "signed or otherwise authenticated by an arbitrator who concurs with the award."[124]

8.5.3.3 Time Limits May Not Apply to Challenges to the Existence or Enforceability of the Arbitration Agreement

As § 8.4.4.2, *supra*, explains, lack of an enforceable arbitration agreement is a basis on which to vacate an award. But a growing number of courts have held that the consumer may seek to oppose confirmation of an award on this basis even if the deadline for seeking *vacatur* has passed.[125] According to the First Circuit:

> We find no indication that Congress intended for a party to be found to have waived the argument that there was no written agreement to arbitrate if that party failed to raise the argument within the time period established by section 12. . . . We thus conclude that, as a general matter, section 12, as well as section 2 and the other enforcement provisions of the FAA, do not come into play unless there is a written agreement to arbitrate. Thus, if there is no such agreement, the actions of the arbitrator have no legal validity. It follows that one is not required to mount a collateral challenge to such an ineffectual action, for if the agreement to arbitrate does not exist, there is no obligation to arbitrate—and a noncontracting person's failure to appear at the arbitration hearing does not create such an obligation. . . . A party that contends that it is not bound by an agreement to arbitrate can therefore simply abstain from participation in the proceedings, and raise the inexistence of a written contractual agreement to arbitrate as a defense to a proceeding seeking confirmation of the arbitration award, without the limitations contained in section 12, which are only applicable to those bound by a written agreement to arbitrate.[126]

121 *See* MBNA Am. Bank v. Credit, 132 P.3d 898 (Kan. Ct. App. 2006); MBNA Am. Bank v. Barben, 111 P.3d 663 (Kan. Ct. App. 2005) (table) (text available at 2005 WL 1214244).

122 Unif. Arbitration Act § 19(a) (2000).

123 Unif. Arbitration Act § 2(a) (2000).

124 Unif. Arbitration Act § 19(a) (2000).

125 *See* MCI Telecommunications Corp. v. Exalon Indus., Inc., 138 F.3d 426 (1st Cir. 1998); Danner v. MBNA Am. Bank, 2007 WL 1219747 (Ark. Apr. 26, 2007); MBNA Am. Bank v. Blanks, 2007 WL 2713361 (Ark. Ct. App. Sept. 19, 2007); MBNA Am. Bank v. Boata, 2007 WL 2089678 (Conn. July 31, 2007); CACV of Colo., L.L.C. v. Corda, 2005 WL 3664087 (Conn. Super. Ct. Dec. 16, 2005) (in five related cases declining to confirm awards against consumers when the bank failed to present sufficient evidence that a valid agreement to arbitrate existed); MBNA Am. Bank v. Credit, 132 P.3d 898 (Kan. Ct. App. 2006); NCO Portfolio Mgmt., Inc. v. Chouest, 2008 WL 1970319 (La. Ct. App. Apr. 29, 2008); Arrow Overall Supply Co. v. Peloquin Enterprises, 323 N.W.2d 1 (Mich. 1982); MBNA Am. Bank v. Forsmark, 2005 WL 2401444 (Mich. Ct. App. Sept. 29, 2005); Bank of Am. v. Dahlquist, 2007 WL 404471 (Mont. Feb. 7, 2007); MBNA Am. Bank v. Cornock, No. 03-C-0018 (N.H. Super. Ct. Mar. 20, 2007), *available at* www.consumerlaw.org/unreported; *In re* Matarasso, 56 N.Y.2d 264 (1982); MBNA Am. Bank v. Nelson, 15 Misc. 3d 1148(A) (Civ. Ct. 2007) (table); MBNA Am. Bank v. Straub, 815 N.Y.S.2d 450 (Civ. Ct. 2006); Worldwide Asset Purchasing, L.L.C. v. Karafotias, 801 N.Y.S.2d 721 (Civ. Ct. 2005); FIA Card Services, Nat'l Ass'n v. Thompson, 2008 WL 624904 (N.Y. Dist. Ct. Mar. 10, 2008); MBNA Am. Bank v. Christianson, 659 S.E.2d 209 (S.C. Ct. App. 2008); MBNA Am. Bank v. Engen, 128 Wash. App. 1050 (2005) (allowing the consumer to contest an arbitration award after the award was confirmed when the consumer alleged no arbitration agreement); *see also* MBNA Am. Bank v. Gorman, 147 Cal. App. 4th Supp. 1 (2007) (while appellate court did not address the issue, the trial court had denied confirmation because no enforceable arbitration agreement existed, even though time to vacate the award had elapsed); *cf.* Dewitt v. Collins, 2004 WL 102514 (Mich. Ct. App. Jan. 22, 2004) (certain situations allow the consumer to challenge the confirmation beyond the time period, but not allowed in other situations). *But see* Webb v. MBNA Am. Bank, 2005 WL 2648019 (E.D. Ark. Oct. 13, 2005); MBNA Am. Bank v. Bailey, 2007 WL 3355482 (Conn. App. Ct. Nov. 20, 2007) (consumer can not raise lack of arbitration agreement in confirmation proceeding if consumer did not object to arbitration proceeding, even if consumer did not participate in arbitration proceeding); MBNA Am. Bank v. Swartz, 2006 WL 1071523 (Del. Ch. Ct. Apr. 13, 2006); MBNA Am. Bank v. Saleba, 69 Mass. App. Ct. 1102 (2007); MBNA Am. Bank v. Hart, 710 N.W.2d 125 (N.D. 2006); CACV v. Kogler, 2006 WL 2790398 (Ohio Ct. App. Sept. 29, 2006) (but Ohio also requires that the creditor file a copy of the arbitration agreement as a precondition to confirmation); Brust v. MBNA Am. Bank, 2005 WL 1047583 (Tex. App. June 2, 2005); MBNA Am. Bank v. Orr, 2008 WL 699248 (Wash. Ct. App. Mar. 17, 2008); *cf.* MBNA Am. Bank v. Stehly, 2008 WL 141675 (N.Y. Sup. Ct. Jan. 11, 2008) (when consumer did not appear in the confirmation proceeding, judge can not raise lack of arbitration agreement).

126 MCI Telecommunications Corp. v. Exalon Indus., Inc., 138 F.3d 426 (1st Cir. 1998).

Of course, the right to raise the lack of a binding arbitration agreement can be lost if the consumer participates in the arbitration proceeding without objection. This requirement raises a proof problem for the consumer in the subsequent court confirmation to substantiate that the consumer did in fact object to the enforceability of the arbitration agreement. Failure to provide such proof may result in the award being confirmed.[127]

One basis for arguing that the lack of a binding arbitration agreement can be raised in the confirmation proceeding irrespective of any time limits to seek to vacate is that this issue goes to the subject matter jurisdiction of the arbitrator, a defense that, under state law, can be raised at any time, even in the confirmation hearing after the deadline to vacate the award has passed.[128] In addition, some state arbitration statutes require the party seeking confirmation to file a copy of the arbitration agreement, the award, and other documents, implicitly conditioning confirmation on the existence of an enforceable agreement.[129] Failure to do so results in dismissal, although perhaps not dismissal with prejudice.[130]

Protecting the right to challenge the existence of the arbitration agreement at any time benefits creditors as well as alleged debtors. In several recent cases consumers have been persuaded by debt counselors that they should file arbitration proceedings with providers not specified in the creditor's arbitration agreement. These alternative providers charge the consumer a fee and typically issue an award on behalf of the consumer voiding the alleged debt. When the consumer seeks to confirm such an award in court, creditors have argued that the award is unenforceable, because the arbitrator had no jurisdiction to decide the dispute. For example, the Montana Supreme Court found that a credit card issuer could challenge confirmation of an award made by an arbitration service provider not specified in the arbitration agreement, even though the ninety-day period had lapsed for the card issuer to object.[131] The award was invalid ab initio.

There is another reason why consumers must be able to vacate an award in a confirmation proceeding after the time period to seek to vacate would appear to have elapsed. As explained in § 8.4.2, *supra*, the time period to seek to vacate an award begins when the consumer has proper notice of the award. The UAA provides for proper notice by delivery by the arbitrator personally or by registered mail or "as provided in the agreement."[132] NAF arbitration awards are typically not delivered personally or by registered mail, and instead rely on the "as provided in the agreement" language. To argue that notice can instead be provided by using a different method, as specified in the agreement, presupposes the existence of an agreement. A challenge to the enforceability of the arbitration agreement is challenging the very existence of an enforceable agreement to modify the notice requirement. Thus the enforceability challenge can be recast as simply arguing that the consumer did not receive proper notice of the award and thus still can seek to vacate the award. When notice was not delivered personally or by registered mail, a court thus must first determine if there is an enforceable agreement before it determines whether such a challenge is timely.[133] If it finds there is no enforceable agreement, then the challenge to the agreement's enforceability is not time-barred (because the award was never properly delivered), and the award must be vacated.[134]

New York Civil Practice Rule 7503(c) specifies that a party seeking arbitration can provide a notice to the other party specifying the agreement pursuant to which arbitration is sought and the name and address of the party serving the notice, and stating that unless the party served applies to stay the arbitration within twenty days after such service he shall thereafter be precluded from objecting that a valid agreement did not exist. Such notice or demand shall be served in the same manner as a summons or by registered or certified mail, return receipt requested. But if the notice is not proper, the provision is not effective.[135]

127 *See* MBNA Am. Bank v. Gilbert, 2007 WL 3171824 (Ark. Ct. App. Oct. 31, 2007).

128 MBNA Am. Bank v. Boata, 2007 WL 2089678 (Conn. July 31, 2007); MBNA Am. Bank v. Credit, 132 P.3d 898 (Kan. Ct. App. 2006); Bank of Am. v. Dahlquist, 2007 WL 404471 (Mont. Feb. 7, 2007). *But see* MBNA Am. Bank v. Bailey, 2007 WL 3355482 (Conn. App. Ct. Nov. 20, 2007) (consumer can not raise lack of arbitration agreement in confirmation proceeding if consumer did not object to arbitration proceeding, even if consumer did not participate in arbitration proceeding).

129 *See* Ohio Rev. Code Ann. § 2711.14 (West).

130 *See, e.g.*, Worldwide Asset Purchasing, L.L.C. v. Karafotias, 801 N.Y.S.2d 721 (Civ. Ct. 2005) (denying motion to confirm arbitration award "in the absence of any evidentiary proof in admissible form to support confirmation of the award," but granting petitioner leave to renew); MBNA Am. Bank v. Berlin, 2005 WL 3193850, at *2 (Ohio Ct. App. Nov. 30, 2005) (trial court did not err by dismissing creditor's petition to confirm when creditor failed to include appropriate documentation but did err in dismissing the application with prejudice).

131 Bank of Am. v. Dahlquist, 2007 WL 404471 (Mont. Feb. 7, 2007) (when procedure outlined in the parties' arbitration agreement for selecting an arbitrator is not followed, a party is not required to challenge the resulting arbitration award within the FAA's ninety-day time limitation because it is void ab initio); *see also* Buczek v. Trans Union L.L.C., 2006 WL 3666635, at *2 (S.D. Fla. Nov. 9, 2006) (dismissing consumer's argument that debt had been eliminated by arbitration award, when the agreement with the creditor had not provided for arbitration; award was "of no force and effect"); *cf.* MBNA Am. Bank v. Bodalia, 2006 WL 1793211 (Ala. Civ. App. June 30, 2006) (granting MBNA's motion to vacate award issued by alternative service provider). *But see* Citibank v. Wood, 862 N.E.2d 576 (Ohio Ct. App. 2006).

132 Unif. Arbitration Act §§ 8(a), 12(b) (1955).

133 MBNA Am. Bank v. Credit, 132 P.3d 898 (Kan. Ct. App. 2006).

134 MBNA Am. Bank v. Credit, 132 P.3d 898 (Kan. Ct. App. 2006).

135 Lucas v. MBNA, 2008 WL 44325 (N.Y. Sup. Ct. Jan. 2, 2008).

8.5.3.4 Creditor's Failure to Produce Arbitration Agreement and Any Applicable Assignment

Some states or state courts require that the creditor produce the arbitration agreement as a precondition to confirmation. As this requirement is an affirmative one for the creditor, the consumer need not move to vacate and there is no issue as to the time period to seek to vacate expiring; the creditor must comply whenever it brings a confirmation action.

For example, Connecticut and Ohio require the party seeking confirmation of an award to file a copy of the arbitration agreement, the award, and other documents.[136] When the application for confirmation is not accompanied by all the required documentation, it must be dismissed, although perhaps not dismissed with prejudice.[137] On the other hand, if such documentation is presented, the burden may shift to the consumer to challenge that evidence.[138]

Courts should require the creditor to produce the contract, any applicable assignment of the contract, and the arbitration agreement,[139] or simply demand to see the documentation.[140] For example, a New York court has laid out the requirements that should be met before a court can confirm an MBNA/NAF award, under either New York law or the FAA:

> (1) A written agreement to arbitrate must be included with the petition to confirm.
> (2) The bank must establish that the credit card agreement—and the arbitration clause in it—are binding on the cardholder (an affidavit by a person with personal knowledge and the relevant supporting documents will suffice).
> (3) The bank must show that the notice of arbitration was properly served, either as provided under state law or as provided in the arbitration agreement.
> (4) The court must take into account issues such as whether the petition to confirm/vacate is timely and whether a court previously compelled the arbitration.[141]

Other courts have said it is not enough for the attorney to state on information and belief that the arbitration agreement exists.[142]

An assignee of the original creditor must provide proof of assignment of that particular account. It is not enough that the assignee show that there has been a general assignment; rather, a clear assignment chain for the particular account must be shown between the original creditor and the company seeking the confirmation. Furthermore it is not enough that the arbitrator issued the award to that party, thereby assuming a proper assignment.[143]

8.5.4 Effect on Confirmation When Consumer Objects to, or Fails to Participate in, Arbitration

The implications of participating in, objecting to, or simply ignoring arbitration proceedings need to be considered, and these effects vary by jurisdiction. A consumer who participates in an arbitration proceeding without objecting to the arbitrator's jurisdiction risks that a court will find that she has waived the right to argue, in opposing confirmation of an award, that she is not bound by the arbitration clause.[144] Thus if the consumer does participate in the arbitration proceeding, it is important to make it clear that the consumer is doing so only under protest, and that she disputes that she is bound by an agreement to arbitrate.[145] In

136 Conn. Gen. Stat. § 52-421(a); Ohio Rev. Code Ann. § 2711.14 (West).

137 MBNA Am. Bank v. Berlin, 2005 WL 3193850 (Ohio Ct. App. Nov. 30, 2005) (strict compliance is required as a matter of subject matter jurisdiction); *cf.* Chase Manhatten Bank USA v. Myers, 2008 WL 62995 (Ohio Ct. App. Feb. 28, 2008) (creditor must attach credit card agreement, but it need not be signed); Hillco Receivables, L.L.C. v. Barton, 2007 WL 2812908 (Ohio Ct. App. Sept. 28, 2007) (same); MBNA Am. Bank v. Harper, 2007 WL 2812906 (Ohio Ct. App. Sept. 28, 2007) (same); NCO Portfolio Mgmt., Inc. v. McGill, 2006 WL 2041476 (Ohio Ct. App. July 21, 2006) (same).

138 *See* MBNA Am. Bank v. O'Brien, 858 N.E.2d 1220 (Ohio Ct. App. 2006) (*pro se* consumer apparently did not present any evidence challenging documentation).

139 MBNA Am. Bank v. Straub, 815 N.Y.S.2d 450, 452–457 (Civ. Ct. 2006); Worldwide Asset Purchasing v. Karafotias, 801 N.Y.S.2d 721 (Civ. Ct. 2005). *But see* Parks v. MBNA Am. Bank, 204 S.W.3d 305 (Mo. Ct. App. 2006) (burden is on the consumer to first allege that there is no binding arbitration agreement).

140 *See* MBNA Am Bank v. Swartz, 2006 WL 1071523 (Del. Ch. Ct. Apr. 13, 2006); *cf.* MBNA Am. Bank v. Boyce, 723 N.W.2d 449 (Iowa Ct. App. 2006) (trial court had dismissed ten MBNA motions to confirm when MBNA had not produced a written agreement to arbitrate; the appellate court overturned these rulings when the consumers had never opposed the confirmation proceedings).

141 MBNA Am. Bank v. Straub, 815 N.Y.S.2d 450, 452–457 (Civ. Ct. 2006); *see also* MBNA Am. Bank v. Nelson, 15 Misc. 3d 1148(A) (Civ. Ct. 2007) (table); Citibank v. Martin, 807 N.Y.S.2d 284 (Civ. Ct. 2005) (setting forth the levels of proof required to support summary judgment on question of whether debtor owes debt).

142 Worldwide Asset Purchasing v. Karafotias, 801 N.Y.S.2d 721 (Civ. Ct. 2005).

143 *Id.*

144 *See, e.g.*, Garner v. MBNA Am. Bank, 2006 WL 2354939 (N.D. Tex. Aug. 14, 2006); Webb v. MBNA Am. Bank, 2006 WL 618186 (E.D. Ark. Mar. 10, 2006) (compelling arbitration of Fair Debt Collection Practices Act case when consumer had previously participated in arbitration of debt collection case initiated by a buyer of an MBNA debt); MBNA Am. Bank v. Saleba, 69 Mass. App. Ct. 1102 (2007).

145 *See, e.g.*, MBNA Am. Bank v. Felton, 2004 WL 2898632 (Conn. Super. Ct. Nov. 8, 2004); MBNA Am. Bank v. Barben,

most jurisdictions raising this objection before the arbitrator should be sufficient to preserve the argument, and the consumer need not also raise this objection by seeking a stay of arbitration in a court proceeding.[146]

Courts in some jurisdictions have held, in various ways, that an award obtained without the participation of the consumer can not be confirmed. The UAA, revised UAA, and the FAA all provide that a party can go to court to compel the other party to submit to arbitration.[147] A number of courts find this procedure to be the proper one to follow when the consumer does not willingly participate in the collection using arbitration.

In Pennsylvania arbitration awards obtained without the consumer's participation can not be judicially confirmed. In *Bank One Delaware v. Mitchell*, a Pennsylvania trial court held that, if a creditor proceeds to arbitration without the consumer's participation, and without a court's determination that the arbitration clause is valid, the creditor can not later obtain judicial confirmation of the award.[148] Rather, if the consumer does not participate, the creditor must bring a court action to obtain an order that the arbitration clause applies to the dispute and that the consumer must arbitrate the dispute. The *Mitchell* court viewed the motion to compel arbitration as the proper procedure to follow if one party does not participate; the alternative procedure specified by the NAF rules, of going forward without both parties, was found to be invalid, because there was no jurisdiction to proceed.

After *Mitchell*, the Pennsylvania Supreme Court codified this requirement in the state's Rules of Civil Procedure.[149] A creditor can seek to confirm an award in Pennsylvania only if the consumer either attended a hearing before an arbitrator or signed a writing after the claim was filed agreeing to submit the claim to an arbitrator. If not, the creditor must have first obtained a court order compelling the consumer to proceed to arbitration, pursuant to procedures also spelled out in the rules.[150] The motion to confirm the award must contain factual allegations that the motion complies with these requirements.[151] In Virginia some courts have held that an award obtained without the consumer's participating in a hearing can not be confirmed.[152]

Courts in other jurisdictions have held that, if the consumer *objects* to arbitration, the creditor must get a court order compelling arbitration if the consumer fails to participate. The Kansas Supreme Court and the Kentucky Court of Appeals have both held that, because any challenge to the existence of a valid agreement to arbitrate must be decided by a court, a cardholder's objection to arbitration triggers the creditor's responsibility to seek court intervention to compel arbitration.[153] On this basis, the courts refused to confirm an award issued in an arbitration proceeding that was conducted over the cardholder's objection.

8.5.5 Defects in the Form of the Confirmation Proceeding

8.5.5.1 Creditor's Petition to Confirm Is Untimely

There is much confusion as to when a creditor must file a confirmation action. Under the FAA[154] and several state statutes,[155] the deadline is one year from delivery of the award. California has a four-year limit.[156] Neither the revised UAA nor the UAA sets a time limit to confirm an award. An Indiana appellate court has decided to use the FAA's one-year time period when the Indiana arbitration procedures (based on the UAA) do not specify a time limit, even though the general limitations period to collect a debt in Indiana is much longer.[157] The revised UAA commentary states that states should use their general statute of limitations for the filing and execution of a judgment in a state.[158]

There is similar confusion as to the consequences of a creditor failing to meet the applicable deadline. It would appear in most states that the confirmation action will be dismissed as untimely.[159] Some states allow the creditor to bring a common law action to collect on the arbitration

---

111 P.3d 663 (Kan. Ct. App. 2005) (table) (text available at 2005 WL 1214244).

146 Holcim (Tex.) Ltd. P'ship v. Humboldt Wedag, Inc., 211 S.W.3d 796 (Tex. App. 2006). *But see* Garner v. MBNA Am. Bank., 2006 WL 2354939 (N.D. Tex. Aug. 14, 2006).

147 9 U.S.C. § 4; Unif. Arbitration Act UAA § 2 (1955); Unif. Arbitration Act § 7 (2000).

148 Bank One Del. v. Mitchell, 70 Pa. D. & C.4th 353 (C.P. 2005), *aff'd sub nom.* Bank One v. Mitchell, 897 A.2d 512 (Pa. 2006) (table).

149 Pa. R. Civ. P. 1326–1331.

150 Pa. R. Civ. P. 1327.

151 Pa. R. Civ. P. 1328(c).

152 *E.g.*, CACV v. Rubin, No. GV06-004208-00 (Va. Dist. Ct. Apr. 21, 2006).

153 MBNA Am. Bank v. Credit, 132 P.3d 898, 901 (Kan. 2006); Fischer v. MBNA Am. Bank, 2007 WL 779295 (Ky. Ct. App. Mar. 16, 2007).

154 9 U.S.C. § 9.

155 *See, e.g.*, Conn. Gen. Stat. § 52-417; N.Y. C.P.L.R. 7510 (McKinney); Ohio Rev. Code Ann. § 2711.09 (West); *see also* MBNA Am. Bank v. Terry, 2006 WL 513952 (Ohio Ct. App. Mar. 3, 2006).

156 Cal. Civ. Proc. Code § 1288 (West).

157 MBNA Am. Bank v. Rogers, 838 N.E.2d 475 (Ind. Ct. App. 2005).

158 Unif. Arbitration Act § 22 cmt. 2 (2000).

159 *See* MBNA Am. Bank v. Rogers, 838 N.E.2d 475 (Ind. Ct. App. 2005) (dismissing petition to confirm as untimely: "Having elected the benefits of the streamlined summary proceeding, MBNA may not complain that the limited time to preserve the arbitration award for later enforcement in a court of law deprives it of the applicable statute of limitations for the commencement of an action."); MBNA Am. Bank v. Terry, 2006 WL 513952 (Ohio Ct. App. Mar. 3, 2006); *see also* Asset Acceptance, L.L.C. v. Sisson, 832 N.Y.S.2d 797 (Sup. Ct. 2007). *But see* NCO Portfolio Mgmt. Inc. v. Lewis, 2007 WL 2229251 (Ohio Ct. App. Aug. 6, 2007). *See generally* National

award,[160] but in that case the consumer should be able to raise all available substantive defenses and counterclaims, and will not be limited to the statutory *vacatur* grounds.

8.5.5.2 Creditor Filed Petition to Confirm in the Wrong Court

The consumer can object to the creditor's choice of court and venue for the confirmation proceeding. As described in National Consumer Law Center, *Consumer Arbitration Agreements* § 11.2.1,[161] there is almost never federal jurisdiction to confirm a consumer collection action. Any confirmation action brought in federal court without an independent basis for federal jurisdiction will be dismissed.[162] Moreover not all courts in a state will be authorized by the state to hear confirmation proceedings.[163]

The confirmation action should be brought in state court in the state of the consumer's residence. Any attempt to confirm the award other than in the state where the consumer resides will run afoul of the federal Fair Debt Collection Practices Act (FDCPA),[164] the Federal Trade Commission Act, and state deceptive practices (UDAP) law.[165] Consumer attorneys sometimes note NAF's address in Minnesota and question whether it is proper for an arbitration award in Minnesota to be confirmed in another state. But typically the arbitration proceeding is administered from Minnesota, but any in-person hearing will take place in the state of the consumer's residence.

The UAA and revised UAA allow creditors to seek to confirm awards in a court specified in the arbitration agreement, the court in the county where the award was made, or a court in the county where the consumer resides.[166] Because arbitration agreements will rarely specify a particular court, proper venue will generally be in the county where the consumer resides.

In addition, the FDCPA allows an attorney to bring an action to collect on a consumer debt only in the judicial district where the consumer signed the contract or presently resides.[167] If the case is brought elsewhere in the state, the attorney is liable under the FDCPA.[168] Even in cases brought when the FDCPA does not apply (such as when the creditor is the claimant), UDAP precedent indicates it is unfair to bring a consumer collection action in a distant venue.[169]

In the rare case in which federal court jurisdiction is proper, the FAA and FDCPA will determine venue. The FAA states that, if no court is specified in the agreement, then application to confirm the award must be sought in the federal district court where the award was made.[170] The United States Supreme Court has held that venue is proper either in the district where the award was made or in any district proper under the general venue statute.[171] But the FDCPA requires the action to be brought in the county where the consumer resides, and this more specific requirement should control.

8.5.5.3 When Entity Confirming Award Not Entity Receiving the Award

According to one court, it is "not uncommon for the arbitration award to be rendered in favor of the alleged creditor and for the petition seeking confirmation of that award to be brought by a different entity. The court should be loath to confirm such an award and enter a judgment without a proper explanation for this change of identity, supported by evidentiary proof."[172] Even in a case when an award was entered for MBNA, the court refused to confirm

---

Consumer Law Center, Consumer Arbitration Agreements § 11.2.3.2 (5th ed. 2007).

160 *See* National Consumer Law Center, Consumer Arbitration Agreements § 11.2.3.2 (5th ed. 2007); *see also* MBNA Am. Bank v. Canfora, 2007 WL 2318095 (Ohio Ct. App. Aug. 15, 2007).

161 (5th ed. 2007).

162 *See* Austin v. MBNA Am., 2006 WL 3496655 (M.D. Ala. Dec. 4, 2006); Watson v. MBNA Am. Bank, 2005 WL 1875778 (W.D.N.C. Aug. 1, 2005); Garcia v. MBNA Am. Bank, 2005 WL 1653639 (D. Or. July 6, 2005); Stafford v. Chase Manhattan Bank U.S.A., 2005 WL 1330874 (M.D.N.C. June 3, 2005); Miles v. MBNA Am. Bank, 2005 WL 1220842 (E.D. Wash. May 23, 2005); Fischer v. MBNA Am. Bank, 2005 WL 1168388 (W.D. Ky. May 17, 2005); Mesdag v. MBNA Am. Bank, 2005 WL 418549 (D. Or. Feb. 17, 2005); Mellado v. MBNA Am. Bank, 2004 WL 2937224 (N.D. Tex. Dec. 17, 2004); Kearns v. MBNA Am. Bank, 2004 WL 2512742 (N.D. Tex. Nov. 5, 2004); MBNA Am. Bank v. Shnitzer, 2004 WL 1717670 (D. Or. July 30, 2004); *see also* FIA Card Services, Nat'l Ass'n v. Gachiengu, 2008 WL 336300 (S.D. Tex. Feb. 5, 2008).

163 *See* MBNA Am. Bank v. Bodalia, 949 So. 2d 935 (Ala. Civ. App. 2006); MBNA Am. Bank v. Torchia, Nos. 0442CV0163, 0442CV0164 (Mass. Dist. Ct. Jan. 14, 2005), *available at* www.consumerlaw.org/unreported; MBNA Am. Bank v. Hansen, 745 N.W.2d 609 (Neb. Ct. App. 2008) (only district courts, not county courts, have jurisdiction to hear confirmation actions); MBNA Am. Bank v. Coe, 770 N.Y.S.2d 588 (City Ct. 2003); Citibank S.D. v. Wood, 862 N.E.2d 576 (Ohio Ct. App. 2006) (municipal court does not have jurisdiction, only common pleas courts).

164 15 U.S.C. § 1692i.

165 National Consumer Law Center, Unfair and Deceptive Acts and Practices § 5.1.1.4 (6th ed. 2004 and Supp.).

166 Unif. Arbitration Act § 18 (1955); Unif. Arbitration Act § 27 (2000).

167 15 U.S.C. § 1692i.

168 *See* § 8.7.3, *infra*.

169 National Consumer Law Center, Unfair and Deceptive Acts and Practices § 5.1.1.4 (6th ed. 2004 and Supp.); *see also* Barquis v. Merchants Collection Ass'n, 7 Cal. 3d 94 (1972); Yu v. Signet Bank/Virginia, 69 Cal. App. 4th 1377 (1999).

170 9 U.S.C. § 9.

171 Cortez Byrd Chips, Inc. v. Bill Harbert Constr. Co., 529 U.S. 193, 120 S. Ct. 1331, 146 L. Ed. 2d 171 (2000).

172 FIA Card Services, Nat'l Ass'n v. Thompson, 2008 WL 624904 (N.Y. Dist. Ct. Mar. 10, 2008).

an award in the name of MBNA's successor, FIA Card Services.[173] The court found a letter from the Comptroller of the Currency regarding the name change to be inadequate evidence, when that letter references other documents substantiating the change but those documents were not attached, and when the letter was not introduced with a proper foundation.[174]

8.5.5.4 Seeking an Amount in Excess of the Award

A confirmation application should only seek to confirm the exact amount of the arbitration award. There is no statutory authority for a court to confirm anything other than the award, such as interest that might accrue after the award. Any attempt to confirm a larger amount should be dismissed. If state procedure allows the creditor in the same proceeding to confirm the arbitration amount and seek additional recovery, then the consumer should have all available substantive defenses and counterclaims to that additional amount.

8.5.5.5 Other Requirements for Confirmation

In New York, a corporation seeking to confirm the award must plead that it is a corporation authorized to do business in New York, and provide proof to that effect.[175] New York courts have also stated that the creditor must produce proof of timely notice to the consumer of the arbitration hearing.[176]

8.6 What If a Default Has Already Been Entered in the Confirmation Proceeding?

If the consumer has already defaulted in the confirmation proceeding, state rules similar to Federal Rule of Civil Procedure 60 allow the consumer to seek to re-open the confirmation proceeding even well after it has been held. A detailed discussion of setting aside default judgments is found in § 13.2, *infra*.

173 *Id.*

174 *Id.*

175 MBNA Am. Bank v. Nelson, 15 Misc. 3d 1148(A) (Civ. Ct. 2007) (table); *cf.* MBNA Am. Bank v. McArdle, 2007 WL 1229214 (Ohio Ct. App. Apr. 27, 2007) (while a foreign corporation in Ohio can not seek confirmation of an award unless it has a license to transact business in the state, this requirement does not apply to a national bank).

176 MBNA Am. Bank v. Turull, 842 N.Y.S.2d 146 (Sup. Ct. 2007); Worldwide Asset Purchasing v. Karafotias, 801 N.Y.S.2d 721 (Civ. Ct. 2005).

8.7 Affirmative Challenges to Debt Collection Practices Related to the Arbitration

8.7.1 Potential Defendants

Creditor use of arbitration to collect debts naturally leads to the question whether any conduct in connection with that arbitration process violates federal or state debt collection law. It is important to understand the status of various potential defendants, because available claims will vary depending on the nature of the defendant.

One type of party is the originating creditor, such as MBNA. That creditor can then sell the debt to a debt purchaser, who may purchase the debt before the consumer's default or, more commonly for credit card debt, after the default. The arbitration to collect on the debt can be in the name of any of these creditors, but the creditor can also hire various parties to handle the arbitration process, such as a collection law firm, collection agency, or process server.

The arbitration agreement will specify an arbitration service provider to administer the arbitration, such as the NAF, and the arbitration will be conducted by an arbitrator from the service provider's panel. In general there will be arbitral immunity for both the arbitrator and the arbitration service provider, at least as to their conduct of the arbitration proceeding.[177] They may face liability for breach of contract or for deceptive advertising, and the like, however.[178]

8.7.2 Practices Subject to Challenge

Almost any deceptive, unfair, or oppressive collection tactic in connection with a debt collection arbitration is potentially subject to challenge. Thus it should be actionable if a creditor or collector threaten to collect using an arbitration proceeding if there is no intent to follow through with that threat.[179] Nevertheless, filing for arbitration is relatively inexpensive and it may be difficult to prove that this threat is false. Of course, the threat is deceptive if the creditor has no right to proceed to arbitration, either because there is no agreement to arbitrate such disputes or because the agreement is not enforceable. In a recent case an action was allowed to proceed against MBNA's attorney, when that attorney brought an arbitration collection action on behalf of

177 *See* National Consumer Law Center, Consumer Arbitration Agreements § 11.6 (5th ed. 2007); *see also* Park v. Columbia Credit Services, Inc., 2007 WL 1847142 (W.D. Mo. June 25, 2007) (arbitrator has immunity even when consumer challenges authority of arbitrator to hear the proceeding).

178 *See* National Consumer Law Center, Consumer Arbitration Agreements § 11.6 (5th ed. 2007).

179 National Consumer Law Center, Fair Debt Collection § 5.5.2.11 (6th ed. 2008).

MBNA after MBNA had sold the debt to another creditor.[180] Similarly, the threat is deceptive if the creditor never proceeds to arbitration for that class of debts.

In addition, whether before or after the creditor or collector obtains an arbitration award, it is deceptive for a creditor or collector to imply that it can immediately seek to garnish wages or seize property based on the arbitration award.[181] Instead, the creditor must first confirm the award, and only then seek such post-judicial remedies based on the judgment obtained confirming the order. It should also be deceptive for a creditor or collector to imply that it will confirm any arbitration award resulting from an arbitration collection proceeding, if in fact it has no intent to confirm such an award.

A recent action certified in part as a class action alleges that the law firm Wolpoff & Abramson, as a collection attorney for MBNA, misrepresented the character, amount or legal status of debts, threatened action that can not be taken or was not intended to be taken, and used deceptive representations to collect a debt.[182] The plaintiffs argued, among other things, that notices sent to consumers at least until 2005 stated that "unless you have agreed otherwise, an In-person Participatory Hearing will be held in the Judicial District where you reside," when in fact documentary hearings were always held unless the consumer affirmatively requested a participatory hearing.

A class action against Wolpoff & Abramson alleges the law firm sought and recovered excessive attorney fees in NAF arbitrations.[183] Another potential claim might involve arbitrations being brought by attorneys not admitted to practice in the state where the consumer resides. Although the parties to an arbitration do not have to be represented by attorneys, state law may prohibit attorneys from appearing if not admitted in that state.

8.7.3 The Federal Fair Debt Collection Practices Act

The FDCPA does not apply to creditors collecting their own debts, but only to collection agencies, collection attorneys, and those purchasing a debt after the consumer's default.[184] As such, the Act applies to threats or other deceptive conduct made by an attorney, collection agency, or credit card debt buyer.[185] But the Act does not apply to MBNA or other credit card issuers.[186] While abusive and harassing behavior of an individual hired to personally serve the arbitration notice to the consumer may be actionable under state law,[187] at least one court has found that that person is not covered by the FDCPA.[188]

The FDCPA prohibits unfair and deceptive conduct generally, enumerates a number of prohibited practices, and establishes a number of other requirements, such as notice of verification rights. If the potential defendant is within the scope of the Act, then the Act should be able to remedy most forms of collection abuse involved in the arbitration proceeding.

The FDCPA provides for actual damages, plus statutory damages of up to $1000 and attorney fees.[189] Class actions may be brought under the Act. A recent example is the partial class certification in *Karnette v. Wolpoff & Abramson, L.L.P.*,[190] an action brought on behalf of Virginia consumers against the law firm routinely utilized by MBNA in its collection using arbitration.

8.7.4 State Law Claims

Even if not covered by the FDCPA, deceptive collection practices by employees of the creditor initiating the debt (such as MBNA or another credit card issuer) should be actionable under state debt collection or deceptive practices laws, and perhaps even as a tort.[191] Even if the FDCPA applies to a potential defendant, it still may be preferable to bring only state law claims if state court is viewed as a more favorable forum than federal court. For example, when the consumer's collection harassment claim may be forced into arbitration, state courts are often more receptive to claims that the arbitration requirement is unconscionable.

8.7.5 Must the Consumer's Debt Harassment Claim Be Sent to Arbitration?

In response to a consumer's affirmative court action claiming debt collection abuse related to debt collection arbitration, the defendant may attempt to compel arbitration,

180 Kelly v. Wolpoff & Abramson, L.L.P., 2007 WL 2381536 (D. Colo. Aug. 17, 2007).

181 *See* Worch v. Wolpoff & Abramson, L.L.P., 477 F. Supp. 2d 1015 (E.D. Mo. 2007) (allowing the allegation to go to trial).

182 Karnette v. Wolpoff & Abramson, L.L.P., 2007 WL 922288 (E.D. Va. Mar. 23, 2007).

183 Bontempo v. Wolpoff & Abramson, L.L.P., 2007 WL 3174050 (W.D. Pa. Oct. 29, 2007).

184 *See* National Consumer Law Center, Fair Debt Collection § 4.2 (6th ed. 2008).

185 *See* Worch v. Wolpoff & Abramson, L.L.P., 2006 WL 1523240 (E.D. Mo. June 1, 2006); *see also* Karnette v. Wolpoff & Abramson, L.L.P., 444 F. Supp. 2d 640 (E.D. Va. 2006).

186 *See, e.g.*, Park v. Columbia Credit Services, Inc., 2007 WL 1847142 (W.D. Mo. June 25, 2007).

187 *See* § 8.7.4, *infra*.

188 Worch v. Wolpoff & Abramson, L.L.P., 477 F. Supp. 2d 1015 (E.D. Mo. 2007).

189 National Consumer Law Center, Fair Debt Collection (6th ed. 2008).

190 2007 WL 922288 (E.D. Va. Mar. 23, 2007).

191 *See* National Consumer Law Center, Fair Debt Collection (6th ed. 2008); *see also* Kelly v. Wolpoff & Abramson, L.L.P., 2007 WL 2381536 (D. Colo. Aug. 17, 2007) (state deceptive practices claim could proceed against MBNA's attorney).

arguing that it is included within the creditor's arbitration clause. A consumer may oppose arbitration of such a claim on several grounds.

First, the language of the arbitration clause may indicate that the clause is applicable only to certain parties, and thus not applicable to others, such as collection attorneys or collection agencies. Courts have interpreted MBNA's clause as not applying to collection attorneys and collectors unless the collector is named as a co-defendant with MBNA.[192] Likewise, it is unclear whether attorneys and third-party collection agencies are "agents" of MBNA (thus falling within the arbitration clause's language) or whether they are independent contractors not covered by the arbitration clause.[193] The Discover Card arbitration provision, at least at one time, did not even mention agents or assignees, and a court therefore found the clause did not apply to an action brought against a collection law firm collecting on a Discover Card debt.[194]

If a debt buyer wishes to take advantage of its status as an assignee, a court should require that it provide documentation that it is in fact an assignee. Similarly, MBNA's clause provides that it covers actions "arising from or relating" to the credit card agreement, and an action based on the tortious behavior of collectors may not arise from or relate to the credit card agreement.[195] In short, before a defendant can seek to take advantage of an arbitration clause, the defendant should have to demonstrate both that it is a party that can take advantage of the clause and that the debt collection harassment claim is covered by the clause.

In addition, even if the agreement applies to the creditor, collector, or attorney, the agreement may not be enforceable, for reasons discussed throughout this manual—for example, because the consumer never agreed to arbitration, or because the clause is unconscionable.[196]

If the action is brought on a classwide basis, the class can argue that any limitation on classwide arbitration procedure makes the clause unconscionable, and also that NAF's involvement in the case should preclude it from administering the action. The action becomes viable if the court throws out the arbitration agreement completely or only limits it so that classwide arbitration is available before an entity other than NAF.

8.7.6 *Preclusive Effect of Creditor's Arbitration Action on Debt*

If the consumer previously participated in an arbitration proceeding or other debt collection proceeding the collector may also attempt to argue, under the doctrines of claim preclusion, res judicata, or a similar theory, that the consumer was required to bring any counterclaims in that proceeding rather than in a separate case. While an arbitration proceeding may have the same preclusive effect as a court proceeding,[197] courts generally find that a consumer's debt harassment claims are not precluded by a collection lawsuit on the debt.[198] Thus a court has rejected a collection attorney's defense of claim preclusion based on a prior collection arbitration proceeding.[199] But the result may be different if the federal FDCPA action is really an attack on the arbitration award, which should have been brought instead as a motion to vacate the award.[200]

8.8 Government Enforcement Action Against Using Arbitration for Collection

Challenges to collection using arbitration can be initiated through a private action, or through a government enforcement agency suing the creditor or the arbitration service provider. Such an action would avoid the practical problems of a private attorney realizing sufficient recovery from an action to justify the time and costs involved with such a major challenge. There is also no question that a government initiated action can remain in court, and need not be referred to arbitration pursuant to the creditor's arbitration clause with consumers.[201] Moreover, an action for injunctive relief,

192 Karnette v. Wolpoff & Abramson, L.L.P., 444 F. Supp. 2d 640 (E.D. Va. 2006); Bontempo v. Wolpoff & Abramson, 2006 WL 3040905 (W. D. Pa. Oct. 24, 2006). *But see* Nazar v. Wolpoff & Abramson, 2007 WL 528753 (D. Kan. Feb. 15, 2007) (arbitrator decides whether arbitration agreement applies to collector when agreement states that issues as to the applicability of the arbitration agreement are to be determined by the arbitrator).

It is important to carefully distinguish the nature of the parties, such as whether they are collectors or assignees. *See* Hoefs v. CACV of Colorado, L.L.C., 365 F. Supp. 2d 69 (D. Mass. 2005) (MBNA clause applies to assignees and collectors named as co-defendants with the assignee because the clause explicitly applies to "us" and also collectors named as co-defendants with "us," and "us" includes assignees).

193 *See* National Consumer Law Center, Consumer Arbitration Agreements § 7.4 (5th ed. 2007); *see also* Montgomery v. Fla. First Fin. Group, Inc., 2007 WL 1789115 (M.D. Fla. Apr. 19, 2007).

194 Nazar v. Wolpoff & Abramson, L.L.P., 2007 WL 2875377 (D. Kan. Oct. 3, 2007).

195 *See* National Consumer Law Center, Consumer Arbitration Agreements § 7.3.3 (5th ed. 2007).

196 *See id.* Chs. 5, 6.

197 *See id.* § 11.8.

198 *See* National Consumer Law Center, Fair Debt Collection § 7.4.2 (6th ed. 2008); *see also* Kelly v. Wolpoff & Abramson, L.L.P., 2007 WL 2381536 (D. Colo. Aug. 17, 2007) (proceedings related to MBNA collection arbitration does not preclude FDCPA claim against MBNA's attorney).

199 Karnette v. Wolpoff & Abramson, L.L.P., 2007 WL 922288 (E.D. Va. Mar. 23, 2007).

200 Nazar v. Wolpoff & Abramson, L.L.P., 530 F. Supp. 2d 1161 (D. Kan. 2008); Nickoloff v. Wolpoff & Abramson, L.L.P., 511 F. Supp. 2d 1043 (C.D. Cal. 2007).

201 *See* Equal Employment Opportunity Comm'n v. Waffle House,

civil penalties, and perhaps even restitution will not be affected by the ninety-day period to vacate existing judgments.

The Federal Trade Commission (FTC) can bring enforcement actions against creditors and arbitration service providers to challenge unfair or deceptive acts or practices. The FTC has successfully issued rules and engaged in enforcement actions against overreaching creditor remedies found in consumer adhesion contracts,[202] and collecting on debts using arbitration is a similar practice. Nevertheless, Congress has explicitly denied the FTC the ability to bring enforcement actions against banks, credit unions, or savings and loans associations. Instead, authority to bring enforcement actions against these entities is reserved for federal banking agencies.

This exemption is significant because, at present, creditors using arbitration to collect on debts tend to be national banks, whose unfair practices are policed by the Office of the Comptroller of the Currency (OCC), not the FTC. Complaints about national banks' collecting on debts via arbitration should be addressed to the OCC. While the OCC states that it has the authority and willingness to stop any unfair practice by a national bank, critics are skeptical. The National Consumer Law Center would like to be kept informed of the OCC's responsiveness to complaints about national banks.

State attorneys general can also challenge unfair actions using arbitration to collect on debts. Unlike the FTC, state attorneys general typically are authorized to sue banks operating in their state and, like the FTC, are generally empowered to stop unfair or deceptive practices. A national bank sued by a state will claim that OCC regulation preempts state laws. The law in this area is only now developing,[203] but it is hard to see how a bank can avail itself of state laws to collect on its debts and to confirm its arbitration awards, but then claim that state law does not apply to determine if its arbitration procedures are unfair or deceptive.

Inc., 534 U.S. 279, 122 S. Ct. 754, 151 L. Ed. 2d 755 (2002).

202 *See* Am. Fin. Services Ass'n v. Fed. Trade Comm'n, 767 F.2d 957 (D.C. Cir. 1985); *see also* National Consumer Law Center, Unfair and Deceptive Acts and Practices § 5.1.3 (6th ed. 2004 and Supp.).

203 *See* National Consumer Law Center, Unfair and Deceptive Acts and Practices § 2.5.3 (6th ed. 2004 and Supp.).

Chapter 9 Criminal and Civil Collection of Dishonored Checks

9.1 Introduction

A troublesome debt collection tactic is to threaten consumers with prosecution under criminal dishonored check statutes. When a consumer writes a check which is dishonored (bounced) because the consumer's account has insufficient funds (NSF) or credit to cover the check, or was closed, the person holding the check may threaten to initiate a dishonored check criminal prosecution against the consumer.

Civil dishonored check statutes, discussed in § 9.3, *infra*, give collectors additional leverage. These statutes reward bounty hunters by making consumers whose checks are dishonored liable for statutory or multiple damages, attorney fees, and other changes.

Even though these statutes evidence a public policy to discourage people from writing checks that will be dishonored, many creditors and collectors encourage consumers to do just that. Some debt collectors solicit postdated checks from financially distressed consumers, knowing that the possibility of a dishonored check prosecution provides the collector with powerful collection leverage.[1] Payday lenders, who provide small, short term loans at three-digit interest rates, commonly use this method of coercion.[2] Banks have recently entered the high-cost loan business by offering "overdraft loans," in which consumers are encouraged to write checks without money in the bank.[3]

There are a variety of situations in which dishonored checks are written. On the one hand is the professional criminal check kiter. More often, such checks are written by a financially desperate parent buying food without funds, a consumer who expects the check not to be cashed, a consumer who makes an inadvertent error in balancing a checkbook and can not immediately cover the check, or a person who expected the check to be covered by a deposited check that bounced.[4] In some states with legalized gambling ca-

1 *See, e.g.*, United States v. Cent. Adjustment Bureau, Inc., 667 F. Supp. 370 (N.D. Tex. 1986) (collector violated 15 U.S.C. § 1692f(3) by soliciting postdated checks with the purpose of threatening criminal prosecution), *aff'd*, 823 F.2d 880 (5th Cir. 1987) (per curiam); Strong v. Nat'l Collection Sys., 19 Clearinghouse Rev. 47 (E.D. Ark. 1985) (settlement agreement) (collector agreed not to resume use of a letter threatening criminal prosecution of consumers who had sent the collector postdated checks which were dishonored for insufficient funds); *In re* G.C. Services Corp., 83 F.T.C. 1521, 1525 (Fed. Trade Comm'n 1974) (complaint alleged that collection agency solicited postdated checks and later threatened criminal prosecution if the check was dishonored); National Consumer Law Center, Fair Debt Collection § 5.6.4 (6th ed. 2008).

2 *See, e.g.*, Turner v. E-Z Check Cashing, 35 F. Supp. 2d 1042 (M.D. Tenn. 1999) (payday lender violated deceptive practices (UDAP) statute by threatening groundless criminal dishonored check prosecution as means of collecting debt); Hamilton v. York, 987 F. Supp. 953 (E.D. Ky. 1997); *In re* Dorsey, 373 B.R. 528 (Bankr. N.D. Ohio 2007) (automatic stay did not bar criminal prosecution arising from check to payday lender); Watson v. State, 235 Ga. App. 381, 509 S.E.2d 87 (1998) (payday lenders who used criminal dishonored check prosecutions to collect violated state criminal RICO statute; predicate offenses were multiple perjuries, in swearing out dishonored check complaints stating that checks were given for merchandise, when lender had no merchandise to sell); State v. McWilliams, 2008 WL 442520 (Mont. Feb. 28, 2008) (affirming conviction; statute barring payday loan licensees from initiating criminal dishonored check prosecutions did not apply to private arrangement when non-licensee creditor lent $1000 secured by postdated $1250 check); State v. Widener, 2007 WL 293133 (Ohio Ct. App. Feb. 2, 2007) (affirming larceny by deception conviction arising from nonpayment of payday loan; when consumer realized she could not pay, she stopped payment in order to save bank NSF check charges, and so informed payday lender); *see also* Smith v. Cash Store Mgmt., Inc., 195 F.3d 325 (7th Cir. 1999) (payday lender could lawfully assert that "your check is security for the loan" when check entitled holder to seek remedies, including interest, costs, and collection expenses, under civil dishonored check statute).

3 *See* National Consumer Law Center, The Cost of Credit: Regulation, Preemption, and Industry Abuses § 7.5.6 (3d ed. 2005 and Supp.); National Consumer Law Center, Truth in Lending § 2.5.7 (6th ed. 2007).

4 On a nationally administered test, 99% of 17-year-olds and 84% of adults were not able to correctly balance a sample checking account. National Assessment of Educ. Progress, Consumer Math (1975). One percent of checks are dishonored; of those 71.2% are for insufficient funds, 2.7% drawn on uncollected funds, 4.4% drawn on closed accounts, 2.7% stop payment orders, 4.9% missing endorsements, and 14.1% for other reasons, including bank errors. *Statement of Preston Martin to House Banking Subcommittee*, 70 Fed. Res. Bull. 319 (1984). One of 5245 returned checks (two of every one million checks written) is a loss to a bank. W. Stafeil, Bank Admin. Instit., The Impact of Exception Items on the Check Collection System: A

sino markers, which authorize the casino to access any present or future bank account of the debtor, are treated as checks and can lead to dishonored check prosecution if the account contains insufficient funds.[5]

Often the holder of a dishonored check is a retailer who accepted or cashed the check, but there is an active debt buyer industry that purchases dishonored checks. Some companies guarantee to merchants that checks customers write will be paid, and then purchase and try to collect any checks that are dishonored.[6] Some collection agencies specialize in collecting dishonored checks for merchants.

Another volume in this series, *Consumer Banking and Payments Law*,[7] addresses other issues regarding dishonored checks, including wrongful dishonor, the circumstances in which checks are and are not payable, electronic re-presentment of dishonored checks, and the consumer's right to stop payment on a check.

9.2 Criminal Dishonored Check Laws

9.2.1 Introduction

This section discusses the scope, limitations, and validity of criminal dishonored check laws as well as defenses to prosecution under those laws. This summary should aid the civil practitioner in counseling clients who have written or endorsed checks not covered by sufficient funds. Familiarity with the limitations of criminal dishonored check laws should ease the fear of prosecution in many instances and may provide a basis for a civil claim against the collector who threatens prosecution. This discussion is intended, however, only as a general guide to issues that should be researched under applicable state laws in the event of a prosecution or threat of prosecution. Because the dishonored check criminal statutes are frequently changed by state legislatures, counsel should be particularly careful in determining which decisions apply to the current statute.

9.2.2 Defenses Based on Constitutional Rights

Most state constitutions contain a prohibition against imprisonment for debt,[8] although this is not a protection explicitly provided by the United States Constitution. Some state dishonored check laws have been declared facially unconstitutional under such provisions.[9] Other courts have construed dishonored check statutes to require proof of fraudulent intent in order to save them from unconstitutionality.[10]

Quantitative Description (1970).

5 Fleeger v. Bell, 95 F. Supp. 2d 1126 (D. Nev. 2000) (casino marker fits definition of "check or draft" in Nevada's criminal dishonored check statute), *aff'd*, 2001 WL 1491252 (9th Cir. Nov. 26, 2001); Shamburger v. Grand Casino of Miss., Inc., 84 F. Supp. 2d 794 (S.D. Miss. 1998) (when bank responds NSF, markers turned over to district attorney who sends out letter required by dishonored check statute, but does not actually prosecute); TeleRecovery, Inc. v. Rayborn, 814 So. 2d 688 (La. Ct. App. 2002) (casino markers were checks and covered by NSF check law, but denying multiple damages when collector failed to comply with notice requirements).

6 *See* Volden v. Innovative Fin. Sys., Inc., 440 F.3d 947 (8th Cir. 2006) (check guarantee service is debt collector covered by Fair Debt Collection Practices Act (FDCPA)).

7 National Consumer Law Center, Consumer Banking and Payments Law §§ 2.5, 2.6 (3d ed. 2005 and Supp.).

8 *See* Comment, *Imprisonment for Debt and the Constitution*, 1970 Law & Soc. Order 658. *See generally* § 12.10, *infra*.

9 Burnam v. Commonwealth, 228 Ky. 410, 15 S.W.2d 256 (1929) (dishonored check law unconstitutional when element of fraud deleted and debtor not permitted indigency defense required by state constitution); State v. Nelson, 58 S.D. 562, 237 N.W. 766 (1931) (dishonored check law unconstitutional when punishment was for failing to pay postdated check); *see also* People v. Vinnola, 177 Colo. 405, 494 P.2d 826 (1972) (modified dishonored check law was unconstitutionally vague, violated protections against imprisonment for debt, and offended equal protection requirements). *But see* State v. Avery, 111 Kan. 588 (1922); State v. Taylor, 73 S.W.2d 378 (Mo. 1934). *See generally* Wanda Ellen Wakefield, Annotation, *Constitutionality of "Bad Check Statute,"* 16 A.L.R.4th 631 (1982).

10 People v. Felgar, 58 P.3d 1122 (Colo. Ct. App. 2002) (check fraud statute must be construed to allow only permissive inference, not mandatory presumption, which would be unconstitutional; reversing check fraud conviction when jury was given mandatory presumption instruction); Neidlinger v. State, 88 S.E. 687 (Ga. Ct. App. 1916) (implying fraud as element of offense to avoid unconstitutional construction; no fraud when a postdated check was given, as postdating implies insufficient present funds); State v. Wilkens, 95 P.3d 135 (Kan. Ct. App. 2004) (table) (text available at 2004 WL 1784607) (rebuttable presumption of intent to defraud not unconstitutional); State v. Tsoi, 111 Wash. App. 1016 (2002) (table) (text available at 2002 WL 662884) (instruction that jury was permitted but not required to infer knowledge from writing NSF check was not unconstitutional "so long as the proven facts support the instruction"; conviction affirmed when defendant business owner wrote fifteen NSF checks after being notified by bank of overdrawn account); *see also* State v. Owen, 935 P.2d 183 (Idaho Ct. App. 1997) (Idaho's theft by deception and theft by false promise statutes did not violate state constitutional prohibition of "imprisonment for debt except in case of fraud," even though the offenses did not require proof of all elements of common law fraud, when each included "some deception" or "express or implied misrepresentation" or "a scheme to defraud"); State v. Allison, 607 N.W.2d 1 (S.D. 2000) (statute criminalizing failure to return military property not unconstitutional imprisonment for debt, as intent requirement is implied, accidental loss or destruction not a crime; also state's entrustment of property to militia members is not a debtor-creditor relationship); State v. Robinson, 602 N.W.2d 730 (S.D. 1999) (both statute and due process required that jury be instructed that presumption of knowledge of insufficient funds is rebuttable and state still bears burden of proof beyond reasonable doubt); Colin v. State, 168 S.W.2d 500 (Tex. Crim. App. 1943) (dishonored check prosecution not imprisonment for debt because fraudulent intent required). *But see* Dirk v. State, 305 So. 2d 187 (Fla. 1974)

Even when such statutes are facially constitutional, they may be applied in an unconstitutional manner in particular collection cases.[11] For example, the practice of not processing dishonored check cases in return for a $500 payment was held to deny equal protection to an indigent defendant who was unable to pay, went to trial, and was sentenced to jail. The court rejected an argument that this practice was a legitimate form of plea bargaining.[12]

9.2.3 *Checks That Are Postdated or Given for Preexisting Debts*

Many courts have held that dishonored check laws do not apply to postdated checks.[13] There are a number of reasons for this position. First, a postdated check implicitly represents that the check writer lacks sufficient present funds to cover the check.[14] Second, a postdated check is not payable

---

(upholding constitutionality of criminal NSF statute against challenges based on vagueness and existence of presumption); *cf.* Carter v. Lowry, 169 Ga. 515, 151 S.E. 23 (1929) (presumption of fraud established by dishonored check law does not offend due process).

11 *See* Knight v. Constantino, 2006 WL 1529567 (S.D. Ind. May 31, 2006) (consumer stated Fourth and Fourteenth Amendment claims arising from dishonored check prosecution when she alleged that check was postdated and had been paid within ten days of notice of dishonor, either of which excluded it from Indiana's criminal dishonored check statute, and that investigator's affidavit knowingly misstated these facts); Helton v. Dixon, 2006 WL 751239 (E.D. Ky. Mar. 21, 2006) (fact issues in section 1983 action alleging malicious prosecution arising from NSF check charges). *See generally* J. Potuto, *And Mussolini Had the Trains Running on Time: A Review of the Bad Check Offense and the Law Enforcement Debt Collector*, 65 Neb. L. Rev. 242 (1986) (critique of Neb. law and dishonored check criminal diversion plan).

12 Watson v. State, 235 Ga. App. 381, 509 S.E.2d 87 (1998) (separate concurrence argued that majority did not go far enough; "The root of the problem lies in our statutory framework that subjects one who 'bounces' a check to criminal penalties.").

13 *See* Knight v. Constantino, 2006 WL 1529567 (S.D. Ind. May 31, 2006) (postdated check explicitly excluded from coverage of Indiana criminal dishonored check statute; consumer stated Fourth Amendment claim with allegation that investigator's affidavit knowingly misrepresented that check was not postdated); Banderas v. State, 372 So. 2d 489 (Fla. Dist. Ct. App. 1979); State v. Stooksberry, 872 S.W.2d 906 (Tenn. 1994) (postdated check was not a check or a sight draft within the meaning of the worthless check statute); State v. Braham, 567 S.E.2d 624 (W. Va. 2002) (West Virginia dishonored check statute explicitly did not apply to postdated checks; postdated check may support larceny by fraudulent scheme conviction, but fraudulent intent not shown merely by NSF check); *see also* Jones v. Kunin, 2000 WL 3442107 (S.D. Ill. May 1, 2000) (intent to defraud not shown for purposes of civil dishonored check statute when debtor gave postdated check to payday lender). *But see* State v. McFadden, 467 N.W.2d 578 (Iowa 1991) (postdated check may support larceny conviction unless there is "an understanding between the parties" that check not cashable when received; note that court retreated from this position in State v. Hogrefe, 557 N.W.2d 871 (Iowa 1996)); State v. Harris, 913 S.W.2d 348 (Mo. Ct. App. 1995) (state must show that intent to defraud existed at time check was written; check writer's testimony that she intended to pay on date shown on check disbelieved when balances were very low at all relevant times, and check writer had ceased to communicate with bank); State v. Papillon, 389 N.W.2d 553 (Neb. 1986) (conviction can not be based on postdated check when both check writer and payee were aware that check was postdated, even though check writer closed account shortly before the postdated date); State v. Kelm, 672 A.2d 1261 (N.J. Super. Ct. App. Div. 1996) (state must show knowledge that funds would be insufficient on date of check; when account had negative balances for a month, knowledge was shown); State v. Hammond, 498 N.W.2d 126 (N.D. 1993) (postdating no defense unless postdated check is "knowingly received as such"); State v. Widener, 2007 WL 293133 (Ohio Ct. App. Feb. 2, 2007) (affirming larceny by deception conviction when consumer stopped payment on check given for payday loan after realizing she could not pay, and so informed lender; no contest plea precludes review of merits other than denial of initial motion to dismiss); Tucker v. Lakeshore Chevrolet, Inc., 2004 WL 2251807 (Ohio Ct. App. Oct. 7, 2004) (probable cause sufficient to defeat malicious prosecution claim, even if check writer told car dealer funds were insufficient, car dealer said check would never be cashed, and gave permission to stop payment when real purchaser returned to close deal; check presented and criminal charges pursued after real purchaser reneged); State v. Brotzman, 108 Wash. App. 1042 (2001) (postdated check may support conviction for larceny by check); *cf.* State v. Washington, 700 So. 2d 1068 (La. Ct. App. 1997) (intent to defraud found, notwithstanding defendant's testimony that she told car dealer she did not have funds in account to cover check, and car dealer promised to hold it for thirty days, when she neither paid check nor returned car for six months, and when she returned car it had 19,000 miles on it); State v. Harris, 977 S.W.2d 127 (Tenn. Ct. App. 1998) (affirming conviction; although dishonored check statute does not apply to postdated checks, it does apply to check that defendant signed but left blank as to date and all other respects). *See generally* John D. Perovich, Annotation, *Application of "Bad Check" Statute with Respect to Postdated Checks*, 52 A.L.R.3d 464 (1973); 32 Am. Jur. 2d *False Pretenses* § 70 (2007).

14 People v. Abbott, 638 P.2d 781 (Colo. 1981); People v. Cundiff, 16 Ill. App. 3d 267, 305 N.E.2d 735 (1973); State v. Mucci, 594 S.E.2d 411 (N.C. Ct. App. 2004) (check writer telling payee to hold check for a few days is proof that payee knew balance insufficient); State v. Boyd, 2003 WL 21060863 (Ohio Ct. App. May 9, 2003) (evidence insufficient to support larceny by check when defendant handed over undated check and told payee's employee to call him before cashing; "poor business practices" not sufficient); Commonwealth v. Kelinson, 199 Pa. Super. 135, 184 A.2d 374 (1964); Harmon v. State, 2005 WL 1743744 (Tex. App. July 25, 2005) ("taking without effective consent" element of theft not shown when buyer of cattle, who was allowed to take them before writing check, informed seller that he would need time to raise funds to cover postdated check, apparently a usual practice); *see also In re* Greer, 2002 WL 1558544 (Bankr. D. Colo. July 12, 2002) (NSF check not fraudulent misrepresentation when tenant told landlord check would bounce, but would be covered later; landlord presented check immediately; awarding costs and fees to tenant; landlord's nondischargeability claim "not substantially justified"); *cf.* People v. Pugh, 127 Cal. Rptr. 2d 770 (Ct. App. 2002) (giving postdated check not

on demand, a commercial law requirement for checks.[15] In addition, a postdated check is little different from a promissory note for which nonpayment may not be prosecuted under dishonored check laws.[16] Other states hold that a postdated check becomes a check on the date the check specifies,[17] or allow the defense only if the payee is made aware of the current lack of funds.[18] Giving two checks to the same person, one postdated and one not, c[illegible] inference that there were sufficient funds to cover the [illegible] that was not postdated.[19]

Courts may likewise exclude checks given for preexisting debts from the application of dishonored check laws.[20] A

larceny when seller was informed of insufficient funds, and buyer believed he could cover, but larceny shown when buyer took possession of property and told seller to resubmit check, knowing that bank balance was insufficient); People v. Meller, 185 Colo. 389, 524 P.2d 1366 (1974) (in absence of a representation that check is good, a postdated check implies that the payee has notice of the check writer's lack of funds—but only if the payee knew in fact that the check was postdated); People v. Gerber, 115 Misc. 2d 222, 453 N.Y.S.2d 998 (Crim. Ct. 1982). *But see* State v. Spitko, 2 Conn. Cir. 99, 195 A.2d 577 (1963); People v. Weathington, 2003 WL 23003363 (Cal. Ct. App. Dec. 22, 2003) (simply postdating check insufficient to show payee's knowledge; affirming conviction when payee checked with bank and was told balance sufficient, after which check writer withdrew funds); State v. McWilliams, 2008 WL 442520 (Mont. Feb. 28, 2008) (drawee's consent to take postdated checks not a defense to criminal prosecution of check writer; while drawee may have consented to take the checks and refrain from depositing them immediately, this was not consent to nonpayment); *cf.* State v. Hogrefe, 557 N.W.2d 871 (Iowa 1996) (theft by deception conviction proper when check writer was in financial trouble and jury could reasonably find he did not intend to pay, but reversing conviction on other grounds).

15 People v. Kubitz, 37 Misc. 2d 453, 235 N.Y.S.2d 971 (County Ct. 1963); State v. Stooksberry, 872 S.W.2d 906 (Tenn. 1994). *But see* State v. Taylor, 73 S.W.2d 378 (Mo. 1934) (even if postdated check is not a check, it is a draft, for which statute allowed prosecution); State v. McWilliams, 2008 WL 442520 (Mont. Feb. 28, 2008) (postdated check is payable on demand and meets Uniform Commercial Code definition of check).

16 State v. Stout, 8 Ariz. App. 545, 448 P.2d 115 (1968); Bivens v. State, 153 Ga. App. 631 (1980); State v. Eikelberger, 72 Idaho 245, 239 P.2d 1069 (Idaho 1951); Gibbs v. Commonwealth, 273 S.W.2d 583 (Ky. Ct. App. 1954). *But see* State v. McFadden, 467 N.W.2d 578 (Iowa 1991); State v. Wyman, 945 S.W.2d 74 (Mo. Ct. App. 1997) (intent to defraud shown, not merely failure to perform future promise to deposit money into account, when car buyer who gave seller postdated check falsely stated that she already had financing).

17 State v. Fitanides, 683 A.2d 534 (N.H. 1996) (New Hampshire treats postdated check as having been written on the day of its date; check writer was guilty if he or she knew check would not be paid; when bank balance was insufficient for two months after date, evidence was sufficient); *see also* Uribe v. Correa, 862 So. 2d 883, 885 n.2 (Fla. Dist. Ct. App. 2003) (treble damages under civil dishonored check statute are not available if postdated check is deposited before its date); *cf.* Young v. State, 594 S.E.2d 667 (Ga. Ct. App. 2004) (postdated NSF check inadequate to support theft by deception charge; distinguishing case in which check writer does not tell payee check is postdated and lies about current state of bank account).

18 People v. Weathington, 2003 WL 23003363 (Cal. Ct. App. Dec. 22, 2003) (if payee knows of insufficient funds, conviction barred no matter how fraudulent the promise to cover, but simply postdating check insufficient to show payee's knowledge; affirming conviction when payee checked with bank, was told balance sufficient, after which check writer withdrew funds); State v. Wamsley, 2003 WL 1869927 (Ohio Ct. App. Apr. 14, 2003) (affirming conviction; check writer gave postdated check on Friday and told payee that sufficient funds would be available on Monday but check was never covered; intent is question of fact); *see also* People v. Pugh, 127 Cal. Rptr. 2d 770 (Ct. App. 2002) (giving postdated check not larceny when seller was informed of insufficient funds and buyer believed he could cover, but larceny shown when buyer took possession of property and told seller to resubmit check, knowing that bank balance was insufficient); State v. Stewart, 921 A.2d 933 (N.H. 2007) (reversing conviction because of improper jury instructions; state must show that check writer knew or believed that check would not be paid when presented to bank, not just that funds were insufficient at time check was written); *cf.* State v. Jones, 2008 WL 564723 (Ohio Ct. App. Mar. 3, 2008) (affirming conviction when defendant told payee to hold check for one day but balances were insufficient for weeks and check was never covered); Thompson v. Adcox, 63 S.W.3d 783 (Tenn. Ct. App. 2001) (postdated check becomes check, for purposes of civil dishonored check statute, on postdated date, even though criminal prosecution would not be allowed).

19 People v. Abbott, 638 P.2d 781 (Colo. 1981).

20 *See* Schmidt v. Slaughter, Clearinghouse No. 51,961 (M.D. Ga. 1996) (collection lawyer's letter violated FDCPA by falsely threatening criminal prosecution when criminal process was not available because check was given for an existing debt and thus was not covered by the Georgia criminal dishonored check law); Holder v. State, 529 S.E.2d 907 (Ga. Ct. App. 2000) (NSF check given to independent contractor at end of week for that week's work was for "present consideration" when interval between work and payment was short, but check for payee's share of business's earnings was not, when payee had not parted with anything of value in return for check); State v. Ripley, 889 So. 2d 1214 (La. Ct. App. 2004) (NSF check for antecedent debt will support conviction only if it is precondition for provision of future services; lessor made "considered business decision" to give lessee time to seek investors); Johnson v. State, 2005 WL 3387763 (Tex. App. Dec. 13, 2005) (reversing theft of services conviction when NSF check for day care was written at time when there was large arrearage and after the services were terminated); *cf.* Wenger v. Aceto, 2008 WL 787313 (Mass. Mar. 27, 2008) (noting open question of Massachusetts law whether larceny by check requires showing that payee parted with something of value or whether check for past services is sufficient). *But see* State v. Madani, 910 S.W.2d 362 (Mo. Ct. App. 1995) (statute requires only proof of intent to defraud, not proof that defendant received anything of value; when dishonored check written to cover debt for two previous dishonored checks served to "stall creditor and frustrate prosecution," intent was sufficiently shown); Merchant v. State, 4 P.3d 184 (Wyo. 2000) (writing NSF check to pay preexisting debt violates Wyoming dishonored check statute, which specifically refers to check "to pay a debt"); Bailey v. State, 408 P.2d 244 (Wyo. 1965) (crime was issuing a worthless check for "any obligation," so statute applied when check given for a preexisting debt); *cf.* People v. Gutierrez, 1 P.3d 241 (Colo. Ct. App. 1999) (NSF check written to pay preexisting debt violates Colorado dishonored check statute); Huse v. State, 180 S.W.3d 847 (Tex. App. 2005)

payee who accepts a check for a preexisting debt gives up nothing of value in return (an express requirement of some dishonored check statutes).[21] In addition, no intent to defraud can be implied from giving such a check,[22] and a payee who solicits such a check may not in fact have been defrauded.[23]

Other courts, however, have held that if the check writer seeks a respite from collection efforts, this is sufficient return to support a dishonored check conviction.[24] If the payment of an arrearage is a condition for the continuing provision of goods or services that will generally be sufficient to support a conviction.[25]

9.2.4 Other Limitations and Defenses

Other exceptions or defenses may be available under certain statutes or circumstances.[26] The advocate should always investigate whether the payment method in question meets the statutory definition of a check. The state's dishonored check law may not, for example, cover certain types of electronic payment methods. The use of electronic media may, however, support charges of wire fraud.[27]

There can be no fraud, an essential element in most states, when the payee of the check was informed of the check writer's financial distress or insufficient funds balance.[28] It

---

(upholding theft of services conviction when NSF check for antecedent services induced payee to continue to provide services). *See generally* F. M. English, Annotation, *Construction and Effect of "Bad Check" Statute with Respect to Check in Payment of Pre-existing Debt*, 59 A.L.R.2d 1159 (1958); 32 Am. Jur. 2d *False Pretenses* § 68 (2007).

21 Ellerbee v. State, 569 S.E.2d 902 (Ga. Ct. App. 2002) (reversing theft by deception conviction; wholesaler did not part with cars in reliance on false statement when failing used car business already possessed cars at time check was written; later promises to pay did not misrepresent any past or present fact); Holder v. State, 242 Ga. App. 479, 529 S.E.2d 907 (2000) (NSF check given to member of membership organization for "business growth" not for present consideration when payee had paid for membership sometime in the past and had not parted with anything of value in return for check); State v. Campbell, 543 P.2d 1171 (Idaho 1975) (state may not rely on presumption of fraud, but must prove it when dishonored check was given for preexisting debt); State v. Blasi, 312 A.2d 135 (N.J. 1973) (prosecution can not be based on presentment of check to pay preexisting debt).

22 Phillips v. State, 24 Ala. App. 456, 136 So. 480 (1931); Berry v. State, 153 Ga. 169, 111 S.E. 669 (1922) ("evident purpose was to escape the importunate duns of his creditor, and to get temporary respite therefrom," not to take anything of value); State v. Blasi, 64 N.J. 51, 312 A.2d 135 (1973); State v. Davis, 26 N.M. 523, 194 P. 882 (N.M. 1921); *see also* Lowery v. City of Boaz, 393 So. 2d 534 (Ala. Crim. App. 1981); State v. Durbin, 83 Ohio App. 3d 156, 614 N.E.2d 799 (1992) (limiting situations in which intent to defraud can be found when check is given for preexisting debt). *But see* People v. Nibur, 238 A.D. 233 (1933) (prosecution may be based on delivery of NSF check for preexisting indebtedness, but here there was insufficient evidence of intent); State v. Lowenstein, 109 Ohio St. 393, 142 N.E. 897 (1924).

23 Driskell v. State, 47 Ga. App. 741, 171 S.E. 389 (1933); *see also* Ellerbee v. State, 569 S.E.2d 902 (Ga. Ct. App. 2002) (reversing theft by deception conviction; wholesaler did not part with cars in reliance on false statement when failing used car business already possessed cars at time check was written; later promises to pay did not misrepresent any past or present fact).

24 *See* State v. Madani, 910 S.W.2d 362 (Mo. Ct. App. 1995) (statute requires only proof of intent to defraud, not proof that defendant received anything of value; when dishonored check written to cover debt for two previous dishonored checks served to "stall creditor and frustrate prosecution," intent was sufficiently shown); Silverberg v. Mirenberg, 746 N.Y.S.2d 742 (Civ. Ct. 2001) (check written for third party's antecedent debt is given for value; temporary cessation of legal action against third party was sufficient); State v. Bergsmark, 2004 WL 2426236 (Ohio Ct. App. Oct. 29, 2004) (need not show that "monetary benefit" was obtained; "any type of advantage," including creditor's belief that debt is paid, is sufficient); State v. Suber, 798 N.E.2d 684 (Ohio Ct. App. 2003) (temporary respite from collection action sufficient to show detriment from dishonored check written to cover previous dishonored checks); State v. Wamsley, 2003 WL 1869927 (Ohio Ct. App. Apr. 14, 2003) (same); State v. Brotzman, 108 Wash. App. 1042 (2001) (post-dated check written for preexisting debt will support larceny conviction; "brief reprieve" from collection efforts is sufficient); State v. Alams, 93 Wash. App. 754, 970 P.2d 367 (1999).

25 *See* Huse v. State, 180 S.W.3d 847 (Tex. App. 2005) (upholding theft of services conviction when NSF check for antecedent services induced payee to continue to provide services). *But cf.* State v. Ripley, 889 So. 2d 1214 (La. Ct. App. 2004) (NSF check for antecedent debt will support conviction only if it is precondition for provision of future services; not satisfied when lessor made "considered business decision" to give lessee time to seek investors); Johnson v. State, 2005 WL 3387763 (Tex. App. Dec. 13, 2005) (reversing theft of services conviction; no showing that NSF check for past services, written at time when there was large arrearage, had resulted in provision of any additional services).

26 *See* 32 Am. Jur. 2d *False Pretenses* §§ 62–74 (2007).

27 United States v. Schwartz, 2005 WL 834869 (E.D. Pa. Apr. 11, 2005) (bank fraud and wire fraud convictions were supported by NSF electronic payments to credit card company); United States v. Bistrian, 2005 WL 477998 (E.D. Pa. Mar. 1, 2005) (upholding wire fraud conviction when defendant used NSF checks to purchase luxury cars; wire element supported by exchange of e-mails with dealership, fraud element supported by knowing use of NSF check).

28 Jones v. Kunin, 2000 WL 3442107 (S.D. Ill. May 1, 2000) (no intent to defraud shown when payday lender solicited postdated checks, and it was "clear under the circumstances" that borrower did not have sufficient funds); Turner v. E-Z Check Cashing, 35 F. Supp. 2d 1042 (M.D. Tenn. 1999) (Tennessee law did not allow dishonored check prosecution when holder knew check writer did not have enough funds on deposit to cover checks; payday lender's knowledge presumed as borrower's lack of cash is basis for transaction); People v. Poyet, 6 Cal. 3d 530, 99 Cal. Rptr. 758, 492 P.2d 1150 (1972); People v. Meller, 185 Colo. 389, 524 P.2d 1366 (1974); White v. State, 27 Ga. App. 774, 110 S.E. 40 (1921); People v. McLaughlin, 123 Ill. App. 3d 24, 462 N.E.2d 875 (1984) (intent to defraud not shown beyond reasonable doubt when defendant told payee that check would be good when presented and requested that presentment be delayed); Gibbs v. Commonwealth, 273 S.W.2d 583 (Ky. Ct. App. 1954); *see also In re* Greer, 2002 WL 1558544 (Bankr. D.

may be a defense that the check writer reasonably expected the check to be paid when it was written or presented,[29] but courts have often found that such a belief was unreasonable or that the defense's evidence was insufficient to rebut a statutory presumption of intent.[30] In addition, some statutes

Colo. July 12, 2002) (NSF check not fraudulent misrepresentation when tenant told landlord check would bounce, but would be covered later, yet landlord presented check immediately); *cf.* People v. Weathington, 2003 WL 23003363 (Cal. Ct. App. Dec. 22, 2003) (if payee knows of insufficient funds, conviction barred no matter how fraudulent the promise to cover, but simply postdating check insufficient to show payee's knowledge; affirming conviction when payee checked with bank and was told balance sufficient, after which check writer withdrew funds); People v. Chrysler, 639 N.Y.S.2d 213 (App. Div. 1996) (intent element of dishonored check offense may be negated by "an understanding" that a "check is not to be cashed until the check writer advises the payee that the check is good," but finding criminal intent when check writer said check would be good in a day or two, but it was written on closed account); State v. Sneed, 908 S.W.2d 408 (Tenn. Ct. App. 1995) (dishonored check statute does not apply if payee or holder "knows or has good and sufficient reason to believe" that check writer had insufficient funds, but finding that payee here did not know). *But see* State v. Kelm, 672 A.2d 1261 (N.J. Super. Ct. App. Div. 1996) (upholding conviction even though check writer told payee she would have to wait "a few days" when account had negative balances for entire month); Tucker v. Lakeshore Chevrolet, Inc., 2004 WL 2251807 (Ohio Ct. App. Oct. 7, 2004) (probable cause sufficient to defeat malicious prosecution claim, even if check writer told car dealer funds were insufficient, car dealer said check would never be cashed, and gave permission to stop payment when real purchaser returned to close deal; check presented and criminal charges pursued after real purchaser reneged); State v. Wallace, 138 P.3d 599 (Utah Ct. App. 2006) (not a defense to dishonored check charge that check writer told payee funds were insufficient, or that there was an agreement to delay cashing).

29 Parrot Heads, Inc. v. Dep't of Bus. & Prof'l Regulation, 741 So. 2d 1231 (Fla. Dist. Ct. App. 1999) (state must show that check writer knew that funds were insufficient); State v. Harris, 2005 WL 757584 (Minn. Ct. App. Apr. 5, 2005) (intent must be shown as of time check written; reversing conviction when check presented six weeks after it was written, at which time account was closed, and there was no evidence of time or circumstances of closure); People v. Nibur, 238 A.D. 233 (1933) (reversing conviction when check writer told payee that account had insufficient funds and made reasonable efforts to obtain funds to deposit before check was presented); *cf.* Hegar v. State, 11 S.W.3d 290 (Tex. App. 1999) (evidence of other recent returned checks was relevant to prove intent because "guilty intent cannot be inferred from the mere act of giving a check in exchange for goods"). *But see* State v. Mathisen, 356 N.W.2d 129 (N.D. 1984) (no "good faith" defense to violation of dishonored check statute; innocent impression that there were sufficient funds on deposit is not a defense). *See generally* 32 Am. Jur. 2d *False Pretenses* §§ 66–67 (2007); W. L. Heyman, Annotation, *Reasonable Expectation of Payment as Affecting Offenses Under "Worthless Check" Statutes*, 9 A.L.R.3d 719 (1966).

30 Weathington v. Wong, 2008 WL 718477 (N.D. Cal. Mar. 14, 2008) (finding sufficient evidence of intent to defraud and knowledge of insufficiency in light of several bounced checks, withdrawal of funds after check was written, and prior incidents when defendant withdrew funds after checks written); Blackford v. Wal-Mart, 912 F. Supp. 537 (S.D. Ga. 1996) (reckless disregard for the state of check writer's checking account was sufficient to make out the knowledge element of Georgia dishonored check statute; distinguishing between "Russian roulette" approach and "an occasional arithmetic mistake"); Delevie v. State, 454 So. 2d 1044 (Ala. Crim. App. 1984) (showing that check had been presented and that payment had been refused is prima facie evidence of check writer's intent to defraud); Wells v. State, 807 So. 2d 132 (Fla. Dist. Ct. App. 2002) (affirming conviction of concert promoter who wrote dishonored checks for performers' travel, intending to cover checks from concert revenue, which failed to materialize); Walker v. State, 467 N.E.2d 1248 (Ind. Ct. App. 1984) (when statute stipulates that proof that check was issued and that payment was refused is prima facie evidence of intent, burden shifted to defendant to show lack of knowledge); Baber v. Commonwealth, 2004 WL 1364283 (Ky. June 17, 2004) (fraudulent intent shown even though balance sufficient to pay check in question, when bank followed usual procedure of cashing largest item first, leaving no funds to pay this check, and defendant could have honored the check to avoid prosecution); Crawley v. Commonwealth, 2003 WL 22149310 (Ky. Sept. 19, 2003) (affirming theft by deception conviction; failure to cover within ten days created rebuttable presumption of intent; defendant used credit card "courtesy checks" and testified that he had checked with credit card issuer before doing so); State v. Mosby, 956 So. 2d 843 (La. Ct. App. 2007) (knowledge of insufficiency shown when bank statement showed sufficient funds on day check written, but insufficient funds next day and negative balance for two weeks thereafter); State v. Washington, 700 So. 2d 1068 (La. Ct. App. 1997) (finding intent to defraud, notwithstanding defendant's testimony that she intended to cover check, when defendant wrote $5000 check as down payment for car but neither paid check nor returned car for six months, when she returned car with 19,000 miles on it); Commonwealth v. Garcia, 863 N.E.2d 94 (Mass. App. Ct. 2007) (affirming conviction when defendant's story of cashing checks for man named Cash Money "strains credulity"); People v. Thompson, 2003 WL 22928739 (Mich. Ct. App. Dec. 11, 2003) (failure to cover within five days sufficient to support conviction, even though insufficient funds resulted from bank error, other checks were covered on second presentment, and check was covered after various failures of communication with payee); State v. Carroll, 2000 Mo. App. LEXIS 1219 (Mo. Ct. App. Aug. 10, 2000) (intent to pay negated when bank officer testified to negative balances over several month period), *aff'd in part, rev'd in part on other grounds*, 41 S.W.3d 878 (Mo. 2001); State v. Harris, 913 S.W.2d 348 (Mo. Ct. App. 1995) (check writer's testimony that she intended to pay on date of postdated check disbelieved when balances were very low at all relevant times, and check writer had ceased to communicate with bank); State v. Stewart, 921 A.2d 933 (N.H. 2007) (reversing conviction because of improper jury instructions; state must show that check writer knew or believed that check would not be paid when presented to bank, not just that funds were insufficient at time check was written); State v. Olsen, 590 S.E.2d 477 (N.C. Ct. App. 2004) (table) (text available at 2004 WL 77836) (evidence of negative or insufficient balances at relevant time sufficient to show that defendant, partner in a small business who wrote all the checks, knew funds insufficient); State v. Mucci, 594 S.E.2d 411 (N.C. Ct. App. 2004) (evidence that other checks bounced during same time period is probative of knowledge; check writer's request that payee hold check for a

make it a defense that the check is paid within a statutory period after notice of dishonor.[31]

The manner in which the dishonoring of the check occurs is also relevant. Some courts hold that the necessary element of fraud is lacking when the dishonored check was cashed at the bank at which the checking account was maintained, as the bank holding the account is charged with knowledge of the account balance.[32] Different rules may apply to checks drawn on closed or nonexistent accounts, or to stop payments.[33]

When the check is in fact paid by the drawee bank, the consumer can not be prosecuted under a dishonored check statute. For example, in one case a consumer wrote checks that she did not have funds to cover. However her credit union had issued her a card by which it guaranteed payment of any checks she wrote, and it in fact paid her checks. The court held that, because the checks had been paid, the consumer could not be prosecuted under a dishonored check statute.[34]

Some states, in addition to larceny by check statutes, have statutes forbidding "larceny by deception" or by "false promise,"[35] or obtaining property by false pre-

few days is proof that she knew balance insufficient); State v. Weller, 2007 WL 4305884 (Ohio Ct. App. Dec. 11, 2007) (bounced paychecks of start-up business; when funds moved around between bank accounts in manner suggestive of check kiting, evidence showed more than a failed business venture); State v. Bound, 2004 WL 2806430 (Ohio Ct. App. Dec. 1, 2004) (evidence sufficient to sustain dishonored check and theft by deception convictions when owner of failing business wrote eleven dishonored checks, and was able to cover only seven of them during statutory period); State v. Bergsmark, 2004 WL 2426236 (Ohio Ct. App. Oct. 29, 2004) (knowledge and intent shown if defendant "has no reasonable ground to believe" funds sufficient; here owner of failing business continued to write NSF checks after bank informed him that overdrafts would not be covered); Penn v. State, 684 P.2d 562 (Okla. Crim. App. 1984) (defendant's testimony that he thought there were sufficient funds to cover checks merely created questions of fact for the jury); State v. Dickinson, 528 S.E.2d 675 (S.C. Ct. App. 2000) (defendant's testimony of intent to pay disbelieved when check was for $20,000 and bank officer testified that balance in account never exceeded $1000; defendant also gave false address); Whitaker v. State, 2003 WL 21402386 (Tex. App. June 18, 2003) (affirming larceny by check conviction when account was $700 overdrawn at time check written and check not paid until after arrest); Leon v. State, 102 S.W.3d 776 (Tex. App. 2003) (affirming conviction of chief executive officer of small company on theft by deception charge on basis of NSF company checks he allowed to be signed by another while he was ill; intent to deprive shown by fact that checks dishonored within thirty days and not paid within ten days after notice); Womack v. State, 2001 WL 1383179 (Tex. App. Nov. 8, 2001) (bank records properly admitted to show intent, knowledge and absence of mistake: records showed numerous four-figure NSF checks and three months of large negative balances); Hartman v. Commonwealth, 2004 WL 237715 (Va. Ct. App. Feb. 10, 2004) (presumption of knowledge not rebutted by defendant's testimony that he was poor bookkeeper but did not intend to steal; evidence of other overdrafts was probative); State v. Brotzman, 108 Wash. App. 1042 (2001) (affirming conviction when defendant wrote postdated check believing she would receive income from pending business transaction, which fell through; future deal was "a mere expectancy"); State v. Alams, 970 P.2d 367 (Wash. Ct. App. 1997) (when check was written on account closed because of numerous overdrafts, debtor's testimony that he thought he had enough money to cover the check was disbelieved); Cox v. State, 964 P.2d 1235 (Wyo. 1998) (intent to defraud was sufficient to support dishonored check conviction when debtor failed to repay within five days of notice of dishonor, even though he paid within ten days and account on which $1500 check was written contained over $1200; court states that defendant "did not present any evidence of a reasonable expectation that the check would be paid on presentation"); *see also* Ingram v. State, 2005 WL 16290 (Tex. App. Jan. 5, 2005) (evidence sufficient to sustain NSF check theft of services conviction, based on long period of negative balances before and after date of check, check written so shortly before services rendered that payee could not discover it was NSF, and account transfers suggesting check kiting).

31 Knight v. Constantino, 2006 WL 1529567 (S.D. Ind. May 31, 2006) (defense to Indiana dishonored check charge that check was paid within ten days of notice; consumer stated Fourth Amendment claim with allegation that investigator's affidavit knowingly misrepresented that check was not paid); Lapp v. State, 100 P.3d 862 (Wyo. 2004) (failure to cover within five days is evidence of intent to defraud, an essential element; reversing conviction when payee's testimony "vague" as to when check writer paid); *cf.* State v. Mosby, 956 So. 2d 843 (La. Ct. App. 2007) (intent to defraud shown in light of evidence of statutory notice and nonpayment); Glaze v. State, 230 S.W.3d 258 (Tex. App. 2007) (probable cause to arrest sufficiently alleged when notice was given and check not covered within statutory period); Vance v. Commonwealth, 2007 WL 737557 (Va. Ct. App. Mar. 13, 2007) (nonpayment after notice creates presumption of intent to defraud; notice sent to address on check is sufficient, even if returned undelivered); Huff v. State, 992 P.2d 1071 (Wyo. 1999) (insufficient funds and failure to make good within five days after statutory notice is evidence of intent to deceive). *But cf.* State v. Wilkens, 95 P.3d 135 (Kan. Ct. App. 2004) (table) (text available at 2004 WL 1784607) (rebuttable presumption of intent to defraud if not repaid within seven days of proper notice; mailing sufficient even though defendant testified to non-receipt; rejecting constitutional challenge to jury instruction regarding presumption). *See generally* Nat'l Ass'n of Credit Mgmt., Manual of Credit & Commercial Laws § 17-3 (98th ed. 2007).

32 *See* Bruce I. McDaniel, Annotation, *Cashing Check at Bank at Which Account Is Maintained as a Violation of Bad Check Statutes*, 75 A.L.R.3d 1080 (1977). *But see* State v. Suber, 798 N.E.2d 684 (Ohio Ct. App. 2003) (check tendered to bank, drawn on account at that same bank, sufficient to support larceny by check when there was "a chain of instruments sure to be dishonored," that is, a classic check kite).

33 *But cf.* Sykes v. Commonwealth, 593 S.E.2d 545 (Va. Ct. App. 2004) (statutory presumption of intent to defraud, which arises from check drawn on nonexistent account, also applies to closed account; five-day notice not required; presumption rebuttable; check writer may prove that account closed without his or her knowledge).

34 Goldyn v. Hayes, 444 F.3d 1062 (9th Cir. 2006) (granting federal habeas corpus relief).

35 *See* State v. Hogrefe, 557 N.W.2d 871 (Iowa 1996) (postdated check which check writer told payee was not presently cashable may be promise with present intent not to perform, supporting

tenses,[36] which may be applied to NSF checks. The requirements of these statutes may be more flexible than those of dishonored check statutes, but generally require some evidence of a promise made with the present intent not to perform.

9.2.5 Dishonored Checks and Bankruptcy

A creditor may seek to use a dishonored check prosecution to gain an advantage in a consumer's bankruptcy. The bankruptcy automatic stay generally does not affect a criminal prosecution.[37] Other sections of the Bankruptcy Code,

larceny by deception conviction when check writer was in financial trouble, but conviction reversed on other grounds); Crawley v. Commonwealth, 2003 WL 22149310 (Ky. Sept. 19, 2003) (affirming theft by deception conviction; failure to cover within ten days was sufficient; defendant used credit card "courtesy checks" and testified that he had checked with credit card issuer before doing so); Tanner v. Commonwealth, 2008 WL 344191 (Ky. Ct. App. Feb. 8, 2008) (affirming theft by deception conviction when defendant member of limited liability corporation signed blank checks to be filled out and used by another member); Commonwealth v. Kaplan, 877 N.E.2d 642 (Mass. App. Ct. 2007) (although mere failure to make good on commercial transaction does not establish the criminal intent required for larceny, sufficiently shown when retailer stopped payment on check to wholesaler, sold the goods to innocent purchasers, promised to cover, but did not); State v. Widener, 2007 WL 293133 (Ohio Ct. App. Feb. 2, 2007) (affirming larceny by deception conviction arising from nonpayment of payday loan; consumer's no contest plea precludes review of merits other than denial of initial motion to dismiss); State v. Bound, 2004 WL 2806430 (Ohio Ct. App. Dec. 1, 2004) (evidence sufficient to sustain dishonored check and theft by deception convictions based on credit application and purchase of goods on credit during time defendant was passing bad checks); State v. Farah, 2003 WL 22511079 (Ohio Ct. App. Nov. 6, 2003) (defendant could be convicted of misdemeanor theft even after acquittal for larceny by check; gave blank check on closed account as security for loan of gaming chips, and left owing money); State v. Taylor, 2003 WL 366779 (Ohio Ct. App. Feb. 21, 2003) (larceny by deception shown in check kiting scheme: opening account with worthless check and drawing on it when funds become available before check dishonored); Ingram v. State, 2005 WL 16290 (Tex. App. Jan. 5, 2005) (evidence sufficient to sustain theft of services conviction based on NSF check: long period of negative balances before and after check date, check written so shortly before services rendered that payee could not discover it was bad, and account transfers suggested check kiting); Leon v. State, 102 S.W.3d 776 (Tex. App. 2003) (affirming conviction of chief executive officer of small company for theft by deception on basis of NSF company checks he allowed to be signed by another while he was ill; intent to deprive shown by fact that checks dishonored within thirty days and not paid within ten days after notice); *see also* United States v. Bistrian, 2005 WL 477998 (E.D. Pa. Mar. 1, 2005) (knowingly passing NSF check was "scheme to defraud" sufficient to sustain wire fraud conviction when checks were for entire purchase price of new Porsche or Mercedes); *cf.* State v. Henninger, 130 Idaho 638, 945 P.2d 864 (Ct. App. 1997) (theft by unauthorized control not shown when defendant told dealer he would have $5000 tomorrow, signed promissory note due in twenty-four hours, and drove off with truck, in which seller retained security interest, but if charge had been theft by false promise or deception, such a charge would be supported by lies told in persuading dealer to accept note). *But see* Brady v. State, 599 S.E.2d 313 (Ga. Ct. App. 2004) (conviction for theft by deception not supported by evidence when defendant told car dealer he would have funds in a few days and took truck, but later wrote an NSF check, because at time dealer parted with truck all the misrepresentations concerned future events); Young v. State, 594 S.E.2d 667 (Ga. Ct. App. 2004) (postdated NSF check insufficient to support theft by deception; distinguishing case in which check writer does not tell payee check is postdated, and lies about current state of bank account); Ellerbee v. State, 569 S.E.2d 902 (Ga. Ct. App. 2002) (reversing theft by deception conviction; wholesaler did not part with cars in reliance on false statement when failing used car business already possessed cars at time check was written; later promises to pay did not misrepresent any past or present fact; representation as to future insufficient); Mizioler v. State, 2003 WL 22023915 (Tex. App. Aug. 27, 2003) (reversing theft by deception conviction, because matter was "contractual dispute" and only evidence of deception was "failure to perform": during a "heated confrontation" after business hours, on lot which also contained car dealer's home, dealer gave angry customer a check for his money back, then stopped payment the next morning); State v. Braham, 567 S.E.2d 624 (W. Va. 2002) (postdated NSF check alone insufficient to support larceny by fraudulent scheme conviction; must show fraudulent intent at time check written; defendant should have been allowed to present evidence of his reasons for stopping payment).

36 State v. Rogers, 485 S.E.2d 619 (N.C. 1997) (finding writing of worthless check on closed account in exchange for property to be sufficient without more to support conviction for obtaining property by false pretenses); State v. Pardue, 624 S.E.2d 434 (N.C. Ct. App. 2006) (table) (text available at 2006 WL 91362) (" '[T]he writing and passing of a worthless check in exchange for property, standing alone, is sufficient to uphold a conviction for obtaining property under false pretenses.' " (citations omitted)). *But see* Shropshire v. Commonwealth, 577 S.E.2d 521 (Va. Ct. App. 2003) (reversing larceny by false pretenses conviction when defendant took possession of car before he paid with dishonored check and returned car at some point after check dishonored; no evidence of sales contract, note, etcetera, to indicate that seller parted with title; "mere possession" was not sufficient).

37 *See In re* Swain, 325 B.R. 264 (B.A.P. 8th Cir. 2005) (neither creditor nor prosecutor violated automatic stay or discharge injunction when debtor covered a dishonored check in response to a notice from the prosecutor shortly before filing for bankruptcy—but then trustee filed a preference action requiring the creditor to turn the debtor's payment over to bankruptcy estate; creditor notified prosecutor, who went forward with criminal charges; creditor's notice to prosecutor not "action to collect a debt" and prosecutor not agent of creditor because not under creditor's control); Dovell v. Guernsey Bank, 2007 WL 2269839 (S.D. Ohio Aug. 9, 2007) (exception is absolute; bankruptcy court can not consider motivation behind criminal case); *In re* Pickett, 321 B.R. 663 (Bankr. D. Vt. 2005) (criminal prosecution for NSF check does not violate automatic stay or discharge injunction; provision of Bankruptcy Code making exception for criminal prosecution does not include exception for bad faith); *In re* Dennison, 321 B.R. 378 (Bankr. D. Conn. 2005) (automatic stay does not bar criminal prosecution for NSF check, even if intended to collect a debt; rejecting motivation

however, allow the court to distinguish between "true criminal prosecutions" and "debt collection actions in sheep's clothing," which may be enjoined to promote bankruptcy's goals of evenhanded treatment for all creditors and a breathing space for debtors.[38]

Another exception to the automatic stay allows negotiation of checks which were delivered prepetition.[39]

Bankruptcy courts differ on the question of whether a payday lender's presentation of a postdated check for payment violates the automatic stay.[40] But even if the postpetition presentment of a check and the creditor's receipt of funds from the debtor's account fall within this exception to the automatic stay, the debtor should be able to recover the funds as the postpetition transfer is avoidable under section 549 of the Bankruptcy Code.[41]

Creditors may also argue that an NSF check is a fraudulent misrepresentation, which makes a debt nondischargeable if the creditor proves fraud in a timely action brought in the bankruptcy case. Many decisions however find factual grounds to deny nondischargeability.[42]

9.2.6 Diversion Programs

The use of taxpayers' resources and the state's criminal powers to collect civil debts has been criticized on public policy and constitutional grounds.[43] As one court noted,

test of earlier cases); *In re* Bibbs, 282 B.R. 876 (Bankr. E.D. Ark. 2002) (bankruptcy automatic stay does not bar criminal proceeding even if underlying purpose was debt collection; allowing probation revocation in multiple dishonored check cases to go forward); *In re* Byrd, 256 B.R. 246 (Bankr. E.D.N.C. 2000) (expressing reservations about Nevada's "diversion program," but holding that prosecution to collect dishonored checks written to a casino is unaffected by automatic stay or bankruptcy discharge); *cf. In re* Dorsey, 373 B.R. 528 (Bankr. N.D. Ohio 2007) (criminal prosecution did not violate automatic stay; creditor's motive is relevant, but debtor here did not meet burden of showing that payday lender's primary motive was debt collection, as it routinely prosecuted NSF checks to deter this conduct).

38 *In re* Reisen, 2004 WL 764628 (Bankr. N.D. Iowa Mar. 4, 2004) (concluding that dishonored check prosecution may be enjoined if "principal motivation" is collection of prepetition debt, but no automatic stay violation here when retailer's clerical error prevented collector from learning of bankruptcy); Shepard v. Piggly Wiggly (*In re* Shepard), 2000 WL 33743081 (Bankr. M.D. Ga. Jan. 6, 2000) (prosecution may be enjoined if brought in bad faith, and it would be no defense to criminal prosecution that it was brought for the purpose of collecting a debt; enjoining criminal prosecution for dishonored check to retailer); *see also In re* Perry, 312 B.R. 717 (Bankr. M.D. Ga. 2004) (criminal prosecution will be enjoined only if brought in bad faith, and "it would be no defense to the criminal prosecution that it was brought for the purpose of collecting a debt"; here prosecution not enjoined because no evidence that "debt collection defense" unavailable to contractor accused of misappropriating funds given him by home owners to pay subcontractors); *cf. In re* Batt, 322 B.R. 776 (Bankr. N.D. Ohio 2005) (reluctantly recognizing "motivation test" but noting strong presumption in favor of criminal prosecution; there was a heavy burden on debtor to show improper motive for prosecution; improper motive not shown when creditor testified that its usual practice was to prosecute those who gave NSF checks). *But see In re* Simonini, 2003 WL 21500197 (4th Cir. July 1, 2003) (automatic stay inapplicable regardless of motive, and district court did not have power to enjoin prosecution); Dovell v. Guernsey Bank, 2007 WL 2269839 (S.D. Ohio Aug. 9, 2007) (vacating injunction against criminal prosecution; exception of criminal prosecutions from automatic stay is absolute).

39 11 U.S.C. § 362(b)(11); *see In re* Roete, 936 F.2d 963 (7th Cir. 1991).

40 *Permitted*: *In re* Thomas, 428 F.3d 735 (8th Cir. 2005) (automatic stay makes exception for presentment of negotiable instrument); *In re* Blasco, 352 B.R. 888 (Bankr. N.D. Ala. 2006) (payday lender's attempt to cash check after petition date not stay violation; check was negotiable instrument); *In re* Mehaffey, 2005 WL 831805 (Bankr. N.D. Iowa Apr. 8, 2005) (same).

Forbidden: *In re* Wolfe, 2005 WL 579690 (Bankr. N.D. Iowa Feb. 2, 2005) (willful violation of stay); *see also In re* Hagood, 2007 WL 772556 (Bankr. N.D. Ala. Mar. 9, 2007) (payday lender violated discharge injunction by cashing check given prepetition to secure debt that was discharged in bankruptcy).

41 *See In re* Thomas, 311 B.R. 75 (Bankr. W.D. Mo. 2004), *aff'd*, 428 F.3d 735 (8th Cir. 2005); *In re* Franklin, 254 B.R. 718 (Bankr. W.D. Tenn. 2000); *see also* National Consumer Law Center, Consumer Bankruptcy Law and Practice § 10.4.2.6.6 (8th ed. 2006 and Supp.).

42 *See In re* Hermes, 340 B.R. 369 (Bankr. C.D. Ill. 2006) (presumption of fraud under Illinois law rebutted by farmer's testimony that he expected check to be covered by his line of credit; debt was dischargeable); *In re* Bullock, 317 B.R. 885 (Bankr. M.D. Ala. 2004) (debtor gave automobile dealer two checks and told him to hold them for two weeks; dishonor of one check was not sufficient to show "intentional misrepresentation of past or existing fact" sufficient to deny discharge; promissory fraud was not shown either as it requires the lack of intent to pay at time; awarding attorney fees to debtor because dealer's position "not substantially justified"); *In re* Barsamian, 318 B.R. 508 (Bankr. W.D. Wis. 2004) (writing NSF check is not, without more, a false representation); *In re* Sanchez, 277 B.R. 904 (Bankr. N.D. Ill. 2002) (NSF check written by small business and failure to cover upon demand not sufficient to make out prima facie case that debt resulted from false representation; nonpayment may have been "the unexpected result of the financial difficulties that drove the debtor to bankruptcy"); *In re* Greer, 2002 WL 1558544 (Bankr. D. Colo. July 12, 2002) (landlord's nondischargeability complaint not substantially justified when tenant told landlord that check would bounce, but that he would be able to cover it later, yet landlord presented it immediately); *cf. In re* Dansereau, 274 B.R. 686 (Bankr. W.D. Tex. 2002) (payday lender subject to Rule 11 sanctions and reduction of claims to $1 for repeatedly asserting that its NSF checks were priority claims, when reasonable inquiry would show they were not). *But see In re* Bell, 2006 WL 3082110 (Bankr. D. Kan. Oct. 30, 2006) (state default judgment for treble damages on NSF check nondischargeable as "actual fraud").

43 *See, e.g.*, State v. Henninger, 130 Idaho 638, 945 P.2d 864 (Ct. App. 1997) (strong public policy against using criminal court to collect civil debt); J. Potuto, *And Mussolini Had the Trains Running on Time: A Review of the Bad Check Offense and the Law Enforcement Debt Collector*, 65 Neb. L. Rev. 242 (1986); *see also* Victory Distributors, Inc. v. Ayer Div. of the Dist. Ct. Dep't, 755 N.E.2d 273 (Mass. 2001) (upholding small town

"[T]he justice of the peace . . . is not a collection bureau. If he acts as a collection bureau, or if he utilizes the criminal processes of the court to collect a civil debt, he is perverting the functions of this small claims court and bringing disrespect upon the entire judicial process."[44]

A particularly questionable practice is the use of privately operated diversion programs to process dishonored checks for prosecutors' offices. One program sent out letters saying that a criminal complaint had been received—even though no complaint had issued and the prosecutor had not evaluated the case—and informing the consumer that payment of the check, a fee, and a program fee for an educational class would prevent prosecution.[45] A court found this program to be a debt collector within the meaning of the Fair Debt Collection Practices Act (FDCPA), and found the use of sheriff's letterhead to be a violation of the FDCPA and state law.[46]

In another case the Eleventh Circuit reversed a trial court's holding that this program was an arm of the state, and thus immune to FDCPA claims. The appellate court noted that (1) the state's attorney's office exercised very little control over the program's operations, that is, did not screen cases before letters were sent, (2) that the program was not paid for by state funds, and (3) that the state would not be liable for judgments against the program.[47]

Amendments made to the FDCPA in 2006 provide a exemption for check diversion debt collectors who meet its requirements.[48] One court has also held that the program does not violate the Due Process or Equal Protection provisions of the United States Constitution.[49]

9.3 Civil Dishonored Check Statutes

Many states have enacted civil dishonored check laws, which encourage bounty hunters by providing for attorney fees and multiple or inflated damages.[50] Many of these

---

district court's refusal to issue criminal complaints for large retailer's NSF checks, citing lack of resources and the inappropriateness of using criminal court to collect civil debts).

44 State *ex rel.* Richardson v. Edgeworth, 214 So. 2d 579, 588 (Miss. 1968) (wrongful death claim alleging that gross abuse of criminal process to collect very small checks was proximate cause of consumer's suicide); *see also In re* Frederic-Braud, 973 So. 2d 712 (La. 2008) (suspending justice of the peace for, *inter alia*, allowing constable to use her signature stamp on dishonored check notices, and to demand unauthorized fees and misrepresent existence of arrest warrants; justice "permitted her judicial authority to be used in an extra-judicial manner"); *In re* Fusilier, 837 So. 2d 1257 (La. 2003) (suspending judge for activities creating "an appearance of impropriety" and "abandoning his role as neutral arbiter," including his dishonored check program; by working for complainant merchants judge created situation in which "his impartiality could reasonably be questioned" when he presided over criminal trial; also procedural shortcuts created risk that innocent consumers would be prosecuted).

45 Liles v. Am. Corrective Counseling Services, 131 F. Supp. 2d 1114 (S.D. Iowa 2001); *see also* National Consumer Law Center, Fair Debt Collection § 1.5.2 (6th ed. 2008).

46 Gradisher v. Check Enforcement Unit, 210 F. Supp. 2d 907 (W.D. Mich. 2002) (partial summary judgment for consumer class), *related opinion at* Gradisher v. County of Muskegon, 255 F. Supp. 2d 720 (W.D. Mich. 2003) (dismissing due process claims raised in separate suit), *aff'd*, 108 Fed. Appx. 388 (6th Cir. 2004) (table); *see also* Passa v. City of Columbus, 2006 WL 642492 (S.D. Ohio Mar. 9, 2006) (finding named plaintiffs to have standing to bring FDCPA, UDAP, and other claims against payday lenders who use diversion program), *later decision at* 2007 WL 3125130 (S.D. Ohio Oct. 24, 2007) (city is debt collector within meaning of FDCPA), *further decision at* 2008 WL 687168 (S.D. Ohio Mar. 11, 2008) (confirming arbitration award dismissing FDCPA and UDAP claims against lender); Liles v. Am. Corrective Counseling Services, 131 F. Supp. 2d 1114 (S.D. Iowa 2001) (denying summary judgment; issue of material fact whether program was a collector under FDCPA or Iowa debt collection statute); *In re* Reisen, 2004 WL 764628 (Bankr. N.D. Iowa Mar. 4, 2004) (diversion program was private collector, not instrumentality of government); *cf. In re* Simonini, 282 B.R. 604 (W.D.N.C. 2002) (enjoining criminal prosecution; purpose of Nevada's dishonored check diversion program is debt collection), *vacated on other grounds*, 69 Fed. Appx. 169 (4th Cir. 2003) (district court did not have power to enjoin prosecution). *But see* Silvernail v. County of Kent, 385 F.3d 601 (6th Cir. 2004) (diversion program not a denial of due process).

47 Rosario v. Am. Corrective Counseling Services, 506 F.3d 1039 (11th Cir. 2007).

48 *See* National Consumer Law Center, Fair Debt Collection § 4.3.12 (6th ed. 2008).

49 Hamilton v. Am. Corrective Counseling Services, 2006 WL 3332828 (N.D. Ind. Nov. 14, 2006).

50 The following is a list of civil dishonored check laws. Practitioners should use this list only as a starting point in researching the legality of a claim for a civil dishonored check penalty. Authority for a charge is sometimes hidden in a criminal statute or in the state's commercial code.

ALABAMA: Ala. Code § 6-5-285.

ALASKA: Alaska Stat. § 09.68.115.

ARIZONA: Ariz. Rev. Stat. Ann. § 12-671.

ARKANSAS: Ark. Code Ann. §§ 21-6-411 (fees collected by prosecuting attorneys), 4-60-103 (civil dishonored check remedies); *see also* Ark. Code Ann. §§ 5-37-302 (criminal offense), 5-37-303 (notice requirements), 5-37-305 (penalties), 5-37-306 (criminal offense).

CALIFORNIA: Cal. Civil Code § 1719 (West) (requires notice to check writer); Cal. Fin. Code § 23035(b), (c)(6) (West) (forbidding use of criminal process or Cal. Civ. Code § 1719 (West) for payday loans); *see also* Cal. Penal Code §§ 476aa (restitution), 1001.60 to 1001.67 (diversion program) (West); Palmer v. Stassinos, 348 F. Supp. 2d 1070 (N.D. Cal. 2004) (interpreting Cal. Civ. Code § 1719 (West) as not allowing interest).

COLORADO: Colo. Rev. Stat. § 13-21-109.

CONNECTICUT: Conn. Gen. Stat. § 52-565a.

DELAWARE: Del. Code Ann. tit. 6, § 1301A.

DISTRICT OF COLUMBIA: D.C. Code § 28-3152.

FLORIDA: Fla. Stat. § 68.065; *see* F & A Dairy Products, Inc. v. Imperial Food Distributors, Inc., 798 So. 2d 803 (Fla. Dist. Ct. App. 2001) (when check writer presented no evidence that nonpayment resulted from economic hardship, nor that treble damages would result in economic hardship, court must award

statutes provide for a flat fee even in the absence of a contractual basis for the charge.[51]

---

treble damages pursuant to civil dishonored check statute); *see also* Fla. Stat. § 832.08 (diversion program).

GEORGIA: Ga. Code Ann. §§ 13-6-15 (damages for writing dishonored checks), 16-9-20(i), (j) (service charges; part of criminal statute); *see also* Ga. Code Ann. § 16-9-21 (criminal statute).

GUAM: Guam Code Ann. tit. 20, § 6104.

HAWAII: Haw. Rev. Stat. § 490:3-506; *see also* Haw. Rev. Stat. § 480F-4 (payday lender not allowed to use this procedure).

IDAHO: Idaho Code Ann. §§ 1-2301A, 28-22-105.

ILLINOIS: 720 Ill. Comp. Stat. § 5/17-1a; 810 Ill. Comp. Stat. § 5/3-806.

INDIANA: Ind. Code §§ 34-24-3-1, 26-2-7-5, 26-2-7-6; *see also* Ind. Code §§ 35-43-5-5 (criminal statute; provides for service charges), 26-1-3.1-502.5 (surcharge after dishonor), 24-4.5-3-202(f) (U.C.C.C. provision limiting charges).

IOWA: Iowa Code § 554.3513; *see also* Iowa Code § 625.22 (costs and attorney fees in action to recover for dishonored check).

KANSAS: Kan. Stat. Ann. §§ 60-2610, 60-2611; *see also* Kan. Stat. Ann. §§ 16a-2-501 (certain NSF charges permitted by U.C.C.C.), 21-3707 (criminal statute, but provides that payment of service charges after notice will prevent prosecution).

KENTUCKY: Ky. Rev. Stat. Ann. § 514.040(1)(e) (West); *see also* Ky. Rev. Stat. Ann. § 514.040(4)–(5) (West) (criminal statute).

LOUISIANA: La. Rev. Stat. Ann. §§ 9:2782 to 9:2782.2; *see* Cole Builders L.L.C. v. JJ Properties of W. Monroe, L.L.C., 961 So. 2d 569 (La. Ct. App. 2007) (award of double damages, costs, and attorney fees is mandatory when requirements of civil dishonored check statute are met); *see also* La. Rev. Stat. Ann. § 14:71 (criminal statute providing for mandatory restitution).

MAINE: Me. Rev. Stat. Ann. tit. 14, §§ 6071–6073.

MARYLAND: Md. Code Ann., Com. Law §§ 15-802 to 15-803 (West).

MASSACHUSETTS: Mass. Gen. Laws ch. 93, § 40A.

MICHIGAN: Mich. Comp. Laws § 600.2952; *see also* Mich. Comp. Laws §§ 600.2953 (retail fraud), 750.131 to 750.134 (criminal NSF check statutes).

MINNESOTA: Minn. Stat. § 604.113; *see also* Minn. Stat. §§ 609.535 (criminal statute, but provides notice and opportunity to pay to avoid prosecution), 628.69 (diversion program).

MISSISSIPPI: Miss. Code Ann. § 11-7-12; *see also* Miss. Code Ann. §§ 97-19-55 to 97-19-81 (criminal NSF check statutes).

MISSOURI: Mo. Rev. Stat. § 570.123; *see also* Mo. Rev. Stat. §§ 408.505(8) (check for payday loan not subject to criminal prosecution unless written on account closed by consumer before check was written, or consumer stops payment), 570.120 (criminal statute, but also provides that recipient may, without seeking criminal charges, collect a service fee).

MONTANA: Mont. Code Ann. § 27-1-717; *see also* Mont. Code Ann. § 31-1-722 (payday lender may not seek damages under section 27-1-717).

NEBRASKA: Neb. Rev. Stat. § 28-611 (criminal statute; provides for fees and requires notice to check writer).

NEVADA: Nev. Rev. Stat. §§ 205.0832(1)(i), 205.132 to 205.134, 205.380 (criminal statutes; provide for notice to check writer), 205.466 (restitution/diversion program).

NEW HAMPSHIRE: N.H. Rev. Stat. Ann. §§ 544-B:1 to 544-B:3, 358-C:5 (allows a $25 check collection charge in consumer credit transactions); *see also* N.H. Rev. Stat. Ann. §§ 507:7, 638:4 (criminal statute providing for mandatory restitution, including costs and protest fee).

NEW JERSEY: N.J. Stat. Ann. § 2A:32A-1 (West).

NEW MEXICO: N.M. Stat. § 56-14-1.

NEW YORK: N.Y. Gen. Oblig. Law §§ 11-104, 11-105, 5-328 (McKinney) (processing fee by holder of dishonored check); *see also* N.Y. Penal Law §§ 190.00 to 190.15 (McKinney) (criminal statute).

NORTH CAROLINA: N.C. Gen. Stat. § 6-21.3; *see also* N.C. Gen. Stat. §§ 14-107.2 (worthless check diversion program), 25-3-505 (evidence of dishonor), 25-3-506 (collection of processing fee for returned checks).

NORTH DAKOTA: N.D. Cent. Code §§ 6-08-16 to 6-08-16.2 (includes both criminal penalties and provisions for civil action and penalties).

OHIO: Ohio Rev. Code Ann. §§ 2307.60, 2307.61 (West) (civil action for "anyone injured in person or property by a criminal act," including a theft offense); *see also* Ohio Rev. Code Ann. §§ 1315.40, 1315.41 (West) (limiting check collection charges of check cashers and prohibiting damages under section 2307.61).

OKLAHOMA: Okla. Stat. tit. 12, § 937 (attorney fees in actions to collect on NSF checks).

OREGON: Or. Rev. Stat. § 30.701.

PENNSYLVANIA: 42 Pa. Cons. Stat. § 8304.

RHODE ISLAND: R.I. Gen. Laws §§ 6-42-3, 6-42-4 (defenses).

SOUTH CAROLINA: S.C. Code Ann. § 34-11-75; *see also* S.C. Code Ann. §§ 34-11-60, 34-11-70, 34-11-80 to 34-11-100 (criminal statutes).

SOUTH DAKOTA: S.D. Codified Laws §§ 21-57-1 to 21-57-7; *see also* S.D. Codified Laws § 21-1-14. Note that section 21-57-2 prohibits holder or assignee from asserting liability under section 21-57-1 unless a court has so ruled, and that section 21-57-3 includes significant defenses.

TENNESSEE: Tenn. Code Ann. §§ 47-29-101 to 47-29-103.

TEXAS: Tex. Bus. & Com. Code Ann. § 3.506 (Vernon) (processing fee by holder of dishonored check); Tex. Crim. Proc. Code Ann. §§ 102.007 (fee for collecting and processing sight order), 102.0071 (justice court dishonored check collection fee) (Vernon); *see also* Tex. Penal Code Ann. § 31.06 (Vernon) (presumption for theft by check).

UTAH: Utah Code Ann. §§ 7-15-1, 7-15-2, 7-23-105 (treble damages not available to payday lender; other section 7-15-1 remedies are); *see* Checkrite Recovery Services v. King, 52 P.3d 1265 (Utah 2002) (construing Utah statute to allow check collector to recover costs of collection including attorney fees, not just court costs, after filing suit on dishonored check).

VERMONT: Vt. Stat. Ann. tit. 9, § 2311.

VIRGINIA: Va. Code Ann. §§ 8.01-27.1 (additional recovery in certain civil actions concerning checks), 8.01-27.2 (civil recovery), 6.1-118.1 (recovery of costs); *see also* Va. Code Ann. §§ 18.2-181 to 18.2-185 (criminal statutes).

WASHINGTON: Wash. Rev. Code §§ 62A.3-515, 31.45.082 (payday lender may recover collection costs, pursuant to section 62A.3-515, but not attorney fees or other interest or damages).

WEST VIRGINIA: W. Va. Code § 55-16-1.

WISCONSIN: Wis. Stat. § 943.245.

WYOMING: Wyo. Stat. Ann. § 1-1-115.

51 *See, e.g.*, N.H. Rev. Stat. Ann. § 358-C:5 ($25 check collection charge by a creditor or debt collector permitted "unless otherwise expressly authorized by written agreement with the consumer"); Ohio Rev. Code Ann. § 1319.16 (West) (permitting

Civil dishonored check statutes are strictly construed, and minor or technical errors may suffice to defeat recovery.[52] They may apply only to NSF checks, not checks on which the consumer stops payment, or the statute may impose additional preconditions to recovery for a stop payment.[53] The debtor's attorney should also investigate whether the payment method the debtor used is covered by the statute, as some civil dishonored check statutes may not be written to encompass certain electronic payment methods. Courts have rejected collector attempts to apply civil theft[54] and shoplifting[55] statutes to NSF check cases.

The relationship between the civil dishonored check law and criminal law remedies will vary from state to state. The statute may bar a civil dishonored check claim if the check writer has already paid the face amount of the check plus any penalties required by the criminal dishonored check statute.[56]

Some civil dishonored check statutes exclude postdated checks.[57] In addition, states that specifically regulate payday lending often restrict the use of criminal or civil dishonored

---

collection agency to impose check collection charge of $30 or 10% of amount of the check, whichever is greater, plus the amount of any charge imposed by the financial institution on the holder of the check); *see also* Int'l Bureau of Fraud Control, Ltd. v. Clayton, 188 Ill. App. 3d 703, 135 Ill. Dec. 920, 544 N.E.2d 416 (1989) (collector of NSF checks was governed by state statute limiting fees of collection agencies to $10 in non-litigation collection); Merrel v. Research & Data Inc., 3 Kan. App. 2d 48, 589 P.2d 120 (1979) (noting that state dishonored check criminal statute authorizes $3 service charge for dishonored checks, but $5 fee for a collection agency collecting dishonored checks was justified; signs disclosing the fee in the stores when the checks were cashed created a valid contract).

52 The Group, Inc. v. Spanier, 940 P.2d 1120 (Colo. Ct. App. 1997) (reversing award of treble damages to collector; collector must comply strictly with civil dishonored check statute; notice was defective when it sought attorney fees when statute only allowed "costs of collection" if check "assigned for collection to a person licensed as a collection agency"); Stadler v. Devito, 931 P.2d 573 (Colo. Ct. App. 1996) (strictly construing notice requirements of Colorado statute; notice insufficient when creditor did not make further efforts to find correct address when certified mail sent to incorrect address was returned "unknown"; creditor acted unlawfully in proceeding with treble damages claim); Commercial Med. Accounts v. Mackintosh, 662 N.E.2d 659 (Ind. Ct. App. 1996) (multiple damages and attorney fees were properly denied under civil dishonored check when plaintiff failed to prove it sent notice of dishonor, a statutory requirement); Royal Air, Inc. v. Pronto Delivery Serv., Inc., 917 So. 2d 1197 (La. Ct. App. 2005) (La. Rev. Stat. Ann. § 9:2782.2, which provides double damages for wrongful stop payment, is penal and must be strictly construed; it requires showing of intent to defraud or absence of "justifiable dispute" as to the obligation and multiple damages properly denied when dispute was justifiable as customer stopped payment when repaired airplane malfunctioned during test flight); Wright & Moreno L.L.C. v. Clement, 891 So. 2d 704 (La. Ct. App. 2004) (strictly construing statute providing multiple damages for wrongful stop payment to be inapplicable to NSF check); Redden v. Ripley, 862 So. 2d 469 (La. Ct. App. 2003) (civil dishonored check law does not apply to checks drawn on "uncollected" rather than "insufficient" funds; penal statute, narrowly construed; bank negligently failed to credit cashier's check deposited by check writer before writing check); TeleRecovery of La., Inc. v. Rayborn, 814 So. 2d 688 (La. Ct. App. 2002) (denying multiple damages because creditor failed to comply with notice requirements); Sanders v. Mitchell, 810 So. 2d 1276 (La. Ct. App. 2002) (denying multiple damages and attorney fees; dishonored check statute is harsh remedy and must be strictly complied with; notice letter gave debtor fifteen days instead of fifteen business days, and failed to set forth statutory penalties); F. Christiana & Co. v. Matt's Grocery, Inc. No. 2, 674 So. 2d 419 (La. Ct. App. 1996) (Louisiana statute that allowed attorney fees in dishonored check cases is "penal" and must be strictly construed; failure to comply exactly with statute barred the award of statutory attorney fees); *see also* Collection Bureau Services, Inc. v. Morrow, 87 P.3d 1024 (Mont. 2004) (collector can not seek penalties under civil dishonored check statute after debtor has defaulted on payment plan without sending new demand letter; FDCPA violation to demand statutory damages without new notice); Rufener v. Lunau, 2004 WL 639851 (Ohio Ct. App. Mar. 19, 2004) (denying statutory damages and attorney fees; notice provision of demand letter not conspicuous; same typeface as rest of letter). *But see* Charles v. Check Rite, Ltd., 1998 U.S. Dist. LEXIS 22512 (D. Ariz. Dec. 14, 1998) (adopting strained interpretation of state dishonored check law to allow collector to demand penalty before complying with statutory notice requirements); *cf.* Fisk v. Basile, 2001 WL 1159602 (Conn. Super. Ct. Aug. 28, 2001) (requiring clear and convincing evidence for treble damages under civil theft statute; declining to award treble damages because of insufficient proof that debtor did not intend to pay back loan or cover checks).

53 Francis v. Snyder, 389 F. Supp. 2d 1034 (N.D. Ill. 2005) (collector's threat to use Illinois statute that did not apply to stop payments was threat of action that could not legally be taken); Jenkins v. Union Corp., 999 F. Supp. 1120 (N.D. Ill. 1998) (when Illinois law permitted imposition of fee for NSF check but not for stop payment, collector's attempt to collect $25 fee for stop payment check was unauthorized); Uribe v. Correa, 862 So. 2d 883 (Fla. Dist. Ct. App. 2003) (civil dishonored check statute applies to checks on which check writer stops payment only if intent to defraud shown; trial court must resolve allegation that payee obtained check by fraud before it can order penalties under civil dishonored check statute); Pro Car Care, Inc. v. Johnson, 118 P.3d 815 (Or. Ct. App. 2005) (civil dishonored check statute applies only if payment stopped "without reasonable cause"; not shown when customer reasonably believed she had reasonable cause when vehicle failed to start shortly after leaving repair shop, even though problem turned out not to be repair shop's fault).

54 *See* Rocano v. Harris, 2007 WL 1827955 (Conn. Super. Ct. June 1, 2007) (denying multiple damages under civil theft statute because issuing dishonored check does not amount to larceny).

55 *See* Johnson v. Riddle, 305 F.3d 1107 (10th Cir. 2002) (FDCPA case; Utah courts will not apply civil shoplifting statute to NSF checks, because specific Utah statute dealing with dishonored checks limits penalty to $15).

56 *See* Dobbs v. State, 229 S.W.3d 651 (Mo. Ct. App. 2007) (payee of dishonored check may recover under either civil or criminal statute, but not both).

57 *See* Nance v. Ulferts, 282 F. Supp. 2d 912 (N.D. Ind. 2003) (Indiana's civil dishonored check statute explicitly excludes postdated checks; FDCPA violation when payday lender sought treble damages under that statute).

check laws by lenders, and may require that borrowers be informed of this restriction.[58] Regardless of the existence of a specific statutory exemption, a debtor who gives a postdated check to a payday lender does not have intent to defraud, which many civil dishonored check statutes require.[59]

Some courts have found authority for service charges on returned checks in a provision of Article 2 of the Uniform Commercial Code (UCC)[60] that allows a person in the position of the seller to recover incidental damages for nonpayment of the price of goods.[61] Courts that are less anxious to find authority for returned check charges correctly hold that UCC Article 3, not Article 2, applies to collection of dishonored checks that have been sold to a third party.[62] Another justification that some courts have accepted is that signs posted at the merchant's place of business can create an implied contract to pay a fee for a dishonored check.[63]

Because of the growth of the debt buying industry, collection attempts may continue on a dishonored check many years after the check was written. UCC Article 3 requires

58 *See, e.g.*, Cal. Fin. Code § 23036 (West) (forbidding both criminal prosecution and application of civil multiple damages law; borrower must be informed of this restriction); Haw. Rev. Stat. § 480F-4 (may not recover under civil multiple damages provision); Ind. Code § 24-4.5-7-406 ("small loan" statute; explicitly forbidding treble damages, attorney fees, prejudgment interest, or damages for dishonored checks "under any statute other than this chapter" and requiring that loan agreements conspicuously disclose this prohibition); Mont. Code Ann. § 31-1-722 (may recover $30 fee for NSF check, but may not recover under civil multiple damages provision); Ohio Rev. Code Ann. §§ 1315.40, 1315.41 (West) (limiting check collection charges and barring multiple damages under civil dishonored check statute); *see also* Payday Today, Inc. v. Indiana Dep't of Fin. Institutions, 2006 WL 148943 (N.D. Ind. Jan. 17, 2006) (upholding the constitutionality of small loan law that forbids payday lenders to threaten or bring criminal charges or contract for attorney fees and limits the fees they can charge for dishonored checks); Neidow v. Cash in a Flash/Merrillville, 841 N.E.2d 649 (Ind. Ct. App. 2006) (denying multiple damages for default judgment against consumer who wrote check on closed account); Cash in a Flash, Inc./Hobart v. Hoffman, 841 N.E.2d 644 (Ind. Ct. App. 2006) (same); Payday Today, Inc. v. McCullough, 841 N.E.2d 638 (Ind. Ct. App. 2006) (to recover multiple damages and attorney fees under dishonored check or civil theft statute, payday lender must show either fraud on a financial institution, defined to require fraudulent intent at the time check was written, or common law fraud; fraud not shown as customer stopped payment on checks given as security for loan).

59 Jones v. Kunin, 2000 WL 3442107 (S.D. Ill. May 1, 2000); *see also* Nance v. Ulferts, 282 F. Supp. 2d 912 (N.D. Ind. 2003) (Indiana's civil dishonored check statute explicitly excludes postdated checks; FDCPA violation when payday lender sought treble damages under that statute; no claim under civil theft statute when consumer failed to allege pecuniary loss). *But see* Montclair v. L.O.I., Inc., 246 Fed. Appx. 535 (9th Cir. 2007) (collection agency-assignee of payday loan check can seek $500 penalty under civil dishonored check law; provisions denying penalty to payday lender licensees not applicable, because agency not a licensee); *cf.* Smith v. Cash Store Mgmt., Inc., 195 F.3d 325 (7th Cir. 1999) (opining, in context of Truth in Lending issue, that payday lender could seek remedies under civil dishonored check statute that allows interest, costs and collection expenses); Thompson v. Adcox, 63 S.W.3d 783 (Tenn. Ct. App. 2001) (postdated check becomes check, for purposes of civil dishonored check statute, on postdated date, even though criminal prosecution would not be allowed).

60 U.C.C. § 2-710.

61 *See* Freyermuth v. Credit Bureau Services, 248 F.3d 767 (8th Cir. 2001); Tuttle v. Equifax Check Services, 190 F.3d 9 (2d Cir. 1999) ($20 service charge); Martsolf v. JBC Legal Group, 2008 WL 275719 (M.D. Pa. Jan. 30, 2008) (U.C.C. permits assignee to demand $30 incidental damages); Abels v. JBC Legal Group, 434 F. Supp. 2d 763 (N.D. Cal. 2006) (if assignee acquired all payee's rights in check, it can seek U.C.C. Article 2 incidental damages in an amount that would be reasonable if imposed by original seller); Lee v. Sec. Check, L.L.C., 203 F. Supp. 2d 657 (N.D. Miss. 2000) ($30 service charge permitted as incidental damages under U.C.C. when collector put itself in position of seller); Charles v. Check Rite, Ltd., 1998 U.S. Dist. LEXIS 22512 (D. Ariz. Dec. 14, 1998) ($25 fee was incidental damages under U.C.C. Article 2).

62 U.C.C. § 3-310(b)(3); U.C.C. § 3-310 cmt. 3 (a person other than the original seller who holds the check can only use U.C.C. Article 3 remedies); *see* Semper v. JBC Legal Group, 2005 WL 2172377 (W.D. Wash. Sept. 6, 2005) (law firm that purchased dishonored check debts for purpose of collection was not "seller" under U.C.C. Article 2, so was not entitled to incidental damages, and its demand for these damages violated FDCPA); Ballard v. Equifax Check Serv., 27 F. Supp. 2d 1201 (E.D. Cal. 1998) (only seller, not check guarantee service, can claim U.C.C. Article 2 incidental damages [note that California has since enacted statutory authority for $25 to $35 charges]); People *ex rel.* Spitzer v. Boyajian Law Offices, Prof'l Corp., 851 N.Y.S.2d 72 (Sup. Ct. 2007) (table) (text available at 2007 WL 3118767) (debt buyers could not claim U.C.C. damages, as they did not sell goods nor incur the kind of incidental damages, such as stopping delivery or caring for goods, contemplated by U.C.C. Article 2); *cf.* Newman v. Checkrite Cal., Inc., 912 F. Supp. 1354, 1368 (E.D. Cal. 1995) (finding it unnecessary to reach issue). *But see* Abels v. JBC Legal Group, 434 F. Supp. 2d 763 (N.D. Cal. 2006) (distinguishing *Ballard*; if assignee acquired all payee's rights in check, it can seek U.C.C. Article 2 incidental damages in an amount that would be reasonable if imposed by original seller, as well as U.C.C. Article 3 damages).

63 *See* Merrel v. Research & Data Inc., 589 P.2d 120 (Kan. Ct. App. 1979) ($5 fee for a collection agency collecting dishonored checks was justified, even though it exceeded that allowed by state dishonored check criminal statute, when signs disclosing the fee in the stores where the checks were cashed created a valid contract); CybrCollect, Inc. v. North Dakota Dep't of Fin. Institutions, 703 N.W.2d 285 (N.D. 2005) (electronic collector of NSF checks could debit consumers' accounts for statutory fee, without written authorization, when amount of fee and fact it would be electronically debited were posted on signs at participating merchants). *But cf.* Irwin v. Mascott, 96 F. Supp. 2d 968 (N.D. Cal. 1999) (even if collector could show that consumers were properly notified of service charge, charge would be a penalty, not liquidated damages, and thus forbidden by California law); Ballard v. Equifax Check Services, 27 F. Supp. 2d 1201 (E.D. Cal. 1998) (rejecting argument that consumer had entered into contract for a dishonored check charge when there was no evidence of an oral agreement, a customary practice, or a sign posted).

suit to be brought on a check within three years after its dishonor or ten years after the date on the check, whichever occurs first.[64]

9.4 Affirmative Remedies for Abuse of Dishonored Check Laws

The overwhelming majority of courts that have addressed the issue have concluded that dishonored checks are "debts" as defined by the Fair Debt Collection Practices Act (FDCPA), that consumers who write such checks meet the FDCPA's definition of "consumer," and that collectors of such checks meet its definition of "collector."[65] These courts have rightly concluded that the FDCPA is not limited

64 U.C.C. § 3-118; *see also* Martsolf v. JBC Legal Group, 2008 WL 275719 (M.D. Pa. Jan. 30, 2008) (threatening suit on dishonored check after statute of limitations has expired is FDCPA violation); Dunaway v. JBC & Associates, Inc., 2005 WL 1529574 (E.D. Mich. June 20, 2005) (threatening time-barred suit or criminal prosecution on check is FDCPA violation).

65 Fed. Trade Comm'n v. Check Investors, Inc., 502 F.3d 159 (3d Cir. 2007) (checks are FDCPA debts, check writers are consumers, and collectors to whom NSF checks are assigned meet FDCPA definition of debt collector); Volden v. Innovative Fin. Sys., Inc., 440 F.3d 947 (8th Cir. 2006); Snow v. Jesse L. Riddle, Prof'l Corp., 143 F.3d 1350 (10th Cir. 1998) (dishonored check meets FDCPA definition of debt); Duffy v. Landberg, 133 F.3d 1120 (8th Cir. 1998) (dishonored check is a debt covered by the FDCPA; check guarantee company is debt collector); Charles v. Lundgren & Associates, Prof'l Corp., 119 F.3d 739 (9th Cir. 1997) (dishonored check is a debt covered by FDCPA); Radi v. Bennett Law Offices, 117 F.3d 1426 (9th Cir. 1997) (table) (text available at 1997 WL 367868) (check is a debt as defined by FDCPA); Draper v. CRA Sec. Sys., Inc., 117 F.3d 1424 (9th Cir. 1997) (table) (text available at 1997 WL 367869) (dishonored check is a debt within meaning of FDCPA); Ryan v. Wexler & Wexler, 113 F.3d 91 (7th Cir. 1997) (dishonored check is debt covered by FDCPA); Bass v. Stolper, Koritzinsky, Brewster & Neider, S.C., 111 F.3d 1322 (7th Cir. 1997) (check written to purchase consumer goods is debt as defined by FDCPA even though check was later dishonored for insufficient funds); Broadnax v. Greene Credit Serv., 106 F.3d 400 (6th Cir. 1997) (table) (text available at 1997 WL 14777) (FDCPA applies to collection activity on check issued to pay commercial obligation when payee altered it and cashed it at supermarket to buy groceries); Gary v. Goldman & Co., 180 F. Supp. 2d 668 (E.D. Pa. 2002) (dishonored check is debt under FDCPA); Wiegand v. JNR Adjustment Co., 2002 U.S. Dist. LEXIS 7292 (D. Minn. Apr. 22, 2002) (attempting to collect from the checking account owner the amounts of stolen, forged checks that were subsequently dishonored was attempting to collect a "debt" within the FDCPA, notwithstanding the underlying theft and the purported absence of a consensual transaction between the merchant and the putative debtor); Rogers v. Simmons, 2002 U.S. Dist. LEXIS 5457 (N.D. Ill. Mar. 28, 2002) (dishonored check written to casino was issued for purposes of entertainment and was a "debt" within FDCPA); Armstrong v. Rose Law Firm, Prof'l Ass'n, 2002 U.S. Dist. LEXIS 4039 (D. Minn. Mar. 7, 2002) (FDCPA contains no fraud or tort exception that would exclude dishonored check from definition of a "debt"); Winterstein v. CrossCheck, Inc., 149 F. Supp. 2d 466, 470 (N.D. Ill. 2001) (check guarantee company is debt collector under FDCPA); Gradisher v. Check Enforcement Unit, Inc., 133 F. Supp. 2d 988 (W.D. Mich. 2001) (collection of amount owed to another because of a dishonored check is debt collection under FDCPA); Connor v. Automated Accounts, Inc., 202 F.R.D. 265 (E.D. Wash. 2001) (there is no "fraud exception" to the FDCPA; it is irrelevant whether class members might have intended their checks to be dishonored); Irwin v. Mascott, 96 F. Supp. 2d 968 (N.D. Cal. 1999) (FDCPA covers dishonored checks, regardless of consumers' intent or knowledge when they wrote the checks); Caron v. Charles E. Maxwell, Prof'l Corp., 48 F. Supp. 2d 932 (D. Ariz. 1999) (FDCPA is not limited to collection of debts arising out of an offer or extension of credit and applies to collection of dishonored checks); Price v. Surety Acceptance Corp., 1999 U.S. Dist. LEXIS 22418 (D. Ariz. Aug. 13, 1999) (a check meets FDCPA definition of debt); Ballard v. Equifax Check Services, 27 F. Supp. 2d 1201 (E.D. Cal. 1998) (check authorization/guarantee company that purchases dishonored checks from merchants and then seeks to collect from consumers is a debt collector as defined by FDCPA); Ditty v. CheckRite, Ltd., 973 F. Supp. 1320 (D. Utah 1997) (dishonored check is a debt under FDCPA, and Act's coverage extends to abusive check collection practices); Ernst v. Jesse L. Riddle, Prof'l Corp., 964 F. Supp. 213 (M.D. La. 1997) (dishonored check for consumer goods is a debt under FDCPA); Johnson v. CRA Sec. Sys., 963 F. Supp. 859 (N.D. Cal. 1997) (dishonored check is a "debt" whose collection is subject to FDCPA); Byes v. Telecheck Recovery Serv., Inc., 1997 WL 736692 (E.D. La. Nov. 24, 1997) (claim on dishonored, allegedly forged check is covered by the FDCPA even though the plaintiff from whom the collector sought payment may not have been a consumer); Rosales v. Nat'l City Corp., 1997 U.S. Dist. LEXIS 23923 (D. Mass. Aug. 31, 1997) (dishonored check is a "debt" whose collection is subject to FDCPA); Fulcher v. Wexler, 1997 U.S. Dist. LEXIS 4229 (D. Conn. Feb. 24, 1997) (dishonored check for consumer goods is a debt covered by FDCPA); Ganske v. Checkrite, Ltd., 1997 WL 33810208 (W.D. Wis. Jan. 6, 1997) (dishonored check is a "debt" whose collection is subject to FDCPA); Narwick v. Wexler, 901 F. Supp. 1275 (N.D. Ill. 1995) (dishonored check for consumer items is a debt under FDCPA); Keele v. Wexler, 1995 WL 549048 (N.D. Ill. Sept. 12, 1995) (dishonored check is a "debt" whose collection is subject to FDCPA); *In re* Schrimpsher, 17 B.R. 999 (Bankr. N.D.N.Y. 1982) (collector of checks was a "debt collector"); *see also* John F. LeFevre, Att'y, Fed. Trade Comm'n, Informal Staff Letter to James A. Cathcart, Chief, California Bureau of Collection & Investigative Services (Aug. 24, 1981); John F. LeFevre, Att'y, Fed. Trade Comm'n, Informal Staff Letter to E.A. Fleming, Check-It Services (Apr. 1, 1982); John F. LeFevre, Att'y, Fed. Trade Comm'n, Informal Staff Letter to Paul H. Green, Chief Executive Officer, Cross Check, Inc. (Sept. 17, 1996); Laureen France, Investigative Specialist, Fed. Trade Comm'n, Informal Staff Letter to Judith Klayman, Evergreen Legal Services (Nov. 22, 1988) (check guarantee service covered). *But see* Krevsky v. Equifax Check Serv., Inc., 85 F. Supp. 2d 479 (M.D. Pa. 2000) (dishonored check is not a debt under the FDCPA because payment by check does not involve the extension of credit; overruled by Fed. Trade Comm'n v. Check Investors, Inc., 502 F.3d 159 (3d Cir. 2007)); Bezpalko v. Gilfillan, Gilpin & Brehman, 1998 WL 321268 (E.D. Pa. June 17, 1998) (same); Goodman v. S. Credit Recovery, Inc., 1998 WL 240403 (E.D. La. May 12, 1998) (check is not an FDCPA debt); Alexander v. Moore & Associates, Inc., 553 F. Supp. 948 (D. Haw. 1982) (finding check guarantee service for landlords

to debts that arise from credit transactions.[66] They have also recognized that the FDCPA does not contain a fraud or tort exception that would exclude dishonored checks from the definition of "debt."[67]

The following acts by check collectors violate the Fair Debt Collection Practices Act (FDCPA) and state deceptive practices (UDAP) statutes:

- Falsely threatening to initiate a criminal prosecution on a dishonored check;[68]
- Threatening to impose civil dishonored check penalties when the statute does not allow it;[69]

---

and other creditors not to be debt collector; service did not collect on debts owed to another as it collected on the amount it had paid to the landlord).

66 *See* Pollice v. Nat'l Tax Funding, Ltd. P'ship, 225 F.3d 379 (3d Cir. 2000) (rejecting *dicta* in Zimmerman v. HBO Affiliate Group, 834 F.2d 1163 (3d Cir. 1987) that FDCPA covers a debt only if the obligation involves a credit agreement or the deferral of payment).

67 *See* Armstrong v. Rose Law Firm, Prof'l Ass'n, 2002 U.S. Dist. LEXIS 4039 (D. Minn. Mar. 7, 2002); Connor v. Automated Accounts, Inc., 202 F.R.D. 265 (E.D. Wash. 2001).

68 *Finding FDCPA violations*: Fed. Trade Comm'n v. Check Investors, Inc., 502 F.3d 159 (3d Cir. 2007) (false threats of criminal prosecution and civil suit violate FDCPA; writers of NSF checks are consumers within meaning of FDCPA); Dunaway v. JBC & Associates, Inc., 2005 WL 1529574 (E.D. Mich. June 20, 2005) (threatening to file criminal charges when statute of limitations has run or when collector does not intend to take this action is FDCPA violation); McHugh v. Check Investors Inc., 2003 WL 21283288 (W.D. Va. May 21, 2003) (awarding statutory damages and lodestar fees for FDCPA violations and actual and punitive damages for intentional infliction of emotional distress when collector threatened immediate arrest for dishonored check debt not owed); Gradisher v. Check Enforcement Unit, 210 F. Supp. 2d 907 (W.D. Mich. 2002) (diversion program's letter on sheriff's letterhead misrepresented collector's relationship with sheriff and the likelihood of prosecution, in violation of FDCPA and state collection law); Davis v. Commercial Check Control, Inc., 1999 U.S. Dist. LEXIS 1682 (N.D. Ill. Feb. 12, 1999) (statement in computer-generated dunning letter sent by collector of NSF checks that "various penal codes allow criminal prosecution" and "we may proceed to file your check with local law enforcement" violated FDCPA when out of 20,000 checks not one had been referred for criminal prosecution). *But see* Guidry v. Clare, 442 F. Supp. 2d 282 (E.D. Va. 2006) (imposing Rule 11 sanctions against consumer who brought FDCPA and state tort claims after criminal dishonored check case *nolle prossed*; creditor had legal and factual basis for dishonored check claim). *See generally* National Consumer Law Center, Fair Debt Collection §§ 5.5.2, 5.5.7, 5.5.8, 5.5.10, 5.5.13, 8.3.2, 10.2, 10.6.3, 11.2, 11.3 (6th ed. 2008).

Finding UDAP violations: Turner v. E-Z Check Cashing, 35 F. Supp. 2d 1042 (M.D. Tenn. 1999) (payday lender's threat of criminal dishonored check prosecution was UDAP violation; there was no basis for prosecution as lender knew borrowers did not have enough funds on deposit to cover checks); Hamilton v. York, 987 F. Supp. 953 (E.D. Ky. 1997) (payday lender's threat of criminal dishonored check prosecution was UDAP violation because debt was usurious and unenforceable); Papadopoulos v. Josem, 2002 WL 194494 (Conn. Super. Ct. Jan. 11, 2002) (allowing plaintiff to go forward with claims of negligence, malicious prosecution, and UDAP violation against her former attorney who allowed a criminal dishonored check prosecution to go forward, resulting in her public arrest and brief incarceration, even though she had covered the NSF check); *see also* Fed. Trade Comm'n v. Check Investors, Inc., 502 F.3d 159 (3d Cir. 2007) (false threats of criminal prosecution and civil suit violates Federal Trade Commission Act).

69 Veach v. Sheeks, 316 F.3d 690, 693 (7th Cir. 2003) (demanding treble damages, court costs, and attorney fees before suit violates FDCPA); Picht v. Jon R. Hawks, Ltd., 236 F.3d 446 (8th Cir. 2001) (penalty under dishonored check statute discretionary with court; violation of Minnesota law and thus FDCPA when collector used garnishment procedure intended only for collection of definite sum); Gearing v. Check Brokerage Corp., 233 F.3d 469 (7th Cir. 2000) (check broker was not subrogee, so could not take advantage of damage provisions of Illinois dishonored check law, when it bought dishonored checks with proviso that it could sell them back after sixty days, because this escape clause meant that it would not bear the loss if the check could not be collected; its attempt to collect damages under Illinois dishonored check law violated FDCPA); Duffy v. Landberg, 215 F.3d 871 (8th Cir. 2000) (collector violated FDCPA by referring to $100 penalty, when Minnesota dishonored check statute made amount of penalty discretionary with court, and by threatening attorney fees, which were only available for larger checks); Hunt v. Check Recovery Services, Inc., 478 F. Supp. 2d 1157 (N.D. Cal. 2007) (remedies of California civil dishonored check statute, Cal. Civ. Code § 1719 (West), are exclusive; collector violated FDCPA when it demanded both section 1719 damages and pre-judgment interest); Abels v. JBC Legal Group, 434 F. Supp. 2d 763 (N.D. Cal. 2006) (denying debt buyer's motion to dismiss FDCPA claim; California statute allowing $25 dishonored check charge not retroactive; fact issues whether assignee could recover under U.C.C.); Francis v. Snyder, 389 F. Supp. 2d 1034 (N.D. Ill. 2005) (payday loan collector violated FDCPA by threatening suit under statute allowing $25 or collection costs, when statute applied only to checks that are returned because check writer has no account or insufficient funds or credit, not when check writer stops payment); Semper v. JBC Legal Group, 2005 WL 2172377 (W.D. Wash. Sept. 6, 2005) (law firm that purchased dishonored check debts for purpose of collection was not "seller" within meaning of Washington dishonored check law and not entitled to statutory damages meant to reimburse merchants for incidental damages); Brumbelow v. Law Offices of Bennett & Deloney, Prof'l Corp., 2005 WL 1566689 (D. Utah June 21, 2005) (FDCPA claim stated when law firm demanded sum for "settlement" and "covenant not to sue" in excess of sum permitted by state civil dishonored check law); Palmer v. Stassinos, 348 F. Supp. 2d 1070 (N.D. Cal. 2004) (denial of motion to dismiss; seeking interest on dishonored check, not allowed by California NSF check law, is FDCPA violation); Nance v. Ulferts, 282 F. Supp. 2d 912 (N.D. Ind. 2003) (Indiana's civil dishonored check statute explicitly excludes postdated checks; FDCPA violation when payday lender sought treble damages under that statute); Sonmore v. CheckRite Recovery Services, 187 F. Supp. 2d 1128 (D. Minn. 2001) (FDCPA violations when collector referred to $100 penalty but amount of penalty was discretionary and defenses were available); Jones v. Kunin, 2000 WL 34402017 (S.D. Ill. May 1, 2000) (consumer stated FDCPA claim against payday lender that threatened liability under Illinois civil dishonored check law which requires "intent to defraud" when lender solicited postdated checks and it was "clear under the

- Threatening suit on a dishonored check after the statute of limitations has expired.[70]

Consumers may also have claims under state debt collection statutes for these acts.[71] Initiation of a dishonored check prosecution without probable cause may be actionable as a tort such as malicious prosecution, intentional infliction of emotional distress, or abuse of process, making the collector liable for actual and punitive damages.[72]

circumstances" that borrower did not have sufficient funds); Ballard v. Equifax Check Services, Inc., 27 F. Supp. 2d 1201 (E.D. Cal. 1998) (collector's incorrect statement that dishonored check service charge was allowed by California law was false representation within the meaning of FDCPA); Jenkins v. Union Corp., 999 F. Supp. 1120 (N.D. Ill. 1998) (when Illinois law permitted imposition of fee for NSF check but not for stop payment, collector's attempt to collect $25 fee for stopped check was unauthorized); Collection Bureau Services, Inc. v. Morrow, 87 P.3d 1024 (Mont. 2004) (FDCPA violation to demand statutory damages without new notice after consumer defaulted on payment plan negotiated with NSF check collector); *see also* Johnson v. Riddle, 305 F.3d 1107 (10th Cir. 2002) (FDCPA case; Utah courts will not apply civil shoplifting statute to NSF checks, because specific Utah statute dealing with dishonored checks limited penalty to $15); People *ex rel.* Spitzer v. Boyajian Law Offices, Prof'l Corp., 851 N.Y.S.2d 72 (Sup. Ct. 2007) (table) (text available at 2007 WL 3118767) (violations of state debt collection law by collector of NSF checks: misstated provisions of New York dishonored check law, and demanded damages to which not entitled); *cf.* Armstrong v. Rose Law Firm, 2002 WL 461705 (D. Minn. Mar. 22, 2002) (letter violated FDCPA by not clearly stating amount of debt when it lumped together check amount and statutory service charge and called it "amount referred," but reference to additional penalty of "up to" $100 not a violation when this correctly stated Minnesota law); Irwin v. Mascott, 96 F. Supp. 2d 968 (N.D. Cal. 1999) (certifying class; even if collector could show that consumers were properly notified of service charge, charge would be a penalty, not liquidated damages, and thus forbidden by California law); Havens-Tobias v. Eagle, 2003 WL 1601461 (Ohio Ct. App. Mar. 28, 2003) (UDAP claim would lie against creditor who referred claim to collector while blocking consumer's attempts to cover NSF check; no tort or UDAP claim against attorney who reasonably relied on incomplete information from creditor). *But see* Volden v. Innovative Fin. Sys., Inc., 440 F.3d 947 (8th Cir. 2006) (electronically debiting statutory dishonored check fee without written permission of account holder not FDCPA violation; although it violated automated clearing house rules and breached contract between clearing house and check guarantee service, it was permitted by state law so long as check fee conspicuously disclosed by sign at place where check written); Havens-Tobias v. Eagle, 127 F. Supp. 2d 889 (S.D. Ohio 2001) (no violation of FDCPA by seller's collection attorney when seller refused to accept face amount of NSF check and instead chose to sue, because Ohio statute provided for civil recovery from one who commits theft offense including passing dishonored checks); Wells v. McDonough, 1999 U.S. Dist. LEXIS 15535 (N.D. Ill. Sept. 29, 1999) (statement in collection letter that "you are or may be in violation of your state laws defining and governing the issuance of bad checks" was not a misrepresentation when Illinois dishonored check law allowed a service charge of up to $25 even if demand by certified mail was not made, and collector demanded only $25 charge); Charles v. Check Rite, Ltd., 1998 U.S. Dist. LEXIS 22512 (D. Ariz. Dec. 14, 1998) (collector did not violate FDCPA by demanding penalty before complying with statutory notice requirements). *See generally* National Consumer Law Center, Fair Debt Collection § 11.3 (6th ed. 2008) (UDAP claims against debt collectors).

70 Martsolf v. JBC Legal Group, 2008 WL 275719 (M.D. Pa. Jan. 30, 2008); Dunaway v. JBC & Associates, Inc., 2005 WL 1529574 (E.D. Mich. June 20, 2005).

71 Gradisher v. Check Enforcement Unit, 210 F. Supp. 2d 907 (W.D. Mich. 2002) (diversion program's letter on sheriff's letterhead misrepresented collector's relationship with sheriff and the likelihood of prosecution, in violation of FDCPA and state collection law); People *ex rel.* Spitzer v. Boyajian Law Offices, Prof'l Corp., 851 N.Y.S.2d 72 (Sup. Ct. 2007) (table) (text available at 2007 WL 3118767) (violations of state debt collection law by collector of NSF checks: misstated provisions of New York dishonored check law, and demanded damages to which not entitled).

72 National Consumer Law Center, Fair Debt Collection § 10.6.1 (6th ed. 2008); *see* Alexander v. Manheim Services Corp., 2007 WL 2026455 (S.D. Miss. July 9, 2007) (car dealer stated claims for abuse of process, malicious prosecution, wrongful repossession, negligence, defamation, civil conspiracy; genuine issues of fact whether auto auction agreed to hold check, but cashed it prematurely and swore out criminal complaint when it bounced); McHugh v. Check Investors Inc., 2003 WL 21283288 (W.D. Va. May 21, 2003) (awarding actual and punitive damages for intentional infliction of emotional distress when collector threatened immediate arrest for dishonored check debt not owed); Hayfield v. Home Depot, U.S.A., Inc., 168 F. Supp. 2d 436 (E.D. Pa. 2001) (consumer stated a claim for punitive damages when retailer vigorously prosecuted criminal dishonored check charges although customer had shown that check was refused not for insufficient funds but because of negligent misprint by check printing company); Wal-Mart Stores v. Patterson, 816 So. 2d 1 (Ala. 2001) (checking account owner who was arrested and charged after his ex-wife forged his signature stated claim for negligence and malicious prosecution when Wal-Mart accepted a check signed with a man's name that was presented by a woman); Papadopoulos v. Josem, 2002 WL 194494 (Conn. Super. Ct. Jan. 11, 2002) (allowing plaintiff to go forward with claims of negligence, malicious prosecution, and UDAP violation against her former attorney who allowed a criminal dishonored check prosecution to go forward, resulting in her public arrest and brief incarceration, even though she had covered the NSF check); *see also* West v. Bruno's Inc., 837 So. 2d 303 (Ala. Civ. App. 2002) (Alabama dishonored check statute grants civil and criminal immunity to holder of "worthless negotiable instrument" who follows statutory procedure; consumer raised genuine issue of fact whether store held "worthless" check when she showed store manager a bank statement and bank computer printout indicating that check had been paid leaving balance in account; allowing consumer to go forward with malicious prosecution and other tort claims arising from *nol prossed* dishonored check prosecution). *But see* Guidry v. Clare, 442 F. Supp. 2d 282 (E.D. Va. 2006) (imposing Rule 11 sanctions against consumer who brought FDCPA and state tort claims after criminal dishonored check case *nolle prossed*; creditor had legal and factual basis for dishonored check claim); Ross v. Creel Printing & Publ'g Co., 122 Cal. Rptr. 2d 787 (Ct. App. 2002) (creditor's conduct not outrageous enough to support claim of intentional infliction of emotional distress: prosecution for NSF check written by debtor in his official capacity as chief executive officer of corporation); Blue Moon Cycle v.

It may be unethical in some states for a lawyer to threaten or initiate criminal dishonored check proceedings solely to collect a civil debt for fees.[73] In extreme cases a collector may be criminally liable for threatening criminal prosecution on a dishonored check charge.[74]

A payday lender who used dishonored check prosecutions as a collection device was convicted of violating Georgia's criminal RICO statute. The predicate offenses were perjuries and swearing that the checks had been written for "merchandise," when the lender had no merchandise to sell.[75]

Jenkins, 642 S.E.2d 637 (Ga. 2007) (reversing false arrest and malicious prosecution judgments arising from criminal prosecution of agent who physically delivered NSF company check, signed by company president; Georgia dishonored check law provides immunity to holder who sends proper notices, also criminalizes "delivery" of NSF check); Watson v. Gore Bros., Inc., 2003 WL 22064051 (Tex. App. Sept. 4, 2003) (no intentional infliction of emotional distress, because no outrageous conduct; no malicious prosecution because creditor had probable cause to prosecute when farmer knowingly wrote NSF checks, informed creditor that checks would not be covered until certain milk payments received, and checks were never covered).

73 *See* Papadopoulos v. Josem, 2002 WL 194494 (Conn. Super. Ct. Jan. 11, 2002) (allowing plaintiff to go forward with claims of negligence, malicious prosecution, and UDAP violation against her former attorney who allowed her to be arrested for bouncing a check for his fees, even though she had covered the NSF check). *See generally* Gregory G. Sarno, Annotation, *Initiating, or threatening to initiate, criminal prosecution as a ground for disciplining counsel*, 42 A.L.R.4th 1000 (1985); National Consumer Law Center, Fair Debt Collection § 11.5.3 (6th ed. 2008).

74 State v. Ross, 573 N.W.2d 906 (Iowa 1998) (fraudulent telemarketer's conviction for extortion supported by evidence that he threatened criminal prosecution and public humiliation of elderly victim who stopped payment on her check when she realized she was being defrauded).

75 Watson v. State, 509 S.E.2d 87 (Ga. Ct. App. 1998).

Chapter 10 Medical Debt

10.1 Introduction

10.1.1 The Problem of Medical Debt

Rationing and denial of health care services to low-income Americans continue to be perennial problems. About 47 million Americans, or nearly 16% of the United States' population, lack health insurance.[1] When consumers are uninsured or their insurance coverage is inadequate, the result is medical debt.

The amount of medical debt burdening low-income consumers is enormous. According to one study, 46% of uninsured consumers have outstanding medical debts.[2] Another study reported that medical debtors have an average of almost $9000 in medical bills.[3] There may be racial disparities in the distribution of medical debt, as people of color make up a disproportionate share of the uninsured.[4]

One study found that 27% of bankruptcies involved medical bills of over $1000, and about half of all bankruptcies are caused in part by medical reasons, such as illness or injury, medical debt, or lost work due to medical reasons.[5] Out of pocket medical costs for "medical bankruptcy" debtors averaged nearly $12,000.[6] Most startling, this study found that 75% of medical bankruptcy debtors had health insurance coverage at the onset of illness.[7] In fact, having health insurance is no guarantee against medical debt, especially for the "underinsured," that is, patients with inadequate insurance coverage or with high co-payment or deductibles.[8]

Medical debt is especially onerous because it is often sudden, unplanned, and unavoidable, and debtors may be vulnerable due to illness or infirmity. The problem is further exacerbated by the fact that, not only is medical care extremely expensive, but uninsured consumers are often charged several times more for the same medical services as private insurers or Medicaid, thus adding to their debt burden.[9]

Low-income consumers may have a variety of health law and consumer law defenses to debt collection efforts by doctors, hospitals, and their collection agencies. This chapter focuses on the consumer law defenses that may be available. Other resources should be consulted regarding health law defenses.[10]

10.1.2 Aggressive Debt Collection

Many hospitals and health care providers are quick to send unpaid medical bills to collections. Some hospitals

1 Carmen DeNavas-Walt, Bernadette D. Proctor, Jessica Smith, United States Census Bureau, Income, Poverty, and Health Insurance Coverage in the United States: 2006 (Aug. 2007).

2 Dennis Andrulis, Lisa Duchon, Carol Pryor & Nanette Goodman, Access Project, Paying for Health Care When You're Uninsured (Jan. 2003); *see also* Sara R. Collins, Commonwealth Fund, Gaps in Health Insurance: An All-American Problem: Findings from the Commonwealth Fund Biennial Health Insurance Survey (Apr. 2006) (21% of adults under age 65 had medical debt); Robert W. Seifert, Access Project, Home Sick: How Medical Debt Undermines Housing Security (Nov. 2005) (finding that 46% of low-income clients of Volunteer Income Tax Assistance sites had medical debt).

3 Access Project, The Consequences of Medical Debt: Evidence from Three Communities (Feb. 2003).

4 *See* Michelle M. Doty, Jennifer Edwards, & Alyssa Holmgren, Commonwealth Fund, Seeing Red: Americans Driven Into Debt by Medical Bills (Aug. 2005) (52% of African Americans reported difficulties paying medical bills versus 34% of Hispanics and 28% of whites); SEIU Hosp. Accountability Project, Why the Working Poor Pay More (Mar. 2003) (finding the greatest number of "self-pay" or uninsured patients who were discharged from hospitals in Cook County, Illinois came from high minority areas).

5 David U. Himmelstein, Elizabeth Warren, Deborah Thorne & Steffie Woolhandler, *Illness and Injury as Contributors to Bankruptcy*, Health Affairs—Web Exclusive (Feb. 2, 2005), *available at* http://content.healthaffairs.org/cgi/reprint/hlthaff.w5.63v1.

6 *Id.*

7 *Id.*

8 Cathy Schoen, Michelle M. Doty, Sara R. Collins & Alyssa L. Holmgren, *Insured But Not Protected: How Many Adults Are Underinsured?*, Health Affairs—Web Exclusive (June 2005), *available at* http://content.healthaffairs.org/cgi/content/abstract/hlthaff.w5.289; *see also* Sara R. Collins, Commonwealth Fund, Gaps in Health Insurance: An All-American Problem: Findings from the Commonwealth Fund Biennial Health Insurance Survey (Apr. 2006) (18% of consumers who had health insurance owed medical debt they could not pay); Robert W. Seifert, Access Project, Home Sick: How Medical Debt Undermines Housing Security (Nov. 2005) (41% of medical debtors surveyed had insurance at the time bills were incurred).

9 *See* § 10.5.5.2, *infra*.

10 Alan Alop, Defending Hospital Collection Cases (rev. ed. 2005), *available at* www.illinoislegaladvocate.org/index.cfm?fuseaction=home.dsp_content&contentID=728; Nat'l Health Law Program, An Advocate's Guide to the Medicaid Program (2001).

have reduced the amount of time they wait before sending unpaid bills to collection agencies, from the traditional 150 to 210 days to as little as 30 to 60 days.[11] Studies have found that about one-third of uninsured consumers have been contacted by a collection agency.[12] Advocates for the uninsured assert that hospitals engage in debt collection in part to prevent the consumers from returning to their hospitals.[13]

Medical debt collection agencies can be especially aggressive. Documented tactics include liens on homes,[14] wage garnishments,[15] and bank account attachments.[16] The use of bank account garnishment by medical bill collectors can be especially egregious. For instance, medical collectors in Minnesota regularly use that state's unusual provision permitting debt collectors to seize bank accounts without seeking a judgment or even court authorization.[17] In New York state collection agencies have been collecting decades-old hospital collection judgments using electronic service of garnishment orders.[18]

Some hospitals have been even known to use the tactic of a *capeas* or body attachment.[19] One hospital that engaged in aggressive debt collection techniques lost its tax-exempt status as a result.[20] Health care providers have also been known to agree to payment plans, only to sue the patients months or years later for the amount of the debt.[21] The issue of aggressive medical debt collection has drawn the attention of Congress.[22]

In response to negative publicity, the American Hospital Association (AHA), a private trade association, has issued guidance to hospitals on billing and collection practices.[23] In particular, the AHA recommended that hospitals make information on their price lists publicly available, provide financial counseling to low-income uninsured patients, es-

11 Jennifer Steinhauer, *Will Doctors Make Your Credit Sick?*, N.Y. Times, Feb. 4, 2001 (quoting American Collector's Association); *see also* Access Project, The Consequences of Medical Debt: Evidence from Three Communities (Feb. 2003).

12 Lisa Duchon, et al., Commonwealth Fund, Security Matters: How Instability in Health Insurance Puts U.S. Workers at Risk (Dec. 2001); *see also* Sara R. Collins, et al., Commonwealth Fund, The Affordability Crisis in U.S. Health Care: Findings from the Commonwealth Fund Biennial Health Insurance Survey (Mar. 2004) (21% of adults under age 65 report being contacted by a collection agency over medical bills); Jessica H. May & Peter J. Cunningham, Ctr. for Studying Health System Change, Tough Trade-Offs: Medical Bills, Family Finances, and Access to Care (June 2004) (more than 60% of consumers with medical bill problems reported having been contacted by a collection agency).

13 Terry Carter, *Who Pays Hefty Hospital Tabs? Suits Claim Tax-Exempt Status Creates Duty to Provide Affordable or Free Care for Needy*, A.B.A. J., Jan. 2005, at 14; *see also* Glenn Howatt, *The Sting of Debt Collectors*, Minnesota Star Tribune, Dec. 19, 2004 (quoting Minnesota Attorney General Mike Hatch, who accused aggressive hospitals of "sending a message to the community" that "the best way to prevent these [uninsured] people from coming back is to pound them").

14 Elisabeth Benjamin, Amy Chung & Renee Philips, Health Law Unit—Legal Aid Soc'y of N.Y., State Secret 2005: How Government Statutes and Hospitals' Voluntary Efforts Fail to Protect Uninsured Patients (Jan. 2005) (finding that 15 out of 31 New York City not-for-profit hospitals use liens on patients' homes as a collection tactic); Conn. Ctr. for a New Economy, Yale, Don't Lien on Me (Sept. 2003) (finding that Yale-New Haven Hospital placed liens on an estimated 7.5% of owner-occupied homes in New Haven during the past nine years).

15 Elisabeth Benjamin, Amy Chung & Renee Philips, Health Law Unit—Legal Aid Soc'y of N.Y., State Secret 2005: How Government Statutes and Hospitals' Voluntary Efforts Fail to Protect Uninsured Patients (Jan. 2005) (finding that 27 out of 31 New York City not-for-profit hospitals use wage garnishments as a collection tactic); Steve Tripoli & Chi Chi Wu, National Consumer Law Center, Unhealthy Pursuits: How the Sick and Vulnerable Are Harmed by Abusive Medical Debt Collection Tactics (Dec. 2005), *available at* www.consumerlaw.org/issues/medical_debt/content/medicaldebt.pdf; *see, e.g.*, Hillcrest Med. Ctr. v. Monroy, 38 P.3d 931 (Okla. Civ. App. 2001) (upholding stay on hospital's garnishment of patient's wages due to hardship and ordering lower court to determine whether already garnished wages should be refunded).

16 Elisabeth Benjamin, Amy Chung & Renee Philips, Health Law Unit—Legal Aid Soc'y of N.Y., State Secret 2005: How Government Statutes and Hospitals' Voluntary Efforts Fail to Protect Uninsured Patients (Jan. 2005) (finding that 24 out of 31 New York City not-for-profit hospitals use bank account attachments as a collection tactic).

17 Minnesota Attorney General's Office, Compliance Review of Fairview Health Services (Jan. 31, 2005).

18 Lucette Lagnado, *Cold Case Files: Dunned for Old Bills, Poor Find Some Hospitals Never Forget*, Wall St. J., June 8, 2004, at A1.

19 Lucette Lagnado, *Hospitals Try Extreme Measures to Collect Their Overdue Debts*, Wall St. J., Oct. 30, 2003, at A1 (documenting how one Illinois hospital sought 164 arrest warrants for medical debtors since 1995).

A *capeas* or body attachment is an arrest warrant that creditors or collection agencies obtain when a debtor fails to show up for a court hearing.

20 Lucette Lagnado, *Hospital Found "Not Charitable" Loses Its Status as Tax Exempt*, Wall St. J., Feb. 19, 2004 (describing how the Illinois Department of Revenue revoked the tax exempt status of Provena Covenant Medical Center, in part because of Provena's aggressive use of lawsuits and other debt collection methods to collect from uninsured patients).

21 *See, e.g.*, Valley Hosp. v. Laubshire, 2007 WL 1342187 (N.J. Super. Ct. App. Div. May 9, 2007) (hospital sued patient despite the fact patient had made monthly payments on the debt for seven years pursuant to statements sent by the hospital); Univ. Ortho & Sports v. Pleasant, 2007 WL 867625 (Ohio Ct. App. Mar. 23, 2007) (provider's agreement to accept payment plan did not bar provider from suing patient later).

22 Internal Revenue Service, Hospital Compliance Project—Interim Report (July 2007), *available at* www.irs.gov/pub/irs-tege/eo_interim_hospital_report_072007.pdf; Minority Staff, Senate Fin. Comm., Tax-Exempt Hospitals: Discussion Draft (July 18, 2007), *available at* http://grassley.senate.gov/releases/2007/07182007.pdf.

23 Bd. of Trustees of the Am. Hosp. Ass'n, Hospital Billing and Collection Practices—Statement of Principles and Guidelines (Dec. 2003), *available at* www.aha.org/aha/content/2004/pdf/guidelinesfinalweb.pdf.

A list of hospitals that have confirmed their commitment to these guidelines is available at www.aha.org/aha/content/2004/pdf/cocweblist.pdf (last visited Apr. 2008).

tablish policies regarding helping patients to apply for public assistance or hospital-based charity care, establish policies to offer discounts to low-income patients who do not receive charity care, and define standards for third-party debt collectors acting on their behalf.[24]

There may be some question as to whether hospitals are actually following the AHA guidelines or guidelines of similar trade groups. For example, the New York state hospital trade group issued voluntary guidelines in early 2004, but the majority of New York City hospitals have not followed some or even all of these guidelines.[25] One American Hospital Association guideline of particular concern is the recommendation to define standards for third-party debt collection. In several instances, hospital officials have disavowed any knowledge of debt collection abuse, or have otherwise indicated they are not monitoring or reviewing the activities of third party collectors acting on their behalf.[26]

10.1.3 Practical Considerations

A very effective method to deal with medical debt is to find someone else to pay for it. Advocates should make sure that their clients have applied for any assistance programs to which they are entitled. This may include government or private programs, such as Medicaid,[27] Medicare Savings Programs,[28] an overlooked insurance source,[29] pharmacy assistance programs,[30] church or social service assistance programs, or low-cost dental care from dental school programs.

If a client is low or moderate income, make sure to inquire about charity or "free care" eligibility. These programs arise from the implicit duty of not-for-profit hospitals, because of their charitable status, to provide a certain amount of free care to low-income patients. In some states this obligation is explicit. Low-income patients are often not informed about these free care or charity programs, or given information on other forms of financial assistance (including Medicaid).[31] Ironically, many hospitals will count an unpaid medical debt as "charity care" despite the fact the hospital or a debt collector continues to attempt to collect the debt.[32] One limitation of charity care programs is that they may only cover hospital bills, leaving the patient still owing significant debts to a physician or other health care provider.

Informal negotiation over medical debt can be especially effective.[33] Hospitals and other medical providers may be more willing to reduce bills because of the fact that these bills are often several times more than both what the hospital's actual costs are, as well as what the hospital would receive from Medicaid or Medicare.[34] Any settlement to pay medical bills should of course be documented in writing.[35] If medicals bills have adversely affected the consumer's credit report,[36] any settlement should require the provider or collector to remove or correct this negative information. Sample language is available in another manual in this series.[37]

24 Bd. of Trustees of the Am. Hosp. Ass'n, Hospital Billing and Collection Practices—Statement of Principles and Guidelines (Dec. 2003), *available at* www.aha.org/aha/content/2004/pdf/guidelinesfinalweb.pdf.

25 Elisabeth Benjamin, Amy Chung & Renee Philips, Health Law Unit—Legal Aid Soc'y of N.Y., State Secret 2005: How Government Statutes and Hospitals' Voluntary Efforts Fail to Protect Uninsured Patients (Jan. 2005).

26 Minnesota Attorney General's Office, Compliance Review of Fairview Health Services (Jan. 31, 2005) (finding that not-for-profit hospital had no internal controls over its debt collection activities); Jonathan Cohn, *Uncharitable?*, N.Y. Times Magazine, Dec. 19, 2004, at 51 (quoting former head of Medicare stating "90 percent of the hospital CEO's in the U.S. had no idea what the collection offices were doing").

27 Note that individuals who qualify for Medicaid can get retroactive benefits to cover medical expenses incurred up to three months before the date of application. 42 U.S.C. § 1396a(a)(34); 42 C.F.R. § 435.914.

28 These programs help low-income Medicare recipients pay for Medicare premiums and can save eligible individuals over $1100 per year. Some programs may also cover co-insurance and deductibles for certain people. To learn more, see www.medicare.gov/publications/pubs/pdf/10126.pdf (last visited Mar. 2008).

29 Overlooked insurance sources can include workers' compensation, home owner's insurance, automobile insurance, or insurance from a current or former employer or spouse.

30 One example is the Partnership for Prescription Assistance, whose website is located at www.pparx.org/Intro.php (last visited Apr. 2008).

31 *See* Elisabeth Benjamin, Amy Chung & Renee Philips, Health Law Unit—Legal Aid Soc'y of N.Y., State Secret 2005: How Government Statutes and Hospitals' Voluntary Efforts Fail to Protect Uninsured Patients, Jan. 2005 (noting that out of 31 New York City nonprofit hospitals, 25 failed to post signs informing patients about charity care assistance, 17 would not provide information about charity care assistance unless the patient asked to speak to upper management, 18 would not provide this information over the phone, and 13 did not provide this information in person); Robert W. Seifert, Access Project, Home Sick: How Medical Debt Undermines Housing Security (Nov. 2005) (78% of patients not offered financial assistance).

32 *See* Internal Revenue Service, Hospital Compliance Project—Interim Report (July 2007), *available at* www.irs.gov/pub/irs-tege/eo_interim_hospital_report_072007.pdf (in survey of 487 tax-exempt hospitals, 44% admitted they included some bad debt as "uncompensated care" for the purposes of reporting community benefits expenditures).

33 One expert estimated that less than one out of twenty uninsured patients actually negotiates over a hospital bill. *A Review of Hospital Billing and Collection Practices Before the Subcomm. on Oversight and Investigations of the H. Comm. on Energy and Commerce*, 108th Cong. (2004) (statement of Gerard Anderson, Professor, Bloomberg Sch. of Pub. Health, Johns Hopkins Univ.).

34 *See* § 10.5.5.2, *infra.*

35 A payment plan, especially if it is not written, may not be an adequate defense if the provider decides to later sue on the debt. *See, e.g.*, Univ. Ortho & Sports v. Pleasant, 2007 WL 867625 (Ohio Ct. App. Mar. 23, 2007) (provider's agreement to accept payment plan not binding because no additional consideration provided).

36 *See* § 10.3.4, *infra.*

37 National Consumer Law Center, Fair Credit Reporting Appx. J.9 (6th ed. 2006 and Supp.); *see also id.* § 12.6.4.

Medical debt is generally unsecured debt, and less of a priority than essential expenses such as food, housing costs (rent or mortgage), utilities, or other secured debt (for example, car payments).[38] Clients should be advised to pay the higher priority bills first.[39] Clients should be advised to very careful about converting medical debt into secured debt, for example, by taking out a second mortgage to pay for medical bills.[40] They should also be careful not to use credit cards to pay medical bills, which has become a common practice.[41] Credit card lenders are notorious for abusive practices, such as charging extraordinarily high penalty interest rates and fees.[42] Moreover, unlike a health care provider, patients will not be able to negotiate with a credit card lender to reduce a bill because of discriminatory pricing.

A non-monetary consideration that is unique to medical debt is whether the debtor will be able to continue to get care from the particular facility. In non-emergency situations, hospitals and other providers are usually allowed to turn away a patient because of prior debt.[43] They may also require that the patient pay a deposit before services will be provided.[44] However, there may be "safety net" facilities nearby, such as a public hospital or a community health center. In emergency situations, the debtor should be able to obtain care from a hospital regardless of past debt under the Emergency Medical Treatment and Active Labor Act (EMTALA), an "anti-dumping" statute.[45] Also, Medicaid prohibits providers from denying services to Medicaid recipients on the basis of outstanding debts for co-payments or deductibles.[46]

10.1.4 Finding Out the Extent of the Debt

Another problem with medical debt is the fact that a single incident will often create debts owed to a variety of actors. For example, a single hospital visit can result in bills from the ambulance service, the hospital itself, the surgeon, the anesthesiologist, and medical equipment providers. Most medical debt is owed to hospitals, but significant numbers of debtors report owing amounts to doctors, ambulances services, pharmacies and others.[47] Thus, even if an uninsured patient is able to obtain charity care or negotiate a settlement to cover a hospital bill, she may still owe significant debts to a physician or other healthcare provider.

A practical issue for some medical debtors is that they may not be aware of owing debt to all these creditors. Previously, attorneys could obtain a fairly complete inventory of medical debt by pulling the debtor's credit report. However a provision added in 2003 to the Fair Credit Reporting Act prohibited credit bureaus from including the identity of medical creditors/collectors unless the information does not disclose either the specific provider or nature of the medical services.[48]

38 These considerations are discussed in more detail in NCLC Guide to Surviving Debt (2008). This publication is available from NCLC's Publications Department at (617) 542-9595.

39 This advice is especially important given that one-third of medical debtors had trouble paying their rent or mortgage due to medical bills. These debtors are at risk of eviction or foreclosure because they may have paid their medical bills instead of the rent or mortgage. Access Project, The Consequences of Medical Debt: Evidence from Three Communities (Feb. 2003).

40 In 1997, 10% of home equity lines of credit and 2% of closed-end home equity loans were used in part to pay medical debt. Glenn B. Canner, Thomas A. Durkin & Charles A. Luckett, *Recent Developments in Home Equity Lending*, Fed. Reserve Bull. (Apr. 1998).

A study of bankruptcy filers found that 15% of home owners in the group who had taken out a second or third mortgage cited medical bills as a reason for doing so. Even worse, follow up interviews revealed that among home owners with high cost home loans (interest rates greater than 12% or points and fees 8% or greater), nearly 14% cited a medical reason for taking out the loan. David U. Himmelstein, Elizabeth Warren, Deborah Thorne & Steffie Woolhandler, Illness and Injury as Contributors to Bankruptcy, Health Affairs—Web Exclusive (Feb. 2, 2005), *available at* http://content.healthaffairs.org/cgi/reprint/hlthaff.w5.63v1.

41 *See* § 10.4.5, *infra*.

42 *See* National Consumer Law Center, The Cost of Credit: Regulation, Preemption, and Industry Abuses § 11.7 (3d ed. 2005 and Supp.).

43 Access Project, The Consequences of Medical Debt: Evidence from Three Communities (Feb. 2003) (one-third of medical debtors in study reported that providers refused or delayed care due to prior medical bills).

Patients themselves are often deterred from seeking medical care because of debt to a facility or provider. *See* Hugh F. Daly, Leslie M. Oblak, Robert W. Seifert & Kimberly Shellenberger, *Into the Red to Stay in the Pink: The Hidden Cost of Being Uninsured*, Health Matrix: Journal of Law—Medicine (Winter 2002).

44 One study found that 30% of consumers with prior medical bills were asked to pay upfront. Access Project, The Consequences of Medical Debt: Evidence from Three Communities (Feb. 2003).

45 42 U.S.C. § 1395dd; *see* § 10.3.2, *infra*.

46 Beeker v. Olzewski, 415 F. Supp. 2d 734 (E.D. Mich. 2006).

The court did note that recently enacted amendments to Medicaid may have an impact on this prohibition. *Id.*

47 In a recent study of bankruptcy filers, among those who reported owing medical debt, hospital bills were the biggest expense for 42.5%, while doctors' bills were the biggest for 20%. David U. Himmelstein, Elizabeth Warren, Deborah Thorne & Steffie Woolhandler, Illness and Injury as Contributors to Bankruptcy, Health Affairs—Web Exclusive (Feb. 2, 2005), *available at* http://content.healthaffairs.org/cgi/reprint/hlthaff.w5.63v1; *see also* Carol Pryor & Deborah Gurewich, Access Project, Getting Care But Paying the Price: How Medical Debt Leaves Many in Massachusetts Facing Tough Choices (Feb. 2004) (79% of medical debtors owed amounts to hospitals, 47% owed amounts to doctors, and 24% owed amounts to ambulance services); Robert W. Seifert, Access Project, Home Sick: How Medical Debt Undermines Housing Security (Nov. 2005) (70% of medical debtors owed debt to hospitals, 44% owed debt to physicians, 20% owed debt to a lab, and 13% owed debt to an ambulance service).

48 15 U.S.C. § 1681c(a)(6); *see* § 10.3.4, *infra*.

One way to find out more information about a debtor's medical bill is to request the full invoice that itemizes individual charges from the hospital. Federal health care privacy regulations require that hospitals provide a copy of medical records and other health information to patients at their request.[49] Practitioners may want to specifically ask for "Form HCFA-1450" or "UB-92," which is a form used by hospitals and other institutions to complete a Medicare claim.

Practitioners may attempt to obtain more information by requesting verification under the Fair Debt Collection Practices Act (FDCPA). However, collection agencies are not required to give itemized billing statements pursuant to a request for verification under the FDCPA.[50] If the debtor has insurance but owes medical debt due to co-payments or deductibles, another way to obtain more information is to obtain the Explanation of Benefits (EOB) from the debtor's insurance company. Once a debtor has a copy of his or her bill, the next big hurdle is deciphering it.[51] Medical bills are notorious for being incomprehensible, and have been described as no less than Kafkaesque.[52] Patients sometimes refuse to pay bills because they fail to itemize the amounts sought or explain what the charges were for.[53]

10.2 Applicability of FDCPA to Abusive Medical Collection Agencies

10.2.1 General

The full panoply of laws that protect consumers from abusive debt collection tactics are available to patients who have been subject to such tactics by health care providers and their collectors. These laws are discussed in detail in other manuals in this series.[54] This chapter will summarize the major laws that protect consumers and any nuances in the application of those laws to medical collection situations.

The Fair Debt Collection Practices Act clearly applies to medical debt.[55] There have been many instances of medical collection agencies and even providers violating the FDCPA's prohibitions against harassment,[56] deception[57] and unfair

49 45 C.F.R. § 164.502(a)(2); *see* § 10.3.3, *infra.*

50 Recker v. Cent. Collections Bureau, 2005 WL 2654222 (S.D. Ind. Oct. 17, 2005) (computer printout setting forth amount of debts, medical services provided, and dates that debts were incurred were sufficient for verification under FDCPA); Zaborac v. Mut. Hosp. Services, 2004 WL 2538643 (S.D. Ind. Oct. 7, 2004); *see also* Clark v. Capital Credit & Collection Services, 2004 WL 1305326 (D. Or. Jan. 23, 2004) (debt collector not required to investigate whether psychotherapy bills were covered by insurance in verifying debt), *aff'd in part, rev'd in part,* 460 F.3d 1162 (9th Cir. 2006), *aff'd in relevant part,* 198 Fed. Appx. 623 (9th Cir. 2006).

51 For tips on how to read a hospital bill, see *Decoding Your Hospital Bills: You Can Find And Fix Costly Errors,* Consumer Reports, Jan. 2003, at 19.

52 Katie Hafner, *Treated for Illness, Then Lost in Labyrinth of Bills,* N.Y. Times, Oct. 31, 2005.

53 *See, e.g.,* Univ. of Wis. Med. Found. v. Turner, 735 N.W.2d 195 (Wis. Ct. App. 2007) (*pro se* patient held liable for bill despite his confusion over the bill and questions as to whether services were actually provided for all of the charges).

54 National Consumer Law Center, Fair Debt Collection (6th ed. 2008); National Consumer Law Center, Fair Credit Reporting (6th ed. 2006 and Supp.); National Consumer Law Center, Unfair and Deceptive Acts and Practices (6th ed. 2004 and Supp.).

55 *E.g.,* Pipiles v. Credit Bureau, 886 F.2d 22 (2d Cir. 1989); Campion v. Credit Bureau Services, Inc., 2000 U.S. Dist. LEXIS 20233 (E.D. Wash. Sept. 19, 2000); Finnegan v. Univ. of Rochester Med. Ctr., 21 F. Supp. 2d 223 (W.D.N.Y. 1998); Creighton v. Emporia Credit Services, 981 F. Supp. 411 (E.D. Va. 1997); Adams v. Law Offices of Stuckert & Yates, 926 F. Supp. 521 (E.D. Pa. 1996) (even though the consumer and the physician expected the consumer's insurer to pay the bill, still considered consumer's debt because the consumer was ultimately responsible for paying); Bingham v. Collection Bureau, 505 F. Supp. 864 (D.N.D. 1981); Roger J. Fitzpatrick, Att'y, Div. of Credit Practices, Fed. Trade Comm'n, Informal Staff Letter to Thomas Isgrigg, Vice President, U.S. Credit Bureau Inc. (Dec. 22, 1992); Fed. Trade Comm'n, Official Staff Commentary to FDCPA § 803(5), 53 Fed. Reg. 50,097 (Dec. 13, 1988); *see* National Consumer Law Center, Fair Debt Collection § 4.4.2.2 (6th ed. 2008).

56 *See, e.g.,* Baruch v. Healthcare Receivable Mgmt., Inc., 2007 WL 3232090 (E.D.N.Y. Oct. 30, 2007) (aggressive dunning by medical debt collector, including repeated letters, calls, and threats, over debt for which provider had agreed to not to bill patient and accept whatever Medicaid paid); Flamm v. Sarner & Assoc., 2006 WL 43770 (E.D. Pa. Jan. 3, 2006) (process server hired by collection attorney repeatedly showed up to debtor's workplace, informed debtor's supervisor that debtor owed large debt to doctor, and made accusations in loud and aggressive tone to administrative assistant that plaintiff was "sneaky little thief" who "stole thousands of dollars from a doctor"); Clark v. Capital Credit & Collection Services, 2004 WL 1305326 (D. Or. Jan. 23, 2004) (dispute over psychotherapy bills; collection agency employee was rude, argumentative and condescending), *aff'd in relevant part, rev'd in part,* 460 F.3d 1162 (9th Cir. 2006), *aff'd in part,* 198 Fed. Appx. 623 (9th Cir. 2006); Joseph v. J.J. MacIntyre Companies, 238 F. Supp. 2d 1158 (N.D. Cal. 2002) (barrage of phone calls to disabled senior citizen, despite requests to stop), *later opinion at* 281 F. Supp. 2d 1156 (N.D. Cal. 2003) (collector's motion for summary judgment denied). *See generally* Steve Tripoli & Chi Chi Wu, National Consumer Law Center, Unhealthy Pursuits: How the Sick and Vulnerable Are Harmed by Abusive Medical Debt Collection Tactics (Dec. 2005), *available at* www.consumerlaw.org/issues/medical_debt/content/medicaldebt.pdf.

57 *See, e.g.,* Lester E. Cox Med. Ctr. v. Huntsman, 408 F.3d 989 (8th Cir. 2005) (FDCPA violation to use letterhead bearing name that appeared to be third-party collection agency, when agency was owned by hospital); Alarcon v. TransUnion Mktg., 2007 WL 1201624 (N.D. Ohio Apr. 20, 2007) (patient stated claim for provider's use of "flat rating," that is, use of letterhead creating false impression that a collection agency is dunning the patient); Carlson v. Long Island Jewish Med. Ctr., 378 F. Supp.

debt collection practices.[58] There have also been examples when these medical bill collectors:

- Failed to provide consumers with appropriate notices under the FDCPA;[59]
- Sued consumers in an inappropriate forum;[60]
- Failed to abide by a cease communications request;[61]
- Falsely threatened imminent legal action;[62] and
- Demanded repayment of illegal and excessive collection fees not authorized by contract or state law.[63]

FDCPA claims may be asserted in individual suits against the collection agency, as one of several counts in a broader health services class action, or as a counterclaim or third party complaint in a collection suit filed by a collection agency or a health care provider.

10.2.2 Coverage of Various Actors in Medical Debt Collection

The fact that the FDCPA applies primarily to collection agencies and collection lawyers, and usually not to creditors, is not so significant in the health care field because hospitals and doctors are major users of collection agencies.[64] In addition, health care providers sell debts to debt buyers,[65]

2d 128 (E.D.N.Y. 2005) (use of fictitious name may violate FDCPA); Alexander v. Unlimited Progress Corp., 2004 WL 2384645 (N.D. Ill. Oct. 20, 2004) (agency collecting dentist bill; deceptive to demand immediate payment of the debt after consumer filed for bankruptcy); Avila v. Van Ru Credit Corp., 1995 WL 41425 (N.D. Ill. Jan. 31, 1995) (class certification in an FDCPA case involving, *inter alia*, attempts to collect debts arising from student loans and medical or hospital bills by deceptively using attorney's letterhead); Robinson v. Credit Serv. Co., 1991 WL 186665 (D.N.J. Sept. 16, 1991) (dunning a parent of a twenty-year-old child for the child's medical bill may misrepresent the parent's liability, in violation of FDCPA); Weiss v. Collection Ctr., Inc., 667 N.W.2d 567 (N.D. 2003) (consumers stated FDCPA claim against clinic's collector for sending letter informing consumers that collector had obtained information from DMV about consumer's vehicle; letter could be read by unsophisticated consumer as threat to seize vehicle).

58 Mikula v. Great Lakes Fin. Services, 2004 WL 1656556 (N.D. Ill. July 22, 2004) (FDCPA claim against hospital for balance billing in violation of hospital's preferred provider agreement with insurer); Carroll v. Butterfield Health Care, 2003 WL 22462604 (N.D. Ill. Oct. 29, 2003) (nursing home's violated Medicaid law by requiring personal guarantee of patient's son-in-law; son-in-law stated FDCPA claim against attorney-collector for suing on illegal guarantee); Edwards v. McCormick, 136 F. Supp. 2d 795 (S.D. Ohio 2001) (demanding payment of medical bill from non-debtor spouse and threatening forced sale of home contrary to state exemption law violated FDCPA); Finnegan v. Univ. of Rochester Med. Ctr., 21 F. Supp. 2d 223 (W.D.N.Y. 1998) (denying motion to dismiss when collector continued to attempt to collect debt it knew was disputed and reported the debt to credit reporting agency); *cf.* Zaborac v. Mut. Hosp. Serv., 2004 WL 2538643 (S.D. Ind. Oct. 7, 2004) (debt collector violated FDCPA's prohibition against communicating with consumer known to be represented by counsel; bona fide error defense allowed).

59 Cinelli v. MCS Claims Services, Inc., 236 F.R.D. 118 (E.D.N.Y. 2006) (class action settlement of FDCPA claim that verification letter from hospital's debt collector that failed to inform debtors that disputes over validity of the debt must be in writing); Finnegan v. Univ. of Rochester Med. Ctr., 21 F. Supp. 2d 223 (W.D.N.Y. 1998) (consumer stated FDCPA claim against hospital collection agency for failing to send validation notice); Jones v. Ginn, Clearinghouse No. 48,160 (N.D. Ohio 1992) (consent judgment) (in settlement of case, hospital's debt collectors enjoined from sending statement failing to disclose that notice is attempt to collect debt and that information obtained will be used for that purpose).

60 Tedrow v. Cowles, 2007 WL 2688276 (S. D. Ohio Sept. 12, 2007) (class certification of FDCPA and UDAP action alleging that attorney for hospital filed collection actions in Ohio county where patients neither resided nor received services); Jack Mailman & Leonard Flug, D.D.S. v. Whaley, 2002 WL 31988623 (N.Y. Civ. Ct. Nov. 25, 2002) (venue improper under state or federal statute when Brooklyn consumers were sued in Staten Island court; court expresses disapproval of attorney-collector's practice of bringing large volume of collection cases there and orders collector to bring future suits in the county where the debtor resides); Jones v. Ginn, Clearinghouse No. 48,160 (N.D. Ohio 1992) (consent judgment) (in case settlement hospital's debt collectors enjoined from bringing civil suit against consumers in a distant forum, that is, a state court located in state other than that in which consumer resides).

61 Barton v. Revenue Corp., 2007 WL 892994 (N.D. Ohio Mar. 21, 2007); Clark v. Capital Credit & Collection Services, 2004 WL 1305326 (D. Or. Jan. 23, 2004), *aff'd in relevant part, rev'd in part*, 460 F.3d 1162 (9th Cir. 2006), *aff'd in part*, 198 Fed. Appx. 623 (9th Cir. 2006).

62 Cambron v. Med. Data Systems (*In re* Cambron), 2007 WL 4287376 (M.D. Ala. Dec. 5, 2007) (deceptive to imply that medical debt collector could garnish wages or seize assets to recover time-barred debts); Bankston v. Phycom Corp., 2007 WL 4170627 (N.D. Cal. Nov. 19, 2007); Kreek v. Phycom Corp., 2007 WL 1229315 (N.D. Cal. Apr. 25, 2007).

63 Shula v. Lawent, 359 F.3d 489 (7th Cir. 2004) (agency collecting doctor's bill; deceptive to demand specific amount of court costs in absence of court order when Illinois law made award of costs discretionary); Adams v. A & S Collection Associates, Inc., 2007 WL 2206935 (D. Conn. July 23, 2007) (doctor's bill added a 49% collection fee and 18% interest in violation of state law), *subsequent proceeding at* 2007 WL 2206936 (D. Conn. July 30, 2007); Foster v. D.B.S. Collection Agency, 463 F. Supp. 2d 783 (S.D. Ohio 2006) (debt collector filed improperly filed lawsuits without legal capacity, sought attorney fees in violation of state law, and sued spouses of medical debtors without showing necessaries doctrine applied).

64 *See* Robert M. Hunt, Fed. Reserve Bank of Philadelphia, *Collecting Consumer Debt in America*, Bus. Rev., at 13 (2d Quarter 2007), *available at* www.philadelphiafed.org/files/br/2007/q2/hunt_collecting-consumer-debt.pdf ("health-care providers represented the most important group of customers [for debt collectors], accounting for more than a quarter of all revenues"); Ass'n of Credit & Collection Professionals, White Paper—Healthcare Billing and Collections: The Industry Perspective (May 2004) (three-fifths of ACA members engaged in billing and collections for healthcare providers).

65 *See* ACA Int'l, Healthcare Collection, Servicing and Debt Purchasing Practices: Statement of Principles and Guidelines, Ass'n of Credit & Collection Professionals (Feb. 22, 2007) (discussing "debt sale agreements" with healthcare providers);

who are also covered under the FDCPA.[66] Some providers are also transferring medical debt to lenders, such as banks or finance companies.[67] These debts may be in default and, if so, the lenders should be covered by the FDCPA.[68] Yet it is unclear that these lenders are giving the notices required under the FDCPA.

Debt collectors sometimes provide services to hospitals in addition to collection activities, such as providing admission and registration support, collecting financial information from patients to support a Medicaid or charity care application, providing customer support on billing questions, and conducting follow up with insurance companies.[69] These activities would not be covered under the FDCPA.[70] However medical billing companies may be subject to state laws[71] or other regulatory schemes.[72] There are even state agencies that act as medical debt collectors;[73] they would not be subject to the FDCPA.[74]

While hospitals and doctors are generally "creditors" not subject to the FDCPA,[75] there are a number of instances in which they have formed in-house or affiliated collection entities. These entities may be subject to the FDCPA. An example of one such entity was described in detail in *Orenbuch v. North Shore Health Systems*.[76] In *Orenbuch*, a group of hospitals formed Regional Claims Recovery Service (RCRS), a debt collection agency that was an unincorporated subdivision of a corporation that provided the hospitals' administrative support. RCRS had its own employees and computer system at a separate location. RCRS also actively marketed its services to hospitals outside the North Shore family and used its own letterhead. It was undisputed that RCRS was subject to the FDCPA.[77]

Other examples of similar entities have been described in Federal Trade Commission (FTC) informal staff letters.[78] For example, the FTC discussed the example of a nonprofit hospital that created a separate collection organization to collect debts for itself and other health care providers.[79] The FTC has stated that if a hospital and a debt collection agency do share common ownership, the agency should indicate its affiliation with the hospital when collecting the hospital's debts unless the agency is functionally independent of the hospital.[80] However, if an affiliated collection agency is

---

see also Hosp. & Doctors Serv. Bureau v. Mitchell, 2007 WL 1136080 (N.J. Super. Ct. App. Div. Apr. 18, 2007) (hospital's nonprofit status did not bar it from assigning medical bills to debt buyer).

There are even debt buyers that specialize in the purchase of medical debt. See, for example, www.medclr.com (last visited Feb. 2008) (debt buyer specializing in purchase of medical debt). For more on debt buyers, see § 1.4, *supra*.

66 National Consumer Law Center, Fair Debt Collection § 4.2 (6th ed. 2008).

67 Brian Grow & Robert Berner, Fresh Pain for the Uninsured, Bus. Week, Nov. 21, 2007; *see, e.g.*, Katiuzhinsky v. Perry, 62 Cal. Rptr. 3d 309 (Ct. App. 2007) (example of a specialized medical financing company to which hospitals sell accident victims' debts at a 50% discount; finance company then waits until tort recovery to collect full amount of debt).

68 National Consumer Law Center, Fair Debt Collection § 4.2 (6th ed. 2008).

69 Ass'n of Credit & Collection Professionals, White Paper—Healthcare Billing and Collections: The Industry Perspective (May 2004).

70 Dickard v. Okla. Mgmt. Services for Physicians, L.L.C., 2007 WL 3025020 (W.D. Ark. Oct. 15, 2007) (company that provided billing service was not debt collector under FDCPA because debt was not in default when bill was sent); Healey v. Jzanus, Inc., 2006 WL 898067 (E.D.N.Y. Apr. 4, 2006) (FDCPA did not apply when service that both engaged in debt collection and processed Medicaid claims sent letter to debtor, because letter sought information for Medicaid application and debt was not in default).

71 *See, e.g.*, Flores v. Rawlings Co., L.L.C., 117 Haw. 153 (Haw. 2008) (provider of "claims recovery services" was a collection agency under Hawaii law even though it asserted that it did not collect "debts"; Hawaii statute covers entity that collects "claims or money due on accounts" for another).

72 *See, e.g.*, Office of Inspector General, United States Dep't of Health & Human Services, Compliance Program Guidance for Third-Party Medical Billing Companies, 63 Fed. Reg. 70,138 (Dec. 18, 1998).

73 Mike Bevel, *State Passes Bill Enabling It to Act As Debt Collector for Medical Bills* (May 14, 2007), *available at* InsideARM.com.

74 *See* National Consumer Law Center, Fair Debt Collection § 4.3.4 (6th ed. 2008).

75 Sabeta v. Baptist Hosp., Inc., 410 F. Supp. 2d 1224 (S.D. Fla. 2005) (FDCPA does not apply to hospital collecting its own debts in its own name); Kolari v. N.Y. Presbyterian Hosp., 382 F. Supp. 2d 562 (S.D.N.Y. 2005) (same), *vacated in part on other grounds*, 455 F.3d 118 (2d Cir. 2006); Carlson v. Long Island Jewish Med. Ctr., 378 F. Supp. 2d 128 (E.D.N.Y. 2005) (use of fictitious name may violate FDCPA); Burton v. William Beaumont Hosp., 373 F. Supp. 2d 707 (E.D. Mich. 2005) (FDCPA does not apply to hospital collecting its own debts in its own name); Hutt v. Albert Einstein Med. Ctr., 2005 WL 2396313 (E.D. Pa. Sept. 28, 2005) (same); Cargile v. Baylor Health Care Sys., 2005 WL 2445482 (N.D. Tex. Aug. 10, 2005) (same); Darr v. Sutter Health, 2004 WL 2873068 (N.D. Cal. Nov. 20, 2004) (same); *see* National Consumer Law Center, Fair Debt Collection § 4.3.2 (6th ed. 2008).

76 250 F. Supp. 2d 145 (E.D.N.Y. 2003).

77 *Id.* (finding no violation of the FDCPA for failure to disclose the relationship between RCRS and affiliated hospitals); *see* Carlson v. Long Island Jewish Med. Ctr., 378 F. Supp. 2d 128 (E.D.N.Y. 2005) (case also involving Regional Claims Recovery Service); *see also* Healy v. Jzanus, Ltd., 2002 WL 31654571 (E.D.N.Y. Nov. 20, 2002) (FDCPA applied to unincorporated association called "Medicaid Recovery Services" that sought information for Medicaid application, but also included in its letters a "balance due" and statement that "this is an attempt to collect a debt").

78 See National Consumer Law Center, Fair Debt Collection § 3.2.5 (6th ed. 2008), for a discussion of the legal status of FTC informal staff letters.

79 Norman E. Oliver, Att'y, Div. of Credit Practices, Fed. Trade Comm'n, Informal Staff Letter to Joan M. Healy, Att'y (Dec. 2, 1981) (noting that the use of an attorney letterhead by the collector's staff attorney without indicating the attorney's employment by the collector would violate the FDCPA subjecting the collector and the attorney to liability).

80 Jonathan D. Jerison, Att'y, Div. of Credit Practices, Fed. Trade

actually staffed and run by another collection agency, it should operate under the name of the collection agency, as it controls the employees.[81]

Even if a health care provider does not use a separate entity or affiliate to collect its debts, the provider's own conduct might subject it to the FDCPA. For example, if a hospital's internal bill collector misrepresents that he or she is calling from a collection agency or a private law firm, both the employee and the hospital are covered by the FDCPA.[82] Indeed, one FTC informal staff letter indicated that a hospital staff attorney's plan to send collection letters on letterhead, implying that he was a private practitioner without disclosing his hospital employment, would violate the FDCPA and subject both the hospital and the attorney to FDCPA liability.[83] A hospital that operated its collection division under a separate name instead of its true name was found to be a debt collector under the FDCPA, and to have violated section 1692a(6) by sending a dunning letter using the fictitious name.[84]

10.3 Other Federal Statutes Applicable to Medical Debt

10.3.1 Truth in Lending

Many hospitals will offer payment plans to consumers who owe large amounts of medical debt. Under certain circumstances, these plans will be covered by the federal Truth in Lending Act (TILA).[85] A non-credit transaction, such as the typical medical bill, can be converted to a credit transaction subject to TILA if several requirements are met.

First, the creditor and the consumer must enter into an agreement that gives the consumer the right to defer payment of the debt.[86] Second, the agreement must provide for the imposition of a finance charge or payment of the debt in more than four installments.[87] Note that the imposition of late charges can not be equated with finance charges to bring the agreement under TILA; if the debt is still structured as an account receivable that is due in full, the imposition of late charges will not make it a credit transaction subject to TILA.[88] If there is a payment plan, there must be a written agreement reflecting payment terms, not simply "an informal workout arrangement," to bring it within the scope of TILA.[89]

Finally, the consumer must be able to show that the creditor "regularly" extends consumer credit. The Federal Reserve Board has defined "regularly" to mean that the creditor must have extended credit more than twenty-five times in the preceding calendar year (or more than five times for transactions secured by a dwelling).[90]

Comm'n, Informal Staff Letter to William E. Roach, Jr., Att'y, Gardner, Carton & Douglas (Nov. 8, 1983).

81 *Id.*; Orenbuch v. N. Shore Health Sys., 250 F. Supp. 2d 145 (E.D.N.Y. 2003) (not deceptive to use name under which affiliated but functionally separate collector was licensed; disclosure of corporate affiliation not required).

82 Lester E. Cox Med. Ctr. v. Huntsman, 408 F.3d 989 (8th Cir. 2005) (use of fictitious name violated FDCPA); Alarcon v. TransUnion Mktg., 2007 WL 1201624 (N.D. Ohio Apr. 20, 2007) (patient stated claim for provider's use of "flat rating," that is, use of letterhead creating false impression that a collection agency is dunning the patient); Sabeta v. Baptist Hosp., Inc., 410 F. Supp. 2d 1224 (S.D. Fla. 2005) (granting leave to amend to allege use of fictitious name); Carlson v. Long Island Jewish Med. Ctr., 378 F. Supp. 2d 128 (E.D.N.Y. 2005) (denying hospital's motion to dismiss FDCPA claim when plaintiff alleged use of fictitious name); Cargile v. Baylor Health Care Sys., 2005 WL 2445482 (N.D. Tex. Aug. 10, 2005) (granting leaving to amend to allege use of fictitious name with respect to collection of debts against plaintiffs). *But see* Medica Self-Insured v. Tenet Healthcare Corp., 2007 WL 1385589 (D. Minn. May 4, 2007) (hospital entity that used fictitious name to collect debts but disclosed that it was hospital's collection department was not debt collector under FDCPA). *See generally* National Consumer Law Center, Fair Debt Collection § 4.2.5 (6th ed. 2008).

83 Alan D. Reffkin, Att'y, Div. of Credit Practices, Fed. Trade Comm'n, Informal Staff Letter to James E. McDonald, Esq. (Apr. 10, 1980).

84 Lester E. Cox Med. Ctr. v. Huntsman, 408 F.3d 989 (8th Cir. 2005).

85 15 U.S.C. §§ 1601–1640; *see* National Consumer Law Center, Truth in Lending Ch. 2 (6th ed. 2007); *cf.* Jack Mailman & Leonard Flug, D.D.S. v. Whaley, 2002 WL 31988623 (N.Y. Civ. Ct. Nov. 25, 2002) (consumer credit transaction within meaning of state consumer credit statute; imposition of service charge showed that time payments were contemplated).

86 15 U.S.C. § 1602(e); Regulation Z, 12 C.F.R. § 226.2(a)(14) (definition of "credit"); *see* Pollice v. Nat'l Tax Funding, 225 F.3d 379 (3d Cir. 2000) (installment payment agreement entered into between consumer and collection agency to repay delinquent water bills was credit transaction subject to TILA). *See generally* National Consumer Law Center, Truth in Lending § 2.2.4.1 (6th ed. 2007); National Consumer Law Center, The Cost of Credit: Regulation, Preemption, and Industry Abuses § 10.5.2.3 (3d ed. 2005 and Supp.).

87 15 U.S.C. § 1602(f)(1); Regulation Z, 12 C.F.R. § 226.2(a)(17)(i)(A); *see* National Consumer Law Center, Truth in Lending § 2.3.4 (6th ed. 2007 and Supp.).

88 Regulation Z, 12 C.F.R. § 226.4(c)(2); Fed. Reserve Bd., Official Staff Commentary to 12 C.F.R. § 226.4(c)(2)-1 (reprinted in National Consumer Law Center, Truth in Lending Appx. C (6th ed. 2007)); *see* Bright v. Ball Mem'l Hosp. Ass'n, 616 F.2d 328 (7th Cir. 1980) (because the entire lump sum was due, and there was no new formal written arrangement for time payments, a .75% per month charge was a "late charge."). *See generally* National Consumer Law Center, Truth in Lending § 3.9.3.4 (6th ed. 2007).

89 Bright v. Ball Mem'l Hosp. Ass'n, 616 F.2d 328 (7th Cir. 1980); Finnegan v. Univ. of Rochester Med. Ctr., 21 F. Supp. 2d 223 (W.D.N.Y. 1998) (arrangement with hospital to hold off on collection while debtor pursued Social Security appeal was an "informal workout agreement," not an extension of credit for purposes of TILA); *see* National Consumer Law Center, Truth in Lending § 2.3.4.3 (6th ed. 2007).

90 Regulation Z, 12 C.F.R. § 226.2(a)(17)(i); *see* National Consumer Law Center, Truth in Lending § 2.3.3 (6th ed. 2007).

In addition to the above factors to establish TILA coverage, the credit arrangement must be "consummated," that is offered by the creditor and accepted by the consumer.[91] The hospital's mere offer of an installment plan is insufficient to establish TILA coverage.[92]

If TILA does cover the a medical bill payment plan, the creditor will be required to clearly disclose certain terms of that credit to the consumer prior to consummation.[93] When the TILA applies to a payment plan for a medical debt and the creditor fails to make key TILA disclosures, the creditor will be liable to the consumer for actual damages, statutory damages (twice the finance charge, but no less than $100 nor more than $1000), and attorney fees.[94] Suit may be brought to recover TILA damages within one year of the violation,[95] or, in most states, TILA violations may be raised at any time as a recoupment or counterclaim to the provider's collection suit.[96]

Increasingly, hospitals are offering loans or lines of credit to pay for medical services. Many times this credit is extended by a separate lender, not the provider—although the provider may be acting as a loan broker and subject to state laws governing that activity.[97] These credit arrangements would clearly be subject to TILA, and practitioners should examine whether proper disclosures were made.[98] In some cases lenders may characterize the credit as "open-end" credit, that is, a reusable credit line, when it is really closed-end credit, because the disclosure requirements for open-end credit are much weaker. Practitioners may want to challenge such spurious open-end credit arrangements.[99] On the other hand, if the credit is truly open-end but is accessed using a card or other device, it may constitute a "credit card" under TILA.[100]

Certain insurers may pay for a patient's medical bills under the theory that the payments are a "loan" to the patient.[101] This arrangement is a form of subrogation, so that the insurer can recover the payments should the patient receive funds in, for example, a tort lawsuit.[102] If these loans involve a finance charge or a written agreement to repay in four or more installments, TILA should apply.

10.3.2 EMTALA

If a debtor was refused treatment at an emergency room because of medical debt, a counterclaim may exist pursuant to the Emergency Medical Treatment and Active Labor Act (EMTALA).[103] EMTALA is a federal statute that prohibits hospitals from turning away a patient in need of emergency medical treatment because, among other things, the patient may not be able to pay for the care.[104] EMTALA should prohibit a hospital from turning away a patient in need of emergency care because of prior bills owed to that hospital.[105]

EMTALA prohibits delay in providing medical screening or care in order to inquire about payment for care.[106] However, the Unites States Department of Health and Human Services has issued a regulation under EMTALA permitting hospitals to employ "reasonable registration processes," which include asking about payment, so long as the inquiry does not delay treatment or screening.[107] A number of courts have interpreted this regulation to allow hospitals to seek the signature of patients on consent forms that include a provision (usually hidden) requiring patients' agreement to pay for the medical care provided.[108]

---

91 Regulation Z, 12 C.F.R. § 226.2(a)(13); Fed. Reserve Bd., Official Staff Commentary to 12 C.F.R. § 226.2(a)(13) (reprinted in National Consumer Law Center, Truth in Lending Appx. C (6th ed. 2007)); *see* National Consumer Law Center, Truth in Lending § 4.3.2 (6th ed. 2007).

92 *E.g.*, Bright v. Ball Mem'l Hosp. Ass'n, 616 F.2d 328 (7th Cir. 1980) (no evidence that consumer accepted hospital's payment plan offer, so TILA did not apply).

93 See National Consumer Law Center, Truth in Lending Ch. 4 (6th ed. 2007), for a description of disclosures required for closed-end credit. Disclosures for open-end credit are discussed in Chapter 5 of the same manual.

94 *Id.* Ch. 8.

95 *Id.* § 7.2.

96 15 U.S.C. § 1640(e); *see also* National Consumer Law Center, Truth in Lending § 7.2.5 (6th ed. 2007).

97 *See* § 10.4.5, *infra*.

98 *See, e.g.*, Jones v. People's Heritage Bank, 433 F. Supp. 2d 1328 (S.D. Ga. 2006) (dental credit plan charged hidden administrative fee withheld from amount paid to dentist; court held hidden fee was not a finance charge because plaintiff did not pay more because she paid by credit, but rather because she did not pay at inception of work; court ignores fact that only a patient paying in cash could pay at inception and that therefore the additional amount owed is related to use of credit).

99 See National Consumer Law Center, Truth in Lending § 5.2.3 (6th ed. 2007), for a discussion of challenging spurious open-end credit.

100 15 U.S.C. § 1602(k); *see* National Consumer Law Center, Truth in Lending § 5.2.4.1 (6th ed. 2007).

101 *See, e.g.*, Flores v. Rawlings Co., L.L.C., 117 Haw. 153 (Haw. 2008).

102 *See* § 10.4.6, *infra*.

103 42 U.S.C. § 1395dd.

104 *See* St. Anthony Hosp. v. United States Dep't of Health & Human Services, 309 F.3d 680 (10th Cir. 2002) (Congress enacted the EMTALA to address the problem of hospital emergency rooms "refusing to accept or treat patients with emergency conditions if the patient does not have medical insurance"; citing H.R. Rep. No. 99-241, pt. 1, at 27 (1985)); Battle v. Mem'l Hosp., 228 F.3d 544 (5th Cir. 2000) (EMTALA's purpose "to prevent 'patient dumping,' which is the practice of refusing to treat patients who are unable to pay").

105 *See* Ziegler v. Elmore County Health Care Auth., 56 F. Supp. 2d 1324 (M.D. Ala. 1999) (denying hospital's motion for summary judgment on EMTALA claim of child whose recovery was delayed and suffering prolonged after being turned away from emergency room because mother owed bill).

106 42 U.S.C. § 1395dd(h).

107 42 C.F.R. § 489.24(d)(4)(iv).

108 Parker v. Salina Reg'l Health Ctr., Inc., 463 F. Supp. 2d 1263 (D. Kan. 2006); Sabeta v. Baptist Hosp., Inc., 410 F. Supp. 2d 1224

EMTALA applies to private hospitals which accept Medicare or Medicaid, and to certain public hospitals.[109] EMTALA provides for a private cause of action against hospitals,[110] but not physicians,[111] who violate its provisions.[112] The patient may obtain any remedies available under applicable tort law in the state where the hospital is located, such as actual damages, attorney fees and, in some states, punitive damages.[113] However, the patient must allege "personal harm" from the EMTALA violation that would be compensable under that state's personal injury law. Thus a number of courts have held that economic injury due to debt collection or discriminatory pricing is not actionable under EMTALA.[114] Violation of EMTALA might be challenged using a state deceptive practices (UDAP) statute.[115]

Some states may have emergency admission requirements that are more detailed or stricter than the federal statute.[116] Note that EMTALA does not provide for *free care*—if an uninsured patient does receive treatment, the patient may be held liable for medical bills.[117] Indeed, in several dozen cases challenging uninsured patients' medical bills as excessive, the courts have dismissed EMTALA claims.[118]

10.3.3 Debt Collection and Privacy of Medical Information

Practitioners should look out for potential violations of medical privacy rules by providers when they send medical information to debt collectors. The United States Department of Health and Human Services (HHS) has issued rules

(S.D. Fla. 2005); Grant v. Trinity Health Mich., 390 F. Supp. 2d 643 (E.D. Mich. 2005); Kolari v. N.Y. Presbyterian Hosp., 382 F. Supp. 2d 562 (S.D.N.Y. 2005), *vacated in part on other grounds*, 455 F.3d 118 (2d Cir. 2006); Burton v. William Beaumont Hosp., 373 F. Supp. 2d 707 (E.D. Mich. 2005); Amato v. UPMC, 371 F. Supp. 2d 752 (W.D. Pa. 2005); Hutt v. Albert Einstein Med. Ctr., 2005 WL 2396313 (E.D. Pa. Sept. 28, 2005); Feliciana v. Thomas Jefferson Univ. Hosp., 2005 WL 2397047 (E.D. Pa. Sept. 28, 2005).

109 EMTALA applies to public hospitals operated by subdivisions of the state such as counties and municipalities, but not hospitals operated by the state itself, which have Eleventh Amendment immunity. *See* Root v. New Liberty Hosp. Dist., 209 F.3d 1068 (8th Cir. 2000) (public hospital operated by local hospital district may be sued under EMTALA, which preempts state sovereign immunity statute); Drew v. Univ. of Tenn. Reg'l Med. Ctr. Hosp., 2000 U.S. App. LEXIS 8936 (6th Cir. May 1, 2000) (Eleventh Amendment barred EMTALA suit against the state university hospital, which is an arm of the state); Lebron v. Ashford Presbyterian Cmty. Hosp., 975 F. Supp. 407 (D. P.R. 1997) (University of Puerto Rico is a state entity protected from EMTALA liability by Eleventh Amendment).

110 42 U.S.C. § 1395dd(a).

111 *See* Eberhardt v. City of Los Angeles, 62 F.3d 1253 (9th Cir. 1995); King v. Ahrens, 16 F.3d 265 (8th Cir. 1994) (no cause of action against individual physician); Delaney v. Cade, 986 F.2d 387 (10th Cir. 1993) (plain language of statute indicates actions may be brought against hospitals but not doctors); Baber v. Hosp. Corp. of Am., 977 F.2d 872 (4th Cir. 1992) (no cause of action against individual physician); Gatewood v. Wash. Healthcare Corp., 933 F.2d 1037 (D.C. Cir. 1991).

112 42 U.S.C. § 1395dd(d)(2).

113 42 U.S.C. § 1395dd(d)(2).

114 Harrison v. Christus St. Patrick Hosp., 430 F. Supp. 2d 591 (W.D. La. 2006); Sabeta v. Baptist Hosp., Inc., 410 F. Supp. 2d 1224 (S.D. Fla. 2005); Grant v. Trinity Health Mich., 390 F. Supp. 2d 643 (E.D. Mich. 2005) (EMTALA claim dismissed because damages for "personal harm" only encompass mental distress and bodily harm); Kolari v. N.Y. Presbyterian Hosp., 382 F. Supp. 2d 562 (S.D.N.Y. 2005); Burton v. William Beaumont Hosp., 373 F. Supp. 2d 707 (E.D. Mich. 2005); Amato v. UPMC, 371 F. Supp. 2d 752 (W.D. Pa. 2005); Quinn v. BJC Health Sys., 364 F. Supp. 2d 1046 (E.D. Mo. 2005); Valencia v. Miss. Baptist Med. Ctr., 363 F. Supp. 2d 867 (S.D. Miss. 2005); Feliciana v. Thomas Jefferson Univ. Hosp., 2005 WL 2397047 (E.D. Pa. Sept. 28, 2005); Hutt v. Albert Einstein Med. Ctr., 2005 WL 2396313 (E.D. Pa. Sept. 28, 2005); Nash v. Lee Mem'l Health Sys., 2005 WL 2043642 (M.D. Fla. Aug. 25, 2005); Kabeller v. Orlando Reg'l Healthcare Sys., Inc., 2005 WL 1925717 (M.D. Fla. Aug. 11, 2005); Cargile v. Baylor Health Care Sys., 2005 WL 2445482 (N.D. Tex. Aug. 10, 2005); Gardner v. N. Miss. Health Services, Inc., 2005 WL 1312753 (N.D. Miss. May 31, 2005); Jakubiec v. Sacred Heart Health Sys., Inc., 2005 WL 1261443 (N.D. Fla. May 26, 2005); Wright v. St. Dominic Health Services, Inc., 2005 WL 743339 (S.D. Miss. Mar. 5, 2005); Peterson v. Fairview Health Services, 2005 WL 226168 (D. Minn. Feb. 1, 2005); Kizzire v. Baptist Health Sys., Inc., 343 F. Supp. 2d 1074 (N.D. Ala. 2004), *aff'd on other grounds*, 441 F.3d 1306 (11th Cir. 2006). *But see* Fotia v. Palmetto Behavioral Health, 317 F. Supp. 2d 638 (D.S.C. 2004) (plaintiff sufficiently alleged "personal harm" to sustain claim for retaliatory firing for revealing hospital's EMTALA violation; only his damages were limited to those damages available in personal injury claims).

A number of courts subsequently held that the analysis of "personal harm" in *Fotia* is limited to cases brought under the "whistleblower" provisions of EMTALA. Burton v. William Beaumont Hosp., 373 F. Supp. 2d 707 (E.D. Mich. 2005); Jakubiec v. Sacred Heart Health Sys., Inc., 2005 WL 1261443 (N.D. Fla. May 26, 2005).

115 Coast Plaza Doctors Hosp. v. UHP Healthcare, 129 Cal. Rptr. 2d 650 (Ct. App. 2002) (hospital stated a claim for violation of California UDAP law with allegation that health maintenance organization caused patients to be transferred in violation of EMTALA).

116 *See, e.g.*, Mass. Gen. Laws ch. 111, § 70E (detailed requirements for safe and comfortable transfer); N.Y. Pub. Health Law § 2805-b (McKinney) (certain general hospitals may not transfer for inability to pay; violation of this section, or preventing access to required services, is a misdemeanor).

117 Emergency Physicians Integrated Care v. Salt Lake County, 167 P.3d 1080 (Utah 2007) (EMTALA requires provision of emergency care but does not prevent the provider from seeking payment from patient or, in this case, county that had statutory duty to care for inmates).

118 *See, e.g.*, Harrison v. Christus St. Patrick Hosp., 430 F. Supp. 2d 591 (W.D. La. 2006); Sabeta v. Baptist Hosp., Inc., 410 F. Supp. 2d 1224 (S.D. Fla. 2005); Grant v. Trinity Health Mich., 390 F. Supp. 2d 643 (E.D. Mich. 2005).

One of these cases noted that EMTALA does not prohibit discriminatory pricing. Quinn v. BJC Health Sys., 364 F. Supp. 2d 1046 (E.D. Mo. 2005).

governing the privacy of medical information pursuant to the Health Insurance Portability and Accountability Act (HIPAA) of 1996.[119] The HIPAA privacy rule applies to health care providers, as well as health plans and clearinghouses.[120] In general, the HIPAA privacy rule permits health care providers to disclose individually identifiable health information only in certain circumstances, unless the individual's written consent is obtained.[121] These circumstances include, among others, treatment, payment, and health care operations activities.[122]

The HIPAA privacy rule does generally permit the disclosure of medical information without the consumer's consent in order to collect payment for services.[123] The disclosure is limited to certain parties, including the provider's "business associates," which presumably would include third-party collection agencies.[124] However, the health care provider must make reasonable efforts to disclose only the minimum amount of protected health information needed to accomplish the intended purpose of the disclosure.[125] Thus, the provider should not disclose the consumer's entire medical record to the debt collector, unless it can specifically justify why the entire record is reasonably needed for debt collection. Furthermore, the HIPAA privacy rule permits the debt collector to disclose protected health information in order to obtain payment, but the collector may only disclose the minimum information necessary to do so.[126] One interesting issue is whether the collector can attach a list of medical expenses to a complaint in a collection action without violating the HIPAA rules.

Note that the HIPAA rules do not provide for a private right of action, but patients might be able to seek relief under some state deceptive practices (UDAP) statutes.[127] Some states may have health information privacy laws that are more protective than the HIPAA privacy rule.[128] Conduct that violates HIPAA might also violate state laws protecting patient-physician confidentiality or constitute common law torts, such as invasion of privacy.[129] Finally, patients can seek relief for a HIPAA violation with the HHS's Office of Civil Rights.[130]

10.3.4 Credit Reporting Issues and Medical Debt

Another way in which medical debt affects consumers is through their credit histories. Providers will often send a medical debt to a collection agency, which results in a derogatory item on the consumer's credit report[131] and a resulting decrease of the consumer's credit score.[132] A study by Federal Reserve Board researchers found that 52% of all accounts reported by collection agencies consisted of medical debt.[133] A study of medical debtors found that, of those surveyed who knew the answer, three out of five reported that their medical debts had shown up in their credit reports.[134] Some of these black marks were for small dollar amounts: 16% of the medical debts showing up on credit reports were

119 Pub. L. No. 104-191, 110 Stat. 1936 (1996).
The HIPAA privacy rule may be found in 45 C.F.R. parts 160 and 164. A summary of the HIPAA privacy rule is available from the HHS's Office of Civil Rights, which is responsible for its implementation. United States Dep't of Health & Human Services, Office of Civil Rights, Summary of the HIPAA Privacy Rule (May 2003), *available at* www.hhs.gov/ocr/privacysummary.pdf (last visited Apr. 2008).

120 45 C.F.R. § 160.102.

121 45 C.F.R. § 164.502.

122 45 C.F.R. §§ 164.502, 164.506.

123 45 C.F.R. §§ 164.502, 164.506; Zaborac v. Mut. Hosp. Services, 2004 WL 2538643 (S.D. Ind. Oct. 7, 2004) (permissible disclosure under HIPAA to obtain "payment" includes debt collection activities).
An exception to this rule is psychotherapy notes, which may not be disclosed without the patient's authorization for payment purposes. 45 C.F.R. § 164.508(a)(2).

124 The HHS's Office of Civil Rights has stated that the HIPAA privacy rule does not prevent health care providers from using third-party collection agencies. *See* United States Dep't of Health & Human Services, Does the HIPAA Privacy Rule Prevent Health Plans and Providers from Using Debt Collection Agencies?, *available at* www.hhs.gov/hipaafaq/providers/smaller/268.html (last visited Apr. 2008). Note that the provider must include certain provisions in its contract with a business associate such as a debt collection agency, including safeguards for the health information used or disclosed by that business associate. In addition, the provider may not contractually authorize its business associate to make any use or disclosure of protected health information that would violate the HIPAA privacy rule. 45 C.F.R. § 164.504(e).

125 45 C.F.R. §§ 164.502(b), 164.514(d).

126 Zaborac v. Mut. Hosp. Services, 2004 WL 2538643 (S.D. Ind. Oct. 7, 2004) (discussing interaction between HIPAA and FDCPA's debt verification requirement).

127 Acara v. Banks, 470 F.3d 569 (5th Cir. 2006). *See generally* National Consumer Law Center, Unfair and Deceptive Acts and Practices § 3.2.7 (6th ed. 2004 and Supp.).

128 For a summary of state health information privacy laws, see Health Privacy Project, State Health Privacy Laws (2d ed. 2002), *available at* www.healthprivacy.org.

129 Franklin Collection Serv., Inc. v. Kyle, 955 So. 2d 284 (Miss. 2007) (collection agency disclosed patient's medical information in lawsuit pleading; no claim for violation of patient-physician confidentiality but invasion of privacy claim survived summary judgment "by barest thread"); *see* National Consumer Law Center, Fair Credit Reporting § 10.5 (6th ed. 2006 and Supp.).

130 United States Dep't of Health & Human Services, Office of Civil Rights, How to File A Health Information Privacy Complaint With The Office For Civil Rights, *available at* www.hhs.gov/ocr/privacyhowtofile.htm (last visited Apr. 2008).

131 *See* National Consumer Law Center, Fair Credit Reporting § 3.3.3.8 (6th ed. 2006 and Supp.).

132 *See id.* § 14.5.2.1.

133 Robert Avery, Paul Calem, Glenn Canner & Raphael Bostic, *An Overview of Consumer Data and Credit Reporting*, Fed. Reserve Bull., at 69 (Feb. 2003).

134 Robert W. Seifert, Access Project, Home Sick: How Medical Debt Undermines Housing Security (Nov. 2005).

for under $500.[135] Medical debt also sometimes is reported on the credit reports of spouses or other relatives.[136]

The impact of medical debt on a consumer's credit report is especially egregious when the medical debt is one which an insurer arguably should have paid. Disputes between health insurers, providers, and consumers occur frequently, and can be of extended duration. Many medical bills are referred to collection agencies during these disputes but are ultimately paid by insurers.[137] A consumer's credit history and credit score may be damaged as a result of a debt being sent to collections during a dispute, or even if the insurer is simply slow in paying the bill.[138] Consumers in these situations may want to file a written dispute with the credit bureaus.[139] Filing a written dispute with the credit bureau provides a cause of action under the Fair Credit Reporting Act (FCRA) against the furnisher of the information, if the furnisher fails to undertake a reasonable investigation of the dispute.[140] In addition, whenever reaching a settlement over medical bills that have adversely affected the consumer's credit record, practitioners should obtain the agreement of the provider or collector to remove or correct this negative information.[141]

The FCRA contains several restrictions on medical information contained in credit reports. The FCRA prohibits credit bureaus from furnishing for employment purposes, or in connection with a credit or insurance transaction, a credit report that contains medical information, unless the consumer consents.[142] The consent for employment and credit purposes (but not for insurance) must be written, must be specific, and must describe the use of the information.[143] In addition, the medical information must be relevant to the employment or credit transaction at issue.[144]

The FCRA also prohibits credit bureaus from including the name, address, or telephone number of medical information furnishers unless the bureau formats the information so that it does not disclose either the specific provider or the nature of the medical services.[145] In order to help credit bureaus comply with this requirement, health care providers and medical information furnishers must notify credit bureaus of their status as such.[146]

The FCRA also prohibits creditors from obtaining or using a consumer's medical information in connection with evaluating creditworthiness, unless permitted by regulation.[147] The regulations generally permit the use of financial information related to a medical condition (in other words, medical debts) so long as the creditor does not treat the consumer less favorably on the basis of the medical condition.[148] Another manual in this series provides more information on the FCRA's provisions regarding medical information.[149]

---

135 *Id.*

For examples of the impact of credit reporting of medical debt, see generally Steve Tripoli & Chi Chi Wu, National Consumer Law Center, Unhealthy Pursuits: How the Sick and Vulnerable Are Harmed by Abusive Medical Debt Collection Tactics (Dec. 2005), *available at* www.consumerlaw.org/issues/medical_debt/content/medicaldebt.pdf.

136 *See, e.g.*, Dunn v. Lehigh Valley Ctr. for Sight, 2003 WL 22299275 (E.D. Pa. Sept. 30, 2003) (provider entitled to report delinquent medical debt on credit report of spouse because spouse also liable for debt under Pennsylvania necessaries statute); Bickford v. Onslow Mem'l Hosp. Found., 855 A.2d 1150 (Me. 2004) (alleging claims for intentional infliction of emotional distress, as well as for defamation and tortuous interference with an economic advantage, over hospital wrongfully reporting to credit bureau that plaintiff owed bills for services to ex-wife's daughter, to whom plaintiff had no legal relationship).

137 *See, e.g.*, Chamberlain v. Farm Bureau Mut. Ins. Co., 137 P.3d 1081 (Kan. Ct. App. 2006) (accident victim's insurer refused to pay full amount of provider's charges because insurer believed they exceeded customary and usual charges, resulting in harm to victim's credit record); *see also* Jennifer Steinhauer, *Will Doctors Make Your Credit Sick?*, N.Y. Times, Feb. 4, 2001; Consumer Fed'n of Am. & Nat'l Credit Reporting Ass'n, Credit Score Accuracy and Implications for Consumers 31 (Dec. 17, 2002), *available at* www.consumerfed.org/121702CFA_NCRA_Credit_Score_Report_Final.pdf.

138 *E.g.*, Witherwax v. Transcare, 801 N.Y.S.2d 782 (Sup. Ct. 2005) (table) (provider failed to bill insurer and instead sent bill to collection agency resulting in negative items on patient's credit report); Angelucci v. Fairmont Gen. Hosp., 618 S.E.2d 373 (W. Va. 2005) (hospital failed to submit bills to insurer and then sent bill to collection agency resulting in negative items on patient's credit report).

139 *See* Bickford v. Onslow Mem'l Hosp. Found., 855 A.2d 1150 (Me. 2004) (noting that medical billing dispute reflected in credit report could have been addressed through FCRA's dispute resolution procedures).

For more information on submitting an FCRA dispute, see National Consumer Law Center, Fair Credit Reporting § 4.5.2 (6th ed. 2006 and Supp.).

140 National Consumer Law Center, Fair Credit Reporting § 6.10 (6th ed. 2006 and Supp.).

If the furnisher does correct the consumer's credit report, however, there is no cause of action under the FCRA. *See, e.g.*, Krieg v. U.M.C. Hosp., 2007 WL 57560 (9th Cir. Jan. 9, 2007) (no FCRA violation when hospital took back account from collection agency, resulting in correction to patient's credit report, after it received information that patient's medical bills would be paid by federal and state government agencies). *But cf.* Witherwax v. Transcare, 801 N.Y.S.2d 782 (Sup. Ct. 2005) (table) (dismissing state law claim for defamation of credit because patient was liable on debt); Angelucci v. Fairmont Gen. Hosp., 618 S.E.2d 373 (W. Va. 2005) (dismissing state law claim for wrongful and malicious credit reporting because patient liable for debt).

141 Sample language to do so is available in another manual in this series. National Consumer Law Center, Fair Credit Reporting § 12.6.4, Appx. J.9 (6th ed. 2006 and Supp.).

142 15 U.S.C. § 1681b(g); *see* National Consumer Law Center, Fair Credit Reporting § 5.4.1.2 (6th ed. 2006 and Supp.).

143 15 U.S.C. § 1681b(g)(1)(B)(ii).

144 15 U.S.C. § 1681b(g)(1)(B)(i).

145 15 U.S.C. § 1681c(a)(6).

There is an exception to this prohibition for insurance companies other than property and casualty insurers. 15 U.S.C. § 1681c(a)(6).

146 15 U.S.C. § 1681s-2(a)(9).

147 15 U.S.C. § 1681b(g)(2)(5).

148 National Consumer Law Center, Fair Credit Reporting § 5.4.1.5 (6th ed. 2006 and Supp.).

149 *Id.* § 5.4.1.

In addition to being furnishers of information to credit bureaus, health care providers may be users of credit reports. Some hospitals have been ordering the credit reports of patients, including patients who apply for or are eligible for charity care.[150] These hospitals claim that they ordered the patients' credit reports to verify income and thus their eligibility for charity care. However credit reports do not contain information about a consumer's income,[151] causing concern that these hospitals were instead looking for lines of credit that the applicants could use to pay hospital bills. In addition, credit bureaus are developing specialized health care credit scores that rely on hospital payment records.[152]

A provider must have a permissible purpose under the FCRA in order to access a patient's credit report.[153] One court has held that a dentist had a permissible purpose in ordering the credit report of a potential patient as a "legitimate business need" under the FCRA.[154]

10.3.5 Nursing Home Law

If the medical debt is owed to a nursing home facility, regulations governing that industry may provide a defense or cause of action. The federal Nursing Home Reform Law (NHRL) prohibits a facility from requiring a resident's family or friends to become financially responsible for expenses.[155] The NHRL regulations also require that nursing facilities inform consumers of all charges, including (for Medicaid recipients) those charges not covered by Medicaid.[156]

While the NHRL prohibits a facility from requiring relatives to accept responsibility for expenses, the NHRL does not prohibit the facility from asking relatives to *voluntarily* agree to be financially responsible.[157] The tricky issue is, of course, whether such agreement is truly voluntary or whether it is obtained by using a form contract that includes a boilerplate financial responsibility provision that the relative does not read or comprehend.[158] In addition, the NHRL does not prohibit a resident's representative who has legal access to the resident's income or assets from agreeing to use those funds to pay for care.[159]

The NHRL does not provide for a private right of action, but violation of this law may be actionable under a state UDAP statute.[160] State laws may provide additional protections, such as requirements for financial disclosure and restrictions on transfer or discharge for nonpayment.[161] State

150 Sarah Bernstein, *Why Hospitals Want Your Credit Report*, Wall St. Journal, Mar. 18, 2008; Phuong Cat Le, *Harborview Checks On Charity Patients' Credit: Hospital Quietly Tests Need For Financial Help*, Seattle Post-Intelligencer, Feb. 27, 2007.

151 *See* National Consumer Law Center, Fair Credit Reporting § 3.2.3 (6th ed. 2006 and Supp.).

152 Michelle Andrews, *Worries About Healthcare Credit Scores*, On Health & Money—U.S. News and World Report On-Line (Apr. 10, 2008), *available at* www.usnews.com/blogs/on-health-and-money/2008/4/10/worries-about-healthcare-credit-scores.html; Sarah Bernstein, *Why Hospitals Want Your Credit Report*, Wall St. J., Mar. 18, 2008.

153 *See* National Consumer Law Center, Fair Credit Reporting Ch. 7 (6th ed. 2006 and Supp.).

154 Wallace v. Finkel, 2006 WL 1731149 (M.D. Ala. June 22, 2006).

Note that the court did not engage in an analysis of what exactly was the dentist's business need, as the court appeared to place the burden on the consumer to show that the defendant's reason for obtaining the report was impermissible. *See* National Consumer Law Center, Fair Credit Reporting § 7.2.8 (6th ed. 2006 and Supp.) (discussing legitimate business need permissible purpose for obtaining a credit report).

155 42 U.S.C. § 1395i-3(c)(5)(A)(ii); 42 U.S.C. § 1396r(c)(5)(A)(ii) (Medicaid Act); Carroll v. Butterfield Health Care, 2003 WL 22462604 (N.D. Ill. Oct. 29, 2003) (nursing home violated NHRL by requiring personal guarantee from patient's son-in-law; son-in-law stated FDCPA claim against attorney-collector for suing on illegal guarantee); *see* National Consumer Law Center, Unfair and Deceptive Acts and Practices § 5.11.3.2.2 (6th ed. 2004 and Supp.).

156 42 C.F.R. § 483.10(b)(5), (6).

For more information regarding the NHRL and its regulations, see Eric M. Carlson, Long-Term Care Advocacy (2003).

157 Podolsky v. First Healthcare Corp., 58 Cal. Rptr. 2d 89 (Ct. App. 1996).

158 Katherine C. Pearson, *The Responsible Thing to Do About "Responsible Party" Provisions in Nursing Home Agreements: A Proposal for Change on Three Fronts*, 37 U. Mich. J.L. Reform 757 (2004).

159 42 U.S.C. § 1395i-3(c)(5)(B)(ii); 42 U.S.C. § 1396r(c)(5)(B)(ii) (Medicaid Act); *see* Bishop Wicke Health Ctr. v. Gorel, 2007 WL 2318097 (Conn. Super. Ct. July 27, 2007) (nursing home could sue representative for breach of contract for failing to maintain resident's eligibility for Medicaid, but NHRL barred *quantum meruit* and unjust enrichment claims against third party).

160 *See* Podolsky v. First Healthcare Corp., 58 Cal. Rptr. 2d 89 (Ct. App. 1996) (while nursing home was not prohibited from asking relatives to voluntarily agree to be financially responsible, lack of consideration for voluntary agreement and failure to inform relatives of their rights under NHRL was deceptive in violation of California UDAP law); National Consumer Law Center, Unfair and Deceptive Acts and Practices § 5.11.3.1 (6th ed. 2004 and Supp.); *cf.* Haven Health Ctr. of Lichfield Hills v. Parente, 2007 WL 123602 (Conn. Super. Ct. Jan. 8, 2007) (son of nursing home patient, who alleged that he signed only as his mother's power of attorney and that he was never given a copy of the preprinted contract, could bring UDAP claim against nursing home). *But see* Carroll v. Butterfield Health Care, 2003 WL 22462604 (N.D. Ill. Oct. 29, 2003) (no UDAP claim under Illinois law against nursing home that unlawfully required guarantee; guarantor failed to show substantial injury because he did not alleged that he was coerced into admitting patient to that home, or that he had no choice of alternative facilities).

161 *See, e.g.*, Fla. Stat. § 400.022 (financial disclosures and billing); La. Rev. Stat. Ann. § 40:2010.8 (financial disclosures; discharge or transfer); Minn. Stat. § 144.6501 (may not require co-signer to assume personal liability; must disclose this requirement in bold capitals); Oak Crest Vill. v. Murphy, 841 A.2d 816 (Md. 2004) (provision of continuing care retirement community contract that prohibited resident from divesting assets below certain amount violated Maryland Nursing Home Patient's Bill of Rights); Northfield Care Ctr. v. Anderson, 707 N.W.2d 731

statutes vary widely as to the existence and scope of a private remedy for violations.[162]

10.3.6 Protections Against Balance Billing

Medicaid programs often reimburse providers at rates less than what private insurers pay and far less than "list charges."[163] State Medicaid programs prohibit health care providers from engaging in the practice of "balance billing," or collecting additional amounts from Medicaid patients to make up for the difference in rates, when the service in question is a covered benefit.[164] The Medicare Act contains a similar provision;[165] however, there is no private right of action to bring an affirmative suit under this provision of the Medicare Act.[166] A patient might be able to assert the prohibition against balance billing under a state deceptive practices (UDAP) law or as a defense to a collection action.[167]

The prohibition against balance billing applies when the provider submits a claim for Medicaid payment, even if Medicaid denies the claim.[168] Some cases have barred providers from recovering against a patient when the provider fails to timely bill Medicaid,[169] or even for failing to assist the patient in applying for Medicaid.[170] The Medicaid balance billing prohibitions may prevent providers and insurers from placing a lien on the tort recoveries of Medicaid beneficiaries and attempting to collect amounts greater than what Medicaid pays.[171] Also, Medicaid law prohibits pro-

(Minn. Ct. App. 2006) (state law permits nursing home to solicit voluntary agreement for relative to be financially responsible, but only to the extent that the patient's income or assets are misapplied or relative acted in bad faith).

162 *See* Mass. Gen. Laws ch. 111, § 70E ("in addition to any other action allowed by law or regulation" civil cause of action for malpractice); Mich. Comp. Laws § 333.20203 (guidelines only; do not expand or limit rights under other law; no civil or criminal liability for non-compliance); Minn. Stat. § 144.6501 (nursing home contracts are consumer contracts within meaning of consumer protection statutes). *But see* Darviris v. Petros, 812 N.E.2d 1188 (Mass. 2004) (violation of Mass. Gen. Laws ch. 111, § 70E, not UDAP statute, despite regulation making violations of certain statutes per se UDAP violations).

163 See § 10.5.5.2, *infra*, for an explanation of the differing rates paid by Medicaid, private insurers, and how they are far less than the "list charges" assessed against uninsured patients.

164 42 U.S.C. § 1396a(a)(25)(c); 42 C.F.R. § 447.15; Spectrum Health Continuing Care Group v. Anna Marie Bowling Irrevocable Trust, 410 F.3d 304 (6th Cir. 2005) (nursing home violated Medicaid's balance billing prohibition by seeking recovery from patient's tort settlement after accepting Medicaid funds for care of patient); Evanston Hosp. v. Hauck, 1 F.3d 540 (7th Cir. 1993) (once hospital accepts Medicaid or Medicare payment, it is barred from pursuing the patient for any balance, and it can not avoid this prohibition by returning the payment to the government); Olszewski v. Scripps Health, 135 Cal. Rptr. 2d 1 (Cal. 2003) (federal Medicaid law preempted state hospital lien law that permitted lien for customary charges).

For more on Medicaid law and the prohibition against balance billing (also called the "payment in full" defense), see Nat'l Health Law Program, An Advocate's Guide to the Medicaid Program (2001 ed.).

165 42 U.S.C. § 1395cc(a)(1)(A).

166 Wentz v. Kindred Hospitals E., L.L.C., 333 F. Supp. 2d 1298 (S.D. Fla. 2004) (no private right of action to enforce Medicare's balance billing prohibition, but patient could proceed with breach of contract claim that charges were "unlawful" and thus violated the provider's contract); Wogan v. Kunze, 623 S.E.2d 107 (S.C. Ct. App. 2005) (no private right of action under Medicare Act for physician's failure to file Medicare claim).

167 Smallwood v. Cent. Peninsula Gen. Hosp., 151 P.3d 319 (Alaska 2007) (patients could challenge hospital's balance billing in violation of Medicaid regulations as UDAP violation and as third party beneficiary of agreement between state and hospital); Wentz v. Kindred Hospitals E., L.L.C., 333 F. Supp. 2d 1298 (S.D. Fla. 2004) (no private right of action to enforce Medicare's balance billing prohibition, but patient could proceed with breach of contract claim that charges were "unlawful" and thus violated the provider's contract); Mikula v. Great Lakes Fin. Services, 2004 WL 1656556 (N.D. Ill. July 22, 2004) (balance billing in violation of hospital's preferred provider agreement with insurer actionable under FDCPA); *see* National Consumer Law Center, Unfair and Deceptive Acts and Practices § 3.2.7 (6th ed. 2004 and Supp.); *cf.* Fla. Health Sciences Ctr., Inc. v. Elsenheimer, 952 So. 2d 575 (Fla. Dist. Ct. App. 2007) (challenge to Medicaid balance billing under state debt collection statute; class action status denied for lack of commonality or typicality). *But see* Richmond v. Higgins, 435 F.3d 825 (8th Cir. 2006) (no FDCPA violation for debt collection activities that may have violated Medicaid balance billing provisions, because plaintiff's attorney failed to raise issue until six months after first debt collection attempt).

168 Banks v. Sec'y, Indiana Family & Soc. Services Admin., 997 F.2d 231 (7th Cir. 1993) (provider is precluded from seeking payment from patient after submitting claim to Medicaid, whether Medicaid pays the claim or denies it); Serafini v. Blake, 213 Cal. Rptr. 207 (Ct. App. 1985) (provider can not bill Medicaid patient for claims denied by Medicaid due to provider error).

169 Layton Physical Therapy Co. v. Palozzi, 149 Ohio App. 3d 332, 777 N.E.2d 306 (2002) (when patient was eligible for Medicaid, and Medicaid approved the treatments, provider could not sue patient or parents for covered services; failure to timely bill Medicaid did not make services "uncovered" for billing purposes); *cf.* Evanston Hosp. v. Hauck, 1 F.3d 540 (7th Cir. 1993) (once hospital accepts Medicaid or Medicare payment, it is barred from pursuing the patient for any balance, and it can not avoid this by returning the payment to the government); Picker v. Castro, 776 N.Y.S.2d 433 (App. Term 2003) (provider's refusal to fill-out insurance paperwork violated duty of good faith and fair dealing; provider precluded from recovering fees from patient). *But see* Wentz v. Kindred Hospitals E., L.L.C., 333 F. Supp. 2d 1298 (S.D. Fla. 2004) (provider returned Medicare payment so it could seek recovery against patient's personal injury settlement).

170 Mount Sinai Hosp. v. Kornegay, 347 N.Y.S.2d 807 (Civ. Ct. 1973) (when hospital failed to submit Medicaid application it was barred from seeking payment from the patient); *see* Alan Alop, Defending Hospital Collection Cases (rev. ed. 2005), *available at* www.illinoislegaladvocate.org/index.cfm?fuseaction=home.dsp_content&contentID=728.

171 Manjusha P. Kulkarni, Nat'l Health L. Program, Fact Sheet: State and Provider Liens Asserted Against the Recoveries of Medicaid and Medicare Beneficiaries (June 2004).

viders from denying services to Medicaid recipients on the basis of outstanding debts for co-payments or deductibles.[172]

The flip side of balance billing protections is that Medicaid and Medicare beneficiaries must assign their right to payment from any liable third party to the Medicaid or Medicare program, so that the program will have a lien against beneficiaries' tort recoveries.[173] However, the amount of this lien may not exceed the portion of the tort recovery allocated to medical expenses.[174]

There are similar protections against balance billing for services covered by worker's compensation and other government programs.[175] Providers may also be precluded from balance billing patients with private insurance under state law,[176] or under their contracts with insurers.[177] Some in-

---

A provision in the Medicare regulations that similarly prohibited liens against beneficiaries' tort recoveries was eliminated in 2003; thus it appears such liens are permissible with respect to Medicare beneficiaries under certain conditions. *Id.*; *see* § 10.7, *infra* (discussing provider and insurer liens on tort recoveries).

172 Beeker v. Olzewski, 415 F. Supp. 2d 734 (E.D. Mich. 2006).
The court did note that recently enacted amendments to Medicaid law may have an impact on this prohibition. *Id.*

173 *Id.*

174 Arkansas Dep't of Health & Social Services v. Ahlborn, 547 U.S. 268, 126 S. Ct. 1752, 164 L. Ed. 2d 459 (2006).

175 Haw. Rev. Stat. § 386-27(b)(2); Va. Code Ann. § 65.2-601.1; Rutherford v. Ralph Hutton & Associates, 2004 WL 1119676 (Cal. Ct. App. May 20, 2004) (hospital's balance billing by attempting to enforce lien against personal injury recovery was forbidden by hospital's contract with county government program to provide medical care to indigent and uninsured patients); Am. Family Mut. Ins. Co. v. Centura Health-St. Anthony Centura Hosp., 46 P.3d 490 (Colo. Ct. App. 2002) (workers' compensation statute prescribes amount hospital may charge; hospital must return to auto insurance company the difference between permitted charge and PIP benefits paid out while workers compensation case being contested); Rivera v. Veterans Mem'l Med. Ctr., 818 A.2d 731 (Conn. 2003) (class action alleging violations of Connecticut UDAP law, abuse of process, and breach of the implied covenant of good faith and fair dealing over hospital's collection activities for medical services that were covered by workers' compensation); Pub. Health Trust v. Dade County Sch. Bd., 693 So. 2d 562 (Fla. Dist. Ct. App. 1996); Valley Rehab. & Med. Services v. Cash, 789 N.Y.S.2d 869 (Dist. Ct. 2004) (New York worker's compensation law permits provider to recover against patient only if patient fails to prosecute claim for worker's compensation or board determines patient's condition is not covered by program; otherwise provider must collect fees from the carrier); Daughters of Charity Health Services of Waco v. Linnstaedter, 226 S.W.3d 409 (Tex. 2007) (when workers' compensation insurer reimbursed hospital, labor code limits on charges barred hospital from filing property code lien against tort recovery from at-fault driver). *But see* Alaska Native Tribal Health Consortium v. Settlement Funds Held for or to Be Paid on Behalf of E.R. *ex rel.* Ridley, 84 P.3d 418 (Alaska 2004) (hospital that provided free care to Alaska natives could place lien on tort recoveries; federal statute that forbade Indian Health Service facilities to charge patients did not prohibit them from recovering under Alaska lien law); Allen & Norman, L.L.C. v. Chauvin, 916 So. 2d 1071 (La. Ct. App. 2005) (provider not prohibited by Louisiana workers' compensation law from balance billing by placing lien on tort recovery of patient).

176 Gianetti v. Siglinger, 900 A.2d 520 (Conn. 2006) (health plan agreement and Connecticut law forbade balance billing; affirming trial court's award of $26,000 and attorney fees of $40,000 under Connecticut UDAP statute for physician's repeated violation of both agreement and law); Valley Hosp. v. Kroll, 847 A.2d 636 (N.J. Super. Ct. Law Div. 2003) (New Jersey law prohibited hospital from balance billing difference between "list charges" and amount covered by private Medigap insurance); McArthur Chiropractic Ctr. v. Randall, 852 N.E.2d 198 (Ohio Ct. App. 2006) (Ohio law requires providers to seek compensation for services covered by insurance solely from insurer; if provider was under contract with patient's insurer, he could not recover against patient); Grandview/Southview Hospitals v. Monie, 2005 WL 737393 (Ohio Ct. App. Apr. 1, 2005) (noting that Ohio law requires providers to seek compensation for covered services solely from insurer except for co-pays and deductibles); Parmatown Spinal & Rehab. Ctr. v. Lewis, 2003 WL 22208786 (Ohio Ct. App. Sept. 25, 2003) (Ohio law prohibits health care providers from balance billing patients with insurance; but patient in this case waived protections of the law when she instructed insurer not to pay provider's claims); Seminole Family Med. Clinic v. Southern, 116 P.3d 191 (Okla. Civ. App. 2005) (noting Oklahoma State Board of Health rule requiring contracts between health maintenance organizations (HMOs) and providers to hold patients harmless if HMO does not pay claim; in this case, patient failed to show she was covered by HMO during relevant time period of services); *cf.* Richmond v. Caban, 754 N.E.2d 871 (Ill. App. Ct. 2001) (hospital could choose whether to bill HMO or place lien on tort recovery; note however that lien may be invalid under provision of HMO statute that forbids provider to have recourse against plan members for anything except co-pays, deductibles, and non-covered services; open question regarding interaction between HMO statute and lien statute).

177 Mikula v. Great Lakes Fin. Services, 2004 WL 1656556 (N.D. Ill. July 22, 2004) (FDCPA claim alleged against hospital for balance billing in violation of hospital's preferred provider agreement with insurer); Lutheran Gen. Hosp., Inc. v. Printing Indus. of Illinois/Indiana Employee Benefit Trust, 24 F. Supp. 2d 846 (N.D. Ill. 1998) (when hospital's agreement with employee benefit plan forbade it to dun patients for services covered by plan, and patient had properly authorized hospital to bill plan, hospital was forbidden to bill patient for covered services; remanded on issue of whether all services were covered); Parnell v. Adventist Health Sys./West, 109 P.3d 69 (Cal. 2005) (provider who agreed to accept insurer's reimbursement as "payment in full" for medical services could not assert lien on patient's tort recovery, despite state law permitting lien, because patient did not owe debt to provider); Constantine v. MCG Health, Inc., 619 S.E.2d 718 (Ga. Ct. App. 2005) (hospital that was paid by insurer could not return payment and then claim lien on patient's tort recovery; contract between hospital and insurer forbade billing patient, even though state law provided that lien was against the tort cause of action and not against the patient personally); Lopez v. Morley, 817 N.E.2d 592 (Ill. App. Ct. 2004) (lien not permitted but court notes that hospital's contract could have provided that insurance payment would not extinguish debt); Richmond v. Caban, 754 N.E.2d 871 (Ill. App. Ct. 2001) (hospital could choose whether to bill HMO or place lien on tort recovery; note however that lien may be invalid under provision of HMO statute that forbids provider

surers have even filed lawsuits against providers who balanced billed their members.[178] On the other hand, patients have sued their insurers for providers' balance billing, based on the insurers' guarantees that they would not be billed for amounts other than co-payments and deductibles.[179] One tactic used by providers is to decline billing an insurer or Medicaid/Medicare to avoid these balance billing prohibitions, in anticipation of recovering greater amounts (full list charges) from tort settlements.[180]

to have recourse against plan members for anything except co-pays, deductibles and non-covered services; open question regarding interaction between HMO statute and lien statute); N.C. v. A.W., 713 N.E.2d 775 (Ill. App. Ct. 1999) (HMO contract forbade balance billing; acceptance of HMO payment canceled debt; lien not permitted); Midwest Neurosurgery, Prof'l Corp. v. State Farm Ins. Companies, 686 N.W.2d 572 (Neb. 2004) (when provider had agreed with HMO to accept specific amount, this was the "amount due"; provider could not place lien on personal injury recovery for its undiscounted bill; note that this depended on precise wording of the contract provisions); Dorr v. Sacred Heart Hosp., 597 N.W.2d 462 (Wis. Ct. App. 1999) (lien was void when auto accident victim was covered by HMO, contract between the hospital and the HMO, as well as a provision of state statute, forbade the hospital to bill the patient for services covered by HMO; allegation that hospital refused to present claim to HMO and sought lien instead sufficient to state a claim for breach of contract, UDAP, and racketeering); *see also* Rutherford v. Ralph Hutton & Associates, 2004 WL 1119676 (Cal. Ct. App. May 20, 2004) (hospital's balance billing by attempting to enforce lien against personal injury recovery was forbidden by hospital's contract with county government program to provide medical care to indigent and uninsured patients). *But see* Watts v. Promina Gwinnett Health Sys., Inc., 242 Ga. App. 377, 530 S.E.2d 14 (2000) (patient's payment of bill waived claim that charge violated hospital's contract with HMO); Rogalla v. Christie Clinic, 794 N.E.2d 384 (Ill. App. Ct. 2003) (subrogation clause in plan's contract with hospital did not conflict with ban on balance billing; hospital's claim was against a fund, that is, the personal injury recovery, not the plan member).

See § 10.7.2, *infra*, for other cases in which providers have sought liens against patients' tort recoveries even after payment of medical bills by insurers.

178 Prospect Med. Group, Inc. v. Northridge Emergency Med. Group, 39 Cal. Rptr. 3d 456 (Ct. App.) (managed care insurer had standing to litigate reasonableness of balanced billed charges to its subscribers, but California law did not prohibit balance billing by emergency room physicians who did not have contract with insurer), *review granted*, 136 P.3d 167 (Cal. 2006); *see also* Press Release, Horizon Blue Cross Blue Shield of New Jersey Granted Preliminary Injunctive Relief Against Vanguard Anesthesia Associations (Jan. 2007) (HMO obtained injunction against providers over balance billing of its members).

179 Cohen v. Health Net, 29 Cal. Rptr. 3d 46 (Ct. App. 2005) (suit preempted by Employee Retirement Income Security Act).

180 *See, e.g.*, Whittaker v. Lee Mem'l Health Sys., 177 Fed. Appx. 892 (11th Cir. 2006) (patient had viable third party beneficiary contract claim against hospital that declined insurance payments in order to seek lien against patient's automobile insurance policy); Wentz v. Kindred Hospitals E., L.L.C., 333 F. Supp. 2d 1298 (S.D. Fla. 2004) (provider returned Medicare payment so it could seek recovery against patient's personal injury settlement); Constantine v. MCG Health, Inc., 619 S.E.2d 718 (Ga. Ct. App. 2005) (hospital that was paid by insurer attempted to return payment and then claim lien on patient's tort recovery); Elaine Hopkins, *Woman: St. Francis Saved My Life—But Ruined My Credit*, Peoria J. Star, Jan. 20, 2001, at A1.

See § 10.7.2, *infra*, for a discussion of provider liens on tort settlements after receiving insurance payments.

10.4 State Remedies for Medical Debt Collection Abuses

10.4.1 General

The most suitable remedies for medical debt collection harassment often utilize state debt collection statutes, state unfair and deceptive acts and practices (UDAP) statutes, the tort of intentional infliction of emotional distress and other state remedies.[181] These remedies may allow suit directly against the health care provider as well as against a collection agency for abusive collection tactics. In addition to private remedies, state regulators can take action against financial misconduct by regulated professionals.[182]

10.4.2 State Debt Collection Statutes

State debt collection statutes were passed mostly in the 1960s and 1970s to protect consumers against abusive debt collection practices.[183] The statutes often apply to both creditors and collection agencies.[184] They may have a broader definition of collection agency than the FDCPA, covering other entities such as medical billing providers.[185] They often provide for private actions, attorney fees, and actual damages (and sometimes statutory damages).[186]

181 *See, e.g.*, Joseph v. J.J. MacIntyre Companies, 238 F. Supp. 2d 1158 (N.D. Cal. 2002) (claims for state and federal debt collection violations, UDAP, and common law torts; barrage of phone calls to disabled senior citizen, despite requests to stop), *later opinion at* 281 F. Supp. 2d 1156 (N.D. Cal. 2003) (collector's motion for summary judgment denied).

182 Havsy v. Washington State Dep't of Health, 123 Wash. App. 1030 (2004) (state board sanctioned doctor in part for misleading patients about the price of treatment, failing to inform patient of the high cost of a certain procedure and that insurance would not cover that procedure, and using a "small-print" form to obtain patient's agreement to be liable for charges; doctor's conduct breached fiduciary duty to patient).

183 *See* National Consumer Law Center, Fair Debt Collection § 11.2 (6th ed. 2008).

184 *Id.* § 11.2.3, Appx. E.

185 *See, e.g.*, Flores v. Rawlings Co., L.L.C., 117 Haw. 153 (Haw. 2008) (provider of "claims recovery services" was a collection agency under Hawaii law even though it asserted that it was not covered under FDCPA because it did not collect "debts"; Hawaii statute covers entity that collects "claims or money due on accounts" for another).

186 *See* National Consumer Law Center, Fair Debt Collection § 11.2.5 (6th ed. 2008).

10.4.3 State UDAP Statutes

State UDAP statutes often proscribe unfair or deceptive debt collection tactics.[187] In some states, UDAP statutes provide for recovery of double or treble actual damages as well as attorney fees. Thus, a harassed consumer with substantial actual damages might recover more under the UDAP statute than the FDCPA.[188]

A UDAP claim may be available for unfair or deceptive practices by providers beyond collection issues.[189] For example, Connecticut courts have held that failure to inform indigent patients of the availability of free care under Hill-Burton or the state free care statute may constitute a violation of the Connecticut Unfair Trade Practices Act.[190]

UDAP actions may be useful to challenge hospital discriminatory pricing practices, when hospitals charge uninsured patients several times the amounts that are paid by private insurers, Medicaid, or Medicare for the same procedures.[191] There have been several cases which have met with some success,[192] including settlements of class actions.[193] On the other hand, a number of other courts have found discriminatory pricing not actionable under UDAP statutes,[194] and some have expressed a judicial reluctance or

---

187 *See id.* § 11.3.3; *see also* National Consumer Law Center, Unfair and Deceptive Acts and Practices §§ 2.2.2, 2.3.10, 5.1.1 (6th ed. 2004 and Supp.).

188 For examples of UDAP cases involving medical debt collection, see Joseph v. J.J. MacIntyre Companies, 238 F. Supp. 2d 1158 (N.D. Cal. 2002) (state debt collection, UDAP and tort claims for barrage of phone calls to disabled senior citizen), *later opinion at* 281 F. Supp. 2d 1156 (N.D. Cal. 2003) (collector's motion for summary judgment denied) and Ahmad v. Yale New Haven Hosp., 38 Conn. L. Rptr. 238 (Super. Ct. 2004) (use of aggressive debt collection against patients who were eligible for—but never informed of—free or discounted care is actionable under UDAP statute), *later proceeding at* 2006 WL 337335 (Conn. Super. Ct. Jan. 25, 2006) (denying class certification), *clarified*, 2006 WL 895037 (Conn. Super. Ct. Mar. 24, 2006).

189 *See, e.g.*, Palmer v. St. Joseph Healthcare, P.S.O., Inc., 77 P.3d 560 (N.M. Ct. App. 2003) (Medicare law did not preempt UDAP and common law claims against HMO that raised premiums and cut back services shortly after promising that these would not change for a year; detailed discussion of Medicare preemption); Froemming v. Perez, 2006 WL 704479 (Tex. App. Mar. 22, 2006) (upholding trial court's decision in favor of plaintiff in UDAP action; patient alleged that orthodontist agreed to a discounted price for braces, then reneged on agreement and attempted to extract more money by refusing to complete treatment). *But see* SWA, Inc. v. Straka, 2003 WL 21434637 (Ohio Ct. App. June 19, 2003) (daughter who did not sign nursing home admission agreement not a consumer within meaning of UDAP, because no transaction with home; when home sued daughter for mother's care, remedy for baseless suit was motion for sanctions, not UDAP counterclaim); Trevino v. Christus Santa Rosa Healthcare Corp., 2002 WL 31423711 (Tex. App. Oct. 30, 2002) (improperly triaged patient gave birth in the bathroom, hospital billed her for labor and delivery; billing for services not performed not a UDAP violation when that section of statute applies only to repairs of goods).

190 Yale New Haven Med. Ctr. v. Mitchell, 683 A.2d 1362 (Conn. Super. Ct. 1995) (correcting opinion at 662 A.2d 178); *see also* Ahmad v. Yale New Haven Hosp., 38 Conn. L. Rptr. 238 (Super. Ct. 2004) (finding private right of action under Connecticut free care statute; failure to inform eligible patients of free care availability may violate both free care statute and UDAP statute), *later proceeding at* 2006 WL 337335 (Conn. Super. Ct. Jan. 25, 2006) (denying class certification), *clarified*, 2006 WL 895037 (Conn. Super. Ct. Mar. 24, 2006). *But see* Martinez v. Yale New Haven Hosp., 2005 WL 2364901 (Conn. Super. Ct. Sept. 1, 2005) (striking UDAP claims because plaintiffs failed to allege how violation of charity care statute related to entrepreneurial or business aspect of hospital services).

191 *See* § 10.5.5.2, *infra*.

192 Hill v. Sisters of St. Francis Health Services, 2006 WL 3783415 (N.D. Ill. Dec. 20, 2006) (denying dismissal of UDAP and unconscionability claims for discriminatory pricing); *In re* Sutter Health Uninsured Pricing Cases, 2005 WL 1842582 (Cal. Super. Ct. July 16, 2005) (same); Servedio v. Our Lady of the Resurrection Med. Ctr., Clearinghouse No. 55,626 (Ill. Cir. Ct. Cook County Jan. 6, 2005); Turner v. Legacy Health Sys., 2006 WL 657176 (Or. Cir. Ct. Oct. 4, 2005) (granting class certification in case challenging discriminatory pricing under Oregon UDAP statute); *see also* Mary Jo Feldstein, *BJC Overpayment Case is Class-Action*, St. Louis Post-Dispatch, Mar. 7, 2007 (class action certification granted in discriminatory pricing case against St. Louis area hospital); *cf.* Colomar v. Mercy Hosp., Inc., 461 F. Supp. 2d 1265 (S.D. Fla. 2006) (while fact that uninsured patients paid more than insurers for same services alone would not give rise to UDAP clam, allegations that hospital's prices were excessive in comparison to other hospitals and in comparison to actual cost of services would support viable UDAP claim).

193 *In re* Tenet Healthcare Cases II, 2005 WL 1949562 (Cal. Super. Ct. Aug. 8, 2005); *see also* Steven Carter, *Providence Health System Will Offer Refunds To Uninsured*, Portland Oregonian, June 24, 2006; Keith Darcé, *Scripps To Settle Uninsured Billing Suit*, San Diego Union-Tribune, Feb. 1, 2008; *Consejo Announces Major Settlement With HMA Hospitals*, Managed Care Wkly. Dig. 57, Feb. 26, 2007; Bob Egelko, *Hospital Chain Agrees To Settlement: Catholic Healthcare West Says It Will Pay $423 Million Refund*, San Francisco Chronicle, Jan. 12, 2007; David Phelps, *Uninsured Patients May Get Discounts: Allina and Fairview Settled a Class-Action Suit Claiming That People Without Health Coverage Paid Too Much For Medical Care*, Minneapolis Star-Tribune, Mar. 17, 2007.

The *Sutter Health*, *Legacy Health*, and *Resurrection Medical* cases all settled as well. Dale Kasler, *Sutter Health Deal Gets OK*, Sacramento Bee, Dec. 13, 2006; *Legacy Uninsured Lawsuit Settlement Approved*, Portland Bus. J., Mar. 6, 2007; Mark Taylor, *Legal Harbinger? Consumer Fraud Settlement May Lead To More*, Modern Healthcare, June 20, 2005 (*Servedio* case); *cf.* Class Settlement Agreement and Release, *In re* Columbia HCA Healthcare Corp. Billing Practices Litig., Civ. No. 3-98-MDL-1227 (M.D. Tenn. Apr. 2003) (settlement of class action alleging ERISA and UDAP violations for billing for medical services not rendered, for exaggerated patient illness, for unnecessary treatment, as well as excessive, unreasonable, or impermissibly high amounts).

194 Morrell v. Wellstar Health Sys., Inc., 633 S.E.2d 68 (Ga. Ct. App. 2006) (discriminatory pricing was not deceptive or confusing in violation of Georgia UDAP statute); Cox v. Athens Reg'l Med. Ctr., Inc., 631 S.E.2d 792 (Ga. Ct. App. 2006) (same); Rockford Mem'l Hosp. v. Havrilesko, 858 N.E.2d 56 (Ill. App. Ct. 2006) (excessive charges were not unfair under Illinois UDAP statute; plaintiffs failed to sufficiently plead

even hostility to the concept that discriminatory pricing is an unfair practice.[195]

Some courts have dismissed UDAP claims citing state statutes that require hospitals to disclose their charges to consumers or file them with state agencies. For example, the court in *Cox v. Athens Regional Medical Center*[196] based its decision in part on the fact that Georgia law provided patients with the right to request a copy of hospital charges, and that Georgia policy was to encourage market forces to control health care costs by providing information so that consumers could make cost-effective decisions by comparison shopping.

The problem with this reasoning is that comparison shopping is often difficult when medical decisions are involved, especially in emergency situations. Note that two of the plaintiffs in *Cox* received treatment, respectively, for a burned hand and in the emergency room. Would it have been realistic for them to go "comparison shopping"?

Other courts have held that UDAP claims for discriminatory pricing failed because the patients never paid the charges, and thus did not suffer actual damages.[197] However some UDAP statutes permit patients to seek injunctive relief.[198]

Other practices that could be challenged under UDAP statutes may include health care providers that violate prohibitions against balance billing[199] or who misrepresent that the patient's insurance will pay all charges, then subsequently balance bill. UDAP actions may lie against providers who pressure non-responsible relatives to accept liability for medical bills.[200] However UDAP actions against insurers over balance billing may be preempted by ERISA.[201] Even providers have brought UDAP claims against insurers.[202]

---

claim that hospital deceptively concealed facts about billing practices); Mercy Health Partners of Southwest Ohio v. Miller, 2005 WL 2592674 (Ohio Ct. Com. Pl. Sept. 30, 2005) (discriminatory pricing not unfair practice under Ohio UDAP statute and plaintiff failed to allege any statements about hospital pricing that were misleading); Nygaard v. Sioux Valley Hosp. & Health Sys., 731 N.W.2d 184 (S.D. 2007) (discriminatory pricing not deceptive practice; note that South Dakota UDAP statute does not prohibit "unfair" practices).

195 DiCarlo v. St. Mary's Hosp., 2006 WL 2038498 (D.N.J. July 19, 2006) ("For a court to presume to address [the problems of discriminatory pricing] would be rushing in where angels fear to tread"; relying on *Kolari* even after reversal); Kolari v. N.Y. Presbyterian Hosp., 382 F. Supp. 2d 562 (S.D.N.Y. 2005) ("This orchestrated assault on scores of nonprofit hospitals, necessitating the expenditure of those hospitals' scarce resources to beat back meritless legal claims, is undoubtedly part of the litigation explosion that has been so well-documented in the media."), *vacated in relevant part*, 455 F.3d 118 (2d Cir. 2006) (trial court abused its discretion in exercising supplemental jurisdiction over state law claims after dismissing federal claims).

196 631 S.E.2d 792 (Ga. Ct. App. 2006); *see also* Morrell v. Wellstar Health Sys., Inc., 633 S.E.2d 68 (Ga. Ct. App. 2006) (discriminatory pricing was not deceptive or confusing in violation of Georgia UDAP statute); *cf.* Banner Health v. Med. Sav. Ins. Co., 163 P.3d 1096 (Ariz. Ct. App. 2007) (because hospital was required to file its rates with state agency, the rates could not be challenged as unconscionable or unreasonable, despite the fact that rates were 400% of hospital's costs and hospital only charged full rates to 2% of patients).

197 Urquhart v. Manatee Mem'l Hosp., 2007 WL 781738 (M.D. Fla. Mar. 13, 2007) (while breach of contract and UDAP claim challenging discriminatory pricing were viable, failure to allege actual injury from practice required dismissal); Freeman Health Sys. v. Wass, 124 S.W.3d 504 (Mo. Ct. App. 2004) (discriminatory pricing claim failed to allege ascertainable loss required as element under Missouri UDAP statute, because patients had not paid the amount hospital charged); *cf.* Lester E. Cox Med. Ctr. v. Huntsman, 2003 WL 22004998 (W.D. Mo. Aug. 5, 2003) (UDAP claim for overcharging; ascertainable damages not shown, as amount of alleged overcharge was much less than amount owing on bill and litigation expenses in contesting the bill not recoverable as damages), *aff'd*, 408 F.3d 989 (8th Cir. 2005).

198 Smallwood v. Cent. Peninsula Gen. Hosp., 151 P.3d 319 (Alaska 2007) (patient did not suffer actual damages from hospital's balance billing but could seek injunctive relief under state UDAP statute). *See generally* National Consumer Law Center, Unfair and Deceptive Acts and Practices § 8.6.2 (6th ed. 2004 and Supp.).

199 Smallwood v. Cent. Peninsula Gen. Hosp., 151 P.3d 319 (Alaska 2007) (patients could challenge hospital's balance billing in violation of Medicaid regulations as UDAP violation and as third party beneficiary of agreement between state and hospital); Gianetti v. Siglinger, 900 A.2d 520 (Conn. 2006) (affirming trial court's award of $26,000 and attorney fees of $40,000 under UDAP statute for physician's repeated violation of health plan agreement and Connecticut law prohibiting balance billing); *see also* Rivera v. Veterans Mem'l Med. Ctr., 818 A.2d 731 (Conn. 2003) (class action alleging violations of Connecticut UDAP law, abuse of process, and breach of the implied covenant of good faith and fair dealing over hospital's balance billing and collection efforts when workers' compensation covered medical services). *But see* Olszewski v. Scripps Health, 135 Cal. Rptr. 2d 1 (Cal. 2003) (no UDAP claim against provider that filed lien for customary charges pursuant to California law; court held that California lien law was preempted by federal Medicaid law but provided safe harbor defense against UDAP claim); Wogan v. Kunze, 623 S.E.2d 107 (S.C. Ct. App. 2005) (patient's widow failed to state UDAP claim for balance billing in violation of Medicare Act because statute did not permit her to sue in representative capacity; in this case, patient paid for prescription drug out of pocket). *See generally* § 10.3.6, *supra* (protections against balance billing).

200 Podolsky v. First Healthcare Corp., 58 Cal. Rptr. 2d 89 (Ct. App. 1996) (nursing home violated UDAP law by soliciting relatives for voluntary agreement to be financially responsible for patient, due to lack of consideration for voluntary agreement and failure to inform relatives of their rights under federal law to refuse agreement). *But see* Carroll v. Butterfield Health Care, 2003 WL 22462604 (N.D. Ill. Oct. 29, 2003) (no state UDAP claim against nursing home that required guarantee in violation of federal law).

For examples of pressuring non-responsible relatives, see § 10.5.3.2, *infra*.

201 Cohen v. Health Net, 29 Cal. Rptr. 3d 46 (Ct. App. 2005); *see* National Consumer Law Center, Unfair and Deceptive Acts and Practices § 5.11.7 (6th ed. 2004 and Supp.).

202 Bell v. Blue Cross, 31 Cal. Rptr. 3d 688 (Ct. App. 2005) (when state law requires HMOs to pay out-of-network emergency

Some state UDAP statutes exempt transactions between consumers and physicians or members of learned professions in general.[203] These exemptions have defeated several UDAP cases over discriminatory pricing.[204] These exemptions may not, however, apply to a transaction with a service provider such as a health maintenance organization (HMO).[205] These exemptions also should not apply to debt collectors working on behalf of medical professionals.[206]

In other states there is an exemption for the professional aspects of medical care, but not the entrepreneurial aspects, so misrepresentations about billing would probably not be exempt.[207] Health care providers might also be excluded from UDAP coverage under state laws that exempt businesses governed by a regulatory body.[208]

10.4.4 *State Medical Debt Protections*

10.4.4.1 Comprehensive Medical Debtor Protection Laws

Several states, recognizing the special burden created by health care debts and the problem of discriminatory pricing, have enacted medical debtor protection laws. These states include California, Connecticut, Illinois, and New York. In addition, the Minnesota Attorney General's Office has reached an agreement with Minnesota hospitals providing for similar protections.[209]

Connecticut passed the first medical debtor protection law, in part in response to reports of aggressive debt collection by Yale New Haven Hospital. This law prohibits a hospital that receives "free bed funds," that is, charity care funds, from suing a medical debtor unless it determines that the debtor is not eligible for the free bed funds.[210] The law also requires hospitals to include information about free bed funds and other free care programs in all bills and collection notices.[211] A Connecticut court has held there is a private right of action to enforce this section under the pre-2003 version of this statute.[212]

---

room physicians for services rendered to insureds, physician could bring UDAP claim against insurer for insurer's failure to pay a "reasonable and customary value" for such services); Coast Plaza Doctors Hosp. v. UHP Healthcare, 129 Cal. Rptr. 2d 650 (Ct. App. 2002) (hospital alleged sufficient facts to state a claim for violation of state UDAP law with allegation that HMO caused patients to be transferred in violation of EMTALA).

203 *See, e.g.*, Ohio Rev. Code Ann. § 1345.01 (West) (transactions between attorneys, physicians, or dentists and their clients or patients). *See generally* National Consumer Law Center, Unfair and Deceptive Acts and Practices § 2.3.10 (6th ed. 2004 and Supp.).

204 DiCarlo v. St. Mary's Hosp., 2006 WL 2038498 (D.N.J. July 19, 2006) (no UDAP claim for discriminatory pricing because state UDAP statute exempts medical professionals); Shelton v. Duke Univ. Health Sys., 633 S.E.2d 113 (N.C. Ct. App. 2006) (no UDAP claim for discriminatory pricing because state UDAP statute exempts medical professionals).

205 Summa Health Sys. v. Viningre, 749 N.E.2d 344 (Ohio Ct. App. 2000) (HMO made misrepresentations about financial aspects of patient's care).

206 Foster v. D.B.S. Collection Agency, 463 F. Supp. 2d 783 (S.D. Ohio 2006) (also noting in dicta that Ohio UDAP exemption for medical professionals does not apply to hospitals); *cf.* Freeman Health Sys. v. Wass, 124 S.W.3d 504 (Mo. Ct. App. 2004) (medical goods and services are merchandise within meaning of UDAP statute).

207 Janusauskas v. Fichman, 826 A.2d 1066 (Conn. 2003) (UDAP claim will lie for entrepreneurial matters such as solicitation of business and billing practices, but not for professional "competence or strategy"; when advertising not false, informed consent is malpractice question, not UDAP violation); Haynes v. Yale-New Haven Hosp., 699 A.2d 964 (Conn. 1997) (state UDAP statute applies to "entrepreneurial aspects" such as "solicitation and billing practices," but not to professional negligence or competency issues; extensive collection of cases); Henderson v. Gandy, 623 S.E.2d 465 (Ga. 2005) (state UDAP statute apples to entrepreneurial aspects of health care but not to malpractice); Simmons v. Stephenson, 84 S.W.3d 926 (Ky. Ct. App. 2002) (UDAP claim will lie for "entrepreneurial, commercial or business aspects" of health care, but not "misconduct in the actual performance of medical services or the actual practice of medicine"; no UDAP violation when surgeon told patient to come back in six months, when patient required immediate additional surgery to correct faulty result); Darviris v. Petros, 812 N.E.2d 1188 (Mass. 2004) (collection of cases from various states; UDAP statute applies to "entrepreneurial, commercial or business" aspects of health care, such as advertising and billing; does not apply to failure to obtain informed consent, which is malpractice); Nelson v. Ho, 564 N.W.2d 482 (Mich. Ct. App. 1997) (UDAP statute, which makes no specific reference to medicine or law, applies only to business or commercial aspects of practice). *But see* DiCarlo v. St. Mary's Hosp., 2006 WL 2038498 (D.N.J. July 19, 2006) (no UDAP claim for discriminatory pricing because New Jersey UDAP statute exempts medical professionals even with respect to entrepreneurial matters; court relies on *Macedo v. Dello Russo*); Macedo v. Dello Russo, 840 A.2d 238 (N.J. 2004) (learned professionals beyond reach of New Jersey UDAP statute when operating in their professional capacities; misrepresentation of licensure not a UDAP violation); Phillips v. A Triangle Women's Health Clinic, 573 S.E.2d 600 (N.C. Ct. App. 2002) (much broader learned profession exemption; misrepresentation of professional qualifications not a UDAP violation), *aff'd*, 597 S.E.2d 669 (N.C. 2003) (per curiam). *See generally* National Consumer Law Center, Unfair and Deceptive Acts and Practices § 2.3.10 (6th ed. 2004 and Supp.).

208 Burton v. William Beaumont Hosp., 373 F. Supp. 2d 707 (E.D. Mich. 2005) (hospital's discriminatory pricing practices exempted from Michigan UDAP law under regulated industries exception). *But see* Smallwood v. Cent. Peninsula Gen. Hosp., 151 P.3d 319 (Alaska 2007) (UDAP claim against hospital for balance billing was not barred because hospital was governed by Medicaid regulations). *See generally* National Consumer Law Center, Unfair and Deceptive Acts and Practices § 2.3.3 (6th ed. 2004 and Supp.).

209 Press Release, Minnesota Attorney General's Office, Attorney General Lori Swanson and Minnesota Hospitals Announce Continuation of Medical Billing Agreement (Apr. 4, 2007).

210 Conn. Gen. Stat. § 19a-673b.

211 Conn. Gen. Stat. § 19a-509b.

212 Ahmad v. Yale New Haven Hosp., Inc., 38 Conn. L. Rptr. 238 (Super. Ct. 2004), *later proceeding at* 2006 WL 337335 (Conn.

Hospitals are prohibited from collecting from certain uninsured patients more than the actual cost of services, and thus can not collect the list price or "gross charges," which are much higher.[213] Patients are eligible for this "uninsured patient discount" if they have an income at or below 250% of the poverty level and have been turned down for state-administered assistance or Medicare.[214] A hospital does not violate this section if it bills for, but does not actually collect, more than the uninsured patient discount; however, the statute might be raised as defense to debt collection, as grounds for injunctive relief, and possibly to define public policy for UDAP claim.[215] Furthermore, a hospital can not sue a debtor unless it has determined whether the debtor qualifies for this uninsured patient discount.[216]

If a hospital has information that a debtor qualifies for free beds funds, the uninsured patient discount, or any other program that could reduce a medical debt, the hospital's debt collectors must cease collection, even if there is a judgment against the debtor, until a determination is made regarding eligibility for these programs.[217] Finally, the law provides an increased homestead exemption for hospital debts, limits the amount of pre-judgment and post-judgment interest, and prohibits wage garnishment, bank account executions, and lien foreclosures if a medical debtor is complying with a court-ordered installment payment plan.[218]

California prohibits discriminatory pricing for uninsured or underinsured patients whose income is under 350% of the federal poverty level ("financially qualified patients").[219] Hospitals can not charge financially qualified patients more than what they receive from Medicare, Medicaid, or another government program.[220] California's law also requires hospitals to have a written financial assistance policy, which must be based on income and must cover all financially qualified patients.[221] Hospitals are required to provide payment plans for financially qualified patients who receive a discount, and the payment plan must be interest free.[222]

California's law provides debt collection protections for medical debt. Hospitals can not sue uninsured or underinsured patients within the first 150 days after sending them the initial bill, and such time periods are extended during appeals.[223] They also can not report negative information to a credit bureau during that time frame.[224] Hospitals can not use wage garnishments or home liens against financially qualified patients or foreclose on the patient's home.[225] They can not send a bill to collections while a patient is applying for financial assistance, negotiating over a bill, or in a payment plan unless the collector agrees to comply with the law's requirements for providing discounts, financial assistance and payment plans.[226]

California's law requires hospitals to have written policies defining when a debt is forwarded for collection, who has authority to send a debt into collections, standards for debt collection, and to obtain the agreement of debt collectors to adhere to these standards.[227] Finally, the law provides for a number of mandatory notices regarding the hospital's financial assistance policies, as well as advising patients about Medicaid availability and their debt collection rights under federal and California law.[228]

Other California laws also address medical debt. California prohibits health facilities from detaining a patient for nonpayment of a medical debt.[229] It also requires hospitals to make a copy of their "charge description masters" publicly available.[230] The charge description master is the schedule of the "retail" prices for services or items charged by the hospital.[231] The intent of the disclosure was both to enable consumers to comparison shop and to provide an impetus for hospitals to limit their markups.[232] Finally, California prohibits county hospitals from adding interest to a medical debt and from enforcing liens against the family home while the debtor or his dependent children reside there.[233]

Super. Ct. Jan. 25, 2006) (denying class certification), *clarified*, 2006 WL 895037 (Conn. Super. Ct. Mar. 24, 2006).

213 Conn. Gen. Stat. § 19a-673; *see* § 10.5.5.2, *infra* (discussing how hospitals often charge the uninsured several times more than insurers because the uninsured are charged "gross charges" but insurers receive large discounts).

214 Conn. Gen Stat. § 19a-673(a)(4).

215 Ahmad v. Yale New Haven Hosp., Inc., 38 Conn. L. Rptr. 238 (Super. Ct. 2004), *later proceeding at* 2006 WL 337335 (Conn. Super. Ct. Jan. 25, 2006) (denying class certification), *clarified*, 2006 WL 895037 (Conn. Super. Ct. Mar. 24, 2006).

216 Conn. Gen. Stat. § 19a-673b.

217 Conn. Gen. Stat. § 19a-673d.

218 Conn. Gen. Stat. §§ 37-3a(b), 52-352b(t), 52-356a, 52-356d.

219 Cal. Health & Safety Code §§ 127400–127446 (West).

220 Cal. Health & Safety Code § 127405(d) (West).

221 Cal. Health & Safety Code § 127405(a) (West).

222 Cal. Health & Safety Code §§ 127405(b), 127425(g) (West).

223 Cal. Health & Safety Code § 127425(d) (West).

224 Cal. Health & Safety Code § 127425(d) (West).

225 Cal. Health & Safety Code § 127425(f)(1) (West).
However, a debt collector is permitted to use wage garnishments upon court order, as well as home liens. Cal. Health & Safety Code § 127425(f)(2) (West). The collector can not foreclose upon a home lien while the debtor, debtor's spouse, or debtor's minor child resides in the home.

226 Cal. Health & Safety Code § 127425(e) (West).

227 Cal. Health & Safety Code § 127425(a), (b) (West).

228 Cal. Health & Safety Code §§ 127410, 127420, 127430 (West).

229 Cal. Health & Safety Code § 1285 (West).

230 Cal. Health & Safety Code § 1339.51(a)(1) (West).

231 Cal. Health & Safety Code § 1339.51(b)(1) (West).
See § 10.5.5.2, *infra*, regarding hospital pricing issues.

232 This statute revealed startling disparities between what hospitals charge for certain items and services. For example, it revealed that one hospital charged $9.00 for a single tablet of Tylenol and another charged $5.50, whereas another hospital charged just 12 cents—the retail price of Tylenol is about 8 or 9 cents a tablet. For a series of blood tests called a "comprehensive metabolic panel," one hospital charged $1733 while another charged $576 and a third only charged $97. Lucette Lagnado, *Medical Markup: California Hospitals Open Books, Showing Huge Price Differences*, Wall St. J., Dec. 27, 2004.

233 Cal. Welf. & Inst. Code § 17401 (West).

New York's medical debtor protection law prohibits discriminatory pricing by hospitals that receive state charity care funding.[234] Hospitals can not charge uninsured patients whose income is under 300% of the federal poverty level more than what the hospitals receive from Medicare, Medicaid or the highest volume payor for that hospital.[235] New York's law requires that hospitals have a written financial assistance policy, and sets forth the actual sliding scale and discount rates that hospitals must provide.[236] Patients with income under the federal poverty threshold can only be required to pay a nominal amount, while those with incomes of 100% to 150% of poverty can be required to pay up to 20% of the amount paid by insurers.[237] In addition, hospitals are required to provide for payment plans, for which the monthly payment can not exceed 10% of the patient's gross monthly income and for which interest is limited to the rate on a 90-day Treasury bill plus 0.5%.[238]

New York's law also provides debt collection protections for medical debt. If a patient is eligible for Medicaid or is applying for financial assistance, the hospital can not send the bill to collections during the application process.[239] Hospitals must provide a thirty-day notice to patients before referring a bill to a debt collector.[240] The New York law does not prohibit home liens for medical debt, but it does prohibit foreclosures on the patient's home.[241] Debt collectors must obtain the consent of the hospital to institute a lawsuit over medical bills.[242] In addition, collectors must follow the hospital's financial assistance policies and provide information on such policies.[243] Finally, the New York law requires hospitals to provide notices of their financial assistance policies.[244]

Illinois has a Fair Patient Billing Act that provides protections for medical debtors in billing and collections. The law requires that hospitals include certain information in their bills, such as a brief description of the services provided, the dates of service, the amount owed for such services, contact information for billing inquiries, a description of how an uninsured patient can apply for financial assistance, and a notice that the patient can obtain an itemized bill.[245] The Illinois law also requires hospitals to establish procedures for billing inquiries and disputes, including providing a telephone number for inquiries and disputes, and requiring the hospitals to return telephone calls about bills within two business days.[246] The law does not set forth what kind of investigation or action the hospital must undertake in order to resolve a billing dispute.

The Illinois law prohibits hospitals from suing uninsured patients who have "clearly demonstrated" insufficient income and assets to pay.[247] Furthermore, hospitals can only institute a collection lawsuit after the hospital has provided the patient with opportunities to: (1) apply for financial assistance; (2) avail themselves of a payment plan; and (3) assess the accuracy of a bill.[248] If the circumstances suggest the patient is eligible for charity care, the hospital must provide sixty days for the patient to apply before instituting a lawsuit.[249] If the patient is already in a payment plan, the hospital can only sue if the patient has failed to make payments.[250] Hospitals can not sue patients who have applied for Medicaid until the application is denied.[251] Debt collectors can not sue a patient without the approval of an authorized hospital employee.[252] Hospitals can not refer a bill to a debt collector without providing an opportunity for the patient to request a reasonable payment plan with the first thirty days after the initial bill.[253] Finally, a separate Illinois law restricts the percentage of a personal injury recovery that may be subject to a lien by certain health care providers.[254]

10.4.4.2 Special Medical Debt Exemption Statutes

States sometimes have special provisions in their exemption or other statutes that protect medical debtors. North Carolina forbids wage garnishment for a health care debt if either: (a) the debtor's income does not exceed 200% of poverty; (b) the debtor is making payments of 10% of disposable income; or (c) the debtor is making reasonable efforts to obtain payment from a third-party payor. When garnishment is permitted the creditor must first make reasonable efforts to obtain payment from a third-party payor, and comply with special notice and hearing requirements.[255]

Kansas forbids wage garnishments for two months after the return to employment of a debtor after an illness of the debtor or of a family member which has kept the debtor out

This protection has been limited to medical debts incurred by indigent patients. Joseph v. J.J. MacIntyre Companies, 238 F. Supp. 2d 1158 (N.D. Cal. 2002).

234 N.Y. Pub. Health Law § 2807-k(9-a) (McKinney).

235 N.Y. Pub. Health Law § 2807-k(9-a)(a) (McKinney).

236 N.Y. Pub. Health Law § 2807-k(9-a)(b) (McKinney).

237 N.Y. Pub. Health Law § 2807-k(9-a)(b) (McKinney).

238 N.Y. Pub. Health Law § 2807-k(9-a)(d) (McKinney).

239 N.Y. Pub. Health Law § 2807-k(9-a)(h) (McKinney).

240 N.Y. Pub. Health Law § 2807-k(9-a)(h) (McKinney).

241 N.Y. Pub. Health Law § 2807-k(9-a)(h) (McKinney).

242 N.Y. Pub. Health Law § 2807-k(9-a)(h) (McKinney).

243 N.Y. Pub. Health Law § 2807-k(9-a)(h) (McKinney).

244 N.Y. Pub. Health Law § 2807-k(9-a)(c) (McKinney).

245 210 Ill. Comp. Stat. § 88/20.

246 210 Ill. Comp. Stat. § 88/25.

247 210 Ill. Comp. Stat. § 88/35.

248 210 Ill. Comp. Stat. § 88/30(a)(1).

249 210 Ill. Comp. Stat. § 88/30(a)(3).

250 210 Ill. Comp. Stat. § 88/30(a)(4).

251 210 Ill. Comp. Stat. § 88/30(a)(5).

252 210 Ill. Comp. Stat. § 88/30(c).

253 210 Ill. Comp. Stat. § 88/30(b).

254 770 Ill. Comp. Stat. § 23/10(a) (limiting the total amount of all provider liens to forty percent of the patients' recovery).
For more on the ability of medical providers to seek liens on personal injury recovery, see § 10.7, *infra*.

255 N.C. Gen. Stat. § 131E-49.

of work for two or more weeks.[256] Virginia prohibits health care providers from collecting any debts arising from medical treatment, or referring those debts to a collector, if a claim has been made for workers' compensation[257] or compensation for crime victims.[258]

Nevada[259] and Ohio[260] forbid execution on the primary residence for health care debts during the lifetime of the debtor and certain specified dependents. In these states, a lien may be created which may be foreclosed only after the residence ceases to be occupied by the protected persons. Louisiana provides a homestead exemption for the full value of the home for debts arising from catastrophic or terminal illness or injury.[261] West Virginia provides a larger homestead exemption for debts resulting from "catastrophic illness or injury."[262]

New Jersey prohibits collection activities against patients found eligible for charity care.[263] In addition, New Jersey has established a Hospital Care Payment Commission to which hospitals can voluntarily assign medical debts.[264] The commission has the power to set off state tax refunds and other state refunds to collect medical debts,[265] but the hospital must agree to first determine whether patients are eligible for charity care.[266] Texas prohibits providers from recovering from a patient the amount that would have been paid by an insurer, if the reason for non-coverage is that the provider failed to bill the insurer in a timely manner.[267] Ohio has a special provision protecting children and former spouses for whom a family court has ordered the other ex-spouse to provide health insurance. If the required health insurance is not provided, Ohio law prohibits any provider or collection agency from seeking to collect medical bills that should have been covered by such health insurance, if the former spouse or children provides a copy of the relevant court order and reasonable help in locating the responsible party.[268]

Many states have statutes detailing the rights of health care patients, often called patients' bills of rights. Although these statutes generally focus on issues such as privacy and informed consent, they may also be useful in a debt collection case. Massachusetts, for example, requires providers to provide itemized bills and explanations of charges and, upon request, information about financial aid and free care.[269] Florida's HMO Act prohibits unfair or deceptive trade practices, but is not privately enforceable.[270]

10.4.5 State Loan Broker Laws

A common debt collection tactic by health care providers is to take on the role of loan brokers, steering patients toward lenders to borrow money to pay off medical bills.[271] Medical bills are a significant source of credit card and home-secured debt.[272] For providers, the advantages of this

---

256 Kan. Stat. Ann. § 60-2310.

257 Va. Code Ann. § 65.2-601.1.

258 Va. Code Ann. § 19.2-368.5:2.

259 Nev. Rev. Stat. § 21.095 provides that the primary dwelling (including a mobile home) and land may not be executed upon for a medical bill during the lifetime of the debtor, debtor's spouse, a joint tenant who was a joint tenant at the time judgment was entered, or debtor's dependent disabled adult child, or during the minority of any child of the debtor.

260 Ohio Rev. Code Ann. §§ 2329.66(A)(1)(a), 2329.661 (West) provide that, for debts for health care services or supplies, the homestead exemption has no dollar limitation. *See* Edwards v. McCormick, 136 F. Supp. 2d 795 (S.D. Ohio 2001) (threatening forced sale of home contrary to state exemption is FDCPA violation); Wickliffe Country Place v. Kovacs, 765 N.E.2d 975 (Ohio Ct. App. 2001) (remanding for determination whether services provided by nursing home were "health care services and supplies," in which case lien would be precluded).

261 La. Rev. Stat. Ann. § 20:1; *see In re* Collet, 351 B.R. 395 (Bankr. W.D. La. 2006) (debtors not entitled to unlimited homestead exemption for catastrophic illness, because not all of the credit card cash advances they borrowed were used to pay medical expenses).

262 W. Va. Code § 38-9-3(b) provides a blanket $5000 exemption which increases to $7500 for hospital or medical expenses for catastrophic illness or injury.

263 N.J. Admin. Code § 10:52-11.14.

264 N.J. Stat. Ann. §§ 17B:30-41 to 17B:30-57 (West).

265 N.J. Stat. Ann. § 17B:30-45 (West).

In return, hospitals let the state keep fifty percent of the amount collected, plus administrative and collection costs. N.J. Stat. Ann. § 17B:30-44 (West).

266 N.J. Stat. Ann. § 17B:30-47 (West).

267 Tex. Civ. Prac. & Rem. Code Ann. §§ 146.002, 146.003 (Vernon) (provider must submit bill within either eleven months or the time specified in any contract with insurer).

268 Ohio Rev. Code Ann. § 1349.01 (West).

Also, the provider or collection agency may not report to any credit bureau, and the credit bureau may not report, any information about the nonpayment in the file of the former spouse.

269 Mass. Gen. Laws ch. 111, § 70E.

270 Electrostim Med. Services, Inc., 2007 WL 470481 (M.D. Fla. Feb. 13, 2007).

However patients could bring claims under common law or other theories based on the same allegations. *Id.*

271 For examples of health care providers acting as loan brokers, see Brian Grow and Robert Berner, *Fresh Pain for the Uninsured*, Bus. Week, Nov. 21, 2007; Steve Tripoli & Chi Chi Wu, National Consumer Law Center, Unhealthy Pursuits: How the Sick and Vulnerable are Harmed by Abusive Medical Debt Collection Tactics (Dec. 2005), *available at* www.consumerlaw.org/issues/medical_debt/content/medicaldebt.pdf; Jones v. Peoples' Heritage Bank, 433 F. Supp. 2d 1328 (S.D. Ga. 2006) (dentist arranged financing with lender offering credit program specially designed for dental bills).

272 See § 10.1.3, *supra*, regarding the use of home loans to pay down medical debt. One survey has found that medical bills contribute to the credit card debt of 29% of low-income and middle-income borrowers. Cindy Zeldin & Mark Rukavina, Demos & Access Project, Borrowing to Stay Healthy: How Credit Card Debt is Related to Medical Expenses (Jan. 2007). This same study also found that consumers with medical debt had a higher level of credit card debt than those without ($11,623 versus $7964). *See, e.g., In re* Collet, 351 B.R. 395 (Bankr. W.D. La. 2006) (bankruptcy filing by consumer who

practice are obvious: they get their money right away, while offloading the burden of pursuing payments to third parties. Patients, however, may become burdened by the high interest rates charged by some lenders, as well as by losing the ability to negotiate a reduction in the bill on the basis of discriminatory pricing.[273]

Hospitals that steer patients toward lenders may be violating state laws that regulate loan brokers. Some of these laws require loan brokers to obtain a license from state banking departments, which presumably many health care providers have not done.[274] A few states also cap the loan rates that can be charged.[275] For-profit hospitals that act as loan brokers may also violate state credit services organizations laws.[276]

In some cases, patients may not be aware that their medical bills have been transferred to a third party lender. The "authorization" for such a transfer may be buried in the fine print of the hospital's admissions form.[277] Such lenders often charge high interest rates, and the contractual basis to charge such rates is questionable.

Some credit programs designed for medical bills also entail automatic deductions from a patient's wages, and thus involve employers offering the programs.[278] This practice may also expose the employers to loan brokering issues. If the wage assignments are not cancelable at the option of the employee, they might also violate the Federal Trade Commission's Credit Practices Rule.[279]

10.4.6 State Tort Law

In some cases of medical debt collection, state tort law may provide a cause of action. The tort of intentional infliction of emotional distress has widespread recognition and is often applied in the debt collection context.[280] The advantage of this tort is the likelihood of recovery of punitive damages in an egregious case in which the collector's malice is readily apparent. Some courts permit large punitive damage awards against tortfeasors who make large profits in hopes of deterring similar misconduct by others.[281] The difficulty with this tort is that it is available in many states only for clearly outrageous conduct resulting in very severe distress.[282] The courts often impose a greater duty of care upon debt collectors who are dealing with people known to be disabled or convalescing.[283]

---

borrowed cash advances from credit cards in part to pay medical expenses).

273 *See* § 10.5.5.2, *infra*.

274 Ala. Code §§ 5-19-1 to 5-19-31 (requiring brokers of loans of $2000 or less to obtain a license); Ariz. Rev. Stat. Ann. §§ 6-601 to 6-615 (requiring loan brokers to obtain a license); Iowa Code §§ 535C.1 to 535C.14 (prohibiting loan brokers from collecting advance fees and requiring written loan brokerage agreements); Neb. Rev. Stat. §§ 45-189 to 45-191.11 (requiring loan brokers to file disclosure and brokerage agreements with the state and to pay a filing fee to the state; prohibiting loan brokers from collecting advance fees; and requiring brokers to provide borrowers with disclosures and written agreements); N.J. Stat. Ann. §§ 17:11C-1 to 17:11C-50 (West) (requiring loan brokers to obtain a license); N.D. Cent. Code § 13-04.1-02 (requiring loans brokers to obtain a license).

275 For example, Massachusetts requires small loan brokers to obtain a license from the state Division of Banks and prohibits them from brokering loans that charge over 23% annual interest. Mass. Gen. Laws ch. 140, § 96. Pennsylvania requires brokers of loans under $25,000 to be licensed and caps rates at 24% per year. 7 Pa. Cons. Stat. §§ 6201–6219; *see also* Ga. Code Ann. §§ 7-3-1 to 7-3-29 (requiring brokers of loans of $3000 or less to obtain a license and capping interest rates); R.I. Gen. Laws § 19-14.1-1 (requiring loan brokers to obtain a license and capping interest rates); Tex. Fin. Code Ann. § 342.051 (Vernon) (requiring persons who engage in the business of negotiating loans to obtain a license and capping interest on those loans as specified under Tex. Fin. Code Ann. § 342.201 (Vernon)).

276 *See* National Consumer Law Center, Fair Credit Reporting Ch. 15 (6th ed. 2006 and Supp.).

277 *See, e.g.*, Brian Grow & Robert Berner, *Fresh Pain for the Uninsured*, Bus. Week, Nov. 21, 2007.

278 Sarah Bernstein, *In New Health Plan, Patients Pay Their Share—Or Else*, Wall St. J., Mar. 13, 2006 (describing UnitedHealth Group's OnePay plan, which uses automatic wage deduction and imposes 7.5% interest rate to repay loans used to pay deductibles and co-payments; notes that UnitedHealth chartered its own bank for OnePay).

279 16 C.F.R. § 444; *see* National Consumer Law Center, Unfair and Deceptive Acts and Practices § 5.1.1.2.2 (6th ed. 2004 and Supp.).

The FTC rule does not apply to banks, but many banks are governed by comparable rules. *Id.*

280 *See, e.g.*, Bickford v. Onslow Mem'l Hosp. Found., 855 A.2d 1150 (Me. 2004) (alleging claims for intentional infliction of emotional distress, as well as for defamation and tortuous interference with an economic advantage, over hospital wrongfully reporting to credit bureau that plaintiff owed bills for services to ex-wife's daughter, to whom plaintiff had no legal relationship).

281 *See* National Consumer Law Center, Fair Debt Collection § 6.5 (6th ed. 2008).

282 *See, e.g.*, Ziegler v. Elmore County Health Care Auth., 56 F. Supp. 2d 1324 (M.D. Ala. 1999) (mother whose sick child was denied treatment at hospital because she owed past-due bill failed to state claim for outrage, when child recovered fully and mother alleged no ill effects from her emotional distress); Weiss v. Collection Ctr., Inc., 667 N.W.2d 567 (N.D. 2003) (consumer stated claim for FDCPA violation but not intentional inflection of emotional distress; letter which could be read by unsophisticated consumer as threat to seize vehicle for $255 clinic bill not extreme and outrageous); Froemming v. Perez, 2006 WL 704479 (Tex. App. Mar. 22, 2006) (plaintiff could recover under state UDAP statute, but not for tort of mental anguish, when orthodontist agreed to give plaintiff a discounted price for braces, then reneged on agreement and attempted to extract more money by refusing to complete treatment for plaintiff's daughter).

283 *See* National Consumer Law Center, Fair Debt Collection § 10.2 (6th ed. 2008).

10.4.7 Other State Common Law Claims

Other state common law claims may be applicable in particular instances of medical debt collection. These claims may include:

- Breach of contract;[284]
- Breach of the covenant of good faith and fair dealing, which is incorporated into health care contracts[285]—this duty may require that charges not set forth specifically in an agreement be reasonable;[286]
- Breach of fiduciary duty;[287]
- Unconscionability;[288]
- Fraud;[289]

284 Urquhart v. Manatee Mem'l Hosp., 2007 WL 781738 (M.D. Fla. Mar. 13, 2007) (hospital's excessive charges could be challenged as breach of contract); Colomar v. Mercy Hosp., Inc., 461 F. Supp. 2d 1265 (S.D. Fla. 2006) (same); Wentz v. Kindred Hospitals E., L.L.C., 333 F. Supp. 2d 1298 (S.D. Fla. 2004) (when provider returned Medicare payment so it could seek recovery against patient's personal injury settlement, patient could proceed with breach of contract claim that charges were "unlawful" and thus violated the provider's contract); Servedio v. Our Lady of the Resurrection Med. Ctr., Clearinghouse No. 55,626 (Ill. Cir. Ct. Cook County Jan. 6, 2005) (consumer permitted to proceed on breach of contract claim for hospital's discriminatory pricing charging uninsured patients several times more than private and public insurers); Turner v. Legacy Health Systems, 2006 WL 657176 (Or. Cir. Ct. Oct. 4, 2005) (granting class certification in case challenging discriminatory pricing as breach of contract). *But see* Harrison v. Christus St. Patrick Hosp., 430 F. Supp. 2d 591 (W.D. La. 2006) (no breach of contract or fiduciary duty claim, or unjust enrichment claim, for discriminatory pricing); DiCarlo v. St. Mary's Hosp., 2006 WL 2038498 (D.N.J. July 19, 2006) (no breach of contract or fiduciary duty claim for discriminatory pricing); Burton v. William Beaumont Hosp., 373 F. Supp. 2d 707 (E.D. Mich. 2005) (same); Morrell v. Wellstar Health Sys., Inc., 633 S.E.2d 68 (Ga. Ct. App. 2006) (same); Cox v. Athens Reg'l Med. Ctr., Inc., 631 S.E.2d 792 (Ga. Ct. App. 2006) (same); Morgan v. State, 787 N.Y.S.2d 356 (App. Div. 2004) (dismissing breach of contract claim for discriminatory pricing); Shelton v. Duke Univ. Health Sys., 633 S.E.2d 113 (N.C. Ct. App. 2006) (no breach of contract or fiduciary duty claim for discriminatory pricing); Nygaard v. Sioux Valley Hosp. & Health Sys., 731 N.W.2d 184 (S.D. 2007) (no breach of contract or fiduciary duty claim for discriminatory pricing).

285 Rivera v. Veterans Mem'l Med. Ctr., 818 A.2d 731 (Conn. 2003) (class action alleging violations of state UDAP law, abuse of process, and breach of the implied covenant of good faith and fair dealing over hospital's balance billing and collection efforts when workers' compensation covered medical services); Picker v. Castro, 776 N.Y.S.2d 433 (App. Term 2003) (provider's refusal to fill out insurance paperwork violated duty of good faith and fair dealing; provider precluded from recovering fees from patient).

286 Greenfield v. Manor Care, Inc., 705 So. 2d 926 (Fla. Dist. Ct. App. 1997) (contract with nursing home included duty of good faith and fair dealing, which required that when no price term specified, only reasonable price could be charged), *overruled on other grounds by* Knowles v. Beverly Enterprises, 898 So. 2d 1 (Fla. 2004). *But see* Kizzire v. Baptist Health Sys., 441 F.3d 1306 (11th Cir. 2006) (claim of breach of duty of good faith and fair dealing dismissed on res judicata grounds; all claims relating to price of care were compulsory counterclaims in hospital's collection action); Urquhart v. Manatee Mem'l Hosp., 2007 WL 781738 (M.D. Fla. Mar. 13, 2007) (no breach of duty of good faith and fair dealing over discriminatory pricing).

287 Havsy v. Washington State Dep't of Health, 123 Wash. App. 1030 (2004) (licensing board sanctions affirmed in case in which doctor breached fiduciary duty to patient by misleading patient about the price of treatment, failing to inform patient of the high cost of a certain procedure and that insurance would not cover that procedure, and using a "small-print" form to obtain patient's agreement to be liable for charges). *But see* Harrison v. Christus St. Patrick Hosp., 430 F. Supp. 2d 591 (W.D. La. 2006) (no breach of contract or fiduciary duty claim, or unjust enrichment claim, for discriminatory pricing); DiCarlo v. St. Mary's Hosp., 2006 WL 2038498 (D.N.J. July 19, 2006) (no breach of contract or fiduciary duty claim for discriminatory pricing); Morrell v. Wellstar Health Sys., Inc., 633 S.E.2d 68 (Ga. Ct. App. 2006) (same); Cox v. Athens Reg'l Med. Ctr., Inc., 631 S.E.2d 792 (Ga. Ct. App. 2006) (same); Shelton v. Duke Univ. Health Sys., 633 S.E.2d 113 (N.C. Ct. App. 2006) (no breach of contract or fiduciary duty claim for discriminatory pricing); Nygaard v. Sioux Valley Hosp. & Health Sys., 731 N.W.2d 184 (S.D. 2007) (no breach of contract or fiduciary duty claim for discriminatory pricing). *See generally* Mark A. Hall & Carl E. Schneider, *Patients as Consumers: Courts, Contracts, and The New Medical Marketplace*, 106 Mich. L. Rev. 642 (Feb. 2008).

288 *See* Hill v. Sisters of St. Francis Health Services, 2006 WL 3783415 (N.D. Ill. Dec. 20, 2006) (denying dismissal of UDAP and unconscionability claims for discriminatory pricing); Phoenix Baptist Hosp. & Med. Ctr. v. Aiken, 877 P.2d 1345 (Ariz. Ct. App. 1994) (husband signed contract when wife had just had heart attack, husband was distraught, could not read contract without his reading glasses, which he did not have with him, and contract was not explained to him; court held that this was contract of adhesion, sent case back to trial court for factual findings whether husband reasonably expected his separate property to be covered, and whether contract was unconscionable); *In re* Sutter Health Uninsured Pricing Cases, 2005 WL 1842582 (Cal. Super. Ct. July 16, 2005) (denying dismissal of UDAP and unconscionability claims for discriminatory pricing). *See generally* National Consumer Law Center, Unfair and Deceptive Acts and Practices §§ 4.3, 4.4 (6th ed. 2004 and Supp.); Mark A. Hall & Carl E. Schneider, *Patients as Consumers: Courts, Contracts, and The New Medical Marketplace*, 106 Mich. L. Rev. 642 (Feb. 2008); George A. Nation, *Obscene Contracts: The Doctrine of Unconscionability and Hospital Billing of the Uninsured*, 94 Ky. L.J. 101–137 (2005–2006).

289 Martinez v. Yale New Haven Hosp., 2005 WL 2364901 (Conn. Super. Ct. Sept. 1, 2005) (informing patients that only option was to pay charges, despite availability of charity care funds, not actionable as fraud but actionable as negligent misrepresentation); Summa Health Sys. v. Viningre, 140 Ohio App. 3d 780, 749 N.E.2d 344 (2000) (fraud judgment affirmed when HMO told patient who had been injured by HMO's misreading of test that she would not be required to pay for further testing and surgery, but then negotiated malpractice settlement making no mention of bills, and billed her for the surgery). *But see* SWA, Inc. v. Straka, 2003 WL 21434637 (Ohio Ct. App. June 19, 2003) (misrepresentations in nursing home admission materials not actionable when incorrect statement caused no damage to patient or family); Mercy Health Partners of Southwest Ohio v. Miller, 2005 WL 2592674 (Ohio Ct. Com. Pl. Sept. 30, 2005) (discriminatory pricing not actionable as fraud under Ohio law).

- Limitations on collection fees;[290]
- Usury;[291]
- Malicious prosecution;[292] and
- Other common law claims.[293]

10.4.8 Claims Based on Hospital's Charitable Status

10.4.8.1 General

Many hospitals are organized as not-for-profit corporations, and have tax-exempt status under state law and the Internal Revenue Code. As such, they have an implicit duty to provide a certain amount of free care to low-income patients; in some states this obligation is explicit. Engaging in collection activities against low-income patients while failing to inform them of their eligibility to apply for charity care may be actionable under state laws prohibiting unfair and deceptive acts and practices.[294] Such conduct might also constitute a breach of the hospital's charitable duty under state tax law.[295] However, several dozen federal courts have rejected the theory the such conduct violates a charitable trust based upon the tax-exempt status of the hospital under section 501(c)(3) of the Internal Revenue Code.[296]

A few hospitals still have obligations under the Hill-Burton Act,[297] a federal law that provided hospitals with construction and renovation grant funds. In return, hospitals were obligated to provide a certain amount of uncompensated care for twenty years. While most hospitals are no longer bound by this obligation, a few still are.[298] Failure to comply with the Hill-Burton Act may give rise to a claim.[299]

290 *E.g.*, HCA Health Services, Inc. v. Peters, Clearinghouse No. 44,663 (D. Va. 1989) (when parent assumed financial responsibility for emergency care for child and signed contract before admittance which was open-ended, speculative, and under the complete control of health care provider, court held unenforceable as unreasonable provision for 25% collection attorney fees); *see* National Consumer Law Center, Fair Debt Collection § 11.8 (6th ed. 2008).

291 *Cf.* Egge v. Healthspan Services Co., 115 F. Supp. 2d 1126 (D. Minn. 2000) (usury not shown when consumer never paid debt; illegal interest was never collected, an essential element under Minnesota statute).

292 *See, e.g.*, Rutherford v. Ralph Hutton & Associates, 2004 WL 1119676 (Cal. Ct. App. May 20, 2004) (malicious prosecution action brought against hospital over its attempt to enforce lien against personal injury recovery when balance billing was forbidden by hospital's contract with county aid program). *See generally* National Consumer Law Center, Fair Debt Collection § 10.6 (6th ed. 2008).

293 Joseph v. J.J. MacIntyre Companies, 238 F. Supp. 2d 1158 (N.D. Cal. 2002) (barrage of phone calls to disabled senior citizen; consumer stated claims for intrusion on seclusion and tort-in-se), *later opinion at* 281 F. Supp. 2d 1156 (N.D. Cal. 2003) (collector's motion for Fry judgment denied); Bickford v. Onslow Mem'l Hosp. Found., 855 A.2d 1150 (Me. 2004) (alleging claims for defamation and tortuous interference with economic advantage, over hospital's wrongful credit reporting); *cf.* Muse v. Charter Hosp., Inc., 452 S.E.2d 589 (N.C. Ct. App. 1995) (malpractice judgment proper when hospital's policy of requiring patients to be discharged when their insurance was used up "interfered with" treating physician's medical judgment), *aff'd*, 342 N.C. 403 (1995) (per curiam).

294 Martinez v. Yale New Haven Hosp., 2005 WL 2364901 (Conn. Super. Ct. Sept. 1, 2005) (informing patients that their only option was to pay charges, despite availability of charity care funds, may be actionable as negligent misrepresentation); Ahmad v. Yale New Haven Hosp., 38 Conn. L. Rptr. 238 (Super. Ct. 2004) (finding private right of action under Connecticut free care statute; failure to inform eligible patients of free care availability may violate both free care statute and UDAP statute), *later proceeding at* 2006 WL 337335 (Conn. Super. Ct. Jan. 25, 2006) (denying class certification), *clarified*, 2006 WL 895037 (Conn. Super. Ct. Mar. 24, 2006); *see* § 10.4.3, *supra* (UDAP section).

295 Alan Alop, Defending Hospital Collection Cases (rev. ed. 2005), *available at* www.illinoislegaladvocate.org/index.cfm?fuseaction=home.dsp_content&contentID=728; *cf.* Hill v. Sisters of St. Francis Health Services, 2006 WL 3783415 (N.D. Ill. Dec. 20, 2006) (allegation that discriminatory pricing violated state's charitable organization exemption supported claim that hospital violated UDAP statute); Ahmad v. Yale New Haven Hosp., 38 Conn. L. Rptr. 238 (Super. Ct. 2004) (action alleging violations of free care statute did not violate rule that beneficiaries may not sue to enforce charitable trust), *later proceeding at* 2006 WL 337335 (Conn. Super. Ct. Jan. 25, 2006) (denying class certification), *clarified*, 2006 WL 895037 (Conn. Super. Ct. Mar. 24, 2006). *But see* Servedio v. Our Lady of the Resurrection Med. Ctr., Clearinghouse No. 55,626 (Ill. Cir. Ct. Cook County Jan. 6, 2005) (dismissing plaintiff's claim that hospital's discriminatory pricing violated charitable obligation under Illinois revenue code; no private right of action under revenue code).

New York law specifically prohibits patients from using the fact that a hospital receives state charity care funds as a legal defense in a hospital collection action. N.Y. Pub. Health Law § 2807-k(14) (McKinney).

296 *See* § 10.4.8.2, *infra*.

297 42 U.S.C. § 291c.

298 Hospitals that have Hill-Burton obligations are identified on-line at www.hrsa.gov/hillburton/hillburtonfacilities.htm.

299 Yale New Haven Hosp. v. Gargiulo, 1999 WL 989422 (Conn. Super. Ct. Oct. 18, 1999) (special defense of failure to mitigate sufficiently alleged: hospital failed to advise patient of Hill-Burton or other aid programs, or to assist her in applying); *see also* Flagstaff Med. Ctr. v. Sullivan, 962 F.2d 879 (9th. Cir. 1992) (court applied state contract law to hold that indigent patients are third party beneficiaries of contract between HHS and hospital which accepted Hill-Burton funds; eligible patients who were denied such care may be granted relief from debt to hospital); Davis v. Ball Mem'l Hosp., 640 F.2d 30 (7th Cir. 1980) (regulation created an entitlement to uncompensated care); Creditor's Serv. Inc. v. Schaffer, 659 P.2d 694 (Colo. 1982); Yale New Haven Hosp. v. Mitchell, 683 A.2d 1362 (Conn. Super. Ct. 1995) (correcting opinion at 662 A.2d 178) (failure to notify indigent patients of the availability of free care under Hill-Burton or the Connecticut Hospital Bed fund is a defense to a hospital debt collection suit; case remanded to trial court for factual findings on issue whether failure to notify was also unfair trade practice); Hosp. Ctr. at Orange v. Cook, 177 N.J. Super. 289, 426 A.2d 526 (Super. Ct. App. Div. 1981)

10.4.8.2 Not-for-Profit Hospital Litigation Cases

Earlier this decade, several dozen class action lawsuits challenging hospital billing practices were filed in an orchestrated campaign. The suits were based on a number of legal claims but primarily focused on the theory that the hospitals had violated contracts with the federal government, to which the plaintiffs were third-party beneficiaries, to provide charitable care in exchange for federal tax-exempt status.[300] The suits also included claims under the Emergency Medical Treatment and Active Labor Act (EMTALA), the Fair Debt Collection Practices Act (FDCPA), as well as state claims for UDAP violations, breach of the duty of good faith and fair dealing, and breach of contract.

Most of the federal claims in these lawsuits were dismissed on the pleadings. The courts uniformly dismissed claims for breach of contract or charitable trust based upon a theory of the hospital's obligations under section 501(c)(3) of the Internal Revenue Code.[301] The courts held that tax-exempt status does not create a contract between the hospital and the Internal Revenue Service, and that even if it did the plaintiffs could not enforce that contract because they were at most incidental beneficiaries. Furthermore, these courts held that there is no private right of action to enforce section 501(c)(3).[302]

Several courts distinguished cases finding a private right of action for patients to enforce the Hill-Burton Act.[303] These courts noted that in the Hill-Burton cases, the hospitals did actually enter into a written agreement with the government and received funds under that agreement. Furthermore the courts noted that Hill-Burton provided a private right of action to litigants.

The courts also uniformly dismissed claims for violation of a charitable trust, holding that there was no intent to establish a charitable trust and, even if there were, the plaintiffs would have no right to enforce it.[304] The courts

(hospital's failure to comply with Hill-Burton a bar to suit for services rendered). *But see* White v. Moses Taylor Hosp., 841 F. Supp. 629 (M.D. Pa. 1992) (*Flagstaff* decision considered and rejected; private right of action only to compel future compliance by hospital).

300 Harrison v. Christus St. Patrick Hosp., 430 F. Supp. 2d 591 (W.D. La. 2006); Sabeta v. Baptist Hosp., Inc., 410 F. Supp. 2d 1224 (S.D. Fla. 2005); Grant v. Trinity Health Mich., 390 F. Supp. 2d 643 (E.D. Mich. 2005); McCoy v. E. Texas Med. Ctr., 388 F. Supp. 2d 760 (E.D. Tex. 2005); Bobo v. Christus Health, 227 F.R.D. 479 (E.D. Tex. 2005); Kolari v. N.Y. Presbyterian Hosp., 382 F. Supp. 2d 562 (S.D.N.Y. 2005), *vacated in part on other grounds*, 455 F.3d 118 (2d Cir. 2006); Quinn v. BJC Health Sys., 364 F. Supp. 2d 1046 (E.D. Mo. 2005); Valencia v. Miss. Baptist Med. Ctr., 363 F. Supp. 2d 867 (S.D. Miss. 2005); Nash v. Lee Mem'l Health Sys., 2005 WL 2043642 (M.D. Fla. Aug. 25, 2005); Kabeller v. Orlando Reg'l Healthcare Sys., Inc., 2005 WL 1925717 (M.D. Fla. Aug. 11, 2005); Cargile v. Baylor Health Care Sys., 2005 WL 2445482 (N.D. Tex. Aug. 10, 2005); Gardner v. N. Miss. Health Services, Inc., 2005 WL 1312753 (N.D. Miss. May 31, 2005); Jakubiec v. Sacred Heart Health Sys., Inc., 2005 WL 1261443 (N.D. Fla. May 26, 2005); Wright v. St. Dominic Health Services, Inc., 2005 WL 743339 (S.D. Miss. Mar. 5, 2005); Schmitt v. Protestant Mem'l Med. Ctr., 2005 WL 4157466 (S.D. Ill. Feb. 23, 2005); Peterson v. Fairview Health Services, 2005 WL 226168 (D. Minn. Feb. 1, 2005); Ferguson v. Centura Health Corp., 358 F. Supp. 2d 1014 (D. Colo. 2004); Burton v. William Beaumont Hosp., 347 F. Supp. 2d 486 (E.D. Mich. 2004); Kizzire v. Baptist Health Sys., Inc., 343 F. Supp. 2d 1074 (N.D. Ala. 2004), *aff'd on other grounds*, 441 F.3d 1306 (11th Cir. 2006); Darr v. Sutter Health, 2004 WL 2873068 (N.D. Cal. Nov. 20, 2004).

301 Harrison v. Christus St. Patrick Hosp., 430 F. Supp. 2d 591 (W.D. La. 2006); Sabeta v. Baptist Hosp., Inc., 410 F. Supp. 2d 1224 (S.D. Fla. 2005); Grant v. Trinity Health Mich., 390 F. Supp. 2d 643 (E.D. Mich. 2005); McCoy v. E. Texas Med. Ctr., 388 F. Supp. 2d 760 (E.D. Tex. 2005); Bobo v. Christus Health, 227 F.R.D. 479 (E.D. Tex. 2005); Kolari v. N.Y. Presbyterian Hosp., 382 F. Supp. 2d 562 (S.D.N.Y. 2005), *vacated in part on other grounds*, 455 F.3d 118 (2d Cir. 2006); Quinn v. BJC Health Sys., 364 F. Supp. 2d 1046 (E.D. Mo. 2005); Valencia v. Miss. Baptist Med. Ctr., 363 F. Supp. 2d 867 (S.D. Miss. 2005); Nash v. Lee Mem'l Health Sys., 2005 WL 2043642 (M.D. Fla. Aug. 25, 2005); Kabeller v. Orlando Reg'l Healthcare Sys., Inc., 2005 WL 1925717 (M.D. Fla. Aug. 11, 2005); Cargile v. Baylor Health Care Sys., 2005 WL 2445482 (N.D. Tex. Aug. 10, 2005); Gardner v. N. Miss. Health Services, Inc., 2005 WL 1312753 (N.D. Miss. May 31, 2005); Jakubiec v. Sacred Heart Health Sys., Inc., 2005 WL 1261443 (N.D. Fla. May 26, 2005); Wright v. St. Dominic Health Services, Inc., 2005 WL 743339 (S.D. Miss. Mar. 5, 2005); Schmitt v. Protestant Mem'l Med. Ctr., 2005 WL 4157466 (S.D. Ill. Feb. 23, 2005); Peterson v. Fairview Health Services, 2005 WL 226168 (D. Minn. Feb. 1, 2005); Ferguson v. Centura Health Corp., 358 F. Supp. 2d 1014 (D. Colo. 2004); Burton v. William Beaumont Hosp., 347 F. Supp. 2d 486 (E.D. Mich. 2004); Kizzire v. Baptist Health Sys., Inc., 343 F. Supp. 2d 1074 (N.D. Ala. 2004), *aff'd on other grounds*, 441 F.3d 1306 (11th Cir. 2006); Darr v. Sutter Health, 2004 WL 2873068 (N.D. Cal. Nov. 20, 2004).

302 While claims based on a theory that a hospital violated its tax-exempt status have almost uniformly failed, one court has held that such a violation could be used to show that the hospital's practices violated public policy, which was an issue under that state's UDAP statute. *See* Hill v. Sisters of St. Francis Health Services, 2006 WL 3783415 (N.D. Ill. Dec. 20, 2006).

303 Sabeta v. Baptist Hosp., Inc., 410 F. Supp. 2d 1224 (S.D. Fla. 2005); Grant v. Trinity Health Mich., 390 F. Supp. 2d 643 (E.D. Mich. 2005); McCoy v. E. Texas Med. Ctr., 388 F. Supp. 2d 760 (E.D. Tex. 2005); Kolari v. N.Y. Presbyterian Hosp., 382 F. Supp. 2d 562 (S.D.N.Y. 2005), *vacated in part on other grounds*, 455 F.3d 118 (2d Cir. 2006); Quinn v. BJC Health Sys., 364 F. Supp. 2d 1046 (E.D. Mo. 2005); Valencia v. Miss. Baptist Med. Ctr., 363 F. Supp. 2d 867 (S.D. Miss. 2005); Feliciana v. Thomas Jefferson Univ. Hosp., 2005 WL 2397047 (E.D. Pa. Sept. 28, 2005); Hutt v. Albert Einstein Med. Ctr., 2005 WL 2396313 (E.D. Pa. Sept. 28, 2005); Schmitt v. Protestant Mem'l Med. Ctr., 2005 WL 4157466 (S.D. Ill. Feb. 23, 2005); Ferguson v. Centura Health Corp., 358 F. Supp. 2d 1014 (D. Colo. 2004).

304 Harrison v. Christus St. Patrick Hosp., 430 F. Supp. 2d 591 (W.D. La. 2006); Sabeta v. Baptist Hosp., Inc., 410 F. Supp. 2d 1224 (S.D. Fla. 2005); Grant v. Trinity Health Mich., 390 F. Supp. 2d 643 (E.D. Mich. 2005); McCoy v. E. Texas Med. Ctr., 388 F. Supp. 2d 760 (E.D. Tex. 2005); Bobo v. Christus Health,

similarly uniformly dismissed EMTALA claims.[305] Claims under the FDCPA met with mixed success. While these claims were dismissed in two cases,[306] courts in other cases denied dismissal or dismissed without prejudice, permitting plaintiffs to amend their claims.[307]

After dismissal of the federal claims, most of the district courts declined to exercise supplemental jurisdiction over the remaining state law claims. A few courts did rule substantively on the state law claims, dismissing counts for UDAP violations, fraud, breach of contract, and unjust enrichment.[308] However, the Second Circuit rebuked one district court for abusing its discretion in exercising supplemental jurisdiction and dismissing the state law claims.[309] Some of the cases were refiled in state court, where a few met with more success.[310]

An initial settlement of one of these cases was eventually undone. A tentative settlement of unfiled claims against North Mississippi Medical Center unraveled when news of the settlement resulted in a dramatic increase in that hospital's charity care volume, as uninsured patients from both the hospital's area and across the state bypassed other hospitals to seek care at North Mississippi, and workers allegedly dropped their health insurance coverage to take advantage of the settlement.[311] After North Mississippi backed out of the settlement it successfully moved to dismiss the plaintiff's case in federal court.[312]

10.5 Defenses to a Medical Debt Collection Action

10.5.1 General

Practitioners defending consumers sued over medical debt have a number of viable defenses. Aggressive advocacy can often result in very favorable outcomes. Medical debt collectors are accustomed to obtaining default judgments, and are not used to being forced to put on a case.[313] Defending a consumer against a collection action is also important because once a default judgment has entered, res judicata may preclude the consumer from challenging the abuses or unfair practices of medical creditors.[314]

As few medical debt collection suits go to trial, collectors may overlook a necessary element of proof. Practitioners may prevail because of such a failure of proof, as well as by establishing the consumer's defenses and counterclaims.

A medical debt collector may sue under various theories, each with different elements and different burdens of proof. The burdens of proof may also differ from state to state. For example, a medical debt collection suit may be an action for breach of contract, on a promissory note, on an open account

227 F.R.D. 479 (E.D. Tex. 2005); Kolari v. N.Y. Presbyterian Hosp., 382 F. Supp. 2d 562 (S.D.N.Y. 2005), *vacated in part on other grounds*, 455 F.3d 118 (2d Cir. 2006); Quinn v. BJC Health Sys., 364 F. Supp. 2d 1046 (E.D. Mo. 2005); Valencia v. Miss. Baptist Med. Ctr., 363 F. Supp. 2d 867 (S.D. Miss. 2005); Nash v. Lee Mem'l Health Sys., 2005 WL 2043642 (M.D. Fla. Aug. 25, 2005); Kabeller v. Orlando Reg'l Healthcare Sys., Inc., 2005 WL 1925717 (M.D. Fla. Aug. 11, 2005); Cargile v. Baylor Health Care Sys., 2005 WL 2445482 (N.D. Tex. Aug. 10, 2005); Gardner v. N. Miss. Health Services, Inc., 2005 WL 1312753 (N.D. Miss. May 31, 2005); Jakubiec v. Sacred Heart Health Sys., Inc., 2005 WL 1261443 (N.D. Fla. May 26, 2005); Wright v. St. Dominic Health Services, Inc., 2005 WL 743339 (S.D. Miss. Mar. 5, 2005); Schmitt v. Protestant Mem'l Med. Ctr., 2005 WL 4157466 (S.D. Ill. Feb. 23, 2005); Peterson v. Fairview Health Services, 2005 WL 226168 (D. Minn. Feb. 1, 2005); Ferguson v. Centura Health Corp., 358 F. Supp. 2d 1014 (D. Colo. 2004); Burton v. William Beaumont Hosp., 347 F. Supp. 2d 486 (E.D. Mich. 2004); Kizzire v. Baptist Health Sys., Inc., 343 F. Supp. 2d 1074 (N.D. Ala. 2004), *aff'd on other grounds*, 441 F.3d 1306 (11th Cir. 2006); Darr v. Sutter Health, 2004 WL 2873068 (N.D. Cal. Nov. 20, 2004).

305 *See* § 10.3.2, *supra*.

306 Kolari v. N.Y. Presbyterian Hosp., 382 F. Supp. 2d 562 (S.D.N.Y. 2005); Hutt v. Albert Einstein Med. Ctr., 2005 WL 2396313 (E.D. Pa. Sept. 28, 2005).

307 Sabeta v. Baptist Hosp., Inc., 410 F. Supp. 2d 1224 (S.D. Fla. 2005); Cargile v. Baylor Health Care Sys., 2005 WL 2445482 (N.D. Tex. Aug. 10, 2005).

308 Carlson v. Long Island Jewish Med. Ctr., 378 F. Supp. 2d 128 (E.D.N.Y. 2005); Burton v. William Beaumont Hosp., 373 F. Supp. 2d 707 (E.D. Mich. 2005).

309 Kolari v. N.Y. Presbyterian Hosp., 455 F.3d 118 (2d Cir. 2006).

310 *See In re* Sutter Health Uninsured Pricing Cases, 2005 WL 1842582 (Cal. Super. Ct. July 16, 2005) (denying dismissal of UDAP and unconscionability claims for discriminatory pricing); Turner v. Legacy Health Sys., 2006 WL 657176 (Or. Cir. Ct. Oct. 4, 2005) (granting class certification in case challenging discriminatory pricing under breach of contract and UDAP theory); *see also* Press Release, Statement from Dick Scruggs Nonprofit Hospital Litigation, Oct. 11, 2005 (stating that motions to dismiss were denied in eleven state court cases); Steven Carter, *Providence Health System Will Offer Refunds To Uninsured*, Portland Oregonian, June 24, 2006; Bob Egelko, *Hospital Chain Agrees To Settlement: Catholic Healthcare West Says It Will Pay $423 Million Refund*, San Francisco Chronicle, Jan. 12, 2007; David Phelps, *Uninsured Patients May Get Discounts: Allina and Fairview Settled a Class-Action Suit Claiming That People Without Health Coverage Paid Too Much For Medical Care*, Minneapolis Star-Tribune, Mar. 17, 2007.

311 Ceci Connolly, *Tax-Exempt Hospitals' Practices Challenged, 46 Lawsuits Allege That Uninsured Pay the Most*, Wash. Post, Jan. 29, 2005, at A1.

312 Gardner v. N. Miss. Health Services, Inc., 2005 WL 1312753 (N.D. Miss. May 31, 2005).

313 An analysis of collection actions filed by a Connecticut hospital revealed that 70% of the debtors never filed an appearance with the court. Only 9% of debtors were represented by counsel. Connecticut Ctr. for a New Economy, Uncharitable Care: Yale-New Haven Hospital's Charity Care and Collection Practices (Jan. 2003).

314 *See* Kizzire v. Baptist Health Sys., 441 F.3d 1306 (11th Cir. 2006) (discriminatory pricing and other claims dismissed on res judicata grounds; court held claims should have been raised as compulsory counterclaims in hospital's collection suit); Franklin Collection Serv. v. Stewart, 863 So. 2d 925 (Miss. 2003) (res judicata barred challenge by patients that open account theory was not applicable to recover unpaid medical debt).

or an account stated theory, for breach of an implied contract, or for *quantum meruit*. Practitioners should pay attention to the differences in proof required. In particular, if a medical debt collection action is based on an implied contract, on *quantum meruit*, on an account stated, or on a contract without a definite, agreed price, the collector may be required to prove the ordinary and reasonable value of the service provided in order to recover.[315] Proof of the health provider's license may be a necessary element to recover under any theory,[316] as may be proof that the collector is licensed.[317]

10.5.2 Account Stated Actions

Health providers' collection suits frequently are based on an account stated theory. This theory is often inappropriate because there was no prior agreement on the price or value of the services.[318] Furthermore, there is an argument that the account stated theory should be impermissible with respect to consumer debts covered by the Fair Debt Collection Practices Act (FDCPA), because it deprives the consumer of the FDCPA's right to dispute a debt.[319]

Collection suits based on the theory of account stated frequently fail to allege the necessary elements of such an action, subjecting the complaint to dismissal.[320] In some cases, the medical debt will arise from a one-time transaction, which does not give rise to an account stated claim because there was no expectation of ongoing transactions.[321]

315 *See* § 10.5.5, *infra*.

316 *See, e.g.*, Diagnostic Services of S. Fla. v. State Farm Mut. Auto Ins. Co., 877 So. 2d 1 (Fla. Dist. Ct. App. 2004) (Florida statute provides that charges by unlicensed "clinics" are unenforceable, but mobile diagnostic service did not violate law in that it was not "clinic" within the meaning of licensing statute); Reddix v. Chatham County Hosp. Auth., 134 Ga. App. 860, 216 S.E.2d 680 (1975) (hospital required to show licensing; while hospital testified it was licensed, it failed to introduce the license, the best evidence of that fact), *overruled by* Merrill Lynch v. Zimmerman, 285 S.E.2d 181 (Ga. 1981) (testimony of license is sufficient); *cf.* Brockett *ex rel.* Brockett v. Davis, 762 N.E.2d 513 (Ill. App. Ct. 2001) (statute requiring licensing of professional corporations not intended to protect public against unqualified practitioners, statute requiring licensing of health-care professionals is; tortfeasor challenging validity of victim's medical bills may not challenge lack of corporate license, but may raise question whether treatment provided by unlicensed persons).

317 *See generally* §§ 3.6.2, 3.6.3, *supra*.

318 Braude & Margulies, Prof'l Corp. v. Fireman's Fund Ins. Co., 468 F. Supp. 2d 190 (D.D.C. 2007) (claim for account stated requires express or implied agreement as to the amount due; "mere mailing of a bill and the recipient's silence do not reflect an agreement to pay"); Merkle v. Health Options, Inc., 940 So. 2d 1190 (Fla. Dist. Ct. App. 2006) (physician could not recover against insurer of patients that he treated under an account stated claim, because there was no agreement as to the amount due, nor was there an express or implicit promise to pay); Bingham Mem'l Hosp. v. Boyd, 8 P.3d 664 (Idaho Ct. App. 2000) (when critically ill patient never signed contract, cause of action was quasi-contract, not open account, and attorney fees could not be awarded under open account statute); Dreyer Med. Clinic v. Corral, 591 N.E.2d 111 (Ill. App. Ct. 1992) (sending of bill and lack of objection by recipient insufficient to prove account stated; here provider failed to prove several essential elements); N.Y. Ctr. for Neuropsychology & Forensic Behavioral Science, 2007 WL 3391601 (N.Y. Civ. Ct. Nov. 14, 2007) (prima facie case of account stated requires that debtor agree upon the amount owed and to pay the debt); *see* 13 Arthur Linton Corbin, Corbin on Contracts §§ 1312, 1313 (1962–2002 interim edition) ("The rendition of a bill by a doctor . . . may be an offer of compromise or liquidation of the claim; but the mere retention of this bill in silence, unaccompanied by other circumstances, should seldom, if ever, be held an acceptance of the offer."); *see also* Protestant Hosp. Builders v. Goedde, 98 Ill. App. 3d 1028, 424 N.E.2d 1302 (1981); *cf.* Nelson v. First Nat'l Bank of Omaha, 2004 WL 2711032 (Minn. Ct. App. Nov. 30, 2004) (credit card debt did not create an account stated because card issuer did not produce any evidence of consumer's assent to the account, nor could it show an existing relationship from which assent could be implied from the consumer's failure to protest billing statements). *But see* Franklin Collection Serv. v. Stewart, 863 So. 2d 925 (Miss. 2003) (medical bills were open accounts under Mississippi statute); Huntington Hosp. v. Abrandt, 779 N.Y.S.2d 891 (App. Term. 2004) (acceptance of medical services created implied contract to pay; summary judgment for hospital on account stated).

319 15 U.S.C. § 1692g; *see* National Consumer Law Center, Fair Debt Collection § 5.7 (6th ed. 2008).

Note that section 1692g(c) provides that a court may not treat a consumer's failure to dispute a debt under that section as an admission of liability. Thus, to the extent that an account stated action would require the court to construe the consumer's silence as acceptance of a bill, one could argue that section 1692g(c) prohibits such an assumption.

320 Alan Alop, Defending Hospital Collection Cases (rev. ed. 2005), *available at* www.illinoislegaladvocate.org/index.cfm?fuseaction=home.dsp_content&contentID=728; *see* Dreyer Med. Clinic v. Corral, 591 N.E.2d 111 (Ill. App. Ct. 1992) (account stated is method of proving damages; creditor must first prove liability; creditor failed to prove several essential elements); St. Tammany Parish Hosp. v. Burris, 804 So. 2d 960 (La. Ct. App. 2001) (reversing summary judgment for hospital on open account claim when hospital failed to properly identify the patient, named only as "the minor child of" alleged debtor, or to allege that debtor was responsible for child's bill; hospital also failed to prove notice, essential to its claim for attorney fees); *see also* Reddix v. Chatham County Hosp. Auth., 134 Ga. App. 860, 216 S.E.2d 680 (1975), *overruled on other grounds by* Merrill Lynch v. Zimmerman, 285 S.E.2d 181 (Ga. 1981); Culverhouse v. Jackson, 127 Ga. App. 635 (1972); 1A C.J.S. *Account Stated* § 2 (1985); *cf.* Morrison, Cohen, Singer & Weinstein, L.L.P. v. Brophy, 798 N.Y.S.2d 379 (App. Div. 2005) (reversing summary judgment for law firm seeking legal fees when firm had failed to establish that its invoices were properly addressed and mailed or that the debtor agreed to increase in billing rates reflected in invoices); Tully v. Citibank (S.D.), 173 S.W.3d 212 (Tex. App. 2005) (creditor can not collect credit card debt through a suit on a "sworn account" because that theory applies only when title to personal property passes from seller to buyer).

321 Morse L.L.C. v. United Wis. Life Ins. Co., 356 F. Supp. 2d 1296 (S.D. Fla. 2005) (provider failed to state claim for account stated against insurer because provider did not allege expecta-

Another common failing in collection actions alleging an account stated claim is the omission of documentation of the account itself.[322] The way courts interpret and apply the elements of an action on an account may vary widely.[323] Some states require an independent basis for liability in an account stated claim, and consider the accounting to merely establish the amount of the debt.[324] In addition the provider may be required to prove the ordinary and reasonable price of its services.[325] See § 4.7, *supra*, for more on the account stated cause of action.

10.5.3 Defenses to Contract Claims

10.5.3.1 Duress As a Defense

A potential defense to a hospital collection action based on breach of contract is duress. A hospital's requirement that a debtor agree to pay the patient's medical bills in order for the patient to be admitted or discharged may give rise to the complete contractual defense of duress, especially if the debtor is not the patient, but a relative or friend.[326]

Duress consists of the following three elements:[327]

- *The creditor's exercise of coercion.* Coercion is any form of constraint or compulsion improperly exercised upon the debtor. One form of compulsion may be refusal to admit a patient unless a relative or friend agrees to give a third party guarantee. Mandatory emergency admittance statutes such as EMTALA may be critical in these situations, showing that the refusal to admit the patient was unlawful.[328] Another form of constraint may be the act or threat of a hospital detaining a patient by refusing to discharge the patient until a bill is paid.[329] Although coercion directed at one other than the debtor usually does not constitute actionable duress, an exception is often made when the other person is the debtor's close relative.[330]

---

tion of future transactions, and instead the facts reflected a one-time claim that was objected to); Reigelsperger v. Siller, 23 Cal. Rptr. 3d 249 (Ct. App. 2005) (no open book account existed between patient and chiropractor when there was no ongoing doctor-patient relationship or expectation of future transactions), *review granted*, 110 P.3d 289 (Cal. 2005).

322 Reigelsperger v. Siller, 23 Cal. Rptr. 3d 249 (Ct. App. 2005) (dismissing open book account claim in part because there was no evidence of a permanent record showing an open account with debits and credits), *review granted*, 110 P.3d 289 (Cal. 2005); Grandell Rehab. & Nursing Home v. Devlin, 809 N.Y.S.2d 481 (Sup. Ct. 2005) (table) (text available at 2005 WL 3240554) (dismissing action for failure to describe or attach any statement of account and because defendant—the adult son of the patient—disputed liability for his mother's bills); Mercy Franciscan Hosp. v. Willis, 2004 WL 2244809 (Ohio Ct. App. Sept. 24, 2004) (upholding trial court's removal of default when the complaint had failed to attach a copy of an accounting; debtor had moved for relief from default alleging he did "not know what this bill is for").

323 1 Am. Jur. 2d *Accounts and Accounting* § 8 (2007). *See generally* 1 C.J.S. *Account, Action On* §§ 1–38 (1985).

Note that, in some states, an "account stated" claim actually differs from an "open account claim." *See, e.g.*, Ayers v. Cavalry SVP, L.L.C., 876 So. 2d 474 (Ala. Civ. App. 2003) (different statute of limitations under Alabama law for account stated versus open account claim).

324 Dreyer Med. Clinic v. Corral, 591 N.E.2d 111 (Ill. App. Ct. 1992) (account stated is method of proving damages; creditor must first prove liability; creditor failed to prove several essential elements); Citibank (S.D.) v. Martin, 807 N.Y.S.2d 284 (Civ. Ct. 2005) (account stated can not create a liability when none existed). *But see* Berlin v. Pickett, 221 S.W.3d 406 (Mo. Ct. App. 2006) (no express agreement needed for open account claim).

325 St. Luke's Episcopal-Presbyterian Hosp. v. Underwood, 957 S.W.2d 496 (Mo. Ct. App. 1997) (in action on account, hospital must prove reasonableness of charges; testimony of "credit assistant" that charges were in line with those of other hospitals in the area was relevant and should have been admitted); *see also* 1 Am. Jur. 2d *Accounts and Accounting* § 35 (1994); 1 C.J.S. *Account, Action On* §§ 15, 28 (1985).

For more on reasonable value, see generally § 10.5.5, *infra*.

326 *See, e.g.*, Greenfield v. Manor Care, Inc., 705 So. 2d 926 (Fla. Dist. Ct. App. 1997) (surviving spouse allowed to raise defense of imposition when contract provision allowing immediate eviction of resident for nonpayment prevented her from challenging alleged overcharges at time of payment), *overruled on other grounds by* Knowles v. Beverly Enterprises, 898 So. 2d 1 (Fla. 2004). *But see* Heartland Health Sys. v. Chamberlin, 871 S.W.2d 8 (Mo. Ct. App. 1993) (mother of a patient had not signed contract under duress when she believed guarantee was needed to provide treatment to her eighteen-year-old son who was bleeding out his ears and mouth, and had a bone sticking out through the skin).

An unreported case exemplifies how the duress defense can be successfully utilized. A hospital had brought a $56,000 suit against the patient's widow who had signed an agreement believing it was necessary to gain admittance for her husband, who was in great pain and vomiting, while waiting for emergency treatment. He later died in the hospital of cancer. The jury voided the bill. *Jury Voids Dead Man's Hospital Bill*, Wash. Post, May 8, 1979, at C1.

327 The elements may differ by state. *See, e.g.*, Eden Park Mgmt. v. Schrull, 2007 WL 706583 (Conn. Super. Ct. Feb. 14, 2007) (elements of duress are (1) a wrongful act or threat, (2) that left the victim with no reasonable alternative, (3) to which the victim acceded, and (4) the resulting transaction was unfair to the victim; patient failed to demonstrate duress).

328 See § 10.3.2, *supra*, for discussion of EMTALA. *Cf.* Heartland Health Sys. v. Chamberlin, 871 S.W.2d 8, 11 (Mo. Ct. App. 1993) (no duress because the hospital could have withheld its services unless and until mother of patient agreed to pay for services; EMTALA not raised).

329 *See* Gadsden Gen. Hosp. v. Hamilton, 212 Ala. 531, 103 So. 553 (1925) (hospital's threat not to release plaintiff until she paid her bill combined with her resultant stay in the hospital eleven hours after she was medically capable of release, amounted to false imprisonment, even though she was *not* physically restrained); *see also* Williams v. Rentz Banking Co., 112 Ga. App. 384, 145 S.E.2d 256 (1965) (a debtor's signing a note only after bank officials refused to allow debtor to leave the bank can be duress), *rev'd on other grounds*, 114 Ga. App. 718 (1966).

330 *See* Greenfield v. Manor Care, Inc. 705 So. 2d 926 (Fla. Dist. Ct. App. 1997) (surviving spouse allowed to raise defense of

- *The debtor's loss of volition as a result of the coercion.* A hospital's resort to a threat not to admit or discharge a patient may go a long way toward meeting this subjective test, particularly when the patient or the relative or friend refused to sign a note prior to the threat, but did so afterwards.
- *A promissory note or contract must be executed as a result of the wrongful coercion.* When a hospital sues on a note or contract for health care, practitioners should probe their client about the circumstances surrounding the signing of the contract to determine if coercion was applied. Because of the power of hospitals over people's lives, the possibilities for coercion in signing such notes abound. However, many hospitals do not rely on contracts or notes when suing on hospital bills, and the duress defense is available only against a suit on a contract or note.

This defense may be lost if the consumer pays voluntarily after the coercion has ceased.[331] However, the voluntary payment doctrine may not apply if the payment was made out of necessity and the patient had not reasonable alternative, or if deception was involved.[332] Even if a contract is voided for duress, the consumer may be liable in *quantum meruit*.[333]

10.5.3.2 Other Defenses to a Contract Action

When a relative or friend of the patient signs an admission form containing a clause making him or her financially responsible for the patient's bills, the court may find that there was no actual intent to accept financial responsibility.[334] Alternatively, the court may conclude that the contract

---

"imposition" when contract provision allowing immediate eviction of resident for nonpayment prevented her from challenging alleged overcharges at time of payment), *overruled on other grounds by* Knowles v. Beverly Enterprises, 898 So. 2d 1 (Fla. 2004); Bedard v. Notre Dame Hosp., 89 R.I. 195, 151 A.2d 690 (1959) (action for trespass on the case upheld when hospital detained son until bill for son's treatment paid); Robertson v. Shinn Grocery Co., 34 S.W.2d 367 (Tex. Civ. App. 1930) (threat of arrest of son coerced signing of deed of trust).

331 Greene v. Alachua Gen. Hosp., Inc., 705 So. 2d 953 (Fla. Dist. Ct. App. 1998) (when hospital sent bill after patient was out of hospital, and not under pressure greater than that felt by any debtor, defense of imposition not proven); Hall v. Humana Hosp. Daytona Beach, 686 So. 2d 653 (Fla. Dist. Ct. App. 1996) (granting summary judgment against class of patients who had already paid their bills in class action seeking to recover alleged overcharges for pharmaceuticals, medical supplies, laboratory services; patients alleged "imposition," that is, that they had been coerced into signing contract which included price list); *cf.* Watts v. Promina Gwinnett Health Sys., Inc., 242 Ga. App. 377, 530 S.E.2d 14 (2000) (patient's voluntary payment of hospital bill out of proceeds of tort judgment barred claim that charges were unreasonable and not authorized by hospital's agreement with HMO or patient's assignment of benefits).

332 Ramirez v. Smart Corp., 863 N.E.2d 800 (Ill. App. Ct. Feb. 16, 2007).

The voluntary payment doctrine also does not apply to UDAP claims. *Id.*

333 Milford Hosp. v. Champeau, 2001 Conn. Super. LEXIS 1166 (Conn. Super. Ct. Apr. 27, 2001) (duress not shown although wife alleged she was told she "had to" sign contract before admission of her seriously ill husband; even if duress defense made out, couple was liable in *quantum meruit*, and wife was liable under necessaries statute); Galloway v. Methodist Hospitals, Inc., 658 N.E.2d 611 (Ind. Ct. App. 1995) (consumers alleged there was no contract because of "extreme duress" when husband, a lawyer, signed for wife's admission for an obstetrical emergency but did not sign for financial responsibility; however, court found both spouses liable in *quantum meruit*). *See generally* § 10.5.4, *infra*.

334 Carroll v. Butterfield Health Care, 2003 WL 22462604 (N.D. Ill. Oct. 29, 2003) (nursing home's violation of Medicaid law by requiring personal guarantee of patient's son-in-law; son-in-law stated FDCPA but not UDAP claim against attorney-collector for suing on illegal guarantee); Phoenix Baptist Hosp. & Med. Ctr. v. Aiken, 877 P.2d 1345 (Ariz. 1994) (husband signed contract when wife had just had heart attack, husband was distraught, could not read contract without his reading glasses, which he did not have with him, and contract was not explained to him; court held that this was contract of adhesion, sent case back to trial court for factual findings whether husband reasonably expected his separate property to be covered, and whether contract was unconscionable); Samaritan Health Sys. v. Caldwell, 191 Ariz. 479, 957 P.2d 1373 (Ct. App. 1998) (when wife signed admission agreement only as attorney in fact pursuant to husband's durable power of attorney, debt not enforceable against her separate property); Haven Health Ctr. of Lichfield Hills v. Parente, 2007 WL 123602 (Conn. Super. Ct. Jan. 8, 2007) (son of nursing home patient, who alleged that he signed only as his mother's power of attorney and that he was never given a copy of the preprinted contract, could bring UDAP claim against nursing home); Walton v. Mariner Health of Md., 894 A.2d 584 (Md. 2006) (daughter did not agree to be personally liable for mother's nursing home bills by signing admission contract as her mother's agent); Valley Hosp. v. Kroll, 847 A.2d 636 (N.J. Super. Ct. Law Div. 2003) (agreement signed by patient's wife that would require her to pay balance of hospital bill not paid by Medigap insurance was unenforceable as a contract of adhesion); St. John's Episcopal Hosp. v. McAdoo, 405 N.Y.S.2d 935 (Civ. Ct. 1978) (court refused to enforce liability provision that was buried in assignment of insurance benefits form; contract of adhesion; hospital should know contracts will be signed under circumstances when reasonable person too distraught to read whole document); Columbia Hosp. v. Hraska, 72 Misc. 2d 112, 338 N.Y.S.2d 527 (Civ. Ct. 1972); *see also* Wright v. Polk Gen. Hosp., 95 Ga. App. 821, 99 S.E.2d 162 (1957) (no consideration); Baton Rouge Gen. Hosp. v. Superior Cleaners, 231 La. 820, 93 So. 2d (1957) (no intent); *cf.* Podolsky v. First Healthcare Corp., 58 Cal. Rptr. 2d 89 (Ct. App. 1996) (nursing home violated California UDAP law by soliciting relatives for voluntary agreement to be financially responsible for patient, home failed to show consideration for voluntary agreement and failed to inform relatives of their rights under federal law); JML Care Ctr. v. Bishop, 2004 Mass. App. Div. 63 (Dist. Ct. 2004) (longtime friend and assistance signed admission agreement merely to facilitate admission; in this case, nursing home did not attempt to impose liability on friend). *But see* Care Ctr. of Kansas City v. Horton, 173 S.W.3d 353 (Mo. Ct. App. 2005) (daughter was personally liable when she signed admission contract as agent for father, because contract imposed liability on agents); Trocki Plastic Surgery Ctr. v. Bartkowski,

documents simply do not impose personal liability on the relative.[335] A patient who signs a contract in an impaired state may be able to argue that she lacked capacity to enter into a contract at the time of execution.[336] See § 4.5, Ch. 5, *supra*, for more on defenses to a breach of contract claim.

10.5.4 Quantum Meruit

Quantum meruit or implied contract is especially important in the health care context. It may be asserted as a basis for liability after a contract has been invalidated for duress or on other grounds,[337] when consent could not be obtained, or even if consent has been refused.[338] Providers also assert *quantum meruit* claims against insurers of patients whom they treat.[339] The elements of *quantum meruit* are that a

344 N.J. Super. 399, 782 A.2d 447 (Super. Ct. App. Div. 2001) (wife's alleged inability to understand agreement no defense when no allegation of duress, fraud or coercion).

For examples of providers who pressure non-responsible relatives into accepting financial liability, see Health Consumer Alliance, Sick and in Debt: Improper Practices That Cause Medical Debt for Low-Income Californians (Summer 2004).

335 *See, e.g.*, Slovik v. Prime Healthcare Corp., 838 So. 2d 1054 (Ala. Civ. App. 2002) (nursing home's dealings with patient's stepson/personal representative did not amount to contract by which he agreed to be personally liable); Grandell Rehab. & Nursing Home v. Devlin, 809 N.Y.S.2d 481 (Sup. Ct. 2005) (table) (text available at 2005 WL 3240554) (dismissing nursing home's action against adult son of patient when son had never contracted with home, and ordering hearing on sanctions against collection attorney); *cf.* Northfield Care Ctr. v. Anderson, 707 N.W.2d 731 (Minn. Ct. App. 2006) (Minnesota law provides that son who signed admission contract was personally liable, but only to the extent that mother's assets were misapplied).

336 Eden Park Mgmt. v. Schrull, 2007 WL 706583 (Conn. Super. Ct. Feb. 14, 2007) (patient alleged she was confused at the time of signing; allegations sufficient to plead lack of capacity, that is, that patient may not have understood the nature, extent, and consequences of signing the contract). *See generally* § 5.4.1, *supra*.

337 Yale Diagnostic Radiology v. Estate of Harun Fountain, 838 A.2d 179 (Conn. 2004) (minor is liable in *quantum meruit* for necessaries such as medical care; parent is primarily liable, but if parent can not or will not pay, minor is liable); Milford Hosp. v. Champeau, 2001 Conn. Super. LEXIS 1166 (Conn. Super. Ct. Apr. 27, 2001) (even if contract signed by wife were invalid, couple was liable in *quantum meruit* for husband's treatment); Yale New Haven Hosp. v. Gargiulo, 1999 WL 989422 (Conn. Super. Ct. Oct. 18, 1999) (if no express contract between patient and hospital, implied contract to pay reasonable value of the services rendered); Galloway v. Methodist Hosp., Inc., 658 N.E.2d 611 (Ind. Ct. App. 1995) (even if contract, signed by husband at time of wife's admission for obstetrical emergency, was invalid, both spouses were liable in *quantum meruit*); Valley Hosp. v. Kroll, 847 A.2d 636 (N.J. Super. Ct. Law Div. 2003) (agreement signed by patient's wife was unenforceable as a contract of adhesion, but hospital could recover against her in *quantum meruit*; wife not liable because reasonable value of services already paid by insurer); Comm'r of the Dep't of Social Services v. Fishman, 280 A.D.2d 396, 720 N.Y.S.2d 493 (2001) (New York statute provides that furnishing medical benefits by Department of Social Services creates implied contract with responsible relative, here the spouse of nursing home patient); Layton Physical Therapy Co. v. Palozzi, 777 N.E.2d 306 (Ohio Ct. App. 2002) (if parents do not pay for necessaries, here medical care, minor child secondarily liable in quasi-contract); Dallas County Hosp. Dist. v. Wiley *ex rel.* Wiley, 2002 WL 1286515 (Tex. App. June 12, 2002) (lien invalid, but *quantum meruit* claim may go forward); *see also* JML Care Ctr. v. Bishop, 2004 Mass. App. Div. 63 (Dist. Ct. 2004) (*quantum meruit* not available when valid contract in effect, but would be available as equitable remedy if contract were unenforceable); Parmatown Spinal & Rehab. Ctr. v. Lewis, 2003 WL 22208786 (Ohio Ct. App. Sept. 25, 2003) (provider could recover against patient in *quantum meruit* despite the fact that provider had express contract with insurer). *But see* Burton v. William Beaumont Hosp., 373 F. Supp. 2d 707 (E.D. Mich. 2005) (unjust enrichment claim not viable when an express contract governs); Morse L.L.C. v. United Wis. Life Ins. Co., 356 F. Supp. 2d 1296 (S.D. Fla. 2005) (dismissing *quantum meruit* claim because provider had alleged existence of an express contract; *quantum meruit* claim is a "fiction [that] can not be maintained, however, when the rights of the parties are described in an express contract"); Promenade Nursing Home, Inc. v. Lacey, 814 N.Y.S.2d 564 (Civ. Ct. 2005) (table) (text available at 2005 WL 3592001) (existence of written contract precluded claim for *quantum meruit* or other quasi-contract claims); Tully v. Citibank (S.D.), 173 S.W.3d 212 (Tex. App. 2005) (credit card company could not recover using *quantum meruit* theory when it proved the existence of an express contract).

338 Crane v. Native Am. Air Ambulance, 2007 WL 625917 (D. Ariz. Feb. 23, 2007) (patient was liable for air ambulance service bill of $12,825 even though he did not request service and claimed he did not need service); *Ex parte* Univ. of S. Ala. v. Grubb, 737 So. 2d 1049 (Ala. 1999) (patient was liable for her share of bill at hospital which paramedics chose because it had helicopter landing pad, when she accepted treatment there willingly, even though she requested a different hospital where her insurance would have paid 100% of bill); Yale New Haven Hosp. v. Alsever, 2000 Conn. Super. LEXIS 3612 (Conn. Super. Ct. Dec. 22, 2000) (granting summary judgment on quasi-contract liability, but reserving amount of damages for trial when some services allegedly performed over patient's objection); Bingham Mem'l Hosp. v. Boyd, 8 P.3d 664 (Idaho Ct. App. 2000) (patient's estate was liable in implied contract even though critically ill patient did not sign any papers); Novak v. Credit Bureau Collection Serv., 2007 WL 4339450 (Ind. Ct. App. Dec. 13, 2007) (hospital entitled to recover in *quantum meruit* for services provided to unconscious patient who never requested or agreed to services); Credit Bureau Enterprises, Inc. v. Pelo, 608 N.W.2d 20 (Iowa 2000) (patient liable in *quantum meruit* for expenses of involuntary commitment, when treatment was necessary to prevent serious bodily harm or pain, provider reasonably believed that patient would consent if able to do so, and refusal of consent not binding as patient was incompetent), *partially superseded by statute*, Tama County v. Grundy County, 648 N.W.2d 83 (Iowa 2002) (amendments to Iowa law made county of patient's residence liable for involuntary commitment expenses to private hospital).

339 *See, e.g.*, Merkle v. Health Options, Inc., 940 So. 2d 1190 (Fla. Dist. Ct. App. 2006) (physician who provided emergency care to HMO members stated *quantum meruit* and state statutory claims against HMO); River Park Hosp. v. Bluecross/Blueshield of Tenn., 173 S.W.3d 43 (Tenn. 2002) (action for *quantum meruit*, unjust enrichment, and other claims by hospital against HMO, when hospital sought more than HMO's regular reim-

benefit was conferred and accepted, under circumstances such that the recipient should know the provider expected to be paid, and it would be unjust to accept the benefit without paying.[340] The provider may also be required to show the reasonable value of the services rendered.[341] See § 4.8, *supra*, for more on the *quantum meruit* cause of action.

bursement rate for emergency treatment of HMO members); Emergency Physicians Integrated Care v. Salt Lake County, 167 P.3d 1080 (Utah 2007) (physicians who treated county inmates could bring claim in *quantum meruit* against county).

340 Cardiology Associates v. Sussman, 2000 Conn. Super. LEXIS 1544 (Conn. Super. Ct. June 16, 2000) (patient liable in implied contract when provider showed that it provided services under circumstances such that it could expect to be paid, and billed for the fair, reasonable and customary amount); Bingham Mem'l Hosp. v. Boyd, 8 P.3d 664 (Idaho Ct. App. 2000); Parmatown Spinal & Rehab. Ctr. v. Lewis, 2003 WL 22208786 (Ohio Ct. App. Sept. 25, 2003) (elements of claim are that: (1) a benefit was conferred on the recipient, (2) the recipient had knowledge of that benefit, and (3) it would unjust or inequitable to permit the recipient to retain the benefit without compensating the party that conferred the benefit).

341 McMeans v. Med. Liabilities Recoveries, Inc., 2002 WL 31835746 (Cal. Ct. App. Dec. 19, 2002) (hospital lien limited to reasonable value of necessary services, testimony of chief executive officer as to customary rates not probative when she had no personal knowledge of care provided); Milford Hosp. v. Champeau, 2001 Conn. Super. LEXIS 1166 (Conn. Super. Ct. Apr. 27, 2001) (question of reasonableness relevant only to damages, not liability, when hospital asserted claims for *quantum meruit*, unjust enrichment, and spousal liability for necessaries); Yale New Haven Hosp. v. Alsever, 2000 Conn. Super. LEXIS 3612 (Conn. Super. Ct. Dec. 22, 2000) (granting summary judgment to hospital on quasi-contract claim, but only as to liability; amount of damages required trial due to question whether services were necessary or were competently performed; some services apparently provided over patient's objection); Cardiology Associates v. Sussman, 2000 Conn. Super. LEXIS 1544 (Conn. Super. Ct. June 16, 2000) (patient liable in implied contract when provider presented evidence that it provided services and billed for the fair, reasonable, and customary price); William H. Stoll, L.L.C. v. Scarber, 652 S.E.2d 834 (Ga. Ct. App. 2007) (plaintiff in *quantum meruit*—in this case, an attorney—was required to prove the reasonable value of services); Estate of Bonner, 954 S.W.2d 356 (Mo. Ct. App. 1997) (medical provider must prove that services were rendered, were medically necessary, and price was reasonable, but need not present expert evidence on medical necessity unless patient/debtor raised that issue); Valley Hosp. v. Kroll, 847 A.2d 636 (N.J. Super. Ct. Law Div. 2003) (*quantum meruit* claim limited to reasonable value of services by hospital; payments made by Medigap insurer presumed reasonable; patient's wife not liable for additional amounts); Hailey v. MedCorp., 2006 WL 2640238 (Ohio Ct. App. Sept. 15, 2006) (ambulance service entitled to recover only reasonable value of services under *quantum meruit* theory); Temple Univ. Hosp. v. Healthcare Mgmt. Alternatives, Inc., 832 A.2d 501 (Pa. Super. Ct. 2003) (hospital that treated Medicaid-HMO members at a time when it had no contract entitled to recover in *quantum meruit*; must show reasonable value of its services; posted rates not probative when posted rates were 300% of costs and hospital received this amount in only 1–3% of cases); Doe v. H.C.A. Health Services of Tenn., 46 S.W.3d 191 (Tenn. 2001) (patient only liable for reasonable charges when hospital charges were set forth only in a confidential, changing, internal price list); H.E. Butt Grocery Co. v. Rencare, Ltd., 2004 WL 199272 (Tex. App. Feb. 4, 2004) (reasonable value an essential element for *quantum meruit* claim; jury entitled to weigh evidence beyond provider's charges to determine reasonable value); Emergency Physicians Integrated Care v. Salt Lake County, 167 P.3d 1080 (Utah 2007) (if physicians could prove *quantum meruit* claim, they were entitled to the reasonable value of service); *see* Alan Alop, Defending Hospital Collection Cases (rev. ed. 2005), *available at* www.illinoislegaladvocate.org/index.cfm?fuseaction=home.dsp_content&contentID=728. *But see* Huntington Hosp. v. Abrandt, 779 N.Y.S.2d 891 (App. Term. 2004) (summary judgment for hospital on implied contract claim; patient's challenge to hospital's charges based on fact that patient was charged more than other payors not sufficient to create triable issue of fact as to reasonableness of charges).

10.5.5 *Reasonable Value*

10.5.5.1 Burden to Show Reasonable Value

A critical issue in many medical debt collection cases will be the reasonable value of the medical services rendered. An inquiry into the reasonable value may be required even when there is an express contract.[342] However this inquiry

342 Urquhart v. Manatee Mem'l Hosp., 2007 WL 781738 (M.D. Fla. Mar. 13, 2007) (Florida requires amount of open pricing contract to be reasonable; hospital's excessive charges could be challenged as breach of contract); Colomar v. Mercy Hosp., Inc., 461 F. Supp. 2d 1265 (S.D. Fla. 2006) (same); Howard v. Willis-Knighton Med. Ctr., 924 So. 2d 1245 (La. Ct. App. 2006) (whether express or implied contract, charges must be reasonable unless fixed in contract); Estate of Bonner, 954 S.W.2d 356 (Mo. Ct. App. 1997) (medical provider must prove that services were rendered, were medically necessary, and price was reasonable); Castro v. E. End Plastic, Reconstructive & Hand Surgery, 2008 WL 82684 (N.Y. App. Div. Jan. 8, 2008) (provider not entitled to judgment for difference between insurance payment and provider's charges, absent evidence of the reasonable value of services); Hailey v. MedCorp., 2006 WL 2640238 (Ohio Ct. App. Sept. 15, 2006) (ambulance service entitled to recover only reasonable value of services); Turner v. Legacy Health Sys., 2006 WL 657176 (Or. Cir. Ct. Oct. 4, 2005) (when contracts for medical services did not specify price for services, such fees must be reasonable under the circumstances); Doe v. H.C.A. Health Services of Tenn., 46 S.W.3d 191 (Tenn. 2001) (express contract voided because of the lack of specificity in determining the amount of charges, holding that only an implied-in-law contract existed requiring patient to pay reasonable value of services); *cf.* Ramirez v. Smart Corp., 863 N.E.2d 800 (Ill. App. Ct. 2007) (when patients had statutory right to obtain their medical records, hospitals must charge a reasonable amount for copying services). *But see* Martinez v. Yale New Haven Hosp., 2005 WL 2364901 (Conn. Super. Ct. Sept. 1, 2005) (despite fact that contract did not specify price in dollars, court held that contract contained a definite and enforceable standard to determine a liquidated price); Shelton v. Duke Univ. Health Sys., 633 S.E.2d 113 (N.C. Ct. App. 2006) (when contract specified that patient would be charged hospital's "regular" rates, contract was sufficiently definite for hospital to impose chargemaster list prices on the uninsured, despite charging reduced rates to third-party payors); Nygaard v. Sioux

may be foreclosed in states where hospitals are statutorily required to disclose or file their charges.[343]

The provider should bear the burden of proving reasonable value,[344] although some courts have placed the burden on the debtor or held the provider to a very minimal level of prima facie proof.[345] The question of reasonable value is a

Valley Hosp. & Health Sys., 731 N.W.2d 184 (S.D. 2007) (when complaint pleaded that contract stated prices were "fixed," no implied term in contract that prices would be fair and reasonable, despite charging reduced rates to third-party payors).

343 Banner Health v. Med. Sav. Ins. Co., 163 P.3d 1096 (Ariz. Ct. App. 2007) (because hospital was required to file its rates with state agency, the rates could not be challenged as unconscionable or unreasonable, despite the fact that rates were 400% of hospital's costs and hospital only charged full rates to 2% of patients); Morrell v. Wellstar Health Sys., Inc., 633 S.E.2d 68 (Ga. Ct. App. 2006) (rates need not be reasonable; noting that Georgia law provided right for patient to request copy of hospital charges, and that Georgia policy was to encourage market forces to control health care costs by providing information so that consumers could make cost-effective decisions by comparison shopping); Cox v. Athens Reg'l Med. Ctr., Inc., 631 S.E.2d 792 (Ga. Ct. App. 2006) (same).

344 Greenfield v. Manor Care, Inc. 705 So. 2d 926 (Fla. Dist. Ct. App. 1997) (when no price specified, only a reasonable price may be charged), *overruled on other grounds by* Knowles v. Beverly Enterprises, 898 So. 2d 1 (Fla. 2004); Payne v. Humana Hosp. Orange Park, 661 So. 2d 1239 (Fla. Dist. Ct. App. 1995) (when contract allegedly did not specify the price for medical services, patient not bound to pay "unreasonable" charges and stated a claim in a class complaint); Reddix v. Chatham County Hosp. Auth., 134 Ga. App. 860, 216 S.E.2d 680 (1975) (hospital failed to prove reasonableness and value of services), *overruled on other grounds by* Merrill Lynch v. Zimmerman, 285 S.E.2d 181 (Ga. 1981); Culverhouse v. Jackson, 127 Ga. App. 635 (1972) (physician failed to prove ordinary and reasonable value of services); Victory Mem'l Hosp. v. Rice, 493 N.E.2d 117 (Ill. 1986); Fowle v. Parsons, 141 N.W. 1049 (Iowa 1913); Freeman Health Sys. v. Wass, 124 S.W.3d 504 (Mo. Ct. App. 2004) (hospital can not prevail in collection lawsuit without showing reasonable value of services); St. Luke's Episcopal-Presbyterian Hosp. v. Underwood, 957 S.W.2d 496 (Mo. Ct. App. 1997) (in action on account, hospital must prove reasonableness of charges; testimony of "credit assistant" that charges were in line with those of other hospitals in the area was relevant and should have been admitted); Estate of Bonner, 954 S.W.2d 356 (Mo. Ct. App. 1997) (medical provider must prove that services were rendered, were medically necessary, and price was reasonable, but need not present expert evidence on medical necessity unless patient/debtor raised that issue; court properly allowed some charges and disallowed others, after hearing evidence about treatment plan, patient's condition, and so forth); Valley Hosp. v. Kroll, 847 A.2d 636 (N.J. Super. Ct. Law Div. 2003) (*quantum meruit* claim limited to reasonable value of services by hospital; payments made by Medigap insurer presumed reasonable; patient's wife not liable for additional amounts); Hailey v. MedCorp., 2006 WL 2640238 (Ohio Ct. App. Sept. 15, 2006) (in order to recover against patient, ambulance service required to demonstrate reasonable value of services at trial by competent, credible evidence); Piggee v. Mercy Hosp., 186 P.2d 817 (Okla. 1947) (summary judgment inappropriate); Turner v. Legacy Health Sys., 2006 WL 657176 (Or. Cir. Ct. Oct. 4, 2005) (when contracts for medical services did not specify price for services, such fees must be reasonable under the circumstances); Temple Univ. Hosp. v. Healthcare Mgmt. Alternatives, Inc., 832 A.2d 501 (Pa. Super. Ct. 2003) (hospital that treated Medicaid-HMO members at a time when it had no contract entitled to recover in *quantum meruit*; must show reasonable value of its services; posted rates not probative when posted rates were 300% of costs and hospital received this amount in only 1–3% of cases); River Park Hosp. v. Bluecross/Blueshield of Tenn., 173 S.W.3d 43 (Tenn. 2002) (in action for unjust enrichment, both hospital's standard rate and HMO's reimbursement rate were relevant to the determination of a reasonable rate, but not conclusive; case remanded for a determination of a reasonable rate); Doe v. H.C.A. Health Services of Tenn., 46 S.W.3d 191 (Tenn. 2001) (when price not specified in contract, hospital can only require patient to pay "fair value" of goods and services); H.E. Butt Grocery Co. v. Rencare, Ltd., 2004 WL 199272 (Tex. App. Feb. 4, 2004) (reasonable value an essential element for *quantum meruit* claim; jury entitled to weigh evidence beyond provider's charges to determine reasonable value); *see* Alan Alop, Defending Hospital Collection Cases (rev. ed. 2005), *available at* www.illinoislegaladvocate.org/index.cfm?fuseaction=home.dsp_content&contentID=728; *cf* Prospect Med. Group, Inc. v. Northridge Emergency Med. Group, 39 Cal. Rptr. 3d 456 (Ct. App.) (following *Bell*, and noting that hospital's chargemaster prices are not determinative of the reasonable value; insurer permitted to challenge such prices), *review granted*, 136 P.3d 167 (Cal. 2006); Bell v. Blue Cross, 31 Cal. Rptr. 3d 688 (Ct. App. 2005) (under California law that requires HMOs to pay out-of-network emergency room physicians for services rendered to insureds, physicians were entitled to "reasonable and customary value" for such services). *But see* Martinez v. Yale New Haven Hosp., 2005 WL 2364901 (Conn. Super. Ct. Sept. 1, 2005) (despite fact that contract did not specify price in dollars, court held that contract contained a definite and enforceable standard to determine a liquidated price; in this case, patients had brought a breach of contract claim alleging unreasonable price).

345 Sholkoff v. Boca Raton Cmty. Hosp., 693 So. 2d 1114 (Fla. Dist. Ct. App. 1997); Wash. County Mem'l Hosp. v. Hattabaugh, 717 N.E.2d 929 (Ind. Ct. App. 1999) (burden of proof was on consumers who claimed services were not worth what hospital charged; amount billed was prima facie evidence of value of services); Galloway v. Methodist Hospitals, Inc., 658 N.E.2d 611 (Ind. Ct. App. 1995) (amount of bill was prima facie evidence of amount owed in *quantum meruit*; charges were reasonable when they were comparable to other facilities in the area and based upon hospital's budgetary needs); Dawson v. Prager, 76 P.3d 1036 (Kan. 2003) (provider's affidavit that amounts owed constituted co-payments after insurance coverage sufficient to grant summary judgment for provider, despite objection of patient that she paid "regularly" paid co-payments); Trocki Plastic Surgery Ctr. v. Bartkowski, 782 A.2d 447 (N.J. Super. Ct. App. Div. 2001) (reasonableness shown when consumers received bill and did not complain about the charges, nor about the quality of the service); Hahnemann Univ. Hosp. v. Dudnick, 678 A.2d 266 (N.J. Super. Ct. App. Div. 1996) (burden is on patient to show that charges are not "usual, customary and reasonable"; charges were in accord with other teaching institutions in the area and had been approved by state Insurance Commission, charges were reasonable; also that insurance company paid its share without protest was further evidence of reasonableness); Fulton County Health Ctr. v. Jones, 2007 WL 4277583 (Ohio Ct. App. Dec. 7, 2007) (summary judgment for provider on issue of reasonable value when debtor failed to submit evidence contesting it); Dickey v. Burick, 829 N.E.2d

pure question of fact for a jury, and thus should allow the debtor to defeat the collector's motion for summary judgment or directed verdict.[346]

Two factors that courts look at to determine reasonable value are: (1) internal factors of the hospital, including the hospital's cost of operations and its budgetary needs and (2) charges for comparable services by similar hospitals.[347]

A hospital or medical provider often attempts to meet its burden by having a staff member testify as to the above factors. Courts have allowed such testimony, and held it sufficient to establish reasonable value.[348] Some courts have even held that conclusory statements by a hospital employee that the charges were fair and reasonable were sufficient, so long as such statements were uncontroverted.[349] Thus, it is critical for the patient's counsel to challenge such statements by attacking them on cross-examination and by presenting evidence supporting any of the theories discussed in this section.[350] Practitioners should be aware of medical industry

---

1242 (Ohio Ct. App. 2005) (provider's bill was prima facie evidence of amount owed; provider not required to lay foundation that charges were reasonable and necessary unless challenged by debtor).

346 Shellnut v. Randolph County Hosp., 469 So. 2d 632 (Ala. Civ. App. 1985); Reyher v. State Farm Mut. Ins. Co., 171 P.3d 1263 (Colo. Ct. App. 2007) (reasonableness of charges was issue of fact for jury); Fowle v. Parsons, 141 N.W. 1049 (Iowa 1913); Piggee v. Mercy Hosp., 186 P.2d 817 (Okla. 1947) (summary judgment inappropriate); Turner v. Legacy Health Sys., 2006 WL 657176 (Or. Cir. Ct. Oct. 4, 2005) (whether highest rates were "reasonable fees" is fact question for jury); H.E. Butt Grocery Co. v. Rencare, Ltd., 2004 WL 199272 (Tex. App. Feb. 4, 2004) (jury entitled to weigh evidence beyond provider's charges to determine reasonable value; entitled to weigh credibility of employee's testimony regarding specific items, including why provider charged $150 for box of gloves that cost $25; could also consider center's contracts with third-party payors); *cf.* Sisters of the Third Order of Notre Dame v. Summerson, 577 N.E.2d 177 (Ill. App. Ct. 1991). *But see* Dawson v. Prager, 76 P.3d 1036 (Kan. 2003) (provider's affidavit that amounts owed constituted co-payments after insurance coverage sufficient to grant summary judgment for provider, despite objection of patient that she paid "regularly" paid co-payments); Huntington Hosp. v. Abrandt, 779 N.Y.S.2d 891 (App. Term. 2004) (summary judgment for hospital; patient's challenge to hospital's charges based on fact that patient was charged more than other payors not sufficient to create triable issue of fact as to reasonableness of charges).

347 Lifespan Physicians Prof'l Serv. Org. v. Healthcare Value Mgmt., 2006 WL 1549054 (D.R.I. June 5, 2006) ("reasonable and customary" prices are determined by what other hospitals in the area charge); Bell v. Blue Cross, 31 Cal. Rptr. 3d 688 (Ct. App. 2005) (the "reasonable and customary value" for medical services should be based upon the physician's qualifications, nature of services, provider's usual charges, and prevailing provider rates charged in the area); Victory Mem'l Hosp. v. Rice, 493 N.E.2d 117 (Ill. App. Ct. 1986); Howard v. Willis-Knighton Med. Ctr., 924 So. 2d 1245 (La. Ct. App. 2006) (following *Victory Mem'l Hosp.* and *Ellis Hosp.*); Ellis Hosp. v. Little, 409 N.Y.S.2d 459 (App. Div. 1978) (price shown to be fair and reasonable when hospital itemized the services provided, treasurer testified as to relationship of prices to hospital's costs, and officer of another hospital testified as to customary charges in the community); Doe v. HCA Health Services, 46 S.W.3d 191 (Tenn. 2001); *cf.* Majid v. Stubblefield, 589 N.E.2d 1045 (Ill. App. Ct. 1992) (doctor's evidence of rates charged by the only two other practitioners of his specialty in a rural three-county area was sufficient despite patient's evidence of lower rates over a larger, more diverse area).

One court has cautioned that a market analysis comparing prices of other hospitals is not determinative as to whether prices are reasonable. Colomar v. Mercy Hosp., Inc., 461 F. Supp. 2d 1265 (S.D. Fla. 2006) ("if other hospitals grossly overcharge for services relative to their costs, then a mere side-by-side comparison of hospitals' unreasonable charges would make them appear reasonable").

348 Galloway v. Methodist Hosp., 658 N.E.2d 611, 613 (Ind. Ct. App. 1995); St. Luke's Episcopal-Presbyterian Hosp. v. Underwood, 957 S.W.2d 496, 498–499 (Mo. Ct. App. 1997); Ellis Hosp. v. Little, 65 A.D.2d 644, 409 N.Y.S.2d 459, 461 (1978). *But see* McMeans v. Med. Liabilities Recoveries, Inc., 2002 WL 31835746 (Cal. Ct. App. Dec. 19, 2002) (hospital lien limited to reasonable value of necessary services; testimony of chief executive officer as to customary rates not probative when she had no personal knowledge of care provided); Majid v. Stubblefield, 226 Ill. App. 3d 637, 589 N.E.2d 1045 (1992) (court allowed office manager to testify that physician's charges were similar to other physician charges in the region, but suggested that such hearsay testimony was only permissible because it was a small claims court proceeding); Advocacy Org. for Patients & Providers v. Auto Club Ins. Ass'n, 670 N.W.2d 569 (Mich. Ct. App. 2003) (providers' customary charges do not define "reasonable charges" for purposes of no-fault automobile insurance), *aff'd*, 693 N.W.2d 358 (Mich. 2005).

349 *See Ex parte* Univ. of S. Ala. v. Grubb, 737 So. 2d 1049, 1053 (Ala. 1999); Dawson v. Prager, 76 P.3d 1036 (Kan. 2003) (provider's affidavit that amounts owed constituted co-payments after insurance coverage sufficient to grant summary judgment for provider, despite objection of patient that she paid "regularly" paid co-payments); Heartland Health Sys. v. Chamberlin, 871 S.W.2d 8, 11 (Mo. Ct. App. 1993) (hospital employee's assertion that charges were reasonable and customary sufficient to shift burden to patient to challenge necessity and reasonableness of particular items); St. Joseph Hosp. v. Blake, 1989 Ohio App. LEXIS 2838 (Ohio Ct. App. July 19, 1989); *cf.* Univ. of Wis. Med. Found. v. Turner, 735 N.W.2d 195 (Wis. Ct. App. 2007) (*pro se* patient; testimony of accounts manager was sufficient to prove bills were for medical services that were reasonable and necessary).

350 *Cf.* Victory Mem'l Hosp. v. Rice, 143 Ill. App. 3d 621, 493 N.E.2d 117, 120 (1986) (patient is "free to attack the reasonableness of the charges through cross-examination and presentation of this case"). *Compare* Estate of Bonner, 954 S.W.2d 356 (Mo. Ct. App. 1997) (because patient's estate put accuracy of records at issue by cross-examination, trial court acted within discretion in disallowing certain charges) *and* H.E. Butt Grocery Co. v. Rencare, Ltd., 2004 WL 199272 (Tex. App. Feb. 4, 2004) (employee cross-examined regarding method of calculating line items, that is, why dialysis center charged $150 for box of gloves that cost $25; also evidence of center's contracts with other payors, payment structure of other plans, fact that center charged Blue Cross a lump sum charge for same services; take-nothing judgment affirmed) *with* Bingham Mem'l Hosp. v. Boyd, 8 P.3d 664, 669 (Idaho Ct. App. 2000) (appellate court declined to examine reasonableness of award to hospital given

reference guides such as MediCode and the RedBook (for pharmaceuticals and supplies).[351] Note that a challenge to the reasonable value of air transportation ambulance services may be preempted by the Airline Deregulation Act.[352]

10.5.5.2 Discriminatory Pricing: How the Poor Pay More

One of the most potentially powerful ways to prove that a hospital bill is unreasonable is to show that the patient is being charged more than third-party payors such as health maintenance organizations (HMOs), private insurers, and Medicare. This disparity results from "discriminatory" or "variable" pricing, a phenomenon described as follows by the hospitals' own trade group, the American Hospital Association:

> While a hospital charges all patients receiving the same service the same price, what varies dramatically is how much a hospital is actually paid for the care it provides. The Medicare and Medicaid programs set payments that are not only less than charges, but also often less than the actual cost of caring for these patients. Private insurers negotiate discounts from charges on behalf of the enrollees they cover. As pressure increases from private insurers and managed care companies for deeper discounts, charges have increased, as hospitals struggle to balance government under-funding and find the resources to care for those without insurance. But in the absence of health care coverage for all in America, people without insurance face bills reflecting these higher charges, with no one to negotiate on their behalf. They are victims of America's fragmented and inconsistent health care payment system.[353]

The result is that uninsured patients pay several times more than HMOs, insurance companies, and the government. It also results in uninsured individuals paying several times more than the hospital's actual cost of services.[354]

Discriminatory pricing has also been documented in a number of reported cases. In one case involving a dispute between a hospital and an HMO, the chief financial officer (CFO) of a hospital admitted that his hospital received 80% or more of its posted rates no more than 6% of the time.[355] Opposing counsel's expert economist testified that the hospital received the full amount of its posted charges only about 1–3% of the time, and that the posted rates had risen from 172% of actual costs in 1994 to 300% in 1996. He also noted that private insurers typically paid only 112% of costs in 1996, and Medicaid and Medicare paid even less. The hospital's CFO admitted that none of the twelve private insurers who had contracts with the hospital paid published rates.[356]

In another case, the chief executive officer (CEO) of a regional health care system testified that the average markup of hospital services was 2.3 or 2.4 times the cost of providing such services. The defendant hospital in this case used such a markup, yet only received about 39% of its total "chargemaster" (or list price) charges, yielding an actual net profit of 3%. In other words, the hospital had to charge nearly two and a half times its cost in order to receive payments slightly above its costs from most of its payors (insurers). This CEO opined that the chargemaster charges would not be a reasonable amount for a patient who had insurance, but were a reasonable charge for an uninsured patient.[357]

---

failure by patient's estate to challenge amount of charges).

351 Catholic Healthcare West-Bay Area v. Seafarers' Health & Benefits Plan, 2007 WL 160995 (N.D. Cal. Jan. 18, 2007) (upholding insurer's use of MediCode and RedBook to determine reasonable prices to pay hospital).

352 Crane v. Native Am. Air Ambulance, 2007 WL 625917 (D. Ariz. Feb. 23, 2007).

353 Am. Hosp. Ass'n, Alert—Four Related Issues Drawing Media and Congressional Attention—Know Your Organization's Policies (June 10, 2003); *see* SEIU Hosp. Accountability Project, Why the Working Poor Pay More (Mar. 2003) (discussion of discriminatory pricing patterns in Chicago metropolitan area); *see also* Gina Kolata, *Medical Fees are Often Higher for Patients Without Insurance*, N.Y. Times, Apr. 2, 2001, at A1; Irene Wielawski, *Gouging the Medically Uninsured: A Tale of Two Bills*, Health Affairs (Sept.–Oct. 2000).

Discriminatory pricing also occurs with respect to prescription medications. Lindsey Johnson, U.S. Pub. Interest Research Group, Paying the Price: The High Cost of Prescription Drugs for Uninsured Americans (Oct. 2004) (finding that uninsured consumers pay 78% more on average for twelve common prescription drugs than the federal government pays for the same medications).

354 Marilyn Weber Serafini, *Sticker Shock*, Nat'l J., Oct. 18, 2003, at 3180 (chart of average markup of gross charges—what the uninsured pay—from hospitals' cost, showing in some states, hospital charges were 200% over costs).

For a history of how discriminatory pricing developed see *A Review of Hospital Billing and Collection Practices Before the Subcomm. on Oversight and Investigations of the H. Comm. on Energy and Commerce*, 108th Cong. (2004) (statement of Gerard Anderson, Professor, Bloomberg Sch. of Pub. Health, Johns Hopkins Univ.). Dr. Anderson testified how in the mid-1980s, hospital "list charges" were typically only 25% above costs, but now it is common for list charges to be two to four times higher than costs. List charges are also two to four times what most insurers pay, and most insurers pay costs plus or minus 15%. *Id.*; *see also* Jonathan Cohn, *Uncharitable?*, N.Y. Times Magazine, Dec. 19, 2004, at 51 (discussing how discriminatory pricing evolved during the last few decades due to changes to the Medicare program and the demands of managed care insurers for discounts).

355 Temple Univ. Hosp. v. Healthcare Mgmt. Alternatives, Inc., 832 A.2d 501 (Pa. Super. Ct. 2003).

356 *Id.*

357 Howard v. Willis-Knighton Med. Ctr., 924 So. 2d 1245 (La. Ct. App. 2006).

In another example, a court upheld a judgment against patients for full chargemaster prices despite evidence that these charges were 400% of the hospital's costs, only 2% of patients

While legal challenges by medical debtors to discriminatory pricing have met with mixed success,[358] the most effective use of this phenomenon may be as evidentiary proof to establish that the hospital's bill is unreasonably high. The patient can also argue that the hospital's charges to the uninsured are not reasonable in that they are not the "usual and customary" charges, because most patients pay less.[359] (Conversely, one court has held that an insurer's payment of the full price charged by the hospital was sufficient to establish that the price was reasonable.)[360]

Note that the hospital may "charge" every payer the same amount but accept as full payment from third-party payers amounts *less* than the full charges. At least one court has accepted this semantic legerdemain.[361]

were ever charged full prices, and the hospital usually accepted about one-third of its listed prices. Banner Health v. Med. Sav. Ins. Co., 163 P.3d 1096 (Ariz. Ct. App. 2007).

358 *See* Hill v. Sisters of St. Francis Health Services, 2006 WL 3783415 (N.D. Ill. Dec. 20, 2006) (denying dismissal of UDAP and unconscionability claims for discriminatory pricing); *In re* Sutter Health Uninsured Pricing Cases, 2005 WL 1842582 (Cal. Super. Ct. July 16, 2005) (same); Greenfield v. Manor Care, Inc. 705 So. 2d 926 (Fla. Dist. Ct. App. 1997) (reversing dismissal of several claims against nursing home that inflated billing price of pharmaceuticals and other supplies it provided to patients), *overruled on other grounds by* Knowles v. Beverly Enterprises, 898 So. 2d 1 (Fla. 2004); Servedio v. Our Lady of the Resurrection Med. Ctr., Clearinghouse No. 55,626 (Ill. Cir. Ct. Cook County Jan. 6, 2005) (permitting plaintiff to proceed with UDAP challenge against hospital discriminatory pricing practices); Turner v. Legacy Health Sys., 2006 WL 657176 (Or. Cir. Ct. Oct. 4, 2005) (granting class certification in case challenging discriminatory pricing under Oregon UDAP statute); *cf.* Urquhart v. Manatee Mem'l Hosp., 2007 WL 781738 (M.D. Fla. Mar. 13, 2007) (while breach of contract and UDAP claim challenging discriminatory pricing were viable, failure to allege actual injury from practice required dismissal); Colomar v. Mercy Hosp., Inc., 461 F. Supp. 2d 1265 (S.D. Fla. 2006) (while fact that uninsured patients paid more than insurers for same services alone would not give rise to UDAP clam, allegations that hospital's prices were excessive in comparison to other hospitals and in comparison to actual cost of services would support viable UDAP claim); Howard v. Willis-Knighton Med. Ctr., 924 So. 2d 1245 (La. Ct. App. 2006) (discriminatory pricing not sufficient to prove chargemaster prices were not per se unreasonable for the uninsured but might be unreasonable to in certain cases depending on patient's financial circumstances; need for individual consideration defeated class action certification).

Several cases challenging discriminatory pricing, including the *Sutter Health*, *Servedio*, and *Turner* cases have resulted in settlements. *See* § 10.4.3, *supra*.

Unsuccessful challenges include: Kizzire v. Baptist Health Sys., 441 F.3d 1306 (11th Cir. 2006) (discriminatory pricing and other claims dismissed on res judicata grounds; court held claims should have been raised as compulsory counterclaims in hospital's collection suit); Harrison v. Christus St. Patrick Hosp., 430 F. Supp. 2d 591 (W.D. La. 2006) (dismissing breach of contract and fiduciary duty claims, as well as unjust enrichment for discriminatory pricing claim); DiCarlo v. St. Mary's Hosp., 2006 WL 2038498 (D.N.J. July 19, 2006) (no breach of contract, breach of fiduciary duty, or UDAP claims for discriminatory pricing); Banner Health v. Med. Sav. Ins. Co., 163 P.3d 1096 (Ariz. Ct. App. 2007) (discriminatory pricing was not unconscionable or unreasonable because hospital was required to file its rates with state agency); Hillsborough County Hosp. v. Fernandez, 664 So. 2d 1071 (Fla. Dist. Ct. App. 1995) (evidence that hospital entered into contracts with managed care providers for certain discounts was not sufficient to prove that rates charged to uninsured individuals were excessive); Morrell v. Wellstar Health Sys., Inc., 633 S.E.2d 68 (Ga. Ct. App. 2006) (discriminatory pricing was not deceptive or confusing in violation of Georgia UDAP statute); Cox v. Athens Reg'l Med. Ctr., Inc., 631 S.E.2d 792 (Ga. Ct. App. 2006) (same); Thorne v. Doe, 724 So. 2d 242 (La. Ct. App. 1998) (price of certain blood products administered in the hospital was 400% to 500% higher than price for same products for home administration; overcharging not shown, when no showing that plaintiff was billed more than "hospital's established price"); Parnell v. Madonna Rehab. Hosp., Inc., 602 N.W.2d 461 (Neb. 1999) (hospital entitled to lien against settlement proceeds in amount of bill, which represented "usual and customary" charges even though it accepted lower amounts in workers' compensation and Medicaid cases); Shelton v. Duke Univ. Health Sys., 633 S.E.2d 113 (N.C. Ct. App. 2006) (no breach of contract or fiduciary duty claims for discriminatory pricing); Mercy Health Partners of Southwest Ohio v. Miller, 2005 WL 2592674 (Ohio Ct. Com. Pl. Sept. 30, 2005) (discriminatory pricing not unfair practice under Ohio UDAP statute); Nygaard v. Sioux Valley Hosp. & Health Sys., 731 N.W.2d 184 (S.D. 2007) (discriminatory pricing not deceptive practice; note that South Dakota UDAP statute does not prohibit "unfair" practices).

One court has held that discriminatory pricing did not violate the Social Security Act, the equal protection and due process clauses of the state and federal constitutions, or public policy. Methodist Med. Ctr. of Ill. v. Taylor, 140 Ill. App. 3d 713, 489 N.E.2d 351 (1986).

359 Colomar v. Mercy Hosp., Inc., 461 F. Supp. 2d 1265 (S.D. Fla. 2006) (while discriminatory pricing alone would not give rise to UDAP clam, allegations that hospital's prices were excessive in comparison to other hospitals and in comparison to actual cost of services would support viable UDAP claim); Valley Hosp. v. Kroll, 847 A.2d 636 (N.J. Super. Ct. Law Div. 2003) (*quantum meruit* claim limited to reasonable value of services by hospital; payments made by Medigap insurer presumed reasonable; patient's wife not liable for additional amounts); H.E. Butt Grocery Co. v. Rencare, Ltd., 2004 WL 199272 (Tex. App. Feb. 4, 2004) (jury entitled to consider evidence of contracts with other payors, payment structure of other plans, fact that dialysis center charged Blue Cross lump sum charge for same services; evidence supported jury's award of damages in amount lesser than provider's charges). *But see* Huntington Hosp. v. Abrandt, 779 N.Y.S.2d 891 (App. Term. 2004) (discriminatory pricing not sufficient to create triable issue of fact as to reasonableness of charges; summary judgment for hospital).

360 Crane v. Native Am. Air Ambulance, 2007 WL 625917 (D. Ariz. Feb. 23, 2007).

361 Parnell v. Madonna Rehab. Hosp., 602 N.W.2d 461 (Neb. 1999) (phrase "usual and customary charges" means the amount typically billed, not the amount typically received, by medical providers); *see also* Burton v. William Beaumont Hosp., 373 F. Supp. 2d 707 (E.D. Mich. 2005) (no breach of contract claim for discriminatory pricing; court noted that hospital's charges for certain services were uniform regardless of insurance status, but failed to note whether the hospital accepted lower payments for insured).

Discriminatory pricing has been challenged under state laws that prohibit unfair and deceptive acts and practices.[362] A few state attorneys general have also challenged discriminatory pricing as an unfair practice.[363] There also have been proposals to condition the tax-exempt status of hospitals on prohibiting discriminatory pricing.[364]

Discriminatory pricing is also an issue for patients who had health insurance at the time of the hospitalization but are being billed for a co-payment based on a percentage (for example, 20%) of the bill. It is critical to learn what the insurance company has actually paid the hospital. If the hospital discounted the bill in calculating the amount that the insurance company had to pay, it can be argued that the patient should be responsible only for paying 20% of the discounted bill—not 20% of the full charges.[365] Insured patients are also affected by discriminatory pricing when providers "balance bill" them for amounts in excess of what insurers pay,[366] or if their insurers do not have a contract with the provider setting forth negotiated prices, and the insurer refuses to pay the full list or "chargemaster" prices for services, leaving patients liable for the balance.[367]

Hospitals have defended their discriminatory pricing policies by arguing that the Medicaid and Medicare programs require them to charge "uniform rates" (which requirements do not prohibit hospitals from accepting discounted payments) and to make reasonable collection efforts of Medicare co-payments and deductibles. However, the United States Department of Health and Human Services has issued guidance permitting hospitals and other providers to "provide discounts to uninsured and underinsured patients who can not afford their hospital bills and to Medicare beneficiaries who can not afford their Medicare cost-sharing obligations."[368] This guidance should provide significant support for practitioners who are negotiating with providers to seek to reduce the amount of a medical debt.[369]

Another form of inflated pricing occurs when patients receive care at medical clinics considered to be hospital-based. These clinics may charge significant additional "facility" fees, which can double or triple a bill from what patients would pay for the exact same service provided at a non-hospital-based medical practice.[370] Failure to disclose these facility fees could be challenged as deceptive under state UDAP law.[371]

362 *See* § 10.4.3, *supra*.

363 Press Release, Wisconsin Attorney General's Office, Actions Against Hospitals for Overcharging the Uninsured (Nov. 7, 2005) (lawsuits against St. Joseph's Regional Medical Center and Wisconsin Heart Hospital by Wisconsin attorney general alleging discriminatory pricing constitute unfair trade practice); Agreement, *In re* Allina Health Sys., Civ. No. C1-05-4576 (May 2005) (settlement between Minnesota attorney general and Allina Health System that requires Allina to charge uninsured consumers no more than the rate for "most favored insurer" and to reform debt collection practices).

364 Minority Staff, Senate Fin. Comm., Tax-Exempt Hospitals: Discussion Draft (July 18, 2007), *available at* http://grassley.senate.gov/releases/2007/07182007.pdf.

365 *See* McConocha v. Blue Cross & Blue Shield of Ohio, 898 F. Supp. 545 (N.D. Ohio 1995) (in a suit against the *insurer* on this theory, the court ruled that it was reasonable for the patient to expect to have to pay only 20% of the amount the hospital would actually receive as opposed to 20% of full, undiscounted charges); *see also* Corsini v. United HealthCare Services, Inc., 145 F. Supp. 2d 184 (D.R.I. 2001) (holding that an HMO's method of calculating 20% co-payments as a percentage of charges as opposed to discounted fees actually paid, violated the terms of coverage); Everson v. Blue Cross & Blue Shield of Ohio, 898 F. Supp. 532 (N.D. Ohio 1994) (terms of coverage ambiguous as to whether the "reasonable charge" from which co-payments calculated reflected agreed upon discounts; construing the ambiguity against the insurer). *But see* Hoover v. Blue Cross & Blue Shield of Ala., 855 F.2d 1538, 1543 (11th Cir. 1988) (health insurer did not breach its fiduciary duty by requiring members to pay 20% of undiscounted hospital charges); Lefler v. United HealthCare of Utah, Inc., 162 F. Supp. 2d 1310 (D. Utah 2001) (HMO acted reasonably by pegging co-pay percentage to full, undiscounted amounts), *aff'd*, 72 Fed. Appx. 818 (10th Cir. 2003); Crosse v. BCBSD, Inc., 836 A.2d 492 (Del. Super. Ct. 2003) (Blue Cross did not owe fiduciary duty to insureds to pass on discounts and rebates received from providers); *cf.* Ries v. Humana Health Plan, Inc., 1995 WL 669583 (N.D. Ill. Nov. 8, 1995) (breach of fiduciary duty when an HMO put $8947 lien on member's settlement award for treatment of her injuries from a car accident although it settled her medical bills for just $600).

A similar discounting agreement was the subject of the United States Supreme Court's decision in Humana v. Forsyth, 525 U.S. 299, 119 S. Ct. 710, 142 L. Ed. 2d 753 (1999) (Nevada hospital gave discounts of 40% to 96% to an insurance company that owned it, yet the hospital billed patients for co-payments calculated as a percentage of the undiscounted bill).

366 *See* § 10.3.6, *supra*.

367 *See, e.g.*, Prospect Med. Group, Inc. v. Northridge Emergency Med. Group, 39 Cal. Rptr. 3d 456 (Ct. App.) (managed care insurer paid emergency room physicians the Medicare rate for services; physicians who did not have contract with the insurer were permitted to balance bill patients for amounts over Medicare rates), *review granted*, 136 P.3d 167 (Cal. 2006); Chamberlain v. Farm Bureau Mut. Ins. Co., 137 P.3d 1080 (Kan. Ct. App. 2006) (accident victim's insurer refused to pay full amount of provider's charges because insurer believed they exceeded customary and usual charges, resulting in harm to victim's credit record).

368 Letter from Tommy G. Thompson, Sec'y of United States Dep't of Health & Human Services, to Richard J. Davidson, President, Am. Hosp. Ass'n (Feb. 19, 2004).

369 *See, e.g.*, Vince Galloro, *Tenet to Offer Discounts*, Modern Healthcare, Mar. 8, 2004, at 8 (for-profit hospital chain announces implementation of discount rate plan for the uninsured; plan had been on hold for one year pending Department of Health and Human Services guidance.).

370 Julie Appleby, *"Hospital-Based" Clinics Can Charge More*, USA Today, Nov. 16, 2006.

371 Virginia Mason Med. Ctr. v. Executive Risk Ins., 2007 WL 3473683 (W.D. Wash. Nov. 14, 2007) (discussing prior settlement of UDAP lawsuit over facility charges).

10.5.5.3 Overbilling, Error, and Hospital Negligence

Another way to attack the reasonableness of the hospital's charges is to show an error in them. Obtaining the medical records and the pharmacy ledger or record and comparing them to an itemized list of the goods and services allegedly provided to the patient may reveal that some goods and services were not actually provided or were inadvertently billed for twice. Sometimes double-billing occurs because a separately billed service is already included in the charge for another procedure.[372] Overbilling can also result from the hospital's use of the wrong diagnostic related grouping (DRG) code to label, and therefore bill for, a procedure. Practitioners will need to investigate the DRG coding through discovery or obtain expert assistance in this regard.[373] Delays caused by the hospital and infections acquired during hospitalization[374] may also result in a longer stay and a higher bill than are reasonable.

10.5.6 Other Defenses or Counterclaims in Medical Debt Collection Suits

10.5.6.1 Using Affirmative Claims Defensively

Many of the affirmative claims discussed in § 10.4, *supra*, can be asserted as defenses in a medical debt collection suit, including:

- Failure to comply with Hill-Burton Act requirements or other laws creating a duty to provide free or reduced cost care;[375]
- Breach of the hospital's charitable duty under state tax law;[376]
- The provider's acceptance, or even application for, a Medicaid or Medicare payment that by statute or regulation must be considered payment in full;[377]
- Failure of the provider to process public aid applications or to bill Medicaid or Medicare,[378] or to properly bill the patient's insurer;[379]
- Provisions of the provider's contract with an HMO or a state health insurance statute that bar the provider from billing a health maintenance organization (HMO) member for services covered by the HMO;[380]
- Breach of the duty of good faith and fair dealing;[381] and
- Breach of a fiduciary duty.[382]

10.5.6.2 Other Defenses

Defenses that may be available against a medical debt collection suit include:

- Negligently misinforming patient as to extent of insurance coverage;[383]
- The provider's failure to provide a translation of the contract for a non-English speaking consumer;[384] and

372 *See, e.g.*, Lester E. Cox Med. Centers v. Huntsman, 2003 WL 22004998 (W.D. Mo. Aug. 5, 2003) (bill for $1800 "bundle" of supplies resulted in patient being charged for items that were unnecessary for her surgery), *aff'd on other grounds*, 408 F.3d 989 (8th Cir. 2005); *see also Decoding Your Hospital Bills*, Consumer Reports, Jan. 2003, at 19; Peter Davidson, *10 Ways to Avoid Outrageous Hospital Overcharges*, *available at* Bankrate.com.

373 There are some companies that conduct "mini-audits," which consist of expert review of the itemized hospital bill. A list of some of these companies may be found at www.billadvocates.com/affiliates.htm (last visited Apr. 2008).

374 *See* Duke Univ. Med. Ctr., Hospital-Acquired Antibiotic-Resistant Infections Triple Costs and Lengths of Hospitalizations (Sept. 28, 1997).

375 *See* §§ 10.1.3, 10.4.3, *supra*.

376 *See* § 10.4.8.2, *supra*.

377 *See* § 10.3.6, *supra*.

378 *Id.*

379 Grandview/Southview Hospitals v. Monie, 2005 WL 737393 (Ohio Ct. App. Apr. 1, 2005) (upholding trial court's judgment denying recovery to hospital that billed wrong insurance company).

At least one state requires that health care providers bill insurers or patients in a timely manner. Tex. Civ. Prac. & Rem. Code Ann. § 146.002 (Vernon) (provider must submit bill within either eleven months or the time specified in any contract with insurer).

380 *See* § 10.3.6, *supra*.

381 *See* § 10.4.7, *supra*.

382 *Id.*

383 Yale New Haven Hosp. v. Vignola, 2002 WL 377675 (Conn. Super. Ct. Feb. 15, 2002) (at time of admission, patient asked whether treatment was covered by her insurance, and hospital employee stated, incorrectly, that it was; hospital had no duty to ascertain insurance coverage, but when it undertook to advise patient, duty of due care arose); Havsy v. Washington State Dep't of Health, Bd. of Osteopathic Medicine & Surgery, 123 Wash. App. 1030 (2004) (licensing board sanctions affirmed doctor breached fiduciary duty to patient by misleading patient about the price of treatment, failing to inform patient of the high cost of a certain procedure and that insurance would not cover that procedure). *But see* MRI Co-op. v. Berlin, 1993 WL 257078 (Ohio Ct. App. June 30, 1993) (assignment of insurance benefits, which provided that patient would be liable if insurance did not pay, enforced as written, even though provider's employee told patient that his insurance would cover the cost).

384 *See* Alan Alop, Defending Hospital Collection Cases (rev. ed. 2005), *available at* www.illinoislegaladvocate.org/index.cfm?fuseaction=home.dsp_content&contentID=728; National Consumer Law Center, Unfair and Deceptive Acts and Practices § 5.2.1 (6th ed. 2004 and Supp.).

A failure to provide a translation of the contract may also violate Title VI of the Civil Rights Act of 1964, 42 U.S.C. §§ 2000d to 2000d-7, and its implementing regulations. Title VI prohibits discrimination on the basis of race, ethnicity, or national origin by any healthcare provider that receives federal funds (including Medicare and Medicaid). Consumers can file complaints for violation of Title VI with their regional office of the Department of Health & Human Service's Office for Civil Rights. There is, however, no private right of action under Title

- The provider's malpractice, which may be raised as a defense to a debt, even if the consumer did not sue for malpractice.[385]

10.6 Liability for Familial Medical Care Under Necessaries Statutes

Necessaries statutes, which evolved from Married Woman Acts passed by many states at the turn of the century, make spouses liable for each other's medical bills. The typical necessaries statute, as written, imposed liability on husbands for wives' medical bills, but not *vice versa.* Some states have abolished this doctrine or ruled the necessaries statute unconstitutional.[386] But other states have rewritten the necessaries statutes in gender-neutral terms, often believing its historical form violated the Equal Protection Clause, and extended it to impose liability on a wife for her husband's medical expenses.[387] In addition to nec-

VI for this type of violation. Alexander v. Sandoval, 532 U.S. 275, 121 S. Ct. 1511, 149 L. Ed. 2d 517 (2001).

385 Wash. County Mem'l Hosp. v. Hattabaugh, 717 N.E.2d 929 (Ind. Ct. App. 1999) (consumers, who did not sue for malpractice, allowed to introduce evidence that surgery had resulted in permanent damage, as defense to collection suit).

386 *See* Egge v. Healthspan Services Co., 115 F. Supp. 2d 1126 (D. Minn. 2000) (Minnesota's elimination of spousal liability for necessaries in 1997 was not retroactive); Emanuel v. McGriff, 596 So. 2d 578 (Ala. 1992) (striking down doctrine of necessaries as unconstitutional gender discrimination, refusing to extend the doctrine to include wives' liability for husbands' necessaries, and deferring to legislature); Connor v. Southwest Fla. Reg'l Med. Ctr., Inc., 668 So. 2d 175 (Fla. 1995) (common law doctrine of necessaries abolished on equal protection grounds); Condore v. Prince George's County, 289 Md. 516, 425 A.2d 1011 (1981) (based on Maryland's Equal Rights Amendment, court invalidated necessaries statute; extension of statute best determined by legislature); N. Ottawa Cmty. Hosp. v. Kieft, 578 N.W.2d 267 (Mich. 1998) (Married Woman's Property Act and provisions of state constitution which protect married women's separate property were constitutional and prevented the expansion of the common law doctrine of necessaries to make wife liable for husband's medical bills; doctrine of necessaries was abrogated; deferring to the legislature); Account Specialists & Credit Collections, Inc. v. Jackman, 970 P.2d 202 (Okla. Civ. App. 1998) (statute which codified common law doctrine of husband's liability for wife's necessaries was unconstitutional; legislature, not court, should now decide whether to impose liability on both spouses, or on neither); Schilling v. Bedford County Mem'l Hosp., 225 Va. 539, 544, 303 S.E.2d 905, 908 (1983) (necessaries statute is unconstitutional and should be abolished; extension to include wives, if advisable, is for legislature, not courts; rather than repealing the statute, state legislature subsequently extended the statute to impose a reciprocal duty on wives); Med. Ctr. Hosp. v. Lorain, 675 A.2d 1326 (Vt. 1996) (court chose to abolish rather than expand the doctrine; it was not very effective in protecting needy spouses, and the complex social issues involved should be addressed by the legislature); *see also* Govan v. Med. Credit Services, Inc., 621 So. 2d 928 (Miss. 1993) (absent express consent, spouse not responsible to health care provider for other spouse's debts).

387 *E.g.*, Conn. Gen. Stat. § 46b-37 (both spouses jointly liable for family expenses, including reasonable and necessary medical care); 750 Ill. Comp. Stat. § 65/15 (both spouses jointly liable for family expenses, including reasonable and necessary medical care); Mass. Gen. Laws ch. 209, § 1; 23 Pa. Cons. Stat. § 4102; Tex. Fam. Code Ann. § 2.501 (Vernon); Va. Code Ann. §§ 8.01-220.2, 55-37; Wis. Stat. § 765.001(2); *see* Lester E. Cox Med. Centers v. Huntsman, 2003 WL 22004998 (W.D. Mo. Aug. 5, 2003) (husband was liable for wife's medical bill; not FDCPA violation to dun him for bill), *aff'd on other grounds*, 408 F.3d 989 (8th Cir. 2005); *In re* Balthrop, 2005 WL 3691335 (Bankr. E.D. Va. Nov. 28, 2005) (discussing two Virginia necessaries statutes, one applicable to all necessaries, Va. Code Ann. § 55-37, and one specifically applicable to emergency medical care, Va. Code Ann. § 8.01-220.2; only latter statute permits recovery against the marital home); Queen's Med. Ctr. v. Kagawa, 967 P.2d 686 (Haw. 1998) (under gender-neutral spousal liability statute, wife was liable for husband's hospital bill, even though couple were in process of getting a divorce; case remanded to trial court to determine if each charge was necessary and reasonable); Mem'l Hosp. v. Hahaj, 430 N.E.2d 412 (Ind. 1992) (necessaries statute extended to impose liability on both spouses); St. Francis Reg'l Med. Ctr., Inc. v. Bowles, 251 Kan. 334, 836 P.2d 1123 (1992) (necessaries statute violates Equal Protection Clause of Fourteenth Amendment; statute expanded to apply to husbands and wives equally); Pioneer Valley Postal Fed. Credit Union v. Soja, 2002 Mass. App. Div. 193 (Dist. Ct. 2002) (necessaries statute, Mass. Gen. Laws ch. 209, § 1, applies to all spouses' property, not just that held in tenancy by entireties); Hulse v. Warren, 777 S.W.2d 319 (Mo. 1989) (necessaries statute extended to impose liability on both spouses); St. Luke's Episcopal-Presbyterian Hosp. v. Underwood, 957 S.W.2d 496 (Mo. Ct. App. 1997) (wife, who did not sign contract for husband's hospital admission, was liable under doctrine of necessaries; necessity was proven by husband's testimony that he came to hospital because of angina, and underwent bypass surgery); St. Joseph Hosp. v. Rizzo, 676 A.2d 98 (N.H. 1996) (doctrine of necessaries extended to create liability for a wife for her husband's medical treatment); Jersey Shore Med. Center-Fitkin Hosp. v. Estate of Baum, 84 N.J. 137, 151, 417 A.2d 1003, 1010 (1980) (necessaries statute should be expanded to apply to both spouses; joint and several approach); Med. Bus. Associates Inc. v. Steiner, 183 A.D.2d 86, 588 N.Y.S.2d 890 (1992) (necessaries statute violated the Equal Protection Clause; unconstitutionality to be remedied by extending common law rule to both spouses); Forsyth Mem'l Hosp. v. Chisholm, 467 S.E.2d 88 (N.C. 1996); N.C. Baptist Hospitals, Inc. v. Harris, 354 S.E.2d 471 (N.C. 1987) (necessaries statute expanded to apply to both husbands and wives); MRI Co-operative v. Berlin, 1993 WL 257078 (Ohio Ct. App. June 30, 1993) (wife liable under family expense statute if able to pay; remanded to determine ability to pay); Albert Einstein Med. Ctr. v. Gold, 66 Pa. D. & C.2d 347, 349 (C.P. 1974) (quoting Conway v. Dana, 456 Pa. 536, 539, 318 A.2d 324 (1974), court extended necessaries statute to make a wife liable for medical services provided to her husband, though not automatically liable for bill because wife may raise any available defenses); Landmark Med. Ctr. v. Gauthier, 635 A.2d 1145 (R.I. 1994); Richland Mem'l Hosp. v. Burton, 282 S.C. 159, 318 S.E.2d 12 (S.C. 1984) (necessaries statute extended to impose liability on both spouses); Trident Reg'l Med. Ctr. v. Evans, 454 S.E.2d 343 (S.C. Ct. App. 1995); Accounts Mgmt., Inc. v. Lichfield, 576 N.W.2d 233 (S.D. 1998) (widow was liable for

essaries statutes, state Medicaid law imposes liability on a responsible relative, generally the spouse, for payment of nursing home expenses.[388]

Liability for a spouse's medical care becomes a major problem if a prolonged last illness threatens the surviving spouse with impoverishment.[389] There are several arguments that the spouse may use to avoid liability. Imposition of liability upon a spouse even under a gender-neutral statute may violate the Equal Credit Opportunity Act, which prohibits creditors from requiring that both spouses obligate themselves for one spouse's transaction.[390] In states that have not yet ruled on extending the statute to wives, the non-debtor wife can argue that extending the doctrine to her is a task for the legislature, not the court.[391]

In addition, courts in states that continue to recognize the necessaries doctrine may limit the circumstances in which they will impose liability on the non-debtor spouse.[392] Some

late husband's medical bills; medical care was a "necessary" within meaning of statute, making each spouse liable for "all necessaries of life" of the other); Outpatient Diagnostic Ctr. v. Christian, 1997 Tenn. App. LEXIS 305 (Tenn. Ct. App. Apr. 30, 1997) (either spouse is liable for the other's medical bills under common law doctrine of necessaries); Sinai Samaritan Med. Ctr. v. McCabe, 541 N.W.2d 190 (Wis. Ct. App. 1995) (Wis. Stat. § 765.001(2) imposed "mutual duty of support"; each spouse was obligated "in accordance with his or her abilities" to provide adequate maintenance for the other); *see also In re* Olexa, 317 B.R. 290 (Bankr. W.D. Pa. 2004) (detailed analysis of Pennsylvania necessaries statute, 23 Pa. Cons. Stat. § 4102, and cases construing it; statute was amended after enactment of state equal rights amendment), *aff'd*, 476 F.3d 177 (3d Cir. 2007).

Ohio, which recognized common law marriage, made common law spouses liable for each other's necessaries, including last illness expenses. Warren Gen. Hosp. v. Brink, 610 N.E.2d 1128 (Ohio Ct. App. 1992).

388 *See, e.g.*, Robbins v. DeBuono, 218 F.3d 197 (2d Cir. 2000) (New York's practice of attributing income of institutionalized spouse to non-institutionalized spouse required her to deplete her resources so as to be impoverished when spouse died; as to Social Security benefits, practice was forbidden by anti-assignment statute, as to ERISA benefits it was permissible); Comm'r of the Dep't of Soc. Services v. Fishman, 280 A.D.2d 396, 720 N.Y.S.2d 493 (2001) (widow who had assets and income liable in implied contract for husband's nursing home expenses); *In re* Estate of Bergman, 688 N.W.2d 187 (N.D. 2004) (construes impoverished spouse provisions of Medicaid law).

389 For examples of the harsh impact of the necessaries doctrine on surviving spouses, see Steve Tripoli & Chi Chi Wu, National Consumer Law Center, Unhealthy Pursuits: How the Sick and Vulnerable Are Harmed by Abusive Medical Debt Collection Tactics (Dec. 2005), *available at* www.consumerlaw.org/issues/medical_debt/content/medicaldebt.pdf. One court has held that the necessaries doctrine even permits a provider to report medical debt on the credit report of a spouse, despite the fact that the spouse's liability had not been reduced to judgment. Dunn v. Lehigh Valley Ctr. for Sight, 2003 WL 22299275 (E.D. Pa. Sept. 30, 2003).

390 15 U.S.C. § 1691(a)(1); 12 C.F.R. §§ 202.7(d)(1), 202.11(b)(1)(ii); *see* Edwards v. McCormick, 136 F. Supp. 2d 795, 803 n.9 (S.D. Ohio 2001) (stating in dicta that imposition of liability upon spouse probably violates Equal Credit Opportunity Act). *See generally* National Consumer Law Center, Credit Discrimination § 9.3 (4th ed. 2005 and Supp.).

391 *See* Davis v. Baxter County Reg'l Hosp., 855 S.W.2d 303 (Ark. 1993) (common law doctrine of necessaries not superseded or amended and remains in effect; equal protection violation not argued or considered); Medlock v. Ft. Smith Serv. Fin. Corp., 304 Ark. 652, 803 S.W.2d 930 (Ark. 1991); Connor v. Southwest Fla. Reg'l Med. Ctr., Inc., 668 So. 2d 175 (Fla. 1995); Rydstrom v. Bayfront Med. Ctr., 632 So. 2d 143 (Fla. Dist. Ct. App. 1994); Account Specialists & Credit Collections, Inc. v. Jackman, 970 P.2d 202 (Okla. Civ. App. 1998) (statute which codified common law doctrine of husband's liability for wife's necessaries was unconstitutional; legislature, not court, should now decide whether to impose liability on both spouses, or on neither); Med. Ctr. Hosp. v. Lorain, 675 A.2d 1326 (Vt. 1996); Hitchcock Clinic, Inc. v. Mackie, 160 Vt. 610, 648 A.2d 817 (1993).

392 *E.g.*, Schlaefer v. Fin. Mgmt. Serv., 196 Ariz. 336, 996 P.2d 745 (Ct. App. 2000) (debts for necessary medical care presumed to be community debts, but presumption rebutted by proof of valid premarital agreement that each spouse would be responsible for own debts); Samaritan Health Sys. v. Caldwell, 191 Ariz. 479, 957 P.2d 1373 (Ct. App. 1998) (health care debts are community debts, which may be satisfied from community property, but not from separate property of non-debtor spouse); Jewish Home for the Aged, Inc. v. Nuterangelo, 38 Conn. L. Rptr. 408 (Super. Ct. 2004) (state necessaries statute is to be strictly construed; nursing home expenses did not qualify as "hospital expenses" or "services of a physician or dentist," so that nursing home was required to show it qualified under catch-all category of services that "have gone to the support of the family"); N. Shore Cmty. Bank & Trust Co. v. Kollar, 710 N.E.2d 106 (Ill. App. Ct. 1999) (bank loan, even if the proceeds are spent for household needs, was not a "family expense" within the meaning of the Illinois family expense statute; widow not liable on loan taken by deceased husband; attorney fees to the widow); Bartrom v. Adjustment Bureau, Inc., 618 N.E.2d 1 (Ind. 1993); Porter Mem'l Hosp. v. Wozniak, 680 N.E.2d 13 (Ind. Ct. App. 1997) (wife's medical care was necessary, as evidence showed she had coronary disease and spent time in intensive care and her resources were insufficient, as shown by bankruptcy; remanded to trial court to determine husband's ability to pay); MRI Coop. v. Berlin, 1993 WL 257078 (Ohio Ct. App. June 30, 1993) (wife liable under family expense statute if able to pay; remanded to determine ability to pay); Ohio State Univ. Med. Ctr. v. Calovini, 2002 WL 31953905 (Ohio Ct. Cl. Oct. 8, 2002) (wife not liable for husband's medical care; fulltime housewife with no independent means had no ability to pay); Doctors Laves, Sarewitz & Walko v. Briggs, 613 A.2d 506 (N.J. Super. Ct. Law Div. 1992) (when wife separated from husband for five years with no financial interdependence, wife not liable for husband's medical expenses as wife, but liable in *quantum meruit* up to the amount of insurance proceeds paid to her husband's estate for those medical expenses); Ellis Hosp. v. Little, 409 N.Y.S.2d 459 (App. Div. 1978) (social service law that imposes spousal liability provides exemption for homestead "essential and appropriate to the needs of the household" (N.Y. Soc. Serv. Law § 336 (McKinney)); fact question as to widow's ability to pay depends on value of her nonexempt real estate); Roach v. Mamakos, 764 N.Y.S.2d 539 (Sup. Ct. 2003) (ex-husband not liable because alleged creditor, who was wife's father, failed to show that he expected to be paid, had sought payment from wife and that she was unable to pay; also doctrine of necessaries inapplicable when support order defined husband's duty to support, or when separation was fault of debtor

state statutes apply the doctrine only to emergency care,[393] or make separation a defense.[394] The creditor may be required to prove that the services provided were actually a "necessary,"[395] although that may be an easier burden in a medical debt case. Also, the creditor's recovery against the spouse may be limited to the amount owed for medical services, and may not extend to liability for attorney fees, interest, or collection costs.[396] The spouse who incurred the debt may remain primarily liable, and the other spouse may only be secondarily liable.[397] Failure to make a timely claim against the estate of the primary debtor wife may defeat an attempt to collect from the secondarily liable spouse.[398] The creditor may not have to sue the primarily liable debtor spouse separately, however, as long as it has demanded payment unsuccessfully from the primarily liable spouse.[399] Other states hold that the creditor must prove that the secondarily liable spouse had failed to support the primarily liable spouse.[400]

It may be a defense that the financial resources of the spouse who incurred the expenses were sufficient;[401] that the

---

spouse); Raleigh Gen. Hosp. v. Caudill, 591 S.E.2d 315 (W. Va. 2003) (former W. Va. Code § 48-3-22 [now § 48-29-303] made spouses liable for "the reasonable and necessary services of a physician rendered to either spouse while residing together as husband and wife;" court construed this narrowly; widow not liable for hospital costs other than physician's services).

393 Sentara Va. Beach Gen. Hosp. v. LeBeau, 188 F. Supp. 2d 623 (E.D. Va. 2002) (emergency not shown when cancer patient underwent testing to determine results of chemotherapy, and was scheduled for surgery two weeks later).

394 Balyeat Collection Professionals v. Garland, 51 P.3d 1127 (Mont. 2002) (Montana statute provides exception if non-debtor has been abandoned by debtor, or if couple living separately by agreement; remanded for fact finding on abandonment when couple were going through divorce); Roach v. Mamakos, 764 N.Y.S.2d 539 (Sup. Ct. 2003) (doctrine of necessaries inapplicable if support order defined husband's duty to support, or if separation was fault of debtor spouse); THC Piketon v. Edwards, 2007 WL 4305719 (Ohio Ct. App. Dec. 11, 2007) (no liability for spouse of patient if patient has abandoned spouse without cause).

395 Nelson v. First Nat'l Bank of Omaha, 2004 WL 2711032 (Minn. Ct. App. Nov. 30, 2004) (credit card lender failed to show that items purchased on account were household necessities, and thus lender not entitled to summary judgment on liability of spouse); Rienzo v. Parisi, 2008 WL 190488 (N.J. Super. Ct. App. Div. Jan. 24, 2008) (creditor must show that it was the direct provider of necessaries to recover from spouse; loan of money used to pay necessaries does not qualify).

396 N.A.R., Inc. v. Elmer, 141 P.3d 606 (Utah Ct. App. 2006) (interest and attorney fees, provided for in contract for medical services, are not necessaries within the meaning of the Utah Family Expense statute).

397 *In re* Olexa, 476 F.3d 177 (3d Cir. 2007) (contracting spouse primarily liable under Pennsylvania necessaries statute); Bartrom v. Adjustment Bureau, Inc., 618 N.E.2d 1 (Ind. 1993) (absent express contractual liability or authorization under the laws of agency, husband not responsible to health care provider for wife's debts; however, when a shortfall between dependent spouse's necessary expenses and separate funds exists, financially superior spouse becomes secondarily liable through doctrine); Mem'l Hosp. v. Hahaj, 430 N.E.2d 412 (Ind. 1992); St. Francis Reg'l Med. Ctr., Inc. v. Bowles, 251 Kan. 334, 836 P.2d 1123 (1992); Bethany Med. Ctr. v. Niyazi, 890 P.2d 349 (Kan. Ct. App. 1995); Hulse v. Warren, 777 S.W.2d 319 (Mo. 1989); Hawley v. Hawley, 904 S.W.2d 584 (Mo. Ct. App. 1995); Cheshire Med. Ctr. v. Holbrook, 663 A.2d 1344 (N.H. 1995); Rienzo v. Parisi, 2008 WL 190488 (N.J. Super. Ct. App. Div. Jan. 24, 2008) (creditor must seek satisfaction from the primarily liable spouse in order to seek recourse under necessaries doctrine); Med. Bus. Associates Inc. v. Steiner, 183 A.D.2d 86, 588 N.Y.S.2d 890 (1992); Roach v. Mamakos, 764 N.Y.S.2d 539 (Sup. Ct. 2003) (failure to sue primarily liable spouse is fatal to necessaries claim); THC Piketon v. Edwards, 2007 WL 4305719 (Ohio Ct. App. Dec. 11, 2007) (in order to hold spouse liable for medical bills creditor must show that patient is unable to pay the medical bills); Landmark Med. Ctr. v. Gauthier, 635 A.2d 1145 (R.I. 1994); Trident Reg'l Med. Ctr. v. Evans, 454 S.E.2d 343 (S.C. Ct. App. 1995); Anderson Mem'l Hosp. v. Hagen, 443 S.E.2d 399 (S.C. Ct. App. 1994).

398 Collection Bureau of San Jose v. Rumsey, 24 Cal. 4th 301, 99 Cal. Rptr. 2d 792 (2000) (one-year statute of limitations for claims against an estate barred a claim against a widow, under necessaries statute, for husband's last illness expenses); Anderson Mem'l Hosp. v. Hagen, 443 S.E.2d 399 (S.C. Ct. App. 1994); Accounts Mgmt., Inc. v. Nelson, 663 N.W.2d 237 (S.D. 2003) (hospital that failed to make timely claim on father's estate could not sue adult children for necessaries). *But see* Samaritan Health Sys. v. Caldwell, 957 P.2d 1373 (Ariz. Ct. App. 1998) (limitation on claims against estate did not bar suit on community debt against community property in hands of surviving spouse); Aker v. Ft. Wayne Urology, 562 N.E.2d 751 (Ind. Ct. App. 1990); Wesley Long Nursing Ctr. v. Harper, 653 S.E.2d 256 (N.C. Ct. App. 2007) (provider need not seek payment for nursing home expenses from wife's estate first; surviving spouse liable for debt); Fulton County Health Ctr. v. Jones, 2007 WL 4277583 (Ohio Ct. App. Dec. 7, 2007) (summary judgment for provider, despite surviving spouse's argument that provider failed to establish that patient's estate unable to pay bill).

399 Bethany Med. Ctr. v. Niyazi, 890 P.2d 349 (Kan. Ct. App. 1995); Cheshire Med. Ctr. v. Holbrook, 663 A.2d 1344 (N.H. 1995); Trident Reg'l Med. Ctr. v. Evans, 454 S.E.2d 343 (S.C. Ct. App. 1995).

400 Allen v. Keating, 517 N.W.2d 830 (Mich. Ct. App. 1994) (spouses were separated); Smith v. Hernandez, 794 P.2d 772 (Okla. Civ. App. 1990).

401 *In re* Olexa, 476 F.3d 177 (3d Cir. 2007) (creditor may go after other spouse under Pennsylvania necessaries statute only if contracting spouse's assets insufficient); Foster v. DBS Collection Agency, 463 F. Supp. 2d 783 (S.D. Ohio 2006) (debt collector not entitled to sue spouse under Ohio necessaries doctrine when collector failed to establish that the primary debtor was unable to pay debt; collector also failed to obtain assurances from original creditor that spouse was jointly liable); St. Francis Reg'l Med. Ctr., Inc. v. Bowles, 251 Kan. 334, 836 P.2d 1123 (1992); Bethany Med. Ctr. v. Niyazi, 890 P.2d 349 (Kan. Ct. App. 1995); Hawley v. Hawley, 904 S.W.2d 584 (Mo. Ct. App. 1995); Med. Bus. Associates Inc. v. Steiner, 183 A.D.2d 86, 588 N.Y.S.2d 890, 897 (1992); Roach v. Mamakos, 764 N.Y.S.2d 539 (Sup. Ct. 2003) (must show that primarily liable spouse is unable to pay); Promenade Nursing Home, Inc. v. Lacey, 814 N.Y.S.2d 564 (Civ. Ct. 2005) (table) (text available at 2005 WL 3592001) (claim for medical necessaries must show that the primary debtor is unable to pay for the debt out of his own resources; that the creditor relied on the credit of

creditor did not rely on the non-debtor spouse's credit to furnish the necessaries;[402] or that, as at common law, the non-debtor spouse's inability to pay the spouse's debts limits his or her responsibility to do so.[403] The secondarily liable spouse may also raise any defenses available to the other spouse.[404]

Difficult problems may be created by divorce or separation.[405] Divorce decrees often require one spouse to provide health insurance for the other, and for the children. A spouse who fails to comply may be found to be a self-insurer for expenses which should have been covered.[406] Courts are

non-patient spouse in deciding to extend credit; and that the non-patient spouse has the means to pay the debt); THC Piketon v. Edwards, 2007 WL 4305719 (Ohio Ct. App. Dec. 11, 2007) (in order to hold spouse liable for medical bills creditor must show that patient is unable to pay the medical bills); Landmark Med. Ctr. v. Gauthier, 635 A.2d 1145 (R.I. 1994) ("Only if the spouse who received the benefit has insufficient resources to satisfy the debt may the other spouse be liable.").

402 Kent Gen. Hosp., Inc. v. Russell, 1997 Del. Super. LEXIS 336 (Del. Super. Ct. July 14, 1997) (doctrine of necessaries did not apply when hospital relied on wife's individual credit), *aff'd*, 705 A.2d 244 (Del. 1998) (table) (text available at 1998 WL 15010); Med. Bus. Associates Inc. v. Steiner, 183 A.D.2d 86, 588 N.Y.S.2d 890, 897 (1992) (citing Our Lady of Lourdes v. Frey, 152 A.D.2d 73, 75 (1989)); Promenade Nursing Home, Inc. v. Lacey, 814 N.Y.S.2d 564 (Civ. Ct. 2005) (table) (text available at 2005 WL 3592001) (claim for medical necessaries must show that the primary debtor is unable to pay for the debt out of his own resources; that the creditor relied on the credit of non-patient spouse in deciding to extend credit; and that the non-patient spouse has the means to pay the debt).

403 *In re* Olexa, 317 B.R. 290 (Bankr. W.D. Pa. 2004) (pecuniary circumstances of the non-contracting spouse are relevant under Pennsylvania necessaries statute), *aff'd*, 476 F.3d 177 (3d Cir. 2007); Kent Gen. Hosp., Inc. v. Russell, 1997 Del. Super. LEXIS 336 (Del. Super. Ct. July 14, 1997) (doctrine of necessaries did not apply when hospital relied on wife's individual credit), *aff'd*, 705 A.2d 244 (Del. 1998) (table) (text available at 1998 WL 15010); Med. Bus. Associates Inc. v. Steiner, 183 A.D.2d 86, 588 N.Y.S.2d 890, 897 (1992) (citing Our Lady of Lourdes v. Frey, 152 A.D.2d 73, 75 (1989)); Promenade Nursing Home, Inc. v. Lacey, 814 N.Y.S.2d 564 (Civ. Ct. 2005) (table) (text available at 2005 WL 3592001) (claim for medical necessaries must show that the primary debtor is unable to pay for the debt out of his own resources; that the creditor relied on the credit of non-patient spouse in deciding to extend credit; and that the non-patient spouse has the means to pay the debt); *see also* Porter Mem'l Hosp. v. Wozniak, 680 N.E.2d 13 (Ind. Ct. App. 1997) (when medical care was necessary, and debtor-wife's resources insufficient, remanded to trial court to determine husband's ability to pay); Ellis Hosp. v. Little, 409 N.Y.S.2d 459 (App. Div. 1978) (social service law that imposes spousal liability provides exemption for homestead "essential and appropriate to the needs of the household" (N.Y. Soc. Serv. Law § 336 (McKinney)); fact question as to widow's ability to pay depends on value of her nonexempt real estate); MRI Coop. v. Berlin, 1993 WL 257078 (Ohio Ct. App. June 30, 1993) (wife liable under family expense statute if able to pay; remanded to determine ability to pay); Ohio State Univ. Med. Ctr. v. Calovini, 2002 WL 31953905 (Ohio Ct. Cl. Oct. 8, 2002) (wife not liable for husband's medical care; fulltime housewife with no independent means had no ability to pay).

404 St. Francis Reg'l Med. Ctr., Inc. v. Bowles, 251 Kan. 334, 836 P.2d 1123 (1992). *But see* Porter Mem'l Hosp. v. Wozniak, 680 N.E.2d 13 (Ind. Ct. App. 1997) (debtor-wife's discharge in bankruptcy did not eliminate husband's liability under doctrine of necessaries).

405 Yale Univ. Sch. of Med. v. Scianna, 701 A.2d 65 (Conn. Super. Ct. 1997) (when couple was separated and husband was paying support to wife, wife was not liable for husband's medical bills; Connecticut's poorly drafted necessaries statute construed to allow "separation defense" to all recipient spouses, that is, those who are receiving or entitled to receive support from "provider spouse"); Queen's Med. Ctr. v. Kagawa, 967 P.2d 686 (Haw. 1998) (under gender-neutral spousal liability statute, wife was liable for husband's hospital bill, even though couple was in process of getting a divorce; case remanded to trial court to determine if each charge was necessary and reasonable); Proctor v. Taylor, 665 N.E.2d 872 (Ill. App. Ct. 1996) (Illinois's family support statute, 750 Ill. Comp. Stat. § 65/15(a)(3), imposed liability on non-custodial divorced parent for hospital bill of unemancipated minor child); Bartrom v. Adjustment Bureau, 618 N.E.2d 1 (Ind. 1993) (non-debtor spouse has limited liability for necessaries, which continues regardless of separation, as long as a duty to support continues to exist; misconduct by the debtor spouse may eliminate non-debtor spouse's duty); Allen v. Keating, 517 N.W.2d 830 (Mich. Ct. App. 1994) (if spouses separated, burden on creditor to prove that non-debtor husband has failed to support wife; husband not liable if there is an adequate support order, or he has "otherwise provided adequate support"); Balyeat Collection Professionals v. Garland, 51 P.3d 1127 (Mont. 2002) (Montana statute provides exception if non-debtor has been abandoned by debtor, or if couple living separately by agreement; remanded for fact finding on abandonment when couple were going through divorce); Roach v. Mamakos, 764 N.Y.S.2d 539 (Sup. Ct. 2003) (ex-husband not liable because alleged creditor, who was wife's father, failed to show that he expected to be paid, had sought payment from wife, and that she was unable to pay; also doctrine of necessaries inapplicable when support order defined husband's duty to support, or when separation was fault of debtor spouse); Forsyth Mem'l Hosp. v. Chisholm, 467 S.E.2d 88 (N.C. 1996) (separation not a defense when health care provider had no actual notice that spouses were separated; wife transported seriously ill husband to hospital and "admitted" him, without informing hospital of the separation); Potter v. Karivalis, 718 A.2d 823 (Pa. Super. Ct. 1997) (gender-neutral statute upheld against constitutional challenge; incarcerated husband liable for wife's medical expenses under Pennsylvania necessaries statute); Mercy Health Sys. Corp. v. Gauss, 639 N.W.2d 803 (Wis. Ct. App. 2001) (table) (text available at 2001 WL 1632549) (separation not a defense to medical debt of ex-wife incurred during marriage); St. Mary's Hosp. Med. Ctr. v. Brody, 519 N.W.2d 706 (Wis. Ct. App. 1994) (ex-wife liable for husband's medical expenses incurred during the marriage, despite provision in divorce decree that husband should be responsible for those expenses).

406 Ohio Rev. Code Ann. § 1349.01 (West) (ex-spouse who fails to provide court-ordered health insurance liable for uncovered medical bills); Blair v. Blair, 272 Ga. 94, 527 S.E.2d 177 (2000); Tietjens v. Tietjens, 744 N.E.2d 1064 (Ind. Ct. App. 2001) (separation agreement, which became part of divorce decree, required husband to provide health insurance until couple mutually agreed it was no longer necessary; informal agreement, not approved by court, was insufficient, so husband

divided on the question whether a spouse who provides the required level of coverage may nonetheless be liable for expenses not covered.[407]

In some states, there is familial duty of support that extends beyond spouses. This duty may impose joint and several liability on both parents of a minor child,[408] or even secondary liability on adult offspring of an indigent parent.[409] A minor may be held liable for necessaries, and may be sued after reaching the age of majority, if the parents are shown to be unwilling or unable to provide them.[410]

10.7 Health Care Providers' Lien on Personal Injury Recoveries

10.7.1 General

Health care providers may be able to place a lien on a patient's tort recovery from the entity which caused the patient's injuries.[411] The amount of the lien may be regulated

---

was liable for insurance premiums and for bills incurred while wife was uninsured).

407 *Compare In re* Dixon, 245 B.R. 367 (Bankr. W.D. Mo. 2000) (support order in divorce decree replaced husband's common law duty to support) *and* Tietjens v. Tietjens, 744 N.E.2d 1064 (Ind. Ct. App. 2001) (when couple deleted from draft separation agreement the requirement that husband pay medical bills not covered by insurance, husband was not liable) *with* Sheppard & Enoch Pratt Physicians, Prof'l Ass'n v. Sakwa, 725 So. 2d 755 (Miss. 1998) (common law duty to provide necessary medical care survived the divorce decree) *and* McLain v. W. Side Bone & Joint Ctr., 656 So. 2d 119 (Miss. 1995) (provider could recover from father even though he had complied with all medical insurance obligations of divorce decree; father's remedy was to seek divorce court order for reimbursement from mother).

408 Phillips v. Dodds, 867 N.E.2d 1122 (Ill. App. Ct. 2007) (aunt could liable for medical bills of niece under Illinois family expense statute when she accepted niece into her household and stood *in loco parentis*, even though aunt was not niece's legal guardian); Proctor v. Taylor, 665 N.E.2d 872 (Ill. App. Ct. 1996) (Illinois family expense statute imposed liability on non-custodial divorced parent of unemancipated minor child); Schmidt v. Mut. Hosp. Services, Inc., 832 N.E.2d 977 (Ind. Ct. App. 2005) (parents' duty to support child makes them liable for the child's medical bills even when parents had explicitly refused consent to treatment); Sheppard & Enoch Pratt Physicians, Prof'l Ass'n v. Sakwa, 725 So. 2d 755 (Miss. 1998) (common law duty to support made non-custodial father, who had provided health insurance as required by divorce decree, liable for minor daughter's medical expenses not covered by insurance); McLain v. W. Side Bone & Joint Ctr., 656 So. 2d 119 (Miss. 1995) (non-custodial father who had complied with support order by providing health insurance for child liable for expenses not covered by insurance); Estate of Bonner, 954 S.W.2d 356 (Mo. Ct. App. 1997) (conservatorship estate of incompetent mother was liable, under the doctrine of necessaries, for care provided to infant son); Brookdale Hosp. Med. Ctr. v. Lewis, 803 N.Y.S.2d 17 (Civ. Ct. 2005) (table) (text available at 2005 WL 1792593) (non-custodial parent may be held liable for child's medical bills even if the parent did not request the services, if parent has the financial ability and fails to support child).

409 *In re* Marriage of Leni, 50 Cal. Rptr. 3d 886 (Ct. App. 2006) (California imposes statutory duty to support indigent elderly parent, and such obligation becomes a community debt); Boe v. Dep't of Human Services, 844 A.2d 531 (N.J. Super. Ct. App. Div. 2004) (even without statutory lien, which defeated patient's son's right of survivorship in jointly owned house, son was responsible relative who would be liable for mother's state hospital care), *vacated on other grounds*, 873 A.2d 500 (N.J. 2005) (statute adopted extinguishing liens against persons treated at psychiatric facility); Presbyterian Med. Ctr. v. Budd, 832 A.2d 1066 (Pa. Super. Ct. 2003) (nursing home stated claim against adult daughter under Pennsylvania statute that requires adult children "of sufficient ability" to support "indigent" parents); Landmark Med. Ctr. v. Gauthier, 635 A.2d 1145 (R.I. 1994); Accounts Mgmt., Inc. v. Nelson, 663 N.W.2d 237 (S.D. 2003) (deceased father not indigent within meaning of family support statute when estate contained sufficient funds to pay bill; hospital that failed to make timely claim on estate could not sue adult children); Prairie Lakes Healthcare Sys. v. Wookey, 583 N.W.2d 405 (S.D. 1998) (South Dakota statute makes adult child responsible for support of indigent parent, if adult child is financially able); *cf.* Vencor, Inc. v. Gray, 66 P.3d 323 (Mont. 2003) (table) (text available at 2003 WL 329248) (healthcare provider had no standing to sue under statute requiring adult child to support indigent parent; only the county or the parent could sue; but note that statute makes promise to pay for parents' necessaries binding).

410 Williams v. Baptist Health Sys., Inc., 857 So. 2d 149 (Ala. Civ. App. 2003) (parents primarily liable, child secondarily liable; when mother's bankruptcy showed inability to pay, daughter's wages could be garnished after majority); Yale Diagnostic Radiology v. Estate of Harun Fountain, 838 A.2d 179 (Conn. 2004) (minor is liable in *quantum meruit* for necessaries such as medical care; parent is primarily liable, but if parent can not or will not pay, minor is liable; when parent's debts discharged in bankruptcy, hospital could reach estate created by minor's personal injury recovery); Woodberry v. Hammond Lumber Co., 2003 WL 1665251 (Me. Super. Ct. Mar. 10, 2003) (child will be liable for cost of medical care if parents unable or unwilling to provide it); Schmidt v. Prince George's Hosp., 366 Md. 535, 784 A.2d 1112 (2001) (eighteen-year-old could be sued for emergency treatment provided when she was sixteen; parents' unwillingness to pay shown by father's receiving and spending Blue Cross check, instead of forwarding it to provider); Layton Physical Therapy Co. v. Palozzi, 149 Ohio App. 3d 332, 777 N.E.2d 306 (2002) (if parents do not pay for necessaries, here medical care, minor child secondarily liable in quasi-contract); Dallas County Hosp. Dist. v. Wiley *ex rel.* Wiley, 2002 WL 1286515 (Tex. App. June 12, 2002) (hospital could sue minor "by and through" his parent for minor's medical expenses); *cf.* Neb. Health Sys. v. Bear (*In re* Marshall), 634 N.W.2d 300 (Neb. Ct. App. 2001) (hospital's necessaries claim against child not decided on merits because time-barred); State *ex rel.* Packard v. Perry, 655 S.E.2d 548 (W. Va. 2007) (minor may be responsible for his or her own medical expenses under West Virginia doctrine of necessaries).

411 Mercado v. Allstate Ins. Co., 340 F.3d 824 (9th Cir. 2003) (not a UDAP violation for insurer to require that county and lawyer be co-payees of settlement check, when county that provided medical care entitled to a lien, and lawyer had already filed one); *Ex parte* Univ. of S. Ala. v. Garrick, 761 So. 2d 240 (Ala. Civ. App. 1999) (analyzing Alabama's hospital lien statute); Alaska Native Tribal Health Consortium v. Settlement Funds Held for or to Be Paid on Behalf of E.R. *ex rel.* Ridley, 84 P.3d 418

by statute.[412] State law will also prescribe substantive and procedural requirements, and a provider's failure to comply will invalidate the lien.[413] In some cases, a provider's claim will not fall within the scope of the state law.[414]

(Alaska 2004) (hospital that provided free care to Alaska natives could place lien on tort recoveries); McMeans v. Med. Liabilities Recoveries, Inc., 2002 WL 31835746 (Cal. Ct. App. Dec. 19, 2002) (detailed discussion of California lien law); Kenneth F. White, Chartered v. St. Alphonsus Reg'l Med. Ctr., 31 P.3d 926 (Idaho Ct. App. 2001) (hospital lien took priority over attorney fees); Marquez v. Progressive Ins. Co., 944 So. 2d 876 (La. Ct. App. 2006) (Louisiana law entitles hospital to entirety of insurance proceeds, leaving nothing for accident victim); Marvin's Midtown Chiropractic Clinic v. State Farm Mut. Auto. Ins. Co., 142 S.W.3d 751 (Mo. Ct. App. 2004) (enforcing lien agreement that chiropractor required of accident victims); Wyant v. Kenda, 102 P.3d 1260 (Mont. 2004) (tortfeasor's insurer acted permissibly when it named lienor-chiropractor as co-payee of settlement check); Bergan Mercy Health Sys. v. Haven, 260 Neb. 846, 620 N.W.2d 339 (2000) (hospital lien statute not unconstitutional "special legislation," and is not overridden by more general statute providing exemption for personal injury recoveries); Broadway Clinic v. Liberty Mut. Ins. Co., 139 P.3d 873 (Okla. 2006) (Oklahoma physician's lien statute allows recovery from both patient's own automobile insurance policy as well as tortfeasor's insurance); Hermann Hosp. v. Martinez, 990 S.W.2d 476 (Tex. App. 1999) (hospital lien is valid against recovery on any claim brought by injured person "which is attributed to the negligence of another"); Riegleman v. Krieg, 679 N.W.2d 857 (Wis. Ct. App. 2004) ("doctor's lien" document signed by patient and attorney was valid contract). *But cf.* Holeton v. Crouse Cartage Co., 92 Ohio St. 3d 115, 748 N.E.2d 1111 (2001) (workers' compensation subrogation statute was unconstitutional when it allowed fund to reach personal injury recovery even if victim was not made whole and allowed the fund to reach recoveries of third parties, that is, parents and adult children in death cases). *See generally* C. Crocca, Annotation, *Construction, Operation, and Effect of Statutes Giving Hospital Lien Against Recovery from Tortfeasor Causing Patient's Injuries*, 16 A.L.R.5th 262 (1993).

412 *See* 770 Ill. Comp. Stat. § 23/10(a) (limiting the total amount of all provider liens to forty percent of the patient's recovery); HealthOne, Inc. v. Columbia Wesley Med. Ctr., 93 F. Supp. 2d 1152 (D. Kan. 2000) (Kansas hospital lien act allows lien for up to $5000; any additional amounts are subject to "equitable distribution" of settlement amount); Cullimore v. St. Anthony Med. Ctr., 718 N.E.2d 1221 (Ind. Ct. App. 1999) (Indiana hospital lien statute provides that if recovery not sufficient to pay all liens, amount will be proportioned pro rata, leaving enough for patient to get 20%; court held that underlying debt is not extinguished and hospital may sue patient for the balance); King County Rehab, Inc. v. Clackamas County, 164 P.3d 1190 (Or. Ct. App. 2007) (long term care provider's lien limited to cost of care under statute, and did not extend to attorney fees for collection); Daughters of Charity Health Services of Waco v. Linnstaedter, 226 S.W.3d 409 (Tex. 2007) (worker's compensation insurer reimbursed hospital; labor code barred hospital from filing property code lien against tort recovery from at-fault driver); *see also* Shelter Mut. Ins. Co. v. Kennedy, 347 Ark. 184, 60 S.W.3d 458 (Ark. 2001) (insurance company not entitled to subrogation when accident victim not made whole by tort settlement; victim had continuing medical problems, and would require future treatment).

413 *In re* Pratt, 2000 Bankr. LEXIS 94 (B.A.P. 10th Cir. Feb. 15, 2000) (lien filed by physician for certain itemized amounts "up to the final balance" was good only as to the itemized amounts); *In re* Norton, 248 B.R. 131 (Bankr. W.D. Wis. 2000) (financial responsibility form, which required patient to pay provider out of proceeds of any settlement, was merely a promise to pay, not an explicit assignment, and thus did not create lien); *In re* Woodward, 234 B.R. 519 (Bankr. N.D. Okla. 1999) (hospital liens not perfected at time of bankruptcy filing; detailed discussion of Oklahoma procedural requirements for hospital liens); *Ex parte* Infinity S. Ins. Co., 737 So. 2d 463 (Ala. 1999) (failure to strictly comply with statute invalidated hospital lien, but hospital was free to sue patient); County of San Bernardino v. Calderon, 56 Cal. Rptr. 3d 333 (Ct. App. 2007) (hospital's lien did not become effective until it gave notice as required under statute); Mares v. Baughman, 92 Cal. App. 4th 672, 112 Cal. Rptr. 2d 264 (2001) (California statute allowing county that provided medical services a lien against "judgments" does not authorize a lien on a settlement); Wilson v. F.B. McAfoos & Co., 800 N.E.2d 177 (Ill. App. Ct. 2003) (physician's lien not assignable; statutory creation, unknown to common law, must be narrowly construed); Anderson v. Dep't of Mental Health & Developmental Disabilities, 711 N.E.2d 1170 (Ill. App. Ct. 1999) (no lien for Department of Mental Health, when it failed to prove causal connection between treatment it gave and injuries for which patient sued tortfeasor); Sam v. Direct Gen. Ins. Co., 951 So. 2d 482 (La. Ct. App. 2007) (providers who failed to comply with procedural requirements of Louisiana lien statute were not entitled to a share of the tort recovery); Neb. Health Sys. v. Bear (*In re* Marshall), 10 Neb. App. 589, 634 N.W.2d 300 (2001) ("substantial compliance" required; not shown when hospital failed to provide required notices to tortfeasor and court, so lien never perfected). *But see* Via Christi Reg'l Med. Ctr. v. Brown (*In re* Brown), 2007 WL 2029498 (Bankr. D. Kan. July 10, 2007) (hospital's lien attached to settlement funds, notwithstanding the failure of the lien statements to name (and the failure to serve) all of the parties identified); Andrews v. Samaritan Health Sys., 36 P.3d 57 (Ariz. Ct. App. 2001) (untimely recording did not invalidate lien); Stephens v. Parkview Hosp., Inc., 745 N.E.2d 262 (Ind. Ct. App. 2001) (hospital lien valid even though required notice sent to wrong attorney; victim's attorney had actual notice, so no prejudice); St. Francis Hosp. v. Vaughn, 971 P.2d 401 (Okla. Civ. App. 1998) (hospital lien was timely and valid, when attorney received notice of lien after insurance company mailed settlement check, but before attorney received and deposited check).

414 *In re* Pratt, 2000 Bankr. LEXIS 94 (B.A.P. 10th Cir. Feb. 15, 2000) (Oklahoma physicians' lien statute strictly construed; does not allow medical corporation to file physician's lien); St. Anthony's Med. Ctr. v. Metze, 23 S.W.3d 692 (Mo. Ct. App. 2000) (Missouri hospital lien statute did not allow lien against proceeds of wrongful death action, which benefited the survivors, not the estate); Quality Chiropractic, Prof'l Corp. v. Farmers Ins. Co. of Ariz., 51 P.3d 1172 (N.M. Ct. App. 2002) (New Mexico statute allows lien by hospital but not individual providers, so court refuses to enforce "irrevocable lien and assignment" signed by patient as condition of receiving treatment); Dallas County Hosp. Dist. v. Wiley *ex rel.* Wiley, 2002 WL 1286515 (Tex. App. June 12, 2002) (hospital lien statute does not apply to proceeds of "an insurance policy in favor of the injured individual or the injured individual's beneficiary"; no lien against proceeds of action against minor patient's father's uninsured motorist insurance carrier, but *quantum meruit* claim allowed to go forward).

The lien may be reduced if the patient can show unreasonableness.[415] Other issues likely to arise are the scope of the trial court's power to apportion the recovery, or limit further collection action by the health care creditor, and whether the provider's share of a common fund should be reduced by the pro-rated share of attorney fees and other costs.[416]

415 McMeans v. Med. Liabilities Recoveries, Inc., 2002 WL 31835746 (Cal. Ct. App. Dec. 19, 2002) (when hospital permitted to place lien despite payment by insurer, amount of lien limited to reasonable value of necessary services); Phillips v. DeCarlo, 301 Ill. App. 3d 680, 705 N.E.2d 113 (1998) (trial court should have allowed patient to present evidence of unreasonableness; remanded for evidentiary hearing); Temesvary v. Houdek, 301 Ill. App. 3d 560, 703 N.E.2d 613 (1998) (unreasonableness not proven, when patient's expert not familiar with the differences between freestanding nuclear medicine center and hospital, and when lienor sufficiently explained basis for calculation of fees); Riegleman v. Krieg, 679 N.W.2d 857 (Wis. Ct. App. 2004) (treatment was necessary and charges reasonable; independent medical examination concluded that it was not, but court, who heard evidence from provider and patient, found otherwise).

416 *See* Howe v. Scottsdale Ins. Co., 204 F.3d 624 (5th Cir. 2000) (hospital which claimed statutory lien on tort recovery not required to contribute to attorney fees and costs of tort action); IBEW-NECA Southwestern Health & Benefit Fund v. Gurule, 337 F. Supp. 2d 845 (N.D. Tex. 2004) (ERISA preempted New Mexico statute requiring liens to be reduced by pro rata share of attorney fees); Fairfield Mfg. Co. v. Hartman, 132 F. Supp. 2d 1142 (N.D. Ind. 2001) (provision of ERISA agreement allowing subrogation, and making beneficiary responsible for all expenses of recovery including attorney fees, not unconscionable; plan not required to pay share of attorney fees); HealthOne, Inc. v. Columbia Wesley Med. Ctr., 93 F. Supp. 2d 1152 (D. Kan. 2000) (hospital lien is junior to attorney's lien, and priority can not be defeated by prior assignment); Alaska Native Tribal Health Consortium v. Settlement Funds Held for or to Be Paid on Behalf of E.R. *ex rel.* Ridley, 84 P.3d 418 (Alaska 2004) (hospital that provided free care to Alaska natives could place lien on tort recoveries; amount must be reduced by pro rata share of attorney fees); Trevino v. HHL Fin. Services, 945 P.2d 1345 (Colo. 1997) (assignee of health care debt could file lien against tort settlement; no reduction for its share of fees and costs); Holland v. State Farm Mut. Auto. Ins. Co., 513 S.E.2d 48 (Ga. Ct. App. 1999) (lien for accident victim's attorney fees took priority over hospital and Medicaid reimbursement liens; except for this exception, hospital and welfare department took entire amount of plaintiff's recovery); Kenneth F. White, Chartered v. St. Alphonsus Reg'l Med. Ctr., 31 P.3d 926 (Idaho Ct. App. 2001) (hospital lien took priority over attorney fees; no attorney's lien when attorney negotiated settlement without filing suit; common fund doctrine did not apply); Bishop v. Burgard, 764 N.E.2d 24 (Ill. 2002) (ERISA does not preempt Illinois's common fund doctrine when ERISA plan seeks to enforce lien on personal injury proceeds, pursuant to subrogation clause in plan; lien reduced by plan's share of attorney fees); Hillenbrand v. Meyer Med. Group, 308 Ill. App. 3d 381, 720 N.E.2d 287 (1999) (common fund doctrine required healthcare provider which filed physicians' lien against patient's tort settlement to bear its proportionate share of attorney fees incurred in negotiating the settlement); Cullimore v. St. Anthony Med. Ctr., 718 N.E.2d 1221 (Ind. Ct. App. 1999) (Indiana hospital lien statute provides that if recovery not sufficient to pay all liens, amount will be proportioned pro rata, leaving enough for patient to get twenty percent; court held that underlying debt is not extinguished and hospital may sue patient for the balance); Marquez v. Progressive Ins. Co., 944 So. 2d 876 (La. Ct. App. 2006) (under Louisiana law, attorney's lien has precedence over hospital's lien); Wyant v. Kenda, 102 P.3d 1260 (Mont. 2004) (under Montana law, healthcare lien may not be reduced by amount of attorney fees; note however that attorney's lien takes priority over healthcare lien); Mountain W. Farm Bureau Mut. Ins. Co. v. Hall, 38 P.3d 825 (Mont. 2001) (Montana statute which provides that hospitals with lien on personal injury proceeds need not pay share of attorney fees not retroactive; remanded to determine if common fund doctrine applied); Eaton Martinez & Hart v. Univ. Hosp., 934 P.2d 270 (N.M. 1997) (public hospital's lien would not be reduced by its share of costs; court noted that result might be different for private hospital); Martino v. Dyer, 2000 Tenn. App. LEXIS 764 (Tenn. Ct. App. Nov. 22, 2000) (when personal injury judgment sufficient to pay both hospital and attorney, hospital liens should not be reduced by its share of attorney fees; statute giving priority to attorney's lien applied only when proceeds insufficient to go around).

10.7.2 *Hospitals' Ability to Seek a Lien After Receipt of Insurance Payment*

Some providers may seek to place a lien on a tort recovery, even though the services provided were covered by the patient's health maintenance organization (HMO) or insurance plan (which will pay substantially less than the gross charges or list price[417]). Some courts have disapproved this practice, reasoning that once the patient authorizes payment from the HMO, he or she owes no debt to the provider.[418] Other courts, however, have allowed a hospital

417 *See* § 10.5.5.2, *supra*.

418 Satsky v. United States, 993 F. Supp. 1027 (S.D. Tex. 1998) (no debt, no lien; hospital that had accepted discounted payment from insurer as "payment in full" could not place lien on personal injury recovery); Parnell v. Adventist Health Sys./West, 109 P.3d 69 (Cal. 2005) (provider who agreed to accept insurer's reimbursement as "payment in full" for medical services could not assert lien on patient's tort recovery, despite state law permitting lien, because patient did not owe debt to provider); Rutherford v. Ralph Hutton & Associates, 2004 WL 1119676 (Cal. Ct. App. May 20, 2004) (hospital's balance billing by attempting to enforce lien against personal injury recovery was forbidden by hospital's contract with county government program to provide medical care to indigent and uninsured patients); Gianetti v. Siglinger, 900 A.2d 520 (Conn. 2006) (health plan agreement and Connecticut law forbade balance billing; affirming trial court's award of $26,000 and attorney fees of $40,000 under Connecticut UDAP statute for physician's repeated violation of both agreement and law); Constantine v. MCG Health, Inc., 619 S.E.2d 718 (Ga. Ct. App. 2005) (hospital that was paid by insurer could not return payment and then claim lien on patient's tort recovery; contract between hospital and insurer forbade billing patient, even though state law provided that lien was against the tort cause of action and not against the patient personally); Lopez v. Morley, 817 N.E.2d 592 (Ill. App. Ct. 2004) (lien not permitted but court notes that hospital's contract could have provided that insurance payment would not extinguish debt); N.C. by L.C. v. A.W. by R.W., 713 N.E.2d 775 (Ill. App. Ct. 1999) (lien was void when

a lien for the difference between the HMO reimbursement and its customary charges.[419] The outcome of these cases may turn on the precise wording of the contract between the provider and the insurer. Medicaid or Medicare law, as well as state laws that prohibit providers from balance billing patients with private insurance, may also limit the ability of a hospital to assert claims against a tort recovery.[420]

10.7.3 Liens by Insurers or Third-Party Payors

Many HMOs or employee benefit plans include subrogation clauses allowing them to reach a member's tort recovery,[421] even if the recovery is grossly insufficient to compensate the victim—as in the familiar case in which the costs of a lawsuit and the tortfeasor's lack of nonexempt assets mandate a settlement for insurance policy limits.[422] Some clauses even allow the plan to recover more than it spent, for example by placing a lien for the customary charge, even though it pays the provider a discounted rate.[423] Other subrogation arrangements consist of insurers who characterize their payments of a patient's medical bills as a "loan" to the patient.[424] State laws that forbid or limit subrogation[425] may not apply to employee benefit plans, because of

---

automobile accident victim was covered by HMO, which paid hospital the sum agreed upon in contract between hospital and HMO; no lien can exist when there is no underlying debt and patient's debt was extinguished by HMO's payment to hospital); Howard v. Willis-Knighton Med. Ctr., 924 So. 2d 1245 (La. Ct. App. 2006) (certifying classes of insured patients who were charged full list prices instead of discount prices negotiated by their insurers when hospital placed lien on their tort recoveries); Midwest Neurosurgery, Prof'l Corp. v. State Farm Ins. Companies, 686 N.W.2d 572 (Neb. 2004) (when provider had agreed with HMO to accept specific amount, this was the "amount due"; provider could not place lien on personal injury recovery for its undiscounted bill; note that this depended on precise wording of the contract provisions); Dorr v. Sacred Heart Hosp., 597 N.W.2d 462 (Wis. Ct. App. 1999) (lien was void when auto accident victim was covered by HMO, and contract between the hospital and the HMO, as well as a provision of state statute, forbade the hospital to bill the patient for services covered by HMO; patient who alleged this practice had stated sufficient facts to support state UDAP and racketeering claims); *see also* Daughters of Charity Health Services of Waco v. Linnstaedter, 226 S.W.3d 409 (Tex. 2007) (when workers' compensation insurer reimbursed hospital, labor code limits on charges barred hospital from filing property code lien against tort recovery from at-fault driver).

419 Samsel v. Allstate Ins. Co., 59 P.3d 281 (Ariz. 2002) (medical expenses paid by HMO are "actually incurred" within meaning of automobile insurance policy when, although hospital can not bill patient, it has lien on tort recovery for its full charges); Andrews v. Samaritan Health Sys., 36 P.3d 57 (Ariz. Ct. App. 2001) (allowing lien despite "paid in full" language in the HMO contract, when the hospital contract reserved the right of recourse against third parties and a state statute allowed a hospital lien for customary charges); Whiteside v. Tenet Healthcare Corp., 124 Cal. Rptr. 2d 580 (Ct. App. 2002) (hospital that was reimbursed by one insurance company at preferred provider rate could recover from patient's second insurance policy for difference between that and regular rate; contract forbade billing the patient, but specifically permitted billing third-party payors); Watts v. Promina Gwinnett Health Sys., Inc., 242 Ga. App. 377, 530 S.E.2d 14 (2000) (hospital had valid lien on patient's tort recovery, despite HMO contract for fixed rate); Rogalla v. Christie Clinic, Prof'l Corp., 794 N.E.2d 384 (Ill. App. Ct. 2003) (disagreeing with N.C. by L.C. v. A.W. by R.W., 713 N.E.2d 775 (Ill. App. Ct. 1999); provider entitled to seek lien against patient's tort recovery under Illinois Physician Lien Act despite agreement with insurer that provider could not seek payment from patients other than co-payments and deductibles); Richmond v. Caban, 754 N.E.2d 871 (Ill. App. Ct. 2001) (hospital could choose whether to bill HMO or place lien on tort recovery; note however that lien may be invalid under provision of HMO statute that forbids provider to have recourse against plan members for anything except co-pays, deductibles and non-covered services; open question regarding interaction between HMO statute and lien statute).

420 *See* § 10.3.6, *supra*. *See generally* Manjusha P. Kulkarni, Nat'l Health Law Project, Fact Sheet: State and Provider Liens Asserted Against the Recoveries of Medicaid and Medicare Beneficiaries (June 2004).

421 A claim for subrogation under one of these clauses may be considered a "debt" under the Fair Debt Collection Practices Act. Hamilton v. United Health Care, 310 F.3d 385 (5th Cir. 2002), *later opinion at* Hamilton v. Trover Solutions, Inc., 2003 WL 21105100 (E.D. La. May 13, 2003) (subrogation collection company not a debt collector, because debts not delinquent when it obtains them), *aff'd*, 104 Fed. Appx. 942 (5th Cir. 2004).

422 *See, e.g.*, Administrative Comm. for Wal-Mart Stores, Inc. Associates' Welfare Plan v. Salazar, 525 F. Supp. 2d 1103 (D. Ariz. 2007) (ERISA permitted plan to recover from personal injury recovery, even though result was that plan was made whole and accident victim was not); IBEW-NECA Southwestern Health & Benefit Fund v. Gurule, 337 F. Supp. 2d 845 (N.D. Tex. 2004) (subrogation clause provided that plan would be paid first, whether or not victim was made whole, and without regard to any allocation of funds by court); Franks v. Prudential Health Care Plan, 164 F. Supp. 2d 865 (W.D. Tex. 2001); Carpenter v. Wal-Mart Stores, Inc., 252 B.R. 905 (E.D. Va. 2000), *aff'd*, 2002 WL 1162277 (4th Cir. June 3, 2002).

However, if the subrogation clause in an ERISA plan does not give the insurer the right of first reimbursement, the insurer's recovery may be limited by the common law make-whole rule. Barnes v. Indep. Automobile Dealers Ass'n, 64 F.3d 1389 (9th Cir. 1995).

423 Franks v. Prudential Health Care Plan, 164 F. Supp. 2d 865 (W.D. Tex. 2001) (consumer failed to state cause of action in complaint alleging this practice); Rogalla v. Christie Clinic, Prof'l Corp., 794 N.E.2d 384 (Ill. App. Ct. 2003) (HMO entitled to lien on patient's personal injury recovery for more than it paid for patient's share of monthly capitation, that is, flat fee, that HMO paid to provider). *But see* Swanson v. St. John's Reg'l Med. Ctr., 118 Cal. Rptr. 2d 325 (Ct. App. 2002) (California statute limits HMO liens to the amount actually paid to the provider), *overruled on other grounds by* Parnell v. Adventist Health Sys./West, 109 P.3d 69 (Cal. 2005).

424 *See, e.g.*, Flores v. Rawlings Co., L.L.C., 117 Haw. 153 (Haw. 2008).

425 *See, e.g.*, 75 Pa. Cons. Stat. § 1720 (prohibiting insurer subrogation in tort recoveries involving motor vehicles); Va. Code Ann. § 38.2-3405; Shelter Mut. Ins. Co. v. Kennedy, 347 Ark. 184, 60 S.W.3d 458 (Ark. 2001) (insurance company not entitled to subrogation when accident victim not made whole by

preemption by the Employee Retirement Income Security Act (ERISA).[426] ERISA in fact provides employee benefit plans with a cause of action to enforce subrogation provisions.[427]

---

tort settlement); Wheat v. Blue Cross of Cal., 2002 Cal. App. Unpub. LEXIS 448 (Cal. Ct. App. Apr. 29, 2002) (insurer not entitled to subrogation when accident victim not made whole, and its suit seeking reimbursement may amount to malicious prosecution).

Note that state law on this subject varies widely; when the Maryland supreme court in Riemer v. Columbia Med. Plan, 358 Md. 222, 747 A.2d 677 (2000) construed a state statute to forbid subrogation, the legislature immediately amended the statute to permit it.

426 29 U.S.C. § 1144(a); FMC Corp. v. Holliday, 498 U.S. 52, 111 S. Ct. 403, 112 L. Ed. 2d 356 (1990); Wirth v. Aetna U.S. Healthcare, 469 F.3d 305 (3d Cir. 2006); State Farm Mut. Ins. Co. v. Smith, 342 F. Supp. 2d 541 (W.D. Va. 2004) (ERISA preempts Virginia anti-subrogation statute, but only for health insurance plans that are self-funded); Franks v. Prudential Health Care Plan, 164 F. Supp. 2d 865 (W.D. Tex. 2001); Carpenter v. Wal-Mart Stores, Inc., 252 B.R. 905 (E.D. Va. 2000), *aff'd*, 2002 WL 1162277 (4th Cir. June 3, 2002) (unpublished). *But see* Singh v. Prudential Health Care Plan, Inc., 335 F.3d 278 (4th Cir. 2003) (Maryland law prohibiting subrogation was saved from preemption as regulation on insurance; Maryland law subsequently amended to permit subrogation); Bishop v. Burgard, 764 N.E.2d 24 (Ill. 2002) (ERISA does not preempt Illinois's common fund doctrine when ERISA plan seeks to enforce lien on personal injury proceeds, pursuant to subrogation clause in plan; lien reduced by plan's share of attorney fees).

427 Trustees of Teamsters Local Union No. 443 Health Services & Ins. Plan v. Papero, 485 F. Supp. 2d 67 (D. Conn. 2007) (employee benefit plan could proceed with ERISA claim against patient's personal injury attorney, because attorney may be a fiduciary under ERISA and thus liable to the plan for retaining tort recovery funds).

Chapter 11 Defending Consumers Against Collection by Federal Administrative Agencies

11.1 Congress Strengthens Federal Government's Debt Collection Powers

Throughout the 1980s and 1990s, Congress passed numerous laws to strengthen the tools available to the United States when it has a claim against a person. Many in Congress believed that this would help reduce the large budget deficits facing the federal government. Unfortunately much of the increased federal debt collection effort hit financially distressed and low-income households who had been the intended beneficiaries of federal student loan and housing programs and who did not have the resources to repay the claims of the United States, much less balance the federal budget. This chapter surveys the powers, the limitations on those powers, and the programs of the federal bureaucracies which may frequently pursue claims against individuals.

Federal agencies' collection efforts fall into three stages. First, the creditor agency will attempt to collect the claim through its own methods. Second, if a claim has been delinquent for more than 180 days, the creditor agency is to refer the claim to the U.S. Treasury Department, which coordinates centralized collection efforts. These two pre-litigation stages are governed primarily by the Federal Claims Collection Act, as amended by the Debt Collection Improvement Act,[1] and a host of regulations. These efforts can include intercepting the debtor's income tax refund, offsetting the debt against government payments due the debtor, reporting the debt to credit reporting agencies, administratively garnishing wages, offsetting the debt against a federal employee's salary, and hiring private collection agencies and collection attorneys. These first two stages are discussed in § 11.2, *infra*.

The third stage is litigation. Suits to collect federal claims are governed by the Federal Debt Collection Procedures Act[2] as well as the laws that govern nonfederal claims, for example, the Federal Rules of Civil Procedure. Litigation under the Federal Debt Collection Procedures Act is discussed in § 11.3, *infra*.

11.2 Federal Agencies' Non-Litigation Collection Methods

11.2.1 Overview of Federal Collection Laws and Regulations

11.2.1.1 Federal Collection Statutes

The extrajudicial collection of debts by United States administrative agencies is governed primarily by the Federal Claims Collection Act.[3] The Act mandates that federal agencies must attempt to collect overdue obligations, and permits agencies to settle, suspend, terminate collection activity on, or discharge claims when appropriate.

The Claims Collection Act was amended in October 1982, by the Debt Collection Act of 1982.[4] The Debt Collection Act toughened the debt collection and debt prevention procedures available to federal agencies. In particular, it permitted the release to commercial credit reporting agencies of obligors' names, addresses and amounts owing.[5] It also made IRS information about debtors' addresses available to agencies for collection purposes.[6] Later amendments allowed agencies to hire collection agencies and private collection attorneys,[7] and intercept consumers' federal tax refunds and other sums owed by the government to consumers.[8]

In 1996 Congress again strengthened the debt collection powers of federal agencies, in ways that weigh heavily on

1 31 U.S.C. §§ 3701–3720E; *see* § 11.2.1.1, *infra*; *see also* United States v. York, 909 F. Supp. 4, 7 n.1 (D.D.C. 1995) (HUD's administrative offset regulations under Claims Collection Act apply only when government has not obtained a judgment against the debtor).

2 28 U.S.C. §§ 3001–3308; *see* § 11.3, *infra*.

3 31 U.S.C. §§ 3711–3719.

4 Pub. L. No. 97-365, 96 Stat. 1749 (1982).

5 31 U.S.C. § 3711(e); *see* § 11.2.3, *infra*.

6 5 U.S.C. § 552a(b)(12), (m)(2); 26 U.S.C. § 6103(*l*)(3), (6), (8), (m)(2), (p)(4).

7 *See* 31 U.S.C. § 3718; *see* § 11.2.4, *infra*.

8 31 U.S.C. § 3720A; *see* § 11.2.4, *infra*.

some low-income households, by passing the Debt Collection Improvement Act of 1996.[9] This law amended the Claims Collection Act and other federal statutes to:

- Permit administrative offset against formerly exempt Social Security, Black Lung, and Railroad Retirement benefits.[10]
- Allow administrative wage garnishment of up to fifteen percent of disposable pay, "notwithstanding state law."[11] This procedure and its relation to federal wage garnishment limits are discussed in § 12.4.2.1, *infra*.
- Allow creditor agencies to disclose the identity of debtors and the existence of the debt, and require the Treasury Department to adopt regulations concerning the dissemination of information about delinquent debts owed to the government.[12] The Treasury Department initially published notices that it planned to issue proposed regulations on this topic,[13] but withdrew the matter from its docket in 2005.[14] The existing regulations do, however, require creditor agencies to implement procedures to report delinquent debts to credit bureaus.[15] They also allow delinquent debtors' addresses to be reported to other agencies and to collection agencies.[16]
- Deny federal loans, loan insurance, or guarantees, other than disaster loans, to debtors delinquent on federal non-tax claims. This restriction may be waived by an agency head as to an individual debtor or a class of claims.[17] It does not apply if the debt has been discharged in bankruptcy or is being challenged by a timely appeal.[18] It does apply, however, to debts for which the creditor agency has suspended or terminated collection.[19] The debtor can regain eligibility for federal loans, insurance, and guarantees by curing the delinquency or entering into a satisfactory written repayment agreement with the creditor agency.[20]
- Mandate a computer match to locate federal employees who owe debts to federal agencies, so that the debts can be offset against their earnings.[21]
- Increase oversight of agencies' debt collection performance, and provide incentives for more active pursuit of collections.[22]

Key provisions of these laws are reproduced in Appendix E, *infra*.

In addition to these general statutes authorizing federal collection efforts, there are often special statutes governing particular agencies' collections. Neither the Claims Collection Act nor the regulations under it supersede any other applicable statute, the common law, or contract term relating to collection procedure.[23]

11.2.1.2 Regulations Under the Claims Collection Act

The Claims Collection Act calls for the collection of debts to be carried out under guidelines promulgated jointly by the Attorney General and the Secretary of the Treasury.[24] These regulations (the joint regulations)[25] detail the procedures that all agencies must follow in their collection efforts. A second set of regulations sets requirements for administrative wage garnishment and specifies the steps the Treasury Department takes when agencies refer claims to it for centralized offset.[26] In addition, the Treasury Department has posted manuals and guides on-line for agencies to use when referring cases to the Department.[27]

The Claims Collection Act also requires individual creditor agencies to have their own regulations about collecting claims.[28] Virtually all agencies offering direct consumer loans, guaranteeing or insuring consumer loans, or administering benefits programs collect debts under the authority of the Federal Claims Collection Act and have regulations parallel to the joint regulations.[29]

---

9 Pub. L. No. 104-134, ch. 10, 110 Stat. 1321.
10 31 U.S.C. § 3716(c)(3)(A)(i); *see* § 11.2.8, *infra*.
11 31 U.S.C. § 3720D.
12 31 U.S.C. § 3720E.
13 66 Fed. Reg. 62,091 (Dec. 3, 2001).
14 70 Fed. Reg. 27,364 (May 16, 2005).
15 31 C.F.R. § 901.4; *see* § 11.2.3, *infra*.
16 31 C.F.R. § 901.11(b).
17 31 U.S.C. § 3720B.
18 31 C.F.R. § 285.13(d)(2)(ii), (iii).
19 31 C.F.R. § 285.13(d)(3).
20 31 C.F.R. § 285.13(e)(1)(iii), (iv).
21 5 U.S.C. § 5514(a)(1); *see* § 11.2.6, *infra*.
22 31 U.S.C. §§ 3719, 3720C.

23 31 C.F.R. §§ 900.1(c), 901.9(i); *see* Johnson v. All-State Constr., Inc., 329 F.3d 848 (Fed. Cir. 2003) (government retains common law right of setoff); McCall Stock Farms v. United States, 14 F.3d 1562 (Fed. Cir. 1993) (common law offset rights supplement statutory provisions); McBride Cotton & Cattle Corp. v. Veneman, 296 F. Supp. 2d 1125 (D. Ariz. 2003) (upholding broader Agriculture Dep't offset regulations as permissible under separate statute); United States v. York, 909 F. Supp. 4 (D.D.C. 1995), *rev'd on other grounds*, 112 F.3d 1218 (D.C. Cir. 1997); Brumley v. United States, 55 Fed. Cl. 431 (Fed. Cl. 2003); Boers v. United States, 44 Fed. Cl. 725 (Fed. Cl. 1999) (setoff of dairy indemnity payments against Farmer's Home Administration loan was available under either common law or Debt Collection Improvement Act), *aff'd*, 243 F.3d 561 (Fed. Cir. 2000).
24 31 U.S.C. §§ 3711(d)(2); *see also* 31 U.S.C. §§ 3711(g)(10), 3716(b), 3716(c)(B)(5), 3717(h), 3720A(d), 3720B(a) (other authority to adopt regulations).
25 31 C.F.R. pts. 900–904.
These rules superseded a set of rules formerly found at 4 C.F.R. pts. 101–105. *See* 65 Fed. Reg. 70,390 (Nov. 22, 2000).
26 31 C.F.R. pt. 285.
27 These items may be found at http://fms.treas.gov.
28 5 U.S.C. § 5514(b)(1); 31 U.S.C. § 3716(b); *see also* 31 C.F.R. § 285.5(d)(4).
29 *See* § 11.4, *infra* (review of selected agencies' rules).

11.2.1.3 Coverage

The Claims Collection Act is applicable to "claims" and "debts," which are defined as any amount of funds or property that has been determined by an appropriate official of the federal government to be owed to the United States.[30] The statute includes a non-exhaustive list of examples, including funds owed on loans made, insured, or guaranteed by the government, deficiency judgments, overpayments, fines, and penalties.[31] A criminal restitution order meets the definition of "claim."[32]

Most provisions of the Act do not apply to debts arising under the Internal Revenue Code or the tariff laws,[33] or (with some significant exceptions) to debts arising under the Social Security Act.[34]

11.2.2 The Federal Agency Must Make Proper Written Demand for Payment

Until 2000, the joint regulations required federal agencies, in most cases, to make three written demands for payment before taking further action against the debtor, other than charging interest.[35] That requirement has now been reduced to a single demand letter.[36] The demand letter must inform the debtor of the basis for the indebtedness, the debtor's right to seek review within the agency, the standards for imposing interest, penalties, or administrative costs, the date by which payment should be made to avoid late charges and enforced collection (usually thirty days from mailing), and the name, address, and phone number of a contact person or office within the agency.[37]

The joint regulations specify that agencies should take steps to insure that all demand letters are mailed on the same day they are dated,[38] thus insuring the consumer the maximum time to respond before the deadline. In addition, agencies are directed to respond promptly to communications from the debtor.[39] The agency can sue or take other action before sending a written demand when a statute of limitations is about to run or prompt action is necessary to protect the government's interest for other reasons.[40] Courts have held that the agency need not prove that the debtor actually received the notice as long as it was properly sent.[41]

Agencies must give debtors advance notice that litigation may be initiated.[42] Notice to the debtor is also required if the agency or the Treasury Department is going to offset the debt against a payment owed to the debtor.[43] These notices can be combined with the initial demand letter.[44]

---

30 31 U.S.C. § 3701(b)(1).

31 31 U.S.C. § 3701(b)(1)(A), (C), (F).

32 United States v. Harrison, 2007 WL 2332662 (N.D. Tex. Aug. 16, 2007).

33 31 U.S.C. § 3701(d)(1) and (3) make sections 3711(e) and 3716 to 3719 inapplicable to these debts. In addition, section 3720B (denial of federal loans) is inapplicable to tax debts by virtue of section 3720B(a); section 3720D (administrative wage garnishment) is applicable only to nontax debts by virtue of section 3720D(a); and section 3720E (dissemination of information about identity of delinquent debtors) is applicable only to nontax debts by virtue of section 3720E(a). *See also* 31 C.F.R. § 901.12(a) (making all the collection methods set forth by part 901 inapplicable to tax and tariff debts).

34 31 U.S.C. § 3701(d)(2) makes section 3711(e) and 3716 to 3719 inapplicable to debts arising under the Social Security Act, except as provided in 42 U.S.C. §§ 404(f) and 1383(b)(4). Those sections make 31 U.S.C. §§ 3711(f) (probably intended to refer to credit reporting under 31 U.S.C. § 2711(e), see section 31001(k) of Pub. L. No. 104-134, 110 Stat. 1341 (1996)), 3716 (administrative offset), 3717 (interest and penalties on claims), and 3718 (contracts for collection services), plus 5 U.S.C. § 5514 (offset against federal employee's salary) applicable to certain Social Security and SSI overpayments (those which were made after the beneficiary became eighteen years old and are not recoverable by other methods after the debtor stops receiving benefits). In addition, section 3720A (tax intercept) applies to OASDI overpayments if the overpaid individual is not currently receiving Title II benefits (*see* § 3720A(f)(1)). Sections 3720B (denial of federal loans), 3720D (administrative wage garnishment), and 3720E (dissemination of information regarding identity of debtors) are silent as to their application to debts arising under the Social Security Act. *See also* 31 C.F.R. § 901.12(a).

35 4 C.F.R. § 102.2(a), *superseded by* 31 C.F.R. pts. 900–904 (these new regulations were announced in 65 Fed. Reg. 70,390 (Nov. 22, 2000)).

36 31 C.F.R. § 901.2(a), *as adopted by* 65 Fed. Reg. 70,390 (Nov. 22, 2000) ("[g]enerally, one demand letter should suffice," although agencies have discretion to determine the number of demand letters).

37 31 C.F.R. § 901.2(b); *see also* 31 C.F.R. § 285.5(d)(6).

38 31 C.F.R. § 901.2(c).

39 31 C.F.R. § 901.2(e).

40 31 C.F.R. § 901.2(a); *see also* United States v. Golden Elevator, Inc., 868 F. Supp. 1063 (C.D. Ill. 1994) (due process did not require Small Business Administration to give debtor notice of possible administrative remedies or opportunity to exhaust administrative remedies before acceleration and foreclosure; debtor knew of right to accelerate from original contact and had not been "denied administrative consideration" having been given deferments, seasonal payments, and so forth).

41 Shabtai v. United States Dep't of Educ., 2003 WL 21983025 (S.D.N.Y. Aug. 20, 2003); Roth v. United States, 2003 WL 21730094 (D. Minn. July 22, 2003).

42 31 C.F.R. § 901.2(g).

43 31 C.F.R. §§ 285.5(d)(6), 901.3(b)(4); *see* §§ 11.2.6, 11.2.8.3, *infra*; *see also* Omegbu v. United States Dep't of Treasury, 118 Fed. Appx. 989 (7th Cir. 2004) (procedure for offsetting Social Security Disability Income (SSDI) for student loan satisfied due process; one letter to last known address, stating that debt would be referred for offset, and disclosing right to hearing; six years later, debtor approved for SSDI and informed that fifteen percent would be offset); *cf.* Setlech v. United States, 816 F. Supp. 161 (E.D.N.Y. 1993) (for tax refund intercept, notice mailed to last address known to Internal Revenue Service was sufficient even though it was not received by the debtor), *aff'd*, 17 F.3d 390 (2d Cir. 1993) (table).

44 31 C.F.R. §§ 901.2(g), 901.3(b)(4)(iv).

If the agency's demand letter provides insufficient detail, the debtor may want to make a Freedom of Information Act request to obtain information about the claimed debt.[45]

11.2.3 Release of Information to Credit Reporting Agencies

The Claims Collection Act authorizes federal agencies to disclose debtor information to credit reporting agencies.[46] This authority does not apply to tax debts, debts arising under the Social Security Act (other than certain overpayments), or debts for tariffs.[47] Information that may be released is limited to the name, address and Social Security number of the obligor, the amount, status, and history of the claim, and the agency involved.[48]

The agency must verify the validity of the claim prior to releasing information, and the agency must notify the affected individual both that a report will be made and that the individual has a right to administrative review of that action.[49] Obligors are entitled to notice sixty days before information is actually released to a credit reporting agency.[50] The federal agency can not contact a credit reporting agency at all if a repayment plan has been agreed upon or administrative review requested.[51]

An agency planning to release information to a credit reporting agency must establish procedures to update the reported information and to respond to requests from the consumer reporting agency for verification.[52] It must also get satisfactory assurances from the credit reporting agency that the agency is complying with the Fair Credit Reporting Act (FCRA)[53] and other applicable statutes concerning consumer credit information.[54]

If the debtor disputes the debt with the credit reporting agency, the credit reporting agency is required to ask the government agency to reinvestigate the claim.[55] If the government agency does not conduct a reasonable investigation and report back to the credit reporting agency,[56] the alleged debtor may bring an FCRA claim against the government agency.[57]

Prior to the 1982 amendments, agencies were required to comply with the Privacy Act of 1974[58] in making reports to credit reporting agencies. The 1982 amendments specifically excluded reports to credit reporting agencies from Privacy Act requirements.[59]

11.2.4 Contracts with Private Debt Collection Agencies and Collection Lawyers

The Claims Collection Act authorizes agencies to contract with private collection agencies and attorneys to collect debts,[60] except those arising under the Internal Revenue Code and the tariff laws, and certain claims arising under the Social Security Act.[61] Federal agencies can contract with private collection agencies to collect debts owed the federal agency,[62] but the federal agency can not relinquish control of the final determination of the claim.[63] The private collection service is bound by the Fair Debt Collection Practices Act and all other applicable federal and state laws and regulations relating to debt collection practices.[64] The use of

45 5 U.S.C. § 552.

46 31 U.S.C. § 3711(e); *see also* 31 C.F.R. § 901.4.

47 *Tax and tariffs*: 31 U.S.C. § 3701(d)(1) and (3) make section 3711(e) inapplicable to these debts.

Debts arising under Social Security Act: 31 U.S.C. § 3701(d)(2) makes section 3711(e) inapplicable to debts arising under the Social Security Act, except as provided in 42 U.S.C. §§ 404(f) and 1383(b)(4). Those sections make 31 U.S.C. §§ 3711(f) (probably intended to refer to credit reporting under 31 U.S.C. § 2711(e), see section 31001(k) of Pub. L. No. 104-134, 110 Stat. 1341 (1996)) applicable to certain Social Security and SSI overpayments (those which were made after the beneficiary became eighteen years old and are not recoverable by other methods after the debtor stops receiving benefits). *See also* 31 C.F.R. § 901.12(a); 45 C.F.R. § 30.16 (Dep't of Health and Human Services regulation concerning credit reporting); § 11.2.11.3, *infra*.

48 31 U.S.C. § 3711(e)(1)(F).

49 31 U.S.C. § 3711(e)(1)(B), (C).

50 31 U.S.C. § 3711(e)(1)(C).

51 31 U.S.C. § 3711(e)(1)(D).

52 31 U.S.C. § 3711(e)(1)(E).

53 15 U.S.C. § 1681.

54 31 U.S.C. § 3711(e)(1)(E)(iii).

55 15 U.S.C. § 1681i(a)(2).

56 15 U.S.C. § 1681s-2(b); *see also* 31 U.S.C. § 3711(e)(1)(E)(ii).

57 *See* Johnson v. United States Dep't of Defense, 2000 WL 33956225 (D. Minn. Oct. 17, 2000) (dismissing tort claims for failure to exhaust administrative remedies, but allowing FCRA claims to go forward). *See generally* National Consumer Law Center, Fair Credit Reporting §§ 2.3.5.6, 6.2.1, 6.10 (6th ed. 2006 and Supp.); National Consumer Law Center, Fair Debt Collection § 9.6 (6th ed. 2008).

The duties of 15 U.S.C. § 1681s-2(b) fall on any "person" that provides information to a credit reporting agency, and "person" is broadly defined at 15 U.S.C. § 1682a(f) with no exclusion for government agencies.

58 5 U.S.C. § 552a.

59 5 U.S.C. § 552a(b)(12), *as amended by* Pub. L. No. 97-365, § 2, 96 Stat. 1749 (1982).

60 31 U.S.C. § 3718.

61 31 U.S.C. § 3701(d).

62 31 U.S.C. § 3718; *see also* 31 C.F.R. § 901.5; Dep't of the Treasury, Fiscal Year 2006 Report to the Congress, U.S. Government Receivables and Debt Collection Activities of Federal Agencies 11–13 (July 2007), *available at* http://fms.treas.gov (reporting that, in FY 2006, $17.5 billion in federal debts were referred to private collectors, with total collections of $739.6 million).

63 31 U.S.C. § 3718(a)(1); *see also* 31 C.F.R. § 901.5(a)(1), (2).

64 31 U.S.C. § 3718(a)(2); *see also* 31 C.F.R. § 901.5(a)(3).

private collection agencies to collect tax debts is discussed in another manual in this series.[65]

The Attorney General is also authorized to hire private lawyers to collect government debts (for example, student loans, FHA loans).[66] The government agency to which the debt is owed must retain full control over the litigation and the decision to refer a debt.[67] The Act provides that private collection attorneys retained to collect government debts are debt collectors as defined by the Fair Debt Collection Practices Act notwithstanding the exemption in 15 U.S.C. § 1692a(6) for, among other things, officers and employees of the United States.[68] If a consumer asserts a counterclaim in a collection action brought by a private attorney for the government, it must be served on the Attorney General or the local United States attorney as well as on the private attorney.[69] Regulations for the program have been adopted, largely tracking the statute.[70]

11.2.5 Interest, Administrative Charges, and Penalties

The Debt Collection Act requires federal agencies to charge interest on overdue claims of at least the annual average rate the Treasury Department earns on bank accounts into which it deposits taxes and loan repayments that it collects.[71] The interest rate is to be a fixed rate, determined when the agency first notifies the debtor of the amount due.[72] If the contract, a repayment agreement, or another statute establishes a different rate, however, that rate should be imposed instead.[73]

Agencies are also directed to assess charges to cover certain administrative costs of handling overdue claims,[74] and penalties of up to six percent per year on claims more than ninety days late.[75] Penalties accrue from the date of the delinquency,[76] while interest accrues from the date the agency sends a notice.[77]

Interest and administrative charges may not be imposed if a claim is paid within thirty days after the interest first accrues, and this period may be extended by the agency.[78] Agencies must have regulations setting forth the circumstances under which they will suspend the imposition of interest and administrative charges while a review request is pending.[79]

The statute allows agencies to adopt regulations setting forth circumstances in which it is appropriate to waive collection of interest and charges.[80] The joint regulations allow waiver of interest, penalties, and administrative costs, in whole or in part, under the general standards for the compromise of claims,[81] or if it is determined that collection of the charges "is against equity and good conscience or is not in the best interest of the United States."[82]

Interest can not be calculated on interest, penalties, or administrative costs.[83] Interest is allowed only when the underlying claim is a contractual obligation to pay money.[84] The creditor agency must give the debtor a written notice explaining the charges.[85]

The requirements of the Debt Collection Act regarding interest, penalties, and administrative charges do not apply to claims arising under the Social Security Act (with the exception of certain overpayments),[86] the Internal Revenue

---

65 National Consumer Law Center, Fair Debt Collection § 9.10 (6th ed. 2008).

66 31 U.S.C. § 3718(b).

67 31 U.S.C. § 3718(b)(1)(B)(5).

68 31 U.S.C. § 3718(b)(1)(B)(6).

69 31 U.S.C. § 3718(b)(1)(B)(7).

70 28 C.F.R. §§ 11.1 to 11.12.

71 31 U.S.C. § 3717(a)(1); *see* 31 C.F.R. § 901.9.

72 31 U.S.C. § 3717(c); *see* Precision Pine & Timber, Inc. v. United States, 75 Fed. Cl. 80 (Fed. Cl. 2006).

73 31 U.S.C. § 3717(g)(1); 31 C.F.R. § 901.9(b)(2); *see* United States v. Hyundai Merchant Marine Co., 172 F.3d 1187, 1192 (9th Cir. 1999) (Debt Collection Act's interest and penalty provisions do not apply when other statute sets interest rate); United States v. Spann, 797 F. Supp. 980 (S.D. Fla. 1992) (government could not recover six percent interest on student loan because contract set rate at three percent); Westchester Fire Ins. Co. v. United States, 52 Fed. Cl. 567 (Fed. Cl. 2002) (awarding interest based on contractual clause rather than section 3717).

74 31 U.S.C. § 3711(g)(6); 31 C.F.R. §§ 901.1(f), 901.9(c); *see* United States v. A.R.A.Z., Inc., 2007 WL 2693668 (E.D.N.Y. Sept. 10, 2007) (finding authority for "debt management service" charge, but denying claim for it because government failed to justify amount).

75 31 C.F.R. § 901.9(c); *see also* 31 C.F.R. § 285.2(i) (adding fees for tax refund intercept to the debt).

76 31 C.F.R. § 901.9(d); *see* Am. Airlines, Inc. v. United States, 77 Fed. Cl. 672 (Fed. Cl. 2007).

77 31 U.S.C. § 3717(b); *see* Am. Airlines, Inc. v. United States, 77 Fed. Cl. 672 (Fed. Cl. 2007); *cf.* 31 C.F.R. § 901.9(b)(1) (interest accrues from date of delinquency "or as otherwise provided by law").

78 31 C.F.R. § 901.9(g).

79 31 C.F.R. § 901.9(h); *see also* § 11.2.10, *infra* (rules regarding suspension of collection activity).

80 31 U.S.C. § 3717(h).

81 *See* 31 C.F.R. pt. 902.

82 31 C.F.R. § 901.9(g); *see* Titan Wheel Corp. v. United States Envtl. Prot. Agency, 291 F. Supp. 2d 899, 933 (S.D. Iowa 2003) (upholding agency's discretion not to waive interest), *aff'd*, 113 Fed. Appx. 734 (8th Cir. 2004) (table).

83 31 U.S.C. § 3717(f); 31 C.F.R. § 901.9(b)(3).

The regulation creates an exception if the debtor has defaulted on a previous repayment agreement.

84 Thermalon Indus., Ltd. v. United States, 51 Fed. Cl. 464 (Fed. Cl. 2002).

85 31 C.F.R. § 901.9(a).

86 31 U.S.C. § 3701(d)(2) makes section 3717 inapplicable to debts arising under the Social Security Act, except as provided in 42 U.S.C. §§ 404(f) and 1383(b)(4). Those sections make section 3717 (interest and penalties on claims) applicable to certain Social Security and SSI overpayments (those which were made after the beneficiary became eighteen years old and are not recoverable by other methods after the debtor stops receiving benefits).

Code, or the tariff laws,[87] or to claims under contracts executed before October 25, 1982.[88] This latter exception may help debtors with old student loans.[89] For debts not governed by the statute, the government may have a common law right to claim interest.[90]

11.2.6 *Offset Against Federal Employee's Salary*

Federal agencies can collect on debts owed them by a federal employee through an offset against the employee's pay or other compensation.[91] Under a mandate in the 1996 Debt Collection Improvement Act, agencies refer debts to the Treasury Department, which conducts a centralized computer match to identify federal employees who owe debts to the federal government for the purpose of offsetting the debts against their earnings.[92] As of fiscal year 2006, the Treasury Department was processing offsets against salaries paid by the Agriculture, Defense, and Interior Departments, the General Services Administration, and the Postal Service, and was planning to add other agencies in future years.[93]

Salary offset is limited to fifteen percent of the employee's disposable income unless the employee agrees otherwise in writing.[94] Debts can be referred to the Treasury Department for centralized salary offset only within ten years after the agency's right of action accrues, except for judgment debts and as otherwise authorized by law.[95]

Agency employees subject to salary offset are entitled to notice and hearing.[96] The agency that holds the debt must give the employee at least a thirty-day advance written notice, stating the nature and amount of the debt, that the agency plans to use salary offset, that the employee may inspect and copy the agency's record of the debt, that the employee may obtain a review of the debt within the agency, and that the employee may enter into a written contract with the agency to repay the debt.[97] A timely request for a hearing stays collection actions.[98]

In addition, the agency that employs the debtor must give the debtor advance written notice of the date salary deductions will commence and of the amount of the deductions.[99] Another notice, stating the amount of the offset and the identity of the creditor agency, and providing a contact within the creditor agency, is required when the offset occurs, unless this information is included in the first notice.[100]

When employment ends before repayment is completed, an agency may offset the debt against any payments made by the agency of any nature.[101] The statute is not clear whether the fifteen percent limit still applies. The regulation takes the position that the fifteen-percent limitation on salary offset does not apply to final and lump sum payments made to employees leaving federal service.[102]

11.2.7 *Tax Refund Interception*

The federal government may intercept federal income tax refunds to offset a federal agency's claim against a taxpayer.[103] For example, a consumer entitled to a federal income tax refund because of over-withholding of taxes may have that refund intercepted and applied to an old student loan claim by the United States Department of Education, or to an old manufactured home loan claim by the United States Department of Housing and Urban Development.[104] Tax refunds may also be intercepted for past-due state income tax debts that are reported to the Treasury Department by the states.[105] Agencies can continue to use other

87 31 C.F.R. § 901.12(a). *But see* 42 U.S.C. §§ 404(f), 1383(b)(4) (making 31 U.S.C. § 3717 applicable to certain SSI and Title II overpayments).

88 31 U.S.C. § 3717(g)(2); *see* United States v. S. Cal. Edison Co., 300 F. Supp. 2d 964, 992 (E.D. Cal. 2004) (because case involved contract executed before Oct. 25, 1982, no costs are allowed).

89 *See* United States v. Burns, 1992 WL 247438 (S.D. Fla. Sept. 14, 1992) (declining to award costs because student loan debts arose in 1975 and 1977).

90 31 C.F.R. § 901.9(i); *see* Seaboard Lumber Co. v. United States, 48 Fed. Cl. 814 (Fed. Cl. 2001), *aff'd on other grounds*, 308 F.3d 1283 (Fed. Cir. 2002).

91 5 U.S.C. § 5514.

The regulations may be found at 31 C.F.R. § 285.7(d)(iv) and 5 C.F.R. §§ 550.1101 to 550.1109. The joint regulations are inapplicable to salary offset to the extent that they are inconsistent with these regulations. *See* 31 C.F.R. § 901.3(a)(2)(iv).

92 5 U.S.C. § 5514(a)(1); *see* § 11.2.1.1, *supra*.

93 Dep't of the Treasury, Fact Sheet, Delinquent Debt Collection, Fiscal Year 2006 (Mar. 7, 2007), *available at* http://fms.treas.gov; *see also* 41 C.F.R. §§ 105-56.024 to 105-56.033 (GSA regulation for offsets against its employees' salaries).

94 5 U.S.C. § 5514(a)(1).

95 31 C.F.R. § 285.7(d)(3)(ii); *see also* 31 U.S.C. § 3716(e)(1).

96 5 U.S.C. § 5514(a)(2).

97 5 U.S.C. § 5514(a)(2); 31 C.F.R. § 285.7(d)(3); 5 C.F.R. § 550.1104(d) (specifying details that agencies must include in their notices).

98 5 U.S.C. § 5514(a)(2); *see* Ramirez v. Dep't of the Army, 86 M.S.P.B. 211 (Merit Sys. Prot. Bd. 2000) (creditor agency can not deduct debt from retirement pay until it has completed hearing requested by debtor).

99 31 C.F.R. § 285.7(i).

100 31 C.F.R. § 285.7(i)(2).

101 5 U.S.C. § 5514(a)(1).

102 31 C.F.R. § 285.7(a)(6).

103 Authority to intercept tax refunds as a means of collecting debts owed to the federal government was added to the Federal Claims Collection Act, 31 U.S.C. § 3720A, and the Internal Revenue Code, 26 U.S.C. § 6402(d), by the Deficit Reduction Act, Pub. L. No. 98-369, § 2653, 98 Stat. 1153 (1984). *See also* 42 U.S.C. § 664 (directing the Dep't of Health and Human Services to notify the Dep't of the Treasury to intercept tax refund payments for past due support).

104 *See, e.g.*, Ingram v. Cuomo, 51 F. Supp. 2d 667 (M.D.N.C. 1999) (manufactured home loan).

105 26 U.S.C. § 6402(e); 31 C.F.R. § 285.8; *see* Dep't of the Treasury, Fiscal Year 2006 Report to the Congress, U.S. Gov-

collection methods, such as wage garnishment, even while the Treasury Department is intercepting a tax refund.[106] The best way for consumers to avoid a tax intercept is to adjust their income tax withholding, so that there is no refund to intercept.

Intercept is only allowed for debts that are referred to the Treasury Department for offset within ten years after the agency's right of action accrues, except for judgment debts or as otherwise allowed by law.[107] Intercept is not allowed as a means of collecting Social Security and SSI overpayments from people who are still receiving Social Security benefits.[108]

Tax refund interception is governed not by the general administrative offset regulations,[109] but by a separate set of tax intercept regulations.[110] Agencies participating in the tax intercept program must also adopt their own regulations.[111]

The statute[112] provides that, before referring a debt to the Treasury Department for tax intercept, the creditor agency must:

- Notify the borrower that the agency intends to take such action;[113]
- Give the consumer at least sixty days to present evidence that the debt is not past due or legally enforceable;[114]
- Consider any evidence and determine that an amount is past due and legally enforceable;[115]
- Satisfy relevant Treasury Department regulations;[116] and
- Certify to the Treasury Department that the agency has made reasonable efforts to obtain payment of the debt.[117]

Treasury Department regulations also require that, prior to intercept, the debtor be given the opportunity to enter into a repayment agreement[118] and that, in most cases, the creditor agency disclose the debt to a credit reporting agency before referring the debt to the IRS for interception.[119]

A parallel section of the Internal Revenue Code requires the Internal Revenue Service (IRS) to intercept the tax refund check upon notice from any federal agency.[120] The IRS is required to remit the intercepted amount to the creditor agency and to send notification of the offset to the taxpayer.[121] Unlike the notice sent by the creditor agency, this notice must be sent at the time of each intercept.[122] The notice must advise any non-debtor spouse who filed a joint tax return with the debtor of the steps to take to secure his or her proper share of the tax refund.[123]

If the taxpayer owes more than one debt, the tax refund will be applied against the debts in the order in which they accrued.[124] Courts have disagreed about whether the government can proceed with a setoff to collect a dischargeable debt when the debtor files bankruptcy and claims the tax refund as exempt.[125] The taxpayer whose refund has been

---

ernment Receivables and Debt Collection Activities of Federal Agencies 14, 16 (July 2007), *available at* http://fms.treas.gov (reporting that, in FY 2006, federal tax intercepts collected $216 million in state income taxes, and that thirty-seven states and territories, plus the District of Columbia, are participating).

106 31 C.F.R. § 285.2(b)(5).

107 31 C.F.R. § 285.2(d)(1)(ii); *see also* 31 U.S.C. § 3716(e)(1).

108 31 U.S.C. §§ 3701(d)(2), 3720A(f); *see also* 31 C.F.R. § 285.2(b)(4), (d)(1)(v).

Additional restrictions imposed by Social Security statutes are that the overpayment must have occurred after the beneficiary reached age eighteen and the debt must not be recoverable by other means. 42 U.S.C. §§ 404(f), 1383(b).

109 *See* 31 C.F.R. § 901.3(a)(iii) (general administrative offset regulation inapplicable to debts arising under or payments made under Internal Revenue Code).

110 31 C.F.R. § 285.2.

111 31 C.F.R. § 285.2(c); 26 C.F.R. § 301.6402-6(b); *see* United States Dep't of Agric. v. Huff (*In re* Huff), 343 B.R. 136, 142 (W.D. Pa. 2006).

112 31 U.S.C. § 3720A(b).

113 *See* 31 C.F.R. § 285.2(d)(1)(iii)(B) (requiring "reasonable attempt" to give notice); *see also In re* Shortt, 277 B.R. 683 (Bankr. N.D. Tex. 2002) (notice of intent to set off tax refund, sent to debtors' last known address, sufficient even though never received; debtors had not notified creditor of address change); *cf.* United States Dep't of Agric. v. Huff (*In re* Huff), 343 B.R. 136 (W.D. Pa. 2006) (creditor agency need only give notice once, before initial submission of debt to Treasury Department, not every year before taxes are intercepted).

114 31 C.F.R. § 285.2(d)(1)(iii)(C).

115 *See, e.g.*, Ingram v. Cuomo, 51 F. Supp. 2d 667 (M.D.N.C. 1999) (deficiency due after manufactured home repossession and sale was "past due and legally enforceable" even though it had not been reduced to judgment); Abbe v. Bochert, 2001 Ohio App. LEXIS 2618 (Ohio Ct. App. June 13, 2001) (if obligor is up-to-date on payments of current support and court-ordered installments toward arrearage, and no amount is past due, then despite existence of debt tax refund offset is not authorized, but *pro se* litigant failed to preserve issue for review).

116 26 C.F.R. § 301.6402-6.

117 31 U.S.C. § 3720A(b)(5); 31 C.F.R. § 285.2(d)(iii).

118 31 C.F.R. § 285.2(d)(1)(iii)(D).

119 26 C.F.R § 301.6402-6(c)(6).

120 26 U.S.C. § 6402(d) (interception of non-child support claims); 26 U.S.C. § 6402(c) (offset of past-due support).

121 26 U.S.C. § 6402(d)(1)(C); 26 C.F.R. § 301.6402-6(h); 31 C.F.R. § 285.2(f).

122 26 C.F.R. § 301.6402-6(h)(1) (requiring notice of amount and date of offset); *see* United States Dep't of Agric. v. Huff (*In re* Huff), 343 B.R. 136 (W.D. Pa. 2006).

123 31 C.F.R. § 285.2(f); *see* Ingram v. Cuomo, 51 F. Supp. 2d 667 (M.D.N.C. 1999) (spouse's claim to portion of refund is not defense to creditor agency's claim, but should be asserted through Internal Revenue Service procedures).

124 26 U.S.C. § 6402(d)(2).

125 *In re* Beaucage, 342 B.R. 408 (D. Mass. 2006) (set-off allowed); United States v. Killen (*In re* Killen), 249 B.R. 585 (D. Conn. 2000) (no offset of tax refund for Dep't of Hous. & Urban Dev. loan when tax refund claimed exempt); *In re* Pigott, 330 B.R. 797 (Bankr. S.D. Ala. 2005) (setoff allowed); *In re* Lyle, 324 B.R. 128 (Bankr. N.D. Cal. 2005) (tax refund never became part of child support obligor's bankruptcy estate; obligor had no right to receive refund because statute required IRS to reduce it by amount of support debt before sending it out); *In re* Bourne, 262 B.R. 745 (Bankr. E.D. Tenn. 2001) (setoff allowed); Stewart

intercepted is prohibited from suing the IRS over the tax intercept; recourse is limited to action against the federal agency requesting the offset.[126]

In *Sorenson v. Secretary of the Treasury of the United States*,[127] the United States Supreme Court held that the earned income credit portion of a federal tax refund is subject to interception for overdue child support, along with the rest of the refund. The Court allowed the interception despite the argument that the earned income tax credit was more like a government benefit than a tax overpayment. Consumers can avoid offset of the earned income tax credit, however, by using it to decrease the amount of federal income tax withheld from earnings by the employer, or having it paid bit-by-bit throughout the year as part of the consumer's paycheck, so that it will not form part of a tax refund that would be subject to intercept.[128]

11.2.8 Administrative Offset Against Federal Benefits and Other Payments

11.2.8.1 General

The Debt Collection Improvement Act significantly expanded federal agencies' ability to offset non-tax debts against federal benefits and other payments due the debtor.[129] Most administrative offsets are handled centrally by the Treasury Department, but individual agencies also have authority to make offsets,[130] including *ad hoc* non-centralized offsets.[131] In addition, a number of decisions recognize a common law right of offset on the part of federal agencies.[132] Offset is only allowed for claims that have been outstanding for ten years or less.[133]

The Treasury Department may charge a fee for the cost of the offset procedure, which may be added to the debt.[134] The statute allows the Secretary of the Treasury to enter into reciprocal agreements with states so that debts owed to states can also be offset against federal payments.[135]

11.2.8.2 Benefits Against Which Debts Can Be Offset

While debts can be offset against any type of federal payment, such as payments under federal contracts, the effect of the offset program on benefit payments is of most concern to low-income debtors.[136] Debts can not be offset

v. Army & Air Force Exch. Serv., 253 B.R. 51 (Bankr. E.D. Ark. 2000) (no violation of automatic stay to hold tax refund pending determination of right to setoff); *see also* United States v. Luongo, 259 F.3d 323 (5th Cir. 2001) (IRS may set off tax refund against earlier tax liability, even though old debt has been discharged in bankruptcy and debtor claimed refund as exempt). *See generally* National Consumer Law Center, Consumer Bankruptcy Law and Practice §§ 9.4.3, 10.4.2.6.4.3 (8th ed. 2006 and Supp.).

126 26 U.S.C. § 6402(f); 26 C.F.R. § 301.6402-6(*l*); 31 C.F.R. § 285.2(j); *see* Greenland v. Van Ru Credit Corp., 2006 WL 2884458 (W.D. Mich. Oct. 10, 2006) (granting Treasury Department's motion to dismiss); *In re* Cannon, 2005 WL 3278003 (Bankr. E.D. Ark. Oct. 31, 2005) (dismissing claim based on interception of tax refund against Internal Revenue Service, but allowing debtor to amend to state claim against creditor agency).

127 475 U.S. 851, 106 S. Ct. 1600, 89 L. Ed. 2d 855 (1986); *see also* Bosarge v. United States Dep't of Educ., 5 F.3d 1414 (11th Cir. 1993) (refusing to create a "public policy exception" to bar intercept of refunds consisting of earned income credit to repay student loan); *In re* Allen, 266 B.R. 713 (Bankr. N.D. Iowa 2001) (earned income credit may be intercepted for debts owed to HUD and United States Dep't of Agric., even though exempt public benefit under Iowa law; state exemptions not applicable to tax refund intercepts).

128 *See* Internal Revenue Serv., Employer's Tax Guide, Circular E.
The employee needs to fill out a W-5 form called the "Earned Income Credit Advance Payment Certificate" to get advance payment of the earned income credit.

129 31 U.S.C. § 3716.

130 31 C.F.R. § 901.3(b)(4)(iii)(C), (c).

131 31 C.F.R. § 901.3(c); *see* § 11.2.8.3, *infra*.

132 Johnson v. All-State Constr., Inc., 329 F.3d 848 (Fed. Cir. 2003) (government retains common law right of setoff); Amoco Production Co. v. Fry, 118 F.3d 812 (D.C. Cir. 1997) (government has common law offset rights); McCall Stock Farms v. United States, 14 F.3d 1562 (Fed. Cir. 1993) (common law offset rights supplement statutory provisions); United States v. York, 909 F. Supp. 4 (D.D.C. 1995), *rev'd on other grounds*, 112 F.3d 1218 (D.C. Cir. 1997); Brumley v. United States, 55 Fed. Cl. 431 (Fed. Cl. 2003); Boers v. United States, 44 Fed. Cl. 725 (Fed. Cl. 1999) (setoff of dairy indemnity payments against Farmer's Home Administration loan was available under either common law or Debt Collection Improvement Act), *aff'd*, 243 F.3d 561 (Fed. Cir. 2000).

133 31 U.S.C. § 3716(e)(1); *see* Lewis v. United States Dep't of Agric., 245 Fed. Appx. 330 (5th Cir. 2007) (when agency has not accelerated debt, ten-year period runs from date each unpaid installment became due); Seward v. United States Dep't of Agric., 229 F. Supp. 2d 557, 569, 570 (S.D. Miss. 2002) (interpreting debt as "outstanding" at least from the point it became delinquent); *see also* Brumley v. United States, 55 Fed. Cl. 431 (Fed. Cl. 2003) (discussing government's argument that partial payment extends the ten-year period, but deciding case on other grounds because a separate statute allowed setoff without regard to length of time debt was outstanding); § 11.2.11.2, *infra*, (discussion of the ten-year limitation in the context of student loan collections).

134 31 C.F.R. § 285.4(g).

135 31 U.S.C. § 3716(h)(1); *see* 31 C.F.R. § 285.6, *adopted by* 72 Fed. Reg. 1283 (Jan. 11, 2007) (interim rules for pilot project to use administrative offset against federal non-tax payments to collect delinquent debts owed to states); *Hearing Before the Permanent Subcomm. on Investigations of the Senate Homeland Security & Gov't Affairs Comm.*, 110th Cong. (Nov. 14, 2007) (statement of Comm'r Kenneth R. Papaj, Fin. Mgmt. Serv., U.S. Dep't of the Treasury), *available at* www.treas.gov/news/reports/testimony-nov14-2007.html (reporting on reciprocal agreements with New Jersey and Maryland as part of pilot program).

136 Offset against benefit payments is governed by 31 C.F.R.

against federally insured student loan payments and other payments made by the Department of Education under Title IV of the Higher Education Assistance Act,[137] veterans benefits, benefits under Part C of the Black Lung Act, or "tier 2" Railroad Retirement benefits.[138] The Secretary of the Treasury also has general authority to exempt any means-tested payments from offset when so requested by the agency administering the program, and may also exempt other benefits if offset would substantially interfere with or defeat the purposes of the program.[139]

Administrative offset is allowed against Social Security benefits, benefits under Part B of the Black Lung Act, and some Railroad Retirement benefits, notwithstanding the general protection from assignment and execution that these benefits enjoy.[140] Offset against these benefits is limited to fifteen percent of the "monthly covered benefit payment."[141] Further, $9000 per year ($750 per month) is exempt.[142] In computing whether any portion of benefits is available for offset, amounts already being deducted to repay overpayments are not counted as received by the debtor.[143] The amount of Social Security benefits available for offset is also reduced by any Medicare insurance premiums that are deducted from the debtor's Social Security check.[144] Thus, if a debtor's $850 monthly Social Security benefit amount is reduced by a $45 monthly Medicare premium and a $50 monthly deduction to repay an overpayment, leaving the debtor with a $755 monthly check, only the amount in excess of $750—in this example, $5—will be available for offset.

Under the statute, the $9000 annual exemption figure is to be reduced by the amount of any federal benefits the debtor receives during the same year that are not subject to offset.[145] Thus, if a debtor received $5000 in veterans benefits, which are not subject to offset, plus $7000 in Social Security benefits, the $5000 in veterans benefits would be subtracted from the $9000 exemption, leaving only a $4000 exemption to be applied to the Social Security benefits. The Treasury Department has, however, deferred implementation of this provision because of its complexity.[146]

Some courts have allowed setoff against an Equal Access to Justice Act (EAJA) fee award that was granted for the debtor's attorney's work on the debtor's Social Security disability benefits case.[147] The more sensible view is that, because EAJA fees are intended to compensate the claimant's attorney and not to generate income for the claimant, they can not be offset to collect debts owed by the claimant, but a decision taking this position[148] was abrogated by the Tenth Circuit.[149] That decision, however, left open the question whether the attorney might have a lien on the EAJA award that would take priority over the offset.[150]

11.2.8.3 Offset Procedures

There are a number of regulations regarding standards and procedures for administrative offset. The most extensive are the joint regulations,[151] which focus on the steps creditor agencies must take prior to offset, and a set of Treasury Department regulations that govern its implementation of centralized administrative offset.[152] In addition, agencies are required to adopt their own regulations before they collect claims by administrative offset.[153] Many agencies, such as the Department of Housing and Urban Development (HUD) and the Department of Veterans Affairs (VA), have promulgated their own regulations.[154]

Federal agencies are required to refer debts over 180 days delinquent to the Secretary of the Treasury in order to pursue centralized administrative offset.[155] Before submitting the debt to the Treasury Department for offset, the creditor agency must give the debtor notice of the claim, an opportunity to inspect and copy the relevant records, an opportu-

§ 285.4. Offset against other federal payments is governed by 31 C.F.R. § 285.5.

137 31 U.S.C. § 3716(c)(1)(C).

138 See 63 Fed. Reg. 44,986 (Aug. 21, 1998), which lists these benefit programs as not subject to offset. *Cf.* 31 U.S.C. § 3716(c)(3)(A)(i) (allowing offset against payments due under Part B of Black Lung Benefits Act and Railroad Retirement benefits other than tier 2 benefits). The *Federal Register* also lists SSI benefits as not subject to offset, although 31 U.S.C. § 3716(c)(3) expressly overrides 42 U.S.C. § 1383(d)(1), which protects SSI benefits. At current benefit levels, SSI benefits will always fall below the $9000 threshold for offset. Veterans' benefits are protected from offset by 38 U.S.C. §§ 5301 and 5314 except for debts arising from veterans' benefit overpayments.

139 31 U.S.C. § 3716(c)(3)(B); 31 C.F.R. § 901.3(b)(6).

140 31 U.S.C. § 3716(c)(3)(a).

141 31 C.F.R. § 285.4(e)(1)(ii); *see also* 31 C.F.R. § 285.4(b) (defining "monthly covered benefit payment" as a "covered benefit payment payable to a payee on a recurring basis at monthly intervals that is not expressly limited in duration, at the time the first payment is made, to a period of less than 12 months").

142 31 U.S.C. § 3716(C)(3)(a)(ii).

143 31 U.S.C. § 3716(C)(3)(a)(ii).

144 31 C.F.R. § 285.4(b) (definition of "covered benefit payment"); *see also* Section Analysis (b), 63 Fed. Reg. 44,986, 44,987 (Aug. 21, 1998).

145 31 U.S.C. § 3716(c)(3)(A)(ii)(I).

146 63 Fed. Reg. 44,986, 44,987 (Aug. 21, 1998).

147 Manning v. Astrue, 2007 WL 4443228 (10th Cir. Dec. 20, 2007); McCarty v. Astrue, 505 F. Supp. 2d 624 (N.D. Cal. 2007); Reeves v. Barnhart, 473 F. Supp. 2d 1173 (M.D. Ala. 2007); Dewey v. Astrue, 2007 WL 2013599 (D. Kan. July 9, 2007).

148 Dixon-Townsell v. Barnhart, 445 F. Supp. 2d 1283 (N.D. Okla. 2006).

149 Manning v. Astrue, 2007 WL 4443228 (10th Cir. Dec. 20, 2007).

150 *Id.* at *3 n.3.

151 31 C.F.R. § 901.3.

152 31 C.F.R. pt. 285.

153 31 U.S.C. § 3716(b).

154 *See* § 11.2.11.4, *infra*.

155 31 C.F.R. §§ 285.12(c), (d), 901.3(b)(1).

nity for administrative review, and an opportunity to enter into a payment agreement.[156] If an employee requests a review of the debt and a question of credibility or veracity is raised, the joint regulations provide for an oral hearing.[157] When an oral hearing is not required, the agency must allow the debtor a "paper hearing," that is, a review of the written record.[158]

Once the claim has been submitted to the Treasury Department but before offset occurs, the disbursing official must give the debtor a second notice stating the date the offset will begin and other information.[159] A third notice, with similar information, is required at the time of the offset.[160] A debtor who is unsure about how to contact the creditor agency can get contact information by calling the Treasury Offset Program Call Center at (800) 304-3107.

Administrative offsets must be implemented in a manner that meets due process requirements.[161] Agencies are required to establish procedures for providing the debtor with appropriate procedural protections.[162] However, agencies can also conduct their own *ad hoc* offsets, without going through the Treasury Department,[163] and in exigent circumstances can do so without giving notice or providing a prior opportunity for a review hearing.[164]

11.2.8.4 Defenses to Offsets

A consumer may be able to attack a tax intercept or other administrative offset when the statutory and regulatory preconditions to intercept have not been met. The joint regulations provide that "the failure of an agency to comply with the provisions of this chapter shall not be available as a defense to any debtor."[165] However, this regulation can be interpreted to mean that failure to comply with the regulations is not a defense to the underlying debt, but can still be a basis for quashing the particular collection method.[166] Even if the regulation is interpreted to bar raising noncompliance with the joint regulations as a defense to the offset itself, it should be remembered that many agencies have their own regulations about offset procedures. Failure of the creditor agency to follow its own regulations may be a defense.[167] In addition, many of the steps required by the

---

156 31 U.S.C. § 3716(a); *see* Frew v. Van Ru Credit Corp., 2006 WL 2261624 (E.D. Pa. Aug. 7, 2006) (remanding case to agency because of failure to give debtor hearing she requested); Christensen v. United States, 2006 WL 744296 (W.D. Mo. Mar. 23, 2006) (denying government's motion for summary judgment when notice was deficient in that it did not say that debt would be collected by way of administrative offset); § 11.2.2, *supra*; *see also* 31 C.F.R. § 901.3(b)(4)(ii), (e).

157 31 C.F.R. § 901.3(e).

158 31 C.F.R. § 901.3(e).

159 31 C.F.R. § 285.4(f)(1).

160 31 C.F.R. § 285.4(f)(2); *see also* 31 C.F.R. § 901.3(b)(3).

161 *See* Allison v. Madigan, 951 F.2d 869 (8th Cir. 1991) (upholding Farmer's Home Administration 1990 regulations for administrative offset of farmer loans against due process challenge); Old Republic Ins. Co. v. Fed. Crop Ins. Corp., 947 F.2d 269 (7th Cir. 1991) (agency's informal hearing procedures afforded debtor due process); Moseanko v. Dockter, 944 F.2d 418 (8th Cir. 1991) (describing history of due process litigation regarding setoff against farmer subsidies and allowances); McBride Cotton & Cattle Corp. v. Veneman, 296 F. Supp. 2d 1125 (D. Ariz. 2003) (upholding offset procedures even though only individual debtors, not corporate debtors, received notice and opportunity to object); United States v. Golden Elevator, Inc., 868 F. Supp. 1063 (C.D. Ill. 1994) (due process did not require Small Business Administration to give debtor notice of possible administrative remedies or opportunity to exhaust administrative remedies before acceleration and foreclosure; debtor knew of right to accelerate from original contact and had not been "denied administrative consideration" having been given deferments, seasonal payments, and so forth); Glover v. Brady, 1994 U.S. Dist. LEXIS 13211 (S.D.N.Y. Sept. 13, 1994) (manner of giving notice of setoff meets due process requirements if it is reasonably calculated to provide actual notice); Setlech v. United States, 816 F. Supp. 161 (E.D.N.Y. 1993) (reasonable efforts to give pre-offset notice satisfy due process requirements), *aff'd*, 17 F.3d 390 (2d Cir. 1993) (table); Atwater v. Roudebush, 452 F. Supp. 622 (N.D. Ill. 1976) (government's informal conference with debtor before setting off FHA debt against his final salary check did not meet due process requirements); *see also* Omegbu v. United States Dep't of Treasury, 118 Fed. Appx. 989 (7th Cir. 2004) (procedure for offsetting Social Security disability benefits for student loan satisfied due process; one letter to last known address, stating that debt would be referred for offset, and disclosing right to hearing; six years later, debtor approved for SSDI and informed that fifteen percent would be offset); McCarty v. Astrue, 505 F. Supp. 2d 624 (N.D. Cal. 2007) (agency's offset notice satisfied due process); Sibley v. Diversified Collection Services, Inc., 1997 U.S. Dist. LEXIS 23583 (N.D. Tex. June 10, 1997) (failure to offer borrowers an in-person hearing and failure to notify them of several possible defenses to administrative wage garnishment did not deny them due process); Wagner v. Duffy, 700 F. Supp. 935 (N.D. Ill. 1988) (state procedure for intercept of state and federal income tax refunds to enforce support orders violated due process notice requirements by failing to give unsophisticated defendants notice of common defenses); Knisky v. Bowman, 656 F. Supp. 1540 (W.D. Mich. 1987) (state tax intercept procedure not violative of due process); § 12.7.4, *infra*.

162 31 C.F.R. § 901.3(b)(4), (5).

163 31 C.F.R. § 901.3(c).

164 31 C.F.R. § 901.3(b)(4)(iii)(C).

165 31 C.F.R. § 900.8; *see In re* Zandford, 2006 WL 3533230 (Bankr. D. Del. Nov. 27, 2006) (agency's failure to refer debt to Treasury Dep't is not a defense to the debt).

166 *See* Ramirez v. Dep't of the Army, 86 M.S.P.B. 211 (Merit Sys. Prot. Bd. 2000) (creditor agency can not deduct debt from retirement pay until it has complied with its own regulations by completing hearing requested by debtor); *cf. In re* Zandford, 2006 WL 2036990 (Bankr. D. Del. July 18, 2006) (agency's failure to refer debt to Treasury Department within 180 days was not defense to claim), *reconsideration denied*, 2006 WL 3533230 (Bankr. D. Del. Nov. 27, 2006) (elaborating on reasons).

167 *See* Ramirez v. Dep't of the Army, 86 M.S.P.B. 211 (Merit Sys. Prot. Bd. 2000). *But cf.* Brannum v. Gaddy, 2003 WL 252135 (D.C. Cir. Feb. 3, 2003) (agency's failure to follow statutory notice requirements exactly not a defense, when debtor received actual notice); Lewis v. Glickman, 104 F. Supp. 2d 1311 (D.

joint regulations are duplicated in the statute, and failure to follow the steps that the statute requires before offset should be a defense to the offset.

The regulations state that the failure of a benefits recipient to receive the notices required before and at the time of the offset does not affect the validity of the offset of benefits.[168] The regulations also take the position that a disbursing agency's failure to give notice of offset against a recurring payment does not affect the validity of the offset.[169] These positions seem to conflict with due process and may be attacked on those grounds. Further, to the extent that the regulations set forth due process requirements, failure to comply with them or to follow other procedures that would afford due process would be a defense to the offset.[170]

Another potential defense is that the debt is not in fact past due[171] or legally enforceable.[172] For example, the debtor might be current on payments, the debt may have been discharged in bankruptcy, the government may be estopped by its conduct from enforcing the debt, the agency may have failed to credit the debtor's payments, or the debt may not have been properly assigned from a private party to the government.[173] Under the statutory scheme, these claims should be raised through the creditor agency's appeal system when the creditor agency notifies the debtor that it intends to implement an offset or refer the claim to the Treasury Department for centralized offset.

11.2.9 Installment Plans and Other Compromises

Installment repayment plans are specifically authorized, if the debtor documents an inability to pay in a lump sum.[174] The amounts and schedule of payments should bear a reasonable relation to the size of the debt and the debtor's ability to pay.[175] The regulations require that installment agreements provide for payment in full within three years or less whenever possible.[176]

In addition, the joint regulations establish specific procedures for federal agencies to compromise claims.[177] A compromise of a debt in excess of $100,000 must be approved by the Justice Department.[178] Any compromise reached must have some relationship to anticipated possible recovery through further administrative or judicial proceedings.

Agencies may compromise a debt if the debtor is unable to pay the full amount in a reasonable time or the government is unable to collect the debt in full within a reasonable time by enforced collection proceedings.[179] In determining whether the debtor is unable to pay, the agency must verify the debtor's financial circumstances through a sworn financial statement and a credit report and must consider the debtor's health, age, present and potential income, assets, and prospects.[180]

Claims may be also be compromised when the cost of collection does not justify the enforced collection of the full amount of the debt,[181] or if there are significant doubts about the agency's chances of winning a lawsuit.[182] Statutory penalties, forfeitures, or claims normally imposed "as an aid to enforcement and to compel compliance" may also be compromised if the ends of enforcement and compliance are served by the compromise.[183]

Kan. 2000) (flawed preliminary hearing not prejudicial when debtor subsequently had full evidentiary hearing and administrative appeal; agency's violation of own rule concerning stay not prejudicial when its right to offset was ultimately upheld), *aff'd*, 2002 U.S. App. LEXIS 13269 (10th Cir. July 3, 2002).

168 31 C.F.R. § 285.4(f)(3).

169 31 C.F.R. § 285.5(g)(1).

170 *See* § 11.2.8.3, *supra*.

171 31 U.S.C. § 3716(c)(6); 31 C.F.R. § 901.3(b); *see* Abbe v. Bochert, 2001 Ohio App. LEXIS 2618 (Ohio Ct. App. June 13, 2001) (if obligor up-to-date on payments of current support and court-ordered installments toward arrearage, and no amount is past due, then despite existence of debt tax refund offset can not be authorized, but *pro se* litigant failed to preserve issue for review); *see also* Davis v. North Carolina Dep't of Human Res., 505 S.E.2d 77 (N.C. 1998) (interception of federal tax refund was improper when father was current on payments ordered by the court following adjudication of paternity; intercept would be allowed if department obtained opinion of Attorney General that the court-ordered support plan was inadequate for collection of the arrears). *But cf.* Ingram v. Cuomo, 51 F. Supp. 2d 667 (M.D.N.C. 1999) (deficiency due after manufactured home repossession and sale was "past due and legally enforceable" even though it had not been reduced to judgment).

172 Seward v. United States Dep't of Agric., 229 F. Supp. 2d 557 (S.D. Miss. 2002) (Dep't of Agriculture equitably estopped from using offset to collect on farm loan); *In re* Norton, Clearinghouse No. 51,290 (United States Dep't of Hous. & Urban Dev. Bd. of Contract Appeals 1996) (HUDBCA No. 94-A-NY-S732) (lender's failure to give notice of private sale of manufactured home to debtor at last known address barred deficiency claim and thus tax intercept and entitled consumer to U.C.C. § 9-507 damages from HUD). *But cf.* Ingram v. Cuomo, 51 F. Supp. 2d 667 (M.D.N.C. 1999) (claim need not have been reduced to judgment in order to be "past due and legally enforceable"); Blake v. Cisneros, 837 F. Supp. 834 (S.D. Tex. 1993) (divorce court order did not release debtor, as divorce courts do not have jurisdiction to interfere with creditor's right to collect from either divorcing party).

173 *See, e.g.*, National Consumer Law Center, Student Loan Law (3d ed. 2006 and Supp.).

174 31 C.F.R. § 901.8(a).

175 31 C.F.R. § 901.8(b).

176 31 C.F.R. § 901.8(b).

177 31 C.F.R. pt. 902; *see also* 31 U.S.C. § 3711(a)(2).

If the principal amount of the debt exceeds $100,000 (or such other amount as the Attorney General may direct), the authority to accept a compromise rests with the Attorney General. 31 C.F.R. § 902.1(b).

178 31 C.F.R. § 902.1.

179 31 C.F.R. § 902.2(a)(1), (2).

180 31 C.F.R. § 902.2(b), (c), (g).

181 31 C.F.R. § 902.2(a)(3), (e).

182 31 C.F.R. § 902.2(a)(4), (d).

183 31 C.F.R. § 902.3; *see also* 31 C.F.R. § 901.9(g).

11.2.10 Suspension, Termination, and Discharge of Claims

The former joint regulations allowed agencies to forego offset in light of the debtor's circumstances, or if offset would substantially interfere with or defeat the purposes of the program authorizing the payments against which offset was contemplated.[184] The revised regulations adopted in 2000 do not contain this provision. The statute and the revised regulations do, however, allow for suspension or termination of collection activity or discharge of the indebtedness in certain circumstances.[185]

An agency has authority to suspend collection activity on a debt when the it can not locate the debtor, the debtor's financial condition is expected to improve, or the debtor has requested waiver or review of the debt.[186] In determining whether to suspend collection activity based on the debtor's financial condition, the agency is to take a debtor's future prospects into account, and determine whether the applicable statute of limitations or the ten-year limit on offsets is close and whether the debtor will pay interest.[187]

Of more benefit to low-income debtors is the authority of agencies to terminate collection activity. Termination is allowed when:

- The agency is unable to collect any substantial amount through its own efforts or the efforts of others;
- The agency is unable to locate the debtor;
- Costs of collection are anticipated to exceed the amount recoverable;
- The debt is legally without merit or can not be substantiated or enforcement is barred by the applicable statute of limitations; or
- The debt has been discharged in bankruptcy.[188]

After terminating collection activity on a debt, an agency may still sell the debt,[189] offset it against future income or assets that the debtor acquires, or resume collection if the debtor's status changes or a new collection tool becomes available.[190] The agency can also screen future applicants for prior indebtedness,[191] and can deny loans, licenses, and other federal benefits and privileges.[192] Debts on which the agency has terminated collection activity are to be sold using competitive procedures if the Secretary of the Treasury determines that sale is in the best interests of the United States.[193]

184 4 C.F.R. § 102.3(a)(2), *superseded by* 31 C.F.R. pts. 900–904 (as adopted by 65 Fed. Reg. 70,390 (Nov. 22, 2000)).
185 31 U.S.C. § 3711(a)(3); 31 C.F.R. pt. 903; *see* § 11.2.10, *infra*.
186 31 C.F.R. § 903.2(a), (b); *see also* 31 U.S.C. § 3711(a)(3).
187 31 C.F.R. § 903.2(b).
188 31 U.S.C. §§ 903.3(a), 3711(a)(3).
189 *See* 31 U.S.C. § 3711(i)(1) (authority to sell debts).
190 31 C.F.R. § 903.3(b).
191 31 C.F.R. § 903.3(b)(4).
192 31 U.S.C. § 3720B; 31 C.F.R. § 285.13(d)(3).
193 37 U.S.C. § 3711(i)(2).

If a creditor agency has taken all appropriate steps to collect a debt, it may discharge the debt.[194] Before discharging a debt, the creditor agency must try to sell it if the Treasury Department determines that sale is in the best interests of the United States.[195] Once discharged, however, a debt can not be sold, and further collection action is precluded.[196]

11.2.11 Federal Agencies' Implementation of Collection Requirements

11.2.11.1 Survey of Selected Agencies

This section briefly describes the actions of selected federal agencies to implement the debt collection authority and requirements already described. Additional limitations or defenses provided by those agencies' enabling statutes and regulations are beyond the scope of this discussion.

11.2.11.2 Department of Education: Student Loans

One of the most pervasive debt collection programs run by the federal government involves student loans. Through the last two decades, Congress kept increasing the Department of Education's arsenal of collection tools to deal with delinquent student loans. In doing so, Congress had in mind employed college graduates not paying their student loans. Congress largely ignored the tremendous problem created by the fact that thousands of fraudulent vocational schools spawned by the federal student loan program had generated millions of student loans in which the students had the defense of the school's fraud. Department of Education student loan collection efforts and the complex issues arising in vocational school fraud/student loan cases are analyzed in detail in NCLC's *Student Loan Law*.[197]

Congress has granted the Department of Education additional debt collection powers, including administrative wage garnishment,[198] exemption from statutes of limitations,[199] and authority to collect reasonable collection fees.[200] Ad-

194 31 C.F.R. § 903.5.
195 31 U.S.C. § 3711(i)(2).
196 31 C.F.R. § 903.5.
197 (3d ed. 2006 and Supp.).
198 20 U.S.C. § 1095a; *see* Savage v. Scales, 310 F. Supp. 2d 122 (D.D.C. 2004) (authority for administrative wage garnishment at 20 U.S.C. § 1095a overrides state law restrictions on garnishment; due process is satisfied by mailing of notice, even if not received); National Consumer Law Center, Student Loan Law § 5.3 (3d ed. 2006 and Supp.).
199 20 U.S.C. § 1091a, *as amended by* Pub. L. No. 102-26, 105 Stat. 123 (1991).
200 *See* Black v. Educ. Credit Mgmt., 459 F.3d 796 (7th Cir. 2006) (rejecting constitutional challenge to regulation allowing percentage-based collection fees); *see also* Gingo v. United States Dep't of Educ., 149 F. Supp. 2d 1195 (E.D. Cal. 2000) (chal-

ministrative wage garnishments to collect student loans may be initiated by the Department of Education or by guaranty agencies. Separate statutory authority applies depending on which entity is garnishing. The Higher Education Act (HEA) garnishment authority should apply only when guaranty agencies are garnishing.[201] The Debt Collection Improvement Act covers Department of Education garnishments.[202] Although there are some differences between the two statutes, the most significant is no longer relevant. Prior to Congressional changes in 2005, the Higher Education Act administrative wage garnishment statute and regulations allowed garnishment "only" up to ten percent of "disposable pay" compared to a 15% limit in the Debt Collection Improvement Act. As of July 1, 2006, the HEA limit was increased to 15%.[203]

The HEA provides only that the amount deducted may not exceed 15%.[204] The Department's regulations specify that the amount that can be garnished is the *lesser* of 15% of disposable income or the amount that exceeds thirty times the prevailing minimum wage (the amount permitted by 15 U.S.C. § 1673).[205] 15 U.S.C. § 1673 also limits total garnishments to 25% of disposable income, so that a student loan garnishment plus other garnishments should not exceed 25% of income. Student loans are also denied discharge in bankruptcy except upon showing of undue hardship.[206] There are, however, a number of grounds on which debtors can seek forgiveness or restructuring of student loan debts under Department of Education regulations.[207]

The Department also has authority to offset Social Security benefits (except SSI benefits) and many other federal benefits to collect student loan debts.[208] The Supreme Court, in *Lockhart v. United States*,[209] held that there was no statute of limitations on the offset of Social Security benefits to pay a student loan.

When collection agencies or attorneys are collecting a student loan, the student is protected by the Fair Debt Collection Practices Act (FDCPA).[210] Private guaranty agencies are also covered by the FDCPA unless they obtained the debt before it went into default or fall into the exemption for fiduciaries because of their relationship to the government.[211] State guaranty agencies will likely be exempted under the FDCPA's exclusion for state employees.[212]

Whether FDCPA claims can be asserted against collectors of student loans other than the Department of Education is analyzed in more detail in NCLC's *Fair Debt Collection* §§ 4.2.3, 4.3.8, and 4.4.2.2.[213] Whether private collectors of student loans are subject to claims under state debt collection laws is discussed in § 11.2.2 of that manual.

11.2.11.3 Department of Health and Human Services

The debt collection regulations of the Department of Health and Human Services (HHS) are similar to the joint regulations.[214] They authorize administrative offset, credit bureau reports, installment payment agreements, tax intercepts, administrative wage garnishment, transfer to the Treasury Department for centralized collection, offset against

lenge to 18.5% collection costs, which greatly exceeded actual cost, failed to state a claim; no private right of action under Higher Education Act; guarantee agency not a state actor within meaning of section 1983); *In re* Evans, 322 B.R. 429 (Bankr. W.D. Wash. 2005). *See generally* National Consumer Law Center, Student Loan Law § 4.4 (3d ed. 2006 and Supp.).

201 20 U.S.C. § 1095a.

202 31 U.S.C. § 3720(D).

203 20 U.S.C. § 1095a(a)(1); 34 C.F.R. § 682.410(b)(9)(i)(A). *See generally* National Consumer Law Center, Student Loan Law § 5.3 (3d ed. 2006 and Supp.).

204 20 U.S.C. § 1095a(a)(1).

205 34 C.F.R. § 682.410(b)(9)(i)(A).

The minimum wage can be found in 29 U.S.C. § 206(a)(1). The ongoing changes in the minimum wage and their effect on the amount of wages that can be garnished are discussed in § 12.4.1.4, *infra*.

206 11 U.S.C. § 523(a)(8); *see* National Consumer Law Center, Consumer Bankruptcy Law and Practice § 14.4.3.8 (8th ed. 2006 and Supp.).

207 *See, e.g.*, National Consumer Law Center, Student Loan Law § 6.2 (closed school discharge), § 6.3 (false certification discharge), § 6.4 (unpaid refund discharge), § 6.6 (disability discharge), § 8.2 (loan consolidation), Ch. 9 (borrower's claims against the school) (3d ed. 2006 and Supp.).

208 *See* National Consumer Law Center, Student Loan Law § 5.4 (3d ed. 2006 and Supp.).

209 546 U.S. 142, 126 S. Ct. 699, 163 L. Ed. 2d 557 (2005).

210 Peter v. GC Services Ltd. P'ship, 310 F.3d 344 (5th Cir. 2002) (collection agency's use of the Department of Education name on collection letter to student loan borrower violates FDCPA); *see* 31 U.S.C. § 3718(a)(2).

The Department of Education and the student loan lender are exempt under different provisions of the FDCPA, 15 U.S.C. §§ 1692a(6)(C) and (A) respectively. *See, e.g.*, Arroyo v. Solomon & Solomon, Prof'l Corp., 2001 U.S. Dist. LEXIS 21908 (E.D.N.Y. Nov. 7, 2001) (FDCPA claim can be based on collector's misleading communications about debtor's rights under Higher Education Act (HEA); such a claim is not preempted by HEA); Kort v. Diversified Collection Services, Inc., 2001 U.S. Dist. LEXIS 11701 (N.D. Ill. July 31, 2001) (consumer stated claim against private collector, when wage withholding notice could lead unsophisticated consumer to believe that withholding would occur sooner than legally permitted).

211 Brannan v. United Student Aid Funds, Inc., 94 F.3d 1260 (9th Cir. 1996); Sibley v. Diversified Collection Services, Inc., 1997 U.S. Dist. LEXIS 23583 (N.D. Tex. June 10, 1997) (ruling on defendants' motion to dismiss). *But see* Pelfrey v. Educ. Credit Mgmt. Co., 71 F. Supp. 2d 1161 (N.D. Ala. 1999), *aff'd*, 208 F.3d 945 (11th Cir. 2000) (per curiam); Davis v. United Student Aid Funds, Inc., 45 F. Supp. 2d 1104 (D. Kan. 1998) (nonprofit student loan guaranty agency was a fiduciary and therefore not a debt collector). *See generally* National Consumer Law Center, Student Loan Law § 4.5.3.5 (3d ed. 2006 and Supp.).

212 15 U.S.C. § 1692a(6)(C); *see* National Consumer Law Center, Fair Debt Collection §§ 4.2.3, 4.3.8 (6th ed. 2008).

213 (6th ed. 2008).

214 45 C.F.R. pts. 30–33.

federal employees' salaries, compromise of debts, suspension and termination of collection activities, and referral to collection agencies.

Interest is not charged on debts arising from payments to beneficiaries under Titles II, XVI, and XVIII of the Social Security Act, except for certain overpayments.[215] The Secretary may waive collection of interest, administrative costs, and penalties in certain circumstances.[216]

Debts arising from payments to beneficiaries under Titles II, XVI, and XVIII of the Social Security Act are not to be reported to credit reporting agencies or referred to collection agencies except for certain overpayments.[217] For debts of less than $20,000, the Secretary has authority to compromise the debt or terminate or suspend collection if the debtor is unable to pay, or if collection would not be cost-effective.[218] Larger debts can also be compromised, but only with Department of Justice approval.

The Social Security Administration has a separate set of rules that allow it to use credit reports, administrative offsets, and administrative wage garnishment to recover Title II[219] and Supplemental Security Income[220] overpayments. In addition, Social Security Administration regulations allow it to reduce Title II benefits by up to ten percent a month to recover Title II or SSI overpayments.[221] The recipient may request that less be withheld from the monthly benefit.[222] The entire amount of a retroactive award may be offset to recover an overpayment.[223] The agency has extensive regulations about waiver of overpayments and the procedure for seeking a waiver.[224]

11.2.11.4 Department of Housing and Urban Development

The debt collection regulations of the Department of Housing and Urban Development (HUD) authorize administrative and salary offsets,[225] administrative wage garnishment,[226] compromise of claims,[227] liquidation of collateral,[228] disclosure of defaults to credit reporting agencies,[229] and contracts with outside collection services.[230] The regulations detail the procedures HUD must follow in the use of offsets,[231] as well as procedures for review.[232]

11.2.11.5 Department of Veterans Affairs

The debt collection regulations of the Department of Veterans Affairs (VA) permit disclosure to a credit reporting agency that an individual owes an obligation to the United States.[233] The VA regulations regarding administrative offset set forth additional standards for collection efforts.[234] They explicitly state, however, that the Department's failure to comply with the standards shall not be available as a defense to any debtor.[235] The Department of Veterans Affairs has statutory authority to offset benefit overpayments against veterans benefits.[236]

Waiver of benefit overpayments and loan debts is authorized when recovery would be against equity and good conscience as defined by VA regulations.[237] In deciding whether to waive all or part of a debt, the agency must weigh the relative fault of the veteran and the agency and consider whether full repayment would result in undue hardship, or waiver would result in unjust enrichment, whether collection would defeat the purpose of the benefit program, and whether the veteran detrimentally relied on an agency error.[238] Waiver

---

215 31 U.S.C. § 3701(d)(2); 31 C.F.R. § 901.12(a); *cf.* 20 C.F.R. § 422.303 (Social Security Administration will charge interest, penalties, and collection costs when authorized by the joint regulations); 45 C.F.R. § 30.13(d).

Title II refers to Old Age, Survivors, and Disability insurance benefits; Title XVI refers to Supplemental Security Income for Aged, Blind, and Disabled (SSI); Title XVIII refers to Health Insurance for Aged and Disabled (Medicare).

216 45 C.F.R. § 30.18.

217 45 C.F.R. § 30.13(a); 20 C.F.R. §§ 422.305, 422.301(a)(2), 404.527(a), 416.590(a); 42 U.S.C. § 404(f) (referring to 31 U.S.C. § 3711(f) but probably means 31 U.S.C. § 3711(e)).

218 45 C.F.R. §§ 30.22, 30.24, 30.26, 30.31, 30.32.

219 20 C.F.R. §§ 404.501 to 404.545, 422.301 to 422.445 (reporting to credit bureaus, administrative offset, administrative wage garnishment; note that according to 20 C.F.R. §§ 404.527 and 415.590(a) these steps are allowed only if the overpayment occurred after the beneficiary became eighteen, the beneficiary is no longer entitled to benefits, and the Social Security Administration has determined that the overpayment is not otherwise recoverable).

220 20 C.F.R. §§ 416.581 to 416.590.

221 42 U.S.C. § 1320b-17(b)(1); 20 C.F.R. §§ 416.571, 416.573(b)(1).

The ten percent cap does not apply if the debt involved fraud, willful misrepresentation, or concealment of information. 42 U.S.C. § 1320b-17(b)(2); 20 C.F.R. § 416.571.

222 20 C.F.R. § 416.571.

223 20 C.F.R. § 416.573(a).

224 20 C.F.R. §§ 404.506 to 404.512.

225 24 C.F.R. § 17.72(b).

226 24 C.F.R. § 17.170.

227 24 C.F.R. §§ 17.65, 17.73.

228 24 C.F.R. § 17.72(c).

229 24 C.F.R. § 17.76(b).

230 24 C.F.R. § 17.77.

231 24 C.F.R. §§ 17.100 to 17.118 (administrative offsets); 24 C.F.R. §§ 17.125 to 17.140 (salary offsets); 24 C.F.R. §§ 17.150 to 17.161 (tax refund or other federal payment intercept).

232 24 C.F.R. §§ 17.152, 17.153; *see* Ingram v. Cuomo, 51 F. Supp. 2d 667 (M.D.N.C. 1999) (upholding agency hearing's decision that debt was past due and legally enforceable).

233 38 C.F.R. §§ 1.901 to 1.995.

234 38 C.F.R. §§ 1.911, 1.912, 1.912a; *see also* 38 C.F.R. §§ 1.980 to 1.995 (offset against federal employees' salaries).

235 38 C.F.R. § 1.901.

236 38 U.S.C. §§ 5301, 5314.

237 38 C.F.R. §§ 1.962 to 1.965.

238 *See* Reyes v. Nicholson, 21 Vet. App. 370 (Vet. App. 2007) (upholding Secretary's interpretation of waiver authority; affirming denial of waiver); Mueller v. Nicholson, 20 Vet. App. 510 (Vet. App. 2006) (table) (text available at 2006 WL 176517) (affirming agency decision waiving half of loan guarantee indebtedness; repayment not against equity and good

is not permitted if there is fraud, misrepresentation, or bad faith.[239]

The veteran has the right to dispute the existence or the amount of the debt, request waiver of collection, and have a hearing on the waiver request.[240] The veteran also has the right to appeal the Department's decision on either the existence or amount of the debt.[241] Judicial review is, however, deferential: an agency decision will be reversed only if arbitrary and capricious.[242]

There is no deadline for disputing the existence or amount of the debt, but the veteran has only 180 days from the notice of the debt to request waiver of collection.[243] If, within thirty days after the date of notification of the debt, the debtor submits a written dispute of the existence or amount of the debt or requests waiver, offset against current benefits is stayed until the matter is resolved.[244]

With respect to debts arising from VA-guaranteed home loans, the Department does not attempt to collect deficiency judgments after foreclosure from veterans except in cases involving fraud, misrepresentation, or bad faith.[245] When a veteran sells a VA-financed home, the Department has special rules for releasing the veteran from further liability on the mortgage debt.[246]

The National Veterans Legal Services Project has published a manual to assist veterans and their representatives in dealing with VA benefits and debt issues.[247]

11.2.11.6 Department of Agriculture

The collection of loan repayments to the Department of Agriculture is governed by rules reflecting the provisions of the Debt Collection Act.[248] In early 2008, the Department overhauled these rules.[249] The agency must give the debtor written notice thirty days before exercising administrative offset, explaining the proposed action and the method of obtaining review.[250] The debtor may request, in writing, a review of the agency's determination that the debt exists and the propriety of the administrative offset.[251] The debtor may avoid offset by submitting a repayment plan acceptable to the agency.[252] There are similar provisions for advance notice, hearings, and written repayment agreements when salary offset is proposed.[253] The Department has also adopted separate offset regulations for some of its programs under the authority of certain agriculture statutes.[254]

---

conscience, but full repayment would cause undue hardship); Jordan v. Brown, 10 Vet. App. 171 (Vet. App. 1997) (affirming waiver of half of overpayment; remarried widow reported change in name and address, may have orally reported remarriage; "significant fault" on part of widow, who had been informed that checks received after remarriage must be returned); Cullen v. Brown, 5 Vet. App. 510 (Vet. App. 1993) (vacating and remanding agency denial of waiver when agency failed to consider key factors, such as, relative fault when disabled veteran, who advised VA of mistake but kept checks, would have had zero income if he returned the checks, and undue hardship when veteran's financial statement indicated income inadequate for basic needs).

239 *See* Zyglewicz v. Nicholson, 20 Vet. App. 127 (Vet. App. 2005) (table) (text available at 2005 WL 1239147) (agency had "plausible basis" for finding bad faith after three years of unreported income); Senin v. Nicholson, 19 Vet. App. 510 (Vet. App. 2005) (table) (text available at 2005 WL 1004489) (fault but not fraud shown when unreported income came from college trust funds for veteran's children; affirming waiver of one half of overpayment), *aff'd*, 117 Fed. Appx. 87 (Fed. Cir. 2006); Kelly v. Nicholson, 19 Vet. App. 510 (Vet. App. 2005) (table) (text available at 2005 WL 1076699) (substantial underreporting of income over a period of years sufficient to bar waiver).

240 38 C.F.R. § 1.911(c).

Offset is limited to fifteen percent of net monthly payment. 38 C.F.R. § 1.912a(e)(3).

241 38 C.F.R. § 1.911(c).

242 Mueller v. Nicholson, 20 Vet. App. 510 (Vet. App. 2006) (table) (text available at 2006 WL 176517); Kinslow v. Nicholson, 20 Vet. App. 132 (Vet. App. 2005) (table) (text available at 2005 WL 1545135) (not arbitrary and capricious); Zyglewicz v. Nicholson, 20 Vet. App. 127 (Vet. App. 2005) (table) (text available at 2005 WL 1239147) ("plausible basis" for finding). *But see* Steward v. Nicholson, 20 Vet. App. 227 (Vet. App. 2005) (table) (text available at 2005 WL 3028821) (vacating and remanding denial of waiver of mortgage guarantee debt; agency should make findings regarding circumstances of foreclosure); King v. Principi, 19 Vet. App. 160 (Vet. App. 2004) (table) (text available at 2004 WL 3111063) (vacating denial of waiver); Cullen v. Brown, 5 Vet. App. 510 (Vet. App. 1993) (vacating and remanding denial of waiver when agency failed to consider key factors).

243 38 U.S.C. § 5302.

244 38 C.F.R. § 1.912a(c); *see* Ginish v. Prinicipi, 2003 WL 21191195 (Vet. App. May 16, 2003) (finding that VA wrongfully offset VA benefits while veteran's dispute of the debt was pending).

The length of the stay depends on various factors listed in the regulation. The VA has the authority to begin offset immediately if deferring offset would jeopardize collection.

245 38 U.S.C. § 3703(e)(1).

This protection applies to loans secured on or after January 1, 1990. *See also* 38 C.F.R. §§ 1.964, 1.965.

246 38 U.S.C. § 3713; *see also* 38 C.F.R. §§ 1.964, 1.965.

247 Veterans Benefits Manual (2007).

For information about ordering this manual, visit the website of the National Veterans Legal Services Program, www.nvlsp.org, or the website of LexisNexis, which publishes the manual, http://bookstore.lexis.com.

248 7 C.F.R. pt. 3; *see* United States Dep't of Agric. v. Huff (*In re* Huff), 343 B.R. 136 (W.D. Pa. 2006) (discussing notice requirements for tax intercept to repay Rural Housing Service loan); Lewis v. Glickman, 104 F. Supp. 2d 1311 (D. Kan. 2000) (agency's offset decision upheld despite its dilatoriness and multiple procedural violations when debtor failed to show prejudice), *aff'd*, 2002 U.S. App. LEXIS 13269 (10th Cir. July 3, 2002).

249 73 Fed. Reg. 1 (Jan. 2, 2008).

250 7 C.F.R. § 3.25; *see also* 7 C.F.R. § 3.26 (exceptions to the advance notice requirement).

251 7 C.F.R. §§ 3.23(f), 3.29.

252 7 C.F.R. § 3.28.

253 7 C.F.R. §§ 3.51 to 3.68.

254 7 C.F.R. pt. 792 (Farm Services Agency), pt. 1403 (Commodity Credit Corp. and, by cross-reference, Farm Services Agency);

The Department's rules do not apply to collection of Food Stamp debts owed by individual recipients.[255] Collection of those debts is the obligation of states when administering their Food Stamp programs.[256]

11.2.12 Debtor Remedies for Illegal Agency Collection Practices

11.2.12.1 Overview

The joint regulations expressly prohibit raising agency misconduct as a defense to a claim: "[T]he failure of an agency to comply with the provisions of this chapter shall not be available as a defense to any debtor."[257] But there are a number of judicial remedies available to those illegally harassed for debts they owe to federal agencies.

If the debtor seeks review of a tax refund intercept, federal tax law prevents federal courts from exercising jurisdiction over the Treasury Department.[258] That statute, however, does not preclude federal court jurisdiction over the agency to which the offset was paid.[259]

11.2.12.2 *Bivens* Suit

Individual federal employees may be found liable for violation of constitutional rights when their conduct "violates clearly established statutory or constitutional rights of which a reasonable person would have known."[260] In *Bivens v. Six Unknown Agents of the Federal Bureau of Narcotics*,[261] the United States Supreme Court determined that a federal employee otherwise entitled to qualified immunity from suit loses this defense in the face of unreasonable conduct.[262] The Court effectively created a private cause of action for damages for constitutional violations.[263] The Supreme Court has refused, however, to extend *Bivens* to permit suits against federal agencies (as opposed to federal employees).[264]

A *Bivens* remedy does not lie when (1) Congress has provided an equally effective alternative remedy and declared it to be a substitute for recovery under the Constitution, or (2) in the absence of affirmative action by Congress, "special factors counsel hesitation."[265] A *Bivens* suit is not allowed even when the remedy Congress has created offers the plaintiff significantly less protection.[266] Several circuits applying these criteria have concluded that a *Bivens* remedy is not available against the Internal Revenue Service (IRS), because the remedies in the Internal Revenue Code are adequate.[267] Some courts have, however, left the door open

---

see 60 Fed. Reg. 43,705 (Aug. 23, 1995) (citing statutory authority for these regulations); *see also* McBride Cotton & Cattle Corp. v. Veneman, 296 F. Supp. 2d 1125 (D. Ariz. 2003) (upholding scope of offset authority of 7 C.F.R. § 1403.7 as permissible under agriculture statute).

255 7 C.F.R. § 3.1(c)(1); *see also* 73 Fed. Reg. 1, 1 (Jan. 2, 2008).

256 *See* 7 C.F.R. § 273.18 (setting forth requirements for states' Food Stamp debt collections).

257 31 C.F.R. § 900.8; *see* § 11.2.8.4, *supra*.

258 26 U.S.C. § 6402(f); *see* Albert v. OSI Educ. Services, 2004 WL 483166 (D. Minn. Mar. 11, 2004).

259 26 U.S.C. § 6402(f).

260 Harlow v. Fitzgerald, 457 U.S. 800, 818, 102 S. Ct. 2727, 73 L. Ed. 2d 396 (1982).

261 Bivens v. Six Unknown Agents of the Fed. Bureau of Narcotics, 403 U.S. 388, 91 S. Ct. 1999, 29 L. Ed. 2d 619 (1971), *on remand*, 456 F.2d 1339 (2d Cir. 1972).

262 "Reasonableness" is to be measured objectively by reference to law clearly established at the time of the incident in question. Harlow v. Fitzgerald, 457 U.S. 800, 818, 102 S. Ct. 2727, 73 L. Ed. 2d 396 (1982); *see also* Hanlon v. Berger, 526 U.S. 808, 119 S. Ct. 1706, 143 L. Ed. 2d 978 (1999).

263 *See* Hernandez v. Mitchell, 612 F.2d 61, 65 (2d Cir. 1979); Shiraishi v. United States, 2007 WL 2263071 (D. Haw. Aug. 3, 2007) (borrower stated *Bivens* claim for denial of due process against Farm Service employee whose delay in processing homestead application caused farmer to lose opportunity to leaseback farm, but claim barred by res judicata because same issues raised in foreclosure proceeding); Wahad v. Fed. Bureau of Investigation, 994 F. Supp. 237, 239 (S.D.N.Y. 1998); Taylor v. Internal Revenue Serv., 915 F. Supp. 1015, 1019 (N.D. Iowa 1996), *aff'd*, 106 F.3d 833 (8th Cir. 1997).

264 Fed. Deposit Ins. Corp. v. Meyer, 510 U.S. 471, 114 S. Ct. 996, 127 L. Ed. 2d 308 (1994), *on remand*, 51 F.3d 900 (9th Cir. 1995); *see also* Dye v. United States, 516 F. Supp. 2d 61 (D.D.C. 2007) (*Bivens* allows actions against individual agents, but not the government itself).

265 Carlson v. Green, 446 U.S. 14, 18–19, 100 S. Ct. 1468, 64 L. Ed. 2d 15 (1980).

266 Bush v. Lucas, 462 U.S. 367, 388–390, 103 S. Ct. 2404, 76 L. Ed. 2d 648 (1983); *see also* Schweicker v. Chilicky, 487 U.S. 412, 425, 108 S. Ct. 2460, 101 L. Ed. 2d 370 (1988) (plaintiffs complaining of wrongful acts by Social Security administrators must confine their complaints to the procedures provided by the Social Security Act); Hudson Valley Black Press v. Internal Revenue Serv., 409 F.3d 106 (2d Cir. 2005) (comprehensiveness of statutory scheme, not adequacy of remedies, is determinative); Murrhee v. Principi, 364 F. Supp. 2d 782 (C.D. Ill. 2005) (no *Bivens* claim for due process violations in veterans' pension matter; remedial scheme provided by statute); Stewart v. Barnhart, 2005 WL 3088543 (W.D. Ky. Nov. 14, 2005) (no *Bivens* action for wrongful termination of Social Security benefits).

267 *See, e.g.*, Godt v. Internal Revenue Serv., 2008 WL 656264 (7th Cir. Mar. 12, 2008) (unpublished) (no *Bivens* action for "relatively trivial" misconduct by individual IRS agents); Hudson Valley Black Press v. Internal Revenue Serv., 409 F.3d 106 (2d Cir. 2005); Adams v. Johnson, 355 F.3d 1179 (9th Cir. 2004) (no *Bivens* remedy if statute provides "some mechanism of relief"; *Bivens* claim will not lie for any allegedly unconstitutional actions by IRS); Giles v. Volvo Trucks of N. Am., 2008 WL 509178 (M.D. Pa. Feb. 20, 2008) (*Bivens* action will not lie for constitutional violations in the investigation, assessment, or collection of taxes); Al-Sharif v. Bradley, 2008 WL 410364 (S.D. Ga. Feb. 20, 2008) (tax code provides adequate remedies); Caton v. Hutson, 2007 WL 4731010 (M.D. Fla. Nov. 19, 2007) (unpublished) (tax code provides exclusive remedy for wrongful assessment or collection by IRS employees); Foley v. Comm'r, 2007 WL 806521 (N.D. Cal. Mar. 15, 2007) (no *Bivens* action for misconduct by IRS agents; 26 U.S.C. § 7433 was exclusive

for claims of Fourth Amendment violations,[268] or egregious government misconduct.[269]

Regardless of *Bivens*, consumers may be able to seek injunctive relief against federal actors when their due process rights under specific federal laws have been violated.[270] In addition, sovereign immunity can be expressly waived by statute, giving a consumer a right to seek money damages in circumstances in which a *Bivens* suit would be unavailable.[271]

remedy when, because of misreading of Social Security number, one taxpayer was accused of earning—and not reporting—income earned by another); Celauro v. Internal Revenue Serv., 411 F. Supp. 2d 257 (E.D.N.Y. 2006) (no *Bivens* claim against IRS agents, because statutory remedies adequate), *aff'd*, 214 Fed. Appx. 95 (2d Cir. 2007); *see also* § 11.2.12.6, *infra*.

The relevant statutes may be found at 26 U.S.C. §§ 7422, 7432, 7433; 28 U.S.C. § 1346.

268 Meredith v. Erath, 342 F.3d 1057 (9th Cir. 2003) (allowing *Bivens* action to go forward with claims of excessive force arising from IRS's early morning armed raid on residence and business premises); Nat'l Commodity & Barter Ass'n v. Gibbs, 886 F.2d 1240 (10th Cir. 1989) (First or Fourth Amendment violations—here, seizures of membership lists—would support *Bivens* action; remanding on question of qualified immunity); Cameron v. Internal Revenue Serv., 773 F.2d 126 (7th Cir. 1985) (*Bivens* action might lie if agents ransacked a home); *see also* Taxacher v. Torbic, 2000 U.S. Dist. LEXIS 15193 (W.D. Pa. Feb. 23, 2000), *aff'd*, 251 F.3d 154 (3d Cir. 2000) (table). *But see* Hudson Valley Black Press v. Internal Revenue Serv., 409 F.3d 106 (2d Cir. 2005) (*Bivens* action will not lie for First and Fourth Amendment claims alleging IRS attack on publication that criticized its treatment of minority taxpayers); Adams v. Johnson, 355 F.3d 1179 (9th Cir. 2004) (*Bivens* claim will not lie for any allegedly unconstitutional actions by IRS); Dahn v. United States, 127 F.3d 1249 (10th Cir. 1997) (citing *Gibbs* for proposition that IRS agents not subject to *Bivens* actions).

269 Cameron v. Internal Revenue Serv., 773 F.2d 126 (7th Cir. 1985) ("lawless vendetta" not shown here); Rutherford v. United States, 702 F.2d 580 (5th Cir. 1983) (*Bivens* action would be appropriate if taxpayer showed a "vendetta" which required lengthy and expensive litigation to undo; remanding to district court to determine if agent's conduct so egregious as to deprive taxpayer of substantive due process); *see also* Connor v. Matthews, 134 F. Supp. 2d 797 (N.D. Tex. 2001) (taxpayer failed to allege egregious misconduct within *Rutherford* exception).

270 *See, e.g.*, Atwater v. Roudebush, 452 F. Supp. 622 (N.D. Ill. 1976) (denying government's motion for summary judgment on due process claim for injunctive relief regarding offset of Federal Housing Administration debt against salary).

271 Irwin v. Dep't of Veterans Affairs, 498 U.S. 89, 111 S. Ct. 453, 112 L. Ed. 2d 435 (1990); United States v. Mitchell, 445 U.S. 535, 538, 100 S. Ct. 1349, 63 L. Ed. 2d 607 (1980) (waiver of sovereign immunity can not be implied but must be unequivocally expressed); *see also* Donovan v. Gober, 5 F. Supp. 2d 142 (W.D.N.Y. 1998) (Department of Veterans Affairs has waived sovereign immunity so suit for money damages caused by unconstitutional administrative offset may be filed against it even though such a suit could not be brought under *Bivens*).

11.2.12.3 Suit Under Privacy Act

An obligor is entitled to an injunction and costs for violations of the Privacy Act.[272] If a violation is intentional or willful, the remedy is an award of at least $1000 or any greater sum which represents actual damages.[273] To recover, a consumer must show that the violations have adversely affected the obligor.[274] A two-year statute of limitations applies. For injunctive relief, the statute of limitations begins to run at the time of the violation; for monetary awards, it begins at the time of discovery of the misconduct.[275]

11.2.12.4 Administrative Procedures Act

The Administrative Procedures Act (APA) provides that "final agency actions for which there is no other adequate remedy in a court are subject to judicial review."[276] This language might be broadly construed to cover a case of agency misconduct in debt collection.[277] An APA action is also available to review an agency's determination to offset a debt against a tax refund or other government payment.[278] Generally, administrative remedies must be exhausted be-

272 5 U.S.C. § 552a(g).

273 Doe v. Chao, 540 U.S. 614, 124 S. Ct. 1204, 157 L. Ed. 2d 1122 (2004) (actual damages must be shown; leaving open the question, on which the circuit courts are split, whether emotional distress is sufficient); Rice v. United States, 245 F.R.D. 3 (D.D.C. 2007) (proof of actual damages requires more than adverse effect; open question whether emotional distress sufficient; issue not decided here as alleged distress not sufficiently severe when plaintiffs did not seek medical attention).

274 Rice v. United States, 245 F.R.D. 3 (D.D.C. 2007) (allegation that plaintiffs suffered "anger, dismay, anxiety and fear" from release of personal information sufficient to show "adverse effect" and confer standing).

275 Note that the Privacy Act precludes a *Bivens* action for damages. Sullivan v. U.S. Postal Serv., 944 F. Supp. 191 (W.D.N.Y. 1996) (citing Bush v. Lucas, 462 U.S. 367, 368, 103 S. Ct. 2404, 76 L. Ed. 2d 648 (1983)).

276 5 U.S.C. § 704.

277 *See* Standifer v. Sec. Exch. Comm'n, 2008 WL 513352 (N.D. Ga. Feb. 22, 2008).

278 *See* Anand v. United States Nat'l Sec. Agency, 2006 WL 3257430 (N.D.N.Y. Nov. 9, 2006) (APA action may lie for agency's failure to comply with Debt Collection Improvement Act, but debtor here failed to exhaust administrative remedies, and agency's threats to use collection methods were not final actions); Lewis v. Glickman, 104 F. Supp. 2d 1311 (D. Kan. 2000), *aff'd*, 2002 U.S. App. LEXIS 13269 (10th Cir. July 3, 2002); Ingram v. Cuomo, 51 F. Supp. 2d 667 (M.D.N.C. 1999); *cf.* Sheehy v. Johanns, 2007 WL 656429 (W.D.N.Y. Feb. 27, 2007) (review is available only of agency's determination to accelerate loans, which debtor appealed within agency, not unappealed agency decision to institute administrative offsets). *But cf.* Greenland v. Van Ru Credit Corp., 2006 WL 2884458 (W.D. Mich. Oct. 10, 2006) (APA does not allow court to review Treasury Department's tax refund interception); Shabtai v. United States Dep't of Educ., 2003 WL 21983025 (S.D.N.Y. Aug. 20, 2003) (injunction against offset not available unless Secretary of Education acted outside authority).

fore judicial review is sought.[279] When a plaintiff has a strong interest in immediate review, however, a balancing test will be applied to determine if the exhaustion of remedies requirement can be waived.[280]

11.2.12.5 Federal Tort Claims Act

The Federal Tort Claims Act (FTCA)[281] may provide an avenue for redress against a federal agency for negligence or certain intentional torts committed by its employees. The FTCA acts as a statutory waiver of the United States' sovereign immunity for tortious conduct, but the numerous exceptions to this waiver work to bar claims against federal employees for certain torts.[282] Although a plaintiff can not recover both under the FTCA and on a *Bivens* claim, the two can be joined in a single action.[283] The government may seek to sever the FTCA claim and try it first, but this result would defeat Congress's intent in providing two complementary remedies, and would raise Seventh Amendment concerns by depriving the plaintiff of the right to a jury trial.[284]

The basic elements of a cause of action under the FTCA are set forth in 28 U.S.C. § 1346(b). That section specifies six conditions which must be met in order to impose liability on the United States under the Act: (1) the claim must be for money damages; (2) the damage claim must be for injury or loss of property, or for personal injury or death; (3) the damage must have been caused by a negligent or wrongful act or omission; (4) the wrongful actor must have been a federal employee; (5) the employee must have been acting within the scope of his employment; and (6) the circumstances must be such that, if the United States were a private person, liability would be imposed under the law of the place of where the wrongful act or omission occurred.[285]

Although many exceptions to governmental liability for intentional torts are enumerated in the Act, intentional infliction of emotional distress is not among them, and is therefore actionable.[286] Further, negligent infliction of emotional harm may be asserted as a claim if such a cause of action is available under state law.[287] The statute likewise does not enumerate an exception for invasion of privacy claims,[288] so such a claim is also actionable as long as it is recognized under local law.[289]

Several exceptions to the FTCA are likely to be significant in debt collection matters. The waiver of sovereign immunity does not apply to the assessment or collection of any tax,[290] leaving taxpayers with only the limited remedies found in the Internal Revenue Code.[291] The Act does not

279 Anand v. United States Nat'l Sec. Agency, 2006 WL 3257430 (N.D.N.Y. Nov. 9, 2006) (dismissing challenge to federal collection efforts due to failure to exhaust agency remedies).

280 West v. Bergland, 611 F.2d 710 (8th Cir. 1979); *see also* McCarthy v. Madigan, 503 U.S. 140, 146, 112 S. Ct. 1081, 117 L. Ed. 2d 291 (1992); Kendrick v. Carlson, 995 F.2d 1440, 1447 (8th Cir. 1993).

281 28 U.S.C. §§ 2671–2680, *as amended by* the Federal Employees Liability Reform and Tort Compensation Act of 1988 (FELRTCA, or the Westfall Act), Pub. L. No. 100-694, 102 Stat. 4564 (1988).

See Lester Jayson & Robert Longstreth, Handling Federal Tort Claims Administrative and Judicial Remedies (2001 with annual updates) for more detail about FTCA claims.

282 28 U.S.C. § 2680(h).

Note that the FTCA does not prevent issuance of injunctive or other equitable relief. B.C. Morton Int'l Corp. v. Fed. Deposit Ins. Corp., 305 F.2d 692, 695 (1st Cir. 1962); Corbin v. Fed. Reserve Bank, 458 F. Supp. 143, 146 (S.D.N.Y. 1978), *aff'd*, 629 F.2d 233 (2d Cir. 1980).

It also does not bar suit against individual employees for constitutional torts. Castro v. United States, 34 F.3d 106, 110 (2d Cir. 1994).

283 *See* Ortiz v. Pearson, 1999 U.S. Dist. LEXIS 22450 (S.D.N.Y. Nov. 5, 1999), *adopted by* 88 F. Supp. 2d 151 (S.D.N.Y. 2000).

284 *Id.*

285 *See* Fed. Deposit Ins. Corp. v. Meyer, 510 U.S. 471, 114 S. Ct. 996, 127 L. Ed. 2d 308 (1994).

286 *See* Truman v. United States, 26 F.3d 592 (5th Cir. 1994); Sheehan v. United States, 896 F.2d 1168 (9th Cir. 1990) (Cal. law); Hart v. United States, 894 F.2d 1539, 1548 (11th Cir. 1990) (Fla. law); DeFord v. Sec'y of Labor, 700 F.2d 281, 290 (6th Cir. 1983); Gross v. United States, 676 F.2d 295 (8th Cir. 1982), *after remand*, 723 F.2d 609 (8th Cir. 1983); Wilkinson v. United States, 2007 WL 3544062 (D.N.D. Nov. 9, 2007) (awarding damages for intentional infliction of emotional distress, also trespass and conversion, against Bureau of Indian Affairs, which wrongfully leased out Indians' land, at request of Farm Service Agency, after default on farm loans). *But see* Harris v. Taxpayer Advocate Serv. I.R.S.—United States, 2006 WL 536194 (N.D. Tex. Feb. 24, 2006) (no waiver of immunity for IRS).

287 D'Ambra v. United States, 354 F. Supp. 810 (D.R.I. 1973), *aff'd in part, vacated in part on other grounds*, 481 F.2d 14 (1st Cir. 1973); *see also* Olivas v. United States, 506 F.2d 1158 (9th Cir. 1974); Ginaitt v. Harounian, 806 F. Supp. 311 (D.R.I. 1992); Ellington v. United States, 404 F. Supp. 1165 (M.D. Fla. 1975). *See generally* National Consumer Law Center, Fair Debt Collection § 10.2 (6th ed. 2008) (state recognition of tort of negligent infliction of emotional distress).

288 28 U.S.C. § 2680(h); Mundy v. United States, 983 F.2d 950, 953 (9th Cir. 1993); O'Donnell v. United States, 891 F.2d 1079 (3d Cir. 1989) (Pa. law); Doe v. DiGenova, 779 F.2d 74, 87 (D.C. Cir. 1985), *on remand*, 642 F. Supp. 624 (D.D.C. 1986), *later proceedings at* 851 F.2d 1457 (D.C. Cir. 1988); Black v. Sheraton Corp. of Am., 564 F.2d 531 (D.C. Cir. 1977); Flowers v. United States, 348 F.2d 910 (10th Cir. 1965); Lopez-Pacheco v. United States, 627 F. Supp. 1224 (D. P.R. 1986), *aff'd*, 815 F.2d 692 (1st Cir. 1987) (mem.); Fagot v. Fed. Deposit Ins. Corp., 584 F. Supp. 1168, 1176 (D. P.R. 1984). *But see* Dolan v. United States, 2008 WL 362556 (D. Or. Feb. 8, 2008) (invasion of privacy claim that arose from physical attack barred by assault and battery exception; must "look beyond the labels").

289 Hurwitz v. United States, 884 F.2d 684 (2d Cir. 1989) (plaintiff could not assert invasion of privacy claim under FTCA when New York did not recognize this cause of action, as a private person would not be liable on this claim in New York). *See generally* National Consumer Law Center, Fair Debt Collection § 10.3 (6th ed. 2008) (state recognition of tort of invasion of privacy).

290 28 U.S.C. § 2680(c); *see* § 11.2.12.9, *infra*.

291 26 U.S.C. §§ 6330, 7422, 7432, 7433; *see* § 11.2.12.9, *supra*.

waive sovereign immunity for assault, battery, false imprisonment, false arrest, malicious prosecution, abuse of process, libel, slander, misrepresentation, deceit, or interference with contract rights.[292] However, sovereign immunity *is* waived for the first six of these torts if committed by a United States investigative or law enforcement officer.[293]

The waiver of sovereign immunity also does not apply to federal employees' discretionary acts.[294] A discretionary act is defined as one that includes an element of choice, grounded in considerations of public policy.[295] Because the waiver of sovereign immunity applies only to actions which would be tortious if done by a private actor, it does not allow due process or equal protection claims, which concern government action.[296]

Suits brought under the FTCA must be brought against the United States itself, rather than against specific agencies or employees, or will be dismissed on jurisdictional grounds.[297] In addition, any claim asserted under the Act must first be brought before the agency in question, unless it is asserted as a cross-claim, counterclaim or third party complaint.[298]

Apart from the exclusions set forth in the statute, applicable state law usually governs affirmative defenses under the FTCA. However, the statutes of limitations are fixed by federal law, which also determines whether or not the period of limitations may be tolled.[299]

In 1988, the Supreme Court held, in *Westfall v. Ervin*,[300] that a federal employee was *not* immune from personal liability for state common law torts unless his conduct was not only within the scope of his employment but also was in exercise of governmental discretion. Congress worked swiftly to overturn this decision by enacting amendments to the FTCA known collectively as the Federal Employees Liability Reform and Tort Compensation Act (FELRTCA) or "Westfall amendments."[301] This legislation specifically immunizes employees from personal liability for damages resulting from common law torts committed within the ambit of their federal jobs.[302] The exclusive remedy for such torts is an action against the United States itself under the FTCA.[303] The *Westfall* amendments also permit the United

292 28 U.S.C. § 2680(h); *see* Conard v. Evans, 193 Fed. Appx. 945 (11th Cir. 2006) (affirming dismissal of claims for false arrest, libel, and slander based on student loan collection tactics); Pauly v. United States Dep't of Agric., 348 F.3d 1143 (9th Cir. 2003); Lawrence v. United States, 340 F.3d 952 (9th Cir. 2003); Standifer v. Sec. Exch. Comm'n, 2008 WL 513352 (N.D. Ga. Feb. 22, 2008) (FTCA claims arising from Securities Exchange Commission receivership barred by exception for claims of interference with contract rights); Dolan v. United States, 2008 WL 362556 (D. Or. Feb. 8, 2008) (invasion of privacy claim that arose from physical attack barred by assault and battery exception); Avery v. United States, 2008 WL 347904 (D.D.C. Feb. 7, 2008) (defamation claim alleging false reporting of student loan information barred by intentional torts exception); Burgess v. United States Dep't of Educ., 2006 WL 1047064 (D. Vt. Apr. 17, 2006) (dismissing defamation claim); Gayton v. United States, 2006 WL 408562 (N.D. Cal. Feb. 17, 2006) (neither employee nor United States liable for assault by non-law enforcement employee); Nogueras-Cartagena v. United States, 172 F. Supp. 2d 296 (D. P.R. 2001), *aff'd*, 75 Fed. Appx. 795 (1st Cir. 2003); Zolman v. United States, 170 F. Supp. 2d 746 (W.D. Mich. 2001) (defamation claim barred); Bickley v. United States Dep't of the Treasury, 2000 U.S. Dist. LEXIS 2141 (W.D. Va. Jan. 18, 2000), *aff'd*, 225 F.3d 653 (4th Cir. 2000) (table).

293 28 U.S.C. § 2680(h).

294 28 U.S.C. § 2680(a); *see* Palay v. United States, 349 F.3d 418 (7th Cir. 2003) (declining to dismiss pleading when facts not yet developed that would show whether discretionary function exception applied).

295 Lawrence v. United States, 340 F.3d 952 (9th Cir. 2003); Standifer v. Sec. Exch. Comm'n, 2008 WL 513352 (N.D. Ga. Feb. 22, 2008) (FTCA claims arising from Securities Exchange Commission receivership barred by discretionary function exception); Littell v. United States, 191 F. Supp. 2d 1338 (M.D. Fla. 2002); Nogueras-Cartagena v. United States, 172 F. Supp. 2d 296 (D. P.R. 2001), *aff'd*, 75 Fed. Appx. 795 (1st Cir. 2003).

296 Lewis v. Glickman, 104 F. Supp. 2d 1311 (D. Kan. 2000), *aff'd*, 2002 U.S. App. LEXIS 13269 (10th Cir. July 3, 2002).

297 28 U.S.C. § 2679(a); *see* Rivera v. United States, 928 F.2d 592, 609 (2d Cir. 1991); Gilles v. United States, 906 F.2d 1386 (10th Cir. 1990); Curtis v. Treasury Dep't, 2007 WL 460646 (N.D. Cal. Feb. 7, 2007); Gayton v. United States, 2006 WL 408562 (N.D. Cal. Feb. 17, 2006).

298 28 U.S.C. § 2675(a); *see, e.g.*, Palay v. United States, 349 F.3d 418 (7th Cir. 2003) (dismissing one of plaintiff's two claims because it was not sufficiently stated in his administrative claim); Lowery v. United States Dep't of Educ., 499 F. Supp. 2d 928 (N.D. Ohio 2007) (plaintiff bears burden of proof on presentation issue; allegation that letters were sent at unspecified time to unnamed employees of Department of Education telling them they were dunning wrong person not sufficient); Ortiz-Romany v. United States, 497 F. Supp. 2d 285 (D. P.R. 2007) (filing suit just fifteen days after filing administrative claim and before agency ruled does not constitute exhaustion of administrative remedies); Martin v. Sallie Mae, Inc., 2007 WL 4305607 (S.D. W. Va. Dec. 7, 2007) (negligence claim against Army, alleging failure to pay student loans as agreed, barred by failure to present claim); Curtis v. Treasury Dep't, 2007 WL 2854274 (N.D. Cal. Sept. 27, 2007) (sending a facsimile of draft complaint to employees of agency not sufficient presentation to satisfy Federal Tort Claims Act, because doing so would not "trigger an administrative process"); Burgess v. United States Dep't of Educ., 2006 WL 1047064 (D. Vt. Apr. 17, 2006) (dismissing FTCA suit regarding collection of government debt because plaintiffs did not allege that they presented their claim in writing to agency).

299 *See* 28 U.S.C. § 2401(b).

300 484 U.S. 292, 108 S. Ct. 580, 98 L. Ed. 2d 619 (1988).

301 Pub. L. No. 100-694, 102 Stat. 4564 (1988).

302 Note that FELCRTA does not prevent injunctive or equitable relief or suit for constitutional violations against individuals.

303 *See* United States v. Smith, 499 U.S. 160, 111 S. Ct. 1180, 113 L. Ed. 2d 134 (1991); McHugh v. Univ. of Vt., 966 F.2d 67 (2d Cir. 1992); Rivera v. United States, 928 F.2d 592 (2d Cir. 1991); Nogueras-Cartagena v. United States, 172 F. Supp. 2d 296 (D. P.R. 2001) (ordering United States substituted as defendant in place of individual FBI and IRS agents and prosecutors when plaintiffs failed to prove actions outside official capacity), *aff'd*, 75 Fed. Appx. 795 (1st Cir. 2003); Connor v. Matthews, 134 F.

States to use any defenses available to it independently, including the numerous exceptions to liability set forth in the FTCA, even though the defenses would not have been available to the employee.[304]

11.2.12.6 Violation of Bankruptcy Stay

If the debtor has filed bankruptcy, a government creditor may violate bankruptcy law by, for example, freezing a bank account in violation of the automatic stay, or attempting to collect a discharged debt. Available relief includes compensatory damages, including damages for mental anguish, the return of improperly intercepted funds, and, if the misconduct is willful or in bad faith, attorney fees.[305]

11.2.12.7 Fair Debt Collection Practices Act

Debt collection by United States officers and employees is excluded from the provisions of the Fair Debt Collection Practices Act (FDCPA).[306] However, private collection agencies and collection attorneys hired by the government are bound by the FDCPA and all other applicable legislation regulating debt collection practices.[307] Claims under that statute may be appropriate if a collector has, for example, misrepresented the government's rights in connection with collection of a claim.

11.2.12.8 State Agencies

A state agency, such as a state welfare department, engaged in a joint federal-state program may be subject to state restrictions on its collection processes.[308] In addition, federal employees may be sued under 42 U.S.C. § 1983 if they have conspired with state officials to violate a debtor's constitutional rights.[309]

11.2.12.9 Remedies for Abuses by IRS

Tax practice is a highly complex subject, beyond the scope of this manual, but practitioners should be aware of the special problems presented by the Internal Revenue Service (IRS) debt collection. Most of the remedies for abusive collection conduct by the federal government do not apply to federal tax collection. The FTCA explicitly exempts from its waiver of sovereign immunity the assessment or collection of any tax.[310] The Anti-Injunction Act and the

---

Supp. 2d 797 (N.D. Tex. 2001) (action against individual IRS agent is action against United States, and barred by sovereign immunity); Marsden v. Fed. Bureau of Prisons, 856 F. Supp. 832, 836 (S.D.N.Y. 1994).

304 28 U.S.C. §§ 2674, 2680(h); *see* Fair v. Swenson, 753 F. Supp. 875 (D. Colo.), *aff'd*, 947 F.2d 953 (10th Cir. 1991) (table).

305 *In re* Harchar, 371 B.R. 254 (N.D. Ohio 2007) (chapter 13 debtors stated claim for violation of automatic stay when Internal Revenue Service (IRS) froze their accounts, resulting in denial of earned income credit refunds to low-income family); *In re* Bryant, 340 B.R. 569 (Bankr. N.D. Tex. 2006) (IRS's post-discharge attempt to collect interest on tax debt paid in chapter 13); *In re* Atkins, 279 B.R. 639 (Bankr. N.D.N.Y. 2002) (awarding $30,000 compensatory damages when government dunned consumer for fourteen years and intercepted three tax refunds, although debt discharged in bankruptcy and mortgaged home voluntarily surrendered to Farmer's Home Administration). *But see In re* Rivera Torres, 432 F.3d 20 (1st Cir. 2005) (sovereign immunity not waived as to emotional distress damages; reversing award of emotional distress damages for IRS attempts to collect discharged debt), *on remand*, *In re* Torres, 377 B.R. 428 (Bankr. D. P.R. 2007) ("money recovery" in the section of bankruptcy law waiving sovereign immunity not as broad as "money damages" and does not include pecuniary loss awarded here). *See generally* National Consumer Law Center, Consumer Bankruptcy Law and Practice § 9.6 (8th ed. 2006 and Supp.).

306 15 U.S.C. § 1692a(6)(C); *see* National Consumer Law Center, Fair Debt Collection § 4.3.4 (6th ed. 2008); *see also* Greenland v. Van Ru Credit Corp., 2006 WL 2884458 (W.D. Mich. Oct. 10, 2006); Frew v. Van Ru Credit Corp., 2006 WL 2261624 (E.D. Pa. Aug. 7, 2006); Kenney v. Barnhart, 2006 WL 2092607, at *9 (C.D. Cal. July 26, 2006).

The Department of the Treasury, and perhaps other agencies, have adopted guidelines for employee collection efforts based on the FDCPA. Department of the Treasury Manual Supp., No. 5G-243 (Dec. 26, 1979).

Collection agencies and attorneys hired by the United States are subject to the FDCPA. 31 U.S.C. § 3178(a)(2); *see* § 11.3.6, *infra*.

307 31 U.S.C. § 3718(a)(2)(B), (b)(1)(B)(6); *see also* 31 C.F.R. § 901.5(a)(3). *See generally* § 11.2.4, *infra*.

308 *See, e.g.*, Wyatt v. Commonwealth, 463 A.2d 64 (Pa. Commw. Ct. 1983) (state welfare worker's false implication to client that welfare would be repaid from exempt Social Security lump-sum payment not a "fair means" of debt collection).

309 Melo v. Hafer, 912 F.2d 628, 638 (3d Cir. 1990), *aff'd*, 502 U.S. 21, *on remand* 13 F.3d 736 (3d Cir. 1994); *see* National Consumer Law Center, Fair Debt Collection § 9.12 (6th ed. 2008); § 12.3, *infra*.

310 8 U.S.C. § 2680(c); Asemani v. Internal Revenue Serv., 2006 WL 41265 (3d Cir. Jan. 6, 2006); Fishburn v. Brown, 125 F.3d 979 (6th Cir. 1997) (sovereign immunity bars FTCA action against IRS); Munaco v. United States, 502 F. Supp. 2d 614 (E.D. Mich. 2007) (FTCA exception for tax collection barred conversion and slander of title claims against IRS, which placed lien on property four months after delinquent taxpayer had sold it to innocent third party); Harris v. Taxpayer Advocate Serv. I.R.S.—United States, 2006 WL 536194 (N.D. Tex. Feb. 24, 2006) (mag.), *adopted*, 2006 WL 1305285 (N.D. Tex. Mar. 31, 2006); Brewer v. Comm'r, 430 F. Supp. 2d 1254 (S.D. Ala. 2006) (no waiver of sovereign immunity for common law or constitutional torts in tax collection); Harris v. United States, 2005 WL 518977 (S.D. Tex. Jan. 18, 2005); Morrison v. United States Dep't of Agric., 2001 U.S. Dist. LEXIS 7419 (S.D. Ohio May 1, 2001) (sovereign immunity bars FTCA action by farmer against IRS challenging setoff of sum owed to farmer by Agricultural Stabilization and Conservation Service), *aff'd*, 2001 U.S. App. LEXIS 23754 (6th Cir. Oct. 26, 2001); Bilger v. United States, 2001 U.S. Dist. LEXIS 3236 (E.D. Cal. Jan. 9, 2001) (broadly construing FTCA's tax exception to apply to any acts of IRS employees in course of their duties). *But see* Tekle *ex rel.* Tekle v. United States, 457 F.3d 1088 (9th Cir. 2006)

Declaratory Judgment Act generally forbid injunctions and declaratory judgments against the IRS.[311] Actions under 42 U.S.C. § 1983 will not lie for deprivation of rights under color of federal law.[312]

All circuits that have considered *Bivens* actions against IRS agents have applied the *Schweiker v. Chilicky*[313] criteria, and concluded that the remedies provided in the Internal Revenue Code are usually adequate, despite their limitations.[314] *Bivens* suits are thus barred, with a possible exception for extreme cases: a "lawless and arbitrary vendetta" for which the statute provides no adequate remedy, or violations of the First or Fourth Amendments.[315] Some

(allowing FTCA action to go forward against IRS and narcotics agents who allegedly used excessive force against taxpayers' eleven-year-old son; FTCA exception for certain willful torts not applicable to law enforcement officers; tax collection exemption not mentioned); *cf.* Nogueras-Cartagena v. United States, 172 F. Supp. 2d 296 (D. P.R. 2001) (allowing malicious prosecution case against United States to go forward; claims arose from IRS and FBI's investigation and unsuccessful criminal prosecution of alleged violations of tax law; no discussion of exemption for assessment of collection of tax), *aff'd*, 75 Fed. Appx. 795 (1st Cir. 2003).

311 26 U.S.C. § 7421; 28 U.S.C. § 2201; *see* Godt v. Internal Revenue Serv., 2008 WL 656264 (7th Cir. Mar. 12, 2008) (unpublished) (Anti-Injunction Act bars action in which taxpayer is "trying to evade collection"); United States v. Berk, 374 B.R. 385 (D. Mass. 2007) (claims for injunctive or declaratory relief, here seeking to enjoin real estate foreclosure, barred by Anti-Injunction Act); Sterner v. United States Drug Enforcement Agency, 467 F. Supp. 2d 1017 (S.D. Cal. 2006) (Anti-Injunction Act protects actions "that may culminate in the assessment or collection of taxes"; refusing to enjoin IRS seizure of doctor's confidential patient records, but would consider injunction against dissemination for non-tax purposes); O'Meara v. Waters, 464 F. Supp. 2d 474 (D. Md. 2006) (irreparable harm exception to Anti-Injunction Act not shown; taxpayer denied face-to-face hearing could have appealed to Tax Court, or paid tax and sued for refund); Lindsey v. United States, 448 F. Supp. 2d 37 (D.D.C. 2006); Celauro v. Internal Revenue Serv., 411 F. Supp. 2d 257 (E.D.N.Y. 2006), *aff'd*, 214 Fed. Appx. 95 (2d Cir. 2007); Babington v. Comm'r, 2005 WL 2001165 (M.D. Fla. July 6, 2005) (no showing that government can not prove entitlement to tax); March v. Harper, 2002 WL 1396510 (D. Haw. May 14, 2002) (exceptions to Anti-Injunction Act very narrow; not shown here by *pro se* taxpayer challenging wage garnishment); People *ex rel.* Ervin v. Dist. Dir., 170 F. Supp. 2d 1040 (E.D. Cal. 2001) (Anti-Injunction Act bars suit to enjoin collection of tax; taxpayer unable to prove exceptions, that is, that government can not under any circumstances prevail on the merits, and plaintiff lacks adequate remedy at law and will suffer irreparable harm).

312 Rogers v. Vicuna, 264 F.3d 1 (1st Cir. 2001); Johnson v. Internal Revenue Serv., 2001 U.S. Dist. LEXIS 15931 (E.D. Pa. Aug. 20, 2001).

313 487 U.S. 412, 108 S. Ct. 2460, 101 L. Ed. 2d 370 (1988).

314 Godt v. Internal Revenue Serv., 2008 WL 656264 (7th Cir. Mar. 12, 2008) (unpublished) (no *Bivens* action for "relatively trivial" misconduct by individual IRS agents); Hudson Valley Black Press v. Internal Revenue Serv., 409 F.3d 106 (2d Cir. 2005); Adams v. Johnson, 355 F.3d 1179 (9th Cir. 2004); Shreiber v. Mastrogiovanni, 214 F.3d 148 (3d Cir. 2000) (no *Bivens* cause of action against IRS agents because statutory remedies adequate); Dahn v. United States, 127 F.3d 1249 (10th Cir. 1997) (IRS agents not subject to *Bivens* actions); Fishburn v. Brown, 125 F.3d 979 (6th Cir. 1997); Vennes v. An Unknown Number of Unidentified Agents, 26 F.3d 1448 (8th Cir. 1994) (no *Bivens* remedy for overzealous tax assessment or collection); Wages v. Internal Revenue Serv., 915 F.2d 1230 (9th Cir. 1990) (even if taxpayer stated claim for constitutional violation, *Bivens* action not available because statutory remedies adequate); Baddour, Inc. v. United States, 802 F.2d 801 (5th Cir. 1986) (no *Bivens* remedy, when tax code provides adequate remedies for improper levy); Cameron v. Internal Revenue Serv., 773 F.2d 126 (7th Cir. 1985) (tax code remedies generally adequate, but *Bivens* action might lie if agents "ransacked a home" or engaged in "lawless vendetta"); Giles v. Volvo Trucks of N. Am., 2008 WL 509178 (M.D. Pa. Feb. 20, 2008) (*Bivens* action will not lie for constitutional violations in the investigation, assessment, or collection of taxes); Al-Sharif v. Bradley, 2008 WL 410364 (S.D. Ga. Feb. 20, 2008) (tax code provides adequate remedies); Caton v. Hutson, 2007 WL 4731010 (M.D. Fla. Nov. 19, 2007) (unpublished) (tax code provides exclusive remedy for wrongful assessment or collection by IRS employees); Foley v. Comm'r, 2007 WL 806521 (N.D. Cal. Mar. 15, 2007) (no *Bivens* action for misconduct by IRS agents; 26 U.S.C. § 7433 is exclusive remedy when, because of misreading of Social Security number, one taxpayer was accused of earning—and not reporting—income earned by another); Jones v. Internal Revenue Serv., 216 F. Supp. 2d 955 (D. Neb. 2002) (*Schweiker* rule bars *Bivens* action against IRS agents), *aff'd*, 60 Fed. Appx. 642 (8th Cir. 2003); People *ex rel.* Ervin v. Dist. Dir., 170 F. Supp. 2d 1040 (E.D. Cal. 2001) (Internal Revenue Code remedies "comprehensive and exclusive"); Beech v. Comm'r, 190 F. Supp. 2d 1183 (D. Ariz. 2001) (IRS remedies are adequate so *Bivens* claim is precluded), *aff'd*, 2002 WL 1302256 (9th Cir. June 13, 2002); *see also* Celauro v. Internal Revenue Serv., 411 F. Supp. 2d 257 (E.D.N.Y. 2006) (no *Bivens* remedy because statutory remedies adequate), *aff'd*, 214 Fed. Appx. 95 (2d Cir. 2007); Schadl v. Kupinse, 2001 U.S. Dist. LEXIS 10351 (D. Conn. Mar. 29, 2001) (tax code remedies adequate); *cf.* Rogers v. Vicuna, 264 F.3d 1 (1st Cir. 2001) (noting conflict on question whether tax code remedies adequate, but declining to reach this question when search and seizure reasonable within meaning of Fourth Amendment). *But see* Meredith v. Erath, 182 F. Supp. 2d 964 (C.D. Cal. 2001) (allowing *Bivens* action to go forward with claims of excessive force and improper detention, arising from IRS's early morning armed raid on residence and business premises), *rev'd in part on other grounds*, 342 F.3d 1057 (9th Cir. 2003).

315 Nat'l Commodity & Barter Ass'n v. Gibbs, 886 F.2d 1240 (10th Cir. 1989) (*Bivens* available for First or Fourth Amendment violations by IRS); Cameron v. Internal Revenue Serv., 773 F.2d 126 (7th Cir. 1985) (*Bivens* action might lie if agents ransacked a home or engaged in "lawless vendetta;" not shown here); Rutherford v. United States, 702 F.2d 580 (5th Cir. 1983) (*Bivens* action would be appropriate if taxpayer showed a "vendetta" which required lengthy and expensive litigation to undo;); Williamson v. Sena, 2006 WL 1308290 (D.N.M. Mar. 28, 2006) (recognizing exception for violations of Fourth Amendment but not Fifth, Ninth, or Tenth Amendments), *aff'd*, 230 Fed. Appx. 815 (10th Cir. 2007); Meredith v. Erath, 182 F. Supp. 2d 964 (C.D. Cal. 2001) (allowing *Bivens* action to go forward with claims of excessive force and improper detention, arising from IRS's early morning armed raid on residence and business premises), *rev'd in part on other grounds*, 342 F.3d 1057 (9th Cir. 2003); Connor v. Matthews, 134 F. Supp. 2d 797

courts have been willing to apply a standard Fourth Amendment analysis—probable cause, particularity, scope of search, and so forth—in *Bivens* challenges to searches and seizures by the IRS.[316]

In most cases, the only remedies available to aggrieved taxpayers are those found in the Internal Revenue Code. Taxpayers may seek a refund of an incorrectly assessed tax, but must first pay the disputed amount and pursue an administrative claim for refund and may recover only the amount of the tax, not expenses incurred in, for example, mortgaging one's house to pay the tax, or pursuing administrative and judicial remedies.[317] Taxpayers may sue for actual damages resulting from reckless, intentional, or negligent disregard of Internal Revenue statutes or regulations in the collection[318]—but not the assessment[319]—of taxes, or for failure to release a lien.[320] Note however that many of the standards governing IRS agents' conduct are found in agency rulings or an agency manual, which are neither statutes nor regulations within the meaning of this section.[321] However, the tax code does include restrictions on

---

(N.D. Tex. 2001) (taxpayer failed to allege egregious misconduct which might fit within *Rutherford* exception). *But see* Hudson Valley Black Press v. Internal Revenue Serv., 409 F.3d 106 (2d Cir. 2005) (*Bivens* action will not lie for First and Fourth Amendment claims alleging IRS attack on publication that criticized its treatment of minority taxpayers); Adams v. Johnson, 355 F.3d 1179 (9th Cir. 2004) (*Bivens* claim will not lie for any allegedly unconstitutional actions by IRS).

316 Rogers v. Vicuna, 264 F.3d 1 (1st Cir. 2001) (no reasonable expectation of privacy, so no warrant needed when vehicles seized from driveway clearly visible and accessible from public street); Leveto v. Lapina, 258 F.3d 156 (3d Cir. 2001) (search was reasonable; note that this case predates Shreiber v. Mastrogiovanni, 214 F.3d 148 (3d Cir. 2000), which may take a narrower view); Meredith v. Erath, 182 F. Supp. 2d 964 (C.D. Cal. 2001) (detailed Fourth Amendment analysis of IRS's early morning armed raid on residence and business premises), *rev'd in part on other grounds*, 342 F.3d 1057 (9th Cir. 2003); Taxacher v. Torbic, 2000 U.S. Dist. LEXIS 15193 (W.D. Penn. Feb. 23, 2000) (detailed discussion of qualified immunity; no violation of clearly established right when search met Fourth Amendment reasonableness standards), *aff'd*, 251 F.3d 154 (3d Cir. 2000) (table); *see also* Tekle *ex rel.* Tekle v. United States, 457 F.3d 1088 (9th Cir. 2006) (allowing *Bivens* and FTCA actions to go forward against IRS and narcotics agents who allegedly used excessive force against and unreasonably detained taxpayers' eleven-year-old son); Clarke v. Fiske, 2005 WL 3617731 (W.D. Tex. Sept. 20, 2005) (no Fourth Amendment claim against police or IRS, when arrest warrant was valid, damage to house not unreasonable when police believed arrestee was within and was evading them, and IRS agent did not enter until after damage done), *aff'd*, 2007 WL 1725527 (5th Cir. June 14, 2007).

317 26 U.S.C. § 7422; 28 U.S.C. § 1346; *see* McMillen v. United States Dep't of the Treasury, 960 F.2d 187 (1st Cir. 1991) (payment of disputed amount a prerequisite to challenge to tax assessment); Al-Sharif v. Bradley, 2008 WL 410364 (S.D. Ga. Feb. 20, 2008) (action for refund fails because taxpayer has not fully paid the disputed amounts); Ross v. United States, 460 F. Supp. 2d 139 (D.D.C. 2006) (replevin action will not lie for property seized by IRS; only remedies are refund under section 7422 or damages under section 7433; both barred by failure to exhaust administrative remedies); Babington v. Comm'r, 2005 WL 2001165 (M.D. Fla. July 6, 2005) (taxpayers must pay tax and exhaust administrative remedies); Vaughn v. Internal Revenue Serv., 2001 U.S. Dist. LEXIS 10871 (E.D. Mich. June 22, 2001) (no cause of action for taxpayer who mortgaged house to pay incorrectly assessed sum which was subsequently returned), *adopted by* 2001 U.S. Dist. LEXIS 11432 (E.D. Mich. July 18, 2001); Macleod v. Internal Revenue Serv., 2000 U.S. Dist. LEXIS 12322 (S.D. Cal. Aug. 7, 2000) (taxpayers must pay disputed amount in full and exhaust administrative remedies); *see also* Skillo v. United States, 68 Fed. Cl. 734 (Fed. Cl. 2005) (court of claims may hear tax matter only if it is action for refund; payment of tax and exhaustion of remedies required).

318 26 U.S.C. § 7433; *see* Nogueras-Cartagena v. United States, 125 Fed. Appx. 323 (1st Cir. 2005) (section 7433, like the FTCA, requires a showing of exhaustion of administrative remedies); Foley v. Comm'r, 2007 WL 806521 (N.D. Cal. Mar. 15, 2007) (26 U.S.C. § 7433 is exclusive remedy when, because of misreading of Social Security number, one taxpayer was accused of earning—and not reporting—income earned by another); Ross v. United States, 460 F. Supp. 2d 139 (D.D.C. 2006) (section 7433 is exclusive remedy for misconduct in collection of taxes; replevin action will not lie for property seized by IRS); Turner v. United States, 429 F. Supp. 2d 149 (D.D.C. 2006) (even if section 7433 administrative remedies futile, which was not shown here, court has no power to excuse compliance with statutory exhaustion requirement); Harris v. Taxpayer Advocate Serv. I.R.S.—United States, 2006 WL 536194 (N.D. Tex. Feb. 24, 2006) (section 7433 applies only to collection of tax; no cause of action for intentional torts occurring in dispute over claim for expedited tax return); Sepp v. United States, 2006 WL 213995 (D. Ariz. Jan. 25, 2006) (sections 7432 and 7433 are waivers of sovereign immunity, which must be narrowly construed); Devore v. United States, 110 F. Supp. 2d 1320 (D. Nev. 2000) (section 7433 provides only remedy for taxpayer who alleges that lien was filed, in violation of IRS regulations, after he claimed due process hearing); United States v. Kaigler, 109 F. Supp. 2d 736 (N.D. Ohio 2000) (dismissing section 7433 counterclaim because taxpayer failed to allege which section of statute or regulation violated); *cf.* Macleod v. Internal Revenue Serv., 2000 U.S. Dist. LEXIS 12322 (S.D. Cal. Aug. 7, 2000) (giving taxpayers who failed to state a *Bivens* or FTCA claim an opportunity to replead under 26 U.S.C. § 7433).

319 Brewer v. Comm'r, 430 F. Supp. 2d 1254 (S.D. Ala. 2006); Vaughn v. Internal Revenue Serv., 2001 U.S. Dist. LEXIS 10871 (E.D. Mich. June 22, 2001) (damages only for improper collection, not negligent assessment), *adopted by* 2001 U.S. Dist. LEXIS 11432 (E.D. Mich. July 18, 2001).

320 26 U.S.C. § 7432; *see* Kabakjian v. United States, 92 F. Supp. 2d 435 (E.D. Pa. Apr. 12, 2000) (burden on taxpayers to show actual economic damages from delayed release of lien; not shown when taxpayers alleged one denial of a credit card application; emotional distress damages not recoverable), *aff'd*, 267 F.3d 208 (3d Cir. 2001). *But cf.* Parker v. Comm'r, T.C. Memo 2005-294, 2005 WL 3501575 (U.S. Tax Ct. Dec. 22, 2005) (placing, and refusing to release, lien on exempt property, here Indian lands, neither abuse of discretion nor denial of due process when no attempt to levy; no requirement that filed liens "explicitly exclude" exempt property).

321 Shwarz v. United States, 234 F.3d 428 (9th Cir. 2000) (IRS manual and policy statement not statutes or regulations within meaning of section 7433; no cause of action for violation);

collection calls at inconvenient times and places; contacts with taxpayers represented by attorneys; contacts at the taxpayer's place of employment; and harassment and abuse.[322]

If liability is shown, the United States is liable for the plaintiff's "actual, direct economic damages" plus "the costs of the action," except that, in suits alleging negligent disregard of a provision of the Internal Revenue Code, damages may not exceed $100,000.[323] In a suit alleging disregard of a provision of the Internal Revenue Code, if the taxpayer's position is found to be frivolous or groundless, the taxpayer may be required to pay a penalty of up to $10,000.[324]

The Internal Revenue Code also provides for notice and an administrative hearing, with an appeal to the Tax Court, for taxpayers threatened with a levy.[325] These sections contain strict procedural requirements—often including short time limits—and failure to exhaust administrative remedies will bar any subsequent judicial review.[326]

Special issues relating to the Internal Revenue Service's use of private debt collection agencies to collect delinquent taxes are discussed in a different NCLC manual.[327]

11.3 Federal Debt Collection Procedures Act

11.3.1 Civil Procedure and Exemptions for Collection of Federal Government's Claims

In 1990 Congress passed the Federal Debt Collection Procedures Act.[328] Congress intended the Act to create a

---

United States v. Meisner, 2007 WL 1290088 (D. Neb. May 2, 2007) (IRS manual does not have force of law; no private right of action for failure to follow its procedures); Sachs v. United States, 2001 U.S. Dist. LEXIS 17279 (E.D. Mich. Aug. 20, 2001) (no cause of action for violation of IRS manual or revenue rulings), *aff'd*, 2003 U.S. App. LEXIS 103374 (6th Cir. Feb. 21, 2003).

322 26 U.S.C. § 6304.

323 26 U.S.C. § 7433(b). *But see In re* Klauer, 362 B.R. 31 (Bankr. M.D. Fla. 2006) (denying costs and attorney fees when IRS's challenge to dischargeability, though unsuccessful, was "substantially justified"; legitimate question whether complex tax shelter was willful tax evasion).

324 26 U.S.C. § 6673(b).

325 26 U.S.C. § 6330; *see* Barry v. United States, 2007 WL 276622 (11th Cir. Jan. 31, 2007) (district court lacked subject matter jurisdiction over due process challenge to IRS administrative hearing; even for constitutional issues, appeal to Tax Court is only remedy); Weber v. Internal Revenue Serv., 2007 WL 316460 (W.D. Wis. Jan. 8, 2007) (district court lacks subject matter jurisdiction over due process claim alleging IRS refusal of face-to-face hearing to hearing-impaired taxpayer); Bartschi v. Tracy, 2001 U.S. Dist. LEXIS 16333 (D. Ariz. Sept. 5, 2001) (dismissing claim of improper levy procedure for lack of jurisdiction, as it may be brought only under 26 U.S.C. § 6330); Skillo v. United States, 68 Fed. Cl. 734 (Fed. Cl. 2005) (dismissing due process claim; petition to Tax Court, with ninety-day limitations period, is only remedy for taxpayer who disagrees with deficiency assessment). *But cf.* Boyd v. Comm'r, 451 F.3d 8 (1st Cir. 2006) (procedural protections that are required for levy do not apply to offset of tax refund).

326 Al-Sharif v. Bradley, 2008 WL 410364 (S.D. Ga. Feb. 20, 2008) (failure to exhaust remedies pursuant to section 7433 is jurisdictional); Dye v. United States, 516 F. Supp. 2d 61 (D.D.C. 2007) (denying actions for refund and money damages when taxpayer did not exhaust remedies pursuant to section 7433); Munaco v. United States, 502 F. Supp. 2d 614 (E.D. Mich. 2007) (exhaustion requirements apply to third party who seeks refund of sum paid to release improper lien and clear title to property); United States v. Berk, 374 B.R. 385 (D. Mass. 2007) (section 7432(d) and 7433(d) claims alleging failure to release lien, and misconduct by Internal Revenue Service agents, both barred by failure to exhaust administrative remedies); Ross v. United States, 460 F. Supp. 2d 139 (D.D.C. 2006) (barring section 7422 refund action and section 7433 claim for damages because of failure to exhaust administrative remedies); Lindsey v. United States, 448 F. Supp. 2d 37 (D.D.C. 2006) (requirement for exhaustion of administrative remedies before pursuing section 7422 action for refund is jurisdictional; section 7433 claim for damages that fails to allege exhaustion fails to state claim); Turner v. United States, 429 F. Supp. 2d 149 (D.D.C. 2006) (even if section 7433 administrative remedies had been futile, court has no power to excuse compliance with statutory exhaustion requirement); Ulloa v. United States, 2005 WL 2739105 (N.D.N.Y. Oct. 24, 2005) (thirty-day period to seek judicial review of collection hearing includes holidays; court must dismiss claim of *pro se* petitioner who believed the New Year holiday was excluded); Knight v. United States, 2000 U.S. Dist. LEXIS 5645 (S.D. Ga. Mar. 21, 2000) (claims time-barred, even though taxpayer testified he never received notice of disallowance and IRS could not produce proof of mailing; other claims barred due to failure to exhaust administrative remedies because claims not made in writing, although presented orally to problem resolution officer); Rosenberg v. United States, 72 Fed. Cl. 387 (Fed. Cl. 2006) (payment of tax and administrative claim for refund were required, even though several circuits had held that IRS had no power to tax communications services in question), *aff'd*, 223 Fed. Appx. 985 (Fed. Cir. 2007). *But see* Pennoni v. United States, 79 Fed. Cl. 552 (Fed. Cl. 2007) (section 7422 procedures for seeking tax refund not applicable to claim that IRS improperly used garnishment to recoup amount of allegedly improper refund; taxpayer may sue in Court of Claims alleging illegal exaction); Greenberg v. Internal Revenue Serv., 2006 WL 2808086 (W.D. Ark. Aug. 14, 2006) (denying IRS motion to dismiss for failure to exhaust administrative remedies when taxpayer alleged non-receipt of penalty or levy notices and first learned of problem when Social Security garnished); *cf.* Kabakjian v. United States, 92 F. Supp. 2d 435 (E.D. Pa. Apr. 12, 2000) (exhaustion requirement "strict but not mindless"; taxpayers allowed to go forward), *aff'd*, 267 F.3d 208 (3d Cir. 2001).

327 National Consumer Law Center, Fair Debt Collection § 9.10 (6th ed. 2008).

328 Pub. L. No. 101-647, tit. XXXVI, 104 Stat. 4933 (codified at 28 U.S.C. §§ 3001–3308); *see also* Schueler v. Rayjas Enterprises, Inc., 847 F. Supp. 1147 (S.D.N.Y. 1994) (appendix contains government's statement and section by section analysis of the bill which became the Federal Debt Collections Procedures Act).

new statutory framework for the judicial enforcement of most debts owed *to* the U.S. government. The sponsors believed this would facilitate the collection of U.S. government debts and serve to reduce the federal budget deficit.[329]

Rather than defer to state judicial remedies as does Rule 64 of the Federal Rules of Civil Procedure, the Federal Debt Collection Procedures Act (Procedures Act) establishes a federal judicial collection scheme that in large part preempts and replaces state law when the United States is collecting a debt it originated or guaranteed.[330] Alleged debtors in such actions, however, are entitled, under the Procedures Act, to their choice of either federal bankruptcy or state homestead and personal property exemptions.[331]

The Procedures Act only governs debts owed to the United States.[332] It does not govern debts that arise from contracts to which the government was not an original party,[333] or debts that will inure to the economic benefit of a private party rather than the government.[334] It does not apply to or affect the offset programs discussed earlier in this chapter.[335] It does not curtail the government's rights under other federal and state laws to collect certain types of debts, including fines, penalties, assessments, restitution, or forfeitures arising in a criminal case, and taxes and other amounts that can be collected in the same manner as taxes.[336] For those debts, the government is not required to proceed under the Procedures Act, but may choose instead to proceed under state law.[337]

The Procedures Act became effective May 28, 1991.[338] It applied to pending suits[339] and judgments,[340] but did not apply to judgments entered more than ten years before enactment.[341]

11.3.2 Pre-Judgment Remedies

The Procedures Act establishes both pre-judgment and post-judgment remedies. The pre-judgment remedies are attachment, receivership,[342] garnishment (of non-earnings), and sequestration of income from property.[343] These rem-

329 H.R. Rep. No. 101-736, at 23, *reprinted in* 1990 U.S.C.C.A.N. 6630, 6631; *see* United States v. Bongiorno, 106 F.3d 1027 (1st Cir. 1997) (goal of statute was reduction of U.S. deficit).

330 28 U.S.C. § 3001(a), (b); *see* Markham v. Fay, 74 F.3d 1347 (1st Cir. 1996); Mahler v. United States Dep't of Justice, 2001 U.S. Dist. LEXIS 19266 (S.D. Fla. Oct. 5, 2001) (procedural requirements of Florida's Enforcement of Foreign Judgments Act explicitly preempted by Federal Debt Collection Procedures Act).

331 28 U.S.C. § 3014; *see* § 11.3.4, *infra.*

332 Fed. Trade Comm'n v. Nat'l Bus. Consultants, Inc., 376 F.3d 317 (5th Cir. 2004) (judgment in favor of Federal Trade Commission is covered even though recovery will be used in part for consumer redress); *cf.* United States v. Veal, 2005 WL 1532748 (W.D. Mo. June 28, 2005) (debt was owed "to the U.S." under Procedures Act even though only a small fraction of damages were payable to the government in discrimination action brought by government on behalf of aggrieved women).

333 28 U.S.C. § 3002(3)(B); *see* Sobranes Recovery Pool I, L.L.C. v. Todd & Hughes Constr. Corp., 2007 WL 4181680 (5th Cir. Nov. 28, 2007) (Procedures Act does not apply to judgment obtained by Federal Deposit Insurance Corp. on note between private party and failed bank); United States v. Commercial Tech., Inc., 354 F.3d 378, 382 n.4 (5th Cir. 2003).

334 United States v. Bongiorno, 106 F.3d 1027 (1st Cir. 1997) (Procedures Act does not apply to child support restitution order because it would inure to economic benefit of other parent rather than United States); *cf.* United States v. Rostoff, 164 F.3d 63 (1st Cir. 1999) (restitution debts may be collected by the Procedures Act if they are owed to the United States). *But cf.* United States v. Abdelhadi, 327 F. Supp. 2d 587, 601 n.21 (E.D. Va. 2004) (Procedures Act may be available to enforce order that convicted criminal defendant make restitution to third party).

335 28 U.S.C. § 3003(c)(6); *see* Borsarge v. United States Dep't of Educ., 5 F.3d 1414 (11th Cir. 1993) (student loan debtor could not take advantage of state exemptions incorporated by Procedures Act to protect income tax refund from offset).

336 28 U.S.C. § 3003(b); *see* United States v. Mays, 430 F.3d 963 (9th Cir. 2005) (by specifically importing Procedures Act's procedures into Mandatory Victims Restitution Act, Congress clearly meant to make those procedures available to benefit victims connected with criminal cases); Sequoia Prop. & Equip. Ltd. P'ship v. United States, 100 Fed. Appx. 638 (9th Cir. 2004) (government can collect tax debts either under Procedures Act or Internal Revenue Code); United States v. Hawkins, 392 F. Supp. 2d 757 (W.D. Va. 2005) (that the defendant was current on the monthly installments due pursuant to her Mandatory Victims Restitution Act payment schedule did not prevent the government from obtaining a debtor's examination pursuant to the Procedures Act to independently enforce the restitution order); United States v. Debbi, 2005 WL 1020557 (S.D.N.Y. Apr. 29, 2005) (restitution order was treated as tax lien for collection purposes, and Procedures Act allowed delinquent taxes to be collected through levying of Employee Retirement Income Security Act plans); United States v. Patiwana, 267 F. Supp. 2d 301 (E.D.N.Y. 2003); *see also* 18 U.S.C. § 3613(a) (allowing government the option of proceeding under the Procedures Act to collect criminal fines).

337 United States v. Carney, 796 F. Supp. 700 (E.D.N.Y. 1992) (Procedures Act left Internal Revenue Service free to choose whether to use it or state law—here, the New York Debtor-Creditor Law's broader definition of "fraudulent transfer"—to collect taxes); *see also* United States v. Golden Elevator, Inc., 868 F. Supp. 1063 (C.D. Ill. 1994) (allowing government the option of proceeding under state law even for a debt not listed in 28 U.S.C. § 3003(b); having chosen state law to foreclose on mortgage, government could not seek the ten percent surcharge allowed by the Procedures Act).

338 28 U.S.C. § 3001 nn.

339 28 U.S.C. § 3001 nn.; *see also* United States v. Gelb, 783 F. Supp. 748 (E.D.N.Y. 1991) (fraudulent conveyance provisions of 28 U.S.C. §§ 3304–3308 apply retroactively).

340 United States v. Armstrong, 2005 WL 937857 (N.D. Tex. Apr. 21, 2005) (Procedures Act applies to judgments on debts owed to the United States issued after May 29, 1981).

341 28 U.S.C. § 3005; *see* Pierce v. United States, 232 B.R. 333 (E.D.N.C. 1999) (Procedures Act applies to judgment entered in 1985 and allows wage garnishment even though state law would preclude garnishment after ten years).

342 United States v. Brosseau, 2005 WL 94550 (N.D. Tex. Jan. 14, 2005) (under Procedures Act, court may appoint a receiver only at government's request, not at request of judgment debtor).

343 28 U.S.C. §§ 3102–3105; *see* United States v. Cap Quality Care,

edies are only available upon a showing of extraordinary circumstances, for example, the debtor is about to leave the United States or dispose of property, and the debtor is entitled to notice of the right to a prompt post-seizure hearing to assert the absence of grounds for the remedy, the lack of a valid claim, a defense or an exemption.[344]

11.3.3 Post-Judgment Remedies

The Procedures Act's post-judgment remedies provide for judgment liens, notice of exempt property rights, execution of judgments, installment payment orders against self-employed persons or persons concealing substantial earnings, and garnishment, including garnishment of earnings.[345] Another provision of the Act provides for setting aside fraudulent conveyances.[346]

Judgment liens are effective for twenty years, unless satisfied, and may be renewed for another twenty years.[347] Until the judgment lien is satisfied, the debtor is ineligible for grants or loans made, insured, guaranteed or financed directly or indirectly by the federal government, although agencies have authority to promulgate regulations for waiver of this provision.[348]

Wage (and perhaps bank account) garnishments may be continuous,[349] and wage garnishment is allowed even if the debtor is in a state that does not allow it.[350] While the Procedures Act allows garnishment of up to 25% of the debtor's disposable earnings, several courts have held that this is a maximum, and the court has discretion to reduce the amount in light of the debtor's circumstances.[351]

A judgment debtor who disputes the government's right to a particular post-judgment remedy may file a motion to quash.[352] The District Court must conduct a hearing on the motion as soon as practicable, but the issues are limited to the validity of any claim of exemption and the government's compliance with the Procedures Act's requirements.[353] A judgment debtor objecting to a writ of garnishment must meet certain procedural requirements.[354]

The Procedures Act allows the government to recover a surcharge of up to ten percent of the debt to cover the costs of processing and handling the litigation and enforcement of the claim.[355] This surcharge can only be recovered, however, in proceedings seeking pre-judgment or post-judgment remedies, not in a suit on the underlying debt.[356] The surcharge

---

Inc., 400 F. Supp. 2d 295 (D. Me. 2005) (denying federal government's request for pre-judgment remedies of receivership or sequestration under Procedures Act as defendant was not currently "liable for a debt" because the government had not obtained a judgment for the fines and penalties sought in its criminal prosecution).

344 28 U.S.C. § 3101(b), (d); *see also* Nat'l Labor Relations Bd. v. E.D.P. Med. Computer Sys., Inc., 6 F.3d 951 (2d Cir. 1993) (pre-judgment garnishment warranted when property at risk of disappearing; Procedures Act complies with due process); United States v. Teeven, 862 F. Supp. 1200 (D. Del. 1992) (detailed and heavily fact-specific discussion of what government must show "with particularity" to demonstrate probable validity of debt, and "compelling circumstances" to justify pre-judgment remedies; debtors have burden of going forward at post-seizure hearing).

345 28 U.S.C. §§ 3201–3205; United States v. Santee Sioux Tribe, 254 F.3d 728 (8th Cir. 2001) (allowing execution upon bank accounts bearing defendant's federal tax identification number); United States v. Runnells, 335 F. Supp. 2d 724 (E.D. Va. 2004) (ordering document production so that court can decide whether to order installment payments from self-employment earnings).

346 28 U.S.C. §§ 3301–3308; *cf.* United States v. Goforth, 465 F.3d 730 (6th Cir. 2006) (husband's monthly transfers to wife for household expenses not fraudulent transfers); United States v. Loftis, 2007 WL 2428558 (N.D. Tex. Aug. 27, 2007) (debtor does not have right to jury trial on government's fraudulent transfer claim).

347 28 U.S.C. § 3201(c).

348 28 U.S.C. § 3201(e).

349 28 U.S.C. § 3205(a).

350 Pierce v. United States, 232 B.R. 333 (E.D.N.C. 1999) (government can continue to garnish debtor's wages despite state law prohibiting enforcement of judgment against personal property more than ten years after date of judgment).

351 United States v. Ogburn, 499 F. Supp. 2d 28 (D.D.C. 2007); United States v. Crowther, 473 F. Supp. 2d 729, 731 (N.D. Tex. 2007); United States v. George, 144 F. Supp. 2d 161 (E.D.N.Y. 2001); United States v. Kaye, 93 F. Supp. 2d 196, 199 (D. Conn. 2000). *But see* United States v. Hanhardt, 353 F. Supp. 2d 957 (N.D. Ill. 2004) (court does not have authority to reduce garnishment of pension below twenty-five percent).

352 28 U.S.C. § 3202(d).

353 28 U.S.C. § 3202(d) (issues may be somewhat broader if the judgment is a default judgment); *see* United States v. Pugh, 75 Fed. Appx. 546 (8th Cir. 2003) (requiring hearing on exemptions, government's compliance with Procedures Act, and debtor's claim that balance of debt had already been reduced); United States v. Greenberg, 2006 WL 3791373 (D. Vt. Dec. 22, 2006).

354 28 U.S.C. § 3205(c)(5); *see* United States v. Crowther, 473 F. Supp. 2d 729 (N.D. Tex. 2007) (judgment debtor failed to meet procedural requirements imposed by section 3205(c)(5) when he filed blank exemption form and separate request for hearing, and did not disclose substance of his objection until hearing).

355 28 U.S.C. § 3011; *see* Bd. of Governors of the Fed. Reserve Sys. v. Pharaon, 169 F.3d 110 (2d Cir. 1999) (government entitled to ten-percent surcharge, and interest on surcharge, after it sought a pre-judgment restraining order against dissipation of assets); United States v. Jean-Baptiste, 2007 WL 3197390 (E.D.N.Y. Oct. 26, 2007); United States v. Goo, 2002 WL 31934169 (Haw. Nov. 18, 2002) (allowing surcharge in addition to foreclosure expenses).

356 United States v. Rostoff, 164 F.3d 63 (1st Cir. 1999) (government can not assess surcharge in an action to determine the amount of the debt); United States v. Sackett, 114 F.3d 1050 (10th Cir. 1997) (surcharge is available only for pre-judgment or post-judgment proceedings); United States v. George, 144 F. Supp. 2d 161 (E.D.N.Y. 2001) (government entitled to surcharge based on post-judgment enforcement proceedings only once it brings such proceedings, and interest on surcharge runs from date it is imposed, not from date of judgment); United States v. Mauldin, 805 F. Supp. 35 (N.D. Ala. 1992) (surcharge can not be assessed against debtor in suit on student loan debt when government did not use any of the Procedures Act's pre-judgment or post-judgment remedies).

is not applicable when the government is awarded attorney fees or the law on which the claim is based provides any other amount to cover such costs.[357]

11.3.4 Property Exempt from Seizure

The law provides debtors with a choice between the federal exemptions provided in the Bankruptcy Code[358] or the combination of state exemptions and non-Bankruptcy Act federal exemptions.[359] The level of exemptions was one of the greatest contrasts between the House and Senate bills leading to the Procedures Act. The Senate had chosen a list of exemptions similar to, but even slightly more limited than, those in the Bankruptcy Code.[360] The House bill was more generous, providing, for example, a homestead exemption of $70,000 to $99,999.99.[361]

The compromise allows the debtor to choose between the Bankruptcy Act homestead exemption or the state homestead exemption (which in a few states exempts the full value of the homestead).[362] In addition, the remedies available to the United States can be enforced against property co-owned by the debtor and another person only to the extent allowed by the law of the state where the property is located.[363] This provision appears to allow debtors who choose the bankruptcy exemptions to exempt entireties property in states that recognize that doctrine.

A non-debtor has the right to move for an order denying, limiting, conditioning, regulating, extending, or modifying the use of any enforcement procedure.[364] The government can also join third parties and pursue fraudulent transfers of assets.[365]

The Procedures Act does not supersede or modify the federal garnishment protections of seventy-five percent of earnings or thirty times the minimum wage, whichever is greater.[366] In addition, federal Bankruptcy Code[367] or state personal property exemptions[368] may provide an additional protection for earnings and savings. The exemptions provided by the Procedures Act do not restrict the government's ability to collect criminal restitution debts.[369]

357 28 U.S.C. § 3011(b).

358 11 U.S.C. § 522(d); *see* National Consumer Law Center, Consumer Bankruptcy Law and Practice Ch. 10 (8th ed. 2006 and Supp.).

359 28 U.S.C. § 3014; *see* Connell v. United States, 2003 WL 21508244 (9th Cir. June 30, 2003) (debtor may use state exemptions, but his insurance settlement is still not exempt); United States v. Neff, 2007 WL 776532 (D.N.D. Mar. 12, 2007) (debtors may claim state homestead exemption). *But cf.* United States v. Sawaf, 74 F.3d 119 (6th. Cir. 1996) (anti-alienation provision of Employee Retirement Income Security Act (ERISA) would not stop IRS from using Procedures Act garnishment to attach taxpayer's interest in an ERISA pension fund to satisfy judgment for back taxes); United States v. Dixon, 2007 WL 163245 (D. Kan. Jan. 18, 2007) (Procedures Act allows government to garnish retirement plans whether interests are future, vested or contingent; future possibility of a survivor annuity election does not make retirement plan exempt). *See generally* § 12.5.10.2, *infra.*

360 *See* S. 84, 101st Cong. § 3401 (1989), *reprinted in* 135 Cong. Rec. S14,685 to S14,697 (daily ed. Nov. 3, 1989).

361 H.R. 5640, 101st Cong. § 3014 (1989).

362 28 U.S.C. § 3014(a); *see* Ch. 12, *infra* (discussion of state exemption law); Appx. F, *infra* (summaries of state exemption laws).

The Fifth Circuit has ruled that these fairly generous exemptions are not available to a debtor who is subject to a disgorgement order entered by consent in a securities fraud action, as such an order does not meet the statute's definition of "debt." Sec. Exch. Comm'n v. AMX Int'l, Inc., 7 F.3d 71 (5th Cir. 1993); *see also* Pierce v. United States, 232 B.R. 333 (E.D.N.C. 1999) (wages can be garnished under Procedures Act even though judgment would be too old for garnishment under state law).

363 28 U.S.C. §§ 3010(a), 3014(a)(2)(B) (debtors who choose the state exemptions plus federal nonbankruptcy exemptions can also exempt their interest in entireties or community property if allowed by state law); *see* United States v. Sprint Equities NY, Inc., 92 Fed. Appx. 841 (2d Cir. 2004); Fischre v. United States, 852 F. Supp. 628 (W.D. Mich. 1994) (federal lien can only attach to debtor's contingent survivorship interest in entireties property); *see also* United States v. Sowada, 2003 WL 22902613 (E.D. La. Dec. 8, 2003) (requiring government to give notice and opportunity for hearing to spouse before garnishing community property; government can reach property co-owned by debtor and spouse because state law allows it); *cf.* United States v. Coluccio, 51 F.3d 337 (2d Cir. 1995) (bail bond posted by mother for son was not subject to seizure under Procedures Act).

364 28 U.S.C. § 3013; *see* United States v. Kollintzas, 501 F.3d 796 (7th Cir. 2007) (non-party who has interest in the target property may participate in case without formally intervening); United States v. Tedder, 2004 WL 415270 (W.D. Wis. Feb. 26, 2004).

365 28 U.S.C. § 3304; *see* Fed. Trade Comm'n v. Nat'l Bus. Consultants, Inc., 376 F.3d 317 (5th Cir. 2004); *In re* Phillips & Hornsby Litig., 306 F. Supp. 2d 631 (M.D. La. 2004).

366 28 U.S.C. § 3003(c)(4); 15 U.S.C. § 1673(a); *see also* United States v. Hanhardt, 353 F. Supp. 2d 957 (N.D. Ill. 2004) (government's legal claim to garnishment of twenty-five percent of defendant's annuity payments to satisfy restitution order was superior to defendant's other financial obligations).

Note that the dollar amount will change as the federal minimum wage is adjusted. *See* § 12.4.1.4, *infra.*

367 11 U.S.C. § 522(d)(5) ($1075 interest in any property, plus up to $10,125 of any unused portion of $20,200 homestead exemption, as adjusted for inflation effective April 1, 2007).

368 *See* § 12.5.3, *infra.*

369 18 U.S.C. § 3613(a)(2), (f); *see* Paul Revere Ins. Group v. United States, 500 F.3d 957 (9th Cir. 2007) (state exemptions apply when government uses state procedures to collect criminal restitution); United States v. Phillips, 2002 WL 31489546 (6th Cir. Nov. 6, 2002); United States v. Laws, 352 F. Supp. 2d 707 (E.D. Va. 2004); *see also* United States v. Novak, 476 F.3d 1041 (9th Cir. 2007) (Employee Retirement Income Security Act (ERISA) does not prevent garnishment of retirement funds for criminal restitution once defendant has a current, unilateral right to receive payment); United States v. First Bank & Trust, 477 F. Supp. 2d 777 (E.D. Tex. 2007) (ERISA-qualified plan not exempt from garnishment for criminal restitution); United States v. James, 312 F. Supp. 2d 802 (E.D. Va. 2004) (criminal restitution laws override ERISA protections); United States v. Tyson, 265 F. Supp. 2d 788 (E.D. Mich. 2003) (allowing

11.3.5 Distant Filing of Collection Suits Possible

Perhaps the most draconian measure in the Procedures Act is the establishment of nationwide service of process,[370] with the resulting specter that the federal government could sue in a forum thousands of miles from the alleged debtor's current residence. Federal courts have interpreted this part of the Procedures Act to mean that a court can acquire personal jurisdiction over a debtor even if the debtor does not have the "minimum contacts" with the forum state that *International Shoe Co. v. Washington*[371] requires. Instead, the court can exercise personal jurisdiction as long as the debtor has minimum contacts anywhere within the United States.[372] One court has held, however, that an additional inquiry—an analysis of personal jurisdiction under the five-factor "reasonableness" test enunciated in *Asahi Metal Industries Co. v. Superior Court*[373]—is necessary after establishing that the debtor has minimum contacts with the United States.[374] This test requires analysis of: (1) the burden that the exercise of jurisdiction will impose on the defendant; (2) the interests of the forum state in adjudicating the case; (3) the plaintiff's interest in obtaining convenient and effective relief; (4) the interstate judicial system's interest in obtaining the most efficient resolution of the controversy; and (5) the shared interest of the states in furthering substantive social policies.[375]

The nationwide service provision is somewhat ameliorated by the defendant's right to transfer the case to the district where he or she resides[376] and the requirement that the debtor be given notice of the right to transfer.[377] However the defendant has only twenty days after receiving the notice to request the transfer.[378] Also, the Procedures Act's transfer provision does not allow defendants to transfer actions to the defendant's home district in all cases. For example, a sentencing court's continuing jurisdiction over criminal restitution overrides a defendant's right under the Procedures Act to transfer a case to their home district.[379] One court found the Procedures Act transfer provision inapplicable to a fraudulent conveyance action commenced under subchapter D of the Procedures Act as opposed to actions brought pursuant to "[s]ubchapters B and C of Procedures Act *only*, which relate to pre-judgment and post-judgment collection remedies."[380]

11.3.6 Impact on Low-Income Consumers

The impact of this law on low-income consumers, for example, student loan or federal housing loan borrowers or recipients of federal benefit overpayments, is not clear. The rhetoric surrounding this bill and its predecessors often focused on wealthy drug dealers, scofflaws, and professionals, such as doctors and lawyers, avoiding their just debts.[381] However, many of the provisions sought by the U.S. Attorneys (the main proponents and drafters of the original bill)[382] would have affected low-income and moderate-income citizens most heavily, if they were sued by the federal government. The strengthening of the exemptions in the House may have deflected much of the impact on low-income households by protecting more of their income and property. Indeed, some of the litigation since the Procedures Act's passage has been by debtors seeking to establish that the Act covers them so that they can take advantage of its exemptions.[383] Because the government can seize income, benefits, and tax refunds without going to court,[384] the Procedures Act may not give it much additional leverage against low-income debtors who do not have substantial nonexempt assets.

government to garnish ERISA fund in proceeding under Procedures Act to satisfy criminal restitution order); United States v. Sowada, 2003 WL 22902613 (E.D. La. Dec. 8, 2003) (government can garnish ERISA plan funds for satisfaction of criminal fines and penalties); United States v. Grico, 2003 WL 21244024 (E.D. Pa. May 22, 2003) (ERISA funds not exempt for criminal fine; court also says ERISA funds are generally reachable under Procedures Act).

370 28 U.S.C. § 3004(b).

371 326 U.S. 310, 66 S. Ct. 154, 90 L. Ed. 95 (U.S. 1945).

372 Reese Bros., Inc. v. U.S. Postal Serv., 477 F. Supp. 2d 31, 40 (D.D.C. 2007); United States v. Sutton, 2005 WL 281162, at *1 (D. Conn. Jan. 10, 2005).

373 480 U.S. 102, 113–114, 107 S. Ct. 1026, 94 L. Ed. 2d 92 (1987).

374 2005 WL 281162 (D. Conn. Jan. 10, 2005).

375 *Id.*

376 28 U.S.C. § 3004(b)(2); *see* United States v. Allison, 2007 WL 2491192 (W.D.N.C. Aug. 29, 2007) (ordering transfer). *But cf.* United States v. Nash, 175 F.3d 440 (6th Cir. 1999) (finding a district court's failure to grant a transfer to be a legal error, but finding the error harmless).

377 28 U.S.C. § 3101(d).

378 28 U.S.C. § 3004(b)(2).

379 United States v. Tedder, 2004 WL 415270 (W.D. Wis. Feb. 26, 2004); *see also* United States v. Furkin, 165 F.3d 33 (7th Cir. 1998) (table) (text available at 1998 WL 846873) (upholding a district court's decision to deny a transfer request for collection proceedings brought to enforce the criminal judgment entered by that court).

380 United States v. Sutton, 2005 WL 281162 (D. Conn. Jan. 10, 2005); *see also* United States v. Klearman, 1998 WL 122250 (E.D. Pa. Mar. 10, 1998).

381 *See, e.g.*, 136 Cong. Rec. S17,595 (daily ed. Oct. 27, 1990).

382 H.R. Rep. No. 101-736, at 26, *reprinted in* 1990 U.S.C.C.A.N. 6630, 6634.

383 *See, e.g.*, Borsarge v. United States Dep't of Educ., 5 F.3d 1414 (11th Cir. 1993) (student loan debtor sought to protect tax refund by establishing that Procedures Act, which incorporated state exemptions, applied); Sec. Exch. Comm'n v. AMX Int'l, Inc., 7 F.3d 71 (5th Cir. 1993) (securities fraud debtor sought to protect home by establishing that Procedures Act governed disgorgement order).

384 *See* § 11.2, *supra*.

Chapter 12 Protecting Debtors from Creditors' Post-Judgment Remedies

12.1 Introduction

This chapter examines collection devices, including wage garnishment, levy upon personal and real property, and debtor examinations, that are available to a creditor that has recovered a judgment against a debtor. The chapter focuses upon asserting state and federal restrictions on these remedies to protect the debtor's essential property and income. The chapter also addresses the prohibition on imprisonment for debt that is found in most states' constitutions or statutes.

A debtor who possesses *only* exempt assets is referred to as "judgment proof" or "collection proof." While a judgment may be taken against such a person, there is no way for the creditor to compel collection of the judgment from the debtor's income or assets unless the debtor's circumstances change. Evaluating whether a debtor has income or assets that a creditor can reach is important both at the outset of a collection defense case and at the point when a creditor is attempting to execute upon a judgment.[1]

This chapter examines basic principles of interpretation of exemption laws and the due process limitations on garnishment. It then analyzes the federal and state laws that protect debtors' wages, property, and other income, including the question whether these assets retain their exempt character when deposited in a bank account. The chapter concludes by examining the extent to which a creditor can reach funds in a jointly held bank account, whether debtors can waive exemptions, interstate collection issues, imprisonment for debt, and debtor's examinations. The right of a bank to set off a debt against a debtor's deposit account is discussed in another manual in this series.[2]

1 *See* §§ 2.1, 2.3.7, *supra* (case acceptance and strategy considerations).

2 National Consumer Law Center, Consumer Banking and Payments Law § 4.3 (3d ed. 2005 and Supp.).

12.2 General Principles

12.2.1 Exemption Laws Must Be Liberally Construed in Favor of the Debtor

State and federal exemption laws, which exclude a wide variety of income and property from seizure by creditors, are a fundamental safeguard for the protection of low-income persons. Exemption laws are designed to protect debtors and their families from destitution, and to afford debtors a means of financial rehabilitation.

Exemption laws were established to protect a limited amount of a debtor's property from a forced sale for the payment of debts. The courts have enumerated the following purposes: (1) to provide the debtor with enough money to survive; (2) to protect the debtor's dignity; (3) to afford a means of financial rehabilitation; (4) to protect the family unit from impoverishment; and (5) to spread the burden of a debtor's support from society to his creditors.[3]

Exemptions are to be liberally construed in favor of the debtor and the debtor's family.[4] Courts recognize the strong

3 *See, e.g.*, *In re* Johnson, 880 F.2d 78, 83 (8th Cir. 1989) (Minn. law); *In re* Kester, 339 B.R. 749 (B.A.P. 10th Cir. 2006) (homesteads protected "for the benefit of society and of the family—to protect the family from destitution and society from the danger of her citizens becoming paupers"), *aff'd*, 493 F.3d 1208 (10th Cir. 2007); *In re* Dwyer, 305 B.R. 582, 585 (Bankr. M.D. Fla. 2004) (protect families from destitution and relieve state of support burden); N. Side Bank v. Gentile, 129 Wis. 2d 208, 385 N.W.2d. 133 (Wis. 1986); W. Vukowich, *Debtors Exemption Rights*, 62 Geo. L.J. 779 (1974).

4 Wilder v. Inter-Island Stream Navigation Co., 211 U.S. 239, 29 S. Ct. 58, 53 L. Ed. 164 (1908); *In re* Irish, 403 F.3d 611 (8th Cir. 2005); *In re* Drenttel, 403 F.3d 611 (8th Cir. 2005) (liberally construing Minnesota statute, which was silent regarding location of homestead, to exempt newly acquired Arizona home); *In re* Casserino, 379 F.3d 1069 (9th Cir. 2004) (Or. law); *In re* Perry, 345 F.3d 303 (5th Cir. 2003) (Texas homestead law); *In re* Vigil, 2003 WL 22024830 (10th Cir. Aug. 26, 2003) (Wyo. law); *In re* Cobbins, 227 F.3d 302 (5th Cir. 2000) (Miss. law) (liberal construction required, but mobile home not exempt unless debtor also owns land); *In re* Colwell, 196 F.3d 1225 (11th Cir. 1999) (Fla. law); *In re* Crockett, 158 F.3d 332 (5th Cir. 1998) (Tex. law); *In re* McDaniel, 70 F.3d 841 (5th Cir. 1995) (Tex. law); *In re* Johnson, 880 F.2d 78, 83 (8th Cir. 1989) (Minn.

public policy in favor of the preservation of the home,[5] "the

law); Tignor v. Parkinson, 729 F.2d 977, 981 (4th Cir. 1984) (Va. law); *In re* Perry, 357 B.R. 175 (B.A.P. 1st Cir. 2006) (allowing exemption when it was impossible to tell whether homestead declaration or bankruptcy petition filed first); *In re* Carlson, 303 B.R. 478 (B.A.P. 10th Cir. 2004) (Utah law); *In re* Winters, 2000 Bankr. LEXIS 648 (B.A.P. 10th Cir. June 26, 2000); *In re* Kwiecinski, 245 B.R. 672 (B.A.P. 10th Cir. 2000); *In re* Bechtoldt, 210 B.R. 599 (B.A.P. 10th Cir. 1997) (Wyo. law); *In re* Webb, 214 B.R. 553 (E.D. Va. 1997); Levin v. Dare, 203 B.R. 137 (S.D. Ind. 1996) (liberally construing ambiguous statute to hold property exempt); Marine Midland Bank v. Surfbelt, Inc., 532 F. Supp. 728 (W.D. Pa. 1982); *In re* Morse, 237 F. Supp. 579 (S.D. Cal. 1964); *In re* Bailey, 172 F. Supp. 925 (D. Neb. 1959); *In re* Bading, 376 B.R. 143 (Bankr. W.D. Tex. 2007) (homesteads are "a favorite of the law"; liberal construction required); *In re* Prestwood, 322 B.R. 463 (Bankr. S.D. Fla. 2005) (liberally construing Florida homestead exemption to apply when debtor maintained extensive ties to California but sufficiently demonstrated intent to live in Florida); *In re* Jones, 318 B.R. 841 (Bankr. S.D. Ohio 2005); *In re* Rutland, 318 B.R. 588 (Bankr. M.D. Ala. 2004); *In re* Yettaw, 316 B.R. 560 (Bankr. M.D. Fla. 2004) (recreational vehicle occupied as residence was exempt); *In re* Buchberger, 311 B.R. 794 (Bankr. D. Ariz. 2004) (liberally construing motor vehicle exemption to include all-terrain vehicle); *In re* Roberge, 307 B.R. 442 (Bankr. D. Vt. 2004) (liberal interpretation of Vermont exemptions to protect "family group"; married couple living apart, each with a child, were two family groups, who could each claim full set of exemptions); *In re* Hughes, 306 B.R. 683, 686 (Bankr. M.D. Ala. 2004); *In re* Dwyer, 305 B.R. 582, 585 (Bankr. M.D. Fla. 2004); *In re* Wilson, 305 B.R. 4 (Bankr. N.D. Iowa 2004); *In re* Moore, 269 B.R. 864 (Bankr. D. Idaho 2001); *In re* Stratton, 269 B.R. 716 (Bankr. D. Or. 2001); *In re* Marples, 266 B.R. 202 (Bankr. D. Idaho 2001); *In re* Atkinson, 258 B.R. 769 (Bankr. D. Idaho 2001); *In re* Siegle, 2000 Bankr. LEXIS 1627 (Bankr. D. Mont. Dec. 6, 2000), *amended by* 257 B.R. 591 (Bankr. D. Mont. 2001); *In re* Moore, 251 B.R. 380 (Bankr. W.D. Mo. 2000) (liberally construing motor vehicle exemption to include recreational all-terrain vehicles when statute did not specifically exclude them); *In re* Longstreet, 246 B.R. 611 (Bankr. S.D. Iowa 2000); *In re* Hasse, 246 B.R. 247 (Bankr. E.D. Va. 2000) (construing Virginia's exemption for individual retirement accounts); *In re* Bogue, 240 B.R. 742 (Bankr. E.D. Wis. 1999); *In re* Simpson, 238 B.R. 776 (Bankr. S.D. Ill. 1999); *In re* Cain, 235 B.R. 812 (Bankr. M.D.N.C. 1998); *In re* Shaffer, 228 B.R. 892 (Bankr. N.D. Ohio 1998); *In re* Robertson, 227 B.R. 844 (Bankr. S.D. Ind. 1998) (Indiana courts have a longstanding practice of construing exemption statutes liberally in favor of debtors); *In re* Rhines, 227 B.R. 308 (Bankr. D. Mont. 1998); *In re* Gallegos, 226 B.R. 111 (Bankr. D. Idaho 1998); *In re* Black, 225 B.R. 610 (Bankr. M.D. La. 1998); *In re* Hankel, 223 B.R. 728 (Bankr. D.N.D. 1998) (homestead statutes, like all exemption statutes, are to be liberally interpreted); *In re* Clifford, 222 B.R. 8 (Bankr. D. Conn. 1998) (exemption statutes, here the tools of trade exemption, are to be interpreted liberally); *In re* Brockhouse, 220 B.R. 623 (Bankr. C.D. Ill. 1998); *In re* Lazin, 217 B.R. 332 (Bankr. M.D. Fla. 1998) (liberally construing Florida exemption for annuity contracts); *In re* Ward, 210 B.R. 531 (Bankr. E.D. Va. 1997); *In re* Evans, 190 B.R. 1015 (Bankr. E.D. Ark. 1995), *aff'd*, 108 F.3d 1381 (8th Cir. 1997) (table); *In re* Powell, 173 B.R. 338 (Bankr. E.D. Ky. 1994); *In re* Galvin, 158 B.R. 806 (Bankr. W.D. Mo. 1993); *In re* Maylin, 155 B.R. 605 (Bankr. D. Me. 1993); *In re* Miller, 103 B.R. 65 (Bankr. N.D.N.Y. 1989); *In re* Thexton, 39 B.R. 367 (Bankr. D. Kan. 1984); *In re* Lind, 10 B.R. 611 (Bankr. D.S.D. 1981); *In re* Avery, 514 So. 2d 1380 (Ala. 1987); Fleet v. Zwick, 994 P.2d 480 (Colo. Ct. App. 1999); *In re* Marriage of Gedgaudas, 978 P.2d 677 (Colo. Ct. App. 1999); Wilmington Trust Co. v. Barry, 338 A.2d 575 (Del. Super. Ct. 1975), *aff'd*, 359 A.2d 664 (Del. 1976) (mem.); Goldenberg. v. Sawczak, 791 So. 2d 1078 (Fla. 2001); Havoco of Am., Ltd. v. Hill, 790 So. 2d 1018 (Fla. 2001) (constitutional homestead exemption is liberally construed); Broward v. Jacksonville Med. Ctr., 690 So. 2d 589 (Fla. 1997); Schuler v. Wallace, 61 Haw. 590, 607 P.2d 411 (Haw. 1980); LPP Mortgage, Ltd. v. Meurer, 2004 WL 57585 (Iowa Ct. App. Jan. 14, 2004) (homestead exemption statutes are broadly construed); Redmond v. Kester, 159 P.3d 1004 (Kan. 2007); Bohl v. Bohl, 234 Kan. 227, 670 P.2d 1344 (1983); Celco, Inc. v. Davis Van Lines, 226 Kan. 366, 598 P.2d 188 (1979); Dwyer v. Cempellin, 673 N.E.2d 863 (Mass. 1996) (discussion of public policy of homestead exemptions and liberal construction in favor of debtor); Household Fin. Corp. v. Ellis, 107 N.C. App. 262, 419 S.E.2d 592 (1992), *aff'd*, 429 S.E.2d 716 (N.C. 1993) (per curiam); Morgan Keegan Mortgage Co. v. Candelaria, 951 P.2d 1066 (N.M. Ct. App. 1997); Meadow Wind Healthcare Ctr. v. McInnes, 2000 Ohio App. LEXIS 3415 (Ohio Ct. App. July 24, 2000); *In re* Anderson, 932 P.2d 1110 (Okla. 1996); Beck v. Lapsley, 593 S.W.2d 410, 413 (S.D. 1999); Pierce v. Wash. Mut. Bank, 226 S.W.3d 711 (Tex. App. 2007) (history of homestead laws; principle of liberal construction); P.I.E. Employees Fed. Credit Union v. Bass, 759 P.2d 1144 (Utah 1988); Homeside Lending, Inc. v. Miller, 31 P.3d 607 (Utah Ct. App. 2001); Mercier v. Partlow, 149 Vt. 523, 546 A.2d 787 (1988); Macumber v. Shafer, 637 P.2d 645 (Wash. 1981); *In re* Elliott, 74 Wash. 2d 600, 446 P.2d 347 (Wash. 1968); Cowart v. Pan Am. Bank, 2000 Wash. App. LEXIS 2132 (Wash. Ct. App. Nov. 3, 2000); Schwanz v. Teper, 66 Wis. 2d 157, 223 N.W.2d 896 (Wis. 1974); *see also* Iowa State Bank & Trust Co. v. Michel, 683 N.W.2d 95 (Iowa 2004) (homestead rights are jealously guarded by the law). *But see In re* McWilliams, 296 B.R. 424 (Bankr. E.D. Va. 2002) (strictly construing recording requirements of Virginia homestead exemption statute); *cf. In re* Oakley, 344 F.3d 709, 712 (7th Cir. 2003) (Ind. law) (dismissing rule of liberal construction even though state courts use it); *In re* Jackson, 2001 Bankr. LEXIS 525 (Bankr. E.D. Va. Mar. 30, 2001) (homestead exemption statute is liberally construed, but its procedural requirements are construed strictly, so homestead deed untimely).

5 *See, e.g., In re* Perry, 357 B.R. 175 (B.A.P. 1st Cir. 2006) (noting important public policy of protecting home and allowing exemption when it was impossible to tell whether homestead declaration or bankruptcy petition filed first); *In re* Kester, 339 B.R. 749 (B.A.P. 10th Cir. 2006) (homesteads protected "for the benefit of society and of the family—to protect the family from destitution and society from the danger of her citizens becoming paupers"), *aff'd*, 493 F.3d 1208 (10th Cir. 2007); *In re* McCollum, 363 B.R. 789 (E.D. La. 2007); United States v. Neff, 2007 WL 776532 (D.N.D. Mar. 12, 2007) (history of North Dakota homestead law; noting important public policy served by homestead; ambiguous language in loan documents does not waive homestead exemption); Fix v. First State Bank of Roscoe, 359 B.R. 755 (D.S.D. 2007) (strong public policy in favor of South Dakota homesteads; waivers permitted but must be very clear; invalid here as against public policy); *In re* Walsh, 359 B.R. 389 (Bankr. D. Mass. 2007) (Massachusetts homestead declaration protects entire family, not just individual who files); *In re* Hughes, 306 B.R. 683, 686 (Bankr. M.D. Ala. 2004) (rule of

necessary shelter and personal property required for [families'] welfare in difficult economic circumstances,"[6] and the assurance of "the basic necessities."[7] Courts have the equitable power to stay executions upon terms and conditions that are just, such as installment payments.[8] If it is possible to construe an exemption statute in ways that are both favorable and unfavorable to the debtor, the favorable method should be chosen.[9]

Conversely, as garnishment is a harsh remedy, created by statute in derogation of common law, garnishment statutes are strictly construed. A creditor's failure to comply strictly with all procedural requirements of the statute will result in quashing the garnishment.[10] Exceptions to exemption laws are narrowly construed.[11]

Even though exemption laws are entitled to a liberal construction, exemptions may not be construed to aid wrongdoing.[12] Courts often distinguish between exempt

liberal construction applies especially to laws protecting homestead); First Ala. Bank v. Renfro, 452 So. 2d 464 (Ala. 1984); Fleet v. Zwick, 994 P.2d 480 (Colo. Ct. App. 1999) ("it has long been the policy of this state to preserve the home for the family, even at the sacrifice of just demands, because the preservation of the home is deemed of paramount importance"); Havoco of Am., Ltd. v. Hill, 790 So. 2d 1018 (Fla. 2001); *In re* Bly, 456 N.W.2d 195 (Iowa 1990) (homestead exemption "not for the benefit of the husband or wife alone, but for the family of which they are a part"; exemption protected against a drug forfeiture); Dwyer v. Cempellin, 424 Mass. 26, 673 N.E.2d 863 (1996) ("the value of securing to householders a home for the family regardless of the householder's financial condition"); *In re* Martin, 875 P.2d 417 (Okla. 1994) ("the beneficent spirit of protecting the family home"); Pierce v. Wash. Mut. Bank, 226 S.W.3d 711 (Tex. App. 2007) (history of homestead laws); *see also* Ash-Will Farms, L.C. v. Leachman Cattle Co., L.L.C., 2006 WL 3827453 (D. Mont. Dec. 27, 2006) (refusing on equitable grounds to order marshalling, which would have required government creditor to enforce debt against homestead and leave nonexempt property for other creditors; causing farmers to lose their homestead would be "an injustice").

6 *In re* Brockhouse, 220 B.R. 623 (Bankr. C.D. Ill. 1998).

7 *In re* Hazelhurst, 228 B.R. 199 (Bankr. E.D. Tenn. 1998).

8 *See, e.g.*, Quality Carpets v. Carter, 587 A.2d 254 (N.H. 1991); Keystone Sav. Ass'n v. Kitsock, 633 A.2d 165 (Pa. Super. Ct. 1993) (court in which execution proceedings are pending has inherent right to stay proceedings when it is necessary to protect the rights of the parties); *see also* United States v. Ogburn, 499 F. Supp. 2d 28 (D.D.C. 2007) (court has discretion to suspend continuing garnishment for criminal restitution or order amount less than the statutory twenty-five percent; suspension proper when debtor's spouse unemployed and couple had small children); Gerber v. Holcomb, 2006 WL 3019731 (Tenn. Ct. App. Oct. 25, 2006) (courts have authority to order wage garnishment in amount lower than statutory maximum).

9 *In re* Perry, 357 B.R. 175 (B.A.P. 1st Cir. 2006) (allowing exemption when it was impossible to tell whether homestead declaration or bankruptcy petition filed first, because clerks' time stamps indicated same minute); *In re* Kimble, 344 B.R. 546 (Bankr. S.D. Ohio 2006) (liberally construing Ohio exemption of "an interest" to include future interest, here a remainder interest owned by debtors who in manufactured home on property with permission of life tenant); *In re* Brockhouse, 220 B.R. 623 (Bankr. C.D. Ill. 1998); *In re* Snyder, 149 P.3d 26 (Mont. 2006) (liberally construing homestead to include sale proceeds, even if no homestead declaration filed before sale; noting inconsistency in statutes that exempt proceeds but require that declaration include statement that owner resides on property).

10 Moory v. Quadras, Inc., 970 S.W.2d 275 (Ark. 1998) (garnishment is a purely statutory remedy, and the statute must be strictly construed; writ of garnishment may be issued only by the county court which rendered the judgment); Williams v. Espirito Santo Bank, 656 So. 2d 212 (Fla. Dist. Ct. App. 1995); Requena v. Salomon, Smith, Barney, Inc., 2002 WL 356696 (Tex. App. Mar. 7, 2002) (writ of garnishment properly dissolved when service on debtor not made "as soon as practicable" after service on garnishee; statutory requirements must be strictly complied with); Watkins v. Peterson Enterprises, 973 P.2d 1037 (Wash. 1999) (garnishment is a harsh remedy and creditor must strictly follow statutory procedure); Bartel v. Zucktriegal, 47 P.3d 581 (Wash. Ct. App. 2002); Layne v. West Virginia Child Support Enforcement Div., 518 S.E.2d 357 (W. Va. 1998) (garnishment of disability benefits to collect child support arrearage allowed only if exact statutory procedure is followed); *see also* ARL Credit Services, Inc. v. Piper, 736 N.W.2d 771 (Neb. Ct. App. 2007) (because garnishment in aid of execution was unknown to common law, statute must be strictly construed; debtor may assert head of household's "in lieu of homestead" exemption to protect garnished bank account).

11 *In re* Skinner, 2001 WL 1699660 (Bankr. M.D.N.C. Aug. 7, 2001); Havoco of Am., Ltd. v. Hill, 790 So. 2d 1018, 1021 (Fla. 2001); Cross v. Strader Constr. Co., 768 So. 2d 465 (Fla. Dist. Ct. App. 2000) (mechanic's lien exception to homestead exemption strictly construed; contractor's judgment in *quantum meruit* not a mechanic's lien); Carrel v. Carrel, 791 S.W.2d 831 (Mo. Ct. App. 1990) (exceptions to maximum garnishment restrictions must be narrowly construed).

12 *In re* Fin. Federated Title & Trust, Inc., 347 F.3d 880 (11th Cir. 2003) (Fla. law) (home purchased with traceable proceeds of Ponzi scheme not exempt); *In re* Beverly, 374 B.R. 221 (9th Cir. B.A.P. 2007) (Cal. law) (discussing limits of exemption planning—intent is critical, size also important); *In re* Addison, 368 B.R. 791 (8th Cir. B.A.P. 2007) (limits of exemption planning; fraudulent transfer criteria applicable; fraud shown when debtor, faced with large liability, used "large percentage" of nonexempt assets to pay down mortgage on homestead and buy individual retirement accounts); Dowling v. Davis, 2006 WL 2331070 (M.D. Fla. Aug. 10, 2006) (intent to hinder creditors not sufficient to trigger fraud exception to Florida homestead exemption; must show homestead purchased with proceeds of fraud or egregious conduct; sufficiently alleged here when funds allegedly obtained by fraud on third party, not objecting creditor), *later decision at* 2007 WL 1839555 (M.D. Fla. June 26, 2007) (partial summary judgment for debtors; fraud not shown; noting the narrowness of Florida fraud exception); *In re* Osland, 2006 WL 503240 (D. Minn. Mar. 1, 2006) (more than conversion of nonexempt assets to exempt must be shown; not shown here when debtor took out second mortgage in direct violation of state family court order); *In re* Hawkins, 377 B.R. 761 (Bankr. S.D. Fla. 2007) (fraud or egregious conduct not shown when debtor borrowed money, paid much of it back, and discharged remaining debt in bankruptcy); *In re* Keck, 363 B.R. 193 (Bankr. D. Kan. 2007) (homestead exemption reduced when debtors used large credit card advances to pay down mortgage and make home improvements; equitable lien when specific cash advances could be traced to homestead);

property purchased or improved with the proceeds of wrongdoing, and exempt property purchased with nonexempt, but legitimately possessed, funds. The former is generally nonexempt, and some courts enable a creditor to execute on the property by recognizing an equitable lien in favor of the creditor, at least up to the amount of the traceable funds.[13] In the latter case the property may be

In re Gosman, 362 B.R. 549 (Bankr. S.D. Fla. 2007) (encumbering homestead without creditor's permission, although breach of contract, not "fraud or egregious conduct" sufficient to justify lien on homestead); *In re* Huie, 2007 WL 2317152 (Bankr. E.D. Tex. Aug. 8, 2007) (homestead purchased with fraudulently obtained funds nonexempt up to the amount of those funds); *In re* Romano, 353 B.R. 738 (Bankr. D. Mass. 2006) (creditor failed to prove homestead purchased with proceeds of embezzlement; constructive trust denied); *In re* Hecker, 316 B.R. 375 (Bankr. S.D. Fla. 2004) (homestead purchased with traceable proceeds of fraud subject to equitable lien in favor of victim); *In re* McGinnis, 306 B.R. 279 (Bankr. W.D. Mo. 2004) (very narrow fraud exception to Kansas homestead exemption; debtors with "some legitimate reasons" for moving to Kansas could claim exemption despite evidence of intent to hinder creditors; after involuntary bankruptcy filed, debtors purchased house with $88,000 cash in brown paper bag); *In re* Burghart, 2004 WL 2026805 (Bankr. D. Kan. Jan. 15, 2004) (investing nonexempt funds in exempt asset not fraud on creditor unless creditor has claim, that is, a constructive trust, in specific nonexempt asset; not fraudulent transfer to use year-end bonus to pay down debt on family truck); *In re* Baker, 273 B.R. 892 (Bankr. D. Wyo. 2002) (Wyoming annuities exemption excepts transfers to hinder creditors; sale of nonexempt property and purchase of annuities on eve of bankruptcy, placing all assets beyond reach of creditors, went beyond "exemption planning" and was fraudulent); *In re* Pich, 253 B.R. 562 (Bankr. D. Idaho 2000) (using building as residence in violation of zoning laws did not in itself preclude homestead exemption, but debtor was estopped by his rezoning application, which was an implicit representation that he would not live there); *In re* Ziegler, 239 B.R. 375 (Bankr. C.D. Ill. 1999) ("sale" of homestead to close relative, while debtors continued to live there and pay mortgage); *In re* Sholdan, 218 B.R. 475 (Bankr. D. Minn. 1998) (was fraudulent transfer under Minnesota law for ninety-year-old in fragile health and faced with large personal injury judgment to quietly invest life savings in a house, move into it, and immediately file for bankruptcy just before dying; homestead exemption did not protect house from judgment creditor), *aff'd*, 217 F.3d 1006 (8th Cir. 2000); James v. Thaggard, 795 So. 2d 738 (Ala. Civ. App. 2001) (denying homestead exemption on grounds of equity and good conscience when borrower falsely represented he was unmarried, but then defended foreclosure on grounds that wife had not signed mortgage); Battin v. Bayside Fin. Corp., 2004 WL 2307102 (Cal. Ct. App. Oct. 14, 2004) (homestead exemption prevents fixing of lien, even for debt nondischargeable in bankruptcy because of fraud; proceeds also protected); Hoyman v. Coffin, 976 P.2d 311 (Colo. Ct. App. 1998) (when solo practitioner manipulated one-person corporation so as to pay herself nothing during period of garnishment, and large sum on day after garnishment expired, court found this conduct fraudulent, and allowed garnishment of entire amount, plus costs and attorney fees); Havoco of Am., Ltd. v. Hill, 790 So. 2d 1018 (Fla. 2001) (expressing willingness to impose equitable lien when proceeds of fraud are invested in homestead, but not otherwise); Willis v. Red Reef, Inc., 921 So. 2d 681 (Fla. Dist. Ct. App. 2006) (equitable lien on homestead only if purchased with proceeds of fraud or egregious conduct; here, transfer was arguably fraudulent, but creditor had no specific claim on funds, that is, they had not been stolen from creditor; equitable lien denied); Brose v. Brose, 750 So. 2d 717 (Fla. Dist. Ct. App. 2000) (homestead could be sold for alimony obligation, when purchase was attempt to place assets beyond reach of ex-wife; note that in Havoco of Am., Ltd. v. Hill, 790 So. 2d 1018, 1028 n.12 (Fla. 2001) the Florida Supreme Court declined to express an opinion as to the validity of this approach); Lackey v. Lackey, 691 So. 2d 990 (Miss. 1997) (exemption for insurance proceeds would not protect beneficiaries of a policy purchased with funds stolen by a fiduciary; remanding for determination whether policy was bought with stolen money); Maki v. Chong, 75 P.3d 376 (Nev. 2003) (fraud exception to Nevada homestead exemption; home purchased with traceable proceeds of fraud subject to equitable lien for benefit of victim); Coppler & Mannick, Prof'l Corp. v. Wakeland, 117 P.3d 914 (N.M. 2005) (owner's tortious and malicious conduct—tearing out fixtures and vandalizing home when faced with imminent foreclosure—constituted "extraordinary circumstances" sufficient to warrant equitable lien on homestead); Skelton v. Wash. Mut. Bank, 61 S.W.3d 56 (Tex. App. 2001) (widow had no claims on homestead, and mortgage not invalidated by lack of her signature, when couple agreed husband alone should apply for mortgage because of wife's bad credit record, and husband falsely informed lender he was single); Leibman v. Grand, 981 S.W.2d 426 (Tex. App. 1998) (Texas exemption for annuities made exception if premium payments were made in fraud of creditors; annuity not exempt when husband, who was grossly delinquent in various obligations resulting from divorce, sold nonexempt property and purchased annuity); *see also In re* Eilbert, 162 F.3d 523 (8th Cir. 1998) (when elderly widow purchased annuity with a single payment consisting of almost the entire proceeds of her husband's estate, at a time when a substantial personal injury suit was pending against estate, and chose a "retirement date" two months after her payment, this was not an exempt "pension, annuity or similar plan" making payments "on account of age" because widow had unfettered discretion as to when payments would begin); *In re* Ross-Tucker, 2005 WL 3263932 (Bankr. D.D.C. Nov. 28, 2005) (trustee may surcharge exempt homestead for funds concealed by debtor who settled lawsuit without trustee's authorization); *In re* Maronde, 332 B.R. 593 (Bankr. D. Minn. 2005) (homestead exemption limited under 11 U.S.C. § 522(o) when debtor paid down home equity line with proceeds of nonexempt property on eve of bankruptcy); *cf.* Devan Lowe, Inc. v. Stephens, 842 So. 2d 703 (Ala. Civ. App. 2002) (garnishment laws construed liberally to prevent fraud).

13 *In re* Chew, 496 F.3d 11 (1st. Cir. 2007) (Mass. law) (exempt property, purchased with combination of clean money and proceeds of fraud or breach of fiduciary duty, is nonexempt up to the amount of traceable proceeds of wrongdoing); *In re* Fin. Federated Title & Trust, Inc., 347 F.3d 880 (11th Cir. 2003) (Fla. law) (home purchased with traceable proceeds of Ponzi scheme not exempt); Anderson v. Sullivan, 2007 WL 2288142 (D.N.D. Aug. 7, 2007) (Fla. law) (equitable lien on homestead purchased with funds misappropriated from a trust); *In re* Romano, 353 B.R. 738 (Bankr. D. Mass. 2006) (creditor failed to prove homestead purchased with proceeds of embezzlement; constructive trust denied); *In re* Hecker, 316 B.R. 375 (Bankr. S.D. Fla. 2004); *In re* Scott Wetzel Services, 293 B.R. 791 (Bankr. M.D. Fla. 2003) (refusing to dismiss claim of constructive trust on annuities ex-wife purchased with court-ordered payments that ex-husband made with misappropriated funds); *In re* Lin-

exempt, or the transaction may be analyzed using the state's law regarding fraudulent transfers.[14]

sey, 296 B.R. 582 (Bankr. D. Mass. 2003) (lien on homestead for amount of traceable stolen funds spent on improvements); *In re* Thiel, 275 B.R. 633 (Bankr. M.D. Fla. 2001) ("fraudulent or egregious act" shown when mortgage paid down with proceeds of debtor-husband's fraud; equitable lien on homestead property could be imposed even if joint-owner wife was innocent); Synod of S. Atl. Presbyterian Church v. Magpusao (*In re* Magpusao), 265 B.R. 492 (Bankr. M.D. Fla. 2001) (allowing equitable lien on home bought with funds stolen by wife when husband knowingly benefited from her fraud); European Am. Bank v. Lapes (*In re* Lapes), 254 B.R. 501 (Bankr. S.D. Fla. 2000) (homestead purchased with proceeds directly traceable to fraud is not exempt); Havoco of Am., Ltd. v. Hill, 790 So. 2d 1018 (Fla. 2001) (expressing willingness to impose equitable lien when proceeds of fraud are invested in homestead, but not otherwise); Willis v. Red Reef, Inc., 921 So. 2d 681 (Fla. Dist Ct. App. 2006) (equitable lien on homestead only if purchased with proceeds of fraud or egregious conduct; no equitable lien when transfer was arguably fraudulent, but creditor had no specific claim on funds, that is, they had not been stolen from creditor); Lackey v. Lackey, 691 So. 2d 990 (Miss. 1997) (exemption for insurance proceeds would not protect beneficiaries of policy purchased with funds stolen by fiduciary); Maki v. Chong, 75 P.3d 376 (Nev. 2003) (home purchased with traceable proceeds of fraud subject to equitable lien for benefit of victim); Paulman v. Pemberton (*In re* Paulman), 246 Wis. 2d 909, 633 N.W.2d 715 (Ct. App. 2001) (homestead exemption did not protect home purchased with funds converted from judgment creditor); *see also In re* Keck, 363 B.R. 193 (Bankr. D. Kan. 2007) (allowing equitable lien on homestead when debtor's large credit card cash advances could be traced to homestead); *cf. In re* Mazon, 368 B.R. 906 (Bankr. M.D. Fla. 2007) (debtors concealed and dissipated nonexempt property; trustee could surcharge exempt retirement accounts but not homestead, when dissipated property could not be traced to homestead); Sell v. Sell, 949 So. 2d 1108 (Fla. Dist. Ct. App. 2007) (ex-husband's conduct in evading court orders, for which he was jailed for contempt, sufficiently reprehensible to support equitable lien on homestead). *But see In re* Laing, 329 B.R. 761 (Bankr. M.D. Fla. 2005) (denying equitable lien when debtor was, at most, a "net recipient" and not an "active participant" in Ponzi scheme); *In re* Crum, 294 B.R. 402 (Bankr. M.D. Fla. 2003) (denying equitable lien when creditor unable to show that proceeds of fraud used to buy or improve homestead; account into which proceeds deposited contained enough legitimate funds to cover expenditures on homestead); *cf.* Williams v. Aloisi, 271 B.R. 676 (M.D. Fla. 2002) (home would be protected if ex-wife did not know, at the time of purchase, that funds she received from ex-husband to buy it were derived from fraud); *In re* Deerey, 371 B.R. 525 (Bankr. M.D. Fla. 2007) (purchase of homestead with illegally obtained funds not sufficient to support equitable lien; must be proceeds of fraud or egregious conduct, narrowly defined); Partridge v. Partridge, 790 So. 2d 1280 (Fla. Dist. Ct. App. 2001) (ex-husband's failure to sell homestead to pay alimony not the sort of conduct that justifies foreclosure of equitable lien).

14 *Exempt*: *In re* Chauncey, 454 F.3d 1292 (11th Cir. 2006) (refusing to impose equitable lien on homestead when debtor, after large judgment entered against her, used nonexempt personal injury settlement to pay down mortgage on homestead); Cadle Co. v. Newhouse, 2001 U.S. App. LEXIS 21852 (2d Cir. Oct. 11, 2001) (New York earnings exemption continued to protect husband's earnings, if needed for reasonable living expenses, even after fraudulent transfer to non-debtor wife); Shaia v. Meyer (*In re* Meyer), 244 F.3d 352 (4th Cir. 2001) (debtor-husband's use of nonexempt funds, an inheritance, to pay off mortgages on home owned with non-debtor wife in tenancy by the entireties not fraudulent transfer; home was exempt); *In re* Bradley, 294 B.R. 64 (B.A.P. 8th Cir. 2003) (home purchased during period of financial distress with proceeds of fair, arms-length sale of nonexempt property was exempt); *In re* Osland, 2006 WL 503240 (D. Minn. Mar. 1, 2006) (more than conversion of nonexempt assets to exempt must be shown; taking out second mortgage in direct violation of state family court order is insufficient); *In re* Soza, 358 B.R. 903 (S.D. Tex. 2006) (purchase of exempt annuity with nonexempt, but legitimately owned, funds not sufficient to show fraud); *In re* Hodes, 287 B.R. 561 (D. Kan. 2002) (investing proceeds of nonexempt assets in improvements to homestead did not defeat exemption of homestead or of funds prepaid to builder); *In re* Hawkins, 377 B.R. 761, 767 (Bankr. S.D. Fla. 2007) (no grounds for equitable lien if debtor merely borrowed money, used it to buy home, and failed to repay it); *In re* Gosman, 362 B.R. 549 (Bankr. S.D. Fla. 2007) (encumbering homestead without creditor's permission, although breach of contract, not "fraud or egregious conduct" sufficient to justify lien on homestead); *In re* Peres, 2007 WL 2766776 (Bankr. N.D. Tex. Sept. 18, 2007) (conversion of nonexempt property to exempt property not fraudulent absent actual intent to defraud creditors); *In re* Agnew, 355 B.R. 276 (Bankr. D. Kan. 2006) (trustee failed to show fraudulent transfer; unlimited Kansas homestead available; land swap involving family farmland was part of elderly mother's estate planning); *In re* Moreno, 352 B.R. 455 (Bankr. N.D. Ill. 2006) (transfer to tenancy by entireties not fraudulent; move to "gang free" neighborhood was legitimate family purpose); *In re* Tolson, 338 B.R. 359 (Bankr. C.D. Ill. 2005) (transfer of property to tenancy by entireties not fraudulent if legitimate family purpose shown, here, estate planning); *In re* Vangen, 334 B.R. 241 (Bankr. W.D. Wis. 2005) (retirement-related annuities purchased with nonexempt funds considered exempt given no extrinsic evidence of fraud); *In re* McClung, 327 B.R. 690 (Bankr. M.D. Fla. 2005) (repairs to homestead with funds removed, without creditor permission, from account pledged as collateral did not constitute fraudulent or egregious conduct sufficient to justify lien on homestead); *In re* McGinnis, 306 B.R. 279 (Bankr. W.D. Mo. 2004) (debtors with "some legitimate reasons" for moving to Kansas could claim exemption in house purchased with sales proceeds of Missouri home and various nonexempt assets, despite evidence of intent to hinder creditors); *In re* Burghart, 2004 WL 2026805 (Bankr. D. Kan. Jan. 15, 2004) (investing nonexempt funds in exempt asset not fraud on creditor unless creditor has constructive trust on specific nonexempt asset; not fraudulent transfer to use year-end bonus to pay down debt on family truck); *In re* Rodriguez, 282 B.R. 194 (Bankr. N.D. Tex. 2002) (not fraud within meaning of exception to Texas homestead exemption when transfers—from mortgagor to ex-wife to debtor—arguably violated due on sale clause of mortgage); *In re* McCabe, 280 B.R. 841 (Bankr. N.D. Iowa 2002) (conversion of nonexempt to exempt property not per se fraudulent, even if done to put property beyond reach of creditors; debtor could exempt costly shotgun purchased on eve of bankruptcy); *In re* Lowery, 262 B.R. 875 (Bankr. M.D. Fla. 2001) (addition of parcels to their citrus farm and transfer of parcels from trust to joint tenancy by financially distressed married couple were not fraudulent); *In re* Simms, 243 B.R. 156 (Bankr. S.D. Fla. 2000) (use of nonexempt proceeds of sale of homestead to purchase

Some exemption statutes specifically exclude transfers in fraud of creditors, but this exception may be narrowly construed.[15] In jurisdictions in which the homestead exemption is found in the state constitution, homesteads may be

exempt annuity not fraudulent when debtors bought it because of advancing age and ill health, did not conceal the transaction, and though in debt were not subject to collection pressure); *In re* Coates, 242 B.R. 901 (Bankr. N.D. Tex. 2000) (Texas fraudulent transfer statute applies only to personal property, so homestead purchased with proceeds of sale of nonexempt property in order to defeat creditors was exempt but motor vehicle was not); *In re* Hendricks, 237 B.R. 821 (Bankr. M.D. Fla. 1999) (home owned in tenancy by entireties exempt, even though purchased by wife with her nonexempt cash at a time when she was threatened by a large judgment; homestead exemption in constitution is not affected by change in fraudulent conveyance statute); *In re* Young, 235 B.R. 666 (Bankr. M.D. Fla. 1999) (sale of nonexempt property in Illinois and purchase of Florida homestead not sufficient to show fraud); Havoco of Am., Ltd. v. Hill, 790 So. 2d 1018 (Fla. 2001) (homestead purchased to protect assets from creditors is exempt; fraudulent transfer laws do not apply); Conseco Services L.L.C. v. Cuneo, 904 So. 2d 438 (Fla. Dist. Ct. App. 2005) (purchase of homestead with nonexempt funds at time when litigation imminent not sufficient to justify lien on homestead); Nadrich v. Nadrich, 872 So. 2d 994 (Fla. Dist. Ct. App. 2004) (evidence insufficient to support equitable lien on ex-husband's new homestead; not shown to be acquired as "instrument of fraud" or "means of escaping support obligation"); Robles v. Robles, 860 So. 2d 1014 (Fla. Dist. Ct. App. 2003) (equitable lien on homestead for delinquent alimony improper when failure of husband's law practice impaired ability to pay and there was no showing of affirmative fraudulent or reprehensible conduct); Smith v. Smith, 761 So. 2d 370 (Fla. Dist. Ct. App. 2000) (homestead could not be sold to foreclose lien awarded to ex-wife to compensate for injuries inflicted by abusive husband, because homestead was not purchased with proceeds of fraud, nor was purchase part of financial manipulations to avoid support obligation); Russell v. Black, 2000 Mass. Super. LEXIS 350 (Mass. Super. Ct. July 28, 2000) (filing a declaration of homestead at time when home owner is threatened with lawsuit not a fraudulent transfer); Gilchinsky v. Nat'l Westminster Bank, 732 A.2d 482 (N.J. 1999) (rollover of funds from New York employer's ERISA plan to New Jersey individual retirement account (IRA) was fraudulent, and IRA was nonexempt, when moving funds to New Jersey would help debtor avoid collection of a New York judgment for funds embezzled from employer); *see also* Evans v. Wolinsky, 347 B.R. 9 (D. Vt. 2006) (transfer of entireties property to wife individually, at time when no joint debts, not fraudulent; no harm to creditors when property was already exempt before transfer); *In re* Siervo, 2006 WL 3068841 (Bankr. S.D. Fla. Apr. 3, 2006) (use of sales proceeds of nonexempt asset to pay down homestead mortgage when bankruptcy imminent not prima facie evidence of fraud); *In re* Dismore, 2005 WL 419709 (Bankr. M.D. Fla. Jan. 4, 2005) (transfer of asset from exempt tenancy by entireties status into name of non-debtor spouse is not fraudulent transfer).

Not exempt: *In re* Eilbert, 162 F.3d 523 (8th Cir. 1998) (when elderly widow purchased annuity with a single payment consisting of almost the entire proceeds of her husband's estate, at a time when a substantial personal injury suit was pending against estate, and chose a "retirement date" two months after her payment, this was not an exempt "pension, annuity or similar plan" making payments "on account of age" because widow had unfettered discretion as to when payments would begin); *In re* Addison, 368 B.R. 791 (B.A.P. 8th Cir. 2007) (fraudulent transfer criteria applicable; fraud shown when debtor, faced with large liability, used large percentage of nonexempt assets to pay down mortgage on homestead and buy individual retirement accounts); *In re* Kelley, 2007 WL 2492732 (M.D. Fla. Aug. 30, 2007) (fraudulent transfer shown when debtor repaid sum borrowed against exempt life insurance when bankruptcy imminent and debtor insolvent); *In re* Sissom, 366 B.R. 677 (Bankr. S.D. Tex. 2007) (when "badges of fraud" present, homestead nonexempt up to amount of proceeds of sale of nonexempt stock used to purchase homestead); *In re* Orgeron, 2006 WL 335438 (Bankr. W.D. Mo. Feb. 2, 2006) (individual retirement account is exempt except for contributions made in contemplation of bankruptcy); *In re* Lacount, 342 B.R. 809 (Bankr. D. Mont. 2005) (sale of nonexempt assets to pay down mortgage on homestead was fraudulent transfer within meaning of bankruptcy law; homestead exemption reduced by amount of transfers); *In re* Baker, 273 B.R. 892 (Bankr. D. Wyo. 2002) (Wyoming annuities exemption excepts transfers to hinder creditors; sale of nonexempt property and purchase of annuities on eve of bankruptcy, placing all assets beyond reach of creditors, went beyond "exemption planning" and was fraudulent); *In re* Ziegler, 239 B.R. 375 (Bankr. C.D. Ill. 1999) ("sale" of homestead to close relative, while debtors continued to live there and pay mortgage, was fraudulent); *In re* Sholdan, 218 B.R. 475 (Bankr. D. Minn. 1998) (it was fraudulent transfer under Minnesota law for ninety-year-old in fragile health and faced with large personal injury judgment to quietly invest life savings in a house, move into it, and immediately file for bankruptcy just before dying; homestead exemption did not protect house from judgment creditor), *aff'd*, 217 F.3d 1006 (8th Cir. 2000); Brose v. Brose, 750 So. 2d 717 (Fla. Dist. Ct. App. 2000) (homestead could be sold for alimony obligation, when purchase was attempt to place assets beyond reach of ex-wife); Gilchinsky v. Nat'l Westminster Bank, 732 A.2d 482 (N.J. 1999) (rollover of funds from New York employer's ERISA plan to New Jersey individual retirement account was fraudulent, and individual retirement account was nonexempt, when moving funds to New Jersey would help debtor avoid collection of New York judgment for funds embezzled from employer); Leibman v. Grand, 981 S.W.2d 426 (Tex. App. 1998) (Texas exemption for annuities made exception if premium payments were made in fraud of creditors; annuity not exempt when husband, who was grossly delinquent in various obligations resulting from divorce, sold nonexempt property and purchased annuity).

15 *In re* Soza, 358 B.R. 903 (S.D. Tex. 2006) (Texas annuity exemption excepts payments made "in fraud of creditors," but purchase of exempt annuity with nonexempt, but legitimately owned, funds not sufficient to show fraud); *In re* Moreno, 352 B.R. 455 (Bankr. N.D. Ill. 2006) (when there are legitimate and illegitimate reasons for transfer of property to tenancy by entireties, sole intent can not be shown; here debtors showed "legitimate family reasons" for selling house owned in joint tenancy and buying one in tenancy by entireties five days before large judgment against husband, as new neighborhood was safer for children); *In re* Tolson, 338 B.R. 359 (Bankr. C.D. Ill. 2005) (Illinois does not protect property transferred into tenancy by entireties with the sole intent to avoid the payment of existing debts; not shown when financially troubled couple was doing estate planning and lawyer drafted husband's will at same time as deed). *But cf. In re* Kelley, 2007 WL 2492732 (M.D. Fla. Aug. 30, 2007) (fraudulent transfer shown when insolvent

treated more favorably than other property in analyzing possibly fraudulent transfers.[16]

The 2005 amendments to the Bankruptcy Code made a number of changes regarding the exemptions a debtor may claim in a bankruptcy case.[17] Three new provisions limit debtors from taking full advantage of state homestead exemptions: (1) section 522(o), which deals with prepetition conversion of nonexempt property with fraudulent intent; (2) section 522(p), which covers acquisitions of homestead property within 1215 days of the bankruptcy filing; and (3) section 522(q), which relates to the commission of certain bad acts by the debtor.

12.2.2 Proceeds from Sale of Exempt Property

Exemption statutes are not intended to restrict debtors' freedom to dispose of exempt property as they wish.[18] Creditors have no right to complain of the disposition of exempt property. Transfers of exempt property can not be attached by creditors.[19] Many decisions hold that the proceeds of the sale of exempt property deposited in a bank account are exempt, although commingling with nonexempt funds may present a problem of tracing for some courts.[20] Some states also explicitly protect real and personal property that is purchased with exempt benefit payments.[21]

Some state statutes protect the proceeds of the sale of a homestead[22] or compensation for damage to or destruction

debtor paid back sum borrowed against exempt life insurance when bankruptcy imminent).

16 *In re* Mazon, 368 B.R. 906 (Bankr. M.D. Fla. 2007) (trustee can not surcharge homestead, when dissipated property could not be traced to homestead; noting that homestead exemption "enjoys a special place in the hierarchy of rights given to Florida citizens"); *In re* Potter, 320 B.R. 753 (Bankr. M.D. Fla. 2005) (legislative acts may limit statutory exemptions but not constitutional exemptions); Torgelson v. Real Property Known As 17138 880th Ave., 734 N.W.2d 279 (Minn. Ct. App. 2007) (constitutional homestead exemption bars forfeiture for state offenses); State v. One 1965 Red Chevrolet Pickup, 37 P.3d 815 (Okla. 2001) (homestead exemption found in state constitution protects against state criminal law forfeiture, but statutory personal property exemption does not).

17 *See* National Consumer Law Center, Consumer Bankruptcy Law and Practice § 10.2.3.4 (8th ed. 2006 and Supp.).

18 *In re* Dismore, 2005 WL 419709 (Bankr. M.D. Fla. Jan. 4, 2005) (transfer of certificate of deposit to wife not fraudulent because certificate was exempt property to which creditors had no claim); Howard v. Calhoun, 155 Fla. 689, 21 So. 2d 361 (1945); Goebel v. Brandley, 174 S.W.3d 359 (Tex. App. 2005) (purchase of savings bonds for children by payroll deduction was transfer of exempt property, in this case unpaid wages, which could not be fraudulent transfer); Moore v. Neyland, 180 S.W.2d 658 (Tex. Civ. App. 1944).

19 *In re* Matthews, 360 B.R. 732 (Bankr. M.D. Fla. 2007) (transfer from one form of exempt property to another not fraudulent); Anderson v. Odell, 51 Mich. 492, 16 N.W. 870 (1883); *see also* Burns v. Miller, Hiersche, Martens & Hayward, Prof'l Corp., 948 S.W.2d 317 (Tex. App. 1997) (statute barring orders requiring turnover of the "proceeds" or a "disbursement" of property exempt under any other statute protects disbursements from spendthrift trust).

20 *In re* Castro, 2006 WL 4005571 (Bankr. S.D. Fla. Oct. 24, 2006) (proceeds exempt in bank account; fact that bad credit would make new home purchase problematical not sufficient to negate intent to reinvest); *In re* Dezonia, 347 B.R. 920 (Bankr. M.D. Fla. 2006) (proceeds of voluntary or involuntary sale of homestead, here foreclosure surplus, are exempt if intended to be used for new homestead, and not commingled with other funds); *In re* Barbe, 2006 WL 2403826 (Bankr. E.D. La. Feb. 17, 2006) (insurance proceeds for property destroyed by hurricane will be exempt if property was exempt); *In re* Alam, 336 B.R. 320 (Bankr. N.D. Ohio 2005) (settlement proceeds from lawsuit for disability benefits exempt, as are investment account funds traceable to settlement proceeds), *aff'd, remanded for factual findings*, 359 B.R. 142 (B.A.P. 6th Cir. 2006); McKernan Co. v. Gregory, 643 N.E.2d 1370 (Ill. App. Ct. 1994); *cf. In re* Nye, 210 B.R. 857 (D. Colo. 1997) (proceeds from sale of exempt home could have been exempt if debtor had met burden of proof). *But see In re* Fouracre, 358 B.R. 384 (Bankr. D. Ariz. 2006) (refusing to trace; proceeds of homestead lost exemption when commingled with other funds in bank account); *In re* Carelock, 2006 WL 3708688 (Bankr. S.D. Ga. Jan. 13, 2006) (Georgia law does not exempt proceeds of exempt property); *In re* Roberts, 2005 WL 1924180 (Bankr. M.D. La. Aug. 10, 2005) (annuity not exempt under Louisiana law even though purchased with distribution from exempt 401k plan); *In re* Simpson, 238 B.R. 776 (Bankr. S.D. Ill. 1999) (insurance payment for damage to vehicle did not fall within exemption for debtor's "interest in motor vehicle"); *cf. In re* White, 377 B.R. 633 (Bankr. D. Ariz. 2007) (proceeds in bank account lost exemption when used for stock trading and not reinvested in homestead within eighteen months). *See generally* W. Vukowich, *Debtors Exemption Rights*, 62 Geo. L.J. 779, 826 (1974).

21 *See, e.g., In re* Baker, 2006 WL 2079919 (Bankr. M.D. Ala. July 25, 2006) (Alabama workers' compensation exemption protects motor vehicle purchased with traceable proceeds of workers' compensation settlement); *In re* Gardiner, 332 B.R. 891 (Bankr. S.D. Cal. 2005) (asset acquired, in part, with workers' compensation award retained exempt status, subject to tracing requirements); Faro v. Porchester Holdings, Inc., 792 So. 2d 1262 (Fla. Dist. Ct. App. 2001); *see also* § 12.5.5, *infra. But see In re* Duemey, 347 B.R. 875 (Bankr. S.D. Ohio 2006) (vehicle purchased for debtor by ex-husband, to satisfy his debt for back child support, not exempt child support); *In re* Christensen, 149 P.3d 40 (Nev. 2006) (wage exemption does not protect property purchased with exempt wages).

22 *In re* McCollum, 363 B.R. 789 (E.D. La. 2007) (Louisiana homestead exemption protects proceeds of voluntary sale); *In re* Takes, 334 B.R. 642 (N.D. Iowa 2005) (returned entrance deposit from retirement community was exempt as proceeds of homestead), *aff'd on other grounds*, 478 F.3d 902 (8th Cir. 2007); *In re* Bading, 376 B.R. 143 (Bankr. W.D. Tex. 2007) (when homestead sold as two parcels, debtor could exempt proceeds of both sales); *In re* VanSickle, 350 B.R. 897 (Bankr. D. Idaho 2006) (Oregon homestead exemption, which protects proceeds of sale of homestead if reinvested in homestead within one year, will protect payments made by buyers pursuant to promissory note, when house sold ten months earlier, provided funds are timely reinvested); *In re* Dezonia, 347 B.R. 920 (Bankr. M.D. Fla. 2006) (proceeds of voluntary or involuntary sale of homestead, here foreclosure surplus, exempt if intended to be used for new homestead, and not commingled with other

of the homestead.[23] Some of these jurisdictions, however,

funds); *In re* Seeley, 341 B.R. 277 (Bankr. W.D. Mo. 2006) (homestead exemption not lost when property placed on market, when debtor testified that proceeds would be used for new homestead; if sale had been completed, proceeds would be exempt); *In re* Ballato, 318 B.R. 205 (Bankr. M.D. Fla. 2004) (ex-husband could claim homestead exemption in proceeds of marital home sold by court order during property division; non-occupancy not a bar when it was required by restraining order); *In re* Cumberbatch, 302 B.R. 675 (Bankr. C.D. Cal. 2003) (court-ordered sale of home during property division was "forced sale to satisfy a money judgment" within meaning of California statute allowing automatic exemption, for six months, for proceeds); *In re* Willoughby, 2003 WL 22849766 (Bankr. C.D. Ill. Dec. 2, 2003) (wife's court-ordered payment to husband as compensation for award to her of former marital home was exempt as proceeds of homestead); *In re* Kalnynch, 284 B.R. 149 (Bankr. M.D. Fla. 2002) (ex-wife, who received house, ordered to pay $15,000 to husband when house sold or refinanced; husband could exempt this as proceeds of homestead); *In re* Miller, 246 B.R. 564 (Bankr. E.D. Tenn. 2000) (Tennessee homestead exemption survives in proceeds of involuntary sale of residence); *In re* Simms, 243 B.R. 156 (Bankr. S.D. Fla. 2000) (proceeds of sale of home retain exemption if rolled over into exempt annuity without fraudulent intent); *In re* Duffy, 240 B.R. 60 (Bankr. D. Nev. 1999) (Nevada homestead exemption protects proceeds of sale of homestead, whether or not debtor intends to reinvest in new homestead); Battin v. Bayside Fin. Corp., 2004 WL 2307102 (Cal. Ct. App. Oct. 14, 2004) (proceeds of sale of homestead exempt, even for debt that was nondischargeable in bankruptcy for fraud); Gen. R.A.C., Inc. v. Coldwell Banker Residential Real Estate, Inc., 876 So. 2d 606 (Fla. Dist. Ct. App. 2004) (buyer's deposit, held in escrow by realtor, was proceeds of seller's homestead, exempt for reasonable time); *In re* Estate of Hamel, 821 So. 2d 1276 (Fla. Dist. Ct. App. 2002) (deceased was in process of selling condominium at time of death, and executor closed sale shortly thereafter; proceeds exempt in hands of adult daughters); Braunger v. Karber, 563 N.W.2d 1 (Iowa 1997) (proceeds of sale of homestead in the hands of the buyers are exempt for reasonable time after sale if seller intends to use them to buy new homestead); *In re* Snyder, 149 P.3d 26 (Mont. 2006) (proceeds exempt for eighteen months even though no homestead declaration filed at time of sale); Morgan Keegan Mortgage Co. v. Candelaria, 951 P.2d 1066 (N.M. Ct. App. 1997) (homestead exemption protected $20,000 of proceeds of private sale conducted with court's permission before foreclosure judgment; exemption would have applied to proceeds of foreclosure sale, and public policy favored voluntary sales during foreclosure to maximize debtor's return); Upton v. Household Fin. Indus. Loan Co., 102 Wash. App. 220, 6 P.3d 1231 (2000) (homestead exemption protects surplus resulting from foreclosure sale, but holder of second mortgage has priority over home owner's homestead rights); *In re* Sweet, 944 P.2d 414 (Wash. Ct. App. 1997) (Washington's homestead exemption protects surplus paid to home owners after non-judicial foreclosure); *see also In re* May, 329 B.R. 789 (Bankr. D.N.H. 2005) (when house sold during bankruptcy, debtor receives up to amount of homestead exemption from proceeds); *cf. In re* Kujan, 286 B.R. 216 (Bankr. D. Conn. 2002) (Connecticut exempts proceeds of forced sale, but not voluntary sale; ex-wife who quitclaimed house to husband could not exempt husband's obligation to pay her when youngest child reached eighteen or house sold). *But see In re* Polimino, 345 B.R. 708 (B.A.P. 10th Cir. 2006) (no homestead exemption in proceeds of refinancing; refinancing not a sale within meaning of Colorado statute exempting sales proceeds); *In re* Schlakman, 2007 WL 1482011 (Bankr. S.D. Fla. Jan. 16, 2007) (debtor could not exempt proceeds of former marital home, located in New York, despite intention to reinvest in Florida home; proceeds exempt only if property was located in Florida); *In re* Wiley, 352 B.R. 716 (Bankr. D. Idaho 2006) (debtors could not claim homestead exemption in both their remaining property and the proceeds of eminent domain taking of one corner); Schalebaum v. Town of Wolfeboro (*In re* Schalebaum), 273 B.R. 1 (Bankr. D.N.H. 2001) (New Hampshire homestead exemption does not cover proceeds of voluntary sale of homestead); *In re* Herrell, 210 B.R. 386 (Bankr. N.D. Fla. 1997) (ex-wife's right to receive a sum from ex-husband, at a date more than one year after property division, secured by a lien on the former marital home, was not proceeds from sale of a homestead, within meaning of Minnesota homestead exemption); Dep't of Revenue *ex rel.* Vickers v. Pelsey, 779 So. 2d 629 (Fla. Dist. Ct. App. 2001) (intent to use funds to build and repair a homestead does not make funds exempt; department could levy on funds obtained as mortgage loan on vacant and presently uninhabitable property, which debtor intended to rehabilitate for use as his home); Homeside Lending, Inc. v. Miller, 31 P.3d 607 (Utah Ct. App. 2001) (proceeds of refinancing not sale proceeds within meaning of Utah exemption statute); *cf. In re* Lares, 188 F.3d 1166 (9th Cir. 1999) (Idaho exempts homestead and sale proceeds from "attachment, execution or forced sale," but not from bank's contractual setoff); *In re* Jones, 327 B.R. 297 (Bankr. S.D. Tex. 2005) (under Texas law asset, other than new homestead, purchased with proceeds of homestead sale not exempt); *In re* Schissler, 250 B.R. 697 (Bankr. W.D. Mo. 2000) (Missouri homestead exemption did not protect funds awarded to husband in lieu of specific marital property in divorce which granted house to wife); Kim v. First Fed. Bank of Cal., 2002 WL 1579602 (Cal. Ct. App. July 17, 2002) (no homestead exemption in surplus proceeds of foreclosure sale, when automatic exemption did not protect against sale pursuant to mortgage, and declared homestead exemption unavailable because declaration filed after lien had attached); Beck v. Lapsley, 593 N.W.2d 410 (S.D. 1999) (if home owners over the age of seventy, who are entitled to exempt entire value of homestead, sell home, they may claim only the standard $30,000 exemption in the proceeds).

23 *In re* Murphy, 367 B.R. 711 (Bankr. D. Kan. 2007) (deceptive practices and breach of warranty causes of action, arising from sale of defective mobile home, exempt under Kansas homestead law); *In re* Crooks, 351 B.R. 783 (Bankr. S.D. Fla. 2006) (Florida homestead exemption protects insurance proceeds that compensate for damage to or destruction of homestead; no homestead when debtors did not own and owner did not reside in house on date of storm, but proceeds exempt because received in trust for owner and mortgage lender, to be used only for repairs); *In re* Barbe, 2006 WL 2403826 (Bankr. E.D. La. Feb. 17, 2006) (insurance proceeds for exempt property destroyed by hurricane are exempt); *In re* Hoffpauir, 258 B.R. 447 (Bankr. D. Idaho 2001) (Idaho exemption statute protects fire insurance proceeds of destroyed property); *In re* Gilley, 236 B.R. 441 (Bankr. M.D. Fla. 1999) (settlement proceeds from lawsuit against pesticide manufacturer whose product contaminated homestead farmland exempt, because debtor planned to spend proceeds on efforts to clean up land), *aff'd*, 211 F.3d 131 (11th Cir. 2000) (table); *In re* Estate of Tolson, 690 N.W.2d 680 (Iowa 2005) (insurance proceeds for water damage to homestead are exempt for reasonable time if used to repair or

require proof of intent to purchase another homestead with the proceeds, or require that the proceeds be so used within a certain period of time.[24]

---

replace). *But see In re* Thurston, 2007 WL 1860892 (Bankr. D. Mass. June 27, 2007) (Massachusetts homestead exemption does not extend to proceeds of claim for damage to property); *In re* Foor, 259 B.R. 899 (Bankr. C.D. Ill. 2000) (cause of action for termite damage that occurred before debtors owned house not protected by homestead exemption); *cf. In re* MacNeal, 2007 WL 917255 (Bankr. S.D. Fla. Mar. 22, 2007) (TILA, HOEPA, and usury claims, arising from purchase of homestead, were personal property, not covered by Florida homestead exemption); *In re* Schubert, 218 B.R. 603 (Bankr. N.D. Okla. 1998) (Oklahoma homestead exemption exempts compensation for damage to homestead property but not home owners' cause of action against sellers and inspector over undisclosed defects in the property); *In re* Bradley, 212 B.R. 998 (Bankr. M.D. Ala. 1997) (homestead exemption did not exempt home owners' cause of action against sellers and realtor for concealment of termite damage before current owners owned home, as this was not analogous to fire insurance proceeds for damage to home).

24 *In re* Konnoff, 356 B.R. 201 (B.A.P. 9th Cir. 2006) (Ariz. law) (analysis of interaction between bankruptcy law and state homestead sunset; proceeds exempt on petition date lose exemption if not timely reinvested); *In re* Smith, 342 B.R. 801 (B.A.P. 9th Cir. 2006) (Arizona proceeds lose exemption if not invested in new homestead within eighteen months; when period expired during bankruptcy, proceeds became part of bankruptcy estate); *In re* Barnes, 307 B.R. 731 (B.A.P. 10th Cir. 2004); *In re* White, 377 B.R. 633 (Bankr. D. Ariz. 2007) (use of proceeds for stock trading negated intent to reinvest; result might be different if used for "critical" living expenses such as rent or healthcare); *In re* Presto, 376 B.R. 554 (Bankr. S.D. Tex. 2007) (exemption for homestead proceeds ends with purchase of new homestead; leftover funds not exempt); *In re* Bading, 376 B.R. 143 (Bankr. W.D. Tex. 2007) (when debtor had to sell homestead as two parcels because creditor refused to release clearly invalid lien on second parcel, time began to run only upon second sale); *In re* Perpinan, 2007 WL 2345019 (Bankr. N.D. Cal. Aug. 15, 2007) (purported reinvestment was sham; homestead exemption lost and bankruptcy discharge denied); *In re* Gauthier, 2007 WL 1580100 (Bankr. S.D. Fla. May 30, 2007) (exemption lost when proceeds used for "living expenses"; note that here concealment of funds was sufficient to deny discharge); *In re* Wynn, 369 B.R. 605 (Bankr. D. Or. 2007) (money spent on rent was reinvested in homestead); *In re* Zavala, 366 B.R. 643 (Bankr. W.D. Tex. 2007) (proceeds of homestead became nonexempt when not reinvested in homestead within six months); *In re* Lane, 364 B.R. 760 (Bankr. D. Or. 2007) (when house sold postpetition, proceeds remained exempt as to prepetition debts, whether or not reinvested; if proceeds in hand on petition date, exemption could be lost); *In re* Russow, 357 B.R. 133 (Bankr. N.D. Iowa 2007) (proceeds of old homestead rolled over into new one are exempt as to preexisting debts); *In re* Fouracre, 358 B.R. 384 (Bankr. D. Ariz. 2006) (proceeds lost exemption, even though debtors, whose bad credit prevented purchase in own name, used funds for earnest money and down payment on purchase of home by relatives, with whom debtors resided in both old and new home); *In re* Letterman, 356 B.R. 540 (Bankr. D. Kan. 2006) (no homestead exemption in house lot or fire insurance proceeds when debtor neither occupied homestead on petition date, nor testified to intention to use proceeds to rebuild); *In re* VanSickle, 350 B.R. 897 (Bankr. D. Idaho 2006) (Oregon homestead exemption, which protects proceeds if reinvested in homestead within one year, protects payments made by buyers pursuant to promissory note, when house sold ten months earlier, provided funds are timely reinvested); *In re* Dezonia, 347 B.R. 920 (Bankr. M.D. Fla. 2006) (proceeds of voluntary or involuntary sale of homestead, here foreclosure surplus, are exempt if intended to be used for new homestead, and not commingled with other funds); *In re* Seeley, 341 B.R. 277 (Bankr. W.D. Mo. 2006) (homestead not lost when property placed on market when debtor testified that proceeds would be used for new homestead; court notes that if sale had been completed, proceeds would be exempt); *In re* Castro, 2006 WL 4005571 (Bankr. S.D. Fla. Oct. 24, 2006) (proceeds exempt in bank account; fact that bad credit would make new home purchase problematical not sufficient to negate intent to reinvest, but funds lost exemption when dissipated postpetition for living expenses); *In re* Jones, 327 B.R. 297 (Bankr. S.D. Tex. 2005) (under Texas law, proceeds from homestead sale not reinvested in new homestead within six months not exempt); *In re* Strasser, 303 B.R. 841 (Bankr. D. Ariz. 2004); *In re* Willoughby, 2003 WL 22849766 (Bankr. C.D. Ill. Dec. 2, 2003) (wife's court-ordered payment to husband as compensation for award to her of former marital home, was exempt when husband intended to invest it in new home); *In re* Kalnynch, 284 B.R. 149 (Bankr. M.D. Fla. 2002) (delay in acquiring new homestead not fatal); *In re* Ginther, 282 B.R. 16 (Bankr. D. Kan. 2002) (proceeds exempt only if used for purchase of Kansas homestead, not when debtors moved to Colorado); *In re* Binko, 258 B.R. 515 (Bankr. S.D. Fla. 2001) (proceeds exempt when debtors showed good faith and due diligence in seeking less expensive home and proceeds not commingled with other funds, although debtors spent some on rental housing while house hunting); *In re* Delson, 247 B.R. 873 (Bankr. S.D. Fla. 2000) (Florida homestead proceeds exempt only if there is intention to purchase another homestead within reasonable time); *In re* Ziegler, 239 B.R. 375 (Bankr. C.D. Ill. 1999) (homestead proceeds not exempt without showing of intent to buy another homestead); *In re* Roberts, 215 B.R. 197 (Bankr. D. Neb. 1997) (intention to sell the homestead property was not abandonment when Nebraska law made proceeds exempt for six months); Fleet v. Zwick, 994 P.2d 480 (Colo. Ct. App. 1999) (when proceeds of sale of homestead were placed in separate bank account, use of some funds for nonexempt purpose did not destroy exempt status of remaining funds); Town of Lake Park v. Grimes, 963 So. 2d 940 (Fla. Dist. Ct. App. 2007) (burden on debtors to show good faith intent to reinvest; not shown here); Rossano v. Britesmile, Inc., 919 So. 2d 551 (Fla. Dist. Ct. App. 2005) (intent to reinvest shown when homestead proceeds were escrowed prior to closing on new homestead); Braunger v. Karber, 563 N.W.2d 1 (Iowa 1997) (creditor sought to garnish proceeds of sale of homestead in the hands of the buyers; because Iowa law made proceeds exempt for a "reasonable time" after sale if used to buy a new homestead, and sellers intended to purchase new homestead, proceeds were exempt); *In re* Snyder, 149 P.3d 26 (Mont. 2006) (proceeds exempt for eighteen months even though no homestead declaration filed at time of sale); *see also* Zibman v. Tow (*In re* Zibman), 268 F.3d 298 (5th Cir. 2001) (Texas homestead exemption protects proceeds of sale only if reinvested in another Texas homestead within six months); Fong v. Town of Bay Harbor Islands, 864 So. 2d 76 (Fla. Dist. Ct. App. 2003) (no lien against homestead for code violations, but if homestead sold and proceeds not reinvested within six months, town may file lien against proceeds); *In re* Estate of Tolson, 690 N.W.2d 680 (Iowa 2005) (insurance proceeds for water damage to homestead exempt for reasonable time if used to repair or replace).

12.2.3 *Constitutional Validity of Exemption Statutes*

12.2.3.1 Impairment of Contracts

Exemption laws do not unconstitutionally impair the obligation of contracts, nor take creditors' property without due process, even when an increase in the exemption amount applies to debts incurred before the change.[25] The contract and due process clauses do not bar every state law that affects a contractual relationship. The reservation of certain essential attributes of sovereign power,[26] such as the right to declare exemptions, and to modify them in response to economic changes, must be read into every contract. As one court noted, "Inflation is an economic reality; as long as it continues, the legislature has a legitimate interest in making corresponding reforms to outdated and unrealistic state laws."[27]

To balance the legitimate expectations of contracting parties with the reserved police power of the state, the Supreme Court has articulated a three-part test for impairment of contract claims. First, does the statute substantially impair the contract? If so, does it serve a "significant and legitimate" public purpose, such as "remedying a broad and general social or economic problem?" Finally, does it adjust "the rights and responsibilities of the contracting parties" based upon "reasonable conditions . . . appropriate to the public purpose"?[28]

25 *In re* Selzer, 104 F.3d 234 (9th Cir. 1996) (retroactive application of statute allowing exemption of individual retirement accounts does not impair contracts); Reliance Ins. Co. v. Ziegler, 938 F.2d 781 (7th Cir. 1991) (application of new exemption statute to cases pending on date of enactment not denial of due process; court should apply the law in effect at the time it renders its decision, unless this would result in manifest injustice); *In re* Little, 2007 WL 2791122 (N.D.N.Y. Sept. 24, 2007) (application of New York's increased homestead exemption to preexisting debt not unconstitutional impairment of contract); *In re* Brown, 2007 WL 2120380 (Bankr. N.D.N.Y. July 23, 2007) (application of increased homestead amount not impairment of contract); *In re* Evans, 362 B.R. 275 (Bankr. D.S.C. 2006) (bankruptcy law required application of amended homestead amount, in effect on the petition date, to debt that preceded increase; considering the choice of law provisions of the bankruptcy law and the mobility of the population, no reasonable creditor could assume that a certain set of exemptions would apply); *In re* Fouracre, 358 B.R. 384 (Bankr. D. Ariz. 2006) (proceeds lost exemption when commingled with other funds in bank account or not invested in new homestead within eighteen months); *In re* Betz, 273 B.R. 313 (Bankr. D. Mass. 2002); *In re* Larson, 260 B.R. 174 (Bankr. D. Colo. 2001) (impairment of contract not substantial when change affected only the remedy, and creditors could reasonably expect exemption amounts to change with time); *In re* Johnson, 69 B.R. 988 (Bankr. D. Minn. 1987) (application of increased homestead exemption to existing unsecured debt not impairment of contract or taking; bank could not reasonably expect that exemption laws would remain unchanged; bank also had not relied on this possibility when, at time of loan, it was fully secured); *In re* Punke, 68 B.R. 936 (Bankr. N.D. Iowa 1987) (application of new exemption amounts to preexisting debts neither impairment of contract nor taking; when inflation is economic reality, reform of outdated and unrealistic laws, which will realize rather than disturb creditors' reasonable expectations); *In re* Hockinson, 60 B.R. 250 (Bankr. N.D. Ill. 1986) (increased exemption amount is "minimal alteration" of contractual relationship; no substantial impairment); *In re* Starns, 52 B.R. 405 (S.D. Tex. 1985) (1983 amendments to Texas homestead law could be applied regardless of date when homestead acquired); *In re* Barnhart, 47 B.R. 277 (Bankr. N.D. Tex. 1985) (Texas's increased homestead exemption applies to existing judgment liens; sovereign's power to change laws is read into all contracts); Homeside Lending, Inc. v. Miller, 31 P.3d 607 (Utah Ct. App. 2001); Macumber v. Shafer, 637 P.2d 645 (Wash. 1981) (increasing exemption only modified remedy; reasonable exercise of police power in response to cost of living increases); *see also In re* Stewart, 246 B.R. 134 (Bankr. D.N.H. 2000) (application of federal bankruptcy law to exempt individual retirement account that was created before state exemption was adopted does not violate contract clause, which only limits states, not federal government); *In re* Bartlett, 168 B.R. 488 (Bankr. D.N.H. 1994) (New Hampshire's constitutional prohibition against retroactive statutes applies only to substantive rights, not remedies; creditor has no "vested substantive right" in lower exemption amount). *But see In re* Sticha, 60 B.R. 717 (Bankr. D. Minn. 1986) (preexisting lien was property interest; application of new exemption amounts would be taking); *In re* Fossum, 59 B.R. 820 (Bankr. D. Minn. 1986) (applying new amounts to preexisting debt would violate contract and takings clauses); Builders Supply Co. v. Pine Belt Sav. & Loan Ass'n, 369 So. 2d 743, 745 (Miss. 1979); *cf. In re* Bassin, 637 F.2d 668 (9th Cir. 1980) (interpreting California homestead exemption's scope in line with state law decisions finding, based on Contract Clause of constitution, that increased exemption can not apply to preexisting debts); *In re* Echevarren, 2 B.R. 215 (Bankr. D. Idaho 1980) (increased exemption amount may be used if "reasonable" and "does not destroy the value of the contract by destroying any meaningful remedy," but retroactive application of increase in homestead from $10,000 to $25,000 would unconstitutionally impair contract).

26 El Paso v. Simmons, 379 U.S. 497, 85 S. Ct. 577, 13 L. Ed. 2d 496 (1965); Home Bldg. & Loan Ass'n v. Blaisdell, 290 U.S. 398, 54 S. Ct. 231, 78 L. Ed. 413 (1934) (upholding Depression-era statute that extended period for redemption from foreclosure); *In re* Barnhart, 47 B.R. 277 (Bankr. N.D. Tex. 1985); Macumber v. Shafer, 637 P.2d 645 (Wash. 1981) ("it is presumed that parties contract with knowledge that reservation of essential attributes of sovereign power is written into all contracts").

27 *In re* Punke, 68 B.R. 936, 941 (Bankr. N.D. Iowa 1987); *see also In re* Little, 2007 WL 2791122 (N.D.N.Y. Sept. 24, 2007) (when homestead exemption so unreasonably low as to be "tantamount to no exemption," legislature recognized need to "review and update"; application of new amount to preexisting debt not unconstitutional); *In re* Brown, 2007 WL 2120380 (Bankr. N.D.N.Y. July 23, 2007) (amendment to take account of "economic reality").

28 Energy Reserves Group, Inc. v. Kan. Light & Power Co., 459 U.S. 400, 103 S. Ct. 697, 74 L. Ed. 2d 569 (1983); *see also* Allied Structural Steel Co. v. Spanaus, 438 U.S. 234, 98 S. Ct. 2716, 57 L. Ed. 2d 727 (1979); Home Bldg. & Loan Ass'n v. Blaisdell, 290 U.S. 398, 54 S. Ct. 231, 78 L. Ed. 413 (1934).

On the first criterion—whether the statute substantially impairs the contract—severity of impact is a key question. "Minimal alteration" of contract rights will end the inquiry at step one; "severe impairment" will require a "careful examination of the nature and purpose" of the state legislation.[29] Courts distinguish between statutes that affect the "core purpose" of a contract and those that merely modify the remedy, such as increased exemptions that place more of an asset off limits.[30] The latter will not be a substantial impairment, unless a very large or unexpected change "destroy[s] the value of the contract by destroying any meaningful remedy."[31]

The reasonable expectations of the parties are highly significant.[32] "State regulation that restricts a party to the gains that it reasonably expected from a contract does not necessarily constitute a substantial impairment."[33] If, for example, exemption amounts are updated to account for inflation, "the reasonable expectations of creditors are realized, not disturbed, by the increased statutory exemption."[34]

One important factor in determining reasonableness is the extent of regulation of the subject matter at the time the contract is formed.[35] Because exemption laws have been in existence for many decades, and have changed periodically to accommodate increased prices, a creditor may not reasonably rely upon their remaining frozen.

The other two criteria closely resemble the familiar "rational relationship to a proper public purpose" balancing test applied in due process and equal protection cases. Courts have generally held that state legislatures may properly shield debtors from total destitution, respond to economic crises, or amend unrealistic statutes to allow for changed prices, and that reasonable exemption statutes are a rational means to these ends.[36]

---

29 Allied Structural Steel Co. v. Spanaus, 438 U.S. 234, 98 S. Ct. 2716, 57 L. Ed. 2d 727 (1979) (severity of impact on contract rights defines "height of the hurdle" that state legislation must clear; when law regarding employee pension rights had severe impact on employer's rights, public purpose was insufficient to save it); Med. Soc'y of N.J. v. Mottola, 320 F. Supp. 2d 254 (D.N.J. 2004) (health care consumer information law which required disclosure of malpractice settlements did not impair contracts, as confidentiality agreements; confidentiality was "collateral aspect" of agreements whose core purpose was to settle disputes; even if impairment serious, statute saved by "legitimate public purpose").

30 *In re* Larson, 260 B.R. 174 (Bankr. D. Colo. 2001) (impairment of contract not substantial when change in exemption amount affected only the remedy); *In re* Bartlett, 168 B.R. 488 (Bankr. D.N.H. 1994) (state constitutional prohibition against retroactive statutes does not apply to remedies such as exemption amount); Macumber v. Shafer, 637 P.2d 645 (Wash. 1981) (increased exemption amounts merely modified remedy); *see also* Hellinger v. Farmers Ins. Exch., 111 Cal. Rptr. 2d 268 (Ct. App. 2001) (no unconstitutional impairment of contract when statute reviving certain time-barred earthquake claims affected only the remedy for breach of contract); Dardeen v. Heartland Manor, Inc., 710 N.E.2d 827 (Ill. 1999) (statute eliminating treble damages merely changed the damages recoverable; no vested right in a particular remedy or procedure); W. Des Moines State Bank v. Mills, 482 N.W.2d 432 (Iowa 1992) (retroactive application of statute eliminating special notice requirement for homestead waivers did not impair contract; statute simply governed procedure for waiver).

31 *In re* Echevarren, 2 B.R. 215, 217 (Bankr. D. Idaho 1980) (retroactive application of increase in homestead from $10,000 to $25,000 would unconstitutionally impair contract).

32 *In re* Little, 2007 WL 2791122 (N.D.N.Y. Sept. 24, 2007) (no substantial impairment; when creditor made loan in 2004, amendment of unreasonably low homestead exemption to account for inflation was foreseeable); *In re* Brown, 2007 WL 2120380 (Bankr. N.D.N.Y. July 23, 2007) (change in unreasonably low homestead exemption foreseeable); *In re* Evans, 362 B.R. 275 (Bankr. D.S.C. 2006) (considering the choice of law provisions of the bankruptcy law and the mobility of the population, no reasonable creditor could assume that a certain set of exemptions would apply); *In re* Larson, 260 B.R. 174 (Bankr. D. Colo. 2001) (creditors could reasonably expect exemption amounts to change with time); *In re* Johnson, 69 B.R. 988 (Bankr. D. Minn. 1987) (bank could not reasonably expect exemption statutes to remain unchanged and did not rely on this assumption when, at time of loan, it appeared to be fully secured); *In re* Punke, 68 B.R. 936 (Bankr. N.D. Iowa 1987) (when inflation is an economic reality, legislation that adjusts for it will realize, rather than disturb, creditors' expectations); *see also* Allstate Ins. Co. v. Kim, 829 A.2d 611 (Md. 2003) (abolition of parent-child immunity in motor vehicle cases covered by compulsory insurance law not impairment of contract, as change was predictable, industry was heavily regulated, and insurers failed to show severe impact).

33 Energy Reserves Group, Inc. v. Kan. Light & Power Co., 459 U.S. 400, 103 S. Ct. 697, 74 L. Ed. 2d 569 (1983) (quoting El Paso v. Simmons, 379 U.S. 497, 85 S. Ct. 577, 13 L. Ed. 2d 496 (1965)).

34 *In re* Punke, 68 B.R. 936, 941 (Bankr. N.D. Iowa 1987); *see also* *In re* Little, 2006 WL 1524594 (Bankr. N.D.N.Y. Apr. 24, 2006) (application of new amount to preexisting debt not impairment of contract); Macumber v. Shafer, 637 P.2d 645 (Wash. 1981).

35 Energy Reserves Group, Inc. v. Kan. Light & Power Co., 459 U.S. 400, 103 S. Ct. 697, 74 L. Ed. 2d 569 (1983) (natural gas highly regulated); *In re* Evans, 362 B.R. 275 (Bankr. D.S.C. 2006) (noting heavily regulated nature of debt collection and bankruptcy; not unconstitutional impairment of contract to apply increased homestead exemption that was in effect on petition date to preexisting debt); *In re* Johnson, 69 B.R. 988 (Bankr. D. Minn. 1987) (exemption laws had long history); *In re* Punke, 68 B.R. 936 (Bankr. N.D. Iowa 1987) (detailed history of Iowa homestead law); *In re* Barnhart, 47 B.R. 277 (Bankr. N.D. Tex. 1985); *see also* Hellinger v. Farmers Ins. Exch., 111 Cal. Rptr. 2d 268 (Ct. App. 2001) (insurance); Allstate Ins. Co. v. Kim, 829 A.2d 611 (Md. 2003) (heavy regulation of insurance industry).

36 Home Bldg. & Loan Ass'n v. Blaisdell, 290 U.S. 398, 54 S. Ct. 231, 78 L. Ed. 413 (1934) (upholding Depression-era statute that extended period for redemption from foreclosure); *In re* Little, 2006 WL 1524594 (Bankr. N.D.N.Y. Apr. 24, 2006) (application of increased exemption to preexisting debt not impairment of contract because inflation had obstructed statutory purpose); *In re* Johnson, 69 B.R. 988 (Bankr. D. Minn. 1987) (changes in homestead exemption were reasonable response to "catastrophic" situation in agriculture); *In re* Punke, 68 B.R. 936 (Bankr. N.D. Iowa 1987) (legislature has legitimate interest in reforming "outdated and unrealistic" exemption

12.2.3.2 Due Process and the Taking of Property

Most courts agree that application of increased exemption amounts is not a taking of property without just compensation in violation of due process.[37] A statutory "program adjusting the benefits and burdens of economic life to promote the common good" will be more deferentially reviewed than will a physical taking.[38] Courts will first decide whether an economic expectancy is solid enough to be treated as a property right protected by the takings clause and, if so, whether a statute's impact is sufficiently serious to constitute a taking. As with impairment of contract claims, reasonable expectations are a key issue.[39]

An unsecured creditor's hope that a debtor's nonexempt property will be sufficient to cover the debt is generally not a property right.[40] A security interest, or a lien that has attached to specific property, such as a judgment lien recorded against real estate, is more likely to be protected.[41] Even if a property right is found, courts will weigh the severity of the impact against the public purpose served by the statute, and may find a permissible adjustment of economic benefits and burdens, rather than a taking.[42]

Whether garnishment and execution procedures comply with due process requirements is discussed in § 12.3, *infra*.

12.2.3.3 Equal Protection

Exemption statutes' distinctions among different types of creditors and among debtors in different circumstances have generally been upheld against equal protection challenges.[43] The Supreme Court has adopted a balancing test for equal protection claims. If the statutes involves a suspect classification, such as race, gender, or national origin, or a fundamental right, such as the right to vote, or the freedom of speech or religion, then it will be subject to strict scrutiny. If it does not, then it need only have a rational relationship to a proper legislative purpose.[44] No court has held that

amounts to account for inflation); *In re* Barnhart, 47 B.R. 277 (Bankr. N.D. Tex. 1985) (long tradition of liberal construction of homestead statutes); Macumber v. Shafer, 637 P.2d 645 (Wash. 1981) (reasonable response to increased cost of living). *But see In re* Sticha, 60 B.R. 717 (Bankr. D. Minn. 1986) (preexisting lien was property interest; application of new exemption amounts would be taking); *In re* Fossum, 59 B.R. 820 (Bankr. D. Minn. 1986) (applying new amounts to preexisting debt would be taking); Builders Supply Co. v. Pine Belt Sav. & Loan Ass'n, 369 So. 2d 743, 745 (Miss. 1979).

37 *In re* Brown, 2007 WL 2120380 (Bankr. N.D.N.Y. July 23, 2007) (increase of homestead amount made unrealistic by inflation simply adjusted economic benefits and burdens and served important public purpose; no unconstitutional taking); *In re* Larson, 260 B.R. 174 (Bankr. D. Colo. 2001) (security interest is property, but impairment, which resulted from "adjustment of benefits and burdens," not severe enough to equal taking); *In re* Bartlett, 168 B.R. 488 (Bankr. D.N.H. 1994) (judicial liens; impairment was reasonable in light of public policy of bankruptcy and exemption laws; creditor did not have property right in assumption that collateral would be sufficient to pay off loan); *In re* Punke, 68 B.R. 936 (Bankr. N.D. Iowa 1987) (statute adjusted benefits and burdens; change was within reasonable expectations of creditors). *But see In re* Sticha, 60 B.R. 717 (Bankr. D. Minn. 1986) (security interest in specific property); *In re* Fossum, 59 B.R. 820 (Bankr. D. Minn. 1986) (same).

38 Pa. Cent. Transp. Co. v. City of New York, 438 U.S. 104, 98 S. Ct. 2646, 57 L. Ed. 2d 631 (1978).

39 *In re* Betz, 273 B.R. 313 (Bankr. D. Mass. 2002); *In re* Larson, 260 B.R. 174 (Bankr. D. Colo. 2001) (security interests were property but impairment here, which resulted from an adjustment of economic benefits and burdens, did not have sufficient impact to be a taking); *In re* Johnson, 69 B.R. 988 (Bankr. D. Minn. 1987) (bank could not reasonably expect that exemption laws would remain unchanged and had not relied on this possibility when, at time of loan, it was fully secured; increased exemption not a taking); *In re* Punke, 68 B.R. 936 (Bankr. N.D. Iowa 1987) (application of new exemption amounts to preexisting debts not taking).

40 *In re* Johnson, 69 B.R. 988 (Bankr. D. Minn. 1987). *But see In re* Bassin, 637 F.2d 668 (9th Cir. 1980) (unsecured claims).

41 *In re* Larson, 260 B.R. 174 (Bankr. D. Colo. 2001) (security interest is property); *In re* Sticha, 60 B.R. 717 (Bankr. D. Minn. 1986) (security interest in specific property); *In re* Fossum, 59 B.R. 820 (Bankr. D. Minn. 1986) (same). *But see In re* Bartlett, 168 B.R. 488 (Bankr. D.N.H. 1994) (judicial liens; creditor did not have property right in assumption that collateral would be sufficient to pay off loan).

42 *See, e.g.*, *In re* Brown, 2007 WL 2120380 (Bankr. N.D.N.Y. July 23, 2007) (adjustment of homestead amount made unrealistic by inflation served important public purpose); *In re* Larson, 260 B.R. 174 (Bankr. D. Colo. 2001) (security interests were property but impairment here, which resulted from an adjustment of economic benefits and burdens, did not have sufficient impact to be a taking).

43 St. Ann's Hosp. v. Arnold, 672 N.E.2d 743 (Ohio Ct. App. 1996) (greater restrictions on garnishment for health care debts reasonable in light of public policy of encouraging people to seek needed medical care); Wooster Cmty. Hosp. v. Anderson, 670 N.E.2d 563 (Ohio Ct. App. 1996) (greater protection of health care debtors was reasonable because of life or death necessity of health care, and the extra burdens imposed by paying back a debt while also suffering health problems); *In re* Davis, 681 N.W.2d 452 (S.D. 2004) (increased homestead exemption for persons age seventy or over not arbitrary, nor denial of equal protection, but unlimited exemption violated state constitutional requirement that exemptions be reasonable); *see also In re* Patterson, 216 B.R. 413 (C.D. Ill. 1998) (exception of wages from wildcard exemption does not violation state constitution's prohibition of special laws); Accounts Mgmt., Inc. v. Williams, 484 N.W.2d 297 (S.D. 1992) (state wage garnishment exemption did not violate privileges and immunities clause of state constitution by favoring wage earners over others). *But see* Cmty. Physical Therapy v. Wayt, 639 N.E.2d 515 (Ohio Ct. App. 1994) (statute placing greater restrictions on garnishment for health care debts was unconstitutional because it had no rational relationship to any governmental purpose).

44 Heller v. Doe, 509 U.S. 312, 319–320, 113 S. Ct. 2637, 125 L. Ed. 2d 257 (1993) (rational relationship standard very deferential to state legislatures); Williamson v. Lee Optical, 348 U.S. 483, 75 S. Ct. 461, 99 L. Ed. 563 (1955); *see also* Am. Fed'n of Gov't Employees v. United States, 195 F. Supp. 2d 4, 10–12 (D.D.C. 2002) (extensive collection of cases defining suspect classes), *aff'd*, 330 F.3d 513 (D.C. Cir. 2003).

creditors are a suspect class, or that there is a fundamental right to a specific collection method.[45] Courts have generally recognized exemption statutes as rational means to achieve proper legislative purposes.[46]

12.2.3.4 State Constitutional Issues

In many states certain exemptions, most commonly the homestead exemption, are found in the state constitution. A constitutional exemption will be less subject to waiver or loss than a statutory exemption.[47] Some courts have also struck down statutory exemptions that were more generous than those in the state constitution.[48] Unlimited exemptions may violate state constitutional provisions for "reasonable" exemptions, but can usually be saved by reading in a requirement that the amount exempted be reasonably necessary for the support of the debtor and dependents.[49]

12.3 Due Process Protections from Garnishment or Execution on Exempt Property

12.3.1 Introduction

Garnishment is a frequently used debt collection technique in which the collector seizes money someone owes to the debtor. For example, a creditor may seize the debtor's wages directly from the employer or attach the debtor's deposits in a bank account directly from the bank. Similarly, creditors may execute on property in the debtor's possession, such as a car or household goods, by obtaining an order for it to be seized and sold.

Until 1969, collectors often used these techniques even before obtaining judgments on the underlying debts. In 1969 the Supreme Court struck down a state pre-judgment wage garnishment statute as unconstitutional on its face.[50] The practical result is that garnishments today are used commonly to enforce only post-judgment debts. Some states allow *ex parte* pre-judgment property attachments, but these statutes have generally been held unconstitutional unless they are limited to exigent circumstances and include substantial procedural safeguards.[51]

---

45 Bowden Bldg. Corp. v. Tennessee Real Estate Comm'n, 15 S.W.3d 434 (Tenn. Ct. App. 1999) (right to sell property not fundamental right triggering strict scrutiny; statute requiring corporation to use licensed real estate broker reviewed under "rational relationship" standard); *see also* Sharp v. Park 'N Fly of Tex., 969 S.W.2d 572 (Tex. App. 1998) ("in examining classifications of economic or property interests, the court employs a rational basis test"); *In re* Honeycutt, 908 P.2d 976 (Wyo. 1995) (construing state constitution; using rational relationship standard to uphold statute denying exemption to privately funded individual retirement account, but exempting employer-sponsored plans).

46 *See* §§ 12.2.3.1, 12.2.3.2, *supra.*

47 *In re* Box, 340 B.R. 782 (S.D. Tex. 2006); Gonzales v. Ameriquest Mortgage, 2005 WL 3333259 (W.D. Tex. Dec. 8, 2005) (borrower entitled to claim homestead exemption despite disclaimer that property was not his homestead when borrower owned only one piece of residential property and lived there); *In re* Hendricks, 237 B.R. 821 (Bankr. M.D. Fla. 1999) (homestead exemption in constitution is not affected by change in fraudulent conveyance statute); Havoco of Am., Ltd. v. Hill, 790 So. 2d 1018 (Fla. 2001) (legislature is powerless to subject constitutional homestead exemption to fraudulent transfer statute); Torgelson v. Real Property Known As 17138 880th Ave., 734 N.W.2d 279 (Minn. Ct. App. 2007) (constitutional homestead exemption bars forfeiture for state offenses); Household Fin. Corp. v. Ellis, 107 N.C. App. 262, 419 S.E.2d 592 (1992) (statute unconstitutional to extent it limits the claiming of constitutional exemptions to twenty days after service of notice), *aff'd*, 429 S.E.2d 716 (N.C. 1993) (per curiam); State v. One 1965 Red Chevrolet Pickup, 37 P.3d 815 (Okla. 2001) (home but not vehicle exempt from state criminal law forfeiture; homestead exemption found in state constitution, motor vehicle exemption and forfeiture provisions are statutory). *But cf.* Dominguez v. Castaneda, 163 S.W.3d 318 (Tex. App. 2005) (debtor owning two residential properties bound by warranty that parcel not homestead).

48 *In re* Holt, 894 F.2d 1005 (8th Cir. 1990) (statutory exemptions are contrary to, and therefore limited by, the lower ceilings in the Arkansas Constitution).

49 *In re* Cross, 255 B.R. 25 (Bankr. N.D. Ind. 2000) (unlimited exemptions violate state constitution unless debtor shows exemption is needed for necessities of life); Citizens' Nat'l Bank v. Foster, 668 N.E.2d 1236 (Ind. 1996) (state constitution provided for "reasonable" exemptions for debtors; exemption for individual retirement accounts, which were limited by federal tax law, was constitutional, but unlimited exemption for life insurance naming the insured's spouse as beneficiary was questionable; debtor must show "reasonable necessity" of amount claimed); Estate of Jones by Blume v. Kvamme, 529 N.W.2d 335 (Minn. 1995) (exemption for individual retirement accounts and certain employee benefits that had no limit on amount and no reference to needs of debtor and family violated Minnesota constitutional provision requiring "reasonable exemptions"); *In re* Davis, 681 N.W.2d 452 (S.D. 2004) (increased homestead exemption for persons seventy or over permissible, but unlimited exemption violated state constitutional requirement of reasonable exemptions; legislature must provide cap); *see also In re* Craig, 545 N.W.2d 764 (N.D. 1996) (limitation of $100,000 per item, $200,000 total for life insurance policies and certain retirement funds was reasonable within meaning of state constitution, which would bar an unlimited exemption); *In re* Bannourah, 201 B.R. 954 (Bankr. S.D. Ind. 1996) (state insurance policy exemption, construed so as to avoid state constitutional problem, exempted amount required to afford the necessities of life). *But see In re* Reiland, 377 B.R. 232 (Bankr. D. Minn. 2007) (unlimited exemption for disability insurance can not be saved; reasonable exemption must prescribe dollar amount, objective criteria, or reference to other statute creating limits).

50 Sniadach v. Family Fin. Corp., 395 U.S. 337, 89 S. Ct. 1820, 23 L. Ed. 2d 349 (1969).

51 Connecticut v. Doehr, 501 U.S. 1, 111 S. Ct. 2105, 115 L. Ed. 2d 1 (1991) (Connecticut statute allowing *ex parte* prejudgment attachment of realty in absence of exigent circumstances and without bond is unconstitutional); *In re* Foust, 310 F.3d 849 (5th Cir. 2002) (construing Mississippi pre-judgment replevin statute

Post-judgment garnishment and execution must still comply with federal due process standards. The major due process concern is to allow debtors to assert that certain of their assets are exempt from execution, and thus may not be taken. In general, the due process clause requires notice of exemptions and right to a hearing on exemptions.

12.3.2 The Constitutional Balancing of Interests

Although it is clear that debtors have a significant property interest in assets which are exempt from garnishment,[52] and that garnishment involves state action sufficient to invoke Fourteenth Amendment protections,[53] it is only since the late 1970s that courts have seriously considered the due process rights of judgment debtors. The relative dearth of earlier litigation and analysis was largely the result of a 1924 Supreme Court decision, *Endicott-Johnson v. Encyclopedia Press*,[54] which held that a judgment debtor has had his day in court and has, in effect, been given "notice of what will follow, no further notice being necessary to advance justice."[55] Thus the view of many courts was that the original service and proceedings in an action on a debt provided all the process the debtor was constitutionally due.[56]

The blanket application of *Endicott* has, however, been seriously undermined by the influence of more recent Supreme Court due process decisions analyzing property deprivation in general and pre-judgment garnishment in particular.[57] In addition, there is a growing judicial recognition that the garnishment involved in *Endicott*, which was decided before the legislative creation of most federal property exemptions and which did not refer to the possibility of exemptions, is facially distinguishable from modern garnishment cases involving potentially exempt property.[58]

Since the Third Circuit's decision in *Finberg v. Sullivan*,[59] the erosion of *Endicott* has proceeded rapidly. Although *Endicott* has not been expressly overruled, all seven federal circuit courts of appeal that have considered post-judgment garnishment or execution on potentially exempt property in

---

to save its constitutionality; pre-seizure hearing required "where feasible"; denial of due process here, because complaint was "skeletal" and no showing that hearing not feasible); McLaughlin v. Weathers, 170 F.3d 577 (6th Cir. 1999) (Tennessee pre-judgment attachment statute not unconstitutional on its face, when attachment available only under "specified exigent circumstances" and procedure was available to challenge issuance of writ); Tri-State Dev. Ltd. v. Johnston, 160 F.3d 528 (9th Cir. 1998) (Washington's pre-judgment attachment statute was unconstitutional on its face, when attachment could be obtained *ex parte* without showing of exigent circumstances); Puerto Rican Am. Ins. v. Burgos-Diaz, 2005 WL 1643299 (D. P.R. June 30, 2005) (Puerto Rico's pre-judgment remedy statute satisfies *Doehr* criteria, if construed to require either "extraordinary circumstances" or a prior interest in the subject property, and a likelihood of success on the merits); Gem Plumbing & Heating Co. v. Rossi, 867 A.2d 796 (R.I. 2005) (Rhode Island mechanics' lien statute, as amended to provide prompt hearing to challenge lien, satisfies due process); Shawmut Bank v. Costello, 643 A.2d 194 (R.I. 1994) (pre-judgment remedy statute unconstitutional when *ex parte* writ issued with no showing of exigent circumstances and no requirement that creditor post bond); Van Blaricom v. Kronenberg, 50 P.3d 266 (Wash. Ct. App. 2002) (attorney may be liable for section 1983 violation for using Washington pre-judgment statute that is unconstitutional as applied when no exigent circumstances); *see also* Frasher v. Fox Distrib. of S.W. Fla., Inc., 813 So. 2d 1017 (Fla. Dist. Ct. App. 2002) (affidavit insufficient to support pre-judgment attachment, on both due process and state statutory grounds, when affiant failed to allege personal knowledge of removal, concealment, and so forth); State *ex rel.* Goldberg v. Mahoning County Probate Ct., 753 N.E.2d 192 (Ohio 2001) (judge's pre-judgment order to seize property of attorney accused of stealing settlement proceeds was unconstitutional because no affidavit, bond, or ruling by independent magistrate).

52 Dionne v. Bouley, 757 F.2d 1344 (1st Cir. 1985); Mayers v. N.Y. Cmty. Bancorp, Inc., 2005 WL 2105810 (E.D.N.Y. Aug. 31, 2005) (exemption for Social Security benefits in bank account is property right protected by due process clause), *later decision at* 2006 WL 2013734 (E.D.N.Y. July 18, 2006) (denying defendants' motion for interlocutory appeal).

53 *See, e.g.*, Sniadach v. Family Fin. Corp., 395 U.S. 337, 89 S. Ct. 1820, 23 L. Ed. 2d 349 (1969); Mayers v. N.Y. Cmty. Bancorp, Inc., 2005 WL 2105810 (E.D.N.Y. Aug. 31, 2005) (procedure for pre-garnishment bank account freeze was state action; state coercion present because bank that disregarded notice could be sanctioned for contempt), *later decision at* 2006 WL 2013734 (E.D.N.Y. July 18, 2006) (denying defendants' motion for interlocutory appeal); Doyle v. Schultz, 97 F. Supp. 2d 763 (W.D. La. 2000) (creditor and attorney were state actors when they set in motion state execution procedure which was unconstitutional as applied); Alaska Dep't of Revenue v. Maxwell, 6 P.3d 733 (Alaska 2000) (child support order void for denial of due process when obligor was given no opportunity to be heard before issuance of administrative order).

54 266 U.S. 285, 45 S. Ct. 61, 69 L. Ed. 288 (1924).

55 *Endicott*, 266 U.S. at 288.

56 For decisions expressly relying on *Endicott*, see Haines v. Gen. Motors Corp., 603 F. Supp. 471 (S.D. Ohio 1983); Ortiz v. Valdez, 971 P.2d 1076 (Colo. Ct. App. 1998) (holding Colorado's post-judgment garnishment scheme acceptable, even though it resulted in freezing non-debtor's exempt Social Security funds for at least five weeks); Pitts v. Dallas Nurseries Garden Ctr., 545 S.W.2d 34 (Tex. App. 1976).

57 *See, e.g.*, N. Ga. Finishing Inc. v. Di-Chem, Inc., 419 U.S. 601, 95 S. Ct. 719, 42 L. Ed. 2d 751 (1975); Mitchell v. W.T. Grant Co., 416 U.S. 600, 94 S. Ct. 1895, 40 L. Ed. 2d 406 (1974); Fuentes v. Shevin, 407 U.S. 67, 92 S. Ct. 1983, 32 L. Ed. 2d 556 (1972); Sniadach v. Family Fin. Corp., 395 U.S. 337, 89 S. Ct. 1820, 23 L. Ed. 2d 349 (1969).

58 Adkins v. Rumsfield, 464 F.3d 456 (4th Cir. 2006) (although *Endicott* not overruled, Supreme Court has "significantly revised" approach to due process in garnishment cases; here, court applies *Matthews* balancing test and concludes that Armed Forces Former Spouses' Protection Act procedure for enforcing state domestic relations orders provides due process); Dionne v. Bouley, 757 F.2d 1344 (1st Cir. 1985); Dorwart v. Caraway, 966 P.2d 1121 (Mont. 1998) (distinguishing *Endicott* and questioning its continuing validity; Montana post-judgment procedure violates due process by failing to require prompt post-seizure notice of exemptions and procedure for claiming them).

59 634 F.2d 50 (3d Cir. 1980).

the last sixteen years have recognized the significant property interests of judgment debtors and have applied balancing-of-interests analyses to determine the extent of debtors' due process rights to notice and hearing.[60] This approach has also expressly been adopted by virtually all federal district courts considering the issue after the *Finberg* decision.[61]

The most prevalent due process analysis for post-judgment garnishment and execution procedures relating to exempt property is the balancing test set out by the Supreme Court in 1976 in *Matthews v. Eldridge*.[62] Under this three-pronged approach, a court considering the process due when a person is deprived of property must weigh:

- The competing interests involved and the effect of state action on these interests;
- The risk of erroneous deprivation of property under the existing system and the probable value of additional or substitute procedures; and
- The cost and administrative burden of the new procedures in comparison to their probable value.

---

60 Aacen v. San Juan County Sheriff's Dep't, 944 F.2d 691 (10th Cir. 1991) (due process violation when notice failed to reveal existence of exemptions other than homestead exemption, or how to claim them); Reigh v. Schleigh, 784 F.2d 1191 (4th Cir. 1986) (new garnishment statute complied with due process); McCahey v. L.P. Investors, 774 F.2d 543 (2d Cir. 1985) (procedures satisfied due process); Dionne v. Bouley, 757 F.2d 1344 (1st Cir. 1985) (finding due process violation); Duranceau v. Wallace, 743 F.2d 709 (9th Cir. 1984) (procedures satisfied due process); Finberg v. Sullivan, 634 F.2d 50 (3d Cir. 1980) (finding due process violation); Brown v. Liberty Loan Corp. of Duval, 539 F.2d 1355 (5th Cir. 1976) (procedures satisfied due process); *see also* Adkins v. Rumsfield, 464 F.3d 456 (4th Cir. 2006) (applying *Matthews* balancing test and concluding that Defense Department may implement state domestic relations garnishment orders without giving them more than facial scrutiny); *cf.* Walsh v. Wal-Mart Stores, Inc., 836 F.2d 1152 (8th Cir. 1988) (no claim stated against employer for due process noncompliance in a garnishment proceeding; claim was against creditor).

61 *See, e.g.*, Mayers v. N.Y. Cmty. Bancorp, Inc., 2005 WL 2105810 (E.D.N.Y. Aug. 31, 2005) (finding plaintiffs sufficiently stated due process claim challenging New York's post-judgment garnishment procedure after rebalancing interests in light of technological changes), *later decision at* 2006 WL 2013734 (E.D.N.Y. July 18, 2006) (denying defendants' motion for interlocutory appeal); Hutchinson v. Cox, 784 F. Supp. 1339 (S.D. Ohio 1992) (due process requires that judgment debtor be informed, during post-judgment execution, of available exemptions and right to hearing); Jacobson v. Johnson, 798 F. Supp. 500 (C.D. Ill. 1991); Cristiano v. Courts of the Justice of the Peace, 669 F. Supp. 662 (D. Del. 1987) (Justice of the Peace courts' process for garnishment of wages invalid for failure to provide prompt post deprivation hearing and sufficient notice of procedure for challenge); Follette v. Cooper, 658 F. Supp. 514 (N.D.N.Y. 1987); Follette v. Vitanza, 658 F. Supp. 492 (N.D.N.Y. 1987) (failure to give notice of federal wage garnishment exemptions and state procedures to assert them unconstitutional); Davis v. Paschall, 640 F. Supp. 198 (E.D. Ark. 1986); Fry's Food Stores v. CBM, Inc., 636 F. Supp. 168 (D. Ariz. 1986) (supplementary process statute unconstitutional); Green v. Harbin, 615 F. Supp. 719 (D. Ala. 1985); Neeley v. Century Fin. Co., 606 F. Supp. 1453 (D. Ariz. 1985) (garnishment statute unconstitutional; *Endicott* applies only when no exemptions possible); Clay v. Fisher, 584 F. Supp. 730 (S.D. Ohio 1984); Harris v. Bailey, 574 F. Supp. 966 (W.D. Va. 1983); Phillips v. Robinson Jewelers, Inc., Clearinghouse No. 31,761 (W.D. Okla. 1983); Deary v. Guardian Loan Co., 534 F. Supp. 1178 (S.D.N.Y. 1982); Simler & Jackson v. Jennings, 23 Ohio Op. 3d 554 (S.D. Ohio 1982) (mag.); Betts v. Coltes, 467 F. Supp. 544 (D. Haw. 1979); Betts v. Tom, 431 F. Supp. 1369 (D. Haw. 1977); Dorwart v. Caraway, 966 P.2d 1121 (Mont. 1998) (Montana post-judgment procedure violates U.S. and Montana due process clauses by failing to require prompt post-seizure notice of exemptions, procedure for claiming them, and availability of hearing); *see also* Roy v. Smith, 735 F. Supp. 313 (C.D. Ill. 1990) (wages); Kirby v. Sprouls, 722 F. Supp. 516 (C.D. Ill. 1989) (state statute violated due process requirements when it failed to require notice of garnishment proceeding, notice of exemption rights under state and federal law, notice of debtor's right to exercise those rights and a prompt hearing); Burris v. Mahaney, 716 F. Supp. 1051 (M.D. Tenn. 1989); Jones v. Marion County Small Claims Ct., 701 F. Supp. 1414 (S.D. Ind. 1988) (state statute for garnishment of bank accounts violated due process requirements of prompt notice and hearing); Imperial Bank v. Pim Elec., Inc., 39 Cal. Rptr. 3d 432 (Ct. App. 1995); Cole v. Goldberger, Pederson & Hochron, 95 Misc. 2d 720, 410 N.Y.S.2d 950 (Sup. Ct. Special Term 1978); Bell v. Beightler, 2003 WL 116146 (Ohio Ct. App. Jan. 14, 2003) (upholding procedures for garnishment of prison inmate's account; administrative hearing on exemptions is sufficient); Layne v. West Virginia Child Support Enforcement Div., 518 S.E.2d 357 (W. Va. 1998) (due process requires notice and an opportunity for hearing before disability benefits can be garnished for child support arrearage). *But see* Haines v. Gen. Motors Corp., 603 F. Supp. 471 (S.D. Ohio 1983) (*Endicott* is controlling); *cf.* Huggins v. Pataki, 2002 WL 1732804 (E.D.N.Y. July 11, 2002) (New York's bank account garnishment procedure, which requires creditor to send notice to debtor after account is frozen, is constitutional even though bank could have determined that account consisted entirely of directly-deposited Social Security funds, and even though creditor failed to send the required notice); *In re* Thelen, 156 B.R. 786 (Bankr. W.D. Mich. 1993) (*Endicott* still good law, no notice or hearing required for seizure of clearly nonexempt property; distinguishing cases requiring notice of possible exemptions).

Earlier decisions generally rejected due process challenges but had no uniform rationale for doing so. *See, e.g.*, First Nat'l Bank v. Hasty, 410 F. Supp. 482 (E.D. Mich. 1976) (rejecting pre-garnishment hearing under *Mitchell*); Phillips v. Bartolomie, 46 Cal. App. 3d 346, 121 Cal. Rptr. 56 (1975) (debtor may be required to file exemption claim); Raigoza v. Sperl, 34 Cal. App. 3d 560, 110 Cal. Rptr. 296 (1973) (statute contained sufficient due process protections); Warner/Elektra/Atlantic Corp. v. B. & B. Record & Tape Merchandisers, 570 P.2d 1320 (Colo. Ct. App. 1977) (no exemption issue); Wilson v. Grimes, 232 Ga. 388, 207 S.E.2d 5 (1974); Bittner v. Butts, 514 S.W.2d 556 (Mo. 1974); Plaza Hotel Associates v. Wellington Associates, 84 Misc. 2d 777, 378 N.Y.S.2d 859 (Sup. Ct. Special Term 1975); Hehr v. Tucker, 256 Or. 254, 472 P.2d 797 (1970); Pitts v. Dallas Nurseries Garden Ctr., 545 S.W.2d 34 (Tex. App. 1976); Dep't of Social & Health Services v. Gerlack, 25 Wash. App. 541, 612 P.2d 382 (1980); *see also* McCahey v. L.P. Investors, 774 F.2d 543, 547 n.5 (2d Cir. 1985).

62 424 U.S. 319, 96 S. Ct. 893, 47 L. Ed. 2d 18 (1976).

A creditor has a clear interest in the prompt and inexpensive satisfaction of judgments it has obtained,[63] and a state has a parallel interest in seeing that the judgment which it has issued is given effect. However, the creditor has no interest whatsoever in the debtor's exempt property, and depriving a debtor of exempt assets may both endanger the debtor's subsistence and frustrate the legislative policies upon which the exemptions are based.

The strength of creditor and debtor property interests may be modified, at least in part, by the facts of a particular case. For example, creditor interests appear to be stronger when garnishment for child support is being sought than in the case of other judgments.[64] On the debtor's side of the equation, some courts have suggested that bank accounts containing exempt funds deserve even stronger protection than a debtor's wages because the garnishment of such an account may deprive the debtor of *all* money needed immediately for food and shelter, whereas a partial wage garnishment would still leave the debtor with most of his or her salary.[65]

Applying the *Matthews* tests, courts generally hold that post-judgment garnishment and execution must comply with four procedural requirements. These standards are discussed in the next four subsections.

12.3.3 Prompt Post-Garnishment Notice Is Required

Courts applying the *Matthews* analysis have almost uniformly ruled that state laws violate due process when they allow garnishment without any notice (other than the actual notice the debtor gets when, for example, he or she receives a smaller pay check).[66] The reason for this is fairly clear: a notice requirement places little burden on a creditor and gives the debtor an opportunity to challenge any improper garnishment.

63 McCahey v. L.P. Investors, 774 F.2d 543, 549 (2d Cir. 1985) (creditor has interest in reaching bank accounts and other liquid assets because this is lowest-cost method of satisfying judgments).

64 This observation, while frequently not acknowledged by courts, seems to be borne out by the results in child support cases. *See, e.g.*, DeTienne v. DeTienne, 815 F. Supp. 394 (D. Kan. 1993) (Social Security disability benefits are subject to garnishment for child support and alimony); *see also* Green v. Harbin, 615 F. Supp. 719 (D. Ala. 1985) (consent decree does not reach child support).

65 Reigh v. Schleigh, 595 F. Supp. 1535 (D. Md. 1984), *rev'd on other grounds*, 784 F.2d 1191 (4th Cir. 1986); Harris v. Bailey, 574 F. Supp. 966 (W.D. Va. 1983). *But cf.* Neeley v. Century Fin. Co., 606 F. Supp. 1453 (D. Ariz. 1985) (wages entitled to greater protection than other assets).

66 *See* Dionne v. Bouley, 757 F.2d 1344 (1st Cir. 1985); Jones v. Marion County Small Claims Ct., 701 F. Supp. 1414 (S.D. Ind. 1988) (state statute for garnishment of bank accounts violated due process requirements of prompt notice and hearing); Reigh v. Schleigh, 595 F. Supp. 1535 (D. Md. 1984), *rev'd on other grounds*, 784 F.2d 1191 (4th Cir. 1986); Clay v. Fisher, 584 F. Supp. 730 (S.D. Ohio 1984); Deary v. Guardian Loan Co., 534 F. Supp. 1178 (S.D.N.Y. 1982); E.J. McKernan Co. v. Gregory, 643 N.E.2d 1370 (Ill. App. Ct. 1994) (former version of Illinois non-wage garnishment law was unconstitutional because it failed to provide notice and hearing regarding possible exemptions, prior to issuance of garnishment summons); Dorwart v. Caraway, 966 P.2d 1121 (Mont. 1998); Cole v. Goldberger, Pederson & Hochron, 95 Misc. 2d 720, 410 N.Y.S.2d 950 (Sup. Ct. Special Term 1978); *see also* Doyle v. Schultz, 97 F. Supp. 2d 763 (W.D. La. 2000) (Louisiana procedure for executing on judgments was unconstitutional as applied, when house was seized pursuant to Texas judgment without notice that judgment had been domesticated); CBM v. Sevier, 910 P.2d 654 (Ariz. Ct. App. 1996) (when creditor sought to garnish one spouse's wages for pre-marital debt, in a community property state, non-debtor spouse should be joined in the garnishment action, to give that spouse notice and opportunity to be heard on what property each spouse had contributed to community); Romero v. Star Markets, 922 P.2d 1018 (Haw. Ct. App. 1996) (when procedure for collecting workers' compensation awards was to move for entry of court judgment, employer who had already participated in administrative hearing must be served with motion; employee's *ex parte* garnishment violated due process); *cf.* Sheppard v. Welch, 2005 WL 1656873 (S.D. Ind. July 5, 2005) (child support obligor stated due process claim when prosecutor issued wage and bank account garnishment orders without the required notice to obligor), *later decision at* 2006 WL 3134869 (S.D. Ind. Oct. 3, 2006) (summary judgment for state; no section 1983 violation when lack of notice was "random and unauthorized" and state post-deprivation remedy was adequate); Savage v. Scales, 310 F. Supp. 2d 122 (D.D.C. 2004) (due process requires only reasonable effort to provide notice; sending notice of administrative garnishment for student loan to last known address is sufficient); First Resolution Inv. Corp. v. Seker, 795 A.2d 868 (N.J. 2002) (notice procedure permitting ordinary mail if certified mail "unclaimed" satisfied due process, but court recommends rule revisions, including a requirement that creditor show how it obtained debtor's "last known address"). *But see* Brown v. Liberty Loan Corp., 539 F.2d 1355 (5th Cir. 1976) (primarily but not exclusively addressing pre-garnishment notice); *cf.* Day v. Idaho Dep't of Corrections, 1999 U.S. App. LEXIS 34125 (9th Cir. Dec. 27, 1999) (prison's withdrawal of money from inmate account for court garnishment not denial of due process in absence of evidence that state court failed to give notice of garnishment or opportunity to be heard); Malowney v. Fed. Collection Deposit Group, 193 F.3d 1342 (11th Cir. 1999) (no case or controversy regarding constitutionality of Florida statute, when Florida court had already dissolved garnishment of exempt funds and repeat garnishment was unlikely); Roush v. Basham, 1998 U.S. App. LEXIS 12903 (4th Cir. June 18, 1998) (no denial of due process when child support enforcement agency was simply negligent, and state court had already ordered return of improperly garnished wages); Farrar v. Glantz, 2000 U.S. Dist. LEXIS 6502 (N.D. Ill. Apr. 25, 2000) (no due process violation when computer error prevented consumer from receiving notice of small claims proceeding; simple negligence is not sufficient, and state court proceeding enabled consumer to prevent taking of any property); Price v. Sec'y of Revenue & Taxation, 664 So. 2d 802 (La. Ct. App. 1995) (under community property law, wages of non-debtor wife could be garnished without notice for tax debt of husband's corporation).

Nevertheless, a number of courts have ruled that due process does not require notice *prior* to garnishment.[67] This position is based on the fear that, in cases involving the garnishment of bank accounts or moveable property, a debtor might remove the property to defeat a valid garnishment. However a prior notice requirement has also been rejected in some wage garnishment cases,[68] even though there can be no reason to fear that unpaid wages will be concealed or removed. In the case of wage garnishment, the only burden placed on the creditor by prior notice would be a minor delay in the commencement of the garnishment while the debtor is given an opportunity to defend his or her wages.

Instead of pre-garnishment notice, the courts have required that notice be contemporaneous with, or immediately follow, the garnishment. Exactly what this means in practice is unclear. For example, a district court in Hawaii required notice *and a hearing* within two days of garnishment.[69] The Second Circuit upheld a rule allowing the mailing of notice within four days of garnishment.[70] Another court has found twenty days between garnishment and notice to be clearly too long.[71] Because there will of necessity be a delay from when the debtor receives notice of a garnishment until the debtor can obtain a hearing, it is important for the debtor to receive notice as soon as possible.

A related procedural protection would be to require the creditor, in seeking a writ of garnishment, to file an affidavit with a judicial officer, stating that the assets to be garnished are not exempt. One court held, in the wage garnishment context, that the absence of such a requirement was a "substantial defect," although it found the garnishment procedure as a whole to meet due process requirements.[72]

A recent district court decision, *Mayers v. New York Community Bankcorp*,[73] takes a fresh look at the constitutionality of freezing the debtor's bank account in light of technological changes. In particular, the court noted that the Social Security Administration's requirement that beneficiaries receive payments electronically, unless they specifically opt out, has increased the risk and severity of erroneous deprivation and decreased the burden of determining whether bank accounts contain only exempt funds. Balancing these factors, along with the government's interest in avoiding clogging up the courts with exemption claims, the *Mayers* court held that the plaintiffs had the right to proceed on their claim that the New York bank account garnishment procedures denies debtors procedural due process by allowing accounts that contain only exempt electronically deposited Social Security funds to be frozen upon service of the garnishment order.

---

67 *See, e.g.*, Nat'l Labor Relations Bd. v. E.D.P. Med. Computer Sys., Inc., 6 F.3d 951 (2d Cir. 1993) (*ex parte* writ justified by extraordinary situation); McCahey v. L.P. Investors, 774 F.2d 543 (2d Cir. 1985) (bank account); Dionne v. Bouley, 757 F.2d 1344 (1st Cir. 1985) (bank account); Finberg v. Sullivan, 634 F.2d 50 (3d Cir. 1980) (bank account); Brown v. Liberty Loan Corp., 539 F.2d 1355 (5th Cir. 1976) (wages); Carter v. Welch, 1999 U.S. Dist. LEXIS 6705 (S.D. Ala. Mar. 12, 1999) (due process requirements satisfied by Alabama procedure, which offered a pre-deprivation hearing before taking funds from inmate account to satisfy court-ordered restitution), *adopted by* 1999 U.S. Dist. LEXIS 6771 (S.D. Ala. Apr. 27, 1999); Nelson v. Silverman, 888 F. Supp. 1041 (S.D. Cal. 1995) (Internal Revenue Service may levy on wages or real property without pre-seizure notice or hearing; post-seizure procedures are sufficient to satisfy due process); Roy v. Smith, 735 F. Supp. 313 (C.D. Ill. 1990) (wages); Ortiz v. Valdez, 971 P.2d 1076 (Colo. Ct. App. 1998) (following *Endicott*; Colorado's post-judgment garnishment scheme acceptable, even though it resulted in non-debtor's exempt Social Security funds being frozen for at least five weeks); First Union Nat'l Bank v. Knyal, 874 So. 2d 716 (Fla. Dist. Ct. App. 2004) (pre-garnishment notice not required for post-judgment garnishment); Collection Professionals, Inc. v. Logan, 695 N.E.2d 1344 (Ill. App. Ct. 1998) (amended Illinois post-judgment garnishment statute provided due process of law when it required debtors to be notified of garnishment, exemptions, procedure for claiming them, and hearing within two days of service of garnishment summons); Leger v. Comm'r of Revenue, 654 N.E.2d 927 (Mass. 1995) (tax collection an exception to rule which requires pre-seizure notice for liens on real estate); *see also* Huggins v. Pataki, 2002 WL 1732804 (E.D.N.Y. July 11, 2002) (New York's bank account garnishment procedure, which requires creditor to send notice to debtor after account is frozen, is constitutional even though bank could have determined that account consisted entirely of directly-deposited Social Security funds, and even though creditor failed to send the required notice); *cf.* Kennedy v. Comm'r of Social Security, 1999 U.S. App. LEXIS 34031 (6th Cir. Dec. 21, 1999) (Social Security recipient failed to state due process claim for state's failure to follow state procedures in garnishing exempt funds, when he did not allege that state failed to provide meaningful post-deprivation process). *But see* Doyle v. Schultz, 97 F. Supp. 2d 763 (W.D. La. 2000) (Louisiana procedure for executing on judgments unconstitutional as applied when it allowed seizure for out-of-state judgment before notifying debtors that judgment had been domesticated); Alaska Dep't of Revenue v. Maxwell, 6 P.3d 733 (Alaska 2000) (child support order void for denial of due process when obligor was given no opportunity to be heard before issuance of administrative order).

68 Brown v. Liberty Loan Corp., 539 F.2d 1355 (5th Cir. 1976); Roy v. Smith, 735 F. Supp. 313 (C.D. Ill. 1990); Betts v. Coltes, 467 F. Supp. 544 (D. Haw. 1979); *see also* Raigoza v. Sperl, 34 Cal. App. 3d 560, 110 Cal. Rptr. 296 (1973); Wilson v. Grimes, 232 Ga. 388, 207 S.E.2d 5 (1974); Hehr v. Tucker, 256 Or. 254, 472 P.2d 797 (1970).

69 Betts v. Tom, 431 F. Supp. 1369 (D. Haw. 1977).

70 McCahey v. L.P. Investors, 593 F. Supp. 319 (E.D.N.Y. 1984), *aff'd*, 774 F.2d 543 (2d Cir. 1985). *But see* Mayers v. N.Y. Cmty. Bancorp, Inc., 2005 WL 2105810 (E.D.N.Y. Aug. 31, 2005) (suggesting *McCahey* should be re-evaluated in light of technological changes), *later decision at* 2006 WL 2013734 (E.D.N.Y. July 18, 2006) (denying defendants' motion for interlocutory appeal).

71 Neeley v. Century Fin. Co., 606 F. Supp. 1453 (D. Ariz. 1985).

72 Brown v. Liberty Loan Corp., 539 F.2d 1355, 1369 (5th Cir. 1976); *see also* Betts v. Tom, 431 F. Supp. 1369 (D. Haw. 1977) (affidavit required for *ex parte* garnishments). *See generally* N. Ga. Finishing Inc. v. Di-Chem, Inc., 419 U.S. 601, 95 S. Ct. 719, 42 L. Ed. 2d 751 (1975).

73 2005 WL 2105810 (E.D.N.Y. Aug. 31, 2005), *later decision at* 2006 WL 2013734 (E.D.N.Y. July 18, 2006) (denying defendants' motion for interlocutory appeal).

12.3.4 Notice Must Inform Debtor of Exemptions

Numerous cases have set out a consistent set of guidelines as to exactly what a garnishment notice must state in order to satisfy due process. The notice must inform the debtor that garnishment has occurred, must describe major legal exemptions from garnishment, and must tell the debtor what procedures the debtor can follow to contest the garnishment.[74] Disclosing this information places little burden on creditors or the state because the information can be included in a preprinted form. These disclosures, on the other hand, are very important to a debtor who often does not know of the existence of exemptions or how to contest improper garnishment.

The courts have not required garnishment notices to list exhaustively all the potential legal exemptions, because this would place an excessive burden on creditors who would have to change the notice whenever federal or state exemption law changed,[75] because the notice would be too complicated to be understood by most debtors,[76] and because composing notices is widely regarded as a legislative task.[77] However, notices violate due process if they do not at least include mention of some of the most important exemptions.[78] In particular, notices apparently must list the potential availability of exemptions for Social Security,[79] TANF benefits,[80] and wage payments.[81] Other exemptions which may have to be listed include SSI, veterans benefits, unemployment compensation, workers' compensation, alimony and child support, pensions, personal property, and lump-sum state exemptions.[82] The list will vary from state to state.

12.3.5 Notice Must Inform Debtor of Procedures to Contest Garnishment

In utility termination cases, the Supreme Court held that notice of the customer's right to dispute a municipal utility's actions was not meaningful unless the notice included a statement of the procedure which the customer should use to challenge the deprivation of services.[83] Federal courts have

74 Aacen v. San Juan County Sheriff's Dep't, 944 F.2d 691 (10th Cir. 1991); McCahey v. L.P. Investors, 774 F.2d 543 (2d Cir. 1985) (reference to exemptions and fact that procedures exist, and suggestion to contact legal aid society, is sufficient); Dionne v. Bouley, 757 F.2d 1344 (1st Cir. 1985); Finberg v. Sullivan, 634 F.2d 50 (3d Cir. 1980); *In re* Pontes, 310 F. Supp. 2d 447 (D.R.I. 2004) (tax sale notice must advise debtor of right of redemption); Jacobson v. Johnson, 798 F. Supp. 500 (C.D. Ill. 1991); Neeley v. Century Fin. Co., 606 F. Supp. 1453 (D. Ariz. 1985); Reigh v. Schleigh, 595 F. Supp. 1535 (D. Md. 1984), *rev'd on other grounds*, 784 F.2d 1191 (4th Cir. 1986); Clay v. Fisher, 584 F. Supp. 730 (S.D. Ohio 1984); Harris v. Bailey, 574 F. Supp. 966 (W.D. Va. 1983); Deary v. Guardian Loan Co., 534 F. Supp. 1178 (S.D.N.Y. 1982); Betts v. Tom, 431 F. Supp. 1369 (D. Haw. 1977); Collection Professionals, Inc. v. Logan, 695 N.E.2d 1344 (Ill. App. Ct. 1998) (amended Illinois post-judgment garnishment statute provided due process of law when it required debtors to be notified of garnishment, exemptions, procedure for claiming them, and hearing within two days of service of garnishment summons); Dorwart v. Caraway, 966 P.2d 1121 (Mont. 1998); *see also* Zeppieri v. New Haven Provision Co., 163 F. Supp. 2d 126 (D. Conn. 2001) (Connecticut post-judgment bank execution statute met due process standards by requiring bank to send exemption claim form to debtor promptly after receiving execution); Hutchinson v. Cox, 784 F. Supp. 1339 (S.D. Ohio 1992) (denial of due process not to inform judgment debtor of exemptions and right to hearing during post-judgment execution); Roy v. Smith, 735 F. Supp. 313 (C.D. Ill. 1990); Kirby v. Sprouls, 722 F. Supp. 516 (C.D. Ill. 1989); State of Washington v. Thompson, 339 Ark. 417, 6 S.W.3d 82 (Ark. 1999) (child support obligor who missed deadline was nonetheless allowed a hearing when notice was "confusing and inconsistent" as to procedure for requesting hearing); Imperial Bank v. Pim Elec., Inc., 39 Cal. Rptr. 3d 432 (Ct. App. 1995) (due process satisfied when notice of possible exemptions given at time of seizure); First Union Nat'l Bank v. Knyal, 874 So. 2d 716 (Fla. Dist. Ct. App. 2004) (Florida procedure requires notice of right to exemptions, procedure for claiming them, and right to hearing); First Resolution Inv. Corp. v. Seker, 795 A.2d 868 (N.J. 2002) (rejecting constitutional challenge to New Jersey notice procedure but recommending rule changes to give debtors more information about how to contest garnishment); *cf.* Resler v. Messerli & Kramer, Prof'l Ass'n, 2003 WL 193498 (D. Minn. Jan. 23, 2003) (allegation that garnishment notice failed to disclose certain state exemptions stated claims under Fair Debt Collection Procedures Act and state law).

75 *See* Dionne v. Bouley, 757 F.2d 1344 (1st Cir. 1985); Reigh v. Schleigh, 595 F. Supp. 1535 (D. Md. 1984), *rev'd on other grounds*, 784 F.2d 1191 (4th Cir. 1986).

76 Reigh v. Schleigh, 595 F. Supp. 1535 (D. Md. 1984), *rev'd on other grounds*, 784 F.2d 1191 (4th Cir. 1986).

77 Neeley v. Century Fin. Co., 606 F. Supp. 1453 (D. Ariz. 1985); *see also* Brown v. Liberty Loan Corp., 539 F.2d 1355 (5th Cir. 1976).

78 Aacen v. San Juan County Sheriff's Dep't, 944 F.2d 691 (10th Cir. 1991) (due process violation when notice of exemptions listed only the homestead exemption and failed to reveal existence of others, or how to claim them). *But see* Reigh v. Schleigh, 595 F. Supp. 1535 (D. Md. 1984) (mere notice that there are federal and state exemptions was sufficient), *rev'd on other grounds*, 784 F.2d 1191 (4th Cir. 1986).

79 Harris v. Bailey, 574 F. Supp. 966 (W.D. Va. 1983).

80 Betts v. Tom, 431 F. Supp. 1369 (D. Haw. 1977).

81 Neeley v. Century Fin. Co., 606 F. Supp. 1453 (D. Ariz. 1985); *see also* Roy v. Smith, 735 F. Supp. 313 (C.D. Ill. 1990).

82 Aacen v. San Juan County Sheriff's Dep't, 944 F.2d 691 (10th Cir. 1991) (due process violation when notice of exemptions listed only the homestead exemption and failed to reveal existence of others, or how to claim them); McCahey v. L.P. Investors, 774 F.2d 543 (2d Cir. 1985) (discussing and upholding New York statute); Hutchinson v. Cox, 784 F. Supp. 1339 (S.D. Ohio 1992) (denial of due process for judgment debtor not to be informed during post-judgment execution that personal property exemptions were allowed by law and that debtor could obtain a hearing to claim exemption); Green v. Harbin, 615 F. Supp. 719 (D. Ala. 1985) (consent decree).

83 Memphis Light, Gas & Water Div. v. Craft, 436 U.S. 1, 98 S. Ct. 1554, 56 L. Ed. 2d 30 (1978); *see also* Mullane v. Cent. Hanover Bank & Trust Co., 339 U.S. 306, 70 S. Ct. 652, 94 L. Ed. 865 (1950) (discussing notice requirements).

applied this principle to garnishment and execution notices by requiring that the notices state what action a debtor may take to contest the procedure.[84]

But a few courts have held that a mere citation to the statute or court rule governing procedures to contest garnishment is a sufficient description of those procedures.[85] The Second Circuit upheld a garnishment notice which told the debtor that procedures were available to challenge garnishment, cited the procedures without explanation, and told the debtor to contact either the creditor or an attorney, including legal aid. The court found no due process violation in that case even though the debtor had contacted the creditor, as the notice advised, and the creditor continued the garnishment process, denying receiving the welfare check stub which the debtor sent him to prove the exemption. A far more effective procedure to enable the debtor to protect exempt property is a garnishment notice that contains the form the state's courts use to claim an exemption, specifies the court clerk and deadline to file an exemption claim, and advises the debtor to consult an attorney.[86]

12.3.6 Debtor Has a Right to a Prompt Hearing

Due process also requires that debtors have the right to obtain a hearing to contest a garnishment or execution within a reasonable period after it has occurred.[87] The courts have widely recognized that delays can impose severe hardship on debtors, and that statutes allowing significant delay prior to a hearing are unconstitutional. As with the timing of notice of garnishment or execution, however, no particular reasonable time before a hearing has been agreed upon. The Third Circuit held that a court rule allowing fifteen days before a hearing on a debtor's petition allowed too much time to elapse,[88] and cases rejecting longer periods are common.[89] One district court required a hearing within two days of garnishment.[90]

Moreover, several courts have strongly criticized statutory provisions which allow discretionary continuances or pre-hearing delays pending discovery.[91] At least one court has ruled that such provisions violate due process, apparently even in the absence of evidence that the provisions were actually invoked.[92] But other courts do not strike down statutes as violating due process on their face, but require proof that the debtor was excessively delayed in his or her attempt to obtain a hearing to contest the garnishment or execution.[93] Consequently, to be safe, consumer attorneys

84 *See* § 12.3.4, *supra*; *see also* Clay v. Fisher, 584 F. Supp. 730 (S.D. Ohio 1984) (due process requires prompt and adequate notice and hearing on exemption claims).

85 McCahey v. L.P. Investors, 774 F.2d 543 (2d Cir. 1985); Neeley v. Century Fin. Co., 606 F. Supp. 1453 (D. Ariz. 1985); *see also* Burris v. Mahaney, 716 F. Supp. 1051 (M.D. Tenn. 1989) (judgment debtor attributed with notice of contents of garnishment document served on employer which stated debtor had right to court hearing and directed her to clerk for forms, but which debtor did not read in its entirety).

86 *See, e.g.*, First Resolution Inv. Corp. v. Seker, 795 A.2d 868 (N.J. 2002) (rejecting constitutional challenge, but ordering Civil Practice Committee to revise form notice to provide further information to debtor about how to challenge garnishment).

87 *See, e.g.*, Dionne v. Bouley, 757 F.2d 1344 (1st Cir. 1985); Finberg v. Sullivan, 634 F.2d 50 (3d Cir. 1980); Brown v. Liberty Loan Corp., 539 F.2d 1355 (5th Cir. 1976); Kirby v. Sprouls, 722 F. Supp. 516 (C.D. Ill. 1989) (constitutional right to opportunity for hearing "within a meaningful time"); Jones v. Marion County Small Claims Ct., 701 F. Supp. 1414 (S.D. Ind. 1988) (state statute for garnishment of bank accounts violated due process requirements of prompt notice and hearing); Neeley v. Century Fin. Co., 606 F. Supp. 1453 (D. Ariz. 1985); Reigh v. Schleigh, 595 F. Supp. 1535 (D. Md. 1984), *rev'd on other grounds*, 784 F.2d 1191 (4th Cir. 1986); Alaska Dep't of Revenue v. Maxwell, 6 P.3d 733 (Alaska 2000) (child support order void for denial of due process, when obligor was given no opportunity to be heard before issuance of administrative order); Dorwart v. Caraway, 966 P.2d 1121 (Mont. 1998); *see also* Jordan v. Fox, Rothschild, O'Brien & Frankel, 20 F.3d 1250 (3d Cir. 1994) (absent pre-judgment waiver, obtaining execution on confessed judgment without providing any means of securing predeprivation hearing or prompt post-seizure relief deprives debtor of due process); Highsmith v. Dep't of Pub. Aid, 803 N.E.2d 652 (Ill. App. Ct. 2004) (administrative hearing on attachment of investment account for child support arrears inadequate when departmental rule excluded non-documentary proof of ownership); Collection Professionals, Inc. v. Logan, 695 N.E.2d 1344 (Ill. App. Ct. 1998) (right to hearing on post-judgment garnishment within twenty-one to thirty days is sufficient); Flowers v. Flowers, 799 N.E.2d 1183 (Ind. Ct. App. 2003) (due process requires that child support obligor must be allowed to attend hearing on income withholding); Sommer v. Maharaj, 843 N.E.2d 649 (Mass. App. Ct. 2006) (judgment debtor and wife had due process right to hearing on question whether accounts were exempt individual retirement accounts), *review granted*, 854 N.E.2d 441 (Mass. 2006); *cf.* McCahey v. L.P. Investors, 774 F.2d 543 (2d Cir. 1985) (absence of mandatory time limit for hearing did not violate due process without evidence that debtor could not, in fact, receive prompt hearing). *But see* Ortiz v. Valdez, 971 P.2d 1076 (Colo. Ct. App. 1998) (Colorado's post-judgment garnishment scheme found acceptable, even though it resulted in freezing of non-debtor's exempt Social Security funds for at least five weeks).

88 Finberg v. Sullivan, 634 F.2d 50 (3d Cir. 1980). *But see* Reigh v. Schleigh, 595 F. Supp. 1535 (D. Md. 1984) (court should not specify exact timetable), *rev'd on other grounds*, 784 F.2d 1191 (4th Cir. 1986).

89 Neeley v. Century Fin. Co., 606 F. Supp. 1453 (D. Ariz. 1985) (thirty-four days with possible continuance); Clay v. Fisher, 584 F. Supp. 730 (S.D. Ohio 1984) (five weeks); Harris v. Bailey, 574 F. Supp. 966 (W.D. Va. 1983) (two months). *But see* Green v. Harbin, 615 F. Supp. 719 (D. Ala. 1985) (consent decree apparently allowing up to three weeks before hearing a contested motion to dissolve garnishment).

90 Betts v. Tom, 431 F. Supp. 1369 (D. Haw. 1977).

91 Finberg v. Sullivan, 634 F.2d 50 (3d Cir. 1980); Neeley v. Century Fin. Co., 606 F. Supp. 1453 (D. Ariz. 1985); *see also* Green v. Harbin, 615 F. Supp. 719 (D. Ala. 1985).

92 Neeley v. Century Fin. Co., 606 F. Supp. 1453 (D. Ariz. 1985).

93 McCahey v. L.P. Investors, 774 F.2d 543 (2d Cir. 1985) (refus-

should develop a full factual record before challenging the statute, so that the existence in actual practice of unconstitutional delays will be unquestioned.

12.4 Protection of Debtors' Wages

12.4.1 Federal Wage Garnishment Protections

12.4.1.1 Purposes of Consumer Credit Protection Act Wage Garnishment Restrictions

The federal Consumer Credit Protection Act (CCPA) wage garnishment provisions[94] exempt a portion of a consumer's earnings from garnishment and prohibit employers from firing a worker due to garnishment resulting from a single indebtedness. Prior to these federal protections, debtors had few protections under state law against garnishment abuses.[95]

As a means to "relieve countless honest debtors driven by economic desperation from plunging into bankruptcy in order to preserve their employment and insure a continued means of support for themselves and their families,"[96] Congress enacted the CCPA garnishment provisions, effective in 1970. The statute lists three purposes for its garnishment restrictions:

- Reduction of predatory extensions of credit;[97]
- Increased job stability;[98] and
- Increased uniformity in bankruptcy laws and protections.[99]

ing to find statute that did not specify time for hearing unconstitutional on its face, when a prompt hearing was allowed and the debtor failed to use proper procedure to contest the garnishment); Reigh v. Schleigh, 595 F. Supp. 1535 (D. Md. 1984), *rev'd on other grounds*, 784 F.2d 1191 (4th Cir. 1986).

94 15 U.S.C. §§ 1671–1677 (reprinted in Appx. B.1, *infra*); *see* Annotation, *Validity, Construction and Application of Secs. 301–307 of Consumer Credit Protection Act (15 U.S.C.S. Secs. 1671–1677) Placing Restrictions on Garnishment of Individuals' Earnings*, 14 A.L.R. Fed. 447 (1973).

95 W. Douglas, Points of Rebellion 48 (1970) ("[T]oday's garnishment proceedings are as destructive and vicious as the debtors' dungeons. . . . In many states the percentage of wages garnished has been so high that a man and his family are often reduced to a starvation level.").

One proposal would have completely abolished garnishment. H.R. 1040, 90th Cong. (1968), *reprinted in* 1968 U.S.C.C.A.N. 1978; *see also* § 12.4.1.4, *infra* (some states ban garnishment).

96 H.R. Rep. No. 1040, 90th Cong. (1968), *reprinted in* 1968 U.S.C.C.A.N. 1979.

97 15 U.S.C. § 1671(a)(1); *see also* Brown v. Liberty Loan Corp., 392 F. Supp. 1023, 1032 (M.D. Fla. 1974) (federal garnishment restrictions were directed "towards abuses of garnishment procedures by consumer financial lenders, such as loan companies"), *rev'd on other grounds*, 539 F.2d 1355 (5th Cir. 1976).

98 15 U.S.C. § 1671(a)(2).

99 15 U.S.C. § 1671(a)(3).

12.4.1.2 Scope of Federal Wage Garnishment Protections

The CCPA protects earnings which are "subject to garnishment." The statute defines garnishment as any legal or equitable procedure through which the earnings of any individual are required to be withheld for payment of debt.[100] The term "subject to garnishment" has been interpreted broadly to relate to any seizure flowing from judicial action,[101] thus applying to proceedings in aid of execution and attachment proceedings.[102] Most wage garnishments are made by court order, with a creditor seeking to satisfy a claim against an employee by reaching an employee's earnings before they are paid.

The CCPA garnishment provisions do not apply to seizures pursuant to a contractual agreement, such as a wage assignment.[103] However, the Federal Trade Commission's Credit Practices Rule broadly prohibits contractual wage assignment provisions unless they are revocable.[104] The CCPA garnishment provisions do apply to wage assignments resulting from a judicial order.[105]

100 15 U.S.C. § 1672(c).

101 Western v. Hodgson, 494 F.2d 379, 382 (4th Cir. 1974); Igbal v. Mucci, 852 A.2d 195 (N.J. Super. Ct. App. Div. 2004) (order requiring debtor to make installment payments to judgment creditor is same as garnishment and can not exceed CCPA limits); Lough v. Robinson, 675 N.E.2d 1272 (Ohio Ct. App. 1996) (child support order was a garnishment within meaning of CCPA and Ohio law); *see also* Caulley v. Caulley, 806 S.W.2d 795 (Tex. 1991) (reversing, on state law grounds, lower court's ruling that federal garnishment protections do not apply to order to turn future wages over to receiver who would pay 90% as alimony arrearages and 10% to former husband). *But see* United States v. Jaffe, 417 F.3d 259 (2d Cir. 2005) (criminal restitution order that directs restitution payments but does not restrain use of specific funds not covered by CCPA); Frankel v. Frankel, 886 A.2d 136 (Md. Ct. Spec. App. 2005) (CCPA does not limit amount of child support, only amount collectible by garnishment).

102 Hodgson v. Hamilton Mun. Court, 349 F. Supp. 1125, 1139 (S.D. Ohio 1972).

103 *See, e.g.*, Western v. Hodgson, 494 F.2d 379 (4th Cir. 1974); Liedka v. Liedka, 101 Misc. 2d 305, 423 N.Y.S.2d 788 (Fam. Ct. 1979); *see also* Sears, Roebuck & Co. v. A. T. & G. Co., 66 Mich. App. 359, 239 N.W.2d 614 (1976) (federal law does not restrict employer's deduction from debtor's earnings to pay debt to employer).

104 16 C.F.R. § 444.2(a)(3); *see* § 12.4.5, *infra*; *see also* National Consumer Law Center, Unfair and Deceptive Acts and Practices §§ 5.1.1.2, 5.1.1.3 (6th ed. 2004 and Supp.).

105 Voss Products, Inc. v. Carlton, 147 F. Supp. 2d 892 (E.D. Tenn. 2001) (order of wage assignment entered in divorce case pursuant to defendant's agreement was garnishment); Donovan v. Hamilton County Mun. Court, 580 F. Supp. 554, 556 (S.D. Ohio 1984) (wage assignment for support issued pursuant to a decree of divorce or dissolution was a garnishment under 15 U.S.C. § 1672(c)); Koethe v. Johnson, 328 N.W.2d 293, 297 (Iowa 1982) (court-ordered wage assignment to satisfy child support obligation was "garnishment" and governed by CCPA); Carrel v. Carrel, 791 S.W.2d 831 (Mo. Ct. App. 1990) (involuntary wage assignment ordered by court as part of contempt order in marriage dissolution case is garnishment).

An early decision held that set off against a federal employee's salary by a federal agency to collect a debt was not restricted by the CCPA.[106] However, federal statutes now incorporate the CCPA restrictions, or greater restrictions, for federal debt collections.[107] In addition, a 1977 amendment clarified that the statute applies not only to court-ordered garnishments, but also when "any State (or officer or agency thereof) . . . make[s], execute[s], or enforce[s] any order or process,"[108] so set-offs by state agencies are covered by the CCPA restrictions.[109]

Some courts have held that the CCPA wage protections only protect against garnishment, and do not operate as an exemption when the debtor files bankruptcy.[110] In practice this rule means that a debtor who is owed accrued, unpaid wages at the time of filing bankruptcy can not use the CCPA to exempt them. The federal wildcard exemption or a state exemption may apply, however.[111]

The CCPA protections do not apply to actions to collect state or federal taxes,[112] but the Internal Revenue Code itself exempts a portion of income from seizure that may be more generous than the CCPA for families and less generous for individuals without dependents.[113] One court has held that the job protection provision in the CCPA, protecting employees from job termination for their first garnishment, does apply to an Internal Revenue Service levy on wages.[114]

The CCPA garnishment protections apply to debt incurred for a business, as well as a consumer, purpose.[115] One court held that the CCPA did not prevent or limit the amount of the attachment of the salary of a polluter to fund sewage treatment for his property, however. The court held that the order requiring him to pay for the cleanup was not a judgment, so the CCPA did not apply.[116] Another court held that the CCPA garnishment provisions did not apply to a state's suit seeking reimbursement for the cost of incarceration from a prisoner's accumulated disability pension payments.[117]

12.4.1.3 Earnings Subject to CCPA Garnishment Protections

12.4.1.3.1 Wages, vacation pay, and payments to independent contractors

The CCPA garnishment provisions protect consumers from garnishment of "earnings," which means compensation paid or payable for personal services, whether denominated as wages, salary, commission, bonus, or other periodic payment pursuant to a pension or retirement program.[118] The key question is whether payments are compensation "for personal services."[119] For example, vacation pay is

106 Atwater v. Roudebush, 452 F. Supp. 622 (N.D. Ill. 1976).

107 *See* §§ 11.2.6, 11.3.3, *supra*.

108 15 U.S.C. § 1673(c).

109 Shine v. Iowa Dep't of Human Services, 592 N.W.2d 684 (Iowa 1999); *see* § 11.2.6, *supra* (federal salary offsets).

110 *See, e.g.*, *In re* Riendeau, 293 B.R. 832 (D. Vt. 2002), *aff'd on other grounds*, 336 F.3d 78 (2d Cir. 2003).

111 *In re* Robinson, 241 B.R. 447 (9th Cir. 1999) (interpreting Oregon's protection of wages as an exemption applicable in bankruptcy); *In re* Irish, 311 B.R. 63 (B.A.P. 8th Cir. 2004) (federal garnishment operate as a bankruptcy exemption because they are incorporated into Iowa exemption law; debtor can stack this exemption with another exemption for $1000 in wages or tax refunds); *In re* Jones, 318 B.R. 841 (Bankr. S.D. Ohio 2005) (federal garnishment limits operate as bankruptcy exemption because they are incorporated into Ohio's exemption statute). *But see In re* Thum, 329 B.R. 848 (C.D. Ill. 2005); *cf. In re* Sikes, 2004 WL 2028021 (Bankr. W.D. Ky. Sept. 8, 2004) (stating that Kentucky statute protecting wages does not apply in bankruptcy; statement is *dicta* because issue was protection of tax refund, not wages).

112 15 U.S.C. § 1673(b).

113 26 U.S.C. § 6334(d) provides for weekly exemption of the standard deduction provided by 26 U.S.C. § 63(c) and the deduction provided for personal exemptions in 26 U.S.C. § 151 divided by 52. Other exemptions are provided by 26 U.S.C. § 6334, including exemption of many government benefits and specified personal property.

114 Martin v. Hawkeye Int'l Trucks, Inc., 782 F. Supp. 1320 (S.D. Iowa 1991).

115 Midlantic Nat'l Bank/North v. Reif, 732 F. Supp. 354 (E.D.N.Y. 1990).

116 Friends of the Sakonnet v. Dutra, 125 B.R. 69 (D.R.I. 1991) (CCPA not meant to be used by polluters to avoid court orders to comply with federal and state environmental laws).

117 State Treasurer v. Gardner, 583 N.W.2d 687 (Mich. 1998).

118 15 U.S.C. § 1672(a); United States v. Armstrong, 2005 WL 937857 (N.D. Tex. Apr. 21, 2005) (Social Security retirement benefits deposited in bank account not "earnings" and not protected by CCPA); *In re* Rangel, 317 B.R. 553 (Bankr. D. Kan. 2004) (tax refund not earnings within meaning of state garnishment exemption); *see also In re* Duncan, 140 B.R. 210, 213 (Bankr. E.D. Tenn. 1992) (state garnishment exemption protected insurance salesman's commissions earned on renewals of policies he had originally sold); Riggs Nat'l Bank v. Simplicio, 54 U.S.L.W. 2457 (D.C. Super. Ct. 1986) (D.C. statute modeled after CCPA protected real estate agent's commissions); Ward v. Ward, 164 N.J. Super. 354, 396 A.2d 365 (Super. Ct. Ch. Div. 1978); Villano v. Villano, 98 Misc. 2d 774, 414 N.Y.S.2d 625 (Sup. Ct. 1979). *But see* Funk v. Utah State Tax Comm'n, 839 P.2d 818 (Utah 1992) (because of their nonperiodic nature, tax refunds did not constitute disposable earnings and were not protected).

119 Shearin v. Beaman, 323 B.R. 917 (E.D.N.C. 2004) (North Carolina exemption of earnings for personal services would exempt portion of year-end bonus, but not interest in capital account of partnership), *aff'd*, 126 Fed. Appx. 640 (4th Cir. 2005) (per curiam); *In re* Sheeran, 369 B.R. 910 (Bankr. E.D. Va. 2007) (earnings of solo law firm were result of personal services; debtor could claim wage exemption); *In re* Hidy, 364 B.R. 679 (Bankr. W.D. Mo. 2007) (payments for unused sick leave and vacation, required by employment contract, were for personal services); *In re* Smith, 284 B.R. 460 (Bankr. W.D. Mo. 2002) (accounts receivable from sales of old cars restored by debtors not exempt earnings; debtors were selling a product, that is, the cars, not a service, and sale price included purchase of cars and parts, as well as debtors' labor); *In re* Marples, 266 B.R. 202 (Bankr. D. Idaho 2001); *In re* Atkinson, 258 B.R. 769

"earnings" within the scope of the statute and is thus protected.[120]

Many courts have found that payments to independent contractors are not "earnings" and are not protected by the CCPA, or by state statutes using similar language.[121] How-

(Bankr. D. Idaho 2001) (doctor's accounts receivables are compensation for personal services so are protected as earnings); Brock v. Westport Recovery Corp., 832 So. 2d 209 (Fla. Dist. Ct. App. 2002) (key question is whether work is like "a salaried job" or "running a business"; "draws" taken by vice-president of family corporation from profits not "compensation for personal services or labor" within meaning of Florida statutes); Genesee County Friend of the Court v. Gen. Motors Corp., 464 Mich. 44, 626 N.W.2d 395 (2001); Gerry Elson Agency Inc. v. Muck, 509 S.W.2d 750, 753 (Mo. Ct. App. 1974); Porter v. Ward, 2007 WL 2874308 (Ohio Ct. App. Oct. 2, 2007) (inmate's earnings for prison labor not wages within meaning of state garnishment statute); Ighnat v. Ighnat, 1989 WL 34733 (Ohio Ct. App. Apr. 11, 1989) (profit-sharing proceeds were "earnings" protected by CCPA and Ohio law, even when garnishment was for child support and alimony); Gen. Elec. Capital Corp. v. ICO, Inc., 230 S.W.3d 702 (Tex. App. 2007) (severance pay in hands of employer was exempt current wages, but exemption lost when paid over to employee); *see also* Bueno v. Pyle, 2001 WL 1544455 (10th Cir. Dec. 5, 2001) (Colorado garnishment limitation applies only to earnings; state tax authorities could garnish prison inmate's account, which contained gifts); United States v. Crawford, 2006 WL 2458710 (E.D. Cal. Aug. 22, 2006) (annuities funded by deductions from deceased father's salary not protected by CCPA; not personal earnings of debtor); Aetna Cas. & Surety Co. v. Rodco Auto Body, 965 F. Supp. 104 (D. Mass. 1996) (debtor's voluntary contributions to individual retirement account were not earnings protected by garnishment limitations of CCPA); John Hancock Mut. Life Ins. Co. v. Frost Nat'l Bank, 393 F. Supp. 204 (E.D. Tenn. 1974) (proceeds of life insurance policy were not "earnings," as term is used in 15 U.S.C. § 1672(a), because such proceeds were not payment for "personal services"), *aff'd*, 516 F.2d 901 (6th Cir. 1975) (table); *In re* Christy, 306 B.R. 611 (Bankr. C.D. Ill. 2004) (genuine issue of fact what part of receivables of two-physician professional corporation was attributable to personal services of debtor-physician and therefore exempt as wages or salary under Illinois law); *In re* Nelson, 2003 WL 22331776 (Bankr. D. Colo. Oct. 1, 2003) (judgment for tortious interference with prospective economic relation, calculated as amount of earnings lost, was not earnings under Colorado exemption statute because plaintiff performed no personal services); Cadle Co. v. G & G Associates, 757 So. 2d 1278 (Fla. Dist. Ct. App. 2000) (evidentiary hearing required to determine if sums held by employer for "expense reimbursement," "reimbursement for investment," and "capital account" were earnings under Florida statute); Rooney v. Rooney, 669 N.W.2d 362 (Minn. Ct. App. 2003) (church was employer and payor within meaning of child support garnishment statute; it required members to give up all individual property, and provided for their needs; obligor was doing work for the church); Bartel v. Zucktriegal, 47 P.3d 581 (Wash. Ct. App. 2002) (judgment creditor could garnish employee's compensation that was disguised by collusive employer).

120 *In re* Hidy, 364 B.R. 679 (Bankr. W.D. Mo. 2007) (payments for unused sick leave and vacation, required by employment contract, were for personal services); Bd. of Educ. of E. Hartford v. Booth, 654 A.2d 717 (Conn. 1995) (Connecticut definition of earnings covers accumulated sick leave and a deferred salary increase payable at termination); Riley v. Kessler, 441 N.E.2d 638 (Ohio 1982); *see also* Montgomery Ward Credit Corp. v. Brewer, Clearinghouse No. 44,517 (D. Minn. 1989) (state law intended to exempt severance pay from garnishment). *But see In re* Henrickson, 2007 WL 703620 (Bankr. D. Alaska Mar. 5, 2007) (exemption for property traceable to "weekly net wages" protects only amount accrued during one work week, not accrued vacation pay and tax refund); *cf. In re* Marples, 266 B.R. 202 (Bankr. D. Idaho 2001) (questioning whether car awarded by random drawing among employees who met sales goal was "earnings"); *In re* Johnson, 199 B.R. 155 (Bankr. W.D. Ky. 1995) (severance pay not earnings within meaning of Kentucky exemption statute).

121 *See* Resolution Trust Corp. v. Texas Moline, Ltd., 96 F. Supp. 2d 644 (S.D. Tex. 2000) (management, accounting, and investment banking fees paid to independent contractor not protected by Texas wage exemption; debtor was principal of financial firm, had own office, and employed others to do much of the work); *In re* Lawrence, 219 B.R. 786 (E.D. Tenn. 1998) (Tennessee garnishment statute did not protect accounts receivable of podiatrist; it is not an exemption statute, but simply a restriction on use of a wage deduction order to reach earnings in hands of employer), *aff'g* 205 B.R. 115 (Bankr. E.D. Tenn. 1997); *In re* Siegel, 214 B.R. 329 (W.D. Tenn. 1997) (Tennessee statute limiting garnishment of wages does not provide exemption for lawyers' accounts receivable); *In re* Smith, 284 B.R. 460 (Bankr. W.D. Mo. 2002) (accounts receivable from sales of old cars restored by debtors not exempt earnings; debtors were selling a product, that is, the cars, not a service, and sale price included purchase of cars and parts, as well as debtors' labor); *In re* Welty, 217 B.R. 907 (Bankr. D. Wyo. 1998) (earnings of business owner who paid himself what was left after settling expenses of the business were not exempt earnings under federal or Wyoming law); *In re* Harrison, 216 B.R. 451 (Bankr. S.D. Fla. 1997) ("deferred wages" due to dentist after dissolution of his professional association were not exempt earnings for personal services, when he exercised substantial control over management of the practice, amount of the two dentists' paychecks was determined by amount of money on hand on payday, and the "deferred wages" were intended as return on his investment); *In re* Zamora, 187 B.R. 783 (Bankr. S.D. Fla. 1995) (courts will look behind labels "employee" and "independent contractor" to determine whether debtor has an arrangement "like a job" or is in control of business, with power to decide how much to draw for salary; income from solo law practice and marina owned by debtor was not exempt); Corto v. Nat'l Scenery Studios, Inc., 705 A.2d 615 (D.C. 1997) (producer's share of box office receipts of theatrical production was not exempt "wages" for "personal services"); Vining v. Siegal, 731 So. 2d 826 (Fla. Dist. Ct. App. 1999) (proceeds of one-man dental practice not earnings within meaning of Florida garnishment exemption); Coward v. Smith, 6 Kan. App. 2d 863, 636 P.2d 793 (1981); Friedt v. Moseanko, 498 N.W.2d 129 (N.D. 1993) (earnings do not include "business profits"; milk distributor's payments to dairy farmer not exempt); Campbell v. Stucki, 220 S.W.3d 562 (Tex. App. 2007) (Texas exemption for current wages does not protect earnings of independent contractor); Devore v. Cent. Bank & Trust, 908 S.W.2d 605 (Tex. App. 1995) (earnings of attorney in private practice not exempt, but earnings from a professional corporation might be); *see also In re* Osworth, 234 B.R. 497 (B.A.P. 9th Cir. 1999) (despite broad language, Oregon statute did not protect the accounts receivable of self-employed real estate agent); *In re* Branscum, 229 B.R. 32 (Bankr. M.D. Fla. 1999) (Florida's earnings ex-

ever, other courts applying state wage exemption laws that track the language of the CCPA garnishment provisions have found that the protections do extend to independent contractors.[122] Claiming protection under a state exemption seems the best course if available for contractors.

12.4.1.3.2 *Non-periodic payments*

Especially difficult problems are raised by non-periodic payments which result from employment, such as profit sharing, incentive payments, deferred compensation, and tax refunds. Some courts simply conclude that non-periodic earnings are not protected.[123] Others consider whether the payments in question are the kind of regular, predictable compensation which workers depend upon for day-to-day living.[124]

---

emption does not protect earnings of private investigator, who was independent contractor); *In re* Segall, 1998 Bankr. LEXIS 209 (Bankr. S.D. Fla. Jan. 26, 1998) (realtor's commissions were not exempt earnings when realtor was paid only commissions, paid own self-employment taxes, had to pay "franchise fee" for use of office and equipment, and controlled his own schedule); *In re* Lee, 204 B.R. 78 (Bankr. M.D. Fla. 1996) (insurance agent who was free to make own business decisions and was responsible for all expenses was independent contractor, so earnings not exempt); Gerry Elson Agency Inc. v. Muck, 509 S.W.2d 750, 755 (Mo. Ct. App. 1974) (CCPA does not protect earnings of trucker who leased truck from shipper and was paid fixed percentage of revenue from shipments); *In re* Galvez, 990 P.2d 187 (Nev. 1999) (real estate agent's lump sum commissions paid at closing were not "earnings" within meaning of Nevada exception, which protects only periodic payments); Gentek Bldg. Products, Inc. v. Check, 590 N.W.2d 282 (Wis. Ct. App. 1999) (unpublished) (commissions earned by seller of building products who was described in contract as "independent contractor" and who received no other compensation not "earnings" protected by Wisconsin statute). *But cf.* Davidson Tex., Inc. v. Garcia, 664 S.W.2d 791 (Tex. App. 1984) (debtor was employee, not independent contractor, and therefore fully protected from garnishment, because of level of control exercised by employer).

122 *In re* Carter, 182 F.3d 1027 (9th Cir. 1999) (entertainer who was sole shareholder of corporation which arranged her contracts, paid business expenses, and so forth, could claim California exemption for earnings; remanding to determine whether large lump sum paid to self on eve of bankruptcy was earnings); *In re* Pruss, 235 B.R. 430 (B.A.P. 8th Cir. 1999) (solo practice attorney's accounts receivable that were attributable to her personal services fall within Nebraska statute's protection for "compensation paid or payable for personal services, whether denominated as wages, salary, commission, bonus or otherwise"); Bargas v. Nye (*In re* Nye), 210 B.R. 857 (D. Colo. 1997) (Colorado exemption statute explicitly protects payments received by independent contractor for labor or services); Mass. Mut. Life Ins. Co. v. Shoemaker, 849 F. Supp. 30 (S.D. Tex. 1994) (Texas amended its exemption statute to allow commissions to be treated more like wages); *In re* Sheeran, 369 B.R. 910 (Bankr. E.D. Va. 2007) (earnings of solo law firm were result of personal services; debtor could claim wage exemption); *In re* Jones, 318 B.R. 841 (Bankr. S.D. Ohio 2005) (CCPA, which Ohio incorporates into its state exemptions, protects earnings of independent contractor if attributable to personal services); *In re* Parsons, 252 B.R. 480 (Bankr. W.D. Mo. 2000) (Missouri wage exemption applies to earnings of real estate broker insofar as funds were compensation for her personal services), *aff'd*, 280 F.3d 1185 (8th Cir. 2002) (approving method of calculating percentage of income attributable to personal services); *In re* Pettit, 224 B.R. 834 (Bankr. M.D. Fla. 1998) (Florida exemption for head of household's earnings protects earnings of "independent contractor" salesman who worked for one company, received fixed amount of monthly compensation, and did not own or control company; debtor's activities were essentially a job, not running a business); *In re* Price, 195 B.R. 775 (Bankr. D. Kan. 1996) (real estate agent's commissions were exempt earnings, even though contract described her as an independent contractor, when she had invested no capital in the business, performed all services personally, and worked for one broker, which exercised considerable control over her work); *In re* Sexton, 140 B.R. 742 (Bankr. S.D. Iowa 1992); *In re* Duncan, 140 B.R. 210 (Bankr. E.D. Tenn. 1992); Harrington v. Dyer, 937 A.2d 77 (Conn. Super. Ct. 2007) (commissions of independent contractor real estate salesperson were earnings, exempt from pre-judgment garnishment); Riggs Nat'l Bank v. Simplicio, 54 U.S.L.W. 2457 (D.C. Super. Ct. 1986) (District of Columbia statute protected real estate agent's commission even though realtor was independent contractor); California-Peterson Currency Exch., Inc. v. Friedman, 316 Ill. App. 3d 610, 736 N.E.2d 616 (2000) (earnings of independent contractor, described by employer as "agent" or "outside contractor," protected by Illinois garnishment limitations); Decision Point, Inc. v. Reece & Nichols Realtors, Inc., 144 P.3d 706 (Kan. 2006) (realtors' commissions were earnings, assignment of which was forbidden by U.C.C.C.); Smythe, Cramer Co. v. Guinta, 762 N.E.2d 1083 (Ohio Mun. Ct. 2001) (realtor's commissions personal earnings within meaning of state and federal garnishment statutes).

123 *In re* Annis, 229 B.R. 802 (B.A.P. 10th Cir. 1999) (tax refund was not "earnings for personal services" within meaning of Oklahoma hardship exemption), *aff'd*, 232 F.3d 749 (10th Cir. 2000); *In re* Dickerson, 227 B.R. 742 (B.A.P. 10th Cir. 1998) (earned income credit is not earnings within meaning of Oklahoma hardship exemption); Pallante v. Int'l Venture Investments, Ltd., 622 F. Supp. 667 (N.D. Ohio 1985) (lump sum severance payment under voluntary separation plan not earnings because not periodic); *In re* Minton, 348 B.R. 467 (Bankr. S.D. Ohio 2006) (tax refund not earnings under federal or Ohio definition, because not periodic); *In re* Demars, 279 B.R. 548 (Bankr. W.D. Mo. 2002) (tax refund not exempt earnings); *In re* Fishbein, 245 B.R. 36 (Bankr. D. Md. 2000) (tax refunds are not wages within meaning of Maryland's wage garnishment limitations); *In re* Galvez, 990 P.2d 187 (Nev. 1999) (Nevada wage exemption does not protect real estate agent's non-periodic lump sum commission); *see also In re* Benn, 491 F.3d 811 (8th Cir. 2007) (tax refunds not exempt under Missouri law; opt-out statute that allows exemptions pursuant to "the law of Missouri" refers only to statutes, not common law that denied attachment of tax refunds in the hands of taxing authorities); *In re* Rangel, 317 B.R. 553 (Bankr. D. Kan. 2004) (tax refund not exempt as "earnings" under Kansas law; not periodic and has lost "direct connection" to wages); *In re* Sikes, 2004 WL 2028021 (Bankr. W.D. Ky. Sept. 8, 2004) (tax refund not exempt as "earnings" under Kentucky wage garnishment statute).

124 Shearin v. Beaman, 323 B.R. 917 (E.D.N.C. 2004) (North Carolina exemption of earnings for personal services exempts portion of year-end bonus, but not interest in capital account of partnership), *aff'd*, 126 Fed. Appx. 640 (4th Cir. 2005) (per curiam); *In re* Lawton, 261 B.R. 774 (Bankr. M.D. Fla. 2001)

In *Kokoszka v. Belford*,[125] in holding that an income tax refund was not "earnings" under the CCPA, the United States Supreme Court stated that it agreed with a court of appeals opinion that earnings are limited to periodic payment of compensation. However the statute itself defines earnings to include any "bonus,"[126] which would not be a periodic payment. The Supreme Court's statement has been characterized as *dictum*, in that the issue before the Court was not the scope of the earnings exemption but whether Congress intended the wage garnishment protections to override the bankruptcy laws.[127]

The Michigan Supreme Court has concluded that the only question under the CCPA is whether the payment is compensation for personal services, and it is irrelevant whether it is periodic, predictable, or non-discretionary.[128] Thus profit-sharing payments, a "signing bonus" awarded to each employee as a result of union wage negotiations, and "recognition awards" made to certain salaried employees who were not eligible for regular pay increases were all protected as "earnings."

Even if a non-periodic payment is not protected under a state wage garnishment statute, some other state statute may protect it. For example, Mississippi provides specific exemptions for state and federal tax refunds, with an additional exemption for federal refunds attributable to the earned income tax credit.[129]

(stock options offered to employees not exempt wages because neither tied to individual performance nor provided in lieu of conventional compensation); *In re* Stroup, 221 B.R. 537 (Bankr. M.D. Fla. 1997) ("deferred compensation" paid to physician upon leaving medical group was not earnings within meaning of Florida exemption, when amount was determined by income of entire group, so was more like severance pay or a dividend on the physician part-owner's financial investment, rather than payment for personal services); Cadle Co. v. G & G Associates, 757 So. 2d 1278 (Fla. Dist. Ct. App. 2000) (evidentiary hearing required to determine if various sums held by employer for "expense reimbursement," "reimbursement for investment," and "capital account" were earnings within meaning of Florida statute exempting head of household's earnings from garnishment); Meyer Jewelry Co. v. Johnson, 581 N.W.2d 734 (Mich. Ct. App. 1998) (profit sharing payment was "payment for work and labor" within meaning of this section; plan was offered to employees and was part of their compensation package); *see also In re* Kramer, 339 B.R. 761 (Bankr. D. Colo. 2006) (stock purchased by payroll deductions as part of compensation package not exempt earnings under Colorado exemption statute; stock was personal property); Bohrer v. DeHart, 969 P.2d 801 (Colo. Ct. App. 1999) ("distribution" from two-person corporation to "employee" who owned and controlled corporation, was in fact earnings for personal services, and thus could be reached by writ of continuing garnishment).

125 417 U.S. 642, 651, 94 S. Ct. 2431, 41 L. Ed. 2d 374 (1974).

126 15 U.S.C. § 1672(a).

127 Genesee County Friend of the Court v. Gen. Motors Corp., 626 N.W.2d 395, 401 n.7 (Mich. 2001).

128 *Id.*

129 Miss. Code Ann. § 85-3-1(h)–(j).

12.4.1.4 Calculating the Amount of Wages Protected

12.4.1.4.1 Calculation rules

The CCPA garnishment provisions set a ceiling on the amount of a debtor's disposable earnings that may be garnished. This subsection discusses these rules. However state restrictions on garnishment, discussed in § 12.4.3, *infra*, should be checked in every case, as they may provide greater protection for the debtor.

The "disposable earnings" protected by the CCPA are that part of the employee's earnings remaining after the deduction of any amount required by law to be withheld. These deductions include federal, state, and local taxes, Social Security, and other governmental retirement programs required by law.[130] Deductions such as those for union dues, health and life insurance, charitable contributions, voluntary wage assignments, and savings bonds are usually not considered required by law to be withheld when calculating the exemption.[131] One court has held, however, that payments into a 401(k) retirement plan should be deducted from gross wages to determine disposable income, because these payments are not considered earnings in the first place, at least for federal income tax purposes.[132]

A Department of Labor fact sheet states that deductions employers make to repay themselves for salary advances extended to workers or merchandise purchased by workers are not required by law to be withheld.[133] Such a deduction may be treated as a garnishment entitled to priority under state law, however.[134] It can also be argued that an amount withheld by the employer to repay itself does not meet the federal definition of "earnings,"[135] because it is neither "paid" nor "payable."

130 15 U.S.C. § 1672(b); *see also* Marshall v. Dist. Ct., 444 F. Supp. 1110 (E.D. Mich. 1978); First Nat'l Bank v. Hasty, 415 F. Supp. 170 (E.D. Mich. 1976), *aff'd*, 573 F.2d 1310 (6th Cir. 1977) (table); DiZazzo v. DiZazzo, 1992 WL 98124 (Conn. Super. Ct. Apr. 23, 1992) (voluntary 401(k) contributions and health insurance premiums were not required to be withheld so were "disposable earnings"; those amounts may be deducted from "earnings" under state exemption law but only to extent reasonable in light of support needs of beneficiaries under support order); Sears, Roebuck & Co. v. A. T. & G. Co., 239 N.W.2d 614 (Mich. Ct. App. 1976) (deduction from debtor's earnings to pay debt to employer was not a deduction required by law to be withheld, but employer's deduction has priority under state law).

131 Dep't of Labor, Fact Sheet #30, *available at* www.dol.gov/esa/regs/compliance/whd/whdfs30.htm.

132 *In re* Robinson, 240 B.R. 70 (Bankr. N.D. Ala. 1999).

133 *Id.*

134 Sears, Roebuck & Co. v. A. T. & G. Co., 66 Mich. App. 359, 239 N.W.2d 614 (1976) (deduction from debtor's earnings to pay debt to employer takes priority over judgment creditor's garnishment).

135 15 U.S.C. § 1672(a).

An existing garnishment for child support should not be treated as a deduction from income. Instead, after the disposable earnings are calculated, the court should determine whether the child support garnishment and any creditors' garnishments fall within the statutory percentages.[136]

The maximum amount of disposable earnings that may be garnished is the lesser of:

- Twenty-five percent of the disposable earnings for that workweek; or
- The amount by which disposable earnings for that week exceed thirty times the federal minimum hourly wage.

In 2007, Congress adopted a law increasing the federal minimum wage from $5.15 to $5.85 per hour as of July 24, 2007, from $5.85 to $6.55 per hour as of July 24, 2008, and from $6.55 to $7.25 per hour as of July 24, 2009.[137]

12.4.1.4.2 Wage garnishment calculations from July 24, 2008, to July 23, 2009

With a minimum wage of $6.55 per hour in effect during the period July 24, 2008 to July 23, 2009, no garnishment can be made if an employee's disposable earnings are $196.50 or less for the week in question. When an employee's disposable earnings exceed $196.50 but are less than $262.00, only the amount over $196.50 can be garnished. For example, an employee's gross earnings in a particular week are $250.00. After deductions required by law, the disposable earnings are $220.00. Because only the amount over $196.50 may be garnished when disposable earnings are less than $262.00, only $23.50 may be garnished and $196.50 must be paid to the employee.

When an employee's disposable earnings are $262.00 or more in a given week, up to 25% of those earnings can be garnished. For example, an employee's gross earnings in a particular week are $350.00. After deductions required by law, the disposable earnings are $320.00. In this week, 25% of disposable earnings, or $80.00 could be garnished. $240.00 must paid to the employee.

12.4.1.4.3 Wage garnishment calculations as of July 24, 2009

After July 23, 2009, with a minimum wage of $7.25 per hour in effect, no garnishment can be made if an employee's disposable earnings are $217.50 or less for the week in question. When an employee's disposable earnings exceed $217.50 but are less than $290.00, only the amount over $217.50 can be garnished. For example, an employee's gross earnings in a particular week are $250.00. After deductions required by law, the disposable earnings are $220.00. Because only the amount over $217.50 may be garnished when the disposable earnings are less than $290.00, only $2.50 may be garnished and $217.50 must be paid to the employee.

When an employee's disposable earnings are $290.00 or more in a given week, up to 25% of those earnings can be garnished. For example, an employee's gross earnings in a particular week are $350.00. After deductions required by law, the disposable earnings are $320.00. In this week, 25% of disposable earnings, or $80.00 could be garnished. $240.00 must be paid to the employee.

12.4.1.4.4 Calculations when worker is not paid weekly

Some additional calculations are necessary when a worker is not paid weekly, but instead is paid bi-weekly, semi-monthly, or monthly. Department of Labor regulations specify how to perform these calculations for these irregular pay periods:

- Assume a calendar month consists of four and one-third workweeks;
- Multiply the number of workweeks or fractions thereof in the irregular pay period times 30 times the minimum hourly wage (which is $196.50 from July 24, 2008 to July 23, 2009, and $217.50 as of July 24, 2009).[138]

---

136 Comptroller v. First Ala. Bank, 642 So. 2d 1349 (Ala. Civ. App. 1993) (child support order against debtor is considered a prior garnishment and is to be deducted from income available for garnishment rather than from gross income to determine disposable earnings); *In re* Marriage of Herrick, 640 N.E.2d 969, 973 (Ill. App. Ct. 1994); Koethe v. Carmel Heights Apartments, 328 N.W.2d 293 (Iowa 1982) (court-ordered assignment of wages to meet child support obligation must be treated as a prior garnishment, not as a deduction from gross income, when determining disposable income); Union Pac. R.R. v. Trona Valley Fed. Credit Union, 57 P.3d 1203 (Wyo. 2002).

137 Pub. L. No. 110-28, §§ 8101–8104, 121 Stat. 112 (2007).
The minimum wage had been $4.25 per hour from 1991 (Pub. L. No. 101-157, § 2, 103 Stat. 938) until Oct. 1, 1996, when it increased to $4.75 per hour by virtue of the Small Business Protection Act, Pub. L. No. 104-188, § 2104, 110 Stat. 1755, which amended the Fair Labor Standards Act, 29 U.S.C. § 206. The same Act also enacted an increase, effective October 1, 1997, to $5.15 per hour. The Washington, D.C. and regional offices of the Wage and Hour Division of the United States Department of Labor may be phoned for information on the current minimum wage. This information is also available on the Department of Labor's website at www.dol.gov/dol/topic/wages/index.htm. The Department of Labor regulations, 29 C.F.R. Part 870, which are reprinted in Appx. B.2, *infra*, still refer to the pre-1997 minimum wage levels. Calculations using the 2007 minimum wage level may be found in the Department of Labor's Fact Sheet #30, available at www.dol.gov/esa/regs/compliance/whd/whdfs30.htm.

138 29 C.F.R. § 870.10(c) (reprinted in Appx. B.2, *infra*); Dep't of Labor Fact Sheet #30 (includes examples based on 2007 increase to minimum wage), *available at* www.dol.gov/esa/regs/compliance/whd/whdfs30.htm; *see also* Koethe v. Johnson, 328 N.W.2d 293 (Iowa 1982) (describing formula for bi-weekly pay period; decision also holds that, when garnishment order arrives in middle of pay period, before entire period's pay is earned, full pay for entire period should be used in CCPA calculations).

Consequently, from July 24, 2008 to July 23, 2009, the CCPA garnishment provisions allow to be garnished the lesser of:

(1) 25% of disposable earnings for the pay period, or
(2) the amount by which disposable earnings for the pay period exceed $393.00 for a bi-weekly pay period, $425.75 for a semi-monthly period, and $851.50 for a monthly period.

Starting on July 24, 2009, the maximum amount allowed to be garnished is the lesser of:

(1) 25% of disposable earnings for the pay period, or
(2) the amount by which disposable earnings for the pay period exceed $435.00 for a bi-weekly pay period, $471.25 for a semi-monthly period and $942.50 for a monthly period.

An employee is entitled to a full exemption even if the employee does not work the full pay period. For example, if an employee with a weekly pay period works only 10 hours at $10.00 per hour after the allowable deductions, all $100.00 of the earnings are exempt for that week.[139]

12.4.1.4.5 Child support and alimony

The CCPA garnishment provisions offer debtors fewer protections when the debt involves a court order for child support or alimony.[140] The maximum amount of disposable income that may be garnished for child support or alimony payments may not exceed:

- 50% for a debtor also supporting another spouse or child;[141]
- 55% for such a debtor if support is twelve weeks or more in arrears;
- 60% for a debtor not supporting another spouse or child;
- 65% for such a debtor if support is twelve weeks or more in arrears.[142]

12.4.1.4.6 Multiple garnishments

When there is more than one garnishment, the priority among them is determined by state law.[143] Some states give

139 *See, e.g.*, First Nat'l Bank v. Columbia Credit Corp., 499 P.2d 1163 (Colo. 1972).

140 Marriage of Eklofe, 586 N.W.2d 357 (Iowa 1998) (Iowa's $800 per year limitation on garnishment of certain low income debtors' wages applied to wage garnishment for alimony, but not child support; discussion of complicated interrelationship of garnishment and family support law, which has changed since case was decided); *In re* Prade, 734 N.E.2d 430 (Ohio Ct. App. 1999) (court has power to order family support in amount greater than that which may be collected by garnishment; approving garnishment of 75% of after-tax income of father who was serving life prison term for murdering children's mother); Albrecht v. Albrecht, 1999 Ohio App. LEXIS 622 (Ohio Ct. App. Feb. 23, 1999) (garnishment of 30% of income was permitted as "child support" when obligor was liquidating arrears, after children were emancipated); Gest v. Gest, 1998 Ohio App. LEXIS 1798 (Ohio Ct. App. Apr. 29, 1998) (federal and state limitations on garnishment for family support apply only to garnishment; court could order spousal and child support and provision of medical insurance for children, which added up to more than 60% of obligor's income, provided wage assignment did not exceed 60%); Laws v. Laws, 758 A.2d 1226 (Pa. Super. Ct. 2000) (maximum child support garnishment under CCPA could be based on obligor's earning capacity rather than lower actual earnings); *see also* Cameron v. Hughes, 825 P.2d 882 (Alaska 1992) (creditor may levy against otherwise exempt property, for example, workers' compensation and Social Security benefits, for past-due child support because of compelling public policy of enforcing child support obligations); *In re* Flores Children v. Flores, 1987 WL 19752 (Ohio Ct. App. Nov. 6, 1987) (Railroad Retirement benefits, though sole source of income, are subject to garnishment under federal and state law and regulations when garnishment is to pay delinquent child support); *cf.* Naedel v. Naedel, 115 Md. App. 347, 693 A.2d 60 (1997) (narrowly construing family support exception to CCPA garnishment limitation: alimony obligation that arose from a voluntary agreement, which was then "incorporated but not merged in" the divorce decree, and was non-modifiable by the court, was neither "ordered by a court" nor "subject to judicial review," so 25% limitation would apply); Carrel v. Carrel, 791 S.W.2d 831 (Mo. Ct. App. 1990) (family support exception to CCPA garnishment limits did not apply to court-ordered wage assignment to satisfy obligation to pay spouse's attorney fees in marriage dissolution case); Cashin v. Cashin, 186 N.J. Super. 183, 451 A.2d 1331 (Super. Ct. Ch. Div. 1982) (construing award of counsel fees in divorce action as support, so allowing higher percentage of wages to be garnished). *But see* Nadrich v. Nadrich, 872 So. 2d 994 (Fla. Dist. Ct. App. 2004) (wage garnishment that exceeded ex-husband's total earnings violated state and federal statutes).

141 Bitzer v. Bitzer, 986 S.W.2d 122 (Ark. Ct. App. 1999) (husband was "supporting" second wife, within meaning of CCPA, when he earned slightly larger income and was obligated on mortgage of house (even though she owned house) and she was supporting a child from her previous marriage, so garnishment by first wife was limited to 55% of disposable income); Rios v. Mireles, 937 P.2d 840 (Colo. Ct. App. 1996) (when debtor owed a support judgment to his second ex-wife but had not paid, he was not "supporting another spouse" within meaning of the CCPA, so first ex-wife could garnish up to 50%); Ctr. for Gastrointestinal Med., Inc. v. Willitts, 623 A.2d 752 (N.H. 1993) (no more than 50% of father's wages could be garnished to satisfy a child support order, due to his obligation to support minor child in his custody, even though he was found to have intentionally restricted his income).

142 15 U.S.C. § 1673(b)(2); *see also* Champion Int'l Corp. v. Ayars, 587 F. Supp. 1274 (D. Conn. 1984); DiZazzo v. DiZazzo, 1992 WL 98124 (Conn. Super. Ct. Apr. 23, 1992) (65% of disposable earnings, not 60%, may be garnished when child support or alimony in arrears).

143 Long Island Trust Co. v. United States Postal Serv., 647 F.2d 336 (2d Cir. 1981); Voss Products, Inc. v. Carlton, 147 F. Supp. 2d 892 (E.D. Tenn. 2001); Koethe v. Carmel Heights Apartments, 328 N.W.2d 293 (Iowa 1982); *see also* Sears, Roebuck & Co. v. A. T. & G. Co., 66 Mich. App. 359, 239 N.W.2d 614 (1976) (deduction from debtor's earnings to pay debt to employer takes priority over judgment creditor's garnishment).

priority to the garnishment that is prior in time.[144] Other states require creditors to take turns garnishing a debtor's earnings, so a later garnishment may take priority over an earlier one.[145] Between creditor garnishments and garnishments for support, however, the state may give priority to those for support, regardless of their timing.[146] As a result, a debtor who is subject to a support garnishment that consumes 25% or more of his or her disposable earnings will be immune from creditor garnishment.[147]

12.4.1.5 Remedies for Excessive Wage Garnishment

There are no specified penalties for court orders allowing excessive wage garnishments. Congress intended the court issuing the garnishment to abide by the provisions of the Act, by stating that "no court of the United States . . . may make, execute or enforce any order or process in violation of this section."[148] The debtor, and probably the debtor's employer, can litigate the propriety of the garnishment in the court that issued it, and appeal from that court's decision.[149]

While the Wage and Hour Division of the Department of Labor has authority to interpret and enforce the wage garnishment restrictions,[150] the CCPA does not give debtors an explicit private right of action under the CCPA for excessive wage garnishment orders.[151] A district court has suggested that monies erroneously paid over to a judgment creditor may be recovered, and a misuse of process or a failure to correct an erroneous garnishment could entitle an employee to damages from the creditor, the debtor's employer, or both.[152] And, of course, garnishing excess wages may vio-

144 *See, e.g.*, Long Island Trust Co. v. United States Postal Serv., 647 F.2d 336 (2d Cir. 1981); Koethe v. Carmel Heights Apartments, 328 N.W.2d 293 (Iowa 1982).

145 *See, e.g.*, Bohrer v. DeHart, 969 P.2d 801 (Colo. Ct. App. 1999).

146 *See, e.g.*, Long Island Trust Co. v. United States Postal Serv., 647 F.2d 336 (2d Cir. 1981); Voss Products, Inc. v. Carlton, 147 F. Supp. 2d 892 (E.D. Tenn. 2001); Lough v. Robinson, 675 N.E.2d 1272 (Ohio Ct. App. 1996); Union Pac. R.R. v. Trona Valley Fed. Credit Union, 57 P.3d 1203 (Wyo. 2002).

147 Long Island Trust Co. v. United States Postal Serv., 647 F.2d 336 (2d Cir. 1981); Voss Products, Inc. v. Carlton, 147 F. Supp. 2d 892 (E.D. Tenn. 2001); Gen. Motors Acceptance Corp. v. Metro. Opera Ass'n, 98 Misc. 2d 307, 413 N.Y.S.2d 818 (App. Term 1978); Lough v. Robinson, 675 N.E.2d 1272 (Ohio Ct. App. 1996) (if child support garnishment exceeds 25% of disposable earnings, creditor garnishments forbidden); Union Pac. R.R. v. Trona Valley Fed. Credit Union, 57 P.3d 1203 (Wyo. 2002); *see also* Igbal v. Mucci, 852 A.2d 195 (N.J. Super. Ct. App. Div. 2004) (when more than 25% of judgment debtor's income was being garnished for child support, court could not order installment payments on ordinary creditor's judgment, because this could lead to wage execution).

148 15 U.S.C. § 1673(c); *see also* Dyche v. Dyche, 570 S.W.2d 293 (Mo. 1978) (courts have the responsibility to enforce the garnishment protections created by the federal statute and any state statute supplementing it).

149 Union Pac. R.R. v. Trona Valley Fed. Credit Union, 57 P.3d 1203 (Wyo. 2002); *see also* Prof'l Credit Collections v. Smith, 933 P.2d 307 (Okla. 1997) (ex-wife who opened default judgment and quashed wage garnishment for ex-husband's debt on grounds of improper service, at which point creditor voluntarily dismissed action, was a prevailing party in an action on open account, entitled to attorney fees at trial and appellate levels); *cf.* Guidry v. Sheet Metal Workers Nat'l Pension Fund, 856 F.2d 1457 (10th Cir. 1988) (debtor who failed to raise objections to state court garnishment in accord with state procedure can not raise them in federal suit), *rev'd on other grounds*, 493 U.S. 365 (1990).

150 15 U.S.C. § 1676.

151 Colbert v. Roling, 2005 WL 3302212 (W.D. Mo. Dec. 5, 2005) (no private right of action under CCPA and therefore no federal right to support claim under 42 U.S.C. § 1983), *aff'd*, 233 Fed. Appx. 587 (8th Cir. 2007); Pressman v. Neubardt, 2002 WL 31780183 (S.D.N.Y. Dec. 12, 2002) (no federal private cause of action for violation of 15 U.S.C. § 1673); Perkins v. Metro. Water Reclamation Dist., 1990 U.S. Dist. LEXIS 12594 (N.D. Ill. Sept. 24, 1990) (no private cause of action against employer for garnishing more than allowed by CCPA); Burris v. Mahaney, 716 F. Supp. 1051 (M.D. Tenn. 1989) (no private cause of action under 15 U.S.C. § 1673 or 42 U.S.C. § 1983 for excessive wage garnishment); Whitney v. Chicago Transit Auth., 1987 U.S. Dist. LEXIS 4564 (N.D. Ill. June 2, 1987) (no private cause of action against employer for violating CCPA); Follette v. Vitanza, 658 F. Supp. 492 (N.D.N.Y. 1983) (debtor can not bring section 1983 claim to enforce federal limits on wage garnishment); Western v. Hodgson, 359 F. Supp. 194 (S.D. W.Va. 1973), *aff'd on other grounds*, 494 F.2d 379 (4th Cir. 1973); Oldham v. Oldham, 337 F. Supp. 1039 (N.D. Iowa 1972) (granting unopposed motion to dismiss cause of action alleging wage garnishment in violation of CCPA); *see also* Williams v. M.R.C. Polymers, 2000 U.S. Dist. LEXIS 2726 (N.D. Ill. Feb. 23, 2000) (suggesting that there is no private right of action); Winslow v. Bauer, 585 F. Supp. 1048 (D. Colo. 1984) (private cause of action can not be founded on section 1671, which merely sets forth Congressional purposes).

152 Cowart v. David J. Axelrod & Associates, 2004 WL 1013352 (N.D. Ill. Apr. 27, 2004) (allowing employee—who was not the judgment debtor—to amend complaint to add common law wrongful garnishment and conversion claims against employer who withheld wages without court order, based on garnishment notice with wrong name); Betts v. Coltes, 467 F. Supp. 544 (D. Haw. 1979); Giles v. Gen. Motors Corp., 802 N.E.2d 858 (Ill. App. Ct. 2003) (employee stated claims for gross negligence or wanton and willful misconduct against employer who continued to withhold wages for 2.5 years after expiration of court order; court order not a defense when it included termination date); *see also* Zaleski v. Collection Bureau, 664 N.W.2d 32 (Neb. Ct. App. 2003) (reversing dismissal of claim asserting statutory private cause of action against creditor and custodians of bank account for wrongful garnishment of exempt wages on deposit); § 12.6, *infra*; *cf.* First Va. Bank v. Randolph, 110 F.3d 75 (D.C. Cir. 1997) (sovereign immunity protects government from any liability to judgment creditor for refusing, mistakenly or otherwise, to withhold federal employee's wages after employee moved to quash garnishment order). *But cf.* Broughton v. Magnetic Ticket & Label Corp., 2006 WL 181669 (M.D. Tenn. Jan. 24, 2006) (employer owed no duty to child support obligor; even if delay in remitting funds withheld from wages was proximate cause of obligor being jailed for contempt, obligor failed to state a claim for negligent or intentional infliction of emotional distress).

late other federal or state debt collection laws.[153] In addition, wrongful garnishment or attachment may give rise to a claim for malicious prosecution or abuse of process,[154] in which case punitive damages may be available.[155]

153 *See In re* Culley, 347 B.R. 115 (B.A.P. 10th Cir. 2006) (table) (affirming $10,000 punitive damages for garnishment in violation of bankruptcy discharge when there was evidence of actual intent to harass and intimidate debtor, who was creditor's ex-spouse); *In re* Tuecke, 2006 WL 3000028 (Bankr. N.D. Iowa Oct. 10, 2006) (debtors entitled to actual damages, costs, attorney fees, and punitive damages for postpetition wage garnishment after actual notice of bankruptcy; disregard for debtors' rights was "blatant" and creditor was "a sophisticated player in the credit industry"); *see also* Todd v. Weltman, Weinberg & Reis. Co. L.P.A., 434 F.3d 432 (6th Cir. 2006) (consumer stated FDCPA claim against collection firm that regularly filed affidavits alleging reasonable belief that bank accounts contained nonexempt funds, with no knowledge whether this was true; here, account contained only exempt Social Security and disability payments). *See generally* Joel E. Smith, Annotation, *Recovery of Damages for Mental Anguish, Distress, Suffering . . . In Action For Wrongful . . . Garnishment . . .*, 83 A.L.R.3d 598 (1978); National Consumer Law Center, Fair Debt Collection §§ 5.6.1–5.6.3 (6th ed. 2008); § 12.6 *infra*.

154 *See* Todd v. Weltman, Weinberg & Reis. Co. L.P.A., 434 F.3d 432 (6th Cir. 2006) (action for wrongful garnishment may lie even if underlying debt is valid); Pinsky v. Duncan, 79 F.3d 306 (2d Cir. 1996) (wrongful attachment may give rise to cause of action for malicious prosecution or abuse of process, but not without evidence of malice and lack of probable cause); Cordero v. Calvary SpVI L.L.C., 2004 WL 1244107 (N.D. Ill. June 3, 2004) (consumer stated claim against creditor's lawyers and process servers, who caused wages to be garnished based on false affidavit of service); Ky. Farm Bureau Mut. Ins. Co. v. Burton, 922 S.W.2d 385 (Ky. Ct. App. 1996) (Kentucky law provides cause of action for wrongful garnishment; if plaintiff proves additional elements of malice and probable cause, common law cause of action for malicious prosecution is available, but judgment creditor's defense of good faith reliance on advice of counsel prevails here). *But cf.* Brown v. Kennard, 94 Cal. App. 4th 40, 113 Cal. Rptr. 2d 891 (2001) (litigation privilege prevents abuse of process claim based on wrongful post-judgment execution proceeding unless it is repeated). *See generally* National Consumer Law Center, Fair Debt Collection § 10.6 (6th ed. 2008).

155 *In re* Culley, 347 B.R. 115 (B.A.P. 10th Cir. 2006) (table) (affirming $10,000 punitive damages award for garnishment in violation of bankruptcy discharge; evidence of actual intent to harass and intimidate debtor, who was creditor's ex-spouse); *In re* Tuecke, 2006 WL 3000028 (Bankr. N.D. Iowa Oct. 10, 2006) (awarding punitive damages for postpetition wage garnishment after actual notice of bankruptcy; disregard for rights was "blatant" and creditor was "a sophisticated player in the credit industry"); Addair v. Huffman, 195 S.E.2d 739 (Va. 1973) (assessing compensatory and punitive damages against owner of collection agency in tort action arising from wrongful wage garnishment); *see also In re* See, 301 B.R. 549 (Bankr. N.D. Iowa 2003) (sanctions, including punitive damages, for bank's violation of automatic stay in continuing to garnish exempt wages despite knowledge of bankruptcy and exempt status of funds); Thomas J. Goger, Annotation, *What Constitutes Malice Sufficient To Justify An Award of Punitive Damages In Action for Wrongful Attachment or Garnishment*, 61 A.L.R.3d 984 (1975).

An employer who pays more to a creditor than the CCPA allows may be liable to the employee under the federal minimum wage laws. The excess amount garnished does not count toward the minimum wage requirement.[156] If the excess amount of the garnishment brings the worker's wages below the minimum wage, the worker has a private cause of action against the employer.[157] The worker may also have a cause of action against the employer under a state wage law, which may apply to any failure to pay wages that are legally due, regardless of whether there is a minimum wage violation.[158] One court awarded costs and attorney fees to an employer as sanctions against an attorney who persistently tried to garnish the wages of an employee against whom no judgment had been taken.[159]

12.4.1.6 Federal Protections Against Employee Discharge for Wage Garnishment

12.4.1.6.1 CCPA discharge prohibition

The preservation of an employee's job is one of the dominant purposes of the CCPA garnishment protections, which provide that no employer may discharge an employee whose earnings have been subject to garnishment for any one indebtedness.[160] The term "one indebtedness" refers to a single debt. Thus an employee may not be discharged regardless of the number of levies or proceedings brought to collect a single debt.[161]

The CCPA restrictions do not protect an employee whose salary has been garnished for more than one debt.[162] That is, the CCPA allows an employer to discharge an employee because there are multiple garnishment orders for different debts. However, if a creditor joins several debts in a court action and obtains one judgment, that one judgment is considered a single indebtedness.[163]

Even in cases of multiple garnishments for multiple debts, the earnings must first be actually "withheld" pursuant to a garnishment order before the employee can be legally discharged. If the employee obtains a release from the creditor after the employer receives a garnishment notice, but before the actual garnishment takes place, then the earnings have not been "withheld," and a discharge would violate the

156 29 C.F.R. § 531.39.

157 29 U.S.C. § 216(b) (authorizing suit for unpaid minimum wages plus additional equal amount as liquidated damages, equitable relief, and attorney fees).

158 *See, e.g.*, 43 Pa. Stat. Ann. § 260.9a (West).

159 Neubauer v. Ohio Remcon, Inc., 2006 WL 772020 (Ohio Ct. App. Mar. 28, 2006).

160 15 U.S.C. § 1674(a).

161 *See* United States Dep't of Labor, Federal Wage Garnishment, WH Publication 1324 at 9 (1978).

162 Cheatham v. Va. Alcoholic Beverage Control Bd., 501 F.2d 1346 (4th Cir. 1974).

163 *See* United States Dep't of Labor, Fact Sheet No. ESA-1078 (1982).

Act.[164] Similarly, if a prior garnishment renders the second garnishment order unenforceable, then a discharge on the basis of the second order would violate the CCPA.[165]

12.4.1.6.2 Criminal and administrative enforcement

The CCPA provides criminal sanctions for wrongful discharge of an employee.[166] The CCPA also provides that its garnishment restrictions are to be enforced by the Secretary of Labor acting through the Wage and Hour Division of the Department of Labor.[167] The Secretary of Labor has the authority to seek injunctive and declaratory relief,[168] and reinstatement of a wrongfully discharged employee.[169] However, enforcement by the Secretary of Labor is discretionary.[170]

12.4.1.6.3 Is there a federal private cause of action?

The Fifth, Eighth, and Ninth Circuits and a number of district courts have held that there is no federal private right of action to enforce the CCPA garnishment protections against employee discharges.[171] These decisions are based on the availability of alternative remedies. Some note the mandate in 15 U.S.C. § 1676 that the Secretary of Labor "shall enforce the provisions of this subchapter," while others rely on adequate private remedies in state statutes. For example, the Uniform Consumer Credit Code (UCCC) expressly provides for a private civil action for a wrongful discharge based upon a wage garnishment.[172] While a few other courts have found that a private right of action must be implied under the CCPA in order to effectively carry out the purposes of the federal legislation,[173] these all predate the Supreme Court's complete reworking of the test for implying such actions.[174]

When the employer is a state or municipal governmental entity, another approach may be used. At least one court has held that an employee discharged because of garnishment proceedings may maintain a private action under 42 U.S.C. § 1983 for deprivation without due process of his or her property interest in continued employment.[175] In this situation a state's Tort Claims Act will not afford immunity to either the governmental entity or its officials.[176]

12.4.1.6.4 Title VII claims

When the CCPA garnishment provisions do not provide an employee with protection from dismissal, or when the CCPA remedies are thought inadequate, another approach to challenging an employee discharge for garnishment is one based on Title VII of the Civil Rights Act of 1964, which prohibits discrimination in employment based on race or certain other characteristics.[177] This statute may also be used

---

164 Donovan v. S. Calif. Gas Co., 715 F.2d 1405 (9th Cir. 1983).

165 Brennan v. Kroger Co., 513 F.2d 961 (7th Cir. 1975).

166 "Whoever willfully violates [the discharge provision] shall be fined not more than $1,000 or imprisoned not more than one year or both." 15 U.S.C. § 1674(b).

167 15 U.S.C. § 1676; *see also* Hodgson v. Consol. Freightways, Inc., 503 F.2d 797, 799 (9th Cir. 1974).

168 *See, e.g.*, Donovan v. Hamilton County Mun. Ct., 580 F. Supp. 554 (S.D. Ohio 1984); Hodgson v. Hamilton Mun. Ct., 349 F. Supp. 1125 (S.D. Ohio 1972).

169 Hodgson v. Consol. Freightways, Inc., 503 F.2d 797 (9th Cir. 1974) (Secretary of Labor's express grant of power to sue under 15 U.S.C. § 1674 provides jurisdictional basis under 28 U.S.C. § 1345 for Secretary's suit seeking reinstatement of employees discharged for multiple wage garnishments); *see also* Martin v. Hawkeye Int'l Trucks, Inc., 782 F. Supp. 1320 (S.D. Iowa 1991) (awarding damages for wrongful termination in suit brought by Secretary on behalf of employee who was discharged because of Internal Revenue Service wage levy).

170 McCabe v. City of Eureka, 664 F.2d 680, 684 n.1 (8th Cir. 1981).

171 LeVick v. Skaggs Companies, Inc., 701 F.2d 777 (9th Cir. 1983); McCabe v. City of Eureka, 664 F.2d 680 (8th Cir. 1981) (noting that a different subchapter of the Act enacted on the same day as part of same law as 15 U.S.C. § 1676 contained a detailed provision for a private right of action); Smith v. Cotton Bros. Baking Co., 609 F.2d 738 (5th Cir. 1980); Stouch v. Williamson Hospitality Corp., 22 F. Supp. 2d 431 (W.D. Pa. 1998) (CCPA's ban on firing worker because of garnishment did not create a private right of action for worker); Western v. Hodgson, 359 F. Supp. 194 (S.D. W.Va. 1973), *aff'd on other grounds*, 494 F.2d 379 (4th Cir. 1974); Simpson v. Sperry Rand Corp., 350 F. Supp. 1057 (W.D. La. 1972), *vacated on other grounds*, 488 F.2d 450 (5th Cir. 1973); Oldham v. Oldham, 337 F. Supp. 1039 (N.D. Iowa 1972); Higgins v. Wilkerson, 63 Lab. Cas. (CCH) ¶ 32,379 (D. Kan. 1970); *see also* Mobile County Personnel Bd. v. City of Satsuma, 513 So. 2d 2 (Ala. Civ. App. 1987) (city employee had no private right to assert 15 U.S.C. § 1674(a) as a bar to his discharge for wage garnishment).

The Sixth Circuit has concurred with this view. Dole v. Hopple Plastics, Inc., 902 F.2d 33, n.1 (6th Cir. 1990) (dicta).

172 U.C.C.C. § 5.202(6) provides for up to six weeks lost wages and reinstatement.

173 Ellis v. Glover & Gardner Constr. Co., 562 F. Supp. 1054 (M.D. Tenn. 1983); Maple v. Citizens Nat'l Bank & Trust Co., 437 F. Supp. 66 (W.D. Okla. 1977); Nunn v. City of Paducah, 367 F. Supp. 957 (W.D. Ky. 1973); *see also* Note, *The Implication of a Private Cause of Action Under Title III of the Consumer Credit Protection Act*, 47 S. Cal. L. Rev. 383, 398–400 (1974).

174 The Supreme Court jurisprudence on this subject is summarized well in Wisniewski v. Rodale, Inc., 510 F.3d 294, 297–301 (3d Cir. 2007).

175 Johnson v. Town of Trail Creek, 771 F. Supp. 271 (N.D. Ind. 1991).

The *Johnson* court did not discuss the Supreme Court's holding, in Middlesex County Sewerage Auth. v. Nat'l Sea Clammers Ass'n, 453 U.S. 1, 101 S. Ct. 2615, 69 L. Ed. 2d 435 (1981), that section 1983 is presumed to provide a remedy unless defendants can show that the statute contains a comprehensive enforcement mechanism whose breadth or scope suggests that Congress viewed that mechanism as the sole means for statutory enforcement. *See also* Gonzaga Univ. v. Doe, 536 U.S. 273, 280 n.8, 122 S. Ct. 2268, 153 L. Ed. 2d 309 (2002).

176 Johnson v. Town of Trail Creek, 771 F. Supp. 271, 275 (N.D. Ind. 1991).

177 Civil Rights Act of 1964, 42 U.S.C. §§ 2000e–2000e-17 (as amended by Equal Employment Opportunity Act of 1972, § 703).

to challenge disciplinary action short of discharge.[178]

Three U.S. circuit courts of appeal[179] and the U.S. Equal Employment Opportunity Commission (EEOC)[180] have recognized that Title VII can be used to challenge the discharge or disciplining of black employees for wage garnishments. An employment practice, such as discharging employees whose wages are garnished, which is facially neutral and evenhandedly applied, with no employer intention to discriminate, may still violate Title VII if the practice has a significantly greater adverse impact on one class (defined by race, color, religion, sex, or national origin) than on another class.[181] These are commonly known as "disparate impact" cases under Title VII.

The seminal Title VII garnishment case, *Johnson v. Pike*,[182] found that a policy of discharge for multiple garnishments had a disparate impact on black workers based on the court's examination of garnishment statistics for the general population.[183] The EEOC has explicitly adopted the reasoning in *Johnson*.[184]

The Fifth Circuit has adopted a different approach, requiring a showing of a statistically significant disparity between the garnishment policy's impact on black and on white employees of the particular employer, not of the general population.[185] The Fifth Circuit approach seems to be at odds with the Supreme Court's view in *Griggs v. Duke Power*,[186] now codified by 42 U.S.C. § 2000e-2k, that accepted statewide statistics in a case involving hiring and the interdepartmental transfer of employees.

The major employer defense to a Title VII discrimination action is "business necessity"—that the practice is necessary to the safe and efficient operation of the business, and that no alternative practice of lesser differential impact would be feasible.[187] Mere employer inconvenience and/or minor expense is not sufficient justification for discharge of the employee whose wages are garnished if such a practice has a disproportionate impact on a protected class of employees. Employers must show a negative relationship between garnishments and job performance and/or safety and efficiency. Conclusory statements are not sufficient evidence of lowered work efficiency.[188] Because Title VII litigation is a complex and fast changing area of the law, an attorney bringing a Title VII action should very carefully analyze the latest case developments.[189]

Because disparate impact litigation is complex, pursuing a claim before the EEOC may be an attractive alternative. Indeed, plaintiffs are required to exhaust their administrative remedies by filing a claim with the EEOC before suing. The statute of limitations for filing a claim with the EEOC varies from 180 to 300 days, depending on whether the state has a work-sharing agreement with the EEOC.[190] The EEOC may be willing to assume that a disparate impact exists, rather than requiring the plaintiff to prove disparate impact. Because the EEOC does not often receive claims based on wage garnishment, the claim should include a cover letter explaining the employee's disparate impact theory.

12.4.1.6.5 State law wrongful discharge claims

Even if federal causes of action can not be maintained, an employee discharged because of a single wage garnishment will probably have a state law tort claim for wrongful discharge. Most states place tort liability on an employer who discharges an employee in violation of specific public policy interests of the state.[191] In some states this tort has

178 Keenen v. Am. Cast Iron Pipe Co., 707 F.2d 1274 (11th Cir. 1983) (reprimand, loss of fringe benefits); Robinson v. City of Dallas, 514 F.2d 1271 (5th Cir. 1975) (suspension).

179 Keenen v. Am. Cast Iron Pipe Co., 707 F.2d 1274 (11th Cir. 1983) (reprimand, loss of fringe benefits); Robinson v. City of Dallas, 514 F.2d 1271 (5th Cir. 1975) (suspension); Wallace v. Debron Corp., 494 F.2d 674 (8th Cir. 1974); *see also* Allan L. Schwartz, Annotation, *Garnishment Discharge Policy of Employer As Unlawful Employment Practice Violative of Title VII of Civil Rights Act of 1964 (42 U.S.C.A. §§ 2000e et seq.)*, 26 A.L.R. Fed. 394 (1976).

180 Equal Employment Opportunity Comm'n, Dec. No. 74-27, Empl. Prac. Guide (CCH) ¶ 6396 (1983); Equal Employment Opportunity Comm'n, Dec. No. 74-34, Empl. Prac. Guide (CCH) ¶ 6407 (1973); Equal Employment Opportunity Comm'n, EEOC Guide to Pre-Employment Inquiries (Aug. 1981), *reproduced in* Fair Empl. Prac. Cas (BNA) ¶ 443:65.

181 Griggs v. Duke Power, 401 U.S. 424, 91 S. Ct. 849, 28 L. Ed. 2d 158 (1971) (requirement of high school diploma for hiring or transfer not shown significantly related to job performance); *see also* 42 U.S.C. § 2000e-2k.

182 332 F. Supp. 490 (C.D. Cal. 1971).

183 *Id.* at 494.

184 Equal Employment Opportunity Comm'n, Dec. No. 74-27, Empl. Prac. Guide (CCH) ¶ 6396 (1983); Equal Employment Opportunity Comm'n, Dec. No. 74-34, Empl. Prac. Guide (CCH) ¶ 6407 (1973).

185 Robinson v. City of Dallas, 514 F.2d 1271, 1273–1274 (5th Cir. 1975); *see also* Keenen v. Am. Cast Iron Pipe Co., 707 F.2d 1274 (11th Cir. 1983).

186 401 U.S. 424, 91 S. Ct. 849, 28 L. Ed. 2d 158 (1981).

Eighteen years after *Griggs*, the United States Supreme Court decided Wards Cove Packing Co. v. Antonio, 490 U.S. 642, 109 S. Ct. 2115, 104 L. Ed. 2d 733 (1989), which set forth a stricter test for disparate impact cases. Congress restored the *Griggs* standards in 1991 by adopting 42 U.S.C. § 2000e-2k.

187 Barbara Lindemann, Paul Grossman, et al, Employment Discrimination Law 191–193 (3d ed. 1996).

188 *See* Wallace v. Debron Corp., 494 F.2d 674 (8th Cir. 1974); Johnson v. Pike, 332 F. Supp. 490 (C.D. Cal. 1971); Equal Employment Opportunity Comm'n, Dec. No. 74-27, Empl. Prac. Guide (CCH) ¶ 6396 (1983); Equal Employment Opportunity Comm'n, Dec. No. 74-34, Empl. Prac. Guide (CCH) ¶ 6407 (1973).

189 *See, e.g.*, Lex Lawson, Employment Discrimination (2d ed. 1996); Barbara Lindeman, Paul Grossman, et al, Employment Discrimination Law (3d ed. 1996).

190 Advocates should check with their regional EEOC office or check the EEOC's website, www.eeoc.gov.

191 Henry H. Perritt, Employee Dismissal Law and Practice §§ 7.01 to 7.12 (5th ed. 2006 looseleaf with annual updates).

been specifically recognized in the context of discharge because of wage garnishment.[192]

Many courts have held that a public policy embodied in federal as well as state statutes can form the basis for this tort.[193] An important advantage of a state law tort claim is that punitive damages as well as compensatory damages may be available.[194]

12.4.2 Special Federal Wage Garnishment Provisions for Particular Categories of Creditors or Debtors

12.4.2.1 Wage Garnishment Restrictions When Federal Agency or Student Loan Guaranty Agency Is Creditor

The federal Debt Collection Improvement Act,[195] enacted April 26, 1996, empowers federal agencies to which delinquent debts are owed to garnish debtors' wages "notwithstanding any provision of state law."[196] The amount deducted is limited to fifteen percent of disposable wages.[197] The statute does not mention the CCPA exemption of thirty times the minimum wage,[198] but the statute's specific preemption of state law, compared to its silence about other federal law, indicates an intention that the CCPA limitation should apply. Most of the CCPA limitations are incorporated in the Treasury Department's implementing regulations.[199]

Agencies have the authority to institute the garnishment administratively, without ever suing the debtor. The creditor agency must provide the debtor with notice thirty days in advance and with the opportunity to request a hearing or negotiate a payment plan.[200] If a debtor has been involuntarily separated from employment, no garnishment may take place until the debtor has been reemployed continuously for twelve months.[201]

The Act forbids the dismissal, refusal to employ, or discipline of an employee whose wages are garnished pursuant to the Act.[202] A private right of action is available, with mandatory attorney fees to a prevailing worker and, in the discretion of the court, reinstatement, back pay, and punitive damages.[203]

A separate statute, the Higher Education Act,[204] governs wage garnishments to collect student loan debts owed to the Department of Education or a federal student loan guaranty agency. This statute is discussed in detail in another manual in this series.[205] The amount garnished is limited to fifteen percent of disposable pay unless the debtor consents to a larger garnishment.[206] Department of Education regulations in addition specify that the amount that can be garnished is the *lesser* of fifteen percent of disposable income or the amount that exceeds thirty times the prevailing minimum wage.[207] One court has held that this statute does not abrogate the state's sovereign immunity, so wages owed by state governmental employers can not be garnished.[208]

---

192 Greeley v. Miami Valley Maint. Contractors, 551 N.E.2d 981 (Ohio 1990) (state statute that prohibited discharge because of wage garnishment order but did not provide a private cause of action set forth the state's public policy, so worker who was discharged because his employer was ordered to withhold a portion of his wages for child support could bring wrongful discharge claim).

193 *See, e.g.*, Faulkner v. United Technologies Corp., 240 Conn. 576, 693 A.2d 293 (1997) (recognizing tort claim for discharging employee who refused to violate federal fraud standards); Wheeler v. Caterpillar Tractor Co., 108 Ill. 2d 502, 485 N.E.2d 372 (1985) (public policy embodied in federal standards for handling of radioactive materials can be basis for wrongful discharge tort); Kulch v. Structural Fibers, Inc., 677 N.E.2d 308 (Ohio 1997); Thompson v. St. Regis Paper Co., 102 Wash. 2d 219, 685 P.2d 1081 (1984) (recognizing public policy exception to employment at will doctrine; federal Foreign Corrupt Practices Act can be basis of public policy). *But see* Griffin v. Mullinix, 947 P.2d 177 (Okla. 1997) (only state statute, not federal, can be basis for public policy underlying wrongful discharge claim).

194 Wheeler v. Caterpillar Tractor Co., 108 Ill. 2d 502, 485 N.E.2d 372 (1985).

195 Pub. L. No. 104-134, § 31001(o)(1), 110 Stat. 1321 (1996); *see* § 11.2.1.1, *supra*.

196 31 U.S.C. § 3720D; 31 C.F.R. pt. 285 (implementing regulations); *see* Frew v. Van Ru Credit Corp., 2006 WL 2261624 (E.D. Pa. Aug. 7, 2006) (Debt Collection Improvement Act overrides Pennsylvania restrictions on wage garnishment); *see also* § 11.2.1.1, *supra*.

197 31 U.S.C. § 3720D(b)(1); *see* Christensen v. United States, 2006 WL 744296 (W.D. Mo. Mar. 23, 2006) (declining to decide whether retirement payments are subject to this limit).

198 *See* § 12.4.1, *supra*. This limitation would be relevant for part-time employees, as reducing a part-time employee's wages by 15% could leave the employee with less than thirty times the minimum wage.

199 31 C.F.R. § 285.11(i).

200 31 U.S.C. § 3720D(b)(2), (4), (5); *see* Christensen v. United States, 2006 WL 744296 (W.D. Mo. Mar. 23, 2006) (fact issues preclude summary judgment for government on claim that agency instituted garnishment without opportunity for hearing).

201 *See* Kort v. Diversified Collection Services, Inc., 2001 U.S. Dist. LEXIS 11701 (N.D. Ill. July 31, 2001) (denial of motion to dismiss; collection agency's letter was misleading in stating that debtor had to submit written documentation of exemption).

202 31 U.S.C. § 3720D(e).

203 31 U.S.C. § 3720D(e)(2).

204 20 U.S.C. § 1091a; *see also* Savage v. Scales, 310 F. Supp. 2d 122 (D.D.C. 2004) (Higher Education Act (HEA) preempts District of Columbia garnishment statute, which requires pre-garnishment notice; HEA post-garnishment procedure adequate to provide due process); Nelson v. Diversified Collection Services, Inc., 961 F. Supp. 863 (D. Md. 1997) (upholding constitutionality of administrative wage garnishment procedures).

205 National Consumer Law Center, Student Loan Law (3d ed. 2006).

206 20 U.S.C. § 1095a(a)(1).

207 34 C.F.R. § 682.410(b)(9)(i)(A).

208 U.S. Student Aid Funds, Inc. v. South Carolina Dep't of Health & Envtl. Control, 588 S.E.2d 599 (S.C. 2003).

12.4.2.2 Garnishment of Federal Employees' Wages

Sovereign immunity protected federal government employees from garnishment[209] until 1994, when Congress authorized garnishment of the paychecks of civilian and military federal employees.[210] That law provided that the CCPA protections, and any more protective state exemptions, were available to federal employees.[211] This statute did not, however, authorize the garnishment of federal pension benefits.[212]

Federal agencies must honor wage garnishment orders in the same manner and to the same extent as if the agency were a private employer. However the agency may deduct an administrative fee from the amount it sends the creditor, even if the fee would not be allowed by state law.[213]

Offset of a federal employee's salary to repay a federal debt is discussed in a different chapter of this manual.[214]

12.4.2.3 Debt Collection Against Military Personnel

The military has adopted regulations placing special restrictions on garnishment. No garnishment will be allowed if "the exigencies of military service" prevented the servicemember from being present at the judicial proceeding at which judgment was rendered, or if the Servicemembers Civil Relief Act[215] has not been complied with.[216] Garnishment is limited to the lesser of twenty-five percent or the amount permitted by a more protective state statute.[217] Another federal statute forbids the garnishment of civilian seafarers' wages, except for family support.[218]

Historically, the payment by military personnel of just, personal debts in a timely fashion was a military concern.[219] Consequently, creditors were generally successful in obtaining the assistance of commanding officers in collecting delinquent debts owed by subordinate military personnel.[220] Federal regulations, however, place restrictions on when the military will assist debt collectors.[221] These regulations adopt some of the protections provided to consumers by other laws. For example, the prohibition of third party contacts by debt collection agencies in the Fair Debt Collection Practices Act[222] is adopted, as well as a broader prohibition of any third party contacts prohibited by state law.[223]

In addition, creditors seeking the assistance of the military in collecting debts must submit documentation that the transaction complied with the Truth in Lending Act.[224] They must also certify that they have complied with standards of fairness prescribed by the regulations, which include limitations on interest rates and late charges, and a general right to cancel contracts for personal goods or services.[225] Protections under the Servicemembers Civil Relief Act are discussed in Chapter 7, *supra*.

12.4.3 State Restrictions on Wage Garnishment

Every state has a statute that limits the amount of wages that a creditor can garnish. Some of these statutes duplicate the protections of the Consumer Credit Protection Act,[226] which limits most creditors to the lesser of twenty-five percent of weekly wages or the amount by which the debtor's disposable earnings exceed thirty times the minimum wage per week.[227] However, many states set higher amounts that may not be garnished by creditors, thus offering more protection for the debtor. The state statute may also exempt more types of income than the federal statute.[228]

---

209 *See, e.g.*, May Dep't Stores v. Walton, 572 F.2d 1275 (8th Cir. 1978) (Veterans Administration employees may not be garnished); *see also* 6 Am. Jur. 2d *Attachment & Garnishment* § 179 (1999).

210 Hatch Act Reform Amendments of 1993, Pub. L. No. 103-94, § 9, 110 Stat. 1321 (codified at 5 U.S.C. § 5520a) (allowing garnishment of federal employees' wages, including employees of executive, judicial and legislative agencies, members of congress and military personnel); *see* § 11.2.6, *supra*.

211 5 U.S.C. § 5520a(b); *see* S. Rep. No. 103-57 at 6, *reprinted in* 1993 U.S.C.C.A.N. 1802, 1807.

212 *See* 5 U.S.C. § 5520a(a)(4)(A).

213 5 U.S.C. § 5520a; *see* Hadley Mem. Hosp. v. Kynard, 981 F. Supp. 690 (D.D.C. 1997) (upholding $75 fee).

214 *See* § 11.2.6, *supra*.

215 50 U.S.C. app. §§ 501–596 (discussed in Ch. 7, *supra*).

216 32 C.F.R. § 112.4.

Section 113.6 prescribes a procedure for determining whether the exigencies of military service prevented the debtor's presence in court.

217 32 C.F.R. § 113.4.

218 46 U.S.C. § 11109; *see* Beneficial La., Inc. v. Wilson, 862 So. 2d 1049 (La. Ct. App. 2003) (debtor, a welder, worked 78% of the time on derrick barges, the rest in employer's fabrication yard on land; seaman status not lost by doing some work on land).

219 Cabell, Fed. Trade Comm'n, Report Of The Presiding Officer On The Proposed Trade Regulation Rule On Credit Practices 316 (1978); *see* 32 C.F.R. § 112.4 (1995).

220 Williams, Fed. Trade Comm'n, Staff Report On The Proposed Trade Regulation Rule On Credit Practices 395–396 (1980).

221 32 C.F.R. §§ 112–113.

222 15 U.S.C. § 1692c(b) (discussed in National Consumer Law Center, Fair Debt Collection §§ 5.3.5–5.3.7 (6th ed. 2008)).

This restriction is incorporated by 32 C.F.R. § 112.4(c)(4) ("contact by a debt collector with third parties, such as commanding officers, for aiding debt collection is prohibited without a court order, or the debtor's prior consent").

223 32 C.F.R. § 112.4(c)(3).

224 32 C.F.R. § 113.6(a)(1).

225 32 C.F.R. § 113.6.

Standards of fairness are set forth in appendix B to 32 C.F.R. § 113.

226 15 U.S.C. §§ 1671–1677; *see* § 12.4.1, *supra*.

227 *See* § 12.4.1.4, *supra*.

228 *See* § 12.4.1.3, *supra*.

Many states protect a higher multiple of either the federal or state minimum wage.[229] A model for a higher exemption is section 5.105 of the Uniform Consumer Credit Code (UCCC), which provides for a weekly exemption of forty instead of thirty times the minimum hourly wage. The National Conference of Commissioners on Uniform State Laws, which drafted the UCCC, believed the federal exemption "scarcely leave[s] enough for a family to subsist on, much less any disposable income which might encourage a debtor to accommodate his creditors without resorting to bankruptcy."[230]

Minnesota, New Mexico, North Dakota, South Dakota, and Vermont (in the case of debts arising from consumer credit transactions) protect forty rather than thirty times the federal minimum wage, and New Hampshire protects fifty times the federal minimum wage. Always examine whether a state law protects a multiple of the federal or the state minimum wage, because state minimums are often significantly higher. For example, Connecticut protects forty times the state minimum wage of $7.65 per hour,[231] Maine protects forty times its state minimum wage of $7.00 per hour (effective October 1, 2007),[232] and Illinois protects forty-five times the state minimum wage of $7.75 per hour (effective July 1, 2008).[233]

North Carolina completely exempts the wages of the head of the household to the extent needed for family support.[234] Texas exempts current wages for personal services, except for court-ordered child support payments.[235] Pennsylvania allows wage garnishment only in very limited circumstances.[236]

229 *See, e.g.*, Conn. Gen. Stat. § 52-361a; Me. Rev. Stat. Ann. tit. 9-A, § 5-105; Minn. Stat. §§ 571.922, 550.136; N.M. Stat. § 35-12-7; N.D. Cent. Code § 32-09.1-03; S.D. Codified Laws § 21-18-51; Vt. Stat. Ann. tit. 12, § 3170. *See generally* Appx. F, *infra*.

230 Note, *State Variations of the UCCC*, 48 Denver L.J. 239, 258 (1971).

231 Conn. Gen. Stat. §§ 31-58, 52-361a.

232 Me. Rev. Stat. Ann. tit. 9-A, § 5-105; Me. Rev. Stat. Ann. tit. 26, § 664.

233 735 Ill. Comp. Stat. § 5/12-803; 820 Ill. Comp. Stat. § 105/4(a). The Illinois minimum wage is scheduled to increase to $8.00 per hour on July 1, 2009, and to $8.25 per hour on July 1, 2010.

234 N.C. Gen. Stat. § 1-362; *see also* Livingston v. Naylor, 920 A.2d 34 (Md. Ct. Spec. App. 2007) (wages exempt under North Carolina law but not Maryland law; when North Carolina judgment was domesticated in Maryland and employer did business in both states, Maryland court could order garnishment only of portion of wages debtor earned while working in Maryland); *cf. In re* Connelly, 276 B.R. 421 (Bankr. W.D.N.C. 2002) (unmarried debtor with no dependents could not exempt earnings as necessary for support of family).

235 Tex. Prop. Code Ann. § 42.001 (Vernon).

236 42 Pa. Cons. Stat. § 8127; *see* Tenuto v. Transworld Sys., Inc., 2000 U.S. Dist. LEXIS 14344 (E.D. Pa. Sept. 29, 2000) (certifying Fair Debt Collection Practices Act class action for Pennsylvania consumer debtors who received a dunning notice referring to wage garnishment).

Alaska exempts $438.00 of weekly net earnings, increased to $688.00 if the debtor's wages are the sole support of the household.[237] Illinois allows only 15% of weekly earnings to be garnished.[238] Missouri allows only 10% of the wages of the head of the household to be garnished.[239] A former Ohio statute put greater limits on garnishment for health care debts than for other types of debts, but courts split on its constitutionality and it has now been repealed.[240]

Courts may have discretion to limit garnishment, especially in cases of hardship.[241] Kansas forbids wage garnishment for two months after recovery of the debtor or a family member from an illness which has prevented the debtor from working at his usual employment for two weeks.[242]

237 Alaska Stat. §§ 09.38.030, 09.38.115; Alaska Admin. Code tit. 8, § 95.030.

238 735 Ill. Comp. Stat. § 5/12-803. *But see* Wienco v. Scene Three, Inc., 29 F.3d 329 (7th Cir. 1994) (interpreting separate statute, 735 Ill. Comp. Stat. § 5/2-1402(c)(1), as allowing order requiring debtor himself to turn over 25% of earnings to creditor; court fails to mention amendment to section 5/2-1402(c)(2) effective seven months before decision that explicitly exempts amounts protected by garnishment statute).

239 Mo. Rev. Stat. § 525.030.

240 Ohio Rev. Code Ann. § 2716.051 (West) (repealed in 1995). *Compare* St. Ann's Hosp. v. Arnold, 672 N.E.2d 743 (Ohio Ct. App. 1996) (classification was reasonable, in light of public policy of encouraging people to seek needed medical care) *and* Wooster Cmty. Hosp. v. Anderson, 670 N.E.2d 563 (Ohio Ct. App. 1996) (classification was rational: health care debtors are different from others because of the life or death necessity of health care, and the extra burdens imposed by paying back a debt while also suffering health problems) *with* Cmty. Physical Therapy v. Wayt, 639 N.E.2d 515 (Ohio Ct. App. 1994) (statute was unconstitutional because it had no rational relationship to any governmental purpose).

241 Midlantic Nat'l Bank/North v. Reif, 732 F. Supp. 354 (E.D.N.Y. 1990) (ordering reduction of wage garnishment due to hardship, as allowed by N.Y. C.P.L.R. § 5231 (McKinney)); LaFreniere-Nietz v. Nietz, 547 N.W.2d 895 (Minn. Ct. App. 1996) (statute permitted garnishments of less than statutory maximum; court which allowed garnishment for child support arrearage and forbade further garnishments properly exercised its equitable powers, when larger garnishment might cause father to lose car or apartment, which would likely result in losing job, and father's financial problems were adversely affecting his visitation with child); Hillcrest Med. Ctr. v. Monroy, 38 P.3d 931 (Okla. Civ. App. 2001) (judgment debtor may file motion for statutory hardship exemption at any time until continuing garnishment terminates; trial court had power to order refund of sums already garnished); Gerber v. Holcomb, 2006 WL 3019731 (Tenn. Ct. App. Oct. 25, 2006) (garnishment statute sets maximum; creditor has no "statutory entitlement" to that sum; trial court did not abuse discretion in ordering lesser amount). *But see* Hartford Postal Employees Credit Union v. Rosemond, 635 A.2d 876 (Conn. App. Ct. 1994) (power to "modify" wage execution does not include power to vacate it; issuance of wage execution was "mandatory" if judgment debtor did not keep up installment payments); *cf.* United States v. Anderson, 2007 WL 2703160 (W.D. Okla. Sept. 13, 2007) (Oklahoma garnishment exemptions for "undue hardship" not applicable to federal garnishment for criminal restitution).

242 Kan. Stat. Ann. § 60-2310.

California exempts "the portion of the judgment debtor's earnings which the judgment debtor proves is necessary for the support of the judgment debtor or the judgment debtor's family supported in whole or in part by the judgment debtor."[243] Arizona allows the garnishment to be reduced to 15% in case of "extreme economic hardship" and forbids garnishment if the debt is "subject to an effective agreement for debt scheduling between the judgment debtor and a qualified debt counseling organization."[244]

Vermont allows an increased exemption if the debtor shows that weekly expenditures "reasonably incurred" for the maintenance of the debtor or his or her dependents exceed the statutorily exempt amount.[245] Connecticut allows garnishment only after a judgment debtor has failed to comply with an installment payment order, and allows for modification of the amount upon motion by the debtor.[246] Some states provide additional protection for certain present or former recipients of needs-tested benefits.[247]

Some states have allowed debtors to use a separate exemption, usually a wildcard exemption, to protect the portion of wages that is subject to garnishment.[248] State domestic relations law defining marital or community property will determine when, if at all, one spouse's wages may be garnished for an individual debt of the other.[249] Whether state wage exemptions follow wages after deposit is discussed in § 12.6, *infra*.

243 Cal. Civ. Proc. Code § 706.051 (West); *see* United States v. Arevalo, 2007 WL 2220969 (N.D. Cal. Aug. 1, 2007) ("necessary for support" does not mean "bare subsistence"; includes "the conveniences of refined society," here cable television and cell phone).

244 Ariz. Rev. Stat. Ann. § 12-1598.10(B)(5), (C), (F).

245 Vt. Stat. Ann. tit. 12, § 3170(b)(3).

246 Conn. Gen. Stat. § 52-361a.

247 *See* § 12.5.5, *infra*.

248 *See* § 12.5.6, *infra* (discussion of wildcard exemptions).

249 State *ex rel.* Indus. Comm'n. v. Wright, 43 P.3d 203 (Ariz. Ct. App. 2002) (spouse's wages are community property, which can not be reached for individual debt; may be made individual property by pre-nuptial agreement; when couple amended agreement after husband incurred a debt, change was fraudulent transfer and husband's wages could be garnished); *see, e.g.*, M.P. Allen Gen. Contractors, Inc. v. Kervin, 2002 WL 265060 (Cal. Ct. App. Feb. 26, 2002) (when married couple separated, wife's wages her separate property; may not be garnished for debt incurred by husband alone during marriage); Schultz v. Sykes, 638 N.W.2d 76 (Wis. Ct. App. 2001) (non-debtor spouse's wages were marital property and could be garnished); *see also* Action Collection Serv., Inc. v. Seele, 69 P.3d 173 (Idaho Ct. App. 2003) (wages are community property; when each spouse has equal right to manage property, wife's wages can be garnished for pre-marital debt); *cf.* United States v. Wahlen, 459 F. Supp. 2d 800 (E.D. Wis. 2006) (court may order criminal forfeiture of marital property, including innocent spouse's individual retirement account and gifts and inheritance she received that were commingled with other marital property).

12.4.4 Relation Between Federal and State Wage Garnishment Protections

The federal Consumer Credit Protection Act[250] explicitly provides that its garnishment restrictions do not limit the operation of state laws that exempt a larger share of a debtor's wages from garnishment.[251] Nor does the CCPA limit the operation of any state laws that prohibit employee discharge in cases in which the CCPA does not prohibit discharge.[252] Congress enacted the CCPA to maximize debtor protections,[253] only preempting state law that is less protective of debtors.[254]

Even if portions of a state law conflict with the federal provisions, the federal law will only preempt those portions that are less protective than the CCPA.[255] If the state law and the CCPA use different formulas to calculate the maximum amount that can be garnished, the formula that protects the most wages in the particular case must be used.[256] For example, a court held that New York wage garnishments

250 See § 12.4.1, *supra*, for a discussion of the federal restrictions on wage garnishment.

251 15 U.S.C. § 1677; *see, e.g.*, *In re* Irish, 311 B.R. 63, 65 n.2 (B.A.P. 8th Cir. 2004); *In re* Duncan, 140 B.R. 210, 213 n.2 (Bankr. E.D. Tenn. 1992) (section 1677 "allows states to enact statutes that would prohibit garnishments altogether or place a greater limit on garnishments than required under the Act"); *In re* Sanders, 69 B.R. 569 (Bankr. E.D. Mo. 1987) (Missouri's 10% limitations applied to prepetition income); Liedka v. Liedka, 101 Misc. 2d 305, 423 N.Y.S.2d 788 (Fam. Ct. 1979).

252 15 U.S.C. § 1677.

253 *See, e.g.*, *In re* Kokoszka, 479 F.2d 990 (2d Cir. 1973), *aff'd sub nom.* Kokoszka v. Belford, 417 U.S. 642 (1974); Anderson v. Anderson, 404 A.2d 275, 280 (Md. 1979).

254 *See, e.g.*, Evans v. Evans, 429 F. Supp. 580 (W.D. Okla. 1976); Crane v. Crane, 417 F. Supp. 38 (E.D. Okla. 1976); Hodgson v. Hamilton Mun. Ct., 349 F. Supp. 1125 (S.D. Ohio 1972); Knight v. Knight, 658 So. 2d 478 (Ala. Civ. App. 1994) (federal law allowing up to 65% of wages to be garnished for alimony or child support did not preempt Alabama law which limited such garnishments to 25%); *In re* Marriage of Herrick, 640 N.E.2d 969 (Ill. App. Ct. 1994) (when garnishment for attorney fees, on top of existing garnishment for support, would exceed statutory limit of 25% of debtor's wages, second garnishment must be abated; federal law preempted state law which would have allowed this second garnishment); Benson v. Richardson, 537 N.W.2d 748 (Iowa 1995) (federal CCPA did not preempt Iowa's more protective treatment of wages, which remained exempt for ninety days in checking or savings account, so long as reasonably traceable).

255 Hodgson v. Hamilton Mun. Ct., 349 F. Supp. 1125 (S.D. Ohio 1972); Hodgson v. Cleveland Mun. Ct., 326 F. Supp. 419 (N.D. Ohio 1971); Phillips v. Gen. Fin. Corp., 297 So. 2d 6 (Fla. 1974); *In re* Marriage of Herrick, 640 N.E.2d 969 (Ill. App. Ct. 1994); Kropf v. Kropf, 538 N.W.2d 496 (Neb. 1995) (when Nebraska law did not limit amount of Social Security benefits which could be garnished for support of ex-wife, CCPA limits applied).

256 Midlantic Nat'l Bank/North v. Reif, 732 F. Supp. 354 (E.D.N.Y. 1990); Evans v. Evans, 429 F. Supp. 580 (W.D. Okla. 1976).

must comply both with a state law that limited garnishment to 10% of gross wages and with the CCPA's limit of 25% of disposable income.[257]

State limits on wage garnishment that do not directly conflict with the CCPA will be applied in addition to the federal protections.[258] Combining state and federal restrictions can result in "stacking" of restrictions and significantly greater protections. For example, in Ohio a former state law allowed garnishment of $17\frac{1}{2}$% of the month's earnings and prohibited more than one wage garnishment every thirty days. Federal courts held that these restrictions had to be applied in combination with the CCPA, which limits garnishments to 25% of the disposable earnings for the pay period.[259] Thus, if the debtor was paid on a weekly basis, only 25% of his or her disposable earnings for that week could be garnished, plus there could be only one wage garnishment every thirty days.

Combining state and federal garnishment restrictions can protect significantly more of a worker's pay than either set of restrictions standing alone. Some states protect a greater percentage of wages when the debt arises from a consumer credit transaction.[260] State personal property exemptions may protect wages once deposited in a bank account.[261] In addition, some states have enacted legislation stronger than the CCPA by prohibiting discharge for multiple garnishments for multiple debts.[262] All of these protections must be applied in addition to the basic federal restrictions.

The Secretary of Labor has the authority to exempt from the CCPA provisions any state that provides garnishment restrictions which are "substantially similar" to those provided under the federal statute.[263] Virginia is the only jurisdiction currently exempted.[264]

12.4.5 Wage Assignments

Wage assignments can affect debtors in ways similar to wage garnishments. The Federal Trade Commission's Credit Practices Rule prohibits wage assignments in connection with the extension of credit to consumers in or affecting commerce.[265] There are three exceptions:

- The assignment by its terms is revocable at the will of the debtor;
- The assignment is a payroll deduction plan or preauthorized payment plan of the sort used in credit unions; or
- The assignment applies only to wages already earned at the time of the assignment. (This last exception allows a borrower to assign the portion of his or her monthly salary that has already been earned at the time credit is extended.[266])

The restrictions apply to all types of compensation paid or payable to an individual for personal services, whether denominated wages, salary, commissions, bonuses, or otherwise, and also apply to periodic payments under pension, retirement, and disability programs.[267] A contract term that violates the Credit Practices Rule is unenforceable.[268] These restrictions apply only to consumer credit debts, however, and states may require wage assignments in other contexts such as family support.[269] Many states also have statutes that restrict wage assignments.[270]

In addition, federal law prohibits enlisted members of the Army, Navy, Air Force, or Marine Corps from assigning their pay, similarly defined to include retirement pay, and provides that any assignment is void.[271] The law allows commissioned officers to assign their pay accounts when due and payable pursuant to regulations prescribed by the secretary of the military service in question,[272] but no such regulations have been adopted.

257 Midlantic Nat'l Bank/North v. Reif, 732 F. Supp. 354 (E.D.N.Y. 1990).

258 Hodgson v. Hamilton Mun. Ct., 349 F. Supp. 1125 (S.D. Ohio 1972); Hodgson v. Cleveland Mun. Ct., 326 F. Supp. 419 (N.D. Ohio 1971).

259 Hodgson v. Hamilton Mun. Ct., 349 F. Supp. 1125 (S.D. Ohio 1972); Hodgson v. Cleveland Mun. Ct., 326 F. Supp. 419 (N.D. Ohio 1971).

260 Iowa, Maine, and Vermont. *See* Appx. F, *infra*.

261 *See* § 12.5.3, *infra*.

262 *See, e.g.*, Unif. Consumer Credit Code § 5.106 (prohibiting employer from discharging any employee because of garnishment to pay a judgment arising from a consumer credit sale, consumer lease, or consumer loan); *see also* Edwin T. Gania, Annotation, *Discharge Based on Garnishment*, 41 A.L.R.5th 32 (1996).

263 15 U.S.C. § 1675; 29 C.F.R. § 870.51.

264 29 C.F.R. § 870.57.

265 16 C.F.R. § 444.2(a)(3).

266 16 C.F.R. § 444.2(a)(3); *see* Scott, Fed. Trade Comm'n, Informal Staff Opinion Letter (Mar. 1, 1985).

267 16 C.F.R. § 444.1(h).

268 *In re* Raymond, 103 B.R. 846 (Bankr. W.D. Ky. 1989) (security interest that violates credit practices rule is unenforceable); *In re* Boyer, 63 B.R. 153 (Bankr. E.D. Mo. 1986) (same); Free Bridge Auto Sales v. Fitzgerald, 48 Va. Cir. 1 (1999) (waiver of exemptions that violates credit practices rule is unenforceable).

269 *See, e.g.*, *In re* Marriage of Mease, 92 P.3d 1148 (Mont. 2004) (court may order wage assignment for family support).

270 *See* Decision Point, Inc. v. Reece & Nichols Realtors, Inc., 144 P.3d 706 (Kan. 2006) (state U.C.C.C. forbids assignment of wages, here realtors' commissions).

271 37 U.S.C. §§ 701(c) (prohibiting assignment of pay of enlisted members of Army, Navy, Air Force, or Marine Corps; any assignment is void), 101 (defining "pay" to include retirement pay); 38 U.S.C. § 5301(a)(1), (3) (prohibiting assignment of payment of benefits due or to become due under any law administered by Secretary of Veterans Affairs).

272 37 U.S.C. § 701(a).

12.5 Protection of Other Exempt Income and Property

12.5.1 Introduction

State and federal exemption laws provide fundamental protections for low-income debtors and their families. Every state has a general exemption law that protects a variety of income and property from judgment creditors. In addition, many federal and state statutes that deal with a particular type of income or asset, such as Social Security benefits or state employees' pensions, include their own exemption provision. Special exemption rules are also sometimes found in statutes dealing with a certain types of debt, such as tax debts.

Some states provide two exemption schemes, one in bankruptcy and another for judgment debts.[273] The differences may be significant. One bankruptcy court, however, has held that Michigan's "bankruptcy only" exemptions are preempted by bankruptcy law.[274] Another court found New York's "bankruptcy only" exemptions permissible.[275] The Bankruptcy Code provides a federal exemption scheme in bankruptcy for states that do not provide their own bankruptcy exemptions.[276]

Under exemption statutes property listed as collateral in a security agreement, mortgage, or deed of trust usually is *not* protected from the creditor who took it as collateral.[277] Such creditors are referred to as secured creditors. Secured creditors usually pursue any valuable collateral as their first collection option. Typical secured transactions are car loans and mortgages to purchase a home. Exemption statutes provide protection against general or unsecured creditors, for example, most bank credit cards, most retailers who issue their own credit cards,[278] tort creditors, landlords, utilities, and medical providers. Even with secured debts, exemption statutes often come into play if a creditor tries to collect a deficiency judgment after having sold the collateral.

Different state procedures exist for asserting exemptions. Due process requires that debtors be given notice of the methods available for asserting major exemptions.[279] Some states require debtors to assert the protections provided by the exemption statutes affirmatively.[280] This requirement is not universal, however,[281] and there is a strong argument that depriving a debtor of a federal exemption because of failure to meet a state procedural requirement violates federal law.[282] Some states may provide a method for a debtor to identify exempt property prior to its seizure. In Massachusetts and a few other states a homestead exemption must have been filed with the recorder of deeds *before* the debt was incurred.[283]

---

273 *See In re* Watts, 298 F.3d 1077 (9th Cir. 2002) (briefly discussing California's complex bankruptcy/nonbankruptcy, automatic/non-automatic exemptions); *In re* Reaves, 285 F.3d 1152 (9th Cir. 2002) (bankruptcy debtor using California bankruptcy exemptions could exempt her car, even though, before she filed bankruptcy, state court had denied her the California nonbankruptcy exemption for the vehicle); *In re* Petrozelli, 139 B.R. 241 (Bankr. E.D. Cal. 1992) (discussing California's dual exemption scheme). *But cf.* MPM Fin. Group, Inc. v. Morton, 2007 WL 1452536 (Ky. Ct. App. May 18, 2007) (Kentucky exemption statute that incorporates federal bankruptcy exemptions applies to all debtors whether in bankruptcy or not; it and another Kentucky statute provide complementary exemption schemes, one a floor and the other a ceiling).

274 *In re* Wallace, 347 B.R. 626 (Bankr. W.D. Mich. 2006).

275 *In re* Brown, 2007 WL 2120380 (Bankr. N.D.N.Y. July 23, 2007).

276 11 U.S.C. § 522; *see* National Consumer Law Center, Consumer Bankruptcy Law and Practice Ch. 10 (8th ed. 2006 and Supp.).

277 *See* § 12.5.2.7, *supra.*

278 Some retailers, however, purport to take a security interest in items purchased with their own credit card. *See* National Consumer Law Center, Repossessions § 3.6 (6th ed. 2005 and Supp.).

279 *See* § 12.3, *supra.*

280 *See* Mayer v. Quy Van Nguyen, 211 F.3d 105 (4th Cir. 2000); Zeppieri v. New Haven Provision Co., 163 F. Supp. 2d 126 (D. Conn. 2001) (exemption of Social Security funds in bank account is not self-executing); Shrestha v. State Credit Adjustment Bur., 117 F. Supp. 2d 142 (D. Conn. 2000) (no violation of Fair Debt Collection Practices Act to garnish account when Connecticut wildcard exemption was not "self-executing" because debtor had to identify property to which it would apply).

281 *See, e.g.*, Balanof v. Niosi, 791 N.Y.S.2d 553 (App. Div. 2005) (requirement that debtor assert exemptions does not apply when property "easily identifiable" as exempt); *cf.* Cal. Civ. Proc. Code § 704.080(e) (West) (first $1000 to $3000 of deposit account is exempt without making a claim; to execute upon excess over this amount, judgment creditor must make claim that it does not consist of exempt funds).

282 *See* § 12.6.7, *infra.*

283 *In re* Garran, 338 F.3d 1 (1st Cir. 2003) (only one homestead declaration per parcel; wife's later filing superseded husband's "disabled person" filing; exemptions could not be stacked); *In re* Perry, 357 B.R. 175 (B.A.P. 1st Cir. 2006) (Mass. law) (homestead declaration must be filed before bankruptcy petition; when it was impossible to tell which filed first, because clerks' time stamps showed same minute, principle of liberal interpretation applied and exemption allowed); *In re* Hildebrandt, 320 B.R. 40 (B.A.P. 1st Cir. 2005) (homestead exemption lost when unmarried couple, who had purchased house as tenants in common and recorded homestead, then conveyed house to one tenant without reserving homestead); *In re* Tofani, 365 B.R. 338 (Bankr. D. Mass. 2007) (homestead declaration, filed when debtor no longer resided on premises, was valid; debtor co-owned house with ex-wife, paid for upkeep, spent significant time visiting his children there, and credibly testified that he intended to buy and live in house after child support obligations terminated; intent to occupy sufficiently shown); *In re* Cook, 2007 WL 2238397 (Bankr. E.D. Va. July 31, 2007) (debtor lost opportunity to exempt her tax refunds when she failed to file homestead deed within five days after meeting of creditors); *In re* Shepard, 2007 WL 1385725 (Bankr. D.N.M. May 7, 2007) (California automatic homestead not available; no homestead declaration filed, and debtors were living and working out-of-state); *In re* Ruggio, 345 B.R. 30 (Bankr. D. Mass.

Each state's exemption laws are cited and summarized in Appendix F, *infra*. The full text of most of these statutes is reprinted in 14 *Collier on Bankruptcy* (15th ed. revised). A thorough analysis of exemptions provided under the Bankruptcy Code for debtors filing bankruptcy is found in Chapter 10 of NCLC's *Consumer Bankruptcy Law and Practice*.[284]

12.5.2 Homestead Exemptions

12.5.2.1 Dollar Amounts or Acreage Protected

Homestead exemptions are designed to protect the home for the debtor and the debtor's family. The only states that do not provide for homestead exemptions are Delaware, Maryland, New Jersey, and Pennsylvania.[285] The remaining states each set a different amount that is exempt. For example, New Hampshire allows $100,000; New York allows $50,000; Florida does not set a dollar amount but allows up to 160 acres outside a municipal area and a half acre within a municipal area.[286] Some states provide a larger homestead exemption for elderly or disabled persons.[287] When a statute

2006) (denying exemption because homestead declaration filed postpetition); *In re* Guido, 344 B.R. 193 (Bankr. D. Mass. 2006) (second mortgage took priority over homestead rights when it was executed before filing of homestead declaration, but not recorded until after); *In re* Vasques, 337 B.R. 255 (Bankr. D. Mass. 2006) (daughter could claim homestead in house deeded to her by parents, with life estate reserved for mother; daughter, who resided with mother, was family member, covered by mother's homestead declaration); *In re* Vizard, 327 B.R. 515 (Bankr. D. Mass. 2005) (homestead exemption lost when homestead conveyed to wife from husband and wife without reservation of homestead); *In re* Melber, 315 B.R. 181 (Bankr. D. Mass. 2004) (husband who owned homestead property conveyed it to self and wife as tenants by entireties without reserving homestead and without wife's signature; two wrongs made a right; exemption survived); *In re* Farrenkopf, 305 B.R. 382 (Bankr. D. Mass. 2004) (wife may claim homestead exemption in property for which husband has filed homestead declaration; only one owner may file, but exemption protects whole family); *In re* Heretakis, 293 B.R. 82 (Bankr. D. Mass. 2003) (increased homestead exemption would apply when homestead declaration filed before effective date of increase, but writs of attachment filed after that date); *In re* Govoni, 289 B.R. 500 (Bankr. D. Mass. 2002) (no homestead exemption for contiguous lot that contained home's septic system, because debtor failed to include that lot in homestead declaration); *In re* Cassesse, 286 B.R. 472 (Bankr. D. Mass. 2002) (ex-wife, who owned house jointly with ex-husband, not covered by his homestead declaration, because after divorce she was no longer family within meaning of statute); Title Trust Deed Serv. Co. v. Pearson, 33 Cal. Rptr. 3d 311 (Ct. App. 2005) (distinguishing between automatic and declared homestead under California law; the latter, but not former, may have priority over judgment lien); Kim v. First Fed. Bank, 2002 WL 1579602 (Cal. Ct. App. July 17, 2002) (no declared exemption when homestead declaration was recorded after judgment lien had already attached; automatic exemption does not protect from sale pursuant to mortgage or deed of trust; sale proceeds not exempt); Shamban v. Masidlover, 705 N.E.2d 1136 (Mass. 1999) (disabled person who filed declaration of homestead claiming $200,000 exemption, but failed to include statutorily required evidence of disability, could claim only standard $100,000 exemption); Patel v. Amresco SBA Holdings, Inc., 867 N.E.2d 337 (Mass. App. Ct. 2007) (homestead not exempt when debt pre-dated homestead and debtor filed homestead declaration after creditor made demand but before it sued); *In re* Snyder, 149 P.3d 26 (Mont. 2006) (liberally construing statute to allow debtor to claim homestead in sale proceeds, even if no homestead declaration filed before sale); *see also In re* Alley, 354 B.R. 783 (Bankr. W.D. Va. 2006) (Virginia statute allows homestead filing up to five days after meeting of creditors; filing was timely when forms and fee delivered to clerk within that time, even though sent back for noncompliance with local rule concerning form); *In re* Swyzd, 346 B.R. 290, 291 n.1 (Bankr. D. Mass. 2006) (criticizing Massachusetts statute, which purports to protect debtors' homes, but protection "may be easily and inadvertently lost by statutory language and conditions that are hyper-technical and often counter-intuitive"), *aff'd*, 370 B.R. 882 (B.A.P. 1st Cir. 2007); *In re* Shelton, 343 B.R. 545 (Bankr. W.D. Va. 2006) (under new statute debtor has five days after rescheduled creditors' meeting actually takes place to file); Russell v. Black, 2000 Mass. Super. LEXIS 350 (Mass. Super. Ct. July 28, 2000) (unliquidated malpractice claim not a prior debt, within meaning of Massachusetts's prior debt exception to homestead); Sanches v. Telles, 960 S.W.2d 762 (Tex. App. 1997) (property was not homestead, even though owner had lived there for eight years, when owner had not filed a homestead deed and had pledged property for bail bond, signing a statement that the property was not homestead). *But see* Siewak v. AmSouth Bank, 2007 WL 141186 (M.D. Fla. Jan. 16, 2007) (failure to file homestead notice not fatal to homestead claim; procedure is voluntary, not mandatory); *In re* Mariano, 311 B.R. 335 (Bankr. D. Mass. 2004) (debtor may file valid homestead declaration after levy and execution, if property has not yet been sold); *In re* Allman, 286 B.R. 402 (Bankr. D. Ariz. 2002) (Arizona statute amended; filing of homestead declaration no longer required); Cowart v. Pan Am. Bank, 2000 Wash. App. LEXIS 2132 (Wash. Ct. App. Nov. 3, 2000) (Washington property automatically acquires homestead status if it is occupied as residence; judgment creditor may acquire a lien against the value in excess of the homestead exemption only by strictly complying with filing procedure); *cf. In re* Gaudreault, 315 B.R. 1 (Bankr. D. Mass. 2004) (debtor in involuntary bankruptcy may obtain Massachusetts homestead by filing declaration after petition and before order for relief).

284 (8th ed. 2006); *see also* W. Vukowich, *Debtor's Exemption Rights,* 62 Georgetown L.J. 779 (1974).

285 *See* Appx. F, *infra*.

286 Braswell v. Braswell, 890 So. 2d 379 (Fla. Dist. Ct. App. 2004) (discussing method of calculating half acre, here considering rights in common areas of condo complex).

287 *In re* Bush, 346 B.R. 207 (Bankr. S.D. Cal. 2006) (explaining method of calculating income, for California statute granting enhanced homestead exemption to low-income debtors age 55 and older: sole proprietor of small business may deduct cost of goods and any legitimate business expenses, but not "investment losses"); *In re* Sweitzer, 332 B.R. 614 (Bankr. C.D. Cal. 2005) (investment losses may be deducted in calculating gross income to determine eligibility for enhanced homestead exemption available to debtors age fifty-five or over with gross annual income below $15,000); *In re* Rolland, 317 B.R. 402 (Bankr.

caps the value of an exempt parcel of land, but not its acreage, there is no limit on the size of the parcel.[288]

The dollar amount of the homestead exemption generally refers to the debtor's equity in the property. For example, if a $200,000 property is encumbered by a $190,000 mortgage, then a $10,000 homestead exemption will make it completely exempt.[289] If the area or value of the homestead exceeds the statutory cap, and division is not feasible, for example, a quarter acre homestead in a suburb with one acre zoning, the homestead may be sold and the debtor will receive the exempt amount.[290] Subject to area and value limitations a landowner may be able to exempt more than one parcel, if used for homestead purposes, though noncontiguous parcels may present a problem.[291]

C.D. Cal. 2004) (debtors not entitled to increased exemption for "physically or mentally disabled"; must show inability to engage in gainful employment; wife, although diagnosed with depression, claimed monthly income from self-employment and monthly expense for self-employment tax); *In re* LaHaye, 2003 WL 22764771 (Bankr. N.D. Cal. Sept. 10, 2003) (standard for disability same as for Social Security disability; burden of proof on objector; when evidence inconclusive, enhanced exemption allowed); *In re* Davis, 681 N.W.2d 452 (S.D. 2004) (increased homestead for the elderly permissible, but unlimited exemption violates state constitutional requirement of reasonableness). *But see In re* Collet, 351 B.R. 395 (Bankr. W.D. La. 2006) (Louisiana's enhanced homestead exemption for debts "arising directly" from "catastrophic or terminal illness or injury" did not apply when part of borrowed money used for family living expenses while debtor recovered from surgery).

288 *In re* Gregory, 229 B.R. 168 (Bankr. N.D. Ohio 1999).

289 *See, e.g.*, KLC, Inc. v. Trayner, 426 F.3d 172 (2d Cir. 2005) (after payment of consensual and statutory liens, but not judgment liens, debtor entitled to foreclosure sale proceeds up to amount of exemption); *In re* Cox, 315 B.R. 850, 858 (B.A.P. 8th Cir. 2004) (Iowa law) (homestead exemption applies to equity in the residence, that is, value of home minus amount of consensual liens); Martone-Rosato v. Guardiano-Neizwanger, 2001 Conn. Super. LEXIS 1294 (Conn. Super. Ct. Apr. 11, 2001) (lien may be placed against property if owner's equity exceeds statutory exemption), *aff'd*, 802 A.2d 927 (Conn. App. Ct. 2002) (table); Kipp v. Sweno, 629 N.W.2d 468 (Minn. Ct. App. 2001) (remanding to determine if equity exceeded cap); Baumann v. Chaska Bldg. Ctr., Inc., 621 N.W.2d 795 (Minn. Ct. App. 2001) (cap on homestead exemption applies to owner's equity, not fair market value); Miller Constr. Co. v. Coltran, 43 P.3d 67 (Wash. Ct. App. 2002) (in determining whether equity is available to satisfy judgment lien, only liens senior to the judgment lien may be considered); *see also In re* Anderson, 378 B.R. 296 (Bankr. W.D. Wash. 2007) (judgment lien can attach to homestead only if there is equity in excess of homestead amount); *In re* DeLavern, 337 B.R. 239 (Bankr. W.D. Wash. 2005) (filing a judgment creates lien on value of homestead in excess of exemption; when debtors' equity was less than exemption amount, judgment creditor was unsecured); *In re* Contrevo, 153 P.3d 652 (Nev. 2007) (judgment lien can not attach to fully exempt property). *But see In re* Watts, 298 F.3d 1077 (9th Cir. 2002) (creditor may file lien on property in which debtor has no nonexempt equity, and execute once equity is created by appreciation of home and pay down of mortgage).

290 *In re* Bradley, 294 B.R. 64 (B.A.P. 8th Cir. 2003) (allowing debtors to select which quarter acre was homestead, the value of which would be paid to them out of proceeds); Siewak v. AmSouth Bank, 2007 WL 141186 (M.D. Fla. Jan. 16, 2007) (fact issue whether property could be divided, or must be sold and proceeds apportioned); *In re* Quraeshi, 289 B.R. 240 (S.D. Fla. 2002) (when half acre was 19% of total acreage, debtor allowed to exempt 19% of net proceeds of sale); *In re* Bradley, 301 B.R. 546 (Bankr. W.D. Ark. 2003) (formula for allocating sales proceeds if zoning or subdivision covenant prevents division); *see also In re* McCabe, 299 B.R. 564 (Bankr. N.D. Iowa 2003) (no "equitable exception" to Iowa's half acre limit for urban homestead; partition will result in parcels of low value).

291 *In re* Stenzel, 301 F.3d 945 (8th Cir. 2002) (fact question whether contiguous parcel sporadically used for agriculture was "used and occupied" as homestead); *In re* Fiffy, 293 B.R. 550 (B.A.P. 1st Cir. 2003) (later-purchased contiguous parcels homestead if "used and occupied" for residence; family recreation is sufficient); United States v. Neff, 2007 WL 776532 (D.N.D. Mar. 12, 2007) (two parcels exempt; separated by rough country road, and farmed together); Painewebber Inc. v. Murray, 260 B.R. 815 (E.D. Tex. 2001) (three tracts used for residence, agriculture and family recreation were exempt; when parcels noncontiguous, more than aesthetic enjoyment must be shown, but activity need not make a profit); *In re* Mohammed, 376 B.R. 38 (Bankr. S.D. Fla. 2007) (contiguous lot may be exempt, if within the area limitations and not used for business purposes); *In re* Irene, 359 B.R. 435 (Bankr. W.D.N.Y. 2007) (condominium owner's deeded parking space exempt; applying New York Real Property Law definition of condominium unit); *In re* Haseltine, 2007 WL 2932807 (Bankr. D.N.H. Oct. 25, 2007) (second lot used for "homestead purposes" need not be contiguous, key issue is use; here, contiguous lot with barn and horses was homestead); *In re* Goff, 2007 WL 1434895 (Bankr. W.D. La. May 11, 2007) (homestead exemption for three contiguous lots: debtors' home, garage apartment, and vacant lot); *In re* McManus, 2006 WL 2846861 (Bankr. W.D. La. Mar. 29, 2006) (Louisiana homestead exemption protects contiguous parcels up to statutory size limit); *In re* Hughes, 306 B.R. 683 (Bankr. M.D. Ala. 2004) (homestead exemption protected tract of land that debtors used for parking and as children's playground and that was adjacent to leased land on which their mobile home stood); *In re* Baker, 307 B.R. 860 (Bankr. N.D. Tex. 2003) (noncontiguous land must be used for "comfort, convenience or support" of the family; cattle grazing and hunting sufficient; placing land in conservation reserve does not eliminate homestead); *In re* Hunter, 295 B.R. 882 (Bankr. W.D. Ark. 2003) (later-purchased, contiguous land was homestead when area limitations not exceeded, but here homestead was lost by abandonment); *In re* Allman, 286 B.R. 402 (Bankr. D. Ariz. 2002) (contiguous parcel exempt, if within dollar limit and not used for non-homestead purpose); *In re* Carey, 282 B.R. 118 (Bankr. D. Mass. 2002) (Massachusetts homestead exemption covers entire property, including home business, storage space and rental property, subject only to dollar limitation; debtors could exempt entire owner-occupied three-decker; court notes that the rent used to pay mortgage is "as necessary as the furnace"); *In re* Edwards, 281 B.R. 439 (Bankr. D. Mass. 2002) (burden of proof on objector; homestead use shown when contiguous lot was bought "for privacy," had some landscaping and a dog run, and children played there; possibility of future development or sale did not destroy exemption); *In re* Kyllonen, 264 B.R. 17 (Bankr. D. Minn. 2001) (contiguous parcels could be exempted, but when land was urban, area limit applied); *In re* Webb, 263 B.R. 788 (Bankr. W.D. Tex. 2001) (when land rented to tenants unrelated to owner, rural homestead lost;

If the state's homestead law is silent about its application to real estate located outside the state, a court may construe it to protect such property.[292] The problem of extraterritoriality has become critical because of recent amendments to bankruptcy law.[293]

12.5.2.2 Who May Claim Homestead Exemption

Frequently homestead exemptions are available only to heads of households but not to individuals. "Head of household" is generally defined as a married person or anyone supporting a dependent.[294] A homestead exemption may

distinguishing case of rental for share of crops); *In re* Zantman, 261 B.R. 41 (Bankr. D. Idaho 2001) (contiguous parcels, acquired at different times, were exempt when debtors raised farm animals and planned to plant oats; so long as land used as one parcel it is homestead, even if zoning law permitted division); Davis v. Davis, 864 So. 2d 458 (Fla. Dist. Ct. App. 2003) (rural homestead not limited to debtor's residence; if it comprises not more than 160 acres of contiguous land it may include income-producing property, here a mobile home park); Michels v. Kozitza, 610 N.W.2d 368 (Minn. Ct. App. 2000) (Minnesota exemption protects only land contiguous to land on which residence is located, even if noncontiguous land is "agricultural homestead" for tax purposes; court notes that this rule fails to recognize realities of modern farming, but statutory language is unambiguous). *But see In re* Wilson, 347 B.R. 880 (E.D. Tenn. 2006) (Tennessee exemption for property owned and used as "principal place of residence" did not protect contiguous parcel used for family purposes; debtors "resided" only on parcel with house); *In re* Williams, 345 B.R. 853 (Bankr. N.D. Ohio 2006) (Ohio exemption for "one parcel" will not protect noncontiguous land); *cf. In re* Olsen, 322 B.R. 400 (Bankr. E.D. Wis. 2005) (homestead exemption not applicable to contiguous parcel that was not "reasonably necessary" for homestead purposes).

292 *In re* Drenttel, 403 F.3d 611 (8th Cir. 2005) (debtor who had just moved to Arizona could claim Minnesota exemption for new home); *In re* Dubravsky, 374 B.R. 467 (Bankr. D.N.H. 2007) (New Hampshire law allows claim of homestead in out-of-state property, here former marital home from which debtor was excluded by divorce decree); *In re* Williams, 369 B.R. 470 (Bankr. W.D. Ark. 2007) (Iowa law is silent concerning extraterritoriality; debtors may claim Iowa exemption for Arkansas home); *In re* Stone, 329 B.R. 860 (Bankr. N.D. Iowa 2005) (Iowa debtor could claim homestead in Wisconsin house, in amount of Wisconsin exemption); *In re* Franklino, 329 B.R. 363 (Bankr. D.R.I. 2005) (homestead exemption may be applicable to remainder interest in out-of-state property if claimant shows intent to occupy property when it becomes available); *In re* Woodruff, 2005 WL 1139891 (Bankr. W.D. Mo. Apr. 28, 2005) (liberally construing Missouri statute, which is silent about extraterritorial application, to allow debtor to claim homestead in Mississippi house); *In re* Nelms, 2005 WL 318802 (Bankr. E.D. Mich. Feb. 4, 2005) (status of real property determined by law of jurisdiction where property located; Michigan debtors can not claim tenancy by entireties exemption in property in Louisiana, which does not recognize tenancy by entireties); *In re* Stratton, 269 B.R. 716 (Bankr. D. Or. 2001) (surveying cases on both sides of question); *see also In re* Jarski, 301 B.R. 342 (Bankr. D. Ariz. 2003) (debtor with residence in California may be able to claim Arizona homestead in Arizona house; issue discussed but not decided). *But see In re* Schlakman, 2007 WL 1482011 (Bankr. S.D. Fla. Jan. 16, 2007) (debtor could not exempt proceeds of former marital home, located in New York, despite intention to reinvest in Florida home; proceeds exempt only if property was located in Florida); *In re* Giffune, 343 B.R. 883 (Bankr. N.D. Ill. 2006) (complex discussion of choice of law; Illinois allows tenancy by entireties only in homesteads, Michigan in all real property; Illinois debtor not entitled to tenancy by entireties exemption for non-homestead property in Michigan); *In re* Ginther, 282 B.R. 16 (Bankr. D. Kan. 2002) (proceeds exempt only if used for purchase of Kansas homestead; not exempt when debtors moved to Colorado); *see also* Appx. F, *infra* (summarizing extraterritoriality and other aspects of state exemption laws).

293 *See* § 12.5.2.6, *infra.*

294 Richardson v. Klaesson, 210 F.3d 811 (8th Cir. 2000) (debtor-family trust which owned house and rented it to debtor-couple could not claim homestead exemption because it was neither married nor head of household; couple could exempt only their interest, here a tenancy at will); *In re* Roberts, 219 B.R. 235 (B.A.P. 8th Cir. 1998) (any married person, whether or not supporting a dependent and even if separated from spouse, may claim the Nebraska homestead exemption); *In re* Allison, 209 B.R. 494 (D. Neb. 1997) (Nebraska homestead exemption which defined head of family to include anyone living with an adult son or daughter "unable to support themselves," applied to debtor whose adult daughter had less than a high school education, could not find work nearer than forty miles away, had no reliable transportation, and needed to spend part of her time caring for ill family members); *In re* Holt, 357 B.R. 917 (Bankr. M.D. Ga. 2006) (debtors could claim homestead exemption in mobile home occupied by twenty-two-year-old daughter and minor grandson, as daughter was dependent); *In re* Uhrich, 355 B.R. 783 (Bankr. D. Neb. 2006) (two single persons resided in jointly owned house with their minor child and the minor niece of one of them; partner who had an income was head of house; niece did not qualify other partner as head of second household, because not the child of a deceased sibling as required by Nebraska definition); *In re* Townsend, 344 B.R. 915 (Bankr. W.D. Mo. 2006) (Missouri head of household wildcard exemption, which refers to "family," is available to debtor living with same-sex partner and partner's two children, when partners had changed last names to indicate commitment, shared parenting and household duties, and debtor was economic support of household and made financial decisions); *In re* Morris, 340 B.R. 78 (Bankr. W.D. Ark. 2006) (allowing head of household exemption when debtor's frail, low-income mother was a dependent; criteria are duty to support, which need not be legal, dependency, which need not be total, and position of authority; exemption, once established, continued after mother's death); *In re* Warnock, 323 B.R. 249 (Bankr. W.D. Ark. 2005) (debtor qualified as head of household when she lived in and co-owned home with seventy-nine-year-old mother and had assumed duty of supporting mother); *In re* Sandvik, 2004 WL 3383656 (Bankr. D.N.D. Dec. 1, 2004) (debtor not head of household; sister, who lived rent-free with debtor, not dependent when capable of self-support); *In re* White, 287 B.R. 232 (Bankr. E.D. Mo. 2002) (widow with no dependents may not claim head of household exemption); *In re* Plaster, 271 B.R. 202 (Bankr. M.D. Fla. 2001) (debtor-niece not head of household when, although she assisted her aunt and paid some household bills, "continuing personal authority, responsibility and obligation" not shown); *In re* Kimball, 270 B.R. 471 (Bankr. W.D. Ark. 2001) (divorced debtor with no dependents not entitled to "married or head of household" exemption amount); *In re* Billings, 262 B.R.

survive the death of the home owner, to protect the home from his or her debts in the hands of a surviving spouse or other close relative or dependent.[295]

88 (Bankr. N.D. Cal. 2001) (California allows larger homestead exemption for one who is part of "family unit," which may include adult relative unable to support self; debtor could claim exemption when adult daughter had epilepsy, could not drive, and was irregularly employed at low-paying jobs); *In re* Thorpe, 251 B.R. 723 (Bankr. W.D. Mo. 2000) (no head of household exemption when couple was separated and had no dependents); *In re* Davis, 228 B.R. 242 (Bankr. D.S.D. 1999) (wife could not claim head of household $6000 personal property exemption when husband earned slightly more than she did, even though she handled most of day-to-day management of household because husband's work required frequent absences from home); *In re* Hankel, 223 B.R. 728 (Bankr. D.N.D. 1998) (son was not head of household when mother was not financially dependent on him and he provided only minimal physical assistance); *In re* Roush, 215 B.R. 592 (Bankr. D. Neb. 1997) (two single adults, who both had minor children and lived together in a house they occupied as joint tenants, qualified as heads of households and could each claim a homestead exemption for his or her interest in the property); Tri-State Delta Chemicals, Inc. v. Wilson, 55 S.W.3d 304 (Ark. Ct. App. 2001) (Arkansas allows homestead exemption only if owner is married or head of household; house became homestead when owner married and lived there with wife; exemption survived divorce); Duran v. Henderson, 71 S.W.3d 833 (Tex. App. 2002) (father, adult daughter, and her child were family for purpose of increased Texas homestead exemption when all three relied on father's Social Security check, and daughter cared for incapacitated father; father had "at least a moral obligation" to provide for daughter and granddaughter); *see also* Painewebber Inc. v. Murray, 260 B.R. 815 (E.D. Tex. 2001) (land claimed as "rural homestead of a family" must be used to support family; tracts used for residence, agriculture, and family recreation were exempt).

295 *In re* Collins, 2005 WL 3506356 (Bankr. C.D. Ill. Nov. 30, 2005) (widow who inherited marital home could stack her exemption, as owner, with deceased husband's exemption, which protected surviving spouse and minor child); *In re* Spann, 2005 WL 3200400 (Bankr. C.D. Ill. Nov. 29, 2005) (surviving spouse who continues to reside in marital home may stack own homestead exemption with that of deceased spouse; right not terminated by remarriage); *In re* Beltramini, 2005 WL 3200428 (Bankr. C.D. Ill. Nov. 29, 2005) (same); Traeger v. Credit First Nat'l Ass'n, 864 So. 2d 1188 (Fla. Dist. Ct. App. 2004) (protection applies to all heirs, even those who would not inherit under intestacy laws); *In re* Estate of Hamel, 821 So. 2d 1276 (Fla. Dist. Ct. App. 2002) (debtor was in process of selling condo at time of death, and executor closed sale shortly thereafter; proceeds exempt in hands of adult daughters); Thompson v. Laney, 766 So. 2d 1087 (Fla. Dist. Ct. App. 2000) (homestead exemption survives owner's death if property passes to spouse or lineal descendent); *In re* Estate of Tolson, 690 N.W.2d 680 (Iowa 2005) (homestead exemption survived when property left to adult children); Parker v. Gates, 2000 Tex. App. LEXIS 8485 (Tex. App. Dec. 21, 2000) (Texas law allows homestead to descend free and clear of decedent's debts, if surviving spouse, minor child, or unmarried adult child resides there; not shown when adult daughter rented apartment and owned business in another city even though she moved in after mother's death). *But cf. In re* Joseph, 262 B.R. 33 (Bankr. W.D.N.Y. 2001) (widow not permitted to claim both her own homestead exemption and that of husband who had died in 1980; New York statute which allows survival of homestead exemption for protection of spouse and children applies only to decedent's debts, not individual debts of the survivor).

12.5.2.3 Distinctions Between Rural and Urban Homesteads

Many states distinguish between rural and urban homesteads, exempting much more land,[296] and sometimes allowing much higher value,[297] for rural homesteads. Some states also provide a separate exemption for personal property used in agriculture.[298]

The urban/rural distinction presents difficult problems when land uses are changing, municipalities are expanding into formerly unincorporated areas, and farmers turn to non-agricultural work to sustain themselves. Courts will generally consider first the character of the area, then whether the individual parcel is used for traditionally rural activities that support the family.[299]

296 *See, e.g.*, Ark. Code Ann. § 16-66-210 (quarter acre or eighty acres); La. Rev. Stat. Ann. § 20:1 (five acres or 200 acres); Tex. Prop. Code Ann. § 41.002 (Vernon) (ten acres or 100 acres for individual, 200 acres for family).

297 *See, e.g.*, Minn. Stat. § 510.02 ($750,000 agricultural, otherwise $300,000).

298 *See* § 12.5.3, *infra*.

299 *In re* Perry, 345 F.3d 303, 315–319 (5th Cir. 2003) (rural homestead may be exempt under former version of statute even if used for non-agricultural purposes, here a campground); *In re* Bouchie, 324 F.3d 780 (5th Cir. 2003) (detailed history of Texas's recently amended rural homestead definition; land was rural when it was within jurisdiction of a municipality but did not receive specified municipal services); Painewebber Inc. v. Murray, 260 B.R. 815 (E.D. Tex. 2001) (factors include municipal services, location of the land, presence of platted streets; rural homestead was exempt when contiguous and noncontiguous tracts used for residence, recreation, gardening, hunting, woodcutting, and fishing); *In re* Engstrom, 370 B.R. 205 (Bankr. D. Minn. 2007) ("rural" not synonymous with "agricultural"; low-density use and lack of subdivisions were sufficiently rural to permit exemption of five-acre lot not used for farming); *In re* Baker, 307 B.R. 860 (Bankr. N.D. Tex. 2003) (noncontiguous land must be used for "comfort, convenience or support" of the family; cattle grazing and hunting sufficient; placing land in conservation reserve does not eliminate homestead); *In re* Rodriguez, 282 B.R. 194 (Bankr. N.D. Tex. 2002) (property was rural because it lacked the enumerated municipal services); *In re* McLachlan, 266 B.R. 220 (Bankr. M.D. Fla. 2001) (home owner in rural area could exempt contiguous lot with palm grove from which he occasionally sold palm trees; land can be part of rural homestead even though it is income producing); *In re* Kyllonen, 264 B.R. 17 (Bankr. D. Minn. 2001) (homestead not rural, despite debtors' small-scale ginseng crop, when both debtors had full-time non-agricultural jobs, neighborhood was suburban and zoned "rural residential," main land use was houses, and any farming was hobby; if character of the area is unclear, court will look at parcel's use); *In re* Webb, 263 B.R. 788 (Bankr. W.D. Tex. 2001) (noncontiguous parcels rented to tenants unrelated to debtor not rural homestead; distinguishing farmland rented for share of crops); *In re* Cole, 205 B.R. 382 (Bankr. E.D. Tex. 1997) (when land not occupied by residence was pasture land, homestead was rural under former version of

12.5.2.4 Nontraditional Homesteads, Manufactured Homes, and Interests Less Than Fee Simple

Homestead exemptions should be construed to extend beyond the traditional single-family home owned in fee simple, because these nontraditional dwellings serve the same purpose as traditional homesteads.[300] A number of state homestead statutes make specific provision for mobile or manufactured homes, and other courts construe their exemptions liberally to include these dwellings.[301] A Florida court has held that a resident of a cooperative "owns" the unit within the meaning of the Florida exemption even though the resident actually owns shares in the cooperative association and then leases the unit.[302] Some courts allow homestead exemptions in nontraditional homesteads such as recreational vehicles,[303] watercraft,[304] and office space.[305]

---

statute even though located within city limits); Davis v. Davis, 864 So. 2d 458 (Fla. Dist. Ct. App. 2003) (rural homestead may include non-agricultural income-producing property, here a mobile home park); Baumann v. Chaska Bldg. Ctr., Inc., 621 N.W.2d 795 (Minn. Ct. App. 2001) (court should look first to character of area, then to use of parcel); *see also* Iowa State Bank & Trust Co. v. Michel, 683 N.W.2d 95 (Iowa 2004) (land was agricultural within meaning of statute regulating waiver of homestead exemption when landowners pastured horses and grew feed for them there, even though neither worked the land themselves nor received income from agriculture; key question is whether land is "suitable for farming"); *cf.* Marketic v. U.S. Bank, 436 F. Supp. 2d 842 (N.D. Tex. 2006) (Texas statute forbids foreclosure of home equity loan against property designated as agricultural for tax purposes as of date of foreclosure, even though not so designated at time of loan).

300 *In re* Carlson, 303 B.R. 478 (B.A.P. 10th Cir. 2004) (Utah law) (liberally construing homestead exemption to include mobile home on land not owned by debtor); *In re* Greene, 346 B.R. 835 (Bankr. D. Nev. 2006) (if debtor actually owns and occupies land, "mode of occupation" is irrelevant; here debtor lived in travel trailer, and had signed contracts to improve land and build house); *In re* Yettaw, 316 B.R. 560 (Bankr. M.D. Fla. 2004) (debtor could claim homestead in inoperable, but possibly repairable, recreational vehicle (RV) in space rented month-to-month in RV park). *See generally* W. Vukowich, *Debtors Exemption Rights*, 62 Geo. L.J. 779, 798 (1974).

301 *In re* Carlson, 303 B.R. 478 (B.A.P. 10th Cir. 2004) (Utah law) (liberally construing homestead exemption to include mobile home on land not owned by debtor); *In re* Thornton, 269 B.R. 682 (W.D. Mo. 2001) (mobile home placed on foundation and connected to well and septic system was real property entitled to homestead exemption instead of smaller statutory exemption for mobile home); *In re* MacLeod, 295 B.R. 1 (Bankr. D. Me. 2003) (mobile home is exempt personal property under Maine law, which exempts real or personal property used as a residence); Gold v. Schwartz, 774 So. 2d 879 (Fla. Dist. Ct. App. 2001) (constitutional homestead exemption, which protects "land and improvements thereon," covered mobile home that was permanently affixed to land); *cf. In re* Rogers, 225 B.R. 755 (Bankr. D. Idaho 1998) (a mobile home is not a "household good" for purposes of avoiding a non-possessory, non-purchase money security interest, when Idaho law allows claim of homestead in mobile home). *But see In re* Cobbins, 227 F.3d 302 (5th Cir. 2000) (mobile home on land not owned by debtor was not exempt under Mississippi law as "land and buildings," nor as personal property, when statute enumerated types of property exempted, and mobile homes were not listed); *In re* Kelly, 334 B.R. 772 (Bankr. D. Mass. 2005) (debtor who was neither elderly nor disabled could not claim homestead in mobile home when term "manufactured homes" had been added to elderly and disabled exemption, but not to general homestead provision); *In re* White, 287 B.R. 232 (Bankr. E.D. Mo. 2002) (debtor who lives in mobile home on land owned by another may claim only personal property exemption in home).

302 S. Walls, Inc. v. Stilwell Corp., 810 So. 2d 566 (Fla. Dist. Ct. App. 2002); *see also* Maher v. Harris Trust & Sav. Bank, 506 F.3d 560 (7th Cir. 2007) (shares in cooperative where couple resided are personal property covered by Illinois homestead exemption and can be owned in tenancy by entireties).

303 *In re* Greene, 346 B.R. 835 (Bankr. D. Nev. 2006) (allowing debtor to claim homestead exemption on land where he debtor lived in travel trailer, when he had signed contracts to improve land and build house); *In re* Yettaw, 316 B.R. 560 (Bankr. M.D. Fla. 2004) (debtor, who had sold home and purchased inoperable recreational vehicle, set up in month-to-month rental space in park, could claim homestead); *In re* Irwin, 293 B.R. 28 (Bankr. D. Ariz. 2003) ("mobile home" in Arizona exemption includes self-propelled motor home, when debtors were Arizona residents and occupied it as their only residence); *In re* Bubnak, 176 B.R. 601 (Bankr. M.D. Fla. 1994) (motor home in park, with permanent utility hookups, had sufficient permanency to qualify as Florida homestead); *cf. In re* Scott, 233 B.R. 32 (Bankr. N.D.N.Y. 1998) (New York homestead may be established in land with a motor home on it if debtor can show actual physical presence and intent to reside there permanently, but not shown here). *But see In re* Andiorio, 237 B.R. 851 (Bankr. M.D. Fla. 1999) (no homestead exemption for recreational vehicle (RV) which stood on land rented month-to-month in park, but hookups were easily removable, RV had tires, and was maintained and insured for highway travel; physical permanency an essential characteristic of Florida homestead); *In re* Kirby, 223 B.R. 825 (Bankr. M.D. Fla. 1998) (Florida homestead exemption did not protect motor home used as principal residence when there was no "permanency"; motor coach was not attached to land, and debtors neither owned nor leased land in Florida).

304 *In re* Mead, 255 B.R. 80 (Bankr. S.D. Fla. 2000) (allowing debtors to claim homestead in motorboat, which was their only home, when boat was tied up in leased space and equipped with living space, and debtors used marina address for drivers license and voter registration); *In re* Ross, 210 B.R. 320 (Bankr. N.D. Ill. 1997) (allowing homestead exemption in charter fishing boat on which owner lived during fishing season); Miami County Day Sch. v. Bakst, 641 So. 2d 467 (Fla. Dist. Ct. App. 1994) (houseboat moored in rented marina slip was exempt; analogous to mobile home in park). *But see In re* Hacker, 260 B.R. 542 (Bankr. M.D. Fla. 2000) (motorboat can never be homestead, because it is self-propelled and designed for transportation, not residence); *In re* Brissont, 250 B.R. 413 (Bankr. M.D. Fla. 2000) (cabin cruiser can not qualify for homestead exemption); *In re* Walter, 230 B.R. 200 (Bankr. S.D. Fla. 1999) (no homestead exemption for motor boat, although it was debtors' primary residence, when it was a recreational vehicle, capable of travel, and not designed as a permanent residence); Norris v. Thomas, 215 S.W.3d 851 (Tex. 2007) (houseboat can never be Texas homestead; law requires land or a structure that can be affixed to land), *followed by In re* Norris, 499 F.3d 443 (5th Cir. 2007).

305 *In re* Turner, 2005 WL 1397150 (Bankr. W.D. Mo. June 1,

One court has articulated these criteria for a nontraditional homestead: (1) the debtor's intent to make the nontraditional abode his homestead; (2) whether the debtor has no other residence; (3) whether the evidence establishes a continuous habitation; (4) whether the debtor maintains at least a possessory right associated with the land establishing a physical presence; (5) whether the nontraditional abode has been physically maintained to allow long-term habitation versus mobility; (6) whether the physical configuration of the abode permits habitation (the physical characteristics of the home are otherwise immaterial).[306]

Sometimes the debtor will have only a remainder interest in the home, while a parent or some other relative holds a life estate. Some courts apply the rule of liberal construction to protect the holder of the remainder interest.[307] Some courts allow homestead exemptions when the property is owned by a trust,[308] or when the debtor has some equitable interest in the property.[309] Courts have also applied home-

---

2005) (zoning violation not bar to homestead claim in commercial storage facility which debtor owned and occupied as his principal residence); *see also In re* Pich, 253 B.R. 562 (Bankr. D. Idaho 2000) (debtor living in office at site of failed business venture could have claimed homestead, even though residential use forbidden, but was estopped by having applied for light industrial zoning, thus impliedly representing that he would not live there); *In re* Laube, 152 B.R. 260 (Bankr. W.D. Wis. 1993) (tractor trailer cab, in which trucker slept, received visitors, completed trucking forms, and ate some meals, was "dwelling" within meaning of Wisconsin homestead exemption, even though it did not have a bathroom or cooking facilities).

306 *In re* Yettaw, 316 B.R. 560 (Bankr. M.D. Fla. 2004).

307 *In re* Stenzel, 301 F.3d 945 (8th Cir. 2002) (one-third remainder interest in property, in which mother held life estate, was sufficient to support homestead exemption; remanding to determine whether property "occupied and used" as homestead, when debtor resided on contiguous parcel and his agricultural use of subject parcel was sporadic); *In re* Vasques, 337 B.R. 255 (Bankr. D. Mass. 2006) (daughter could claim homestead in house deeded to her by parents, with life estate reserved for mother; daughter, who resided with mother, was family member, covered by mother's homestead declaration); *In re* Kimble, 344 B.R. 546 (Bankr. S.D. Ohio 2006) (debtors who owned remainder interest, and resided in mobile home on property with permission of life tenant, could claim exemption; "interest" in Ohio exemption statute includes future interests); *In re* Wycuff, 332 B.R. 297 (Bankr. N.D. Ohio 2005) (husband's dower interest in wife's property was property interest within meaning of homestead statute; spouses could stack their exemptions); *In re* Franklino, 329 B.R. 363 (Bankr. D.R.I. 2005) (homestead exemption may be applicable to remainder interest in out-of-state property if claimant shows intent to occupy property when it becomes available); *In re* Cain, 235 B.R. 812 (Bankr. M.D.N.C. 1998) (allowing debtor to claim homestead exemption in home where he resided with mother, when mother owned life estate and he owned remainder); *In re* Hankel, 223 B.R. 728 (Bankr. D.N.D. 1998) (North Dakota homestead exemption protects son's future interest in house where he resided with his elderly mother, who held a life estate); *cf. In re* Plaster, 271 B.R. 202 (Bankr. M.D. Fla. 2001) (owner of remainder interest may not claim homestead unless head of household; not shown here although debtor assisted her aunt, the life tenant, and paid some household bills). *But see In re* Pettit, 231 B.R. 101 (Bankr. M.D. Fla. 1999) (Florida's homestead exemption did not protect future interest when debtor resided with mother, who had deeded property to debtor but reserved a life interest for herself); *see also In re* Mazoue, 240 B.R. 878 (E.D. La. 1999) (Louisiana homestead exemption did not apply to debtor's one-quarter interest in residence in which he, mother, and brother lived, when mother and brother also held fractional interests and mother held life estate in entire property).

308 *In re* Kester, 493 F.3d 1208 (10th Cir. 2007) (allowing homestead exemption when property owned by self-settled, revocable trust); *In re* Cocke, 371 B.R. 554 (Bankr. M.D. Fla. 2007) (liberally construing homestead exemption to protect property owned by trust, when debtors resided on property, had right to exclude others, and all other rights of ownership except right to divide up property; key issue is whether debtors had legal or equitable right to use property as residence); Cutler v. Cutler *ex rel.* Estate of Cutler, 2007 WL 601866 (Fla. Dist. Ct. App. Feb. 28, 2007) (property was homestead even though long-time owner conveyed it to an irrevocable trust for estate planning purposes, reserving a life estate); Callava v. Feinberg, 864 So. 2d 429 (Fla. Dist. Ct. App. 2003) (judgment debtor may claim Florida homestead exemption in her residence, although property titled in trustee, as debtor has "beneficial interest"); *see also In re* Bogetti, 349 B.R. 14 (E.D. Cal. 2006) (debtors entitled to homestead exemption, but not lien avoidance; property owned by self-settled spendthrift trust which is unenforceable under California law); *cf. In re* Swyzd, 370 B.R. 882 (B.A.P. 1st Cir. 2007) (debtor may claim homestead exemption in house owned by a trust when, at time homestead filed, debtor had succeeded parents as trustee and was only beneficiary, so debtor held both legal and equitable interests); *In re* Alexander, 346 B.R. 546 (Bankr. M.D. Fla. 2006) (Florida statute requires occupancy and a legal or equitable interest that gives right to occupy; here debtor could claim homestead in property owned by revocable trust of which he was sole trustee and primary beneficiary); Duran v. Henderson, 71 S.W.3d 833 (Tex. App. 2002) (transfer of homestead to family trust did not make it vulnerable to creditors, when Texas fraudulent transfer law does not apply to transfer of exempt property). *But see In re* Estarellas, 338 B.R. 538 (Bankr. D. Conn. 2006) (Connecticut homestead exemption protects "owner-occupied" real property; equitable interest not sufficient; no exemption for property owned by revocable, self-settled, spendthrift trust); *In re* Barnes, 275 B.R. 889 (Bankr. E.D. Cal. 2002) (motor home in which debtors resided not homestead because owned by an irrevocable trust); *In re* Bosonetto, 271 B.R. 403 (Bankr. M.D. Fla. 2001) (Florida homestead exemption does not apply to property owned by trust).

309 *In re* Cadengo, 370 B.R. 681 (Bankr. S.D. Tex. 2007) ("any sort of title, legal or equitable" will support homestead exemption; allowing homestead claim when parents' divorce decree required father to deed house to debtor, who resided there, when she reached majority, which he had not done); Coy v. Mango Bay Prop. & Investments, Inc., 963 So. 2d 873 (Fla. Dist. Ct. App. 2007) (right to occupy is sufficient; once acquired, homestead not lost by court order awarding possession to other spouse; ex-husband entitled to hearing on claim of homestead in former marital home, titled in wife alone); Redmond v. Kester, 159 P.3d 1004 (Kan. 2007) (debtors who occupy and intend to occupy property as homestead may base claim on many kinds of property interests, including cotenancy, equitable title, executory contract to purchase, leasehold estate, and life estate; "equitable interest" is sufficient). *But see In re* LaVelle, 350 B.R. 505 (Bankr. D. Idaho 2005) (no homestead claim for land

stead exemptions to homes tied up in probate,[310] homes being purchased under an installment contract,[311] and even rental homes.[312] Courts have been less willing to recognize a homestead exemption in property owned by a partnership.[313]

Courts vary widely in their treatment of interests created by property division in divorce.[314] Joint tenancies also raise

occupied under oral at-will sublease from company wholly owned by husband, which was tenant under lease from L.L.C. seventy percent owned by debtors; lease terminable at will was not "ownership interest"; no homestead claim for interest in a legal entity, here the L.L.C.); *cf. In re* Hart, 332 B.R. 439 (D. Wyo. 2005) (occupancy plus some legal or equitable interest necessary for statutory homestead exemption; mere occupant not entitled to assert exemption over interests of owner or one with superior title); *In re* Perpinan, 2006 WL 3507943 (Bankr. N.D. Cal. Dec. 4, 2006) (California homestead requires both occupancy and ownership; no exemption when alleged ownership arose from sham transaction; debtor purchased interest from mother, with check she never cashed, and shortly thereafter deeded his interest back to her).

310 *In re* Dougan, 350 B.R. 892 (Bankr. D. Idaho 2006) (mother's will, which was still in probate, left home to debtor daughter who resided there, with mother's permission, during mother's lifetime; possessory interest, plus equitable interest arising from will, were sufficient ownership and occupation to support homestead exemption); *In re* Robertson, 227 B.R. 844 (Bankr. S.D. Ind. 1998) (liberally construing Indiana exemptions to allow homestead exemption in house which had been left to debtor by his deceased landlord, even though landlord's estate was still in probate).

311 *In re* Stone, 329 B.R. 860 (Bankr. N.D. Iowa 2005) (house being purchased on contract for deed, occupied by debtor's fiancée and children); *In re* Hunter, 295 B.R. 882 (Bankr. W.D. Ark. July 29, 2003) (homestead established when married person or head of household occupies property as home; "contract for deed" sufficient); *In re* Sorrell, 292 B.R. 276 (Bankr. E.D. Tex. 2002) (buyers could claim homestead in house they were buying under contract for deed, under which seller retained title until payments completed); Redmond v. Kester, 159 P.3d 1004 (Kan. 2007) (Kansas homestead may be based on wide variety of property interests, including executory contract to purchase); *see also In re* Hodes, 402 F.3d 1005 (10th Cir. 2005) (homestead exemption for funds prepaid to builder pursuant to binding contract for addition to homestead); *In re* McKown, 2003 WL 22119193 (Bankr. C.D. Ill. Sept. 8, 2003) (debtor may claim homestead exemption in property purchased at sheriff's sale when she had paid the sale price and moved in and sale was confirmed, even though deed not yet issued). *But cf. In re* Page, 289 B.R. 484 (Bankr. S.D. Ga. 2003) (seller had no homestead exemption in property she was selling under contract for deed, when purchasers were living in house and making payments; seller's interest was security interest, which gave her no right to occupy property).

312 *In re* Takes, 478 F.3d 902 (8th Cir. 2007) (leasehold that can be sold, here created by paying entrance fee to assisted living community, is property right that will support a homestead exemption, but ordinary landlord-tenant relationship is not); *In re* Casserino, 379 F.3d 1069 (9th Cir. 2004) (security deposit and prepaid rent for leased residential premises are protected by Oregon homestead exemption); *In re* Carlson, 303 B.R. 478 (B.A.P. 10th Cir. 2004) (Utah law) (liberally construing homestead exemption to include mobile home on land not owned by debtor); *In re* Wynn, 369 B.R. 605 (Bankr. D. Or. 2007) (proceeds of former marital home spent on rent exempt); *In re* Coffey, 339 B.R. 689 (Bankr. N.D. Ind. 2006) ($7500 prepaid rent was exempt "leasehold"; rental was for one year, and Indiana law made tenant liable for entire sum, even when payable monthly; funds were exempt "leasehold"); *In re* Rutland, 318 B.R. 588 (Bankr. M.D. Ala. 2004) (Alabama homestead protects tenancy in rented apartment; prepaid rent is exempt); *In re* McAtee, 154 B.R. 346, 347 (Bankr. D. Fla. 1993) (debtors who had house on public land, which they rented on ninety-nine-year lease, may claim homestead exemption); *In re* Bartlett, 153 B.R. 881, 883 (Bankr. D. Neb. 1993) (allowing homestead in house situated on leased land); *In re* Buzzell, 110 B.R. 440 (Bankr. D. Neb. 1990) (life estate or leasehold interest sufficient; mobile home on rented land is exempt); Redmond v. Kester, 159 P.3d 1004 (Kan. 2007) (Kansas homestead may be based on wide variety of property interests, including leasehold); Capitol Aggregates, Inc. v. Walker, 448 S.W.2d 830 (Tex. Civ. App. 1969) (debtor whose mobile home was on land rented month-to-month entitled to homestead exemption). *But see In re* Eagle, 373 B.R. 609 (B.A.P. 8th Cir. 2007) (no homestead exemption in leased property; "ownership interest" required); *In re* LaVelle, 350 B.R. 505 (Bankr. D. Idaho 2005) (no homestead claim for land occupied under oral at-will sublease from company wholly owned by husband, which was tenant under lease from L.L.C. seventy percent owned by debtors; lease terminable at will was not "ownership interest"); *In re* Tenorio, 107 B.R. 787, 788 (Bankr. S.D. Fla. 1989); Savage v. Pierson, 157 P.3d 697 (Nev. 2007) (prepaid rent not exempt under homestead or dwelling exemptions that cover land, mobile home, cooperative unit or condominium; right to possession not sufficient; equity must be shown).

313 *In re* Hoggarth Bros., 2004 WL 903814 (D.N.D. Apr. 22, 2004) (farm couples resided on land owned by husbands' farm partnership; wives had no homestead rights); *In re* Shepard, 2007 WL 1385725 (Bankr. D.N.M. May 7, 2007) (partners may not claim homestead exemption in home owned by partnership; trusts distinguished; partnership interest not an identifiable interest in specific piece of partnership property); *In re* Lyle, 355 B.R. 161 (Bankr. D. Ariz. Dec. 13, 2006) (no homestead exemption for property owned by partnership owned by debtors; rights in partnership were personal, not real property); *In re* Monsivais, 274 B.R. 263 (Bankr. W.D. Tex. 2002) (no homestead exemption for home owned by family partnership); *In re* Cole, 205 B.R. 382 (Bankr. E.D. Tex. 1997) (homestead was abandoned when land was transferred from natural person to a "family limited partnership").

314 *In re* Johnson, 375 F.3d 668 (8th Cir. 2004) (lien on former marital home, to assure ex-wife's payment of husband's share of value, not an interest in land within meaning of Minnesota homestead exemption); *In re* Sacharko, 356 B.R. 786 (B.A.P. 1st Cir. 2007) (table) (text available at 2007 WL 128775) (no homestead exemption for forty percent interest in former marital home, now occupied by ex-wife and couple's minor daughter; Rhode Island homestead requires occupancy); *In re* Dubravsky, 374 B.R. 467 (Bankr. D.N.H. 2007) (allowing homestead exemption for former marital home, although debtor was excluded by divorce decree, when home to be sold at later date and proceeds divided); *In re* Dixon, 327 B.R. 421 (Bankr. E.D. Mo. 2005) (husband could not claim homestead exemption for $15,000 ex-wife owed him pursuant to divorce decree when no evidence linked lump sum specifically to debtor's equity in marital home); *In re* Ballato, 318 B.R. 205 (Bankr. M.D. Fla. 2004) (ex-husband could claim homestead exemption for his share of proceeds of marital home, sold by court order during

problems, including whether more than one exemption may be claimed and, if not, how should the one be divided.[315]

12.5.2.5 Occupancy

The establishment of a homestead generally requires actual occupancy, with intent to make the property one's home.[316] This requirement may be a problem for a debtor

property division); *In re* Willoughby, 2003 WL 22849766 (Bankr. C.D. Ill. Dec. 2, 2003) (wife's court-ordered payment to husband as compensation for award of former marital home was exempt as proceeds of homestead); *In re* Kujan, 286 B.R. 216 (Bankr. D. Conn. 2002) (ex-wife who had quitclaimed her share of house to husband at divorce could not claim homestead exemption in her right to receive payment when youngest child reached eighteen or house was sold; she had no right to occupy or buy property and sum might be paid without selling house); *see also In re* Cumberbatch, 302 B.R. 675 (Bankr. C.D. Cal. 2003) (court-ordered sale of home during property division was "forced sale to satisfy a money judgment" within meaning of California statute allowing automatic exemption for six months in proceeds).

315 *In re* Garran, 338 F.3d 1 (1st Cir. 2003) (couple could not stack exemptions; wife's filing of homestead declaration, which protected entire household, superseded husband's earlier homestead declaration); *In re* Rabin, 359 B.R. 242 (B.A.P. 9th Cir. 2007) (Cal. law) (because married couple entitled to only one homestead exemption, registered domestic partners, living together in house they co-owned, are entitled to only one); *In re* Duncan, 294 B.R. 339 (B.A.P. 10th Cir. 2003) (spouses may stack their homestead exemptions, but wife who had no ownership interest on petition date had no exemption); Abernathy v. LaBarge (*In re* Abernathy), 259 B.R. 330 (B.A.P. 8th Cir. 2001) (debtor who owned one-third interest in property, in joint tenancy with non-debtor sisters, could claim entire amount of Missouri homestead exemption), *aff'd*, 2001 WL 1104482 (8th Cir. Sept. 20, 2001); Vinson v. Dakmak, 347 B.R. 620 (E.D. Mich. 2006) (Michigan homestead amount is aggregate maximum; co-owners may not stack); *In re* Limperis, 370 B.R. 859 (Bankr. S.D. Fla. 2007) (married couple, subject to $125,000 Bankruptcy Code cap for homestead acquired within 1215 days, could claim an exemption apiece and stack them for total exemption of $250,000); *In re* Wynn, 369 B.R. 605 (Bankr. D. Or. 2007) (separated couple who sold marital home could allocate exemption between themselves as they chose, so long as total did not exceed cap); *In re* Ewbank, 359 B.R. 807 (Bankr. D.N.M. 2007) (New Mexico statute, permitting stacking of exemptions for "homestead owned jointly by two persons," did not require joint tenancy; tenancy in common was sufficient); *In re* Strobbe, 2007 WL 2562611 (Bankr. D. Mont. Aug. 31, 2007) (owner of undivided one-sixth entitled to exempt one-sixth of statutory exemption amount); *In re* Kleinfeldt, 2007 WL 2138748 (Bankr. D. Vt. July 23, 2007) (part owner entitled to proportionate share of homestead exemption); *In re* Belcher, 2006 WL 3069708 (Bankr. S.D. Ill. Oct. 20, 2006) (married couple lived in house owned by wife alone; husband, who otherwise qualified for homestead, could claim exemption and stack it with wife's); *In re* Rasmussen, 349 B.R. 747 (Bankr. M.D. Fla. Sept. 8, 2006) (applying state homestead law to conclude that each spouse is entitled to $125,000 homestead allowed by bankruptcy law for property acquired during 1215-day lookback period; couple may stack exemptions); *In re* Collins, 2005 WL 3506356 (Bankr. C.D. Ill. Nov. 30, 2005) (widow who inherited marital home could stack her exemption, as owner, with deceased husband's exemption, which protected surviving spouse and minor child); *In re* Nguyen, 332 B.R. 393 (Bankr. W.D. Mo. 2005) (debtor could claim whole $15,000 exemption in her half interest in home owned in joint tenancy with non-debtor domestic partner); *In re* Lindstrom, 331 B.R. 267 (Bankr. E.D. Mich. 2005) (married couple may claim only one homestead exemption); *In re* Norton, 327 B.R. 193 (Bankr. D. Vt. 2005) (joint tenant, not married to co-tenant, who owned one-half interest in property could claim one-half of Vermont homestead amount); *In re* Taylor, 320 B.R. 214 (Bankr. N.D. Ga. 2005) (debtor who owned residence jointly with non-debtor husband limited to single $10,000 homestead exemption); *In re* Green, 319 B.R. 913 (Bankr. M.D. Ga. 2004) (when residence titled in name of one spouse, Georgia statute allows double homestead exemption of $20,000; marital separation of debtor and spouse not relevant); *In re* LaHaye, 2003 WL 22764771 (Bankr. N.D. Cal. Sept. 10, 2003) (debtor could claim entire exemption for her half-interest in property); *In re* Cunningham, 276 B.R. 314 (Bankr. D. Mass. 2002) (debtor may claim a homestead interest in all of a triple decker, occupied by her and her two sisters, in which she owns a two-thirds interest); *In re* Smith, 254 B.R. 751 (Bankr. W.D. Mo. 2000) (debtor who co-owned home with his sister could not claim entire statutory homestead exemption when sister had also filed bankruptcy and claimed the exemption); Kipp v. Sweno, 683 N.W.2d 259 (Minn. 2004) (married couple entitled to only one exemption, but individual debtor can claim entire exemption to protect his survivorship interest); *In re* Arnold, 73 P.3d 861 (Okla. 2003) (married couple may claim only one 160-acre rural homestead); *see also In re* Lezday, 373 B.R. 164 (Bankr. M.D. Fla. 2007) (judgment creditor can attach debtor's interest in jointly owned property, but fact question whether this debtor owned half interest or something else, when his name was placed on deed for estate planning purposes and other joint owner paid entire purchase price); Toma v. Toma, 163 P.3d 540 (Okla. 2007) (homestead exemption prevented creditor from foreclosing on lien on homestead owned by debtor and non-debtor in joint tenancy with right of survivorship; when debtor predeceased non-debtor, creditor lost lien); *cf.* Boe v. Dep't of Human Services, 844 A.2d 531 (N.J. Super. Ct. App. Div. 2004) (mother and son owned house in joint tenancy with right of survivorship; statutory lien for state hospital treatment that attached during her lifetime defeated son's right of survivorship), *appeal dismissed as moot*, 873 A.2d 500 (N.J. 2005) (statute adopted extinguishing liens against persons treated at psychiatric facility); Million v. Slayden, 2001 WL 1329288 (Tex. App. Oct. 30, 2001) (homestead exemption does not protect one joint owner from partition and sale sought by other joint owner).

316 *In re* Casserino, 379 F.3d 1069 (9th Cir. 2004) (Or. law) (occupancy, not legal title, is basis for homestead; Oregon exemption protects prepaid rent and security deposits for leased premises, because loss would likely result in eviction); *In re* Sacharko, 356 B.R. 786 (B.A.P. 1st Cir. 2007) (table) (text available at 2007 WL 128775) (no homestead exemption for forty percent interest in former marital home, now occupied by ex-wife and couple's minor daughter; Rhode Island homestead requires occupancy); *In re* Wilson, 341 B.R. 21 (B.A.P. 9th Cir. 2006) (Washington homestead generally requires occupancy, or failing that at least an equitable interest; denying exemption when husband was barred from house by court order prepetition, and declared homestead was filed after divorce decree had already divested husband of interest in the property); *In re* Kelley, 300 B.R. 11 (B.A.P. 9th Cir. 2003) (Cal. law) (automatic

who seeks to claim a homestead in a recently acquired or less than full-time home. Courts will consider the duration and the reason for the occupancy, the existence of another residence, and other indicia of residency such as the location of bank accounts, business, and voting or motor vehicle registration.[317] The analysis is similar but not identical to the

homestead requires intent to reside permanently; not shown when owner moved into apartment, visited home "occasionally" to repair damage, and rented it to cousin; declared homestead continued, because no new homestead established, but would not protect against forced sale); Feucht v. Pierce, 2006 WL 3354507 (D.S.D. Nov. 15, 2006) (no homestead exemption for wife who had moved out of home jointly owned with estranged husband; intent to return that is "merely possible" or contingent on other event, here husband's departure or couple's reconciliation, is insufficient); *In re* Schuster, 2006 WL 2711800 (D. Mont. Sept. 21, 2006) (residence required with some exceptions for temporary absence with intent to return; not shown here as debtor had not resided in condominium for ten years, but intended to return when his dog died); *In re* Majewski, 362 B.R. 67 (Bankr. D. Conn. 2007) (Connecticut defines homestead as "owner-occupied real property . . . used as a primary residence," but entire property need not be so used; debtor may exempt three-unit building when he lives in one unit and rents out the other two); *In re* Meltzer, 2007 WL 543922 (Bankr. S.D. Tex. Feb. 16, 2007) (property was homestead when debtor used address on bankruptcy forms, received homestead tax exemption, and family friend testified that debtor lived there); *In re* Letterman, 356 B.R. 540 (Bankr. D. Kan. 2006) (no homestead exemption in house lot or fire insurance proceeds; debtor neither occupied homestead on petition date, nor testified to intention to use proceeds to rebuild); *In re* Crooks, 351 B.R. 783 (Bankr. S.D. Fla. 2006) (debtors living in house they did not yet own on date of hurricane; insurance proceeds not proceeds of homestead because debtors did not own, and owner did not occupy house; but proceeds exempt because received by debtors in trust for owner and mortgage lender, to be used for repairs); *In re* Dougan, 350 B.R. 892 (Bankr. D. Idaho 2006) (mother's will, which was still in probate, left home to debtor daughter who resided there, with mother's permission, during mother's lifetime; possessory interest, plus equitable interest arising from will, were sufficient ownership and occupation to support homestead exemption); *In re* Greene, 346 B.R. 835 (Bankr. D. Nev. 2006) (if debtor actually owns and occupies land, "mode of occupation" is irrelevant; here debtor lived in travel trailer, and had signed contracts to improve land and build house); *In re* Fodor, 339 B.R. 519 (Bankr. M.D. Fla. 2006) (alien who had married citizen and applied for change of status, which was granted postpetition, could not lawfully intend to reside permanently on petition date, so not entitled to exemption); *In re* Ronk, 2006 WL 2385240 (Bankr. N.D. Tex. June 19, 2006) (Texas homestead exemption requires intent to occupy, and overt acts evidencing that intent; statement of intent not sufficient when debtors had done nothing to make property habitable); *In re* Reed, 331 B.R. 44 (Bankr. D. Conn. 2005) (property used as residence by debtor or debtor's dependent qualified for homestead exemption); *In re* Simmons, 308 B.R. 559 (Bankr. M.D. Ala. 2004) (husband could not exempt his half-interest in marital home, when couple were separated and husband lived in apartment); *In re* Hughes, 306 B.R. 683 (Bankr. M.D. Ala. 2004) (land used for parking and children's play was exempt even though debtors' dwelling was located on contiguous leased parcel); *In re* Brown, 299 B.R. 425 (Bankr. N.D. Tex. 2003) (vacation timeshare that debtors who resided on military base used for two weeks per year is not homestead under Florida law so is not exempt under federal bankruptcy exemptions); *In re* Walter, 230 B.R. 200 (Bankr. S.D. Fla. 1999) (Canadian citizens who did not have permanent visas could not claim Florida homestead, because they could not intend to permanently reside there); Phillips v. Phillips, 2004 WL 503905 (Conn. Super. Ct. Feb. 25, 2004) (must be actually occupied as principal residence; not shown when debtor owned and paid bills for house occupied by relatives, but ate and slept in another house he shared with wife and used that address on drivers license); Wilcox v. Marriot, 230 S.W.3d 266 (Tex. App. 2007) (possession and use of property by owner who resides there with family are sufficient to make it homestead "in law and in fact"); Gibson v. Fauber, 2004 WL 2002560 (Tex. App. Sept. 8, 2004) (debtor occupied home with mother, later with wife, lived elsewhere only when incarcerated or working at out of town jobs); Houghton v. Miller, 118 P.3d 293 (Utah Ct. App. 2005) (property not "primary personal residence" at time when judgment lien attached; debtor had filed homestead declaration and caused repairs to be begun, but was living elsewhere). *But see* *In re* Foster, 348 B.R. 58 (Bankr. E.D.N.C. 2006) (debtor could claim homestead in property rendered uninhabitable by hurricane damage in 1999 when he showed intent to return; he was living in camper, paying property taxes, storing personal belongings on property, and seeking financial help to finance repairs); *In re* Lindsey, 2006 WL 4112666 (Bankr. M.D. Fla. Dec. 13, 2006) (allowing homestead exemption for debtor who was entitled to exclusive possession of home acquired shortly before parties separated, even though she had not yet moved in); *cf.* *In re* Maloney, 311 B.R. 525 (Bankr. W.D. Mo. 2004) (moving back into abandoned homestead after petition filed and creditors' meeting held was too late to establish new homestead); Gonzalez v. Toews, 4 Cal. Rptr. 3d 434 (Ct. App. 2003) (judgment debtor who moves into property after it has been levied upon can not assert homestead exemption to defeat sale).

317 *In re* Robinson, 295 B.R. 147 (10th Cir. 2003) (must show "overt acts of preparation followed within a reasonable time by actual occupancy or good faith attempt to occupy"; debtor's visit with small overnight bag on eve of bankruptcy filing not sufficient when house owned by debtor's late father was unoccupied and deteriorating or occupied by unsatisfactory tenants); *In re* Cunningham, 354 B.R. 547 (D. Mass. 2006) (proceeds of homestead were exempt when debtors had filed homestead declaration and were residing there on petition date; debtors moved and sold homestead postpetition; bankruptcy law that determines exemptions as of petition date preempted Massachusetts law that would terminate homestead upon voluntary sale); Wechsler v. Carrington, 214 F. Supp. 2d 1348 (S.D. Fla. 2002) (Florida homestead requires actual occupation; when debtor had bought condominium, but was still living in hotel on date judgment was recorded, condominium not exempt; burden of proof on objector); *In re* Meltzer, 2007 WL 543922 (Bankr. S.D. Tex. Feb. 16, 2007) (property was homestead; debtor used address on bankruptcy forms, received homestead tax exemption, and family friend testified that debtor lived there); *In re* Siehler, 2006 WL 2034385 (Bankr. M.D. Fla. Apr. 27, 2006) (debtor could not claim homestead exemption in parent's house in which she owned one-third interest; intent to reside there permanently not shown when she had not changed driver's license and voter registration and admitted that she would return to marital home if she reconciled with husband); *In re* Wilson, 338 B.R. 315 (Bankr. W.D. Ky. 2006) (no homestead exemption in property not listed by debtors as their address for bankruptcy petition; offices of debtors' company located on property, and no evidence of permanent or continuous residence); *In re* Stone,

determination of residency for other legal purposes.[318] A homestead claim may also be possible in land where one plans to make a home, if substantial steps have been taken to prepare the land for occupancy.[319]

329 B.R. 860 (Bankr. N.D. Iowa 2005) (Iowa debtor could claim homestead in Wisconsin house being purchased on contract for deed when home occupied by fiancée and children and debtor intended to move to Wisconsin); *In re* Prestwood, 322 B.R. 463 (Bankr. S.D. Fla. 2005) (allowing Florida homestead exemption when debtor maintained extensive ties to California but sufficiently demonstrated intent to live in Florida); *In re* McGinnis, 306 B.R. 279 (Bankr. W.D. Mo. 2004) (physical presence in Kansas, part of the time in rental housing while finding and buying new house, was sufficient to support Kansas homestead, even though mail was being forwarded to debtors' Missouri attorney); *In re* McClamrock, 2004 WL 229521 (Bankr. M.D.N.C. Feb. 5, 2004) (residence was place where debtor ate, slept, received her mail, and used address on drivers license and bankruptcy petition; leaving former home to escape abusive husband not abandonment, but failure to return for years after he left showed that absence not temporary); *In re* MacLeod, 295 B.R. 1 (Bankr. D. Me. 2003) (mobile home park not park owner's homestead when occupied only one let and rented out the other nineteen); *In re* Page, 289 B.R. 484 (Bankr. S.D. Ga. 2003) (seller had no homestead exemption in property she was selling under contract for deed, when purchasers were living in house and making payments; seller's interest was security interest, which gave her no right to occupy property); *In re* Wipperling, 286 B.R. 106 (Bankr. N.D. Iowa 2002) (allowing debtor to claim homestead in newer mobile home he was living in "as best he could" during set up and renovation, that is, he had to fetch water from uninhabitable older home, because plumbing in new one not yet functional); *In re* Whitehead, 278 B.R. 597 (Bankr. M.D. Fla. 2002) (debtor who bought home in Florida and eventually found work there, but maintained various ties with former home in Indiana, including a temporary job, bank accounts, and physician, was entitled to Florida homestead exemption because evidence was equally balanced and party who challenged exemption bore burden of proof); *In re* Marsico, 278 B.R. 1 (Bankr. D.N.H. 2002) (couple who lived and operated seasonal businesses in New Hampshire, but lived in New Jersey during off-season, not entitled to New Hampshire homestead exemption; "vacation or seasonal" occupancy not sufficient); *In re* Roberts, 280 B.R. 450 (Bankr. D. Mass. 2001) (intent to occupy not shown when at time of filing debtor had left marital home); *In re* Moore, 269 B.R. 864 (Bankr. D. Idaho 2001) (debtor could not claim homestead in business property when she lived elsewhere); *In re* Sparfven, 265 B.R. 506 (Bankr. D. Mass. 2001) (denying Florida homestead exemption when debtor moved back and forth between Florida and Rhode Island); Konover Constr. Co. v. Silberstein, 2003 WL 21805576 (Conn. Super. Ct. July 22, 2003) (house was homestead, even though debtor spent about half of her nights at assisted living facility she owned; she had bought house with husband, used address for drivers license and voter registration, and been served with process there for this action); Kendall Builders, Inc. v. Chesson, 149 S.W.3d 796 (Tex. App. 2004) (allowing Texas homestead even though wife and children remained in California while Texas home being remodeled, when husband began working in Texas, both spouses registered to vote, obtained drivers licenses and opened checking account in Texas, shipped their car there and registered it, and donated to local charities, and contractor knew that family intended to live in house).

318 *In re* Marsico, 278 B.R. 1 (Bankr. D.N.H. 2002) (debtors established residency for purpose of bankruptcy filing, but not for homestead exemption).

319 *In re* Tofani, 365 B.R. 338 (Bankr. D. Mass. 2007) (debtor could claim homestead in home co-owned with ex-wife, who resided there with children; debtor paid for upkeep, spent significant time visiting his children there, and credibly testified that he intended to buy and live in house after child support obligations terminated); *In re* Kleb, 2007 WL 1760925 (Bankr. S.D. Tex. June 19, 2007) (debtor, who lived in temporary housing, could claim homestead in inherited land where he maintained vegetable garden, hunted for food, and had drawn up plans for house; overt acts of homestead use plus intent to reside sufficiently shown); *In re* Ronk, 2006 WL 2385240 (Bankr. N.D. Tex. June 19, 2006) (Texas homestead requires intent to occupy, and overt acts evidencing that intent; statement of intent not sufficient when debtors had done nothing to make property habitable); *In re* McGinnis, 306 B.R. 279 (Bankr. W.D. Mo. 2004) (physical presence in Kansas, part of the time in rental housing while finding and buying new house, was sufficient to support Kansas homestead, even though mail was being forwarded to debtors' Missouri attorney); *In re* Wipperling, 286 B.R. 106 (Bankr. N.D. Iowa 2002) (allowing debtor to claim homestead in newer mobile home he was living in "as best he could" during set up and renovation, that is, he had to fetch water from uninhabitable older home, because plumbing in new one not yet functional); *In re* Moore, 269 B.R. 864 (Bankr. D. Idaho 2001); Holland v. Alker, 2006 WL 1041785 (Tex. App. Apr. 20, 2006) (unpublished) (no homestead exemption for vacant land without evidence of actions to use, improve, or occupy); Kendall Builders, Inc. v. Chesson, 149 S.W.3d 796 (Tex. App. 2004) (allowing Texas homestead even though wife and children remained in California while Texas home being remodeled); *see also In re* Hodes, 287 B.R. 561 (D. Kan. 2002) (debtors could claim homestead in funds prepaid to builder who was constructing addition to home). *But see In re* Sacharko, 356 B.R. 786 (B.A.P. 1st Cir. 2007) (table) (text available at 2007 WL 128775) (Rhode Island homestead exemption requires occupancy; no homestead exemption for ex-husband's interest in former marital home that would not vest until child turned nineteen); Wechsler v. Carrington, 214 F. Supp. 2d 1348 (S.D. Fla. 2002) (Florida homestead requires actual occupation; when debtor had bought condominium, but was still living in hotel on date judgment was recorded, condominium not exempt); *In re* Bace, 364 B.R. 166 (Bankr. S.D.N.Y. 2007) (property on which debtor was building home not homestead because not "principal residence" when debtor was living in apartment and listed that address on bankruptcy papers); *In re* Gott, 2006 WL 2843008 (Bankr. W.D. La. Aug. 31, 2006) (no homestead exemption for vacant land; homestead lost when debtor stated intention to surrender mobile home to lender, even though she intended to put other home on site); *In re* Gandy, 327 B.R. 807 (Bankr. S.D. Tex. 2005) (federal homestead exemption requires actual occupancy; denying homestead when debtor had cleared land, arranged for utilities and bought a trailer, but not moved in); *In re* Estad, 295 B.R. 905 (Bankr. D. Minn. 2003) (exemption in newly built home only as of date family moved in; did not protect against lien that attached while house was under construction); *cf. In re* Brooks, 233 B.R. 696 (Bankr. N.D. Tex. 1999) (actual occupation or preparation to occupy are essential to Texas homestead; no exemption when debtor had "always intended" to build on parcel someday).

A homestead can be lost by abandonment, either by living elsewhere[320] or by using it for non-homestead pur-

320 *Abandonment shown*: *In re* Sacharko, 356 B.R. 786 (B.A.P. 1st Cir. 2007) (table) (text available at 2007 WL 128775) (Rhode Island homestead requires occupancy; no homestead exemption for ex-husband's interest in former marital home that would not vest until child turned nineteen); *In re* Kelley, 300 B.R. 11 (B.A.P. 9th Cir. 2003) (Cal. law) (automatic homestead requires intent to reside permanently; not shown when owner moved into apartment, visited home "occasionally" to repair damage, and rented it to cousin; declared homestead continued, because no new homestead established, but would not protect against forced sale); Feucht v. Pierce, 2006 WL 3354507 (D.S.D. Nov. 15, 2006) (no homestead exemption for wife who had moved out of home jointly owned with estranged husband; intent to return that is "merely possible" or contingent on other event, here husband's departure or couple's reconciliation, is insufficient); *In re* Schuster, 2006 WL 2711800 (D. Mont. Sept. 21, 2006) (residence required with some exceptions for temporary absence, with intent to return; not shown here when debtor had not resided in condominium for ten years, but intended to return when his dog died); Huggins v. Pierce, 2000 U.S. Dist. LEXIS 20615 (W.D. Tex. June 21, 2000) (debtor's deceased parents' home not his homestead when debtor employed abroad, intended to continue that employment, had resided in home only for brief visits, had placed home on market, agreed to split proceeds with siblings, and changed his mailing address); *In re* Naputi, 2007 WL 1864075 (Bankr. D. Idaho June 28, 2007) (six months absence without filing homestead declaration creates rebuttable presumption of abandonment; debtors left home to help sister care for terminally ill husband, but remained for over a year after his death; claim that hiring freeze prevented return to former jobs not sufficient to rebut presumption); *In re* Gaines, 2007 WL 1228157 (Bankr. M.D. Fla. Apr. 18, 2007) (homestead once established lost only by abandonment; intent to abandon shown here when debtor stayed away five years, failed to maintain property so mobile home was removed by city, and provided no support for assertion he left because of serious illness); *In re* Herding, 2007 WL 397276 (Bankr. D.S.D. Jan. 31, 2007) (debtor, originally excluded from home by family court order, showed intent not to return when he stopped making mortgage payments and, in settlement negotiations, offered house to wife); *In re* Letterman, 356 B.R. 540 (Bankr. D. Kan. 2006) (no homestead exemption in house lot or fire insurance proceeds; debtor neither occupied homestead on petition date, nor testified to intention to use proceeds to rebuild); *In re* Gott, 2006 WL 2843008 (Bankr. W.D. La. Aug. 31, 2006) (debtor lost homestead exemption in lot when she moved out of manufactured home located on it and indicated intent to surrender home to secured lender, even though she intended to put another home on site); *In re* Boward, 334 B.R. 350 (Bankr. D. Mass. 2005) (wife could not exempt her share of proceeds of marital home when she had moved out of state, found a job, and quitclaimed her share of house to husband); *In re* Maloney, 311 B.R. 525 (Bankr. W.D. Mo. 2004) (debtor moved out when she married, lived elsewhere for seventeen years; could not show intent to return, which must exist at time of leaving); *In re* Simmons, 308 B.R. 559 (Bankr. M.D. Ala. 2004) (husband living in apartment while divorce pending could not exempt his half-interest in marital home; Alabama homestead requires actual occupancy); *In re* McClamrock, 2004 WL 229521 (Bankr. M.D.N.C. Feb. 5, 2004) (leaving former home to escape abusive husband not abandonment, but failure to return for years after he left showed that absence not temporary); *In re* Pierce, 2003 WL 22860034 (Bankr. D. Vt. Dec. 1, 2003) (wife abandoned her interest in former marital home when, after husband entered nursing home, she returned to parents, bought house as joint tenant with them, used that address for drivers license and bankruptcy petition, and claimed it as homestead in bankruptcy case); *In re* Chase, 2003 WL 22454876 (Bankr. D.N.H. Oct. 14, 2003) (temporary and involuntary absence resulting from incarceration or restraining order not abandonment, but failure to return after restraining order ended showed establishment of new home); *In re* Hunter, 295 B.R. 882 (Bankr. W.D. Ark. July 29, 2003) (homestead abandoned when parcel containing house was sold, and remaining parcel used to raise livestock; debtor resided elsewhere and spent night on parcel only when attending foalings); *In re* Holman, 286 B.R. 882 (Bankr. D. Minn. 2002) (ex-wife, who moved out and obtained divorce prepetition lost any homestead right she might have had as result of husband's continued occupancy); *In re* Klaiber, 265 B.R. 290 (Bankr. M.D. Fla. 2001) (temporary absence for health, economic or family reasons not abandonment, but abandonment shown when debtor put house on market, took out-of-state job, and gave out-of-state address for tax and banking records); *In re* Weza, 248 B.R. 470 (Bankr. D.N.H. 2000) (debtor New Hampshire resident could not claim homestead in Massachusetts property owned in tenancy by entireties with his estranged wife); *In re* Burns, 218 B.R. 897 (Bankr. N.D. Ind. 1998) (actual residence, not legal domicile, determines availability of homestead exemption; ninety-eight-year-old debtor who resided with daughter because of his poor health could not claim homestead exemption in his former home); *In re* Cole, 205 B.R. 382 (Bankr. E.D. Tex. 1997) (homestead was abandoned when land was transferred from natural person to a "family limited partnership"); Parker v. Johnson, 368 Ark. 190 (Ark. 2006) (homestead abandoned when newly divorced couple sold marital home; husband's hope of repurchase not sufficient to negate abandonment); Phillips v. Phillips, 2004 WL 503905 (Conn. Super. Ct. Feb. 25, 2004) (debtor owned and paid bills for house occupied by son and other relatives, but ate and slept in another house he shared with wife and used that address on drivers license); Meadow Groves Mgt. v. McKnight, 689 So. 2d 315 (Fla. Dist. Ct. App. 1997) (homestead exemption in mobile home lost when owner evicted from rental lot); Stewart v. Bader, 907 A.2d 931 (N.H. 2006) (prison inmate serving life sentence without possibility of parole could not claim homestead; absence not temporary); Jones, Givens, Gotcher & Bogan, Prof'l Corp. v. Berger, 46 P.3d 698 (Okla. 2002) (once homestead established, it survives until owner relinquishes it; abandonment shown by leaving with intent not to return; may consider reasons for and duration of absence, whether home put on market or new home purchased; establishing another homestead is sufficient); Barrera v. State, 2005 WL 1691037 (Tex. App. July 21, 2005) (intent not to return shown by acquisition of new homestead); Lares v. Garza, 153 S.W.3d 97 (Tex. App. 2004) (owner who had formerly lived and worked on property was living in mother's house and renting property to a business).

Abandonment not shown: *In re* Tofani, 365 B.R. 338 (Bankr. D. Mass. 2007) (debtor could claim homestead in home co-owned with ex-wife, who resided there with children, when debtor paid for upkeep, visited his children there, and intended to buy and live in house after child support obligations terminated); *In re* Melito, 357 B.R. 684 (Bankr. D. Mass. 2007) (homestead statute requires a writing to terminate homestead; declining to consider whether abandonment also terminates it, as debtors here merely vacated home to accommodate prospective buyer whose financing then fell through); *In re* Caudill,

poses.[321] (Note, however, that one state, Texas, specifically

2007 WL 3171745 (Bankr. S.D. Tex. Oct. 25, 2007) (abandonment not shown when property was listed for sale but debtor resided there at all relevant times); United States v. Neff, 2007 WL 776532 (D.N.D. Mar. 12, 2007) (abandonment not shown when farmer moved to town to care for frail eighty-eight-year-old mother, leaving many belongings in farmhouse, which was neglected but needed only minor repairs); *In re* Ledzey, 2007 WL 295213 (Bankr. M.D. Fla. Jan. 30, 2007) (intent to discontinue homestead not shown when debtor lived on property, but a scrivener's error, corrected as soon as discovered, caused deed to be recorded transferring property); *In re* Foster, 348 B.R. 58 (Bankr. E.D.N.C. 2006) (debtor could claim homestead in property rendered uninhabitable by hurricane damage in 1999 when she was living in camper, paying property taxes and storing personal belongings on property, and seeking financial help from son to finance repairs; intent to return is key); *In re* Seeley, 341 B.R. 277 (Bankr. W.D. Mo. 2006) (presumption of abandonment rebutted when debtor intended, at time of removal, to return once health problems and children's problems with school system were resolved); *In re* Huddleston, 2005 WL 2271859 (Bankr. C.D. Ill. Sept. 7, 2005) (debtors who vacated two-story residence because of health problems able to claim homestead when they demonstrated good faith intent to sell home and to invest proceeds in one-story homestead within a reasonable period of time); Devine v. Devine, 2005 WL 1926038 (Bankr. N.D. Iowa Aug. 5, 2005) (farmers intending to return to farming could claim homestead in farmhouse even though living in rented apartment and working off-farm); *In re* Woodruff, 2005 WL 1139891 (Bankr. W.D. Mo. Apr. 28, 2005) (non-occupancy creates presumption of abandonment which may be rebutted by evidence that, at the time debtor vacated residence, he intended to return); *In re* Nguyen, 332 B.R. 393 (Bankr. W.D. Mo. 2005) (same); *In re* Baker, 307 B.R. 860 (Bankr. N.D. Tex. 2003) (intention to sell or even pending sale not abandonment); *In re* Marrama, 307 B.R. 332 (Bankr. D. Mass. 2004) (once homestead filed, creditor alleging abandonment must provide "unequivocal evidence"; not shown when owner was living in unheated summer cottage in Maine and leasing home to tenants; owner testified he intended to move back when lease expired), *aff'd on other grounds*, 316 B.R. 418 (B.A.P. 1st Cir. 2004); *In re* Murphy, 292 B.R. 403 (Bankr. D.N.D. 2003) (debtor rented home to tenants while attending graduate school out-of-state, but was on leave of absence and continued to receive medical benefits from North Dakota job, and paid taxes and insurance on house, in which she had left personal property); *In re* Patterson, 275 B.R. 578 (Bankr. D. Colo. 2002) (presumption of abandonment rebutted here when family fled from vandalism and stalking, left belongings in the house, did significant renovations, kept up mortgage payments, and returned when stalker left the area); *In re* Kimball, 270 B.R. 471 (Bankr. W.D. Ark. 2001) (once homestead established, it survives divorce; abandonment not shown when debtor lived in homestead on date of petition, even though she had listed house for sale as required by divorce decree); *In re* Owens, 269 B.R. 794 (Bankr. N.D. Ill. 2001) (debtor met burden of showing that prolonged absence was not abandonment when she left state to care for mother during long illness, but kept in touch with Illinois employer and hoped to resume her job upon return); *In re* Laing, 242 B.R. 538 (Bankr. S.D. Fla. 1999) (homestead may be lost by abandonment but no intent to abandon when debtor lived with girlfriend and rented out homestead, then returned to homestead); *In re* Anderson, 240 B.R. 254 (Bankr. W.D. Tex. 1999) (abandonment not shown under federal bankruptcy exemption when debtor in army rented out house, but listed it as her home in military records, and intended to return there); *In re* Sebio, 237 B.R. 1 (Bankr. D. Mass. 1999) (summer home was exempt when owner filed homestead declaration for it and subsequently moved there for year-round occupancy); *In re* Harrison, 236 B.R. 788 (Bankr. M.D. Fla. 1999) (homestead not abandoned when debtor co-owner was living elsewhere because of divorce but house was on market and debtor intended to invest her share of proceeds in new homestead); *In re* Lazin, 221 B.R. 982 (Bankr. M.D. Fla. 1998) (payment of year's rent on Pennsylvania apartment did not defeat claim of homestead in Florida condominium when debtor was living in condominium and had moved to Florida for health reasons); *In re* Simpson, 206 B.R. 230 (Bankr. E.D. Okla. 1997) (Oklahoma property was exempt homestead even though owner worked in Texas during the work week and when required to work weekends, because owner had lived on property for a year, intended to retire there, and had never rented the property or turned off the utilities); LPP Mortgage, Ltd. v. Meurer, 2004 WL 57585 (Iowa Ct. App. Jan. 14, 2004) (intent to return shown when debtor lost job and worked out-of-state after divorce, but home was occupied by relatives, debtor visited most weekends, and he testified that employer planned to open facility in Iowa); Lamkin v. Flanagan, 865 So. 2d 916 (La. Ct. App. 2004) (paying taxes and making repairs sufficient to maintain homestead exemption when debtor testified he intended to return to home, even though because of health problems he spent only two or three nights there over seven years); Farstveet v. Rudolph, 630 N.W.2d 24 (N.D. 2000) (no abandonment when debtor went into hospital and nursing home, even though relatives lived in home and sold belongings to pay medical bills); Meadow Wind Health Care Ctr. v. McInnes, 2000 Ohio App. LEXIS 3415 (Ohio Ct. App. July 24, 2000) (question of fact whether homestead abandoned during nursing home stay, when debtor used nursing home address for mail and voting, but eventually returned home); Holden v. Cribb, 561 S.E.2d 634 (S.C. Ct. App. 2002) (homestead not abandoned when home owner in jail because no intent to make jail his permanent home); Pierce v. Wash. Mut. Bank, 226 S.W.3d 711 (Tex. App. 2007) (if new homestead not established, abandonment is fact question; must show voluntary departure and manifestation of intent not to return); Gibson v. Fauber, 2004 WL 2002560 (Tex. App. Sept. 8, 2004) (debtor lived elsewhere only when incarcerated or working at out-of-town jobs); Wilcox v. Marriott, 103 S.W.3d 469 (Tex. App. 2003) (factual question of owner's intent to use property as homestead precludes summary judgment); Estate of Montague v. Nat'l Loan Investors, Ltd. P'ship, 70 S.W.3d 242 (Tex. App. 2001) (debtors did not abandon homestead despite their declaration that it was not homestead when they continued to live there and never left it without returning); *In re* Estate of Casida, 13 S.W.3d 519 (Tex. App. 2000) (abandonment not shown when home owner traveled a lot, but returned several times a year, and did not remove furnishings from home or acquire other real estate).

321 *Exemption lost*: *In re* Holt, 357 B.R. 917 (Bankr. M.D. Ga. 2006) (no homestead exemption in contiguous lot with house occupied by unrelated tenants; house was not residence of debtor or dependent); *In re* Radtke, 344 B.R. 690 (Bankr. S.D. Fla. 2006) (when debtor's home and rental recreational vehicle sites were both located on same parcel, and parcel could not be divided, it had to be sold and proceeds allocated between homestead and bankruptcy estate); *In re* MacLeod, 295 B.R. 1 (Bankr. D. Me. 2003) (mobile home park owned by debtor not homestead when nineteen lots were rented out and twentieth occupied by owner); *In re* Carpenter, 278 B.R. 102 (Bankr. N.D.

exempts a "business homestead," that is, property used for both residential and business purposes.)[322] Moving out and putting a homestead on the market is probative on the issue of abandonment, but problems arise when a debtor who must relocate or seek a less expensive home must move out before a sale is completed; some courts have held that it is the acquisition of a new homestead, not moving out of the old, that terminates the homestead.[323] Most courts hold that

Miss. 2001) (noncontiguous parcel used mainly for commercial purposes not homestead, even though debtor sometimes kept a few cows there); *In re* Pich, 253 B.R. 562 (Bankr. D. Idaho 2000) (application for light industrial zoning, which barred residential use, estopped debtor from claiming homestead, although he was living in office at site); *In re* Bell, 252 B.R. 562 (Bankr. M.D. Fla. 2000) (homestead exemption did not protect commercial building on same parcel of land as residence; if land could not be subdivided, it must be sold, and the proceeds apportioned); *In re* Tsoupas, 250 B.R. 466 (Bankr. D.N.H. 2000) (debtors who resided in four-unit apartment building, in which husband owned a half interest, could claim homestead only in the part they occupied, as measured by percentage of floor space); *In re* Sears, 246 B.R. 881 (Bankr. S.D. Iowa 2000) (debtors may claim as homestead their house, and one garage of small value, but not buildings used for salvage and repair business), *aff'd*, 246 B.R. 341 (B.A.P. 8th Cir. 2000); *In re* Kang, 243 B.R. 666 (Bankr. N.D. Tex. 1999) (shopkeeper who owned strip mall could claim business homestead in his shop and adjacent parking, but not rest of mall); *In re* Welty, 217 B.R. 907 (Bankr. D. Wyo. 1998) (Wyoming homestead exemption did not protect lots where debtor did not reside and which debtor owned individually, while contiguous lot with residence was owned jointly with spouse); *In re* Pietrunti, 207 B.R. 18 (Bankr. M.D. Fla. 1997) (when debtors subdivided their property into four lots and rented out homes on three of them, Florida homestead exemption protected only the fourth lot occupied by debtors' home); Lares v. Garza, 153 S.W.3d 97 (Tex. App. 2004) (owner who had formerly lived and worked on property was living in mother's house and renting the property to a business).

Property exempt: *In re* Kwiecinski, 245 B.R. 672 (B.A.P. 10th Cir. 2000) (Wyoming homestead exemption protected both of two contiguous parcels, one of which included owner's farmhouse, when owner used both parcels); *In re* Majewski, 362 B.R. 67 (Bankr. D. Conn. 2007) (Connecticut defines homestead as "owner-occupied real property . . . used as a primary residence"; entire property need not be so used; debtor may exempt three-unit building when he lives in one unit and rents out other two); *In re* Irene, 359 B.R. 435 (Bankr. W.D.N.Y. 2007) (deeded parking space exempt although debtor with home law office allowed occasional use by clients; incidental business use does not eliminate homestead); *In re* McBratney, 2007 WL 2684072 (Bankr. D. Kan. Sept. 7, 2007) (use of part of tract to provide income for family does not eliminate homestead; debtor who depended on tenants' rent to pay mortgage could exempt whole owner-occupied four-unit building); *In re* Ensenat, 2007 WL 2029332 (Bankr. S.D. Fla. May 24, 2007) (partially detached unit, occupied by family members, was exempt, even though it might, in future, be rented to strangers); *In re* Springman, 328 B.R. 251 (Bankr. D.D.C. 2005) (renting out two bedrooms of single-family home and "incidental" business use does not destroy homestead); *In re* Sadler, 327 B.R. 654 (Bankr. N.D. Iowa 2005) (farm buildings, here a machine shed, may be exempted as "appurtenant to" the homestead); *In re* McCambry, 327 B.R. 469 (Bankr. D. Kan. 2005) (renting portion of homestead constituted only incidental business use which did not affect debtors' homestead claim); *In re* Myers, 323 B.R. 11 (Bankr. D.N.H. 2005) (debtor entitled to homestead protection in both units of duplex when second unit occupied by dependent elderly mother and not used for production of income); *In re* Shell, 295 B.R. 129 (Bankr. D. Alaska 2003) (allowing debtor to exempt entire owner-occupied six-unit building; rental income also exempt under Alaska Stat. § 9.38.030(b)); *In re* Carey, 282 B.R. 118 (Bankr. D. Mass. 2002) (Massachusetts homestead exemption covers entire property, including home business, storage space and rental property, subject only to dollar limitation; debtors could exempt entire owner-occupied triple decker; court notes that the rent used to pay mortgage is "as necessary as the furnace"); *In re* Brizida, 276 B.R. 316 (Bankr. D. Mass. 2002) (homestead exemption in entire triple decker, when debtors occupied one floor and rented other two to tenants); *In re* Lowery, 262 B.R. 875 (Bankr. M.D. Fla. 2001) (use of part of qualified homestead for commercial purposes does not destroy homestead status; debtors could exempt home and citrus farm); *In re* Haning, 252 B.R. 799 (Bankr. M.D. Fla. 2000) (Florida homestead exemption protected garage, located on same parcel as residence, which owner used for a used car business, but would be lost if owner rented out part of property to another for business purposes); *In re* Trigonis, 224 B.R. 152 (Bankr. D. Nev. 1998) (allowing Nevada homestead exemption on four-unit building, when owner resided in one unit and rented out the other three); *In re* Ruggles, 210 B.R. 57 (Bankr. D. Vt. 1997) (debtor could exempt duplex as homestead when she resided in one-half and rented the other); Davis v. Davis, 864 So. 2d 458 (Fla. Dist. Ct. App. 2003) (rural homestead may include non-agricultural income-producing property, here a mobile home park); *see also* Siewak v. AmSouth Bank, 2007 WL 141186 (M.D. Fla. Jan. 16, 2007) (question of fact whether business use eliminated homestead exemption); *In re* Klaus, 228 B.R. 475 (Bankr. N.D. Okla. 1999) (one-quarter of property was commercial, so $5000 exemption for mixed residential and commercial property applied).

322 *See In re* Jay, 432 F.3d 323 (5th Cir. 2005) (property where debtors worked but did not reside was not homestead).

Prior to a statutory amendment in 2000, the Texas "business homestead" was applicable to property used for an occupation to support the household without regard to residential use. *See, e.g.*, *In re* John Taylor Co., 935 F.2d 75 (5th Cir. 1991) (property used for manufacturing and selling of bedding supplies exempt).

323 Parks v. Buckeye Retirement Co., L.L.C., 2006 WL 1662945 (S.D. Tex. June 9, 2006) (old homestead not lost, even if put on market, until new one established; here, debtors testified that if they could not get financing to build on subject parcel they would sell it and use proceeds for new homestead); *In re* Younger, 373 B.R. 111 (Bankr. D. Idaho 2007) (property not shown to be abandoned before sale when debtor spent some nights on property, and removed his belongings only when purchaser gave him one week to do so); *In re* Melito, 357 B.R. 684 (Bankr. D. Mass. 2007) (debtors who were living in apartment could claim homestead exemption in home vacated to accommodate prospective buyer whose financing then fell through); *In re* Seeley, 341 B.R. 277 (Bankr. W.D. Mo. 2006) (presumption of abandonment rebutted when property put on market but debtor planned to use proceeds to acquire nearby homestead); *In re* Huddleston, 2005 WL 2271859 (Bankr. C.D. Ill. Sept. 7, 2005) (debtors who vacated two-story residence because of health problems and put home on the market able to claim homestead when they demonstrated good faith intent to sell home and invest proceeds in one-story homestead within a

a spouse who flees domestic conflict or is excluded by a restraining order does not abandon the homestead.[324]

reasonable period of time); *In re* White, 293 B.R. 1 (Bankr. N.D. Iowa 2003) (once established, homestead exemption may be transferred from one residence to another; no abandonment when debtors lived for short time in an apartment due to "timing problems" with sale of one house and purchase of next); *In re* Wagenbach, 232 B.R. 112 (Bankr. C.D. Ill. 1999) (proceeds exempt even though debtors moved out of home before closing, when they continued to maintain old home and intended to use proceeds to buy new home); McMillan v. Aru, 773 So. 2d 355 (Miss. Ct. App. 2000) (sheriff's sale permanently enjoined when sellers had moved out and judgment creditor attached after closing but before deed recorded; homestead exemption survived until deed executed, after which sellers had no interest left); Barrera v. State, 2005 WL 1691037 (Tex. App. July 21, 2005) (intent not to return shown by acquisition of new homestead; strong showing of abandonment when furniture moved to new house, new address used for business, taxes, mail, and drivers license); Kendall Builders, Inc. v. Chesson, 149 S.W.3d 796 (Tex. App. 2004) (new home in Texas was homestead within meaning of mechanics lien law when husband began working in Texas, and both spouses registered to vote, obtained drivers licenses, opened checking account, and registered car there, even though wife and children remained in California during remodeling); Cadle Co. v. Harvey, 46 S.W.3d 282 (Tex. App. 2001) (complicated series of transactions, including leasing home to another for two years, ending up with lease with option to buy, did not create gap in homestead exemption); *see also In re* Presto, 376 B.R. 554 (Bankr. S.D. Tex. 2007) (exemption for homestead proceeds ends with purchase of new homestead; leftover funds not exempt).

324 *In re* Dubravsky, 374 B.R. 467 (Bankr. D.N.H. 2007) (leaving home when required by divorce decree not abandonment; home here to be sold at later date and proceeds divided); *In re* Tofani, 365 B.R. 338 (Bankr. D. Mass. 2007) (debtor could claim homestead in home co-owned with ex-wife, who resided there with children; intent to occupy sufficiently shown when debtor paid for upkeep, spent significant time visiting his children there, and testified that he intended to buy and live in house after child support obligations terminated); *In re* Lindsey, 2006 WL 4112666 (Bankr. M.D. Fla. Dec. 13, 2006) (allowing homestead exemption; debtor not residing on premises because she feared for safety of self and children while ex-husband lived nearby); *In re* Gott, 2006 WL 2843008 (Bankr. W.D. La. Aug. 31, 2006) (homestead exemption not lost when debtor fled abusive husband, who continued to harass her after leaving home; but lost when debtor surrendered mobile home, leaving land vacant); *In re* MacFarlane, 325 B.R. 908 (Bankr. M.D. Fla. 2005) (intent to abandon not shown when domestic violence order barred debtor from home); *In re* Ballato, 318 B.R. 205 (Bankr. M.D. Fla. 2004) (ex-husband excluded by restraining order could claim homestead exemption in his share of sale proceeds of former marital home); *In re* McClamrock, 2004 WL 229521 (Bankr. M.D.N.C. Feb. 5, 2004) (leaving former home to escape abusive husband not abandonment, but failure to return for years after he left showed that absence not temporary); *In re* Chase, 2003 WL 22454876 (Bankr. D.N.H. Oct. 14, 2003) (temporary and involuntary absence resulting from incarceration or restraining order not abandonment, but failure to return after restraining order ended showed establishment of new home); *In re* Detko, 290 B.R. 494 (Bankr. D. Vt. 2003) (living in Florida for six months, opening bank account and obtaining driver's license there, and putting house on market not abandonment when debtor was fleeing violent alcoholic ex-husband); *In re* Taylor, 280 B.R. 294 (Bankr. D. Mass. 2002) (debtor wife who left home because of marital problems could claim homestead); *In re* Webber, 278 B.R. 294 (Bankr. D. Mass. 2002) (debtor husband excluded by restraining order; continued occupation by wife and children sufficient to maintain homestead); Phillips v. Fuller, 814 So. 2d 885 (Ala. Civ. App. 2001) (homestead not abandoned by wife who fled abusive husband); Coy v. Mango Bay Prop. & Investments, Inc., 963 So. 2d 873 (Fla. Dist. Ct. App. 2007) (homestead, once acquired, not lost by court order awarding possession to other spouse; ex-husband entitled to hearing on claim of homestead in former marital home, titled in wife alone); Chrissikos v. Chrissikos, 2002 WL 342653 (Tex. App. Mar. 6, 2002) (wife moved out during divorce); *see also In re* Herding, 2007 WL 397276 (Bankr. D.S.D. Jan. 31, 2007) (debtor, originally excluded from home by family court order, showed intent not to return when he stopped making mortgage payments and, in settlement negotiations, offered house to wife). *But see In re* Wilson, 341 B.R. 21 (B.A.P. 9th Cir. 2006) (Wash. law) (no automatic homestead when court order had barred husband from occupancy; declared homestead came too late when it was filed after divorce decree had divested husband of interest in property); *In re* Holman, 286 B.R. 882 (Bankr. D. Minn. 2002) (ex-wife had abandoned homestead when she moved out nineteen months prepetition, and divorce was final four months prepetition; when marriage dissolved, wife lost any homestead right she might have had as result of husband's continued occupancy); Parker v. Johnson, 368 Ark. 190 (Ark. 2006) (homestead abandoned when newly divorced couple sold marital home; husband, who left house when wife filed for divorce, had kept key and maintained premises, but his hope of repurchase not sufficient to negate abandonment).

12.5.2.6 Homestead Exemption Limits in Bankruptcy

The extreme variation in state homestead amounts, and the existence of states with high or unlimited homestead exemptions and narrow fraud exceptions,[325] led to concern about the use of homestead exemptions to shelter unreasonable amounts from creditors. The 2005 amendments to the Bankruptcy Code limit debtors from taking full advantage of state homestead exemptions.[326] Section 522(o) of the Code limits a debtor's state homestead exemption when the debtor converted nonexempt property into exempt homestead property within ten years before the filing of the petition with the intent to hinder, delay, or defraud a creditor.[327]

325 *See, e.g.*, Havaco of Am. v. Hill, 790 So. 2d 1018 (Fla. 2001).

326 *See* National Consumer Law Center, Consumer Bankruptcy Law and Practice § 10.2.3.4 (8th ed. 2006 and Supp.).

327 *See In re* Presto, 376 B.R. 554 (Bankr. S.D. Tex. 2007) (when funds leftover from homestead purchase spent on improvements with actual intent to hinder creditors, $125,000 cap applied); *In re* Anderson, 374 B.R. 848 (Bankr. D. Kan. Oct. 2, 2007) (use of nonexempt funds to pay down mortgage on homestead within ten years before bankruptcy could be covered by section 522(o), but trustee must show intent to hinder or defraud); *In re* Maronde, 332 B.R. 593 (Bankr. D. Minn. 2005) (homestead exemption limited when debtor paid down home equity line with proceeds of nonexempt property on eve of bankruptcy). *But cf. In re* Hinton, 378 B.R. 371 (Bankr. M.D. Fla. 2007) (cap does not apply to property owned in tenancy by entirety).

In addition, two new provisions cap state homestead exemptions at $125,000. Section 522(p) of the Code applies to homestead property acquired during the 1215-day period before filing a petition for bankruptcy.[328] However the monetary cap does not apply to any interest transferred from a debtor's previous principal residence to the debtor's current principal residence if both are in the same state.[329] Section 522(q) of the Code limits a debtor's homestead exemption if the debtor has been convicted of felonies or owes debts arising from certain unlawful conduct.[330]

Another issue created by the 2005 amendments to the Bankruptcy Code is the extraterritorial effect of state exemption laws. Section 522(b)(3)(A), enacted to close the "mansion loophole"—that is, to prevent wealthy debtors from immunizing their entire fortune by moving to a state with an unlimited homestead exemption and a narrow fraud exception and buying a mansion there with all funds available to them—has created serious problems for ordinary debtors who happen to have moved within 180 days before bankruptcy. They are required to apply the exemption law—not the exemption amounts—of the state where they resided for the 735 days preceding the 180 days before they filed for bankruptcy. If these requirements make the debtor ineligible to take advantage of any state's exemptions, the debtor may use the federal exemptions.[331] At least one court, however, has held that debtors who are allowed to claim the state exemptions—even if this results in a zero exemption for their property in the new state—are barred from using the federal exemptions.[332] Note that this provision applies only to ordinary state exemptions, not the exemption for property owned in tenancy by entireties.[333]

12.5.2.7 Special Rules for Certain Types of Debts

Some states forbid execution on a primary dwelling for health care debts during the lifetime of the debtor, the debtor's spouse, or certain dependents; instead, a lien is created which may be enforced if the property is sold.[334]

---

328 *In re* Khan, 375 B.R. 5 (B.A.P. 1st Cir. 2007) (homestead was "acquired" when home was transferred from trust of which debtor and brother were both trustees and beneficiaries to same brothers as joint tenants; decision here turned on specific provisions of the trust); *In re* Rogers, 354 B.R. 792 (N.D. Tex. 2006) (debtor entitled to full Texas homestead in property she inherited outside the lookback period, even though first occupied as homestead during that time); *In re* Anderson, 374 B.R. 848 (Bankr. D. Kan. 2007) (debtor who paid down mortgage on home he had owned for many years did not "acquire" a homestead within meaning of section 522(p)); *In re* Limperis, 370 B.R. 859 (Bankr. S.D. Fla. 2007) (married couple, subject to $125,000 cap for homestead acquired within 1215 days, could claim an exemption apiece and stack them for total exemption of $250,000); *In re* Lyons, 355 B.R. 387 (Bankr. D. Mass. 2006) (homestead exemption was neither capped nor barred by bankruptcy amendments; filing homestead declaration in 2004, just before attachment was recorded, was not acquisition or transfer of any interest in property, when debtor had owned and lived in house since 1977); *In re* Zecher, 2006 WL 3519316 (Bankr. D. Mass. Dec. 6, 2006) (applying cap to property which, in course of refinancing, had been transferred back and forth between debtor, as individual, and limited liability partnership of which he was sole partner); *In re* Virissimo, 332 B.R. 201 (Bankr. D. Nev. 2005); *In re* Kaplan, 331 B.R. 483 (Bankr. S.D. Fla. 2005). *But see In re* Buonopane, 359 B.R. 346 (Bankr. M.D. Fla. 2007) (cap for homesteads acquired within 1215 days of bankruptcy does not apply to property owned in tenancy by entireties); *In re* Mcnabb, 326 B.R. 785 (Bankr. D. Ariz. 2005).

329 11 U.S.C. § 522(p)(2)(b); *see In re* Wayrynen, 332 B.R. 479 (Bankr. S.D. Fla. 2005) (debtor entitled to full homestead exemption even though debtors purchased properties within forty-month period when funds came from proceeds of first homestead bought prior to forty-month period, plus appreciation due to increased property values). *But see In re* Leung, 356 B.R. 317 (Bankr. D. Mass. 2006) (exception for interest transferred from "previous permanent residence" in same state not applicable when property transferred from tenancy by entireties to wife alone and back to tenancy by entireties, with last transfer occurring during lookback period); *In re* Buonopane, 344 B.R. 675 (Bankr. M.D. Fla. 2006) (no "same-state transfer" exception, when debtor moved into first of two Florida homes during lookback period).

330 *In re* Lawson, 340 B.R. 444 (Bankr. D. Mass. 2006) (provision capping homestead for debts arising from criminal act does not require conviction; debtor's admission of facts in state court criminal proceeding is sufficient).

331 *In re* Nickerson, 375 B.R. 869 (Bankr. W.D. Mo. 2007) (Kansas exemptions have no extraterritorial effect; Missouri debtors required to use Kansas exemption law may claim federal exemptions); *In re* Adams, 375 B.R. 532 (Bankr. W.D. Mo. 2007) (Florida exemptions have no extraterritorial effect; when bankruptcy choice of law rules required Missouri debtors to use Florida exemption law, debtors could claim federal exemptions because no state exemptions available); *In re* Tate, 2007 WL 81835 (Bankr. D. Or. Jan. 8, 2007) (Texas homestead law has no extraterritorial effect; when use of Texas law resulted in no exemption for Oregon home, debtor could use federal exemptions).

332 *In re* Katseanes, 2007 WL 2962637 (Bankr. D. Idaho Oct. 9, 2007) (Utah exemptions have no extraterritorial effect; when Utah exemptions "available," even though they result in no exemption for Idaho home, debtor could not use federal exemptions).

333 *In re* Schwarz, 362 B.R. 532 (Bankr. S.D. Fla. 2007) (debtor barred from using Florida homestead exemption could exempt tenancy by entireties property).

334 *See, e.g.*, Nev. Rev. Stat. § 21.095 (protecting debtor, spouse, joint tenant who was a joint tenant at the time judgment was entered, dependent disabled adult child, or minor child during minority); Ohio Rev. Code Ann. §§ 2329.66(A)(1)(a), 2329.661 (West) (protecting debtor, surviving spouse, or minor child); *see also* Edwards v. McCormack, 136 F. Supp. 2d 795 (S.D. Ohio 2001) (lawyer-collector violated Fair Debt Collection Practices Act and Ohio Consumer Sales Practices Act by threatening health-care debtors with foreclosure on real property, because foreclosure forbidden by Ohio statute); *In re* Estate of Borg, 2007 WL 2034285 (Minn. Ct. App. July 17, 2007) (unpublished) (estate recovery of Medicaid benefits; when home occupied by daughter who cared for mother for several years before mother's last hospitalization, lien may be imposed, but not foreclosed upon, while daughter resides there); Wickliffe

Frequently debts for child support or alimony may be enforced against the homestead, and the sale of a home may be ordered as part of the property division during a divorce.[335] Nonetheless, some courts hold that proceeds of a homestead sale may not be used to satisfy unsecured a debt for attorney fees that arises from divorce or some other family law matter.[336]

Most state homestead exemptions do not protect against criminal law forfeitures.[337] An Illinois statute which was

Country Place v. Kovacs, 765 N.E.2d 975 (Ohio Ct. App. 2001) (remanding for factual development to determine whether nursing home provided health care services); Meadow Wind Healthcare Ctr. v. McInnes, 2000 Ohio App. LEXIS 3415 (Ohio Ct. App. July 24, 2000) (question of fact whether services of nursing home were "health care services or supplies"; if debtor shows that home provided any health care service or supply, statute will apply). *But see In re* Collet, 351 B.R. 395 (Bankr. W.D. La. 2006) (Louisiana's enhanced homestead exemption for debts "arising directly" from "catastrophic or terminal illness or injury" did not apply when part of borrowed money used for family living expenses while debtor recovered from surgery).

335 *In re* Jarski, 301 B.R. 342 (Bankr. D. Ariz. 2003) (attorney fees in child support matters were child support; lien could attach to homestead); Wallace v. Wallace, 922 So. 2d 1008 (Fla. Dist. Ct. App. 2006) (lien may be placed on homestead to secure ex-wife's "special equity" granted to compensate for funds she spent on renovation); Dep't of Revenue *ex rel.* Greene v. Bush, 838 So. 2d 653 (Fla. Dist. Ct. App. 2003) (homestead exemption does not protect against claim for child support); Hieke v. Hieke, 782 So. 2d 443 (Fla. Dist. Ct. App. 2001) (homestead exemption did not protect against ex-wife's equitable lien on home, because it was an ownership interest); Brose v. Brose, 750 So. 2d 717 (Fla. Dist. Ct. App. 2000) (homestead could be sold for alimony obligation, when it was purchased with proceeds of financial manipulations intended to put assets beyond reach of ex-wife); Kautzman v. Kautzman, 618 N.W.2d 500 (N.D. 2000) (homestead could be sold to foreclose equitable lien awarded to ex-wife in response to husband's wrongful financial manipulations); *In re* Marriage of Maresh, 78 P.3d 157 (Or. Ct. App. 2003) (homestead exemption did not bar sheriff's sale to foreclose lien imposed by divorce decree; statute not specific, but power of court to achieve fair division of property would be undermined if spouse with lien could not enforce it against house); Pearson v. Pearson, 169 Vt. 28, 726 A.2d 71 (1999) (homestead statute, which is intended to protect family home against creditors, does not prevent family court encumbrance to give effect to property division in divorce judgment); *In re* Marriage of Foley, 930 P.2d 929 (Wash. Ct. App. 1997) (homestead exemption did not apply when court ordered sale or refinancing of former marital home, to enable husband, who received home, to pay wife her share of community property); *see also In re* Bingham, 344 B.R. 648 (Bankr. W.D. Okla. 2006) (attorney's lien may attach to otherwise exempt property, including homestead, divided up in divorce). *But see* Cannon v. Cannon, 254 B.R. 773 (S.D. Fla. 2000) (lien created by divorce judgment can not attach to homestead property; homestead exemption arises from state constitution, and support obligation not listed among exceptions); Dyer v. Beverly & Tittle, Prof'l Ass'n, 777 So. 2d 1055 (Fla. Dist. Ct. App. 2001) (ex-wife's attorney fees were connected to support obligation so as to create equitable lien on homestead, but homestead exemption barred forced sale when no showing of fraudulent or egregious conduct by husband); Smith v. Smith, 761 So. 2d 370 (Fla. Dist. Ct. App. 2000) (no forced sale of homestead when homestead not purchased with proceeds of fraud nor as part of financial juggling to avoid support obligation, even though wife's equitable lien was awarded to compensate for physical injuries inflicted by abusive husband); Anderson v. Veblen Premium Pork, Inc., 2000 Minn. App. LEXIS 891 (Minn. Ct. App. Aug. 22, 2000) (creditor could not foreclose on husband's homestead based on ex-wife's assignment of lien created by divorce court to secure husband's obligations to her, as this would be attempt by creditor to evade the exemption); *cf. In re* Tendal, 323 B.R. 254 (Bankr. N.D. Iowa 2005) (court ordered wife to hold husband harmless for certain credit card debts; no lien on homestead; court had power to impose lien, but no indication that it did so). *See generally* Jane Massey Draper, Annotation, *Enforcement of a Claim for Alimony or Support, or for Attorney's Fees or Costs in Connection Therewith, Against Exemptions*, 52 A.L.R.5th 221 (1997).

336 Harleaux v. Harleaux, 154 S.W.3d 925 (Tex. App. 2005) (court may not order attorney fees, arising from dispute over sale of marital home, paid from proceeds of homestead); *In re* Marriage of Banks, 887 S.W.2d 160 (Tex. App. 1994) (ordering payment of unsecured creditors—including attorney fees—from proceeds of homestead would "circumvent the constitutional and statutory provisions" that protect the homestead from general creditors); *see also* Johnson v. Johnson, 2005 WL 3440773 (Tex. App. Dec. 16, 2005) (attorney fees were not child support therefore lien on homestead not permitted). *But see In re* Bingham, 344 B.R. 648 (Bankr. W.D. Okla. 2006) (attorney's lien may attach to otherwise exempt property, including homestead, divided up in divorce); *In re* Jarski, 301 B.R. 342 (Bankr. D. Ariz. 2003) (attorney fees in child support matters were child support; lien could attach to homestead); Sell v. Sell, 949 So. 2d 1108 (Fla. Dist. Ct. App. 2007) (ex-husband's share of homestead proceeds could be reached for wife's attorney fees; husband's egregious evasion of court orders resulted in jailing for contempt).

337 United States v. One Parcel of Real Prop. Known As 16614 Cayuga Rd., 2003 WL 21437207 (10th Cir. June 23, 2003) (Oklahoma homestead exemption does not bar federal forfeiture of homestead used as marijuana farm); United States v. Lampien, 89 F.3d 1316 (7th Cir. 1996) (Wisconsin homestead exemption did not protect against federal government lien pursuant to restitution provisions of Victim Witness Protection Act (VWPA); even if exemption applies to debt arising from criminal conduct, it would be preempted by VWPA); United States v. One Single Family Residence at 2200 S.W. 28th Ave., Ft. Lauderdale, Fla., 204 F. Supp. 2d 1361 (S.D. Fla. 2002) (federal forfeiture law preempts state homestead exemptions); *In re* Brewer, 209 B.R. 575 (Bankr. S.D. Fla. 1996) (federal drug forfeiture law preempts state homestead exemption); *In re* Smith, 176 B.R. 221 (Bankr. N.D. Ala. 1995) (homestead exemption does not apply in state drug forfeiture proceeding); Lot 39, Sec. C, N. Hills Subdivision v. State, 85 S.W.3d 429 (Tex. App. 2002) (Texas constitutional homestead exemption does not protect against criminal law forfeiture); Tellevik v. Real Prop. in Pierce County, 921 P.2d 1088 (Wash. Ct. App. 1996) (Washington's homestead exemption does not protect against drug forfeiture); *see also In re* Hutchins, 306 B.R. 82 (Bankr. D. Vt. 2004) (lien for husband's federal criminal fines encumbered his interest in real property even though it would have been protected by state entireties doctrine). *But see* Mathieu v. City of Lauderdale Lakes, 961 So. 2d 363 (Fla. Dist. Ct. App. 2007) (liens for municipal code violations may not be foreclosed against homestead property); Torgelson v. Real Prop.

construed to provide such protection[338] was amended to eliminate it.[339] The Florida exemption has, however, been construed to exempt homesteads against a lien for court-ordered restitution in a criminal case.[340] Federal criminal law preempts any state homestead or tenancy by entireties exemption that would protect the debtor's property against a federal restitution or forfeiture order.[341]

Mortgages, deeds of trust, and mechanics liens based on contracts are usually considered waivers or exclusions from homestead protections.[342] In some states, however, both spouses must sign when a married couple is involved.[343]

Known As 17138 880th Ave., 734 N.W.2d 279 (Minn. Ct. App. 2007) (constitutional homestead exemption bars forfeiture for state offenses); State v. One 1965 Red Chevrolet Pickup, 37 P.3d 815 (Okla. 2001) (homesteads exempt, personal property not exempt from state criminal forfeiture, when homestead exemption found in state constitution, but forfeiture provisions and personal property exemptions are statutory).

338 People v. One Residence, 621 N.E.2d 1026 (Ill. App. Ct. 1993) (homestead exemption applied to "involuntary taking of property for any purpose" including forfeiture pursuant to state controlled substances statute).

339 735 Ill. Comp. Stat. § 5/12-903.5.

340 Ergos v. State, 670 So. 2d 1079 (Fla. Dist. Ct. App. 1996); *see also* Matthieu v. City of Lauderdale Lakes, 961 So. 2d 363 (Fla. Dist. Ct. App. 2007) (liens for municipal code violations may not be foreclosed against homestead property); Fong v. Town of Bay Harbor Islands, 864 So. 2d 76 (Fla. Dist. Ct. App. 2003) (no lien against homestead for continuing code violations). *But see* United States v. Jaffe, 417 F.3d 259 (2d Cir. 2005) (Florida homestead preempted by federal law; federal court restitution order that may require sale of exempt homestead is valid).

341 United States v. Hyde, 497 F.3d 103 (1st Cir. 2007); United States v. Fleet, 498 F.3d 1225 (11th Cir. 2005); United States v. Wagoner Real Estate, 278 F.3d 1091 (10th Cir. 2002) (federal forfeiture law preempted Oklahoma homestead exemption); United States v. Lampien, 89 F.3d 1316 (7th Cir. 1996) (Wisconsin homestead exemption did not protect against federal government lien pursuant to restitution provisions of Victim Witness Protection Act (VWPA); even if exemption applies to debt arising from criminal conduct, it would be preempted by VWPA); Wang v. Wang, 2007 WL 2460729 (M.D. Fla. Aug. 24, 2007). *But cf.* United States v. Lee, 232 F.3d 556 (7th Cir. 2000) (when property was neither used in the commission of a crime nor purchased with proceeds thereof, tenancy by entireties protects innocent spouse against forfeiture of even guilty spouse's share).

342 Vogel v. Veneman, 276 F.3d 729 (5th Cir. 2002) (homestead exemption does not apply to refinancing of original purchase money debt); *In re* Anderson, 308 B.R. 25 (B.A.P. 8th Cir. 2004) (Minnesota homestead exemption does not protect against voluntary liens); United States v. Berk, 374 B.R. 385 (D. Mass. 2007) (homestead exemption does not protect against mortgage); *In re* Hart, 332 B.R. 439 (D. Wyo. 2005) (denying homestead exemption when wife quitclaimed house to husband with waiver of homestead); Cavazos v. Munoz, 305 B.R. 661 (S.D. Tex. 2004) (mechanics lien was good, as to home owners, when contractor complied with all procedural requirements except the lien affidavit, which serves to protect third parties); *In re* Liberman, 244 B.R. 557 (E.D.N.Y. 2000) (New York homestead exemption does not protect against foreclosure of purchase money mortgage), *aff'd*, 225 F.3d 646 (2d Cir. 2000) (table); *In re* Evans, 2005 WL 3845700 (Bankr. N.D. Fla. Dec. 21, 2005) (Florida homestead exemption does not protect against mortgage, and bankruptcy discharge eliminates only personal liability; foreclosure permitted after discharge); *In re* Rubino, 2004 WL 1701105 (Bankr. N.D. Iowa May 28, 2004) (Iowa homestead exemption does not protect against debt "incurred for work done or material furnished exclusively for the improvement of the homestead," here semi-permanent above-ground pool); *In re* St. Onge, 317 B.R. 39 (Bankr. D.N.H. 2004) (second mortgage will encumber homestead if signed by both spouses with formalities required for conveyance of land); *In re* Desroches, 314 B.R. 19 (Bankr. D. Mass. 2004) (homestead exemption subordinate to second mortgage signed by both spouses with words of grant and mortgage covenants, even though it did not explicitly release homestead); Knolls Condo. Ass'n v. Harms, 781 N.E.2d 261 (Ill. 2002) (homestead exemption not a defense against eviction action brought by condominium association for unpaid fees); Wells Fargo Home Mortgage, Inc. v. Newton, 646 N.W.2d 888 (Minn. Ct. App. 2002) (when proceeds of refinancing used partly to pay off old mortgage and partly for other purposes, only the sum used to pay off mortgage will be treated as purchase money, excluded from homestead protection); Homeside Lending, Inc. v. Miller, 31 P.3d 607 (Utah Ct. App. 2001); *In re* Trustee's Sale of Real Prop. of Ervin, 134 Wash. App. 1047 (2006) (second mortgage takes priority over homestead exemption in distribution of proceeds of first mortgage foreclosure); Upton v. Household Fin. Indus. Loan Co., 102 Wash. App. 220, 6 P.3d 1231 (2000) (deed of trust beneficiary's interest in real property and its proceeds is superior to homestead exemption); *see also In re* Wade, 354 B.R. 876 (Bankr. N.D. Iowa 2006) (Iowa homestead real estate may be pledged, but may be sold only if deficiency remains after all non-homestead collateral is sold); *cf.* Chase Manhattan Mortgage Corp. v. Cook, 141 S.W.3d 709 (Tex. App. 2004) (bank failed to prove that loan used to pay off mechanic's lien, so lien on homestead not permitted by Texas law). *But cf. In re* Strother, 328 B.R. 818 (B.A.P. 10th Cir. 2005) (contractor who failed to perfect statutory mechanics' lien, but instead obtained judgment lien, could not prevent lien avoidance under bankruptcy law); *In re* Sorrell, 292 B.R. 276 (Bankr. E.D. Tex. 2002) (falsified mechanic's lien documents did not override homestead exemption); Cross v. Strader Constr. Co., 768 So. 2d 465 (Fla. Dist. Ct. App. 2000) (contractor's judgment in *quantum meruit* not a mechanic's lien so does not fall within exception to homestead exemption); Iowa State Bank & Trust Co. v. Michel, 683 N.W.2d 95 (Iowa 2004) (applying Iowa restrictions against waiver of homestead exemption by consensual mortgage of agricultural land); Earls v. Chase Bank of Tex., 59 P.3d 364 (Mont. 2002) (mortgage void when regulated lender failed to obtain written waiver of homestead rights required by former Montana statute); Brooks v. Northglen Ass'n, 141 S.W.3d 158 (Tex. 2004) (fees imposed by covenants running with land and in effect at time of purchase may be enforced by foreclosure on homestead, but increased fees allowed by statute may not); Nat'l Loan Investors, Ltd. P'ship v. Taylor, 79 S.W.3d 633 (Tex. App. 2002) (lender who financed finishing and set up of mobile home failed to comply with requirements for lien on homestead, but home owners judicially estopped from denying lien after they listed it on secured creditors schedule in bankruptcy).

343 Hoover v. Wisecarver, 2006 WL 2583735 (S.D. Miss. Sept. 7, 2006) (Mississippi's two-signature requirement applies only if spouses living together in homestead, not when wife had moved out and filed for divorce at time she conveyed property); Wells Fargo Home Mortgage, Inc. v. Dietz, 2005 WL 758595 (D.

Some states forbid or restrict encumbrances of the homestead.[344] Condominium or subdivision fees may be a lien on

Minn. Mar. 30, 2005) (purchase money mortgage signed by only one of two joint tenants, here a married couple, does not confer rights in non-signing spouse's interest; creditor entitled to only half of sales proceeds); *In re* Miller, 352 B.R. 908 (Bankr. M.D. Fla. 2006) (under Alabama law purported conveyance of homestead property, signed by only one spouse, was entirely void, not just as to amount of homestead exemption; property was owned in joint tenancy, and occupied by non-signing spouse); *In re* Davila, 2006 WL 2578868 (Bankr. S.D. Tex. Aug. 31, 2006) (lien for home improvement loan could not attach to homestead because loan documents signed by wife alone); *In re* Reyerson, 2006 WL 1452805 (Bankr. N.D. Iowa May 17, 2006) (lien for ex-husband's debt could not attach to homestead, when wife, who owned undivided half interest, had not waived homestead exemption); *In re* St. Onge, 317 B.R. 39 (Bankr. D.N.H. 2004) (second mortgage will encumber homestead if signed by both spouses with formalities required for conveyance of land); *In re* Melber, 315 B.R. 181 (Bankr. D. Mass. 2004) (husband who owned homestead property conveyed it to self and wife as tenants by entireties without reserving homestead and without wife's signature; two wrongs made a right; exemption survived); *In re* Desroches, 314 B.R. 19 (Bankr. D. Mass. 2004) (homestead exemption subordinate to second mortgage signed by both spouses with words of grant and mortgage covenants, even though it did not explicitly release homestead); *In re* Jakab, 293 B.R. 621 (Bankr. D. Vt. 2003) (mortgage of homestead void for lack of wife's signature); Phillips v. Fuller, 814 So. 2d 885 (Ala. Civ. App. 2001) (homestead not abandoned by wife who fled from abusive husband; mortgage invalid without her signature); Nat'l Bank of Alaska v. Ketzler, 71 P.3d 333 (Alaska 2003) (if non-signing spouse's name is on title, one-signature deed is void on its face; otherwise non-signer must sue within one year); Taylor v. Maness, 941 So. 2d 559 (Fla. Dist. Ct. App. 2006) (contract of sale, signed by owner-husband but not non-owner wife, could not be enforced by specific performance; wife not tortiously interfering with contract because homestead law gave her "absolute legal right" to refuse); Martin v. Martin, 720 N.W.2d 732 (Iowa 2006) (two-signature requirement continues to apply during period of separation while divorce action is in progress; one-signature deed void even though parties were in process of getting divorce, home was owned by husband before marriage, and was awarded to him in divorce); Beal Bank v. Siems, 670 N.W.2d 119 (Iowa 2003) (if at time mortgage is signed, married owner resides on property and claims homestead, both spouses must sign, even if other spouse neither resides nor claims homestead there); Wells Fargo Bank v. Hudson, 2007 WL 3085791 (Iowa Ct. App. Oct. 24, 2007) (mortgage invalid because wife did not sign; "equitable mortgage" not available when statute was clear, and lender had actual knowledge that property was homestead and borrower was married); Peterson v. Lenz, 2004 WL 2793331 (Minn. Ct. App. Dec. 7, 2004) (waiver of homestead filed while divorce pending, to enable wife's lawyer to file attorney's lien, was invalid without husband's signature); Wells Fargo Home Mortgage, Inc. v. Chojnacki, 668 N.W.2d 1 (Minn. Ct. App. 2003) (two signatures required on all except purchase money mortgages; loan secured by mobile home not purchase money when part of proceeds paid off seller's lien; creditor failed to show ratification by non-signing wife; mortgage was void); Wells Fargo Home Mortgage, Inc. v. Newton, 646 N.W.2d 888 (Minn. Ct. App. 2002) (specific requirement for both spouses' signatures on mortgage of homestead trumps general provision of married women's act allowing wife to manage separate property; wife's attempt to mortgage homestead without husband's signature invalid, but wife liable on promissory note); Peterson v. Hinz, 605 N.W.2d 414 (Minn. Ct. App. 2000) (attempt to impose attorney's lien on homestead property, when wife had not signed the homestead waiver, was frivolous); Terminix Int'l, Inc. v. Rice, 904 So. 2d 1051 (Miss. 2004) (two-signature requirement did not apply to arbitration agreement in contract with exterminator, as contract did not affect wife's ownership interest in home); Snoddy v. Snoddy, 791 So. 2d 333 (Miss. Ct. App. 2001) (house became homestead when couple lived there during marriage, even though it was separate property of husband; husband's attempted conveyance was void when wife did not sign); Thurman v. Thurman, 770 So. 2d 1015 (Miss. Ct. App. 2000) (if couple are married and living together, valid deed of trust requires both signatures); Besnilian v. Wilkinson, 25 P.3d 187 (Nev. 2001) (one spouse may not alienate homestead property without consent of the other); Cadle Co. v. Ortiz, 227 S.W.3d 831 (Tex. App. 2007) (mechanic's lien on property titled in wife's name alone invalid when husband did not sign; homestead exemption waived if married person deliberately misrepresents self as single, but burden of proof on creditor; not shown here); Mashburn Trucking v. Martin, 2000 Tex. App. LEXIS 514 (Tex. App. Jan. 24, 2000) (invalidating mechanic's lien on homestead, because only one spouse signed the contract for work and material on which it is based); Equitable Bank v. Chabron, 238 Wis. 2d 708, 618 N.W.2d 262 (Ct. App. 2000). *But see In re* Whaley, 353 B.R. 209 (E.D. Tenn. 2006) (non-owner non-debtor wife's homestead right did not bar trustee's sale of home; wife's $5000 homestead exemption would be paid out of proceeds); *In re* Hoggarth Bros., 2004 WL 903814 (D.N.D. Apr. 22, 2004) (farm couples resided on land owned by farm partnership; because non-partner wives owned no interest in land, mortgage signed only by partner-husbands was valid); James v. Thaggard, 795 So. 2d 738 (Ala. Civ. App. 2001) (husband could not avoid mortgage on grounds that wife had not signed, when she lived, worked, and claimed a homestead on a residence in another state, and had never resided on the mortgaged property); Skelton v. Wash. Mut. Bank, 61 S.W.3d 56 (Tex. App. 2001) (widow had no claims on homestead, and mortgage not invalidated by lack of her signature, when couple agreed husband alone should apply for mortgage, because of wife's bad credit record, and husband falsely informed lender he was single); Charter One Bank v. Estate of Spillane, 807 A.2d 452 (Vt. 2002) (lack of signature renders mortgage voidable, not void; when husband took out home equity line, then first wife died and husband and second wife divorced and remarried after date of last advances, wives' rights were extinguished by death or divorce); Jones v. Estate of Jones, 646 N.W.2d 280 (Wis. 2002) (broad language in premarital agreement allowing spouses to manage separate property waived homestead rights; when husband deeded house to wife and wife deeded it to another, second deed valid without husband's signature).

344 United States v. Candelario-Gomez, 2007 WL 1480658 (W.D.N.C. May 18, 2007) (Texas homestead exemption bars United States from executing on homestead for defaulted bail, even though relative who posted bail gave real estate note and deed of trust); United States v. Neff, 2007 WL 776532 (D.N.D. Mar. 12, 2007) (homestead exemption may not be waived for chattel debt; creditor also failed to show waiver was knowing and voluntary); Marketic v. U.S. Bank, 436 F. Supp. 2d 842 (N.D. Tex. 2006) (statute forbids foreclosure of home equity loan against property designated as agricultural for tax purposes as of date of foreclosure, even though not so designated at time

the homestead if a covenant running with the land and providing for this lien was in place when the property was bought.[345]

12.5.2.8 Preexisting Debts

Some states do not protect a homestead against debts which predate the acquisition of the homestead.[346] A debt incurred after the statute's effective date will be subject to the homestead law, however, even if it is incurred pursuant to a line of credit that predated the statute.[347] Some courts have construed statutes that increase the amount of the homestead exemption to apply to debts incurred before the change.[348] Other states, however, refuse to apply a homestead exemption, or an amended version of it, to debts that arose before its effective date.[349] The result may be different

---

of loan); Box v. State Bank, 340 B.R. 782 (S.D. Tex. 2006) (Texas forbids home equity loan that is conditioned upon paying off unsecured debt to same lender; shown here, despite disclaimer in loan documents); *In re* Cadengo, 370 B.R. 681 (Bankr. S.D. Tex. 2007) (homestead waiver ineffective when creditor had actual knowledge of homestead use); *In re* Kleibrink, 346 B.R. 734 (Bankr. N.D. Tex. 2006) (creditor's compliance with procedure for fixing mechanics' lien on homestead sufficient to make loan good against home owner), *aff'd*, 2007 WL 2438359 (N.D. Tex. Aug. 28, 2007); *In re* Hebert, 301 B.R. 19 (Bankr. N.D. Iowa 2003) (statement in personal guarantee of corporate debt that guarantors "waive the benefit of all homestead laws" not sufficient to comply with Iowa law; homestead waiver must specifically describe piece the property to which it applies); LaSalle Bank v. White, 217 S.W.3d 573 (Tex. App. 2006) (Texas constitution invalidates home equity loan secured by homestead property designated for agricultural use); Florey v. Estate of McConnell, 212 S.W.3D 439 (Tex. App. 2006) (lien to secure attorney fee not among exceptions to Texas's ban on loans secured by homestead; when husband accused of murdering wife gave deed of trust to defense attorney, wife's estate could invalidate the lien); Chase Manhattan Mortgage Corp. v. Cook, 141 S.W.3d 709 (Tex. App. 2004) (bank failed to prove that loan used to pay off mechanic's lien; lien on homestead forbidden by Texas Const. art. IVI, § 50(a) with certain exceptions); *see also In re* Meltzer, 2007 WL 543922 (Bankr. S.D. Tex. Feb. 16, 2007) (loan secured by homestead permitted if loan proceeds to pay property taxes on homestead, but lien invalid when used to pay federal income taxes and gambling debts); *In re* Ferrari, 2006 WL 3247120 (Bankr. D. Alaska Oct. 25, 2006) (refusing to apply marshalling of assets to homestead; Internal Revenue Service, which could recover against exempt or nonexempt property, takes nonexempt property, leaving debtor with homestead and nongovernmental creditor with nothing); *In re* Wade, 354 B.R. 876 (Bankr. N.D. Iowa 2006) (Iowa homestead real estate may be pledged, but may be sold only if deficiency remains after all non-homestead collateral is sold); Robinson v. Saxon Mortgage Services, Inc., 2007 WL 2214439 (Tex. App. Aug. 1, 2007) (waiver was valid, despite minor errors in paperwork, when documents showed permissible refinancing to pay mortgage and mechanics' liens).

345 Sloan v. Owners Ass'n of Westfield, Inc., 167 S.W.3d 401 (Tex. App. 2005) (lien created by subdivision restrictions came into existence before homestead established; lien for subdivision fees, late fees, and attorney fees incurred in litigation over restrictions); *cf.* Andres v. Indian Creek Phase III-B Homeowner's Ass'n, 901 So. 2d 182 (Fla. Dist. Ct. App. 2005) (subdivision covenant did not create continuing lien for attorney fees).

346 *In re* Takes, 478 F.3d 902 (8th Cir. 2007) (new homestead exempt insofar as purchased with exempt proceeds of former homestead that pre-dated the debt, but nonexempt as to balance of purchase price); *In re* Russow, 357 B.R. 133 (Bankr. N.D. Iowa 2007) (proceeds of old homestead rolled over into new homestead exempt as to preexisting debts); *In re* Ruggio, 345 B.R. 30 (Bankr. D. Mass. 2006) (denying exemption because homestead declaration filed postpetition); *In re* Guido, 344 B.R. 193 (Bankr. D. Mass. 2006) (second mortgage executed before filing of homestead declaration, but not recorded until after takes priority over homestead rights); *In re* Whelan, 325 B.R. 462 (Bankr. M.D. Fla. 2005) (judgment lien, recorded against debtors who owned no real property, attached to homestead purchased four years later); *In re* Allen, 301 B.R. 55 (Bankr. S.D. Iowa 2003) (debtors owned and lived in House A, then bought and moved to House B while renting out House A, then sold House B and moved back to House A; homestead exemption did not protect House A against debt incurred while debtors lived in House B); *In re* Estad, 295 B.R. 905 (Bankr. D. Minn. 2003) (did not protect against lien that attached while new house under construction; not homestead until family actually moved in); *In re* White, 293 B.R. 1 (Bankr. N.D. Iowa 2003) (Iowa homestead exemption does not protect against preexisting debts, but may be transferred from one residence to another; no interruption in homestead here even though debtors lived briefly in an apartment between selling one house and purchasing the next); *In re* Norkus, 256 B.R. 298 (Bankr. S.D. Iowa 2000) (Iowa homestead exemption does not protect against debts incurred before homestead acquired); *In re* Nienhaber, 2000 Bankr. LEXIS 1880 (Bankr. E.D. Ky. July 19, 2000) (homestead exemption does not apply when homestead acquired after debt created); Kamerick v. Marion County Bank, 2003 WL 23006949 (Iowa Ct. App. Dec. 24, 2003) (wife's guarantee of farm loan before she acquired homestead was a preexisting debt not protected by homestead exemption); Amresco SBA Holdings, Inc., 867 N.E.2d 37 (Mass. App. Ct. 2007) (debt preexisted homestead when debtor filed homestead declaration after creditor made demand but before it sued; homestead not exempt); Walsh v. Yarossi, 2006 WL 3493476 (Mass. Land Ct. Dec. 5, 2006) (home owner, who was defendant in personal injury action, filed homestead after pre-judgment attachment but before judgment; lien was preexisting debt within meaning of exception to homestead statute).

347 Alessandro v. People's Bank (*In re* Alessandro), 254 B.R. 521 (Bankr. D. Conn. 2000) (Connecticut's new homestead statute, which applies prospectively only, applies to credit extended after its effective date on preexisting line of credit that was terminable at will); *In re* Caraglior, 251 B.R. 778 (Bankr. D. Conn. 2000) (Connecticut homestead exemption protects against debts for balances accrued after its effective date on credit cards issued before that date).

348 *In re* Little, 2006 WL 1524594 (Bankr. N.D.N.Y. Apr. 24, 2006) (increased exemption applied to preexisting debt); Homeside Lending, Inc. v. Miller, 31 P.3d 607 (Utah Ct. App. 2001) (statute set amount debtor could claim as homestead exemption "at the time of sale"); Macumber v. Shafer, 637 P.2d 645 (Wash. 1981); *see also* § 12.2.3.1, *supra*.

349 *In re* Tardugno, 262 B.R. 168 (Bankr. D. Mass. 2001) (Massachusetts statute which increased exemption does not apply retroactively; when statute became effective after debtor filed bankruptcy, lower exemption applied); *In re* Skjetne, 213 B.R.

in bankruptcy.[350]

12.5.2.9 Entireties Property

Although the rule is not universal,[351] many jurisdictions, either by statute or under common law, protect the marital home against seizure for the debts of one spouse.[352] While

274 (Bankr. D. Vt. 1997) (under Vermont law, increase in homestead exemption does not apply to preexisting debts, but result is different when debtor files bankruptcy); *In re* Corson, 206 B.R. 17 (Bankr. D. Conn. 1997) (Connecticut's homestead exemption, which applies prospectively only, did not protect home when debtor incurred debt before statute's effective date, and creditor sued and obtained lien afterwards); Builders Supply Co. v. Pine Belt Sav. & Loan Ass'n, 369 So. 2d 743, 745 (Miss. 1979); *see also* § 12.2.2, *supra* (constitutional issues in application of amended exemption statutes to preexisting debts).

350 *In re* Weinstein, 164 F.3d 677 (1st Cir. 1999); *In re* Mayer, 167 B.R. 186 (B.A.P. 9th Cir. 1994) (exemption amount in effect on date of bankruptcy filing applies); *In re* Dubois, 306 B.R. 423 (Bankr. D. Me. 2004) (Maine statute providing that increase in homestead exemption was prospective only was preempted by bankruptcy law that provided short list of debts that can be collected from exempt property; new exemption amount applied to preexisting debt); *In re* Betz, 273 B.R. 313 (Bankr. D. Mass. 2002) (debtor entitled to increased state exemption in effect on bankruptcy filing date, even as to preexisting debts that were specifically excepted by state statute); *In re* Homonoff, 261 B.R. 551 (Bankr. D.R.I. 2001) (bankruptcy law uses exemptions as of date of filing even though Rhode Island statute denies homestead protection against debts which predate either the enactment of the statute or the acquisition of the homestead); *In re* Strandberg, 253 B.R. 584 (Bankr. D.R.I. 2000); *In re* Ballirano, 233 B.R. 11 (Bankr. D. Mass. 1999) (federal bankruptcy law preempted prior Massachusetts statute's preexisting debt exception to homestead exemption); *In re* Skjetne, 213 B.R. 274 (Bankr. D. Vt. 1997) (applying state exemption law that was in effect on date of bankruptcy filing, even as to debts incurred prior to amendment). *But see In re* Ruggio, 345 B.R. 30 (Bankr. D. Mass. 2006) (denying exemption because homestead declaration filed postpetition).

351 *In re* Nelms, 2005 WL 318802 (Bankr. E.D. Mich. Feb. 4, 2005) (Michigan debtors can not claim tenancy by entireties exemption for property located in Louisiana, which does not recognize tenancy by entireties); *In re* Arwood, 289 B.R. 889 (Bankr. E.D. Tenn. 2003); Kaplan v. First Options of Chicago, 189 B.R. 882, 891 (E.D. Pa. 1995) (New Jersey law does not protect entireties real estate from claim by creditor of one spouse against that spouse's interest in the property).

352 *DELAWARE*: *In re* Kelly, 316 B.R. 629 (D. Del. 2004) (permitting debtor to exempt property held as tenants by the entirety with non-debtor spouse); *In re* Mintz, 2005 WL 758813 (Bankr. D. Del. Mar. 31, 2005) (allowing exemption of residence held as tenants by the entirety when trustee unable to show debtors had any joint debts).

FLORIDA: *In re* Sinnreich, 391 F.3d 1295 (11th Cir. 2004) (Fla. law) (real and personal property held in tenancy by entireties with non-debtor spouse is exempt); United States v. Lee, 232 F.3d 556 (7th Cir. 2000) (Fla. law) (when property was neither used in the commission of a crime nor purchased with proceeds thereof, tenancy by entireties protects innocent spouse against forfeiture of even guilty spouse's interest); *In re* Ramsurat, 361 B.R. 246 (Bankr. M.D. Fla. 2006) (to create Florida tenancy by entireties, couple must be married at time property conveyed; no tenancy by entireties when sale closed before marriage); *In re* Mitchell, 344 B.R. 171 (Bankr. M.D. Fla. 2006) (if property deeded to married couple, tenancy by entireties is presumed; when property was deeded to couple and son, one joint tenant was the entireties and the other was the son); *In re* Willoughby, 212 B.R. 1011 (Bankr. M.D. Fla. 1997) (tenancy by the entireties protects homestead from individual debts of husband, even debt for child support from prior marriage).

ILLINOIS: Maher v. Harris Trust & Sav. Bank, 506 F.3d 560 (7th Cir. 2007) (Illinois allows tenancy by entirety in property maintained or intended as homestead by both husband and wife; rejecting creditor's argument that shares in cooperative where couple resided were personal property that could not be owned in tenancy by entireties); *In re* Eichorn, 338 B.R. 793 (Bankr. S.D. Ill. 2006) (filing of joint bankruptcy neither severs tenancy by entireties, nor "merges" bankruptcy estates; tenancy by entireties property remains exempt as to debt of individual spouse); *cf. In re* Moreno, 352 B.R. 455 (Bankr. N.D. Ill. Sept. 20, 2006) (property could not be reached for individual debts under Illinois statute that applies when property is transferred into tenancy by entireties with sole intent to avoid payment of existing debts when house owned in joint tenancy was sold and new house purchased in tenancy by entireties; "legitimate family purpose" shown as debtors believed new neighborhood was safer for children); *In re* Tolson, 338 B.R. 359 (Bankr. C.D. Ill. 2005) (property could not be reached for individual debts under Illinois statute that applies when property is transferred into tenancy by entireties with sole intent to avoid payment of existing debts when financially troubled couple engaged in estate planning and lawyer drafted husband's will at same time as deed).

IOWA: *In re* Powers, 286 B.R. 726 (Bankr. N.D. Iowa 2002) (homestead right of husband and wife can not be split, so can not be executed upon for non-joint debt).

KENTUCKY: *In re* Brinley, 403 F.3d 415 (6th Cir. 2005) (Ky. law) (explaining how to apply Bankruptcy Code lien avoidance provisions to property owned in tenancy by entireties with non-debtor spouse).

MARYLAND: Schlossberg v. Barney, 380 F.3d 174 (4th Cir. 2004) (Md. law) (spouse who files individual bankruptcy can exempt property held in tenancy by entireties with non-debtor spouse); *In re* Greathouse, 295 B.R. 562 (Bankr. D. Md. 2003) (if no joint debts and no tax debts, property owned in tenancy by entireties completely exempt).

MASSACHUSETTS: *In re* Snyder, 249 B.R. 40 (B.A.P. 1st Cir. 2000) (Mass. law) (husband has 100% interest in home owned as tenancy by entireties), *aff'd*, 248 F.3d 1127 (1st Cir. 2001) (table) (text available at 2001 U.S. App. LEXIS 16685). *But cf. In re* Hidler, 192 B.R. 790 (Bankr. D. Me. 1996) (when Massachusetts tenancy by the entirety was created before the passage of the tenancy by the entireties statute, common law applied and property could be sold for individual debt of husband).

MICHIGAN: *In re* Raynard, 354 B.R. 834 (B.A.P. 6th Cir. Oct. 25, 2006) (Mich. law) (in or out of chapter 13, tenancy by entireties property exempt from creditors of individual spouse); *In re* Spears, 313 B.R. 212 (W.D. Mich. 2004) (filing of bankruptcy by one spouse does not sever tenancy by entireties; entireties property may be reached only for joint debts). *But cf.* United States v. Craft, 535 U.S. 274, 122 S. Ct. 1414, 152 L. Ed. 2d 437 (2002) (Internal Revenue Service not bound by Michigan law that forbids one spouse to alienate property without consent of the other; husband's interest in entireties property was a property interest to which tax lien could attach).

MINNESOTA: O'Hagen v. United States, 86 F.3d 776 (8th Cir. 1996) (Minnesota law forbade one spouse to unilaterally sever joint tenancy; when husband, but not wife, owed delinquent taxes, Internal Revenue Service could levy on and attempt to sell only his survivorship interest); *In re* Johnson, 207 B.R. 878 (Bankr. D. Minn. 1997) (when non-debtor wife continued to reside in house owned by couple in joint tenancy and debtor husband had lived elsewhere for more than six months, which was long enough to lose his homestead exemption under Minnesota law, wife's exemption protected property from debts of husband, wife, or both).

MISSOURI: Brown v. Eads (*In re* Eads), 271 B.R. 371 (Bankr. W.D. Mo. 2002); *In re* Brown, 234 B.R. 907 (Bankr. W.D. Mo. 1999) (under Missouri law, real and personal property of married couple is presumed to be owned in tenancy by the entireties, and thus exempt from claims of individual creditors).

NORTH CAROLINA: N.C. Gen. Stat. § 39-13.6; *In re* Payne, 2004 WL 2757907 (Bankr. M.D.N.C. Nov. 15, 2004) (property owned in tenancy by entireties fully exempt if no joint creditors; because couple did not claim homestead exemption, each debtor entitled to "in lieu of homestead" wildcard).

OHIO: First Fed. Sav. & Loan Ass'n v. Dus, 2003 WL 21545126 (Ohio Ct. App. July 10, 2003) (lien could not attach to real property owned in tenancy by entireties for husband's individual debt; divorce changed tenancy by entireties into joint tenancy, but lien still did not attach because it came into existence while parties were married).

PENNSYLVANIA: *In re* Olexa, 476 F.3d 177 (3d Cir. 2007) (entireties property can not be reached even though debts were for necessaries, as necessaries statute refers only to spouse's separate property).

RHODE ISLAND: *In re* Pearlman, 2005 WL 1331256 (Bankr. D.R.I. Apr. 18, 2005) (commercial property exempt and bankruptcy estate's interest limited to value of contingent expectancy interest when property held as tenants by the entirety); *In re* Strandberg, 253 B.R. 584 (Bankr. D.R.I. 2000) (when property owned in tenancy by entireties, debtor-husband may claim entire homestead exemption; Rhode Island law allows only one owner to claim exemption, which can not be divided).

VERMONT: Evans v. Wolinsky, 347 B.R. 9 (D. Vt. 2006) (entireties property can not be reached by creditors, so transfer to wife individually, at time when no joint debts, not fraudulent); *In re* Hutchins, 306 B.R. 82 (Bankr. D. Vt. 2004) (Vermont recognizes entireties doctrine but lien for federal criminal fine can attach to husband's interest).

VIRGINIA: *In re* Thomas, 312 F.3d 145 (4th Cir. 2002) (Va. law) (even in joint bankruptcy, entireties property may be reached only by joint creditors); *In re* Sampath, 314 B.R. 73 (Bankr. E.D. Va. 2004) (deed to married couple grants tenancy by entireties, even if deed silent as to marital status; adding daughter to deed did not sever tenancy by entireties; couple's share could not be reached for individual debt of husband); *In re* Zella, 196 B.R. 752 (Bankr. E.D. Va. 1996) (proceeds of sale of real estate owned by married couple as "tenancy by the entireties" were, like the real estate, exempt from the claims of one spouse's creditors), *aff'd*, 202 B.R. 712 (E.D. Va. 1996); *In re* Scialdone, 197 B.R. 225 (Bankr. E.D. Va. 1995) (real property held in tenancy by the entirety was exempt from attachment by creditor of only one spouse; tenancy by the entirety can be created only by explicit language in the deed); Sterrett v. Sterrett, 401 Pa. 583, 166 A.2d (1960); Rogers v. Rogers, 512 S.E.2d 821 (Va. 1999) (when creditors had federal court judgment against husband and state judgment against wife, both apparently resulting from the same transactions, entireties property could not be attached; only a joint judgment against husband and wife could be satisfied from entireties property).

the scope of this protection varies from state to state, most states base the protection on the theory that the interests of both husband and wife extend to the whole of the property.[353] For as long as the marriage continues, the estate can not be severed, terminated, or partitioned by either spouse without the other's consent.[354] The estate is severed, however, by divorce or the death of one spouse,[355] or the transfer of the property by both spouses to some other form of ownership.[356] In the case of divorce, the tenancy by entireties becomes a tenancy in common.[357] If one spouse dies, the property passes to the other in its entirety.[358]

353 *In re* Thomas, 312 F.3d 145 (4th Cir. 2002); *In re* Raynard, 354 B.R. 834 (B.A.P. 6th Cir. Oct. 25, 2006) (Mich. law); *In re* Snyder, 249 B.R. 40 (B.A.P. 1st Cir. 2000) (Mass. law), *aff'd*, 248 F.3d 1127 (1st Cir. 2001) (table) (text available at 2001 U.S. App. LEXIS 16685); *see also In re* Giffune, 343 B.R. 883 (Bankr. N.D. Ill. 2006).

354 *In re* Brinley, 403 F.3d 415 (6th Cir. 2005) (explaining how to apply Bankruptcy Code lien avoidance provisions to property owned in tenancy by entireties with non-debtor spouse), *cert. denied*, 546 U.S. 1149 (2006); *In re* Thomas, 312 F.3d 145 (4th Cir. 2002); *In re* Raynard, 354 B.R. 834 (B.A.P. 6th Cir. Oct. 25, 2006) (Mich. law); *In re* Snyder, 249 B.R. 40 (B.A.P. 1st Cir. 2000) (Mass. law), *aff'd*, 248 F.3d 1127 (1st Cir. 2001) (table) (text available at 2001 U.S. App. LEXIS 16685); *In re* Spears, 313 B.R. 212 (W.D. Mich. 2004) (filing of bankruptcy by one spouse does not sever tenancy by entireties); *In re* Levinson, 372 B.R. 582 (Bankr. E.D.N.Y. 2007); *In re* Eichorn, 338 B.R. 793 (Bankr. S.D. Ill. 2006) (filing of joint bankruptcy neither severs tenancy by entireties, nor "merges" bankruptcy estates; tenancy by entireties property remains exempt as to debt of individual spouse); *see also* § 12.5.2.7, *supra* (state requirements that both spouses sign mortgage).

355 *In re* Snyder, 249 B.R. 40 (B.A.P. 1st Cir. 2000) (Mass. law), *aff'd*, 248 F.3d 1127 (1st Cir. 2001) (table) (text available at 2001 U.S. App. LEXIS 16685); *In re* Ballato, 318 B.R. 205 (Bankr. M.D. Fla. 2004) (divorce turned tenancy by entireties into tenancy in common, but did not destroy homestead exemption, which protects any interest in land); *In re* Ryan, 282 B.R. 742 (D.R.I. 2002).

356 *See In re* Stanke, 234 B.R. 439 (Bankr. W.D. Mo. 1999) (tenancy by entireties severed, and protection lost, when couple transferred property to tax planning trust, with provisions inconsistent with tenancy by entireties).

357 *In re* Snyder, 249 B.R. 40 (B.A.P. 1st Cir. 2000) (Mass. law), *aff'd*, 248 F.3d 1127 (1st Cir. 2001) (table) (text available at 2001 U.S. App. LEXIS 16685); *In re* Hutchins, 306 B.R. 82 (Bankr. D. Vt. 2004); *In re* Shannis, 229 B.R. 234 (Bankr. M.D. Fla. 1999); *In re* LaBorde, 231 B.R. 162 (Bankr. W.D.N.Y. 1999) (under New York law, divorce severed tenancy by entireties; when husband, after divorce, deeded his half-interest in home to former wife, she took subject to judgment liens against former husband).

358 *In re* Thomas, 312 F.3d 145 (4th Cir. 2002); *In re* Snyder, 249 B.R. 40 (B.A.P. 1st Cir. 2000) (Mass. law), *aff'd*, 248 F.3d 1127 (1st Cir. 2001) (table) (text available at 2001 U.S. App. LEXIS 16685).

Entireties property can be reached by a creditor if both husband and wife owe the debt.[359] In some states, a judgment creditor can place an attachment on the debtor spouse's interest in the property, and enforce it if and when the debtor spouse survives the death of the other spouse.[360] In some states the judgment creditor can also sell or force the sale of this contingent future expectancy interest.[361] A significant benefit of tenancy by entireties is that some of the restrictions on the use of state exemptions, created by recent amendments to bankruptcy law, do not apply to the tenancy by entireties exemption.[362]

359 *In re* Kartman, 354 B.R. 70 (Bankr. W.D. Pa. 2006) (when creditor seeks to levy on entireties property key issue is whether both spouses liable); *In re* Kartman, 354 B.R. 70 (Bankr. W.D. Pa. 2006) (if creditor has claim for joint debt, tenancy by entireties property not exempt in individual spouse's bankruptcy); *In re* Guzior, 347 B.R. 237 (Bankr. E.D. Mich. 2006) (in bankruptcy, tenancy by entireties property is nonexempt to the amount of joint debt minus the homestead exemption); Rogers v. Rogers, 512 S.E.2d 821 (Va. 1999). *But see In re* Olexa, 317 B.R. 290 (Bankr. W.D. Pa. 2004) (wife alone filed for bankruptcy, but debts were for necessaries within meaning of Pennsylvania law; because necessaries statute referred only to spouse's separate property, entireties property could not be reached), *aff'd*, 476 F.3d 177 (3d Cir. 2007); *cf. In re* Curda-Derickson, 668 N.W.2d 736 (Wis. Ct. App. 2003) (debts incurred during marriage presumed to be for family purposes, but exception for tort of one spouse; judgment for husband's conversion could be satisfied only from his separate property or interest in marital property).

360 *In re* Ryan, 282 B.R. 742 (D.R.I. 2002); *In re* Levinson, 372 B.R. 582 (Bankr. E.D.N.Y. 2007) (refusing to avoid judgment lien on entireties property; debtor's interest extends to 100% of property's value).

361 *In re* Ryan, 282 B.R. 742 (D.R.I. 2002); *In re* Arwood, 289 B.R. 889 (Bankr. E.D. Tenn. 2003) (trustee can sell debtor-spouse's survivorship interest in property owned in tenancy by entireties with non-debtor spouse); Kipp v. Sweno, 683 N.W.2d 259 (Minn. 2004) (husband's survivorship interest can be sold, but he can claim entire $200,000 homestead exemption); *see also In re* Weza, 248 B.R. 470 (Bankr. D.N.H. 2000) (debtor-husband's interest in Massachusetts property held by common law tenancy by entireties could be sold by husband's creditor, and both husband and wife dispossessed, subject to survivorship rights of wife).

362 *In re* Hinton, 378 B.R. 371 (Bankr. M.D. Fla. 2007) (cap does not apply to property owned in tenancy by entirety); *In re* Schwarz, 362 B.R. 532 (Bankr. S.D. Fla. 2007) (debtor barred by choice-of-law provisions from claiming Florida homestead could exempt tenancy by entireties property); *In re* Buonopane, 359 B.R. 346 (Bankr. M.D. Fla. 2007) (cap for homesteads acquired within 1215 days of bankruptcy does not apply to property owned in tenancy by entireties). *See generally* § 12.5.2.6, *supra*.

12.5.3 Exemptions for Personal Property

12.5.3.1 Purpose

Every state has statutes which exempt a debtor's basic possessions. The purpose of these statutes is to allow debtors to retain basic necessities for living. The specific items exempted under each state statute differ, usually as a result of the antiquity of the statutes, geography, and the local economy. For example, states in the north frequently exempt a certain amount of products that are to be used as fuel. Other states with a strong agricultural community allow for a certain amount of crops and farm animals to be retained, in order to allow the debtor to continue to earn a living. Exemptions for personal property generally do not apply to purchase money debts[363] or criminal forfeitures.[364]

12.5.3.2 General Scope

Most statutes exempt necessary household goods, construed to include not just what is needed for bare subsistence, but items generally found in the home and used to facilitate day-to-day living.[365] The question of what is necessary will depend on local usage, and may change over time. For example, televisions and VCRs have become so common that they are likely to be considered necessary.[366]

363 *See* Coonts v. Potts, 316 F.3d 745 (8th Cir. 2003); *In re* Johnson, 179 B.R. 800 (Bankr. E.D. Va. 1995) (when consumer borrowed money from credit union for stated purpose of buying car, but never listed lien on title certificate, debt was purchase money and car was not exempt); *see also In re* Rushdi, 174 B.R. 126 (Bankr. D. Idaho 1994) (when borrowers refinanced several debts, some purchase money, some not, new security interests were all non-purchase money).

364 State v. One 1965 Red Chevrolet Pickup, 37 P.3d 815 (Okla. 2001) (exemption from "every other species of forced sale" not broad enough to shield personal property from criminal forfeiture).

365 *In re* Goss, 352 B.R. 309 (Bankr. E.D. Okla. 2006) (large commercial-type safe not a household good; even if family needed safe place for papers, this safe went beyond what was reasonably necessary; cow used for breeding not exempt under statute exempting "milk cow"); *In re* LaJuerrne, 2004 WL 2192515 (Bankr. D. Kan. July 9, 2004) (using broad definition of household goods, many items in collection of automotive memorabilia are exempt); *In re* Heath, 318 B.R. 115 (Bankr. W.D. Ky. 2004) ("functional nexus" test exempts items that foster or help enable daily existence in the household; rifle for deer hunting exempt but not tanning bed); *In re* Latham, 182 B.R. 479 (Bankr. W.D. Va. 1995) (exempt furniture must be used for day to day living in debtors' home; furniture of beach house which was sometimes used for family vacations and sometimes rented out was not exempt); *see also* New Century Fin. Services, Inc. v. Arellano, 2006 WL 3344985 (N.J. Super. Ct. App. Div. Nov. 30, 2006) (safe deposit box not protected by exemption for "goods and chattels"; creditor entitled to court order to open box to see if it contained nonexempt property).

366 Planned Parenthood of Columbus/Willamette, Inc. v. Am. Coa-

Utah added microwaves to its list of exempt household goods in 1997.[367]

Some states have amended their exemption statutes to cover computers or other electronics.[368] One court, while declining to exempt a "relatively sophisticated" and "not inexpensive" computer system as "home furnishings," left the door ajar by comparing home computers today with televisions in the '50s, which evolved from an "expensive curiosity" to "a virtual necessity which can be purchased for relatively little."[369] Shortly thereafter, that court exempted a computer system used by members of a debtor's family for schoolwork.[370]

Courts have varied widely in their treatment of small amenities such as entertainment, hobby, and sports equipment,[371] jewelry,[372] and knick-

---

lition of Life Activists, 2007 WL 4118597 (S.D. Ohio Nov. 16, 2007) (personal computers, printers, software, VCR, stereo and at least one television are exempt); *In re* Biancavilla, 173 B.R. 930 (Bankr. D. Idaho 1994) (television and VCR were exempt; recreational equipment and computer system were not household goods, but computer system was tool of trade); *see also In re* Doss, 298 B.R. 866 (Bankr. W.D. Tenn. 2003) (big screen television was household good within meaning of bankruptcy lien avoidance provision); *In re* Hicks, 276 B.R. 84 (Bankr. W.D. Va. 2001) (television and VCR exempt); *In re* Elst, 210 B.R. 790 (Bankr. E.D. Wis. 1997) (second television set falls within federal bankruptcy exemption for household goods, because it provided entertainment for family and guests in the house); *In re* Sydlowski, 186 B.R. 907 (Bankr. N.D. Ohio 1995) (television, VCR and, for debtor with custody of child, a video game); *In re* Kinnemore, 181 B.R. 516 (Bankr. D. Idaho 1995) (television and VCR); *In re* French, 177 B.R. 568 (Bankr. E.D. Tenn. 1995) (VCR).

367 Utah Code Ann. § 78-23-5.

368 *See, e.g.*, Iowa Code § 627.6(5) (radios, televisions, record, tape, compact disc, or DVD players, satellite dishes, cable television equipment, computers, software, printers, and so forth); Nev. Rev. Stat. § 21.090(1)(b) (electronics).

369 *In re* Larson, 203 B.R. 176 (Bankr. W.D. Okla. 1996) (rejecting creditor's argument that home furnishings exemption should apply only to bare necessities of survival; it includes items "reasonably necessary to the maintenance of a home").

370 *In re* Ratliff, 209 B.R. 534 (Bankr. W.D. Okla. 1997) (computer and printer used by children and one debtor who was a student, to do schoolwork, was exempt under "household and kitchen furniture" exemption); *accord In re* Hicks, 276 B.R. 84 (Bankr. W.D. Va. 2001) (computer used for educational purposes was exempt); *In re* Andrews, 225 B.R. 485 (Bankr. D. Idaho 1998) (one computer is reasonably necessary to household, so is exempt under Idaho exemptions); *see* § 12.5.3.4, *infra*; *see also In re* Rhines, 227 B.R. 308 (Bankr. D. Mont. 1998) (computer exempt as household good under federal bankruptcy exemptions); *In re* Crawford, 226 B.R. 484 (Bankr. N.D. Ga. 1998) (computer used for educational purposes was household good under federal bankruptcy exemptions); *cf. In re* Liston, 206 B.R. 235 (Bankr. W.D. Okla. 1997) (computer not exempt as home furnishing). *But see* CSC Holdings, Inc. v. Sam's Electronics, Inc., 2006 WL 1620242 (W.D. Okla. June 8, 2006) (computer is not household good; note that debtor provided no evidence of how computer would be used when moved from business premises to home); *In re* Irwin, 232 B.R. 151 (Bankr. D. Minn. 1999) (Minnesota exemption for household appliances did not cover computer, which is not usually thought of as an appliance and was not included in statute's list of entertainment and information items that were exempt).

371 Crockett v. Lowe (*In re* Crockett), 158 F.3d 332 (5th Cir. 1998) (jet ski was not exempt under Texas exemption for "athletic and sporting equipment, including bicycles," which had been construed in other bankruptcy cases to exclude sailboats and motorboats); *In re* Lucas, 77 B.R. 242 (B.A.P. 9th Cir. 1987) (golf clubs, camera equipment, and exercise bicycle fall within California household property exemption); *In re* LaJuerrne, 2004 WL 2192515 (Bankr. D. Kan. July 9, 2004) (many but not all items in collection of automotive memorabilia exempt); *In re* Schreiber, 231 B.R. 17 (Bankr. D. Me. 1999) (pop-up camper was not household good within meaning of Maine law, because there was no nexus between camper and "daily use, maintenance or upkeep of the debtor's household"); *In re* Gallegos, 226 B.R. 111 (Bankr. D. Idaho 1998) (horse was household pet, within meaning of Idaho exemption, when it was kept as a companion, to be ridden by debtor's young daughter, even though it was kept outside rather than in house); *In re* Lynch, 139 B.R. 868 (Bankr. N.D. Ohio 1992) (household goods are "items of personal property reasonably necessary for the day-to-day existence of people in their homes"; sound system and recordings were household goods, but not cameras); *see also* Fraley v. Commercial Credit, 189 B.R. 398 (W.D. Ky. 1995) (goods need not be "essential for survival" to be household goods; stereo, aquarium and camcorder (the modern equivalent of a photo album) were household goods under federal bankruptcy exemption); *In re* Doss, 298 B.R. 866 (Bankr. W.D. Tenn. 2003) (big screen television was household good within meaning of bankruptcy lien avoidance provision); *In re* Elst, 210 B.R. 790 (Bankr. E.D. Wis. 1997) (under federal bankruptcy exemptions, bicycle was not a household good because it was not used in and around the house); *In re* French, 177 B.R. 568 (Bankr. E.D. Tenn. 1995) (camera and accessories used to take family pictures and VCR used for personal entertainment were household goods under federal bankruptcy exemptions); *cf. In re* Hirsch, 338 B.R. 193 (Bankr. W.D.N.Y. 2006) (coin collection exempt up to face value of coins under New York exemption for cash; to extent numismatic value exceeded face value, collection would be sold and exempt amount paid to debtors). *But see In re* Thomas, 2005 WL 2429963 (Bankr. C.D. Ill. Sept. 21, 2005) (pool table not household goods for purposes of lien avoidance under 11 U.S.C. § 522(f)); *In re* Hicks, 276 B.R. 84 (Bankr. W.D. Va. 2001) (movie and video cameras and pool table not exempt as household goods).

372 CSC Holdings, Inc. v. Sam's Electronics, Inc., 2006 WL 1620242 (W.D. Okla. June 8, 2006) (watch was exempt, ring was not; both worn regularly, but debtor provided evidence of small value only of watch); *In re* Stegall, 2007 WL 1125635 (Bankr. S.D. Iowa Apr. 3, 2007) (former Iowa exemption for ring "owned and received by the debtor . . . on or before the date of marriage" would not exempt replacement diamond, bought after original was lost; note that statute has been amended to delete the operative language); *In re* Urie, 2006 WL 533514 (Bankr. W.D. Mo. Jan. 31, 2006) (Missouri's $1500 exemption for "wedding ring" covers engagement ring and may be stacked with $500 jewelry exemption to fully exempt $2000 ring); *In re* Hazelhurst, 228 B.R. 199 (Bankr. E.D. Tenn. 1998) (some jewelry may be exempted as "necessary and proper wearing apparel," depending on value, how often it is worn, and for what occasions; diamond engagement ring from former husband, which debtor no longer wore, was not exempt, but

knacks.[373] Some states specifically list firearms as exempt,[374] and in other states some courts have found them covered by more general exemptions.[375] Lawnmowers and other equipment for maintaining the property are often found to fall within an exemption for household appliances or furnishings.[376] Most states provide an exemption for health aids and one court has allowed a mobility-impaired debtor to exempt a modified van, up to the value of the modifications, and stack that exemption with the motor vehicle exemption.[377]

Many statutes provide an exemption for motor vehicles.[378] In some states the exempt amount is increased if

amethyst ring inherited from grandmother and worn about once a week was exempt); *In re* Wilson, 213 B.R. 413 (Bankr. D.R.I. 1997) (championship football ring which player wore daily was "held primarily for personal use" and was exempt when ring had significant sentimental value and had not been bought as investment); *In re* Meyer, 211 B.R. 203 (Bankr. E.D. Va. 1997) (Virginia exemption for wearing apparel protected cuff links and inexpensive watch that had been bought for everyday wear rather than investment purposes); *In re* Lynch, 139 B.R. 868 (Bankr. N.D. Ohio 1992) (watch and diamond and ruby jewelry not exempt as household goods); Merrill Lynch Interfunding, Inc. v. Argenti, 2001 Conn. Super. LEXIS 1992 (Conn. Super. Ct. July 20, 2001) (diamond ring given to wife on twelfth anniversary was neither wedding nor engagement ring and is not necessary apparel when it was large, expensive, and not worn regularly); *In re* Winters, 40 P.3d 1231 (Wyo. 2002) (mother's wedding ring that unmarried debtor inherited not exempt as wedding ring under Wyoming law). *But see In re* Weeden, 306 B.R. 449 (Bankr. W.D.N.Y. 2004) (diamond engagement ring not exempt); *In re* Tiberia, 227 B.R. 26 (Bankr. W.D.N.Y. 1998) (diamond ring given to fiancée at time of engagement, and not used in wedding ceremony, was not a "wedding ring" within meaning of New York exemption); *cf. In re* Peterson, 280 B.R. 886 (Bankr. S.D. Ala. 2001) (items bought to enhance prestige or display wealth, such as expensive jewelry, not exempt; mink coat not exempt because "monetary value clearly outweighs utility value"; less expensive of two watches exempt).

373 *In re* Lucas, 77 B.R. 242 (B.A.P. 9th Cir. 1987) (applying California household property exemption; Hummel figurines exempt); *In re* Pullman, 317 B.R. 324 (Bankr. E.D. Va. 2004) (sports memorabilia that were not received from ancestor not heirlooms despite intent to pass them on to children); *In re* LaJuerrne, 2004 WL 2192515 (Bankr. D. Kan. July 9, 2004) (extensive collection of automotive memorabilia; many but not all items exempt); *cf. In re* Lebovitz, 360 B.R. 612 (B.A.P. 6th Cir. 2007) (Tennessee's unlimited exemption for "necessary and proper" wearing apparel protects "serviceable apparel appropriate to the work performed by debtor" even if some jewelry included; "luxury items," ranging in price from $1000 to $8000, were not necessary and proper).

374 *See In re* McCabe, 280 B.R. 841 (Bankr. N.D. Iowa 2002) (when exemption for one firearm had no cap, debtor could exempt costly shotgun bought on eve of bankruptcy); *In re* Maynard, 139 P.3d 803 (Mont. 2006) (statute protects required military equipment plus one gun; debtor not in National Guard or militia may use wildcard to exempt second gun). *But see In re* Lawson, 2006 WL 2130650 (E.D. Okla. June 21, 2006) (Oklahoma firearms exemption applies only to guns for personal or household use, not to valuable collection held for investment or used in business as bail bondsman); *cf. In re* Brown, 189 B.R. 653 (Bankr. M.D. La. 1995) (Louisiana exemption for arms and military accoutrements applied only to weapons kept for military purposes, not those kept for hunting or collectibles).

375 *In re* Heath, 318 B.R. 115 (Bankr. W.D. Ky. 2004) (in rural area where adult son hunted deer for family table, one rifle suitable for deer hunting was exempt household good); *In re* Karaus, 276 B.R. 227 (Bankr. D. Neb. 2002) (firearm kept for self defense is household good, but gun collection acquired for historical or aesthetic interest is not exempt as "immediate personal possession"); *In re* Mason, 254 B.R. 764 (Bankr. D. Idaho 2000) (firearm may be exempt as household good, even though Idaho also has separate exemption for firearms; use of firearm for hunting or home defense favors exemption); *In re* Rhines, 227 B.R. 308 (Bankr. D. Mont. 1998) (rifle and shotgun were household goods under federal bankruptcy exemptions when debtor regularly hunted and game was main source of meat for family); *In re* Crawford, 226 B.R. 484 (Bankr. N.D. Ga. 1998) (rifle kept to defend home was household good under federal bankruptcy exemptions); *In re* Maynard, 139 P.3d 803 (Mont. 2006) (debtors may exempt one gun under firearms exemption and another under wildcard); *see also In re* Shell, 295 B.R. 129 (Bankr. D. Alaska 2003) (only one gun may be exempted under Alaska's household goods exemption); *In re* Raines, 161 B.R. 548 (Bankr. N.D. Ga. 1993) (handgun kept for defense had sufficiently strong "functional nexus" with the home to make it an exempt household good under federal bankruptcy exemptions), *aff'd*, 170 B.R. 187 (N.D. Ga. 1994). *But see In re* Debias, 1999 U.S. App. LEXIS 29860 (10th Cir. Nov. 15, 1999) (handgun not an exempt household good under Colorado law because it was "not akin" to any items on statutory list of exempt items); *cf. In re* McGreevy, 955 F.2d 957 (4th Cir. 1992) (shotgun and rifle used primarily for sport away from home do not support and facilitate day-to-day living within the home so do not fall within federal bankruptcy exemption for household goods); *In re* French, 177 B.R. 568 (Bankr. E.D. Tenn. 1995) (revolver kept for self defense was not a household good under federal bankruptcy exemptions when debtor lived with sister who already owned a handgun for that purpose, nor was shotgun when husband testified that wife needed it to protect home in his absence, but wife did not know how to load or fire it).

376 *In re* Irwin, 232 B.R. 151 (Bankr. D. Minn. 1999) (Minnesota exemption for household appliances, televisions, radios, and phonographs covered lawn mower, which was necessary to maintain home); *In re* Andrews, 225 B.R. 485 (Bankr. D. Idaho 1998) (hand tools were reasonably necessary household goods); *In re* Payne, 215 B.R. 889 (Bankr. N.D. Okla. 1997) (both riding lawn mower and push lawn mower were exempt under "household and kitchen furniture" exemption as both were reasonably necessary to keep lawn acceptable and avoid nuisance citation by municipality).

377 *In re* Hellen, 329 B.R. 678 (Bankr. N.D. Ill. 2005) (doctor-recommended modifications to van to enable patient to drive entitled to exemption as "professionally prescribed heath aids" even though no written prescription). *But see In re* Khan, 375 B.R. 5 (Bankr. M.D. Fla. 2007) (unmodified van, approved for a handicapped parking permit, not an exempt health aid; must be "uniquely suited" to accommodate disability); *In re* McCashen, 339 B.R. 907 (Bankr. N.D. Ohio 2006) (even if unmodified van could be health aid—which is debatable—not exempt when neither professionally prescribed nor medically necessary; no health aid exemption for only model of van roomy enough for morbidly obese debtor).

378 *In re* Bell, 333 B.R. 839 (Bankr. W.D. Mo. 2005) (amended Missouri statute covering "any motor vehicle in the aggregate" allows debtors to split the exemption between two vehicles; here

the debtor or a family member is disabled.[379]

debtors stacked head of household, two wildcard, one motor vehicle and part of another motor vehicle exemption to exempt one vehicle, and applied balance of second motor vehicle exemption to second vehicle); *In re* Scott, 332 B.R. 377 (Bankr. E.D. Mo. 2005) (Missouri's amended motor vehicle exemption, "any vehicle in the aggregate," may be split to protect two vehicles); *In re* Lund, 2005 WL 3620335 (Bankr. W.D. Mo. Dec. 9, 2005) (motorcycle is exempt but not motorized bicycle); *In re* Bailey, 326 B.R. 750 (Bankr. S.D. Iowa 2004) (Iowa motor vehicle exemption would cover classic Ford, disassembled and currently inoperable, being rebuilt for investment; when essential parts were present, it was "self-propelled vehicle" within statutory definition); *In re* Vicknair, 315 B.R. 822 (Bankr. E.D. La. 2004) (history of Louisiana's frequently amended motor vehicle exemption; specific exemption for one motor vehicle per household, with $7500 cap, trumps general tools of trade exemption; bus driver may not exempt bus as tool of trade); *In re* Buchberger, 311 B.R. 794 (Bankr. D. Ariz. 2004) ("personal, family or household" purposes include recreation; applying rule of liberal construction and definition in transportation statute to exempt all terrain vehicle); *In re* Sleeth, 300 B.R. 351 (Bankr. D. Ariz. 2003) (motor home is motor vehicle); Schilling v. Tran, 287 B.R. 887 (W.D. Ky. 2002) (allowing husband and wife to stack motor vehicle exemptions to exempt one vehicle; when title listed both spouses in alternative each had ownership interest); *In re* Moore, 251 B.R. 380 (Bankr. W.D. Mo. 2000) (when Missouri motor vehicle exemption did not explicitly exclude recreational all terrain vehicles, principle of liberal construction required inclusion); *cf. In re* Belsome, 434 F.3d 774 (5th Cir. 2005) (Louisiana's specific exemption for motor vehicle trumps general tools of trade exemption; school bus exempt only up to amount of motor vehicle exemption); *In re* Savoie, 351 B.R. 392 (Bankr. W.D. La. 2006) (former Louisiana statute, now amended, allowed exemption only for one vehicle per household used for work or commuting; debtors could exempt either pickup or family car). *But cf. In re* Carelock, 2006 WL 3708688 (Bankr. S.D. Ga. Jan. 13, 2006) (insurance proceeds, which debtor intended to use to replace totaled car, not exempt because Georgia law does not exempt proceeds of exempt property); *In re* Hill, 310 B.R. 294 (Bankr. W.D. La. 2004) (Louisiana motor vehicle exemption applies only to vehicle used for work or commuting; retired or unemployed debtor may not exempt vehicle); *In re* Barbera, 285 B.R. 355 (Bankr. D.R.I. 2002) (Rhode Island motor vehicle exemption does not cover boat, when definition of vehicle in state transportation law includes operation on highway); *In re* Simpson, 238 B.R. 776 (Bankr. S.D. Ill. 1999) (Illinois exemption for debtor's "interest in a motor vehicle" did not exempt insurance proceeds for "totaled" vehicle); *In re* Struckhoff, 231 B.R. 69 (Bankr. E.D. Mo. 1999) (Missouri exemption for "any motor vehicle" covers exemption of only one motor vehicle when other exemptions refer to "one or more" or use the plural; statute has been amended); *In re* Drewes, 217 B.R. 978 (D.N.H. 1998) (motorcycle is not protected by exemption for "automobile").

379 *See In re* Sleeth, 300 B.R. 351 (Bankr. D. Ariz. 2003) (applying enhanced exemption for "physically disabled" when debtor had serious heart disease and qualified for Social Security disability payments); *see also In re* Hellen, 329 B.R. 678 (Bankr. N.D. Ill. 2005) (mobility-impaired debtor could claim "professionally prescribed health aids" exemption up to value of modifications to van and stack this exemption with motor vehicle exemption). *But see In re* Coleman, 209 B.R. 739 (Bankr. D. Colo. 1997) (Colorado's $3000 "elderly or disabled" exemption for a motor vehicle did not protect a motor vehicle used by an able-bodied debtor to transport an arguably disabled dependent to medical treatment).

12.5.3.3 Tools of the Trade

A useful exemption found in many state statutes protects "tools of a trade." Some states also have an exemption for property used in agriculture.[380]

In defining tools of the trade many states apply a use test, and reject a narrower definition of tools as inanimate objects that augment or extend the limits of human ability or power.[381] Texas exempts motor vehicles only if they are

380 Painewebber, Inc. v. Murray, 260 B.R. 815 (E.D. Tex. 2001) (when rural homestead used for agriculture debtor could exempt tractor, riding mower, and pick-up truck under agricultural exemption, in addition to the one vehicle per licensed driver allowed by motor vehicle exemption); *In re* Larson, 260 B.R. 174 (D. Colo. 2001) (livestock used for breeding is exempt); *In re* Miller, 370 B.R. 914 (Bankr. D. Minn. 2007) (farm wife who worked full-time off-farm was engaged in farming when she kept farm books, delivered meals to field, ran errands, drove tractor, and sometimes worked in fields); *In re* Hintzman, 2007 WL 80964 (Bankr. D. Minn. Jan. 8, 2007) (debtors not engaged in farming; four-year history of unprofitable farming, statement of intent to return, but no arrangements to resume); Devine v. Devine, 2005 WL 1926038 (Bankr. N.D. Iowa Aug. 5, 2005) (farming equipment exempt); *In re* Thompson, 311 B.R. 822 (Bankr. D. Kan. 2004) (criteria for determining whether debtors are farmers; husband worked at least forty hours on farm, in addition to full-time off-farm employment, and wife, also employed off-farm, devoted "considerable energy and personal resources" to farming; intention to make a profit must be shown, but expectation need not be reasonable; farm equipment was exempt); *In re* Kieffer, 279 B.R. 290 (Bankr. D. Kan. 2002) (allowing husband and wife to stack their exemptions for farm equipment when wife shared work on farm in addition to her off-farm employment, couple made business decisions together, and wife had signed notes for purchase of farm equipment); *In re* Larson, 260 B.R. 174 (Bankr. D. Colo. 2001) (debtors were "engaged in agriculture as principal occupation" even though they were working in trucking business in attempt to save unprofitable family farm; husband and wife could each stack an agricultural exemption with a tools of trade exemption for farm implements and livestock).

381 *In re* Gregory, 245 B.R. 171 (B.A.P. 10th Cir. 2000) (Wyo. law) (Air Force security officer's practice pistol was not a means of carrying on his trade, when he had another pistol which he actually carried while on duty, and employer did not require practice pistol), *aff'd*, 246 F.3d 681 (10th Cir. 2000); *In re* Siegel, 214 B.R. 329 (W.D. Tenn. 1997) (lawyer in solo practice could exempt computer system as tool of trade; rejecting test whether item is "uniquely suited" to use in the trade, in favor of fact-based consideration of the role of computers in a modern law office); *In re* Hively, 358 B.R. 752 (Bankr. C.D. Ill. 2007) (cargo trailer used to haul food and cooking equipment by caterers who cooked at events was exempt; when value was less than statutory cap, trailer qualified as "tool of small value"); *In re* Savoie, 351 B.R. 392 (Bankr. W.D. La. 2006) (to qualify for Louisiana tools of trade exemption motor vehicle must be used by debtor or household; no exemption for semi-trailers owned by debtor but driven by independent contractor drivers); *In re* Giles, 340 B.R. 543 (Bankr. E.D. Pa. 2006) (applying use test

"peculiarly adapted" to use in a particular trade, but applies a more flexible use test for other property.[382]

A tools of the trade exemption may be used in some jurisdictions to exempt a vehicle which is necessary to the debtor's livelihood—although something more than commuting must often be shown.[383] A computer system was found to be a tool of a trade, when the employer furnished software so the debtor could work at home, even though work at home was not mandatory.[384]

---

for federal bankruptcy exemption; standard motor vehicle was tool of trade for artisan who made hats and sold at craft fairs; public transportation not a reasonable alternative for buying materials and attending shows); *In re* Gray, 303 B.R. 632 (Bankr. W.D. Mo. 2003) (applying use test; horses and cattle used to teach riding and roping are tools of trade of riding and rodeo skills instructor); *In re* Shell, 295 B.R. 129 (Bankr. D. Alaska 2003) (tools and equipment used to maintain owner-occupied multiple dwelling were exempt tools of a trade); *In re* VanWinkle, 265 B.R. 247 (Bankr. D. Colo. 2001) (independent truck driver may exempt truck); *In re* Aurelio, 252 B.R. 102 (Bankr. N.D. Miss. 2000) (property that is reasonably necessary for the performance of debtor's occupation; restaurant equipment qualifies, but not proceeds of its sale in absence of evidence of intent to resume the business); *In re* Nipper, 243 B.R. 33 (Bankr. E.D. Tenn. 1999) (Tennessee tools of trade exemption is meant to apply to hand tools of small value, not capital assets or major pieces of machinery such as independent trucker's tractor-trailer); *In re* Mackey, 209 B.R. 251 (Bankr. E.D. Okla. 1997) (Oklahoma tools of the trade exemption should be broadly construed to include not only small, handheld things, but also any other property which is "reasonably necessary, convenient or suitable for [the owner's] trade or profession"; allowing independent truck driver to exempt up to $5000 limit for value of Peterbilt truck); *In re* Carson, 184 B.R. 587 (Bankr. N.D. Okla. 1995) (Oklahoma tools of trade exemption protects lawyer's computer system, as computers are "truly necessary" to the "efficient and modern practice of law" in the community). *But see In re* Rollins, 2007 WL 2428079 (Bankr. W.D. Mo. Aug. 17, 2007) (certificates of deposit used to post statutorily required security by debtor credit repair service not tool of trade; Missouri has broad tools of trade exemption, but unclear whether cash or certificate of deposit could ever be covered); *In re* Gentry, 297 B.R. 553 (Bankr. C.D. Ill. 2003) (Illinois exemption is construed narrowly to cover only artisans' "tools of modest value"; self-employed contractor may not exempt Bobcat regardless of its use); *cf. In re* White, 234 B.R. 388 (Bankr. W.D. Tex. 1999) (custom software which debtor computer programmers had created and licensed to their employer was not a tool, but a product, of their trade, and thus was not exempt).

382 *In re* Juhasz, 208 B.R. 32 (Bankr. S.D. Tex. 1997) (ordinary Porsche used to call on customers and deliver jewelry and collectibles was not a tool of the trade when there was no modification which adapted it for particular use as a delivery vehicle); *In re* Baldowski, 191 B.R. 102 (Bankr. N.D. Tex. 1996) (property need not be "peculiarly adapted" to the trade, but must be "tools" or "apparatus"; ordinary dishes, cutlery, tables exempt as tools of the trade of a café owner); *cf.* Goffney v. Prime Bank, 2002 WL 122155 (Tex. App. Jan. 31, 2002) (criminal defense lawyer could not exempt certificates of deposit occasionally pledged to post bail for clients; debtor could practice criminal law without them, and certificates were not "used with sufficient regularity to indicate actual use").

383 *In re* Lyall, 191 B.R. 78 (E.D. Va. 1996) (car must be necessary, not merely convenient or useful, in debtor's occupation to qualify as exempt tool of the trade), *on remand*, 193 B.R. 767 (Bankr. E.D. Va. 1996) (automobile is "necessary" within meaning of the Virginia "tools of a trade" exemption if debtor would be unable to compete effectively without it; when self-employed architect used car frequently to visit job sites and attend meetings with municipal officials, it was exempt); *In re* Taylor, 2005 WL 846222 (Bankr. D. V.I. Apr. 7, 2005) (motor vehicle not a tool of a trade unless it is itself used a tool, for example, as a taxi or a tow truck); *In re* Vicknair, 315 B.R. 822 (Bankr. E.D. La. 2004) (Louisiana's motor vehicle exemption, with $7500 cap, trumps general tools of trade exemption; bus driver may not exempt her bus as tool of trade); *In re* Black, 280 B.R. 258 (Bankr. D. Colo. 2002) (self-employed building contractor may exempt truck used to tow equipment and transport tools to worksites, as otherwise debtor could not practice his occupation); *In re* VanWinkle, 265 B.R. 247 (Bankr. D. Colo. 2001) (independent truck driver may exempt truck); *In re* Heimbouch, 246 B.R. 895 (Bankr. D. Neb. 2000) (Nebraska exemption for motor vehicle used in connection with business did not exempt farmer's classic Corvette, although sometimes used for farm business, when farmer also owned pickup trucks and jeep); *In re* Black, 225 B.R. 610 (Bankr. M.D. La. 1998) (tools of trade exemption would protect truck which debtor did not personally drive when debtor depended on income from truck for her living, but denying exemption because truck's size brought it within former statute's definition of nonexempt "luxury automobile"); *In re* Clifford, 222 B.R. 8 (Bankr. D. Conn. 1998) (tools of trade of building contractor included pickup truck used to transport workers and materials to job sites, lift truck, crawler loader, and fax machine used for bidding, all of which were necessary to enable debtor to compete as contractor); *In re* Rawn, 199 B.R. 733 (Bankr. E.D. Cal. 1996) (car would be "tool of the trade" only if debtor's occupation was "uniquely dependent on" its use, for example, a realtor who showed houses to prospective buyers); *In re* Erwin, 199 B.R. 628 (Bankr. S.D. Tex. 1996) (more than "general value and use in business" was required to make a car a tool of the trade; when debtor was a constable who served process, but any four-door car, including a rental, would serve, car was not exempt); *see also In re* McCoy, 2006 WL 2868611 (E.D. Va. Oct. 3, 2006) (motor vehicle not exempt tool of trade under federal bankruptcy exemptions unless "specially suited" or "peculiarly adapted" to debtor's business; tax deduction for business use of vehicle not probative on this issue), *aff'd*, 219 Fed. Appx. 326 (4th Cir. 2007); *In re* White, 352 B.R. 633 (Bankr. E.D. La. 2006) (vehicle used for commuting not exempt tool of trade under federal bankruptcy exemptions); *In re* Giles, 340 B.R. 543 (Bankr. E.D. Pa. 2006) (standard motor vehicle was tool of trade under federal bankruptcy exemptions for artisan who made hats and sold at craft fairs; public transportation not a reasonable alternative for buying materials and attending shows). *But see* Neb. Rev. Stat. § 25-1556 (explicitly exempting motor vehicle required to get to work).

384 *In re* Biancavilla, 173 B.R. 930 (Bankr. D. Idaho 1994); *see also In re* Siegel, 214 B.R. 329 (W.D. Tenn. 1997) (lawyer in solo practice could exempt computer system as tool of trade); *In re* Carson, 184 B.R. 587 (Bankr. N.D. Okla. 1995) (Oklahoma tools of trade exemption protects lawyer's computer system). *But see In re* Hoffpauir, 258 B.R. 447 (Bankr. D. Idaho 2001) (computer not tool of trade when debtor wife sometimes worked at home, but no evidence that this was required; evidence that employer supplied software or equipment would be probative).

Some states limit the tools of the trade to the debtor's principal occupation.[385] Wyoming has construed this to limit only the number of exemptions: the debtor may exempt the tools of one part-time occupation, or several, up to the $2000 cap, but may not claim an exemption for each trade.[386] A debtor who is not currently practicing a trade but intends to return to it may be able to claim a tools of the trade exemption, depending on the strength of the evidence.[387]

385 *In re* Lampe, 278 B.R. 205 (B.A.P. 10th Cir. 2002) (Kan. law) (spouses could stack exemptions when farming was principal occupation, even though both spouses also worked off-farm), *aff'd*, 331 F.3d 750 (10th Cir. 2003); *In re* Kieffer, 279 B.R. 290 (Bankr. D. Kan. 2002) (wife's principal occupation was farming, even though she also worked off the farm); *In re* Zink, 177 B.R. 713 (Bankr. D. Kan. 1995) (construing Kansas "principal occupation" language to allow exemption for tools of only that occupation); Seel v. Wittman, 173 B.R. 734 (D. Kan. 1994) (lawn mower used in side business not exempt). *But see In re* Thompson, 311 B.R. 822 (Bankr. D. Kan. 2004) (may exempt tools of more than one occupation, as long as activity "has a legitimate business or profit motive," but one $7500 cap applies to total for all trades; even if principal occupation test applied, farm equipment was exempt when husband farmed at least forty hours a week and wife devoted "considerable energy and personal resources" to farm).

386 *In re* Bechtoldt, 210 B.R. 599 (B.A.P. 10th Cir. 1997) (Wyo. law) (allowing debtor who worked primarily as plumber but also as painter to exempt painting tools).

387 Planned Parenthood of Columbus/Willamette, Inc. v. Am. Coalition of Life Activists, 2007 WL 4118597 (S.D. Ohio Nov. 16, 2007) (minister not presently serving as pastor may claim books as tools of trade, when he writes and plans someday to return to preaching; considerations are whether debtor has reasonable prospect of returning to trade, time away, and any other circumstances, here, involvement in a lawsuit); *In re* Miller, 370 B.R. 914 (Bankr. D. Minn. 2007) (intent to return shown; thirty-five years of farming, and "definite arrangements" to resume); *In re* Hintzman, 2007 WL 80964 (Bankr. D. Minn. Jan. 8, 2007) (intent to return not shown; four years unprofitable farming, no arrangements to resume, simple statement of intent not enough); *In re* Goss, 352 B.R. 309 (Bankr. E.D. Okla. 2006) (farm equipment not exempt when farmer was retired or, at most, farming only as "hobby"); Devine v. Devine, 2005 WL 1926038 (Bankr. N.D. Iowa Aug. 5, 2005) (debtors who were living and working off farm could exempt farming equipment when intent to return to farming sufficiently shown); *In re* Thompson, 311 B.R. 822 (Bankr. D. Kan. 2004) (farmers who raised game birds sold entire stock "to make ends meet," but intended to resume as soon as they could raise the necessary money; equipment was exempt); *In re* Lund, 2003 WL 21673545 (Bankr. N.D. Iowa July 14, 2003) (farm equipment exempt even though couple who had farmed for decades did not plant crop because bank cut off credit; factors include intensity of past farming and sincerity and reasonableness of intent to resume; that profits are "speculative" is not fatal); *In re* Aurelio, 252 B.R. 102 (Bankr. N.D. Miss. 2000) (tools of trade exemption did not cover proceeds of sale of equipment, when no intent to invest in new equipment and resume business); *In re* Mausser, 225 B.R. 667 (Bankr. N.D. Iowa 1998) (debtors not actively engaged in farming must show something more than mere intent to resume, such as long previous involvement in farming, or some actions such as renting land, to claim Iowa exemption for farm equipment for debtors "engaged in farming"); Girgis v. Macaluso Realty Co., 778 So. 2d 1210 (La. Ct. App. 2001) (temporary non-use of tools does not eliminate exemption); Landry v. Landry, 917 A.2d 1262 (N.H. 2007) (incarcerated debtor could exempt mechanics' tools; had worked as mechanic before imprisonment and intended to do so upon release); *see also In re* Lampe, 278 B.R. 205 (B.A.P. 10th Cir. 2002) (farming remained debtors' principal occupation even though they were facing farm foreclosure and had taken outside jobs, when they continued to farm and would do so on other land even if foreclosure went through), *aff'd*, 331 F.3d 750 (10th Cir. 2003); *In re* Banke, 275 B.R. 317 (Bankr. N.D. Iowa 2002) (court considers intensity of past business, sincerity of intent to return, prospects for return, lapse of time, and any other circumstances; boat not tool of trade of fishing guide when not used for twelve years, during which time debtor worked full time at other occupation).

12.5.3.4 Tenancy by the Entireties in Personal Property

Some states recognize tenancy by the entireties, which protects marital property from attachment for individual debts of one spouse, in personal as well as real property.[388]

388 *DISTRICT OF COLUMBIA*: Morrison v. Potter, 764 A.2d 234 (D.C. 2000) (married couples' joint checking accounts presumed to be held in tenancy by entireties; standard joint tenancy language in account agreement does not rebut presumption); Roberts & Lloyd, Inc. v. Zyblut, 691 A.2d 635 (D.C. 1997) (property owned by married couple presumed to be owned in tenancy by the entirety, even if words of conveyance would have created ordinary joint tenancy).

FLORIDA: *In re* Sinnreich, 391 F.3d 1295 (11th Cir. 2004) (Fla. law) (real and personal property held in tenancy by entireties with non-debtor spouse is exempt); *In re* Kepley, 352 B.R. 526 (Bankr. M.D. Fla. 2006) (funds in bank account owned in tenancy by entireties can not be reached for individual debts; here, no suggestion that funds belonged only to debtor or were placed in account for purpose of hindering creditors); *In re* Kossow, 325 B.R. 478 (Bankr. S.D. Fla. 2005) (noting disagreement among Florida courts as to breadth of *Beal Bank* presumption and concluding it applies to all personal property acquired in accordance with the unities of an entireties estate); Beal Bank v. Almand & Associates, 780 So. 2d 45 (Fla. 2001) (couple with two names on account presumed to own it by entireties unless expressly disclaimed; signature card for joint tenancy not express disclaimer unless couple was offered entireties account and declined); *see also In re* Hill, 197 F.3d 1135 (11th Cir. 1999) (transfer to tenancy by the entireties may be attacked as fraudulent transfer, but due process requires that non-debtor spouse be made a party to this proceeding); *In re* Koesling, 210 B.R. 487 (Bankr. N.D. Fla. 1997) (Florida recognizes tenancy by the entireties in personal property; couple met burden of proof of intent when ownership of promissory note was in both names, and husband testified as to intent; note that *Beal Bank* removes the burden of proof from the debtors); Nunez v. Fernandez, 724 So. 2d 182 (Fla. Dist. Ct. App. 1999) (judgment debt of one spouse may not be set off against mortgage and promissory note owned by couple in tenancy by entireties); *cf.* Thomas J. Konrad & Associates v. McCoy, 705 So. 2d 948 (Fla. Dist. Ct. App. 1998) (creditor of husband sought to garnish couple's bank account owned by tenancy of entireties; remanding to decide whether husband's transfer of his separate funds into joint account, after judgment had been entered against him, was

A number of states hold that, when a married couple jointly owns personal property, a presumption arises that it is owned by the entireties.[389] Documentation such as a bank signature card that states that the asset is held as a joint tenancy does not necessarily rebut this presumption.[390] The general rules governing entireties property are discussed in § 12.5.2.9, *supra*.

fraudulent). *But see* Xayavong v. Sunny Gifts, Inc., 891 So. 2d 1075 (Fla. Dist. Ct. App. 2004) (*Beal Bank* presumption that married couple's property owned in tenancy by the entireties does not apply to motor vehicles when title statute unambiguously prescribes how to create co-ownership interest); *cf. In re* Pereau, 2007 WL 907545 (Bankr. M.D. Fla. Mar. 13, 2007) (listing six "unities" needed for tenancy by entireties; unity of interest not present when settlement check covered husband's injuries and wife's loss of consortium, two distinct claims).

MARYLAND: Cruickshank-Wallace v. County Banking & Trust Co., 885 A.2d 403 (Md. Ct. Spec. App. 2005) (Maryland recognizes tenancy by entireties in personal property, but here, tax refunds arising from husband's individual earnings not owned in tenancy by entireties, even though couple filed joint returns and had agreed that their property would be owned in tenancy by entireties).

MICHIGAN: Zavradinos v. JTRB, Inc., 2007 WL 2404612 (Mich. Ct. App. Aug. 23, 2007) (married couple's property presumed owned in tenancy by entireties unless otherwise "expressly provided").

MISSOURI: *In re* Booth, 309 B.R. 568 (Bankr. W.D. Mo. 2004) (presumption of tenancy by entireties rebutted when vehicle purchased during marriage was titled in husband alone; no tenancy by entireties in vehicles purchased before marriage); *In re* Walker, 279 B.R. 544 (Bankr. W.D. Mo. 2002) (despite Missouri presumption that married couples own their property by entireties, tax refund of debtor and sole wage-earner wife was her individual property and could be garnished by her individual creditors); *In re* Thorpe, 251 B.R. 723 (Bankr. W.D. Mo. 2000) (Missouri permits ownership of personalty by entireties, but requirements not satisfied even though motor vehicle was acquired during marriage); *In re* Brown, 234 B.R. 907 (Bankr. W.D. Mo. 1999) (under Missouri law, real and personal property of married couple is presumed to be owned in tenancy by the entireties, and thus exempt from claims of individual creditors); *see also* Scott v. Union Planters' Bank, 196 S.W.3d 574 (Mo. Ct. App. 2006) (bank not liable to wife for allowing husband to withdraw entire sum in bank account, but court notes that this decision is not meant to "disturb settled law" that an execution for a judgment against one spouse can not affect a bank account held in tenancy by entireties).

PENNSYLVANIA: 78 Arch St. Associates v. Blatstein (*In re* Blatstein), 192 F.3d 88, 96 (3d Cir. 1999) (in Pennsylvania, real or personal property of married couple is presumed to be owned in tenancy by entireties); DiFlorido v. DiFlorido, 459 Pa. 641, 331 A.2d 174 (1975) (household goods are presumed to be entireties property); Cohen v. Goldberg, 431 Pa. 192, 244 A.2d 763 (1968) (money held in joint bank account was entireties property).

RHODE ISLAND: *In re* Homonoff, 261 B.R. 551 (Bankr. D.R.I. 2001) (personal property may be owned by entireties, but only if that intent clearly appears in conveyance; not shown here).

TENNESSEE: Avenell v. Gibson, 2005 WL 458733 (Tenn. Ct. App. Feb. 28, 2005) (1988 change in bank account attachment procedure did not change long-standing rule that presumes that married couple's bank account is held in tenancy by entireties, notwithstanding account agreement describing joint tenancy).

VERMONT: McNeilly v. Geremia, 249 B.R. 576 (B.A.P. 1st Cir. 2000) (proceeds of entireties real estate in Rhode Island that were transferred to Vermont bank account owned in tenancy by entireties were exempt under Vermont law, which applied even though debtors were in Rhode Island).

VIRGINIA: *In re* Thomas, 312 F.3d 145 (4th Cir. 2002) (even in joint bankruptcy entireties property may be reached only by joint creditors); *In re* Potter, 274 B.R. 224 (Bankr. E.D. Va. 2002) (personal property in Virginia may be owned by entireties, but documents must either use the words "tenancy by entireties" or describe owners as husband and wife; not applicable when stock titled to couple's two names, in joint tenancy with right of survivorship, and no mention of marital status); *In re* Massey, 225 B.R. 887 (Bankr. E.D. Va. 1998) (under Virginia law, personal property could be owned in tenancy by entirety, even if it was not proceeds of sale of entireties real estate; when brokerage account described shares as owned by couple "as tenants by entirety," this was sufficient); Rogers v. Rogers, 512 S.E.2d 821 (Va. 1999) (when creditors had federal court judgment against husband and state judgment against wife both apparently resulting from the same transactions, entireties property could not be attached; only a joint judgment against husband and wife could be satisfied from entireties property). *But cf.* Rue & Associates, Inc. v. White, 2006 WL 2022184 (Va. Cir. Ct. July 18, 2006) (married couple's bank accounts were joint tenancy, not tenancy by entireties, when papers did not specify tenancy by entireties).

WYOMING: *In re* Welty, 217 B.R. 907 (Bankr. D. Wyo. 1998) (intangibles, here a business, could be held in tenancy by entirety, but documents must show clear intent to create this type of ownership).

Other states do not recognize tenancy by entireties in personal property, for example: *In re* Gillette, 248 B.R. 845 (Bankr. M.D. Fla. 1999) (Florida debtors could not hold tenancy by entireties in investment account located in Wisconsin, which does not recognize tenancy by entireties); Lurie v. Sheriff of Gallatin County, 999 P.2d 342 (Mont. 2000) (tenancy by entireties not recognized in Montana, even for property moved to Montana from a state that does recognize it); *see also* § 12.7.1, *infra*.

389 78 Arch St. Associates v. Blatstein (*In re* Blatstein), 192 F.3d 88, 96 (3d Cir. 1999); *In re* Hinton, 378 B.R. 371 (Bankr. M.D. Fla. 2007) (property of married couple presumed to be held in tenancy by entireties; when individual tax refunds deposited in bank account or used to purchase certificate of deposit held in tenancy by entireties, refunds were exempt); *In re* Pereau, 2007 WL 907545 (Bankr. M.D. Fla. Mar. 13, 2007) (*Beal Bank* presumption applies to all property, not just bank accounts, but tenancy by entireties not shown here, because no unity of interest); *In re* Kossow, 325 B.R. 478 (Bankr. S.D. Fla. 2005) (presumption that all personal property of married couple is held as tenancy by the entireties as long as acquired in accordance with unities of possession, interest, title, and time with right of survivorship); Beal Bank v. Almand & Associates, 780 So. 2d 45 (Fla. 2001) (recognizing presumption; creditor has burden of rebutting it); Avenell v. Gibson, 2005 WL 458733 (Tenn. Ct. App. Feb. 28, 2005) (bank accounts of married couples presumed held as tenancy by the entireties).

390 Matthews v. Cohen, 2007 WL 4557244 (M.D. Fla. Dec. 21, 2007) (*Beal Bank* presumption not overcome; debtors checked "joint tenancy with survivorship" box on stock certificate; check box for "other" provided, but none for "tenancy by

12.5.4 Exemptions for Bank Accounts

Some states provide for a small amount of money held in a bank account to be exempt, ranging from $100 up to $7500.[391] Also, some states codify the rule that exempt property, for example, Social Security income, that is deposited in a bank account continues to be exempt if it is not so commingled with nonexempt funds as to be untraceable.[392] Some state statutes which provide for prepaid college tuition trust funds also exempt all or part of these funds from creditors of the donor, the prospective student, or both.[393]

Wildcard exemptions are also often available to protect some amount of cash. Attempts to treat cash as an exempt household good or tangible personal property have failed, however.[394]

12.5.5 Protection of Benefit Payments

12.5.5.1 General

Most government benefit payments are exempt under the laws governing the assistance program. In addition, many state exemption laws repeat all or some of the federal exemptions for types of benefits.[395]

In general government benefits continue to be exempt after payment to the beneficiary.[396] In at least a few states exemption protection is also given to real or personal property purchased with benefit payments.[397]

---

entireties"); Morrison v. Potter, 764 A.2d 234 (D.C. 2000) (married couples' joint checking accounts presumed to be held in tenancy by entireties; standard joint tenancy language in account agreement does not rebut presumption); Beal Bank v. Almand & Associates, 780 So. 2d 45 (Fla. 2001); Zavradinos v. JTRB, Inc., 2007 WL 2404612 (Mich. Ct. App. Aug. 23, 2007) (married couple's property presumed owned in tenancy by entireties; checking "joint tenancy with right to survival" box on brokerage account paperwork not sufficient to rebut; must specify "and not in tenancy by entireties"); Avenell v. Gibson, 2005 WL 458733 (Tenn. Ct. App. Feb. 28, 2005) (1988 change in bank account attachment procedure did not change long-standing rule that presumes that married couple's bank account is held in tenancy by entireties, notwithstanding account agreement describing joint tenancy).

While *Beal Bank* dealt with a bank signature card, it probably overrules other Florida cases holding that the form of ownership stated on a title or other ownership document is conclusive, for example: *In re* Mastrofino, 247 B.R. 330 (Bankr. M.D. Fla. 2000) (no tenancy by entireties in car that was titled to "husband or wife" and could be sold by either co-owner, nor in bank account when signature card created joint tenancy and permitted withdrawal on one signature).

391 *In re* Schapiro, 246 B.R. 751 (Bankr. W.D.N.Y. 2000) (when will left a specific sum of money this amount was currency within meaning of New York exemption and beneficiary could exempt $2500). *But cf. In re* Cordy, 254 B.R. 413 (Bankr. N.D. Ohio 2000) (Ohio exemption for "money on deposit in a bank, savings and loan institution, credit union, public utility, landlord or other person" covers only bank accounts and security deposits; U.S. savings bonds and cash surrender value of life insurance policy not exempt).

392 *See* § 12.6, *infra*.

393 *See, e.g.*, Fla. Stat. § 222.22; N.Y. C.P.L.R. 5205(j) (McKinney); Ohio Rev. Code Ann. § 2329.66(A)(16) (West); Wis. Stat. § 815.18(3)(o); *see also In re* Cheatham, 309 B.R. 631 (Bankr. M.D. Ala. 2004) (prepaid affordable college tuition contract, pursuant to Ala. Code §§ 16-33C-1 to 16-33C-13, belongs to children, and is not part of parent's bankruptcy estate). *But see In re* Addison, 368 B.R. 791 (B.A.P. 8th Cir. 2007) (prepaid tuition accounts were property of debtor, not beneficiary, when debtor could change beneficiary at will; note that recent change in bankruptcy law exempts portion of such accounts); *In re* Quackenbush, 339 B.R. 845 (Bankr. S.D.N.Y. 2006) (funds placed by father in trust for daughter's education several years before enactment of tuition savings account statute not protected by this statute, and under gifts to minors law, ceased to be held in trust when beneficiary reached majority, so were nonexempt property of daughter); *In re* Darby, 212 B.R. 382 (Bankr. M.D. Ala. 1997) (Alabama exemption for spendthrift trusts did not protect prepaid college tuition contracts purchased from state agency when parent could cancel at any time and get refund), *later opinion at* 226 B.R. 126 (Bankr. M.D. Ala. 1998) (father held tuition contracts in trust, so funds were not available to father's creditors).

394 *In re* Oakley, 344 F.3d 709 (7th Cir. 2003) (cash was not "tangible personal property" within meaning of Indiana exemption, so was protected only by $100 exemption for intangibles); *In re* Moss, 258 B.R. 427 (Bankr. W.D. Mo. 2001) ($1000 cash could not be exempted as household good but $400 could be exempted under wildcard exemption), *aff'd on other grounds*, 266 B.R. 697 (B.A.P. 8th Cir. 2001), *aff'd*, 289 F.3d 540 (8th Cir. 2002); *see also In re* Young, 297 B.R. 492 (Bankr. E.D. Tex. 2003) (interest in a trust fund, inherited from father, not personal property within meaning of Texas personal property exemption); Cartwright v. Deposit Guar. Nat'l Bank, 675 So. 2d 847 (Miss. 1996) (exemption for "tangible" personal property did not protect funds in bank account).

395 *See* Appx. F, *infra*.

396 *See* § 12.6, *infra*.

397 *See, e.g.*, *In re* Williams, 171 B.R. 451 (D.N.H. 1994) (workers' compensation lump sum deposited in bank account remained exempt, as did car purchased with lump sum; workers' compensation proceeds are "meant to be put to useful purposes"); *In re* Baker, 2006 WL 2079919 (Bankr. M.D. Ala. July 25, 2006) (Alabama workers' compensation exemption protects motor vehicle purchased with traceable proceeds of workers' compensation settlement); *In re* Gardiner, 332 B.R. 891 (Bankr. S.D. Cal. 2005) (asset acquired, in part, with workers' compensation award retained exempt status, subject to tracing requirements); *In re* Ladomer, 215 B.R. 265 (Bankr. S.D. Fla. 1997); *In re* Nelson, 179 B.R. 811 (Bankr. W.D. Va. 1994) (mobile home and lot purchased with workers' compensation funds); Broward v. Jacksonville Med. Ctr., 690 So. 2d 589 (Fla. 1997). *But see In re* Irwin, 371 B.R. 344 (Bankr. C.D. Ill. 2007) (workers' compensation settlement funds remained exempt in money market account used only for workers' compensation, but lost exemption when used to pay down lien on motor vehicle); *In re* Duemey, 347 B.R. 875 (Bankr. S.D. Ohio 2006) (vehicle purchased for debtor by ex-husband, to satisfy his debt for back child support, not exempt child support); *In re* Rajkovic, 289 B.R. 197 (Bankr. M.D. Fla. 2002) (workers' compensation funds lost exemption when large lump sum transferred to

12.5.5.2 Public Assistance Benefits

The purpose of the Temporary Assistance to Needy Families program, the successor to the Aid to Families with Dependent Children program, is to help states provide assistance to needy families so that children may be cared for in their own homes or in the homes of relatives.[398] It would be contrary to the purpose of the Act to allow creditors to attach payments received under the Act. Generally, public assistance grants are exempt under state statutes.[399]

At least five states exempt the wages, as well as the benefits, of certain present or former recipients of means-tested benefits. Rhode Island exempts all wages of a debtor who is, or within one year was, "an object of relief from any state, federal, or municipal corporation or agency."[400] Minnesota forbids all wage garnishments for six months after a return to employment and termination of public benefits for a debtor who had been a recipient of needs-based assistance or an inmate in a correctional institution.[401] Vermont forbids wage garnishments if a debtor was, within two months of the garnishment hearing, a welfare recipient.[402] New York forbids garnishment of the wages of a debtor who receives public assistance or would qualify for public assistance if the amount of the garnishment were subtracted from his or her wages.[403] Connecticut exempts wages earned by recipients under an incentive earnings or similar program.[404]

12.5.5.3 Social Security and SSI Benefits

12.5.5.3.1 Nature of the protection

The Social Security Act provides that Social Security and SSI benefits are not transferable or assignable, and forbids "execution, levy, attachment, garnishment or other legal process" to reach benefits paid or payable to recipients.[405] These benefits are exempt both before and after payment to the beneficiary,[406] and regardless of whether the creditor is a state or a private entity.[407]

Nonetheless, Social Security and certain other federal benefits may, within limits, be administratively offset for debts, including student loans, owed to the federal government.[408] Additionally, child support and alimony may be collected from certain types of Social Security benefits.[409]

12.5.5.3.2 "Other legal process"

While the Social Security Act's prohibition of execution, levy, attachment, and garnishment needs little interpretation, the meaning of "other legal process" is less clear. In *State of Washington Department of Social & Health Services v. Guardianship Estate of Keffeler*, the Supreme Court interpreted this term to refer to "process much like the processes of execution, levy, attachment, and garnishment."[410] It

debtor's closely held corporation and used to purchase limousine; funds "invested in a business venture" were no longer used to rehabilitate worker or save him from poverty while disabled); *In re* Burchard, 214 B.R. 494 (Bankr. D. Neb. 1997) (proceeds of personal injury judgment remained exempt while they were "cash or cash equivalent," but exemption did not protect personal property bought with the proceeds); Holsman v. Holsman, 49 S.W.3d 795 (Mo. Ct. App. 2001) (in absence of evidence that gift was not intended, depositing workers' compensation lump sum in couple's joint account made it marital property that could be divided up at divorce); SSM Health Care Sys. v. Bartel, 914 S.W.2d 8 (Mo. Ct. App. 1995); *In re* Christensen, 149 P.3d 40 (Nev. 2006) (wage exemption does not protect property purchased with exempt wages); Gray v. Gray, 922 P.2d 615 (Okla. 1996) (veterans disability funds lost quality of moneys when used to purchase property; specially adapted vehicle was jointly acquired property which could be divided up by divorce judgment).

398 42 U.S.C. § 601.

399 *See, e.g.*, *In re* Wilson, 305 B.R. 4 (Bankr. N.D. Iowa 2004) (Iowa exemption for public assistance benefits covers "safety net" farm payments based on amount of crops grown, limited to farmers with gross income less than $2.5 million); *In re* Herald, 294 B.R. 440 (Bankr. W.D.N.Y. 2003) (proceeds of workers' compensation settlement covered by state exemption for disability benefits); Creditors Discount & Audit v. Frame, 21 Clearinghouse Rev. 1109 (Ill. Cir. Ct. 1987) (Aid to Families with Dependent Children (AFDC) recipient's agreement to pay judgment creditor out of AFDC proceeds void as against public policy); MacQuarrie v. Balch, 285 N.E.2d 103 (Mass. 1972); Guardian Loan Co. v. Baylis, 112 N.J. Super. 44, 270 A.2d 304 (Dist. Ct. 1970); Consumer Credit Corp. v. Lewis, 313 N.Y.S.2d 879 (Dist. Ct. 1970). *But see In re* Boyett, 250 B.R. 822 (Bankr. S.D. Ga. 2000) (federal crop loss disaster relief payment not covered by Georgia's "local public assistance benefits" exemption); Asset Acceptance Corp. v. Hughes, 706 N.W.2d 446 (Mich. Ct. App. 2005) (state homestead property tax credit not a public assistance benefit).

400 R.I. Gen. Laws § 9-26-4(8).

401 Minn. Stat. § 550.37(14); Bar-Meir v. N. Am. Die Casting Ass'n, 2003 WL 22015444 (Minn. Ct. App. Aug. 26, 2003) (debtor failed to show that funds in account were either exempt benefits or earnings of a benefit recipient).

402 Vt. Stat. Ann. tit. 12, § 3170.

403 N.Y. Soc. Serv. Law § 137-a (McKinney).

404 Conn. Gen. Stat. § 52-352b(d).

405 42 U.S.C. §§ 407(a), 1383(d)(1).

406 Philpott v. Essex County Welfare Bd., 409 U.S. 413, 93 S. Ct. 590, 34 L. Ed. 2d 608 (1973); Hambrick v. First Sec. Bank, 336 F. Supp. 2d 890 (E.D. Ark. 2004) (protects all benefits, lump sum as well as periodic payments); Binder & Binder, Prof'l Corp. v. Barnhart, 281 F. Supp. 2d 574 (E.D.N.Y. 2003) (anti-alienation clause prevented attachment of attorney's charging lien to SSI benefits recovered in proceeding when attorney represented claimant), *vacated on other grounds*, 399 F.3d 128 (2d Cir. 2005) (jurisdictional grounds).

407 Bennett v. Arkansas, 485 U.S. 395, 108 S. Ct. 1204, 99 L. Ed. 2d 455 (1988); Philpott v. Essex County Welfare Bd., 409 U.S. 41, 93 S. Ct. 590, 34 L. Ed. 2d 608 (1973).

408 *See* § 11.2.1.1, *supra*.

409 *See* § 12.5.10.3, *supra*.

410 537 U.S. 371, 385, 123 S. Ct. 1017, 154 L. Ed. 2d 972 (2003), *on remand*, Guardianship Estate of Keffeler *ex rel.* Pierce v. State, 88 P.3d 949 (Wash. 2004) (finding no denial of equal protection when all representative payees required to use funds

stated that the term, "at a minimum, would seem to require utilization of some judicial or quasi-judicial mechanism, though not necessarily an elaborate one, by which control over property passes from one person to another in order to discharge or secure discharge of an allegedly existing or anticipated liability."[411] The Court therefore concluded that it is not "other legal process" for a state official to obtain an appointment as representative payee for a foster child who was receiving state services, and use the benefits to reimburse the state.[412] The Court noted that the state did not have a claim of debt against the foster child, so was not using its representative payee status to obtain repayment of a debt.[413] Further, the state's actions were explicitly permitted by Social Security regulations, and the process of becoming a representative payee is not similar enough to execution, levy, attachment, and garnishment, the acts specified in section 407, to qualify as "other legal process."[414]

The implications of *Keffeler* outside the context of the appointment of representative payees are not yet clear. Cases holding that recipients may not be ordered to turn over future checks or income from future checks to creditors clearly satisfy *Keffeler*'s requirements, because they bar a judicial remedy that accomplishes the same result as garnishment or attachment.[415] The state's seizure of exempt funds from inmate accounts for prison or mental hospital expenses should also still be considered "other legal process,"[416] especially when the state requires that the inmate deposit the funds in that account.[417] This type of seizure is a means of collecting a debt owed by the inmate, and it involves using a state statute or regulation to transfer the beneficiary's funds to the state.

A number of courts have held that "other legal process" includes the set off of exempt funds in bank accounts.[418]

---

for current maintenance; procedure for appointing representative payee sufficient to satisfy due process).

411 State of Washington Dep't of Social & Health Services v. Guardianship Estate of Keffeler, 537 U.S. 371, 385, 123 S. Ct. 1017, 154 L. Ed. 2d 972 (2003).

412 *Id.*; Kolbeson v. State of Washington Dep't of Social & Health Services, 118 P.3d 901 (Wash. Ct. App. 2005) (state hospital as representative payee could take involuntary patient's benefits to pay for hospitalization; procedure for determining amount due was not "other legal process"); *see also* Gean v. Hattaway, 330 F.3d 758 (6th Cir. 2003); Mason v. Sybinski, 280 F.3d 788 (7th Cir. 2002) (state hospital, as representative payee for SSI recipient, used funds to pay hospital; no deprivation of due process when procedure for appointing representative payee met due process standards; no taking when patient received food, shelter, and medical care in return; use of funds complied with Social Security Administration regulations); King v. Shafer, 940 F.2d 1182 (8th Cir. 1991) (Social Security regulations specifically permitted appointment of hospital official as representative payee, and use of benefits for hospital expenses); Nau v. State, 2007 WL 3378345 (Colo. Ct. App. Nov. 15, 2007) (state hospital superintendent appointed fiduciary for incompetent beneficiaries; use of Veterans Administration benefits and state old age benefits for current charges not violation of anti-alienation provisions of statutes, nor taking without due process).

413 State of Washington Dep't of Social & Health Services v. Guardianship Estate of Keffeler, 537 U.S. 371, 386, 123 S. Ct. 1017, 154 L. Ed. 2d 972 (2003).

414 *Id.*; *cf. In re* J.G., 652 S.E.2d 266 (N.C. Ct. App. 2007) (anti-alienability statute does not prevent state court from ordering state agency that has custody of minor child to use child's Social Security benefits in certain way for benefit of child).

415 Park Hope Nursing Home v. Eckelberger, 185 Misc. 2d 617, 713 N.Y.S.2d 918 (Sup. Ct. 2000) (Medicaid and Social Security recipient refused to pay patient-paid amount; nursing home entitled to judgment but not to order requiring turnover of future checks); First Nat'l Bank & Trust Co. of Ada v. Arles, 816 P.2d 537 (Okla. 1991) (creditor brought contempt action to enforce installment payment agreement resulting from judgment on defaulted bank loan; claim denied when debtor's only income was exempt benefits); *see also* State v. Eaton, 99 P.3d 661 (Mont. 2004) (Social Security benefits may not be counted as income for state criminal restitution order set at twenty percent of "net income"; if benefits counted, restitution order would be "other legal process"); *cf.* Hoult v. Hoult, 373 F.3d 47 (1st Cir. 2004) (close question whether it was "other legal process" for court to order judgment debtor to deposit all his income, including exempt benefits, in one bank account, from which he could withdraw only court-approved sum for living expenses; not reached because parties agreed to omit Social Security benefits from order).

416 Bennett v. Arkansas, 485 U.S. 395, 108 S. Ct. 1204, 99 L. Ed. 2d 455 (1988) (statute that permitted state to seize exempt benefits to pay for cost of imprisonment was preempted by anti-alienation clause); Crawford v. Gould, 56 F.3d 1162 (9th Cir. 1995) (withdrawal of Social Security funds from mental patient's trust accounts, in which they were required to deposit all funds received, was "other legal process" in violation of anti-assignment clause; authorization form, even if signed, was not meaningful consent when it did not explain that benefits were exempt); Brinkman v. Rahm, 878 F.2d 263 (9th Cir. 1989) (deducting exempt benefit funds from patient's hospital accounts to pay for care was other legal process; court specifically did not reach question whether benefits could be counted in determining ability to pay); Tidwell v. Schweiker, 677 F.2d 560 (7th Cir. 1982) (mental patients asked to sign agreement placing benefits in account from which they would be seized for hospital expenses; not told that funds were exempt or agreement was voluntary; even if agreement was revocable and voluntary, this was forbidden "transfer or assignment"); *see also* Nelson v. Heiss, 271 F.3d 891 (9th Cir. 2001) (anti-alienation clause violated when prison allowed inmate, whose account was funded with veterans benefits, to draw against insufficient funds and then put a hold on his account to cover overdraft); State *ex rel.* Nixon v. McClure, 969 S.W.2d 801 (Mo. Ct. App. 1998) (federal civil service pension could not be seized for prison reimbursement).

417 *See* Lopez v. Wash. Mut. Bank, 302 F.3d 900 (9th Cir.), *as amended by* 311 F.3d 928 (9th Cir. 2002) (bank's collection of amounts owed under overdraft checking account plan from direct-deposited Social Security benefits was equivalent to voluntary payment because plaintiffs continued direct deposits after incurring overdrafts, so not barred by section 407; distinguishing *Nelson v. Heiss*, because rules for prison account not voluntarily accepted).

418 Tom v. First Am. Credit Union, 151 F.3d 1289 (10th Cir. 1998); Marengo v. First Am. Bank, 152 F. Supp. 2d 92 (D. Mass. 2001); *In re* Capps, 251 B.R. 73 (Bankr. D. Neb. 2000); *see* § 12.6, *infra*; *cf.* Hambrick v. First Sec. Bank, 336 F. Supp. 2d

These holdings are also consistent with the Supreme Court's definition in *Keffeler*, because a bank when making a setoff is transferring funds from the debtor to itself to repay a debt. Unlike the representative payee procedure in *Keffeler*, a setoff is almost identical to "execution, levy, attachment, [or] garnishment" on a bank account.[419] The bank is able to use the right of set off as an alternative to the judicial process only because it is wearing two hats—one as the creditor and the other as the holder of the consumer's deposit. But that dual status should not enable the bank to avoid the protections of the anti-alienability clause. The only reason a court is not involved is because of the bank's dual status.

In *Lopez v. Washington Mutual Bank,* however, the Ninth Circuit held that when a bank covered checks for which a depositor had insufficient funds, it could set off the overdraft fees against the consumer's Social Security benefits that were subsequently deposited into the account.[420] The court stressed that the fees were not a separate, preexisting debt, but were related to the operation of the depositor's checking account. Because the depositor could have directed the Social Security Administration to deposit the benefits elsewhere, the court treated each deposit to the account after the overdraft as a voluntary payment of the debt. A class of California consumers challenged this practice as a violation of several California consumer protection statutes, but a jury verdict for the consumers was reversed on appeal and is now before the state supreme court.[421]

There are critical distinctions between *Lopez* and the usual bank setoff. In *Lopez,* the debt was incurred in the same account, so the bank could be said to have been simply balancing the account: the debit created by the overdraft was simply balanced by the credit of the deposit. In the more typical bank setoff, the bank is setting off an unrelated debt against a deposit account. The protection of exempt funds in bank accounts is discussed in more detail in § 12.6, *infra.*

An express or implied threat to use a judicial or quasi-judicial process to seize exempt funds is also "other legal process." Thus, while a state may bill beneficiaries or their representative payees for state hospital expenses,[422] it may not threaten a lawsuit, a tax refund intercept, or other collection methods to compel the turnover of exempt benefits.[423] Likewise, a creditor's threat to garnish exempt Social Security funds is a violation of not only the Fair Debt Collection Practices Act (FDCPA), but also section 407.[424]

12.5.5.3.3 Exceptions

Some courts hold that exempt benefits may be considered as income for various purposes,[425] such as setting the amount of family support payments[426] or determining eligibility or benefit levels for Medicaid or other public assistance.[427] Courts have held that to do so is not "other legal

890 (E.D. Ark. 2004) (open question whether setoff is "other legal process"; court does not reach question because genuine issue of fact whether account was closed at time Social Security funds direct deposited).

419 *See* Tom v. First Am. Credit Union, 151 F.3d 1289 (10th Cir. 1998) (noting that there is no relevant difference between setoff and garnishment).

420 Lopez v. Wash. Mut. Bank, 302 F.3d 900, 905 (9th Cir.), *as amended by* 311 F.3d 928 (9th Cir. 2002) (distinguishing Nelson v. Heiss, 271 F.3d 891 (9th Cir. 2001), on ground that prisoners there did not voluntarily open accounts with the prison, did not have the option of receiving benefits directly, and did not voluntarily execute agreements about treatment of the funds).

421 Miller v. Bank of Am., 2004 WL 3153009 (Cal. App. Dep't Super. Ct. Dec. 30, 2004) (finding bank liable for violation of Consumer Legal Remedies Act and for fraudulent business practices), *rev'd*, 51 Cal. Rptr. 3d 223 (Ct. App. 2006), *review granted*, 154 P.3d 997 (Cal. 2007).

422 Kriegbaum v. Katz, 909 F.2d 70 (2d Cir. 1990) (repeated billings permitted); Fetterusso v. State of New York, 898 F.2d 322 (2d Cir. 1990) (billing procedure not "other legal process" because no express or implied threat of legal sanctions).

423 King v. Shafer, 940 F.2d 1182 (8th Cir. 1991) (threat of legal action is "other legal process"; what the state may not do, it may not threaten to do); Kriegbaum v. Katz, 909 F.2d 70 (2d Cir. 1990) ("special proceeding" to remove conservator who refused to turn over funds is "other legal process").

424 Hogue v. Palisades Collection, Inc., 494 F. Supp. 2d 1043 (S.D Ohio 2007) (allowing debt collection and consumer protection claims to go forward; noting that creditors could use other methods to determine whether nonexempt funds present); Jordan v. Thomas & Thomas, 2007 WL 2838474 (S.D. Ohio Sept. 26, 2007) (FDCPA claim stated; frozen account contained only exempt Social Security funds; genuine issue of fact whether collector's attorneys conducted investigation or had reasonable cause to believe account contained nonexempt funds); Albright v. Allied Int'l Credit Corp., 2003 WL 22350928 (C.D. Cal. Aug. 25, 2003) (post-*Keffeler* decision); *cf.* Lee v. Javitch, Block, & Rathbone, 2007 WL 3332706 (S.D. Ohio Nov. 7, 2007) (denying summary judgment on FDCPA and UDAP claims; Ohio statute cited in *Todd* has been amended to require only "reasonable cause to believe"; genuine issue of fact as to reasonable cause when large-volume collection firm did crude screening, that is, eliminated debtors aged over sixty-five with no employer or trade lines listed on credit report). *But see* Parker v. Wetch & Abbot, P.L.C., 2006 WL 4846042 (S.D. Iowa July 11, 2006) (freeze of account containing exempt benefits did not violate anti-alienation clause of Social Security Act, state or federal fair debt collection acts, or state consumer protection law); Smith v. Levine, 2006 WL 3704622 (Cal. Ct. App. Dec. 18, 2006) (litigation privilege barred abuse of process claim arising from levy on non-debtor's account, and conversion claim arising from refusal to return improperly seized funds).

425 *In re* Sohn, 300 B.R. 332 (Bankr. D. Minn. 2003) (income from exempt sources, here the earned income credit, must be counted in calculating disposable income for chapter 13 bankruptcy). *But see* State v. Eaton, 99 P.3d 661 (Mont. 2004) (Social Security benefits may not be counted in calculating income for purposes of state criminal restitution order set at twenty percent of "net income").

426 *See* § 12.5.10.3, *infra.*

427 Wojchowski v. Daines, 498 F.3d 99 (2d Cir. 2007) (allocation of institutionalized spouse's Social Security income to community spouse does not violate anti-alienation clause; *Robbins v. DeBuono* has no continuing validity in light of *Keffeler*); Johnson

process" even if it requires recipients to spend benefits. Thus, a threat of eviction from a homeless shelter was not other legal process, when the agreement to pay rent, in an amount based on exempt benefits income, was treated as voluntary.[428]

Exempt benefits may also be used to compensate guardians and attorneys in guardianship proceedings involving the beneficiary.[429] Courts are divided, however, on the questions of how to treat Social Security benefits when dividing marital property at divorce,[430] and whether a judgment may be taken against a person whose only income is exempt benefits.[431]

Applications for Social Security disability or SSI benefits often result in long delays, followed by the award of a large lump sum of retroactive benefits. If a disability insurer or the state has paid benefits to enable the disabled person to survive the delay, an overpayment often results. The Social Security Act allows the Social Security Administration to withhold a recipient's retroactive SSI award to reimburse the state for public assistance benefits it provided while the recipient's SSI application was pending.[432] On the other hand, courts have refused to allow disability insurers to recoup overpayments from the lump-sum award, regardless of any agreement with the beneficiary.[433] Courts have,

v. Wing, 12 F. Supp. 2d 311 (S.D.N.Y. 1998) (calculating resident's share of payments for homeless shelter), *aff'd*, 178 F.3d 611 (2d Cir. 1999); Estate of Palmer v. Dep't of Pub. Aid, 760 N.E.2d 80 (Ill. App. Ct. 2001) (Social Security and veterans benefits may be considered in setting amount of Medicaid, but state may not seek to recoup overpayments from estate which contains only exempt public benefits); State Cent. Collection Unit v. Stewart, 438 A.2d 1311 (Md. 1981) (ability to pay for mental hospital services); *In re* Estate of Tomeck, 872 N.E.2d 236 (N.Y. 2007) (allocation of institutionalized spouse's Social Security income to community spouse does not violate anti-alienation clause). *But see* Robbins v. DeBuono, 218 F.3d 197 (2d Cir. 2000) (New York Medicaid program's practice of attributing institutionalized person's Social Security income to non-institutionalized spouse was "other legal process"; note that Ruck v. Novello, 295 F. Supp. 2d 258 (W.D.N.Y. 2003) holds that this decision has no continuing validity in light of *Keffeler*).

428 Johnson v. Wing, 12 F. Supp. 2d 311 (S.D.N.Y. 1998), *aff'd*, 178 F.3d 611 (2d Cir. 1999).

429 *In re* Guardianship of Huseman, 831 N.E.2d 1147 (Ill. App. Ct. 2005).

430 Leathers v. Leathers, 166 P.3d 929 (Ariz. Ct. App. 2007) (ordering husband to pay "one half the value" of his Social Security as spousal maintenance did not violate anti-alienation clause); *In re* Marriage of Crook, 813 N.E.2d 198 (Ill. 2004) (court may not consider one spouse's Social Security in determining division of community property); *In re* Marriage of Wojcik, 838 N.E.2d 282 (Ill. App. Ct. 2005) (exempt veterans' disability benefits may not be considered marital property, divided up, or used as a setoff, in allocating property at divorce); *In re* Marriage of Hulstrom, 794 N.E.2d 980 (Ill. App. Ct. 2003) (anti-alienation clause barred provision of marital property division that would pool and divide in half the spouses' Social Security benefits); Severs v. Severs, 837 N.E.2d 498 (Ind. 2005) (SSDI benefits are not a marital asset and may not be divided at divorce); Young v. Young, 931 So. 2d 541 (La. Ct. App. 2006) (SSDI benefits are not community property); Depot v. Depot, 893 A.2d 995 (Me. 2006) (Social Security benefits, or their present value, are not marital property and may not be divided, nor may marital property be transferred to offset Social Security benefits; in determining a fair distribution of property, however, court must consider "all relevant factors" including expected receipt of benefits); Webster v. Webster, 716 N.W.2d 47 (Neb. 2006) (court may neither directly divide Social Security benefits nor adjust property division to compensate for unequal Social Security); Neville v. Neville, 791 N.E.2d 434 (Ohio 2003) (although Social Security benefits can not be divided as marital property, parties' future Social Security may be considered, along with all other assets, in making equitable division of marital property); Simmons v. Simmons, 634 S.E.2d 1 (S.C. 2006) (family court erred in approving property settlement that called for division of husband's Social Security benefits); *see also* Griffin v. Griffin, 872 N.E.2d 653 (Ind. Ct. App. 2007) (Veterans Administration disability benefits may not be divided nor considered in property division; here, after being ordered to split military retirement with ex-wife, husband waived retirement benefits to receive disability); Halstead v. Halstead, 596 S.E.2d 353 (N.C. Ct. App. 2004) (military disability pay, unlike military retirement pay, may not be treated—directly or indirectly—as marital asset in division of property); Ghrist v. Ghrist, 2007 WL 1372690 (Tex. App. May 11, 2007) (ex-husband waived military retirement benefits to receive Veterans Administration disability; anti-alienation clause prevented any consideration of these benefits in property division; wife entitled only to half of remaining retirement benefits).

431 Bressmer v. Fed. Express Corp. Long Term Disability Plan, 2000 U.S. App. LEXIS 11024 (2d Cir. May 16, 2000) (insurer could have judgment for overpayments resulting from delayed SSDI application, but could not satisfy it from exempt benefits); Provident Life & Cas. Co. v. Crean, 804 So. 2d 236 (Ala. Civ. App. 2001) (insurer seeking judgment for overpayment must prove that beneficiary has nonexempt income); Russo v. Russo, 474 A.2d 473 (Conn. App. Ct. 1984) (divorce court may order ex-husband to pay certain debts even if his income comes from exempt Social Security benefits, when he also had other potential sources of income available); State Cent. Collection Unit v. Stewart, 438 A.2d 1311 (Md. 1981) (state suing for mental hospital reimbursement; could have judgment, in case state discovered or debtor acquired nonexempt income, but could not satisfy it from exempt benefits); Tookes v. N.Y.C. Parking Violations Bureau, 663 N.Y.S.2d 28 (App. Div. 1997) (garnishment of benefits forbidden, but voluntary payment plan to recover seized car was permissible, even though only income was exempt benefits); Park Hope Nursing Home v. Eckelberger, 185 Misc. 2d 617, 713 N.Y.S.2d 918 (Sup. Ct. 2000) (Medicaid and Social Security recipient refused to pay patient-paid amount; nursing home entitled to judgment but not to order requiring turnover of future checks); Cont'l Cas. Co. v. Hunt, 913 P.2d 292 (Okla. 1996) (no judgment to recover insurance overpayments from retroactive Social Security disability; lawsuit, threat of lawsuit or judgment is "other legal process"); First Nat'l Bank & Trust Co. of Ada v. Arles, 816 P.2d 537 (Okla. 1991) (creditor brought contempt action to enforce installment payment agreement resulting from judgment on defaulted bank loan; denied when debtor's only income was exempt benefits).

432 42 U.S.C. § 1383(g).

433 Mote v. Aetna Life Ins. Co., 435 F. Supp. 2d 827 (N.D. Ill. 2006) (insurer seeking to recover disability overpayment may not have constructive trust on account containing Social Security disabil-

however, allowed the insurer to set off this overpayment against future benefits, that is, to reduce or discontinue benefits until the overpayment is made up.[434] This is not "other legal process," because the insurer or the state does not take control of the benefits.

12.5.5.4 FEMA Disaster Relief Assistance

One of the primary federal programs available to help individual victims of disaster is the Individuals and Households Program (IHP), administered by the Federal Emergency Management Agency (FEMA).[435] The IHP consists of housing assistance,[436] which may be used to pay for rent, repair, or housing construction, and other needs assistance,[437] which may be provided to replace personal property (clothing, furnishings, appliances, and so forth) or to meet other disaster-related necessary expenses (for example, medical, dental, funeral, or transportation costs).

The implementing federal regulation makes all assistance provided through the IHP "exempt from garnishment, seizure, encumbrance, levy, execution, pledge, attachment, release or waiver."[438] The regulation also prohibits recipients from transferring or assigning their rights under the program. However these limitations do not apply to FEMA's recovery of assistance fraudulently obtained or misapplied.

12.5.5.5 Other Benefits and Payments

Veterans benefits administered by the Department of Veterans Affairs are generally exempt even after deposit in a checking account.[439] Student loan proceeds are exempt.[440] In some states, tax refunds which consist of the "earned income tax credit" may be exempt as earnings, as support, or as public assistance benefits.[441] Many states also exempt

ity payments; anti-alienation clause of Social Security Act trumps statute allowing recovery of overpayments); Cont'l Cas. Co. v. Hunt, 913 P.2d 292 (Okla. 1996) (no money judgment to recover private insurance overpayments from lump sum retroactive Social Security disability; question is not whether agreement mentioned exempt funds, but whether recovery would come from exempt funds). *But see* Smith v. Accenture U.S. Group Long-Term Disability Ins. Plan, 2006 WL 2644957 (N.D. Ill. Sept. 13, 2006) (insurer seeking to recover disability overpayment arising from receipt of Social Security disability benefits may reach bank account in which SSDI benefits are commingled with nonexempt funds; because this is a "lien by agreement," tracing is not necessary).

434 Revells v. Metro. Life Ins. Co., 261 F. Supp. 2d 1359 (M.D. Ala. 2003); Stuart v. Metro. Life Ins. Co., 664 F. Supp. 619 (D. Me. 1987) (recoupment agreement allowing this practice does not violate section 407(a)), *aff'd*, 849 F.2d 1534 (1st Cir. 1988); Poisson v. Allstate Life Ins. Co., 640 F. Supp. 147 (D. Me. 1986) (same); *In re* Morin, 2006 WL 2085224 (Bankr. D.N.J. July 11, 2006) (erroneously paid disability retirement payments could be set off against retirement benefits when debtor becomes eligible for retirement, notwithstanding ERISA anti-alienation clause; here, however, benefits were exempted by N.J. exemption for certain trusts); *see also* Eubanks v. Prudential Ins. of Am., 336 F. Supp. 2d 521 (M.D.N.C. 2004) (ERISA's anti-alienation provision does not forbid insurer from setting off present benefits to recoup previous overpayment); Hurd v. Ill. Bell Tel. Co., 136 F. Supp. 125 (D. Ill. 1955) (provision in private pension plan to reduce benefits when Social Security increased not transfer or assignment), *aff'd*, 234 F.2d 942 (7th Cir. 1955).

435 The IHP is statutorily authorized under the Robert T. Stafford Disaster Relief and Emergency Assistance Act. 42 U.S.C. §§ 5121–5206. The Stafford Act authorizes the President to issue major disaster declarations thereby triggering the assistance available through the Act. Through executive orders the President has delegated responsibility for administering the major provisions of the Act to FEMA. *See* Exec. Order No. 12673, 54 Fed. Reg. 12,571 (Mar. 23, 1989).

436 42 U.S.C. § 5174(c); 44 C.F.R. § 206.117(b).

437 42 U.S.C. § 5174(e); 44 C.F.R. § 206.119(a), (b).

438 44 C.F.R. § 206.110(g).

439 38 U.S.C. § 5301; Porter v. Aetna Cas. & Surety Co., 370 U.S. 159, 82 S. Ct. 1231, 8 L. Ed. 2d 407 (1962) (deposited Veterans Administration benefits retain exempt characteristic so long as they remain subject to demand and use for needs of recipient for maintenance and support, and not converted to permanent investment); *In re* Strong, 8 P.3d 763 (Mont. 2000) (Veterans Administration disability benefits can not be treated as marital property or otherwise counted in division of property upon divorce, but can be considered in child support determination); Tookes v. N.Y.C. Parking Violations Bureau, 663 N.Y.S.2d 28 (App. Div. 1997) (affirming order forbidding garnishment of disability benefits, but reversing order deeming judgment satisfied; a payment plan which debtor agreed to in order to get his seized car back was voluntary and permissible even though debtor's only source of income was disability benefits); *see also* Funeral Fin. Services, Inc. v. United States, 234 F.3d 1015 (7th Cir. 2000) (anti-alienation provisions of statutes governing National Service Insurance and veterans benefits violated when beneficiaries assigned benefits to funeral home, which assigned them to lender, for advance to pay for funeral); Palmer v. Dep't of Pub. Aid, 760 N.E.2d 80 (Ill. App. Ct. 2001) (Social Security and veterans benefits may be considered in setting amount of Medicaid, but state may not seek to recoup overpayments from estate which contains only exempt public benefits). *But cf.* Lawson v. Clarke, 2007 WL 2778259 (W.D. Wash. Sept. 21, 2007) (military retirement pay may be seized, pursuant to state law, to pay for incarceration expenses); Loving v. Sterling, 680 A.2d 1030 (D.C. 1996) (state may consider veteran's disability benefits as income for purposes of setting amount of child support); New York State Crime Victims' Bd. *ex rel.* K.A.S. v. Wendell, 815 N.Y.S.2d 438 (Sup. Ct. 2006) (military retirement pay not exempt veterans' benefits).

440 20 U.S.C. § 1095a(d).

441 *See In re* James, 406 F.3d 1340 (11th Cir. 2005) (tax refund attributable to earned income tax credit was "paid or payable as public assistance to needy persons" within meaning of Alabama exemption statute); Flanery v. Mathison, 289 B.R. 624 (W.D. Ky. 2003) (Kentucky exemption for "all public benefits" covers tax refund attributable to earned income credit); *In re* Brasher, 253 B.R. 484 (M.D. Ala. 2000) (earned income credit falls within Alabama exemption for "all amounts paid or payable as public assistance to needy persons"); *In re* Tomczyk, 295 B.R. 894 (Bankr. D. Minn. 2003) (tax refund attributable to earned income credit covered by Minnesota exemption for "all relief based on need"; credit similar to programs listed in statute, because intended to assist working poor); *In re* Sharp, 286 B.R.

crime victims' compensation.[442] The Tennessee exemption for certain benefits on account of disability, or for lost earning power, has been construed to enable a widow to exempt payments received as the surviving spouse of a federal nuclear weapons worker who died of occupational disease.[443] Alimony and child support are generally exempt in the hands of the recipient, at least so far as necessary for support.[444]

627 (Bankr. E.D. Ky. 2002) (Kentucky exemption for "all public benefits" covers tax refund attributable to earned income credit); *In re* Sanderson, 283 B.R. 595 (Bankr. M.D. Fla. 2002) (recently amended Fla. Stat. § 222.25 exempts tax refunds attributable to earned income credit, even after deposit and commingling, but not ordinary tax refunds); *In re* Longstreet, 246 B.R. 611 (Bankr. S.D. Iowa 2000) (earned income credit is exempt as "public assistance benefit"); *In re* Ray, 1999 Bankr. LEXIS 1807 (Bankr. N.D. Ill. June 23, 1999) (earned income credit is public assistance within meaning of Illinois exemption statute); *In re* Fish, 224 B.R. 82 (Bankr. S.D. Ill. 1998) (earned income credit was exempt under Illinois exemption for "public assistance"); *In re* Brockhouse, 220 B.R. 623 (Bankr. C.D. Ill. 1998) (earned income credit was exempt "public assistance benefit" within meaning of Illinois statute); *In re* Barnett, 214 B.R. 632 (Bankr. W.D. Okla. 1997) (earned income credit was "earnings from personal services" which qualify for state hardship exemption); *see also In re* Walsh, 298 B.R. 894 (Bankr. D. Colo. 2003) (Colorado exemption for "earned income credit" applies to specific program that enables low income taxpayers to get back sum that may exceed tax refund, and not to various other tax credits, here the adoption credit, that are available to taxpayers with incomes below specific level). *But see In re* Benn, 491 F.3d 811 (8th Cir. 2007) (anticipated tax refunds not exempt under Missouri law; no discussion of earned income credit issue); *In re* Collins, 170 F.3d 512 (5th Cir. 1999) (earned income credit was not exempt under Louisiana law exempting benefits "under this title," that is, Louisiana public assistance law); *In re* Trudeau, 237 B.R. 803 (B.A.P. 10th Cir. 1999) (earned income credit was neither earnings nor public assistance within meaning of Wyoming exemption statutes); *In re* George, 1997 U.S. Dist. LEXIS 22829 (N.D. Okla. Aug. 7, 1997), *adopting* 1997 U.S. Dist. LEXIS 22830 (N.D. Okla. May 28, 1997) (earned income credit was not "support" exempt under Oklahoma law); *In re* Builder, 368 B.R. 10 (Bankr. D. Ariz. 2007) (Arizona exemption for "assistance granted under this title" and "money paid or payable under this title" did not exempt federal earned income credit; distinguishing cases from states with broader public assistance exemptions); *In re* Demars, 279 B.R. 548 (Bankr. W.D. Mo. 2002) (earned income credit not exempt "local public assistance"); *In re* Garrett, 225 B.R. 301 (Bankr. W.D.N.Y. 1998) (tax refunds consisting of state and federal earned income credit, and state child care and real property tax credits, were not protected by exemption for Social Security, unemployment or local public assistance, but first $2500 could be exempted under New York exemption for "cash"); *In re* McCourt, 217 B.R. 998 (Bankr. S.D. Ohio 1997) (earned income credit was not exempt under Ohio exemption for Aid to Dependent Children); *In re* Rutter, 204 B.R. 57 (Bankr. D. Or. 1997) (earned income credit was not exempt under Oregon exemptions for "general" or "public" assistance, which refer to specific Oregon welfare programs, or for "spousal support, child support or separate maintenance"); *In re* Goertz, 202 B.R. 614 (Bankr. W.D. Mo. 1996) (earned income credit was not exempt under Missouri exemption for "local public assistance benefits"); *In re* Beagle, 200 B.R. 595 (Bankr. N.D. Ohio 1996) (earned income credit was not protected by Ohio exemptions for Aid to Families with Dependent Children and disability funds; it had been exempt under former provision exempting "poor relief" which was repealed when Ohio eliminated general relief); *In re* Kurilich, 199 B.R. 161 (Bankr. N.D. Ohio 1996) (tax refund attributable to earned income credit was not exempt under Ohio's public assistance exemption, which was narrowed by Ohio's elimination of the general relief category of welfare); *cf. In re* Sohn, 300 B.R. 332 (Bankr. D. Minn. 2003) (earned income credit must be counted in calculating disposable income for chapter 13 bankruptcy); *In re* Crampton, 249 B.R. 215 (Bankr. D. Idaho 2000) (federal tax credit for education benefits a wide range of taxpayers, including the affluent, so is not exempt as public assistance benefit); Asset Acceptance Corp. v. Hughes, 706 N.W.2d 446 (Mich. Ct. App. 2005) (state homestead property tax credit not a public assistance benefit). *See generally* § 12.4.1.3.2, *supra*.

442 *See* Appx. F, *infra*. *But see In re* Seymour, 285 B.R. 57 (Bankr. N.D. Ga. 2002) (interpreting Georgia exemption for crime victim reparation to cover only payments for bodily injury or loss of earning power, not restitution for financial loss).

443 *In re* Luttrell, 313 B.R. 751 (Bankr. E.D. Tenn. 2004).

444 Harbaugh v. Sweet (*In re* Harbaugh), 257 B.R. 485 (E.D. Mich. 2001) (installment payments ordered by court in return for certain marital property that were necessary for ex-wife's support were exempt alimony, not property settlement, under federal exemptions); *In re* Kleinsmith, 361 B.R. 504 (Bankr. S.D. Iowa 2006) (credit union forbidden to set off accounts containing only exempt child support); *In re* Palidora, 310 B.R. 164 (Bankr. D. Ariz. 2004) (court-ordered child support from former spouse exempt in hands of recipient and remains exempt in bank account); *In re* Edwards, 255 B.R. 726 (Bankr. S.D. Ohio 2000) (Ohio exemption for right to receive child support applies to arrearage, but only so far as necessary for support of debtor and dependents); Holmes v. Wooley, 792 A.2d 1018 (Del. Super. Ct. 2001) (child support funds being garnished from husband's wages and routed to wife via state agency could not be attached for debt owed by wife to husband; Delaware does not exempt child support, but provides that recipient is fiduciary for children); *In re* Marriage of Comley, 32 P.3d 1128 (Kan. 2001) (funds paid into court by ex-husband's employer to satisfy support order may not be garnished for ex-wife's attorney fees); Balanof v. Niosi, 791 N.Y.S.2d 553 (App. Div. 2005) (holding alimony exempt so far as needed for support and limiting attempt by wife's lawyer to garnish alimony payments for attorney fees). *But see In re* Duemey, 347 B.R. 875 (Bankr. S.D. Ohio 2006) (vehicle purchased for debtor by ex-husband, to satisfy his debt for back child support, not exempt child support); *In re* Hageman, 260 B.R. 852 (Bankr. S.D. Ohio 2001) (lump sum distribution from ex-husband's retirement plan was nonexempt property settlement, not exempt alimony, when separation agreement provided that neither spouse would owe support to the other); *cf. In re* Evert, 342 F.3d 358 (5th Cir. 2003) (promissory note executed by ex-husband during property division not exempt "alimony, support or separate maintenance under bankruptcy code"; for exemption claim, unlike nondischargeability, court will not look beyond the labels to distinguish support from property division); *In re* Delmoe, 365 B.R. 124 (Bankr. S.D. Ohio 2007) (Ohio exemption for "an allowance or other maintenance to the extent reasonably necessary for the support of the person or any of the person's dependents" refers only to legally required support; no exemption for trust voluntarily created by late father's will to pay allowance to adult daughter); Schwartz v. Haas, 739 A.2d 1188

The purpose of the unemployment compensation and workers' compensation laws is to provide a substitute for wages lost during a period of unemployment not the fault of the employee. State statutes generally exempt this income.[445] As with other exempt benefits, garnishment may be permitted for child support or alimony.[446]

(Vt. 1999) (family court properly set off sum owed by ex-wife as part of property division against ex-husband's alimony obligation; alimony is exempt under Vermont law, but ex-wife here is not a "debtor" within meaning of the exemption statute).

445 Iowa Code § 96.15(3) (unemployment compensation, so long as not commingled with other funds, remains exempt from any remedy whatsoever for the collection of all debts); Strong v. Laubach, 371 F.3d 1242 (10th Cir. 2004) (Okla. law) (workers' compensation settlement, including bi-weekly payments, lump sum and annuity, is fully exempt); Johnson v. Iannacone, 314 B.R. 779 (D. Minn. 2004) (Minnesota exemption for "any claim for [workers' compensation] covered lump sum as well as periodic payments); Gagne v. Christians, 172 B.R. 50 (D. Minn. 1994) (lump sum workers' compensation settlement, which served the same purpose as periodic payments, exempt under Minnesota law); *In re* Arsenault, 318 B.R. 616 (Bankr. D.N.H. 2004) (New Hampshire protects workers' compensation "regardless of the form" into which benefits converted, so long as traceable; lump-sum workers' compensation remained exempt in bank account held as "Totten trust" for worker's son, when worker controlled funds and son's rights accrued only on father's death); *In re* Harrelson, 311 B.R. 618 (Bankr. M.D. Fla. 2004) (large lump-sum workers' compensation settlement invested in money market account, treasury bonds, and mutual fund shares remained exempt, because still could be drawn upon to provide for living expenses or medical care), *aff'd*, 143 Fed. Appx. 238 (11th Cir. 2005); *In re* Herald, 294 B.R. 440 (Bankr. W.D.N.Y. 2003) (proceeds of workers' compensation settlement covered by state exemption for disability benefits); *In re* Meyer, 211 B.R. 203 (Bankr. E.D. Va. 1997) (noting statutory protection for unemployment benefits and workers' compensation benefits even if deposited and commingled); Kruger v. Wells Fargo Bank, 521 P.2d 441 (Cal. 1974) (unemployment compensation and disability benefits deposited into bank account retain their exemption); *see also In re* Lindsay, 261 B.R. 209 (Bankr. S.D. Ohio 2001) (annuity purchased to fund structured settlement of workers' compensation claim fully exempt under Ohio law); Kaliner v. Murphy (*In re* Murphy), 2000 Bankr. LEXIS 59 (Bankr. E.D. Pa. Jan. 19, 2000) (annuity purchased to fund monthly workers' compensation payments to totally disabled worker was a disability benefit, exempt under federal bankruptcy exemptions); *In re* Anderson, 932 P.2d 1110 (Okla. 1996) (Oklahoma law allows one $50,000 exemption for each interest in a claim for personal injury, death, or workers' compensation; two exemptions permissible when plaintiff's work injury resulted in a workers' compensation claim, and a malpractice judgment against the doctor who performed "unauthorized surgery); *cf. In re* Bonuchi, 322 B.R. 868 (Bankr. W.D. Mo. 2005) (workers' compensation loses exemption upon payment to worker, but annuity that funds structured settlement of tort and workers' compensation claims is exempt as annuity "payable upon disability"); Fla. Asset Fin. Corp. v. Utah Labor Comm'n, 147 P.3d 1189 (Utah 2006) (Utah statute does not protect benefits after payment to worker; worker may assign benefits after receipt, but may not order commission to pay directly to creditor).

446 *See* Gunhammer v. Bowen, 2007 WL 2123786 (D.S.D. July 20, 2007) (allowing income withholding for child support from unemployment compensation).

12.5.6 Wildcard Exemptions and Stacking

Some states provide for a "wildcard" exemption that exempts any property specified by the debtor up to a certain amount.[447] In some states wildcard exemptions may be used to exempt wages that are not otherwise protected.[448]

447 *In re* Oakley, 344 F.3d 709 (7th Cir. 2003) (cash was not "tangible personal property" within meaning of Indiana exemption; protected only by $100 exemption for intangibles); *In re* Oglesby, 333 B.R. 788 (Bankr. S.D. Ohio 2005) (Ohio exemption for "any property" covers real or personal property; may be applied to one item or split among several); *In re* Anzalone, 318 B.R. 127 (Bankr. C.D. Ill. 2004) (real estate commissions, paid or to be paid to debtor, were "personal property" which could be exempted under Illinois wildcard exemption); *In re* Payne, 2004 WL 2757907 (Bankr. M.D.N.C. Nov. 15, 2004) (property owned in tenancy by entireties fully exempt if no joint creditors; because couple claimed entireties exemption, not homestead exemption, each debtor entitled to "in lieu of homestead" wildcard); *In re* Latham, 317 B.R. 733 (Bankr. E.D. Tenn. 2004) (enforceable contract for sale of real property turns seller's interest into personal property; debtor could claim personal property exemption for his share of sale proceeds when buyers had received warranty deed); *In re* Sharp, 286 B.R. 627 (Bankr. E.D. Ky. 2002) (debtor may use wildcard to exempt part of tax refund; may also use exemption for public benefits to exempt portion attributable to earned income credit); *In re* McDonald, 279 B.R. 382 (Bankr. D.D.C. 2002) (D.C. "unused homestead" exemption exempts the difference between $8075 and the homestead amount claimed); Schalebaum v. Town of Wolfeboro (*In re* Schalebaum), 273 B.R. 1 (Bankr. D.N.H. 2001) (New Hampshire wildcard, which includes cash, protects proceeds of voluntary sale of homestead); *In re* Foor, 259 B.R. 899 (Bankr. C.D. Ill. 2000) (Illinois wildcard would exempt cause of action against sellers of house for undisclosed termite damage); *In re* Ball, 201 B.R. 204 (Bankr. N.D. Ill. 1996) (Illinois's $2000 wildcard exemption may be used to exempt debtor's share of Truth in Lending Act class action claim); *In re* Miller, 198 B.R. 500 (Bankr. N.D. Ohio 1996) (Ohio's wildcard exemption may be used to avoid liens on real property); *In re* Arnold, 193 B.R. 897 (Bankr. W.D. Mo. 1996) (wildcard exemption may be used to exempt bank accounts); *In re* Scrams, 172 B.R. 297 (Bankr. D. Neb. 1994) (Nebraska's wildcard "in lieu of homestead" exemption may be used to exempt a car, up to the $2500 limitation); ARL Credit Services, Inc. v. Piper, 736 N.W.2d 771 (Neb. Ct. App. 2007) (debtor may use head of household's "in lieu of homestead" exemption to protect bank account); *cf.* Oakley v. Freeland, 344 F.3d 709 (7th Cir. 2003) (cash is "intangible property," for which there is a $100 cap, not "tangible personal property" within meaning of Indiana's $4000 wildcard exemption). *But see In re* Young, 297 B.R. 492 (Bankr. E.D. Tex. 2003) (interest in a trust fund, inherited from father, not personal property within meaning of Texas personal property exemption); *In re* Siegle, 2000 Bankr. LEXIS 1627 (Bankr. D. Mont. Dec. 6, 2000), *amended by* 257 B.R. 591 (Bankr. D. Mont. 2001) (interpreting Montana's exemption statute to allow exemption only of property that falls within a listed category, without a wildcard).

448 *In re* Irish, 311 B.R. 63 (B.A.P. 8th Cir. 2004); *In re* Robinson, 240 B.R. 70 (Bankr. N.D. Ala. 1999) (state constitutional wildcard exemption could be used to protect future wages not

Inside or outside of bankruptcy, the possibility of stacking a wildcard exemption with another exemption should be considered.[449] For example, Georgia's wildcard exemption, which allows debtors to apply any unused portion of the homestead exemption to other property, could be stacked with the $200 per item exemption for household goods to enable debtors to exempt the entire value of their appliances and living room set.[450]

In addition, many states allow married couples to claim two exemptions and to stack them.[451] If the couple is living

protected by statutory wildcard exemption); *In re* Johnson, 57 B.R. 635 (Bankr. N.D. Ill. 1986) (permitting wildcard exemption for "any other property" to be stacked with eighty-five percent exemption for wages to preserve all of debtor's wages from garnishment; statute was later amended to restrict use of wildcard to protect wages); *In re* Avery, 514 So. 2d 1380 (Ala. 1987) ($3000 state personal property exemption could be applied to future wages; note that this exemption was amended in 1988 so that it no longer applies to wages); Bank of Am. v. Stine, 839 A.2d 727 (Md. 2003) (wage garnishment within ninety days of bankruptcy may be avoided as preferential transfer, and debtor can then use Maryland wildcard "cash or other property" exemption to exempt the funds thus recovered; note that outside of bankruptcy, Maryland statute explicitly forbids use of wildcard exemption to protect nonexempt wages). *But see In re* Ealy, 2007 WL 1077792 (Bankr. N.D. Ill. Apr. 6, 2007) (state exemption inapplicable to garnished wages recovered by bankruptcy trustee as preferential transfer); *In re* Royer, 2006 WL 978878 (Bankr. C.D. Ill. 2006) (neither wildcard nor wage exemption protects accrued earnings, here commissions, in hands of employer from turnover in bankruptcy case); *In re* Ealy, 355 B.R. 685 (Bankr. N.D. Ill. 2006) (sums deducted from wages pursuant to garnishment order not exempt; noting change in statute barring use of wildcard exemption for wages); *In re* Patterson, 216 B.R. 413 (Bankr. C.D. Ill. 1998) (upholding amended statute as constitutional); *In re* Youngblood, 212 B.R. 593 (Bankr. N.D. Ill. 1997); *In re* Andres, 212 B.R. 306 (Bankr. N.D. Ill. 1997); *In re* Franklin, 210 B.R. 560 (Bankr. N.D. Ill. 1997).

449 *See, e.g., In re* Irish, 311 B.R. 63 (B.A.P. 8th Cir. 2004) (debtor school teacher may stack exemption for seventy-five percent of wages with exemption for "accrued wages or tax refund" to exempt July and August salary that accrued at end of school year in June); Little v. Reaves (*In re* Reaves), 256 B.R. 306 (B.A.P. 9th Cir. 2000) (motor vehicle exemption may be stacked with wildcard and unused portion of homestead exemptions), *aff'd on other grounds*, 285 F.3d 1152 (9th Cir. 2002); *In re* Bezares, 377 B.R. 413 (Bankr. M.D. Fla. 2007) (newly enacted "in lieu of homestead" exemption may be stacked with existing wildcard exemption); *In re* Urie, 2006 WL 533514 (Bankr. W.D. Mo. Jan. 31, 2006) (Missouri exemption for "any motor vehicle . . . in the aggregate" may be split between two vehicles and stacked with wildcard exemption; wedding ring exemption may be stacked with jewelry exemption); *In re* Bell, 333 B.R. 839 (Bankr. W.D. Mo. 2005) (married couple could stack head of household, two wildcard, one motor vehicle and part of another motor vehicle exemption to exempt one vehicle, and apply balance of second motor vehicle exemption to second vehicle); *In re* Gagnon, 2005 WL 1331142 (Bankr. D.N.H. June 1, 2005) (New Hampshire wildcard exemption of $1000 plus up to $7000 in unused exemptions may be applied to one piece of property or spread over several); *In re* Payne, 2004 WL 2757907 (Bankr. M.D.N.C. Nov. 15, 2004) (couple who exempted home under bankruptcy code exemption for entireties property could use North Carolina "unused homestead" exemption to protect other property); Price v. Manufacturers & Traders Trust Co. (*In re* Price), 266 B.R. 572 (Bankr. W.D.N.Y. 2001) (New York law exempts 90% of wages and $2500 in cash in hand; cash exemption may be used to protect the 10% of wages not protected by the wage exemption); Vaillancourt v. Granite Group (*In re* Vaillancourt), 260 B.R. 66 (Bankr. D.N.H. 2001) (New Hampshire wildcard exemption for "any property" may be stacked with homestead or personal property exemptions); *In re* Rutter, 247 B.R. 334 (Bankr. M.D. Fla. 2000) (debtor may stack Florida's constitutional personal property exemption with its statutory motor vehicle exemption to exempt entire equity in his truck); *In re* Bova, 205 B.R. 467 (Bankr. E.D. Pa. 1997) (debtor could stack state exemption for payments "on account of personal bodily injury" with exemption for "compensation of loss of future earnings" when debtor could show that part of personal injury damages were for loss of earning power, and that the amount was "reasonably necessary" for the support of debtor or dependents); Landry v. Landry, 917 A.2d 1262 (N.H. 2007) (wildcard and unused portion of certain other exemptions may be stacked with tools of trade exemption to fully exempt mechanic's tools); *In re* Anderson, 932 P.2d 1110 (Okla. 1996) (liberally construing Oklahoma law, which allows one $50,000 exemption for each interest in a claim for personal injury, death, or workers' compensation, to allow two exemptions when plaintiff's work injury resulted in a workers' compensation claim and a malpractice judgment against the doctor who performed "unauthorized surgery"). *But see In re* Thornton, 269 B.R. 682 (W.D. Mo. 2001) (debtors who resided in mobile home not permitted to stack homestead exemption with exemption for "mobile home used as principal residence"; when home was permanently attached, homestead exemption applied); *In re* Hughes, 244 B.R. 448 (Bankr. D.S.D. 1999) (refusing to allow stacking of "additional personal property" exemption to protect proceeds of sale of homestead which exceeded homestead limit); *In re* Struckhoff, 231 B.R. 69 (Bankr. E.D. Mo. 1999) (Missouri exemption for "any" motor vehicle allows exemption of only one vehicle per debtor, so if debtor's interest in the car is worth less than the statutory $1000, the balance may not be applied to other vehicle or personal property).

450 *In re* Ambrose, 179 B.R. 982 (Bankr. S.D. Ga. 1995).

451 *In re* Duncan, 294 B.R. 339 (B.A.P. 10th Cir. 2003) (spouses may stack homestead exemptions, but wife who had no ownership interest on petition date not entitled to exemption); *In re* Lampe, 278 B.R. 205 (B.A.P. 10th Cir. 2002) (Kan. law) (spouses could stack exemptions in farm equipment purchased with funds from couple's joint account, when wife signed notes, and state law presumes equal ownership by husband and wife), *aff'd*, 331 F.3d 750 (10th Cir. 2003); Planned Parenthood of Columbus/Willamette, Inc. v. Am. Coalition of Life Activists, 2007 WL 4118597 (S.D. Ohio Nov. 16, 2007) (debtor and non-debtor spouse may stack aggregate and per item household goods exemptions); Schilling v. Tran, 287 B.R. 887 (W.D. Ky. 2002) (allowing husband and wife to stack motor vehicle exemptions to exempt one vehicle; when title listed both spouses in alternative each had ownership interest); *In re* Limperis, 370 B.R. 859 (Bankr. S.D. Fla. 2007) (married couple, subject to federal $125,000 cap for homestead acquired within 1215 days, could claim an exemption apiece and stack them for total exemption of $250,000); *In re* Ewbank, 359 B.R. 807 (Bankr. D.N.M. 2007) (New Mexico statute, permitting stacking of exemptions for "homestead owned jointly by two persons," did not require joint tenancy; tenancy in common was

apart, some courts allow each partner a full complement of exemptions,[452] while others allow an exemption only for the former marital home, or only one exemption per couple for other property.[453] States that recognize domestic partnerships may treat the partners like married couples for exemption purposes.[454]

sufficient); *In re* Bell, 333 B.R. 839 (Bankr. W.D. Mo. 2005) (married couple could stack head of household, two wildcard, one motor vehicle and part of another motor vehicle exemption to exempt one vehicle, and apply balance of second motor vehicle exemption to second vehicle); *In re* Collins, 2005 WL 3506356 (Bankr. C.D. Ill. Nov. 30, 2005) (widow who inherited marital home could stack her exemption, as owner, with deceased husband's exemption, which protected surviving spouse and minor child); *In re* Bippert, 311 B.R. 456 (Bankr. W.D. Tex. 2004) (both spouses sought to exempt cause of action for personal injury to wife alone; court looked to state marital property law and allowed each to exempt their property in claim; claim was wife's separate property except for lost wages, which were community, and loss of consortium, which was husband's separate property); *In re* Perez, 302 B.R. 661 (Bankr. D. Ariz. 2003) (spouse who filed individual bankruptcy could stack own and non-filing spouse's motor vehicle exemptions to protect family car; community property was part of bankruptcy estate, and individual spouse could act on behalf of community); *In re* Hejmowski, 296 B.R. 645 (Bankr. W.D.N.Y. 2003) (couple who filed joint tax return may stack New York's $2500 cash exemptions to protect $5000 in tax return, even if only one spouse earned income that tax year); *In re* Kieffer, 279 B.R. 290 (Bankr. D. Kan. 2002) (spouses could stack exemptions for farm equipment, when wife was co-owner, because equipment purchased with joint funds and wife signed notes); *In re* Hoffpauir, 258 B.R. 447 (Bankr. D. Idaho 2001) (when amended statute eliminated "per household" caps, each spouse could claim exemption in fire insurance proceeds of destroyed household goods); *In re* Guyot, 240 B.R. 326 (Bankr. D. Minn. 1999) (when Minnesota statute allowed exemption of one life insurance contract, each spouse could exempt one contract); *In re* Sherman, 237 B.R. 551 (Bankr. N.D.N.Y. 1999) (when New York's homestead and personal property exemptions refer to "an individual debtor," a married couple may stack two exemptions). *But see In re* Garran, 338 F.3d 1 (1st Cir. 2003) (homestead exemptions may not be stacked; only one spouse may claim homestead exemption for benefit of family, so wife's claim of homestead invalidated husband's earlier claim); *In re* Dawson, 266 B.R. 355 (Bankr. N.D. Tex. 2001) (only one homestead per married couple; once established may not be unilaterally changed or abandoned; husband who moved out of marital home and filed bankruptcy before divorce was final not entitled to homestead claim in his current residence); *In re* Garvin, 262 B.R. 529 (Bankr. D. Mont. 2001) (married debtors could claim only one state exemption in jointly owned motor vehicle); *In re* Soper, 258 B.R. 748 (Bankr. W.D. Mo. 2001) (married couple living together may claim equity in only one home, even though combined equity in house and vacation cabin less than state homestead cap; statute exempts "a dwelling house"); *In re* Nye, 250 B.R. 46 (Bankr. W.D.N.Y. 2000) (one spouse could not claim entire homestead exemption while other spouse claimed in-lieu-of-homestead exemption; each could exempt only his or her own one-half interest); *In re* Jackson, 194 B.R. 867 (Bankr. D. Ariz. 1995) (allowing married debtors to stack their $1500 motor vehicle exemptions to exempt $3000 in one car); Kipp v. Sweno, 683 N.W.2d 259 (Minn. 2004) (only one exemption per homestead, cap to be applied to entire equity in homestead owned in tenancy in common, not debtor-husband's share); *In re* Arnold, 73 P.3d 861 (Okla. 2003) (married couple may claim only one 160-acre rural homestead); *cf. In re* Cassity, 281 B.R. 365 (S.D. Ala. 2001) (spouses could not stack two homestead exemptions when property owned by wife alone; husband's interest too inchoate to support his claim); *In re* Toland, 346 B.R. 444 (Bankr. N.D. Ohio 2006) (husband could not claim exemption in car titled in wife's name; Ohio exemption law requires "an interest" in property; one spouse has no interest in other spouse's property); *In re* Czerneski, 330 B.R. 240 (Bankr. E.D. Wis. 2005) (spouses may stack wildcard exemptions in joint bankruptcy, but when home was wife's separate property under state domestic relations law, husband had no interest, and thus no exemption); *In re* Burnett, 303 B.R. 684 (Bankr. M.D. Ga. 2003) (Georgia law that allows double exemption when couple's home is owned by individual debtor applies only in bankruptcy); *In re* Brinley, 278 B.R. 130 (Bankr. W.D. Ky. 2002) (when property owned by couple in joint tenancy, homestead cap should be applied to entire equity, not to debtor-husband's share), *aff'd in part, rev'd in part on other grounds*, 2003 WL 1825521 (W.D. Ky. Apr. 1, 2003); *In re* Horstman, 276 B.R. 80 (Bankr. E.D.N.C. 2002) (wife may not use her wildcard exemption to exempt husband's car; her ownership interest insufficient, even though car marital property under state domestic relations law); *In re* Joseph, 262 B.R. 33 (Bankr. W.D.N.Y. 2001) (widow not permitted to claim both her own homestead exemption and that of husband who had died in 1980; N.Y. statute which allows survival of homestead exemption for protection of spouse and children applies only to debts of deceased spouse, not individual debts of survivor); *In re* Miller, 255 B.R. 221 (Bankr. D. Neb. 2000) (if truck titled in husband's name, only husband may claim an exemption in it); *In re* Schapiro, 246 B.R. 751 (Bankr. W.D.N.Y. 2000) (New York exemption for cash protected a bequest, but when only husband was beneficiary, couple could claim only one exemption).

452 *In re* Colwell, 196 F.3d 1225 (11th Cir. 1999) (when couple are legitimately living apart, that is, not for purposes of fraud, each is entitled to a homestead exemption); *In re* Roberts, 219 B.R. 235 (B.A.P. 8th Cir. 1998); *In re* Roberge, 307 B.R. 442 (Bankr. D. Vt. 2004) (exemptions intended to protect family group; married debtors living apart, each with a child, were two family groups, each entitled to full set of exemptions); *cf.* Mayo v. Sikes, 2006 WL 1750882 (W.D. La. June 20, 2006) (Louisiana exempts one motor vehicle "per household"; only one exemption allowed when evidence insufficient to show that divorcing couple were living apart on bankruptcy petition date).

453 *In re* Rowe, 236 B.R. 11 (B.A.P. 9th Cir. 1999) (Nevada law allows a married couple, even if living apart, to claim only one homestead exemption); *In re* Dawson, 266 B.R. 355 (Bankr. N.D. Texas 2001) (Texas allows only one homestead per married couple; husband who had moved out of marital home could not claim homestead in new home, even though marital home was separate property of wife); *In re* Thorpe, 251 B.R. 723 (Bankr. W.D. Mo. 2000) (when married couple was living apart without dependents, only one motor vehicle and one wildcard exemption allowed for motorcycle of which husband was sole owner); Kipp v. Sweno, 683 N.W.2d 259 (Minn. 2004) (only one homestead per couple, neither doubled for two debtors nor halved for one; debtor husband may claim entire $200,000 exemption for his survivorship interest).

454 *See In re* Rabin, 359 B.R. 242 (B.A.P. 9th Cir. 2007) (intent of California domestic partnership act was to treat domestic partners as spouses; partners who had merged their finances entitled to only one exemption, same as married couple).

12.5.7 *Exemptions for Pensions and Retirement Benefits*

There is a strong public policy favoring protection of retirement plans, without which the state might have to support people made destitute by deprivation of their retirement income.[455] Therefore, federal law and most states exempt at least a portion of benefits received under various employee retirement or pension plans.[456] Sometimes a state's exemption is found in the statute creating or regulating the retirement or pension plan, rather than in a general exemption law. The exemption may continue after the benefits are paid out.[457] The Social Security Act exempts all benefits paid out under the act and the exemption follows the funds deposited into a checking account.[458]

Generally the courts extend an exemption for employee pension plans to tax-qualified individual retirement accounts.[459] Some courts extend this protection to other good

455 *In re* Seltzer, 104 F.3d 234 (9th Cir. 1996).

456 29 U.S.C. §§ 1056(d)(1) (Employee Retirement Income Security Act (ERISA) retirement benefits), 1051(6) (excluding certain individual retirement accounts from ERISA's protection); *see* Patterson v. Shumate, 504 U.S. 753, 112 S. Ct. 2242, 119 L. Ed. 2d 519 (1992) (ERISA-qualified pension plan funds are not available to creditors in or out of bankruptcy); Guidry v. Sheet Metal Workers Nat'l Pension Fund, 493 U.S. 365, 110 S. Ct. 680, 107 L. Ed. 2d 782 (1990) (ERISA's anti-alienation provisions for pension benefits prohibit their garnishment even when in form of constructive trust); *In re* Sandvik, 2004 WL 3383656 (Bankr. D.N.D. Dec. 1, 2004) (in determining whether individual retirement account exceeds state statutory exemption, court will not count ERISA plan which, under federal law, is not part of bankruptcy estate); *In re* Tomlin, 315 B.R. 439 (Bankr. E.D. Mich. 2004) (individual retirement account is exempt in bankruptcy; ERISA does not preempt Michigan law, enacted when state opted out of federal bankruptcy exemptions); *In re* Handel, 301 B.R. 421 (Bankr. S.D.N.Y. 2003) (anti-alienation clause sufficient to make plan exempt, even though debtor dealt with plan in way that caused it to lose favorable tax treatment); *see also In re* Laher, 496 F.3d 279 (3d Cir. 2007) (TIAA-CREF retirement annuity, which contained anti-alienation clause, is a trust under New York law and is not part of bankruptcy estate); *In re* Hainlen, 365 B.R. 288 (Bankr. S.D. Ga. 2007) (annuity, received as beneficiary of deceased father's retirement plan, included strong anti-alienation clause; plan was trust, under Georgia law, and excluded from bankruptcy estate); *cf.* Mackey v. Lanier Collection Agency & Serv., Inc., 486 U.S. 825, 836, 108 S. Ct. 2182, 100 L. Ed. 2d 836 (1988) (ERISA prohibits assignment or alienation of benefits provided by ERISA pension plans but not ERISA welfare benefit plans); Christensen v. United States, 2006 WL 744296 (W.D. Mo. Mar. 23, 2006) (declining to decide whether federal retirement payments are subject to wage garnishment limits or can be offset to collect federal debts). *But see In re* Haney, 316 B.R. 827 (Bankr. E.D. Pa. 2004) (individual retirement accounts not exempt under federal bankruptcy exemptions, if debtors under age $59\frac{1}{2}$ and not disabled); *cf.* Lampkins v. Golden, 2002 U.S. App. LEXIS 900 (6th Cir. Jan. 17, 2002) (Simplified Employee Pension is not protected by ERISA's exemption provision, and ERISA preempts state exemption law that might have applied to it); Katzenberg v. Lazzari, 2007 WL 1017645 (E.D.N.Y. Mar. 12, 2007) (debt that arises from ERISA plan fiduciary's misappropriate of money from the plan or breach of other duties to the plan may be offset against ERISA benefits owed to the fiduciary); *In re* Radcliffe, 372 B.R. 401 (Bankr. N.D. Ind. 2007) (debt that arises from criminal acts or fiduciary defalcation involving ERISA plan may be set off against ERISA benefits owed to the wrongdoer under the plan, but offset can not be based on corporate officer's personal guarantee of company's obligation to make contributions to plan even though company breached this obligation).

457 *In re* Meyer, 211 B.R. 203 (Bankr. E.D. Va. 1997) (military retirement pay is exempt under federal law because it is not listed among the types of federal employee compensation made subject to garnishment by 5 U.S.C. § 5520, nor listed in regulations as subject to "involuntary allotment"; the pay retains exempt status when directly deposited in Navy Federal Credit Union, but not when transferred to debtor's non-special purpose checking account in another institution); *In re* Bresnahan, 183 B.R. 506 (Bankr. S.D. Ohio 1995) (retirement pension, exempt under Ohio law so far as reasonably necessary for the support of debtor and dependents, retains its exempt character when deposited in checking account); Dowling v. Chicago Options Associates, Inc., 847 N.E.2d 741 (Ill. App. Ct. 2006) (401(k) funds remain exempt after payout if "periodic payments for support" but not if "lump sum available for investment"). *But see* Hoult v. Hoult, 373 F.3d 47 (1st Cir. 2004) (ERISA does not exempt funds in hands of beneficiary; anti-alienation clause not violated by court order requiring judgment debtor to deposit all his income, including ERISA funds, in one bank account, from which he could withdraw only court-approved sum for monthly expenses); *In re* McDonald, 2003 WL 23211570 (Bankr. M.D.N.C. Sept. 27, 2003) (funds in ERISA plan lose exemption when paid to beneficiary; funds borrowed from plan and deposited in credit union not exempt, so credit union could set off account); *In re* Ryzner, 208 B.R. 568 (Bankr. M.D. Fla. 1997) (former police officer's disability payments retain their exempt character when deposited in a bank account, so long as they remain traceable); Briceno v. Briceno, 2007 WL 4146280 (Tenn. Ct. App. Nov. 21, 2007) (ERISA exemption ends once funds are disbursed, so family court may impose constructive trust on pension payments after their payment).

458 Hoult v. Hoult, 373 F.3d 47 (1st Cir. 2004) (anti-alienation provision applies to Social Security benefits paid to beneficiary and deposited in account); *see* §§ 12.5.5, *supra*; 12.6, *infra*.

459 Rousey v. Jacoway, 544 U.S. 320, 125 S. Ct. 1561, 161 L. Ed. 2d 563 (2005) (tax-qualified individual retirement accounts, funded by distributions from employer's pension plan, covered by federal bankruptcy exemption for "similar plan . . . on account of . . . age" when tax penalty for withdrawal before age $59\frac{1}{2}$ was "substantial barrier" to early withdrawal); Premier Capital, Inc. v. Decarolis (*In re* Decarolis), 259 B.R. 467 (B.A.P. 1st Cir. 2001) (tax-qualified retirement plan exempt under New Hampshire law, even if amounts deposited in account exceed tax exempt amount, except if there is fraudulent transfer); Walsh v. McMurry, 2006 WL 2422583 (W.D. Pa. Aug. 18, 2006) (individual retirement account is exempt so far as necessary for support; Supreme Court decision has overruled earlier Third Circuit precedent that denied exemption to individual retirement account if debtor had no present right to payments); *In re* Quinn, 327 B.R. 818 (W.D. Mich. 2005) (state university retirement plan was an exempt trust; strong anti-alienation language in both plan documents and state statute governing retirement system); *In re* Hermes, 239 B.R. 491 (E.D. Mich. 1999) (tax-qualified IRA which allowed withdrawals before age $59\frac{1}{2}$ subject

to a penalty was similar to other plans providing income on account of age, disability, and the like, and was exempt); *In re* Sheeran, 369 B.R. 910 (Bankr. E.D. Va. 2007) (debtor could exempt individual retirement account, into which she had rolled over 401(k) from former employer, except for a sum mistakenly deposited by employer in the 401(k)); *In re* Gill, 2007 WL 2990564 (Bankr. D.D.C. Oct. 11, 2007) (thrift savings plan exempt, under District of Columbia law, if tax-qualified); *In re* True, 340 B.R. 597 (Bankr. N.D. Ohio 2006) (Ohio exemption for property specifically exempted by federal laws other than the bankruptcy act protected funds held in employee's ERISA-qualified tax deferred annuity); *In re* Hartman, 345 B.R. 826 (Bankr. N.D. Ohio 2005) (Ohio individual retirement account exemption protects funds rolled over from ex-husband's plan as required by qualified domestic relations order); *In re* Sforzo, 332 B.R. 294 (Bankr. N.D. Ohio 2005) (ERISA-qualified tax-sheltered annuity exempt under Ohio law); *In re* Booth, 331 B.R. 233 (Bankr. W.D. Pa. 2005) (individual retirement account is exempt so far as necessary for support); *In re* Bashara, 293 B.R. 216 (Bankr. D. Neb. 2003) (tax-qualified individual retirement accounts are "similar plans" under Nebraska statute that exempts pensions, profit sharing and similar plans; exempt insofar as needed for support); *In re* Buzza, 287 B.R. 417 (Bankr. S.D. Ohio 2002) (Ohio exemption for individual retirement accounts not preempted by ERISA because individual retirement accounts not "employee benefit plans"); *In re* McCabe, 280 B.R. 841 (Bankr. N.D. Iowa 2002) (allowing elderly debtors to keep entire individual retirement account, when annual contributions had never exceeded the $2000 permitted by tax code); *In re* Vandeberg, 276 B.R. 581 (Bankr. E.D. Tenn. 2001) (Roth individual retirement account so similar to types of individual retirement accounts included in Tennessee statute that it was exempt before amendment to include Roths); *In re* Maurer, 268 B.R. 335 (Bankr. W.D.N.Y. 2001) (to determine whether state employees deferred compensation plan is a "similar plan" within meaning of New York exemption, court must determine if Internal Revenue Service has found the plan qualified under section 457), *aff'd*, 2002 WL 1012985 (W.D.N.Y. May 13, 2002); *In re* Gurry, 253 B.R. 406 (Bankr. E.D. Va. 2000) (debtor who had both an ERISA plan and an individual retirement account was not entitled to Virginia's unlimited exemption for individual retirement account, and funds in exempt ERISA plan counted against individual retirement account exemption); *In re* Hasse, 246 B.R. 247 (Bankr. E.D. Va. 2000) (Virginia law allows unlimited exemption for individual retirement account only if debtor does not have employer-sponsored retirement plan established pursuant to certain sections of the Internal Revenue Code; plan that was similar but not identical to such plans did not bar exemption for individual retirement account); *In re* Stewart, 246 B.R. 134 (Bankr. D.N.H. 2000) (tax-qualified individual retirement account fully exempt under New Hampshire law, but only as to debts incurred after effective date of statute; this limitation does not apply in bankruptcy); *In re* MacLean, 2000 Bankr. LEXIS 1796 (Bankr. D.N.H. Mar. 1, 2000) (same); *In re* Bogue, 240 B.R. 742 (Bankr. E.D. Wis. 1999) (Wisconsin exemption for retirement plans protects annuities which comply with any section of Internal Revenue Code); *In re* Bruski, 226 B.R. 422 (Bankr. W.D. Wis. 1998) (Wisconsin's exemption for annuities which comply with Internal Revenue Code covers tax-deferred annuity, which would begin paying out at age $59\frac{1}{2}$, even though there was no limit on contributions, but exemption could raise serious problems if used by wealthier debtors to shelter large sums); *In re* Luttge, 204 B.R. 259 (Bankr. S.D. Fla. 1997) (tax-qualified individual retirement account was exempt under Florida law, even though it was not covered by ERISA); *In re* McKown, 203 B.R. 722 (Bankr. E.D. Cal. 1996) (individual retirement account was sufficiently similar to a "pension, profit-sharing, annuity" to be exempt under California law; result would be different if account were being used as "savings account" or to shelter funds from creditors), *aff'd*, 203 F.3d 1188 (B.A.P. 9th Cir. 1997); *In re* Ritter, 190 B.R. 323 (Bankr. N.D. Ill. 1995) (under Illinois statute which exempted private plans "intended in good faith" to provide for retirement, Keogh and individual retirement accounts were exempt, even though debtor had made early withdrawals during period of unemployment, and might do so again, when there was no evidence of lack of good faith at the time the plans were established); *In re* Bates, 176 B.R. 104 (Bankr. D. Me. 1994) (when Maine law exempted pensions, annuities, and "any similar plan" on account of age, disability, an individual retirement account was a "similar plan" even though debtor could pay penalty and take early withdrawal; individual retirement account could be "necessary for debtor's support," even though debtor was still under age $59\frac{1}{2}$); Schwartzman v. Wilshinsky, 57 Cal. Rptr. 2d 790 (Ct. App. 1996) (individual retirement accounts were exempt only to extent necessary to support debtor and dependents; plan funded by employer profit sharing and employee deferred compensation was wholly exempt); Mexic v. Mexic, 808 So. 2d 685 (La. Ct. App. 2001) (Roth individual retirement account was a "tax-deferred arrangement" exempted by Louisiana statute even before amendment to specifically include Roths); C.P. v. Piscataway Twp. Bd. of Educ., 681 A.2d 105 (N.J. Super. Ct. App. Div. 1996) (New Jersey statute which exempted "pension funds" covered tax-qualified individual retirement accounts); *see also In re* Lawrence, 235 B.R. 498 (Bankr. S.D. Fla. 1999) (Florida law permits exemption of non-ERISA-qualified pension plan, if plan is tax-qualified, but this plan is not), *rev'd on other grounds*, 244 B.R. 868 (S.D. Fla. 2000); *In re* Spradlin, 231 B.R. 254 (Bankr. E.D. Mich. 1999) (construing Michigan statutory exemption for "an" individual retirement account to allow debtor to exempt only one of his two individual retirement accounts); *In re* Hawkinson, 222 B.R. 334 (Bankr. D. Minn. 1998) (when Minnesota law capped exemptions for non-ERISA qualified plans at $51,000, and debtor owned three plans, two ERISA-qualified and one not, only the non-ERISA plan would be counted toward the cap); *In re* Outen, 220 B.R. 26 (Bankr. D.S.C. 1998) (individual retirement account was exempt, subject to "reasonable necessity" limitation, whether or not debtor had present right to payments); *In re* Francisco, 204 B.R. 799 (Bankr. M.D. Fla. 1996). *But see* Huisinga v. Kemmerer (*In re* Kemmerer), 251 B.R. 50 (B.A.P. 8th Cir. 2000) (individual retirement annuity into which debtor rolled over 401(k) funds was not exempt under Iowa law that only covered individual retirement accounts); Schoonover v. Karr, 285 B.R. 695 (S.D. Ill. 2002) (account not exempt because not tax-qualified), *aff'd*, 331 F.3d 575 (7th Cir. 2003); *In re* Orgeron, 2006 WL 335438 (Bankr. W.D. Mo. Feb. 2, 2006) (individual retirement account contributions made "in contemplation of bankruptcy"—here within thirty days prepetition—not exempt; balance of individual retirement account is exempt); *In re* Navarre, 332 B.R. 24 (Bankr. M.D. Ala. 2004) (interest in individual retirement account inherited from mother not exempt because no longer tax-qualified; non-spouse beneficiary can not roll over funds into own individual retirement account); *In re* Haney, 316 B.R. 827 (Bankr. E.D. Pa. 2004) (individual retirement accounts not exempt under federal bankruptcy exemptions, if debtors under age $59\frac{1}{2}$ and not disabled); *In re* Sims, 241 B.R. 467 (Bankr. N.D.

faith private retirement plans.[460] One court has held that a "voluntary buy-out" used by an employer to encourage

Okla. 1999) (individual retirement account inherited from father was no longer a retirement planning tool so was not exempt); *In re* Handshaw, 198 B.R. 633 (Bankr. M.D. Fla. 1996) (county retirement benefits were not exempt: state statute preempted by ERISA, and benefits not within ERISA governmental unit exception, when benefits were provided by the National Association of Counties, not directly by the governmental unit; county's own deferred compensation plan was exempt); *cf.* United States v. Infelise, 159 F.3d 300 (7th Cir. 1998) (individual retirement account governed by 26 U.S.C. § 408 could be subjected to forfeiture in criminal case); *In re* Hughes, 293 B.R. 528 (Bankr. M.D. Fla. 2003) (individual retirement account lost exempt status when debtor used funds for loan to his corporation; prompt repayment did not restore exemption).

460 *In re* Martin, 297 B.R. 750 (8th Cir. 2003) (annuities exempted as "employee benefits," but only if funded with wages or other sums derived from employment, including self-employment, and payable on account of age, disability, illness or length of service; not shown when annuity purchased with sale proceeds of farmland); Sawczak v. Goldenberg, 218 F.3d 1264 (11th Cir. 2000) (individual retirement accounts exempt when they fit the Florida statutory definition, were not acquired with proceeds of fraud, and were not a transfer of nonexempt to exempt assets on the eve of bankruptcy); Warfield v. Alaniz, 2007 WL 4287838 (D. Ariz. Dec. 6, 2007) (annuity purchased with funds from debtor's individual retirement account was protected by exemption for individual retirement accounts); *In re* Pepmeyer, 273 B.R. 782 (N.D. Iowa 2002) ("individual retirement annuity" exempt under Iowa law); *In re* Delaney, 268 B.R. 57 (D. Vt. 2001) (remanding to determine whether annuity, payable at specific age or upon disability, is "payable on account of death, disability, retirement, or termination of employment" and whether the funds are necessary for support of debtor); *In re* Deem, 2007 WL 295437 (Bankr. N.D. Ohio Jan. 29, 2007) ("retirement annuity" offered by employer was exempt under Ohio provision for property exempt under nonbankruptcy federal law); *In re* Vangen, 334 B.R. 241 (Bankr. W.D. Wis. 2005) (retirement-related annuities purchased with nonexempt funds considered exempt given no extrinsic evidence of fraud); *In re* Lynch, 321 B.R. 114 (Bankr. S.D.N.Y. 2005) (under New York law annuity exempt so far as needed for support); Rohan v. Bull, 2004 WL 1052778 (Cal. Ct. App. May 11, 2004) (private retirement plans, here an individual retirement account into which debtor rolled over funds from employer's profit-sharing plan, exempt so far as needed for support); Goldenberg v. Sawczak, 791 So. 2d 1078 (Fla. 2001) (proceeds of annuity contract exempt if there is a surrender penalty); Cashio v. Tollin, 712 So. 2d 254 (La. Ct. App. 1998) (annuity was exempt under Louisiana law, whether or not purchased with tax-exempt funds); Lozano v. Lozano, 975 S.W.2d 63 (Tex. App. 1998) (individual retirement account was exempt, whether or not the source of funds, here a rollover from a former employer's plan, was exempt); *see also In re* Henrickson, 277 B.R. 759 (B.A.P. 8th Cir. 2002) (annuities are exempt retirement plans only if contributions "tied to" employment, including self-employment, or come from exempt source); *In re* Ondrey, 1999 U.S. Dist. LEXIS 9287 (W.D.N.Y. June 15, 1999) (American citizen who was employed in Canada could exempt employer-sponsored retirement plan, but retirement savings plan not exempt because debtor could withdraw funds at will); *In re* Tykla, 353 B.R. 437 (Bankr. W.D. Pa. 2006) (state employee's deferred compensation plan is not part of bankruptcy estate because restrictions on transfer are enforceable under "applicable non-bankruptcy law"); *cf. In re* Mooney, 248 B.R. 391 (Bankr. C.D. Cal. 2000) (when debtor rolled over funds from fully-exempt ERISA-qualified employer plan to private individual retirement account which is exempt only "to the extent necessary for the support of debtor and dependents," the lesser exemption applied). *But see* Eilbert v. Pelican, 162 F.3d 523 (8th Cir. 1998) (annuity was not a "similar plan" within meaning of Iowa statute which exempted retirement plans, when debtor had complete control over when and how payments would be made, plan was funded by single lump sum payment by debtor when large personal injury judgment was imminent, and debtor chose to start receiving payments two months after purchase of the annuity), *aff'g* 212 B.R. 954 (B.A.P. 8th Cir. 1997); *In re* Carbaugh, 278 B.R. 512 (B.A.P. 10th Cir. 2002) (investment account containing only distribution from exempt ERISA account not exempt; benefits lost exempt status when distributed; state exemption for benefits "payable from" retirement account lost when benefits paid); Schoonover v. Karr, 285 B.R. 695 (S.D. Ill. 2002) (account not exempt because not tax-qualified), *aff'd*, 331 F.3d 575 (7th Cir. 2003); *In re* Lowe, 252 B.R. 614 (W.D.N.Y. 2000) (profit sharing plan not exempt as pension or similar plan when the amount owed to employee did not depend on length of service, age, disability, or the like; not an exempt spendthrift trust, because employee could access funds as soon as employer declared it payable); *In re* Phillips, 218 B.R. 520 (N.D. Cal. 1998) (purported "private retirement plan" was not "designed or used" for retirement purposes within meaning of California exemption when it was informal, owners retained control over the funds and used them for purposes not related to retirement, and attempts to formalize the plan were made only after a large judgment was imminent); *In re* Green, 2007 WL 1031677 (Bankr. E.D. Tenn. Apr. 2, 2007) (exemption for annuity payable on account of age, illness, length of service, and so forth, refers to product purchased over time to serve as substitute for wages upon retirement or disability; no exemption for annuity that funded structured settlement for wrongful death of debtor's minor son, upon whom debtor was never dependent, even though debtor was now disabled and annuity was only source of income); *In re* Madia, 294 B.R. 177 (Bankr. M.D. Fla. 2003) (Florida uses federal bankruptcy criteria for exempt retirement plans; deferred compensation pursuant to section 457 of Internal Revenue Code not exempt because this section not listed in bankruptcy exemption, and compensation not on account of age, disability, length of service, or the like); *In re* Hughes, 293 B.R. 528 (Bankr. M.D. Fla. 2003) (individual retirement account lost exempt status when debtor used funds for loan to his corporation; prompt repayment did not restore exemption); *In re* Greenfield, 289 B.R. 146 (Bankr. S.D. Cal. 2003) (inherited retirement account from which forty-one-year-old debtor was receiving payments not exempt because not used for retirement purposes); *In re* Hupton, 287 B.R. 438 (Bankr. N.D. Iowa 2002) (retirement annuity inherited from father not exempt; payments not on account of debtor's age, disability, or the like; Iowa does not exempt annuities; not a spendthrift trust because lump sum distribution possible); *In re* Barnes, 275 B.R. 889 (Bankr. E.D. Cal. 2002) (annuity purchased with single lump sum not a retirement plan; plan requires gradual accumulation, also must either be provided by third party such as employer, or be tax-qualified self-employed plan); *In re* Ellis, 274 B.R. 782 (Bankr. S.D. Ill. 2002) (whole life insurance policy that provided for payment of annuity after age sixty-five was neither an annuity nor a retirement plan; annuity was one of several ways to cash in the policy, and plan was not tax-qualified); *In re* Johnson, 274 B.R. 473 (Bankr. E.D. Mich.

early retirement was a "similar plan" within the meaning of a state exemption statute.[461] Note that, if an exemption applies only to tax-qualified plans, the plan will become nonexempt if the funds are used in a transaction prohibited by tax law.[462]

Some courts have extended the exemption to pension and disability benefits awarded to former spouses or domestic partners.[463] But exemptions or anti-alienation provisions will generally not prevent an ex-spouse from claiming pension or retirement benefits pursuant to a divorce decree.[464]

State exemptions seek to balance the need for security in old age against the possible abuse of retirement accounts to

2002) (brokerage account not exempt under Michigan law because not an individual retirement account); *In re* Sutton, 272 B.R. 802 (Bankr. M.D. Fla. 2002) (Keogh plan of solo practice realtor not exempt under Florida law); *In re* Selfe, 260 B.R. 463 (Bankr. E.D. Mo. 2001) (proceeds of Federal Employees' Group Life Insurance policy are life insurance, not a "death benefit plan" exempt under Missouri law; life insurance not exempt); *In re* Collett, 253 B.R. 452 (Bankr. W.D. Mo. 2000) (Missouri exemption for annuity which pays out on account of illness, age, length of service, disability or death, did not protect annuity purchased to comply with testator's instructions that her nephew's inheritance should be paid out in increments); *In re* Kuraishi, 237 B.R. 172 (Bankr. C.D. Cal. 1999) (Keogh plan found to be "self-settled spendthrift trust" and thus not exempt under California law, when same person, a doctor, was employer, employee, and beneficiary); *In re* Cobb, 231 B.R. 236 (Bankr. D.N.J. 1999) (funds from ERISA-qualified thrift plan lost exemption when withdrawn and deposited in regular checking account, when debtor had no intention of rolling them over into another exempt plan); *In re* Rogers, 222 B.R. 348 (Bankr. S.D. Cal. 1998) ("life and health insurance annuity" that was not tax-qualified and was purchased with a single lump sum was not a retirement plan under California law); *In re* Bruce, 224 B.R. 505 (Bankr. M.D. Fla. 1998) (annual payments to lottery winner were not an exempt annuity under Florida law when state paid winnings from income from bonds purchased with income from ticket sales); *In re* Dunn, 215 B.R. 121 (Bankr. E.D. Mich. 1997), *supplemental opinion at* 215 B.R. 848 (Bankr. E.D. Mich. 1997) (annuity savings plan which was funded entirely by voluntary contributions of employee was not exempt under either federal or Michigan law); *cf. In re* Rousey, 347 F.3d 689 (8th Cir. 2003) (individual retirement accounts created by rollover from employee pension fund not exempt under federal bankruptcy exemptions, when no additional contributions after initial lump sum, and depositors could remove funds at will subject only to tax penalty; might be exempt if withdrawals were limited to circumstances such as age or illness); *In re* Thomas, 331 B.R. 798 (Bankr. W.D. Ark. 2005) (individual retirement account and annuity not exempt when they lacked requisite transfer restrictions).

461 *In re* Carlson, 192 B.R. 755 (Bankr. D. Idaho 1996) (exemption for pensions, profit sharing, "similar plans"). *But see In re* Bartholomew, 214 B.R. 322 (Bankr. S.D. Ohio 1997) (severance pay, one year's salary paid to long-term employee whose job was being eliminated, was not a "pension, annuity or similar plan" within meaning of Ohio exemption when lump sum was offered on a one-time basis to small group of employees affected by downsizing).

462 *In re* Plunk, 481 F.3d 302 (5th Cir. 2007) (bankruptcy court could find plan nonexempt because no longer tax-qualified due to disqualifying events); Aebig v. Cox, 2006 WL 1360504 (Mich. Ct. App. May 18, 2006) (debtor's self-directed individual retirement account lost status and exemption as a result of prohibited transaction, that is, lease of property to corporation owned by his wife); Nu-Way Energy Corp. v. Delp, 205 S.W.3d 667 (Tex. App. 2006) (tax qualification and exemption both lost because of complex commercial transaction involving release of personal guarantee of corporate debt).

463 *In re* Metz, 225 B.R. 173 (B.A.P. 9th Cir. 1998) (former wife's share of husband's retirement plan, awarded to her at divorce, was exempt under both ERISA and California law); *In re* Hartman, 345 B.R. 826 (Bankr. N.D. Ohio 2005) (Ohio individual retirement account exemption protects funds rolled over from ex-husband's plan as required by qualified domestic relations order because they are tax-qualified); *In re* Farmer, 295 B.R. 322 (Bankr. W.D. Wis. 2003) (retirement account awarded to wife by qualified domestic relations order was exempt under both ERISA's anti-alienation clause and Wisconsin exemption for retirement accounts); *In re* Seddon, 255 B.R. 815 (Bankr. W.D.N.C. 2000) (anti-alienation provision for federal civil service retirement benefits protects benefits granted to ex-wife by divorce decree); *In re* Lummer, 219 B.R. 510 (Bankr. S.D. Ill. 1998) (Illinois' broadly worded exemption for retirement benefits protects former wife's share of husband's military retirement pay); *In re* Cason, 211 B.R. 72 (Bankr. N.D. Fla. 1997) (anti-alienation provision of Florida's State Retirement System Act, which protects "benefits accrued to any person," exempts half-interest in benefits awarded to state employee's ex-spouse). *But see* Deretich v. City of St. Francis, 128 F.3d 1209 (8th Cir. 1997) (Minnesota exemption for employee benefits does not protect disability insurance benefits which had been awarded to employee's ex-wife as part of divorce settlement); *In re* Wilbur, 126 F.3d 1218 (9th Cir. 1997) (exemption for retirement plans did not protect funds derived from exempt retirement plan, paid to former domestic partner pursuant to court judgment dividing property when partners separated); *In re* Anderson, 269 B.R. 27 (B.A.P. 8th Cir. 2001) (husband's interest in ex-wife's individual retirement account, awarded to him by divorce decree, not exempt retirement plan, because his rights did not arise from employment); *In re* Hageman, 260 B.R. 852 (Bankr. S.D. Ohio 2001) (Ohio's exemption for retirement plans protects only plan participant, not ex-spouse awarded interest in the plan); *In re* Thurman, 255 B.R. 730 (Bankr. M.D. Tenn. 2000) (retirement plans exempt only if they are the debtor's plan, so proceeds of ex-husband's 401K, awarded to debtor in divorce, not exempt when plan was in husband's name only).

464 Harmand v. Harmand, 931 So. 2d 18 (Ala. Civ. App. 2005) (federal civil service retirement benefits may be divided at divorce and Office of Personnel Management may be ordered to pay ex-spouse; here some of the benefits were separate property, because earned after marriage terminated, but couple had separation agreement, and party may bargain away separate property); Erb v. Erb, 747 N.E.2d 230 (Ohio 2001) (anti-alienation provision in police and fire fighters' pension fund did not bar court-ordered payments directly to ex-wife, as divorce decree gave wife property interest in pension; statute has since been amended to expressly permit direct payments). *But see* Smith v. Mo. Local Employees Retirement Sys., 235 S.W.3d 578 (Mo. Ct. App. 2007) (specific statute creating state employees' pension system allowed garnishment for child support but did not mention spousal support; notwithstanding general statute providing that no property was exempt as to spousal maintenance, pension not garnishable for spousal maintenance).

shelter unreasonable amounts from creditors. Some statutes exempt retirement funds so far as "reasonably necessary" for the retiree's needs,[465] while others set limits on the amounts which may be exempted in an individual retirement account.[466] These limits may create a hardship for long-term employees who lose their jobs and must roll over substantial

465 *In re* Davis, 323 B.R. 732 (B.A.P. 9th Cir. 2005) (individual retirement account and Keough not reasonably necessary for support within meaning of California exemption when debtor expected to receive distribution of at least $200,000 pursuant to divorce decree); *In re* Hamo, 233 B.R. 718 (B.A.P. 6th Cir. 1999) (fifty-four-year-old debtor with heart condition allowed to exempt only $20,000 of $96,000 individual retirement account under Ohio law, when debtor was adequately supported by his wife; note that debtor was so secretive regarding other matters that discharge was denied); *In re* Spenler, 212 B.R. 625 (B.A.P. 9th Cir. 1997) (individual retirement account not reasonably necessary for fifty-five-year-old single male debtor's support within meaning of California exemption when debtor's Social Security and ERISA pension would provide over $5000/month after retirement and he was currently earning enough from his medical practice to build up significant retirement fund before retirement); Walsh v. McMurry, 2006 WL 2422583 (W.D. Pa. Aug. 18, 2006) (articulating criteria for determining whether individual retirement account needed for support of debtor or dependents and remanding for fact finding on that issue); Abbate v. Spear, 289 B.R. 62 (E.D. Va. 2003) (ERISA pensions totally exempt, individual retirement accounts exempt insofar as needed to provide $17,500 per year income; if debtor has both individual retirement account and ERISA pension, ERISA must be considered in determining amount of income available); *In re* Booth, 331 B.R. 233 (Bankr. W.D. Pa. 2005) (individual retirement account and annuity both needed for support when husband was disabled, wife's job was low-paying, and husband's disability payments would end when he qualified for Social Security); *In re* Guikema, 329 B.R. 607 (Bankr. S.D. Ohio 2005) (finding tax-sheltered annuity not necessary for support in light of present and future income); *In re* Lynch, 321 B.R. 114 (Bankr. S.D.N.Y. 2005) (New York exempts any annuity so far as needed for support; semi-retired lawyer who received large fee in the form of an annuity could exempt proceeds, which were a "significant part" of his monthly budget); *In re* Rosen, 318 B.R. 166 (Bankr. D. Neb. 2004) (tax-qualified individual retirement account, into which debtor never deposited more than the permitted $2000/year exempt so far as needed for support); *In re* Bashara, 293 B.R. 216 (Bankr. D. Neb. 2003) (tax-qualified individual retirement accounts exempt so far as needed for support; when trustee failed to raise issue, individual retirement account fully exempt); *In re* Conkle, 275 B.R. 530 (Bankr. S.D. Ohio 2002) (denying exemption for tax-deferred annuity in light of debtors' expenses, ability to keep working until age sixty-five, and amount of Social Security and pensions to be received, even though sixty-year-old husband is unemployed and fifty-nine-year-old wife has health problems); *In re* Roselle, 274 B.R. 486 (Bankr. S.D. Ohio 2002) (benefits from private disability policy are exempt only as needed for support; court scrutinizes debtor's lifestyle, concludes that disabled debtor can move from house to apartment and does not need long-term care insurance); *In re* Cluckey, 221 B.R. 192 (Bankr. N.D. Ohio 1998) (entire $23,000 retirement account was "reasonably necessary" for fifty-four-year-old debtor of limited earning power, with no resources for retirement); *In re* Parker, 219 B.R. 972 (Bankr. S.D. Ohio 1998) ($20,000 retirement account was "reasonably necessary" for sixty-seven-year-old man, with significant health problems, but $34,000 retirement account was not reasonably necessary for fifty-eight-year-old woman who was employed despite health problems, had an ERISA-qualified plan at work, and could continue contributing to that plan for a number of years); *In re* Hoppes, 202 B.R. 595 (Bankr. N.D. Ohio 1996) (allowing couple in mid-fifties to exempt $75,000 of a $150,000 individual retirement account when husband had substantial earnings but was close to retirement and had significant health problems, but some of their expenses were not "reasonably necessary"); *In re* Webb, 189 B.R. 144 (Bankr. S.D. Ohio 1995) (allowing fifty-two-year-old debtor to exempt all of individual retirement account as reasonably necessary for support in retirement, when her ability to save for retirement was limited and average Social Security payment would fall far short of her expenses); *In re* Bates, 176 B.R. 104 (Bankr. D. Me. 1994) (allowing fifty-year-old unemployed debtor living in economically "unpromising" area to keep entire $18,000 individual retirement account); McMullan v. Haycock, 54 Cal. Rptr. 3d 660 (Ct. App. 2007) (private pension plans fully exempt; individual retirement accounts exempt so far as needed for support); Rohan v. Bull, 2004 WL 1052778 (Cal. Ct. App. May 11, 2004) (private retirement plans exempt so far as needed for support; allowing debtors aged seventy-seven and seventy-nine, with significant health problems, to fully exempt individual retirement account); Citizens' Nat'l Bank v. Foster, 668 N.E.2d 1236 (Ind. 1996) (exemption for individual retirement accounts, which were limited by federal tax law, met state constitutional requirement that exemptions be reasonable, but exemption for life insurance naming the insured's spouse as beneficiary, which was not limited in amount, was questionable; debtor must show "reasonable necessity" of amount claimed); Steelstone Indus. v. McCrum, 785 A.2d 1256 (Me. 2001) (to claim exemption, debtor must make prima facie case that individual retirement account necessary for support); Associated Bank v. Twaiten, 2007 WL 2245756 (Minn. Ct. App. Aug. 7, 2007) (disability insurance exempt so far as needed for support; "basic necessities" only, not accustomed standard of living); *see also* Estate of Jones by Blume v. Kvamme, 529 N.W.2d 335 (Minn. 1995) (exemption for individual retirement accounts and certain employee benefits that had no limit on the amount and no reference to the needs of the debtor and family violated Minnesota constitutional provision requiring "reasonable exemptions").

466 *See In re* Seltzer, 104 F.3d 234 (9th Cir. 1996) (Nevada's exemption for individual retirement accounts up to a present value of $100,000 did not violate the Contract Clause, even when applied to debts contracted before the enactment of the exemption statute); *In re* Cathcart, 203 B.R. 599 (Bankr. E.D. Va. 1996) (holding most of debtor's individual retirement account exempt under Virginia exemption for retirement accounts sufficient to provide a benefit of $17,500 per year for life starting at age sixty-five); *see also* Premier Capital, Inc. v. Decarolis (*In re* Decarolis), 259 B.R. 467 (B.A.P. 1st Cir. 2001) (tax-qualified retirement plan is exempt under New Hampshire law, even if amounts deposited in account exceed tax exempt amount, except if fraudulent transfer); *In re* Bissell, 255 B.R. 402 (E.D. Va. 2000) (Virginia debtor had individual retirement account, simplified employee pension and ERISA pension; Virginia cap can not be applied to ERISA, and amount in ERISA plan may not be considered in applying cap to other plans); *In re* MacLean, 2000 Bankr. LEXIS 1796 (Bankr. D.N.H. Mar. 1, 2000); *In re* Craig, 545 N.W.2d 764 (N.D. 1996) (limitation of

sums from their former employer's pension fund into an individual retirement account. State courts have reached differing conclusions on the question of whether to treat rollovers as simply transfers from one exempt form to another,[467] or as new contributions to the individual retirement account.[468] Many state legislatures have recently addressed the protection of retirement accounts, so practitioners should be certain that they have the latest version of their state statute.

One court held that an employee's cause of action against an employer who had mismanaged a Keogh plan so that it lost its exempt status, was itself exempt by analogy to the exemption for funds which compensate for the loss or destruction of other exempt property.[469] As with other exempt property, retirement funds may be subject to garnishment for family support obligations,[470] criminal fines or

---

$100,000 per item, $200,000 total applied to life insurance policies, individual retirement accounts, Keoughs and simplified employee pensions; this was reasonable within meaning of the state constitution, which would bar an unlimited exemption).

467 *See In re* Groff, 234 B.R. 153 (Bankr. M.D. Fla. 1999) (funds rolled over from one tax-exempt retirement plan to another were exempt); *In re* Allen, 228 B.R. 132 (Bankr. W.D. Pa. 1998) (transfer of retirement funds from one brokerage house to another was not a "contribution" when tax-exempt status of funds did not change); *In re* Hickox, 215 B.R. 257 (Bankr. M.D. Fla. 1997) (Florida law exempts individual retirement account which was funded with money "traceable to" debtor's 401(k) plan, even though the rollover here was somewhat circuitous: debtor lost her job, deposited funds from her employers' plan first in her bank account and then in her mother's bank account before deciding to create the individual retirement account); McMullan v. Haycock, 54 Cal. Rptr. 3d 660 (Ct. App. 2007) (funds rolled over from pension plan to individual retirement account retained full exemption so far as needed for support); Rohan v. Bull, 2004 WL 1052778 (Cal. Ct. App. May 11, 2004) (individual retirement account into which debtor rolled over funds from employer's profit-sharing plan is exempt so far as needed for support); Ditto v. McCurdy, 978 P.2d 783 (Haw. 1999) (ERISA anti-alienation provision preempts Hawaii statute which would allow garnishment of retirement plan contributions made within three years before filing bankruptcy or becoming a defendant in a lawsuit); Pauk v. Pauk, 648 N.Y.S.2d 134 (App. Div. 1996) (statutory exemption for individual retirement accounts applies to all individual retirement accounts whether funded by rollover from employer's plan or by debtor's own money); 415 E. 52d St. Associates v. Oppenheimer & Co., 638 N.Y.S.2d 300 (App. Div. 1996) (individual retirement account created by rollover from qualified profit sharing plan is exempt); Chapman v. Wells, 557 N.W.2d 725 (N.D. 1996) (when 401(k) which was exempted by ERISA without limitation on amount was rolled over into an individual retirement account, blanket exemption was lost, but North Dakota law exempted up to $100,000, plus additional amounts necessary for the support of the North Dakota resident and resident's dependents); *see also* Warfield v. Alaniz, 2007 WL 4287838 (D. Ariz. Dec. 6, 2007) (annuity purchased with funds from debtor's individual retirement account is protected by exemption for individual retirement accounts); *In re* Pepmeyer, 273 B.R. 782 (N.D. Iowa 2002) ("individual retirement annuity," funded with rollover from individual retirement account, a $2000 inheritance, and $2000 per year contributions from debtor, is exempt under Iowa law). *But see In re* Roberts, 2005 WL 1924180 (Bankr. M.D. La. Aug. 10, 2005) (no exemption for annuity purchased with funds rolled over from 401k; Louisiana exempts funds rolled over from one 401k to another, or one annuity to another, but not from 401k to annuity or vice versa).

468 *In re* Goldman, 192 B.R. 1 (D. Mass. 1996) (Massachusetts statute limiting exemption for funds "deposited in" retirement accounts within five years before bankruptcy applied to funds rolled over into individual retirement account from exempt employee pension fund); Elias Bros. Restaurants v. Acorn Enterprises, 931 F. Supp. 930 (D. Mass. 1996) (funds in individual retirement account that were rolled over from 401(k) plan or other individual retirement account are not exempt); *In re* McCollum, 287 B.R. 750 (Bankr. E.D. Mo. 2002) (Missouri exemption protects only "right to receive" retirement funds; exemption lost when debtor who lost job cashed in her retirement fund and established individual retirement accounts); *see also In re* Barshak, 106 F.3d 501 (3d Cir. 1997) (when debtor who lost job after fifteen years rolled over entire contents of ERISA pension into individual retirement account, Pennsylvania law required rollover to be treated as "contribution" subject to $15,000/year limitation); *In re* Carbaugh, 278 B.R. 512 (B.A.P. 10th Cir. 2002) (investment account containing only distribution from exempt ERISA account not exempt; benefits lost exempt status when distributed; state exemption for benefits "payable from" retirement account lost when benefits paid); *cf. In re* Rousey, 347 F.3d 689 (8th Cir. 2003) (individual retirement accounts created by rollover from employee pension fund not exempt, when no additional contributions after initial lump sum, and depositors could remove funds at will subject only to tax penalty); Phillips v. Bottoms, 260 B.R. 393 (E.D. Va. 2000) (ERISA anti-alienation provision does not protect funds after rollover into individual retirement account, but Virginia exemption will protect as much as is needed to provide annual income of $17,500 at retirement).

469 State Farm Life Ins. Co. v. Swift (*In re* Swift), 129 F.3d 792 (5th Cir. 1997); *see also In re* Alam, 359 B.R. 142 (B.A.P. 6th Cir. 2006) (bank, money market and mutual fund accounts, traceable to settlement of ERISA action against insurer who wrongfully terminated disability benefits, were "benefits paid under a policy of sickness or accident insurance" within meaning of Ohio exemption).

470 Ventura County Dep't of Child Support Services v. Brown, 11 Cal. Rptr. 3d 489 (Ct. App. 2004) (spendthrift trust, exempt as to ordinary creditors, may be reached for delinquent family support); *In re* Marriage of Singer, 2004 WL 2128562 (Cal. Ct. App. Sept. 23, 2004) (individual retirement accounts, which are exempt as to ordinary creditors, may be reached for family support); Siegal v. Siegal, 700 So. 2d 414 (Fla. Dist. Ct. App. 1997) (court could consider amount in ex-spouse's individual retirement account, generally exempt under Florida law, in determining whether ex-spouse could afford to pay sum required to purge contempt for nonpayment of domestic relations obligation); Duke v. Duke, 675 A.2d 822 (R.I. 1996) (statute forbidding attachment of police and firefighters' pensions did not bar family court from ordering withdrawal of pension funds for child support arrearages); *cf.* Carr v. Jonbil, Inc., 666 N.Y.S.2d 193 (App. Div. 1997) (when no qualified domestic relations order had been issued, funds in an ERISA profit-sharing pension plan were exempt under both New York and federal law).

restitution,[471] and delinquent taxes.[472]

The Supreme Court has ruled that state laws that single out Employee Retirement Income Security Act (ERISA) benefits for special protections are preempted by ERISA.[473] While this decision dealt with an employee welfare plan, not an employee pension plan, it interpreted an ERISA preemption provision that is equally applicable to both. On the other hand, an exemption law that is generally applicable to both ERISA and non-ERISA benefits will not be preempted if the court concludes that it has only a tenuous, remote, or peripheral connection to ERISA plans.[474] In addition, if a state enacted an exemption for ERISA plans when it opted out of the federal bankruptcy exemptions, courts have held that the exemption is not preempted.[475]

471 State *ex rel.* Nixon v. Overmyer, 189 S.W.3d 711 (Mo. Ct. App. 2006) (general state exemptions, here, for bank account, do not apply to state action seeking reimbursement for incarceration costs pursuant to Missouri Inmate Reimbursement Act); New York State Crime Victims' Bd. *ex rel.* K.A.S. v. Wendell, 815 N.Y.S.2d 438 (Sup. Ct. 2006) (New York exemption for earned income does not apply to collection of civil restitution judgment pursuant to Son of Sam law); *see also* § 12.5.10.2, *infra* (inapplicability of exemptions to federal restitution).

472 *See* § 12.5.10.2, *infra* (Internal Revenue Service and other federal debts).

473 Mackey v. Lanier Collection Agency & Serv., Inc., 486 U.S. 825, 830, 108 S. Ct. 2182, 100 L. Ed. 2d 836 (1988); *see also* District of Columbia v. Greater Wash. Bd. of Trade, 506 U.S. 125, 113 S. Ct. 580, 121 L. Ed. 2d 513 (1992) (state law that referred to ERISA plans, albeit without using word "ERISA," is preempted); *In re* DiGiulio, 303 B.R. 144 (Bankr. N.D. Ohio 2003) (simplified employee pension plan not exempted by ERISA anti-alienation clause, and Ohio law that would have exempted it is preempted by ERISA).

474 District of Columbia v. Greater Wash. Bd. of Trade, 506 U.S. 125, 113 S. Ct. 580, 583 n.1, 121 L. Ed. 2d 513 (1992); Mackey v. Lanier Collection Agency & Serv., Inc., 486 U.S. 825, 830, 108 S. Ct. 2182, 100 L. Ed. 2d 836 (1988) (general law allowing garnishment not preempted; because ERISA itself does not prohibit garnishment of employee welfare benefits, they may be garnished); *see also* Standard Ins. Co. v. Saklad, 849 P.2d 1150 (Or. Ct. App. 1993) (state law of general applicability not preempted even though it exempted ERISA welfare plan benefits that ERISA itself did not exempt). *But see* Cmty. Bank Henderson v. Noble, 552 N.W.2d 37 (Minn. Ct. App. 1996) (finding Minnesota exemption statute preempted even though it did not refer specifically to ERISA plans).

475 *In re* Schlein, 8 F.3d 745 (11th Cir. 1993) (Florida exemption statute, which referred to provisions of Internal Revenue Code that designate ERISA-qualified plans, would be preempted but is saved because it was enacted as part of state's opt-out of federal bankruptcy exemptions); *In re* Dyke, 943 F.2d 1435, 1446–1450 (5th Cir. 1991) (state law exempting right to receive payments under any stock bonus, pension, profit sharing, or similar plan refers to ERISA plans by description so would be preempted, but is saved because state adopted it when it opted out of federal bankruptcy exemptions); *In re* Tomlin, 315 B.R. 439 (Bankr. E.D. Mich. 2004) (Michigan individual retirement account exemption not preempted because enacted as part of bankruptcy opt-out). *But cf. In re* DiGiulio, 303 B.R. 144 (Bankr. N.D. Ohio 2003) (simplified employee pension plan not exempted by ERISA anti-alienation clause, and Ohio law that would have exempted it is preempted by ERISA; court does not consider whether state exemption was adopted when state opted out).

12.5.8 Exemptions for Insurance Benefits

Almost every state exempts a certain amount of insurance benefits from creditors.[476] States vary widely, however, as to both the amount and the scope of their insurance exemptions. Some states limit the exemption to policies with an annual premium under a certain amount.[477] Others cap the proceeds or the periodic payment that is exempt.[478] Indiana courts, construing the exemption in accordance with a state constitutional requirement of "reasonable" exemptions, hold that only the amount needed to afford the necessities of

476 *See* Appx. F, *infra* (summarizing each state's exemption laws); *see also In re* Payne, 323 B.R. 723 (B.A.P. 9th Cir. 2005) (criteria for deciding whether an annuity is exempt life insurance or a nonexempt investment); *In re* Kennedy, 336 B.R. 600 (B.A.P. 10th Cir. 2005) (table) (text available at 2005 WL 2662328) (Colo. Rev. Stat. § 10-7-106 exemption applicable only when life insurance policy or annuities contain anti-alienation provisions); *In re* Miller, 370 B.R. 914 (Bankr. D. Minn. 2007) (when couple owned several insurance policies, Minnesota law allowed exemption of only one policy per spouse, even though total amount of policies less than exemption cap); *In re* Ashley, 317 B.R. 352 (Bankr. C.D. Ill. 2004) (history of Illinois's "convoluted" insurance exemption provisions; allowing widow to exempt proceeds without showing of need); *In re* Portal, 45 P.3d 891 (N.M. 2002) (uninsured motorist policy is "accident" policy within meaning of New Mexico exemption for "payments of every kind from any life, accident or health insurance policy"); *cf. In re* Besser, 356 B.R. 531 (Bankr. D. Colo. 2006) (Colorado exempts life insurance but not annuities; statute forbidding beneficiaries to encumber, and so forth, benefits in hands of issuer is not an exemption statute, and even if it were, would not protect against debts of owner of annuity). *But see In re* Selfe, 260 B.R. 463 (Bankr. E.D. Mo. 2001) (life insurance not exempt in Missouri); *cf.* Milligan v. Trautmen, 496 F.3d 666 (5th Cir. 2007) (sum received for prepetition surrender and cancellation of insurance policy not exempt); *In re* Andrews, 301 B.R. 211 (Bankr. N.D. Ohio 2003) (annuities "upon the life of any person" are fully exempt under Ohio law, but they must serve same purpose as life insurance, that is, compensate the beneficiary for death of insured and be worth more in hands of beneficiary; not shown when, in case of retiree's early death, beneficiary received same payments as would have gone to retiree).

477 *See, e.g.*, Nev. Rev. Stat. § 21.090(1)(k) (exempting all benefits growing out of life insurance if annual premium does not exceed $15,000); *see In re* Bower, 234 B.R. 109 (Bankr. D. Nev. 1999) (applying former $1000 annual premium cap to aggregate premium for all policies).

478 Mass. Gen. Laws ch. 175, § 110A; *see* Liberty Mut. Ins. Co. v. Rosenthal, 204 F. Supp. 2d 140 (D. Mass. 2002) ($400/week cap on disability insurance benefits applies to aggregate amount, not to each policy; debtor with income from four disability policies could exempt $400 not $1600); *In re* Craig, 545 N.W.2d 764 (N.D. 1996) (limitation of $100,000 per item, $200,000 total applied to life insurance policies, individual retirement accounts, Keoghs and simplified employee pensions; state constitution would bar an unlimited exemption).

life is exempt.[479] Other state statutes explicitly impose this limitation.[480] Life insurance proceeds are *usually* exempt from writs against the insured, but may be nonexempt, or exempt only as needed for support, for debts of the beneficiary.[481]

Tennessee's exemption for accident, health or disability benefits protects uninsured motorist proceeds, and the cap for personal injury judgments does not apply.[482] However, at least two courts have held that an exemption for accident or disability insurance is not broad enough to protect payments to a personal injury tort plaintiff from the tortfeasor's insurance.[483]

The Florida exemption for disability income benefits under any policy or contract of life, health, accident or other insurance has been construed to protect benefits deposited in a bank account, if traceable.[484] Minnesota and Wisconsin achieve the same result by a statutory exemption for funds traceable to certain insurance benefits.[485] Ohio exempts "an interest in" certain monthly or lump sum disability benefits, and this provision has been construed to cover traceable proceeds.[486] Advocates may also argue that the "paid or payable"[487] or "proceeds of" language found in other statutes provides for a continuing exemption.

Another question is whether the policy itself is exempt. Many states exempt the cash value of a life insurance policy.[488] A Texas court has held that the cash value of life

479 Citizens Nat'l Bank v. Foster, 668 N.E.2d 1236 (Ind. 1996) (insurance exemption, construed to avoid unconstitutionality, exempted only the amount needed to afford "the necessities of life"; creditor has burden of showing that claimed exemption is unreasonable); *see also In re* Stinnett, 465 F.3d 309 (7th Cir. 2006) (Indiana exemption for 100% of disability insurance benefits must be construed to exempt only enough to provide "the necessary comforts of life," as state constitution mandates reasonable exceptions); *In re* Bannourah, 201 B.R. 954 (Bankr. S.D. Ind. 1996) (state insurance policy exemption, construed so as to avoid state constitutional problem, exempts amount "required to afford the necessities of life"; allowing thirty-eight-year-old widow, with limited earning ability, and a four-year-old son to keep $200,000).

480 *See, e.g., In re* Morehead, 283 F.3d 199 (4th Cir. 2002) (W. Va. law) (payments from private disability insurance policy exempt only as needed for support of debtor); *In re* Tooker, 174 B.R. 33 (Bankr. D. Vt. 1994) (allowing sixty-two-year-old widow to keep entire amount, about $130,000; factors include age, health, earning ability, special needs, other assets); Sanders v. Sanders, 711 A.2d 124 (Me. 1998) (income from disability policy is exempt only insofar as reasonably necessary for debtor's support); Associated Bank v. Twaiten, 2007 WL 2245756 (Minn. Ct. App. Aug. 7, 2007) (disability insurance exempt so far as needed for "basic necessities" only, not accustomed standard of living; must consider present and future needs, based on age, employment, and general health). *But see In re* Bird, 288 B.R. 546 (Bankr. C.D. Ill. 2002) (widow could fully exempt proceeds of late husband's life insurance; trustee used wrong section of Illinois law when she argued funds were exempt only as needed for support).

481 Plastipak Packaging, Inc. v. DiPasquale, 75 Fed. Appx. 86 (3d Cir. 2003) (Pa. law) (insurance policy naming spouse as beneficiary is exempt as to debts of insured even if purchased with intent to hinder creditors); *In re* Stilwell, 321 B.R. 471 (C.D. Ill. 2005) (applying principle of liberal construction and holding that proceeds of deceased spouse's life insurance are fully exempt); *In re* Fahey, 352 B.R. 288 (Bankr. D. Colo. 2006) (proceeds of group life insurance exempt as to debts of both insured and beneficiary; note that this is more favorable than Colorado's treatment of individual life insurance); *In re* Lewis, 327 B.R. 645 (Bankr. S.D. Ohio 2005) (proceeds of employee's group insurance policy, payable to beneficiary who is actually dependent on employee, exempt both before and after payment, as to debts of insured or beneficiary); *In re* Ashley, 317 B.R. 352 (Bankr. C.D. Ill. 2004) (allowing widow to exempt proceeds without showing of need); *In re* McWhorter, 312 B.R. 695 (Bankr. N.D. Ala. 2004) (proceeds of life insurance policy exempt as to debts of deceased, but not those of beneficiary); *In re* Romp, 249 B.R. 853 (Bankr. E.D.N.C. 2000) (proceeds of insurance policy, exempt for deceased spouse's debts, not exempt for joint debts); Blanton v. Clark, 2002 WL 709958 (Ohio Ct. App. Apr. 19, 2002) (proceeds of deceased spouse's life insurance may be garnished for joint debts, or for debts of surviving spouse); *see also In re* Fick, 249 B.R. 108 (Bankr. W.D.N.C. 2000) (North Carolina exemption for group insurance protects proceeds against creditors of the insured, but not against creditors of the beneficiary). *But see In re* McCall, 2007 WL 3113332 (Bankr. N.D. Ohio Oct. 19, 2007) (Ohio exemption for group insurance makes life insurance exempt as to debts of beneficiary, here surviving spouse); *In re* Bird, 288 B.R. 546 (Bankr. C.D. Ill. 2002) (widow could fully exempt proceeds of late husband's life insurance; trustee used wrong section of Illinois law when she argued funds were exempt only as needed for support); *In re* Kleinman, 272 B.R. 339 (Bankr. D. Md. 2001) (proceeds of life insurance protected from creditors of deceased spouse and those of the beneficiary); § 12.3, *supra*.

482 *In re* Thompkins, 263 B.R. 223 (Bankr. W.D. Tenn. 2001).

483 Kollar v. Miller, 176 F.3d 175 (3d Cir. 1999) (debtors had no "property or other rights" in tortfeasor's insurance); *In re* Jackson, 2007 WL 4179849 (Bankr. N.D. Iowa Nov. 21, 2007) (statute exempts indemnity or benefit only "as to the insured").

484 Parl v. Parl, 699 So. 2d 765 (Fla. Dist. Ct. App. 1997) (remanding to trial court to determine which funds in bank account were traceable to exempt disability benefits).

485 Minn. Stat. § 550.37; Wis. Stat. § 815.18(3)(i)(2); *see* Associated Bank v. Twaiten, 2007 WL 2245756 (Minn. Ct. App. Aug. 7, 2007) (exemption for disability insurance, so far as needed for support, covers traceable proceeds in bank account).

486 *In re* Alam, 336 B.R. 320 (Bankr. N.D. Ohio 2005) (settlement proceeds from lawsuit for disability benefits exempt as benefits paid under sickness and accident insurance; investment account funds traceable to settlement proceeds also exempt), *aff'd*, 359 B.R. 142 (B.A.P. 6th Cir. 2006).

487 This language in the Social Security Act has been interpreted to protect bank accounts traceable to exempt benefits. Philpott v. Essex County Welfare Bd., 409 U.S. 413, 93 S. Ct. 590, 34 L. Ed. 2d 608 (1973); *see* § 12.6.2, *infra*.

488 Milligan v. Trautmen, 496 F.3d 666 (5th Cir. 2007) (cash value of existing policy exempt, but not sum received for prepetition surrender and cancellation of policy); *In re* Vigil, 2003 WL 22024830 (10th Cir. Aug. 26, 2003) (insured may exempt cash surrender value of life insurance policy); *In re* Rice, 2006 WL 2051842 (Bankr. M.D.N.C. June 21, 2006) (exemption for "money or other benefit" provided by fraternal benefit association protects cash surrender value of life insurance policy issued by such association); *In re* Sloss, 279 B.R. 6 (Bankr. D. Mass. 2002) (exemption for insurance policy lost when divorce decree

insurance policies exempted by the state Insurance Code was not subject to the cap on exempt property in the Property Code.[489] Courts have reached differing results—even when construing identical language—on the question of whether a debtor may exempt the cash value of an insurance policy that is payable to close relatives such as parents or adult children who are not dependent on the debtor.[490] One court that allowed the exemption noted society's interest in encouraging adult children to take care of their elderly parents and in alleviating the financial burdens that a parent's death may place on adult children.[491]

Another issue is whether an annuity, or similar product that may pay a beneficiary upon the owner's death, is exempt as life insurance. In general, courts will determine whether the payment serves the same purpose as life insurance, and whether the beneficiary has an unconditional right to payment. Thus an annuity that will pay a beneficiary only if the owner happens to die before payment of a guaranteed amount will not be exempt.[492]

---

made wife, formerly the beneficiary, trustee for the children); *In re* Johnson, 274 B.R. 473 (Bankr. E.D. Mich. 2002) (Michigan statute explicitly exempts cash surrender value of debtor's life insurance if spouse or children are beneficiaries); Technical Chemicals & Products, Inc. v. Porchester Holdings, Inc., 785 So. 2d 636 (Fla. 2001) (cash surrender value of whole life or limited whole life insurance policies fully exempt under Florida statute); Faro v. Porchester Holdings, Inc., 792 So. 2d 1262 (Fla. Dist. Ct. App. 2001) (applying Florida exemption to certificate of deposit bought with proceeds of cash surrender value of insurance policy); *see also* Soc'y of Lloyd's v. Collins, 284 F.3d 727 (7th Cir. 2002) (life insurance policy of which spouse was beneficiary exempt under Illinois law, even as to premium payments made after debt accrued, when no showing of fraudulent intent); *In re* Trautman, 296 B.R. 651 (Bankr. W.D.N.Y. 2003) (mother and daughter's reciprocal life insurance policies both wholly exempt when both filed bankruptcy; beneficiary had "mere expectancy" that was not part of estate); *cf.* Plastipak Packaging, Inc. v. DiPasquale, 75 Fed. Appx. 86 (3d Cir. 2003) (Pa. law) (funds borrowed from policy by insured not exempt because not being held for benefit of beneficiary); *In re* Oxford, 274 B.R. 887 (Bankr. D. Idaho 2002) (unlimited exemption for unmatured life insurance policy merely allows debtor to keep the policy; limited exemption for loan value applies cap to the aggregate of all policies, not to each separate policy). *But see In re* Lowery, 272 B.R. 317 (Bankr. M.D. Fla. 2001) (cash surrender value not exempt when policy insures one spouse but is owned by the other); *In re* Watkins, 267 B.R. 703 (Bankr. E.D. Va. 2001) (Virginia's unlimited exemption for life insurance proceeds, which protects beneficiary but not insured, does not protect cash surrender value, but homestead exemption may apply); *In re* Jacobs, 264 B.R. 274 (Bankr. W.D.N.Y. 2001) (married debtors could not exempt cash surrender value of life insurance policies on each other's lives); Flatau v. Waggoner (*In re* Waggoner), 244 B.R. 492 (Bankr. M.D. Ga. 2000) (debtor may exempt unmatured life insurance policy itself, but may not exempt its cash value); Schenk Boncher & Prasher v. Vanderlaan, 2003 WL 22026405 (Mich. Ct. App. Aug. 28, 2003) (surrender value of policy not exempt; debtor may be ordered to surrender policy and pay proceeds to judgment creditor); *cf. In re* Davis, 275 B.R. 134 (Bankr. D.D.C. 2002) (District of Columbia law permits debtor to exempt cash surrender value of policy on his or her life if spouse, children, or dependents are beneficiaries; cash surrender value is an exempt "proceed or avail" of the policy); Marriage of Gedgaunas, 978 P.2d 677 (Colo. Ct. App. 1999) (creditor ex-wife could garnish so much of cash value of life insurance as was attributable to premium payments made during twenty-four months previous to attachment); Dowling v. Chicago Options Associates, Inc., 847 N.E.2d 741 (Ill. App. Ct. 2006) (Illinois exemption for policy payable to spouse or dependents applies only if policy payable to natural person; no exemption for policy payable to trust which would distribute proceeds to minor children).

489 *In re* Borchers, 192 B.R. 698 (Bankr. W.D. Tex. 1996).

490 *Dependency must be shown*: *In re* Bunting, 322 B.R. 852 (Bankr. C.D. Ill. 2005) (proceeds of mother's insurance policy not exempt in hands of non-dependent adult son; only a spouse may exempt without showing of dependency); *In re* Bunnell, 322 B.R. 331 (Bankr. N.D. Ohio 2005) (life insurance policy not exempt under Ohio law when beneficiary not a dependent); *In re* Peacock, 292 B.R. 593 (Bankr. S.D. Ohio 2002) (Ohio exempts policy payable to "dependent" of debtor; not exempt when beneficiaries, debtor's elderly mother and aunt, neither lived with debtor nor depended on her for income or personal services); *In re* Grace, 273 B.R. 570 (Bankr. S.D. Ill. 2002) (dependents only, but twenty-year-old college student whose mother was subsidizing his education and some other expenses counted as a dependent); *In re* Sommer, 228 B.R. 674 (Bankr. C.D. Ill. 1998) (adult son may exempt insurance on his life, for which his parents are beneficiaries, only if parents are dependent on him); *In re* McLaren, 227 B.R. 810 (Bankr. S.D. Ill. 1998) (Illinois exemption for policies "payable . . . to a child, parent, or other person dependent on the insured" construed to deny exemption when beneficiaries were non-dependent parents or adult children of insured); People *ex rel.* Dir. of Corrections v. Ruckman, 843 N.E.2d 882 (Ill. App. Ct. 2005) (prison inmate could not exempt proceeds of deceased mother's life insurance because he was not mother's dependent); *see also In re* Rief, 2007 WL 2071808 (Bankr. D. Md. July 16, 2007) (exemption for insurance policy of which spouse, children, or dependents were beneficiaries did not cover policy payable to debtor's estate, of which spouse and children were beneficiaries, because they were not beneficiaries of policy; children's life insurance policies not exempt; debtor was neither insured nor dependent of insured).

Dependency need not be shown: *In re* Wandrey, 334 B.R. 427 (Bankr. N.D. Ind. 2005) (dependency not required to claim life insurance policy as exempt); *In re* Bush, 253 B.R. 863 (Bankr. S.D. Ohio 2000) (to claim Ohio exemption, debtor need only show that beneficiaries were her children, not that they were dependent, but result might be different if this were an effort to shelter a substantial inheritance); *In re* Romp, 249 B.R. 853 (Bankr. E.D.N.C. 2000) (insurance policies, the beneficiaries of which are debtor's adult, non-dependent offspring, are exempt); *In re* Shaffer, 228 B.R. 892 (Bankr. N.D. Ohio 1998) (Ohio exemption for insurance policies payable to "the spouse or children, or any persons dependent on" debtor allowed debtor to exempt cash surrender value of policy when beneficiary was his adult, non-dependent, son).

491 *In re* Shaffer, 228 B.R. 892 (Bankr. N.D. Ohio 1998). *But see In re* Peacock, 292 B.R. 593 (Bankr. S.D. Ohio 2003) (Ohio exempts policy payable to "dependent" of debtor; not exempt when beneficiaries, debtor's elderly mother and aunt, neither lived with debtor nor depended on her for income or personal services).

492 *In re* Kukowski, 356 B.R. 712 (B.A.P. 8th Cir. 2006) (annuity

12.5.9 Personal Injury and Other Causes of Action and Judgments

Some states exempt personal injury recoveries. The Maryland exemption for "money payable in the event of sickness, injury or death" was applied to exempt a structured settlement with a present value of $4,000,000 for a debtor who was permanently disabled by his injuries.[493] Oregon places a cap on its exemption, but interprets it to apply to the sum left over after deduction of liens for medical care, public assistance, attorney services, and the like.[494] The North Carolina exemption for "compensation for personal injury" extends to the portion of the settlement allocated to attorney fees.[495] Some states exempt recoveries only so far as reasonably necessary for the support of the debtor.[496]

Courts have reached varying results as to the status of annuities used to fund structured settlements. Florida,[497] New York,[498] Louisiana,[499] Missouri,[500] and Texas[501] courts have applied the annuities exemption, but Oklahoma[502] and North Dakota[503] apply their exemption for personal injury claims. The Eighth Circuit ruled that Minnesota's exemption for "rights of action" for personal injuries to the debtor did not exempt the proceeds of an annuity, purchased by a tortfeasor to fund a structured settlement.[504]

Beneficiaries of structured settlements, who may be financially desperate or impaired by their injuries, are vulnerable to predatory transactions whereby they sell, assign, or pledge a large number of future payments for a much smaller amount in hand. Most annuities funding such settlements include an anti-assignment clause, and some states have enacted structured settlement protection laws. Unscrupulous lenders or asset purchasers devise elaborate schemes to circumvent these requirements, with varying degrees of success.[505]

Some states also exempt compensation for loss of future earnings; this exemption may be stacked with the personal injury exemption if part of the award was for lost earning power.[506] Payments for loss of consortium

---

that guaranteed payment for the longer of 360 months or debtor's lifetime not exempt as annuity, life insurance, and so forth payable to a spouse, children or dependent upon the insured's death; beneficiaries' right to payment not unconditional because debtor might live more than 360 months); *In re* Andrews, 301 B.R. 211 (Bankr. N.D. Ohio 2003) (Ohio exempts annuities to extent needed for support, but annuity "upon the life of any person" is fully exempt if it serves same purpose as life insurance, that is, to compensate the beneficiary for death of insured and is worth more in hands of beneficiary).

493 *In re* Butcher, 189 B.R. 357 (Bankr. D. Md. 1995) (unlimited exemption was reasonable, facially and as applied), *aff'd*, 125 F.3d 238 (4th Cir. 1997). *But see In re* Hernandez, 272 B.R. 178 (Bankr. D. Md. 2001) (personal injury recovery exempt only insofar as it compensates for injury to the person, future medical expenses, and so forth, but not for prepetition medical expenses sought to be discharged in this bankruptcy; giving debtor thirty days to clarify how personal injury settlement allocated).

494 Valley Credit Serv. v. Kelley, 165 Or. App. 169, 994 P.2d 1229 (2000) (exemption for "right to receive" payments for bodily injury; no right to receive sums required to be deducted before payment to victim).

495 *In re* Simmons, 2006 WL 3392943 (Bankr. M.D.N.C. Nov. 22, 2006).

496 *See In re* Gose, 308 B.R. 41 (B.A.P. 9th Cir. 2004); *In re* Constantino, 274 B.R. 580 (Bankr. N.D.N.Y. 2002) (monthly payments under annuity that funded structured settlement were exempt, but not "singular" every five year payments).

497 *In re* Belue, 238 B.R. 218 (Bankr. S.D. Fla. 1999) (annuity purchased to fund structured settlement is exempt under Florida annuities exemption if debtor is beneficiary, even if tortfeasor's insurer is owner).

498 *In re* Tappan, 277 B.R. 491 (Bankr. W.D.N.Y. 2002) (New York exempts annuities if annuitant paid consideration for the contract; debtor's release of personal injury claim in return for structured settlement funded by annuity met this requirement).

499 *In re* Orso, 283 F.3d 686 (5th Cir. 2002) (annuity purchased to fund personal injury settlement resulting from catastrophic accident, and structured to comply with tax code provisions for such annuities, falls within Louisiana exemption for annuities).

500 *In re* Bonuchi, 327 B.R. 428 (Bankr. W.D. Mo. 2005) (annuity "payable on account of disability" and used to fund children's college-related expenses partially exempt; not reasonable to pay all of children's college expenses to the detriment of unsecured creditors).

501 *In re* Alexander, 227 B.R. 658 (Bankr. N.D. Tex. 1998) (structured settlement of wrongful death case, funded by annuity purchased by tortfeasor's insurance carrier, falls within Texas exemption for annuities).

502 *In re* Alexander, 980 P.2d 659 (Okla. 1999) (only structured settlement payments received after bankruptcy filing are property of bankruptcy estate, and those payments are exempt except to the extent they exceed $50,000 exemption).

503 *In re* Kukowski, 356 B.R. 712 (B.A.P. 8th Cir. 2006) (annuity that funded structured settlement is exempt as personal injury settlement).

504 Christians v. Dulas, 95 F.3d 703 (8th Cir. 1996).

505 *Compare* Liberty Life Assurance Co. v. Gilbert, 507 F.3d 952 (6th Cir. 2007) ("loan agreement" with payments of $159,840 for $51,000 loan; annuity payments sent to post office box, and deposited in bank account controlled by lender; assignment was invalid, and this kind of factoring transaction against Virginia public policy) *with* Coffey v. Singer Asset Fin. Co., L.L.C., 223 S.W.3d 559 (Tex. App. 2007) (pledge of future payments as security for loans violated neither anti-assignment clause nor state legislation; public policy does not bar pledge or assignment of structured settlement proceeds). *See generally* National Consumer Law Center, Repossessions § 2.2.8.2 (6th ed. 2005 and Supp.); National Consumer Law Center, The Cost of Credit: Regulation, Preemption, and Industry Abuses § 7.5.8 (3d ed. 2005 and Supp.).

506 *See In re* Whitson, 319 B.R. 614 (Bankr. E.D. Ark. 2005) (allowing debtor to claim federal exemption for loss of future earnings with respect to entire amount of proceeds from settlement of personal injury claim); *In re* Hanson, 226 B.R. 106 (Bankr. D. Idaho 1998) (any award for "loss of future earnings" in sexual harassment suit would be exempt only insofar as debtors could show that funds were reasonably necessary for their support); *In re* Bova, 205 B.R. 467 (Bankr. E.D. Pa. 1997) (debtor could stack state exemption for payments "on account

may also be exempt.[507]

In some states the definition of "personal injury" is narrow, and excludes physical damage resulting from a non-physical wrong.[508] Some state statutes track the federal bankruptcy exemption for personal injury, excluding both pain and suffering and actual pecuniary loss. Courts generally hold that a showing of "appreciable or cognizable" injury will be sufficient to exempt at least part of the award.[509]

---

of personal bodily injury" with exemption for "compensation of loss of future earnings" when part of personal injury damages was for loss of earning power and was "reasonably necessary" for support of debtor or dependents); *In re* Gilbert, 213 B.R. 502 (Bankr. E.D. Ky. 1997) (Kentucky exemption for loss of future wages protected debtors' personal injury recovery, even though debtors were not employed and were receiving government benefits at time of injury; bankruptcy trustee failed to carry burden of proof that debtors had no earning capacity); *In re* Pless, 202 B.R. 664 (Bankr. N.D.N.Y. 1996) (New York allows exemption for $7500 of personal injury judgment; fact question whether debtor is entitled to additional state exemption for "compensation for future earnings . . . to the extent reasonably necessary" for debtor's support). *But cf. In re* Ballard, 238 B.R. 610 (Bankr. M.D. La. 1999) (Louisiana statutes provided no exemption for personal injury cause of action, and earnings exemption was not broad enough to cover tort recovery for loss of future earning capacity).

507 *In re* Bippert, 311 B.R. 456 (Bankr. W.D. Tex. 2004) (allowing husband to exempt loss of consortium claim); *In re* Tosti, 276 B.R. 204 (Bankr. S.D. Ohio 2001) (loss of consortium is personal injury within meaning of Ohio exemption; debtor wife who was named plaintiff in husband's tort case and signed release at settlement is entitled to exemption for her share of proceeds); *In re* Dealey, 204 B.R. 17 (Bankr. C.D. Ill. 1997) (state exemption for bodily injury judgment covers uninjured spouse's loss of consortium claim, thereby allowing two exemptions to married couple); *In re* Turner, 190 B.R. 836 (Bankr. S.D. Ohio 1996) (Ohio exemption of $5000 for payments "on account of personal bodily injury" exempts uninjured spouse's award for loss of consortium, so married co-debtors got one exemption for the injury and one for the loss of consortium). *But see In re* Patton, 200 B.R. 172 (Bankr. N.D. Ohio 1996) (allowing exemption for personal injury, but not loss of consortium).

508 *In re* Cope, 280 B.R. 516 (D. Or. 2001) (remanding to determine whether the "unlawful employment practices" that gave rise to emotional distress damages included physical injury); *In re* Nelson, 2003 WL 22331776 (Bankr. D. Colo. Oct. 1, 2003) (judgment for interference with prospective economic relation does not fall under exemption for damage to person or property when damages were based on lost profits); *In re* Barner, 239 B.R. 139 (Bankr. W.D. Ky. 1999) (when physical injury is shown recovery will be exempt under Kentucky statute except insofar as it compensates for purely mental suffering without physical manifestations, or for actual pecuniary loss); *In re* Hanson, 226 B.R. 106 (Bankr. D. Idaho 1998) (proceeds of pending sexual harassment suit would be exempt under Oregon's "personal bodily injury" exemption only if plaintiff could show "appreciable" physical injury); *In re* Chapman, 223 B.R. 137 (Bankr. N.D. Ill. 1998) (cause of action for defamation, invasion of privacy, and breach of contract, which alleged only emotional injury, was not exempt under Illinois exemption for "personal bodily injury"); *In re* Langa, 222 B.R. 843 (Bankr. C.D. Ill. 1998) (cause of action for employment discrimination, which alleged sexual harassment by inappropriate touching, resulting in emotional suffering, was not exempt under Illinois exemption for "personal bodily injury" because there was no "physical injury or impairment of physical condition"); *In re* Ciotta, 222 B.R. 626 (Bankr. C.D. Cal. 1998) (California exemption for "personal bodily injury" required showing of "appreciable physical injury"; sexual harassment complainant's "discomfort" and "physical distress" resulting from inappropriate touching may be sufficient if proven); *In re* Marshall, 208 B.R. 690 (Bankr. D. Minn. 1997) (exemption for rights of action for "injuries to the person" did not exempt a sexual harassment claim, even if the harassment resulted in physical injury; in order for this exemption to apply "original trauma must be to the debtor's body"); *In re* Crawford, 208 B.R. 924 (Bankr. D. Minn. 1994) (discrimination and defamation claims debtor brought against employer do not fall within exemption for actions for injury to the person); *see also* Sylvester v. Hafif, 220 B.R. 89 (B.A.P. 9th Cir. 1998) (California's exemption of "personal injury" recoveries allows debtor to exempt portion of malpractice recovery against his former attorney that was attributable to claims for emotional distress, but not portion attributable to harassment and wrongful discharge claims; only amounts reasonably necessary for debtor's support are exempt); Miller v. Accelerated Bureau of Collections, 932 P.2d 824 (Colo. Ct. App. 1996) (recovery for Fair Debt Collection Practices Act violations was not exempt; Colorado exemption for "proceeds of any claim for damages for personal injuries suffered by any debtor" did not exempt "punitive damages," intended to punish wrongdoer, not to compensate plaintiff). *But see In re* Walters, 339 B.R. 607 (Bankr. W.D. Va. 2006) (Virginia's exemption for "all causes of action for personal injury" and proceeds of court award or settlement thereof covers any "injury to personal rights," here libel and negligence); *In re* Dobbins, 249 B.R. 849 (Bankr. D. Md. 2000) (Maryland exemption for personal injury covers mental injury, so sexual harassment settlement which compensated for humiliation and depression is exempt); *In re* LoCurto, 239 B.R. 314 (Bankr. E.D.N.C. 1999) (North Carolina exemption for compensation for personal injury, not including pain and suffering or actual pecuniary loss, covered damages for physical results of stress due to wrongful discharge, but not compensation for lost wages); *In re* Webb, 210 B.R. 266 (Bankr. E.D. Va. 1997) (Virginia exemption for personal injury judgments protects settlement in federal gender discrimination lawsuit when hostile work environment resulted in severe depression), *aff'd*, 214 B.R. 553 (E.D. Va. 1997); *cf. In re* Key, 255 B.R. 217 (Bankr. D. Neb. 2000) (proceeds of cause of action for employment discrimination claim are exempt as "proceeds or benefits of personal injury claims" insofar as they compensate for psychological injury rather than back pay, but cause of action itself is not exempt); *In re* Hurst, 239 B.R. 89 (Bankr. D. Md. 1999) (Maryland personal injury exemption does not exempt the portion of the award which compensates for lost wages).

509 *In re* Buscano, 2006 WL 3247118 (Bankr. D. Alaska Oct. 20, 2006) ("cognizable injury" does not require permanent injury; significant lost time from employment, medical care, and so forth sufficient here, but portion of award for pain and suffering is not exempt); *In re* Lawton, 324 B.R. 20 (Bankr. D. Conn. 2005) (federal exemption for payment on account of personal bodily injury did not require permanent injury); *In re* Scotti, 245 B.R. 17 (Bankr. D.N.J. 2000) (debtor who can show "appreciable or cognizable" physical injury is entitled to exemption, even if award includes compensation for pain and suffering); *In re* Barner, 239 B.R. 139 (Bankr. W.D. Ky. 1999) (when physical

Sometimes debtors have tried to fit causes of action into another exemption. One court held that a malpractice action against an attorney for mishandling a child support and alimony claim does not fall within the state exemption for child support and alimony.[510] Colorado's household goods exemption does not cover a cause of action against the tortfeasor who destroyed the goods, but another exemption for a "claim for the loss, destruction, or damage of exempt property" would apply.[511] Other causes of action may be exempt under a state wildcard exemption.[512] In at least some jurisdictions, an unliquidated claim for damages is not subject to garnishment.[513]

injury is shown, recovery is exempt except insofar as it compensates for purely mental suffering without physical manifestations, or for actual pecuniary loss); *see also In re* Reschick, 343 B.R. 151 (Bankr. W.D. Pa. 2006) (entire structured settlement exempt under federal bankruptcy exemptions when debtor's injuries were serious enough to account for entire settlement); *In re* Kelin, 341 B.R. 521 (Bankr. W.D. Pa. 2006) (husband had no property interest in wife's personal injury claim when he was not a party to complaint or retainer and suit did not allege any injuries on his part, so he can not exempt any portion of the recovery); *In re* Hess, 350 B.R. 882 (Bankr. D. Idaho 2005) (finding that medical malpractice settlement proceeds were reasonably necessary for support, so are exempt under Idaho law).

510 *In re* Hice, 223 B.R. 155 (Bankr. N.D. Ill. 1998).

511 *In re* Fager, 274 B.R. 537 (Bankr. D. Colo. 2002).

512 Ball v. Nationscredit Fin. Services Corp., 207 B.R. 869 (N.D. Ill. 1997) (Illinois wildcard exception may be used to exempt a cause of action under the Truth in Lending Act); *In re* Foor, 259 B.R. 899 (Bankr. C.D. Ill. 2000) (cause of action against sellers of house for undisclosed termite damage); *In re* Kelsey, 224 B.R. 495 (Bankr. M.D. Fla. 1998) (Florida's exemption for "personal property" protects debtor's interest in class action lawsuit, up to $1000 statutory cap); *In re* Ball, 201 B.R. 210 (Bankr. N.D. Ill. 1996) (discussing method of setting value of truth in lending claim for purposes of determining how much of it was exempt under a $2000 wildcard exemption); *see also In re* Reschick, 343 B.R. 151 (Bankr. W.D. Pa. 2006) (annuity purchased by insurer to fund structured settlement of personal injury action could be exempted under wildcard exemption, as well as personal injury exemption); *In re* Kelin, 341 B.R. 521 (Bankr. W.D. Pa. 2006) (personal injury settlement not covered by personal injury exemption because actual pecuniary loss was being compensated, but could be exempted under wildcard and unused homestead exemptions). *But see* Howe v. Richardson, 193 F.3d 60 (1st Cir. 1999) (Rhode Island law provides no exemption for causes of action, including personal injury or breach of contract).

513 *In re* Williams, 293 B.R. 769 (W.D. Mo. 2003) (unliquidated and unassignable potential personal injury claim is fully exempt); Keaton v. Ft. Wayne Neurosurgery, 780 N.E.2d 1183 (Ind. Ct. App. 2003). *But cf. In re* Mahony, 374 B.R. 717 (Bankr. W.D. Mo. 2007) (Missouri's common law protection of unliquidated personal injury claims from garnishment or assignment is not an exemption that is available in bankruptcy).

12.5.10 Special Exemption Schemes for Particular Types of Debt

12.5.10.1 Health Care Debts

A few states, recognizing the special burden created by health care debts, have enacted statutes limiting health care debt collection, or otherwise assisting debtors facing health problems. Nevada and Ohio forbid execution on the primary residence for health care debts during the lifetime of the debtor and certain specified dependents; a lien may be created which may be foreclosed only after the residence ceases to be occupied by the protected persons.[514] West Virginia provides a larger homestead exemption for debts resulting from "catastrophic illness or injury."[515]

Kansas forbids wage garnishments for two months after the return to employment of a debtor after an illness of the debtor or a family member which has kept the debtor out of work for two or more weeks.[516] Wyoming exempts from garnishment contributions to a qualified medical savings account (*except* for health care debts) to the extent the contributions are allowable under the Internal Revenue Code.[517]

A now repealed Ohio statute, which limited the percentage of wage garnishment for health care debts, was upheld as a reasonable classification, in light of the public policy of encouraging people to seek needed medical care.[518] Medical debt is discussed in more detail in Ch. 10, *supra*.

12.5.10.2 IRS and Other Federal Debts

The Internal Revenue Service (IRS) collects federal income taxes subject to wage and property exemptions provided in the Internal Revenue Code.[519] It provides exemptions for income that may be more generous for families and

514 Nev. Rev. Stat. § 21.095; Ohio Rev. Code Ann. §§ 2329.66(A)(1)(a), 2329.661 (West); *see* Edwards v. McCormack, 136 F. Supp. 2d 795 (S.D. Ohio 2001) (lawyer-collector violated Fair Debt Collection Practices Act and Ohio deceptive practices statute by threatening foreclosure on real property owned by Ohio health-care debtors); Wickliffe Country Place v. Kovacs, 765 N.E.2d 975 (Ohio Ct. App. 2001) (fact question whether nursing home provided health care services and supplies).

515 W. Va. Code § 38-9-3(b).

516 Kan. Stat. Ann. § 60-2310.

517 Wyo. Stat. Ann. § 1-20-111.

518 St. Ann's Hosp. v. Arnold, 672 N.E.2d 743 (Ohio Ct. App. 1996); Wooster Cmty. Hosp. v. Anderson, 670 N.E.2d 563 (Ohio Ct. App. 1996) (classification was rational: health care debtors are different from others because of the life or death necessity of health care, and the extra burdens imposed by paying back a debt while also suffering health problems). *But see* Cmty. Physical Therapy v. Wayt, 639 N.E.2d 515 (Ohio Ct. App. 1994) (statute was unconstitutional because it had no rational relationship to any governmental purpose).

519 26 U.S.C. § 6334.

less generous for individuals[520] than the federal wage garnishment protections in the Consumer Credit Protection Act.[521] It exempts other income, such as unemployment benefits, workers' compensation, and income to fulfill a child support obligation, from IRS seizure.[522] Certain personal property, for example, wearing apparel, a family's personal effects and furniture, and tools of the trade, is also exempt.[523] A homestead exemption is provided for the principal residence unless a United States district court judge or magistrate approves the levy.[524] Other exemption laws are not applicable to the IRS.[525]

The statute which provides for fines and restitution in federal criminal cases has its own list of exemptions that includes some, but not all, of the property exempted from tax levy. Most nongovernmental pension benefits and Social Security benefits, for example, may be garnished for criminal fines or restitution.[526] While the wage garnishment restrictions of the CCPA apply to collection of judgments for criminal fines and restitution,[527] they do not apply to debts due for federal or state taxes.[528]

---

520 26 U.S.C. § 6334(d) provides for weekly exemption of the standard deduction provided by 26 U.S.C. § 63(c) and the deduction provided for personal exemptions in 26 U.S.C. § 151 divided by fifty-two.

521 15 U.S.C. §§ 1671–1677; *see* § 12.4.1, *supra*.

522 26 U.S.C. § 6334(a).

523 26 U.S.C. § 6334(a).

524 26 U.S.C. § 6334(a)(13) and (e); *see also* Sills v. Dep't of Treasury (*In re* Sills), 82 F.3d 111 (5th Cir. 1996) (tax lien can be placed on home even if home is exempt from levy).

525 26 U.S.C. § 6334(c); *see, e.g.*, United States v. Berk, 374 B.R. 385 (D. Mass. 2007) (state homestead exemption does not protect against federal tax lien); United States v. Hanson, 2005 WL 3116099 (D. Minn. Apr. 21, 2005) (Minnesota homestead exemption does not protect non-debtor wife against sale of homestead for husband's individual tax liability); *In re* Jones, 206 B.R. 614 (Bankr. D. Colo. 1997) (broad anti-alienation provision of federal statute governing thrift savings plans does not protect against federal tax lien and levy).

526 United States v. Novak, 476 F.3d 1041 (9th Cir. 2007) (Employee Retirement Income Security Act (ERISA) plan can be reached for criminal restitution, but cash-out can be required only if beneficiary could take entire amount in lump sum; barred if spousal consent required); United States v. Phillips, 303 F.3d 548 (5th Cir. 2002) (Mandatory Victim Restitution Act empowers government to use procedures of Federal Debt Collection Act to enforce an order; government could garnish retirement account); United States v. Minneman, 2002 WL 467961 (7th Cir. Mar. 26, 2002) (prisoner's installment payment agreement with Bureau of Prisons not a bar to additional collection efforts under Federal Debt Collection Act; government may garnish cash value of life insurance policies); United States v. Bollin, 264 F.3d 391 (4th Cir. 2001) (federal forfeiture law preempts state law garnishment limitations, so entire individual retirement account subject to forfeiture); United States v. Sawaf, 74 F.3d 119 (6th Cir. 1996) (ERISA's anti-alienation provision does not bar using garnishment of taxpayer's interest in an ERISA pension fund for unpaid taxes); United States v. Himebaugh, 2007 WL 1462430 (N.D. Okla. May 17, 2007) (funds held by employer in 100% vested ERISA plan may be garnished for criminal restitution or fine); United States v. First Bank & Trust E. Tex., 2007 WL 1091021 (E.D. Tex. Apr. 9, 2007) (funds held in 401(k) profit sharing plan could be seized for restitution pursuant to Mandatory Victim Witness Restitution Act, notwithstanding ERISA's anti-alienation provisions); Kagan v. United States, 2007 WL 1074899 (S.D.N.Y. Apr. 5, 2007) (SSDI benefits can be garnished for criminal restitution); United States v. Texas Mun. Retirement Sys., 2006 WL 3839165 (E.D. Tex. Dec. 29, 2006) (annuity was not "exempt annuity" pursuant to 26 U.S.C. § 6334(a)(6), so could be garnished for criminal restitution); United States v. Wahlen, 459 F. Supp. 2d 800 (E.D. Wis. 2006) (ERISA plan and individual retirement account subject to criminal forfeiture; individual retirement account of innocent spouse forfeitable when she could not show it was individual property under Wisconsin law); United States v. Lazorwitz, 411 F. Supp. 2d 634 (E.D.N.C. 2005) (ERISA's anti-alienation provisions and tax law do not apply to restitution required by Mandatory Victim Witness Restitution Act); United States v. Laws, 352 F. Supp. 2d 707 (E.D. Va. 2004) (group annuity, bought with proceeds of former federal employee's thrift savings plan, may be garnished for mandatory victim restitution); United States v. James, 312 F. Supp. 2d 802 (E.D. Va. 2004) (ERISA anti-alienation provision does not bar garnishment for federal criminal restitution); United States v. Tyson, 242 F. Supp. 2d 469 (E.D. Mich. 2003) (ERISA pension may be garnished for court-ordered restitution but not for "special assessment"); *In re* Grico, 2003 WL 21244024 (E.D. Pa. May 22, 2003) (ERISA anti-alienation clause does not bar garnishment for criminal fine); United States v. Garcia, 2003 WL 22594362 (D. Kan. Nov. 6, 2003) (tax-qualified individual retirement account not exempt from garnishment for federal criminal fine); United States v. Kemp, 2002 WL 31548868 (N.D. Tex. Nov. 12, 2002) (Debt Collection Act used to collect criminal fine and restitution; same exemptions as IRS; workers' compensation exempt; funds used to pay child support exempt only if support is court-ordered); United States v. Rice, 196 F. Supp. 2d 1196 (N.D. Okla. 2002) (anti-alienation provision in tax-qualified retirement plan not a bar to garnishment for criminal fines or delinquent taxes); United States v. Taylor, 2001 WL 1172185 (N.D. Tex. Sept. 27, 2001) (sale proceeds of house not exempt as "salary, wages or other income necessary to comply with child support order," in criminal restitution matter); United States v. McLain, 1999 U.S. Dist. LEXIS 11087 (E.D. Mich. June 29, 1999) (pension checks may be garnished for federal restitution debt); *In re* Jones, 206 B.R. 614 (Bankr. D. Colo. 1997) (broad statutory anti-alienation provision does not protect thrift savings plan from federal tax lien and levy); *see also* United States v. Anderson, 2007 WL 2703160 (W.D. Okla. Sept. 13, 2007) (Oklahoma garnishment exemptions for "undue hardship" not applicable to federal garnishment for criminal restitution); United States v. Gaudet, 2004 WL 2367734 (E.D. La. Oct. 20, 2004) (husband's pension was being garnished for restitution of funds he stole from pension fund; because wife's rights were derivative of husband's, that is, qualified domestic relations order awarded her a percentage of pension, she could not claim exemption), *aff'd*, 187 Fed. Appx. 410 (5th Cir. 2006); State Treasurer v. Abbott, 660 N.W.2d 714 (Mich. 2003) (not ERISA violation to order prisoner's pension checks sent to prison to pay expenses of imprisonment); Brown v. Ford Motor Co., 797 N.E.2d 546 (Ohio Ct. App. 2003) (state garnishment law does not apply to IRS garnishment; employer who complies is immune from any liability to employee).

527 18 U.S.C. § 3613(a)(3), (f).

528 15 U.S.C. § 1673(b)(1)(C); *see* United States v. Summers, 2007 WL 3085025 (E.D. Pa. Aug. 23, 2007).

Federal agencies have special administrative powers when collecting debts.[529] These include the power of administrative offset of debts against Social Security and certain other otherwise exempt federal benefits.[530] Further, there is a special statutory exemption scheme that applies when a federal agency litigates a debt in court.[531]

12.5.10.3 Alimony, Child Support, and Similar Claims

Many exempt funds may be reached for child support or alimony.[532] The Social Security Act[533] allows child support and alimony to be collected from Social Security benefits and other federal payments as long as the entitlement to the payment is based upon remuneration for employment. Accordingly, several courts have recognized that Social Security Disability (SSD)[534] payments should be considered in calculating child support.[535] Payments such as SSI benefits[536] that are not based on remuneration for employment are still protected, however.[537] Veterans benefits,[538] civil service,[539] military retirement,[540] unemployment compensa-

529 *See* § 11.2, *supra*.

530 § 11.2.1.1, *supra*.

531 *See* § 11.3.4, *supra*.

532 *See, e.g.*, Drachmeister v. Brassart, 93 P.3d 566 (Colo. Ct. App. 2004) (personal injury judgment may be reached for child support even though otherwise exempt); Lanier v. Lanier, 608 S.E.2d 213 (Ga. 2005) (exempt Railroad Retirement income, which may not be divided in marital property division, should nonetheless be counted in determining spousal support obligation); Ausley v. Ausley, 2005 WL 2205922 (Tenn. Ct. App. Sept. 8, 2005) (finding no garnishment when court order did not attach to specific funds and further stating Tennessee law does not protect against garnishment of disability benefits for purposes of paying court ordered alimony). *But see* Crawford v. Haddock, 621 S.E.2d 127 (Va. 2005) (general statute establishing state retirement system allows garnishment for family support debts, but specific statute dealing with group life insurance exempts the proceeds from "levy, garnishment, and other legal process"; insurance proceeds are exempt).

533 42 U.S.C. § 659(a); *see* Knickerbocker v. Norman, 938 F.2d 891 (8th Cir. 1991); Shepherd v. Shepherd, 467 N.W.2d 237 (Iowa 1991); Mariche v. Mariche, 758 P.2d 745 (Kan. 1988); Sharlot v. Sharlot, 494 N.Y.S.2d 238 (App. Div. 1985); Hobson v. Hobson, 901 P.2d 914 (Or. Ct. App. 1995).

534 SSD is the non-means tested benefit program financed from payroll deductions. SSD is a substitute for earned income and represents money that an employee and their employer have paid for the employee's benefit into a common trust fund under the Social Security Act. *See* 42 U.S.C. § 405.

535 *See* Russo v. Russo, 474 A.2d 473 (Conn. App. Ct. 1984) (divorce decree requiring ex-husband to pay certain debts not violation of section 407(a) even if his income came from exempt Social Security disability benefits; order required him to pay own debts with own money; note that husband apparently had other assets); Metz v. Metz, 101 P.3d 779 (Nev. 2004); Burns v. Edwards, 842 A.2d 186 (N.J. Super. Ct. App. Div. 2004).

536 Supplemental Security Income (SSI) benefits are means-tested and are available only when a disabled person's income is insufficient to provide for basic needs. In contrast to SSD payments, SSI benefits are not based on how much one paid into the system, but rather how much one needs to maintain a minimum level of subsistence based on federal standards. *See* Schweiker v. Wilson, 450 U.S. 221, 101 S. Ct. 1074, 67 L. Ed. 2d 186 (1981).

537 Davis v. Office of Child Support Enforcement, 20 S.W.3d 273 (Ark. 2000) (SSI benefits not considered in determining child support); Dep't of Pub. Aid *ex rel.* Lozada v. Rivera, 755 N.E.2d 548 (Ill. App. Ct. 2001) (SSI benefits already paid to recipient exempt from child support order; when only source of income is SSI, order vacated); Becker County Human Services v. Peppel, 493 N.W.2d 573 (Minn. Ct. App. 1992); Metz v. Metz, 101 P.3d 779 (Nev. 2004) (SSI benefits may not be counted in calculating child support); Crespo v. Crespo, 928 A.2d 833 (N.J. Super. Ct. App. Div. 2007) (reversing order requiring payment of child support arrearages by obligor whose only source of income was SSI); Green v. Redd, 2006 WL 2237700 (N.J. Super. Ct. App. Div. Aug. 7, 2006) (SSI income may not be considered in setting child support; when SSI is obligor's only source of income, collection of arrearage must be suspended until he has other income); Burns v. Edwards, 842 A.2d 186 (N.J. Super. Ct. App. Div. 2004) (child support may not be ordered if obligor's only source of income is SSI); Tennessee Dep't of Human Services v. Young, 802 S.W.2d 594 (Tenn. 1990); State *ex rel.* Raybon v. McElrath, 2003 WL 22401276 (Tenn. Ct. App. Oct. 22, 2003) (child support obligation may not be imposed on disabled person whose only source of income is Social Security benefits for disabled adult child of deceased worker; "remuneration for employment" means that of recipient, not deceased parent); *see also* Moore v. Sharp, 532 N.Y.S.2d 811 (App. Div. 1988); Langlois v. Langlois, 441 N.W.2d 286 (Wis. Ct. App. 1989). *But see* Commonwealth *ex rel.* Hale v. Stovall, 2007 WL 1784081 (Ky. Ct. App. June 8, 2007) (unpublished) (obligor whose only income was SSI required to make payment on child support arrearages; ongoing payments suspended, but only because of "bare subsistence" situation—not receipt of benefits); Whitmore v. Kenney, 626 A.2d 1180 (Pa. Super. Ct. 1993).

538 Rose v. Rose, 481 U.S. 619, 107 S. Ct. 2029, 95 L. Ed. 2d 599 (1987) (state court may hold veteran in contempt for failing to pay child support even though his only source of payment is veterans benefits; one purpose of veterans benefits is support of family); Woods v. Nicholson, 2006 WL 3840220 (Vet. App. Dec. 16, 2006) (continuing garnishment of veteran's disability benefits to satisfy family court order was mandatory; no evidence that excessive amount garnished, or indebtedness discharged), *aff'd*, 2007 WL 2282409 (Fed. Cir. Aug. 9, 2007); Loving v. Sterling, 680 A.2d 1030 (D.C. 1996) (amount of veterans disability payments may be considered in determining amount of child support); *In re* Marriage of Wojcik, 838 N.E.2d 282 (Ill. App. Ct. 2005) (although veterans' disability payments may not be considered in allocating marital property at divorce, they should be counted in setting amount of family support); *In re* Pope-Clifton, 823 N.E.2d 607 (Ill. App. Ct. 2005) (bank account containing only funds from veterans' disability benefits may be garnished for child support).

539 Harmand v. Harmand, 931 So. 2d 18 (Ala. Civ. App. 2005) (federal civil service retirement benefits may be divided at divorce and Office of Personnel Management may be ordered to pay ex-spouse; here some of the benefits were separate property, because earned after marriage terminated, but couple had separation agreement, and party may bargain away separate property).

540 42 U.S.C. § 659(a), (h).

tion, and workers' compensation benefits may also be reached.[541] However, veterans disability benefits[542] and workers' compensation provided to pay medical expenses[543] may remain exempt.

12.6 Protection of Exempt Funds That Have Been Paid or Deposited into Bank Accounts

12.6.1 Key Issues

The continuing protection of exempt funds deposited in bank accounts is especially critical today, as paper checks are being replaced by direct deposit and electronic benefit transfer.[544] The key issues are:

- Whether funds remain exempt when paid to the debtor or deposited in a checking, savings, certificate of deposit, or similar account.
- The amount of exempt funds that may be accumulated before they lose protection.
- Whether the exemption is lost by commingling with nonexempt funds of the beneficiary or another.
- The applicability to wages of the general rule that exemptions continue after payment or deposit.
- The effect of electronic fund transfer requirements on exemptions.

These issues are addressed in the subsections that follow. Whether deposited funds are protected against the bank's self-help remedy of set off for debts owed to the bank is addressed in another manual in this series.[545]

541 Moyle v. Dir., Office of Workers' Compensation Programs, 147 F.3d 1116 (9th Cir. 1998) (disability benefits under Longshore and Harbor Workers' Compensation Act can be garnished for alimony or child support); McNabb v. State *ex rel.* Rhodes, 890 So. 2d 1038 (Ala. Civ. App. 2003) (lump-sum workers' compensation may be garnished for child support, up to CCPA limit, here fifty percent for obligor supporting other dependent); Cameron v. Hughes, 825 P.2d 882 (Alaska 1992) (exemption of workers' compensation was intended to protect workers and their families, not to protect workers from their families); Div. of Child Support Enforcement v. Colorado Indus. Claim Appeals Office, 109 P.3d 1042 (Colo. Ct. App. 2004) (workers' compensation lump-sum settlement subject to administrative lien for child support); State *ex rel.* Lisby v. Lisby, 890 P.2d 727 (Idaho 1995) (lump sum workers' compensation could be garnished for child support, but only up to the fifty-five percent limit applicable to weekly earnings; sum for "future medical care" was exempt as "benefits payable for medical, surgical, or hospital care"); Shine v. Iowa Dept of Human Services, 592 N.W.2d 684 (Iowa 1999) (lump sum from workers' compensation fund can be set off for child support arrearages; remanding for fact finding, whether obligor was supporting other dependents, to determine permissible amount of garnishment); Marriage of Carr & Parr, 591 N.W.2d 627 (Iowa 1999) (child support obligor received lump sum workers' compensation; fifty percent garnishment amount was calculated before deduction of attorney fees and costs, even though this left injured worker with nothing); Siciliano v. State, 294 A.D.2d 238, 742 N.Y.S.2d 282 (2002) (workers' compensation is income subject to attachment for family support; lump-sum settlement can be taken by income attachment to satisfy ex-wife's lien for support payments); *see also* Hanley v. Indus. Comm'n, 21 P.3d 850 (Ariz. Ct. App. 2001) (when workers' compensation payments suspended if claimant imprisoned, except when assigned for family support, family court could order state to pay entire amount of prisoner's benefits for child support); Am. Compensation Ins. Co. v. McBride, 107 P.3d 973 (Colo. Ct. App. 2004) (Colorado statute allowing garnishment of workers' compensation temporary or permanent total disability benefits for court-ordered child support applies to benefits arising from injuries that occurred before May 1, 2001, effective date of the statute).

542 *Ex parte* Billeck, 777 So. 2d 105 (Ala. 2000) (amount of disability benefits could not be considered in setting alimony obligation when retiree became disabled and nonexempt retirement benefits decreased because of disability benefits); Griffin v. Griffin, 872 N.E.2d 653 (Ind. Ct. App. 2007) (Veterans Administration disability benefits may not be divided or considered in property division; here, after being ordered to split military retirement with ex-wife, husband waived retirement benefits to receive disability); Scheidel v. Scheidel, 129 N.M. 223, 4 P.3d 670 (Ct. App. 2000) (veterans disability exempt even in family-support case but when husband voluntarily agreed to take disability benefits resulting in decrease in nonexempt retirement benefits, he could be required to compensate ex-wife, so long as disability benefits not required to be used); Ghrist v. Ghrist, 2007 WL 1372690 (Tex. App. May 11, 2007) (ex-husband waived military retirement benefits to receive Veterans Administration disability; anti-alienation clause prevented any consideration of these benefits in property division; wife entitled only to half of remaining retirement benefits); *see also* Halstead v. Halstead, 596 S.E.2d 353 (N.C. Ct. App. 2004) (military disability pay, unlike military retirement pay, may not be treated—directly or indirectly—as a marital asset in division of property). *But see* Woods v. Nicholson, 2006 WL 3840220 (Vet. App. Dec. 16, 2006) (continuing garnishment of veteran's disability benefits to satisfy Family Court order was mandatory; no evidence that excessive amount garnished, or indebtedness discharged), *aff'd*, 2007 WL 2282409 (Fed. Cir. Aug. 9, 2007); *cf. In re* Strong, 8 P.3d 763 (Mont. 2000) (Veterans Administration disability benefits may be considered as part of veteran's earning power when setting child support, but custodial spouse's attorney fees incurred in seeking child support may not be assessed against exempt veterans' benefits).

543 State *ex rel.* Lisby v. Lisby, 890 P.2d 727 (Idaho 1995) (lump sum workers' compensation could be garnished for family support, but amount for "future medical care" remained exempt).

544 *See* National Consumer Law Center, Consumer Banking and Payments Law Chs. 4, 5, 6 (3d ed. 2005 and Supp.) (discussion of electronic benefits payments and electronic fund transfers).

545 National Consumer Law Center, Consumer Banking and Payments Law § 4.3 (3d ed. 2005 and Supp.).

12.6.2 Are Benefits Exempt Once Deposited in Bank Account?

In *Porter v. Aetna Casualty & Surety Co.*,[546] the Supreme Court held that veterans disability benefits deposited in a bank account remained exempt so long as they are readily traceable and "retain the quality as moneys," that is, they are readily available for the day-to-day needs of the recipient and have not been converted into a "permanent investment." This rationale has been widely applied to other exempt benefits, to hold that exempt funds remain exempt in checking,[547] savings,[548] or certificate of deposit[549] accounts so long as these are "usual means of safekeeping" money used for daily living expenses.[550]

The statutes creating federal and state benefit programs, such as veterans benefits,[551] Social Security benefits,[552]

546 370 U.S. 159, 82 S. Ct. 1231, 8 L. Ed. 2d 407 (1962).

547 Porter v. Aetna Cas. & Surety Co., 370 U.S. 159, 82 S. Ct. 1231, 8 L. Ed. 2d 407 (1962); Granger v. Harris, 2007 WL 1213416 (E.D.N.Y. Apr. 17, 2007) (recipient stated section 1983 claim against bank that disbursed funds to creditor, despite knowledge that funds were Social Security funds); Neilson v. McGuire, 2006 WL 1875383 (D. Neb. July 5, 2006) (Social Security and certain other exempt funds remained exempt when commingled with nonexempt funds in bank account); S & S Diversified Services L.L.C. v. Taylor, 897 F. Supp. 549 (D. Wyo. 1995); *In re* Lichtenberger, 337 B.R. 322 (Bankr. C.D. Ill. 2006) (Social Security benefits remain exempt when commingled with other funds in checking account, so long as traceable); *In re* Cornett, 332 B.R. 289 (Bankr. E.D. Ky. 2005) (funds distributed from teacher's retirement account do not lose exemption when deposited in checking account); United Home Foods Dist., Inc. v. Villegas, 724 P.2d 265 (Okla. Civ. App. 1986); *see also* Todd v. Weltman, Weinberg & Reis Co., 434 F.3d 432 (6th Cir. 2006) (consumer stated Fair Debt Collection Practices Act claim against collection firm that regularly filed affidavits alleging reasonable belief that bank accounts contained nonexempt funds, with no knowledge whether this was true; here, account contained only exempt Social Security and disability payments). *But see* Rue & Associates, Inc. v. White, 2006 WL 2022184 (Va. Cir. July 18, 2006) (Social Security benefits lose exemption when commingled with nonexempt funds in joint bank account).

548 Porter v. Aetna Cas. & Surety Co., 370 U.S. 159, 82 S. Ct. 1231, 8 L. Ed. 2d 407 (1962); Younger v. Mitchell, 777 P.2d 789 (Kan. 1989). *But see In re* Stewart, 2006 WL 2666153 (Bankr. S.D. Ind. Sept. 6, 2006) (portion of teacher's salary escrowed for summer vacation was converted into savings account, and was nonexempt).

549 *In re* Smith, 242 B.R. 427 (Bankr. E.D. Tenn. 1999) (proceeds of veteran's life insurance policy remained exempt when widow used them to purchase certificate of deposit, and funds were not commingled with other funds); Jones v. Goodson, 772 S.W.2d 609 (Ark. 1989) (key issue was accessibility: depositor could obtain funds at will, although he would be penalized by loss of some interest); Decker & Mattison Co. v. Wilson, 44 P.3d 341 (Kan. 2002) (proceeds of workers' compensation settlement, deposited in couple's joint account, then used to purchase certificate of deposit remained exempt, when funds were traceable and certificate of deposit a usual means of safekeeping); E.W. v. Hall, 917 P.2d 854 (Kan. 1996). *But see* Feliciano v. McClung, 556 S.E.2d 807 (W. Va. 2001) (lump sum workers' compensation award would remain exempt in ordinary bank account, but purchase of certificate of deposit turns it into nonexempt investment).

550 *In re* Santillannes, 2005 WL 4704994 (D. Idaho Nov. 5, 2005) (debtor could exempt seventy-five percent of wages directly deposited in shared savings account; funds were directly traceable to wages, and retained quality as monies even though pledged as collateral for credit union loan). *But cf. In re* Kramer, 339 B.R. 761 (Bankr. D. Colo. 2006) (wages would remain exempt in bank account, but stock purchased by payroll deductions had undergone "change of character" and become nonexempt personal property); *In re* Duemey, 347 B.R. 875 (Bankr. S.D. Ohio 2006) (vehicle purchased for debtor by ex-husband, to satisfy his debt for back child support, not exempt; child support had lost "quality as monies"); Asset Acceptance Corp. v. Hughes, 706 N.W.2d 446 (Mich. Ct. App. 2005) (Social Security disability benefits lost exempt status when used to pay the rent, therefore tax credit resulting from payment of rent not exempt).

551 *See* Porter v. Aetna Cas. & Surety Co., 370 U.S. 159, 82 S. Ct. 1231, 8 L. Ed. 2d 407 (1962); *see also* Jones v. Goodson, 772 S.W.2d 609 (Ark. 1989) (certificates of deposit purchased with veterans benefits remained exempt; funds were "immediately accessible" even though depositor would forfeit some interest in case of early withdrawal); Younger v. Mitchell, 777 P.2d 789 (Kan. 1989) (veterans benefits deposited into an interest bearing savings account exempt); United Home Foods Dist., Inc. v. Villegas, 724 P.2d 265 (Okla. Civ. App. 1986) (veterans benefits direct deposited into a bank account and used to pay household expenses exempt). *But cf.* Fox v. Fox, 2001 Tenn. App. LEXIS 239 (Tenn. Ct. App. Apr. 11, 2001) (veterans benefits lost "the quality of moneys" when used to purchase land).

552 Philpott v. Essex County Welfare Bd., 409 U.S. 413, 93 S. Ct. 590, 34 L. Ed. 2d 608 (1973); Granger v. Harris, 2007 WL 1213416 (E.D.N.Y. Apr. 17, 2007) (recipient stated section 1983 claim against bank that disbursed funds to creditor, despite knowledge that funds were Social Security funds); S & S Diversified Services L.L.C. v. Taylor, 897 F. Supp. 549 (D. Wyo. 1995) (Social Security old age benefits remained exempt when commingled with other funds in joint account, so long as they are "reasonably traceable"; court warning creditors of sanctions if they attempt to garnish exempt funds); NCNB Fin. Services v. Shumate, 829 F. Supp. 178 (W.D. Va. 1993) (applying first-in first-out accounting rule applied to exempt old age Social Security benefits), *aff'd*, 45 F.3d 427 (4th Cir. 1994) (table); *In re* Lichtenberger, 337 B.R. 322 (Bankr. C.D. Ill. 2006) (Social Security benefits remain exempt when commingled with other funds in checking account, so long as traceable); *In re* Radford, 265 B.R. 827 (Bankr. W.D. Mo. 2000) (lump-sum Social Security disability payment, received by debtor and deposited in bank account, exempted by "paid or payable" language; no need to determine whether funds necessary for support); *In re* Capps, 251 B.R. 73 (Bankr. D. Neb. 2000) (setoff is a "legal procedure" within meaning of the Social Security Act's anti-alienation provision, so bank could not set off debt against account which contained only Social Security benefits); Anderson Boneless Beef v. Sunshine Ctr., 852 P.2d 1340 (Colo. Ct. App. 1993) (creditor not entitled to garnish Social Security and supplemental security income checks deposited by debtor for care and maintenance of beneficiaries); Hatfield v. Christopher, 841 S.W.2d 761 (Mo. Ct. App. 1992) (when recipient cashed his Social Security check, spent part of it and deposited balance in

workers' compensation benefits,[553] and welfare benefits,[554] generally exempt those benefits from attachment by creditors when those benefits are deposited into a bank account as long as the funds are available on demand or for the support of the beneficiary and not converted into a permanent investment. The same reasoning holds that exemptions for payments from retirement funds,[555] private

account commingled with other funds, benefits remained exempt); Collins, Webster & Rouse v. Coleman, 776 S.W.2d 930 (Mo. Ct. App. 1989) (Social Security benefits exempt); Dean v. Fred's Towing, 801 P.2d 579 (Mont. 1990) (Social Security benefits of non-debtor wife remained exempt when commingled in joint account with debtor husband; first-in first-out accounting rule). *But see* Rue & Associates, Inc. v. White, 2006 WL 2022184 (Va. Cir. July 18, 2006) (Social Security benefits lose exemption when commingled with nonexempt funds in joint bank account); *cf.* Lopez v. Wash. Mut. Bank, 302 F.3d 900 (9th Cir.), *as amended by* 311 F.3d 928 (9th Cir. 2002) (bank's collection of amounts owed under overdraft checking account plan from direct-deposited Social Security and SSI benefits was equivalent to voluntary payment because plaintiffs continued direct deposits after incurring overdrafts, so not barred by section 407 of Social Security Act).

553 *In re* Williams, 171 B.R. 451 (D.N.H. 1994) (car; noting that workers' compensation benefits were "meant to be put to useful purposes"); *In re* Baker, 2006 WL 2079919 (Bankr. M.D. Ala. July 25, 2006) (purpose of workers' compensation is to rehabilitate worker, not to pay his antecedent debts; exemption survives in hands of worker and in motor vehicles purchased with traceable proceeds of workers' compensation settlement); *In re* Gardiner, 332 B.R. 891 (Bankr. S.D. Cal. 2005) (asset acquired, in part, with workers' compensation award retains exempt status, subject to tracing requirements); *In re* Arsenault, 318 B.R. 616 (Bankr. D.N.H. 2004) (New Hampshire protects workers' compensation "regardless of the form" into which benefits converted; so long as traceable, lump-sum workers' compensation remained exempt in bank account held as "Totten trust" for worker's son); *In re* Harrelson, 311 B.R. 618 (Bankr. M.D. Fla. 2004) (large lump-sum workers' compensation settlement invested in money market account, treasury bonds and mutual fund shares remained exempt, because still could be drawn upon to provide for living expenses or medical care), *aff'd*, 143 Fed. Appx. 238 (11th Cir. 2005); *In re* Mix, 244 B.R. 877 (Bankr. S.D. Fla. 2000) (workers' compensation settlement remains exempt when deposited in checking account, even if commingled with nonexempt funds, so long as traceable); *In re* Ladomer, 215 B.R. 265 (Bankr. S.D. Fla. 1997) (Florida exemption for workers' compensation benefits protects workers' compensation claim which had been filed but not yet decided, as well as at all later stages, including deposit in a bank account); *In re* King, 208 B.R. 570 (Bankr. M.D. Fla. 1997) (Florida exemption for workers' compensation "due and payable" protects benefits which have been deposited in bank account); *In re* Nelson, 179 B.R. 811 (Bankr. W.D. Va. 1994) (mobile home and lot); Broward v. Jacksonville Med. Ctr., 690 So. 2d 589 (Fla. 1997) (exemption for workers' compensation benefits "due or payable" continued to protect benefits deposited in bank account, so long as traceable); Decker & Mattison Co. v. Wilson, 44 P.3d 341 (Kan. 2002) (proceeds of workers' compensation settlement, deposited in couple's joint account, then used to purchase certificate of deposit remained exempt when funds were traceable and certificate of deposit a usual means of safekeeping); *cf.* *In re* Irwin, 371 B.R. 344 (Bankr. C.D. Ill. 2007) (workers' compensation settlement funds remained exempt in money market account used only for workers' compensation but lost exemption when used to pay down lien on motor vehicle); Fla. Asset Fin. Corp. v. Utah Labor Comm'n, 147 P.3d 1189 (Utah 2006) (Utah is one of a few states that permits assignment of workers' compensation benefits; if worker who has assigned benefits to creditor reneges and orders Labor Commission to pay him, assignee may sue worker but may not compel Labor Commission to pay benefits to assignee). *But see* Mier v. Andrus, 2006 WL 1228892 (W.D. La. May 3, 2006) (Louisiana workers' compensation funds lose exemption upon payment to worker); *In re* Rajkovic, 289 B.R. 197 (Bankr. M.D. Fla. 2002) (workers' compensation funds lost exemption when large lump sum was transferred to debtor's closely held corporation and used to purchase limousine; funds "invested in a business venture" were no longer used to rehabilitate worker or save him from poverty while disabled); *In re* Moore, 203 B.R. 802 (Bankr. S.D. Fla. 1997), *questioned by In re* Ladoner, 215 B.R. 265 (Bankr. S.D. Fla. 1997) (revising interpretation in light of intervening Florida Supreme Court decision); Borrayo v. Lefever, 159 P.3d 657 (Colo. Ct. App. 2006) (Colorado workers' compensation payments lose exemption when paid to worker); SSM Health Care Sys. v. Bartel, 914 S.W.2d 8 (Mo. Ct. App. 1995) (exemption for workers' compensation "payable to" worker did not exempt funds in the hands of the beneficiary); Nat'l Check Bureau v. Carter, 2005 WL 1714200 (Ohio Ct. App. July 22, 2005) (under Ohio law workers' compensation not exempt once paid, but compensation paid by United States to disabled former federal employee was exempt pursuant to federal statute); Feliciano v. McClung, 556 S.E.2d 807 (W. Va. 2001) (lump sum workers' compensation award would remain exempt in ordinary bank account, but purchase of certificate of deposit turns it into nonexempt investment); *cf.* *In re* Sills, 82 F.3d 111 (5th Cir. 1996) (declining to decide whether house purchased with workers' compensation lump-sum settlement was exempt from levy by Internal Revenue Service; even if it were exempt from levy, it remained subject to federal tax lien); *In re* Sanchez, 362 B.R. 342 (Bankr. W.D. Mich. 2007) (bank account containing traceable proceeds of workers' compensation settlement not exempt under federal bankruptcy law as "right to receive" workers' compensation, but exempt so far as needed for support as traceable proceeds of compensation for loss of future earnings); *In re* Bonuchi, 322 B.R. 868 (Bankr. W.D. Mo. 2005) (workers' compensation award paid into annuity not exempt because no longer "payable," however, annuity itself may be exempt under separate statutory provision); Sullo v. Cinco Star, Inc., 755 So. 2d 822 (Fla. Dist. Ct. App. 2000) (exemption lost when worker received large lump sum, bought certificate of deposit, and pledged that certificate of deposit as security for a loan). *See generally* Jay M. Zitter, Annotation, *Validity, Construction, and Effect of Statutory Exemptions of Proceeds of Workers' Compensation Awards*, 48 A.L.R.5th 473 (1997).

554 *See, e.g.*, MacQuarrie v. Balch, 285 N.E.2d 103 (Mass. 1972); Guardian Loan Co. v. Baylis, 112 N.J. Super. 44, 270 A.2d 304 (Dist. Ct. 1970); Consumer Credit Corp. v. Lewis, 313 N.Y.S.2d 879 (Dist. Ct. 1970); First Nat'l Master Charge v. Gilardi, 44 Ohio App. 2d 383, 324 N.E.2d 576 (1975) (poor relief funds retain exemption after deposit into checking account).

555 Beardsley v. Admiral Ins. Co., 647 So. 2d 327 (Fla. Dist. Ct. App. 1994) (commingling exempt federal retirement funds and nonexempt funds did not destroy exemption; funds should be allocated or traced, if possible).

disability insurance policies,[556] or annuities[557] continue after payment or deposit.

The provisions of the Social Security Act, which apply to old age, survivors', and disability benefits[558] and to SSI,[559] explicitly protect both the "right to receive" benefits and funds "paid or payable" from attachment, garnishment, and "other legal process." The "paid or payable" language clearly exempts the funds in the hands of the recipient.[560] The less explicit language governing veterans disability[561] and civil service retirement[562] benefits has also been construed to exempt funds paid to the recipient.

By virtue of explicit statutory language, federally insured student loans, federal educational grants, federal student work assistance, and property traceable to such assistance are exempt from garnishment or attachment, except for educational debts owing to the Department of Education.[563] Similarly, most states apply state exemptions to wages,[564]

---

556 *In re* Alam, 336 B.R. 320 (Bankr. N.D. Ohio 2005) (settlement proceeds from lawsuit for disability benefits exempt as benefits paid under sickness and accident insurance; investment account funds traceable to settlement proceeds also exempt), *aff'd*, 359 B.R. 142 (B.A.P. 6th Cir. 2006); Parl v. Parl, 699 So. 2d 765 (Fla. Dist. Ct. App. 1997).

557 *In re* Lazin, 217 B.R. 332 (M.D. Fla. 1998); *see also In re* Hunt, 250 B.R. 482 (Bankr. E.D.N.Y. 2000) (state employees' pensions). *But see* State *ex rel.* Nixon v. Mahmud, 11 S.W.3d 718 (Mo. Ct. App. 1999) (Missouri exemption for funds "payable to" a participant or beneficiary of a retirement account did not protect funds once disbursed to the beneficiary and deposited in bank account).

558 42 U.S.C. § 407(a).

559 42 U.S.C. § 1383(d)(1).

560 Granger v. Harris, 2007 WL 1213416 (E.D.N.Y. Apr. 17, 2007) (recipient stated section 1983 claim against bank that disbursed funds to creditor, despite knowledge that funds were Social Security funds); *see also* Bennett v. Arkansas, 485 U.S. 395, 108 S. Ct. 1204, 99 L. Ed. 2d 455 (1988); Philpott v. Essex County Welfare Bd., 409 U.S. 413, 93 S. Ct. 590, 34 L. Ed. 2d 608 (1973); Tom v. First Am. Credit Union, 151 F.3d 1289 (10th Cir. 1998); Crawford v. Gould, 56 F.3d 1162 (9th Cir. 1995); Brinkman v. Rahm, 878 F.2d 263 (9th Cir. 1989); S & S Diversified Services L.L.C. v. Taylor, 897 F. Supp. 549 (D. Wyo. 1995); *In re* Lazin, 217 B.R. 332 (Bankr. M.D. Fla. 1998); Hatfield v. Christopher, 841 S.W.2d 761 (Mo. Ct. App. 1992); Collins, Webster & Rouse v. Coleman, 776 S.W.2d 930 (Mo. Ct. App. 1989); Sears, Roebuck & Co. v. Harris, 854 P.2d 921 (Okla. Civ. App. 1993). *But see* Fraser v. Deppe, 770 S.W.2d 479 (Mo. Ct. App. 1989) (repudiated by later decision in *Collins, Webster & Rouse v. Coleman*); Ponath v. Hedrick, 126 N.W.2d 28 (Wis. 1964); *cf. In re* Burke, 251 B.R. 720 (Bankr. D. Minn. 2000) (Federal Crop Loss Disaster Assistance payments not exempt after payment to farmer; statutory language barring attachment and so forth "before payment" intended for convenience of agency, not protection of farmer).

561 38 U.S.C. § 5301 (benefits "due or to become due" and payments "made to, or on account of, a beneficiary"); Porter v. Aetna Cas. & Surety Co., 370 U.S. 159, 82 S. Ct. 1231, 8 L. Ed. 2d 407 (1962); Sears, Roebuck & Co. v. Harris, 854 P.2d 921 (Okla. Civ. App. 1993). *But cf.* Gray v. Gray, 922 P.2d 615 (Okla. 1996) (personal property purchased with veterans benefits not exempt).

562 5 U.S.C. § 8346 ("money mentioned by this subchapter is not . . . subject to execution, levy, attachment, garnishment, or other legal process"); *see* Tom v. First Am. Credit Union, 151 F.3d 1289 (10th Cir. 1998); Waggoner v. Game Sales Co., 702 S.W.2d 808 (Ark. 1986); Missouri *ex rel.* Nixon v. McClure, 969 S.W.2d 801 (Mo. Ct. App. 1998); Joseph v. Giacalone, 637 N.Y.S.2d 771 (App. Div. 1996); *see also* Sears, Roebuck & Co. v. Harris, 854 P.2d 921 (Okla. Civ. App. 1993) (exemption clearly applies to future payments, and court "not particularly impressed" with argument that it does not apply to payments already made).

563 20 U.S.C. § 1095a(d).

564 Cadle Co. v. Newhouse, 2001 U.S. App. LEXIS 21852 (2d Cir. Oct. 11, 2001) (New York earnings exemption continued to protect husband's earnings, if needed for reasonable living expenses, even after fraudulent transfer to account in name of non-debtor wife); *In re* Robinson, 241 B.R. 447 (B.A.P. 9th Cir. 1999) (Oregon's wage protections, which included a garnishment limitation and continuing protection for wages deposited in bank accounts, exempted wages which were accrued but unpaid at time debtors filed bankruptcy); *In re* Santillannes, 2005 WL 4704994 (D. Idaho Nov. 5, 2005) (debtor could exempt seventy-five percent of wages directly deposited in shared savings account; funds directly traceable to wages, and retained quality as monies even though pledged as collateral for credit union loan); *In re* Nye, 210 B.R. 857 (D. Colo. 1997) (Colorado's garnishment limitation explicitly protected earnings after deposit in checking account; debtor, however, failed to carry burden of proof as to origin of funds); Montgomery Ward Credit Corp. v. Brewer, Clearinghouse No. 44,517 (D. Minn. 1989) (seventy-five percent of earnings and all severance pay deposited in joint bank account exempt from garnishment); *In re* Stevenson, 374 B.R. 891 (Bankr. M.D. Fla. 2007) (Florida exemption for head of family's wages explicitly covers traceable funds in bank account, but debtor failed to prove he was head of family); *In re* Urban, 262 B.R. 865 (Bankr. D. Kan. 2001) (Kansas wage exemption protects wages directly deposited in a bank account); *In re* Coolbaugh, 250 B.R. 162 (Bankr. W.D.N.Y. 2000) (New York earnings exemption protects earnings in a checking account if earned for personal services within past sixty days and necessary to debtor's support); *In re* Ryzner, 208 B.R. 568 (Bankr. M.D. Fla. 1997) (former police officer's disability payments retained their exempt character when deposited in a bank account, so long as they remained traceable); *In re* Norris, 203 B.R. 463 (Bankr. D. Nev. 1996) (interpreting "disposable income" exemption to protect earnings commingled with other funds in checking account so long as funds remain traceable and easily withdrawable); *In re* Arnold, 193 B.R. 897 (Bankr. W.D. Mo. 1996) (under Missouri law exempt wages do not lose their exemption by being commingled with other funds in bank account); Miller v. Monrean, 507 P.2d 771 (Alaska 1973) (state exemption law protects earnings after they are received and deposited into bank account); Rutter v. Shumway, 26 P. 321 (Colo. 1891) (state exemption continues to protect wages after their deposit into bank account); E.J. Benson v. Richardson, 537 N.W.2d 748 (Iowa 1995) (Iowa statute provided that exempt wages remain so for ninety days in checking or savings account, if reasonably traceable; exemption applied when debtor husband deposited earnings in account of non-debtor wife; property purchased by wife during ninety days was exempt); Midamerica Sav. Bank v. Miehe, 438 N.W.2d 837 (Iowa 1989); Staton v. Vernon, 229 N.W. 763, 764, 67 A.L.R. 1200 (Iowa 1931) (state exemption continues to protect wages after deposit into bank account); Zaleski v. Collection Bureau of

unemployment compensation,[565] or other exempt funds[566] that have been paid to the debtor or deposited in a bank account. Some general state exemption statutes also specifically protect exempt funds in bank accounts.[567]

Grand Island, 664 N.W.2d 32 (Neb. Ct. App. 2003) (Nebraska forbids garnishment of wages earned within sixty days before date of garnishment; inmate stated claim against collector who garnished "release savings account" into which wages were compulsorily deposited); *see also* Grant Hosp. v. O'Nail, 1997 WL 101657 (Ohio Ct. App. Mar. 4, 1997) (exempt earnings deposited into joint checking account of debtor and spouse would remain exempt, if traceable, but exempt earnings deposited in savings account were not exempt). *But see In re* Sinclair, 417 F.3d 527 (5th Cir. 2005) (Louisiana garnishment limitation not an exemption and does not protect wages deposited directly into bank account); Wienco, Inc. v. Scene Three, Inc., 29 F.3d 329 (7th Cir. 1994) (approving order requiring recalcitrant judgment debtor to turn over 75% of wages, even though Illinois limits garnishment to 15%; rejecting argument that wage garnishment act continues to protect wages after payment to wage earner); *In re* Adcock, 264 B.R. 708 (D. Kan. 2000) (wages electronically deposited in debtors' bank account not protected by Kansas wage exemption, which protects wages only in the hands of the employer); Mass. Mut. Life Ins. Co. v. Shoemaker, 849 F. Supp. 30 (S.D. Tex. 1994) (Texas exemption for "current wages" does not survive deposit); *In re* Cauley, 374 B.R. 311 (Bankr. M.D. Fla. 2007) (Ala. law) (wages lose exemption when commingled with other funds in bank account); *In re* Stewart, 2006 WL 2666153 (Bankr. S.D. Ind. Sept. 6, 2006) (exemption for wages does not apply to wages that teacher had employer place in escrow account, to be paid out during summer vacation); *In re* Thum, 329 B.R. 848 (Bankr. C.D. Ill. 2005) (Illinois limits on garnishment and wage assignment not an exemption under previous version of statute); *In re* Palidora, 310 B.R. 164 (Bankr. D. Ariz. 2004) (Arizona exemption does not protect wages deposited directly into bank account); *In re* Resler, 282 B.R. 246 (Bankr. D. Kan. 2002) (Kansas exemption does not protect wages after electronic direct deposit to worker's checking account); *In re* Lawrence, 205 B.R. 115 (Bankr. E.D. Tenn. 1997) (Tennessee garnishment statute, substantially identical to CCPA, did not protect wages in the hands of the debtor), *aff'd*, 219 B.R. 786 (E.D. Tenn. 1998); Frazer, Ryan, Goldberg, Keyt & Lawless v. Smith, 907 P.2d 1384 (Ariz. Ct. App. 1995) (Arizona statute modeled on CCPA distinguished between exempt wages and nonexempt "monies"; wages became "monies" when deposited in bank account); Brown v. Kentucky Natural Res. & Env't Cabinet, 40 S.W.3d 873 (Ky. Ct. App. 1999) (Kentucky wage garnishment statute, which tracks the CCPA, does not protect wages deposited in bank account); Gen. Elec. Capital Corp. v. ICO, Inc., 230 S.W.3d 702 (Tex. App. 2007) (Texas exemption for current wages lost upon payment to employee); Am. Express Travel Related Services v. Harris, 831 S.W.2d 531 (Tex. App. 1992) (bank account containing wages can be garnished); Thatcher v. Dep't of Social & Health Services, 908 P.2d 920 (Wash. Ct. App. 1996) (earnings which were fifty percent exempt under child support statute lost their exemption as soon as deposited in bank account; same rule as under general garnishment statute); *In re* Walsh, 96 P.3d 1 (Wyo. 2004) (Wyoming garnishment statute protects only accrued and unpaid wages); *cf. In re* Mulvihill, 326 B.R. 459 (Bankr. D. Ariz. 2005) (debtors permitted to exempt seventy-five percent of actual damage award for unpaid wages; exemption would have been lost if amounts had actually been paid to debtor); *In re* Sikes, 2004 WL 2028021 (Bankr. W.D. Ky. Sept. 8, 2004) (stating in *dicta* that Kentucky law limits on wage garnishment to not apply to wages in hands of employee or in bank account); Schmerbeck v. River Oaks Bank, 786 S.W.2d 521 (Tex. App. 1990) (upholding turnover order requiring judgment debtor to deliver paycheck to receiver), *superseded by statute as stated in* Burns v. Miller, Hiersche, Martens & Hayward, 948 S.W.2d 317 (Tex. App. 1997). *See generally* Annotation, *Deposit of exempt funds as affecting debtor's exemption*, 67 A.L.R. 1203 (1930); 31 Am. Jur. 2d *Exemptions* § 45 (2002); W. Vukowich, *Debtors' Exemptions Rights*, 62 Geo. L.J. 779, 836–837 (1974).

565 Kruger v. Wells Fargo Bank, 521 P.2d 441 (Cal. 1974) (unemployment compensation and disability benefits deposited into bank account retain their exemption).

566 *In re* Cornett, 332 B.R. 289 (Bankr. E.D. Ky. 2005) (funds distributed from teacher's retirement fund do not lose exemption when deposited in checking account); *In re* Hunt, 250 B.R. 482 (Bankr. E.D.N.Y. 2000) (state employees' pensions retain exemption when paid to employee and deposited in bank account); *In re* Meyer, 211 B.R. 203 (Bankr. E.D. Va. 1997) (military retirement pay was exempt under federal law and retained exempt status under Virginia law when directly deposited in Navy Federal Credit Union, but lost exempt status when transferred to debtor's checking account in another institution that had not been opened especially for deposit of these funds); Kruger v. Wells Fargo Bank, 521 P.2d 441 (Cal. 1974) (unemployment compensation and disability benefits deposited into bank account retain their exemption); McKernan Co. v. Gregory, 643 N.E.2d 1370 (Ill. App. Ct. 1994) (traceable proceeds of exempt property, the cash value of an insurance policy, remained exempt so long as they were held "for the support of debtor and his family"; exemption would be lost if funds were "transformed into an investment"). *But see* Hooper v. State, 908 P.2d 1252 (Idaho Ct. App. 1995) (earnings in prison inmate's account were not exempt, when they were commingled with funds from outside sources and Department of Correction provided for all inmate's needs); Cmty. Bank v. Noble, 552 N.W.2d 37 (Minn. Ct. App. 1996) (Employee Retirement Income Security Act (ERISA) preempted state statute which exempted pension funds; under ERISA, funds lose their exempt status as soon as disbursed; creditor could seize uncashed pension check).

567 *See, e.g.*, Iowa Code § 96.15(3) (unemployment compensation, so long as not commingled with other funds, remains exempt from any remedy whatsoever for the collection of all debts); Minn. Stat. § 550.37(14), (20) (needs-based assistance is explicitly protected from set off or security interest by bank); Or. Rev. Stat. § 18.348 (exempt funds in bank accounts); Vt. Stat. Ann. tit. 12, § 2740(19) (property traceable to debtor's right to receive a long list of exempt funds, including insurance, crime victims benefits, family support, personal injury recoveries as well as government benefits); *In re* Watts, 2006 WL 3899996 (Bankr. S.D. W. Va. Aug. 17, 2006) (interpreting West Virginia statute to allow weekly exemption of funds on deposit in a financial institution, wages or salary, up to the greater of $1000 or 125% of the federal poverty line divided by the number of pay periods per year); *In re* Sanderson, 283 B.R. 595 (Bankr. M.D. Fla. 2002) (recently amended Fla. Stat. § 222.25 exempts tax refunds attributable to earned income credit, even after deposit and commingling); *In re* Platt, 270 B.R. 773 (Bankr. D. Or. 2001) (Oregon garnishment statute protected bank account containing funds traceable to debtor-husband's earnings so long as funds remained identifiable and accumulation did not exceed $7500); *In re* Christensen, 149 P.3d 40 (Nev. 2006) (Nevada statute recently amended to specify that exemption protects

Interpreting exemption statutes to protect paid or deposited funds is a straightforward construction that accomplishes their purpose of protecting funds necessary for the support of the debtor and the debtor's family.[568] It is also consistent with the general principle that exemption statutes are to be liberally construed.[569] A notable exception to this rule, however, is the holding of several courts that the federal limitations on wage garnishment do not protect earnings once they are deposited in an account.[570] Another limitation is that the exemption, even of Social Security and SSI benefits, may be lost if the funds are accumulated beyond the amount needed for daily care and maintenance.[571]

12.6.3 Commingling of Exempt and Nonexempt Funds

Commingling of exempt funds with nonexempt funds or funds of another raises the problem of traceability. Most courts will continue to protect such funds,[572] generally applying a first-in first-out accounting method.[573] Others, a minority, simply refuse to trace, finding that the exemption was lost when the funds were commingled.[574] The use of an account which is limited to exempt funds should offer protection in such states.

---

earnings deposited in bank account; even before amendment, statute protected deposited earnings). *But see* Schoonover v. Karr, 285 B.R. 695 (S.D. Ill. 2002) (under Illinois law, benefits lose exemption when deposited in bank), *aff'd sub nom. In re* Schoonover, 331 F.3d 575 (7th Cir. 2003) (Illinois exemption and federal anti-alienation clause meant to protect "minimum monthly income of beneficiaries, not "hoards of cash," here over $75,000 in various accounts); Behavior Mgmt. Associates v. Bucilli, 726 N.E.2d 592 (Ohio Ct. App. 1999) (lottery winnings deposited in a checking account were not exempt when statute provided that "no right of any person to a prize award shall be assignable, or subject to garnishment").

568 Porter v. Aetna Cas. & Surety Co., 370 U.S. 159, 162, 82 S. Ct. 1231, 8 L. Ed. 2d 407 (1962).

569 *See* § 12.2, *supra*.

570 *See* § 12.6.6, *infra*.

571 *In re* Schoonover, 331 F.3d 575 (7th Cir. 2003) (Illinois exemption and federal anti-alienation clause meant to protect "minimum monthly income of beneficiaries," not "hoards of cash"—here over $75,000 in various accounts); *In re* Lazin, 217 B.R. 332 (Bankr. M.D. Fla. 1998) (if funds accumulate, court must address question of necessity); *In re* Crandall, 200 B.R. 243 (Bankr. M.D. Fla. 1995) (11th Circuit gives narrow interpretation to "ability to meet basic needs"; disabled SSI recipient whose income barely covered day to day needs allowed to keep only $5000 of $10,000 lump sum retroactive benefit payment); *see also* Citronelle-Mobile Gathering, Inc. v. Watkins, 934 F.2d 1180 (11th Cir. 1991) (refusing to allow multimillionaire who fled to Switzerland to exempt $2300 Social Security commingled in account with $63,000 balance); *In re* Treadwell, 699 F.2d 1050 (11th Cir. 1983) (debtor gave away money to family members). *But see In re* Radford, 265 B.R. 827 (Bankr. W.D. Mo. 2000) (lump-sum Social Security disability payment, received by debtor and deposited in his bank account, exempted by "paid or payable" language; no need to determine whether funds necessary for support); E.W. v. Hall, 917 P.2d 854 (Kan. 1996) (prison inmate's Social Security funds in savings account and certificate of deposit were exempt even though prison was meeting all his daily living needs).

572 *See, e.g.*, Tom v. First Am. Credit Union, 151 F.3d 1289 (10th Cir. 1998); Neilson v. McGuire, 2006 WL 1875383 (D. Neb. July 5, 2006) (Social Security and certain exempt funds remained exempt when commingled with nonexempt funds in bank account; court calculates from bank statements that seventy-five percent of account was Social Security funds); *In re* Nye, 210 B.R. 857 (D. Colo. 1997); *In re* Williams, 171 B.R. 451 (D.N.H. 1994); NCNB Fin. Services v. Shumate, 829 F. Supp. 178 (W.D. Va. 1993), *aff'd*, 45 F.3d 427 (4th Cir. 1994) (table); *In re* Lichtenberger, 337 B.R. 322 (Bankr. C.D. Ill. 2006) (Social Security benefits remain exempt when commingled with other funds in checking account, so long as traceable; choosing first-in first-out tracing method); *In re* Gardiner, 332 B.R. 891 (Bankr. S.D. Cal. 2005) (asset acquired, in part, with workers' compensation award retained exempt status, subject to tracing requirements); *In re* Sanderson, 283 B.R. 595 (Bankr. M.D. Fla. 2002) (recently amended Fla. Stat. § 222.25 exempts tax refunds attributable to earned income credit, even after deposit and commingling); *In re* Mix, 244 B.R. 877 (Bankr. S.D. Fla. 2000) (workers' compensation settlement remains exempt in checking account, even if commingled with nonexempt funds, so long as traceable); *In re* Lazin, 217 B.R. 332 (Bankr. M.D. Fla. 1998); *In re* Ryzner, 208 B.R. 568 (Bankr. M.D. Fla. 1997); *In re* Norris, 203 B.R. 463 (Bankr. D. Nev. 1996); Waggoner v. Game Sales Co., 702 S.W.2d 808 (Ark. 1986); Orlyn v. Novastar Mortgage, Inc., 2006 WL 1102688 (Cal. Ct. App. Apr. 27, 2006) (Social Security and wages commingled in bank account; Social Security automatically exempt; wages not exempt when debtor failed to prove they had been earned with thirty days); Broward v. Jacksonville Med. Ctr., 690 So. 2d 589 (Fla. 1997); Parl v. Parl, 699 So. 2d 765 (Fla. Dist. Ct. App. 1997); Beardsley v. Admiral Ins. Co., 647 So. 2d 327 (Fla. Dist. Ct. App. 1994); Decker & Mattison Co. v. Wilson, 44 P.3d 341 (Kan. 2002) (proceeds of workers' compensation settlement, deposited in couple's joint account, then used to purchase certificate of deposit remained exempt, when funds were traceable and certificate of deposit a usual means of safekeeping); Hatfield v. Christopher, 841 S.W.2d 761 (Mo. Ct. App. 1992); Collins, Webster & Rouse v. Coleman, 776 S.W.2d 930 (Mo. Ct. App. 1989); Dean v. Fred's Towing, 801 P.2d 579 (Mont. 1990); *In re* Christensen, 149 P.3d 40 (Nev. 2006) (commingling does not destroy exemption, so long as funds remain available for day to day use, and reasonably traceable). *But see* Citibank (S.D) v. Five Star Bank, 824 N.Y.S.2d 761 (Sup. Ct. 2006) (exempt funds deposited in joint account several months before were no longer traceable when there were numerous deposits and withdrawals thereafter).

573 *See, e.g.*, S & S Diversified Services L.L.C. v. Taylor, 897 F. Supp. 549 (D. Wyo. 1995); NCNB Fin. Services v. Shumate, 829 F. Supp. 178 (W.D. Va. 1993), *aff'd*, 45 F.3d 427 (4th Cir. 1994) (table); *In re* Lichtenberger, 337 B.R. 322 (Bankr. C.D. Ill. 2006) (using first-in, first-out method to trace Social Security funds commingled in joint checking account); Dean v. Fred's Towing, 801 P.2d 579 (Mont. 1990); *In re* Christensen, 149 P.3d 40 (Nev. 2006) (choosing first-in, first-out after comparing four tracing methods); Lincoln Fin. Services, Inc. v. Miceli, 17 Misc. 3d 1109(A) (Dist. Ct. 2007) (table) (text available at 2007 WL 2917242) (first-in, first-out tracing for Social Security benefits in bank account).

574 *See, e.g.*, *In re* Cauley, 374 B.R. 311 (Bankr. M.D. Fla. 2007)

12.6.4 Protection of Federal Benefits in Electronic Transfer Accounts

In 1996, Congress passed a law, commonly known as "EFT-99,"[575] that requires all federal benefits, salaries, and retirement pay to be electronically deposited in a financial institution, subject to certain hardship waivers. For recipients without bank accounts, the Treasury Department established its own program for low-cost Electronic Transfer Accounts (ETAs) for federal benefit recipients. These accounts are described in more detail in NCLC's *Consumer Banking and Payments Law* § 5.3.[576]

Financial institutions are permitted, but not required, to offer low-cost ETAs to recipients for the direct deposit of federal benefits.[577] Once an institution decides to offer ETAs, however, it must make them available to any federal benefit recipient who requests one, regardless of credit history and without any minimum balance requirement.[578] There are limits on the fees that can be charged and minimum requirements on other terms and conditions for ETAs.

The Treasury requirements for ETA accounts specifically address the protection of exempt funds from attachment and set off.[579] Federal benefits may not be attached. A bank may choose to allow the deposit of funds other than federal benefits in an ETA, however, and these other funds are subject to attachment in the usual way. If the bank allows the deposit of nonexempt funds it must, at the time when the account is opened, explain to the customer that these funds may be attached. If the funds are attached the bank must promptly notify the customer.

12.6.5 Direct Access Card

The Treasury Department has moved closer to its goal of completely electronic delivery of federal benefits by adopting a MasterCard-branded prepaid (stored value) debit card for Social Security and SSI recipients.[580] The Direct Express card will become the standard, default method of providing those benefits, and eventually others, to all new unbanked recipients. The card—"Direct Express"—is also available to banked recipients who do not want benefits deposited into their bank account. This new card is discussed in more detail in another manual in this series.[581]

Funds deposited on the Direct Express card will not be subject to garnishment *or* freezing, except as authorized by *federal* law.[582] Federal law permits garnishment of exempt funds only in very limited circumstances and provides no separate authority to freeze exempt funds. The only private debts for which Social Security funds—but not SSI—may be garnished are child support and alimony.[583] In addition, Social Security (but not SSI) payments may be administratively offset, within limits, to satisfy debts owed to the federal government (such as taxes or student loans),[584] but administrative offsets are deducted from the payment before it is even made, whether that is by direct deposit, a paper check, or the Direct Express card.

12.6.6 Do Federal Wage Protections Apply to Paid or Deposited Earnings?

A paycheck that the employer has drawn but has not yet delivered to the employee is protected by the Consumer Credit Protection Act (CCPA).[585] Ignoring the CCPA's remedial purpose, however, several decisions have held that the CCPA does not protect earnings of a wage earner after the time that they are paid over to the employee, so the exemption is lost once the earnings are deposited in a financial institution.[586] Another court reached a similar con-

(Ala. law) (wages lose exemption when commingled with other funds in bank account); Bernardini v. Cent. Bank, 290 S.E.2d 863 (Va. 1982); Rue & Associates, Inc. v. White, 2006 WL 2022184 (Va. Cir. Ct. July 18, 2006) (Social Security benefits lose exemption when commingled with nonexempt funds in joint bank account); *see also* Idaho Code Ann. § 11-604 (exemptions for insurance, disability and family support are "lost immediately upon the commingling of any of the funds . . . with any other funds"); *In re* Fouracre, 358 B.R. 384 (Bankr. D. Ariz. 2006) (proceeds of homestead lose exemption when commingled with other funds in bank account). *But cf. In re* Meyer, 211 B.R. 203 (Bankr. E.D. Va. 1997) (noting statutory protection for unemployment benefits and workers' compensation benefits even if deposited and commingled).

575 31 U.S.C. § 3332(f)(1).

576 (3d ed. 2005 and Supp.).

577 31 C.F.R. § 208.5; 64 Fed. Reg. 38,510 (July 16, 1999).

578 64 Fed. Reg. 38,510 (July 16, 1999).
The financial institution can, however, deny a recipient an account to someone who has committed fraud or abuse of an ETA account. *Id.*

579 64 Fed. Reg. 38,510, 38,512–38,514 (July 16, 1999).

580 *See* U.S. Dep't of Treasury, Financial Mgmt. Serv., Direct Express Card: Overview, *available at* http://fms.treas.gov/directexpress/index.html.

581 National Consumer Law Center, Consumer Banking and Payments Law § 10.8a (3d ed. 2005 and 2008 Supp.).

582 *See* U.S. Dep't of Treasury, Direct Express Card Program (Dec. 31, 2007) (reprinted in National Consumer Law Center, Consumer Banking and Payments Law Appx. H.5 (3d ed. 2005 and 2008 Supp.)).

583 *See* 42 U.S.C. § 659(a); § 12.5.10.3, *supra*.

584 *See* §§ 11.2.8.2, 12.5.5.3, *supra*.

585 Hodgson v. Christopher, 365 F. Supp. 583 (D.N.D. 1973).

586 Usery v. First Nat'l Bank, 586 F.2d 107 (9th Cir. 1978) (unrealistic to ask bank to determine which deposits traceable to employee pay check, therefore bank not responsible for determining exemptions under the CCPA); United States v. Crawford, 2006 WL 2458710 (E.D. Cal. Aug. 22, 2006) (CCPA protects earnings only in the hands of the employer); Dunlop v. First Nat'l Bank, 399 F. Supp. 855 (D. Ariz. 1975) (wage protections do not apply after deposit into bank); John O. Melby & Co. Bank v. Anderson, 88 Wis. 2d 252, 276 N.W.2d 274 (Wis. 1979) (even when money in checking account was directly traceable to payroll earnings, restrictions of the CCPA restricting garnishments did not apply); *see also* Triple J Saipan, Inc.

clusion but made the distinction between compulsory and non-compulsory deposit of wages, holding that a compulsory direct deposit as a condition of employment renders the earnings subject to the restrictions of the CCPA even after they are deposited in a bank.[587]

State wage exemptions commonly apply to wages after deposit.[588] This state approach should call the federal court approach of not exempting deposited wages into question. For example, the Ohio Supreme Court has held that wages, immune from execution, garnishment, or attachment under state law, retained their exempt character when deposited in a checking account, so long as the source of the funds was known or reasonably traceable.[589] In so holding the court recognized that the purpose of exemption statutes is to "protect funds intended primarily for maintenance and support of the debtor's family."[590] That purpose would be frustrated if wages lost their exempt character upon deposit in an account maintained to pay those expenses.[591]

In an age when cash is no longer the common method of paying bills, such a conclusion is the only sensible one. As one court noted more than half a century ago, "[i]t would be an unreasonable construction to hold that by deposit of the earnings in the bank . . . and [acquiring] in lieu thereof, a credit due him from the bank . . . the exempt character of the funds should be lost."[592] It is also the rule as to veterans benefits,[593] Social Security benefits,[594] welfare benefits,[595] and workers' compensation.[596]

The reasoning in the CCPA decisions is strained compared to the state decisions. The context in which the CCPA cases arose may explain the CCPA courts' failing to follow the usual rule. In apparently the earliest case to rule on the issue, the Secretary of Labor brought an action against the bank where the paycheck was deposited, and would have required the bank to identify the exempt amount and assert the exemptions.[597] The Ninth Circuit was clearly aghast at the notion of placing this kind of burden on the bank, and stressed the novelty of the question, and the difficulty of calculating the exempt amount.[598] Laboring under the mistaken notion that there was no guidance on "whether compensation retains its character as earnings after deposit in the employee's bank account,"[599] the court then strained to find a difference between the congressional purpose in exempting Social Security and veterans benefits (to provide maintenance and support) and the congressional purpose for exempting a portion of wages.

The Ninth Circuit focused on the legislative concern with preserving the stability of the employer-employee relationship, a purpose not directly furthered by extending the exemption to deposited wages. That rationale, of course, ignored the more fundamental purpose of "insuring a continued means of support [of the debtors] and their families," also a specified congressional purpose,[600] and the fundamental historical purpose behind exemptions.[601] It further tortured the plain language of the federal statute, which specifically defines earnings as "compensation *paid* or payable for personal services."[602] The use of the past tense "paid" has been interpreted to mean there is no distinction between exempt funds in the hands of the payor and in the hands of the debtor.[603] To the contrary, the absence of the word "paid" in the relevant exemption statute was critical in another court's refusal to hold wages exempt upon deposit.[604]

As the CCPA was the first federal wage garnishment act, the logical place for those courts to have looked for precedent on whether wages retained their exempt earnings would have been to state wage exemption law, in which precedent did in fact exist.[605] In fact, the similar argument that wages were exempt only while in the employer's hands had been presented—and rejected—before:

> Such a construction would practically frustrate the beneficent objects of the statute . . . think of the court [saying to a debtor]: "Yes, the money was

v. Norita, 2007 WL 4124477 (N. Mar. I. Nov. 16, 2007) (garnishment limitations cease to protect funds upon payment to debtor).

587 Household Fin. Corp. v. Kinder, 3 Ohio Misc. 2d 3, 444 N.E.2d 99 (Mun. Ct. 1982); *see also* § 12.7, *infra.*

588 *See* § 12.6.2, *supra.*

589 Daugherty v. Cent. Trust Co. of Northern Ohio, 504 N.E.2d 1100 (Ohio 1986).

590 *Id.* at 1103.

591 *Id.*

592 Staton v. Vernon, 229 N.W. 763, 764, 67 A.L.R. 1200 (Iowa 1931).

593 *See* § 12.5.5, *supra.*

594 Philpott v. Essex County Welfare Bd., 409 U.S. 413, 93 S. Ct. 590, 34 L. Ed. 2d 608 (1973); *see* § 12.5.5, *supra.*

595 *See* § 12.5.5, *supra.*

596 *See* § 12.5.5.5, *supra.*

597 Usery v. First Nat'l Bank, 586 F.2d 107 (9th Cir. 1978).

598 *Id.* at 109–110 n.8.

599 *Id.* at 110.

600 H.R. 1040, 90th Cong. (1968), *reprinted in* 1968 U.S.C.C.A.N. 1966, 1979.

601 W. Vukowich, *Debtors' Exemptions Rights*, 62 Geo. L.J. 779, 784–786 (1974).

602 15 U.S.C. § 1672(a).

603 Consumer Credit Corp. v. Lewis, 313 N.Y.S.2d 879 (Dist. Ct. 1970).

604 Holmes v. Blazer Fin. Services, Inc., 369 So. 2d 987, 989 (Fla. Dist. Ct. App. 1979) (statute exempted funds "due for personal labor or services"). *But cf.* Brown v. Kentucky Natural Res. & Env't Cabinet, 40 S.W.3d 873 (Ky. Ct. App. 1999) (Kentucky wage garnishment statute, which tracks the CCPA, does not protect wages deposited in bank account).

The Florida statute which *Holmes* construed was later amended to make it clear that wages remained exempt six months after deposit. Further, the Florida Supreme Court has declined to apply the *Holmes* court's reasoning to workers' compensation funds on deposit, holding these benefits exempt even though the statute only covered benefits "due or payable." Broward v. Jacksonville Med. Ctr., 690 So. 2d 589 (Fla. 1997).

605 *See, e.g.*, Rutter v. Shumway, 26 P. 321 (Colo. 1891); Staton v. Vernon, 229 N.W. 763 (Iowa 1931); Annotation, *Deposit of exempt funds as affecting debtor's exemption*, 67 A.L.R. 1203 (1930).

your wages before you received it, and was exempt; but, having received it, it is no longer wages, but capital, and is not exempt. You were entitled to enjoy it before you received it, but not afterwards."[606]

The burden on the banks postulated by those cases, of course, is a phantom one. If the identity of the deposits as wages is not clear from the bank's records, the debtor can be required to come forward to establish the exemption. Any accounting difficulties can be overcome by simple tracing rules such as the first in, first out rule (FIFO). Concerning arguments about tracing difficulties, the Colorado Supreme Court said "[t]his reasoning is altogether too subtle and refined to be applied to a statute requiring a liberal construction," and suggested adopting a FIFO approach.[607] In other situations when tracing of funds is important, courts have felt free to adopt tracing rules which will accomplish the necessary purpose.[608]

Kokoszka v. Belford,[609] cited by the courts that have denied exempt status for deposited wages, is not to the contrary. It held that an income tax refund traceable to wages was not exempt under the act. More on point is *Porter v. Aetna Casualty & Surety Co.*,[610] in which the Supreme Court recognized that the Veterans Administration exemption would be lost when the funds were no longer "subject to demand and use as the needs of the veteran for support and maintenance required."

Given the weaknesses in their reasoning, the cases denying the exempt status of deposited wages under the CCPA should not be considered dispositive. It is to be hoped that in the future some court will take a more rational look at this question under the CCPA. At the very least, these decisions should not be inappropriately used to justify expanding their rule to state wage garnishment exemptions.[611] The federal act does not preempt any state law providing for *greater* protection from garnishment than allowed under the CCPA.[612]

606 Rutter v. Shumway, 26 P. 321, 322 (Colo. 1891).

607 *Id.* "It certainly is quite as reasonable to presume that the money first earned was first expended as to suppose the contrary." *Id.*; *see also In re* Coolbaugh, 250 B.R. 162 (Bankr. W.D.N.Y. 2000) (setting forth rules for tracing New York earnings deposited in bank account); Unif. Exemptions Act, 13 U.L.A. § 9(c) (suggesting alternative tracing rules).

608 *See, e.g.*, *In re* Linklater, 48 B.R. 916 (Bankr. D. Nev. 1985); *In re* Conn, 16 B.R. 454 (Bankr. E.D. Tenn. 1982) (using first-in, first-out rule to determine extent of purchase money security interest).

609 417 U.S. 642, 94 S. Ct. 2431, 41 L. Ed. 2d 374 (1974).

610 370 U.S. 159, 82 S. Ct. 1231, 8 L. Ed. 2d 407 (1962).

611 Benson v. Richardson, 537 N.W.2d 748 (Iowa 1995) (federal CCPA did not preempt Iowa's more protective treatment of wages, which remained exempt for ninety days in checking or savings account, so long as reasonably traceable); *see* § 12.4.4, *supra*.

612 15 U.S.C. § 1677(1); *see* § 12.4.4, *supra*.

12.6.7 Liability for Wrongful Seizure of Bank Account Funds

Judgment creditors and banks may be liable for wrongfully seizing funds from the debtor's bank account. For example, in *Cruthis v. Firstar Bank*,[613] the court upheld a jury determination that the bank had illegally converted funds from debtor's checking account. Acting on a letter from debtor's employer requesting the return of payroll deposits, the bank withdrew funds from the debtor's account without notice. While acknowledging that banks generally have a right to set off, the court stated that the bank could not "offset" debts owed by the depositor to third parties. However, the court also found that the bank's lack of good judgment did not rise to the level of willful and wanton conduct such that it would support the jury's punitive damages award.

The more difficult question arises when a bank takes exempt funds from a depositor's account pursuant to writ of execution or other court order served by the judgment creditor. Courts have been reluctant to impose liability on banks to determine independently whether funds in an account are exempt.[614] However, given the relative ease with which banks can now determine the source of electronic deposits and whether the accounts contain only exempt funds, more diligence may be required of them to satisfy an ordinary standard of care.[615] Indeed, a California

613 822 N.E.2d 454 (Ill. App. Ct. 2005).

614 *See, e.g.*, Gorstein v. World Sav. Bank, 110 Fed. Appx. 9 (9th Cir. 2004) (bank has no duty to determine whether portion of funds in account were exempt); Alexander v. Bank of Am., 2007 WL 3046637 (W.D. Mo. Oct. 17, 2007) (bank not liable for six weeks' freeze of SSDI benefits; only remedy for violation of anti-alienation clause is release of garnishment, no intentional infliction of emotional distress when bank acted "promptly" to release garnishment; court assumes that bank could not know funds were exempt until debtor formally claimed exemption); Parker v. Wetch & Abbot, P.L.C., 2006 WL 4846042 (S.D. Iowa July 11, 2006) (freeze of account containing exempt benefits did not violate anti-alienation clause of Social Security Act, state or federal fair debt collection acts, or state consumer protection law).

615 *See* Granger v. Harris, 2007 WL 1213416 (E.D.N.Y. Apr. 17, 2007) (recipient stated section 1983 claim against bank that disbursed funds to creditor, despite knowledge that funds were Social Security funds; state statute imposing sanctions on bank that failed to comply with restraining order was state compulsion sufficient to allege action under color of state law); Mayers v. N.Y. Cmty. Bancorp, Inc., 2005 WL 2105810 (E.D.N.Y. Aug. 31, 2005) (recent changes in technology, for example, electronic direct deposit of Social Security benefits and ease of identifying deposits as exempt funds, require a re-evaluation of New York procedure allowing pre-judgment freeze of bank accounts), *later decision at* 2006 WL 2013734 (E.D.N.Y. July 18, 2006) (denying defendants' motion for interlocutory appeal); Lincoln Fin. Services, Inc. v. Miceli, 17 Misc. 3d 1109(A) (Dist. Ct. 2007) (table) (text available at 2007 WL 2917242) (ordering return of garnished Social Security funds and ordering creditor to include instructions and form in future restraining notices,

statute requires the garnishee bank to do exactly that.[616]

Creditors and creditors' attorneys who wrongfully seize bank account funds may be subject to common law claims such as conversion, negligence, or intentional infliction of emotional distress and to statutory claims for violations of the Fair Debt Collection Practices Act (FDCPA) and state deceptive practices statutes.[617] A recent decision raises the stakes for attorneys submitting affidavits to initiate bank account garnishments. In *Todd v. Weltman*,[618] a collection attorney had obtained a bank account garnishment order by submitting an affidavit stating that "the affiant has a reasonable basis to believe that the [bank] may have property, other than personal earnings, of the judgment debtor that is not exempt under the law of this state or the United States."[619] In fact, according to the complaint, the bank account contained solely Social Security benefits. The plaintiffs alleged that the collection attorney had not conducted a debtor's exam, undertaken discovery, or had any factual basis for believing that the bank account contained nonexempt funds. The Sixth Circuit denied the attorney's immunity claim, thereby allowing the plaintiff to proceed on his claim that the collection attorney violated the FDCPA by using unfair methods and false, deceptive, and misleading representations to collect the debt.

The freezing of bank accounts containing direct-deposited exempt benefits has become a widespread problem, as debt buyers and large-volume collection firms use garnishment notices knowing that few debtors will succeed in objecting to the garnishment of exempt funds. Some also use bank account garnishments as a discovery tool.[620] This practice results in the freezing—often for weeks or months—of many debtors' clearly exempt and desperately needed benefits, in order to net the occasional debtor who has received an inheritance, lottery win, or other nonexempt windfall.

In years past courts generally held that banks do not have a duty to make an independent evaluation of whether a bank account contains exempt funds, for the purpose of refusing a garnishment order. The courts generally found against the recipient, reasoning that the bank had no duty to determine whether a portion of the funds were exempt.[621] However the

---

allowing bank to report and not restrain Social Security funds).

616 Cal. Civ. Proc. Code § 704.080 (West); *see* Chung v. Bank of Am., 2004 WL 1938272 (Cal. Ct. App. 2004) (bank garnishee had duty to verify whether funds were exempt).

617 *See* Todd v. Weltman, 434 F.3d 432 (6th Cir. 2006); Lee v. Javitch, Block, & Rathbone, 522 F. Supp. 2d 945 (S.D. Ohio 2007) (Ohio statute cited in *Todd* has been amended to require only "reasonable cause to believe"; genuine issue of fact as to reasonable cause when large-volume collection firm did crude screening, that is, eliminated debtors aged over age sixty-five with no employer or trade lines listed on credit report; denying summary judgment on FDCPA and UDAP claims); Hogue v. Palisades Collection, Inc., 494 F. Supp. 2d 1043 (S.D Ohio 2007) (debtor stated claims under federal and Iowa fair debt collection acts, Iowa Uniform Consumer Credit Code, tort claim for abuse of process against creditor and its attorney who continued garnishment after being shown affidavit and bank statements showing that account contained only exempt Social Security benefits); Jordan v. Thomas & Thomas, 2007 WL 2838474 (S.D. Ohio Sept. 26, 2007) (FDCPA claim stated; frozen account contained only exempt Social Security funds; genuine issue of fact whether collector's attorneys conducted investigation or had reasonable cause to believe account contained nonexempt funds); Rahaman v. Weber, 2005 WL 89413 (Minn. Ct. App. Jan. 18, 2005) (procedure for claiming exemption, including damages if creditor seized exempt property, did not preclude common law causes of action for conversion against creditor and its attorneys); *see also* Lee v. Javitch, Block, & Rathbone, 2007 WL 3332706 (S.D. Ohio Nov. 7, 2007) (denying summary judgment on FDCPA and UDAP claims; Ohio statute cited in *Todd* has been amended to require only "reasonable cause to believe"; genuine issue of fact as to reasonable cause when large-volume collection firm did crude screening, that is, eliminated debtors aged over sixty-five with no employer or trade lines listed on credit report). *But see* Beler v. Blatt, Hasenmiller, Liebsker, Moore, L.L.C., 480 F.3d 470 (7th Cir. 2007) (law firm that served citation on bank seeking freeze only of nonexempt property not liable when bank froze account containing only SSI); Parker v. Wetch & Abbot, P.L.C., 2006 WL 4846042 (S.D. Iowa July 11, 2006) (freeze of account containing exempt benefits did not violate anti-alienation clause of Social Security Act, state or federal fair debt collection acts, or state consumer protection law); *cf.* Smith v. Levine, 2006 WL 3704622 (Cal. Ct. App. Dec. 18, 2006) (litigation privilege barred abuse of process claim arising from levy on non-debtor's account, and conversion claim arising from refusal to return improperly seized funds).

618 434 F.3d 432 (6th Cir. 2006).

619 Todd v. Weltman, 434 F.3d 432, 435 (6th Cir. 2006); *see also* Rahaman v. Weber, 2005 WL 89413 (Minn. Ct. App. Jan. 19, 2005); Contact Res. Services, L.L.C. v. Gregory, 806 N.Y.S.2d 407 (City Ct. 2005) (protective order requires creditor to include in pre-judgment restraining notice statement that notice ineffective as to accounts containing only exempt SSI and SSD benefits). *But cf.* Lee v. Javitch, Block, & Rathbone, 522 F. Supp. 2d 945 (S.D. Ohio 2007) (Ohio statute cited in *Todd* has been amended to require only "reasonable cause to believe"; genuine issue of fact as to reasonable cause when large-volume collection firm did crude screening, that is, eliminated debtors aged over age sixty-five with no employer or trade lines listed on credit report; denying summary judgment on FDCPA and UDAP claims).

620 Hogue v. Palisades Collection, Inc., 494 F. Supp. 2d 1043 (S.D Ohio 2007) (noting that creditors could use other methods to determine whether nonexempt funds present; allowing debt collection and consumer protection claims to go forward).

621 *See, e.g.*, Gorstein v. World Sav. Bank, 110 Fed. Appx. 9 (9th Cir. 2004); Alexander v. Bank of Am., 2007 WL 3046637 (W.D. Mo. Oct. 17, 2007) (bank not liable for six weeks' freeze of SSDI benefits; only remedy for violation of anti-alienation clause is release of garnishment, no private right of action for damages; no intentional infliction of emotional distress when bank acted "promptly" to release garnishment; court assumes that bank could not know funds were exempt until debtor formally claimed exemption); Parker v. Wetch & Abbot, P.L.C., 2006 WL 4846042 (S.D. Iowa July 11, 2006) (freeze of account containing exempt benefits did not violate anti-alienation clause of Social Security Act, state or federal debt collection acts, or state consumer protection law).

enormous growth in direct deposit of federal benefits makes it easy for a bank to determine that an account contains exempt funds.[622]

Banks, which receive fees for garnishments, often argue that they perceive a risk of liability or sanctions if they disburse frozen funds to debtors. In actuality, it seems highly unlikely that any court would sanction a bank for refusing to freeze funds that are unequivocally exempt under federal law. To the contrary, the collector's attempt to seize funds which are defined as exempt under federal law would be actionable under a variety of state and federal laws.[623] Indeed some states relieve banks of liability for holding exempt funds pursuant to a garnishment summons.[624]

A few states have updated their garnishment statutes or court rules to address the special problems of direct-deposited benefits. Pennsylvania rules of civil procedure state explicitly that service of the writ will not attach funds in an account in which funds are direct-deposited on a recurring basis, and identified as exempt under state or federal law.[625] A debtor's failure to claim the exemption does not result in waiver.[626] California provides that a modest amount of benefits is exempt without making a claim.[627] Connecticut has a similar provision, and specifically confers immunity on a bank that attempts in good faith to comply with the statute.[628] (In both states, however, the debtor must file a claim to prevent the freezing and turnover of any amount in excess of the modest amount protected by the statute.)

In other states, it is necessary to construe the federal and state statutes and rules harmoniously. The state statutes may define exempt property under state law, prescribe the form for the garnishment summons and the bank's response, and establish a procedure for claiming exemptions. Many of these statutes were enacted long before direct deposit, or even exempt benefits under federal law, existed. Advocates in these states should point out that state statutes can not abrogate a federal right, and that the federal law establishing that the funds are exempt is clear. It would seem improper under federal law to interpret a state statute to mean that funds which are exempt under federal law can lose that protected status just because the consumer fails to follow a state-required procedure.[629] Also, the principle of liberal construction and the public policy served by the benefit programs support a construction that allows banks to disburse funds to debtors that are clearly exempt. A few New York courts have ordered creditors to include in their restraining notices, served on banks to initiate a garnishment, a check box to indicate that the bank holds directly deposited exempt funds, and instructions that such funds should not be restrained.[630]

12.7 Creditor's Right to Seize Funds in a Joint Bank Account May Be Limited to Debtor's Contribution

12.7.1 Introduction

It is not unusual for an individual to list another person, perhaps a relative or friend, jointly on a bank account even though only one of them deposits funds into the account. This listing may be done to facilitate care for an aging parent, hold money in trust for a child, or facilitate management of an account while a member of the armed forces is serving overseas. While listing another person on an account may be simpler than setting up a power of attorney or a trust account, the owner of the funds runs that risk that the other person's creditors will seek to garnish the funds.[631]

622 *See* Mayers v. N.Y. Cmty. Bancorp, Inc., 2005 WL 2105810 (E.D.N.Y. Aug. 31, 2005), *later decision at* 2006 WL 2013734 (E.D.N.Y. July 18, 2006) (denying defendants' motion for interlocutory appeal).

623 Hogue v. Palisades Collection, Inc., 494 F. Supp. 2d 1043 (S.D Ohio 2007) (claim stated for unfair and unconscionable collection practices under FDCPA when collector temporarily garnished consumer's bank account, comprised entirely of federally exempt Social Security funds, and prior to garnishment consumer's attorney had sent collector letter stating funds were exempt and included consumer's sworn affidavit stating that "her sole source of income was Social Security and it was the only source of deposits in her bank account").

624 *See, e.g.*, Fla. Stat. §§ 77.06, 77.13; Haw. Rev. Stat. § 65202; Mich. Comp. Laws § 491.628; Ohio Rev. Code Ann. § 2716.15 (West).

625 Pa. R. Civ. P. 3111.1.

626 Pa. R. Civ. P. 3123.

627 Cal. Civ. Proc. Code § 704.080 (West); *see* Chung v. Bank of Am., 2004 WL 1938272 (Cal. Ct. App. Aug. 26, 2004) (bank garnishee implementing this provision has duty to verify whether funds were exempt).

628 Conn. Gen. Stat. § 52-367b.

629 For example, the Social Security Act, at 42 U.S.C. § 407(a), explicitly says:

> The right of any person to any future payment under this subchapter shall not be transferable or assignable, at law or in equity, and *none of the moneys paid* or payable or rights existing under this subchapter shall be subject to execution, levy, attachment, garnishment, or other legal process, or to the operation of any bankruptcy or insolvency law. (*emphasis added*).

630 Lincoln Fin. Services, Inc. v. Miceli, 17 Misc. 3d 1109(A) (Dist. Ct. 2007) (table) (text available at 2007 WL 2917242) (ordering creditor to include instructions about exempt funds in any future restraining notices against this debtor); Contact Res. Services, Inc. v. Gregory, 806 N.Y.S.2d 407 (City Ct. 2005) (protective order as to specific debtor).

631 *See, e.g.*, Branch Banking Trust Co. v. Bartley, 2006 WL 1113632 (Ky. Ct. App. Apr. 28, 2006) (father sued bank that allowed creditor to garnish non-custodial account containing minor son's funds; bank raised genuine issue of fact on counterclaim that father breached fiduciary duty by setting up ordinary joint account and failing to respond to creditor's garnishment notice); Olbres v. Hampton Co-Op. Bank, 698 A.2d 1239 (N.H. 1997) (certificate of deposit held in trust for debtors'

Some protection is provided for members of the armed forces by the Servicemembers Civil Relief Act, which one court has interpreted to require a judgment creditor to file a non-military affidavit for each joint tenant before executing on a joint account.[632]

Most jurisdictions are in agreement that joint accounts are subject to legal process by the creditor of a single co-depositor,[633] but only to the extent of the debtor-depositor's equitable interest in the funds.[634] In determining what portion of the account represents the debtor's interest, most courts have focused on one or more of three factors: (1) the agreement between the bank and the depositors; (2) the co-depositors' respective net contributions to the account; and (3) statutes defining the rights in jointly held bank accounts.[635]

Some states allow married couples to own personal property, including bank accounts, as tenants by the entireties, which shields marital property from attachment for individual debts.[636] In other states couples' joint accounts are vulnerable.[637] Note that a tenancy by the entireties may be severed by, among other things, transfer to a tax planning trust, and will be severed by divorce.[638]

daughter could be set off by parents' creditor, when trust was tentative trust, that is, statute allowed parents to use the money, and daughter had right of survivorship).

632 Palisades Acquisition, L.L.C. v. Ibrahim, 812 N.Y.S.2d 866 (Civ. Ct. 2006).

633 L. C. Di Stasi, Jr., Annotation, *Attachment-Joint Bank Account*, 11 A.L.R.3d 1465, 1468 (1967).

634 *Id.* at 1469; Blue Cross Blue Shield v. Askanzi, 2007 WL 2874012 (E.D. Mich. Sept. 25, 2007) (rebuttable presumption that owners of joint account made equal contributions; rebutted here by tracing origin of funds); Puerto Rican Am. Ins. v. Burgos-Diaz, 2005 WL 1643299 (D. P.R. June 30, 2005) (mag.) (lifting attachment of joint bank account after elder father established that funds were his and that son's name had been added for convenience); *In re* Kleinsmith, 361 B.R. 504 (Bankr. S.D. Iowa 2006) (no setoff when funds belonged to minor daughter; credit union rules required minor's account to be joint with adult); *In re* Cullen, 329 B.R. 52 (Bankr. N.D. Iowa 2005) (son contributed no funds in joint account held by father and son, therefore son had no property interest in account; set off not permitted when no property interest and insufficient evidence that father intended account to be liable for son's debts); *In re* Magness, 276 B.R. 167 (Bankr. N.D. Miss. 2002) (very close fact question whether bank may set off certificates of deposit held in names of debtor and his parents; bank may not set off funds held in trust for another; nature of funds, not name of account is controlling, but key question is whether bank knew of trust or fiduciary relationship); Universal Mktg. & Entertainment v. Bank One, 53 P.3d 191 (Ariz. Ct. App. 2002) (creditor's garnishment of funds that one business wired to debtor's account to use to buy another business was not conversion when funds were in ordinary unrestricted account); Blanton v. Clark, 2002 WL 709958 (Ohio Ct. App. Apr. 19, 2002) (two signature account may be garnished when debtor could withdraw funds on single signature, but court will "look to the realities of ownership"; funds here were traceable to debtor); Sears Roebuck & Co. v. Cosey, 44 P.3d 582 (Okla. Civ. App. 2002) (presumption of joint ownership may be rebutted even if account agreement allows single signature withdrawal; presumption rebutted when non-debtor mother showed she deposited all the funds); *see also* LSF Franchise REO I, L.L.C. v. Emporia Restaurants, Inc., 152 P.3d 34 (Kan. 2007) (creditor may only reach deposited funds if they are actually owned by debtor; account need not be designated as special, but here debtor failed to prove that accounts consisted of funds for payroll taxes held in trust for taxing authorities); Pinkstaff v. Hill, 827 S.W.2d 747 (Mo. Ct. App. 1992) (cause of action for wrongful garnishment/malicious prosecution stated when party alleged that it explained to garnishee bank that garnished account did not belong to named depositor, but to another party, and that after party intervened, garnishment quashed). *But see* Singleton v. Am. Sec. Bank, 849 So. 2d 72 (La. Ct. App. 2003) (allowing bank to treat all funds in account as belonging to depositor unless notified otherwise; oral notice after setoff insufficient); Enright v. Lehmann, 735 N.W.2d 326 (Minn. 2007) (funds belong to depositors in proportion to contribution; no garnishment of funds contributed by non-debtor, unless creditor can show intent to make gift to debtor). *See generally* 10 Am. Jur. 2d *Banks* §§ 672–676 (1997).

635 7 Am. Jur. Proof of Facts 2d § 311 (1975).

636 *See* § 12.5.3.4, *supra*.

637 United States v. Kollintzas, 501 F.3d 796 (7th Cir. 2007) (government enforcing criminal restitution could seize joint account of defendant and non-debtor wife; wife failed to make timely claim for her contributions); United States v. Armstrong, 2005 WL 937857 (N.D. Tex. Apr. 21, 2005) (holding bank account containing non-debtor wife's Social Security benefits to be community property under Texas law and subject to garnishment for husband's criminal fine); Sullivan v. Cent. Bank, 601 So. 2d 985 (Ala. 1992) (allowing bank to set off husband's debt against checking account that wife had before marriage, which was a joint account with survivorship once she added husband's name to it); Nat'l Union Fire Ins. Co. v. Greene, 195 Ariz. 105, 985 P.2d 590 (Ariz. 1999) (judgment creditor, who obtained judgment in a non-community property state, could garnish bank account of debtor and non-debtor spouse, who had moved to Arizona, a community property state, but non-debtor spouse must be given notice and an opportunity to be heard); Grover v. Bay View Bank, 87 Cal. App. 4th 452, 104 Cal. Rptr. 2d 677 (2001) (under California law creditor may levy on account of non-debtor spouse but must submit affidavit regarding marital relationship; when prescribed procedure not followed, bank could not freeze account and was not liable to creditor when spouse withdrew funds); Fleet Bank of Conn. v. Carillo, 691 A.2d 1068 (Conn. 1997) (judgment creditor of one spouse may obtain bank execution, pursuant to Connecticut statute, against bank account of married couple to which both spouses had contributed; either spouse could withdraw entire balance, so by putting her money in joint account non-debtor wife took risk that husband might use account to pay his individual debts); Enright v. Lehmann, 735 N.W.2d 326 (Minn. 2007) (garnishment of funds contributed by non-debtor spouse allowable only if creditor can show intent to make gift to debtor); Nat'l Bank of Ariz. v. Moore, 122 P.3d 1265 (N.M. Ct. App. 2005) (comparing Arizona and New Mexico garnishment law related to community property bank accounts; Arizona forbids collection of individual debt from community property, New Mexico allows debt to be satisfied from debtor-spouse's half interest; applying New Mexico law to New Mexico bank account owned by Arizona couple); *In re* Diafos, 37 P.3d 304 (Wash. Ct. App. 2001) (if debtor's individual property not sufficient, creditor may be able to reach half of community property for pre-marital debt; creditor allowed to challenge pre-marital agreement).

638 *In re* Stanke, 234 B.R. 439 (Bankr. W.D. Mo. 1999) (tenancy

12.7.2 The Contract Approach

Some courts have found the agreement between the bank and the depositors to be determinative. These agreements (and the laws which regulate them) usually provide that, in the absence of customers' instructions to the contrary, each co-depositor has a right to withdraw any or all of the funds at any time. If, it is reasoned, a single co-depositor has an absolute right to withdraw funds without notice to co-depositors, and is able to use those funds for any purpose (including payment of the debt in question), a creditor should be able to "stand in the depositor's shoes," and attach the entire account.[639] Put more succinctly, an "unqualified contractual right to receive property is itself a property right subject to seizure by levy."[640] However, when it was clear to the bank that the debtor had only limited rights to the funds, the creditor could not assert greater rights.[641]

Some courts have refused to admit evidence of depositors' intent which contradicts the printed deposit agree-

was severed when spouses transferred property to tax planning trust, with provisions inconsistent with tenancy by entireties); *In re* LaBorde, 231 B.R. 162 (Bankr. W.D.N.Y. 1999) (under New York law, divorce severed tenancy by entireties; when husband, after divorce, deeded his half-interest in home to former wife, she took subject to judgment liens against him); *In re* Shannis, 229 B.R. 234 (Bankr. M.D. Fla. 1999) (under Florida law, tenancy by entireties is severed by divorce; property is then owned in tenancy in common, and can be reached by creditors of individual spouse). *But cf.* First Fed. Sav. & Loan Ass'n v. Dus, 2003 WL 21545126 (Ohio Ct. App. July 10, 2003) (divorce turned tenancy by entireties into joint tenancy, but lien for husband's individual debt still would not attach, because debt incurred during marriage).

639 United States v. Nat'l Bank of Commerce, 472 U.S. 713, 105 S. Ct. 2919, 86 L. Ed. 2d 565 (1985); Mottaz v. Union Planters Bank (*In re* Dame), 268 B.R. 529 (Bankr. S.D. Ill. 2001) (bank may set off couple's entire account for business debt guaranteed by wife alone, when agreement gave either party right to withdraw entire amount); *In re* King, 214 B.R. 69 (Bankr. D. Conn. 1997) (under Connecticut law either party to joint account may withdraw the entire amount); Winecoff v. Compass Bank, 876 So. 2d 1145 (Ala. Civ. App. 2003) (bank properly set off joint account for inadvertent overpayment to one depositor; account agreement permitted this; unconscionability of agreement may be raised only as defense, not as a claim for relief when depositors were suing bank); A & B Bolt & Supply, Inc. v. Standard Offshore Services, Inc., 858 So. 2d 509 (La. Ct. App. 2003) (Louisiana law of setoff applies to any funds that debtor can withdraw on single signature except individual retirement accounts and certain other tax deferred funds); Singleton v. Am. Sec. Bank, 849 So. 2d 72 (La. Ct. App. 2003) (bank allowed to treat all funds in account as belonging to depositor unless notified otherwise; oral notice after setoff insufficient); Ingram v. Hocking Valley Bank, 708 N.E.2d 232 (Ohio Ct. App. 1997) (under Ohio law, either party to joint account may withdraw entire amount); Couture v. Pawtucket Credit Union, 765 A.2d 831 (R.I. 2001) (setoff allowed for debt of non-contributing son whose name was on elderly parents' account, but setoff provision in contract might be "so inconspicuous, unclear or unconscionable" as to be unenforceable); *see also* Nichols v. Wray, 925 S.W.2d 785 (Ark. 1996) (joint account is "conclusive evidence" of intent to create joint tenancy with survivorship; extrinsic evidence admitted only to show fraud, undue influence, or similar misconduct); Triplett v. Brunt-Ward Chevrolet, Oldsmobile, Pontiac, Cadillac, GMC Trucks, Inc., 812 So. 2d 1061 (Miss. Ct. App. 2001) (bank had no duty to notify non-debtor joint account holder of garnishment; either holder could, however, intervene and assert non-debtor's ownership of the funds); *cf.* United States v. Kollintzas, 501 F.3d 796 (7th Cir. 2007) (when state law permitted one joint depositor to withdraw entire amount, and wife failed to make timely claim for her contributions, government enforcing criminal restitution could seize joint account of defendant and non-debtor wife). *But see* Citizens Fed. Sav. Bank v. Zierolf, 694 N.E.2d 496 (Ohio Ct. App. 1997) (even though bank protection statute allowed either owner to withdraw entire amount, this statute merely protected bank from liability for wrongful act of joint tenant in withdrawing money; bank's right of setoff was limited to amount of money owned by debtor co-tenant, and presumption of equal ownership was rebuttable).

640 St. Louis Union Trust Co. v. United States, 617 F.2d 1293, 1302 (1980); *see also* Sullivan v. Cent. Bank, 601 So. 2d 985 (Ala. 1992); Mancuso v. United Bank, 818 P.2d 732 (Colo. 1991); Fleet Bank of Conn. v. Carillo, 691 A.2d 1068 (Conn. 1997) (by putting her money in joint account, non-debtor wife took risk that husband might use account to pay his individual debts, as either spouse could withdraw entire balance; husband's judgment creditor can reach the account); Masotti v. Bristol Sav. Bank, 653 A.2d 179 (Conn. 1995); Isaac v. First Nat'l Bank, 647 A.2d 1159 (D.C. 1994); Fisher v. State Bank, 643 N.E.2d 811 (Ill. 1994); Barton v. Hudson, 560 S.W.2d 20 (Ky. Ct. App. 1977); Park Enterprises, Inc. v. Track, 233 Minn. 467, 47 N.W.2d 194 (1951); Deposit Guar. Nat'l Bank v. Pete, 583 So. 2d 180 (Miss. 1991) (joint construction account in name of home owner and contractor subject to garnishment by contractor's judgment creditors to extent contractor was able to write checks on the account for his own use and not limited to paying laborers and materialmen); Farrell v. Coulter, 898 S.W.2d 139 (Mo. Ct. App. 1995) (savings account held by judgment debtor as "revocable trust" funded with her money for the benefit of her minor children was available to judgment creditor when debtor had "such extensive power over the deposit as to justify treating [her] as in substance the unrestricted owner of the deposit"; if she had followed the Transfer to Minors Law and created an irrevocable trust, the money would have been beyond the reach of her creditors); Wrede v. Exch. Bank, 531 N.W.2d 523 (Neb. 1995); Paradis v. Greater Providence Deposit Corp., 651 A.2d 738 (R.I. 1994).

641 *In re* Cullen, 329 B.R. 52 (Bankr. N.D. Iowa 2005) (when debtor son added to non-debtor father's account for emergency purposes, presumption of equal ownership rebutted and setoff for son's debts not permitted); *In re* Nunley, 19 B.R. 785 (Bankr. E.D. Tenn. 1982) (joint account not part of bankruptcy estate, clear that mother was to withdraw funds only for forwarding to son in military); *In re* Garretson, 6 B.R. 127 (Bankr. E.D. Tenn. 1980) (joint account not part of bankruptcy estate; husband was without authority to redeem certificate of deposit); Ross v. Thrift Sav. & Loan Co., 60 Ohio App. 3d 94, 573 N.E.2d 788 (1989) (when account was established by spouses to freeze assets pending their divorce and required two signatures for withdrawal, equal ownership not presumed; bank wrongfully paid husband's creditor on a garnishment order when husband could not withdraw funds on his own signature).

ment.[642] Those that allow extrinsic evidence place the burden of proof on the account holders,[643] at least when there is no claim that the account is entireties property.[644]

Many of the federal cases using this approach are tax collection actions which involve a combination of federal and state law. Thus they are clearly distinguishable from cases involving ordinary creditors, which are decided solely on state law. Furthermore, few states follow a "pure" contract approach. Although by virtue of the contract the entire account is *initially* vulnerable, the nondebtor often has the opportunity to recover his or her share of the money from the attaching creditor. The ultimate result is thus not unlike that obtained in jurisdictions favoring a second method—the contribution approach.

12.7.3 The Net Contribution Approach

In other jurisdictions the net contribution of the joint depositors determines each depositor's proportional ownership rights.[645] This rule is often shaped in part by statute. South Dakota,[646] Nebraska,[647] and Colorado,[648] for example, have by statute adopted this "net contribution rule." In some jurisdictions the presumption that the co-tenants have ownership rights proportionate to their contributions can be rebutted by evidence that one co-tenant's contributions were intended as a gift to the other.[649]

---

642 Grass v. Grass, 706 A.2d 1369 (Conn. App. Ct. 1998) (no joint account created when contract required signatures of both co-tenants but only one signed); Isaac v. First Nat'l Bank, 647 A.2d 1159 (D.C. 1994) (contract will govern in the absence of fraud, duress or mutual mistake); Fisher v. State Bank, 643 N.E.2d 811 (Ill. 1994) (right of setoff governed by contract, not by ownership of funds); Union Planters Nat'l Bank v. Jetton, 856 So. 2d 674 (Miss. Ct. App. 2003) (written contract conclusive and parol evidence inadmissible; when recent widow put sons' names on certificates of deposit and written documents created joint tenancy, certificates of deposit could be set off for son's debt); Kopp v. Bank One, 2003 WL 102609 (Ohio Ct. App. Jan. 10, 2003) (deposit agreement conclusive; evidence of intent not admissible; "realities of ownership" relevant only if depositors not given notice of account rules; account funded solely by non-debtor could be set off for car lease debt that existed when account opened); Robinson v. Delfino, 710 A.2d 154 (R.I. 1998) (when the contract is unambiguous court will not consider extrinsic evidence, except for questions of fraud, undue influence, or lack of capacity); Paradis v. Greater Providence Deposit Corp., 651 A.2d 738 (R.I. 1994) (when contract is unambiguous on face extrinsic evidence not admitted); Allen v. Wachtendorf, 962 S.W.2d 279 (Tex. App. 1998) (extrinsic evidence of intent will not be considered when signature card clearly creates a joint account with right of survivorship); *see also* Dubis v. Zarins (*In re* Teranis), 128 F.3d 469 (7th Cir. 1997) (eighty-year-old widow seeking to avoid probate put her daughter's name on deed to condominium which widow bought with her own money and occupied as her residence; when daughter went bankrupt, condominium could be sold by bankruptcy trustee; court refused to consider extrinsic evidence of widow's mistaken belief that she was granting only right of survivorship); *In re* Estate of White, 105 S.W.3d 524 (Mo. Ct. App. 2003) (language of account documents conclusive in inheritance case; testimony as to depositor's intent relevant only if the documents are ambiguous).

643 *In re* Johnson, 232 B.R. 735 (Bankr. C.D. Ill. 1999) (placing another's name on a bank account creates a presumption that a gift was intended, rebuttable only by "clear and convincing" evidence, but hearing allowed on mother's claim that convenience account was intended, even though there was no written agreement as provided for by Illinois statute regarding trust and payable on death accounts); Watlow Elec. Mfg. Co. v. Wrob, 881 S.W.2d 650 (Mo. Ct. App. 1994) (trial court should have focused on question whether debtor older brother was holding funds, a share of his grandfather's estate, for nondebtor minor brother); Sears Roebuck & Co. v. Cosey, 44 P.3d 582 (Okla. Civ. App. 2002) (presumption of joint ownership may be rebutted even if account agreement allows single signature withdrawal); Mitchell v. Mitchell, 756 A.2d 179 (R.I. 2000) (rebuttable presumption that putting name on joint account shows intent to make a gift, but convenience accounts still recognized). *But see* Watlow Elec. Mfg. Co. v. Wrob, 899 S.W.2d 951 (Mo. Ct. App. 1995) (trial court's finding that debtor-brother was "contributor" and therefore owner of all funds in account was supported by sufficient evidence).

644 *See* §§ 12.5.3.4, 12.7.1, *supra*.

645 *In re* Kolodziejczyk & Rotella v. Wing, 689 N.Y.S.2d 825 (App. Div. 1999) (testimony of mother that she owned money in joint account, and had put her son's name on account only to confer right of survivorship, was sufficient to rebut statutory presumption of joint ownership; money was not "available to" son so as to disqualify him for food stamps); Blanton v. Clark, 2002 WL 709958 (Ohio Ct. App. Apr. 19, 2002) (court will "look to the realities of ownership," but funds here were traceable to debtor); *In re* Estate of Mayer, 664 N.E.2d 583 (Ohio Ct. App. 1995) (when contributing co-tenant died, non-contributor owed the estate the sums she had withdrawn for her own use during his lifetime); *In re* Estate of Tosh, 920 P.2d 1230 (Wash. Ct. App. 1996) (when non-contributor withdrew funds during contributor's lifetime, constructive trust created in favor of contributor's estate); Fireman's Fund Ins. Co. v. Northwest Paving & Constr. Co., 891 P.2d 747 (Wash. Ct. App. 1995) (presumption that funds belong to co-tenants in proportion to amounts deposited by each may be rebutted by clear and convincing evidence of a contrary intent at the time the account was opened).

646 S.D. Codified Laws § 29A-6-103.

647 Neb. Rev. Stat. § 30-2722; *see In re* Overton, 169 B.R. 196 (Bankr D. Neb. 1994) (contract and security agreement allowed bank to set off account for debt of non-contributing account holder, but what was left after setoff belonged to sole depositor, not non-contributor's bankruptcy estate; contract governed relations of account holders with bank, but not with one another); Craig v. Hasting State Bank, 221 Neb. 746, 380 N.W.2d 618 (1986); LaBenz v. LaBenz, 575 N.W.2d 161 (Neb. Ct. App. 1998) (funds in joint account belong to parties in proportion to their net contributions unless there is clear and convincing evidence of contributing tenant's intent to make gift to non-contributor; husband's placement of funds, which he owned at time of marriage, in joint account with wife did not create a presumption of a gift).

648 Colo. Rev. Stat. § 15-15-211(2).

649 Hayden v. Gardner, 238 Ark. 351, 381 S.W.2d 752 (Ark. 1964) (garnishment allowed only to extent of debtor's ownership, which can be established by parol evidence of contributions and intent to make a gift); *In re* Estate of Shea, 848 N.E.2d 185 (Ill.

Absent clear evidence of co-depositors' respective ownership rights, courts typically rely on various presumptions. In some jurisdictions, a judgment debtor presumptively holds the entire account, and unless he or she is able to establish otherwise, all monies in the account may be reached.[650] In other jurisdictions, it is presumed that co-depositors share equally in the ownership of the account.[651]

App. Ct. 2006) (estate rebutted presumption that adding joint tenant was a gift when account owner had discussed, with lawyer and others, need for someone to pay bills, and so forth, if he became disabled); Highsmith v. Dep't of Pub. Aid, 803 N.E.2d 652 (Ill. App. Ct. 2004) (burden on non-debtor to show ownership of funds and lack of donative intent; when father funded account for son's education and son did not choose to be educated, this was at most a conditional gift, and could not be reached for son's child support obligation); Enright v. Lehmann, 735 N.W.2d 326 (Minn. 2007) (funds belong to depositors in proportion to contribution; no garnishment of funds contributed by non-debtor, unless creditor can show intent to make gift to debtor); Craig v. Hasting State Bank, 221 Neb. 746, 380 N.W.2d 618, 623 (1986) (Nebraska presumes that there is no intent to make a gift unless there is clear and convincing evidence of gift); Citizens Fed. Sav. Bank v. Zierolf, 694 N.E.2d 496 (Ohio Ct. App. 1997) (bank's right of set off is limited to amount of money owned by debtor; remanding for fact finding on non-debtor father's "realities of ownership defense"); *see also In re* Sciarra, 175 B.R. 2 (Bankr. D. Conn. 1994) (depositor told bank he wanted funds in certificate of deposit to pass to his brother upon depositor's death; brother's name, but not signature, on the signature card; no intent to make *inter vivos* gift, so certificate of deposit could not be set off for brother's debt); *In re* Estate of Delaney, 819 A.2d 968 (D.C. 2003) (inheritance case; District of Columbia law presumes convenience account, notwithstanding language of signature cards, when one party deposits all the funds); Delta Fertilizer, Inc. v. Weaver, 547 So. 2d 800 (Miss. 1989) (no garnishment of account when mother of debtor deposited all of the funds into the account); Food Services Corp. v. Rheam, 145 S.W.3d 484 (Mo. Ct. App. 2004) (non-debtor tenants may show that debtor contributed nothing, and that they did not intend a gift; remanding to determine debtor's contributions and co-tenants' intentions); *cf.* Giove v. Stanko, 882 F.2d 1316 (8th Cir. 1989) (allowing creditor to garnish certificates of deposit held jointly by debtor and children; rejecting claim that debtor made a gift of the funds to the children which would have shielded the funds from garnishment). *But cf.* Vitacco v. Eckberg, 648 N.E.2d 1010 (Ill. App. Ct. 1995) (Illinois presumes that depositor intends a gift to non-contributing co-tenants, but presumption overcome here by clear and convincing evidence of convenience account when elderly depositor sued his co-tenant after he learned she was writing checks to herself instead of paying his bills).

650 Soc'y of Lloyd's v. Collins, 284 F.3d 727 (7th Cir. 2002) (non-debtor wife rebutted presumption of joint ownership when funds came from her rental property and account was used to pay her debts or joint debts; husband's use of account to pay credit card bill on which wife was jointly liable did not make it subject to garnishment); Ackley State Bank v. Thielke, 920 F.2d 521 (8th Cir. 1990); Harp's Food Stores, Inc. v. Res. Group Services, L.L.C., 2006 WL 2056648 (E.D. Okla. July 21, 2006) (non-debtor ex-wife rebutted presumption of debtor's ownership; only funds in account were deposited by husband to satisfy court order requiring payment to wife upon refinancing of marital home); S & S Diversified Services L.L.C. v. Taylor, 897 F. Supp. 549 (D. Wyo. 1995) (when nondebtor claimed that funds in account came from her annuity, she must prove both ownership of the annuity and her intent in depositing funds in joint account); *In re* Johnson, 232 B.R. 735 (Bankr. C.D. Ill. 1999) (placing another's name on a bank account creates a presumption that a gift was intended, rebuttable only by clear and convincing evidence); Maloy v. Stuttgart Mem'l Hosp., 872 S.W.2d 401 (Ark. 1994) (nondebtor, who contributed all funds to account, failed to rebut presumption with testimony that she intended to avoid probate, enable her children to write checks in an emergency, and shield funds from possible nursing home bills); Traders Travel Int'l, Inc. v. Howser, 753 P.2d 244 (Haw. 1988); Highsmith v. Dep't of Pub. Aid, 803 N.E.2d 652 (Ill. App. Ct. 2004) (burden on non-debtor tenant to show ownership of funds); Hurst v. Curtsinger, 2004 WL 102778 (Ky. Ct. App. Jan. 23, 2004) (rebuttable presumption that debtor owns entire account); Brown v. Kentucky Natural Res. & Env't Cabinet, 40 S.W.3d 873 (Ky. Ct. App. 1999) (rebuttable presumption that debtor owned the whole account; trial court should consider net contributions of each spouse, whether non-debtor spouse was sufficiently removed from other spouse's indebtedness, and what were the spouses' expectations about use of the funds); *In re* Estate of Johnson, 777 N.Y.S.2d 212 (App. Div. 2004) (presumption of joint tenancy rebutted here by clear and convincing evidence of convenience account); Tayar v. Tayar, 618 N.Y.S.2d 35 (App. Div. 1994) (opening of joint account creates presumption that each tenant is possessed of whole account; burden of proof on party seeking to rebut); Jiminez v. Brown, 509 S.E.2d 241 (N.C. 1998) (funds in joint account with minor son were available to creditors "to the extent of debtor's contribution to the account"; funds presumed to be those of debtor, burden on debtor and co-tenants to prove ownership); Sears, Roebuck & Co. v. Cosey, 44 P.3d 582 (Okla. Civ. App. 2002) (presumption of joint ownership rebutted when non-debtor mother showed she deposited all the funds); Baker v. Baker, 710 P.2d 129 (Okla. Civ. App. 1985); Mitchell v. Mitchell, 756 A.2d 179 (R.I. 2000) (rebuttable presumption that putting name on joint account shows intent to make a gift, but convenience accounts still recognized); Russ *ex rel.* Schwartz v. Russ, 734 N.W.2d 874 (Wis. 2007) (depositor to joint account presumed to make gift to co-tenants, absent clear and convincing evidence of other intent); *see also* RPS, Inc. v. Travel-Max Int'l, Inc., 823 So. 2d 243 (Fla. Dist. Ct. App. 2002) (judgment creditor entitled to jury trial on question whether funds in bank account belonged to debtor or to third-party claimant); Food Services Corp. v. Rheam, 145 S.W.3d 484 (Mo. Ct. App. 2004) (non-debtor tenants may show that debtor contributed nothing, and that they did not intend a gift; L. C. Di Stasi, Jr., Annotation, *Joint bank account as subject to attachment, garnishment, or execution by creditor of one of the joint depositors*, 11 A.L.R.3d 1465, 1476 (1967).

651 *See* Blue Cross Blue Shield v. Askanzi, 2007 WL 2874012 (E.D. Mich. Sept. 25, 2007) (rebuttable presumption that owners of joint account made equal contributions; rebutted here by tracing origin of funds); Fed. Deposit Ins. Corp. v. Koffman, 849 F. Supp. 176 (N.D.N.Y. 1994) (citing Brezinski v. Brezinski, 463 N.Y.S.2d 975 (App. Div. 1983)); *In re* Cullen, 329 B.R. 52 (Bankr. N.D. Iowa 2005) (under Iowa law rebuttable presumption exists that joint tenants hold property in equal shares); *In re* Kondora, 194 B.R. 202 (Bankr. N.D. Iowa 1996) (joint accounts presumed to be owned in equal shares by the co-tenants; presumption can be rebutted by clear and convincing evidence; funds may be garnished only to the extent of the debtor's interest in the property); *In re* Baugh, 60 B.R. 102 (Bankr. E.D. Ark. 1986) (in absence of evidence of different contributions to an

Some jurisdictions treat joint accounts held by husband and wife as tenancies by the entireties.[652] Because the deposits belong to them as a unit and not as individuals, attachment or garnishment is precluded altogether when only one spouse is a debtor.[653]

12.8 Waiver of Exemptions

12.8.1 General

Many states prohibit waivers of personal exemptions, considering them to be void and against public policy.[654] The states that do allow waiver generally require that it be in writing, signed by the appropriate parties, and acknowledged.[655] In addition, a Federal Trade Commission (FTC) rule prohibits executory waivers of exemptions in consumer credit contracts.[656]

Another way that otherwise exempt property can become subject to collection remedies is if it is collateral for the debt. Most exemption statutes provide exceptions for property given as collateral in a security agreement, making collateral subject to seizure by the secured creditors.[657] Likewise, the FTC prohibition on waivers of exemptions does not restrict the use of otherwise exempt property as collateral, but there are other federal and state restrictions on collateral for consumer credit contracts.[658]

Courts may also find that exemptions do not shelter income from claims that are related to the acquisition of that income. For example, one court held that an attorney who won a retroactive child support award for a client could

account jointly held by spouses, presumed that one-half of account was a gift to each other, making one-half of the account available to the creditor of one of them); Danielson v. Lazoski, 531 N.W.2d 799 (Mich. Ct. App. 1995); Univ. of Mont. v. Coe, 704 P.2d 1029 (Mont. 1985); Sicari v. First Fid. Bank, 668 N.Y.S.2d 406 (App. Div. 1998) (parties to joint checking account are presumed to be entitled to equal shares); Citibank (S.D) v. Five Star Bank, 824 N.Y.S.2d 761 (Sup. Ct. 2006) (couple failed to rebut presumption of fifty-fifty ownership of account into which both paychecks were deposited, used to pay household and individual bills); Velocity Investments L.L.C./Citibank v. Astoria Fed. Sav. & Loan, 824 N.Y.S.2d 767 (Dist. Ct. 2006) (genuine issue of fact as to ownership of funds in account titled in debtor daughter and non-debtor father; presumption of fifty-fifty ownership, but father testified that daughter's name was on account only so she could write checks for invalid mother if he was "not around"); Vetter v. Hampton, 375 N.E.2d 804 (Ohio 1978); Citizens Fed. Sav. Bank v. Zierolf, 694 N.E.2d 496 (Ohio Ct. App. 1997) (presumption of equal ownership was rebuttable); *see also* Ford Motor Credit Co. v. Astoria Fed., 189 Misc. 2d 475, 733 N.Y.S.2d 583 (Dist. Ct. 2001) (non-debtor co-tenant's failure to respond to notice of garnishment of account was sufficient to rebut presumption that non-debtor owned fifty percent of account, so creditor could seize entire account); L. C. Di Stasi, Jr., Annotation, *Joint bank account as subject to attachment, garnishment, or execution by creditor of one of the joint depositors*, 11 A.L.R.3d 1465, 1477 (1967).

652 *See* § 12.5.3.4, *supra*.

653 *See* L. C. Di Stasi, Jr., Annotation, *Joint bank account as subject to attachment, garnishment, or execution by creditor of one of the joint depositors*, 11 A.L.R.3d 1465, 1484 (1967); § 12.7.1, *supra*.

654 *See, e.g.*, United States v. Neff, 2007 WL 776532 (D.N.D. Mar. 12, 2007) (North Dakota forbids waiver of homestead exemption for chattel debt); *In re* Box, 340 B.R. 782 (S.D. Tex. 2006) (lien against homestead invalid when home equity lender did not strictly comply with constitutional requirements, despite borrowers' acknowledgment that requirements were satisfied); Gonzalez v. Ameriquest Mortgage, 2005 WL 3333259 (W.D. Tex. Dec. 8, 2005) (debtor's statement that property not homestead insufficient to waive homestead protection when debtor owned only one residential property and lived there); Tuxis-Ohr's Fuel, Inc. v. Trio Marketers Inc., 2005 WL 3047266 (Conn. Super. Ct. Oct. 26, 2005) (waiver of homestead in contract, here personal guarantee of a business debt, void as against public policy); DeMayo v. Chames, 972 So. 2d 850 (Fla. 2007) (waiver of homestead in an unsecured agreement is unenforceable); Estate of Montague v. Nat'l Loan Investors, Ltd. P'ship, 70 S.W.3d 242 (Tex. App. 2001) (invalidating debtor's statement that land was not their homestead); *see also In re* Morris, 2007 WL 2120177 (Bankr. N.D. Ala. July 18, 2007) (Alabama statute forbidding waiver of exemptions refers to specific exemptions provided by statute; does not exempt entire value of truck when statute caps exemption at $3000). *But see* Dominguez v. Castaneda, 163 S.W.3d 318 (Tex. App. 2005) (borrower who owned two residential properties bound by warranty that one parcel not homestead).

655 Chelsea State Bank v. Wagner (*In re* Wagner), 259 B.R. 694 (B.A.P. 8th Cir. 2001) (mortgages unenforceable for noncompliance with Iowa requirement that waiver of homestead exemption for agricultural land or buildings be in ten-point boldface type and contain prescribed language); Fix v. First State Bank of Roscoe, 359 B.R. 755 (D.S.D. 2007) (waiver void as against public policy; waivers permitted but must be "so clear that there can be no question concerning the intended effect"; not shown here when settlement agreement for unrelated matter did not mention homestead); *In re* Cadengo, 370 B.R. 681 (Bankr. S.D. Tex. 2007) (homestead waivers strictly limited in Texas; waiver here was ineffective); *In re* Hebert, 301 B.R. 19 (Bankr. N.D. Iowa 2003) (statement in personal guarantee of corporate debt that guarantors "waive the benefit of all homestead laws" not sufficient to comply with Iowa law; homestead waiver must specifically describe piece of property to which it applies); Republic Leasing Corp. v. Farnes, 2000 Minn. App. LEXIS 390 (Minn. Ct. App. Apr. 25, 2000) (homestead exemption may be waived only by "an act which evidences an unequivocal intention to do so"; not shown when settlement agreement required defendants to provide "adequate security" for note, but did not define adequate security); Red River State Bank v. Reierson, 533 N.W.2d 683 (N.D. 1995) (similar North Dakota statute); *see also In re* Peterson, 620 N.W.2d 29 (Minn. 2000) (lawyer suspended from practice for filing attorney's lien against client's homestead without signed waiver of homestead exemption, and attempting to forge waiver while being investigated for ethics violation).

656 16 C.F.R. § 444.2(a)(2); *see* § 12.8.2, *infra*.

657 *See* § 12.5.2.8, *supra*. *But see* United States v. Neff, 2007 WL 776532 (D.N.D. Mar. 12, 2007) (North Dakota forbids waiver of homestead exemption for chattel debt).

658 *See* § 12.8.2, *infra*; *see also* National Consumer Law Center, Repossessions Ch. 3 (6th ed. 2005 and Supp.).

execute upon the award to collect his fee, even though state statutes generally exempted child support from execution.[659]

In some states the debtor may also waive exemptions by failing to assert them, or by failing to assert them properly. Procedural restrictions of this sort should be narrowly construed so that financially strained debtors can take full advantage of exemptions.[660]

12.8.2 FTC Prohibition of Waiver of Exemptions

The FTC's Credit Practices Rule prohibits lenders and retail installment sellers from including waiver of exemption clauses in their consumer contracts.[661] The rule prohibits a clause that: "[c]onstitutes or contains an executory waiver or a limitation of exemption from attachment, execution, or other process on real or personal property held, owned by, or due to the consumer." There is an exception that makes it clear that this provision does not prohibit security interests in exempt property, but because the Credit Practices Rule also prohibits most non-purchase money security interests in household goods[662] this exception will be of little effect.

While there is no private cause of action for violation of an FTC Rule,[663] inclusion of a clause that the FTC has declared unfair will be a violation of most states' unfair and deceptive acts and practices (UDAP) statutes, as long as the creditor is covered by the statute.[664] Such a clause is also unenforceable.[665]

The West Virginia Supreme Court of Appeals found deceptive a contractual provision waiving the consumer's rights to exempt certain property from seizure. The waiver was only "to the extent permitted by law," and West Virginia prohibits such a waiver. The creditor argued that the contractual provision was not deceptive because the provision had no effect as it was not "permitted by law." But the court found the provision misleading and likely to cause confusion or misunderstanding.[666]

12.9 Interstate Collection Efforts

12.9.1 General

In general, a court can execute upon assets only if they are located within the reach of its service of process.[667] Thus the first question to examine in any interstate execution is where the asset at issue is located.

It is easy to tell where a tangible asset such as land or a vehicle is located, whether within the jurisdiction of the court issuing the judgment or outside that court's jurisdiction. For those types of tangible assets, the creditor must go to the state where the asset is located and institute execution there. If the asset is located in a state other than the one that rendered the judgment, the creditor can use the procedures of the Uniform Enforcement of Foreign Judgments Act, discussed in § 12.9.2, *infra*.

The question becomes knotty, though, when an intangible asset such as a bank account or the right to payment of wages is at issue.[668] These two cases are examined in §§ 12.9.3 and 12.9.4, *infra*.

12.9.2 Use of One State's Courts to Enforce Another State's Judgment

As noted in the previous section, to reach out-of-state assets the creditor must apply to a court in that other state. The United States Constitution requires the court in that second state to give full faith and credit to the judgment issued by the first state.[669]

---

659 *In re* Wageman, 25 Kan. App. 2d 682, 968 P.2d 1114 (1998). *But see* Binder & Binder, Prof'l Corp. v. Barnhart, 281 F. Supp. 2d 574 (E.D.N.Y. 2003) (anti-alienation clause of Social Security Act prevents the attachment of attorney's charging lien to SSI benefits recovered in proceeding in which attorney represented claimant), *vacated on other grounds*, 399 F.3d 128 (2d Cir. 2005) (jurisdictional grounds).

660 *In re* Skinner, 2001 WL 1699660 (Bankr. M.D.N.C. Aug. 7, 2001) (minor procedural omission by debtor is not permanent waiver of exemptions); Household Fin. Corp. v. Ellis, 419 S.E.2d 592 (N.C. Ct. App. 1992) (waiver of exemptions by failing to assert them at time of first execution does not prevent debtor from asserting them against subsequent executions; statutory requirement that constitutional exemption be asserted prior to payment of proceeds of sale to creditor is unconstitutional), *aff'd*, 429 S.E.2d 716 (N.C. 1993) (per curiam); *see* § 12.2.1, *supra*.

661 16 C.F.R. § 444.2(a)(2).

The Rule and the accompanying Statement of Basis and Purpose may be found at 49 Fed. Reg. 7740 (Mar. 1, 1984). *See generally* National Consumer Law Center, Unfair and Deceptive Acts and Practices §§ 5.1.1.2, 5.1.1.3, Appx. B.1 (6th ed. 2004 and Supp.).

662 16 C.F.R. § 444.2(a)(4).

663 *See* National Consumer Law Center, Unfair and Deceptive Acts and Practices § 9.1 (6th ed. 2004 and Supp.).

664 *See* National Consumer Law Center, Fair Debt Collection §§ 8.2.2, 11.3 (6th ed. 2008).

665 Free Bridge Auto Sales v. Fitzgerald, 48 Va. Cir. 1 (1999); F & S Fin. v. Jordan, 48 Va. Cir. 580 (1997).

666 Orlando v. Fin. One, 369 S.E.2d 882 (W. Va. 1988).

667 *See* Baker v. Bennett, 644 So. 2d 901 (Ala. 1994) (Alabama courts do not have jurisdiction to issue garnishment orders to reach assets outside its territorial jurisdiction); Desert Wide Cabling & Installation v. Wells Fargo & Co., 958 P.2d 457 (Ariz. Ct. App. 1998) (Arizona writ of garnishment can not be served on California bank). *See generally* Gary Clifford Korn, *Attachment of Bank Deposits in the Electronic Age: The Doctrine of Digitrex*, 100 Banking L.J. 607 (Aug.–Sept. 1983).

668 *Cf.* Koh v. Inno-Pacific Holdings, Ltd., 54 P.3d 1270 (Wash. Ct. App. 2002) (corporation's interest in a partnership is located where the partnership is formally organized).

669 U.S. Const., art. IV, § 1; *see also* Livingston v. Naylor, 920 A.2d 34 (Md. Ct. Spec. App. 2007).

The full faith and credit requirement does not mean that the second state must adopt the practices of the first state regarding the time, manner, and mechanisms for enforcing judgments: "Enforcement measures do not travel with the sister state judgment . . . ; such effects remain subject to the evenhanded control of forum law."[670] So, for example, a creditor that is enforcing a California judgment through the Indiana courts can make use of Indiana collection remedies, not those available in California. If Indiana disallows certain remedies that would be available in California, or gives debtors different protections, the creditor is bound by the Indiana rules.[671]

As a matter of constitutional law, a state's exercise of *in rem* or *in personam* jurisdiction must comport with fair play and substantial justice.[672] Courts have, however, held that this rule does not require a creditor to obtain *in personam* jurisdiction over the debtor in order to enforce a judgment in a state other than the one that issued it. Instead, the presence of the debtor's asset in that second state is sufficient to support jurisdiction.[673]

To regulate the second state's enforcement of the first state's judgment, most states adopt the Uniform Enforcement of Foreign Judgments Act.[674] This Act provides a procedure for registering a judgment in another jurisdiction and initiating execution proceedings on assets located there. The creditor may also have the right to use older procedures such as filing a new suit on the judgment in the second state.

Under the uniform act, the judgment creditor must first file an authenticated copy of the judgment with a court in the state where enforcement is sought.[675] The creditor must also file an affidavit setting forth the name and last known address of the judgment debtor and the judgment creditor.[676] The court is then required to send a prompt notice of the filing of the judgment to the judgment debtor at the address given.[677]

Upon accomplishment of these steps, the creditor can use the same enforcement procedures as would be available for a judgment entered by the courts in that state.[678] However, the uniform law allows the state to specify a limited time period during which the state's enforcement procedures would be available.[679]

If the debtor appeals the underlying judgment or obtains a stay from the court that issued it, the stay applies in the enforcing state as well.[680] In addition, the debtor can seek a stay or an order reopening or vacating the judgment from the court in the enforcing state, following the same procedures that would apply to a judgment issued by that state's courts.[681]

12.9.3 Bank Accounts

While it is clear that to execute upon tangible property, such as land or a vehicle, the creditor must use the courts of

670 Baker v. Gen. Motors Corp., 522 U.S. 222, 235, 118 S. Ct. 657, 139 L. Ed. 2d 580 (1998); *see also* Restatement (Second) of Conflict of Laws § 99 (1971) ("the local law of the forum determines the method by which a judgment of another state is enforced").

671 Mahl v. Aaron, 809 N.E.2d 953 (Ind. Ct. App. 2004).

672 Shaffer v. Heitner, 433 U.S. 186, 207, 97 S. Ct. 2569, 53 L. Ed. 2d 683 (1977); Livingston v. Naylor, 920 A.2d 34, 53 (Md. Ct. Spec. App. 2007); *see also* Goodyear Tire & Rubber Co. v. Ruby, 540 A.2d 482 (Md. 1988) (Maryland court can enforce its judgment by issuing order requiring out-of-state corporation that is doing business in Maryland to garnish Texas employee's wages only if the corporation has sufficient minimum contacts with Maryland); Bianco v. Concepts "100," Inc., 436 A.2d 206 (Pa. Super. Ct. 1981) (Pennsylvania court may issue garnishment against out-of-state insurance company only if the company has sufficient minimum contacts with Pennsylvania to allow personal jurisdiction).

673 Huggins v. Deinhard, 654 P.2d 32 (Ariz. Ct. App. 1982) (Arizona court may enforce registered California judgment against debtor's Arizona bank account without acquiring personal jurisdiction over the debtor); Bank of Babylon v. Quirk, 472 A.2d 21 (Conn. 1984); Tabet v. Tabet, 644 So. 2d 557 (Fla. Dist. Ct. App. 1994); Williamson v. Williamson, 275 S.E.2d 42 (Ga. 1981) (personal jurisdiction over debtor unnecessary as long as debtor has property in the state that can be executed upon); Hexter v. Hexter, 386 N.E.2d 1006 (Ind. Ct. App. 1979); Lenchyshyn v. Pelko Elec., Inc., 281 A.D.2d 42, 723 N.Y.S.2d 285 (2001); Fraser v. Littlejohn, 386 S.E.2d 230, 233 (N.C. Ct. App. 1989); Berger v. Berger, 417 A.2d 921 (Vt. 1980); Koh v. Inno-Pacific Holdings, Ltd., 54 P.3d 1270, 1273 (Wash. Ct. App. 2002); *see also* Shaffer v. Heitner, 433 U.S. 186, 211 n.36, 97 S. Ct. 2569, 53 L. Ed. 2d 683 (1977) (dictum) ("Once it has been determined by a court of competent jurisdiction that the defendant is a debtor of the plaintiff, there would seem to be no unfairness in allowing an action to realize on that debt in a State where the defendant has property, whether or not that State would have jurisdiction to determine the existence of the debt as an original matter"); Restatement (Second) of Conflict of Laws § 60 (1971) (state has power to exercise judicial jurisdiction to affect interests in a chattel in the state even if owner is not within court's personal jurisdiction); *cf.* Electrolines, Inc. v. Prudential Assurance Co., Ltd., 677 N.W.2d 874, 885 (Mich. Ct. App. 2003) (court can not enforce foreign judgment unless it has jurisdiction over the defendant or the defendant's property).

674 According to the website of the National Conference of Commissioners on Uniform State Laws, www.nccusl.org, the District of Columbia, Puerto Rico, the U.S. Virgin Islands, and all states except California, Indiana, Massachusetts, and Vermont have adopted the uniform law.

675 Unif. Enforcement of Foreign Judgments Act (UEFJA) § 2.

676 *Id.* § 3.

677 *Id.* § 3(b).

However, the Act provides that if the creditor mails notice to the judgment debtor and files proof of mailing with the court, any failure of the court to mail the notice does not affect the enforcement proceedings. *Cf.* Doyle v. Schultz, 97 F. Supp. 2d 763 (W.D. La. 2000) (judgment creditor and collection firm may be liable under 42 U.S.C. § 1983 for invoking state procedures that allowed issuance of writ for constructive seizure of home without judicial approval or notice and opportunity for hearing based on out-of-state judgment that was not yet final).

678 Unif. Enforcement of Foreign Judgments Act (UEFJA) § 2.

679 *Id.* § 3(c).

680 *Id.* § 4.

681 *Id.* § 2.

the state where the property is located, the issue becomes more complicated with a bank account. Creditors may argue that the location of the branch bank where the debtor maintains the bank account is not dispositive. Instead, they may argue that execution can issue in any state where any branch or office of the debtor's bank is located, and that the bank then must restrain all the debtor's accounts even if they are located in other states (or countries).

A number of decisions reject this view and treat bank accounts as located in the specific branch bank where the debtor maintains the account. These courts require a creditor that seeks to garnish a debtor's bank account to serve the garnishment on the branch bank where the debtor maintains the account, not on a different office or branch of the bank, particularly one located in a different jurisdiction.[682] Thus, if a consumer maintains an account in a branch bank outside of the state where the court issued the judgment, the collector will have to go to that other state to enforce the judgment on that bank account. It can not go to a branch of the same bank that is located in the state where the judgment was issued to seize bank account proceeds.

682 Det Bergenske Dampskibsselskab v. Sabre Shipping Corp., 341 F.2d 50 (2d Cir. 1965) (each bank branch is a separate business entity, and service on a main office or branch does not restrain an account maintained at a separate branch); Shinto Shipping Co. v. Fibrex & Shipping Co., 425 F. Supp. 1088 (N.D. Cal. 1976) (enforcing California statute that garnishment is effective only as to accounts maintained in branch bank where garnishment order is served), *aff'd on other grounds*, 572 F.2d 1328 (9th Cir. 1978); Nat'l Shipping & Trading Corp. v. Weeks Stevedoring Co., 252 F. Supp. 275 (S.D.N.Y. 1966) (attachment must be served on branch where account is maintained); McCloskey v. Chase Manhattan Bank, 183 N.E.2d 227 (N.Y. 1962) (levy upon bank in New York is ineffective to reach deposits maintained in Oregon branch); Nat'l Union Fire Ins. Co. v. Advanced Employment Concepts, Inc., 269 A.D.2d 101, 703 N.Y.S.2d 3 (2000) (service of execution upon bank office in one jurisdiction is insufficient to reach account in branch bank in different jurisdiction); *see also* Baker v. Bennett, 644 So. 2d 901 (Ala. 1994) (Alabama court can not reach judgment debtor's assets in New York brokerage account by serving brokerage's Alabama office; court can not obtain jurisdiction of out-of-state property by issuing writ to bailee over whom the court has personal jurisdiction); *cf.* Ellis v. Barclays Bank PLC-Miami Agency, 594 So. 2d 826 (Fla. Dist. Ct. App. 1992) (garnishment served on Miami branch of international bank can not reach deposits held in other countries; bank had responded as to all its domestic branches, but court does not comment on whether this was proper or required). *But see* Digitrex, Inc. v. Johnson, 491 F. Supp. 66 (S.D.N.Y. 1980) (terming existing rule "obsolete" in light of banks' use of high-speed computers; service of post-judgment restraining notice on main bank office is effective to restrain an account maintained at a branch; note that Nat'l Union Fire Ins. Co. v. Advanced Employment Concepts, Inc., 269 A.D.2d 101, 703 N.Y.S.2d 3 (2000) essentially limits this decision to its facts); Wilton Enter., Inc. v. Cook's Pantry, Inc., 230 N.J. Super. 126, 552 A.2d 1031 (Super. Ct. App. Div. 1988) (levy served on bank branch is effective as to deposit maintained in another branch, when bank had practice of notifying appropriate branch by telephone, even though it did not follow that practice in this case).

This position is consistent with Article 4 of the Uniform Commercial Code, which provides that "[a] branch or separate office of a bank is a separate bank for the purpose of computing the time within which and determining the place at or to which action may be taken or notices or orders shall be given under this Article and under Article 3." A few jurisdictions also have statutes specifying the effect of service of an execution upon a branch bank.[683]

In fact, not only debtors but also banks would be harmed by any other rule. If service of an execution order at one branch restrained any accounts at any other branches, the bank would be liable to the creditor if it cashed any checks or allowed any withdrawals from any accounts at any branches the moment after the execution was served. Even with computer networks, a bank branch can not be expected to implement a real-time system-wide freeze on the debtor's accounts in all branches.[684]

12.9.4 Wages

Earned but unpaid wages, like bank accounts, are not clearly "located" in a specific state like tangible property is. The question then is whether a court can issue a wage garnishment order that affects wages the consumer earns in a different state.

A court in one state will not have jurisdiction over an employer in another state, and therefore can not issue a garnishment order to an out-of-state employer. However, the creditor may argue that the court can garnish wages earned out of state by serving a garnishment order on an in-state facility of the employer. This argument is based on the theory that the wages owed to the consumer reside wherever the employer has a presence, and can be reached anywhere that the employer can be served. For example, a collector, after obtaining a judgment in Missouri, might seek to garnish the consumer's wages earned at an Indiana Walmart store by serving the order on a Walmart store in Missouri.

This view would dilute "fair play and substantial justice" to meaninglessness, as wages earned for a nationwide corporation in one state could be garnished in any of the forty-nine other states.[685] For example, the Georgia Supreme Court rejected a judgment creditor's attempt to gar-

683 Idaho Code Ann. § 8-507 (general rule is that service of execution on bank office only restrains account maintained in that office, but bank may designate a particular office to receive executions, in which case an execution served on that office restrains all accounts at any branches); Wash. Rev. Code § 6.27.080 (writ naming financial institution attaches deposits in that institution).

684 *See* Gary Clifford Korn, *Attachment of Bank Deposits in the Electronic Age: The Doctrine of Digitrex*, 100 Banking L.J. 607 (Aug.–Sept. 1983) (discussing problems that banks would face).

685 *See* Robert Laurence, *Out of State Garnishments: Work-in-Progress, Offered in Tribute to Dr. Robert A. Leflar*, 50 Ark. L. Rev. 415, 418 (1997) ("this rule is an out-moded doctrine that does not survive modern constitutional analysis").

nish a California debtor's Army pay in Georgia.[686] The court rejected the creditor's argument that, because the employer had a presence in Georgia, Georgia courts could order it to turn over wages regardless of where they were earned.

Likewise, a Maryland court has rejected this view, holding that Maryland courts can enforce foreign judgments only against wages earned in Maryland. Thus a garnishment order issued against a corporation headquartered in Maryland is effective as to an employee's wages earned in Maryland, but not as to wages earned in other states.[687] A law review article points out that any other rule would invite creditors to forum shop to find the most remote jurisdiction with the most liberal garnishment laws and the most grudging exemption laws.[688]

Some cases, however, do allow wages earned out of state to be garnished by serving a garnishment order on an in-state facility of the debtor's employer. These courts hold that such a step is permissible if the garnishment order is issued by the court that issued the original judgment and acquired personal jurisdiction over the debtor at that time.[689] For example, a Texas court held that a Florida divorce court could enforce its alimony order by serving a wage garnishment order on a Florida office of the judgment debtor's employer, even though the debtor had moved to Texas and was working there.[690] The court stressed that the judgment for alimony and the garnishment order were issued by the same court that had rendered the initial judgment against the debtor before he moved to Texas, and that the debtor conceded that the Florida judgment was valid and entitled to full faith and credit. The result might have been different if the Florida court had not acquired *in personam* jurisdiction over the debtor in the first instance.

12.10 Imprisonment for Debt

Imprisonment for debt is prohibited in all or nearly all the states and the District of Columbia.[691] These prohibitions

686 Williamson v. Williamson, 275 S.E.2d 42 (Ga. 1981).

687 Livingston v. Naylor, 920 A.2d 34, 53 (Md. Ct. Spec. App. 2007).

688 Robert Laurence, *Out of State Garnishments: Work-in-Progress, Offered in Tribute to Dr. Robert A. Leflar*, 50 Ark. L. Rev. 415, 421 (1997).

689 *See, e.g.*, Smith v. Lorillard, Inc., 945 F.2d 745 (4th Cir. 1991) (Kentucky court that rendered judgment against Kentucky debtor may serve garnishment order on debtor's employer, who does business in Kentucky, even though debtor has moved to North Carolina and now works there); State *ex rel.* Dep't of Revenue v. Control Data Corp., 713 P.2d 30 (Or. 1986) (debtor had enough contacts with Oregon to allow Oregon court to render judgment against him, and then it could issue a wage garnishment order to his employer's in-state office, even though he now worked for that employer in a different state).

690 Knighton v. Int'l Bus. Mach. Corp., 856 S.W.2d 206 (Tex. App. 1993).

691 *ALABAMA*: Ala. Const. art. I, § 20.
ALASKA: Alaska Const. art. I, § 17.
ARIZONA: Ariz. Const. art. II, § 18.
ARKANSAS: Ark. Const. art. II, § 16.
CALIFORNIA: Cal. Const. art. I, § 10.
CONNECTICUT: It appears that Connecticut abolished imprisonment for debt by repealing a statute that had formerly provided for body attachment. *See* Lee v. BSB Greenwich Mortgage Ltd. P'ship, 2007 WL 2743435, at *5 (Conn. Super. Ct. Aug. 31, 2007).
COLORADO: Colo. Const. art. II, § 12.
DELAWARE: Del. Code Ann. tit. 10, § 5052.
DISTRICT OF COLUMBIA: D.C. Code § 15-320(c).
FLORIDA: Fla. Const. art I § 11.
GEORGIA: Ga. Const. art. I, § 1, ¶ XXIII.
HAWAII: Haw. Const. art. I, § 19.
IDAHO: Idaho Const. art. I, § 15.
ILLINOIS: Ill. Const. art. I, § 14.
INDIANA: Ind. Const. art. I, § 22.
IOWA: Iowa Const. art. I, § 19.
KANSAS: Kan. Const. Bill of Rights § 16.
KENTUCKY: Ky. Const. Bill of Rights § 18.
LOUISIANA: La. Rev. Stat. Ann. § 13:4281 (abolishing writ of *capias ad satisfaciendum*).
MAINE: Me. Rev. Stat. Ann. tit. 14, § 3701.
MARYLAND: Md. Const. art. III, § 38.
MASSACHUSSETTS: Mass. Gen. Laws ch. 224, § 6 (prohibiting arrest on execution in civil action unless creditor proves that debtor intends to leave the state).
MICHIGAN: Mich. Const. art. I, § 21.
MINNESOTA: Minn. Const. art. I, § 12.
MISSISSIPPI: Miss. Const. art. III, § 30.
MISSOURI: Mo. Const. art. I, § 11.
MONTANA: Mont. Const. art. II, § 27.
NEBRASKA: Neb. Const. art. I, § 20.
NEVADA: Nev. Const. art. I, § 14.
NEW HAMPSHIRE: Vt. Nat'l Bank v. Taylor, 445 A.2d 1122 (N.H. 1982) (noting that New Hampshire repealed the last of its statutes authorizing imprisonment for debt in 1971, although writs of *capias* can still be used in some circumstances).
NEW JERSEY: N.J. Const. art. I, § 13
NEW MEXICO: N.M. Const. art. II, § 21.
NEW YORK: N.Y. Debt. & Cred. Law § 109 (McKinney) (providing procedure for insolvent debtor to petition for exemption from arrest and imprisonment).
NORTH CAROLINA: N.C. Const. art. I, § 28.
NORTH DAKOTA: N.D. Const. art. I, § 15.
OHIO: Ohio Const. art. I, § 15.
OKLAHOMA: Okla. Const. art. II, § 13.
OREGON: Or. Const. art. I, § 19.
PENNSYLVANIA: 42 Pa. Con. Stat. § 5108.
RHODE ISLAND: R.I. Const. art. I, § 11.
SOUTH CAROLINA: S.C. Const. art. I, § 19.
SOUTH DAKOTA: S.D. Const. art. VI, § 15.
TENNESSEE: Tenn. Const. art. I, § 18.
TEXAS: Tex. Const. art. I, § 18.
UTAH: Utah Const. art. I, § 16.
VERMONT: Vt. Const. ch. II, § 40.
VIRGINIA: Makarov v. Commonwealth, 228 S.E.2d 573 (Va. 1976) (although there is no state constitutional prohibition, "[I]t is nevertheless established in this state that a person may not be imprisoned, absent fraud, for mere failure to pay a debt arising from contract or for mere failure to pay a judgment for a debt founded on contract. . . . [I]mprisonment of poor debtors offends fundamental principles of justice in today's ordered society.").

represent a break with the rule that had prevailed in England until 1838, which allowed body attachment or a writ of *capias ad satisfaciendum* as a means of enforcing a civil judgment for a debt.[692]

Most states include a prohibition against imprisonment for debt in their state constitutions. In several states there is a statutory rather than a constitutional prohibition.[693] In a few states, the prohibition is not found in any statute or constitutional provision but is recognized by judicial decisions, sometimes based on the repeal of a statute that formerly authorized the practice.[694] The United States Constitution does not include a parallel provision, but a federal statute prohibits federal courts from ordering imprisonment for debt in states where it is prohibited.[695] In interpreting a state constitutional prohibition against imprisonment for debt, every doubt must be resolved in favor of the citizen.[696]

Many of the state prohibitions make an exception for fraud[697] or tort.[698] Some states allow imprisonment for debt when the debtor is about to leave the jurisdiction,[699] or when the debtor "refuses to deliver up his estate for the benefit of his creditors."[700] A number of states restrict the protection to civil actions.[701] It is common for states to interpret their prohibitions not to prohibit imprisonment for nonpayment of family support obligations[702] and fines,[703] and in some states these are explicit exceptions.[704]

Many states apply their prohibition against imprisonment for debt to disallow incarceration on dishonored check charges unless there is a showing that the defendant acted with criminal intent.[705] Only when criminal intent is established will the case fall within the exception for fraud,[706] although intent may be presumed in some states by the failure to pay the check after a notice period expires.[707]

Despite the near universal prohibitions against imprisonment for debt, there may be exceptions in some of the states that amount to the same thing. A critical question is whether a court has the power to order a debtor to make payments on a debt, or apply specific property to the debt, and then hold the debtor in contempt for failing to do so.[708] Some courts hold that this stratagem does not result in imprisonment for debt, reasoning that the debtor is not being punished for owing the debt, but for violating the court order.[709] Typically

WASHINGTON: Wash. Const. art. I, § 17.

WEST VIRGINIA: *See* Boarman v. Boarman, 556 S.E.2d 800, 804 (W. Va. 2001) ("West Virginia has abandoned the Dickensian notion of 'debtor's prison.' ").

WISCONSIN: Wis. Const. art. I, § 16.

WYOMING: Wyo. Const. art. I, § 5.

692 Becky A Vogt, *State v. Allison: Imprisonment for Debt in South Dakota*, 46 S.D. L. Rev. 334, 343 (2001) (describing history of imprisonment for debt).

693 *See, e.g.*, La. Rev. Stat. Ann. § 13:4281 (abolishing writ of *capias ad satisfaciendum*); 42 Pa. Cons. Stat. § 5108.

694 *See, e.g.*, Lee v. BSB Greenwich Mortgage Ltd. P'ship, 2007 WL 2743435, at *5 (Conn. Super. Ct. Aug. 31, 2007) (noting that Connecticut abolished imprisonment for debt by repealing a statute that had formerly provided for body attachment); Makarov v. Commonwealth, 228 S.E.2d 573 (Va. 1976) (although there is no state constitutional prohibition, "[I]t is nevertheless established in this state that a person may not be imprisoned, absent fraud, for mere failure to pay a debt arising from contract or for mere failure to pay a judgment for a debt founded on contract. . . . [I]mprisonment of poor debtors offends fundamental principles of justice in today's ordered society.").

695 28 U.S.C. § 2007.

696 State v. Riggs, 807 S.W.2d 32 (Ark. 1991).

697 *See, e.g.*, Ariz. Const. art. II, § 18; Ind. Const. art. I, § 22.

698 *See, e.g.*, Colo. Const. art. II, § 12. *But see* Cal. Const. art. I, § 10 (explicitly including civil actions for tort in the prohibition).

699 *See, e.g.*, Alaska Const. art. I, § 17; Mass. Gen. Laws ch. 224, § 6; Or. Const. art. I, § 12.

700 Ill. Const. art. I, § 14; *accord* Colo. Const. art. II, § 12; Ky. Const. Bill of Rights § 18; Mont. Const. art. II, § 27; N.D. Const. art. I, § 15; 42 Pa. Con. Stat. § 5108; R.I. Const. art. I, § 11.

701 *See, e.g.*, Iowa Const. art. I, § 19; Ohio Const. art. I, § 15.

702 *See, e.g.*, Mitchell v. Mitchell, 871 N.E.2d 390 (Ind. Ct. App. 2007) (in some circumstances trial court may use contempt to enforce property settlement that is incorporated into divorce decree); Foley v. Mannor, 844 N.E.2d 494 (Ind. Ct. App. 2006) (imprisonment for contempt for failure to pay child support is constitutional, but only when the minor needs support, not after minor becomes emancipated or is adopted); *cf.* Randall v. Randall, 948 So. 2d 71 (Fla. Dist. Ct. App. 2007) (using contempt to enforce equitable distribution order requiring ex-spouse to pay debts owed to third parties would be unconstitutional as imprisonment for debt); *In re* Green, 221 S.W.3d 645 (Tex. 2007) (constitutional prohibition of imprisonment for debt means that contractual agreement to pay spousal support can not be enforced by contempt); *Ex parte* Hall, 854 S.W.2d 656 (Tex. 1993) (order to pay child or spousal support that is authorized by family law is enforceable by contempt, but not shown here).

703 Lavender v. City of Tuscaloosa, 198 So. 459, 461 (Ala. 1940).

704 *See, e.g.*, Md. Const. art. III, § 38 (explicit exception for spousal or child support); Mo. Const. art. 1, § 11 (explicit exception for fines and penalties imposed by law).

705 *See* § 9.2.2, *supra*.

706 *See, e.g.*, State v. Riggs, 807 S.W.2d 32 (Ark. 1991) (striking down statute because it allowed imprisonment upon showing of willful failure to pay rather than fraud).

707 *See* § 9.2, *supra*.

708 *See, e.g.*, 735 Ill. Comp. Stat. § 5/2-1402(c)(2) (allowing court to order a debtor to make installment payments out of nonexempt income); N.J. Stat. Ann. § 2A:17-64 (West) (allowing court to order debtor to pay judgment in installments from nonexempt income). *See generally* Annotation, *Constitutionality, construction, and application of statutes empowering court to require judgment debtor to make payment out of income or by instalments*, 111 A.L.R. 392 (1937 with 2008 Supp.).

709 DeGeorge v. Warheit, 741 N.W.2d 384, 391 (Mich. Ct. App. 2007) (affirming finding of contempt when debtor violated stipulated order not to transfer personal assets without court approval; "the punishment was for [defendant's] violation of the court's order, and not for failure to pay appellees for debts owed on a private contract"); *see also* Mason Furniture Corp. v. George, 362 A.2d 188 (N.H. 1976) (court may, after considering a number of factors, imprison judgment debtor for failing to make installment payment under an existing order); *cf.* Paulis v. Super. Ct., 2004 WL 3704007 (N. Mar. I. June 8, 2004)

these courts allow punishment for contempt only if there is a showing that the debtor has the financial means to comply with the order, on the theory that the contempt order would be punishment for the mere act of owing the debt without such a showing.[710] Some courts only allow a debtor to be held in civil contempt, which means that the debtor must be able to avoid imprisonment by making the payment.[711]

Other jurisdictions, however, recognize that allowing courts to order debtors to pay debts, and then holding them in civil or criminal contempt if they do not, amounts to imprisonment for debt. For example, the highest court in the District of Columbia holds that "contempt in general, and imprisonment in particular, are not appropriate means to enforce a money judgment."[712] The Indiana Supreme Court holds that "refusal to discharge a money judgment is not contempt of court and can not be punished as a contempt of court."[713]

(denying writ of prohibition; even if prohibition against imprisonment for debt is part of Northern Mariana Islands common law, imprisonment of debtor for failing to comply with order to pay $25 per month would not be a violation).

710 Ivy v. Keith, 92 S.W.3d 671 (Ark. 2002) (because of prohibition against imprisonment for debt, indigency is a defense to contempt finding for nonpayment of Rule 11 sanctions); Jensen v. Estate of Gambidilla, 896 So. 2d 917 (Fla. Dist. Ct. App. 2005) (trial court may not use civil contempt to incarcerate former personal representative of estate for failing to return estate property without express finding that contemnor has present ability to comply); Wells v. State, 474 A.2d 846 (Me. 1984) (debtors can not be sentenced to fixed term of confinement for failing to comply with stipulated order that they make payments on a civil debt; court must find that they have the present ability to pay and must allow them to obtain release by making the payments); Yoder v. County of Cumberland, 278 A.2d 379 (Me. 1971) (due process violation to imprison person for noncompliance with order to pay wife's divorce attorney fees without a prior hearing on the reasons for nonpayment); Vt. Nat'l Bank v. Taylor, 445 A.2d 1122 (Vt. 1982) (court can not issue *ex parte* writ of *capias* upon debtor's failure to make payments ordered by the court; debtor must first be given opportunity for hearing on reasons for nonpayment and ability to pay); Britannia Holdings Ltd. v. Greer, 113 P.3d 1041 (Wash. Ct. App. 2005) (not imprisonment for debt to hold a party in contempt for failure to comply with an order entered in supplemental proceedings to deliver money or property to pay a civil debt, as long as it is shown that debtor has ability to pay).

711 *See* Wells v. State, 474 A.2d 846 (Me. 1984).

712 *In re* Estate of Bonham, 817 A.2d 192, 195 (D.C. 2003); *accord* Bahre v. Bahre, 230 N.E.2d 411, 414 (Ind. 1967).

713 Bahre v. Bahre, 230 N.E.2d 411, 414 (Ind. 1967); *accord* Hill v. Paluzzi, 581 S.E.2d 730 (Ga. Ct. App. 2003) (money judgment can be enforced by execution, but not by contempt, even when consent decree requires specific payments); Rosenthal v. Am. Constr. & Realty Co., 247 N.W. 119, 120 (Mich. 1933); McCall v. Cunard, 2008 WL 307706 (Ohio Ct. App. Feb. 1, 2008) (unpublished) (reversing finding that tenant was in contempt for failing to pay rent as ordered by eviction court; contempt proceeding is not a proper method by which to collect a civil judgment); *Ex parte* Hall, 854 S.W.2d 656 (Tex. 1993) (failure to comply with an order to pay a debt is not contempt punishable by imprisonment); *see also* McKenna v. Gray, 438 S.E.2d 901 (Ga. 1994) (in the absence of statutory authority or other extraneous circumstances, contempt is not an available remedy to enforce a money judgment, even if the debtor violates an order requiring payment).

12.11 Debtor's Examinations

States generally make post-judgment discovery proceedings available to creditors to force debtors to answer questions about their assets. The creditor may have the right to issue interrogatories to the debtor, summon the debtor to a debtor's examination to answer questions in person, and issue a subpoena *duces tecum* requiring the debtor to produce assets or records. These proceedings are often called supplementary proceedings.

There are limits on debtor's examinations. A Missouri court held that debtor's examinations are limited statutory creations, so courts do not have authority to compel the attendance of third parties not listed in the statute.[714] In some states a creditor has the right to institute post-judgment supplementary proceedings only after unsuccessfully attempting to execute upon the judgment.[715] A debtor may assert the Fifth Amendment privilege against self-incrimination at a debtor's examination.[716]

Debtor's examinations create particular problems because in most if not all states the debtor can be held in contempt of court for failure to appear for a debtor's examination.[717] Debtors frequently fail to appear at debtor's examinations because the notice is in obtuse legalese, they have no means of transportation to the examination site, or they are unable to miss work without risking job termination. A debtor who has failed to appear for a debtor's examination may feel compelled to pay the debt because of the fear of incarceration. Some states follow a practice of allowing debtors to avoid contempt by rescheduling the examination.

A debtor who fails to appear for a debtor's examination may face either criminal contempt or civil contempt. Crimi-

714 State *ex rel.* Long v. Askren, 874 S.W.2d 466 (Mo. Ct. App. 1994). *But cf.* Imperial Bank v. PIM Elec., Inc., 39 Cal. Rptr. 2d 432, 437 (Ct. App. 1995) (noting that California allows judgment creditor to examine third persons who have property of, or are indebted to, the judgment debtor).

715 *See, e.g.*, Mo. Rev. Stat. § 513.380; N.H. Rev. Stat. Ann. § 498:8; *cf.* Hogue v. Palisades Collection, L.L.C., 494 F. Supp. 2d 1043 (S.D. Iowa 2007) (noting that Nebraska law that formerly required execution to be returned unsatisfied before debtor's examination could be conducted has been amended to delete this requirement; interpreting Iowa law not to require unsuccessful garnishment before debtor's examination could be conducted).

716 State *ex rel.* Heidelberg v. Holden, 98 S.W.3d 116 (Mo. Ct. App. 2003); State *ex rel.* Long v. Askren, 874 S.W.2d 466 (Mo. Ct. App. 1994) (debtor can invoke privilege against self-incrimination to avoid testifying at debtor's examination or producing documents); Empire Wholesale Lumber Co. v. Meyers, 85 P.3d 339 (Or. Ct. App. 2004).

717 *In re* Weick, 127 P.3d 178 (Idaho 2005); Too Easy Entertainment, Inc. v. Seven Arts Pictures, Inc., 943 So. 2d 1194 (La. Ct. App. 2006).

nal contempt is intended as punishment, while civil contempt is intended to coerce compliance. If the contemnor is sentenced to a fixed term of imprisonment, it is considered criminal contempt. With civil contempt, the contemnor can obtain release by complying with the original court order, and so is said to have the keys to the prison in his pocket. A defendant may be entitled to greater constitutional safeguards in the case of criminal contempt than civil contempt. A debtor who does not have the ability to comply with the court's order can not be found in civil[718] or criminal contempt.[719] The state may require special procedures before a debtor may be arrested for failing to appear for a debtor's examination, and if it does, the court must follow them and can not rely on its inherent authority to enforce its orders.[720]

A Virginia decision holds that arresting a debtor for failing to appear at a debtor's examination is not imprisonment for debt when the debtor could obtain his release by answering the creditor's questions and surrendering any assets to which the creditor was entitled.[721] The court reached this conclusion even though the trial court's order also allowed the debtor to obtain his release by paying the underlying judgment.

Even if a debtor's examination is lawful, it can be used improperly and abusively. Scheduling a debtor's examination in a distant venue may violate the Fair Debt Collection Practices Act (FDCPA).[722] It may also constitute abuse of process[723] or lead to a claim of false imprisonment.[724] Debt collectors may also violate the FDCPA by using the possibility of contempt for failure to appear at a debtor's examination as a basis for threatening or implying that nonpayment of a debt will result in imprisonment.[725]

---

718 Johnson & Placke v. Norris, 874 So. 2d 340 (La. Ct. App. 2004).

719 Diaz v. Baca, 203 Fed. Appx. 884 (9th Cir. 2006) (inability to comply is affirmative defense to contempt charge; charge appears to have been criminal contempt because imprisonment was for fixed three-day period); *In re* Weick, 127 P.3d 178 (Idaho 2005) (for indirect criminal contempt for failure to appear at debtor's examination, complainant must prove elements beyond reasonable doubt, but defendant has burden of producing evidence that creates a reasonable doubt as to his ability to comply).

720 Hiber v. Creditors Collection Serv., 961 P.2d 898 (Or. Ct. App. 1998).

721 Early Used Cars, Inc. v. Province, 239 S.E.2d 98 (Va. 1977); *cf.* Dahlz v. County of San Mateo, 2001 U.S. App. LEXIS 3541 (9th Cir. Mar. 2, 2001) (rejecting *pro se* debtor's section 1983 claim against creditor and creditor's attorney for having him arrested for failure to appear for debtor's examination).

722 Flores v. Quick Collect, Inc., 2007 WL 433239 (D. Or. Jan. 31, 2007).

723 *See* National Consumer Law Center, Fair Debt Collection § 10.6.3 (6th ed. 2008).

724 *See id.* § 10.8; *cf.* Hiber v. Creditors Collection Serv., 961 P.2d 898 (Or. Ct. App. 1998) (attorney who obtained arrest warrant for judgment debtor's failure to appear at debtor's examination is not liable for false imprisonment in the absence of malice or bad faith, even though warrant was void because of failure to follow state procedure).

725 *But see* Spinarski v. Credit Bureau, 1996 U.S. Dist. LEXIS 22547 (D.N.M. Sept. 19, 1999) (reference in pre-suit collection letter to possibility of arrest for failure to appear at debtor's examination not FDCPA violation; court accepts what appears to be extremely thin evidence that the collector ever employed this tactic or that judgment debtors were ever arrested).

Chapter 13 Setting Aside or Discharging a Judgment

13.1 Introduction

After a collector obtains a judgment on a debt, consumers have a number of steps they can take to protect their interests, either by undoing the judgment or minimizing its effect. If the consumer has answered the suit and lost on the merits, the consumer can appeal the decision, arguing the court made an error in law or allowed the collector to recover without an adequate evidentiary showing. Generally, the consumer can not appeal if the consumer did not answer the complaint and did not present the issue on appeal to the trial court.

Earlier chapters examine the applicable law and the collector's evidentiary burden.[1] For guidance on appellate procedures, advocates should consult other resources at the state level, because these procedures vary from state to state and from court to court within a state.

This chapter instead examines other approaches to setting aside a collector's judgment or minimizing its impact. Most collection actions end in either a default judgment or a stipulation for judgment. This chapter will consider how the consumer can set aside such judgments, allowing a fresh trial on the merits. Bankruptcy is another option, because a bankruptcy discharge will eliminate many, if not all, of the adverse consequences that a judgment holds for the consumer.

The chapter concludes with a consideration of the advisability of another option—bringing a separate court action challenging the collector's litigation misconduct. Chapter 14, *infra*, offers a more detailed discussion of such separate court actions, in the context of a litigation brought after the consumer *prevails* in the collection action. This chapter examines the advisability of such an action after a judgment for the collector.

If the judgment can not be set aside or otherwise avoided, Chapter 12, *supra*, examines consumer defenses to the collector's attempts at wage garnishment, seizure of funds from the consumer's bank account, placement of liens on the consumer's property, and other creditor post-judgment remedies. Such consumer defenses largely rest on the consumer being able to claim certain income or assets as exempt under federal or state law.

1 *See* Chs. 3, 4, *supra*.

13.2 Setting Aside a Default Judgment

13.2.1 State Standards

Most studies find that over eighty percent of consumer collection actions result in default judgments for the collector.[2] Later, particularly when a creditor initiates post-judgment remedies, consumers may seek legal representation or attempt on their own to reopen the default judgment.

Certain trial judges have little sympathy for even unsophisticated *pro se* defendants who fail to properly answer and contest a collection action, and are loathe to set aside default judgments. But state law is generally favorable to allowing a default judgment to be set aside. For example, the New Jersey Supreme Court has stated that a court should view " 'the opening of default judgments . . . with great liberality,' " and should tolerate " 'every reasonable ground for indulgence . . . to the end that a just result is reached.' "[3] Doubts should be resolved in favor of the consumer who is seeking to reopen the default judgment.[4]

A state's procedure to set aside a judgment is remedial and should be liberally construed so that justice is served.[5] Washington's Supreme Court has stated that it "is the policy of the law that controversies be determined on the merits rather than by default."[6] Similarly, a number of state supreme courts have stated that default judgments are disfavored and the trial court is vested with broad discretion to set them aside.[7] The trial judge's decision will not be disturbed

2 *See* § 1.4.4, *supra*.

3 Mancini v. EDS *ex rel.* N.J. Auto. Full Ins. Underwriting Ass'n, 625 A.2d 484, 486 (N.J. 1993) (citation omitted); *see also* Columbia Recovery Corp. v. Menchaca, 2008 WL 961037 (N.J. Super. Ct. App. Div. Mar. 12, 2008); Asset Acceptance L.L.C. v. Scott, 2007 WL 3145360 (N.J. Super. Ct. App. Div. Oct. 30, 2007).

4 Mancini v. EDS *ex rel.* N.J. Auto. Full Ins. Underwriting Ass'n, 625 A.2d 484 (N.J. 1993).

5 Kay v. Marc Glassman, Inc., 665 N.E.2d 1102 (Ohio 1996).

6 Griggs v. Averbeck Realty, Inc., 599 P.2d 1289, 1292 (Wash. 1979) (quoting Dlouhy v. Dlouhy, 55 Wash. 2d 718 (1960)).

7 *See, e.g.*, Idaho State Police v. Real Prop. Situated in the County of Cassia, 156 P.3d 561 (Idaho 2007); Asset Acceptance, L.L.C. v. Moberly, 241 S.W.3d 329 (Ky. 2007); Kennedy v. Black, 424 A.2d 1250 (Pa. 1981); *see also* Atl. Credit & Fin., Inc. v. Guiliana, 829 A.2d 340 (Pa. Super. Ct. 2003). *But see* Bland v. Hammond, 935 A.2d 457 (Md. Ct. Spec. App. 2007).

on appeal absent an abuse of discretion.[8]

The actual standards to set aside a default judgment will be found in a state's statutes or rules of procedure. Procedures may differ for different level courts within the same state. A good starting point is the Federal Rules of Civil Procedure, because many states pattern their procedures after these rules.

Rule 55(c) of the Federal Rules of Civil Procedure states that a default judgment can be set aside pursuant to Rule 60(b) of the Federal Rules of Civil Procedure, and most states have a parallel rule.[9] The federal version of Rule 60(b) states that a final judgment can be set aside for the following reasons:

(1) Mistake, inadvertence, surprise, or excusable neglect;
(2) Certain newly discovered evidence;
(3) Fraud, misrepresentation, or misconduct by an opposing party;
(4) The judgment is void;
(5) The judgment has been satisfied, released or discharged; it is based on an earlier judgment that has been reversed or vacated; or applying it prospectively is no longer equitable; or
(6) Any other reason that justifies relief.

Most states enumerate similar grounds, but there are variations,[10] so that it is important to carefully parse a particular state's standards.

The federal version of Rule 60(c) requires that a motion under Rule 60(b) be made within a reasonable time and, for reasons (1), (2), and (3), no more than a year after the entry of the judgment. (Some state rules provide only four or six months[11] to make such a motion, instead of one year, while others appear to have no time limit.[12]) Rule 60(d) states that Rule 60(b) and (c) do not limit a court's power to entertain an independent action to relieve a party from a judgment, or set aside a judgment for fraud on the court. Some states also allow a default judgment to be set aside within thirty days, without requiring any special reasons for the action.[13]

One court has estimated that thirty-five states have adopted language substantially the same as the federal rules, eight states have reserved equity or broad powers to revise a final judgment, and the remainder limit the grounds to set aside a judgment to certain specific situations.[14] Maryland is in this last group and Maryland's rules allow for a default judgment to be revised only for fraud, mistake or irregularity, newly discovered evidence, or clerical mistakes,[15] and these terms are strictly applied.[16]

Georgia, Connecticut, and Iowa are other examples of

8 *See* Atl. Credit & Fin. v. Dustrude, 2008 WL 57091 (Minn. Ct. App. Mar. 4, 2008); Mancini v. EDS *ex rel.* N.J. Auto. Full Ins. Underwriting Ass'n, 625 A.2d 484 (N.J. 1993).

9 *See* Conn. Gen. Stat. § 52-212 (motion must be made within four months); Kan. Stat. Ann. § 60-255(b) (default judgment set aside in accordance with Kan. Stat. Ann. § 60-260(b)); N.C. Gen Stat. § 1A-1, Rule 55(d) (default judgment set aside in accordance with N.C. Gen Stat. § 1A-1, Rule 60(b)); S.D. Codified Laws § 15-6-55(c) (default judgment set aside in accordance with S.D. Codified Laws § 15-6-60(b)); Ala. R. Civ. P. 55(c) (motion to set aside default judgment must be made within thirty days after judgment entered, and such motions are thereafter subject to Ala. R. Civ. P. 60)); Alaska R. Civ. P. 55(e) (default judgment may be set aside in accordance with Alaska R. Civ. P. 60(b)); Ariz. R. Civ. P. 55(C) (default judgment may be set aside under Ariz. R. Civ. P. 60(c)); Colo. R. Civ. P. 55(c) (default judgment may be set aside under Colo. R. Civ. P. 60(c)); Del. Sup. Ct. R. Civ. P. 55(c) (default judgment may be set aside under Del. Sup. Ct. R. Civ. P. 60(c)); D.C. Sup. Ct. R. Civ. P. 60(b) (motion to set aside judgment); Fla. R. Civ. P. 1.500(d) (default judgment set aside in accordance with Fla. R. Civ. P. 1.540(b)); Haw. R. Civ. P. 55(c) (default judgment set aside in accordance with Haw. R. Civ. P. 60(b)); Idaho Ct. R. Civ. P. 55(c) (default judgment set aside in accordance with Idaho Ct. R. Civ. P. 60(b)); Ind. R. Civ. P. 55(c) (default judgment set aside in accordance with Ind. R. Civ. P. 60(b)); Ky. R. Civ. P. 55.02 (default judgment set aside in accordance with Ky. R. Civ. P. 60.02); Me. R. Civ. P. 55 (court may set aside default judgment under Me. R. Civ. P. 60(b)); Mass. R. Civ. P. 55 (court may set aside default judgment under Mass. R. Civ. P. 60(b)); Minn. R. Civ. P. 60.02; Miss. R. Civ. P. 55(c) (court may set aside default judgment under Miss. R. Civ. P. 60(b)); Mont. R. Civ. P. 55(c) (court may set aside default judgment under Mont. R. Civ. P. 60(b)); Nev. R. Civ. P. 55(c) (court may set aside default judgment under Nev. R. Civ. P. 60(b)); N.J. R. of Ct. 4:43-3 (default judgment may be set aside in accordance with N.J. R. of Ct. 4:50); N.M. R. 1-055(C) (default judgment may be set aside under N.M. R. 1-060); N.D. R. Civ. P. 60(b); Ohio Civ. R. 55(B) (default judgment may be set aside under Ohio Civ. R. 60(B)); Or. R. Civ. P. 69(c) (default judgment may be set aside under Or. R. Civ. P. 71); S.C. R. Civ. P. 55(c) (default judgment may be set aside under S.C. R. Civ. P. 60); Tenn. R. Civ. P. 55.02 (default judgment set aside under Tenn. R. Civ. P. 60.02); Utah R. Civ. P. 55(c) (default judgment set aside under Utah R. Civ. P. 60(b)); Vt. R. Civ. P. 55(c) (default judgment set aside under Vt. R. Civ. P. 60(b)); Wash. Sup. Ct. Civ. R. 55(c) (default judgment set aside under Wash. Sup. Ct. Civ. R. 60(b)); W. Va. R. Civ. P. 55(c) (default judgment set aside under W. Va. R. Civ. P. 60(6)); Wyo. R. Civ. P. 55(c) (default judgment set aside under Wyo. R. Civ. P. 60(b)).

10 The amount of variation differs by state. *See, e.g.*, N.Y. C.P.L.R. 5015 (McKinney) (time periods are different, lack of jurisdiction is a ground instead of "judgment is void," and "other reason that justifies relief" is not included); Ariz. R. Civ. P. 60(c) (largely following the federal rule, but shortening the one-year period to six months); Ky. R. Civ. P. 60.02 (little variation); Minn. R. Civ. P. 60.02 (requiring "any other reason that justifies relief" to be of an "extraordinary nature"); N.J. R. of Ct. 4:50-1, 4:50-2 (little variation); Ohio Civ. R. 60(B) (deletes "judgment is void" as a ground); W. Va. R. Civ. P. 60(b), (c) (little variation).

11 *See, e.g.*, Cal. Civ. Proc. Code § 473(b) (West) (six months); Conn. Gen. Stat. § 52-212 (four months); Ala. R. Civ. P. 60(b) (four months); Ariz. R. Civ. P. 60(c) (six months).

12 *See, e.g.*, Ark. R. Civ. P. 55(c).

13 *See, e.g.*, Ala. R. Civ. P. 55 (c).

14 *See* Andresen v. Andresen, 564 A.2d 399 (Md. 1989).

15 Md. Rules 2-535 (circuit court), 3-535 (district court, whose jurisdiction is limited to $15,000).

Md. Rule 2-613(g) limits the ability to revise a circuit court judgment only as to relief obtained, but does not so limit a district court judgment.

16 Bland v. Hammond, 935 A.2d 457 (Md. Ct. Spec. App. 2007).

states that are far more restrictive than the federal rules as to the grounds to set aside a judgment. Georgia limits the grounds to lack of jurisdiction; fraud, accident, or mistake or the acts of the adverse party unmixed with the negligence or fault of the movant; or a non-amendable defect which appears upon the face of the record or pleadings, showing that no claim in fact existed.[17] Connecticut sets a strict four-month time limit on reopening a default judgment, and requires a showing of reasonable cause, or that a good cause of action or defense in whole or in part existed, and that the plaintiff or defendant was prevented by mistake, accident or other reasonable cause from making the defense.[18] Iowa has a similar provision, with a sixty-day deadline.[19] But even in these states, the consumer should be able to set aside the judgment after that period if the court lacked jurisdiction to award the judgment, such as when the consumer was never properly served with process.[20]

The rest of this section focuses on state rules similar to the federal rules, and will examine the following grounds for setting aside a default judgment:

- Excusable neglect;
- "Any other reason that justifies relief";
- Fraud, misrepresentation or misconduct by an opposing party, or fraud on the court;
- Improper service of the collection action;
- A judgment issued without jurisdiction;
- Lack of notice as to the hearing on the default judgment; and
- Federal protections for active duty military personnel.

The section concludes with a description of an interesting New York statute that allows a court to vacate numerous default judgments on its own motion in one proceeding.

13.2.2 Excusable Neglect

A common basis for setting aside a default judgment is the consumer's excusable neglect in responding to the complaint. The motion to set aside the judgment must be brought within one year, or within a reasonable time, whichever is less. A reasonable time depends on the totality of circumstances.[21]

The sooner the motion is brought, the stronger will be the consumer's position. For example, a court had little difficulty finding one month to be a reasonable time.[22] When a consumer moves to set aside the default shortly after learning of the judgment, the motion will generally be considered to have been made within a reasonable time.[23]

The consumer must show a reasonable excuse for failing to respond to the complaint. The excuse need not be something beyond the consumer's control. The United States Supreme Court has distinguished "excusable neglect" from "any other reason that justifies relief." Unlike excusable neglect, "any other reason that justifies relief" only applies to factors over which the consumer has no control.[24] The Ohio Supreme Court has defined excusable neglect in the negative by stating that "the inaction of the defendant is not 'excusable neglect' if it can be labeled as a 'complete disregard for the judicial system.' "[25]

Excusable neglect thus includes situations when the consumer had control over the problem, but still did not act. Being out of town for several weeks and not checking one's mail has been found to be excusable neglect.[26] A *pro se* defendant's confusion as to court procedure or ignorance over the consequences of a default can be excusable neglect.[27] Excusable neglect can be found when the consumer, after receiving a complaint, was told to "forget it" by the creditor's attorney.[28] Excusable neglect can be found when the consumer promptly asked an attorney for advice, subsequent court notices went to the attorney, and the attorney never informed the consumer that the attorney was not taking the case.[29] Excusable neglect has also been found when a *pro se* litigant failed to inform the court of his new address.[30] Excusable neglect can be found when the consumer is incarcerated and did not receive notice of the action.[31]

---

17 Ga. Code Ann. § 9-11-60(d).

18 Conn. Gen. Stat. §§ 52-212, 52-212a.

19 Iowa Rule 1.977.

20 *See* § 13.2.4, *infra*.

21 *See* Great Seneca Fin. Corp. v. Dwek, 2008 WL 960453 (N.J. Super. Ct. App. Div. Mar. 31, 2008).

22 Columbia Recovery Corp. v. Menchaca, 2008 WL 961037 (N.J. Super. Ct. App. Div. Mar. 12, 2008); *see also* Gen. Motors Acceptance Corp. v. Deskins, 474 N.E.2d 1207 (Ohio Ct. App. 1984) (motion timely when filed three months after judgment entered and one month after defendant learned of judgment).

23 Dottore v. Feathers, 2007 WL 1461320 (Ohio Ct. App. May 18, 2007).

24 Pioneer Inv. Services Co. v. Brunswick Associates Ltd. P'ship, 507 U.S. 380, 113 S. Ct. 1489, 123 L. Ed. 2d 74 (1993); *see also* Asset Acceptance, L.L.C. v. Moberly, 241 S.W.3d 329 (Ky. 2007).

25 Kay v. Marc Glassman, Inc., 665 N.E.2d 1102, 1105 (Ohio 1996) (citations omitted).

26 Grunke v. Kloskin, 355 N.W.2d 207 (Minn. Ct. App. 1984).

27 *See* TCI Group Life Ins. Plan v. Knoebber, 244 F.3d 691 (9th Cir. 2001) (lack of familiarity with the legal system, while not sufficient in itself to demonstrate excusable neglect, is a relevant consideration; so is depression following spouse's death); Canfield v. Van Atta Buick/GMC Truck, 127 F.3d 248 (2d Cir. 1997) (lack of familiarity with court rules may constitute excusable neglect); Briones v. Riviera Hotel & Casino, 116 F.3d 379 (9th Cir. 1997) (omissions of a *pro se* defendant may constitute excusable neglect); Enron Oil Corp. v. Diakuhara, 10 F.3d 90 (2d Cir. 1993) (error not to consider defendant's *pro se* status in considering whether to set aside a default); Stirm v. Puckett, 1695 P.2d 431 (Idaho 1985) (mental illness).

28 Gen. Motors Acceptance Corp. v. Deskins, 474 N.E.2d 1207 (Ohio Ct. App. 1984).

29 Idaho State Police v. Real Prop. Situated in the County of Cassia, 156 P.3d 561 (Idaho 2007).

30 *In re* Beekman, 1991 WL 179580 (Ohio Ct. App. Sept. 10, 1991).

31 Dottore v. Feathers, 2007 WL 1461320 (Ohio Ct. App. May 18, 2007).

Courts will look for a reasonable excuse for failure to act and due diligence after the consumer realizes action is necessary.[32] While the consumer should act promptly when the consumer becomes aware of the neglect, this does not mean the consumer needs to immediately file a motion, but can instead enter into discussions with the other party.[33] Moreover, courts have stated that it is only a secondary factor whether the consumer showed due diligence in seeking to set aside the default after realizing that such action is necessary.[34]

In cases of excusable neglect courts also look to see if the consumer has a meritorious defense.[35] Concerns about judicial economy prohibit retrying a case in which the consumer has no defense. The meritorious defense must be pleaded with some particularity, more than in responding to the original complaint.[36] Nonetheless, the consumer need only allege a meritorious defense, not prove that the consumer will prevail on that defense.[37] "A proffered defense is meritorious when it is not a sham and when, if true, it states a defense in part, or in whole, to the claims for relief set forth in the complaint."[38]

The consumer's allegation of a meritorious defense certainly can be made by affidavit; there need not be a mini-trial of the facts.[39] Courts may not even require that evidence supporting the defense be presented as part of the motion.[40]

Although a meritorious defense can be almost any valid defense, courts may look more kindly on the consumer's motion when the consumer's defense is apparent on the face of the collector's pleadings, as when the form of the complaint fails to meet state requirements,[41] or when insufficient evidence was presented to support a prima facie case.[42] Similarly, when the consumer claims never to have opened an account, a meritorious defense is established when the collector offers little evidence that the individual opened the account or was otherwise obligated on the account.[43]

Some courts also add that, in determining whether to set aside a judgment, one factor to consider should be whether there is substantial prejudice to the opposing party.[44] But this has been called a secondary factor,[45] just one factor to be weighed among others.[46] Prejudice also must be something more than that the collector may not win on the merits if the judgment is set aside. An example of prejudice sufficient to merit denial of a motion to set aside a default is the plaintiff's death, when the plaintiff's estate would be without a witness if the case had to be relitigated.[47]

13.2.3 "Any Other Reason That Justifies Relief"

Federal Rule of Civil Procedure 60(b)(6) provides that a default judgment can be reopened for "any other reason that justifies relief." There is no one-year limit on the consumer's ability to raise this reason as ground for relief, as long as the motion is brought within a reasonable time. This approach is an attractive alternative for a consumer when more than a year has elapsed, and when it is thus no longer possible to set aside the judgment for excusable neglect.

Nevertheless, state courts and even state rules[48] limit this basis for relief to "extraordinary circumstances"[49] or "exceptional situations,"[50] and use this basis sparingly.[51] It should not be used to undermine the time constraints applicable to Rule 60(b)'s other subsections.[52] As the rule states "any other reason," this section does not include grounds mentioned in the prior sections,[53] such as excusable neglect. The United States Supreme Court, in interpreting the federal rule, finds that the subsection is limited to "extraordinary circumstances" beyond the movant's control, and not just to

32 *See* Atl. Credit & Fin. v. Dustrude, 2008 WL 57091 (Minn. Ct. App. Mar. 4, 2008); Little v. King, 161 P.3d 345 (Wash. 2007).

33 Webb v. Erickson, 655 P.2d 6 (Ariz. 1982).

34 Little v. King, 161 P.3d 345 (Wash. 2007).

35 *See* Idaho State Police v. Real Prop. Situated in the County of Cassia, 156 P.3d 561 (Idaho 2007); Asset Acceptance, L.L.C. v. Moberly, 241 S.W.3d 329 (Ky. 2007); Asset Acceptance L.L.C. v. Scott, 2007 WL 3145360 (N.J. Super. Ct. App. Div. Oct. 30, 2007); Little v. King, 161 P.3d 345 (Wash. 2007).

36 Idaho State Police v. Real Prop. Situated in the County of Cassia, 156 P.3d 561 (Idaho 2007); Meglan, Meglan & Co., Ltd. v. Bostic, 2006 WL 1230687 (Ohio Ct. App. May 9, 2006).

37 Meglan, Meglan & Co., Ltd. v. Bostic, 2006 WL 1230687 (Ohio Ct. App. May 9, 2006); Gen. Motors Acceptance Corp. v. Deskins, 474 N.E.2d 1207 (Ohio Ct. App. 1984).

38 Meglan, Meglan & Co., Ltd. v. Bostic, 2006 WL 1230687, at *3 (Ohio Ct. App. May 9, 2006).

39 Webb v. Erickson, 655 P.2d 6 (Ariz. 1982); Meglan, Meglan & Co., Ltd. v. Bostic, 2006 WL 1230687 (Ohio Ct. App. May 9, 2006).

40 Idaho State Police v. Real Prop. Situated in the County of Cassia, 156 P.3d 561 (Idaho 2007).

41 *See, e.g.*, Atl. Credit & Fin., Inc. v. Guiliana, 829 A.2d 340 (Pa. Super. Ct. 2003).

42 Morales v. Santiago, 217 N.J. Super. 496 (Super. Ct. App. Div. 1987).

43 Columbia Recovery Corp. v. Menchaca, 2008 WL 961037 (N.J. Super. Ct. App. Div. Mar. 12, 2008).

44 *See* Rule v. Capital One Bank, 2007 WL 779135 (Ky. Ct. App. Mar. 16, 2007); Atl. Credit & Fin. v. Dustrude, 2008 WL 57091 (Minn. Ct. App. Mar. 4, 2008); Little v. King, 161 P.3d 345 (Wash. 2007).

45 Little v. King, 161 P.3d 345 (Wash. 2007).

46 Top Value Homes, Inc. v. Harden, 460 S.E.2d 427 (S.C. Ct. App. 1995).

47 Grunke v. Kloskin, 355 N.W.2d 207 (Minn. Ct. App. 1984).

48 *See, e.g.*, Ky. R. Civ. P. 60.02.

49 Pioneer Inv. Services Co. v. Brunswick Associates Ltd. P'ship, 507 U.S. 380, 113 S. Ct. 1489, 123 L. Ed. 2d 74 (1993); Webb v. Erickson, 655 P.2d 6 (Ariz. 1982).

50 *See* N.Y. Hosp. v. Robinson, 1999 WL 34876247 (N.J. Super. Ct. App. Div. May 28, 1999).

51 *See* Asset Acceptance, L.L.C. v. Moberly, 241 S.W.3d 329 (Ky. 2007); Great Seneca Fin. Corp. v. Dwek, 2008 WL 960453 (N.J. Super. Ct. App. Div. Mar. 31, 2008).

52 Asset Acceptance, L.L.C. v. Moberly, 241 S.W.3d 329 (Ky. 2007).

53 Webb v. Erickson, 655 P.2d 6 (Ariz. 1982).

excusable neglect.[54] The circumstances must suggest that the party is faultless in the delay.[55]

The standard though is not an impossible one to meet. The Arizona Supreme Court has quoted the United States Supreme Court approvingly regarding this ground to set aside a judgment. It "vests power in courts adequate to enable them to vacate judgments whenever such action is appropriate to accomplish justice."[56]

The United States Supreme Court found "any other reason that justifies relief" present when an individual's incarceration, ill health, and other factors beyond his reasonable control prevented him from seeking to reopen a default judgment for four years.[57] The Arizona Supreme Court has found exceptional circumstances to set aside a default judgment after four and a half years when the individual had no reason to believe the action was related to that individual, when the summons and writ were confusing, and the individual's mental and physical condition was impaired at the time.[58] Another factor was the lack of notice of the default judgment.[59]

In another case a default judgment was reopened for exceptional circumstances after nine years had passed.[60] The consumer contacted Medicaid about a hospital bill (hospitals may not sue Medicaid recipients), and was told it would be taken care of. Then, on receipt of the default judgment, the consumer contacted the collector's law firm to explain that Medicaid said it would take care of the matter. Nine years later, immediately after the first garnishment of the consumer's wages, the consumer sought to reopen the default. Upon denial, she sought legal assistance. The court in these circumstances found the failure to respond to the complaint to be justified, and allowed the default judgment to be set aside.[61]

Similarly, a trial court found exceptional circumstances to reopen a default judgment two years afterwards when the consumer's alcoholism made her incapable of managing her affairs.[62] On the other hand, another court refused to reopen a default judgment for exceptional circumstances when the consumer was incapacitated for eighteen months, but waited over three years to move to reopen the default.[63]

54 Pioneer Inv. Services Co. v. Brunswick Associates Ltd. P'ship, 507 U.S. 380, 113 S. Ct. 1489, 123 L. Ed. 2d 74 (1993).

55 *Id.*

56 Webb v. Erickson, 655 P.2d 6, 10 (Ariz. 1982) (quoting Klapprott v. United States, 335 U.S. 601, 69 S. Ct. 384, 93 L. Ed. 266 (1949)).

57 Klapprott v. United States, 335 U.S. 601, 69 S. Ct. 384, 93 L. Ed. 266 (1949).

58 Webb v. Erickson, 655 P.2d 6 (Ariz. 1982).

59 *Id.*

60 *See* N.Y. Hosp. v. Robinson, 1999 WL 34876247 (N.J. Super. Ct. App. Div. May 28, 1999).

61 *Id.*

62 *See* Asset Acceptance, L.L.C. v. Moberly, 241 S.W.3d 329 (Ky. 2007) (discussing trial court's decision on consumer's motion.

63 Great Seneca Fin. Corp. v. Dwek, 2008 WL 960453 (N.J. Super. Ct. App. Div. Mar. 31, 2008).

13.2.4 Improper Service of the Complaint

Particularly when debt buyers seek to serve a summons on a consumer years after an account has been closed, it is likely that service will be made at the wrong address, or not sent at all, which should be enough to set aside the default judgment. If service of process is defective, then the court issuing the judgment does not have personal jurisdiction over the consumer, and the judgment is void[64]—grounds under federal Rule 60(b) for setting the judgment aside.[65] Other state rules explicitly provide that lack of jurisdiction is grounds to set aside a judgment; inadequate service means there is no personal jurisdiction.[66] Inadequate service should suffice to set aside a judgment even if a state's rules do not list lack of jurisdiction or a judgment being void as grounds to set aside a judgment. Lack of jurisdiction can be raised at any time to attack a judgment.[67] There is no time limit to challenge a void judgment.[68]

For example, in one case the default judgment was set aside six years after it was issued because of defective service.[69] The consumer did not have to show that the delay

64 Peralta v. Heights Med. Ctr., Inc., 485 U.S. 80, 108 S. Ct. 896, 99 L. Ed. 2d 75 (1988) (due process requires the judgment to be set aside).

65 *See* Wolfe v. Stevens, 965 So. 2d 1257 (Fla. Dist. Ct. App. 2007); First Select Co. v. Mastromattei, 2007 WL 1599664 (Mass. Dist. Ct. May 31, 2007); Dombrowski v. Chute, 2000 WL 562542 (Mass. Dist. Ct. May 5, 2000); Gassett v. Snappy Car Rental, 906 P.2d 258 (Nev. 1995); BB & T v. Taylor, 633 S.E.2d 501 (S.C. 2006).

66 *See* Unifund CCR Partners v. Dale, 801 N.Y.S.2d 782 (City Ct. 2005).

67 Fort Trumbull Conservancy, L.L.C. v. Alves, 815 A.2d 1188 (Conn. 2003); Capital One Bank v. Czekala, 2008 WL 539177 (Ill. App. Ct. Feb. 25, 2008); Young v. Progressive Cas. Ins. Co., 108 Md. App. 233, 671 A.2d 515 (1996); First Select Co. v. Mastromattei, 2007 WL 1599664 (Mass. Dist. Ct. May 31, 2007); Dombrowski v. Chute, 2000 WL 562542 (Mass. Dist. Ct. May 5, 2000). *But see* N.Y. C.P.L.R. § 317 (McKinney) (motion must be made within five years and meritorious defense must be presented).

68 *See, e.g.*, Master Fin., Inc. v. Woodburn, 90 P.3d 1236 (Ariz. Ct. App. 2004); United Bank of Boulder v. Buchanan, 836 P.2d 473 (Colo. Ct. App. 1992); Falkner v. Ameritrust Fed. Sav. & Loan Ass'n, 489 So. 2d 758 (Fla. Dist. Ct. App. 1986); Sarkissian v. Chicago Bd. of Educ., 776 N.E.2d 195 (Ill. 2002); Galbreath v. Coleman, 596 N.W.2d 689 (Minn. Ct. App. 1999); Garcia v. Ideal Supply Co., 874 P.2d 752 (Nev. 1994). *But see* McDaniel v. U.S. Fid. Guar. Co., 478 S.E.2d 868 (S.C. Ct. App. 1996) (motion to set aside default judgment on basis that judgment is void must be brought within reasonable time); Ind. R. of Trial Proc. 60(B)(6) (motion on basis that judgment is void must be filed within a reasonable time); *cf.* Plaza Hollister Ltd. P'ship v. County of San Benito, 84 Cal. Rptr. 2d 715 (Ct. App. 1999) (judgment which is void on its face may be set aside at any time, but motion to set aside judgment not void on the record must be brought within statutory time period).

69 *See* First Select Co. v. Mastromattei, 2007 WL 1599664 (Mass. Dist. Ct. May 31, 2007).

was reasonable.[70] And, while it is prudent to do so, the consumer need not even show a meritorious defense.[71] Once the lack of personal jurisdiction is established, the court has no discretion but to set aside the judgment.[72]

Of course, the consumer's non-receipt of the summons is not the same as defective service. Service is typically proper when notice is made at the consumer's last and usual place of residence, even if the consumer is not at that location at the time.[73] In a number of states service of process is made by mailing the summons and complaint by certified and regular mail. Even if the certified mail is returned, the regular mail constitutes service.[74]

However, mailing the summons is no more than a rebuttable presumption that service has been made.[75] This presumption disappears when there is conflicting evidence. When the consumer advances proof that rebuts the presumption of effective service, the burden shifts to the collector to establish that service was made.[76]

For example, the presumption is rebutted when the consumer lived on 211 Keats Drive and the summons and complaint were mailed to 211 Keats Court. Based on this discrepancy the court should not resolve the matter summarily, but should allow testimony and other evidence.[77]

Courts appear divided about whether a consumer's mere statement, without more, that notice was not received is sufficient to require the court to conduct a hearing and sort through the parties' conflicting evidence.[78] But an affidavit that alleges more than just the lack of notice should be sufficient to raise the issue. A consumer's affidavit that the consumer has never lived at the address listed in the summons should be enough, as should an affidavit from the present occupant of the address listed in the summons, stating that the consumer has never lived at that address.[79] Similarly, proof that the consumer did not reside at the location served at the time of service should be enough for the court to conduct an evidentiary hearing on the matter.

The fact that the collector sent a number of letters to the address that were not returned does not prove that service was proper.[80] Moreover, a skip tracing service's information that someone with the consumer's name lived at the address at the time of the summons is not determinative, particularly when the tracing service also lists the consumer as residing at a different address at the same point in time.[81]

13.2.5 Other Jurisdictional Challenges

The prior subsection discusses when inadequate service leading to a lack of personal jurisdiction is grounds to set a default judgment aside. The judgment can also be set aside when there is any other failure of jurisdiction or when the judgment is void for any other reason. This principle is explicit in the federal rules—that a void judgment can be set aside, and that the one year time limit does not apply to this rationale.[82] Of course, void means more than just that the judgment was erroneous as to the law or the facts.[83] It must be void ab initio. The most common example of such a void judgment is if the court has no jurisdiction over the matter.[84]

Lack of subject matter jurisdiction can be shown when the type of case or the amount awarded is beyond the powers of a court—for example, when a small claims court has authority only to issue judgments up to $10,000 and yet issues an award for $11,000. Lack of subject matter jurisdiction also occurs when the collector does not own the debt, and thus has no standing to sue on the debt.[85]

In some states an assignment of the debt in question must be attached to the complaint if someone other than the original creditor brings the action.[86] If that assignment is not attached, is not signed, is not a proper assignment, or does

70 Capital One Bank v. Czekala, 2008 WL 539177 (Ill. App. Ct. Feb. 25, 2008).

71 Peralta v. Heights Med. Ctr., Inc., 485 U.S. 80, 108 S. Ct. 896, 99 L. Ed. 2d 75 (1988); *see also* Master Fin., Inc. v. Woodburn, 90 P.3d 1236 (Ariz. Ct. App. 2004); Ark. R. Civ. P. 55; D.C. R. Civ. P. 55.

72 *See* First Select Co. v. Mastromattei, 2007 WL 1599664 (Mass. Dist. Ct. May 31, 2007); Enter. Rent-A-Car v. Bigelow, 2004 WL 2360223 (Mass. Dist. Ct. Oct. 18, 2004); Dombrowski v. Chute, 2000 WL 562542 (Mass. Dist. Ct. May 5, 2000).

73 *See* Sears, Roebuck & Co v. Ford, 2006 WL 3425069 (Mass. Dist. Ct. Nov. 27, 2006).

74 *See* N.J. R. of Ct. 6:2-3(d)(1).

75 Asset Acceptance L.L.C. v. Scott, 2007 WL 3145360 (N.J. Super. Ct. App. Div. Oct. 30, 2007).

76 *Id.*

77 *Id.*

78 *Compare* Unifund CCR Partners v. Dale, 801 N.Y.S.2d 782 (City Ct. 2005) (affidavit sufficient to require a hearing) *with* Atl. Credit & Fin. v. Dustrude, 2008 WL 57091 (Minn. Ct. App. Mar. 4, 2008) (mere denial of receipt of service is not enough, without additional evidence).

79 *See* First Select Co. v. Mastromattei, 2007 WL 1599664 (Mass. Dist. Ct. May 31, 2007); *see also* Dombrowski v. Chute, 2000 WL 562542 (Mass. Dist. Ct. May 5, 2000).

80 *See* First Select Co. v. Mastromattei, 2007 WL 1599664 (Mass. Dist. Ct. May 31, 2007).

81 *See id.*

82 Fed. R. Civ. P. 60(b)(4), 60(c).

83 Coleman v. First Star, Inc., 646 S.E.2d 443 (N.C. Ct. App. 2007).

84 *See* Capital One Bank v. Czekala, 2008 WL 539177 (Ill. App. Ct. Feb. 25, 2008).

85 Virtually all cases find no subject matter jurisdiction when the plaintiff lacks standing. *See, e.g.*, Stalley *ex rel.* United States v. Orlando Reg'l Healthcare Sys., Inc., 2008 WL 1759115 (11th Cir. Apr. 18, 2008); Morrison v. Bd. of Educ. of Boyd County, 2008 WL 942047 (6th Cir. Apr. 9, 2008); Faibisch v. Univ. of Minn., 304 F.3d 797 (8th Cir. 2002); Swafford v. Norton, 2008 WL 1759117 (Ala. Civ. App. Apr. 18, 2008); Fort Trumbull Conservancy, L.L.C. v. Alves, 943 A.2d 420 (Conn. 2008); Planning Bd. of Marshfield v. Zoning Bd. of Appeals of Pembroke, 427 Mass. 699 (1998); Horry v. Woodbury, 2008 WL 1721541 (N.C. Ct. App. Apr. 15, 2008); *In re* H.G., 2008 WL 1805516 (Tex. App. Apr. 23, 2008). *But see* Mid-State Trust IX v. Davis, 2008 WL 1838350 (Ohio Ct. App. Apr. 25, 2008).

86 *See* § 3.5, *supra*.

not show a continuous chain of assignments from the original creditor,[87] then this deficiency should be enough for the consumer to obtain a hearing on the motion to set aside a default judgment. The same should be the case when the consumer, after the default judgment, is contacted by another collector claiming ownership of the same debt, placing the first collector's ownership of the debt in doubt.

States sometimes have statutes that limit a party's access to the courts because that party lacks a license, and a debt buyer may not have the required license, or state law may limit the ability of a licensed debt collector to bring collection actions in the state's courts.[88] Bringing an action in violation of these statutes may deprive the court of subject matter jurisdiction over the matter.

When a court views the case being brought in the correct county as jurisdictional, filing the action in an improper venue should also provide a basis to set aside the default judgment. California provides that, if an action is brought in the wrong venue, the consumer can seek to set aside the default judgment on this basis at any time within sixty days after the collector's attempt to enforce that judgment.[89]

13.2.6 The Collector's Misconduct or Fraud on the Court

The federal rules establish two different standards for setting aside a default judgment based upon the collector's misconduct. A collector's fraud, misrepresentation, or misconduct is grounds for setting aside a default judgment, if the consumer acts within one year to set aside the judgment.[90] When there is fraud *on the court*, and not just misconduct affecting the consumer, the judgment can be set aside even after the one-year period.[91]

A good example of collector misconduct affecting the consumer would be a collector's attorney telling the consumer to "forget about" the complaint served by that attorney.[92] Another good example of collector misconduct involves a collector representing to the consumer that it will dismiss the case if the consumer enters into a repayment program. Instead, the collector pursues the case and obtains a default judgment even though the consumer makes payments as agreed. Less clear is whether this conduct would also constitute fraud on the court.

Filing false affidavits with the court would appear to be not just collector misconduct, but also fraud upon the court. For example, filing a false affidavit that the consumer is not on active duty in the military should be considered a fraud on the court. The federal Servicemembers Civil Relief Act provides special relief from default judgments for active duty military personnel,[93] but there are limits as to when such a federal right to reopen the default is available.[94] When that federal statute does not provide relief, the default judgment can still be set aside as a fraud on the court.

State rules may require that certain documentation be presented to the court before a default judgment will be issued. False statements in that documentation should be fraud upon the court. An example might be when an affidavit states certain facts upon the affiant's personal knowledge, when the affiant can not possibly have that personal knowledge.

13.2.7 Improper Notice of the Default Hearing

Obtaining a default judgment is a two step process in many states. The consumer is summoned with a complaint, and failure to respond within a specified time period leads to a default. In many states the collector then must file a motion to turn that default into a judgment. State rules patterned after Federal Rule of Civil Procedure 55(b)(2) require that the collector serve the consumer with written notice of its application for a default judgment, if the consumer has filed an appearance in the case.[95] When the consumer is not sent this second notice, the resulting default judgment can later be set aside.[96] Just as the consumer must be properly served the lawsuit itself, the consumer must also be properly served the motion for a default judgment.

The federal rule and most state rules limit the right to this additional notice to situations in which the consumer has filed an appearance. In a surprising number of default judgments the consumer in fact has filed an appearance, even though the consumer has defaulted. In many states, the consumer must file both an appearance and an answer, and confused, unrepresented consumers may believe that filing an appearance is enough. Merely filing the appearance may not stop a default, but it entitles the consumer to the second notice.

Moreover, some courts have construed "appearance" broadly to include conduct and communications prior to the

87 *See* § 4.3, *supra*.
88 *See* § 3.6, *supra*.
89 *See* Cal. Civ. Proc. Code §§ 585.5, 1812.10 (West).
90 Fed. R. Civ. P. 60(b), 60(c).
91 Fed. R. Civ. P. 60(d).
92 *See* Gen Motors Acceptance Corp. v. Deskins, 474 N.E.2d 1207 (Ohio Ct. App. 1984).

93 *See* § 13.2.8, *infra*.
94 *Id.*
95 The federal rule specifies three days notice, but state rules may require more time. *See, e.g.*, N.Y. C.P.L.R. § 3215(g) (McKinney) (five days); La. Code Civ. P. art. 1702 (seven days); Mass. R. Civ. P. 55 (b)(2) (seven days); Ohio Civ. R. 55 (seven days).
96 *See* Nat'l City Bank of Michigan/Illinois v. Hayden, 2003 WL 193510 (Mich. Ct. App. Jan. 28, 2003); Lindblom v. Prime Hospitality Corp., 90 P.3d 1283 (Nev. 2004); Meglan, Meglan & Co., Ltd. v. Bostic, 2006 WL 1230687 (Ohio Ct. App. May 9, 2006); Asset Acceptance L.L.C. v. Springer, 2004 WL 2526369 (Ohio Ct. App. Nov. 5, 2004); *see also* Reid v. Asset Acceptance, L.L.C., 2006 WL 3028072 (Tex. App. Oct. 25, 2006).

filing of an action, even when the defendant does not make an appearance after the case is commenced.[97] In Texas, notice of the motion for a default judgment must be sent if the consumer answers, and a verified letter from the consumer was found to be such an answer, even though not in proper form as an answer.[98]

Some states require the collector to serve notice of the hearing on the default judgment on the consumer even when the consumer does not file an appearance. In New York if more than one year has elapsed since the entry of default, a defendant (even one who has not filed an appearance) must still be given notice of the hearing for a default judgment.[99] Even if one year has not elapsed, notice must be sent if the action is based upon the nonpayment of a contractual obligation and is not filed in small claims court. If the notice is returned as undeliverable or if the residence is unknown, then it must be mailed to the party's place of employment, if known. If that is unknown, it must be mailed to the last known address.[100]

13.2.8 Servicemembers' Special Protections from Default Judgments

The federal Servicemembers Civil Relief Act provides that a court can vacate any default judgment entered while a servicemember is on active duty or within sixty days after release from active duty.[101] The servicemember must apply to the court to have the judgment vacated within ninety days after they have been terminated or released from military service,[102] and must show a meritorious or legal defense, and that military service materially affected the servicemember's ability to make a defense.[103] State law limits on vacating judgments are inapplicable to this right.[104]

13.2.9 Mass Vacatur

New York has a statute that allows for a large number of defaults in consumer credit transactions to be vacated in one action:

> An administrative judge, upon a showing that default judgments were obtained by fraud, misrepresentation, illegality, unconscionability, lack of due service, violations of law, or other illegalities or when such default judgments were obtained in cases in which those defendants would be uniformly entitled to interpose a defense predicated upon but not limited to the foregoing defenses, and when such default judgments have been obtained in a number deemed sufficient by him to justify such action as set forth herein, and upon appropriate notice to counsel for the respective parties, or to the parties themselves, may bring a proceeding to relieve a party or parties from them upon such terms as may be just. The disposition of any proceeding so instituted shall be determined by a judge other than the administrative judge.[105]

13.3 Setting Aside Stipulated Judgments

13.3.1 General

This section focuses on an unrepresented consumer consenting, after the collection action is brought, to a stipulated judgment in favor of the collector. Stipulated judgments consented to in the original credit documents, known as cognovits or confessions of judgment, are generally illegal,[106] and will not be considered here. Nor will this section discuss settlements reached at arms length when the consumer is represented by an attorney. Such settlements are examined elsewhere in this manual.[107]

When an unrepresented consumer attends a court hearing on the debt a favorite collector technique, sometimes encouraged by judges or other court personnel, is to take the consumer out into the corridor and resolve the matter, without appearing before the judge. This procedure has clear potential

---

97 *See, e.g.*, Lindblom v. Prime Hospitality Corp., 90 P.3d 1283 (Nev. 2004) (pre-suit interactions evinced a clear intent to appear and defend). *But see* Morin v. Burris, 161 P.3d 956 (Wash. 2007).

98 Reid v. Asset Acceptance, L.L.C., 2006 WL 3028072 (Tex. App. Oct. 25, 2006).

99 N.Y. C.P.L.R. § 3215(g)(1) (McKinney).

100 N.Y. C.P.L.R. § 3215(g)(3) (McKinney).

101 50 U.S.C. app. § 521(g).

102 50 U.S.C. app. § 521(g)(2); *see also* Collins v. Collins, 805 N.E.2d 410 (Ind. Ct. App. 2006) (servicemember precluded from moving under the Act to set aside default judgment because he did not do so within ninety days after termination of military service).

103 50 U.S.C. app. § 521(g)(1); *see also* Bernhardt v. Alden Café, 374 N.J. Super. 271, 864 A.2d 421 (Super. Ct. App. Div. 2005) (although trial court's decision to vacate default judgment under section 521(g) is discretionary, it abused that discretion when it refused to set aside default for servicemember whose military status was undisputed and who alleged a meritorious defense).

104 *In re* Marriage of Thompson, 666 N.W.2d 616 (Iowa Ct. App. 2003); *In re* B.T.T., 156 S.W.3d 612 (Tex. App. 2004).

105 N.Y. C.P.L.R. 5015(c) (McKinney).

106 *See* 16 C.F.R. § 444.2(a)(1); National Consumer Law Center, Unfair and Deceptive Acts and Practices § 5.1.1.2.4 (6th ed. 2004 and Supp.); *see also, e.g.*, Ala. Code § 8-9-11; Cal. Civ. Proc. Code § 1132 (West); 735 Ill. Comp. Stat. § 5/2-1301(c); Mass. Gen. Laws ch. 231, § 13A; Minn. Stat. § 53C.08(b) (motor vehicle installment sales); N.J. Stat. Ann. § 2A:16-9 (West); N.Y. C.P.L.R. § 3201 (McKinney); Ohio Rev. Code Ann. § 2323.13(E) (West); Tenn. Code Ann. § 25-2-101; Md. Rules (Dist. Ct.), R. 3.611; N.J. R. of Ct. 4:45-1; Or. R. Civ. P. 73A(2).

107 *See* § 2.9, *supra*.

for abuse as unrepresented consumers go up against sophisticated collection attorneys and then sign documents they do not fully understand, often without fully understanding their options as to contesting the matter in court.

Even though the consumer may have valid defenses, collectors may succeed in obtaining more than they could have obtained from the court just by persuading the consumer to sign a stipulation for judgment drafted by the collector's attorney. The stipulation may be one-sided, including inflated amounts as to the balance due, future interest charges, and attorney fees. The stipulation may even waive exemptions and other consumer rights to resist post-judgment collector remedies.

The same standards for setting aside a default judgment apply to setting aside a stipulation for judgment. State rules generally follow the example of the federal version of Rule 60 which states that "on motion and just terms, the court may relieve a party or its legal representative from a final judgment, order, or proceeding for the following reasons."[108] By its own language, this rule applies to any type of judgment, and not just to default judgments. Consequently, Rule 60 establishes the standards for setting aside a stipulated judgment.

The judgment can be set aside within one year when the judgment was a result of "mistake, inadvertence, surprise, or excusable neglect" and also "fraud, misrepresentation, or misconduct by an opposing party."[109] The stipulated judgment can be set aside even beyond one year when there is fraud upon the court, "any other reason that justifies relief," or if the judgment is void because of lack of jurisdiction or some other reason.

The collector's fraud, misrepresentation, or misconduct can thus be grounds for setting aside the stipulated judgment. This criterion includes misrepresentations as to the nature of the document the consumer is signing, or the implications of signing that document. Also ground to set aside the judgment should be any misrepresentation as to the validity of the consumer's defenses.

Look not only for collector misrepresentations, but also for unethical behavior by the collector's attorney. A state's code of legal ethics will have provisions concerning contacts with unrepresented individuals. For example, commentary to the Florida Bar Rules states that the other side's lawyer "should not give advice to an unrepresented person other than the advice to obtain counsel."[110]

A consumer confused as to the nature of a stipulated judgment that the consumer signs may also seek to set aside that default judgment because of "mistake." Mistake may also apply to an unrepresented and unsophisticated consumer's confusion as to what legal rights are available to raise defenses in the proceeding.

108 Fed. R. Civ. P. 60(b).

109 Fed. R. Civ. P. 60(b), 60(c).

110 Commentary to Rules Regulating the Florida Bar, Rule 4-4.3.

In arguing for an expansive reading of both collector misconduct and fraud upon the court, remember that the consumer is not seeking damages and need not prove all of the elements of fraud. Instead the consumer is seeking equity, so that the consumer can be heard upon the merits, when the collector's misrepresentation prevented that from occurring.

Typically, the question of the collector's misconduct will be one of credibility between the consumer and the collector's attorney as to what was said in the corridor. It may be that ethical rules will require the collector to find a new attorney to handle the motion to set aside the stipulated judgment, because the collector's first attorney will be a witness in the matter.

13.3.2 A Special Case: Mailing Stipulations with the Complaint

A number of cases in Florida in 2007 and 2008 have dealt with a collector's practice of including a stipulated judgment with the initial service of process of the summons and complaint. The process server delivers the summons, complaint, and a cover letter from the collector's attorney and a "stipulation for entry of final judgment execution withheld." The cover letter asks the consumer to contact the law firm to negotiate a payment amount that will be included in the stipulated judgment, which has the judgment amount preprinted. The letter states that if an agreed amount is reached, the consumer will not have to go to court. The Stipulation calls for post-judgment interest of 20.4%, almost double the statutory rate, and for the consumer to waive garnishment defenses. A number of consumers contacted the law firm, were told what amount to include in the stipulation, and signed the stipulation.

Florida courts have had little trouble setting aside such stipulated judgments. The courts point to the fact that the stipulations were illegally included with the court summons, and that this misled the consumer as to the consequences of signing the stipulation, providing grounds to set aside the stipulated judgment.[111] The consumer "was misled as to [the stipulation's] nature, her options and was not informed of important legal rights she was forfeiting by signing same."[112] "Serving the Stipulation and cover letter with the

111 Capital One Bank v. Mullis, 15 Fla. L. Weekly Supp. 262a (Fla. County Ct. Duval County Nov. 28, 2007), *available at* www.consumerlaw.org/unreported; Capital One Bank v. Brannon, 15 Fla. L. Weekly Supp. 84a (Fla. County Ct. Duval County Aug. 17, 2007), *available at* www.consumerlaw.org/unreported.

112 Capital One Bank v. Brannon, 15 Fla. L. Weekly Supp. 84a (Fla. County Ct. Duval County Aug. 17, 2007), *available at* www.consumerlaw.org/unreported; *see* Capital One Bank v. Mullis, 15 Fla. L. Weekly Supp. 262a (Fla. County Ct. Duval County Nov. 28, 2007), *available at* www.consumerlaw.org/unreported.

initial process simulates legal process and gives the document an air of authority and importance even though it is not a true legal pleading."[113] Another ground for setting aside the stipulated judgment was that the stipulation is unconscionable and thus unenforceable.[114]

13.4 Bankruptcy Filing's Ability to Limit the Effect of a Judgment

Bankruptcy offers prompt and permanent relief from a court judgment and is often the simplest way to deal with a collector's judgment. With only a few narrow exceptions, the merits of the collector's claim that led to the judgment are irrelevant. Unless the collector has already obtained a lien on the consumer's property, the bankruptcy discharge wipes out the judgment's effect, without the need for any additional motion filings, either in the court where the judgment was entered or in the bankruptcy court. If the collector has already obtained a judgment lien on the consumer's property, the consumer can ask the bankruptcy court to void the lien if it affects exempt property or for certain other reasons.

The filing of the consumer's initial bankruptcy petition puts into effect the automatic stay. The stay operates as a federal court injunction against a wide range of collection activities, and specifically prohibits any collector action to enforce a judgment entered against the debtor prior to the date of the bankruptcy filing.[115] This prohibition clearly encompasses a stay of attachments, garnishments, and execution sales by judicial officers. It also bars the judgment creditor or its agents from seeking to collect on the judgment by use of dunning letters, phone calls, or any other form of coercion or harassment.

Exceptions to the applicability of the automatic stay are very limited, pertaining mostly to debts that arose out of criminal or family court proceedings.[116] For example, in a chapter 7 bankruptcy, the stay does not apply to collection of child support from the debtor's wages earned after the bankruptcy was filed.

Once notified of a bankruptcy filing, the judgment creditor must take prompt action to terminate any ongoing activities being carried out to collect upon a judgment. The creditor must release attachments of bank accounts and cease garnishing wages. Continuation of any of these collection actions, or initiation of any new actions, can subject the creditor to an action for damages, costs, and attorney fees.[117] Bankruptcy also has the advantage of allowing the debtor to recover wages and other property claimed as exempt and seized in execution of a judgment within the ninety-day preference period preceding the commencement of the bankruptcy case.

There are drawbacks to filing a bankruptcy, but generally not the ones consumers fear. For example, concern over a consumer's credit rating or ability to obtain future loans is often misplaced. So are concerns that the consumer will lose most of that individual's personal property, that bankruptcy will substantially harm the consumer's reputation in the community, or that bankruptcy will lead to other forms of discrimination.

One drawback to a bankruptcy filing may be its cost. A chapter 7 filing costs $299 and a chapter 13 filing costs $274, although these amounts can be paid in installments, and certain low-income households can request a waiver of the chapter 7 fee. The consumer will also have to pay for an attorney, unless such representation is offered by a pro bono panel or a neighborhood legal services office.

Another consideration is deciding *when* to file bankruptcy. Filing too soon will prevent the discharge of debts incurred after the date of filing. A first bankruptcy filing limits the consumer's ability to file a second bankruptcy to discharge debts incurred after the first bankruptcy filing. A consumer can only obtain one chapter 7 bankruptcy discharge every eight years, although a subsequent chapter 13 plan can be filed sooner. It is generally best to wait for all debts to ripen before filing for bankruptcy.

A good resource explaining for consumers how bankruptcy works and the pros and cons of filing bankruptcy is *NCLC Guide to Surviving Debt* Chapter 19.[118] Attorneys new to the bankruptcy area should consider utilizing NCLC's *Bankruptcy Basics*,[119] which leads the attorney step-by-step through every stage of the bankruptcy process, and also provides software to complete the official forms. For the most complete discussion of all consumer bankruptcy issues, see NCLC's *Consumer Bankruptcy Law and Practice*.[120]

113 Capital One Bank v. Mullis, 15 Fla. L. Weekly Supp. 262a (Fla. County Ct. Duval County Nov. 28, 2007), *available at* www.consumerlaw.org/unreported; *see also* Capital One Bank v. Miller, 14 Fla. L. Weekly Supp. 585 (Fla. County Ct. Duval County Oct. 24, 2006); N. Star Capital Acquisitions, L.L.C. v. Krig, 14 Fla. L. Weekly Supp. 166a (Fla. County Ct. Duval County Sept. 13, 2006); Capital One Bank v. Livingston, 13 Fla. L. Weekly Supp. 1203a (Fla. County Ct. Duval County Aug. 10, 2006).

114 Capital One Bank v. Mullis, 15 Fla. L. Weekly Supp. 262a (Fla. County Ct. Duval County Nov. 28, 2007), *available at* www.consumerlaw.org/unreported; Capital One Bank v. Brannon, 15 Fla. L. Weekly Supp. 84a (Fla. County Ct. Duval County Aug. 17, 2007), *available at* www.consumerlaw.org/unreported.

115 11 U.S.C. § 362(a).

116 *See* National Consumer Law Center, Consumer Bankruptcy Law and Practice § 9.4.5 (8th ed. 2006 and Supp.).

117 11 U.S.C. § 362(k).

118 (2008).

119 (2007).

120 (8th ed. 2006 and Supp.) (two volumes).

13.5 Consumer's Separate Suit Challenging Litigation Misconduct

One option that consumer attorneys may utilize after a default or stipulated judgment for the collector is to bring a separate action, in state or federal court, challenging the collector's litigation misconduct. The substance of such a claim is considered in Chapter 14, *infra*. This section focuses only on whether it is advisable to bring those claims after the collector has obtained a judgment.

In general it is best, and may even be required, to bring those claims only after setting aside a default or stipulated judgment in the underlying action. The default or stipulated judgment has adjudicated or should have adjudicated the issue being raised in the subsequent litigation, and judicial economy requires that it not be raised again. But in some states res judicata does not apply to a default judgment.[121] There is also a question whether res judicata prevents an action against the collector's attorney, even when it would prevent an action against the collector.

In addition, the applicability of res judicata will depend on the issue the consumer wishes to litigate. For example, a collector's false representation that it would not pursue a suit if the consumer starts making payments might be viewed as a different issue than was before the court in the default judgment. More on the preclusive effect of a judgment for the collector on the consumer's subsequent affirmative action is found in other NCLC manuals.[122]

Once the default or stipulated judgment is set aside, it no longer has preclusive effect on a separate consumer action against the collector. After the judgment is set aside the consumer must then decide whether to bring claims regarding collection misconduct as a separate action or as a counterclaim in the newly revived collection action. Certain factors in making this decision are examined in § 5.5, *supra*. But an additional factor is that the collector, seeing that the consumer has obtained legal representation and intends to litigate vigorously, may not pursue the collection action. There may be no case in which the consumer can raise a counterclaim, and the consumer will be forced instead to bring an affirmative action.

In any action in federal court, such as one raising the Fair Debt Collection Practices Act (FDCPA), the implications of the *Rooker-Feldman* doctrine must be considered. According to the United States Supreme Court, the doctrine is a narrow one, confined to "cases brought by state-court losers complaining of injuries caused by state-court judgments rendered before the district court proceedings commenced and inviting district court review and rejection of those judgments."[123] The law in this area is quite confused at this moment, and it is unclear whether the doctrine, in the context of an FDCPA claim filed after a default judgment for the collector, poses any additional issues not raised by res judicata. The doctrine may not apply at all when the consumer's subsequent action is against the collector's attorney, and not the collector. These issues are examined in more detail in other NCLC manuals.[124]

There are also practical considerations about whether to bring an affirmative action or whether to first set aside the judgment. Filing a motion to set the default judgment aside gives the collector an opportunity to commit the same or additional violations through its response. Conversely, as in any other derivative suit, the consumer's hasty FDCPA case will guarantee that the collector will give its underlying collection case extra attention, and will make efforts to undo some of its litigation misconduct. It may be better to set aside the judgment, obtain a dismissal of the collection action with prejudice, and then bring the affirmative case for the collector's litigation misconduct.

---

121 Anderson v. Gamache & Myers, Prof'l Corp., 2007 WL 1577610 (E.D. Mo. May 31, 2007) (state court default judgment against plaintiff did not address the issues or claims in plaintiff's case, which was also not the same as plaintiff's Fair Debt Collection Practices Act cause of action); Flores v. Quick Collect, Inc., 2007 WL 433239 (D. Or. Jan. 31, 2007) (issue preclusion does not attach by virtue of a judgment taken by default).

122 *See* National Consumer Law Center, Fair Debt Collection § 7.4.2 (6th ed. 2008); National Consumer Law Center, Truth in Lending § 7.6.5 (6th ed. 2007); National Consumer Law Center, Foreclosures § 10.6.5 (2d ed. 2007 and Supp.).

123 Exxon Mobil Corp. v. Arabia, Inc., 544 U.S. 280, 125 S. Ct. 1517, 161 L. Ed. 2d 454 (2005); *accord* Lance v. Dennis, 546 U.S. 459, 126 S. Ct. 1198, 163 L. Ed. 2d 1059 (2006).

124 *See* National Consumer Law Center, Fair Debt Collection § 7.4.4 (6th ed. 2008); National Consumer Law Center, Foreclosures § 10.6.4 (2d ed. 2007 and Supp.).

Chapter 14 Prevailing Consumers' Post-Judgment Actions

14.1 Attorney Fees for the Prevailing Consumer

14.1.1 Introduction

The American rule is that attorney fees are not recoverable absent contractual or statutory authority. This section enumerates seven ways in which a prevailing *consumer* can receive an attorney fee award.

Other related topics, such as how to calculate that award and the proper procedure for seeking the award, are covered in other NCLC manuals. Because collection actions are usually brought in state court, state law will generally govern the attorney fee award, even when the award is based upon federal counterclaims. As a result, while good resources on these topics include NCLC's *Fair Debt Collection* § 6.8[1] and *Truth in Lending* § 8.9,[2] the most comprehensive discussion will be found in NCLC's *Unfair and Deceptive Acts and Practices* § 8.8.[3] In addition, sample pleadings and other sample documentation concerning attorney fee applications, listed in NCLC's *Consumer Law Pleadings*,[4] are available electronically in Microsoft Word format on that manual's companion website.

This section focuses solely on theories by which a prevailing consumer defendant in a collection action can recover the attorney fees required to defend the case. It does not treat other attorney fee topics.

14.1.2 Right to Fees Based upon the Contract

Carefully parse the attorney fee provision in the credit contract if the collector or consumer has produced this contract for the court. Credit contracts typically provide for attorney fees for a prevailing collector, but occasionally such contracts provide for fees for the prevailing party. The Providian standard form credit card agreement is an important example. Any ambiguity as to whether an attorney fee provision applies only to a prevailing collector or to either prevailing party should be construed in the consumer's favor, as the creditor has drafted the standard form contract.

14.1.3 Consumer's Statutory Right to Fees When Collector Has a Contractual Right to Fees

A number of states, including the populous states of California, Florida, and New York, have legislation that provides for reciprocal attorney fees when a contract provides that one of the parties to the contract is to receive attorney fees.[5] These statutes provide that the court may award fees to the prevailing consumer whenever the credit contract provides for fees to be awarded to the collector.

The consumer may be entitled to fees under such a provision even if the collector dismisses the action with prejudice during the trial.[6] Depending on the terms of the statute, fees may be available for the consumer even if the court has found insufficient evidence of the terms of the contract. The collector's reference in its pleadings to the contract and its invocation of the contract's attorney fee provision should be sufficient to award fees to the consumer under the reciprocal fee statute.[7]

14.1.4 Statutory Right to Fees for the Prevailing Party for Certain Causes of Action

Even when the credit contract does not provide for attorney fees, a number of state statutes provide for attorney fees

1 (6th ed. 2008).

2 (6th ed. 2007).

3 (6th ed. 2004 and Supp.).

4 (Index Guide with Companion Website).

5 Cal. Civ. Code § 1717 (West); Conn. Gen. Stat. § 42-150bb; Fla. Stat. § 57.105(7); Haw. Rev. Stat. § 607-14; Mont. Code Ann. § 28-3-704; N.H. Rev. Stat. Ann. § 361-C:2; N.Y. Gen. Oblig. Law § 5-327 (McKinney); Or. Rev. Stat. § 20.096; Utah Code Ann. § 78-27-56.5; Wash. Rev. Code § 4.84.330; *see also* United Wholesale Supply, Inc. v. Wear, 106 Wash. App. 1042, 45 U.C.C. Rep. Serv. 2d 1068 (2001).

6 Landry v. Countrywide Home Loans, Inc., 731 So. 2d 137 (Fla. Dist. Ct. App. 1999); Credit Card Receivables Fund v. Cleary, 2006 WL 3775899 (Fla. Cir. Ct. Dec. 19, 2006). *But see* Wachovia SBA Lending v. Kraft, 158 P.3d 1271 (Wash. Ct. App. 2007).

7 Credit Card Receivables Fund v. Cleary, 2006 WL 3775899 (Fla. Cir. Ct. Dec. 19, 2006).

for the prevailing party in a collection action, or provide fees for the party prevailing on certain causes of action. Alaska provides that "except as otherwise provided by law or agreed to by thc parties, the prevailing party in a civil case shall be awarded attorney's fees calculated under this rule."[8] A California statute relating to retail sales states: "Reasonable attorney's fees and costs shall be awarded to the prevailing party in any action on a contract or installment account subject to the provisions of this chapter regardless of whether such action is instituted by the seller, holder or buyer."[9]

An Arizona statute provides that in a contested action "arising out of a contract, express or implied, the court may award the successful party reasonable attorney fees."[10] As the statute mentions both express and implied contracts, this statute provides a basis for the consumer to recover even in cases in which the collector does not seek to prove a written contract.

Idaho goes one step further and provides that "in any civil action to recover on an open account, account stated, note, bill, negotiable instrument, guaranty, or contract relating to the purchase or sale of goods, wares, merchandise, or services and in any commercial transaction unless otherwise provided by law, the prevailing party shall be allowed a reasonable attorney's fee to be set by the court, to be taxed and collected as costs."[11] Idaho also provides, when that provision does not apply, that the prevailing party still receives attorney fees if the amount the collector pleaded is less than $25,000.[12]

Oklahoma provides fees to the prevailing party "in any civil action to recover for labor or services rendered, or on an open account, a statement of account, account stated, note, bill, negotiable instrument, or contract relating to the purchase or sale of goods, wares, or merchandise."[13] Arkansas has a similar statute.[14] New Mexico provides for attorney fees for the prevailing party on an action on an open account if the action is filed in the district court, small claims court, or magistrate court.[15] Mississippi has a similar statute.[16]

Oklahoma's Supreme Court has upheld an award for the consumer under its statute when the consumer succeeded in setting aside a default judgment and the collector then voluntarily dismissed the case.[17] While a consumer might not be considered to prevail in a case if the collector dismisses the case before the consumer seeks affirmative relief, the motion to vacate the default judgment is such an attempt at affirmative relief. The key is not whether the consumer obtained a judgment, but whether the consumer had a successful result.[18]

8 Alaska R. Civ. P. 82(a).
9 Cal. Civ. Code § 1811.1 (West).
10 Ariz. Rev. Stat. Ann. § 12-341.01(A).
11 Idaho Code Ann. § 12-120(3).
12 Idaho Code Ann. § 12-120(1).
13 Okla. Stat. tit. 12, § 936.
14 Ark. Code Ann. § 16-22-308.
15 N.M. Stat. § 39-2-2.1.
16 Miss. Code Ann. § 11-53-81.
17 Prof'l Credit Collections, Inc. v. Smith, 933 P.2d 307 (Okla. 2007).

14.1.5 Fee Awards Pursuant to Consumer Counterclaims

The statutes underlying the consumer's counterclaims often provide for fees for a prevailing consumer. Section 5.5.2, *supra*, examines whether to bring various counterclaims. One obvious benefit to bringing such counterclaims is that a prevailing consumer will recover statutory attorney fees for counterclaims under such statutes as the Fair Debt Collection Practices Act (FDCPA), the state unfair and deceptive acts and practices (UDAP) statute, and state debt collection and credit laws.[19] Such fees are awarded whether those statutory causes of action are brought affirmatively or as counterclaims. While the attorney fees may compensate only for time spent litigating the statutory counterclaim, that work is likely to be intertwined with, if not inseparable from, the collection case, allowing the consumer to recover a full attorney fee award.[20]

In addition, an FDCPA or UDAP counterclaim for litigation misconduct may claim as actual damages the attorney fees the consumer must pay to defend a case that the collector should not have brought or the aspect of the case that gave rise to the violation. As discussed in the following subsection, the successful counterclaim will result in compensation for attorney time not only for prosecuting the counterclaim (as a statutory fee award), but also for the time spent defending the collector's inappropriate causes of actions (as actual damages).

14.1.6 A Second Lawsuit to Recover the Consumer's Fees in the Collection Action

When the prevailing consumer can not recover attorney fees in the collection action, the consumer may consider bringing a second action after conclusion of the first, seeking to recover for attorney time spent defending the collection action. Similar to an FDCPA or UDAP counterclaim for litigation misconduct discussed in § 14.1.5, *supra*, an affirmative action under these statutes or a malicious prosecution tort would seek as actual damages the attorney fees incurred in defeating the collection action. The prevailing consumer

18 *Id.*
19 *See* § 5.5, *supra*.
20 *See* National Consumer Law Center, Unfair and Deceptive Acts and Practices § 8.8.11.4 (6th ed. 2004 and Supp.). *See generally* Hensley v. Eckerhart, 461 U.S. 424, 103 S. Ct. 1933, 76 L. Ed. 2d 40 (1983).

in this second action could recover statutory fees to prosecute the second action under an FDCPA or UDAP cause of action, and then recover as actual damages the fees expended in the first case.[21] To perfect the claim for actual damages, the consumer needs to be financially obligated to pay the attorney the fees resulting from the successful defense of the collection case, even if those fees have not been paid. To constitute recoverable actual damages the consumer's fee obligation should be for a sum certain and not for an unliquidated, contingent, or other inchoate amount. In some states these fees, as actual damages, might even be trebled under a UDAP statute or enhanced by punitive damages under a malicious prosecution claim. More on such actions is found later in this chapter.[22]

14.1.7 Fees When Collector Denies the Consumer's Request for Admissions

Chapter 2, *supra*, discusses reasons why the consumer might (or might not) wish to send requests for admissions to a collector, and § 4.2.2.1, *supra*, examines the consequences of a party's denials of requests for admissions. When the collector denies facts that the consumer later proves to be true, and the collector did not have a reasonable basis for that denial, then the collector is liable for the reasonable expenses of the consumer's proof—which would include attorney fees and other expenses.[23]

14.1.8 Attorney Fees for Vexatious Litigation

States typically have rules or statutes dealing with vexatious litigation, providing attorney fees for the party prejudiced by such litigation. For example, Arizona's statute states: "The court shall award reasonable attorney fees in any contested action upon clear and convincing evidence that the claim or defense constitutes harassment, is groundless and is not made in good faith."[24] While this is a difficult standard to meet, there may be cases of egregious collector litigation misconduct that meets this standard.

The collector's knowledge will be critical to the consumer's ability to recover under a state statute for vexatious litigation. A collector who pursues a collection action despite knowing that the consumer does not owe the debt is vulnerable to sanctions. For example, sanctions have been awarded when the collector received a copy of the consumer's credit report, which showed that the debt had been discharged in bankruptcy and thus was not owed, but the collector proceeded with the case anyway.[25]

Confirming that a collector received a copy of the consumer's credit report is a simple matter. The consumer can obtain a copy of the report from the reporting agency,[26] and the inquiry section of the consumer's copy will show who has received a copy of the report during the previous year.[27]

A collector's prompt voluntary dismissal of the case after the consumer's answer is not always enough to avoid sanctions.[28] Debt buyers may bring thousands of cases, counting on default judgments in virtually all of them. The collector's bad faith is not lessened when it brings many invalid cases and then drops the few in which a vigorous defense is offered.

States also may have rules that assess "costs" to a party who engages in certain specific forms of vexatious litigation. For example, Florida provides for a defendant to recover "costs" relating to defending a first action when the plaintiff voluntarily dismissed that action without prejudice, and then brings a similar second action.[29] A state's jurisprudence will determine whether the term "costs" includes attorney fees in that context. In Florida, when the credit contract itself defines "costs" to include attorney fees (for example, when the contract states that the creditor is entitled to "costs, including attorney fees"), the consumer can recover attorney fees when a statute provides for the recovery of "costs."[30]

14.2 Cleaning Up the Consumer's Credit Record

14.2.1 How a Case's Dismissal Is Reported to Credit Bureaus

14.2.1.1 The Credit Reporting System

Consumers have a strong interest in insuring that accurate information is reflected in their credit reports, particularly after they prevail in a collection action. The reports and

21 *See* Lowe v. Elite Recovery Solutions Ltd. P'ship, 2008 WL 324777 (E.D. Cal. Feb. 5, 2008); Venes v. Prof'l Serv. Bureau, Inc., 353 N.W.2d 671 (Minn. Ct. App. 1984); *see also* McKnight v. Benitez, 176 F. Supp. 2d 1301 (M.D. Fla. 2001); Evanauskas v. Strumpf, 2001 U.S. Dist. LEXIS 14326 (D. Conn. June 27, 2001).

22 *See* § 14.4, *infra*.

23 *See* Fed. R. Civ. P. 37(c)(2).

24 Ariz. Rev. Stat. Ann. § 12-341.01(C).

25 Unifund CCR Partners v. Villa, 2008 WL 1733235 (Tex. App. Apr. 16, 2008).

26 How to obtain a copy of the report is explained in National Consumer Law Center, Fair Credit Reporting Ch. 3 (6th ed. 2006 and Supp.). *See also* § 14.2.3.1, *infra*.

27 *See* National Consumer Law Center, Fair Credit Reporting § 3.5.4.1 (6th ed. 2006 and Supp.).

28 *See* Unifund CCR Partners v. Villa, 2008 WL 1733235 (Tex. App. Apr. 16, 2008).

29 *See* Fla. R. Civ. P. 1.420(d).

30 Credit Receivables Fund, Inc. v. Cleary, 2006 WL 3775899 (Fla. Cir. Ct. Dec. 19, 2006); *see also* Wilson v. Rose Printing Co., 624 So. 2d 257 (Fla. 1993).

resulting credit scores determine, among other things, access to credit and insurance and its cost, and even whether employment is offered.[31] When a collection action has been filed the consumer's credit reports ordinarily will contain adverse information about that debt and the collection lawsuit.

Surprisingly, winning the collection action, by itself, may do little or nothing to improve the prevailing consumer's credit report. Instead consumers must take affirmative steps to update their credit report based upon the court judgment. Even that affirmative action may accomplish less than most consumers would expect.

Here are some "facts of life" about the credit reporting system. Credit bureaus are called consumer reporting agencies (CRAs) and their activities are regulated by the Fair Credit Reporting Act (FCRA).[32] The three major agencies, Equifax, Experian, and Trans Union, each maintain records on about 210 million Americans and each *month* receive from creditors and other furnishers about four billion pieces of information concerning approximately 1.5 billion credit accounts and other "tradelines." The agencies do not keep "files" in any traditional sense on those 210 million Americans. Instead, when called upon to prepare a credit report, agency software attempts to match the names and other personal identifiers associated with the substantive information from each tradeline in the computer's massive storage banks and assembles all of the information with matching identifiers to create an individual consumer's credit report.

A credit report is thus a snapshot in time. What a consumer sees one month will not be the same as what the consumer or a creditor sees when requesting the report at a different point in time. A credit report will contain identifying information about the consumer, an inquiries section showing what entities have requested a report on the consumer within the last year, and a public records section showing information on court actions and bankruptcies. A large portion of the report will be a listing of credit accounts, often called tradelines.[33] For each tradeline the report will list information about the account and the creditor, when the account was opened, the last update on the account, the highest amount ever owed, the current balance, the date and amount of the maximum delinquency, and the number of times the consumer has been 30, 60, or 90 days delinquent on the account.

14.2.1.2 Reporting of Court Judgments As Public Records

CRAs hire outside "public record vendors" who search, among other things, court records and furnish that information to the agencies. The public records vendors routinely note and report the filing of collection lawsuits as well as the entry of judgments for the plaintiff. However, the same is not true of information about the case's dismissal. The agency may not receive information about the case's dismissal from the vendor or may not use that information to update preexisting information in the consumer's file.[34] As a result the pendency of a collection action often remains as the latest information that the agencies claim to know, even when the case has concluded in the consumer's favor.

Moreover, the original creditor and subsequent debt buyer typically have no affirmative obligation to send the CRAs information about the court judgment. Instead, that information is provided to the agency by a public record vendor, and not the creditor or collector. The creditor and collector instead have obligations relating to the information that they furnish in the account and collection tradeline sections of the credit report, discussed in the next subsection.

14.2.1.3 Reporting of Court Judgments in Tradelines

There is no private enforcement of the FCRA provision requiring furnishers, such as the original creditor or a subsequent debt buyer, to affirmatively update the information that they provide to a CRA; nor is there private enforcement of the FCRA duty to furnish accurate and complete information in the first place.[35] Furnishers' only privately enforceable legal obligation to accurately report and to correct and update information is triggered by the consumer initiating a formal FCRA dispute, and thereby causing a reinvestigation.[36]

When the original creditor, who regularly furnishes information about the consumer's account, brought the collection action, it is very possible that updated information which reflects the court judgment will be forwarded to the CRA as part of that creditor's regular reporting. However, often the updated information is not provided, and in any event it is hard to predict what information will be sent or how it will relate to the other information already in the file.

When a debt buyer brought the collection action, the original creditor will have long since stopped furnishing information about the account to the CRAs. The debt buyer is much less likely to regularly update information on its

31 *See* National Consumer Law Center, Fair Credit Reporting Ch. 12 (6th ed. 2006 and Supp.).

32 15 U.S.C. §§ 1681–1681x; *see also* National Consumer Law Center, Fair Credit Reporting (6th ed. 2006 and Supp.).

33 National Consumer Law Center, Fair Credit Reporting § 3.7 (6th ed. 2006 and Supp.).

34 *See id.* §§ 4.3.2.5, 4.4.6.4.

35 15 U.S.C. § 1681s-2(a)(1), (2); *see* National Consumer Law Center, Fair Credit Reporting § 6.1.2 (6th ed. 2006 and Supp.).

36 15 U.S.C. § 1681s-2(b); *see* National Consumer Law Center, Fair Credit Reporting § 6.10 (6th ed. 2006 and Supp.).

accounts with the CRAs. As a result, new information will rarely be sent to the CRA after the debt buyer's collection action is dismissed.

The only practical way to update and correct information in the consumer's report after prevailing in a collection action is for the consumer to lodge a formal dispute with the CRA. The consumer should dispute any inaccurate information in the original creditor's tradeline, any collection tradeline reflecting the same debt, and any entry in the public records section of the report reflecting the collection action. The CRA will then ask anyone furnishing disputed information (for example, the original creditor and/or the debt buyer) to reinvestigate that information. This process requires the creditor or debt buyer to correct and update information previously supplied to the CRA, including acknowledging the judgment for the consumer in the collection case. The furnisher is liable for the full range of FCRA private remedies for any breach of its reinvestigation duties.[37]

14.2.2 All Information in a Report Must Be Accurate

A credit report includes both current and historical information about credit accounts. Current information includes how much is currently due and how delinquent that amount is. Historical data includes such information as that the account was more than sixty days delinquent in the past, or that the account involves a repossession or a charge-off. The consumer's interest is to correct both current and historical adverse information.

The consumer should be able to correct the current information in the report. If the court dismisses a collection action with prejudice, then the current information on the account should reflect a zero balance. When the consumer disputes a current balance which is more than zero, the CRA will ask the entity that provided that information to reinvestigate.

No matter what entity reported a positive current balance to the CRA, the existence of the court judgment for the consumer means that the credit report must show a zero balance. If the original creditor was the entity that reported a balance owed, it should either report a zero balance (if it brought the collection action) or a zero balance, sold to another (if it had previously sold the debt). After selling the debt to another, the original creditor is no longer owed any money by the consumer, and thus the account should have a zero balance. Similarly, if the current balance information was furnished by an intermediate debt buyer (that is, one who subsequently resold the account), then that debt buyer should remove the entry, or at least correct the entry to show a zero balance, sold to another.

If the entity that reported the current balance was the debt buyer who brought the collection action, then that debt buyer will have to correct the balance to zero owed because its collection action was dismissed with prejudice and the consumer owes nothing on the account.

On the other hand, it will not be possible to eliminate adverse historical information when the favorable resolution of the collection case does not challenge that history. For example, a judgment for the consumer in a collection case might result from the fact that the court found that the account was paid in full at the time of trial. In that event, the court judgment is consistent with the historical information being reported on the account, such as the fact that payments were late sixty days at some points in the past, that a car was in fact repossessed, or that a debt was in fact charged off. When that historical information is correct, it can remain on the report for seven years, notwithstanding the ultimate result in the collection case.

Of course, the consumer's ability to correct historical information is increased if the court's judgment is accompanied by a decision that indicates not only that the debt action was dismissed, but that the consumer did not owe the debt at all, now or in the past. When the original creditor was the plaintiff in the collection action, the best result would be if the court's order includes a requirement that the creditor contact CRAs to correct the historical information in the consumer's file. If the case is settled instead, the consumer can insist on a similar provision in the settlement.[38]

Short of such an order to correct historical information in the consumer's file, it is helpful if the court issues a decision spelling out that the consumer did not owe the debt at all, now or in the past. For example, the court could find unauthorized use, identity theft, a mistaken identity, or the like, and so indicate in a written decision. The consumer can send this decision to the original creditor (or other entity furnishing the historical information to the CRA), and dispute the accuracy of the historical information with the CRA. Then the consumer can dispute ever being ninety days delinquent because the consumer never owed the debt in the first place.

When asked to reinvestigate the entity furnishing the historical information should change what it reports to reflect the court decision. However, even if the court judgment contains no such findings or details (as is typically the case in a small claims court), the fact that the dismissal is consistent with and confirms the consumer's dispute is highly relevant and should be quite persuasive.

37 *See* National Consumer Law Center, Fair Credit Reporting § 6.10 (6th ed. 2006 and Supp.).

38 *See* § 2.9.2, *supra*.

14.2.3 *How to Dispute Information in the Consumer's File*

14.2.3.1 General

The first step in disputing information in a consumer's credit report is to obtain a copy of that report from at least the three major CRAs. Information in the three reports will be similar, but not identical. For example, sometimes one report will not pick up a lawsuit or judgment, while reports from the other CRAs will do so. The consumer will have to make sure that the information in all three reports is updated.

The consumer is entitled to one free report a year, using any of the three following methods:

- On-line at www.annualcreditreport.com;
- By calling toll free (877) 322-8228; or
- By sending a letter to Annual Credit Report Request Service, P.O. Box 105281, Atlanta, GA 30374-5281.

The consumer may be asked detailed information about existing credit accounts and employment, as a form of identification, in addition to the usual forms of identification.

In addition to a free annual report, consumers have a number of other rights to obtain a consumer report from the "Big Three" nationwide CRAs. The consumer is entitled to a free credit report after an identity theft incident,[39] after a consumer receives notice of an adverse credit action that resulted from the consumer's credit report,[40] if the consumer is unemployed or on public assistance,[41] or if state law so provides.[42] The consumer can also purchase a report relatively inexpensively, or purchase one of the many other more expensive (and largely unnecessary) products that the nationwide CRAs are now marketing. Going to the three CRAs' websites will provide easy access to all of these paid products.

Analyze the report carefully to see which entities supplied what information to the CRA, what information was inaccurate prior to the court judgment, and what information is now inaccurate because the consumer prevailed in the collection action. The consumer's next step is to dispute with the relevant CRA all inaccurate information in the report, as described below.

39 National Consumer Law Center, Fair Credit Reporting § 3.3.5 (6th ed. 2006 and Supp.).

40 *Id.* § 3.3.6.

41 *Id.* § 3.3.7.

42 *Id.* § 3.3.8.

14.2.3.2 Send a Dispute at Least to All Three Major Credit Bureaus

The first and most important step to start the formal FCRA dispute process is to mail a dispute directly to the CRA that produced the inaccurate credit report.[43] Disputing the debt with the collector or original creditor and not the CRA is ineffective for FCRA dispute purposes.[44]

It is usually not enough to dispute an error at one CRA. A creditor furnishing incorrect information to one agency will often furnish the same incorrect information to the other two. Moreover, contrary to expectations, correcting a consumer's file with one agency does not lead to correction at the other two. Even if the consumer receives a report from only one CRA, the consumer should send a written dispute to all three—Experian, Trans Union, and Equifax.

14.2.3.3 Also Notify the Collector and Original Creditor of the Dispute

Consumers, at the same time they notify the CRAs, should directly notify the collector or original creditor furnishing the disputed information. The critical notice of dispute is directed to the CRA, which will then ask the collector or creditor to reinvestigate. But consumers strengthen their position when they also notify the furnisher of the inaccurate information. It is also helpful to put the original creditor on notice of the judgment, if it is not on notice already.

Sending a detailed notice to the collector and original creditor short circuits a favorite ploy by which furnishers attempt to justify an inadequate reinvestigation. The CRA, in forwarding the consumer's dispute to the furnisher, will often reduce the consumer's detailed dispute letter to an

43 *See id.* § 4.5.

Although the CRAs change their phone numbers and addresses frequently, here is contact information for the three major CRAs when requesting a credit report other than the annual free report:

Equifax
P.O. Box 740241
Atlanta, GA 30374-0241.
www.equifax.com
(800) 685-1111

Experian
P.O. Box 2002
Allen, TX 75013
www.experian.com
(888) EXPERIAN (397-3742)

TransUnion
P.O. Box 1000
Chester, PA 19022
www.transunion.com
(800) 888-4213

44 *See* National Consumer Law Center, Fair Credit Reporting §§ 6.10, 10.2.4 (6th ed. 2006 and Supp.).

electronic message, with the underlying dispute translated to a generic two-digit dispute code (for example, "01 not his/hers") and perhaps a short, one-line paraphrase of some aspect of the dispute (for example, "Consumer states belongs to husband only"). Supplying the furnisher directly with a copy of the consumer's dispute to the CRA thwarts any claim by the furnisher that it did not understand the consumer's dispute, based only on the abbreviated notice that it received from the CRA.

14.2.3.4 Form of the Request

Although not required by the FCRA, the consumer's dispute with the CRA should be in writing (and the consumer should keep copies of all correspondence). Telephone disputes do not allow for the presentation of copies of the judgment and other important documents, and do not create an adequate record in the event a consumer follows a failed dispute with litigation.

Sending the request by certified mail, return receipt requested, is highly advisable. The legal mailing presumption will normally not suffice. As a practical matter the CRAs seem to lose track of a large number of disputes received, an unfortunate habit for companies whose business itself is record retention. As a legal matter, a CRA that claims that it never received the dispute will argue that it merely made a mistake, rather than defend the accusation that its procedures themselves are inadequate.

Avoid using the Internet to forward disputes. When consumers make a dispute through a CRA website, they are confined to a "check-box" dispute form, and can not forward the judgment or other documents that are essential to support their claim. Nor can the consumer conveniently send a copy of the dispute to the creditor or debt buyer. It is especially ironic that CRAs regularly raise defenses such as the consumer's lack of detail in the dispute, when the Internet dispute process designed by the CRA prevents the consumer from doing anything more.

When consumers request copies of their credit reports from the three major CRAs, they will receive a dispute form that they will be encouraged to use. As with the Internet dispute forms, these forms provide only a list of "check box" dispute choices, and appear to discourage a more detailed description of the dispute. Consumers using such a form for a dispute should at least supplement it with additional written details and documentary support.

Having the consumer sign the dispute under oath converts the letter into an affidavit, with several resulting benefits. The affidavit provides greater credibility to the consumer's complaint, especially in contrast to the furnisher's automated, unsworn response. The affidavit also advances a claim against the CRA that it failed to forward "all relevant information" to the information furnisher. Moreover, CRAs and furnishers may have policies which give greater weight to consumer affidavits and may therefore more readily accept the consumer's version of the dispute and is more likely to resolve it favorably.

A request for reinvestigation often is just the beginning of a protracted battle with the CRA or furnisher, who may ignore correspondence or fail to follow up as promised. It is good practice for the consumer to establish a file of all correspondence sent and received, and to keep proof that the CRA and furnisher have received the consumer's correspondence.

14.2.3.5 Content of the Dispute Letter

The dispute itself should be detailed and specific and should enclose a court endorsed copy of the judgment from the collection action. The dispute letter might also include the name and telephone numbers of the court clerk and attorney who represented the collector.

Particularly when a court order simply dismisses the case, the consumer might include other documentation prepared for trial that explains why not just the current balance, but also historical information in the consumer report is inaccurate—such as an affidavit that the consumer never had an account with the creditor or that a spouse was never on a credit account. Include all other documentary evidence and information that supports the dispute. A consumer's word alone is rarely sufficient. If the original creditor or collector has ever admitted that any of the disputed information is incorrect, include that admission.

The dispute notice should adequately identify the consumer, fully identify the account or other item being disputed, explain why it is disputed, and explain what the consumer wants the CRA to do. Otherwise, the CRAs may take consumer disputes literally, and do nothing more than what is literally requested. Disputes thus should be both very specific, and also general enough to avoid technical interpretations that evade the thrust of the consumer's dispute.

For example, if the consumer states, "I have never had an MBNA credit card, so delete MBNA account #1234," the CRA may only delete an account with that number, and not other MBNA accounts attributed to the consumer. Illustrating the problem from this example is the fact that many creditors change account numbers after an initial dispute is made; correcting just the old account will not affect these new accounts. Other times, the account number the consumer finds on a periodic statement will be different from the number used in the consumer's file at the CRA.

To prevent these problems, a reinvestigation request should describe the full range of accounts the dispute covers. For example, "I have never had an MBNA credit card. Any MBNA account in my credit file is not mine and should be deleted. This includes account number 1234, as well as any other account you may be reporting, as well as any account that may be reported by any debt collector who is reporting a debt originating from an MBNA account." For First USA accounts, which became Bank One and then Chase accounts, a consumer could state, "I am disputing First USA account #2345. It may also be reported as a Bank One or a J.P. Morgan Chase account."

14.2.3.6 Follow Up

A CRA that receives a consumer dispute will ask each entity furnishing the disputed information to reinvestigate. If that furnisher does not verify the disputed information as correct within thirty days, the CRA must delete that information. After a couple of months, it is important to look at the consumer's report again to see if the disputed information has in fact been changed or improperly reinserted. At the same time, review the inquiries section of the report to see if the collector continues to obtain copies of the consumer's report even after the judgment, when it is no longer a creditor and no longer has a permissible purpose to request the report—a clear FCRA violation.[45]

The process of correcting disputed information is highly problematical. Even though the consumer might send a detailed letter with extensive documentation, the CRA may quickly code all of that information into a short message that is electronically relayed to the entity furnishing the disputed information. The entity furnishing the information, often not fully understanding the consumer's dispute from just the short message, may then claim it has reinvestigated and that the information is correct. The report will then remain unchanged.

14.2.4 When Credit Report Is Still Not Corrected

If the CRA fails to correct the consumer's report, then the consumer has several additional steps to take. First, the consumer can repeat the dispute process, providing additional explanations or details, and see if that works the second time through. New information should be specifically included and referenced, because the CRA may refuse to investigate again on the basis that it has already done so. Submitting such additional disputes will always enhance the value of any subsequent litigation and sometimes may actually correct the inaccuracy.

Another option is to bring an FCRA action against the CRA and the entity that improperly reinvestigated the dispute. Such litigation is examined in NCLC's *Fair Credit Reporting*.[46] The FCRA sets a thirty to forty-five day timeframe to resolve a formal dispute. After that, the failure to correct a patent inaccuracy, particularly one that is irrefutably documented by a copy of the court judgment, constitutes a host of FCRA violations by the credit bureau and the entity that failed in its reinvestigation. An FCRA action has a two-year statute of limitations and may be brought in state or federal court. The consumer can recover actual damages (such as damage to the consumer's credit rating) and attorney fees. If the violation is willful the consumer can also recover statutory and punitive damages.

In addition, if the furnisher is a collection agency or a debt buyer subject to the Fair Debt Collection Practices Act (FDCPA) and communicates information which it knows or should know is false to the CRA, it will be liable for violating the FDCPA, which can result in an award of up to $1000 in statutory damages, actual damages, and attorney fees.[47] This FDCPA violation occurs any time the debt collector/furnisher knowingly communicates false information to a CRA and not just during the formal FCRA reinvestigation process.

14.3 Responding to Renewed Collection on the Same Debt

A debt buyer who loses a collection suit may package the extinguished debt into one of its portfolios and sell the portfolio to another debt buyer. The debt buyer may even continue to seek collection on the debt itself.[48] The consumer has significant remedies to challenge such practices.

Of course the consumer has a complete defense if sued a second time on the same debt after the first case was dismissed with prejudice. The consumer also has good legal claims even when there are only collection contacts on the same debt after the judgment for the consumer, or even if a collector just pulls the consumer's credit report, after a judgment for the consumer.

The first collector has engaged in a clear Fair Debt Collection Practices Act (FDCPA) violation by reselling a debt when the court has dismissed the collection action with prejudice. The second debt buyer may also be liable for various FDCPA violations when it duns the consumer on a nonexistent debt, though it will claim to be nothing more than an innocent victim of its assignor's deception.

Magrin v. Unifund CCR Partners, Inc. is the leading case finding an FDCPA violation when a debt buyer sold the debt after its action on the debt had been dismissed.[49] The Ninth Circuit found that the essential ingredients of liability under the FDCPA for such a claim was that the debt seller sold the extinguished debt knowing that it was misrepresenting the debt's legal status (either by affirmative false representation or by omission of the material fact that the debt had been

45 *See* § 14.3, *infra*.

46 (6th ed. 2006 and Supp.).

47 15 U.S.C. § 1692e(8); *see also* National Consumer Law Center, Fair Debt Collection § 5.5.11 (6th ed. 2008).

48 *See* Centurion Capital Corp. v. Druce, 828 N.Y.S.2d 851 (Civ. Ct. 2006).

49 Magrin v. Unifund CCR Partners, Inc., 52 Fed. Appx. 938 (9th Cir. 2002).

extinguished) and with the knowledge that the second debt buyer would undertake efforts to collect the debt. The FDCPA prohibits deceptive or misleading representations "in connection with the collection of any debt."[50] That the debt buyer selling the debt is not the one collecting on the debt is irrelevant, because the debt buyer's misrepresentation is in connection with the second debt buyer's collection of the debt.

The debt seller is also violating the FDCPA provision requiring a collector, whenever communicating "credit information," to disclose that a known disputed debt is disputed.[51] The debt seller that lost the collection lawsuit can hardly deny that it knew that the consumer disputes the debt. Furthermore, the collector is communicating credit information when it completes the assignment documents selling the debt to the next buyer. Consequently, the debt seller, in assigning the debt, must disclose the fact that the debt is disputed.[52] The debt collector who reports to a credit bureau that the debt is still owed after it loses a collection action also violates the FDCPA by communicating credit information that it knew or should have known was false.[53]

In bringing FDCPA claims against the debt buyer, the consumer can recover up to $1000 in statutory damages, attorney fees to pursue the FDCPA action, plus actual damages.[54] Actual damages will depend on the facts of the case, but should include the cost to the consumer of hiring an attorney to respond to the second debt buyer's collection contacts, plus any aggravation and suffering caused by those contacts. Moreover, a state deceptive practices (UDAP) claim should be able to challenge the same conduct, leading in some states to punitive or treble damages.[55]

In *Magrin*, the second debt buyer's defense was that it too was an innocent victim of the first debt buyer. The consumer may be able to convert that protestation into proof establishing the liability of the first debt buyer (the debt buyer that lost the collection action). In the highly unlikely event that the first debt buyer actually disclosed to its assignee that the debt had been extinguished, the second debt buyer, rather than the assignor, would become the principal target of the FDCPA litigation. More likely, the second debt buyer will produce the assignment documentation proving the first debt buyer's misrepresentations and omissions. Either way, the consumer should be able to establish that one or the other debt buyer is culpable.

When the consumer prevails in the collection action, it is also illegal for the collector to continue to request the consumer's credit report. Consequently, it is prudent to review the inquiries section of the consumer's credit report obtained a number of months after the judgment. (It is best to review a report from the same credit bureau that the collector has used in the past.) After the judgment the collector is no longer the consumer's creditor, and no longer has a permissible purpose to request the consumer's credit report. Requesting a credit report without a permissible purpose is a violation of the Fair Credit Reporting Act.[56]

14.4 Consumer's Follow-Up Lawsuit Relating to Collector's Litigation Misconduct

14.4.1 Scope of This Section

After prevailing in the collection action, the consumer may wish to bring affirmative claims against the collector or the collector's attorney based upon their conduct in the collection action. Chapter 5, *supra*, examines the advisability of bringing such claims as counterclaims in the collection action itself. This section considers such claims brought separately after the conclusion of the litigation, with a focus on claims brought under the federal Fair Debt Collection Practices Act (FDCPA). State deceptive practices act (UDAP), malicious prosecution, and abuse of process claims are also considered.

FDCPA litigation is the topic of another NCLC manual, *Fair Debt Collection*,[57] so this section provides just an overview of a consumer's individual action. FDCPA class actions for litigation misconduct by collection attorneys or collectors will not be treated here at all, and the reader is referred to NCLC's *Fair Debt Collection*, and also to another NCLC manual, *Consumer Class Actions*.[58]

14.4.2 Factors to Consider When Initiating Follow-Up Litigation

14.4.2.1 Relief Sought

The relief the consumer seeks is central to any follow-up action suing the collector or the collector's attorney. Americans' sense of justice and the proper operation of the court system is often deeply offended by collector litigation misconduct. Collectors bring suits when they have no legal right to recover, when they have insufficient evidence that the consumer is liable, or when they seek attorney fees and other charges beyond all reason. The collectors are using the court

50 15 U.S.C. § 1692e.

51 15 U.S.C. § 1692e(8).

52 *See* National Consumer Law Center, Fair Debt Collection § 5.5.11 (6th ed. 2008).

53 15 U.S.C. 1692e(8); *see also* National Consumer Law Center, Fair Debt Collection § 5.5.11 (6th ed. 2008).

54 15 U.S.C. § 1692k(a).

55 *See* National Consumer Law Center, Unfair and Deceptive Acts and Practices Appx. A (6th ed. 2004 and Supp.).

56 *See* National Consumer Law Center, Fair Credit Reporting Ch. 7 (6th ed. 2006 and Supp.).

57 (6th ed. 2008).

58 (6th ed. 2006 and Supp.).

system as a rubber stamp for default judgments, taking advantage of consumers' lack of legal sophistication and inability to afford legal representation.

No matter how offensive these practices are, they may not justify an individual action for litigation misconduct if the litigation is unlikely to lead to meaningful relief. The first consideration in bringing follow-up litigation should be what damages has the consumer suffered from having to defend an abusive and unsuccessful collection action. If the consumer recovered attorney fees by prevailing in the collection action, then that action may have caused the consumer minimal or no out-of-pocket damages. On the other hand, consumers who have paid lawyers money to successfully defend them in collection actions and have not been reimbursed for those attorney fees may have incurred significant damages.

Other consumer damages from the collector's unsuccessful collection action are likely to involve emotional injury, which is compensable as actual damages under the FDCPA.[59] There may be other out-of-pocket damages in addition to attorney fees, such as lost time from work and transportation costs.

The FDCPA provides for statutory damages up to $1000 in addition to actual damages and attorney fees to prosecute the FDCPA claim.[60] Other than their salutary deterrent effect, these statutory damages on their own might not be sufficiently large to justify an FDCPA action when actual damages are not proven, particularly considering the complexity of an FDCPA claim for collection litigation misconduct. A class action seeking actual and statutory damages may be more practical, unless there are individualized facts that preclude class treatment. In cases of egregious litigation misconduct, punitive damages are possible under a tort theory, such as malicious prosecution[61] and, in a few states, under the UDAP statute.[62]

14.4.2.2 Must the Consumer's Claim Have Been Brought As a Compulsory Counterclaim in the Collection Action?

States have different rules on compulsory counterclaims, and case law in this area is examined in NCLC's *Fair Debt Collection* § 7.4.2.[63] Whether an FDCPA claim for litigation misconduct is a compulsory counterclaim will often be determined by the facts. An FDCPA claim for litigation misconduct can be brought subsequently when the second case's defendant was not a party to the first case, as when the consumer sues the creditor's attorney in the second case, rather than the creditor. Beware, though, that some judges have little sympathy for a prevailing consumer suing the other side's attorney.

A consumer's claim can not be a compulsory counterclaim in the collection action when the collector's litigation misconduct did not occur until after the answer to the collection complaint was filed.[64] While some collection litigation misconduct arises upon the filing of the collection complaint, many violations accrue only later on, for example, as a result of misrepresentations made in the course of the litigation, such as false sworn statements submitted in support of summary judgment.

Malicious prosecution claims do not have to be brought as compulsory counterclaims. An element of the claim for malicious prosecution is that the consumer must have prevailed in the underlying litigation. Malicious prosecution can not be raised as a counterclaim in the collection action, because the consumer has not yet prevailed.

14.4.2.3 Choice of Federal or State Court

The consumer who wants to litigate FDCPA claims in federal court will have no choice but to bring a separate action for litigation misconduct. Except under very unusual circumstances, the consumer can not remove a state court collection action to federal court—the existence of a counterclaim based on federal law does not create federal jurisdiction.[65]

On the other hand, the consumer may wish to litigate the follow-up claims in state court. There are important reasons to do so. As described in § 14.4.2.5, *infra*, one consideration in any subsequent lawsuit is whether the consumer's case will be forced into arbitration. State courts in many states are more likely to find an arbitration requirement unenforceable than are federal courts. State courts may also be more concerned about litigation abuses in their own court system.

The consumer who wishes to stay in state court runs the risk, when bringing an affirmative state court FDCPA action, that the case will be removed to federal court. The safer course is either to bring the FDCPA violation as a counterclaim in the collection action, or to bring an affirmative action based upon only state law. State UDAP, debt collection, and tort claims may be available.[66]

59 *See* National Consumer Law Center, Fair Debt Collection § 2.5.2.2 (6th ed. 2008).

60 *See id.* §§ 6.4, 6.8.

61 *See id.* § 10.6.

62 *See* National Consumer Law Center, Unfair and Deceptive Acts and Practices Appx. A (6th ed. 2004 and Supp.).

63 (6th ed. 2008).

64 *See* Fed. R. Civ. P. 13(a) (establishing as an element of a compulsory counterclaim "any claim which at the time of serving the pleading the pleader has against any opposing party").

65 *See, e.g.*, Chase Manhattan Mortgage Corp. v. Smith, 507 F.3d 910 (6th Cir. 2007) (case remanded after consumer improperly removed foreclosure action on basis of FDCPA counterclaim).

66 *See* National Consumer Law Center, Fair Debt Collection Chs. 10, 11 (6th ed. 2008).

14.4.2.4 Timing Considerations

The FDCPA has a one-year limitations period,[67] so a consumer must act quickly in bringing any follow-up litigation, particularly when the one year begins to run early in the collection action. On the other hand, it is dangerous to bring an affirmative FDCPA federal court action while the state court collection action is still pending. A natural response by the federal judge is to defer to the state court, and the state court may view with disfavor the consumer's end-around action in federal court.

As described in an earlier chapter,[68] there are also tactical reasons not to bring FDCPA claims while the state court collection action is pending, but to let the collector's suit run its normal course. The indiscriminate and routine nature of the violations committed by debt buyers helps establish a later-filed FDCPA case. Filing the separate federal action while the state case is continuing disrupts that flow. A pending derivative federal FDCPA suit imbues the state collection case with an exceptional significance that insures that the collector will give it very careful and special treatment that can only strengthen its collection suit and weaken the consumer's FDCPA case. This effect can be particularly dramatic when the federal court case defendant is the state court case collection attorney.

If the one-year limitations period makes a follow-up FDCPA claim impossible, then it may be possible to bring other state claims that generally have longer limitations periods. UDAP statutes typically have limitation periods of two years or more,[69] as will most tort claims. Another approach is to file in federal court within the limitations period, but not serve the complaint on the defendant until as many as four months afterwards.[70]

14.4.2.5 Arbitration Requirements

Credit contracts usually contain a requirement that disputes be settled by binding arbitration. When the consumer sues the collector or the collector's attorney, the defendant will typically seek to enforce the arbitration requirement.

Before enforcing the arbitration requirement, the collector must produce evidence of a binding arbitration agreement applying to the consumer. If the court in the collection action ruled that there is no written agreement applying to the consumer, than the collector in the subsequent litigation is collaterally estopped from claiming the existence of an arbitration provision. When, instead, the collector did not present sufficient evidence of the terms of the contract to prevail in its collection action, and this failure is not treated as collateral estoppel, the collector bears the same burden to prove the terms of the contract when it seeks to enforce that contract's arbitration provision. But a defendant, in a subsequent FDCPA action, is likely to go to greater efforts to offer proof of the terms of a contract applying to the consumer than it did in the initial collection action.

If an arbitration agreement applicable to the consumer is produced, then there are still a number of reasons why that arbitration provision may not be enforceable. These issues are examined in detail in NCLC's *Consumer Arbitration Agreements*,[71] and this subsection just suggests a few of the main themes.

Arbitration agreements are generally viewed as applying to disputes with both the original creditor and the creditor's assignees.[72] Thus a debt buyer is likely to receive protection under the arbitration agreement if it has been assigned rights under the contract. On the other hand, if the debt buyer has been assigned only receivables or choses in action, then it has not been assigned the contract, and can not claim protection under the arbitration agreement.

The ability of a collection attorney to gain protection from the arbitration clause is more complicated. Carefully parse the arbitration agreement to see how it treats agents of the creditor or agents of assignees of the creditor. In addition, courts are divided as to whether a collection attorney is an agent of the collector.[73] The collector's attorney should not be able to invoke an arbitration agreement between the consumer and the creditor that, by its own terms, does not apply to a debt buyer's attorney.[74]

There is also a question as to whether an FDCPA claim for litigation misconduct is one of the types of disputes to which the arbitration requirement applies. Look to see if the language of the arbitration agreement would cover such disputes. Such disputes are certainly outside the parties' expectation as to the arbitration agreement's coverage. That expectation deals more with disputes concerning the original transaction, and not litigation abuse by the creditor's assignee. A number of courts have found similar practices to be outside the scope of an arbitration clause.[75]

There is also extensive case law addressing whether an arbitration clause is unconscionable and therefore unenforceable. Unconscionability may relate to the cost of the arbitration proceeding, the arbitration agreement's limitation on consumer remedies, the fact that the agreement only requires the consumer to litigate disputes and not the collector, and to the procedure by which the arbitration requirement was imposed.[76]

---

67 *See id.* § 6.10.

68 § 5.5.2, *supra*.

69 *See* National Consumer Law Center, Unfair and Deceptive Acts and Practices § 7.3.1 (6th ed. 2004 and Supp.).

70 *See* Fed. R. Civ. P. 4(m).

71 (5th ed. 2007).

72 *See* National Consumer Law Center, Consumer Arbitration Agreements § 7.4.5 (5th ed. 2007).

73 National Consumer Law Center, Fair Debt Collection § 2.8 (6th ed. 2008).

74 National Consumer Law Center, Consumer Arbitration Agreements § 7.4 (5th ed. 2007).

75 *Id.* § 7.3.

76 *Id.* Ch. 6.

14.4.3 *FDCPA's Applicability to Litigation Misconduct*

14.4.3.1 FDCPA's Coverage of Litigation Practices

A wide range of state court collection activity is subject to the FDCPA. The Supreme Court in *Heintz v. Jenkins* confirmed that normal collection litigation is included among the collection activities regulated by the FDCPA.[77] Congress itself has since implicitly reaffirmed that principle twice by amending the FDCPA to exempt "a formal pleading" made in a "legal" or "civil action" from certain disclosure requirements.[78] These exceptions would be meaningless if inclusion of collection litigation were not already the rule.

FDCPA coverage is present whenever the state court plaintiff is a debt buyer or other debt collector pursuing a qualifying consumer debt.[79] The FDCPA can not be used to sue an original creditor, but it can be used to sue that creditor's collection attorney, so long as collecting consumer debts is part of the attorney's "regular" business activities.[80]

14.4.3.2 General Standards As to Actionable Litigation Misconduct

The FDCPA protects consumers from unlawful debt collection practices, regardless of whether a valid debt actually exists.[81] Accordingly, the FDCPA encourages aggrieved consumers to file suit to remedy false, unfair, and abusive collection practices irrespective of the validity of the debt. Consistent with the *Heintz* admonition, the resulting liability inquiry focuses on the method of collection and not the result.

The basis for some of the clearest FDCPA violations is the FDCPA section 1692e prohibition against "any" false or deceptive representations or means made in connection with the collection of a debt. Included among the recited statutory examples illustrating this broad proscription are the "false representation of the character, amount, or legal status of any debt"[82] and "the threat to take any action that cannot legally be taken."[83] At first blush, these violations describe much of the collection litigation initiated by the debt buyer industry.

Literally applied, section 1692e would establish automatic FDCPA violations whenever debt collectors file collection actions that are ultimately unsuccessful. However, the Supreme Court in *Heintz* imposed a restriction on the application of the FDCPA to collection litigation when, in response to this specific prospect, the Court stated that "we do not see how the fact that a lawsuit turns out ultimately to be unsuccessful could, by itself, make the bringing of it an 'action that cannot legally be taken.' "[84] One challenge for consumers in asserting FDCPA claims is determining what additional conditions will meet the Supreme Court's directive that something more than a losing collection case is necessary to establish a derivative FDCPA violation.

An FDCPA action in federal court is a poor vehicle to establish the rules or parameters of state law or to determine whether the consumer owes the debt. Among the criteria for good case selection is not only the obvious need to prove that the defendant collector used a prohibited means to collect the debt, but also, as a practical matter, the ability to show that the collector knew or should have known that the challenged conduct was wrongful.

Although the FDCPA is a strict liability statute,[85] intent and knowledge can always be relevant. For example, one of the recited factors in setting statutory damages is the extent to which the collector's "noncompliance was intentional."[86] In addition, a few specific violations require establishing the collector's knowledge or intent.[87]

Irrespective of the requirements of any specific violation, all debt collectors may raise the affirmative bona fide error defense in which good intentions and the absence of culpable knowledge are two of the necessary elements.[88] The bona fide error defense was given added strength when the Supreme Court in *Heintz* cited it as an available mechanism to defeat the suggestion that litigation coverage "automatically would make liable any litigating lawyer who brought, and then lost, a claim against a debtor."[89]

---

77 514 U.S. 291, 115 S. Ct. 1489, 131 L. Ed. 2d 395 (1995).

78 15 U.S.C. §§ 1692e(11), 1692g(d).

79 15 U.S.C. § 1692a(5), (6).

80 *See* National Consumer Law Center, Fair Debt Collection § 4.2.8 (6th ed. 2008).

81 *See id.* § 4.4.1.

82 15 U.S.C. § 1692e(2)(A).

83 15 U.S.C. § 1692e(5).

84 514 U.S. 291, 295–296, 115 S. Ct. 1489, 131 L. Ed. 2d 395 (1995).

85 *See* National Consumer Law Center, Fair Debt Collection § 5.2.3 (6th ed. 2008).

86 15 U.S.C. § 1692k(b).

87 *See* 15 U.S.C. §§ 1692e(5) (the second clause prohibiting the threat to take any action "that is not intended to be taken"), 1692e(8) (communicating credit information "which is known or which should be known to be false"), 1692f(3) (solicitation of postdated check "for the purpose of threatening or instituting criminal prosecution"), 1692f(6)(B) (threatening repossession of property without a "present intention" to do so), 1692c(a)(1) (communicating with a consumer at a "time or place known or which should be known to be inconvenient"), 1692c(a)(2) (communicating with a consumer "if the debt collector knows the consumer is represented by an attorney"), 1692c(a)(3) (communicating with a consumer at work "if the debt collector knows or has reason to know that the consumer's employer prohibits" such contacts), 1692d(5) (using the telephone "with the intent to annoy, abuse, or harass any person"), 1692j (furnishing forms "knowing that such forms would be used to create the false belief" of third party participation).

88 15 U.S.C. § 1692k(c).

89 514 U.S. 291, 295, 115 S. Ct. 1489, 131 L. Ed. 2d 395 (1995).

14.4.3.3 Examples of Litigation Conduct As FDCPA Violations

State court collection litigation presents recurring examples of FDCPA noncompliance when collectors engage in objectively dishonest, false, and illegal collection methods. These unlawful practices include collector misrepresentation as to its legal entitlement to fees, interest, or other additional charges that are prohibited by established state law,[90] and filing sworn declarations that state that the affiants reviewed certain documents when they in fact have not done so or that misrepresent the specific contents of those documents.[91]

On the other hand, an allegation made "on information and belief" or otherwise when applicable state law imposes no duty of inquiry or due diligence may not be a good basis for a successful FDCPA action, even when the statement turns out to be false. An especially poor candidate for a derivative FDCPA violation is an assertion in the collection proceedings of the collector's entitlement to relief, even if ultimately proven to be unfounded, when the falsity of the assertion was not settled when it was made.

Other established FDCPA violations occur when the collection court plaintiff is not authorized to appear or sue under state law.[92] These violations typically result from the failure of the collection court plaintiff to be properly licensed or registered in accordance with state laws regulating who may file suit in the state.[93] In some states a plaintiff is not allowed to sue based on a contingent assignment of the debt[94] or when the plaintiff is not the real party in interest.[95]

Another recurring affirmative FDCPA claim arising from litigation abuse involves the collector suing on a known time-barred debt.[96] Some collectors "launder" these stale and worthless debts when they sue on time-barred debts, hoping the consumer will either default or not assert the statute of limitations as an affirmative defense in the consumer's answer. But even suing on a time-barred debt may not result in an FDCPA violation. In two recent cases,[97] no FDCPA violation was found when the applicable limitations period was not yet established under state law when the time-barred suits were filed. Both courts excused the resulting violations as bona fide errors because of the unsettled state of the state law when the violation occurred.

90 *See* National Consumer Law Center, Fair Debt Collection §§ 5.5.4.3, 5.6.3 (6th ed. 2008).

91 *See* National Consumer Law Center, Fair Debt Collection Appx. K.2.4.12 (6th ed. 2008).

92 *See id.* § 11.5.2.

93 *See id.* § 5.5.8.5.

94 *See id.* § 5.5.8.6.

95 *See id.* § 11.5.2.

96 *See id.* § 5.5.2.12.3.

97 Pescatrice v. Orovitz, 539 F. Supp. 2d 1375 (S.D. Fla. 2008); McCorriston v. L.W.T., Inc., 536 F. Supp. 2d 1268 (M.D. Fla. 2008).

14.4.4 UDAP Claims for Litigation Misconduct

State deceptive practices (UDAP) statutes are often available to challenge litigation misconduct. Successful UDAP challenges have involved collection cases brought in inconvenient venues, filing actions after the limitations period has run, improper service of process, confusing summons, filing meritless collection actions, and deceptive settlement practices leading to default judgments.[98]

UDAP statutes generally do not require intent or knowledge, and usually there is no bona fide error defense.[99] UDAP statutes in most states are very broad in scope, but in a few states will not apply to creditors, attorneys, or debt collectors.[100] UDAP remedies typically include actual damages, attorney fees, and either minimum, multiple, or punitive damages.

14.4.5 Malicious Prosecution and Abuse of Process

Tort claims have the advantage of applying to any creditor, collector, or collector's attorney, and of providing for punitive damages in appropriate cases. Malicious prosecution and abuse of process are both torts that apply to wrongful use of judicial processes. Malicious prosecution is the more widely accepted, highly developed, and difficult to establish of the two. Both apply to civil proceedings, with malicious prosecution sometimes labeled "wrongful civil prosecution" when applied to civil processes. Both torts are examined in detail in NCLC's *Fair Debt Collection* § 10.6.[101]

Malicious prosecution occurs under the following circumstances:

- A proceeding is instituted;
- The proceeding is without probable cause or possible valid claim;
- The proceeding was instituted either maliciously or for an improper purpose; and
- The proceeding is terminated in favor of the defendant.[102]

Some states impose an additional requirement of "special injury" such as seizure of property.[103]

Abuse of process is often described as the use of "legal process against another in an improper manner to accom-

98 National Consumer Law Center, Unfair and Deceptive Acts and Practices § 5.1.1.4 (6th ed. 2004 and Supp.).

99 *Id.* §§ 4.2.4–4.2.6.

100 *Id.* §§ 2.2.1, 2.2.2, 2.3.9.

101 (6th ed. 2008).

102 National Consumer Law Center, Unfair and Deceptive Acts and Practices § 10.6.2 (6th ed. 2004 and Supp.).

103 *Id.*

plish a purpose for which it was not designed."[104] In contrast to malicious prosecution, the tort of abuse of process is not based on the improper institution of legal proceedings, but on the improper use of process *after* it has been issued to accomplish a purpose for which it was not designed.[105] While courts vary in their listings of the elements of the tort, one common statement is:

- The defendant made an illegal, improper, perverted use of the process, a use neither warranted nor authorized by the process;
- The defendant had an ulterior motive or purpose; and
- Damage resulted to the plaintiff from the irregularity.[106]

Some decisions require actual seizure of property as an element, or that the defendant act willfully, but malice usually is not a required element.[107]

104 *Id.* § 10.6.3.

105 *Id.*

106 *Id.*

107 *Id.*

Query whether it is abuse of process for a collector to use admissions to trick an unrepresented consumer to admit to liability that the consumer disputes. Suing in an improper venue has been found to be abuse of process,[108] as has obtaining and executing upon a default judgment after agreeing to dismiss the case,[109] falsifying an affidavit of service of process,[110] and continuing litigation known to be baseless.[111]

108 *Id.*

109 *See* Goodwin Agency, Inc. v. Chesser, 206 S.E.2d 568 (Ga. Ct. App. 1974).

110 Cordero v. Calvary SpIV L.L.C., 2004 WL 1244107 (N.D. Ill. June 3, 2004); Kappell v. Bartlett, 200 Cal. App. 3d 1457, 246 Cal. Rptr. 815 (1988); Parks v. Neuf, 578 N.E.2d 282 (Ill. App. Ct. 1991).

111 Gen. Elec. Capital Corp. v. MHPG, Inc., 2006 WL 2560314 (Mass. Super. Ct. July 26, 2004).

Appendix A Selected Provisions of the Servicemembers Civil Relief Act

50 U.S.C. App. §§ 501–596

[As enacted by Pub. L. No. 108-189, 117 Stat. 2835 (2003), unless otherwise noted.]

TITLE 50 APPENDIX—WAR AND NATIONAL DEFENSE

Servicemembers Civil Relief Act

§ 501. Short title

This Act [sections 501 to 596 of this Appendix] may be cited as the "Servicemembers Civil Relief Act."

§ 502. Purpose

The purposes of this Act are—

(1) to provide for, strengthen, and expedite the national defense through protection extended by this Act to servicemembers of the United States to enable such persons to devote their entire energy to the defense needs of the Nation; and
(2) to provide for the temporary suspension of judicial and administrative proceedings and transactions that may adversely affect the civil rights of servicemembers during their military service.

Title I—General Provisions

§ 511. Definitions

For the purposes of this Act:

(1) Servicemember

The term "servicemember" means a member of the uniformed services, as that term is defined in section 101(a)(5) of title 10, United States Code.

(2) Military service

The term "military service" means—

(A) in the case of a servicemember who is a member of the Army, Navy, Air Force, Marine Corps, or Coast Guard—

(i) active duty, as defined in section 101(d)(1) of title 10, United States Code, and

(ii) in the case of a member of the National Guard, includes service under a call to active service authorized by the President or the Secretary of Defense for a period of more than 30 consecutive days under section 502(f) of title 32, United States Code, for purposes of responding to a national emergency declared by the President and supported by Federal funds;

(B) in the case of a servicemember who is a commissioned officer of the Public Health Service or the National Oceanic and Atmospheric Administration, active service; and

(C) any period during which a servicemember is absent from duty on account of sickness, wounds, leave, or other lawful cause.

(3) Period of military service

The term "period of military service" means the period beginning on the date on which a servicemember enters military service and ending on the date on which the servicemember is released from military service or dies while in military service.

(4) Dependent

The term "dependent," with respect to a servicemember, means—

(A) the servicemember's spouse;

(B) the servicemember's child (as defined in section 101(4) of title 38, United States Code); or

(C) an individual for whom the servicemember provided more than one-half of the individual's support for 180 days immediately preceding an application for relief under this Act.

(5) Court

The term "court" means a court or an administrative agency of the United States or of any State (including any political subdivision of a State), whether or not a court or administrative agency of record.

(6) State

The term "State" includes—

(A) a commonwealth, territory, or possession of the United States; and

(B) the District of Columbia.

(7) Secretary concerned

The term "Secretary concerned"—

(A) with respect to a member of the armed forces, has the meaning given that term in section 101(a)(9) of title 10, United States Code;

(B) with respect to a commissioned officer of the Public Health Service, means the Secretary of Health and Human Services; and

(C) with respect to a commissioned officer of the National Oceanic and Atmospheric Administration, means the Secretary of Commerce.

(8) Motor vehicle

The term "motor vehicle" has the meaning given that term in section 30102(a)(6) of title 49, United States Code.

(9) Judgment

The term "judgment" means any judgment, decree, order, or ruling, final or temporary.

[As amended by Pub. L. No. 108-454, 118 Stat. 3624 (2004).]

§ 512. Jurisdiction and applicability of Act

(a) Jurisdiction

This Act applies to—

(1) the United States;

(2) each of the States, including the political subdivisions thereof; and

(3) all territory subject to the jurisdiction of the United States.

(b) Applicability to proceedings

This Act applies to any judicial or administrative proceeding commenced in any court or agency in any jurisdiction subject to this Act. This Act does not apply to criminal proceedings.

(c) Court in which application may be made

When under this Act any application is required to be made to a court in which no proceeding has already been commenced with respect to the matter, such application may be made to any court which would otherwise have jurisdiction over the matter.

§ 513. Protection of persons secondarily liable

(a) Extension of protection when actions stayed, postponed, or suspended

Whenever pursuant to this Act a court stays, postpones, or suspends (1) the enforcement of an obligation or liability, (2) the prosecution of a suit or proceeding, (3) the entry or enforcement of an order, writ, judgment, or decree, or (4) the performance of any other act, the court may likewise grant such a stay, postponement, or suspension to a surety, guarantor, endorser, accommodation maker, comaker, or other person who is or may be primarily or secondarily subject to the obligation or liability the performance or enforcement of which is stayed, postponed, or suspended.

(b) Vacation or set-aside of judgments

When a judgment or decree is vacated or set aside, in whole or in part, pursuant to this Act, the court may also set aside or vacate, as the case may be, the judgment or decree as to a surety, guarantor, endorser, accommodation maker, comaker, or other person who is or may be primarily or secondarily liable on the contract or liability for the enforcement of the judgment or decree.

(c) Bail bond not to be enforced during period of military service

A court may not enforce a bail bond during the period of military service of the principal on the bond when military service prevents the surety from obtaining the attendance of the principal. The court may discharge the surety and exonerate the bail, in accordance with principles of equity and justice, during or after the period of military service of the principal.

(d) Waiver of rights

(1) Waivers not precluded

This Act does not prevent a waiver in writing by a surety, guarantor, endorser, accommodation maker, comaker, or other person (whether primarily or secondarily liable on an obligation or liability) of the protections provided under subsections (a) and (b). Any such waiver is effective only if it is executed as an instrument separate from the obligation or liability with respect to which it applies.

(2) Waiver invalidated upon entrance to military service

If a waiver under paragraph (1) is executed by an individual who after the execution of the waiver enters military service, or by a dependent of an individual who after the execution of the waiver enters military service, the waiver is not valid after the beginning of the period of such military service unless the waiver was executed by such individual or dependent during the period specified in section 106 [section 516 of this Appendix].

§ 514. Extension of protections to citizens serving with allied forces

A citizen of the United States who is serving with the forces of a nation with which the United States is allied in the prosecution of a war or military action is entitled to the relief and protections provided under this Act if that service with the allied force is similar to military service as defined in this Act. The relief and protections provided to such citizen shall terminate on the date of discharge or release from such service.

§ 515. Notification of benefits

The Secretary concerned shall ensure that notice of the benefits accorded by this Act is provided in writing to persons in military service and to persons entering military service.

§ 515a. Information for members of the armed forces and their dependents on rights and protections of the Servicemembers Civil Relief Act

(a) Outreach to members

The Secretary concerned shall provide to each member of the Armed Forces under the jurisdiction of the Secretary pertinent information on the rights and protections available to members and their dependents under the Servicemembers Civil Relief Act [50 U.S.C. app. §§ 501–596].

(b) Time of provision

The information required to be provided under subsection (a) of this section to a member shall be provided at the following times:

(1) During the initial orientation training of the member.

(2) In the case of a member of a reserve component, during the initial orientation training of the member and when the member is mobilized or otherwise individually called or ordered to active duty for a period of more than one year.

(3) At such other times as the Secretary concerned considers appropriate.

(c) Outreach to dependents

The Secretary concerned may provide to the adult dependents of members under the jurisdiction of the Secretary pertinent information on the rights and protections available to members and their dependents under the Servicemembers Civil Relief Act.

(d) Definitions

In this section, the terms "dependent" and "Secretary concerned" have the meanings given such terms in section 101 of the Servicemembers Civil Relief Act [50 U.S.C. app. § 511].

[Added by Pub. L. No. 109-163, § 690, 119 Stat. 3337 (2006).]

§ 516. Extension of rights and protections to reserves ordered to report for military service and to persons ordered to report for induction

(a) Reserves ordered to report for military service

A member of a reserve component who is ordered to report for military service is entitled to the rights and protections of this title and titles II and III [of this Appendix] during the period beginning on the date of the member's receipt of the order and ending on the date on which the member reports for military service (or, if the order is revoked before the member so reports, or the date on which the order is revoked).

(b) Persons ordered to report for induction

A person who has been ordered to report for induction under the Military Selective Service Act (50 U.S.C. App. 451 et seq.) is entitled to the rights and protections provided a servicemember under this title and titles II and III [of this Appendix] during the period beginning on the date of receipt of the order for induction and ending on the date on which the person reports for induction (or, if the order to report for induction is revoked before the date on which the person reports for induction, on the date on which the order is revoked).

§ 517. Waiver of rights pursuant to written agreement

(a) In general

A servicemember may waive any of the rights and protections provided by this Act. In the case of a waiver that permits an action described in subsection (b), the waiver is effective only if made pursuant to a written agreement of the parties that is executed during or after the servicemember's period of military service. The written agreement shall specify the legal instrument to which the waiver applies and, if the servicemember is not a party to that instrument, the servicemember concerned. Any such waiver that applies to an action listed in subsection (b) of this section is effective only if it is in writing and is executed as an instrument separate from the obligation or liability to which it applies.

(b) Actions requiring waivers in writing

The requirement in subsection (a) for a written waiver applies to the following:

(1) The modification, termination, or cancellation of—

(A) a contract, lease, or bailment; or

(B) an obligation secured by a mortgage, trust, deed, lien, or other security in the nature of a mortgage.

(2) The repossession, retention, foreclosure, sale, forfeiture, or taking possession of property that—

(A) is security for any obligation; or

(B) was purchased or received under a contract, lease, or bailment.

(c) Prominent display of certain contract rights waivers

Any waiver in writing of a right or protection provided by this Act [sections 501 to 596 of this Appendix] that applies to a contract, lease, or similar legal instrument must be in at least 12 point type.

(d) Coverage of periods after orders received

For the purposes of this section—

(1) a person to whom section 106 [section 516 of this Appendix] applies shall be considered to be a servicemember; and

(2) the period with respect to such a person specified in subsection (a) or (b), as the case may be, of section 106 [section 516 of this Appendix] shall be considered to be a period of military service.

[As amended by Pub. L. No. 108-454, 118 Stat. 3624 (2004).]

§ 518. Exercise of rights under Act not to affect certain future financial transactions

Application by a servicemember for, or receipt by a servicemember of, a stay, postponement, or suspension pursuant to this Act in the payment of a tax, fine, penalty, insurance premium, or other civil obligation or liability of that servicemember shall not itself (without regard to other considerations) provide the basis for any of the following:

(1) A determination by a lender or other person that the servicemember is unable to pay the civil obligation or liability in accordance with its terms.

(2) With respect to a credit transaction between a creditor and the servicemember—

(A) a denial or revocation of credit by the creditor;

(B) a change by the creditor in the terms of an existing credit arrangement; or

(C) a refusal by the creditor to grant credit to the servicemember in substantially the amount or on substantially the terms requested.

(3) An adverse report relating to the creditworthiness of the servicemember by or to a person engaged in the practice of assembling or evaluating consumer credit information.

(4) A refusal by an insurer to insure the servicemember.

(5) An annotation in a servicemember's record by a creditor or a person engaged in the practice of assembling or evaluating consumer credit information, identifying the servicemember as a member of the National Guard or a reserve component.

(6) A change in the terms offered or conditions required for the issuance of insurance.

§ 519. Legal representatives

(a) Representative

A legal representative of a servicemember for purposes of this Act [sections 501 to 596 of this Appendix] is either of the following:

(1) An attorney acting on the behalf of a servicemember.

(2) An individual possessing a power of attorney.

(b) Application

Whenever the term "servicemember" is used in this Act [sections 501 to 596 of this Appendix], such term shall be treated as including a reference to a legal representative of the servicemember.

Title II—General Relief

§ 521. Protection of servicemembers against default judgments

(a) Applicability of section

This section applies to any civil action or proceeding in which the defendant does not make an appearance.

(b) Affidavit requirement

(1) Plaintiff to file affidavit

In any action or proceeding covered by this section, the court, before entering judgment for the plaintiff, shall require the plaintiff to file with the court an affidavit—

(A) stating whether or not the defendant is in military service and showing necessary facts to support the affidavit; or

(B) if the plaintiff is unable to determine whether or not the defendant is in military service, stating that the plaintiff is unable to determine whether or not the defendant is in military service.

(2) Appointment of attorney to represent defendant in military service

If in an action covered by this section it appears that the defendant is in military service, the court may not enter a judgment until after the court appoints an attorney to represent the defendant. If an attorney appointed under this section to represent a servicemember cannot locate the servicemember, actions by the attorney in the case shall not waive any defense of the servicemember or otherwise bind the servicemember.

(3) Defendant's military status not ascertained by affidavit

If based upon the affidavits filed in such an action, the court is unable to determine whether the defendant is in military service, the court, before entering judgment, may require the plaintiff to file a bond in an amount approved by the court. If the defendant is later found to be in military service, the bond shall be available to indemnify the defendant against any loss or damage the defendant may suffer by reason of any judgment for the plaintiff against the defendant, should the judgment be set aside in whole or in part. The bond shall remain in effect until expiration of the time for appeal and setting aside of a judgment under applicable Federal or State law or regulation or under any applicable ordinance of a political subdivision of a State. The court may issue such orders or enter such judgments as the court determines necessary to protect the rights of the defendant under this Act.

(4) Satisfaction of requirement for affidavit

The requirement for an affidavit under paragraph (1) may be satisfied by a statement, declaration, verification, or certificate, in writing, subscribed and certified or declared to be true under penalty of perjury.

(c) Penalty for making or using false affidavit

A person who makes or uses an affidavit permitted under subsection (b) (or a statement, declaration, verification, or certificate as authorized under subsection (b)(4)) knowing it to be false, shall be fined as provided in title 18, United States Code, or imprisoned for not more than one year, or both.

(d) Stay of proceedings

In an action covered by this section in which the defendant is in military service, the court shall grant a stay of proceedings for a minimum period of 90 days under this subsection upon application of counsel, or on the court's own motion, if the court determines that—

(1) there may be a defense to the action and a defense cannot be presented without the presence of the defendant; or

(2) after due diligence, counsel has been unable to contact the defendant or otherwise determine if a meritorious defense exists.

(e) Inapplicability of section 202 procedures

A stay of proceedings under subsection (d) shall not be controlled by procedures or requirements under section 202 [section 522 of this Appendix].

(f) Section 202 protection

If a servicemember who is a defendant in an action covered by this section receives actual notice of the action, the servicemember may request a stay of proceeding under section 202 [section 522 of this Appendix].

(g) Vacation or setting aside of default judgments

(1) Authority for court to vacate or set aside judgment

If a default judgment is entered in an action covered by this section against a servicemember during the servicemember's period of military service (or within 60 days after termination of or release from such military service), the court entering the judgment shall, upon application by or on behalf of the servicemember, reopen the judgment for the purpose of allowing the servicemember to defend the action if it appears that—

(A) the servicemember was materially affected by reason of that military service in making a defense to the action; and

(B) the servicemember has a meritorious or legal defense to the action or some part of it.

(2) Time for filing application

An application under this subsection must be filed not later than 90 days after the date of the termination of or release from military service.

(h) Protection of bona fide purchaser

If a court vacates, sets aside, or reverses a default judgment against a servicemember and the vacating, setting aside, or reversing is because of a provision of this Act, that action shall not impair a right or title acquired by a bona fide purchaser for value under the default judgment.

§ 522. Stay of proceedings when servicemember has notice

(a) Applicability of section

This section applies to any civil action or proceeding in which the plaintiff or defendant at the time of filing an application under this section—

(1) is in military service or is within 90 days after termination of or release from military service; and

(2) has received notice of the action or proceeding.

(b) Stay of proceedings

(1) Authority for stay

At any stage before final judgment in a civil action or proceeding in which a servicemember described in subsection (a) is a party, the court may on its own motion and shall, upon application by the servicemember, stay the action for a period of not less than 90 days, if the conditions in paragraph (2) are met.

(2) Conditions for stay

An application for a stay under paragraph (1) shall include the following:

(A) A letter or other communication setting forth facts stating the manner in which current military duty requirements materially affect the servicemember's ability to appear and stating a date when the servicemember will be available to appear.

(B) A letter or other communication from the servicemember's commanding officer stating that the servicemember's current military duty prevents appearance and that military leave is not authorized for the servicemember at the time of the letter.

(c) Application not a waiver of defenses

An application for a stay under this section does not constitute an appearance for jurisdictional purposes and does not constitute a waiver of any substantive or procedural defense (including a defense relating to lack of personal jurisdiction).

(d) Additional stay

(1) Application

A servicemember who is granted a stay of a civil action or proceeding under subsection (b) may apply for an additional stay based on continuing material affect of military duty on the servicemember's ability to appear. Such an application may be made by the servicemember at the time of the initial application under subsection (b) or when it appears that the servicemember is unavailable to prosecute or defend the action. The same information required under subsection (b)(2) shall be included in an application under this subsection.

(2) Appointment of counsel when additional stay refused
If the court refuses to grant an additional stay of proceedings under paragraph (1), the court shall appoint counsel to represent the servicemember in the action or proceeding.

(e) Coordination with section 201 [section 521 of this Appendix]
A servicemember who applies for a stay under this section and is unsuccessful may not seek the protections afforded by section 201 [section 521 of this Appendix].

(f) Inapplicability to section 301 [section 531 of this Appendix]
The protections of this section do not apply to section 301 [section 531 of this Appendix].

[As amended by Pub. L. No. 108-454, 118 Stat. 3624 (2004).]

§ 523. Fines and penalties under contracts

(a) Prohibition of penalties
When an action for compliance with the terms of a contract is stayed pursuant to this Act, a penalty shall not accrue for failure to comply with the terms of the contract during the period of the stay.

(b) Reduction or waiver of fines or penalties
If a servicemember fails to perform an obligation arising under a contract and a penalty is incurred arising from that nonperformance, a court may reduce or waive the fine or penalty if—

(1) the servicemember was in military service at the time the fine or penalty was incurred; and

(2) the ability of the servicemember to perform the obligation was materially affected by such military service.

§ 524. Stay or vacation of execution of judgments, attachments, and garnishments

(a) Court action upon material affect determination
If a servicemember, in the opinion of the court, is materially affected by reason of military service in complying with a court judgment or order, the court may on its own motion and shall on application by the servicemember—

(1) stay the execution of any judgment or order entered against the servicemember; and

(2) vacate or stay an attachment or garnishment of property, money, or debts in the possession of the servicemember or a third party, whether before or after judgment.

(b) Applicability
This section applies to an action or proceeding commenced in a court against a servicemember before or during the period of the servicemember's military service or within 90 days after such service terminates.

§ 525. Duration and term of stays; codefendants not in service

(a) Period of stay
A stay of an action, proceeding, attachment, or execution made pursuant to the provisions of this Act by a court may be ordered for the period of military service and 90 days thereafter, or for any part of that period. The court may set the terms and amounts for such installment payments as is considered reasonable by the court.

(b) Codefendants
If the servicemember is a codefendant with others who are not in military service and who are not entitled to the relief and protections provided under this Act, the plaintiff may proceed against those other defendants with the approval of the court.

(c) Inapplicability of section
This section does not apply to sections 202 and 701 [sections 522 and 591 of this Appendix].

§ 526. Statute of limitations

(a) Tolling of statutes of limitation during military service
The period of a servicemember's military service may not be included in computing any period limited by law, regulation, or order for the bringing of any action or proceeding in a court, or in any board, bureau, commission, department, or other agency of a State (or political subdivision of a State) or the United States by or against the servicemember or the servicemember's heirs, executors, administrators, or assigns.

(b) Redemption of real property
A period of military service may not be included in computing any period provided by law for the redemption of real property sold or forfeited to enforce an obligation, tax, or assessment.

(c) Inapplicability to internal revenue laws
This section does not apply to any period of limitation prescribed by or under the internal revenue laws of the United States.

§ 527. Maximum rate of interest on debts incurred before military service

(a) Interest rate limitation

(1) Limitation to 6 percent
An obligation or liability bearing interest at a rate in excess of 6 percent per year that is incurred by a servicemember, or the servicemember and the servicemember's spouse jointly, before the servicemember enters military service shall not bear interest at a rate in excess of 6 percent per year during the period of military service.

(2) Forgiveness of interest in excess of 6 percent
Interest at a rate in excess of 6 percent per year that would otherwise be incurred but for the prohibition in paragraph (1) is forgiven.

(3) Prevention of acceleration of principal
The amount of any periodic payment due from a servicemember under the terms of the instrument that created an obligation or liability covered by this section shall be reduced by the amount of the interest forgiven under paragraph (2) that is allocable to the period for which such payment is made.

(b) Implementation of limitation

(1) Written notice to creditor
In order for an obligation or liability of a servicemember to be subject to the interest rate limitation in subsection (a), the servicemember shall provide to the creditor written notice and a copy of the military orders calling the servicemember to military service and any orders further extending military

service, not later than 180 days after the date of the servicemember's termination or release from military service.

(2) Limitation effective as of date of order to active duty

Upon receipt of written notice and a copy of orders calling a servicemember to military service, the creditor shall treat the debt in accordance with subsection (a), effective as of the date on which the servicemember is called to military service.

(c) Creditor protection

A court may grant a creditor relief from the limitations of this section if, in the opinion of the court, the ability of the servicemember to pay interest upon the obligation or liability at a rate in excess of 6 percent per year is not materially affected by reason of the servicemember's military service.

(d) Interest

As used in this section, the term "interest" includes service charges, renewal charges, fees, or any other charges (except bona fide insurance) with respect to an obligation or liability.

Title III—Rent, Installment Contracts, Mortgages, Liens, Assignment, Leases

§ 531. Evictions and distress

(a) Court-ordered eviction

(1) In general

Except by court order, a landlord (or another person with paramount title) may not—

(A) evict a servicemember, or the dependents of a servicemember, during a period of military service of the servicemember, from premises—

(i) that are occupied or intended to be occupied primarily as a residence; and

(ii) for which the monthly rent does not exceed $2,400, as adjusted under paragraph (2) for years after 2003; or

(B) subject such premises to a distress during the period of military service.

(2) Housing price inflation adjustment

(A) For calendar years beginning with 2004, the amount in effect under paragraph (1)(A)(ii) shall be increased by the housing price inflation adjustment for the calendar year involved.

(B) For purposes of this paragraph—

(i) The housing price inflation adjustment for any calendar year is the percentage change (if any) by which—

(I) the CPI housing component for November of the preceding calendar year, exceeds

(II) the CPI housing component for November of 1984.

(ii) The term "CPI housing component" means the index published by the Bureau of Labor Statistics of the Department of Labor known as the Consumer Price Index, All Urban Consumers, Rent of Primary Residence, U.S. City Average.

(3) Publication of housing price inflation adjustment

The Secretary of Defense shall cause to be published in the Federal Register each year the amount in effect under paragraph (1)(A)(ii) for that year following the housing price inflation adjustment for that year pursuant to paragraph (2). Such publication shall be made for a year not later than 60 days after such adjustment is made for that year.

(b) Stay of execution

(1) Court authority

Upon an application for eviction or distress with respect to premises covered by this section, the court may on its own motion and shall, if a request is made by or on behalf of a servicemember whose ability to pay the agreed rent is materially affected by military service—

(A) stay the proceedings for a period of 90 days, unless in the opinion of the court, justice and equity require a longer or shorter period of time; or

(B) adjust the obligation under the lease to preserve the interests of all parties.

(2) Relief to landlord

If a stay is granted under paragraph (1), the court may grant to the landlord (or other person with paramount title) such relief as equity may require.

(c) Penalties

(1) Misdemeanor

Except as provided in subsection (a), a person who knowingly takes part in an eviction or distress described in subsection (a), or who knowingly attempts to do so, shall be fined as provided in title 18, United States Code, or imprisoned for not more than one year, or both.

(2) Preservation of other remedies and rights

The remedies and rights provided under this section are in addition to and do not preclude any remedy for wrongful conversion (or wrongful eviction) otherwise available under the law to the person claiming relief under this section, including any award for consequential and punitive damages.

(d) Rent allotment from pay of servicemember

To the extent required by a court order related to property which is the subject of a court action under this section, the Secretary concerned shall make an allotment from the pay of a servicemember to satisfy the terms of such order, except that any such allotment shall be subject to regulations prescribed by the Secretary concerned establishing the maximum amount of pay of servicemembers that may be allotted under this subsection.

(e) Limitation of applicability

Section 202 [section 522 of this Appendix] is not applicable to this section.

§ 532. Protection under installment contracts for purchase or lease

(a) Protection upon breach of contract

(1) Protection after entering military service

After a servicemember enters military service, a contract by the servicemember for—

(A) the purchase of real or personal property (including a motor vehicle); or

(B) the lease or bailment of such property,

may not be rescinded or terminated for a breach of terms of the contract occurring before or during that person's military service, nor may the property be repossessed for such breach without a court order.

(2) Applicability

This section applies only to a contract for which a deposit or installment has been paid by the servicemember before the servicemember enters military service.

(b) Penalties

(1) Misdemeanor

A person who knowingly resumes possession of property in violation of subsection (a), or in violation of section 107 of this Act [section 517 of this Appendix], or who knowingly attempts to do so, shall be fined as provided in title 18, United States Code, or imprisoned for not more than one year, or both.

(2) Preservation of other remedies and rights

The remedies and rights provided under this section are in addition to and do not preclude any remedy for wrongful conversion otherwise available under law to the person claiming relief under this section, including any award for consequential and punitive damages.

(c) Authority of court

In a hearing based on this section, the court—

(1) may order repayment to the servicemember of all or part of the prior installments or deposits as a condition of terminating the contract and resuming possession of the property;

(2) may, on its own motion, and shall on application by a servicemember when the servicemember's ability to comply with the contract is materially affected by military service, stay the proceedings for a period of time as, in the opinion of the court, justice and equity require; or

(3) may make other disposition as is equitable to preserve the interests of all parties.

§ 533. Mortgages and trust deeds

(a) Mortgage as security

This section applies only to an obligation on real or personal property owned by a servicemember that—

(1) originated before the period of the servicemember's military service and for which the servicemember is still obligated; and

(2) is secured by a mortgage, trust deed, or other security in the nature of a mortgage.

(b) Stay of proceedings and adjustment of obligation

In an action filed during, or within 90 days after, a servicemember's period of military service to enforce an obligation described in subsection (a), the court may after a hearing and on its own motion and shall upon application by a servicemember when the servicemember's ability to comply with the obligation is materially affected by military service—

(1) stay the proceedings for a period of time as justice and equity require, or

(2) adjust the obligation to preserve the interests of all parties.

(c) Sale or foreclosure

A sale, foreclosure, or seizure of property for a breach of an obligation described in subsection (a) shall not be valid if made during, or within 90 days after, the period of the servicemember's military service except—

(1) upon a court order granted before such sale, foreclosure, or seizure with a return made and approved by the court; or

(2) if made pursuant to an agreement as provided in section 107 [section 517 of this Appendix].

(d) Penalties

(1) Misdemeanor

A person who knowingly makes or causes to be made a sale, foreclosure, or seizure of property that is prohibited by subsection (c), or who knowingly attempts to do so, shall be fined as provided in title 18, United States Code, or imprisoned for not more than one year, or both.

(2) Preservation of other remedies

The remedies and rights provided under this section are in addition to and do not preclude any remedy for wrongful conversion otherwise available under law to the person claiming relief under this section, including consequential and punitive damages.

§ 534. Settlement of stayed cases relating to personal property

(a) Appraisal of property

When a stay is granted pursuant to this Act in a proceeding to foreclose a mortgage on or to repossess personal property, or to rescind or terminate a contract for the purchase of personal property, the court may appoint three disinterested parties to appraise the property.

(b) Equity payment

Based on the appraisal, and if undue hardship to the servicemember's dependents will not result, the court may order that the amount of the servicemember's equity in the property be paid to the servicemember, or the servicemember's dependents, as a condition of foreclosing the mortgage, repossessing the property, or rescinding or terminating the contract.

§ 535. Termination of residential or motor vehicle leases

(a) Termination by lessee

(1) In general

The lessee on a lease described in subsection (b) may, at the lessee's option, terminate the lease at any time after—

(A) the lessee's entry into military service; or

(B) the date of the lessee's military orders described in paragraph (1)(B) or (2)(B) of subsection (b), as the case may be.

(2) Joint leases

A lessee's termination of a lease pursuant to this subsection shall terminate any obligation a dependent of the lessee may have under the lease.

(b) Covered leases

This section applies to the following leases:

(1) Leases of premises

A lease of premises occupied, or intended to be occupied, by a servicemember or a servicemember's dependents for a residential, professional, business, agricultural, or similar purpose if—

(A) the lease is executed by or on behalf of a person who thereafter and during the term of the lease enters military service; or

(B) the servicemember, while in military service, executes the lease and thereafter receives military orders for a permanent change of station or to deploy with a military unit, or as an individual in support of a military operation, for a period of not less than 90 days.

(2) Leases of motor vehicles

A lease of a motor vehicle used, or intended to be used, by a servicemember or a servicemember's dependents for personal or business transportation if—

(A) the lease is executed by or on behalf of a person who thereafter and during the term of the lease enters military service under a call or order specifying a period of not less than 180 days (or who enters military service under a call or order specifying a period of 180 days or less and who, without a break in service, receives orders extending the period of military service to a period of not less than 180 days); or

(B) the servicemember, while in military service, executes the lease and thereafter receives military orders—

(i) for a change of permanent station—

(I) from a location in the continental United States to a location outside the continental United States; or

(II) from a location in a State outside the continental United States to any location outside that State; or

(ii) to deploy with a military unit, or as an individual in support of a military operation, for a period of not less than 180 days.

(c) Manner of termination

(1) In general

Termination of a lease under subsection (a) is made—

(A) by delivery by the lessee of written notice of such termination, and a copy of the servicemember's military orders, to the lessor (or the lessor's grantee), or to the lessor's agent (or the agent's grantee); and

(B) in the case of a lease of a motor vehicle, by return of the motor vehicle by the lessee to the lessor (or the lessor's grantee), or to the lessor's agent (or the agent's grantee), not later than 15 days after the date of the delivery of written notice under subparagraph (A).

(2) Delivery of notice

Delivery of notice under paragraph (1)(A) may be accomplished—

(A) by hand delivery;

(B) by private business carrier; or

(C) by placing the written notice in an envelope with sufficient postage and with return receipt requested, and addressed as designated by the lessor (or the lessor's grantee) or to the lessor's agent (or the agent's grantee), and depositing the written notice in the United States mails.

(d) Effective date of lease termination

(1) Lease of premises

In the case of a lease described in subsection (b)(1) that provides for monthly payment of rent, termination of the lease under subsection (a) is effective 30 days after the first date on which the next rental payment is due and payable after the date on which the notice under subsection (c) is delivered. In the case of any other lease described in subsection (b)(1), termination of the lease under subsection (a) is effective on the last day of the month following the month in which the notice is delivered.

(2) Lease of motor vehicles

In the case of a lease described in subsection (b)(2), termination of the lease under subsection (a) is effective on the day on which the requirements of subsection (c) are met for such termination.

(e) Arrearages and other obligations and liabilities

Rents or lease amounts unpaid for the period preceding the effective date of the lease termination shall be paid on a prorated basis. In the case of the lease of a motor vehicle, the lessor may not impose an early termination charge, but any taxes, summonses, and title and registration fees and any other obligation and liability of the lessee in accordance with the terms of the lease, including reasonable charges to the lessee for excess wear, use and mileage, that are due and unpaid at the time of termination of the lease shall be paid by the lessee.

(f) Rent paid in advance

Rents or lease amounts paid in advance for a period after the effective date of the termination of the lease shall be refunded to the lessee by the lessor (or the lessor's assignee or the assignee's agent) within 30 days of the effective date of the termination of the lease.

(g) Relief to lessor

Upon application by the lessor to a court before the termination date provided in the written notice, relief granted by this section to a servicemember may be modified as justice and equity require.

(h) Penalties

(1) Misdemeanor

Any person who knowingly seizes, holds, or detains the personal effects, security deposit, or other property of a servicemember or a servicemember's dependent who lawfully terminates a lease covered by this section, or who knowingly interferes with the removal of such property from premises covered by such lease, for the purpose of subjecting or attempting to subject any of such property to a claim for rent accruing subsequent to the date of termination of such lease, or attempts to do so, shall be fined as provided in title 18, United States Code, or imprisoned for not more than one year, or both.

(2) Preservation of other remedies

The remedy and rights provided under this section are in addition to and do not preclude any remedy for wrongful conversion otherwise available under law to the person claiming relief under this section, including any award for consequential or punitive damages.

(i) Definitions

(1) Military orders

The term "military orders", with respect to a servicemember, means official military orders, or any notification, certification, or verification from the servicemember's commanding officer, with respect to the servicemember's current or future military duty status.

(2) CONUS

The term "continental United States" means the 48 contiguous States and the District of Columbia.

[As amended by Pub. L. No. 108-454, 118 Stat. 3624 (2004).]

§ 536. Protection of life insurance policy

(a) Assignment of policy protected

If a life insurance policy on the life of a servicemember is assigned before military service to secure the payment of an obligation, the assignee of the policy (except the insurer in connection with a policy loan) may not exercise, during a period of military service of the servicemember or within one year thereafter, any right or option obtained under the assignment without a court order.

(b) Exception

The prohibition in subsection (a) shall not apply—

(1) if the assignee has the written consent of the insured made during the period described in subsection (a);

(2) when the premiums on the policy are due and unpaid; or

(3) upon the death of the insured.

(c) Order refused because of material affect

A court which receives an application for an order required under subsection (a) may refuse to grant such order if the court determines the ability of the servicemember to comply with the terms of the obligation is materially affected by military service.

(d) Treatment of guaranteed premiums

For purposes of this subsection, premiums guaranteed under the provisions of title IV of this Act shall not be considered due and unpaid.

(e) Penalties

(1) Misdemeanor

A person who knowingly takes an action contrary to this section, or attempts to do so, shall be fined as provided in title 18, United States Code, or imprisoned for not more than one year, or both.

(2) Preservation of other remedies

The remedy and rights provided under this section are in addition to and do not preclude any remedy for wrongful conversion otherwise available under law to the person claiming relief under this section, including any consequential or punitive damages.

§ 537. Enforcement of storage liens

(a) Liens

(1) Limitation on foreclosure or enforcement

A person holding a lien on the property or effects of a servicemember may not, during any period of military service of the servicemember and for 90 days thereafter, foreclose or enforce any lien on such property or effects without a court order granted before foreclosure or enforcement.

(2) Lien defined

For the purposes of paragraph (1), the term "lien" includes a lien for storage, repair, or cleaning of the property or effects of a servicemember or a lien on such property or effects for any other reason.

(b) Stay of proceedings

In a proceeding to foreclose or enforce a lien subject to this section, the court may on its own motion, and shall if requested by a servicemember whose ability to comply with the obligation resulting in the proceeding is materially affected by military service—

(1) stay the proceeding for a period of time as justice and equity require; or

(2) adjust the obligation to preserve the interests of all parties.

The provisions of this subsection do not affect the scope of section 303 [section 533 of this Appendix].

(c) Penalties

(1) Misdemeanor

A person who knowingly takes an action contrary to this section, or attempts to do so, shall be fined as provided in title 18, United States Code, or imprisoned for not more than one year, or both.

(2) Preservation of other remedies

The remedy and rights provided under this section are in addition to and do not preclude any remedy for wrongful conversion otherwise available under law to the person claiming relief under this section, including any consequential or punitive damages.

§ 538. Extension of protections to dependents

Upon application to a court, a dependent of a servicemember is entitled to the protections of this title if the dependent's ability to comply with a lease, contract, bailment, or other obligation is materially affected by reason of the servicemember's military service.

* * *

Title V—Taxes and Public Lands

§ 561. Taxes respecting personal property, money, credits, and real property

(a) Application

This section applies in any case in which a tax or assessment, whether general or special (other than a tax on personal income), falls due and remains unpaid before or during a period of military service with respect to a servicemember's—

(1) personal property (including motor vehicles); or

(2) real property occupied for dwelling, professional, business, or agricultural purposes by a servicemember or the servicemember's dependents or employees—

(A) before the servicemember's entry into military service; and

(B) during the time the tax or assessment remains unpaid.

(b) Sale of property

(1) Limitation on sale of property to enforce tax assessment

Property described in subsection (a) may not be sold to enforce the collection of such tax or assessment except by court order and upon the determination by the court that military service does not materially affect the servicemember's ability to pay the unpaid tax or assessment.

(2) Stay of court proceedings

A court may stay a proceeding to enforce the collection of such tax or assessment, or sale of such property, during a period of military service of the servicemember and for a period not more than 180 days after the termination of, or release of the servicemember from, military service.

(c) Redemption

When property described in subsection (a) is sold or forfeited to enforce the collection of a tax or assessment, a servicemember shall have the right to redeem or commence an action to redeem the servicemember's property during the period of military service or within 180 days after termination of or release from military service. This subsection may not be construed to shorten any period provided by the law of a State (including any political subdivision of a State) for redemption.

(d) Interest on tax or assessment

Whenever a servicemember does not pay a tax or assessment on property described in subsection (a) when due, the amount of the tax or assessment due and unpaid shall bear interest until paid at the rate of 6 percent per year. An additional penalty or interest shall not be incurred by reason of nonpayment. A lien for such unpaid tax or assessment may include interest under this subsection.

(e) Joint ownership application

This section applies to all forms of property described in subsection (a) owned individually by a servicemember or jointly by a servicemember and a dependent or dependents.

* * *

§ 570. Income taxes

(a) Deferral of tax

Upon notice to the Internal Revenue Service or the tax authority of a State or a political subdivision of a State, the collection of income tax on the income of a servicemember falling due before or during military service shall be deferred for a period not more than 180 days after termination of or release from military service, if a servicemember's ability to pay such income tax is materially affected by military service.

(b) Accrual of interest or penalty

No interest or penalty shall accrue for the period of deferment by reason of nonpayment on any amount of tax deferred under this section.

(c) Statute of limitations

The running of a statute of limitations against the collection of tax deferred under this section, by seizure or otherwise, shall be suspended for the period of military service of the servicemember and for an additional period of 270 days thereafter.

(d) Application limitation

This section shall not apply to the tax imposed on employees by section 3101 of the Internal Revenue Code of 1986.

§ 571. Residence for tax purposes

(a) Residence or domicile

A servicemember shall neither lose nor acquire a residence or domicile for purposes of taxation with respect to the person, personal property, or income of the servicemember by reason of being absent or present in any tax jurisdiction of the United States solely in compliance with military orders.

(b) Military service compensation

Compensation of a servicemember for military service shall not be deemed to be income for services performed or from sources within a tax jurisdiction of the United States if the servicemember is not a resident or domiciliary of the jurisdiction in which the servicemember is serving in compliance with military orders.

(c) Personal property

(1) Relief from personal property taxes

The personal property of a servicemember shall not be deemed to be located or present in, or to have a situs for taxation in, the tax jurisdiction in which the servicemember is serving in compliance with military orders.

(2) Exception for property within member's domicile or residence

This subsection applies to personal property or its use within any tax jurisdiction other than the servicemember's domicile or residence.

(3) Exception for property used in trade or business

This section does not prevent taxation by a tax jurisdiction with respect to personal property used in or arising from a trade or business, if it has jurisdiction.

(4) Relationship to law of State of domicile

Eligibility for relief from personal property taxes under this subsection is not contingent on whether or not such taxes are paid to the State of domicile.

(d) Increase of tax liability

A tax jurisdiction may not use the military compensation of a nonresident servicemember to increase the tax liability imposed on other income earned by the nonresident servicemember or spouse subject to tax by the jurisdiction.

(e) Federal Indian reservations

An Indian servicemember whose legal residence or domicile is a Federal Indian reservation shall be taxed by the laws applicable to Federal Indian reservations and not the State where the reservation is located.

(f) Definitions

For purposes of this section:

(1) Personal property

The term "personal property" means intangible and tangible property (including motor vehicles).

(2) Taxation

The term "taxation" includes licenses, fees, or excises imposed with respect to motor vehicles and their use, if the license, fee, or excise is paid by the servicemember in the servicemember's State of domicile or residence.

(3) Tax jurisdiction

The term "tax jurisdiction" means a State or a political subdivision of a State.

Title VI—Administrative Remedies

§ 581. Inappropriate use of Act

If a court determines, in any proceeding to enforce a civil right, that any interest, property, or contract has been transferred or acquired with the intent to delay the just enforcement of such right by taking advantage of this Act, the court shall enter such judgment or make such order as might lawfully be entered or made concerning such transfer or acquisition.

§ 582. Certificates of service; persons reported missing

(a) Prima facie evidence

In any proceeding under this Act, a certificate signed by the Secretary concerned is prima facie evidence as to any of the following facts stated in the certificate:

(1) That a person named is, is not, has been, or has not been in military service.

(2) The time and the place the person entered military service.

(3) The person's residence at the time the person entered military service.

(4) The rank, branch, and unit of military service of the person upon entry.

(5) The inclusive dates of the person's military service.

(6) The monthly pay received by the person at the date of the certificate's issuance.

(7) The time and place of the person's termination of or release from military service, or the person's death during military service.

(b) Certificates

The Secretary concerned shall furnish a certificate under subsection (a) upon receipt of an application for such a certificate. A certificate appearing to be signed by the Secretary concerned is prima facie evidence of its contents and of the signer's authority to issue it.

(c) Treatment of servicemembers in missing status

A servicemember who has been reported missing is presumed to continue in service until accounted for. A requirement under this Act that begins or ends with the death of a servicemember does not begin or end until the servicemember's death is reported to, or determined by, the Secretary concerned or by a court of competent jurisdiction.

§ 583. Interlocutory orders

An interlocutory order issued by a court under this Act may be revoked, modified, or extended by that court upon its own motion or otherwise, upon notification to affected parties as required by the court.

Title VII—Further Relief

§ 591. Anticipatory relief

(a) Application for relief

A servicemember may, during military service or within 180 days of termination of or release from military service, apply to a court for relief—

(1) from any obligation or liability incurred by the servicemember before the servicemember's military service; or

(2) from a tax or assessment falling due before or during the servicemember's military service.

(b) Tax liability or assessment

In a case covered by subsection (a), the court may, if the ability of the servicemember to comply with the terms of such obligation or liability or pay such tax or assessment has been materially affected by reason of military service, after appropriate notice and hearing, grant the following relief:

(1) Stay of enforcement of real estate contracts

(A) In the case of an obligation payable in installments under a contract for the purchase of real estate, or secured by a mortgage or other instrument in the nature of a mortgage upon real estate, the court may grant a stay of the enforcement of the obligation—

(i) during the servicemember's period of military service; and

(ii) from the date of termination of or release from military service, or from the date of application if made after termination of or release from military service.

(B) Any stay under this paragraph shall be—

(i) for a period equal to the remaining life of the installment contract or other instrument, plus a period of time equal to the period of military service of the servicemember, or any part of such combined period; and

(ii) subject to payment of the balance of the principal and accumulated interest due and unpaid at the date of termination or release from the applicant's military service or from the date of application in equal installments during the combined period at the rate of interest on the unpaid balance prescribed in the contract or other instrument evidencing the obligation, and subject to other terms as may be equitable.

(2) Stay of enforcement of other contracts

(A) In the case of any other obligation, liability, tax, or assessment, the court may grant a stay of enforcement—

(i) during the servicemember's military service; and

(ii) from the date of termination of or release from military service, or from the date of application if made after termination or release from military service.

(B) Any stay under this paragraph shall be—

(i) for a period of time equal to the period of the servicemember's military service or any part of such period; and

(ii) subject to payment of the balance of principal and accumulated interest due and unpaid at the date of termination or release from military service, or the date of application, in equal periodic installments during this extended period at the rate of interest as may be prescribed for this obligation, liability, tax, or assessment, if paid when due, and subject to other terms as may be equitable.

(c) Affect of stay on fine or penalty

When a court grants a stay under this section, a fine or penalty shall not accrue on the obligation, liability, tax, or assessment for the period of compliance with the terms and conditions of the stay.

§ 592. Power of attorney

(a) Automatic extension
A power of attorney of a servicemember shall be automatically extended for the period the servicemember is in a missing status (as defined in section 551(2) of title 37, United States Code) if the power of attorney—
(1) was duly executed by the servicemember—
(A) while in military service; or
(B) before entry into military service but after the servicemember—
(i) received a call or order to report for military service; or
(ii) was notified by an official of the Department of Defense that the person could receive a call or order to report for military service;
(2) designates the servicemember's spouse, parent, or other named relative as the servicemember's attorney in fact for certain, specified, or all purposes; and
(3) expires by its terms after the servicemember entered a missing status.
(b) Limitation on power of attorney extension
A power of attorney executed by a servicemember may not be extended under subsection (a) if the document by its terms clearly indicates that the power granted expires on the date specified even though the servicemember, after the date of execution of the document, enters a missing status.

* * *

§ 594. Health insurance reinstatement

(a) Reinstatement of health insurance
A servicemember who, by reason of military service as defined in section 703(a)(1) [section 593(a)(1) of this Appendix], is entitled to the rights and protections of this Act [sections 501 to 596 of this Appendix] shall also be entitled upon termination or release from such service to reinstatement of any health insurance that—
(1) was in effect on the day before such service commenced; and
(2) was terminated effective on a date during the period of such service.
(b) No exclusion or waiting period
The reinstatement of health care insurance coverage for the health or physical condition of a servicemember described in subsection (a), or any other person who is covered by the insurance by reason of the coverage of the servicemember, shall not be subject to an exclusion or a waiting period, if—
(1) the condition arose before or during the period of such service;
(2) an exclusion or a waiting period would not have been imposed for the condition during the period of coverage; and
(3) in a case in which the condition relates to the servicemember, the condition has not been determined by the Secretary of Veterans Affairs to be a disability incurred or aggravated in the line of duty (within the meaning of section 105 of title 38, United States Code).
(c) Exceptions
Subsection (a) does not apply to a servicemember entitled to participate in employer-offered insurance benefits pursuant to the provisions of chapter 43 of title 38, United States Code.
(d) Time for applying for reinstatement
An application under this section must be filed not later than 120 days after the date of the termination of or release from military service.
(e) Limitation on premium increases
(1) Premium protection
The amount of the premium for health insurance coverage that was terminated by a servicemember and required to be reinstated under subsection (a) may not be increased, for the balance of the period for which coverage would have been continued had the coverage not been terminated, to an amount greater than the amount chargeable for such coverage before the termination.
(2) Increases of general applicability not precluded
Paragraph (1) does not prevent an increase in premium to the extent of any general increase in the premiums charged by the carrier of the health care insurance for the same health insurance coverage for persons similarly covered by such insurance during the period between the termination and the reinstatement.

[As amended by Pub. L. No. 109-233, § 302, 120 Stat. 406 (2006).]

* * *

§ 596. Business or trade obligations

(a) Availability of non-business assets to satisfy obligations
If the trade or business (without regard to the form in which such trade or business is carried out) of a servicemember has an obligation or liability for which the servicemember is personally liable, the assets of the servicemember not held in connection with the trade or business may not be available for satisfaction of the obligation or liability during the servicemember's military service.
(b) Relief to obligors
Upon application to a court by the holder of an obligation or liability covered by this section, relief granted by this section to a servicemember may be modified as justice and equity require.

Appendix B Federal Wage Garnishment Statute and Regulations

B.1 Federal Statutory Restrictions on Garnishment

15 U.S.C. §§ 1671–1677

[As enacted by Pub. L. No. 90-321, 82 Stat. 163 (1968), unless otherwise noted.]

TITLE 15—COMMERCE AND TRADE

Chapter 41—Consumer Credit Protection

Subchapter II—Restrictions on Garnishment

Title 15—Commerce and Trade

* * *

Chapter 41—Consumer Credit Protection

* * *

Subchapter II—Restrictions on Garnishment

§ 1671. Congressional findings and declaration of purpose

(a) Disadvantages of garnishment

The Congress finds:

(1) The unrestricted garnishment of compensation due for personal services encourages the making of predatory extensions of credit. Such extensions of credit divert money into excessive credit payments and thereby hinder the production and flow of goods in interstate commerce.

(2) The application of garnishment as a creditors' remedy frequently results in loss of employment by the debtor, and the resulting disruption of employment, production, and consumption constitutes a substantial burden on interstate commerce.

(3) The great disparities among the laws of the several States relating to garnishment have, in effect, destroyed the uniformity of the bankruptcy laws and frustrated the purposes thereof in many areas of the country.

(b) Necessity for regulation

On the basis of the findings stated in subsection (a) of this section, the Congress determines that the provisions of this subchapter are necessary and proper for the purpose of carrying into execution the powers of the Congress to regulate commerce and to establish uniform bankruptcy laws.

§ 1672. Definitions

For the purposes of this subchapter:

(a) The term "earnings" means compensation paid or payable for personal services, whether denominated as wages, salary, commission, bonus, or otherwise, and includes periodic payments pursuant to a pension or retirement program.

(b) The term "disposable earnings" means that part of the earnings of any individual remaining after the deduction from those earnings of any amounts required by law to be withheld.

(c) The term "garnishment" means any legal or equitable procedure through which the earnings of any individual are required to be withheld for payment of any debt.

§ 1673. Restriction on garnishment

(a) Maximum allowable garnishment

Except as provided in subsection (b) of this section and in section 1675 of this title, the maximum part of the aggregate disposable earnings of an individual for any workweek which is subjected to garnishment may not exceed

(1) 25 per centum of his disposable earnings for that week, or

(2) the amount by which his disposable earnings for that week exceed thirty times the Federal minimum hourly wage prescribed by section 206(a)(1) of Title 29 in effect at the time the earnings are payable,

whichever is less. In the case of earnings for any pay period other than a week, the Secretary of Labor shall by regulation prescribe a multiple of the Federal minimum hourly wage equivalent in effect to that set forth in paragraph (2).

(b) Exceptions

(1) The restrictions of subsection (a) of this section do not apply in the case of

(A) any order for the support of any person issued by a court of competent jurisdiction or in accordance with an administrative procedure, which is established by State law, which affords substantial due process, and which is subject to judicial review.

(B) any order of any court of the United States having jurisdiction over cases under chapter 13 of Title 11.

(C) any debt due for any State or Federal tax.

(2) The maximum part of the aggregate disposable earnings of an individual for any workweek which is subject to garnishment to enforce any order for the support of any person shall not exceed—

(A) where such individual is supporting his spouse or dependent child (other than a spouse or child with respect to whose support such order is used), 50 per centum of such individual's disposable earnings for that week; and

(B) where such individual is not supporting such a spouse or dependent child described in clause (A), 60 per centum of such individual's disposable earnings for that week;

except that, with respect to the disposable earnings of any individual for any workweek, the 50 per centum specified in clause (A) shall be deemed to be 55 per centum and the 60 per centum specified in clause (B) shall be deemed to be 65 per centum, if and to the extent that such earnings are subject to garnishment to enforce a support order with respect to a period which is prior to the twelve-week period which ends with the beginning of such workweek.

(c) Execution or enforcement of garnishment order or process prohibited

No court of the United States or any State, and no State (or officer or agency thereof), may make, execute, or enforce any order or process in violation of this section.

[As amended by Pub. L. No. 95-30, 91 Stat. 161 (1977); Pub. L. No. 95-598, 92 Stat. 2676 (1978).]

§ 1674. Restriction on discharge from employment by reason of garnishment

(a) Termination of employment

No employer may discharge any employee by reason of the fact that his earnings have been subjected to garnishment for any one indebtedness.

(b) Penalties

Whoever willfully violates subsection (a) of this section shall be fined not more than $1,000, or imprisoned not more than one year, or both.

§ 1675. Exemption for State-regulated garnishments

The Secretary of Labor may by regulation exempt from the provisions of section 1673(a) and (b)(2) of this title garnishments issued under the laws of any State if he determines that the laws of that State provide restrictions on garnishment which are substantially similar to those provided in section 1673(a) and (b)(2) of this title.

[As amended by Pub. L. No. 95-30, 91 Stat. 161 (1977).]

§ 1676. Enforcement by Secretary of Labor

The Secretary of Labor, acting through the Wage and Hour Division of the Department of Labor, shall enforce the provisions of this subchapter.

§ 1677. Effect on State laws

This subchapter does not annul, alter, or affect, or exempt any person from complying with, the laws of any State

(1) prohibiting garnishments or providing for more limited garnishment than are allowed under this subchapter, or

(2) prohibiting the discharge of any employee by reason of the fact that his earnings have been subjected to garnishment for more than one indebtedness.

B.2 Department of Labor Wage Garnishment Regulations, 29 C.F.R. Part 870

The Department of Labor's wage garnishment regulations, 29 C.F.R. Part 870, reprinted below, have ***not*** been amended to reflect Public Law No. 110-28, 121 Stat. 188 (2007), which amended the Fair Labor Standards Act of 1938, 29 U.S.C. § 206(a)(1). The amendment increased the minimum wage to $5.85 an hour, effective July 24, 2007, and to $6.55 an hour, effective July 24, 2008. A further increase to $7.25 an hour will take effect on July 24, 2009. These changes increase the amount of wages protected from wage garnishment, so that, as of July 24, 2008, $196.50 of weekly disposable earnings (thirty times the minimum wage) is protected.

The tables in the wage garnishment regulations have not been revised to reflect these changes. However, the Department of Labor does publish a fact sheet which updates the numbers. It may be found at www.dol.gov/esa/regs/compliance/whd/whdfs30.htm. The first table, found at 29 C.F.R. § 870.10(c)(3), specifies the maximum amount of disposable earnings fully exempt under federal law. To reflect the increased minimum wage, it should be revised to read as follows:

Date	Minimum amount	Weekly amount	Biweekly amount	Semimonthly amount	Monthly rate
July 24, 2008	$6.55	$196.50	$393.00	$425.75	$851.50

If a consumer's disposable earnings are below the levels established in a second table, found at 29 C.F.R. § 870.10(c)(4), but above the levels specified in the first table, then the consumer's disposable earnings are partially exempt. In that case less than twenty-five percent of the earnings may be garnished. To reflect the increased minimum wage, the second table should be revised to read as follows:

Date	Minimum amount	Weekly amount	Biweekly amount	Semimonthly amount	Monthly rate
July 24, 2008	$ 6.55	$262.00	$524.00	$567.66	$1135.32

For higher wages than specified in the second table, the maximum amount to be garnished is twenty-five percent of the consumer's disposable income.

PART 870—RESTRICTION ON GARNISHMENT

AUTHORITY: Secs. 303, 305, 306, 82 Stat. 163, 164; 15 U.S.C. 1673, 1675, 1676, unless otherwise noted.

SOURCE: 35 Fed. Reg. 8226, May 26, 1970, unless otherwise noted.

Subpart A—General

§ 870.1 Purpose and scope.

(a) This part sets forth the procedures and any policies, determinations, and interpretations of general application whereby the Secretary of Labor carries out his duties under section 303 of the CCPA dealing with restrictions on garnishment of earnings, and section 305 permitting exemptions for State-regulated garnishments in certain situations. While the Secretary's duties under section 303 include insuring that certain amounts of earnings are protected, such duties do not include establishing priorities among multiple garnishments, as such priorities are determined by other Federal statutes or by State law.

(b) Functions of the Secretary under the CCPA to be performed as provided in this part are assigned to the Administrator of the Wage and Hour Division (hereinafter referred to as the Administrator), who, under the general direction and control of the Assistant Secretary, Wage and Labor Standards Administration, shall be empowered to take final and binding actions in administering the provisions of this part. The Administrator is empowered to subdelegate any of his duties under this part. Any legal advice and assistance required for administration of this part shall be provided by the Solicitor of Labor.

[35 FR 8226, May 26, 1970, as amended at 44 Fed. Reg. 30684, May 29, 1979]

§ 870.2 Amendments to this part.

The Administrator may, at any time upon his own motion or upon written request of any interested person setting forth reasonable grounds therefor, amend any rules in this part.

Subpart B—Determinations and Interpretations

§ 870.10 Maximum part of aggregate disposable earnings subject to garnishment under section 303(a).

(a) *Statutory provision.* Section 303 (a) of the CCPA provides that, with some exceptions, the maximum part of the aggregate disposable earnings of an individual for any workweek which is subjected to garnishment may not exceed

(1) 25 per centum of his disposable earnings for that week, or

(2) the amount by which his disposable earnings for that week exceed thirty times the Federal minimum hourly wage prescribed by section 6(a)(1) of the Fair Labor Standards Act of 1938, in effect at the time the earnings are payable.

whichever is less. In the case of earnings for any pay period other than a week, the Secretary of Labor shall by regulation prescribe a multiple of the Federal minimum hourly wage equivalent in effect to that set forth in paragraph (2).

(b) *Weekly pay period.* The statutory exemption formula applies directly to the aggregate disposable earnings paid or payable for a pay period of 1 workweek, or a lesser period. Its intent is to protect from garnishment and save to an individual earner the specified amount of compensation for his personal services rendered in the workweek, or a lesser period. Thus:

(1) The amount of an individual's disposable earnings for a workweek or lesser period which may not be garnished is 30 times the Fair Labor Standards Act minimum wage. If an individual's disposable earnings for such a period are equal to or less than 30 times the minimum wage, the individual's earnings may not be garnished in any amount. (When the minimum wage increases, the proportionate amount of earnings which may not be garnished also increases.) On April 1, 1991, the minimum wage increased to $4.25. Accordingly, the amount of disposable weekly earnings which may not be garnished is $127.50 effective April 1, 1991. (For the period April 1, 1990 through March 31, 1991, the amount that may not be garnished is $114 (30 x $3.80).)

(2) For earnings payable on or after April 1, 1991, if an individual's disposable earnings for a workweek or lesser period are more than $127.50, but less than $170.00, only the amount above $127.50 is subject to garnishment. (For earnings payable during the period April 1, 1990, through March 31, 1991, when the Fair Labor Standards Act minimum wage was $3.80, this range computes to more than $114.00, but less than $152.00.)

(3) For earnings payable on or after April 1, 1991, if an individual's disposable earnings for a workweek or lesser period are $170.00 or more, 25 percent of his/her disposable earnings is subject to garnishment. (The weekly figure was $152.00 (40 × $3.80) for the period April 1, 1990 through March 31, 1991.)

(c) *Pay for a period longer than 1 week.* In the case of disposable earnings which compensate for personal services rendered in a pay period longer than 1 workweek, the weekly statutory exemption formula must be transformed to a formula applicable to such earnings providing equivalent restrictions on wage garnishment.

(1) The 25 percent part of the formula would apply to the aggregate disposable earnings for all the workweeks or fractions thereof compensated by the pay for such pay period.

(2) The following formula should be used to calculate the dollar amount of disposable earnings which would not be subject to garnishment: The number of workweeks, or fractions thereof, should be multiplied times the applicable Federal minimum wage and that amount should be multiplied by 30. For example, for the period April 1, 1990 through March 31, 1991 when the Federal minimum wage was $3.80 per hour, the formula should be calculated based on a minimum wage of $3.80 ($3.80 multiplied by 30 equals $114; $114 multiplied by the number of workweeks (or fractions thereof) equals the amount that cannot be garnished). As of April 1, 1991, the $4.25 Federal minimum wage replaces $3.80 in the formula (and the amount which cannot be garnished would then be $127.50 multiplied by the number of workweeks (or fractions thereof)). For purposes of this formula, a calendar month is considered to consist of 4 workweeks. Thus, during the period April 1, 1990 through March 31, 1991 when the Federal minimum hourly wage was $3.80 an hour, the amount of disposable earnings for a 2-week period is $228.00 (2 x 30 x $3.80); for a monthly period, $494.00 (4 x 30 x $3.80). Effective April 1, 1991, such amounts increased as follows: for a two-week period, $255.00 (2 x 30 x $4.25); for a monthly period, $552.50 (4 x 30 x $4.25). The amount of disposable earnings for any other pay period longer than 1 week shall be computed in a manner consistent with section 303(a) of the act and with this paragraph.

(3) Absent any changes to the rate set forth in section 6(a)(1) of the Fair Labor Standards Act, disposable earnings for individuals paid weekly, biweekly, semimonthly, and monthly may not be garnished unless they are in excess of the following amounts:

Date	Minimum amount	Weekly amount	Biweekly amount	Semimonthly amount	Monthly rate
Jan. 1, 1981	$3.35	$100.50	$201.00	$217.75	$435.50
April. 1, 1990	3.80	114.00	228.00	247.00	494.00
April. 1, 1991	4.25	127.50	255.00	276.25	552.50

(4) Absent any changes to the rate set forth in section 6(a)(1) of the Fair Labor Standards Act, if the disposable earnings are less than the following figures, only the difference between the appropriate figures set forth in paragraph (c)(3) of this section and the individual's disposable earnings may be garnished.

Date	Minimum amount	Weekly amount	Biweekly amount	Semimonthly amount	Monthly rate
Jan. 1, 1981	$3.35	$134.00	$268.00	$290.33	$580.67
April. 1, 1990	3.80	152.00	304.00	329.33	658.67
April. 1, 1991	4.25	170.00	340.00	368.33	736.67

For example, in April of 1990, if an individual's disposable earnings for a biweekly pay period are $274.00, the difference between $228.00 and $274.00 (i.e., $46.00) may be garnished.

(5) If disposable earnings are in excess of the figures stated in paragraph (c)(4) of this section, 25% of the disposable earnings may be garnished.

(d) *Date wages paid or payable controlling*. The date that disposable earnings are paid or payable, and not the date the Court issues the garnishment order, is controlling in determining the amount of disposable earnings that may be garnished. Thus, a garnishment order in November 1990, providing for withholding from wages over a period of time, based on exemptions computed at the $3.80 per hour minimum wage then in effect, would be modified by operation of the change in the law so that wages paid after April 1, 1991, are subject to garnishment to the extent described in paragraphs (b) and (c) of this section on the basis of a minimum rate of $4.25 per hour. This principle is applicable at the time of the enactment of any further increase in the minimum wage.

AUTHORITY: Sec. 2, Pub. L. 93-259, 84 Stat. 55

[35 FR 8226 (May 26, 1970), as amended at 40 FR 52610, Nov. 11, 1975; 43 FR 28471, June 30, 1978; 43 FR 30276, July 14, 1978; 44 FR 30685, May 29, 1979; 56 FR 32254, July 15, 1991; 56 FR 40660, Aug. 15, 1991]

§ 870.11 Exceptions to the restrictions provided by section 303(a) of the CCPA and priorities among garnishments.

(a)(1) Section 303(b) of the Consumer Credit Protection Act provides that the restrictions in section 303(a) do not apply to:

(i) Any debt due for any State or Federal tax, or

(ii) Any order of any court of bankruptcy under Chapter XIII of the Bankruptcy Act.

(2) Accordingly the Consumer Credit Protection Act does not restrict in any way the amount which may be withheld for State or Federal taxes or in Chapter XIII Bankruptcy Act proceedings.

(b)(1) Section 303(b) provides the following restrictions on the amount that may be withheld for the support of any person (e.g. alimony or child support):

(A) Where such individual is supporting his spouse or dependent child (other than a spouse or child with respect to whose support such order is issued), 50 per centum of such individual's disposable earnings for that week; and

(B) Where such individual is not supporting such a spouse or dependent child described in clause (A), 60 per centum of such individual's disposable earnings for that week; except that, with respect to the disposable earnings of any individual for any workweek, the 50 per centum specified in clause (A) shall be deemed to be 55 per centum and the 60 per centum specified in clause (B) shall be deemed to be 65 per centum, if and to the extent that such earnings are subject to garnishment to enforce a support order with respect to a period which is prior to the twelve week period which ends with the beginning of such workweek.

(2) Compliance with the provisions of section 303(a) and (b) may offer problems when there is more than one garnishment. In that event the priority is determined by State law or other Federal laws as the CCPA contains no provisions controlling the priorities of garnishments. However, in no event may the amount of any individual's disposable earnings which may be garnished exceed the percentages specified in section 303. To illustrate:

(i) If 45% of an individual's disposable earnings were garnished for taxes, and this garnishment has priority, the Consumer Credit Protection Act permits garnishment for the support of any person of only the difference between 45% and the applicable percentage (50 to 65%) in the above quoted section 303(b).

(ii) If 70% of an individual's disposable earnings were garnished for taxes and/or a Title XIII Bankruptcy debt, and these garnishments have priority, the Consumer Credit Protection Act does not permit garnishment either for the support of any person or for other debts.

(iii) If 25% of an individual's disposable earnings were withheld pursuant to an ordinary garnishment which is subject to the restrictions of section 303(a), and the garnishment has priority in accordance with State law, the Consumer Credit Protection Act permits the additional garnishment for the support of any person of only the difference between 25% and the applicable percentage (50–65%) in the above quoted section 303(b).

(iv) If 25% or more of an individual's disposable earnings were withheld pursuant to a garnishment for support, and the support garnishment has priority in accordance with State law, the Consumer Credit Protection Act does not permit the withholding of any additional amounts pursuant to an ordinary garnishment which is subject to the restrictions of section 303(a).

[44 FR 30685, May 29, 1979]

Subpart C—Exemption for State-Regulated Garnishments

§ 870.50 General provision.

Section 305 of the CCPA authorizes that Secretary to "exempt from the provisions of section 303(a) garnishments issued under the laws of any State if he determines that the laws of that State provide restrictions on garnishment which are substantially similar to those provided in section 303(a)."

§ 870.51 Exemption policy.

(a) It is the policy of the Secretary of Labor to permit exemption from section 303(a) of the CCPA garnishments issued under the laws of a State if those laws considered together cover every case of garnishment covered by the Act, and if those laws provide the same or greater protection to individuals. Differences in text between the restrictions of State laws and those in section 303(a) of the Act are not material so long as the State laws provide the same or greater restrictions on the garnishment of individuals' earnings.

(b) In determining whether State-regulated garnishments should be exempted from section 303(a) of the CCPA, or whether such an exemption should be terminated, the laws of the State shall be examined with particular regard to the classes of persons and of transactions to which they may apply; the formulas provided for determining the maximum part of an individual's earnings which may be subject to garnishment; restrictions on the application of the formulas; and with regard to procedural burdens placed on the individual whose earnings are subject to garnishment.

(c) Particular attention is directed to the fact that subsection (a) of section 303, when considered with subsection (c) of that section, is read as not requiring the raising of the subsection (a) restrictions as affirmative defenses in garnishment proceedings.

§ 870.52 Application for exemption of State-regulated garnishments.

(a) An application for the exemption of garnishments issued under the laws of a State may be made in duplicate by a duly authorized representative of the State. The application shall be filed with the Administrator of the Wage and Hour Division, Department of Labor, Washington, DC 20210.

(b) Any application for exemption must be accompanied by two copies of all the provisions of the State laws relating to the garnishment of earnings, certified to be true and complete copies by the Attorney General of the State. In addition, the application must be accompanied by a statement, in duplicate, signed by the Attorney General of the State, showing how the laws of the State satisfy the policy expressed in § 870.51(a) and setting forth any other matters which the Attorney General may wish to state concerning the application.

(c) Notice of the filing of an application for exemption shall be published in the *Federal Register*. Copies of the application shall be available for public inspection and copying during business hours at the national office of the Wage and Hour Division and in the regional office of the Wage and Hour Division in which the particular State is located. Interested persons shall be afforded an opportunity to submit written comments concerning the application of the State within a period of time to be specified in the notice.

[35 FR 8226, May 26, 1970, as amended at 35 FR 14315, Sept. 11, 1970]

§ 870.53 Action upon an application for exemption.

(a) The Administrator shall grant or deny within a reasonable time any application for the exemption of State-regulated garnishments. The State representative shall be notified in writing of the decision. In the event of denial, a statement of the grounds for the denial shall be made. To the extent feasible and appropriate, the Administrator may afford to the State representative and to any other interested persons an opportunity to submit orally or in writing data, views, and arguments on the issue of whether or not an exemption should be granted and on any subsidiary issues.

(b) If an application is denied, the State representative shall have an opportunity to request reconsideration by the Administrator. The request shall be made in writing. The Administrator shall permit argument whenever the opportunity to do so has not been afforded under paragraph (a) of this section, and may permit argument in any other case.

(c) General notice of every exemption of State-regulated garnishments and of its terms and conditions shall be given by publication in the *Federal Register*.

§ 870.54 Standards governing the granting of an application for exemption.

The Administrator may grant any application for the exemption of State-regulated garnishments whenever he finds that the laws of the State satisfy the policy expressed in § 870.51(a).

§ 870.55 Terms and conditions of every exemption.

(a) It shall be a condition of every exemption of State-regulated garnishments that the State representative have the powers and duties

(1) To represent, and act on behalf of, the State in relation to the Administrator and his representatives, with regard to any matter relating to, or arising out of, the application, interpretation, and enforcement of State laws regulating garnishment of earnings;

(2) To submit to the Administrator in duplicate and on a current basis, a certified copy of every enactment by the State legislature affecting any of those laws, and a certified copy of any decision in any case involving any of those laws, made by the highest court of the State which has jurisdiction to decide or review cases of its kind, if properly presented to the court; and

(3) To submit to the Administrator any information relating to the enforcement of those laws, which the Administrator may request.

(b) The Administrator may make any exemption subject to additional terms and conditions which he may find appropriate to carry out the purposes of section 303(a) of the Act.

§ 870.56 Termination of exemption.

(a) After notice and opportunity to be heard, the Administrator shall terminate any exemption of State-regulated garnishments when he finds that the laws of the State no longer satisfy the purpose of section 303(a) of the Act or the policy expressed in § 870.51(a). Also, after notice and opportunity to be heard, the Administrator may terminate any exemption if he finds that any of its terms or conditions have been violated.

(b) General notice of the termination of every exemption of State-regulated garnishments shall be given by publication in the Federal Register.

§ 870.57 Exemptions.

Pursuant to section 305 of the CCPA (82 Stat. 164) and in accordance with the provisions of this part, it has been determined that the laws of the following States provide restrictions on garnishment which are substantially similar to those provided in section 303(a) of the CCPA (82 Stat. 163); and that, therefore, garnishments issued under those laws should be, and they hereby are, exempted from the provisions of section 303(a) subject to the terms and conditions of §§ 870.55(a) and 870.56:

(a) *State of Virginia.* Effective June 30, 1978, garnishments issued under the laws of the State of Virginia are exempt from the provisions of sections 303(a) and 303(b) of the CCPA under the following additional conditions: (1) Whenever garnishments are ordered in the State of Virginia which are not deemed to be governed by section 34-29 of the Code of Virginia, as amended, and the laws of another State are applied, sections 303(a) and 303(b) of the CCPA shall apply to such garnishments according to the provisions thereof; and (2) whenever the earnings of any individual subject to garnishment are withheld and a suspending or supersedeas bond is undertaken in the course of an appeal from a lower court decision, sections 303(a) and 303(b) of the CCPA shall apply to the withholding of such earnings under this procedure according to the provisions thereof.

[35 FR 18527, Dec. 5, 1970, as amended at 43 FR 28472, June 30, 1978]

Appendix C Selected Federal Exemption Provisions

C.1 Social Security and SSI Benefits

42 U.S.C. §§ 407, 1383

Chapter 7. Social Security

Subchapter II. Federal Old-Age, Survivors, and Disability Insurance Benefits

§ 407. Assignment; amendment of section

(a) The right of any person to any future payment under this subchapter shall not be transferable or assignable, at law or in equity, and none of the moneys paid or payable or rights existing under this subchapter shall be subject to execution, levy, attachment, garnishment, or other legal process, or to the operation of any bankruptcy or insolvency law.

(b) No other provision of law, enacted before, on, or after April 20, 1983, may be construed to limit, supersede, or otherwise modify the provisions of this section except to the extent that it does so by express reference to this section.

(c) Nothing in this section shall be construed to prohibit withholding taxes from any benefit under this subchapter, if such withholding is done pursuant to a request made in accordance with section 3402(p)(1) of the Internal Revenue Code of 1986 [26 U.S.C.A. § 3402] by the person entitled to such benefit or such person's representative payee.

* * *

Subchapter XVI. Supplemental Security Income for Aged, Blind, and Disabled

Part B. Procedural and General Provisions

§ 1383. Procedure for payment of benefits

* * *

(d) Procedures applicable; prohibition on assignment of payments; representation of claimants; maximum fees; penalties for violations

(1) The provisions of section 407 of this title and subsections (a), (d), and (e) of section 405 of this title shall apply with respect to this part to the same extent as they apply in the case of subchapter II of this chapter.

* * *

C.2 Veterans' Benefits

38 U.S.C. § 5301

Part IV. General Administrative Provisions

Chapter 53. Special Provisions Relating to Benefits

§ 5301. Nonassignability and exempt status of benefits

(a)(1) Payments of benefits due or to become due under any law administered by the Secretary shall not be assignable except to the extent specifically authorized by law, and such payments made to, or on account of, a beneficiary shall be exempt from taxation, shall be exempt from the claim of creditors, and shall not be liable to attachment, levy, or seizure by or under any legal or equitable process whatever, either before or after receipt by the beneficiary. The preceding sentence shall not apply to claims of the United States arising under such laws nor shall the exemption therein contained as to taxation extend to any property purchased in part or wholly out of such payments. The provisions of this section shall not be construed to prohibit the assignment of insurance otherwise authorized under chapter 19 of this title, or of servicemen's indemnity.

(2) For the purposes of this subsection, in any case where a payee of an educational assistance allowance has designated the address of an attorney-in-fact as the payee's address for the purpose of receiving a benefit check and has also executed a power of attorney giving the attorney-in-fact authority to negotiate such benefit check, such action shall be deemed to be an assignment and is prohibited.

(3)(A) This paragraph is intended to clarify that, in any case where a beneficiary entitled to compensation, pension, or dependency and indemnity compensation enters into an agreement with another person under which agreement such other person acquires for consideration the right to receive such benefit by payment of such compensation, pension, or dependency and indemnity compensation, as the case may be, except as provided in subparagraph (B), and including deposit into a joint account from which such other person may make withdrawals, or otherwise, such agreement shall be deemed to be an assignment and is prohibited.

(B) Notwithstanding subparagraph (A), nothing in this paragraph is intended to prohibit a loan involving a beneficiary under the terms of which the beneficiary may use the benefit to repay such other person as long as each of the periodic payments made to repay such other person is separately and voluntarily executed by the beneficiary or is made by preauthorized electronic funds transfer pursuant to the Electronic Funds Transfers Act (15 U.S.C. 1693 et seq.).

(C) Any agreement or arrangement for collateral for security for an agreement that is prohibited under subparagraph (A) is also prohibited and is void from its inception.

(b) This section shall prohibit the collection by setoff or otherwise out of any benefits payable pursuant to any law administered by the Secretary and relating to veterans, their estates, or their dependents, of any claim of the United States or any agency thereof against (1) any person other than the indebted beneficiary or the beneficiary's estate; or (2) any beneficiary or the beneficiary's estate except amounts due the United States by such beneficiary or the beneficiary's estate by reason of overpayments or illegal payments made under such laws to such beneficiary or the beneficiary's estate or to the beneficiary's dependents as such. If the benefits referred to in the preceding sentence are insurance payable by reason of yearly renewable term insurance, United States Government life insurance, or National Service Life Insurance issued by the United States, the exemption provided in this section shall not apply to indebtedness existing against the particular insurance contract upon the maturity of which the claim is based, whether such indebtedness is in the form of liens to secure unpaid premiums or loans, or interest on such premiums or loans, or indebtedness arising from overpayments of dividends, refunds, loans, or other insurance benefits.

(c)(1) Notwithstanding any other provision of this section, the Secretary may, after receiving a request under paragraph (2) of this subsection relating to a veteran, collect by offset of any compensation or pension payable to the veteran under laws administered by the Secretary the uncollected portion of the amount of any indebtedness associated with the veteran's participation in a plan prescribed in chapter 73 of title 10.

(2) If the Secretary concerned (as defined in section 101(5) of title 37) has tried under section 3711(a) of title 31 to collect an amount described in paragraph (1) of this subsection in the case of any veteran, has been unable to collect such amount, and has determined that the uncollected portion of such amount is not collectible from amounts payable by that Secretary to the veteran or that the veteran is not receiving any payment from that Secretary, that Secretary may request the Secretary to make collections in the case of such veteran as authorized in paragraph (1) of this subsection.

(3)(A) A collection authorized by paragraph (1) of this subsection shall be conducted in accordance with the procedures prescribed in section 3716 of title 31 for administrative offset collections made after attempts to collect claims under section 3711(a) of such title.

(B) For the purposes of subparagraph (A) of this paragraph, as used in the second sentence of section 3716(a) of title 31—

(i) the term "records of the agency" shall be considered to refer to the records of the department of the Secretary concerned; and

(ii) the term "agency" in clauses (3) and (4) shall be considered to refer to such department.

(4) Funds collected under this subsection shall be credited to the Department of Defense Military Retirement Fund under chapter 74 of title 10 or to the Retired Pay Account of the Coast Guard, as appropriate.

(d) Notwithstanding subsection (a) of this section, payments of benefits under laws administered by the Secretary shall not be exempt from levy under subchapter D of chapter 64 of the Internal Revenue Code of 1986 (26 U.S.C. 6331 et seq.).

(e) In the case of a person who—

(1) has been determined to be eligible to receive pension or compensation under laws administered by the Secretary but for the receipt by such person of pay pursuant to any provision of law providing retired or retirement pay to members or former members of the Armed Forces or commissioned officers of the National Oceanic and Atmospheric Administration or of the Public Health Service; and

(2) files a waiver of such pay in accordance with section 5305 of this title in the amount of such pension or compensation before the end of the one-year period beginning on the date such person is notified by the Secretary of such person's eligibility for such pension or compensation,

the retired or retirement pay of such person shall be exempt from taxation, as provided in subsection (a) of this section, in an amount equal to the amount of pension or compensation which would have been paid to such person but for the receipt by such person of such pay.

C.3 Exception Allowing Enforcement of Child Support Claims Against Social Security and Veterans' Benefits

42 U.S.C. § 659

Chapter 7. Social Security

Subchapter IV. Grants to States for Aid and Services to Needy Families with Children and for Child-Welfare Services

Part D. Child Support and Establishment of Paternity

§ 659. Consent by the United States to income withholding, garnishment, and similar proceedings for enforcement of child support and alimony obligations

(a) Consent to support enforcement

Notwithstanding any other provision of law (including section 407 of this title and section 5301 of Title 38), effective January 1, 1975, moneys (the entitlement to which is based upon remuneration for employment) due from, or payable by, the United States or the District of Columbia (including any agency, subdivision, or instrumentality thereof) to any individual, including members of the Armed Forces of the United States, shall be subject, in like manner and to the same extent as if the United States or the District of Columbia were a private person, to withholding in accordance with State law enacted pursuant to subsections (a)(1) and (b) of section 666 of this title[1] and regulations of the Secretary under such subsections, and to any other legal process brought, by a State agency administering a program under a State plan approved under this part or by an individual obligee, to enforce the legal obligation of the individual to provide child support or alimony.

* * *

C.4 Civil Service and Federal Retirement and Disability Benefits

5 U.S.C. §§ 8130, 8346, 8470

Title 5. Government Organization and Employees

Part III. Employees

Subpart G. Insurance and Annuities

Chapter 81. Compensation for Work Injuries

Subchapter I. Generally

§ 8130. Assignment of claim

An assignment of a claim for compensation under this subchapter is void. Compensation and claims for compensation are exempt from claims of creditors.

* * *

Chapter 83. Retirement

Subchapter III. Civil Service Retirement

§ 8346. Exemption from legal process; recovery of payments

(a) The money mentioned by this subchapter is not assignable, either in law or equity, except under the provisions of subsections (h) and (j) of section 8345 of this title, or subject to execution, levy, attachment, garnishment, or other legal process, except as otherwise may be provided by Federal laws.

* * *

1 [*Editor's Note: 42 U.S.C. § 666 deals with procedures to improve the effectiveness of child support enforcement, including the withholding of payments.*]

Chapter 84. Federal Employees' Retirement System

Subchapter VI. General and Administrative Provisions

§ 8470. Exemption from legal process; recovery of payments

(a) An amount payable under subchapter II, IV, or V of this chapter is not assignable, either in law or equity, except under the provisions of section 8465 or 8467, or subject to execution, levy, attachment, garnishment or other legal process, except as otherwise may be provided by Federal laws.

* * *

C.5 Servicemembers' Pay

37 U.S.C. § 701

Chapter 13. Allotments and Assignments of Pay

§ 701. Members of the Army, Navy, Air Force, and Marine Corps; contract surgeons

(a) Under regulations prescribed by the Secretary of the military department concerned,[2] a commissioned officer of the Army, Navy, Air Force, or Marine Corps may transfer or assign his pay account, when due and payable.

(b) A contract surgeon, or contract dental surgeon, of the Army, Navy, or Air Force, on duty in Alaska, Hawaii, the Philippine Islands, or Puerto Rico, may transfer or assign his pay account, when due and payable, under the regulations prescribed under subsection (a).

(c) An enlisted member of the Army, Navy, Air Force, or Marine Corps may not assign his pay, and if he does so, the assignment is void.

* * *

C.6 Military Annuities and Survivors' Benefits

10 U.S.C. §§ 1440, 1450

Chapter 73. Annuities Based on Retired or Retainer Pay

Subchapter I. Retired Serviceman's Family Protection Plan

§ 1440. Annuities not subject to legal process

Except as provided in section 1437(c)(3)(B) of this title, no annuity payable under this subchapter is assignable or subject to

2 [*Editor's Note: No such regulations have been enacted.*]

execution, levy, attachment, garnishment, or other legal process.

* * *

Subchapter II. Survivor Benefit Plan

§ 1450. Payment of annuity: beneficiaries

* * *

(i) **Annuities exempt from certain legal process.**—Except as provided in subsection (*l*)(3)(B), an annuity under this section is not assignable or subject to execution, levy, attachment, garnishment, or other legal process.

* * *

C.7 Student Assistance

20 U.S.C. § 1095a

Chapter 28. Higher Education Resources and Student Assistance

Subchapter IV. Student Assistance

Part F. General Provisions Relating to Student Assistance Programs

§ 1095a. Wage garnishment requirement

* * *

(d) No attachment of student assistance

Except as authorized in this section, notwithstanding any other provision of Federal or State law, no grant, loan, or work assistance awarded under this subchapter and part C of subchapter I of chapter 34 of Title 42, or property traceable to such assistance, shall be subject to garnishment or attachment in order to satisfy any debt owed by the student awarded such assistance, other than a debt owed to the Secretary and arising under this subchapter and part C of subchapter I of chapter 34 of Title 42.

* * *

C.8 Railroad Retirement Benefits

45 U.S.C. § 231m

Chapter 9. Retirement of Railroad Employees

Subchapter IV. Railroad Retirement Act of 1974

§ 231m Assignability; exemption from levy

(a) Except as provided in subsection (b) of this section and the Internal Revenue Code of 1986 [26 U.S.C.A. § 1 et seq.], notwithstanding any other law of the United States, or of any State, territory, or the District of Columbia, no annuity or supplemental annuity shall be assignable or be subject to any tax or to garnishment, attachment, or other legal process under any circumstances whatsoever, nor shall the payment thereof be anticipated

(b)(1) This section shall not operate to exclude the amount of any supplemental annuity paid to an individual under section 231a(b) of this title from income taxable pursuant to the Federal income tax provisions of the Internal Revenue Code of 1986 [26 U.S.C.A. § 1 et seq.].

(2) This section shall not operate to prohibit the characterization or treatment of that portion of an annuity under this subchapter which is not computed under section 231b(a), 231c(a), or 231c(f) of this title, or any portion of a supplemental annuity under this subchapter, as community property for the purposes of, or property subject to, distribution in accordance with a court decree of divorce, annulment, or legal separation or the terms of any court-approved property settlement incident to any such court decree. The Board shall make payments of such portions in accordance with any such characterization or treatment or any such decree or settlement.

C.9 Merchant Seamen Wages

46 U.S.C. § 11109

Part G. Merchant Seamen Protection and Relief

Chapter 111. Protection and Relief

§ 11109. Attachment of wages

(a) Wages due or accruing to a master or seaman are not subject to attachment or arrestment from any court, except for an order of a court about the payment by a master or seaman of any part of the master's or seaman's wages for the support and maintenance of the spouse or minor children of the master or seaman, or both. A payment of wages to a master or seaman is valid, notwithstanding any prior sale or assignment of wages or any attachment, encumbrance, or arrestment of the wages.

(b) An assignment or sale of wages or salvage made before the payment of wages does not bind the party making it, except allotments authorized by section 10315 of this title.

(c) This section applies to an individual employed on a fishing vessel or any fish processing vessel.

C.10 Longshoremen's and Harbor Workers' Death and Disability Benefits

33 U.S.C. § 916

Chapter 18. Longshore and Harbor Workers' Compensation

§ 916. Assignment and exemption from claims of creditors

No assignment, release, or commutation of compensation or benefits due or payable under this chapter, except as provided by this chapter, shall be valid, and such compensation and benefits shall be exempt from all claims of creditors and from levy, execution, and attachment or other remedy for recovery or collection of a debt, which exemption may not be waived.

C.11 Foreign Service Retirement and Disability Benefits

22 U.S.C. § 4060

Chapter 52. Foreign Service

Subchapter VIII. Foreign Service Retirement and Disability

Part I. Foreign Service Retirement and Disability System

§ 4060. Assignment and attachment of moneys

* * *

(c) Applicability of other provisions of law or remedies
None of the moneys mentioned in this part shall be assignable either in law or equity, except under subsection (a) or (b) of this section, or subject to execution, levy, attachment, garnishment, or other legal process, except as otherwise may be provided by Federal law.

C.12 Compensation for Injury, Death, or Detention of Employees of U.S. Contractors Outside the U.S.

42 U.S.C. § 1717

Chapter 12. Compensation for Injury, Death, or Detention of Employees of Contractors with United States Outside United States

Subchapter II. Miscellaneous Provisions

§ 1717. Assignment of benefits; execution, levy, etc., against benefits

The right of any person to any benefit under subchapter I of this chapter shall not be transferable or assignable at law or in equity except to the United States, and none of the moneys paid or payable (except money paid hereunder as reimbursement for funeral expenses or as reimbursement with respect to payments of workmen's compensation or in the nature of workmen's compensation benefits), or rights existing under said subchapter, shall be subject to execution, levy, attachment, garnishment, or other legal process or to the operation of any bankruptcy or insolvency law.

C.13 Federal Emergency Management Agency Federal Disaster Assistance

44 C.F.R. § 206.110

PART 206—FEDERAL DISASTER ASSISTANCE

Sec.
206.110 Federal assistance to individuals and households.

AUTHORITY: Robert T. Stafford Disaster Relief and Emergency Assistance Act, 42 U.S.C. 5121 through 5206; Reorganization Plan No. 3 of 1978, 43 FR 41943, 3 C.F.R., 1978 Comp., p. 329; Homeland Security Act of 2002, 6 U.S.C. 101; E.O. 12127, 44 FR 19367, 3 C.F.R., 1979 Comp., p. 376; E.O. 12148, 44 FR 43239, 3 C.F.R., 1979 Comp., p. 412; E.O. 13286, 68 FR 10619, 3 C.F.R., 2003 Comp., p. 166.

SOURCE: 67 FR 61452, Sept. 30, 2002; 67 FR 62896, Oct. 9, 2002, unless otherwise noted.

§ 206.110 Federal assistance to individuals and households

(a) Purpose. This section implements the policy and procedures set forth in section 408 of the Robert T. Stafford Disaster Relief and Emergency Assistance Act, 42 U.S.C. 5174, as amended by the

Disaster Mitigation Act of 2000. This program provides financial assistance and, if necessary, direct assistance to eligible individuals and households who, as a direct result of a major disaster or emergency, have uninsured or under-insured, necessary expenses and serious needs and are unable to meet such expenses or needs through other means.

* * *

(g) Exemption from garnishment. All assistance provided under this subpart is exempt from garnishment, seizure, encumbrance, levy, execution, pledge, attachment, release or waiver. Recipients of rights under this provision may not reassign or transfer the rights. These exemptions do not apply to FEMA recovering assistance fraudulently obtained or misapplied.

* * *

Appendix D Federal Trade Commission Credit Practices Rule

16 C.F.R. Part 444

PART 444—CREDIT PRACTICES

AUTHORITY: Sec. 18(a), 88 Stat. 2193, as amended 93 Stat. 95 (15 U.S.C. 57a); 80 Stat. 383, as amended, 81 Stat. 54 (5 U.S.C. 552).

SOURCE: 49 FR 7789, March 1, 1984, unless otherwise noted.

§ 444.1 Definitions

(a) *Lender*. A person who engages in the business of lending money to consumers within the jurisdiction of the Federal Trade Commission.

(b) *Retail installment seller*. A person who sells goods or services to consumers on a deferred payment basis or pursuant to a lease-purchase arrangement within the jurisdiction of the Federal Trade Commission.

(c) *Person*. An individual corporation, or other business organization.

(d) *Consumer*. A natural person who seeks or acquires goods, services, or money for personal, family, or household use.

(e) *Obligation*. An agreement between a consumer and a lender or retail installment seller.

(f) *Creditor*. A lender or a retail installment seller.

(g) *Debt*. Money that is due or alleged to be due from one to another.

(h) *Earnings*. Compensation paid or payable to an individual or for his or her account for personal services rendered or to be rendered by him or her, whether denominated as wages, salary, commission, bonus, or otherwise, including periodic payments pursuant to a pension, retirement, or disability program.

(i) *Household goods*. Clothing, furniture, appliances, one radio and one television, linens, china, crockery, kitchenware, and personal effects (including wedding rings) of the consumer and his or her dependents, provided that the following are not included within the scope of the term "household goods":

(1) Works of art;
(2) Electronic entertainment equipment (except one television and one radio);
(3) Items acquired as antiques; and
(4) Jewelry (except wedding rings).

(j) *Antique*. Any item over one hundred years of age, including such items that have been repaired or renovated without changing their original form or character.

(k) *Cosigner*. A natural person who renders himself or herself liable for the obligation of another person without compensation. The term shall include any person whose signature is requested as a condition to granting credit to another person, or as a condition for forbearance on collection of another person's obligation that is in default. The term shall not include a spouse whose signature is required on a credit obligation to perfect a security interest pursuant to state law. A person who does not receive goods, services, or money in return for a credit obligation does not receive compensation within the meaning of this definition. A person is a cosigner within the meaning of this definition whether or not he or she is designated as such on a credit obligation.

§ 444.2 Unfair credit practices

(a) In connection with the extension of credit to consumers in or affecting commerce, as commerce is defined in the Federal Trade Commission Act, it is an unfair act or practice within the meaning of Section 5 of that Act for a lender or retail installment seller directly or indirectly to take or receive from a consumer an obligation that:

(1) Constitutes or contains a cognovit or confession of judgment (for purposes other than executory process in the State of Louisiana), warrant of attorney, or other waiver of the right to notice and the opportunity to be heard in the event of suit or process thereon.
(2) Constitutes or contains an executory waiver or a limitation of exemption from attachment, execution, or other process on real or personal property held, owned by, or due to the consumer, unless the waiver applies solely to property subject to a security interest executed in connection with the obligation.
(3) Constitutes or contains an assignment of wages or other earnings unless:
   (i) The assignment by its terms is revocable at the will of the debtor, or
   (ii) The assignment is a payroll deduction plan or preauthorized payment plan, commencing at the time of the transaction, in which the consumer authorizes a series of wage deductions as a method of making each payment, or
   (iii) The assignment applies only to wages or other earnings already earned at the time of the assignment.

(4) Constitutes or contains a nonpossessory security interest in household goods other than a purchase money security interest.

§ 444.3 Unfair or deceptive cosigner practices

(a) In connection with the extension of credit to consumers in or affecting commerce, as commerce is defined in the Federal Trade Commission Act, it is:

(1) A deceptive act or practice within the meaning of section 5 of that Act for a lender or retail installment seller, directly or indirectly, to misrepresent the nature or extent of cosigner liability to any person.

(2) An unfair act or practice within the meaning of section 5 of that Act for a lender or retail installment seller, directly or indirectly, to obligate a cosigner unless the cosigner is informed prior to becoming obligated, which in the case of open end credit shall mean prior to the time that the agreement creating the cosigner's liability for future charges is executed, of the nature of his or her liability as cosigner.

(b) Any lender or retail installment seller who complies with the preventive requirements in paragraph (c) of this section does not violate paragraph (a) of this section.

(c) To prevent these unfair or deceptive acts or practices, a disclosure, consisting of a separate document that shall contain the following statement and no other, shall be given to the cosigner prior to becoming obligated, which in the case of open end credit shall mean prior to the time that the agreement creating the cosigner's liability for future charges is executed:

NOTICE TO COSIGNER

You are being asked to guarantee this debt. Think carefully before you do. If the borrower doesn't pay the debt, you will have to. Be sure you can afford to pay if you have to, and that you want to accept this responsibility.

You may have to pay up to the full amount of the debt if the borrower does not pay. You may also have to pay late fees or collection costs, which increase this amount.

The creditor can collect this debt from you without first trying to collect from the borrower. The creditor can use the same collection methods against you that can be used against the borrower, such as suing you, garnishing your wages, etc. If this debt is ever in default, that fact may become a part of *your* credit record.

This notice is not the contract that makes you liable for the debt.

§ 444.4 Late charges

(a) In connection with collecting a debt arising out of an extension of credit to a consumer in or affecting commerce, as commerce is defined in the Federal Trade Commission Act, it is an unfair act or practice within the meaning of section 5 of that Act for a creditor, directly or indirectly, to levy or collect any delinquency charge on a payment, which payment is otherwise a full payment for the applicable period and is paid on its due date or within an applicable grace period, when the only delinquency is attributable to late fee(s) or delinquency charge(s) assessed on earlier installment(s).

(b) For purposes of this section, "collecting a debt" means any activity other than the use of judicial process that is intended to bring about or does bring about repayment of all or part of a consumer debt.

§ 444.5 State exemptions

(a) If, upon application to the Federal Trade Commission by an appropriate State agency, the Federal Trade Commission determines that:

(1) There is a State requirement or prohibition in effect that applies to any transaction to which a provision of this rule applies; and

(2) The State requirement or prohibition affords a level of protection to consumers that is substantially equivalent to, or greater than, the protection afforded by this rule;

Then that provision of the rule will not be in effect in that State to the extent specified by the Federal Trade Commission in its determination, for as long as the State administers and enforces the State requirement or prohibition effectively.

(b) [*Reserved.*]

Appendix E Selected Provisions Governing Collection of Debts Owed to Federal Government

E.1 Debt Collection Improvement Act

The Debt Collection Improvement Act of 1996 was enacted by Pub. L. No. 104-134, § 31001, 110 Stat. 1321. It is principally codified as part of the Claims Collection Act, 31 U.S.C. §§ 3701–3733, relevant portions of which are reprinted below.

TITLE 31—MONEY AND FINANCE

Chapter 37— Claims

Subchapter I— General

* * *

Subchapter I—General

§ 3701. Definitions and application

(a) In this chapter—
(1) "administrative offset" means withholding funds payable by the United States (including funds payable by the United States on behalf of a State government) to, or held by the United States for, a person to satisfy a claim.
(2) "calendar quarter" means a 3-month period beginning on January 1, April 1, July 1, or October 1.
(3) "consumer reporting agency" means—
(A) a consumer reporting agency as that term is defined in section 603(f) of the Fair Credit Reporting Act (15 U.S.C. 1681a(f)); or
(B) a person that, for money or on a cooperative basis, regularly—
(i) gets information on consumers to give the information to a consumer reporting agency; or
(ii) serves as a marketing agent under an arrangement allowing a third party to get the information from a consumer reporting agency.
(4) "executive, judicial, or legislative agency" means a department, agency, court, court administrative office, or instrumentality in the executive, judicial, or legislative branch of Government, including government corporations.
(5) "military department" means the Departments of the Army, Navy, and Air Force.
(6) "system of records" has the same meaning given that term in section 552a(a)(5) of title 5.
(7) "uniformed services" means the Army, Navy, Air Force, Marine Corps, Coast Guard, Commissioned Corps of the National Oceanic and Atmospheric Administration, and Commissioned Corps of the Public Health Service.
(8) "nontax" means, with respect to any debt or claim, any debt or claim other than a debt or claim under the Internal Revenue Code of 1986.
(b)(1) In subchapter II of this chapter and subsection (a)(8) of this section, the term "claim" or "debt" means any amount of funds or property that has been determined by an appropriate official of the Federal Government to be owed to the United States by a person, organization, or entity other than another Federal agency. A claim includes, without limitation—
(A) funds owed on account of loans made, insured, or guaranteed by the Government, including any deficiency or any difference between the price obtained by the Government in the sale of a property and the amount owed to the Government on a mortgage on the property,
(B) expenditures of nonappropriated funds, including actual and administrative costs related to shoplifting, theft detection, and theft prevention,
(C) over-payments, including payments disallowed by audits performed by the Inspector General of the agency administering the program,

(D) any amount the United States is authorized by statute to collect for the benefit of any person,
(E) the unpaid share of any non-Federal partner in a program involving a Federal payment and a matching, or cost-sharing, payment by the non-Federal partner,
(F) any fines or penalties assessed by an agency; and
(G) other amounts of money or property owed to the Government.

(2) For purposes of section 3716 of this title, each of the terms "claim" and "debt" includes an amount of funds or property owed by a person to a State (including any past-due support being enforced by the State), the District of Columbia, American Samoa, Guam, the United States Virgin Islands, the Commonwealth of the Northern Mariana Islands, or the Commonwealth of Puerto Rico.

(c) In sections 3716 and 3717 of this title, the term "person" does not include an agency of the United States Government.

(d) Sections 3711(e) and 3716-3719 of this title do not apply to a claim or debt under, or to an amount payable under—
(1) the Internal Revenue Code of 1986 (26 U.S.C. 1 et seq.),
(2) the Social Security Act (42 U.S.C. 301 et seq.), except to the extent provided under sections 204(f) and 1631(b)(4) of such Act and section 3716(c) of this title, or
(3) the tariff laws of the United States.

(e) In section 3716 of this title—
(1) "creditor agency" means any agency owed a claim that seeks to collect that claim through administrative offset; and
(2) "payment certifying agency" means any agency that has transmitted a voucher to a disbursing official for disbursement.

(f) In section 3711 of this title, "private collection contractor" means private debt collectors under contract with an agency to collect a nontax debt or claim owed the United States. The term includes private debt collectors, collection agencies, and commercial attorneys.

[As enacted by Pub. L. No. 97-258, 96 Stat. 970 (1982), and amended by Pub. L. No. 97-452, § 1(13)(A), 96 Stat. 2469 (1983); Pub. L. No. 103-387, § 5(b), 108 Stat. 4077 (1994); Pub. L. No. 104-134, § 31001, 110 Stat. 1321-359 (1996); Pub. L. No. 104-316, § 115(g)(2)(A), 110 Stat. 3835 (1996); Pub. L. No. 106-169, § 203(b), 113 Stat. 1832 (1999); Pub. L. No. 107-107, § 335, 115 Stat. 1060 (2001).]

§ 3702. Authority to settle claims

(a) Except as provided in this chapter or another law, all claims of or against the United States Government shall be settled as follows:
(1) The Secretary of Defense shall settle—
(A) claims involving uniformed service members' pay, allowances, travel, transportation, payments for unused accrued leave, retired pay, and survivor benefits; and
(B) claims by transportation carriers involving amounts collected from them for loss or damage incurred to property incident to shipment at Government expense.
(2) The Director of the Office of Personnel Management shall settle claims involving Federal civilian employees' compensation and leave.
(3) The Administrator of General Services shall settle claims involving expenses incurred by Federal civilian employees for official travel and transportation, and for relocation expenses incident to transfers of official duty station.
(4) The Director of the Office of Management and Budget shall settle claims not otherwise provided for by this subsection or another provision of law.

(b)(1) A claim against the Government presented under this section must contain the signature and address of the claimant or an authorized representative. The claim must be received by the official responsible under subsection (a) for settling the claim or by the agency that conducts the activity from which the claim arises within 6 years after the claim accrues except—
(A) as provided in this chapter or another law; or
(B) a claim of a State, the District of Columbia, or a territory or possession of the United States.
(2) When the claim of a member of the armed forces accrues during war or within 5 years before war begins, the claim must be received within 5 years after peace is established or within the period provided in paragraph (1) of this subsection, whichever is later.
(3) A claim that is not received in the time required under this subsection shall be returned with a copy of this subsection, and no further communication is required.

(c) One-year limit for check claims.—
(1) Any claim on account of a Treasury check shall be barred unless it is presented to the agency that authorized the issuance of such check within 1 year after the date of issuance of the check or the effective date of this subsection, whichever is later.
(2) Nothing in this subsection affects the underlying obligation of the United States, or any agency thereof, for which a Treasury check was issued.

(d) The official responsible under subsection (a) for settling the claim shall report to Congress on a claim against the Government that is timely presented under this section that may not be adjusted by using an existing appropriation, and that the official believes Congress should consider for legal or equitable reasons. The report shall include recommendations of the official.

(e)(1) The Secretary of Defense may waive the time limitations set forth in subsection (b) or (c) in the case of a claim referred to in subsection (a)(1)(A). In the case of a claim by or with respect to a member of the uniformed services who is not under the jurisdiction of the Secretary of a military department, such a waiver may be made only upon the request of the Secretary concerned (as defined in section 101 of title 37).
(2) Payment of a claim settled under subsection (a)(1)(A) shall be made from an appropriation that is available, for the fiscal year in which the payment is made, for the same purpose as the appropriation to which the obligation claimed would have been charged if the obligation had been timely paid, except that in the case of a claim for retired pay or survivor benefits, if the obligation claimed would have been paid from a trust fund if timely paid, the payment of the claim shall be made from that trust fund.
(3) This subsection does not apply to a claim in excess of $25,000.

[As enacted by Pub. L. No. 97-258, 96 Stat. 970 (1982), and amended by Pub. L. No. 97-452, § 1(14), 96 Stat. 2470 (1983); Pub. L. No. 100-86, § 1004(b), 101 Stat. 659 (1987); Pub. L. No. 104-201, § 608, 110 Stat. 2542 (1996); Pub. L. No. 104-316, § 202(n)(1), 110 Stat. 3843 (1996); Pub. L. No. 105-85, § 1012, 111 Stat. 1874 (1997); Pub. L. No. 106-398, § 1 , 114 Stat. 1654 (2000); Pub. L. No. 107-314, § 635(a), (b), 116 Stat. 2574 (2002); Pub. L. No. 109-163, § 1056(e)(2), 119 Stat. 3440 (2006).]

Subchapter II—Claims of the United States Government

§ 3711. Collection and compromise

(a) The head of an executive, judicial, or legislative agency—

(1) shall try to collect a claim of the United States Government for money or property arising out of the activities of, or referred to, the agency;

(2) may compromise a claim of the Government of not more than $100,000 (excluding interest) or such higher amount as the Attorney General may from time to time prescribe that has not been referred to another executive or legislative agency for further collection action, except that only the Comptroller General may compromise a claim arising out of an exception the Comptroller General makes in the account of an accountable official; and

(3) may suspend or end collection action on a claim referred to in clause (2) of this subsection when it appears that no person liable on the claim has the present or prospective ability to pay a significant amount of the claim or the cost of collecting the claim is likely to be more than the amount recovered.

(b)(1) The head of an executive, judicial, or legislative agency may not act under subsection (a)(2) or (3) of this section on a claim that appears to be fraudulent, false, or misrepresented by a party with an interest in the claim, or that is based on conduct in violation of the antitrust laws.

(2) The Secretary of Transportation may not compromise for less than $500 a penalty under section 21302 of title 49 for a violation of chapter 203, 205, or 207 of title 49 or a regulation or requirement prescribed or order issued under any of those chapters.

(c) A compromise under this section is final and conclusive unless gotten by fraud, misrepresentation, presenting a false claim, or mutual mistake of fact. An accountable official is not liable for an amount paid or for the value of property lost or damaged if the amount or value is not recovered because of a compromise under this section.

(d) The head of an executive, judicial, or legislative agency acts under—

(1) regulations prescribed by the head of the agency; and

(2) standards that the Attorney General, the Secretary of the Treasury, may prescribe.

(e)(1) When trying to collect a claim of the Government under a law except the Internal Revenue Code of 1986 (26 U.S.C. 1 et seq.), the head of an executive, judicial, or legislative agency shall disclose to a consumer reporting agency information from a system of records that a person is responsible for a claim if—

(A) notice required by section 552a(e)(4) of title 5 indicates that information in the system may be disclosed to a consumer reporting agency;

(B) the head of the agency has reviewed the claim and decided that the claim is valid and overdue;

(C) the head of the agency has notified the person in writing—

(i) that payment of the claim is overdue;

(ii) that, within not less than 60 days after sending the notice, the head of the agency intends to disclose to a consumer reporting agency that the person is responsible for the claim;

(iii) of the specific information to be disclosed to the consumer reporting agency; and

(iv) of the rights the person has to a complete explanation of the claim, to dispute information in the records of the agency about the claim, and to administrative repeal or review of the claim;

(D) the person has not—

(i) repaid or agreed to repay the claim under a written repayment plan that the person has signed and the head of the agency has agreed to; or

(ii) filed for review of the claim under paragraph (2) of this subsection;

(E) the head of the agency has established procedures to—

(i) disclose promptly, to each consumer reporting agency to which the original disclosure was made, a substantial change in the condition or amount of the claim;

(ii) verify or correct promptly information about the claim on request of a consumer reporting agency for verification of information disclosed; and

(iii) get satisfactory assurances from each consumer reporting agency that the agency is complying with all laws of the United States related to providing consumer credit information; and

(F) the information disclosed to the consumer reporting agency is limited to—

(i) information necessary to establish the identity of the person, including name, address, and taxpayer identification number;

(ii) the amount, status, and history of the claim; and

(iii) the agency or program under which the claim arose.

(2) Before disclosing information to a consumer reporting agency under paragraph (1) of this subsection and at other times allowed by law, the head of an executive, judicial, or legislative agency shall provide, on request of a person alleged by the agency to be responsible for the claim, for a review of the obligation of the person, including an opportunity for reconsideration of the initial decision on the claim.

(3) Before disclosing information to a consumer reporting agency under paragraph (1) of this subsection, the head of an executive, judicial, or legislative agency shall take reasonable action to locate a person for whom the head of the agency does not have a current address to send the notice under paragraph (1)(C).

(4) The head of each executive agency shall require, as a condition for insuring or guaranteeing any loan, financing,

or other extension of credit under any law to a person, that the lender provide information relating to the extension of credit to consumer reporting agencies or commercial reporting agencies, as appropriate.

(5) The head of each executive agency may provide to a consumer reporting agency or commercial reporting agency information from a system of records that a person is responsible for a claim which is current, if notice required by section 552a(e)(4) of title 5 indicates that information in the system may be disclosed to a consumer reporting agency or commercial reporting agency, respectively.

(f)(1) The Secretary of Defense may suspend or terminate an action by the Secretary or by the Secretary of a military department under subsection (a) to collect a claim against the estate of a person who died while serving on active duty as a member of the Army, Navy, Air Force, Marine Corps, or Coast Guard during a period when the Coast Guard is operating as a service in the Navy if the Secretary determines that, under the circumstances applicable with respect to the deceased person, it is appropriate to do so.

(2) The Secretary of Homeland Security may suspend or terminate an action by the Secretary under subsection (a) to collect a claim against the estate of a person who died while serving on active duty as a member of the Coast Guard if the Secretary determines that, under the circumstances applicable with respect to the deceased person, it is appropriate to do so.

(3) In this subsection, the term "active duty" has the meaning given that term in section 101 of title 10.

(g)(1) If a nontax debt or claim owed to the United States has been delinquent for a period of 180 days—

(A) the head of the executive, judicial, or legislative agency that administers the program that gave rise to the debt or claim shall transfer the debt or claim to the Secretary of the Treasury; and

(B) upon such transfer the Secretary of the Treasury shall take appropriate action to collect or terminate collection actions on the debt or claim.

(2) Paragraph (1) shall not apply—

(A) to any debt or claim that—

(i) is in litigation or foreclosure;

(ii) will be disposed of under an asset sales program within 1 year after becoming eligible for sale, or later than 1 year if consistent with an asset sales program and a schedule established by the agency and approved by the Director of the Office of Management and Budget;

(iii) has been referred to a private collection contractor for collection for a period of time determined by the Secretary of the Treasury;

(iv) has been referred by, or with the consent of, the Secretary of the Treasury to a debt collection center for a period of time determined by the Secretary of the Treasury; or

(v) will be collected under internal offset, if such offset is sufficient to collect the claim within 3 years after the date the debt or claim is first delinquent; and

(B) to any other specific class of debt or claim, as determined by the Secretary of the Treasury at the request of the head of an executive, judicial, or legislative agency or otherwise.

(3) For purposes of this section, the Secretary of the Treasury may designate, and withdraw such designation of debt collection centers operated by other Federal agencies. The Secretary of the Treasury shall designate such centers on the basis of their performance in collecting delinquent claims owed to the Government.

(4) At the discretion of the Secretary of the Treasury, referral of a nontax claim may be made to—

(A) any executive department or agency operating a debt collection center for servicing, collection, compromise, or suspension or termination of collection action;

(B) a private collection contractor operating under a contract for servicing or collection action; or

(C) the Department of Justice for litigation.

(5) Nontax claims referred or transferred under this section shall be serviced, collected, or compromised, or collection action thereon suspended or terminated, in accordance with otherwise applicable statutory requirements and authorities. Executive departments and agencies operating debt collection centers may enter into agreements with the Secretary of the Treasury to carry out the purposes of this subsection. The Secretary of the Treasury shall—

(A) maintain competition in carrying out this subsection;

(B) maximize collections of delinquent debts by placing delinquent debts quickly;

(C) maintain a schedule of private collection contractors and debt collection centers eligible for referral of claims; and

(D) refer delinquent debts to the person most appropriate to collect the type or amount of claim involved.

(6) Any agency operating a debt collection center to which nontax claims are referred or transferred under this subsection may charge a fee sufficient to cover the full cost of implementing this subsection. The agency transferring or referring the nontax claim shall be charged the fee, and the agency charging the fee shall collect such fee by retaining the amount of the fee from amounts collected pursuant to this subsection. Agencies may agree to pay through a different method, or to fund an activity from another account or from revenue received from the procedure described under section 3720C of this title. Amounts charged under this subsection concerning delinquent claims may be considered as costs pursuant to section 3717(e) of this title.

(7) Notwithstanding any other law concerning the depositing and collection of Federal payments, including section 3302(b) of this title, agencies collecting fees may retain the fees from amounts collected. Any fee charged pursuant to this subsection shall be deposited into an account to be determined by the executive department or agency operating the debt collection center charging the fee (in this subsection referred to in this section as the "Account"). Amounts deposited in the Account shall be available until expended to cover costs associated with the implementation and operation of Governmentwide debt collection activities. Costs properly chargeable to the Account include—

(A) the costs of computer hardware and software, word processing and telecommunications equipment, and other equipment, supplies, and furniture;

(B) personnel training and travel costs;

(C) other personnel and administrative costs;
(D) the costs of any contract for identification, billing, or collection services; and
(E) reasonable costs incurred by the Secretary of the Treasury, including services and utilities provided by the Secretary, and administration of the Account.

(8) Not later than January 1 of each year, there shall be deposited into the Treasury as miscellaneous receipts an amount equal to the amount of unobligated balances remaining in the Account at the close of business on September 30 of the preceding year, minus any part of such balance that the executive department or agency operating the debt collection center determines is necessary to cover or defray the costs under this subsection for the fiscal year in which the deposit is made.

(9) Before discharging any delinquent debt owed to any executive, judicial, or legislative agency, the head of such agency shall take all appropriate steps to collect such debt, including (as applicable)—
(A) administrative offset,
(B) tax refund offset,
(C) Federal salary offset,
(D) referral to private collection contractors,
(E) referral to agencies operating a debt collection center,
(F) reporting delinquencies to credit reporting bureaus,
(G) garnishing the wages of delinquent debtors, and
(H) litigation or foreclosure.

(10) To carry out the purposes of this subsection, the Secretary of the Treasury may prescribe such rules, regulations, and procedures as the Secretary considers necessary and transfer such funds from funds appropriated to the Department of the Treasury as may be necessary to meet existing liabilities and obligations incurred prior to the receipt of revenues that result from debt collections.

(h)(1) The head of an executive, judicial, or legislative agency acting under subsection (a)(1), (2), or (3) of this section to collect a claim, compromise a claim, or terminate collection action on a claim may obtain a consumer report (as that term is defined in section 603 of the Fair Credit Reporting Act (15 U.S.C. 1681a)) or comparable credit information on any person who is liable for the claim.

(2) The obtaining of a consumer report under this subsection is deemed to be a circumstance or purpose authorized or listed under section 604 of the Fair Credit Reporting Act (15 U.S.C. 1681b).

(i)(1) The head of an executive, judicial, or legislative agency may sell, subject to section 504(b) of the Federal Credit Reform Act of 1990 and using competitive procedures, any nontax debt owed to the United States that is delinquent for more than 90 days. Appropriate fees charged by a contractor to assist in the conduct of a sale under this subsection may be payable from the proceeds of the sale.

(2) After terminating collection action, the head of an executive, judicial, or legislative agency shall sell, using competitive procedures, any nontax debt or class of nontax debts owed to the United States, if the Secretary of the Treasury determines the sale is in the best interests of the United States.

(3) Sales of nontax debt under this subsection—
(A) shall be for—
(i) cash, or
(ii) cash and a residuary equity or profit participation, if the head of the agency reasonably determines that the proceeds will be greater than sale solely for cash,
(B) shall be without recourse, but may include the use of guarantees if otherwise authorized, and
(C) shall transfer to the purchaser all rights of the Government to demand payment of the nontax debt, other than with respect to a residuary equity or profit participation under subparagraph (A)(ii).

(4)(A) Within one year after the date of enactment of the Debt Collection Improvement Act of 1996, each executive agency with current and delinquent collateralized nontax debts shall report to the Congress on the valuation of its existing portfolio of loans, notes and guarantees, and other collateralized debts based on standards developed by the Director of the Office of Management and Budget, in consultation with the Secretary of the Treasury.
(B) The Director of the Office of Management and Budget shall determine what information is required to be reported to comply with subparagraph (A). At a minimum, for each financing account and for each liquidating account (as those terms are defined in sections 502(7) and 502(8), respectively, of the Federal Credit Reform Act of 1990) the following information shall be reported:
(i) The cumulative balance of current debts outstanding, the estimated net present value of such debts, the annual administrative expenses of those debts (including the portion of salaries and expenses that are directly related thereto), and the estimated net proceeds that would be received by the Government if such debts were sold.
(ii) The cumulative balance of delinquent debts, debts outstanding, the estimated net present value of such debts, the annual administrative expenses of those debts (including the portion of salaries and expenses that are directly related thereto), and the estimated net proceeds that would be received by the Government if such debts were sold.
(iii) The cumulative balance of guaranteed loans outstanding, the estimated net present value of such guarantees, the annual administrative expenses of such guarantees (including the portion of salaries and expenses that are directly related to such guaranteed loans), and the estimated net proceeds that would be received by the Government if such loan guarantees were sold.
(iv) The cumulative balance of defaulted loans that were previously guaranteed and have resulted in loans receivables, the estimated net present value of such loan assets, the annual administrative expenses of such loan assets (including the portion of salaries and expenses that are directly related to such loan assets), and the estimated net proceeds that would be received by the Government if such loan assets were sold.
(v) The marketability of all debts.

(5) This subsection is not intended to limit existing statutory authority of agencies to sell loans, debts, or other assets.

[As enacted by Pub. L. No. 97-258, 96 Stat. 971 (1982), and

amended by Pub. L. No. 97-452, § 1(15), 96 Stat. 2470 (1983); Pub. L. No. 98-216, § 1(5), 98 Stat. 4 (1984); Pub. L. No. 99-514, § 2, 100 Stat. 2095 (1986); Pub. L. No. 101-552, § 8(b), 104 Stat. 2746 (1990); Pub. L. No. 102-365, § 4(a)(4), 106 Stat. 973 (1992); Pub. L. No. 103-272, § 5(i)(1), 108 Stat. 1375 (1994); Pub. L. No. 104-106, § 1089, 110 Stat. 459 (1996); Pub. L. No. 104-134, § 31001(c)(1), (g)(1)(C), (k), (m)(1), (p), 110 Stat. 1321-359 (1996); Pub. L. No. 104-201, § 1010, 110 Stat. 2635 (1996); Pub. L. No. 104-316, § 115(g)(1), 110 Stat. 3834 (1996); Pub. L. No. 109-241, § 902(b)(4), 120 Stat. 566 (2006).]

* * *

§ 3713. Priority of Government claims

(a)(1) A claim of the United States Government shall be paid first when—
(A) a person indebted to the Government is insolvent and—
(i) the debtor without enough property to pay all debts makes a voluntary assignment of property;
(ii) property of the debtor, if absent, is attached; or
(iii) an act of bankruptcy is committed; or
(B) the estate of a deceased debtor, in the custody of the executor or administrator, is not enough to pay all debts of the debtor.
(2) This subsection does not apply to a case under title 11.

(b) A representative of a person or an estate (except a trustee acting under title 11) paying any part of a debt of the person or estate before paying a claim of the Government is liable to the extent of the payment for unpaid claims of the Government.

[As enacted by Pub. L. No. 97-258, 96 Stat. 972 (1982).]

* * *

§ 3716. Administrative offset

(a) After trying to collect a claim from a person under section 3711(a) of this title, the head of an executive, judicial, or legislative agency may collect the claim by administrative offset. The head of the agency may collect by administrative offset only after giving the debtor—
(1) written notice of the type and amount of the claim, the intention of the head of the agency to collect the claim by administrative offset, and an explanation of the rights of the debtor under this section;
(2) an opportunity to inspect and copy the records of the agency related to the claim;
(3) an opportunity for a review within the agency of the decision of the agency related to the claim; and
(4) an opportunity to make a written agreement with the head of the agency to repay the amount of the claim.

(b) Before collecting a claim by administrative offset, the head of an executive, judicial, or legislative agency must either—
(1) adopt, without change, regulations on collecting by administrative offset promulgated by the Department of Justice, the Government Accountability Office, or the Department of the Treasury; or
(2) prescribe regulations on collecting by administrative offset consistent with the regulations referred to in paragraph (1).

(c)(1)(A) Except as otherwise provided in this subsection, a disbursing official of the Department of the Treasury, the Department of Defense, the United States Postal Service, or any other government corporation, or any disbursing official of the United States designated by the Secretary of the Treasury, shall offset at least annually the amount of a payment which a payment certifying agency has certified to the disbursing official for disbursement, by an amount equal to the amount of a claim which a creditor agency has certified to the Secretary of the Treasury pursuant to this subsection.
(B) An agency that designates disbursing officials pursuant to section 3321(c) of this title is not required to certify claims arising out of its operations to the Secretary of the Treasury before such agency's disbursing officials offset such claims.
(C) Payments certified by the Department of Education under a program administered by the Secretary of Education under title IV of the Higher Education Act of 1965 shall not be subject to administrative offset under this subsection.
(2) Neither the disbursing official nor the payment certifying agency shall be liable—
(A) for the amount of the administrative offset on the basis that the underlying obligation, represented by the payment before the administrative offset was taken, was not satisfied; or
(B) for failure to provide timely notice under paragraph (8).
(3)(A)(i) Notwithstanding any other provision of law (including sections 207 and 1631(d)(1) of the Social Security Act (42 U.S.C. 407 and 1383(d)(1)), section 413(b) of Public Law 91-173 (30 U.S.C. 923(b)), and section 14 of the Act of August 29, 1935 (45 U.S.C. 231m)), except as provided in clause (ii), all payments due to an individual under—
(I) the Social Security Act,
(II) part B of the Black Lung Benefits Act, or
(III) any law administered by the Railroad Retirement Board (other than payments that such Board determines to be tier 2 benefits),
shall be subject to offset under this section.
(ii) An amount of $9,000 which a debtor may receive under Federal benefit programs cited under clause (i) within a 12-month period shall be exempt from offset under this subsection. In applying the $9,000 exemption, the disbursing official shall—
(I) reduce the $9,000 exemption amount for the 12-month period by the amount of all Federal benefit payments made during such 12-month period which are not subject to offset under this subsection; and
(II) apply a prorated amount of the exemption to each periodic benefit payment to be made to the debtor during the applicable 12-month period.
For purposes of the preceding sentence, the amount of a periodic benefit payment shall be the amount after any reduction or deduction required under the laws authorizing the program under which such payment is

authorized to be made (including any reduction or deduction to recover any overpayment under such program).

(B) The Secretary of the Treasury shall exempt from administrative offset under this subsection payments under means-tested programs when requested by the head of the respective agency. The Secretary may exempt other payments from administrative offset under this subsection upon the written request of the head of a payment certifying agency. A written request for exemption of other payments must provide justification for the exemption under standards prescribed by the Secretary. Such standards shall give due consideration to whether administrative offset would tend to interfere substantially with or defeat the purposes of the payment certifying agency's program. The Secretary shall report to the Congress annually on exemptions granted under this section.

(C) The provisions of sections 205(b)(1), 809(a)(1), and 1631(c)(1) of the Social Security Act shall not apply to any administrative offset executed pursuant to this section against benefits authorized by title II, VIII, or title XVI of the Social Security Act, respectively.

(4) The Secretary of the Treasury may charge a fee sufficient to cover the full cost of implementing this subsection. The fee may be collected either by the retention of a portion of amounts collected pursuant to this subsection, or by billing the agency referring or transferring a claim for those amounts. Fees charged to the agencies shall be based on actual administrative offsets completed. Amounts received by the United States as fees under this subsection shall be deposited into the account of the Department of the Treasury under section 3711(g)(7) of this title, and shall be collected and accounted for in accordance with the provisions of that section.

(5) The Secretary of the Treasury in consultation with the Commissioner of Social Security and the Director of the Office of Management and Budget, may prescribe such rules, regulations, and procedures as the Secretary of the Treasury considers necessary to carry out this subsection. The Secretary shall consult with the heads of affected agencies in the development of such rules, regulations, and procedures.

(6) Any Federal agency that is owed by a person a past due, legally enforceable nontax debt that is over 180 days delinquent, including nontax debt administered by a third party acting as an agent for the Federal Government, shall notify the Secretary of the Treasury of all such nontax debts for purposes of administrative offset under this subsection.

(7)(A) The disbursing official conducting an administrative offset with respect to a payment to a payee shall notify the payee in writing of—

(i) the occurrence of the administrative offset to satisfy a past due legally enforceable debt, including a description of the type and amount of the payment otherwise payable to the payee against which the offset was executed;

(ii) the identity of the creditor agency requesting the offset; and

(iii) a contact point within the creditor agency that will handle concerns regarding the offset.

(B) If the payment to be offset is a periodic benefit payment, the disbursing official shall take reasonable steps, as determined by the Secretary of the Treasury, to provide the notice to the payee not later than the date on which the payee is otherwise scheduled to receive the payment, or as soon as practical thereafter, but no later than the date of the administrative offset. Notwithstanding the preceding sentence, the failure of the debtor to receive such notice shall not impair the legality of such administrative offset.

(8) A levy pursuant to the Internal Revenue Code of 1986 shall take precedence over requests for administrative offset pursuant to other laws.

(d) Nothing in this section is intended to prohibit the use of any other administrative offset authority existing under statute or common law.

(e) This section does not apply—

(1) to a claim under this subchapter that has been outstanding for more than 10 years; or

(2) when a statute explicitly prohibits using administrative offset or setoff to collect the claim or type of claim involved.

(f) The Secretary may waive the requirements of sections 552a(o) and (p) of title 5 for administrative offset or claims collection upon written certification by the head of a State or an executive, judicial, or legislative agency seeking to collect the claim that the requirements of subsection (a) of this section have been met.

(g) The Data Integrity Board of the Department of the Treasury established under 552a(u) of title 5 shall review and include in reports under paragraph (3)(D) of that section a description of any matching activities conducted under this section. If the Secretary has granted a waiver under subsection (f) of this section, no other Data Integrity Board is required to take any action under section 552a(u) of title 5.

(h)(1) The Secretary may, in the discretion of the Secretary, apply subsection (a) with respect to any past-due, legally-enforceable debt owed to a State if—

(A) the appropriate State disbursing official requests that an offset be performed; and

(B) a reciprocal agreement with the State is in effect which contains, at a minimum—

(i) requirements substantially equivalent to subsection (b) of this section; and

(ii) any other requirements which the Secretary considers appropriate to facilitate the offset and prevent duplicative efforts.

(2) This subsection does not apply to—

(A) the collection of a debt or claim on which the administrative costs associated with the collection of the debt or claim exceed the amount of the debt or claim;

(B) any collection of any other type, class, or amount of claim, as the Secretary considers necessary to protect the interest of the United States; or

(C) the disbursement of any class or type of payment exempted by the Secretary of the Treasury at the request of a Federal agency.

(3) In applying this section with respect to any debt owed to a State, subsection (c)(3)(A) shall not apply.

[Added by Pub. L. No. 97-452, § 1(16)(A), 96 Stat. 2471 (1983), and amended by Pub. L. No. 104-134, § 31001(c)(1), (d)(2), (e), (f), 110 Stat. 1321-359 (1996); Pub. L. No. 106-169, § 251(b)(10), 113 Stat. 1856 (1999); Pub. L. No. 108-271, § 8(b), 118 Stat. 814 (2004).]

§ 3717. Interest and penalty on claims

(a)(1) The head of an executive, judicial, or legislative agency shall charge a minimum annual rate of interest on an outstanding debt on a United States Government claim owed by a person that is equal to the average investment rate for the Treasury tax and loan accounts for the 12-month period ending on September 30 of each year, rounded to the nearest whole percentage point. The Secretary of the Treasury shall publish the rate before November 1 of that year. The rate is effective on the first day of the next calendar quarter.

(2) The Secretary may change the rate of interest for a calendar quarter if the average investment rate for the 12-month period ending at the close of the prior calendar quarter, rounded to the nearest whole percentage point, is more or less than the existing published rate by 2 percentage points.

(b) Interest under subsection (a) of this section accrues from the date—

(1) on which notice is mailed after October 25, 1982, if notice was first mailed before October 25, 1982; or

(2) notice of the amount due is first mailed to the debtor at the most current address of the debtor available to the head of the executive or legislative agency, if notice is first mailed after October 24, 1982.

(c) The rate of interest charged under subsection (a) of this section—

(1) is the rate in effect on the date from which interest begins to accrue under subsection (b) of this section; and

(2) remains fixed at that rate for the duration of the indebtedness.

(d) Interest under subsection (a) of this section may not be charged if the amount due on the claim is paid within 30 days after the date from which interest accrues under subsection (b) of this section. The head of an executive, judicial, or legislative agency may extend the 30-day period.

(e) The head of an executive, judicial, or legislative agency shall assess on a claim owed by a person—

(1) a charge to cover the cost of processing and handling a delinquent claim; and

(2) a penalty charge of not more than 6 percent a year for failure to pay a part of a debt more than 90 days past due.

(f) Interest under subsection (a) of this section does not accrue on a charge assessed under subsection (e) of this section.

(g) This section does not apply—

(1) if a statute, regulation required by statute, loan agreement, or contract prohibits charging interest or assessing charges or explicitly fixes the interest or charges; and

(2) to a claim under a contract executed before October 25, 1982, that is in effect on October 25, 1982.

(h) In conformity with standards prescribed jointly by the Attorney General, the Secretary of the Treasury, and the Comptroller General, the head of an executive, judicial, or legislative agency may prescribe regulations identifying circumstances appropriate to waiving collection of interest and charges under subsections (a) and (e) of this section. A waiver under the regulations is deemed to be compliance with this section.

(i)(1) The head of an executive, judicial, or legislative agency may increase an administrative claim by the cost of living adjustment in lieu of charging interest and penalties under this section. Adjustments under this subsection will be computed annually.

(2) For the purpose of this subsection—

(A) the term "cost of living adjustment" means the percentage by which the Consumer Price Index for the month of June of the calendar year preceding the adjustment exceeds the Consumer Price Index for the month of June of the calendar year in which the claim was determined or last adjusted; and

(B) the term "administrative claim" includes all debt that is not based on an extension of Government credit through direct loans, loan guarantees, or insurance, including fines, penalties, and overpayments.

[Added by Pub. L. No. 97-452, § 1(16)(A), 96 Stat. 2472 (1983), and amended by Pub. L. No. 104-134, § 31001(c)(1), (g)(1)(C), (q), 110 Stat. 1321-359 (1996).)

§ 3718. Contracts for collection services

(a) Under conditions the head of an executive, judicial, or legislative agency considers appropriate, the head of the agency may enter into a contract with a person for collection service to recover indebtedness owed, or to locate or recover assets of, the United States Government. The head of an agency may not enter into a contract under the preceding sentence to locate or recover assets of the United States held by a State government or financial institution unless that agency has established procedures approved by the Secretary of the Treasury to identify and recover such assets. The contract shall provide that—

(1) the head of the agency retains the authority to resolve a dispute, compromise a claim, end collection action, and refer a matter to the Attorney General to bring a civil action; and

(2) the person is subject to—

(A) section 552a of title 5, to the extent provided in section 552a(m); and

(B) laws and regulations of the United States Government and State governments related to debt collection practices.

(b)(1)(A) The Attorney General may make contracts retaining private counsel to furnish legal services, including representation in negotiation, compromise, settlement, and litigation, in the case of any claim of indebtedness owed the United States. Each such contract shall include such terms and conditions as the Attorney General considers necessary and appropriate, including a provision specifying the amount of the fee to be paid to the private counsel under such contract or the method for calculating that fee. The amount of the fee payable for legal services furnished under any such contract may not exceed the fee that counsel engaged in the private practice of law in the area or areas where the legal services are furnished typically charge clients for furnishing legal services in the collection of claims of indebtedness, as determined by the Attorney General, considering the amount, age, and nature of the indebtedness and whether the debtor is an individual or a business entity. Nothing in this subparagraph shall relieve the Attorney General of the competition requirements set forth in title III of the Federal Property and Administrative Services Act of 1949 (41 U.S.C. 251 and following).

(B) The Attorney General shall use his best efforts to enter into contracts under this paragraph with law firms owned and controlled by socially and economically disadvantaged individuals and law firms that are qualified HUBZone small business concerns (as defined in section 3(p) of the Small Business Act), so as to enable each agency to comply with paragraph (3).

(2) The head of an executive, judicial, or legislative agency may, subject to the approval of the Attorney General, refer to a private counsel retained under paragraph (1) of this subsection claims of indebtedness owed the United States arising out of activities of that agency.

(3) Each agency shall use its best efforts to assure that not less than 10 percent of the amounts of all claims referred to private counsel by that agency under paragraph (2) are referred to law firms owned and controlled by socially and economically disadvantaged individuals and law firms that are qualified HUBZone small business concerns. For purposes of this paragraph—

(A) the term "law firm owned and controlled by socially and economically disadvantaged individuals" means a law firm that meets the requirements set forth in clauses (i) and (ii) of section 8(d)(3)(C) of the Small Business Act (15 U.S.C. 637(d)(3)(C)(i) and (ii)) and regulations issued under those clauses;

(B) "socially and economically disadvantaged individuals" shall be presumed to include these groups and individuals described in the last paragraph of section 8(d)(3)(C) of the Small Business Act; and

(C) the term "qualified HUBZone small business concern" has the meaning given that term in section 3(p) of the Small Business Act.

(4) Notwithstanding sections 516, 518(b), 519, and 547(2) of title 28, a private counsel retained under paragraph (1) of this subsection may represent the United States in litigation in connection with legal services furnished pursuant to the contract entered into with that counsel under paragraph (1) of this subsection.

(5) A contract made with a private counsel under paragraph (1) of this subsection shall include—

(A) a provision permitting the Attorney General to terminate either the contract or the private counsel's representation of the United States in particular cases if the Attorney General finds that such action is for the convenience of the Government;

(B) a provision stating that the head of the executive or legislative agency which refers a claim under the contract retains the authority to resolve a dispute regarding the claim, to compromise the claim, or to terminate a collection action on the claim; and

(C) a provision requiring the private counsel to transmit monthly to the Attorney General and the head of the executive or legislative agency referring a claim under the contract a report on the services relating to the claim rendered under the contract during the month and the progress made during the month in collecting the claim under the contract.

(6) Notwithstanding the fourth sentence of section 803(6) of the Fair Debt Collection Practices Act (15 U.S.C. 1692a(6)), a private counsel performing legal services pursuant to a contract made under paragraph (1) of this subsection shall be considered to be a debt collector for the purposes of such Act.

(7) Any counterclaim filed in any action to recover indebtedness owed the United States which is brought on behalf of the United States by private counsel retained under this subsection may not be asserted unless the counterclaim is served directly on the Attorney General or the United States Attorney for the judicial district in which, or embracing the place in which, the action is brought. Such service shall be made in accordance with the rules of procedure of the court in which the action is brought.

(c) The Attorney General shall transmit to the Congress an annual report on the activities of the Department of Justice to recover indebtedness owed the United States which was referred to the Department of Justice for collection. Each such report shall include a list, by agency, of—

(1) the total number and amounts of claims which were referred for legal services to the Department of Justice and to private counsel under subsection (b) during the 1-year period covered by the report;

(2) the total number and amount of those claims referred for legal services to the Department of Justice which were collected or were not collected or otherwise resolved during the 1-year period covered by the report; and

(3) the total number and amount of those claims referred for legal services to private counsel under subsection (b)—

(A) which were collected or were not collected or otherwise resolved during the 1-year period covered by the report;

(B) which were not collected or otherwise resolved under a contract terminated by the Attorney General during the 1-year period covered by the report; and

(C) on which the Attorney General terminated the private counsel's representation during the 1-year period covered by the report without terminating the contract with the private counsel under which the claims were referred.

(d) Notwithstanding section 3302(b) of this title, a contract under subsection (a) or (b) of this section may provide that a fee a person charges to recover indebtedness owed, or to locate or recover assets of, the United States Government is payable from the amount recovered.

(e) A contract under subsection (a) or (b) of this section is effective only to the extent and in the amount provided in an appropriation law. This limitation does not apply in the case of a contract that authorizes a person to collect a fee as provided in subsection (d) of this section.

(f) This section does not apply to the collection of debts under the Internal Revenue Code of 1986 (26 U.S.C. 1 et seq.).

(g) In order to assist Congress in determining whether use of private counsel is a cost-effective method of collecting Government debts, the Attorney General shall, following consultation with the Government Accountability Office, maintain and make available to the Inspector General of the Department of Justice, statistical data relating to the comparative costs of debt collection by participating United States Attorneys' Offices and by private counsel.

[Added by Pub. L. No. 97-452, § 1(16)(A), 96 Stat. 2473 (1983), and amended by Pub. L. No. 98-167, 97 Stat. 1104 (1983); Pub. L. No. 99-514, § 2, 100 Stat. 2095 (1986); Pub. L. No. 99-578, § 1, 100 Stat. 3305 (1986); Pub. L. No. 102-589, § 6, 106 Stat. 5135 (1992); Pub. L. No. 103-272, § 4(f)(1)(M), 108 Stat. 1362 (1994); Pub. L. No. 104-134, § 31001(c)(1), (l), (cc)(1), 110 Stat. 1321-359 (1996); Pub. L. No. 105-135, § 604(e)(1), 111 Stat. 2633 (1997); Pub. L. No. 108-271, § 8(b), 118 Stat. 814 (2004).]

§ 3719. Reports on debt collection activities

(a) In consultation with the Comptroller General of the United States, the Secretary of the Treasury shall prescribe regulations requiring the head of each agency with outstanding nontax claims to prepare and submit to the Secretary at least once each year a report summarizing the status of loans and accounts receivable that are managed by the head of the agency. The report shall contain—

(1) information on—

(A) the total amount of loans and accounts receivable owed the agency and when amounts owed the agency are due to be repaid;

(B) the total amount of receivables and number of claims at least 30 days past due;

(C) the total amount written off as actually uncollectible and the total amount allowed for uncollectible loans and accounts receivable;

(D) the rate of interest charged for overdue debts and the amount of interest charged and collected on debts;

(E) the total number of claims and the total amount collected; and

(F) the number and total amount of claims referred to the Attorney General for settlement and the number and total amount of claims the Attorney General settles;

(2) the information described in clause (1) of this subsection for each program or activity the head of the agency carries out; and

(3) other information the Secretary considers necessary to decide whether the head of the agency is acting aggressively to collect the claims of the agency.

(b) The Secretary shall analyze the reports submitted under subsection (a) of this section and shall report annually to Congress on the management of debt collection activities by the head of each agency, including the information provided the Secretary under subsection (a).

[Added by Pub. L. No. 97-452, § 1(16)(A), 96 Stat. 2473 (1983), and amended by Pub. L. No. 104-134, § 31001(aa)(3), 110 Stat. 1321-380 (1996).]

§ 3720. Collection of payments

(a) Each head of an executive agency (other than an agency subject to section 9 of the Act of May 18, 1933 (48 Stat. 63, chapter 32; 16 U.S.C. 831h)) shall, under such regulations as the Secretary of the Treasury shall prescribe, provide for the timely deposit of money by officials and agents of such agency in accordance with section 3302, and for the collection and timely deposit of sums owed to such agency by the use of such procedures as withdrawals and deposits by electronic transfer of funds, automatic withdrawals from accounts at financial institutions, and a system under which financial institutions receive and deposit, on behalf of the executive agency, payments transmitted to post office lockboxes. The Secretary is authorized to collect from any agency not complying with the requirements imposed pursuant to the preceding sentence a charge in an amount the Secretary determines to be the cost to the general fund caused by such noncompliance.

(b) The head of an executive agency shall pay to the Secretary of the Treasury charges imposed pursuant to subsection (a). Payments shall be made out of amounts appropriated or otherwise made available to carry out the program to which the collections relate. The amounts of the charges paid under this subsection shall be deposited in the Cash Management Improvements Fund established by subsection (c).

(c) There is established in the Treasury of the United States a revolving fund to be known as the "Cash Management Improvements Fund". Sums in the fund shall be available without fiscal year limitation for the payment of expenses incurred in developing the methods of collection and deposit described in subsection (a) of this section and the expenses incurred in carrying out collections and deposits using such methods, including the costs of personal services and the costs of the lease or purchase of equipment and operating facilities.

[Added by Pub. L. No. 98-369, § 2652(a)(1), 98 Stat. 1152 (1984).]

§ 3720A. Reduction of tax refund by amount of debt

(a) Any Federal agency that is owed by a person a past-due, legally enforceable debt (including debt administered by a third party acting as an agent for the Federal Government) shall, and any agency subject to section 9 of the Act of May 18, 1933 (16 U.S.C. 831h), owed such a debt may, in accordance with regulations issued pursuant to subsections (b) and (d), notify the Secretary of the Treasury at least once each year of the amount of such debt.

(b) No Federal agency may take action pursuant to subsection (a) with respect to any debt until such agency—

(1) notifies the person incurring such debt that such agency proposes to take action pursuant to such paragraph with respect to such debt;

(2) gives such person at least 60 days to present evidence that all or part of such debt is not past-due or not legally enforceable;

(3) considers any evidence presented by such person and determines that an amount of such debt is past due and legally enforceable;

(4) satisfies such other conditions as the Secretary may prescribe to ensure that the determination made under para-

graph (3) with respect to such debt is valid and that the agency has made reasonable efforts (determined on a government-wide basis) to obtain payment of such debt; and

(5) certifies that reasonable efforts have been made by the agency (pursuant to regulations) to obtain payment of such debt.

(c) Upon receiving notice from any Federal agency that a named person owes to such agency a past-due legally enforceable debt, the Secretary of the Treasury shall determine whether any amounts, as refunds of Federal taxes paid, are payable to such person. If the Secretary of the Treasury finds that any such amount is payable, he shall reduce such refunds by an amount equal to the amount of such debt, pay the amount of such reduction to such agency, and notify such agency of the individual's home address.

(d) The Secretary of the Treasury shall issue regulations prescribing the time or times at which agencies must submit notices of past-due legally enforceable debts, the manner in which such notices must be submitted, and the necessary information that must be contained in or accompany the notices. The regulations shall specify the minimum amount of debt to which the reduction procedure established by subsection (c) may be applied and the fee that an agency must pay to reimburse the Secretary of the Treasury for the full cost of applying such procedure. Any fee paid to the Secretary pursuant to the preceding sentence may be used to reimburse appropriations which bore all or part of the cost of applying such procedure.

(e) Any Federal agency receiving notice from the Secretary of the Treasury that an erroneous payment has been made to such agency under subsection (c) shall pay promptly to the Secretary, in accordance with such regulations as the Secretary may prescribe, an amount equal to the amount of such erroneous payment (without regard to whether any other amounts payable to such agency under such subsection have been paid to such agency).

(f)(1) Subsection (a) shall apply with respect to an OASDI overpayment made to any individual only if such individual is not currently entitled to monthly insurance benefits under title II of the Social Security Act.

(2)(A) The requirements of subsection (b) shall not be treated as met in the case of the recovery of an OASDI overpayment from any individual under this section unless the notification under subsection (b)(1) describes the conditions under which the Commissioner of Social Security is required to waive recovery of an overpayment, as provided under section 204(b) of the Social Security Act.

(B) In any case in which an individual files for a waiver under section 204(b) of the Social Security Act within the 60-day period referred to in subsection (b)(2), the Commissioner of Social Security shall not certify to the Secretary of the Treasury that the debt is valid under subsection (b)(4) before rendering a decision on the waiver request under such section 204(b). In lieu of payment, pursuant to subsection (c), to the Commissioner of Social Security of the amount of any reduction under this subsection based on an OASDI overpayment, the Secretary of the Treasury shall deposit such amount in the Federal Old-Age and Survivors Insurance Trust Fund or the Federal Disability Insurance Trust Fund, whichever is certified to the Secretary of the Treasury as appropriate by the Commissioner of Social Security.

(g) In the case of refunds of business associations, this section shall apply only to refunds payable on or after January 1, 1995. In the case of refunds of individuals who owe debts to Federal agencies that have not participated in the Federal tax refund offset program prior to the date of enactment of this subsection, this section shall apply only to refunds payable on or after January 1, 1994.

(h)(1) The disbursing official of the Department of the Treasury—

(1) shall notify a taxpayer in writing of—

(A) the occurrence of an offset to satisfy a past-due legally enforceable nontax debt;

(B) the identity of the creditor agency requesting the offset; and

(C) a contact point within the creditor agency that will handle concerns regarding the offset;

(2) shall notify the Internal Revenue Service on a weekly basis of—

(A) the occurrence of an offset to satisfy a past-due legally enforceable non-tax debt;

(B) the amount of such offset; and

(C) any other information required by regulations; and

(3) shall match payment records with requests for offset by using a name control, taxpayer identifying number (as that term is used in section 6109 of the Internal Revenue Code of 1986), and any other necessary identifiers.

(h)(2)[1] The term "disbursing official" of the Department of the Treasury means the Secretary or his designee.

(i) An agency subject to section 9 of the Act of May 18, 1933 (16 U.S.C. 831h), may implement this section at its discretion.

[Added by Pub. L. No. 98-369, § 2653(a)(1), 98 Stat. 1153 (1984), and amended by Pub. L. No. 101-508, § 5129(b), 104 Stat. 1388-287 (1990); Pub. L. No. 102-589, § 3, 106 Stat. 5133 (1992); Pub. L. No. 103-296, § 108(j)(2), 108 Stat. 1488 (1994); Pub. L. No. 104-134, § 31001(u)(1), (v)(1), (w), 110 Stat. 1321-375 (1996).]

§ 3720B. Barring delinquent Federal debtors from obtaining Federal loans or loan insurance guarantees

(a) Unless this subsection is waived by the head of a Federal agency, a person may not obtain any Federal financial assistance in the form of a loan (other than a disaster loan or a marketing assistance loan or loan deficiency payment under subtitle C of the Agricultural Market Transition Act (7 U.S.C. 7231 et seq.)) or loan insurance or guarantee administered by the agency if the person has an outstanding debt (other than a debt under the Internal Revenue Code of 1986) with any Federal agency which is in a delinquent status, as determined under standards prescribed by the Secretary of the Treasury. Such a person may obtain additional loans or loan guarantees only after such delinquency is resolved in accordance with those standards. The Secretary of the Treasury may exempt, at the request of an agency, any class of claims.

(b) The head of a Federal agency may delegate the waiver authority under subsection (a) to the Chief Financial Officer of the agency. The waiver authority may be redelegated only to the

1 So in original.

Deputy Chief Financial Officer of the agency.

[Added by Pub. L. No. 104-134, § 31001(j)(1), 110 Stat. 1321-365 (1996), and amended by Pub. L. No. 106-387, § 1(a), 114 Stat. 1549 (2000).]

* * *

§ 3720D. Garnishment

(a) Notwithstanding any provision of State law, the head of an executive, judicial, or legislative agency that administers a program that gives rise to a delinquent nontax debt owed to the United States by an individual may in accordance with this section garnish the disposable pay of the individual to collect the amount owed, if the individual is not currently making required repayment in accordance with any agreement between the agency head and the individual.

(b) In carrying out any garnishment of disposable pay of an individual under subsection (a), the head of an executive, judicial, or legislative agency shall comply with the following requirements:

(1) The amount deducted under this section for any pay period may not exceed 15 percent of disposable pay, except that a greater percentage may be deducted with the written consent of the individual.

(2) The individual shall be provided written notice, sent by mail to the individual's last known address, a minimum of 30 days prior to the initiation of proceedings, from the head of the executive, judicial, or legislative agency, informing the individual of—

(A) the nature and amount of the debt to be collected;

(B) the intention of the agency to initiate proceedings to collect the debt through deductions from pay; and

(C) an explanation of the rights of the individual under this section.

(3) The individual shall be provided an opportunity to inspect and copy records relating to the debt.

(4) The individual shall be provided an opportunity to enter into a written agreement with the executive, judicial, or legislative agency, under terms agreeable to the head of the agency, to establish a schedule for repayment of the debt.

(5) The individual shall be provided an opportunity for a hearing in accordance with subsection (c) on the determination of the head of the executive, judicial, or legislative agency concerning—

(A) the existence or the amount of the debt, and

(B) in the case of an individual whose repayment schedule is established other than by a written agreement pursuant to paragraph (4), the terms of the repayment schedule.

(6) If the individual has been reemployed within 12 months after having been involuntarily separated from employment, no amount may be deducted from the disposable pay of the individual until the individual has been reemployed continuously for at least 12 months.

(c)(1) A hearing under subsection (b)(5) shall be provided prior to issuance of a garnishment order if the individual, on or before the 15th day following the mailing of the notice described in subsection (b)(2), and in accordance with such procedures as the head of the executive, judicial, or legislative agency may prescribe, files a petition requesting such a hearing.

(2) If the individual does not file a petition requesting a hearing prior to such date, the head of the agency shall provide the individual a hearing under subsection (a)(5) upon request, but such hearing need not be provided prior to issuance of a garnishment order.

(3) The hearing official shall issue a final decision at the earliest practicable date, but not later than 60 days after the filing of the petition requesting the hearing.

(d) The notice to the employer of the withholding order shall contain only such information as may be necessary for the employer to comply with the withholding order.

(e)(1) An employer may not discharge from employment, refuse to employ, or take disciplinary action against an individual subject to wage withholding in accordance with this section by reason of the fact that the individual's wages have been subject to garnishment under this section, and such individual may sue in a State or Federal court of competent jurisdiction any employer who takes such action.

(2) The court shall award attorneys' fees to a prevailing employee and, in its discretion, may order reinstatement of the individual, award punitive damages and back pay to the employee, or order such other remedy as may be reasonably necessary.

(f)(1) The employer of an individual—

(A) shall pay to the head of an executive, judicial, or legislative agency as directed in a withholding order issued in an action under this section with respect to the individual, and

(B) shall be liable for any amount that the employer fails to withhold from wages due an employee following receipt by such employer of notice of the withholding order, plus attorneys' fees, costs, and, in the court's discretion, punitive damages.

(2)(A) The head of an executive, judicial, or legislative agency may sue an employer in a State or Federal court of competent jurisdiction to recover amounts for which the employer is liable under paragraph (1)(B).

(B) A suit under this paragraph may not be filed before the termination of the collection action, unless earlier filing is necessary to avoid expiration of any applicable statute of limitations period.

(3) Notwithstanding paragraphs (1) and (2), an employer shall not be required to vary its normal pay and disbursement cycles in order to comply with this subsection.

(g) For the purpose of this section, the term "disposable pay" means that part of the compensation of any individual from an employer remaining after the deduction of any amounts required by any other law to be withheld.

(h) The Secretary of the Treasury shall issue regulations to implement this section.

[Added by Pub. L. No. 104-134, § 31001(o)(1), 110 Stat. 1321-369 (1996).)

§ 3720E. Dissemination of information regarding identity of delinquent debtors

(a) The head of any agency may, with the review of the Secretary of the Treasury, for the purpose of collecting any delinquent nontax debt owed by any person, publish or otherwise publicly disseminate information regarding the identity of the person and the existence of the nontax debt.

(b)(1) The Secretary of the Treasury, in consultation with the Director of the Office of Management and Budget and the heads of other appropriate Federal agencies, shall issue regulations establishing procedures and requirements the Secretary considers appropriate to carry out this section.

(2) Regulations under this subsection shall include—

(A) standards for disseminating information that maximize collections of delinquent nontax debts, by directing actions under this section toward delinquent debtors that have assets or income sufficient to pay their delinquent nontax debt;

(B) procedures and requirements that prevent dissemination of information under this section regarding persons who have not had an opportunity to verify, contest, and compromise their nontax debt in accordance with this subchapter; and

(C) procedures to ensure that persons are not incorrectly identified pursuant to this section.

[Added by Pub. L. No. 104-134, § 31001(r)(1), 110 Stat. 1321-372 (1996).]

* * *

E.2 Federal Employee Salary Offset Statute

5 U.S.C. § 5514

Title 5. Government Organization and Employees

Part III. Employees

Subpart D. Pay and Allowances

Chapter 55. Pay Administration

Subchapter II. Withholding Pay

§ 5514. Installment deduction for indebtedness to the United States

(a)(1) When the head of an agency or his designee determines that an employee, member of the Armed Forces or Reserve of the Armed Forces, is indebted to the United States for debts to which the United States is entitled to be repaid at the time of the determination by the head of an agency or his designee, or is notified of such a debt by the head of another agency or his designee the amount of indebtedness may be collected in monthly installments, or at officially established pay intervals, by deduction from the current pay account of the individual. The deductions may be made from basic pay, special pay, incentive pay, retired pay, retainer pay, or, in the case of an individual not entitled to basic pay, other authorized pay. The amount deducted for any period may not exceed 15 percent of disposable pay, except that a greater percentage may be deducted upon the written consent of the individual involved. If the individual retires or resigns, or if his employment or period of active duty otherwise ends, before collection of the amount of the indebtedness is completed, deduction shall be made from subsequent payments of any nature due the individual from the agency concerned. All Federal agencies to which debts are owed and which have outstanding delinquent debts shall participate in a computer match at least annually of their delinquent debt records with records of Federal employees to identify those employees who are delinquent in repayment of those debts. The preceding sentence shall not apply to any debt under the Internal Revenue Code of 1986. Matched Federal employee records shall include, but shall not be limited to, records of active Civil Service employees government-wide, military active duty personnel, military reservists, United States Postal Service employees, employees of other government corporations, and seasonal and temporary employees. The Secretary of the Treasury shall establish and maintain an interagency consortium to implement centralized salary offset computer matching, and promulgate regulations for this program. Agencies that perform centralized salary offset computer matching services under this subsection are authorized to charge a fee sufficient to cover the full cost for such services.

(2) Except as provided in paragraph (3) of this subsection, prior to initiating any proceedings under paragraph (1) of this subsection to collect any indebtedness of an individual, the head of the agency holding the debt or his designee, shall provide the individual with—

(A) a minimum of thirty days written notice, informing such individual of the nature and amount of the indebtedness determined by such agency to be due, the intention of the agency to initiate proceedings to collect the debt through deductions from pay, and an explanation of the rights of the individual under this subsection;

(B) an opportunity to inspect and copy Government records relating to the debt;

(C) an opportunity to enter into a written agreement with the agency, under terms agreeable to the head of the agency or his designee, to establish a schedule for the repayment of the debt; and

(D) an opportunity for a hearing on the determination of the agency concerning the existence or the amount of the debt, and in the case of an individual whose repayment schedule is established other than by a written agreement pursuant to subparagraph (C), concerning the terms of the repayment schedule.

A hearing, described in subparagraph (D), shall be provided if the individual, on or before the fifteenth day following receipt of the notice described in subparagraph (A), and in accordance with such procedures as the head of the agency may prescribe, files a petition requesting such a hearing. The timely filing of a petition for hearing shall stay the commencement of collection proceedings. A hearing under subparagraph (D) may not be conducted by an individual under the supervision or control of the head of the agency, except that nothing in this sentence shall be construed to prohibit the appointment of an administrative law judge. The hearing official shall issue a final decision at the earliest practicable date, but not later than sixty days after the filing of the petition requesting the hearing.

(3) Paragraph (2) shall not apply to routine intra-agency adjustments of pay that are attributable to clerical or administrative errors or delays in processing pay documents that have occurred within the four pay periods preceding the adjustment and to any adjustment that amounts to $50 or less, if at the time of such adjustment, or as soon thereafter as practical, the individual is provided written notice of the nature and the amount of the adjustment and a point of contact for contesting such adjustment.

(4) The collection of any amount under this section shall be in accordance with the standards promulgated pursuant to sections 3711 and 3716-3718 of title 31 or in accordance with any other statutory authority for the collection of claims of the United States or any agency thereof.

(5) For purposes of this subsection—

(A) "disposable pay" means that part of pay of any individual remaining after the deduction from those earnings of any amounts required by law to be withheld; and

(B) "agency" includes executive departments and agencies, the United States Postal Service, the Postal Regulatory Commission, the United States Senate, the United States House of Representatives, and any court, court administrative office, or instrumentality in the judicial or legislative branches of the Government, and government corporations.

(b)(1) The head of each agency shall prescribe regulations, subject to the approval of the President, to carry out this section and section 3530(d) of title 31. Regulations prescribed by the Secretaries of the military departments shall be uniform for the military services insofar as practicable.

(2) For purposes of section 7117(a) of this title, no regulation prescribed to carry out subsection (a)(2) of this section shall be considered to be a Government-wide rule or regulation.

(c) Subsection (a) of this section does not modify existing statutes which provide for forfeiture of pay or allowances. This section and section 3530(d) of title 31 do not repeal, modify, or amend section 4837(d) or 9837(d) of title 10 or section 1007(b), (c) of title 37.

(d) A levy pursuant to the Internal Revenue Code of 1986 shall take precedence over other deductions under this section.

[As enacted by Pub. L. No. 89-554, 80 Stat. 477 (1966), and amended by Pub. L. No. 96-54, § 2(a)(2), 93 Stat. 381 (1979); Pub. L. No. 97-258, § 3(a)(12), 96 Stat. 1063 (1982); Pub. L. No. 97-365, § 5, 96 Stat. 1751 (1982); Pub. L. No. 97-452, § 2(a)(2), 96 Stat. 2478 (1983); Pub. L. No. 98-216, § 3(a)(4), 98 Stat. 6 (1984); Pub. L. No. 104-134, tit. III, § 31001(h), 110 Stat. 1321-363 (1996); Pub. L. No. 109-435, § 604(b), 120 Stat. 3241 (2006).]

Appendix F Summaries of State Exemption Laws

What Is Included

This appendix summarizes state exemption statutes. It focuses on statutes that exempt property of consumer debtors from collection by creditors. Statutes that provide special exemption rules for child support or other family support collections, or for other special types of debts, such as reimbursements to the state, are not summarized here.

This appendix also does not summarize exemption provisions found in laws other than the state's general exemption laws. For example, statutes that create or regulate specific assets, such as public or private pensions, workers' compensation, educational savings accounts, insurance, or crime victims' compensation, often contain their own exemption language.

Whenever an asset is not listed as exempt in the state's exemption statute, the statutes that create or regulate that type of asset should also be checked. In addition, this appendix only summarizes prohibitions against waiver of exemptions that are found in the state's exemption statutes, not those in the Federal Trade Commission's Credit Practices Rule or state consumer protection laws.

In addition to exemption statutes, many states protect certain assets by common law doctrines such as ownership by the entireties. These doctrines are not summarized here, but are discussed in §§ 12.5.2.9, 12.5.3.4, *supra*.

Collier on Bankruptcy, volume 14, is another valuable reference on state exemption law. It reprints the full text of state exemption statutes, including most of those summarized here.

Exemptions in Bankruptcy Proceedings

This appendix includes a series of questions and answers for each state designed to help determine the applicable exemption law for purposes of 11 U.S.C. § 522(b)(3)(A) in a debtor's bankruptcy proceeding. Which state's exemption law applies is determined by the debtor's domicile. According to the Bankruptcy Code, the debtor's domicile for exemption purposes is the state in which the debtor's domicile has been located for the 730 days immediately preceding the petition filing date or, if the debtor's domicile has not been located in a single state for the 730-day period, the state in which the debtor was domiciled for the longer portion of the 180 days immediately preceding the 730-day period.[1]

If the domiciliary state, as determined by section 522(b)(3)(A), has not opted out of the federal exemption scheme, or if the statutory opt-out applies only to residents or domiciliaries of that state, the debtor may claim the federal bankruptcy exemptions found in section 522(d). The first question for each state therefore asks whether the state has opted out of the federal bankruptcy exemption scheme. The next question asks whether the state's opt-out is limited to residents or domiciliaries of that state.

If the effect of section 522(b)(3)(A) is to render the debtor ineligible for any exemption, the debtor may also use the federal bankruptcy exemptions found in section 522(d). Such a situation could arise if the exemption law of the debtor's domicile requires the debtor to reside within the state in order to claim an exemption or if the law does not permit an exemption to be taken on property located outside the state. Thus the next question addresses whether the state exemption provisions covering homesteads and personal property may be given extraterritorial effect, thereby permitting an exemption to be used on property not located within the state.

If the language of the state exemption statute indicates that it applies only to property located in that state, or to a debtor domiciled in that state, the response is listed as "no." If the language of the state exemption statute indicates that it applies only to a resident of that state, the response is listed as "probably not," recognizing the possibility that a debtor may maintain a residence in the state even though the bankruptcy case has been filed in the state of the debtor's domicile for venue purposes. If the state exemption statute indicates that it applies to property located outside the state, or if the statute is silent but case law has construed the statute as having extraterritorial effect, the response is listed as "yes." If the statute does not clearly specify its extraterritorial effect and the issue has not been resolved by case law, the response is listed as "uncertain." In some cases, in which the statutory language or case law is inconclusive but suggests a leaning in one direction, the response is listed as "possibly yes," "possibly not," "probably yes," or "probably not."

ALABAMA

Has state opted out of federal bankruptcy exemptions? Yes. Ala. Code § 6-10-11.

Is opt out limited to residents or domiciliaries of the state? Not specified. Alabama Code § 6-10-11: "In cases instituted under [Title 11] there shall be exempt . . . only that property . . . exempt under the laws of Alabama and under [federal laws other than § 522(d)]."

Do state's exemptions have extraterritorial application?

Homestead: No. *See In re* Carter, 213 B.R. 26 (Bankr. N.D. Ala. 1997); Sims v. Cox, 611 So. 2d 339 (Ala. 1992); *see also* Ala. Code § 6-10-2 (limited to "the homestead of every resident of this state").

Personal property: Probably not. Ala. Code § 6-10-6 limited to "the personal property of such resident."

---

1 11 U.S.C. § 522(b)(3)(A).
For a discussion of the domiciliary requirements, see National Consumer Law Center, Consumer Bankruptcy Law and Practice Ch. 10 (8th ed. 2006 and Supp.).

***Wages*: Ala. Code §§ 5-19-15, 6-10-7, 6-10-120.**
Scope: Wages, salaries, or other compensation of laborers or employees, residents of Alabama, for personal services.
Amount: For consumer loans, consumer credit sales and consumer leases, similar to federal exemptions; for all other debts 75% of weekly disposable income is exempt. For consumer loans, disposable earnings are those left after legally required deductions. Disposable earnings do not include voluntary "periodic payments pursuant to a pension, retirement or disability program."
Survival after payment/deposit: Not specified in exemption statute.
Waiver: Permitted. Waiver must be in writing.
***Homestead*: Ala. Const. art. X, §§ 205, 206; Ala. Code §§ 6-10-2 to 6-10-4, 6-10-20, 6-10-41, 6-10-120, 6-10-122.**
Amount: $5000 per individual not exceeding 160 acres is exempt, subject to certain liens. Mobile home explicitly included. If husband and wife own homestead jointly, each may claim the exemption separately "to the same extent and value as an unmarried individual." Exemption available whether debtor owns a fee or less estate, whether in common or in severalty.
Procedural requirements: Any resident may file sworn declaration with office of probate judge in county where property located. (This is not essential to claim of exemption; other procedure exists to claim exemptions after levy.)
Special provisions: If home owner dies, homestead exemption survives during the lifetime of the surviving spouse and the minority of any children. Married person's mortgage, deed or other conveyance of homestead requires signature of spouse, made before an officer authorized to take acknowledgment of deeds. Once a homestead declaration is filed, temporary absence or leasing of homestead will not eliminate the exemption.
Waiver: Yes, by separate instrument in writing. Signature of spouse, if any, required, and must be made before officer authorized to take acknowledgment of deeds.
***Tangible personal property*: Ala. Const. art. X, § 204; Ala. Code §§ 6-10-5, 6-10-6, 6-10-120, 6-10-121, and 6-10-126.**
Household goods: $3000. All personal property, except for wages.
Motor vehicles: See above.
Tools of trade: See above.
Clothing and jewelry: All necessary and proper wearing apparel of debtor and family; not covered by $3000 cap.
Miscellaneous and wildcard: Burial place and church pew; family portraits and books; not covered by $3000 cap.
Waiver: May be waived, in writing, either by separate instrument, or included in note or contract, *except* as to specified essential household goods, tools of trade, vehicle essential to debtor's business, wearing apparel and library.
***Benefits, retirement plans, insurance, judgments, and other intangibles*: Ala. Code § 6-10-8.**
Public benefits: Not specified in exemption statute.
Pensions, retirement plans and annuities: Not specified in exemption statute.
Insurance, judgments or other compensation for injury: Insurance policies, if spouse or children are beneficiaries. Proceeds of insurance in beneficiaries' hands are exempt as to debts of the insured.
Bank accounts: Not specified in exemption statute.
Alimony, child support: Not specified in exemption statute.
Survival after payment or deposit: Not specified in exemption statute.

ALASKA

Has state opted out of federal bankruptcy exemptions? Yes. Alaska Stat. § 09.38.055.
Is opt out limited to residents or domiciliaries of the state? Not specified. Alaska Stat. § 09.38.055: "In a proceeding under [Title 11] only the exemptions in [specified sections of Alaska law] apply."
Do state's exemptions have extraterritorial application?
Homestead: No. Alaska Stat. § 09.38.010 limited to "property in this state."
Personal property: Uncertain.
***Wages*: Alaska Stat. §§ 09.38.030, 09.38.050, 09.38.065, 09.38.105, 09.38.115, 09.38.500; Alaska Admin. Code tit. 8, § 95.030.**
Scope: Money received by an individual for personal services, whether denominated wages, salary, commission or otherwise. For debtor who does not receive income weekly, semi-monthly or monthly, cash and liquid assets up to $1750 per month; increases to $2750 per month if debtor is sole support of household.
Amount: $438 of weekly net earnings is exempt, increases to $688 if individual's wages are sole support of household. Net earnings are gross earnings less sums required by law or court order to be withheld. Dollar amounts under this chapter are adjusted on October 1 of even-numbered years, in accordance with the Consumer Price Index; new amounts reported in Alaska Administrative Code. For debtor who does not receive income weekly, semi-monthly or monthly, cash and liquid assets up to $2750 per month.
Survival after payment/deposit: Not specified in exemption statute.
Waiver: Waiver of exemptions given to unsecured creditor before levy is unenforceable.
***Homestead*: Alaska Stat. §§ 09.38.010, 09.38.060, 09.38.065, 09.38.105, 09.38.115; Alaska Admin. Code tit. 8, § 95.030.**
Amount: $67,500 in a principal residence; multiple owners of single homestead may claim only their *pro rata* share of this amount (that is, only one exemption per homestead); homestead is subject to certain liens. Amount adjusted for Consumer Price Index; new amounts take effect on October 30 of even-numbered years, and must be announced by the preceding June 30 at Alaska Admin. Code tit. 8, § 95.030.
Procedural requirements: Not specified.
Special provisions: Proceeds of a voluntary sale of a homestead are exempt for six months after receipt, if traceable. Proceeds of a sale or taking by eminent domain, or of compensation for damaged or destroyed property, are exempt for twelve months, if traceable.
Waiver: Waiver of exemptions given to unsecured creditor before levy is unenforceable.
***Tangible personal property*: Alaska Stat. §§ 09.38.015, 09.38.020, 09.38.025, 09.38.115; Alaska Admin. Code tit. 8, § 95.030 (reports new amounts adjusted for CPI).**
Household goods: $3750, including household goods, clothing, and family pictures and heirlooms.
Motor vehicles: $3750 in car worth not more than $25,000.
Tools of Trade: $3500.
Clothing and jewelry: Clothing included in household goods, above. Jewelry, $1250.
Miscellaneous and wildcard: Pets: $1250. Health aids, burial plot, no cap.
Waiver: Wavier of exemptions given to unsecured creditor before levy is unenforceable.

***Benefits, retirement plans, insurance, judgments, and other intangibles*: Alaska Stat. §§ 09.38.015, 09.38.017; Alaska Admin. Code tit. 8, § 95.030 (reports new amounts adjusted for CPI).**
Public benefits: Any benefits paid or payable and exempt under federal law. Benefits that are not totally exempt (including unemployment, and certain disability benefits) are treated like cash or liquid assets (see above, under Wages). Senior Care Benefits, pursuant to Alaska Stat. §§ 47.45.300 to 47.45.390 (cash and prescription drug assistance), are fully exempt, but this provision is scheduled to expire on June 30, 2007.
Pensions, retirement plans and annuities: Various public employees retirement plans. Contributions to tax-qualified retirement plan, or benefits paid from plan (except for contributions made within 120 days before filing bankruptcy). This section does not prevent payments from plan to alternate payee under qualified domestic relations order. Certain annuity contracts. Certain other plans are treated like cash or liquid assets (see above, under Wages).
Insurance, judgments or other compensation for injury: Benefits paid or payable for medical or surgical care, to the extent they are or will be used for such care. Award from violent crime victims board (or crime victims act of another jurisdiction). Certain unmatured life insurance and annuity contracts (but if accrued dividends and loan values exceed $12,500, debtor may be required to obtain payment of the lesser of the amount of the creditors claim or the amount by which these values exceed $12,500). Personal injury judgments, family support, and various insurance proceeds are treated like cash or liquid assets (see above under Wages).
Bank accounts: College tuition savings plan pursuant to Alaska Stat. §§ 14.40.802 or 14.40.809(a). Effective July 1, 2008, funds held in an escrow account for real estate taxes and insurance, pursuant to the Mortgage Lending Regulation Act, Alaska Stat. § 6.60.360, are exempt.
Alimony, child support: Child support collections made by child support enforcement agency.
Survival after payment or deposit: Not specified in exemption statute.

ARIZONA

Has state opted out of federal bankruptcy exemptions? Yes. Ariz. Rev. Stat. Ann. § 33-1133.
Is opt out limited to residents or domiciliaries of the state? Yes. Ariz. Rev. Stat. Ann. § 33-1133: "Residents of this state are not entitled to the Federal exemptions provided in 11 U.S.C. § 522(d)."
Do state's exemptions have extraterritorial application?
Homestead: Uncertain. Compare Ariz. Rev. Stat. Ann. § 33-1101 limiting its application to "any person . . . who resides within the state" with Ariz. Rev. Stat. Ann. § 33-1102(A) providing procedure for debtor having more than one residence to select property as exempt. *See In re* Jarski, 301 B.R. 342 (Bankr. D. Ariz. 2003).
Personal property: Uncertain.
***Wages*: Ariz. Rev. Stat. Ann. §§ 33-1131, 33-1132, 12-1598.10(B)(5) and (F).**
Scope: Wages, salary or compensation for personal services, including bonuses and commissions or otherwise, including payments pursuant to a pension or retirement program or a deferred compensation plan.
Amount: Similar to federal. May be reduced to 15% in case of "extreme economic hardship" to debtor or family. Disposable income is calculated by subtracting those amounts required by law to be withheld. Garnishment forbidden if the debt was, at the time of service of the writ, subject to an effective agreement for debt scheduling between the judgment debtor and a qualified debt counseling organization.
Survival after payment/deposit: Not specified in exemption statute.
Waiver: Void and unenforceable.
***Homestead*: Ariz. Rev. Stat. Ann. §§ 33-1101 to 33-1104, 33-1126.**
Amount: $150,000; condominiums, co-ops, and mobile homes (with or without land) explicitly included. Married couple may claim only one exemption. Homestead is subject to certain liens. Debtor who does not claim homestead may exempt prepaid rent or security deposit up to lesser of $1000 or $1\frac{1}{2}$ months rent.
Procedural requirements: No written claim or recording required. (But if debtor owns multiple properties, creditor may require debtor to designate one as homestead.)
Special provisions: Proceeds from sale of homestead are exempt for 18 months.
Waiver: By mortgage or consensual lien, or by declaration of abandonment or waiver, recorded in county where homestead located.
***Tangible personal property*: Ariz. Rev. Stat. Ann. §§ 33-1121.01, 33-1123 to 33-1125, 33-1127 to 33-1130, 33-1132.**
Household goods: $4000 furniture and appliances.
Motor vehicles: $5000 in one vehicle (up to $10,000 if debtor is physically disabled).
Tools of trade: $2500 (does not cover motor vehicle used only for commuting); $2500 farm equipment.
Clothing and jewelry: $500 clothing. $1000 wedding and engagement rings.
Miscellaneous and wildcard: $250 musical instruments; $500 animals; $250 books; a burial plot; miscellaneous items worth $500; materials used for instruction of youth; health aids. *Note*: Husband or wife may each claim personal property exemption, which may be stacked.
Waiver: Void and unenforceable (except for security interests, or recovery of leased property).
***Benefits, retirement plans, insurance, judgments, and other intangibles*: Ariz. Rev. Stat. Ann. § 33-1126.**
Public benefits: Not specified in exemption statute. *See* Ariz. Rev. Stat. Ann. § 46-208.
Pensions, retirement plans and annuities: Certain public and private pensions and tax-qualified retirement plans.
Insurance, judgments or other compensation for injury: $20,000 life insurance proceeds in hands of surviving spouse or child. Cash surrender value of certain insurance policies. Proceeds of fire or other insurance, or any claim for damage to or destruction of, exempt property. Proceeds of health, accident or disability insurance, or similar program of benefits in use by any employer (certain exceptions, but no cap).
Bank accounts: $150 in one bank account.
Alimony, child support: Court-ordered child support or spousal maintenance (no cap).
Survival after payment or deposit: Not specified in exemption statute.

ARKANSAS

Has state opted out of federal bankruptcy exemptions? No. Ark. Code Ann. § 16-66-217.

Is opt out limited to residents or domiciliaries of the state? Not applicable.
Do state's exemptions have extraterritorial application?
Homestead: Probably not. Ark. Code Ann. § 16-66-210 limited to homestead "of any resident of this state." *See* Cherokee Constr. Co. v. Harris, 92 Ark. 260, 122 S.W. 485 (Ark. 1909).
Personal property: Uncertain.
***Wages*: Ark. Code Ann. § 16-66-208.**
Scope: Wages of all laborers and mechanics.
Amount: $25 per week is absolutely exempt; sixty days wages are exempt if debtor's property plus the wages do not exceed the amount exempt under the state constitution (see summary of art. 9 of the state constitution under tangible personal property, *infra*).
Survival after payment/deposit: Not specified in exemption statute.
Waiver: Not specified in exemption statute.
***Homestead*: Ark. Const. art. 9, §§ 3, 4, 5; Ark. Code Ann. §§ 16-66-210, 16-66-212, 16-66-218.**
Amount: Bankruptcy only: $800 for unmarried debtor, $1250 for married. Non-bankruptcy, married or head of household only: 80 acres rural or $\frac{1}{4}$ acre urban, or if this land is not worth $2500, then up to 160 acres rural or one acre urban, up to a value of $2500.
Procedural requirements: None stated. Right not lost by failure to schedule. Non-debtor spouse may claim if debtor fails to do so.
Special provisions: Continues to protect minor children after death of debtor.
Waiver: Not specified in exemption law.
***Tangible personal property*: Ark. Const. art. 9, §§ 1, 2; Ark. Code Ann. §§ 16-66-218, 16-66-219, 16-66-220.**
Household goods: Bankruptcy only: Personal property used as residence or burial plot, if real property not claimed: $800 unmarried or $1250 married. Note: A federal court has held the personal property, motor vehicle and tools of the trade exemptions to be contrary to, and therefore limited by, the lower ceilings in the Arkansas Constitution.[2]
Motor vehicles: Bankruptcy only: $1200.
Tools of trade: Bankruptcy only: $750.
Clothing and jewelry: Wedding bands, necessary wearing apparel.
Miscellaneous and wildcard: Any personal property: $500 married; $200 unmarried.
Waiver: Not specified in exemption statute.
***Benefits, retirement plans, insurance, judgments, and other intangibles*: Ark. Code Ann. §§ 16-66-209, 16-66-218, 16-66-220.**
Public benefits: Not specified in exemption statute. But note that benefits are exempted under various other statutes (cross-referenced in § 16-66-218).
Pensions, retirement plans and annuities: Certain public and private pensions and retirement plans, including IRAs and SEPs. Debtor who chooses state bankruptcy exemptions is limited to $20,000 per debtor or married couple.
Insurance, judgments or other compensation for injury: Moneys paid or payable from life, health and disability insurance.
Bank accounts: Not specified in exemption statute.
Alimony, child support: Not specified in exemption statute.
Survival after payment or deposit: Not specified in exemption statute.

2 *In re* Holt, 894 F.2d 1005 (8th Cir. 1990).

CALIFORNIA

Has state opted out of federal bankruptcy exemptions? Yes. Cal. Civ. Proc. Code § 703.130 (West).
Is opt out limited to residents or domiciliaries of the state? Not specified. Cal. Civ. Proc. Code § 703.130 (West): "[T]he exemptions set forth in [§ 522(d)] . . . are not authorized in this state."
Do state's exemptions have extraterritorial application?
Homestead: Yes. *See In re* Arrol, 207 B.R. 662 (Bankr. N.D. Cal. 1997). *In re* Urban, 361 B.R. 910 (Bankr. D. Mont. 2007).
Personal property: Yes. *See In re* Urban, 361 B.R. 910 (Bankr. D. Mont. 2007).
***Wages*: Cal. Civ. Proc. Code §§ 703.070, 704.070, 706.011, 706.050, 706.051, 706.052 (West).**
Scope: Compensation payable by an employer to an employee for personal services whether denominated as wages, salary, commission, bonus or otherwise. Employee is defined as a public officer or any individual who performs services subject to the right of the employer to control both what shall be done and how it shall be done.
Amount: Same as federal. Larger exemption if debtor can prove need: "the portion of the judgment debtor's earnings which the judgment debtor proves is necessary for the support of the judgment debtor or the judgment debtor's family supported in whole or in part by the judgment debtor is exempt from levy under this chapter."
Survival after payment/deposit: Yes. Paid earnings in bank account 75% exempt (100% if already subjected to withholding order or wage assignment).
Waiver: Not specified in exemption statute.
***Homestead*: Cal. Civ. Proc. Code §§ 487.025, 703.110, 703.040, 704.030, 704.710 to 704.730 (West).**
Amount: $50,000. Increases to $75,000 if debtor is family member and if at least one other family member owns no interest in homestead or only a community property interest. $150,000 for debtors over age 55 if income is under $15,000 (without joint income) or $20,000 (married debtors, joint income) and if sale is involuntary. $150,000 if over age 65 or disabled; may include house, mobile home, boat or condominium. In bankruptcy, the debtor has the option of selecting the $17,425 exemption set forth at Cal. Civ. Proc. Code § 703.140 (West).
Procedural requirements: Yes. See Cal. Civ. Proc. Code §§ 704.910 to 704.995 (West), for declaration of homestead procedure.
Special provisions: Proceeds exempt for six months. Declared homestead continues to protect property after death of owner, if occupied by surviving spouse or specified family member. $2700 exemption for materials purchased in good faith for repair or improvement of homestead. A 2007 amendment allows a debtor not residing in the homestead to claim homestead if a spouse or former spouse resides there, up to the time a court order divides the community property (but note that debtor may still have only one homestead).
Waiver: Prior waivers void (but note that homestead declaration does not limit the right to convey or encumber the property).
***Tangible personal property*: Cal. Civ. Proc. Code §§ 703.110, 703.040, 704.010 to 704.070 (West); Cal. Civ. Code § 703.150 (West).** (In bankruptcy, the debtor has the option of selecting the exemptions set forth at Cal. Civ. Proc. Code § 703.140 (West), which are similar to the federal exemptions.) Some personal property exemptions are adjusted every three years for the cost of

living. New amounts are reported in the California Judicial Forms pamphlet, electronically published in the references and annotations to the exemptions chapter.
Household goods: Ordinary and necessary household furnishings, appliances, wearing apparel and other personal effects. Proceeds from execution sale of items of extraordinary value are exempt in the amount determined by the court to be sufficient to purchase ordinary and necessary replacement. No doubling of exemptions.
Motor vehicles: $2550 aggregate equity in motor vehicle(s); insurance or other compensation for loss or destruction of vehicle exempt for ninety days after receipt.
Tools of trade: $6750. Married couple engaged in same business may stack their exemptions. (Not more than $4850 of this amount for commercial motor vehicle.)
Clothing and jewelry: Ordinary and necessary wearing apparel; $6750 jewelry, heirlooms and works of art.
Miscellaneous and wildcard: Health aids. Family or cemetery plots.
Waiver: Prior waivers void.
***Benefits, retirement plans, insurance, judgments, and other intangibles*: Cal. Civ. Proc. Code §§ 703.080, 704.070 to 704.190 (West).** (In bankruptcy, the debtor has the option of selecting the exemptions set forth at Cal. Civ. Proc. Code § 703.140 (West), which are similar to the federal exemptions.)
Public benefits: Automatic exemption for first $1350 ($2025 for two or more depositors) of directly deposited public benefit funds, or first $2700 ($4050 for two or more depositors) of directly deposited Social Security funds. The rest of the account is exempt insofar as it consists of exempt benefits; the statute provides for notice to the depositor and a procedure for determining the amount of exempt funds. Unemployment benefits (including certain payments from employer, union, or fraternal organization). Welfare benefits (see Cal. Welf. & Inst. Code §§ 10000 to 18996 (West)) or similar aid provided by charitable organization or fraternal benefit society. Relocation benefits for persons displaced by certain eminent domain takings.
Pensions, retirement plans and annuities: Public retirement benefits (except as to family support judgment); certain private retirement plans, including but not limited to SEPs, IRAs, profit sharing plans used for retirement (except as to family support judgments).
Insurance, judgments or other compensation for injury: $10,775 unmatured life insurance policies: separate exemption for each spouse; may be stacked. Health or disability insurance benefits (except as to claim of the health care creditor whose bill was the basis for the claim, or certain family support claims). Personal injury judgment or settlement, so far as needed for support (same exceptions). Wrongful death judgment or settlement if debtor or spouse was dependent on victim, so far as needed for support. Workers' Compensation (except for family support).
Bank accounts: $1350 inmate trust account in correctional or juvenile facility ($300 if debt is for restitution). Financial aid for students of institutions of higher education.
Alimony, child support: Not specified in exemption statute.
Survival after payment or deposit: Yes. See sections covering specific types of benefits.

COLORADO

Has state opted out of federal bankruptcy exemptions? Yes. Colo. Rev. Stat. § 13-54-107.
Is opt out limited to residents or domiciliaries of the state? Yes. Colo. Rev. Stat. § 13-54-107: "[T]he exemptions in [§ 522(d)] are denied to residents of this state. Exemptions authorized to be claimed by residents of this state shall be limited to those exemptions expressly provided by the statutes of this state."
Do state's exemptions have extraterritorial application?
Homestead: No. Colo. Rev. Stat. §§ 38-41-201, 38-41-203 limited to "every homestead in the state of Colorado occupied as a home by the owner." *See In re* Underwood, 342 B.R. 358 (Bankr. N.D. Fla. 2006).
Personal property: No. *See In re* Underwood, 342 B.R. 358 (Bankr. N.D. Fla. 2006).
***Wages*: Colo. Rev. Stat. § 13-54-104.**
Scope: Compensation for personal services; payments to independent contractors are protected. Also includes various insurance, disability, and other benefits.
Amount: Similar to federal, except that thirty times minimum wage refers to *state* minimum wage. Disposable earnings are defined as those left after certain voluntary health insurance deductions, as well as legally required taxes, and so forth. A higher percentage of earnings may be garnished to recover overpayments of certain state benefits.
Survival after payment/deposit: Not specified in exemption statute.
Waiver: Not specified in exemption statute.
***Homestead*: Colo. Rev. Stat. §§ 38-41-201, 38-41-201.6 to 38-41-209.**
Amount: $60,000 in a residence, or $90,000 if owner, spouse or dependent is elderly (defined as age 60 or older) or disabled. Mobile or manufactured homes explicitly included.
Procedural requirements: Filing of homestead declaration permitted but not required. If filed, spouse's signature will be required for sale or encumbrance of property.
Special provisions: Sale or insurance proceeds are exempt for two years. After death of owner, homestead exemption continues to protect surviving spouse and minor children.
Waiver: Permitted.
***Tangible personal property*: Colo. Rev. Stat. §§ 13-54-101 to 13-54-103.**
Household goods: $3000 in household goods; $600 in food and fuel. Nonexclusive list of household goods includes computers, sound systems, cameras, bicycles, fax machines and toys, as well as the usual furniture, dishes, and so forth.
Motor vehicles: $5000 in vehicles or bicycles ($10,000 if elderly or disabled).
Tools of trade: $20,000 in tools of trade. May not be stacked with motor vehicle exemption. $50,000 in farm tools, equipment, and animals; married couple engaged in farming may claim only one farm equipment exemption. May not be stacked with tools of trade exemption.
Clothing and jewelry: $1500 in clothing; $2000 in jewelry.
Miscellaneous and wildcard: $1500 in books and family pictures; one burial site for debtor and each dependent; health aids. $3000 for library of professional person (specifically including clergy).
Waiver: Waived by failure to timely claim.
***Benefits, retirement plans, insurance, judgments, and other intangibles*: Colo. Rev. Stat. §§ 13-54-102 to 13-54-103, 13-64-210.**
Public benefits: Tax refund attributable to earned income credit. *See also* Colo. Rev. Stat. § 26-2-131 (public assistance is exempt).
Pensions, retirement plans and annuities: Military pensions. Various private retirement plans, including ERISA plans and IRAs. For

certain types of debts (child support debt or arrearages, restitution for theft, embezzlement or misappropriation of certain public funds, and certain willful violations of fiduciary duty to a public pension fund), public and private pensions are treated as earnings for calculating garnishment limits.
Insurance, judgments or other compensation for injury: $50,000 in cash surrender value of certain insurance; proceeds of certain life insurance. Insurance proceeds for loss of or damage to exempt property. Crime victim reparation. Personal injury damages (except as to obligations incurred for such injuries or the collection of such damages). Periodic payments to compensate for the loss of future earnings are exempt to the same extent as wages.
Bank accounts: Not specified in exemption statute.
Alimony, child support: Child support payments (but exemption lost if commingled with other funds; if deposited in bank must be in special purpose account).
Survival after payment or deposit: Not specified (except for child support provisions described above).

CONNECTICUT

Has state opted out of federal bankruptcy exemptions? No.
Is opt out limited to residents or domiciliaries of the state? Not applicable.
Do state's exemptions have extraterritorial application?
Homestead: Uncertain.
Personal property: Uncertain.
***Wages*: Conn. Gen. Stat. §§ 52-352b(d), 52-361a.**
Scope: Earnings by reason of personal services, including any compensation payable by an employer to an employee, whether called wages, salary, commission, bonus or otherwise.
Amount: Garnishment is limited to lesser of 25% of debtor's weekly disposable income or amount by which weekly disposable income exceeds forty times the federal or state minimum wage. Disposable income is that left after deductions of taxes, normal retirement contributions, union dues and fees, and health or group life insurance premiums. All wages earned by a public assistance recipient under an incentive earnings program are exempt. No garnishment unless judgment debtor has failed to comply with an installment payment order. Garnishment will be for the statutory maximum, unless the court provides otherwise pursuant to motion for modification. No more than one garnishment at a time. Employer may not discharge or discipline employee for garnishment unless there are more than seven wage executions in one calendar year.
Survival after payment/deposit: Not specified in exemption statute.
Waiver: Not specified in exemption statute.
***Homestead*: Conn. Gen. Stat. §§ 52-352(b)(l), 52-352a, 52-352b(t).**
Amount: $75,000 excluding consensual or statutory liens; $125,000 for money judgment arising out of services provided at a hospital. One residential security deposit, and utility deposits for one residence.
Procedural requirements: Not specified in exemption statute.
Special provisions: Not specified in exemption statute.
Waiver: Not specified in exemption statute.
***Tangible personal property*: Conn. Gen. Stat. §§ 52-352a, 52-352b.**
Household goods: Necessary food, furniture, bedding, and appliances.
Motor vehicles: $3500 (fair market value, less any liens and encumbrances).
Tools of trade: Tools, books, instruments, livestock, and feed, necessary for debtor's occupation, profession, or farming.
Clothing and jewelry: Necessary clothing. Wedding and engagement rings.
Miscellaneous and wildcard: Wildcard $1000 in any property. Health aids, burial plot, certain military items, residential security deposit and utility security deposits.
Waiver: Not specified in exemption statute.
***Benefits, retirement plans, insurance, judgments, and other intangibles*: Conn. Gen. Stat. § 52-352b; *see* §§ 5-171, 52-321(a).**
Public benefits: Public assistance payments, wages of public assistance recipient under incentive program, workers' compensation, Social Security, veterans' and unemployment benefits. *See also* Conn. Gen. Stat. § 17B-86 (various types of state-administered aid exempt).
Pensions, retirement plans and annuities: Certain public and private pensions and retirement plans.
Insurance, judgments or other compensation for injury: Health and disability insurance payments; crime victim reparations, benefits from certain fraternal associations, up to $4000 in accrued dividends or loan value of certain insurance policies. Insurance proceeds on exempt property exempt to same extent as the property.
Bank accounts: Not specified in exemption statute.
Alimony, child support: Court-approved payments for child support; alimony or other support treated as wages.
Survival after payment or deposit: Not specified in exemption statute.

DELAWARE

Has state opted out of federal bankruptcy exemptions? Yes. Del. Code Ann. tit. 10, § 4914.
Is opt out limited to residents or domiciliaries of the state? Yes. Del. Code Ann. tit. 10, § 4913: "[A]n individual debtor domiciled in Delaware is not authorized or entitled to elect the Federal exemptions . . . [in § 522(d)] and may exempt only that property from the estate as set forth is subsection (b) of this section."
Do state's exemptions have extraterritorial application?
Homestead: No exemption.
Personal property: Probably not. Del. Code Ann. tit. 10, § 4902 limited to "every person residing in this state."
***Wages*: Del. Code Ann. tit. 6, § 4345; Del. Code Ann. tit. 10, § 4913.**
Scope: Salaries, commissions and every other form of remuneration paid to an employee for labor or services; does not include payment made for services rendered by self-employed person.
Amount: 85% exempt. For debts arising from retail installment sale, totally exempt for sixty days after default on the contract or installment account. Only one garnishment at a time.
Survival after payment/deposit: Not specified in exemption statute.
Waiver: Not specified in exemption statute.
***Homestead*: Del. Code Ann. tit. 10, § 4914.**
Amount: In bankruptcy only: $50,000 equity in real property or manufactured home which constitutes principal residence.
Procedural requirements: None specified.
Special provisions: None specified.
Waiver: None specified.

***Tangible personal property*: Del. Code Ann. tit. 10, §§ 4902, 4903, 4914, 7323.**
Household goods: Bedding.
Motor vehicles: In bankruptcy only: tools of trade and/or motor vehicle necessary to employment, $15,000. Joint debtors may stack.
Tools of trade: $50 or $75, depending on location. In bankruptcy only: tools of trade and/or motor vehicle necessary to employment, $15,000. Joint debtors may stack.
Clothing and jewelry: Necessary wearing apparel, no cap.
Miscellaneous and wildcard: See above. Also family bible, books and pictures, church pew, burial place, no cap. Additional $500 wildcard for head of family. In bankruptcy only: $25,000.
Waiver: Allowed; both spouses' signatures required.
***Benefits, retirement plans, insurance, judgments, and other intangibles*: Del. Code Ann. tit. 10, §§ 4915, 4916.**
Public benefits: Not specified in exemption statute. *See* Del. Code Ann. tit. 31, § 513 (assistance provided under state public assistance code exempt).
Pensions, retirement plans and annuities: Certain retirement plans, including rollovers. Not exempt from claims of alternate payee under qualified domestic relations order.
Insurance, judgments or other compensation for injury: Not specified in exemption statute. *See* Del. Code Ann. tit. 18, §§ 2725 to 2728 (insurance and annuities).
Bank accounts: Funds held in, or proceeds payable from, Delaware College Investment Plan Account (except when contributions in most recent year exceed $5000 or the average contribution in the two preceding years).
Alimony, child support: Payments received by alternate payee of retirement plan, pursuant to qualified domestic relations order are exempt.
Survival after payment or deposit: Not specified in exemption statute.

DISTRICT OF COLUMBIA

Has state opted out of federal bankruptcy exemptions? No.
Is opt out limited to residents or domiciliaries of the state? Not applicable.
Do state's exemptions have extraterritorial application?
Homestead: Yes (with limitations). D.C. Code § 15-501(a) provides that specified property of a head of family or householder, who resides in the District of Columbia or who earns the major portion of his livelihood there, is exempt "regardless of his place of residence."
Personal property: Yes (with limitations as noted above).
***Wages*: D.C. Code §§ 16-571 to 16-572.**
Scope: Compensation paid or payable for personal services, whether called wages, salary, commission, bonus or otherwise; includes periodic payments pursuant to a pension or retirement program.
Amount: Similar to federal. Only one garnishment at a time.
Survival after payment/deposit: Not specified in exemption statute.
Waiver: Not specified in exemption statute.
***Homestead*: D.C. Code § 15-501(a)(14).**
Amount: Head of family or householder only: Debtor's aggregate interest in real property used as the residence of the debtor or property of the debtor or debtor's dependent in a cooperative that owns property that debtor or dependant uses as a residence.
Procedural requirements: Not specified in exemption statute.
Special provisions: Not specified in exemption statute.
Waiver: Mortgage, deed of trust or sale not valid unless signed by spouse, if debtor is married and living with spouse.
***Tangible personal property*: D.C. Code § 15-501 to 15-503.** (All tangible and intangible personal property exemptions are for householder or head of family only.)
Household goods: $8625 aggregate, single item $425: Household goods, furnishings, wearing apparel, books, animals, crops, musical instruments.
Motor vehicles: $2575 in one vehicle, if used in debtor's business.
Tools of trade: $1625; library and office furniture of professional person, $300.
Clothing and jewelry: Included in household goods exemption.
Miscellaneous and wildcard: $850 any property; unused homestead exemption up to $8075; health aids; family pictures and library, $400.
Waiver: Any sale or encumbrance of exempt property requires spouse's signature if debtor married and living with spouse.
***Benefits, retirement plans, insurance, judgments, and other intangibles*: D.C. Code §§ 15-501 to 15-503.** (All tangible and intangible personal property exemptions are for householder or head of family only.)
Public benefits: Social Security, veterans' benefits, disability, illness or unemployment benefit.
Pensions, retirement plans and annuities: Certain retirement plans.
Insurance, judgments or other compensation for injury: Unmatured life insurance contract; life insurance payments to the extent needed for support; compensation for pain and suffering, actual pecuniary loss, or loss of future earnings; crime victim reparations; certain wrongful death judgments, to the extent needed for support.
Bank accounts: Not specified in exemption statute.
Alimony, child support: Alimony, support or separate maintenance to the extent needed for support. Interest in retirement plan awarded to alternate payee under qualified domestic relations order.
Survival after payment or deposit: Not specified in statute.

FLORIDA

Has state opted out of federal bankruptcy exemptions? Yes, except as to exemptions provided by 11 U.S.C. § 522(d)(10). Fla. Stat. §§ 222.20, 222.201.
Is opt out limited to residents or domiciliaries of the state? Yes. Fla. Stat. §§ 222.20, 222.201: "[R]esidents of this state shall not be entitled to the Federal exemptions provided in § 522(d) [except the exemptions in § 522(d)(10)]." *See In re* Battle, 2006 WL 3702734 (Bankr. W.D. Tex. Dec. 12, 2006).
Do state's exemptions have extraterritorial application?
Homestead: No. *See In re* Schulz, 101 B.R. 301 (Bankr. N.D. Fla. 1989). Procedure for recording a homestead declaration is available only to "any natural person residing in this state." Fla. Stat. § 222.01.
Personal property: No. *See In re* Schulz, 101 B.R. 301 (Bankr. N.D. Fla. 1989).
***Wages*: Fla. Stat. § 222.11.**
Scope: Earnings, defined as compensation paid or payable in money of sum certain for personal services or labor whether called wages, salary, commission or bonus, of a head of family, defined as one who provides more than 50% of the support of a child or

dependant.
Amount: Head of family: $500 per week of disposable earnings exempt, unless debtor has agreed otherwise in writing. Amount garnished may not exceed that allowed by federal law. Disposable earnings are those left over after all deductions required by law. Others: same as federal.
Survival after payment/deposit: Earnings remain exempt for six months in a bank account, even if commingled with other funds, so long as earnings can be traced and properly identified.
Waiver: Wages of head of household in excess of $500 may be garnished with debtor's written permission.
***Homestead*: Fla. Const. art. X, § 4(a)(1); Fla. Stat. §§ 222.01 to 222.03, 222.05.**
Amount: Up to $\frac{1}{2}$ acre inside a municipality or 160 acres outside a municipality is exempt under the Florida Constitution regardless of value, with exceptions for four types of debts (taxes, purchase money debts, services or labor for home repair or improvement, and other labor performed on real property). By statute, a mobile home or modular home may be a homestead, whether or not the home owner owns the land. In addition, if the homestead is outside a municipality and includes less than 160 acres, the debtor may exempt non-homestead land to bring the total up to 160 acres.
Procedural requirements: Permitted but not required to file declaration of homestead, may do so after levy.
Special provisions: None specified in exemption statute.
Waiver: Not specified in exemption statute.
***Tangible personal property*: Fla. Const. art. X, § 4; Fla. Stat. §§ 222.061, 222.07, 222.25.**
Household goods: $1000 in any personal property.
Motor vehicles: Up to $1000 in any one motor vehicle.
Tools of trade: See above.
Clothing and jewelry: See above.
Miscellaneous and wildcard: See above. Professionally prescribed health aids. For a debtor who does not claim or receive the benefits of a homestead exemption, $4000 in any personal property (this exemption does not apply to a debt for child or spousal support).
Waiver: Not specified in exemption statute.
***Benefits, retirement plans, insurance, judgments, and other intangibles*: Fla. Stat. §§ 222.13, 222.14, 222.18, 222.21, 222.22, 222.25; *see* Fla. Stat. § 121.131.**
Public benefits: Earned income tax credit, pursuant to the Internal Revenue Code, or a deposit in a financial institution traceable to an earned income tax credit.
Pensions, retirement plans and annuities: Public pension money received within three months before the attachment; certain tax-qualified retirement plan (except as to claims of alternate payee under qualified domestic relations order).
Insurance, judgments or other compensation for injury: Life insurance proceeds exempt as to creditors of the insured. Cash surrender values of insurance policies or annuities. Disability income benefits under any policy of life, health, accident or other insurance.
Bank accounts: Money paid into or out of a medical savings account or hurricane savings account. Monies paid into or out of prepaid postsecondary education expense trust fund are not subject to attachment, garnishment or legal process by creditors of either purchaser or beneficiary of contract.
Alimony, child support: Pension funds received by alternate payee under qualified domestic relations order.
Survival after payment or deposit: Not specified in exemption statute, except as to tax refunds attributable to earned income tax credit, public pension money received within three months, or payments into or out of medical savings or prepaid college trust fund accounts.

GEORGIA

Has state opted out of federal bankruptcy exemptions? Yes. Ga. Code Ann. § 44-13-100(b).
Is opt out limited to residents or domiciliaries of the state? Yes, with limitation as to prepetition period debtor domiciled in Georgia. Ga. Code Ann. § 44-13-100(b): "an individual debtor whose domicile is in Georgia is prohibited from applying or utilizing [§ 522(d)]"; an " 'individual debtor whose domicile is in Georgia' means an individual whose domicile has been located in Georgia for the 180 days immediately preceding the date of the filing of the bankruptcy petition or for a longer portion of such 180 day period than in any other place." *See In re* Chandler, 362 B.R. 723 (Bankr. N.D. W. Va. 2007).
Do state's exemptions have extraterritorial application?
Homestead: Uncertain. Georgia Code Ann. § 44-13-100 applies to "any debtor who is a natural person."
Personal property: Not specified in exemption statute, but possibly yes. *See In re* Stockburger, 106 F.3d 402 (6th Cir. 1997) (table) (Georgia exemption applies to personal property located in Tennessee because it is the law of the debtor's domicile that controls under § 522(b), not the location of the property).
***Wages*: Ga. Code Ann. § 18-4-20(d)–(f)**
Scope: Compensation paid or payable for personal services, whether called wages, salary, commission, bonus or otherwise, including periodic payments pursuant to a pension or retirement program.
Amount: Similar to federal.
Survival after payment/deposit: Not specified in exemption statute.
Waiver: Not specified in exemption statute.
***Homestead*: Ga. Code Ann. §§ 44-13-1, 44-13-40, and 44-13-100(a)(1).**
Amount: Bankruptcy only: $10,000, or if title to property is in one of two spouses who is a debtor, $20,000 per debtor in any property used as residence or burial plot. Non-bankruptcy: Aggregate of $5000, in real and personal property. May be waived except as to certain essential personal property.
Procedural requirements: None stated. Exemptions may be claimed after judgment.
Special provisions: If debtor fails to claim exemption, spouse or anyone acting on behalf of minor children or dependants may do so.
Waiver: May be waived except as to certain essential personal property.
***Tangible personal property*: Ga. Code Ann. §§ 44-13-1, 44-13-40, 44-13-100.**
Household goods: Any real or personal property in the amount of $5000. Bankruptcy only: up to $300 per item, $5000 total in household goods, clothing, appliances, animals, books, crops or musical instruments.
Motor vehicles: Bankruptcy only: $3500.
Tools of trade: Bankruptcy only: $1500.
Clothing and jewelry: Bankruptcy only: $500 jewelry.
Miscellaneous and wildcard: Bankruptcy only: $600 plus unused amount of $5000 exemption; health aids.

Waiver: Permitted, except as to wearing apparel and $300 worth of household and kitchen furniture and provisions. Waiver may be included in note or contract evidencing indebtedness.

***Benefits, retirement plans, insurance, judgments, and other intangibles*: Ga. Code Ann. §§ 18-4-22, 44-13-100.**

Public benefits: Bankruptcy only: Social Security; veterans' benefits; unemployment, illness or disability benefits; local public assistance.

Pensions, retirement plans and annuities: Certain tax-qualified retirement plans until paid to beneficiary—after payment they are treated like wages. Bankruptcy only: Payments from IRAs, pensions, annuities or similar plans, as needed for support.

Insurance, judgments or other compensation for injury: Bankruptcy only: unmatured life insurance contracts, up to $2000 in accrued dividends or cash or loan value of life insurance; right to receive or property traceable to crime victim reparations, wrongful death award to extent needed for support, personal injury judgment up to $10,000 (not including pain and suffering or actual pecuniary loss), compensation for loss of future earnings of debtor or one on whom debtor is dependent.

Bank accounts: Not specified in exemption statute.

Alimony, child support: Bankruptcy only: alimony, support or separate maintenance to the extent needed for support.

Survival after payment or deposit: Not specified in exemption statute.

HAWAII

Has state opted out of federal bankruptcy exemptions? No.

Is opt out limited to residents or domiciliaries of the state? Not applicable.

Do state's exemptions have extraterritorial application?

Homestead: No. Haw. Rev. Stat. § 651-92(a)(1) applies to one parcel of real property "in the state of Hawaii."

Personal property: Uncertain.

***Wages*: Haw. Rev. Stat. §§ 652-1(a), (b), 651-121, 653-3.**

Scope: Wages, salary, stipend, commissions, annuity or net income under a trust.

Amount: 95% of first $100 earned per month, 90% of the next $100, and 80% of all sums in excess of $200 per month.

Survival after payment/deposit: Wages for thirty days prior to attachment proceedings are exempt.

Waiver: Not specified in exemption statute.

***Homestead*: Haw. Rev. Stat. §§ 651-91 to 651-93, 651-96.**

Amount: $30,000 for married person, head of family or person over 65 and $20,000 for all others; a co-op or long-term lease covered; subject to certain liens. Married couple may claim only one homestead; after decree of separate maintenance or interlocutory decree of divorce, each may claim individual exemption.

Procedural requirements: None stated. May be claimed at time of levy.

Special provisions: Proceeds exempt for six months.

Waiver: Not specified in exemption statute.

***Tangible personal property*: Haw. Rev. Stat. §§ 651-121, 651-122.**

Household goods: Necessary furniture, appliances and books.

Motor vehicles: $2575 (fair market value less liens and encumbrances).

Tools of trade: Tools, implements, one commercial fishing boat, motor vehicle reasonably necessary to, and used by the debtor in his or her trade, business or profession.

Clothing and jewelry: Necessary clothing; $1000 jewelry and watches.

Miscellaneous and wildcard: Burial place. Sales and insurance proceeds of exempt property exempt for six months after receipt.

Waiver: Not specified in exemption statute.

***Benefits, retirement plans, insurance, judgments, and other intangibles*: Haw. Rev. Stat. §§ 651-124, 653-3.**

Public benefits: Not specified in exemption statute.

Pensions, retirement plans and annuities: Pensions, annuities, retirement, disability, death benefits or certain public employees' pension plans pursuant to certain tax-qualified plans. (Except as to claims of alternate payee under qualified domestic relations order or contributions made to a plan within three years before bankruptcy, voluntary or involuntary, or before the date a civil action is initiated against the debtor.)

Insurance, judgments or other compensation for injury: Not specified in exemption statute. *See* Haw. Rev. Stat. § 431:10-232, 431:10-233.

Bank accounts: Not specified in exemption statute.

Alimony, child support: Not specified in exemption statute.

Survival after payment or deposit: Not specified in exemption statute.

IDAHO

Has state opted out of federal bankruptcy exemptions? Yes. Idaho Code Ann. § 11-609.

Is opt out limited to residents or domiciliaries of the state? Not specified. Idaho Code Ann. § 11-609: "In any federal bankruptcy proceeding, an individual debtor may exempt from property of the estate only such property as is specified under the laws of this state."

Do state's exemptions have extraterritorial application?

Homestead: Not specified in exemption statute, but possibly not. *See In re* Halpin, 1994 WL 594199 (Bankr. D. Idaho Nov. 1, 1994) (relying upon secondary authority, finds that Idaho homestead may not be used outside state).

Personal property: Probably not. Idaho Code Ann. § 11-602(1) provides that: "[R]esidents of this state are entitled to the exemptions provided by this act. Nonresidents are entitled to the exemptions provided by the law of the jurisdiction of their residence." Idaho Code Ann. § 11-602(2) provides that the term " 'resident' means an individual who intends to maintain his home in this state."

***Wages*: Idaho Code Ann. §§ 11-206, 11-207.**

Scope: Compensation paid or payable for personal services, whether called wages, salary, commission, bonus or otherwise, including periodic payments from pension or retirement program.

Amount: Similar to federal.

Survival after payment/deposit: Not specified in exemption statute.

Waiver: Not specified in exemption statute.

***Homestead*: Idaho Code Ann. §§ 55-1001 to 55-1008.**

Amount: Lesser of $100,000 or net value of debtor's residence (includes mobile home or unimproved lands on which a residence will be built).

Procedural requirements: If land occupied as residence, homestead exemption is automatic; if owner wishes to claim homestead in land not yet so occupied, must record a declaration of homestead (as well as a declaration of abandonment of any previous home-

stead). Owner who plans to be away from homestead for more than six months must record declaration of homestead.
Special provisions: Sales or insurance proceeds are exempt for one year from the date of the sale or receipt; must show intent to establish new homestead. Married couple may not stack homestead exemptions. Exemption does not protect against judgments obtained before homestead was established.
Waiver: Conveyance or encumbrance of homestead requires signature of both spouses.
***Tangible personal property*: Idaho Code Ann. §§ 11-603 to 11-607.**
Household goods: $500 single item, $5000 aggregate: furniture and appliances reasonably necessary for one household including one firearm, clothing, animals, books and musical instruments.
Motor vehicles: $3000 in one vehicle.
Tools of trade: $1500; a 160-inch water right for irrigation of lands the debtor cultivates.
Clothing and jewelry: Clothing included in $5000 exemption above; $1000 jewelry.
Miscellaneous and wildcard: $800 wildcard; health aids; $1000 in crops from 50 acres of land that the debtor cultivates; up to $500 per item portraits and heirlooms; military items; burial plot.
Waiver: Not specified in exemption statute.
***Benefits, retirement plans, insurance, judgments, and other intangibles*: Idaho Code Ann. §§ 11-603 to 11-607, 55-1011.**
Public benefits: Social Security or veterans' benefits; state, local or federal public assistance; state unemployment (to extent provided for in Idaho Code Ann. § 72-1375). *See also* Idaho Code Ann. § 56-223 (public assistance exempt).
Pensions, retirement plans and annuities: Certain pensions and tax-qualified retirement plans, except as to claims of alternate payee under qualified domestic relations order.
Insurance, judgments or other compensation for injury: Insurance proceeds of exempt property exempt to same extent as the property, for three months after receipt. Benefits payable for medical, surgical or hospital care. Exempt so far as needed for support: benefits payable by reason of disability or illness, personal injury compensation (for injury to self or one on whom dependent), wrongful death compensation (if debtor dependant on victim), life insurance proceeds (if debtor was spouse or dependant of insured).
Bank accounts: Not specified in exemption statute.
Alimony, child support: Certain retirement benefits received by alternate payee pursuant to qualified domestic relations order. Alimony, support or separate maintenance, so far as needed for support.
Survival after payment or deposit: Limited—exemptions for insurance, personal injury compensation, alimony, support, separate maintenance, illness or disability benefits lost if commingled with other funds.

ILLINOIS

Has state opted out of federal bankruptcy exemptions? Yes. 735 Ill. Comp. Stat. § 5/12-1201.
Is opt out limited to residents or domiciliaries of the state? Yes. 735 Ill. Comp. Stat. § 5/12-1201: "[R]esidents of this state shall be prohibited from using . . . [§ 522(d)] except as may be otherwise permitted under the laws of Illinois."
Do state's exemptions have extraterritorial application?
Homestead: Uncertain
Personal property: Uncertain.
***Wages*: 735 Ill. Comp. Stat. §§ 5/12-801, 5/12-803, 5/12-813; 740 Ill. Comp. Stat. § 170/4.**
Scope: Wages, salary, commission or bonus.
Amount: The greater of 85% of disposable income, or 45 times the greater of the federal minimum wage, or, for wage summonses served after January 1, 2006, the wage prescribed by section 4 of the minimum wage law, is exempt. Disposable earnings are those left after all legally required withholding.
Survival after payment/deposit: Not specified in exemption statute.
Waiver: Wage garnishment order may not be issued on confession of judgment.
***Homestead*: 735 Ill. Comp. Stat. §§ 5/12-901 to 5/12-907.**
Amount: $15,000; if property is owned by two or more persons, each may exempt proportionate share of $30,000.
Procedural requirements: Not specified in exemption statute.
Special provisions: Sales proceeds are exempt for one year from the date of the sale. If home owner dies, exemption survives so long as surviving spouse or minor children occupy the homestead. If spouse deserts family, exemption protects spouse who still resides in homestead. Homestead exemption will not protect against drug forfeitures. Insurance proceeds for loss or destruction of homestead, if insured in favor of a person who may claim exemption, are exempt to the extent the building would have been.
Waiver: Must be in writing, and signed by spouse, if any.
***Tangible personal property*: 625 Ill. Comp. Stat. § 45/3A-7; 735 Ill. Comp. Stat. § 5/12-1001.**
Household goods: $4000 in any other property. Right to receive certain benefits (insurance, crime victim reparations, personal injury or wrongful death award) remains exempt for two years after award "accrues"; proceeds of award remain exempt for five years, if traceable. Proceeds of sale of exempt property remain exempt to same extent as property is exempt.
Motor vehicles: $2400 in one motor vehicle.
Tools of trade: $1500
Clothing and jewelry: Necessary clothing.
Miscellaneous and wildcard: Bible, school books and family pictures and health aids; certificate of title to watercraft over 12 feet in length is exempt although the watercraft itself is not exempt. Personal property exemption does not apply if exempt property purchased with intent to convert non-exempt to exempt property, or in fraud of creditors. Property acquired within six months before filing bankruptcy is presumed to have been acquired in anticipation of bankruptcy.
Waiver: Not specified in exemption statute.
***Benefits, retirement plans, insurance, judgments, and other intangibles*: 735 Ill. Comp. Stat. §§ 5/12-1001, 5/12-1006; *see* 820 Ill. Comp. Stat. § 405/1300.**
Public benefits: Social Security, veterans' benefits, unemployment, public assistance. Waivers of exemption void as to unemployment benefits. *See also* 305 Ill. Comp. Stat. § 5/11-3 (financial aid exempt).
Pensions, retirement plans and annuities: Certain public and private pension and retirement plans, including IRAs and SEPs.
Insurance, judgments or other compensation for injury: Proceeds and cash values of insurance policies or annuities payable to spouse, or child, parent, or other dependent of insured; disability, illness or unemployment benefit. Right to receive or property traceable to crime victim reparations, wrongful death (of person on whom debtor was dependent, to extent needed for support), up to

$15,000 personal injury.
Bank accounts: Funds in accounts invested in the Illinois College Savings Pool.
Alimony, child support: Alimony, support or separate maintenance, to the extent needed for support.
Survival after payment or deposit: Sale proceeds of exempt property exempt to same extent as property. Right to receive certain compensation (insurance, crime victim reparations, personal injury or wrongful death) remains exempt for two years after right accrues, property traceable to certain compensation remains exempt for five years if traceable.

INDIANA

Has state opted out of federal bankruptcy exemptions? Yes. Ind. Code § 34-55-10-1.
Is opt out limited to residents or domiciliaries of the state? Yes. Ind. Code § 34-55-10-1: "an individual debtor domiciled in Indiana is not entitled to use . . . [§ 522(d) exemptions]."
Do state's exemptions have extraterritorial application?
Homestead: No. *See* Ind. Code § 34-55-10-2 (applies to the property of a "debtor domiciled in Indiana"). *See In re* West, 352 B.R. 905 (Bankr. M.D. Fla. 2006).
Personal property: No. *See* Ind. Code § 34-55-10-2 (applies to the property of a "debtor domiciled in Indiana"). *See In re* West, 352 B.R. 905 (Bankr. M.D. Fla. 2006).
***Wages*: Ind. Code § 24-4.5-5-105.**
Scope: Earnings of an individual, including wages, commissions, income, rents or profits.
Amount: Similar to federal.
Survival after payment/deposit: Not specified in exemption statute.
Waiver: Not specified in exemption statute.
***Homestead*: Ind. Code §§ 34-55-10-2(c)(1), (2), (5), 34-55-10-2.5, 34-55-10-14.**
Amount: $15,000 subject to certain liens. The exemption is individually available to joint judgment debtors if property held by them as tenants by entireties. Additional exemption for "real estate or tangible personal property" of $8000. As of 2010, and every six years thereafter, the Department of Financial Institutions must establish new exemption amounts, based on changes in the Consumer Price Index.
Procedural requirements: None stated. May claim after judgment.
Special provisions: Not specified in exemption statute.
Waiver: Not specified in exemption statute.
***Tangible personal property*: Ind. Code §§ 34-55-10-2, 34-55-10-2.5.**
Household goods: $8000 in any tangible personal property or non-residential real property and $300 of intangible personal property, including bank accounts and cash[3]; exemptions are subject to certain liens.
Motor vehicles: See above.
Tools of trade: See above.
Clothing and jewelry: See above.
Miscellaneous and wildcard: Health aids (no cap).
Waiver: Not specified in exemption statute.

3 Oakley v. Freeland, 287 B.R. 174 (N.D. Ind. 2002) (cash is "tangible personal property"); Levin v. Dare, 203 B.R. 137 (S.D. Ind. 1996) (when statute was unclear, court followed the Indiana policy of liberal construction for exemption statutes, and held that cash was exempt tangible personal property).

***Benefits, retirement plans, insurance, judgments, and other intangibles*: Ind. Code § 34-55-10-2.**
Public benefits: Not specified in exemption statute.
Pensions, retirement plans and annuities: Certain retirement plans, including rollovers.
Insurance, judgments or other compensation for injury: Not specified in exemption statute.
Bank accounts: Medical savings accounts and certain prepaid tuition and educational savings accounts.
Alimony, child support: Not specified in exemption statute.
Survival after payment or deposit: Not specified in exemption statute.

IOWA

Has state opted out of federal bankruptcy exemptions? Yes. Iowa Code § 627.10.
Is opt out limited to residents or domiciliaries of the state? Not specified, but may be limited to the extent that Iowa law is not applicable to non-resident. Iowa Code § 627.10: "A debtor to whom the law of this state applies on the date of filing of a petition in bankruptcy is not entitled to elect . . . [§ 522(d) exemptions]."
Do state's exemptions have extraterritorial application?
Homestead: Not specified in exemption statute, but probably not. *See In re* Stone, 329 B.R. 860 (Bankr. N.D. Iowa 2005) (relying on Rogers v. Raisor, 60 Iowa 355, 14 N.W. 317 (1882) (proceeds of an Iowa homestead reinvested in a new homestead in another state not exempt under Iowa law)).
Personal property: Probably not. Iowa Code § 627.6 applies to property of a "debtor who is a resident of this state."
***Wages*: Iowa Code §§ 627.6, 642.21, 537.5105.**
Scope: Compensation paid or payable for personal services, whether called wages, salary, commission, bonus or otherwise, including periodic payments from pension or retirement program.
Amount: Maximum garnishment ranges from $250 a year when expected earnings do not exceed $12,000 to 10% of annual earnings when such earnings exceed $50,000. Tax refund is exempt in bankruptcy only, up to $1000 aggregate. In addition, if the debt arises from a consumer credit contract, greater of 75% or 40 times the minimum wage is exempt. The Iowa Consumer Code also provides a procedure for a consumer to seek a reduction in the garnishment amount, if the funds are needed for support of the consumer or the consumer's household.
Survival after payment/deposit: Not specified in exemption statute.
Waiver: Not specified in exemption statute.
***Homestead*: Iowa Code §§ 561.1 to 561.3, 561.20 to 561.22, 627.6(14), 627.9.**
Amount: Up to $\frac{1}{2}$ acre in city or town, otherwise 40 acres; also acreage up to $500 in value; building on the property used for business purposes is exempt up to $300. Only one homestead per household unit (defined as persons who reside together, whether or not related). Homestead purchased with pension money is fully exempt. Up to $500 in the aggregate in: any residential rental deposit, held by landlord as a security deposit; pre-paid rent under an unexpired residential lease; utility security deposits; interest paid on security deposits required by law to be placed in interest-bearing account is also exempt.
Procedural requirements: May select homestead and cause it to be platted, but failure to do so will not destroy exemption.
Special provisions: Homestead liable for debts which predate the

acquisition of the homestead, but exemption passes uninterrupted from old homestead to new, if new homestead acquired with proceeds of old. Homestead purchased with pension money is exempt even as to claims for preexisting debts.

Waiver: Waiver of homestead of agricultural land containing forty acres or more, contained in a contract, must include prescribed language in ten-point boldface type stating that debtor knows of and voluntarily waives homestead rights.

***Tangible personal property*: Iowa Code §§ 627.6, 627.6A.**

Household goods: $7000. Explicitly includes computers, cameras, and a wide range of electronic entertainment equipment (record, tape, CD and DVD players, satellite dishes, cable equipment, and so forth).

Motor vehicles: $7000 in the aggregate of: one motor vehicle and up to $1000 in accrued wages and tax refunds. Exemption for accrued wages available in bankruptcy only. Motor vehicle not exempt as to claim for damages resulting from use of the vehicle.

Tools of trade: $10,000. Farming implements and livestock included, but may not be exempted for deficiency judgment upon foreclosure on agricultural land if debtor exercises the delay of enforcement provisions of Iowa Code § 654.6.

Clothing and jewelry: Clothing and trunks included in household goods exemption. Jewelry: $2000, plus engagement or wedding rings, but if ring acquired by debtor or dependent after the date of marriage and within two years before execution issued or exemption claimed, then limit of $7000 minus any amount claimed under the jewelry exemption.

Miscellaneous and wildcard: One shotgun and either a rifle or a musket; $1000 in books and paintings; professionally prescribed health aids; burial space. Up to $500 aggregate in prepaid rent or security deposits, or utility security deposits.

Waiver: Not specified in exemption statute.

***Benefits, retirement plans, insurance, judgments, and other intangibles*: Iowa Code §§ 627.6, 627.6A, 627.8, 627.9, 627.13; *see* Iowa Code § 96.15.**

Public benefits: Social Security, veterans' benefits, unemployment, or any public assistance benefit. (Waivers of exemption void as to unemployment benefits.) Financial assistance provided under Iowa Code §§ 600.17 to 600.22 (adopted child assistance). *See also* Iowa Code § 239B.6 (family assistance exempt).

Pensions, retirement plans and annuities: Certain pension and retirement plans, including IRAs, SEPs and Roth IRAs; rollovers explicitly included, but above-normal contributions made within one year of bankruptcy excluded. Pensions and retirement plans not exempt if claim is for family support.

Insurance, judgments or other compensation for injury: Disability or illness benefits. Up to $10,000 in accrued dividends, loan or cash surrender value of life insurance policy, if spouse, child, or dependent is beneficiary (except for certain recent contributions to policy). If insured dies, all avails of insurance policies (including life, health, accident or disability) exempt in beneficiaries' hands up to $15,000, as to debts contracted before death of insured. Payments, including a structured settlement, resulting from the wrongful death of a person upon whom debtor or debtor's dependents were dependent, so far as needed for support.

Bank accounts: $1000.

Alimony, child support: Alimony, support or separate maintenance, so far as needed for support.

Survival after payment or deposit: Not specified in exemption statute.

KANSAS

Has state opted out of federal bankruptcy exemptions? Yes, except as to 11 U.S.C. § 522(d)(10) (benefits, alimony, support, maintenance, certain pensions and similar payments). Kan. Stat. Ann. § 60-2312.

Is opt out limited to residents or domiciliaries of the state? Not specified. Kan. Stat. Ann. § 60-2312: "[N]o person, as an individual debtor under the [Bankruptcy Code], may elect exemptions pursuant to [§ 522(d)]."

Do state's exemptions have extraterritorial application?

Homestead: No. *See In re* Spika, 149 B.R. 181 (D. Kan. 1992); *In re* Ginther, 282 B.R. 16 (Bankr. D. Kan. 2002).

Personal property: Probably not. Kan. Stat. Ann. § 60-2304 applies to property of "every person residing in this state."

***Wages*: Kan. Stat. Ann. §§ 60-2310, 60-2311.**

Scope: Compensation paid or payable for personal services, whether called wages, salary, commission, bonus or otherwise.

Amount: Similar to federal. If a debtor is prevented from working at his or her usual employment for two weeks, because of illness of the debtor or a family member, garnishment is forbidden until the expiration of two months after recovery from the illness. No employee may be discharged or disciplined because of wage garnishment. If a debt is assigned to a person or collection agency, the assignee may not use wage garnishment (except for certain child support, tax or court restitution collections).

Survival after payment/deposit: Not specified in exemption statute.

Waiver: Not specified in exemption statute.

***Homestead*: Kan. Stat. Ann. §§ 60-2301, 60-2302.**

Amount: 160 acres of farm land or one acre in a town or city, subject to certain liens. Mobile or manufactured home explicitly included.

Procedural requirements: None stated. May be claimed at time of levy.

Special provisions: Not specified.

Waiver: Sale or encumbrance requires signature of spouse, if any.

***Tangible personal property*: Kan. Stat. Ann. § 60-2304.**

Household goods: Household goods, fuel, food and clothing reasonably necessary at principal residence for one year.

Motor vehicles: $20,000, if used regularly to commute to work; disabled (definition at Kan. Stat. Ann. § 8-1124) no limitations.

Tools of trade: $7500.

Clothing and jewelry: Clothing, see above; $1000 in jewelry.

Miscellaneous and wildcard: Burial space; national guard uniforms and equipment.

Waiver: Not specified in exemption statute.

***Benefits, retirement plans, insurance, judgments, and other intangibles*: Kan. Stat. Ann. §§ 60-2304, 60-2308, 60-2313.**

Public benefits: Public assistance, unemployment, workers' compensation. *See also* Kan. Stat. Ann. § 39-717(c) (assistance under Social Welfare Act is exempt).

Pensions, retirement plans and annuities: Certain pensions and retirement accounts, including tax-qualified IRAs.

Insurance, judgments or other compensation for injury: Life insurance; crime victim compensation; benefits from fraternal organization; certain annuities and death or disability benefits.

Bank accounts: Prepaid college tuition accounts, if the beneficiary is a lineal descendant of the debtor, certain recent contributions excluded; prepaid funeral.

Alimony, child support: Alimony, so far as reasonably necessary to

debtor's support.
Survival after payment or deposit: Not specified in exemption statute.

KENTUCKY

Has state opted out of federal bankruptcy exemptions? No. Ky. Rev. Stat. Ann. § 427.170 (West).
Is opt out limited to residents or domiciliaries of the state? Not applicable.
Do state's exemptions have extraterritorial application?
Homestead: No. Ky. Rev. Stat. Ann. § 427.060 (West) applies to "real or personal property . . . that such debtor or . . . dependent . . . uses as a permanent residence in this state."
Personal property: Probably not. Ky. Rev. Stat. Ann. § 427.010 (West) applies to "personal property of an individual debtor resident in this state."
***Wages*: Ky. Rev. Stat. Ann. §§ 427.005, 427.010(2) (West).**
Scope: Compensation paid or payable for personal services, whether called wages, salary, commission, bonus or otherwise, including periodic payments pursuant to pension or retirement program.
Amount: Similar to federal exemptions.
Survival after payment/deposit: Not specified in exemption statute.
Waiver: Not specified in exemption statute.
***Homestead*: Ky. Rev. Stat. Ann. §§ 427.060, 427.070, 427.100, 427.160 (West).**
Amount: $5000 in real or personal property used as a residence. In bankruptcy, an additional $1000 in real property may be exempted if this sum is not applied to exempt personal property.
Procedural requirements: None stated. May be claimed after judgment.
Special provisions: Does not apply to debts existing at time homestead established. At debtor's death exemption preserved in hands of surviving spouse and minor children.
Waiver: Permitted. Must be in writing, signed by spouse (if any), and recorded like a conveyance of real estate.
***Tangible personal property*: Ky. Rev Stat. Ann. §§ 427.010(1), 427.030, 427.040, 427.150, 427.160 (West).**
Household goods: $3000 in household goods, clothing and jewelry. Explicitly excludes antiques, works of art, jewelry other than wedding rings, and electronic equipment except for one TV and one radio.
Motor vehicles: $2500.
Tools of trade: $300 tools of trade. $3000 farm implements and livestock. $1000 office, library and instruments and $2500 motor vehicle used by professional (for example, clergy, doctor, dentist, attorney, chiropractor, veterinarian); $2500 motor vehicle if used by person who services essential mechanical, electrical or other equipment in general use.
Clothing and jewelry: See above.
Miscellaneous and wildcard: Health aids. Bankruptcy only: $1000 in any real or personal property.
Waiver: Not specified in exemption statute.
***Benefits, retirement plans, insurance, judgments, and other intangibles*: Ky. Rev. Stat. Ann. §§ 427.010(1), 427.110 to 427.125, 427.150, 427.160 (West).**
Public benefits: Not specified in exemption statute. *See* Ky. Rev. Stat. Ann. § 205.220 (West) (public assistance exempt).
Pensions, retirement plans and annuities: Assets of and benefits under profit sharing, annuity or similar plans based on debtor's age, illness, disability, or length of service; certain public pensions; certain tax-qualified retirement plans.
Insurance, judgments or other compensation for injury: Life insurance proceeds; benefits from fraternal organization; crime victim reparations; $7500 personal injury judgments. Compensation for wrongful death or loss of future earnings is exempt to the extent necessary for support of debtor or dependent.
Bank accounts: Not specified.
Alimony, child support: Alimony, support or separate maintenance, to the extent needed for support.
Survival after payment or deposit: Not specified in exemption statute (except that police or firefighter pension is exempt "before or after its order for distribution").

LOUISIANA

Has state opted out of federal bankruptcy exemptions? Yes. La. Rev. Stat. Ann. § 13:3881(B)(1).
Is opt out limited to residents or domiciliaries of the state? Not specified. La. Rev. Stat. Ann. § 13:3881(B)(1): "In cases instituted under [Title 11], there shall be exempt . . . only that property and income which is exempt under the laws of the state of Louisiana and under federal laws other than [§ 522(d)]."
Do state's exemptions have extraterritorial application?
Homestead: Uncertain.
Personal property: Uncertain.
***Wages*: La. Rev. Stat. Ann. § 13:3881.**
Scope: Earnings of any individual. Disposable earnings are those left after legally required deductions, and deductions in usual course of business for retirement, health insurance and life insurance.
Amount: Similar to federal exemptions.
Survival after payment/deposit: Not specified in exemption statute.
Waiver: Not specified in exemption statute.
***Homestead*: La. Rev. Stat. Ann. § 20:1; *see* La. Const. art. 12, § 9.**
Amount: Residence and land, building and appurtenances on contiguous tracts of up to five acres if within a municipality, two hundred acres if not. Up to $25,000, except that for expenses resulting from catastrophic or terminal illness or injury, homestead is exempt up to full value. Some exceptions, including taxes, mortgage, certain criminal restitution. (*Note*: this section, which took effect on January 1, 2000, applies to seizures and judicial sales after that date. Former limits of $15,000 and 160 acres apply to earlier seizures.)
Procedural requirements: Not specified.
Special provisions: Homestead exemption protects surviving spouse and minor children who continue to occupy homestead.
Waiver: Permitted, but requires signature of spouse, if any, recorded in mortgage records. If, however, homestead is separate property of one spouse, that spouse may waive homestead in a mortgage, without the signature of non-owner spouse. Not permitted for rendering of medical treatment, medical services or hospitalization.
***Tangible personal property*: La. Rev. Stat. Ann. § 13:3881.**
Household goods: Clothing, household goods, non-sterling silverware, certain retirement plans; poultry, fowl and one cow for family use; a right of personal servitude of habitation and the usufruct under Article 223 of the Civil Code.

Motor vehicles: $7500 in one vehicle, used by debtor and family for any purpose. Only one motor vehicle per household. $7500 in any vehicle substantially modified, equipped or fitted for adapting its use to physical disability of debtor or family, and used for transporting such disabled person.
Tools of trade: Tools, instruments, books, and one utility trailer used for trade, calling or profession by which debtor earns living. Certain livestock.
Clothing and jewelry: Clothing; $5000 wedding and engagement rings.
Miscellaneous and wildcard: Household pets, family portraits, arms and military accoutrements, musical instruments.
Waiver: Not specified in exemption statute.
***Benefits, retirement plans, insurance, judgments, and other intangibles*: La. Rev. Stat. Ann. § 13:3881.**
Public benefits: Not specified in exemption statute. *See* La. Rev. Stat. Ann. § 46:111 (public assistance exempt). Earned income tax refund.
Pensions, retirement plans and annuities: Pensions, tax-deferred arrangements (defined; includes IRAs, Roth IRA's specifically included, and SEPs), and annuities.
Insurance, judgments or other compensation for injury: Proceeds of any property insurance settlement received as a result of damage caused by a gubernatorially declared disaster to an asset exempt under this section, or held in an escrow account and identified as the proceeds of an exempt asset, is exempt to the same extent as the destroyed or damaged asset.
Bank accounts: Not specified in exemption statute.
Alimony, child support: Not specified in exemption statute.
Survival after payment or deposit: "Proceeds" of exempt pensions, tax-deferred arrangements and annuities are exempt.

MAINE

Has state opted out of federal bankruptcy exemptions? Yes. Me. Rev. Stat. Ann. tit. 14, § 4426.
Is opt out limited to residents or domiciliaries of the state? Not specified. Me. Rev. Stat. Ann. tit. 14, § 4426: "[A] debtor may exempt from property of the debtor's estate under [Title 11], only that property exempt under [11 U.S.C. § 522(b)(2)(A) and (B)]."
Do state's exemptions have extraterritorial application?
Homestead: Uncertain.
Personal property: Uncertain.
***Wages*: Me. Rev. Stat. Ann. tit. 9-A, §§ 5-105, 5-106; Me. Rev. Stat. Ann. tit. 19A, § 2356.**
Scope: Earnings of an individual.
Amount: For consumer credit transaction, maximum garnishment is lesser of 25% of weekly wages, or the amount by which wages exceed 40 times the federal minimum hourly wage. Disposable earnings are those left after legally required deductions.
Survival after payment/deposit: Not specified in garnishment statute.
Waiver: Not specified in garnishment statute.
***Homestead*: Me. Rev. Stat. Ann. tit. 14, § 4422(1).**
Amount: $35,000 in real or personal property used as residence or burial plot, subject to certain exceptions; $70,000 if debtor over 60 or has mental or physical disability that prevents him or her from working and lasts at least twelve months or results in death; $70,000 if minor dependent(s) of debtor have a principal place of residence with debtor. If debtor's interest in the property is held jointly with other person or persons, then the lesser of $35,000 or the debtor's fractional share of $70,000, or if debtor is over 60 or disabled, debtor's fractional share of $140,000. Increased exemptions for elderly or disabled do not apply to liens obtained prior to that provision's effective date, nor to tort judgments involving "other than ordinary negligence on the part of the debtor." Exemption does not protect property that has been fraudulently conveyed.
Procedural requirements: Not specified in exemption statute.
Special provisions: Proceeds from sale of exempt property remain exempt for six months from date of receipt.
Waiver: Not specified in exemption statute.
***Tangible personal property*: Me. Rev. Stat. Ann. tit. 14, §§ 4422(2)–(9), (11), (15), (16).** (Note that Maine's Domestic Relations Code, Me. Rev. Stat. Ann. tit. 19-A, § 2203, which allows seizure and sale of property for family support debts, has its own list of exemptions. It was originally scheduled to sunset on October 1, 1998, but the sunset provision was repealed in 1997 by 1997 Me. Laws ch. 669, § 4.)
Household goods: Household goods, not more than $200 per item; a cook stove, all heating equipment and various fuels; food and provisions for six months, all equipment necessary for harvesting food and material necessary to raise food for one growing season.
Motor vehicles: $5000.
Tools of trade: $5000; one fishing boat, not more than five tons. Farm equipment.
Clothing and jewelry: Clothing, not more than $200 per item; $750 in jewelry and a wedding and engagement ring.
Miscellaneous and wildcard: Books, animals, crops and musical instruments held for personal use but no more than $200 per individual item; health aids. $400 in any personal property and the unused residence exemption but not exceeding $6000 in any type of property that may be exempted as household goods, clothing, furniture or similar items, tools of trade, legal awards, or life insurance benefits.
Waiver: Not specified in exemption statute.
***Benefits, retirement plans, insurance, judgments, and other intangibles*: Me. Rev. Stat. Ann. tit. 14, §§ 4422(10), (11), (13), (14); Me. Rev. Stat. Ann. tit. 3, § 703.**
Public benefits: Social Security, veterans' benefits, unemployment, local public assistance, earned income tax credit or additional child credit. *See also* Me. Rev. Stat. Ann. tit. 22, §§ 3180 (aid to needy persons), 3766 (TANF).
Pensions, retirement plans and annuities: Certain pensions, retirement accounts and annuities, to the extent necessary for support.
Insurance, judgments or other compensation for injury: Property traceable to crime victim reparation, wrongful death judgment, personal injury judgment (up to $12,500), compensation for loss of future earnings. Unmatured life insurance contract; up to $4000 in accrued interest or loan value of life insurance; disability, illness or unemployment benefit.
Bank accounts: Not specified in exemptions statute.
Alimony, child support: Alimony, support or separate maintenance, to extent needed for support.
Survival after payment or deposit: Not specified in exemption statute.

MARYLAND

Has state opted out of federal bankruptcy exemptions? Yes. Md.

Code Ann., Cts. & Jud. Proc. § 11-504 (West).
Is opt out limited to residents or domiciliaries of the state? Not specified. Md. Code Ann., Cts. & Jud. Proc. § 11-504 (West): "In any bankruptcy proceeding, a debtor is not entitled to the federal exemptions provided by § 522(d) of the federal Bankruptcy Code."
Do state's exemptions have extraterritorial application?
Homestead: Yes. *See In re* Grimes, 18 B.R. 132 (Bankr. D. Md. 1982).
Personal property: Yes (exemption provision construed in *In re* Grimes, 18 B.R. 132 (Bankr. D. Md. 1982) also applicable to personal property).
***Wages*: Md. Code Ann., Com. Law § 15-601.1 (West).**
Scope: All monetary remuneration paid to any employee for his or her employment.
Amount: Caroline, Kent, Queen Anne's and Worcester counties follow the federal scheme; in all other counties, the greater of $145 times the number of weeks in which wages earned or 75% of disposable wages is exempt; any medical insurance payment deducted from wages is exempt.
Survival after payment/deposit: Not specified in exemption statute.
Waiver: Not specified in exemption statute.
***Homestead*: Md. Code Ann., Cts. & Jud. Proc. §§ 11-504, 11-507 (West).**
Amount: No explicit homestead exemption. $6000 wild card exemption, which may be applied to any type of property. In bankruptcy, additional $5000 in real or personal property. Both these exemptions are subject to certain liens.
Procedural requirements: None stated.
Special provisions: None stated.
Waiver: Not specified in exemption statute.
***Tangible personal property*: Md. Code Ann., Cts. & Jud. Proc. § 11-504 (West).**
Household goods: $1000 in goods held for family or household use. Additional $5000 in bankruptcy.
Motor vehicles: See *Miscellaneous and wildcard.*
Tools of trade: $5000.
Clothing and jewelry: See above, and *Miscellaneous and wildcard.*
Miscellaneous and wildcard: $6000 in money or property of any kind; health aids. Bankruptcy only: additional $5000 in real or personal property.
Waiver: Certain provisions (including the tangible property, and compensation for injury exemptions) may not be waived "by cognovit note or otherwise."
***Benefits, retirement plans, insurance, judgments, and other intangibles*: Md. Code Ann., Cts. & Jud. Proc. § 11-504 (West).**
Public benefits: Not specified in exemption statute. *See* Md. Code Ann. art. 88A, § 73 (assistance provided under state public assistance program is exempt).
Pensions, retirement plans and annuities: Certain tax qualified retirement plans, except as to claims of alternate payee under qualified domestic relations order.
Insurance, judgments or other compensation for injury: Money payable in the event of injury, sickness or death, or for loss of future earnings, including insurance, judgments, arbitration awards, compensation and relief.
Bank accounts: Not specified in exemption statute.
Alimony, child support: Child support paid or payable in accordance with agreement or court order; spousal support exempt to same extent as wages. Payments from retirement plan to alternate payee under qualified domestic relations order.
Survival after payment or deposit: Not specified in exemption statute.

MASSACHUSETTS

Has state opted out of federal bankruptcy exemptions? No.
Is opt out limited to residents or domiciliaries of the state? Not applicable.
Do state's exemptions have extraterritorial application?
Homestead: Uncertain. Note, however, that Mass. Gen. Laws ch. 188, § 2, requires that a declaration of homestead must be recorded in the registry of deeds for the county or district in which the property is situated or, if a manufactured home, in the city or town clerk's office in the city or town in which the manufactured home is located.
Personal property: Uncertain.
***Wages*: Mass. Gen. Laws ch. 246, § 28.**
Scope: Wages for personal labor or personal services.
Amount: $125 per week is exempt.
Survival after payment/deposit: Not specified in exemption statute.
Waiver: Not specified in exemption statute.
***Homestead*: Mass. Gen. Laws ch. 188, §§ 1, 1A, 4, 6, 7; Mass. Gen. Laws ch. 235, § 34(14).**
Amount: $500,000 in principal family residence; the exemption is not available for debts for taxes, debts arising prior to purchase of the homestead, judgment debts for support of spouse or children. Each debtor who is 62 or older, or disabled, may exempt $500,000 per individual, whether property is owned individually or jointly. These increased figures do not take priority over any lien, right, or interest recorded or filed prior to Nov. 2, 2000. For debtors not claiming an estate of homestead, up to $200 per month for rent.
Procedural requirements: Yes. Must file declaration of homestead. Does not protect against debts incurred before filing. Disabled debtor must file copy of SSI award letter, or physician's certificate stating that debtor meets SSI eligibility requirements, at time of filing homestead declaration.
Special provisions: The homestead estate survives the death of the declarant, for the benefit of a surviving spouse or minor children residing in the homestead.
Waiver: Sale of homestead property or release of homestead requires the signature of the owner and spouse, if any.
***Tangible personal property*: Mass. Gen. Laws ch. 235, § 34; Mass. Gen. Laws ch. 246, § 28.**
Household goods: Necessary clothes and beds, one heating unit, and up to $75 per month for utilities; $3000 in additional necessary household furniture.
Motor vehicles: One motor vehicle, worth up to $700, needed to maintain employment.
Tools of trade: $500.
Clothing and jewelry: See above.
Miscellaneous and wildcard: $200 books; various specified livestock, four tons of hay, $300 in provisions, one pew, military uniforms, one sewing machine not exceeding $200 in value.
Waiver: Not specified in exemption statute.
***Benefits, retirement plans, insurance, judgments, and other intangibles*: Mass. Gen. Laws ch. 246, §§ 28, 28A; Mass. Gen. Laws ch. 32, § 19; Mass. Gen. Laws ch. 235, §§ 34(15), 34A.**
Public benefits: Any sum of money which was received by or is owing to debtor as public assistance. *See also* Mass. Gen. Laws ch. 118, § 10.

Pensions, retirement plans and annuities: Certain pensions and retirement plans, including IRAs; rollovers explicitly covered. Note that sums in excess of 7% of owner's income, deposited within five years before bankruptcy filing or judgment, are not exempt. This exception does not apply to rollovers or transfers.
Insurance, judgments or other compensation for injury: Not specified in exemption statute.
Bank accounts: $100 in shares in a cooperative, $125 in cash and bank deposits on wages due plus an additional $500 in a bank deposit.
Alimony, child support: Not specified in exemption statute.
Survival after payment or deposit: Not specified in exemption statute.

MICHIGAN

Has state opted out of federal bankruptcy exemptions? No.
Is opt out limited to residents or domiciliaries of the state? Not applicable.
Do state's exemptions have extraterritorial application?
Homestead: Uncertain.
Personal property: Uncertain.
***Wages*: Mich. Comp. Laws § 600.5311.**
Scope: Wages.
Amount: Householders may exempt 60% of weekly wages, but not less than $15 per week, and an extra $2 per week per dependent other than a spouse. Other debtors may exempt 40% of weekly wages but not less than $10 per week.
Survival after payment/deposit: Not specified in exemption statute.
Waiver: Not specified in exemption statute.
***Homestead*: Mich. Const. art. X, § 3; Mich. Comp. Laws §§ 559.214, 600.6022 to 600.6024, 600.6027.**
Amount: $3500 not exceeding 40 acres rural or one lot inside city, town, or village, subject to certain liens; an equity of redemption as described in Mich. Comp. Laws § 600.6060. Condominiums occupied as residence explicitly included.
Procedural requirements: If homestead has not been platted and set apart, debtor may designate at time of levy.
Special provisions: After owner's death, exemption protects surviving spouse and minor children.
Waiver: Not specified in exemption statute.
***Tangible personal property*: Mich. Const. art. X, § 3; Mich. Comp. Laws § 600.6023.**
Household goods: $1000 household furniture, utensils, books and appliances; six months of provisions and fuel; certain farm animals; six months supply of feed; tools of trade; certain disability benefits and retirement accounts.
Motor vehicles: Not specified.
Tools of trade: $1000 tools, materials, stock, vehicle for principal business or profession; for householder, certain livestock and feed.
Clothing and jewelry: All clothing.
Miscellaneous and wildcard: All family pictures; all arms required by law to be kept; a pew.
Waiver: Not specified in exemption statute.
***Benefits, retirement plans, insurance, judgments, and other intangibles*: Mich. Comp. Laws § 600.6023.**
Public benefits: Not specified in exemption statute. *See* Mich. Comp. Laws § 400.63 (assistance provided under Social Welfare Act is exempt).
Pensions, retirement plans and annuities: Certain pensions and tax qualified plans, including rollovers (except as to contributions made on eve of bankruptcy, or claims for family support).
Insurance, judgments or other compensation for injury: Insurance benefits paid or payable for illness or disability.
Bank accounts: Householder may claim $1000 in savings and loan, if no homestead claimed.
Alimony, child support: Not specified in exemption statute.
Survival after payment or deposit: Not specified in exemption statute.

MINNESOTA

Has state opted out of federal bankruptcy exemptions? No.
Is opt out limited to residents or domiciliaries of the state? Not applicable.
Do state's exemptions have extraterritorial application?
Homestead: Yes. *See In re* Drenttel, 403 F.3d 611 (8th Cir. 2005).
Personal property: Not specified in exemption statute, but probably yes based on *In re* Drenttel, 403 F.3d 611 (8th Cir. 2005).
***Wages*: Minn. Stat. §§ 550.37(13), (14), (25), 550.136, 571.922.**
Scope: Compensation paid to an employee, who performs personal services for employer who may control both what is done and how it is done, whether called wages, salary, commission, bonus or otherwise, including periodic payments pursuant to pension or retirement plan; compensation for the sale of certain agricultural products from family farm; maintenance as defined in the domestic relations statutes.
Amount: Garnishment limited to lesser of 25% of disposable earnings or amount by which disposable earnings exceed 40 times federal minimum wage. Disposable earnings are those left after all deductions required by law. If the debtor has been a recipient of needs-based assistance, or an inmate of a correctional institution, no garnishment is permitted for six months after return to employment and termination of all public assistance. A separate provision completely exempts proceeds of payments received by a person for labor, skill, material, or machinery contributing to an improvement in real estate. Private right of action for employee terminated because of wage garnishment.
Survival after payment/deposit: Exempt wages remain exempt for 20 days following deposit in financial institution. Statute explicitly protects against banker's right of setoff, and provides for first-in first-out tracing of exempt funds.
Waiver: Not permitted.
***Homestead*: Minn. Stat. §§ 510.01, 510.02, 510.06, 510.07, 550.37(12).**
Amount: $750,000 for a farm, otherwise $300,000; home or house owned and occupied by debtor and land on which such house is situated but only a total of 160 acres outside a platted portion of a city or $\frac{1}{2}$ acre inside a city. Manufactured homes specifically included.
Procedural requirements: None stated. If homestead has not been set apart, it may be claimed at time of levy.
Special provisions: Proceeds exempt for one year. If home owner dies or deserts family, exemption continues to protect spouse and minor children.
Waiver: Not specified in exemption statute.
***Tangible personal property*: Minn. Stat. § 550.37.** (Note that all dollar amounts, except for farm implements and combined farm implements plus tools of trade are indexed, and fluctuate periodically; amounts are adjusted on July 1 of even numbered years.)

Household goods: $9000. Household furniture and appliances, including sound systems, radios and televisions.
Motor vehicles: $4000. If modified for disability, at a cost of no less than $3000: $40,000.
Tools of trade: Farm implements, $13,000. Tools of trade, $10,000. Aggregate of these two exemptions may not exceed $13,000.
Clothing and jewelry: All clothing and one watch. $2450 in aggregate interest in wedding rings or other religious or culturally recognized symbols of marriage exchanged by debtor and spouse at time of marriage, and in the debtor's possession.
Miscellaneous and wildcard: Books and musical instruments; pew and burial place.
Waiver: Household goods exemption may not be waived, except for purchase money security interest, or pawnbroker's possessory interest. Other exemptions may be waived by written waiver in prescribed form.
***Benefits, retirement plans, insurance, judgments, and other intangibles*: Minn. Stat. § 550.37.**
Public benefits: All relief based on need, and the earnings of any recipient, or anyone who has been a benefit recipient or an inmate of a correctional institution within the past six months.
Pensions, retirement plans and annuities: Certain pensions and retirement plans. Employee benefits, present value $60,000.
Insurance, judgments or other compensation for injury: All money arising from any claim for damage to or destruction of exempt property; life insurance proceeds from death of spouse or parent, up to $40,000 with additional $10,000 for each of survivor's dependents; $8000 in accrued interest or loan values of certain life insurance; certain benefits from fraternal associations; rights of action for personal injuries; life insurance accrued dividend or interest, $7600.
Bank accounts: Not specified (but note provisions exempting traceable exempt funds).
Alimony, child support: Not specified in exemption statute.
Survival after payment or deposit: Exemptions for public benefits, or the earnings of recipients, continue for 60 days after deposit in financial institution. First-in, first-out tracing. Other funds (for example, insurance, compensation for damage, and so forth) remain exempt so long as traceable by first-in, first-out method. Burden on debtor to show exempt source.

MISSISSIPPI

Has state opted out of federal bankruptcy exemptions? Yes. Miss. Code Ann. § 85-3-2.
Is opt out limited to residents or domiciliaries of the state? Yes. Miss. Code Ann. § 85-3-4: "[R]esidents of the State of Mississippi shall not be entitled to the federal exemptions . . . [in § 522(d)]."
Do state's exemptions have extraterritorial application?
Homestead: Uncertain.
Personal property: Uncertain.
***Wages*: Miss. Code Ann. § 85-3-4.**
Scope: Wages, salaries or other compensation of laborers or employees.
Amount: Exempt for thirty days after date of service of writ of attachment, execution or garnishment; thereafter similar to federal; $5000 federal tax refund; $5000 state tax refund.
Survival after payment/deposit: Not specified in exemption statute.
Waiver: Not specified in exemption statute.
***Homestead*: Miss. Code Ann. §§ 85-3-21 to 85-3-27, 85-3-1(d).**
Amount: Householder may claim $75,000 of 160 acres owned and occupied as a residence, subject to liens. $30,000 for mobile home used as debtor's residence.
Procedural requirements: Permitted but not required to record declaration of homestead. If this is not done, statute prescribes a formula for determining what land is homestead.
Special provisions: Proceeds of sale or insurance are exempt. Spouses, widows or widowers over 60 may claim exemption on former residence even if they no longer reside there.
Waiver: Not specified in exemption statute.
***Tangible personal property*: Miss. Code Ann. § 85-3-1.**
Household goods: Tangible personal property of the following kinds to a total value of $10,000: household goods (definition similar to that of FTC rule restricting non-possessory security interests), wearing apparel, books, animals or crops, motor vehicles, implements, professional books or tools of a trade, cash on hand, professionally prescribed health aids, and any item of personal property worth less than $200.
Motor vehicles: Included in $10,000 exemption above.
Tools of trade: Included in $10,000 exemption above.
Clothing and jewelry: Included in $10,000 exemption above.
Miscellaneous and wildcard: Included in $10,000 exemption above. Additional $50,000 wildcard exemption for debtors age 70 or older.
Waiver: Not specified in exemption statute.
***Benefits, retirement plans, insurance, judgments, and other intangibles*: Miss. Code Ann. §§ 85-3-1, 85-3-11 to 85-3-19.**
Public benefits: $5000 in earned income tax credit proceeds.
Pensions, retirement plans and annuities: Certain pensions and tax-qualified retirement plans.
Insurance, judgments or other compensation for injury: Sale or insurance proceeds of exempt property; income from disability insurance; certain life insurance proceeds (but not cash surrender or loan value of more than $50,000 resulting from payments or deposits within one year before writ issues); $10,000 personal injury judgments.
Bank accounts: Assets of health savings account.
Alimony, child support: Not specified in exemption statute.
Survival after payment or deposit: Not specified in exemption statute.

MISSOURI

Has state opted out of federal bankruptcy exemptions? Yes. Mo. Rev. Stat. § 513.427.
Is opt out limited to residents or domiciliaries of the state? Not specified. Mo. Rev. Stat. § 513.427: "Every person [seeking] relief under Title 11 . . ., shall be permitted to exempt from property of the estate any property that is exempt from attachment and execution under the law of the state of Missouri or under federal law, other than [§ 522(d)], and no such person is authorized to claim as exempt the property that is specified under [§ 522(d)]."
Do state's exemptions have extraterritorial application?
Homestead: Yes. *In re* Woodruff, 2005 WL 1139891 (Bankr. W.D. Mo. Apr. 28, 2005) (because Missouri exemption law is silent concerning extraterritorial application, and because Missouri's exemptions must be construed liberally, Missouri homestead could be claimed for Mississippi home).
Personal property: Not specified in exemption statute, but probably yes based on *In re* Woodruff, 2005 WL 1139891 (Bankr. W.D.

Mo. Apr. 28, 2005).

***Wages*: Mo. Rev. Stat. § 525.030.**

Scope: Aggregate earnings of an individual.

Amount: Garnishment limited to 10% for head of family; otherwise similar to federal.

Survival after payment/deposit: Not specified in exemption statute.

Waiver: Not specified in exemption statute.

***Homestead*: Mo. Rev. Stat. §§ 513.430(6), 513.475, 513.510.**

Amount: $15,000 in residence and land used in connection with it; exemption for multiple owners may not exceed, in aggregate, $15,000. Mobile home not on or attached to land in which debtor has a fee interest, used as residence and not exceeding $5000 in value is exempt.

Procedural requirements: None stated. Homestead is acquired when deed recorded (or in case of inheritance, when new owner acquires title).

Special provisions: Does not protect against debts that pre-date acquisition of homestead.

Waiver: Spouse must join in any sale or encumbrance.

***Tangible personal property*: Mo. Rev. Stat. §§ 513.430, 513.440.**

Household goods: $3000 in household goods and furnishings, wearing apparel, appliances, books, animals, crops or musical instruments.

Motor vehicles: $3000.

Tools of trade: $3000.

Clothing and jewelry: Clothing included in $1000 household goods exemption. Wedding ring, $1500, other jewelry, $500.

Miscellaneous and wildcard: $600 any property. Additional $1250 wildcard for head of family, plus $350 for each unmarried, dependent, minor child; may not be used to exempt the non-exempt 10% of wages. Professionally prescribed health aids.

Waiver: Not specified in exemption statute.

***Benefits, retirement plans, insurance, judgments, and other intangibles*: Mo. Rev. Stat. §§ 513.430, 513.440.**

Public benefits: Right to receive Social Security, veterans' benefits, unemployment, local public assistance.

Pensions, retirement plans and annuities: Any payment under certain public and private employee benefit plans; money payable to a participant in certain retirement plans, except as to the claims of an alternate payee under a qualified domestic relations order.

Insurance, judgments or other compensation for injury: Unmatured life insurance contracts; accrued dividends and loan values of certain life insurance (in bankruptcy, $150,000 limit); right to receive disability, illness or unemployment benefit. Right to receive, or property traceable to, wrongful death judgment for person on whom debtor was dependent, so far as needed for support.

Bank accounts: Not specified in exemption statute.

Alimony, child support: Right to receive alimony, support or separate maintenance, up to $750 per month. Payments from pension plan to alternative payee under qualified domestic relations order are exempt.

Survival after payment or deposit: Not specified in exemption statute, but note that some exemptions refer to "right to receive" and others to "payments under" or "traceable to."

MONTANA

Has state opted out of federal bankruptcy exemptions? Yes. Mont. Code Ann. § 31-2-106.

Is opt out limited to residents or domiciliaries of the state? Not specified. Mont. Code Ann. § 31-2-106: "An individual may not exempt from the property of the estate in any bankruptcy proceeding the property specified in [§ 522(d)]."

Do state's exemptions have extraterritorial application?

Homestead: Uncertain.

Personal property: Uncertain.

***Wages*: Mont. Code Ann. §§ 25-13-601, 25-13-610, 25-13-614.**

Scope: Same as federal.

Amount: Similar to federal.

Survival after payment/deposit: Yes. Exempt for 45 days after receipt, if traceable by first-in, first-out or "any other reasonable basis for tracing."

Waiver: Waiver of exemptions in unsecured promissory note is unenforceable.

***Homestead*: Mont. Code Ann. §§ 70-32-101 to 70-32-107, 70-32-202, 70-32-216.**

Amount: $250,000 in dwelling house or mobile home and land thereunder. Claimant who owns undivided interest in property is limited to an exemption proportional to claimant's interest.

Procedural requirements: Declaration of homestead must be recorded. But it appears that homestead is protected against debts that precede recording, except mortgages and certain other liens. The main effect of recording a homestead declaration appears to be to require a spouse's signature on any sale or encumbrance thereafter.

Special provisions: Proceeds are exempt for eighteen months following sale, condemnation or destruction of the property.

Waiver: If homestead declaration has been recorded, spouse must join in any sale or encumbrance.

***Tangible personal property*: Mont. Code Ann. §§ 25-13-601, 25-13-608, 25-13-609, 25-13-613.**

Household goods: $600 per item, or $4500 in the aggregate in furniture, appliances, jewelry, wearing apparel, books, firearms and other sporting goods, animals, feed, crops and musical instruments.

Motor vehicles: $2500.

Tools of trade: $3000.

Clothing and jewelry: Included in $4500 household goods exemption.

Miscellaneous and wildcard: Health aids, burial place, property used to carry out government functions.

Waiver: Waiver of exemptions in unsecured promissory note is unenforceable.

***Benefits, retirement plans, insurance, judgments, and other intangibles*: Mont. Code Ann. §§ 25-13-608 to 25-13-610, 25-13-613.**

Public benefits: Social Security, veterans', or local public assistance benefits that debtor has received or is entitled to receive.

Pensions, retirement plans and annuities: Certain public or private pensions or tax-qualified IRAs.

Insurance, judgments or other compensation for injury: Disability or illness benefits; benefits paid for medical, surgical or hospital care, to the extent they are used or will be used to pay for the care; unmatured life insurance policies.

Bank accounts: Shares in certain cooperative associations having up to $500 par value.

Alimony, child support: Maintenance and child support.

Survival after payment or deposit: Proceeds of sale or indemnification for loss of exempt property remain exempt for six months if traceable (that is, first in, first out from bank account). Note that the exemption for certain benefits refers to payments debtor has received or is entitled to receive.

NEBRASKA

Has state opted out of federal bankruptcy exemptions? Yes. Neb. Rev. Stat. § 25-15,105.
Is opt out limited to residents or domiciliaries of the state? Not specified, but may be limited to cases filed in Nebraska. Neb. Rev. Stat. § 25-15,105: "The federal exemptions provided in [§ 522(d)], are hereby rejected by . . . Nebraska. [The Nebraska personal exemptions] apply to any bankruptcy petition filed in Nebraska after April 17, 1980."
Do state's exemptions have extraterritorial application?
Homestead: Uncertain.
Personal property: Uncertain.
***Wages*: Neb. Rev. Stat. § 25-1558, 25-1560 to 25-1563.**
Scope: Earnings paid or payable by an employer to an employee for personal services, whether called wages, salary, commission, bonus or otherwise, including periodic payments from pension or retirement program.
Amount: Head of family, 85% of disposable earnings exempt except for support obligations. Head of family is defined as anyone who actually supports and maintains one or more individuals related to him or her by blood, marriage, adoption or guardianship and whose right to exercise family control and provide for the dependent(s) is based on some moral or legal obligation. All others, similar to federal.
Survival after payment/deposit: Wages appear to be exempt for 60 days under Neb. Rev. Stat. § 25-1560.
Waiver: Assignment, transfer, mortgage or pledge of exempt wages or salary is void and unenforceable.
***Homestead*: Neb. Rev. Stat. §§ 40-101 to 40-103, 40-111 to 40-113, 40-115, 40-116.**
Amount: $60,000 in a dwelling located on up to 160 acres if not in city or village or two contiguous lots if in city or village; available only to heads of households, defined as married persons, surviving spouses, or anyone with a dependent residing with him or her.
Procedural requirements: None stated. May be claimed after judgment, anytime before confirmation of sale.
Special provisions: Proceeds of involuntary sale of homestead are exempt for six months to the same extent as the homestead.
Waiver: Spouse must join in any conveyance or encumbrance.
***Tangible personal property*: Neb. Rev. Stat. §§ 25-1552, 25-1556.**
Household goods: Immediate personal possessions of debtor and family; $1500 household goods, appliances, computers, books and musical instruments.
Motor vehicles: Tools of trade exemption applies to motor vehicle used for work or for commuting.
Tools of trade: $2400.
Clothing and jewelry: All necessary clothing.
Miscellaneous and wildcard: $2500 any personal property except wages. Professionally prescribed health aids.
Waiver: Not specified in exemption statute.
***Benefits, retirement plans, insurance, judgments, and other intangibles*: Neb. Rev. Stat. §§ 25-1552, 25-1553, 25-1556, 25-1559, 25-1563.01, 25-1563.02.**
Public benefits: Not specified in exemption statute. *See* Neb. Rev. Stat. §§ 68-148 (general assistance), 68-1013 (aid to aged, blind, disabled, dependent children, medical assistance). Full amount of any federal or state earned income credit tax refund.
Pensions, retirement plans and annuities: Military disability pensions, and $2000 in property purchased or improved with funds therefrom; certain employee benefits and individual retirement plans, so far as needed for support.
Insurance, judgments or other compensation for injury: Compensation for personal injury or death, whether lump sum or structured settlement, including interest.
Bank accounts: Not specified in exemption statute.
Alimony, child support: Not specified in exemption statute.
Survival after payment or deposit: Note exemption for property traceable to military disability pension.

NEVADA

Has state opted out of federal bankruptcy exemptions? Yes. Nev. Rev. Stat. § 21.090.
Is opt out limited to residents or domiciliaries of the state? Yes. Nev. Rev. Stat. § 21.090: "Any exemptions specified in [§ 522(d)], do not apply to property owned by a resident of this State. . . ."
Do state's exemptions have extraterritorial application?
Homestead: Uncertain.
Personal property: Uncertain.
***Wages*: Nev. Rev. Stat. §§ 21.090, 31.295 to 31.298.**
Scope: Earnings.
Amount: Garnishment may not exceed the lesser of 25% of disposable earnings for the workweek or the amount by which disposable earnings that week exceed 50 times the federal minimum wage.
Survival after payment/deposit: Yes. Earnings are defined to include compensation received by the judgment debtor, in the possession of the judgment debtor, held in accounts in a bank or any other financial institution, or, in the case of a receivable, compensation that is due the judgment debtor.
Waiver: Not specified in garnishment statute.
***Homestead*: Nev. Rev. Stat. §§ 21.090, 21.095, 115.005, 115.010, 115.040.**
Amount: $550,000 in either land and a dwelling or a mobile home, subject to certain liens; land held in spendthrift trust for debtor is exempt. Unlimited exemption if "allodial title" has been established. (Nevada residents can acquire "allodial title" to their land by buying out the property tax right from the government. Then the landowner does not have to pay property tax on the land.) The primary dwelling, including a mobile home, and land may not be executed upon for a medical bill during the lifetime of the debtor, debtor's spouse, a joint tenant who was a joint tenant at the time judgment was entered, or debtor's disabled dependent adult child, or during the minority of any child of debtor. A 2007 amendment added an exemption for sums reasonably deposited with a landlord, to secure the rental or lease of debtor's primary residence (except not exempt as to landlord's claims for rent).
Procedural requirements: Procedure available for filing declaration of homestead. Exemption available even without declaration. Once declaration is filed, spouse must join in any encumbrance or sale.
Special provisions: None specified.
Waiver: Spouse must join in conveyance or encumbrance of declared homestead.
***Tangible personal property*: Nev. Rev. Stat. §§ 21.080, 21.090, 21.100.**
Household goods: $12,000 necessary household goods, furnish-

ings, electronics, wearing apparel, other personal effects and yard equipment.
Motor vehicles: $15,000, no limit if specially equipped for disabled debtor or dependent.
Tools of trade: $10,000 tools of trade; $4500 mining equipment; $4500 farm equipment.
Clothing and jewelry: Jewelry is included in the $5000 wildcard exemption.
Miscellaneous and wildcard: $5000 in private library, works of art, musical instruments and jewelry, all family pictures and keepsakes; health aids; property held in a spendthrift trust; uniforms debtor is legally required to keep, one gun, a collection of metal bearing ores, geological specimens, art curiosities or paleontological remains if the debtor catalogues them and the catalogue is kept near the collection for the free inspection of all visitors; coin collections are not exempt. $1000 in any property, including accounts in a financial institution.
Waiver: Not specified in exemption statute.
***Benefits, retirement plans, insurance, judgments, and other intangibles*: Nev. Rev. Stat. §§ 21.080, 21.090, 21.100.**
Public benefits: Social Security benefits, including without limitation, retirement, survivors, SSI and disability. *See* Nev. Rev. Stat. § 422.291 (assistance awarded pursuant to public welfare administration laws is exempt). Earned income credit or any similar credit pursuant to state law.
Pensions, retirement plans and annuities: Up to $500,000 (present value) in tax-qualified retirement plan.
Insurance, judgments or other compensation for injury: Money or benefits in any manner growing out of life insurance, if premium not more than $15,000 per year (for higher premium, the proportion that $15,000 bears to the premium paid); $16,500 personal injury judgment; wrongful death judgment for person on whom debtor was dependent; compensation for loss of future earnings of debtor or person on whom debtor was dependent, so far as needed for support; criminal restitution.
Bank accounts: Not specified in exemption statute.
Alimony, child support: Court-ordered family support.
Survival after payment or deposit: Not specified in exemption statute.

NEW HAMPSHIRE

Has state opted out of federal bankruptcy exemptions? No.
Is opt out limited to residents or domiciliaries of the state? Not applicable.
Do state's exemptions have extraterritorial application?
Homestead: Yes. *See In re* Weza, 248 B.R. 470 (Bankr. D.N.H. 2000) (New Hampshire homestead may be claimed for property outside state because homestead statute does not limit exemption to property located in New Hampshire; homestead denied, however, because debtor did not currently reside on property).
Personal property: Not specified in exemption statute, but probably yes based on *In re* Weza, 248 B.R. 470 (Bankr. D.N.H. 2000).
***Wages*: N.H. Rev. Stat. Ann. §§ 161-C:11, 512:21.**
Scope: Wages.
Amount: Fifty times federal minimum wage is exempt.
Survival after payment/deposit: Not specified in exemption statute.
Waiver: Not specified in exemption statute.
***Homestead*: N.H. Rev. Stat. Ann. §§ 480:1, 480:3-a, 480:4, 480:5-a, 480:9.**
Amount: $100,000. Manufactured housing explicitly included (but not the underlying land, if owned by another).
Procedural requirements: Procedure available for establishing homestead, but apparently not prerequisite to existence of exemption.
Special provisions: Exemption not lost by conveyance to revocable trust. Homestead right protects surviving spouse.
Waiver: Spouse must join in conveyance or encumbrance, with formalities used for conveyance of land.
***Tangible personal property*: N.H. Rev. Stat. Ann. § 511:2.**
Household goods: $3500 household furniture; beds and bedding; stove, utensils, refrigerator, heating unit; sewing machine; $400 provisions and fuel.
Motor vehicles: $4000.
Tools of trade: $5000.
Clothing and jewelry: Necessary clothing; $500 jewelry.
Miscellaneous and wildcard: Wild card exemption of $1000 plus up to $7000 from unused exemptions for furniture, provisions and fuel, library, tools of trade, motor vehicle and jewelry. Burial place; militia uniforms and arms; $800 in books; various livestock; a meeting-house pew.
Waiver: Not specified in exemption statute.
***Benefits, retirement plans, insurance, judgments, and other intangibles*: N.H. Rev. Stat. Ann. §§ 511:2, 512:21; *see* N.H. Rev. Stat. Ann. §§ 100-A:26, 102:23.**
Public benefits: Not specified in exemption statute. *See* N.H. Rev. Stat. Ann. § 167:25 (public assistance to blind, aged, disabled persons or dependent children is exempt).
Pensions, retirement plans and annuities: Federal pension or bounty funds before payment to debtor; certain tax-qualified retirement plans.
Insurance, judgments or other compensation for injury: Damages for the conversion of exempt property; certain insurance proceeds while in the hands of insurance company.
Bank accounts: Not specified in exemption statute.
Alimony, child support: Not specified in exemption statute.
Survival after payment or deposit: Not specified in exemption statute, but note restrictive language in insurance and military pensions exemptions.

NEW JERSEY

Has state opted out of federal bankruptcy exemptions? No.
Is opt out limited to residents or domiciliaries of the state? Not applicable.
Do state's exemptions have extraterritorial application?
Homestead: No exemption.
Personal property: Uncertain.
***Wages*: N.J. Stat. Ann. §§ 2A:17-50, 2A:17-56, 2A:17-56.9, 2A:17-56.12 (West).**
Scope: Wages, debts, salary, income from trust funds, or profits, due and owing or to become due and owing.
Amount: $48/week is exempt. 90% exempt if debtor's income does not exceed 250% of the poverty level. Employer who discharges employee because of family support garnishment commits disorderly person offense and employee has private right of action for wrongful discharge. For a debt owing to the state, 25% of gross earnings may be garnished, if after the execution debtor's income will not be less than 250% of poverty level.
Survival after payment/deposit: Not specified, but note "due and

owing" language.
Waiver: Not specified in exemption statute.
***Homestead*:** None.
Amount: Not applicable.
Procedural requirements: Not applicable.
Special provisions: Not applicable.
Waiver: Not applicable.
***Tangible personal property*: N.J. Stat. Ann. §§ 2A:17-19, 2A:26-4, 38A:4-8 (West).**
Household goods: $1000 household goods and furniture.
Motor vehicles: Not specified.
Tools of trade: Not specified.
Clothing and jewelry: All necessary clothing.
Miscellaneous and wildcard: $1000 all personal property except clothing. Pay and other benefits due as a result of participation in the state militia.
Waiver: Not specified in exemption statute.
***Benefits, retirement plans, insurance, judgments, and other intangibles*:**
Public benefits: Not specified in exemption statute.
Pensions, retirement plans and annuities: Not specified in exemption statute.
Insurance, judgments or other compensation for injury: Not specified in exemption statute.
Bank accounts: Not specified in exemption statute.
Alimony, child support: Not specified in exemption statute.
Survival after payment or deposit: Not specified in exemption statute.

NEW MEXICO

Has state opted out of federal bankruptcy exemptions? No.
Is opt out limited to residents or domiciliaries of the state? Not applicable.
Do state's exemptions have extraterritorial application?
Homestead: Uncertain.
Personal property: Uncertain.
***Wages*: N.M. Stat. § 35-12-7.**
Scope: Disposable earnings.
Amount: Greater of 75% of disposable earnings or 40 times minimum wage is exempt. Disposable earnings are those left after legally required deductions.
Survival after payment/deposit: Not specified in garnishment statute.
Waiver: Not specified in garnishment statute.
***Homestead*: N.M. Stat. §§ 42-10-9, 42-10-11.**
Amount: $60,000 in land or a dwelling if debtor owns, leases, or purchases the dwelling. Subject to certain liens. If property is jointly owned by two persons, each is entitled to a $60,000 exemption.
Procedural requirements: None specified.
Special provisions: None specified.
Waiver: Not specified in exemption statute.
***Tangible personal property*: N.M. Stat. §§ 42-10-1, 42-10-2, 42-10-10, 53-4-28, 53-10-2.**
Household goods: Furniture and books.
Motor vehicles: $4000.
Tools of trade: $1500.
Clothing and jewelry: Clothing; $2500 jewelry.
Miscellaneous and wildcard: $500 in personal property; married debtors or heads of households may take $500 in cash instead of the personal property; a resident without a homestead may exempt $5000 in real or personal property; health aids; the minimum amount of shares necessary for membership in certain cooperative associations; debtor's interest in the property of an unincorporated association.
Waiver: Not specified in exemption statute.
***Benefits, retirement plans, insurance, judgments, and other intangibles*: N.M. Stat. §§ 42-10-1 to 42-10-5.**
Public benefits: Not specified in exemption statute. *See* N.M. Stat. § 27-2-21 (assistance granted under Public Assistance Act is exempt).
Pensions, retirement plans and annuities: Interests in or proceeds from pension or retirement fund.
Insurance, judgments or other compensation for injury: Cash surrender value of, and payments from accident, health and life insurance and certain annuities, exempt as to debts of both insured and beneficiary; life insurance proceeds exempt as to debts of deceased. Up to $5000 in benefits from benevolent association, as to debts of association member but not recipient.
Bank accounts: Not specified in exemption statute.
Alimony, child support: Not specified in exemption statute.
Survival after payment or deposit: Not specified in exemption statute, but note language regarding retirement plans and insurance.

NEW YORK

Has state opted out of federal bankruptcy exemptions? Yes. N.Y. Debt. & Cred. Law §§ 282, 284 (McKinney).
Is opt out limited to residents or domiciliaries of the state? Yes. N.Y. Debt. & Cred. Law § 282 (McKinney): "[A]n individual debtor domiciled in this state may exempt only [property specified in this statute]."
Do state's exemptions have extraterritorial application?
Homestead: No. *See In re* Crandall, 346 B.R. 220 (Bankr. M.D. Fla. 2006).
Personal property: No. *See In re* Crandall, 346 B.R. 220 (Bankr. M.D. Fla. 2006).

***Wages*: N.Y. C.P.L.R. 5205(d), (e), 5252, 5241 (McKinney); N.Y. Soc. Serv. Law § 137-a (McKinney).**
Scope: Earnings for personal services.
Amount: 90% of earnings rendered 60 days before or any time after delivery of execution to the sheriff or a motion to apply the debtor's earnings to a judgment is exempt; wages received in addition to public assistance are exempt. Garnishment forbidden if debtor is receiving public assistance or would qualify for public assistance if the amount of the garnishment were subtracted from his or her wages. The pay of enlisted personnel and non-commissioned officers in the military is completely exempt, except for family support debts. Employer may not discipline or refuse to hire employee because of wage execution. Private right of action for six weeks lost wages, civil penalty of $500 ($1000 for repeat offense), court may order reinstatement or hiring. Private right of action if employer withholds income after being formally notified by social services official that worker is receiving or eligible for aid.
Survival after payment/deposit: Not specified in exemption statute.
Waiver: Not specified in exemption statute.
***Homestead*: N.Y. C.P.L.R. 5206 (McKinney).**

Amount: $50,000 in the following types of property owned as a principal residence: a lot with a dwelling, a cooperative apartment, a condominium, or a mobile home, unless the judgment was recovered wholly for the purchase price. Security deposit for rental of residence and utility deposits for residence are also exempt.
Procedural requirements: None specified in exemption statute.
Special provisions: Proceeds from a judgment sale are exempt for one year. Protection continues after owner's death, to protect surviving spouse or minor children. Exemption lost if premises not used as residence, except for up to one year absence if homestead is damaged or destroyed.
Waiver: Not specified in exemption statute.
***Tangible personal property*: N.Y. C.P.L.R. 5205 (McKinney); N.Y. Debt. & Cred. Law §§ 282, 283(1) (McKinney).**
Household goods: All stoves and fuel for sixty days; one sewing machine; the family Bible; family pictures, family pew; domestic animals and feed for 60 days to a value of $450; a sixty-day supply of food for the debtor and family; all wearing apparel; household furniture, one refrigerator, one radio, one television, necessary tableware and cooking utensils; wedding ring; necessary working tools not exceeding $600. $5000 aggregate cap when exempting personal property from a bankruptcy estate.
Motor vehicles: $2400 in one vehicle. Bankruptcy only.
Tools of trade: $600 (included in aggregate $5000 above).
Clothing and jewelry: Included in aggregate $5000 above.
Miscellaneous and wildcard: 90% of any unpaid proceeds from the sale of milk if the debtor is a farmer; security deposits; health aids and guide dogs; residential rental or utility security deposits.
Waiver: Not specified in exemption statute.
***Benefits, retirement plans, insurance, judgments, and other intangibles*: N.Y. C.P.L.R. 5205 (McKinney); N.Y. Debt. & Cred. Law §§ 282, 283(1) (McKinney).**
Public benefits: Non-bankruptcy: Note provisions above, forbidding garnishment. Bankruptcy: Right to receive Social Security, unemployment, veterans' benefits, local public assistance.
Pensions, retirement plans and annuities: Any property held in trust for debtor and 90% of income from such trusts—this includes certain retirement plans. Note that there are separate provisions for retirement accounts in bankruptcy exemptions.
Insurance, judgments or other compensation for injury: Judgment for loss or destruction of exempt property remains exempt for one year after judgment is satisfied; certain life insurance, including right to accelerate payment or enter into viatical settlement as provided for in insurance law. In bankruptcy, may also exempt right to receive disability, illness or unemployment benefits, crime victim reparations, wrongful death to extent necessary for support, $7500 personal injury (not including pain and suffering or actual pecuniary loss), loss of future earnings to extent needed for support.
Bank accounts: Funds in a college choice tuition savings program trust fund are fully exempt as to the designated beneficiary, if a minor, and $10,000 is exempt as to the account owner. Additional exemption in bankruptcy for the lesser of $2500 or the amount of certain unused exemptions.
Alimony, child support: Court-ordered family support, to the extent needed for support (this determination to be made by court that made support order).
Survival after payment or deposit: Not specified in exemptions statute.

NORTH CAROLINA

Has state opted out of federal bankruptcy exemptions? Yes. N.C. Gen. Stat. § 1C-1601(f).
Is opt out limited to residents or domiciliaries of the state? Yes. N.C. Gen. Stat. § 1C-1601(f): "The exemptions provided in [§ 522(d)], are not applicable to residents of this State. The exemptions provided by this Article and by other statutory or common law of this State shall apply for purposes of [§ 522(b)]."
Do state's exemptions have extraterritorial application?
Homestead: No. *See In re* Owings, 140 F. 739 (E.D.N.C. 1905).
Personal property: Uncertain.
***Wages*: N.C. Gen. Stat. § 1-362.**
Scope: Earnings for personal services within 60 days before date of court order.
Amount: Exempt to the extent needed for family support.
Survival after payment/deposit: Not specified in exemption statute.
Waiver: Not specified in exemption statute.
***Homestead*: N.C. Const. art. X, § 2; N.C. Gen. Stat §§ 1C-1601(a)(1), (e).**
Amount: $18,500 (for unmarried debtor over age 65, who formerly owned the property in tenancy by entireties or joint tenancy with person now deceased, $37,000) in residence consisting of real or personal property, including a cooperative, subject to certain liens and support claims.
Procedural requirements: None specified in exemption statute.
Special provisions: Exemption survives for the benefit of minor children and unremarried spouse. Sale or encumbrance of homestead requires signatures of both spouses.
Waiver: Exemptions may not be waived before judgment, except by transfer of the property concerned. Waiver after judgment must be in writing and approved by court clerk or judge. May also be waived by failure to claim, after being notified to do so.[4]
***Tangible personal property*: N.C. Gen. Stat. § 1C-1601.**
Household goods: $5000 for debtor plus $1000 per dependent up to an additional $4000. Includes furniture, books, musical instruments, clothing, animals, crops.
Motor vehicles: $3500.
Tools of trade: $2000.
Clothing and jewelry: Clothing included in household goods exemption, above.
Miscellaneous and wildcard: Unused homestead exemption, up to $5000. Professionally prescribed health aids.
Waiver: Exemptions may not be waived before judgment, except by transfer of the property concerned. Waiver after judgment must be in writing and approved by court clerk or judge. May also be waived by failure to claim, after being notified to do so. Exemptions will apply to household goods, notwithstanding any non-purchase money security interest. No exemption for tangible property purchased within 90 days before initiation of collection proceedings or filing of bankruptcy, unless the property was purchased solely with the proceeds of exempt property.
***Benefits, retirement plans, insurance, judgments, and other intangibles*: N.C. Const. art. X, § 5; N.C. Gen. Stat. § 1C-1601.**
Public benefits: Not specified in exemption statute.

4 *But see* Household Fin. Co. v. Ellis, 107 N.C. App. 262, 419 S.E.2d 592 (1992) (section is unconstitutional if it attempts to limit the claiming of constitutional exemptions to twenty days, after notice to designate is served), *aff'd*, 333 N.C. 786 (1993) (per curiam).

Pensions, retirement plans and annuities: Certain tax-qualified retirement plans.
Insurance, judgments or other compensation for injury: Life insurance for the benefit of spouse or children is exempt as to debts of the insured. Compensation for personal injury of debtor or person on whom debtor dependent, or wrongful death of person on whom debtor dependent (except as to claims for medical, legal, funeral, or other services arising from the accident that gave rise to the claim).
Bank accounts: Tax-qualified college savings account, cumulative limit of $25,000. Does not apply to payments within preceding 12 months, unless these were consistent with past pattern of contributions.
Alimony, child support: Alimony and separate maintenance to the extent needed for support of debtor and dependants.
Survival after payment or deposit: Not specified in exemption statute.

NORTH DAKOTA

Has state opted out of federal bankruptcy exemptions? Yes. N.D. Cent. Code § 28-22-17.
Is opt out limited to residents or domiciliaries of the state? Yes. N.D. Cent. Code § 28-22-17: "[R]esidents of this state are not entitled to the federal exemptions provided in [§ 522(d)]. The residents of this state are limited to claiming those exemptions allowable by North Dakota law."
Do state's exemptions have extraterritorial application?
Homestead: Uncertain.
Personal property: Uncertain. Note, however, that certain additional exemptions provided pursuant to N.D. Cent. Code § 28-22-03.1, including motor vehicle and wildcard ("in lieu of homestead") are available only to "resident[s] of this state."
***Wages*: N.D. Cent. Code §§ 28-25-11, 32-09.1-03.**
Scope: Compensation paid or payable for personal services, whether called wages, salary, commission, bonus or otherwise, including military retirement pay, or periodic payments pursuant to a pension or retirement program. Does not include Social Security benefits, or veterans' disability (except for child support garnishment).
Amount: Greater of 75% of disposable earnings or forty times federal minimum wage is exempt with an additional $20 for each dependent living with debtor; earnings for personal services received within sixty days preceding order are totally exempt if debtor can show earnings are necessary for use of a family supported in whole or in part by debtor. Disposable earnings are those left after legally required deductions.
Survival after payment/deposit: Not specified in garnishment statute.
Waiver: Not specified in garnishment statute.
***Homestead*: N.D. Cent. Code §§ 28-22-02, 28-22-03.1(1), 47-18-01, 47-18-04, 47-18-14, 47-18-16.**
Amount: $80,000 in land and dwelling but lots must be contiguous; or a house trailer or mobile home occupied as a residence; exemption subject to certain liens.
Procedural requirements: Procedure available for filing declaration of homestead, but homestead right not impaired by failure to do so.
Special provisions: Sales or insurance proceeds are exempt.
Waiver: Spouse must join in any conveyance or encumbrance.
***Tangible personal property*: N.D. Cent. Code §§ 28-22-01 to 28-22-05.**
Household goods: Fuel and provisions for one year. Head of family may exempt $1000 household and kitchen furniture.
Motor vehicles: $1200, or $32,000 if modified at cost of not less than $1500 to accommodate owner with permanent disability.
Tools of trade: Head of family may exempt $1000 tools of trade, $4500 farming implements and stock, and crops and grain from 160 acres of land occupied by debtor, either as tenant or owner but this exemption subject to certain liens.
Clothing and jewelry: All clothing.
Miscellaneous and wildcard: $7500 in lieu of homestead. Wildcard $2500 for single person, $5000 for head of family, that is, married person or one who resides with certain dependents. Head of family may choose either the wildcard, or the listed head of family exemptions above, and $1500 in books and musical instruments. All family pictures, a pew, $100 in family library.
Waiver: Not specified in exemption statute.
***Benefits, retirement plans, insurance, judgments, and other intangibles*: N.D. Cent. Code §§ 28-22-03.1, 28-22-19.**
Public benefits: Social Security, veterans' disability, aid to dependent children, crime victims' compensation.
Pensions, retirement plans and annuities: Certain pensions and retirement plans, up to $200,000 (more if needed for support).
Insurance, judgments or other compensation for injury: Insurance proceeds of certain exempt property totally exempt. Certain life insurance and annuities payable to spouse or dependent. Right to receive, or property traceable to, compensation for wrongful death of person on whom debtor dependent, $15,000; personal injury to debtor or one on whom debtor dependent (excluding pain and suffering and actual pecuniary loss), $15,000.
Bank accounts: Not specified in exemption statute.
Alimony, child support: Not specified in exemption statute.
Survival after payment or deposit: Apparently yes. Statute lists benefits "paid or payable" or "amounts received from" or "funds traceable to" various benefits; note also language regarding "property traceable to" wrongful death or personal injury compensation.

OHIO

Has state opted out of federal bankruptcy exemptions? Yes. Ohio Rev. Code Ann. § 2329.662 (West).
Is opt out limited to residents or domiciliaries of the state? Yes. Ohio Rev. Code Ann. § 2329.662 (West): "[T]his state specifically does not authorize debtors who are domiciled in this state to exempt the property specified in [§ 522(d)]."
Do state's exemptions have extraterritorial application?
Homestead: No. Ohio Rev. Code Ann. § 2329.66 (West) applies to "every person who is domiciled in this state."
Personal property: No. Ohio Rev. Code Ann. § 2329.66 (West) applies to "every person who is domiciled in this state." *See also* Pallante v. Int'l Venture Investments, Ltd., 622 F. Supp. 667 (N.D. Ohio 1985) (domiciliary of Louisiana may not exempt wages under Ohio exemption statute).
***Wages*: Ohio Rev. Code Ann. §§ 2329.66(A)(13), 2329.661 (West).**
Scope: Personal earnings.
Amount: Similar to federal exemptions. Disposable earnings are those left after legally required deductions.
Survival after payment/deposit: Not specified in exemption statute.
Waiver: Forbidden.

***Homestead*: Ohio Rev. Code Ann. §§ 2329.66(A)(1)(b), 2329.661 (West).**
Amount: $5000 in one parcel of real or personal property used by debtor or dependent as residence, subject to certain liens. For debts for health care services or supplies, the exemption has no dollar limit; this does not preclude the creation of a lien, which may be enforced only when property is sold or otherwise transferred to someone other than a surviving spouse or surviving minor child of debtor.
Procedural requirements: Not specified in exemption statute.
Special provisions: Not specified in exemption statute.
Waiver: Forbidden. Any promise, agreement, or contract that waives the exemption laws of the state is void insofar as it seeks to waive the exemptions.
***Tangible personal property*: Ohio Rev. Code Ann. § 2329.66, 2329.661 (West).**
Household goods: Up to $200 per item in all beds and bedding, up to $300 per item in one cooking unit and one refrigerator or similar unit, up to $200 per item in household goods and jewelry; but one item of jewelry in which debtor has a $400 interest may also be exempted; debtors exempting a homestead may only exempt a total of $1500 in cash, household items, exclusive of cooking unit and refrigerator, and jewelry; debtors not utilizing homestead exemption may exempt a total of $2000 in such items.
Motor vehicles: $1000.
Tools of trade: $750.
Clothing and jewelry: Up to $200 per item in clothing and jewelry, and one piece of jewelry up to $400 (clothing and jewelry are included in $1500 or $2000 caps above, under household goods).
Miscellaneous and wildcard: $400; health aids; notary's seal and official register.
Waiver: Forbidden.
***Benefits, retirement plans, insurance, judgments, and other intangibles*: Ohio Rev. Code Ann. §§ 2329.66, 2329.661, 3334.09, 3334.15 (West).**
Public benefits: Unemployment, workers' compensation, Work First, disability assistance, certain other public benefits.
Pensions, retirement plans and annuities: Certain public and private pensions and retirement plans.
Insurance, judgments or other compensation for injury: Certain life insurance, annuities and group insurance; certain benefits from fraternal organizations; payments from health and disability insurance; wrongful death compensation, for person on whom debtor was dependent so far as needed for support; $5000 personal injury compensation; compensation for loss of future earnings.
Bank accounts: An interest in a tuition credit or a payment subject to a tuition credit contract. Bankruptcy only: $400 in cash, money due or to become due within 90 days, tax refunds, or bank deposits.
Alimony, child support: Child or spousal support or maintenance, as needed for support.
Survival after payment or deposit: Not specified in exemption statute.

OKLAHOMA

Has state opted out of federal bankruptcy exemptions? Yes. Okla. Stat. tit. 31, § 1(B).
Is opt out limited to residents or domiciliaries of the state? Yes. Okla. Stat. tit. 31, § 1(B): "No natural person residing in this state may exempt from the property of the estate in any bankruptcy proceeding the property specified in [§ 522)d)]. . . ."
Do state's exemptions have extraterritorial application?
Homestead: Probably not. Okla. Stat. tit. 31, § 1 applies to "every person residing in the state."
Personal property: Probably not. Okla. Stat. tit. 31, § 1 applies to "every person residing in the state."
***Wages*: Okla. Stat. tit. 12, §§ 1171.1, 1171.2; Okla. Stat. tit. 31, § 1.1.**
Scope: Money earned by a natural person as wages, salary, bonus or commission for personal services.
Amount: Follows federal scheme except debtor who is supporting dependent(s) may exempt a larger percentage on a showing of hardship.
Survival after payment/deposit: Protections apply to earnings within previous 90 days.
Waiver: Not specified in garnishment statute.
***Homestead*: Okla. Const. art. XII, § 1; Okla. Stat. tit. 31, §§ 1, 2, 5.**
Amount: 160 acres not within any city or town, or annexed by a city or town after November 1, 1997, and owned, occupied and used for both residential and commercial agricultural purposes; urban homestead exemption shall not exceed $5000 if more than 25% of the square foot area of the improvements on the land is used for business purposes or if less than 75% of square foot area of the improvements on the land is used as principal residence.
Procedural requirements: None specified in exemption statute.
Special provisions: Temporary rental of the homestead, without acquiring a new homestead, will not eliminate exemption.
Waiver: Not specified in exemption statute.
***Tangible personal property*: Okla. Stat. tit. 31, § 1.**
Household goods: All household furniture, books, portraits and pictures.
Motor vehicles: $7500 in one vehicle.
Tools of trade: $10,000 aggregate in tools of trade and farming implements.
Clothing and jewelry: $4000 clothing, $3000 in wedding and anniversary rings.
Miscellaneous and wildcard: Health aids, a limited number of poultry and livestock, $2000 in guns and a year's supply of provisions; burial place.
Waiver: Not specified in exemption statute.
***Benefits, retirement plans, insurance, judgments, and other intangibles*: Okla. Stat. tit. 31, §§ 1, 7.**
Public benefits: Amount received as earned income tax credit. *See also* Okla. Stat. tit. 56, § 173 (assistance received under certain statutes is exempt).
Pensions, retirement plans and annuities: Military pensions; certain tax-qualified retirement plans.
Insurance, judgments or other compensation for injury: Up to $50,000 personal injury, wrongful death or workers' compensation (no punitive damages).
Bank accounts: Any interest in Oklahoma college tuition savings plan, created pursuant to Okla. Stat. tit. 70, §§ 3970.1 to 3970.12.
Alimony, child support: Right to receive alimony, separate support, or child support, so far as needed for support.
Survival after payment or deposit: Not specified in exemption statute.

OREGON

Has state opted out of federal bankruptcy exemptions? Yes. Or. Rev. Stat. § 18.300.
Is opt out limited to residents or domiciliaries of the state? Yes. Or. Rev. Stat. § 23.305: "[R]esidents of this state shall not be entitled to the [§ 522(d) exemptions]."
Do state's exemptions have extraterritorial application?
Homestead: Yes. *See In re* Stratton, 269 B.R. 716 (Bankr. D. Or. 2001) (Oregon homestead exemption applied to property in California).
Personal property: Probably yes, based on *In re* Stratton, 269 B.R. 716 (Bankr. D. Or. 2001).
***Wages*: Or. Rev. Stat. §§ 18.375, 18.385.**
Scope: Compensation paid or payable for personal services, whether called wages, salary, commission, bonus or otherwise, including periodic payments pursuant to pension or retirement plan. Some independent contractors are covered.
Amount: Greater of 75% of disposable earnings or $183 (after Jan. 1, 2009, $196) is exempt. Disposable earnings are those left over after legally required deductions.
Survival after payment/deposit: Yes, if funds are traceable and not more than $7500 accumulated.
Waiver: Waivers are void.
***Homestead*: Or. Rev. Stat. §§ 18.395, 18.398, 18.402, 18.428.**
Amount: $30,000 in a residence (explicitly covers purchaser's interest in a land sale contract); if two members of household are debtors whose interests in homestead are subject to execution, may not exceed $39,600; can not exceed 160 acres if outside town or city; can not exceed one block if within town or city; homestead exemption subject to certain liens; may exempt $23,000 in a mobile home and land used as residence; if two members of household are debtors whose interest in mobile home and land are subject to execution, the combined exemption may not exceed $30,000. If debtor owns a mobile home but not the land on which it stands, exemptions are $20,000 for individual or $27,000 for multiple owners. Mobile home definition explicitly includes a floating home.
Procedural requirements: None specified in exemption statute.
Special provisions: Proceeds exempt for one year if debtor intends to use them to purchase another homestead. No homestead may be sold for a debt of $3000 or less, except for two or more judgments for the same judgment creditor that total $3000 or more.
Waiver: Not specified in exemption statute.
***Tangible personal property*: Or. Rev. Stat. §§ 18.345, 18.362.**
Household goods: $3000 in household goods, a 60-day supply of fuel and provisions.
Motor vehicles: $2150 (joint debtors may stack).
Tools of trade: $3000 (joint debtors may stack).
Clothing and jewelry: $1800 in wearing apparel, jewelry and other personal items (joint debtors may stack).
Miscellaneous and wildcard: $400 which can be stacked by joint debtors and applied toward any personal property but which can not be used to increase another exemption; $600 in books, pictures and musical instruments (joint debtors may stack), all health aids, $1000 in animals, poultry and 60-day supply of feed, a rifle or shotgun and one pistol, the combined value of which may not exceed $1000.
Waiver: Not specified in exemption statute.
***Benefits, retirement plans, insurance, judgments, and other intangibles*: Or. Rev. Stat. §§ 18.345, 18.348, 18.352, 18.358.**
Public benefits: The right to receive an earned income tax credit under federal law, and all moneys traceable to a payment of an earned income tax credit. Numerous other public benefits are exempted by the statutes establishing the benefit programs. *See, e.g.*, Or. Rev. Stat. § 411.760.
Pensions, retirement plans and annuities: Certain pensions and private retirement plans and annuities, including rollovers from employee pensions to individual accounts.
Insurance, judgments or other compensation for injury: Right to receive, or property traceable to, award under crime victim reparation law; right to receive, or property traceable to, personal injury compensation up to $10,000; right to receive, or property traceable to, compensation for loss of future earnings, to extent needed for support.
Bank accounts: Not specified in exemption statute (except as to survival of exemption in certain exempt funds).
Alimony, child support: Spousal support, child support or separate maintenance, to the extent needed for support.
Survival after payment or deposit: Funds exempt under other specified statutes (including retirement plans, wages, public employees' pensions, vocational rehabilitation, college tuition savings, veterans' loans, public assistance, aid to blind or disabled, old age assistance, Medicaid, benefits for injured inmates, workers' compensation, unemployment, benefits from fraternal organizations, Social Security and veterans' benefits) remain exempt if deposited in bank account, so long as traceable, but exemption lost if more than $7500 accumulated. The limit on accumulation does not apply to funds exempted by 42 U.S.C. § 407 (the anti-alienation provision of the Social Security law).

PENNSYLVANIA

Has state opted out of federal bankruptcy exemptions? No.
Is opt out limited to residents or domiciliaries of the state? Not applicable.
Do state's exemptions have extraterritorial application?
Homestead: No exemption.
Personal property: Uncertain.
***Wages*: 23 Pa. Cons. Stat. § 3703; 42 Pa. Cons. Stat. § 8127.**
Scope: Wages, salaries and commissions of individuals.
Amount: Completely exempt in hands of employer, *except* for certain residential rent or damages, board for four weeks or less, family support, student loan, or criminal fine, restitution, costs. (Support 50%; landlord-tenant 10% or a sum not to place debtor's income below federal poverty guidelines, whichever is less; not specified for other exceptions.) Net wages are those left after legally required deductions, health insurance, and union dues. Garnishment for rent or damages not permitted if lessee is victim of domestic abuse. The Rules of Civil Procedure, Rules 3103 and 3301 through 3304, require notice to debtors of the exemption for income below the poverty guidelines, the guideline amount, and the procedure for preventing garnishment of exempt wages.
Survival after payment/deposit: Exempt "in the hands of the employer."
Waiver: Not specified in garnishment statute.
***Homestead*:** No statutory homestead exemption, but common-law doctrine of tenancy by the entireties protects property owned by husband and wife from debts owed just by one spouse. *See* Sterrett v. Sterrett, 401 Pa. 583, 166 A.2d (1960).

Amount: Not applicable.
Procedural requirements: Not applicable.
Special provisions: Not applicable.
Waiver: Not applicable.
***Tangible personal property*: 42 Pa. Cons. Stat. §§ 8122, 8123, 8124, 8125, 8127.**
Household goods: See *Miscellaneous and wildcard.*
Motor vehicles: See *Miscellaneous and wildcard.*
Tools of trade: See *Miscellaneous and wildcard.*
Clothing and jewelry: All clothing.
Miscellaneous and wildcard: $300 in property including bank notes, money, securities, real property or money due the debtor; the exemption is inapplicable to claims for support, or for board for four weeks or less, or to foreclosure judgments or certain wage claims. Bibles and schoolbooks, sewing machines if not kept for sale or hire, and certain uniforms; tangible personal property on exhibition at any international exhibition held under the auspices of the federal government is exempt in the hands of the authorities of such exhibition or otherwise.
Waiver: Forbidden.
***Benefits, retirement plans, insurance, judgments, and other intangibles*: 42 Pa. Cons. Stat. §§ 8123, 8124, 8125, 8127.**
Public benefits: Unemployment compensation.
Pensions, retirement plans and annuities: Certain public or private pensions and individual retirement plans or annuities, including rollovers. (Except for rollovers, contributions in excess of $15,000 per year not exempt.)
Insurance, judgments or other compensation for injury: Workers' compensation; certain life, health and accident insurance; benefits from fraternal organizations; no-fault auto insurance recoveries.
Bank accounts: See *Miscellaneous and wildcard.*
Alimony, child support: Not specified in exemption statute.
Survival after payment or deposit: Not specified in exemption statute.

PUERTO RICO

Has state opted out of federal bankruptcy exemptions? No.
Is opt out limited to residents or domiciliaries of the state? Not applicable.
Do state's exemptions have extraterritorial application?
Homestead: Uncertain.
Personal property: Uncertain.
***Wages*: P.R. Laws Ann. tit. 32, § 1130.**
Scope: Earnings for personal services within 30 days before levy of execution.
Amount: 75% exempt if debtor can show earnings are necessary for use of family supported wholly or in part by debtor's labor.
Survival after payment/deposit: Not specified in exemption statute.
Waiver: Not specified in exemption statute.
***Homestead*: P.R. Laws Ann. tit. 31, §§ 1851–1855.**
Amount: $15,000 for heads of families, subject to certain mortgages and debts.
Procedural requirements: Head of family who acquires homestead should set forth this fact in the deed, but failure to do so does not destroy exemption.
Special provisions: If home owner dies or deserts family, exemption continues to protect spouse, minor children, and certain other dependents.
Waiver: Not specified in exemption statute.
***Tangible personal property*: P.R. Laws Ann. tit. 32, § 1130.**
Household goods: $100 in chairs, tables, desks and books; necessary household furniture including one sewing machine; $200 in a stove, furniture, beds, bedding; provisions sufficient for one month; iceboxes; $200 in a washing machine, $100 in a radio, $250 in a television and an electric iron.
Motor vehicles: One motor vehicle used in debtor's occupation (except for purchase money and repair debts for the vehicle). Exemption is capped at $6000 for liability for injury to third person by the motor vehicle.
Tools of trade: $300 tools of trade. Various farm animals and their equipment and feed for one month; a water right not to exceed the amount used for land the debtor actually cultivates; $200 in seeds to be planted or sowed within six months; certain mining equipment, aggregate $500.
Clothing and jewelry: All clothing.
Miscellaneous and wildcard: Artwork done by the debtor, family portraits and their necessary frames; $500 in shares of a homestead association if the debtor has no homestead; uniforms the debtor is required to keep and one gun.
Waiver: Not specified in exemption statute.
***Benefits, retirement plans, insurance, judgments, and other intangibles*: P.R. Laws Ann. tit. 32, § 1130.**
Public benefits: Not specified in exemption statute.
Pensions, retirement plans and annuities: Not specified in exemption statute.
Insurance, judgments or other compensation for injury: Certain life insurance.
Bank accounts: Not specified in exemption statute.
Alimony, child support: Not specified in exemption statute.
Survival after payment or deposit: Not specified in exemption statute.

RHODE ISLAND

Has state opted out of federal bankruptcy exemptions? No.
Is opt out limited to residents or domiciliaries of the state? Not applicable.
Do state's exemptions have extraterritorial application?
Homestead: Probably yes. *See In re* Franklino, 329 B.R. 363 (Bankr. D.R.I. 2005) (court accepted without discussion parties stipulation that debtor may claim Rhode Island homestead in property located in Connecticut).
Personal property: Uncertain.
***Wages*: R.I. Gen. Laws § 9-26-4(8).**
Scope: Wages or salary.
Amount: $50 per week is exempt. All wages are exempt if debtor is, or within one year was, "an object of relief from any state, federal, or municipal corporation or agency." Wages due a sailor are completely exempt.
Survival after payment/deposit: Not specified in exemption statute.
Waiver: Not specified in exemption statute.
***Homestead*: R.I. Gen. Laws § 9-26-4.1.**
Amount: $300,000 in land or buildings which debtor has a right to possess by lease or otherwise and occupies or intends to occupy as a principal residence. Significant exceptions: certain liens, debts owed to a federally insured depository institution or a person regulated under title 19 (financial institutions), debt contracted prior to the purchase of the residence. Only one exemption per residence (whether single or multiple owners) and only one prin-

cipal residence per family.
Procedural requirements: None. "Automatic by operation of law."
Special provisions: None specified.
Waiver: Not specified in exemption statute.
***Tangible personal property*: R.I. Gen. Laws § 9-26-4.**
Household goods: Furnishings and family stores of a housekeeper, up to $8600.
Motor vehicles: Motor vehicles with aggregate value up to $10,000.
Tools of trade: Professional's library; tools of trade up to $1200.
Clothing and jewelry: Necessary clothing of debtor and family; $1000 jewelry.
Miscellaneous and wildcard: Books up to $300; one cemetery plot; debts secured by bills of exchange or promissory notes; $50 in holdings in consumer cooperative association.
Waiver: Not specified in exemption statute.
***Benefits, retirement plans, insurance, judgments, and other intangibles*: R.I. Gen. Laws § 9-26-4.**
Public benefits: Not specified in exemption statute. (But note exemption for "other property . . . exempted . . . by general or special acts . . . or by the policy of the law.") *See* R.I. Gen. Laws §§ 40-5.1-15 (assistance provided under Family Independence Act is exempt), 40-6-14 (assistance provided under Public Assistance Act is exempt).
Pensions, retirement plans and annuities: Tax-qualified IRAs, pensions, and retirement annuities, except for certain domestic relations orders.
Insurance, judgments or other compensation for injury: Not specified in exemption statute.
Bank accounts: Account balance in prepaid tuition or tuition savings plan (as defined in R.I. Gen. Laws § 16-7-3).
Alimony, child support: Not specified in exemption statute.
Survival after payment or deposit: Not specified in exemption statute.

SOUTH CAROLINA

Has state opted out of federal bankruptcy exemptions? Yes. S.C. Code Ann. § 15-41-35.
Is opt out limited to residents or domiciliaries of the state? Not specified. S.C. Code Ann. § 15-41-35: "No individual may exempt from the property of the estate in any bankruptcy proceeding the property specified in [§ 522(d)] except as may be expressly permitted by this chapter or by other provisions of law of this State."
Do state's exemptions have extraterritorial application?
Homestead: No. S.C. Code Ann. § 15-41-30 applies to the "real and personal property of a debtor domiciled in this state."
Personal property: No. S.C. Code Ann. § 15-41-30 applies to the "real and personal property of a debtor domiciled in this state."
***Wages*: S.C. Code Ann. §§ 15-39-410, 15-39-420.**
Scope: Personal service earnings are exempt.
Amount: Fully exempt.
Survival after payment/deposit: Not specified in exemption statute.
Waiver: Not specified in exemption statute.
***Homestead*: S.C. Code Ann. § 15-41-30(1); *see* S.C. Const. art. III, § 28.**
Amount: $50,000 in real property or personal property used as residence or in cooperative used as residence or in burial plot. Multiple owners may exempt up to $100,000. Starting July 21, 2007, homestead exemption amounts will be adjusted annually, according to the Consumer Price Index. New amounts will be published each March 1.
Procedural requirements: Not specified in exemption statute.
Special provisions: Not specified in exemption statute.
Waiver: Not specified in exemption statute.
***Tangible personal property*: S.C. Code Ann. § 15-41-30; *see* S.C. Const. art. III, § 28.**
Household goods: $2500 in household furnishings and goods, clothing, appliances, books, animals, crops, musical instruments.
Motor vehicles: $1200 in one motor vehicle.
Tools of trade: $750.
Clothing and jewelry: $500 in jewelry; clothing included in household goods exemption.
Miscellaneous and wildcard: $1000 in cash and liquid assets for those debtors without a homestead; health aids.
Waiver: Not specified in exemption statute.
Special provisions: Dollar amounts are to be adjusted on July 1st each year, to account for changes in the Consumer Price Index.
***Benefits, retirement plans, insurance, judgments, and other intangibles*: S.C. Code Ann. § 15-41-30.**
Public benefits: Right to receive Social Security, unemployment, local public assistance, veterans' benefits.
Pensions, retirement plans and annuities: ERISA pensions; right to receive payment under certain tax-qualified retirement plans.
Insurance, judgments or other compensation for injury: Certain life insurance; right to receive disability, illness or unemployment benefit; right to receive, or property traceable to, award under crime victim reparation law, or payment for bodily injury to debtor, or bodily injury or wrongful death of one on whom debtor is dependent or life insurance proceeds of one on whom debtor was dependent (so far as needed for support).
Bank accounts: Not specified in exemption statute (but note in lieu of homestead exemption).
Alimony, child support: Right to receive alimony, support or separate maintenance.
Survival after payment or deposit: Note that some exemptions specify "right to receive" or "right to receive and property traceable to."

SOUTH DAKOTA

Has state opted out of federal bankruptcy exemptions? Yes. S.D. Codified Laws §§ 43-31-30, 43-45-13.
Is opt out limited to residents or domiciliaries of the state? Yes. S.D. Codified Laws §§ 43-31-30, 43-45-13: "[R]esidents of this state are not entitled to [§ 522(d) exemptions], exemptions which this state specifically does not authorize."
Do state's exemptions have extraterritorial application?
Homestead: Uncertain. Compare S.D. Codified Laws § 43-31-1 which applies to the "homestead of every family, resident in this state," with S.D. Codified Laws § 43-31-2, which defines a homestead as including "two or more houses or mobile homes thus used at different times and places."
Personal property: Uncertain.
***Wages*: S.D. Codified Laws §§ 21-18-2.1, 21-18-51 to 21-18-53.**
Scope: Compensation paid or payable for personal services whether called wages, salary, commission, bonus or otherwise; includes periodic payments from pension or retirement plan.
Amount: Greater of 80% of disposable income or forty times

minimum wage is exempt. Additional exemption of $25/week for each dependent residing with debtor.
Survival after payment/deposit: Not specified in garnishment statute.
Waiver: Not specified in garnishment statute.
***Homestead*: S.D. Codified Laws §§ 43-31-1 to 43-31-6, 43-31-11, 43-31-13, 43-45-3.**
Amount: Dwelling exempt, subject to certain exceptions; mobile home must be larger than 240 square feet at its base and registered in South Dakota at least six months before the claim of exemption; $30,000 in sale proceeds are exempt for one year after receipt but exemption is $170,000 if debtor is 70 or older or the unremarried spouse of such a person; limit of one acre within a town plat and 160 acres outside a town plat; if outside a town plat and acquired under U.S. laws relating to mineral lands, limit is 40 acres; if acquired as a "lode mining claim," limit is five acres.
Procedural requirements: Home owner may have homestead platted, but failure to do so does not destroy exemption.
Special provisions: Upon death of home owner, exemption continues to protect surviving spouse and minor children. New homestead will be exempt to the same extent and in the same manner as the old. Proceeds of sale of homestead exempt for one year.
Waiver: Both spouses must join in conveyance or encumbrance.
***Tangible personal property*: S.D. Codified Laws §§ 43-45-2, 43-45-4.**
Household goods: See *Miscellaneous and wildcard*; provisions and fuel for one year absolutely exempt.
Motor vehicles: See *Miscellaneous and wildcard.*
Tools of trade: See *Miscellaneous and wildcard.*
Clothing and jewelry: All clothing.
Miscellaneous and wildcard: Personal property head of family $6000, others $4000; burial plot; all family pictures, a pew, $200 in a family library.
Waiver: Not specified in exemption statute.
***Benefits, retirement plans, insurance, judgments, and other intangibles*: S.D. Codified Laws §§ 43-45-6, 43-45-15 to 43-45-18.**
Public benefits: Not specified in exemption statute. *See* S.D. Codified Laws § 28-7A-18 (TANF is exempt).
Pensions, retirement plans and annuities: Up to $1 million and the income and distributions therefrom in employee benefit plan. Employee benefit plan is defined as certain tax-qualified plans. In the event that any court of South Dakota finds the exemption excessive, the court is directed to determine what amount is permissible under the state constitution.
Insurance, judgments or other compensation for injury: Life insurance payments to spouse or minor children, exempt from debts of insured and beneficiaries up to $10,000.
Bank accounts: Not specified in exemption statute.
Alimony, child support: Not specified in exemption statute.
Survival after payment or deposit: Not specified in exemption statute.

TENNESSEE

Has state opted out of federal bankruptcy exemptions? Yes. Tenn. Code Ann. § 26-2-112.
Is opt out limited to residents or domiciliaries of the state? Yes (as to "citizens"). Tenn. Code Ann. § 26-2-112: "[C]itizens of Tennessee, . . . are not authorized to claim as exempt the property described in [§ 522(d)]."
Do state's exemptions have extraterritorial application?
Homestead: Uncertain.
Personal property: Uncertain.
***Wages*: Tenn. Code Ann. §§ 26-2-102, 26-2-106 to 26-2-108.**
Scope: Compensation paid or payable for personal services, whether called wages, salary, commission or otherwise, including periodic payments pursuant to pension or retirement program.
Amount: Similar to federal, with additional $2.50 per week exemption for each dependent child under age 16. Disposable earnings are those left after legally required deductions.
Survival after payment/deposit: Not specified in exemption statute.
Waiver: Not specified in exemption statute.
***Homestead*: Tenn. Const. art. 11, § 11; Tenn. Code Ann. §§ 26-2-301 to 26-2-306.**
Amount: $5000 in real property used as principal place of residence including leased property, if leased for more than two years; joint debtors may only exempt $7500 in shared home; subject to sale for payment of public taxes or satisfaction of debt for improvements. For an unmarried individual age 62 or older, the amount is $12,500. For a couple, when one party is age 62 or over, the amount is $20,000. For a couple, when both parties are 62 or older, the amount is $25,000. Exemption protects against some criminal law seizures. For an individual who has one or more minor children in such individual's custody, the amount is $25,000.
Procedural requirements: None stated. Homestead may be set apart at time of levy.
Special provisions: Insurance proceeds also exempt up to $5000. After owner's death, exemption continues to protect spouse and minor children.
Waiver: Not specified in exemption statute.
***Tangible personal property*: Tenn. Code Ann. §§ 8-36-111, 26-2-102 to 26-2-104, 26-2-111, 49-5-909.**
Household goods: See *Miscellaneous and wildcard.*
Motor vehicles: See *Miscellaneous and wildcard.*
Tools of trade: $1900.
Clothing and jewelry: Necessary and proper clothing.
Miscellaneous and wildcard: Personal property to the aggregate value of $4000 (includes cash or bank accounts); health aids; family portraits and pictures, Bible and school books.
Waiver: Not specified in exemption statute.
***Benefits, retirement plans, insurance, judgments, and other intangibles*: Tenn. Code Ann. §§ 8-36-111, 26-2-105, 26-2-110, 26-2-111, 49-5-909.**
Public benefits: Right to receive Social Security, unemployment, veterans' benefits. *See also* Tenn. Code Ann. §§ 71-2-216, 71-3-121, 71-4-117, 71-4-1112 (exempting benefits under various state public assistance statutes).
Pensions, retirement plans and annuities: Public employees' retirement benefits; certain tax-qualified private retirement benefits.
Insurance, judgments or other compensation for injury: Accident, health or disability insurance benefits; certain life insurance; up to $15,000 aggregate in right to receive or property traceable to an award up to $5000 under crime victim reparations law, compensation up to $7500 for personal bodily injury, or up to $10,000 for wrongful death of person on whom debtor was dependent; compensation for loss of future earnings so far as necessary for the support of debtor or dependents.
Bank accounts: See *Miscellaneous and wildcard.*
Alimony, child support: Right to receive certain alimony and child support.

Survival after payment or deposit: Not specified but note language in certain benefit exemptions regarding "right to receive" or "right to receive and property traceable to." State pensions remain exempt in bank account.

TEXAS

Has state opted out of federal bankruptcy exemptions? No.
Is opt out limited to residents or domiciliaries of the state? Not applicable.
Do state's exemptions have extraterritorial application?
Homestead: No. *See In re* Peters, 91 B.R. 401 (Bankr. W.D. Tex. 1988); *see also* Tex. Prop. Code Ann. § 41.002 (Vernon) (which provides a definition of homestead that applies to "all homesteads in this state whenever created"). *See* In re Tate, 2007 WL 81835 (Bankr. D. Or. Jan. 8, 2007).
Personal property: Probably not. *See In re* Peters, 91 B.R. 401 (Bankr. W.D. Tex. 1988).
***Wages*: Tex. Const. art. 16, § 28; Tex. Prop. Code Ann. § 42.001 (Vernon).**
Scope: Wages or commissions for personal services.
Amount: Current wages for personal service are exempt from garnishment. Commissions for personal services also protected, up to 25% of aggregate limitations ($60,000 for a family, $30,000 for an individual).
Survival after payment/deposit: Not specified in exemption statute.
Waiver: Not specified in exemption statute.
***Homestead*: Tex. Const. art. 16, §§ 50, 51; Tex. Prop. Code Ann. §§ 41.001, 41.002 (Vernon).**
Amount: Rural homestead consists of not more than 200 acres for a family or 100 acres for an individual; an urban homestead consists of not more than ten acres (for property sold before January 1, 2000, the prior one-acre exemption applies); includes improvements; must be claimant's home which may include place of business; homestead is subject to certain liens. Urban is defined as within municipal limits and receiving certain municipal services.
Procedural requirements: Procedure available for designation of homestead, but may be done at time of levy.
Special provisions: Proceeds from sale exempt for six months.
Waiver: The Texas Constitution includes detailed restrictions and procedural requirements for loans secured by the homestead. Homestead may not be abandoned without consent of spouse.
***Tangible personal property*: Tex. Prop. Code Ann. §§ 42.001 to 42.005 (Vernon).**
Household goods: Up to $60,000 for a family, $30,000 for a single adult, of the following: household furnishings, provisions, trade implements, clothing, two firearms, sporting equipment, certain animals, certain vehicles, and pets; exemptions not applicable to a child support lien under Family Code.
Motor vehicles: See above.
Tools of trade: See above.
Clothing and jewelry: See above. (Jewelry limited to 25% of aggregate amount.)
Miscellaneous and wildcard: See above. Health aids exempt and not included in cap. Bible, or other book of sacred writings.
Waiver: Not specified in exemption statute.
***Benefits, retirement plans, insurance, judgments, and other intangibles*: Tex. Prop. Code Ann. §§ 42.001, 42.0021, 42.0022 (Vernon).**
Public benefits: Not specified in exemption statute. *See* Tex. Hum. Res. Code Ann. § 31.040 (Vernon) (assistance granted under financial assistance laws is exempt).
Pensions, retirement plans and annuities: Right to assets held in, or to receive payments from, certain pensions or tax-qualified retirement plans. Non-taxable rollovers explicitly included.
Insurance, judgments or other compensation for injury: Certain life insurance.
Bank accounts: Funds held in, or right to receive payments from, certain college tuition savings plans established pursuant to the Education Code; health savings accounts, as defined in Internal Revenue code.
Alimony, child support: Alimony, support or separate maintenance, received or to be received.
Survival after payment or deposit: Not specified in exemption statute.

UTAH

Has state opted out of federal bankruptcy exemptions? Yes. Utah Code Ann. § 78-23-15.
Is opt out limited to residents or domiciliaries of the state? Not specified. Utah Code Ann. § 78-23-15: "No individual may exempt from the property of the estate in any bankruptcy proceeding the property specified in [§ 522(d)]. . . ."
Do state's exemptions have extraterritorial application?
Homestead: No. The exemption provided in Utah Code Ann. § 78-23-3 applies to a homestead "consisting of property in this state."
Personal property: Uncertain.
***Wages*: Utah Code Ann. §§ 70C-7-103, 70C-7-104.**
Scope: Compensation for personal services, whether called wages, salary, commission, bonus or otherwise, including periodic payments pursuant to pension, disability or retirement plan.
Amount: Similar to federal. Disposable earnings are those left after legally required deductions.
Survival after payment/deposit: Not specified in exemption statute.
Waiver: Not specified in exemption statute.
***Homestead*: Utah Const. art. XXII, § 1; Utah Code Ann. §§ 78-23-3, 78-23-4, 78-23-9.**
Amount: Up to $20,000 for an individual or $40,000 for joint owners in the "primary personal residence" defined as a dwelling or mobile home (whether or not debtor owns the land on which mobile home is located) and up to one acre of land "as reasonably necessary to make use of the dwelling or mobile home."
Procedural requirements: Procedure available for filing declaration of homestead; may be filed up to time stated in notice of execution.
Special provisions: Proceeds remain exempt for one year.
Waiver: Spouse must join in conveyance or encumbrance. Waiver of exemptions in favor of unsecured creditor is unenforceable.
***Tangible personal property*: Utah Code Ann. §§ 39-1-47, 78-23-5 to 78-23-11.**
Household goods: Washer, dryer, refrigerator, stove, microwave, sewing machine, carpets, 12 months of provisions, beds and bedding. In addition, $500 exemptions for goods chosen from each of four categories: (1) sofas, chairs, and so forth, (2) kitchen and dining tables and chairs, (3) animals, books and musical instruments, and (4) heirlooms or other items of sentimental value.
Motor vehicles: $2500; specifically excludes recreational or off-road vehicles, except for a motorcycle or van used for daily transportation.

Tools of trade: $3500.
Clothing and jewelry: All clothing, excluding furs and jewelry.
Miscellaneous and wildcard: Health aids; burial plot; military property; family pictures; works of art by debtor. Traceable proceeds of property sold, taken by condemnation, lost, damaged or destroyed remain exempt for one year.
Waiver: Waiver of exemptions in favor of unsecured creditor is unenforceable.
***Benefits, retirement plans, insurance, judgments, and other intangibles*: Utah Code Ann. §§ 78-23-5 to 78-23-11.**
Public benefits: Veterans' benefits; benefits received or to be received from any source on account of disability, illness or unemployment.
Pensions, retirement plans and annuities: Certain tax-qualified retirement plans. Rollovers explicitly included; other contributions within one year of bankruptcy not exempt. Payments from plans for illness or disability fully exempt; others exempt to extent needed for support. Proceeds or benefits of certain trusts of which debtor or dependents are beneficiary.
Insurance, judgments or other compensation for injury: Benefits received or to be received from any source on account of disability, illness or unemployment; proceeds of insurance, judgment or settlement for personal injury or wrongful death; benefits paid or payable for medical, surgical or hospital care, so far as used to pay for that care. Proceeds or benefits of any life insurance paid or payable to debtor upon the death of debtor's spouse or children, provided that policy had been owned by debtor for a continuous unexpired period of one year; proceeds or benefits of any contracts paid or payable to spouse or children upon the death of the debtor, provided that policy has been in existence for continuous unexpired period of one year; proceeds or avails of any unmatured life insurance contracts owned by debtor, excluding any payments made during year before levy or execution. (These sections do not apply to any life insurance pledged as collateral for a loan or other legal obligation.)
Bank accounts: Not specified in exemption statute.
Alimony, child support: Child support; payments from retirement plan to alternate payee under qualified domestic relations order. Alimony and separate maintenance exempt to extent needed for support.
Survival after payment or deposit: Benefits remain exempt after receipt by and in possession of individual, and in any other form in which it is traceable.

VERMONT

Has state opted out of federal bankruptcy exemptions? No.
Is opt out limited to residents or domiciliaries of the state? Not applicable.
Do state's exemptions have extraterritorial application?
Homestead: Yes. *See In re* Oliver, 182 B.R. 699 (Bankr. D. Vt. 1995) (debtor may use Vermont homestead to exempt proceeds of sale of property in another state).
Personal property: Uncertain.
***Wages*: Vt. Stat. Ann. tit. 12, §§ 3170, 3172.**
Scope: Earnings.
Amount: Follows the federal scheme except for consumer credit claims when the greater of 85% of weekly disposable earnings or 40 times federal minimum wage is exempt. No garnishment if debtor was, within two months of the garnishment hearing, a welfare recipient. Court may reduce garnishment amount if debtor shows that weekly expenditures "reasonably incurred" for maintenance of self or dependents exceed the statutorily exempt amount. Garnishment orders may be modified from time to time. Discharge of employee because of garnishment forbidden; discharge within 60 days after garnishment rebuttably presumed to be violation; employee has private right of action for reinstatement, back wages, damages, costs and reasonable attorney fees.
Survival after payment/deposit: Not specified in garnishment statute.
Waiver: Forbidden.
***Homestead*: Vt. Stat. Ann. tit. 27, §§ 101, 107, 109.**
Amount: $75,000 (increased from $30,000 as of January 1, 1997) in land and a dwelling, which may be a permanently sited mobile home, including the rents, issues and profits.
Procedural requirements: Deed or homestead must be recorded; exemption does not protect against debts which precede this declaration, except that new homestead acquired with proceeds of sale of former homestead is exempt as to any debts as to which former homestead was exempt.
Special provisions: None specified.
Waiver: Spouse must join in conveyance or encumbrance.
***Tangible personal property*: Vt. Stat. Ann. tit. 12, §§ 2740, 3023.**
Household goods: $2500 in aggregate value in household furnishings, goods or appliances, books, wearing apparel, animals, crops or musical instruments; one cooking stove, heating appliances, one refrigerator, one freezer, one water heater, sewing machines; various amounts of specified fuel; specified livestock and accessories; health aids; proceeds of exempt property.
Motor vehicles: $2500.
Tools of trade: $5000 tools of trade; $5000 in aggregate value in growing crops.
Clothing and jewelry: A wedding ring; $500 in aggregate value in other jewelry.
Miscellaneous and wildcard: Proceeds of exempt property; $400 aggregate interest in any property plus up to $7000 of unused exemptions for motor vehicles, tools of trade, jewelry, household goods and crop; health aids.
Waiver: Not specified in exemption statute.
***Benefits, retirement plans, insurance, judgments, and other intangibles*: Vt. Stat. Ann. tit. 12, § 2740; *see* Vt. Stat. Ann. tit. 3, § 476.**
Public benefits: Any property traceable to the debtor's right to receive Social Security or veterans' benefits, to the extent reasonably needed for support of debtor or dependents. *See also* Vt. Stat. Ann. tit. 33, § 124 (all moneys granted to persons as assistance are exempt).
Pensions, retirement plans and annuities: Any property traceable to debtor's right to receive certain pension and retirement benefits, to the extent reasonably needed for support of debtor or dependents.
Insurance, judgments or other compensation for injury: Any property traceable to the debtor's right to receive the following, to the extent reasonably needed for the support of debtor and dependents: disability or illness benefits, crime victim's compensation, certain insurance benefits, personal injury (including pain and suffering and actual pecuniary loss) and wrongful death recoveries, compensation for loss of future earnings.
Bank accounts: $700.
Alimony, child support: Any property traceable to debtor's right to

receive alimony, support, or separate maintenance, to the extent needed for support.
Survival after payment or deposit: Yes. Note "property traceable to" language in various benefits exemptions.

VIRGIN ISLANDS

Has state opted out of federal bankruptcy exemptions? No.
Is opt out limited to residents or domiciliaries of the state? Not applicable.
Do state's exemptions have extraterritorial application?
Homestead: Uncertain.
Personal property: Uncertain.
***Wages*: V.I. Code Ann. tit. 5, §§ 521, 522.**
Scope: Wages, salary, commissions or other remuneration for services performed by an employee for his employer, including any remuneration measured partly or wholly by percentages or share of profits, or by other sums based upon work done or results produced and any drawing account made available to an employee by his employer.
Amount: 90% of gross wages in excess of $30 per week is exempt.
Survival after payment/deposit: Not specified in exemption statute.
Waiver: Not specified in exemption statute.
***Homestead*: V.I. Code Ann. tit. 5, § 478.**
Amount: $30,000; rural homestead may not exceed five acres and urban homestead may not exceed $\frac{1}{4}$ of an acre.
Procedural requirements: None stated. Homestead may be claimed at time of levy.
Special provisions: None specified.
Waiver: Spouse must join in encumbrance.
***Tangible personal property*: V.I. Code Ann. tit. 5, § 479.**
Household goods: $3000.
Motor vehicles: None.
Tools of trade: Exempt so far as necessary to carry on trade, occupation or profession by which debtor habitually earns a living.
Clothing and jewelry: Clothing. (Watches and jewelry not exempt.)
Miscellaneous and wildcard: None
Waiver: Not specified in exemption statute.
***Benefits, retirement plans, insurance, judgments, and other intangibles*:**
Public benefits: Not specified in exemption statute. *See* V.I. Code Ann. tit. 34, § 13 (public assistance granted under social welfare laws is exempt).
Pensions, retirement plans and annuities: Not specified in exemption statute.
Insurance, judgments or other compensation for injury: Not specified in exemption statute.
Bank accounts: Not specified in exemption statute.
Alimony, child support: Not specified in exemption statute.
Survival after payment or deposit: Not specified in exemption statute.

VIRGINIA

Has state opted out of federal bankruptcy exemptions? Yes. Va. Code Ann. § 34-3.1.
Is opt out limited to residents or domiciliaries of the state? Not specified. Va. Code Ann. § 34-3.1: "No individual may exempt from the property of the estate in any bankruptcy proceeding the property specified in [§ 522(d)], except as may otherwise be expressly permitted under this title."
Do state's exemptions have extraterritorial application?
Homestead: Yes. Va. Code Ann. § 34-6 sets out the procedure for declaring a homestead for real estate located outside the state. *See also In re* McWilliams, 296 B.R. 424 (Bankr. E.D. Va. 2002) (debtor's claim of Virginia homestead exemption in North Carolina property denied because debtor failed to file homestead deed in both county in which he resided and county in which property was located as required by Virginia law).
Personal property: Uncertain.
***Wages*: Va. Code Ann. §§ 34-17(B), 34-29, 34-32, 34-33.**
Scope: Earnings of an individual.
Amount: Greater of 75% or 40 times federal minimum wage is exempt. Wages of minor fully exempt as to debts of parents. "Homestead exemption," which covers real and personal property, may be used to recover garnished wages. Declaration should be filed after garnishment summons served on employer and before return date of summons.
Survival after payment/deposit: Not specified in exemption statute.
Waiver: Void and unenforceable.
***Homestead*: Va. Code Ann. §§ 34-4, 34-4.1, 34-6, 34-14, 34-18, 34-22.**
Amount: $5000 in any property plus $500 for each dependent; profits derived from homestead property are exempt; exemption subject to certain liens. Additional $2000 in real or personal property for certain disabled veterans.
Procedural requirements: Homestead declaration must be recorded.
Special provisions: None specified.
Waiver: Permitted.
***Tangible personal property*: Va. Code Ann. §§ 34-4, 34-4.1, 34-6, 34-14, 34-18, 34-22, 34-26 to 34-28.**
Household goods: $5000.
Motor vehicles: $2000.
Tools of trade: $10,000. Does not cover motor vehicle used only for commuting. "Occupation" includes enrollment in school or college. For debtor engaged in farming, certain livestock and farming implements.
Clothing and jewelry: $1000 clothing; wedding and engagement rings.
Miscellaneous and wildcard: See homestead exemption above (any real or personal property); family bible; $5000 family portraits and heirlooms; burial place; pets.
Waiver: Permitted, as to property exempted under general ("any real or personal property") homestead exemption, but note that non-possessory security interests are forbidden in certain essential property exempted by Va. Code Ann. §§ 34-26, 34-27, and 34-29.
***Benefits, retirement plans, insurance, judgments, and other intangibles*: Va. Code Ann. §§ 34-26, 34-28.1, 34-34.**
Public benefits: Not specified in exemption statute. *See* Va. Code Ann. § 63.2-506 (public assistance exempt).
Pensions, retirement plans and annuities: *Pensions, retirement plans and annuities*: Retirement plans exempt to the same extent permitted under federal bankruptcy law.
Insurance, judgments or other compensation for injury: Personal injury or wrongful death causes of action or proceeds of judgment or settlement, except as to certain liens.
Bank accounts: Pre-need funeral contract, up to $5000.

Alimony, child support: Not specified in exemption statute.
Survival after payment or deposit: Not specified in exemption statute.

WASHINGTON

Has state opted out of federal bankruptcy exemptions? No.
Is opt out limited to residents or domiciliaries of the state? Not applicable.
Do state's exemptions have extraterritorial application?
Homestead: Uncertain.
Personal property: Uncertain.
***Wages*: Wash. Rev. Code § 6.27.150.**
Scope: Compensation paid or payable for personal services, whether called wages, salary, commission, bonus or otherwise, including periodic payments pursuant to a non-governmental pension or retirement program.
Amount: Similar to federal.
Survival after payment/deposit: Not specified in garnishment statute.
Waiver: Not specified in garnishment statute.
***Homestead*: Wash. Rev. Code §§ 6.13.010 to 63.13.080.**
Amount: $125,000 for dwelling house or mobile home (whether or not permanently affixed) and land, or unimproved land on which debtor intends to place dwelling house or mobile home. If debtor is married, may consist of community property or separate property of either spouse, provided that the same premises can not be claimed separately by the husband and wife with the effect of increasing the exemption in excess of the amount specified by law; homestead exemption subject to certain liens.
Procedural requirements: Homestead is automatic in land occupied as residence; declaration of homestead required to exempt unimproved land on which owner intends to build residence. Declaration of non-abandonment must be recorded if owner who wishes to retain homestead will be absent for more than six months.
Special provisions: Proceeds or insurance remain exempt for one year.
Waiver: Spouse must join in conveyance or encumbrance.
***Tangible personal property*: Wash. Rev. Code §§ 6.15.010 to 6.15.040.**
Household goods: $2700 ($5400 for marital community) household goods, appliances and furniture.
Motor vehicles: $2500 motor vehicle used for personal transportation (two vehicles, aggregate $5000, for community).
Tools of trade: $5000.
Clothing and jewelry: All clothing (but $1000 per individual limit for furs, jewelry or ornaments).
Miscellaneous and wildcard: $1500 books; all family pictures and keepsakes; health aids. $2000 wildcard: may not be used for earnings, not more than $200 for cash, not more than $200 for bank accounts, stocks, or the like.
Waiver: Not specified in exemption statute.
***Benefits, retirement plans, insurance, judgments, and other intangibles*: Wash. Rev. Code §§ 6.15.010 to 6.15.040, 48.18.400 to 48.18.430.**
Public benefits: Not specified in exemption statute. *See* Wash. Rev. Code §§ 74.04.280, 74.08.210 (public assistance exempt).
Pensions, retirement plans and annuities: Certain pensions, annuities and employee benefit plans.
Insurance, judgments or other compensation for injury: $16,150 personal injury judgments; compensation for loss of future earnings, so far as needed for support. Proceeds and avails of life insurance and certain disability insurance fully exempt, as to debts of the insured, or debts of beneficiary existing at time proceeds made available. Insurance proceeds for loss or destruction of exempt property are exempt.
Bank accounts: $200. Prepaid college tuition units (pursuant to Wash. Rev. Code § 28B.95) purchased more than two years prior to the date of a bankruptcy filing or court judgment.
Alimony, child support: Child support, so long as traceable.
Survival after payment or deposit: Yes, as to certain pension and retirement benefits.

WEST VIRGINIA

Has state opted out of federal bankruptcy exemptions? Yes. W. Va. Code § 38-10-4.
Is opt out limited to residents or domiciliaries of the state? Yes. W. Va. Code § 38-10-4: "[T]his state specifically does not authorize persons who are domiciled in this state to exempt the property specified in [§ 522(d)]."
Do state's exemptions have extraterritorial application?
Homestead: Uncertain.
Personal property: Uncertain.
***Wages*: W. Va. Code §§ 38-5A-3, 38-5A-9, 38-5B-12.**
Scope: Salary and wages are given their ordinary meaning, but include compensation measured partly or wholly by commissions, percentages or share of profits, or by other sums based upon work done or results produced, whether or not debtor is given a drawing account.
Amount: Greater of 80% of wages or 30 times federal minimum hourly wage per week is exempt.
Survival after payment/deposit: Not specified in exemption statute, but note that it covers money "due and owing" or "to become due and owing."
Waiver: Not specified in exemption statute.
***Homestead*: W. Va. Const. art. 6, § 48; W. Va. Code §§ 38-9-1 to 38-9-6, 38-10-4.**
Amount: Bankruptcy only: $25,000 in real or personal property or a cooperative that debtor or dependent uses as a residence, or in a burial plot of debtor or dependent; $250,000 for physician's bankruptcy arising from certain medical malpractice judgments. Non-bankruptcy: $5000, which may be claimed by a "husband, wife, parent or other head of household." For all debts and liabilities for hospital or medical expenses incurred for a catastrophic illness or injury as defined, the exemption is $7500. (Enhanced exemption does not apply to debts incurred before July 1, 1996.)
Procedural requirements: None stated. Homestead available "by operation of law."
Special provisions: After debtor's death, exemption continues to protect minor children.
Waiver: Void and unenforceable except as to certain consensual security interests.
***Tangible personal property*: W. Va. Code §§ 38-8-1, 38-8-3, 38-8-10, 38-8-15, 38-10-4, 46A-2-136.**
Household goods: Bankruptcy: household goods and furnishings, clothing, books, animals, musical instruments, up to $400 in any item to an aggregate of $8000. Non-bankruptcy: $8000. For consumer credit transactions and consumer leases, all the property listed in W. Va. Code § 38-8-1, plus all children's books, pictures,

toys and other such personal property of children, and all "medical health equipment used for health purposes" by consumer, spouse or dependent.
Motor vehicles: Bankruptcy: $2400. Non-bankruptcy: $5000.
Tools of trade: Bankruptcy: $1500. Non-bankruptcy: $3000.
Clothing and jewelry: Bankruptcy: $1000 in jewelry. (Clothing included in household goods exemption).
Miscellaneous and wildcard: Bankruptcy: $800 plus any unused household goods exemption; health aids. Non-bankruptcy, head of household: $1000 any personal property. $15,000 cap on non-bankruptcy personal property exemptions including certain bank accounts.
***Benefits, retirement plans, insurance, judgments, and other intangibles*: W. Va. Code §§ 38-8-1, 38-10-4.**
Public benefits: Bankruptcy: Right to receive Social Security, unemployment, veterans' benefits, local public assistance. *See also* W. Va. Code § 9-5-1 (welfare assistance exempt).
Pensions, retirement plans and annuities: Bankruptcy: Certain pensions and retirement plans; any unmeasured life insurance, and up to $8000 in accrued dividends or loan value; right to receive any disability, illness or unemployment benefit; right to receive or property traceable to crime victim reparations, wrongful death of person on whom debtor was dependent, life insurance proceeds as needed for support, up to $15,000 personal injury compensation (not including pain and suffering or actual pecuniary loss), loss of future earnings. Non-bankruptcy: Certain IRA and Simplified Employee Pension funds are exempt.
Insurance, judgments or other compensation for injury: Bankruptcy only: $8000 in loan value or accrued dividends of certain life insurance; $15,000 personal injury; wrongful death payment as needed for support; certain life insurance, as needed for support, compensation for loss of future earnings, as needed for support.
Bank accounts: Bankruptcy: Payments to prepaid college tuition fund. Non-bankruptcy: "[F]unds on deposit in a federally insured financial institution, wages or salary, not to exceed" the greater of $1000 or a figure based on 125% of poverty level.
Alimony, child support: Bankruptcy: Right to receive alimony, support or separate maintenance, to the extent needed for support.
Survival after payment or deposit: Note "property traceable to" language in certain bankruptcy exemptions.

WISCONSIN

Has state opted out of federal bankruptcy exemptions? No.
Is opt out limited to residents or domiciliaries of the state? Not applicable.
Do state's exemptions have extraterritorial application?
Homestead: Uncertain.
Personal property: Probably not. Wis. Stat. § 815.18(5) provides: "A resident is entitled to the exemptions provided by this section. A non-resident is entitled to the exemptions provided by the law of the jurisdiction of his or her residence."
***Wages*: Wis. Stat. §§ 812.30, 812.34, 812.38.**
Scope: Compensation paid or payable for personal services whether called wages, salary, commission, bonus or otherwise, including periodic payments under a pension or retirement program.
Amount: Greater of 80% of disposable earnings or the amount of the federal poverty line adjusted for family size is exempt. Disposable earnings are those left after legally required deductions. Garnishment is forbidden if debtor is eligible to receive need-based public assistance or has received it within six months or if the debtor's household income is below the poverty line. If a 20% garnishment would result in household income below the poverty line, garnishment limited to the amount by which household income exceeds the poverty line. Debtor may petition for relief, if the exemption is "insufficient to acquire the necessities of life for the debtor and his or her dependents." *See also* Wis. Stat. § 815.18(3)(h) (exempting 75% of wages or 30 times minimum wage from execution).
Survival after payment/deposit: Not specified in exemption statute.
Waiver: Not specified in exemption statute.
***Homestead*: Wis. Stat. §§ 815.20, 990.01(13), (14).**
Amount: $40,000 except for mortgages, taxes and certain mechanics liens. Not less than $\frac{1}{4}$ acre, nor more than 40 acres, so far as reasonably necessary to use the dwelling as a home, subject to the value limitation. Married couple may not stack exemptions.
Procedural requirements: None stated. Homestead may be set apart at time of levy.
Special provisions: Sale proceeds exempt for two years, if held with intention to purchase another homestead.
Waiver: Not specified in exemption statute.
***Tangible personal property*: Wis. Stat. §§ 425.106, 815.18.**
Household goods: $5000: household goods, wearing apparel, firearms, Bible, library, pew. For debts that arise from a consumer credit transaction, certain specified household goods are exempt.
Motor vehicles: $1200, plus any unused household goods exemption.
Tools of trade: $7500.
Clothing and jewelry: Clothing and jewelry are included in household goods exemption.
Miscellaneous and wildcard: Provisions for burial.
Waiver: Contractual waiver is void.
***Benefits, retirement plans, insurance, judgments, and other intangibles*: Wis. Stat. § 815.18; *see also* Wis. Stat. §§ 45.03(8)(b), 49.96, 108.13, 614.96.**
Public benefits: Social Security, certain other public assistance, unemployment, veterans' benefits.
Pensions, retirement plans and annuities: Certain public and private pensions and retirement plans.
Insurance, judgments or other compensation for injury: Insurance proceeds for damage to or destruction of exempt property payable to or received by debtor, for two years after date of receipt; unmatured life insurance and up to $150,000 in accrued dividends or loan value, lesser amounts if contract issued or funded within twenty-four months before the earlier of the date the exemption was claimed or the date the action was filed that gave rise to the judgment, life insurance proceeds or wrongful death judgment for person on whom debtor was dependent, to extent needed for support; up to $25,000 personal injury, including pain and suffering and actual pecuniary loss; compensation for loss of future earnings; crime victim reparations; certain fraternal benefits; certain annuities.
Bank accounts: $1000 in bank account, but only to extent account is for personal rather than business use. Tuition units purchased under Wis. Stat. § 14:63 or § 14:64.
Alimony, child support: Child support, family support or maintenance to extent needed for support.
Survival after payment or deposit: Yes, as to property traceable to life insurance proceeds, wrongful death, personal injury, loss of

future earnings, or certain retirement plans and military pensions. Property traceable to exempt property is exempt only if so specified in this section.

WYOMING

Has state opted out of federal bankruptcy exemptions? Yes. Wyo. Stat. Ann. § 1-20-109.

Is opt out limited to residents or domiciliaries of the state? Yes, to the extent that debtor is domiciled in Wyoming for specified period. Wyo. Stat. Ann. § 1-20-109: "[T]he [§ 522(d) exemptions] are not authorized in cases when Wyoming law is applicable on the date of the filing of the petition and the debtor's domicile has been located in Wyoming for the one hundred eighty (180) days immediately preceding the date of the filing of the petition or for a longer portion of the one hundred eighty (180) day period than in any other place."

Do state's exemptions have extraterritorial application?

Homestead: Uncertain.

Personal property: Uncertain.

Wages: Wyo. Stat. Ann. §§ 1-15-408(b), 1-15-511.

Scope: Accrued and unpaid earnings for personal services.

Amount: Similar to federal.

Survival after payment/deposit: No. Note "accrued and unpaid" language.

Waiver: Not specified in garnishment statute.

***Homestead*: Wyo. Const. art. 19, § 9; Wyo. Stat. Ann. §§ 1-20-101 to 1-20-104.**

Amount: $10,000, each occupant entitled to separate exemption; $6000 for a mobile home.

Procedural requirements: Not specified in exemption statute.

Special provisions: After owner's death, exemption continues to protect surviving spouse and minor children.

Waiver: Not specified in exemption statute.

***Tangible personal property*: Wyo. Stat. §§ 1-20-105, 1-20-106.**

Household goods: $2000. May be stacked if two or more persons in residence.

Motor vehicles: $2400 in one vehicle.

Tools of trade: $2000.

Clothing and jewelry: $1000 in necessary clothing; no jewelry except wedding rings.

Miscellaneous and wildcard: Family library and pictures.

Waiver: Not specified in exemption statute.

***Benefits, retirement plans, insurance, judgments, and other intangibles*: Wyo. Stat. Ann. §§ 1-20-110, 1-20-111.**

Public benefits: Not specified in exemptions statute. *See* Wyo. Stat. Ann. § 42-2-113 (public assistance exempt).

Pensions, retirement plans and annuities: Certain public or private pensions, or retirement plans and annuities, "paid or payable."

Insurance, judgments or other compensation for injury: Not specified in exemptions statute.

Bank accounts: Contributions to a qualified medical savings account (except for debts for medical expenses), to the extent that contributions are allowable under the Internal Revenue Code.

Alimony, child support: Not specified in exemptions statute.

Survival after payment or deposit: Note "paid or payable" language in exemption for retirement accounts.

Index

References are to sections

References are to sections

References are to sections

References are to sections

References are to sections

References are to sections

References are to sections

References are to sections

References are to sections

Quick Reference to the Consumer Credit and Sales Legal Practice Series

References are to sections in *all* manuals in NCLC's Consumer Credit and Sales Legal Practice Series. References followed by "S" appear only in a Supplement.

Readers should also consider another search option available at ***www.consumerlaw.org/keyword***. There, users can search all eighteen NCLC manuals for a case name, party name, statutory or regulatory citation, or *any* other word, phrase, or combination of terms. The search engine provides the title, page number and context of every occurrence of that word or phrase within each of the NCLC manuals. Further search instructions and tips are provided on the web site.

The Quick Reference to the Consumer Credit and Sales Legal Practice Series pinpoints where to find specific topics analyzed in the NCLC manuals. References are to individual manual or supplement sections. For more information on these volumes, see *What Your Library Should Contain* at the beginning of this volume, or go to www.consumerlaw.org.

This Quick Reference is a speedy means to locate key terms in the appropriate NCLC manual. More detailed indexes are found at the end of the individual NCLC volumes. Both the detailed contents pages and the detailed indexes for each manual are also available on NCLC's web site, www.consumerlaw.org.

NCLC *strongly recommends,* when searching for PLEADINGS on a particular subject, that users refer to the *Index Guide* accompanying *Consumer Law Pleadings on CD-Rom*, and *not* to this *Quick Reference*. Another option is to search for pleadings directly on the *Consumer Law Pleadings* CD-Rom or on *Consumer Law on the Web*, using the finding tools that are provided on the CD-Rom and website.

The finding tools found on *Consumer Law on the Web* are also an effective means to find statutes, regulations, agency interpretations, legislative history, and other primary source material found on NCLC's website and CD-Roms. Other search options are detailed at page ix, *supra*: *About the Companion Website, Other Search Options.*

Abbreviations

AUS	=	Access to Utility Service (3d ed. 2004 and 2007 Supp.)
Auto	=	Automobile Fraud (3d ed. 2007 and 2008 Supp.)
Arbit	=	Consumer Arbitration Agreements (5th ed. 2007)
Coll	=	Collection Actions (2008)
CBPL	=	Consumer Banking and Payments Law (3d ed. 2005 and 2008 Supp.)
Bankr	=	Consumer Bankruptcy Law and Practice (8th ed. 2006 and 2008 Supp.)
CCA	=	Consumer Class Actions (6th ed. 2006 and 2008 Supp.)
CLP	=	Consumer Law Pleadings, Numbers One Through Thirteen (2007)
COC	=	The Cost of Credit (3d ed. 2005 and 2008 Supp.)
CD	=	Credit Discrimination (4th ed. 2005 and 2008 Supp.)
FCR	=	Fair Credit Reporting (6th ed. 2006 and 2007 Supp.)
FDC	=	Fair Debt Collection (6th ed. 2008)
Fore	=	Foreclosures (2d ed. 2007 and 2008 Supp.)
Repo	=	Repossessions (6th ed. and 2007 Supp.)
Stud	=	Student Loan Law (3d ed. 2006 and 2007 Supp.)
TIL	=	Truth in Lending (6th ed. 2007)
UDAP	=	Unfair and Deceptive Acts and Practices (6th ed. 2004 and 2007 Supp.)
Warr	=	Consumer Warranty Law (3d ed. 2006 and 2008 Supp.)

References are to sections in *all* manuals in NCLC's Consumer Credit and Sales Legal Practice Series

References are to sections in *all* manuals in NCLC's Consumer Credit and Sales Legal Practice Series

References are to sections in *all* manuals in NCLC's Consumer Credit and Sales Legal Practice Series

References are to sections in *all* manuals in NCLC's Consumer Credit and Sales Legal Practice Series

References are to sections in *all* manuals in NCLC's Consumer Credit and Sales Legal Practice Series